3 2894 00181 0538

EAST GREENWICH FREE LIBRARY

MOON

W9-AUE-303

OREGON

JUDY JEWELL & W. C. McRAE

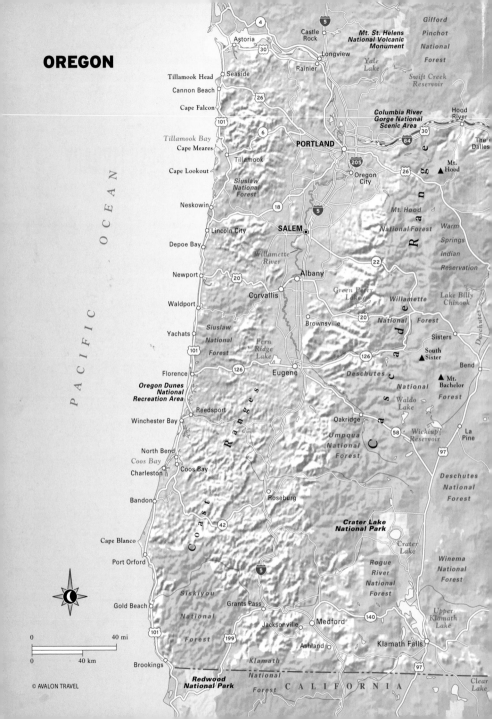

Contents

DISCOVER
Oregon

Truly epic in its breadth, Oregon's landscape is diverse and dramatic. A broad deep-green swath, lush with farmland and studded with old-growth Douglas firs, runs between the rugged Pacific coast and the volcanic peaks of the Cascades. Farther east, you'll find high desert, alpine mountains, and deep river canyons—spectacular country that's largely unexplored by visitors.

But Oregon is much more than a scenic abstraction. In few places has human civilization meshed so agreeably with the natural environment. What helps make Oregon unique is the attitude of its citizens, who are fiercely proud of their state, its culture, and its open spaces. Equal to the great outdoors, the arts are cherished and draw crowds by multitudes. The state also celebrates its historical heritage, ethnic makeup, and straightforward high spirits with a thousand festivals. And the food? Much of Oregon is a huge garden where vegetables, fruit, wine grapes, and farm and ranch products reach perfection. Mighty rivers and 360 miles of Pacific coast provide shellfish, salmon, tuna, and halibut.

Whether it's "three days and four plays" at the Oregon Shakespeare Festival in Ashland, shopping for wild morel mushrooms at the Sisters farmers market, dueling pinot noir tastings in Carlton, or kiteboarding

near Hood River, you'll find that Oregonians engage with everyday life with a verve that's at once intensely local yet tied to a larger, more universal perspective. In Portland, where "organic" and "local" are assumptions, not exceptions, life is rich with the culture and cuisine options of a cosmopolitan center, yet as comfortable and cozy as in a small town.

Oregonians tell a fable about a crossroads on the old Oregon Trail. Pointing south toward the California goldfields was a sign with a drawing of a bag of gold. Pointing north was another sign with the words "To Oregon." The punch line? Only those pioneers who could read continued to Oregon.

Of course, the Oregon Trail is history now, but that doesn't mean that the movement to Oregon is over. The same vaguely agrarian and utopian ideals that drew the pioneers still work magic on a new crop of immigrants eager to move to the Beaver State to open a restaurant, start a software company, or simply seek the good life and a pint of micro-brewed beer.

Planning Your Trip

▶ WHERE TO GO

Portland

Graced by the presence of the Columbia and Willamette Rivers and nearby Mount Hood, Portland is the state's green urban core. Just north of downtown, find the vibrant Pearl District. To the west, Washington Park is home to rose gardens; trails here connect to Forest Park, the nation's largest urban forested park. Cross the Willamette River to the east side to explore its thriving neighborhoods.

Columbia River Gorge and Mount Hood

This is the Pacific Northwest's primal landscape: towering waterfalls, moss-draped rainforests, snowcapped volcanoes—all in a chasm 5 miles wide, 80 miles long, and 3,000 feet deep. The Historic Columbia River Highway ushers travelers to hiking trails. Hood River has a lovely setting at the foot of Mount Hood; drive up the mountain to the landmark Timberline Lodge to more hiking trails and nearly year-round skiing.

IF YOU HAVE . . .

A LONG WEEKEND: Visit Portland with day trips to the Willamette Valley wine country and the Columbia River Gorge.

ONE WEEK: Add a trip down the coast from Astoria to Newport, then head east to Bend and central Oregon's alpine lakes and volcanoes. Return to Portland via Mount Hood.

TWO WEEKS: Add eastern Oregon (catch the Wallowa Mountains in late summer), Crater Lake, and Ashland's Shakespeare Festival.

The Willamette Valley

The historic end of the Oregon Trail, the Willamette Valley is still agriculturally rich, with the emphasis now on wine grapes. Nearly the entire west side of the valley is a wine lover's pilgrimage route. Cycling the wine country adds an active dimension to such a tour. Hike past some of the state's prettiest waterfalls at Silver Falls State Park.

North Coast

Sandy beaches along the northern coastline are separated by headlands, most traced by a hiking trail. Lots of beach towns, ranging from quirky spots that are lost in time to sophisticated resort communities, mean that everyone can find a place to adopt as their own. Vibrant Astoria has a rich history; Cannon Beach is a favorite Portlanders' getaway; and the Three Capes Scenic Loop west of Tillamook provides access to spectacular beaches, including the one at Cape Kiwanda.

Central Coast

The central coast is anchored at its northern end by sprawling Lincoln City and exemplified by Newport, with charming neighborhoods, an active fishing port, and the Oregon Coast Aquarium. At the southern end of the region, Florence and Reedsport are great bases for visits to the Oregon Dunes, which form an otherworldly sand-scape dotted with lakes and bisected by broad estuaries.

South Coast

The south coast feels far from everything, a landscape of mountains, dense forest, wild rivers, and beaches punctuated with dramatic rock formations. West of Coos Bay are wild and beautiful natural areas. Bandon is cozy and full of tourists, many there for the world-class golf courses at Bandon Dunes. The southernmost part of Oregon's coastline may be its most scenic, especially the stretch between Gold Beach and Brookings.

Southern Oregon

Southern Oregon is a land of opposites, ranging from the arts town of Ashland, known for its Shakespeare Festival, to some of the state's most secluded backcountry. The valleys of the North Umpqua and Rogue Rivers are both attractive to hikers and anglers; the Rogue is a top-notch white-water river. Crater Lake is a mesmerizing highlight in Southern Oregon.

Central Oregon

The high desert of central Oregon is cut through by the Deschutes and Crooked Rivers and dotted with volcanic peaks. In Bend, visitors can find good food and a comfortable place to spend the night as well as skiing at nearby Mount Bachelor and easy access to hiking and mountain biking. Raft trips vary from tame floats to the rip-roaring rapids outside Maupin. Visit the Warm Springs

Indian Reservation to get a sense of Native American history and culture.

Northeastern Oregon

You'll hear echoes of the Old West in northeastern Oregon, whether you're touring Chief Joseph's homeland, tracing the steps of Oregon Trail pioneers, or cheering rodeo athletes at the Pendleton Round-Up. Go even further into the past at the John Day Fossil Beds, or explore the geology of Hells Canyon with a boat ride down the Snake River.

Southeastern Oregon

This high-desert region boasts deep blue skies, geologic marvels, and plenty of elbow room. Soak in natural hot springs, view migrating birds at the vast Malheur National Wildlife Refuge, and get to know your fellow travelers at the Frenchglen Hotel. A visit to this corner of Oregon will reconnect you with nature and give you plenty of time and space for reflection.

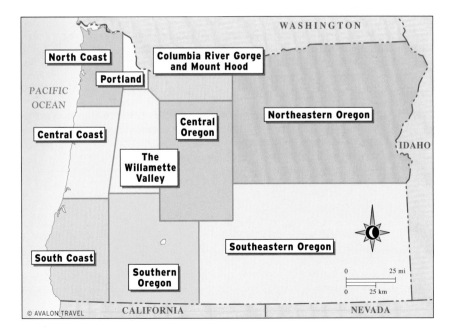

sculpture made of beach trash, Bandon

▶ WHEN TO GO

Although summer weather is usually beautiful, June can be cloudy and cool in the Willamette Valley. When the Willamette Valley heats up, the coast usually remains cool, with morning fog. Trails in the Cascades are often snowy until mid-July—find early summer hikes in the Columbia Gorge or along the Rogue River Trail.

Spring is ideal for touring southeastern Oregon, unless you want to make it all the way to the top of Steens Mountain, which is usually closed by snow until early July.

Autumn's first rains appear in September, but October's weather often starts off clear and beautiful. Even after the rains start, remember that cloudy days with scattered rain are the norm, and that "sun breaks" are common.

Although the mountainous parts of the state accumulate huge amounts of snow during the winter, snowfall is rare on the coast and in the western valleys. Wintertime temperatures are usually above freezing, though the dampness can make it seem colder.

The Best of Oregon

It's almost impossible to cover all of Oregon in a week, so we've crafted a 10-day tour that hits most of the highlights. Although we think it would be a great trip, don't take this itinerary too seriously—and don't hesitate to stay longer at one site or discover your own favorite places along this route. With a mere 10 days to explore the entire state in this itinerary, we couldn't quite get you into the heart of eastern Oregon, but that doesn't mean we don't highly recommend this part of the state. In fact, we like it so much we've devoted an entirely different itinerary to it.

Day 1

Fly into Portland International Airport and either pick up a rental car or take the MAX light rail train into town and arrange to get a rental car in downtown Portland. Spend the afternoon strolling around downtown, visiting Powell's Books and the Pearl District. Spend the night at the Heathman Hotel and dine nearby at old fave Higgins Restaurant & Bar or a slightly longer walk away at trendy Little Bird Bistro.

Day 2

Head northwest out of Portland on U.S. 30 to Astoria. Explore this historic town at the mouth of the Columbia River, including a visit to the replica of Fort Clatsop, which served as Lewis and Clark's winter home in 1805-1806. Then continue south and spend the night in Cannon Beach at the Stephanie Inn.

Day 3

Head south out of town on U.S. 101 and stop for a walk at Oswald West State Park, where you can follow a short trail through an old-growth forest to Short Sands Beach to watch the surfers. Then drive down the coast as far as Yachats and spend the night at Overleaf Lodge. Eat dinner and catch some live music at the Drift Inn Pub.

Wizard Island, Crater Lake National Park

trailside stream in Oswald West State Park

Day 4

Spend the morning exploring the tidepools and old-growth forest around Cape Perpetua. Take a tour of Sea Lion Caves (or just peer down from the road with your binoculars). From the seaside town of Florence, cut east on Route 126 to Eugene, with a detour south to Lorane for a visit to the King Estate Winery tasting room. Spend the night near Eugene's riverside trails at the elegant Inn at the 5th.

Day 5

Drive south along I-5 to Ashland to attend a world-class play. Dine at New Sammy's Cowboy Diner (reserve well in advance) or Amuse, and spend the night at the Ashland Springs Hotel.

Day 6

From Medford, just north of Ashland, drive up the Rogue River on Route 62 through the tiny towns of Prospect and Union Creek to Crater Lake National Park, where you'll spend the night at the Crater Lake Lodge.

Day 7

Head north on U.S. 97 to Bend, visiting the Lava Lands Visitor Center and High Desert Museum on the way. Stay downtown at the Oxford Hotel or a few miles out of town along the Deschutes River at the Mount Bachelor Resort.

Day 8

Continue north to Maupin to meet your raft guide for a daylong float down the Deschutes. At the end of the day, drive up Mount Hood and spend the night at Timberline Lodge.

Day 9

Hike along the Timberline Trail (or spend the morning skiing—even in August) and then drive to Hood River. Take a hike to Upper Horsetail Falls and then continue west to Troutdale, where you'll spend your final night at McMenamins Edgefield, once the county poor farm.

Day 10

It doesn't take long—about 20 minutes—to get from Edgefield to the Portland airport. If you have a late flight, spend the day in Portland, visiting Washington and Forest Parks.

Best Bike Rides

SHORT TRIPS

In downtown Portland, **Waterfront Park and the Eastbank Esplanade** run along either bank of the Willamette River. Cross the Steel Bridge's pedestrian and bike bridge (it's beneath the bridge's main span) at the northern end of the loop, and ride the Hawthorne Bridge's sidewalk at the loop's south end. It's just a couple of miles, pretty flat, and car-free, so it's good for the whole family. If you want to ride farther, continue south on the east side; after passing OMSI, the trail will jog a couple of blocks east and become the **Springwater Corridor,** which runs 21 miles to the town of Boring.

Another family-friendly ride is along the five-mile **Mosier Twin Tunnels** stretch of the Historic Columbia River Highway between Hood River and Mosier. This is a restored portion of the old road, now open only to bike and foot traffic. Park at the Mark O. Hatfield Trailhead at the east end of Hood River, near exit 64 from I-84 ($3 parking fee) or ride up from town (it's a steep approach).

LONGER EXCURSIONS

The **Banks-Vernonia State Trail,** a 21-mile rails-to-trails bike route, runs along the route of an old logging train and includes 80-foot-high railroad trestles, one of which is safety-improved for cyclists. Catch the trail west of Portland; Banks is on Route 47 just south of Route 26. The trail passes through sprawling Stub Stewart State Park, which has a campground and great mountain biking.

Oakridge is known for its network of mountain bike trails, but a challenging 60-mile road ride starts here, too, and goes north along the **Aufderheide National Scenic Byway** to Rainbow, a site on the McKenzie River Highway (Route 126). Near the northern end of the ride, you'll pass Terwilliger Hot Springs. Believe us when we tell you that you'll be too tired to turn around and ride back the way you came, so a car drop is recommended.

Don't plan to ride the 33-mile rim loop around **Crater Lake** too early in the summer, or you'll run into snow. And don't count on riding it too fast, either; most of the ride is above 7,000 feet and you'll be stopping not only to suck air but also to admire the great views of the lake. There's a window, usually in late June, when most of the snow has melted but the road is not yet entirely open to cars. A car-free weekend is held during the third weekend of September.

EPIC ADVENTURES

The **Oregon Coast Bike Route,** a hilly 342-mile ride along busy U.S. 101, is popular for its spectacular ocean views and ample opportunities for eating and sleeping, whether in a hotel bed or in a sleeping bag at a campground.

Cycle Oregon has mapped out some great routes over the years for its weeklong mid-September tours. One of the best makes a 365-mile loop through northeastern Oregon, starting in Baker City, heading east to Halfway, north along Forest Road 39 to Joseph, northwest through Enterprise and Lostine to Elgin, then south along back roads through Cove and Union back to the starting point. Train well for this ride: It's wild, rugged, and beautiful country, and the stretch from Halfway to Joseph climbs over 7,000 feet in 61 miles.

RIDE OREGON

The Oregon Department of Transportation is actively promoting bicycle tourism via an excellent website: www.rideoregonride.com. Here you can find notices of upcoming bicycling events as well as rides along scenic bikeways, mountain trails, and roads. Each ride includes detailed directions and cue sheets, elevation profiles, and maps. Try the 38-mile Covered Bridges Scenic Bikeway out of Cottage Grove, a challenging 79-mile mountain bike ride along the North Umpqua Trail, or a 135-mile figure-8 tour of northeastern Oregon's back roads, starting and ending in La Grande.

The Wine Route

Oregon wines have been in the news ever since the 1980s when a Willamette Valley pinot noir came in second in a blind tasting in France—defeating a field of more expensive and highly esteemed French burgundies. Today, there are over 400 wineries in the state, producing more than 1.7 million cases per year and contributing about $2.7 billion to the state's economy.

Wine grape production now takes place across the state, even in the dry rangelands of eastern Oregon. Planning a trip through Oregon's many wine regions is a good way to explore the state and to track down little-known vintages that don't make it across state lines.

Southern Oregon

Start your wine odyssey in Ashland, where Shakespeare and fine restaurants make good companions for wine exploration. Near town are Ashland Vineyards, famous for the white wine Shakespeare's Love, and Weisinger's Vineyard, which produces fine viognier and cabernet sauvignon. The area's best wines, and the greatest concentration of wineries, are over the ridge in the Applegate Valley. High summer heat here enables the production of red wines such as cabernet and syrah as well as some California-style chardonnays; check out the wines at Valley View Winery or Troon Vineyard. Spend the night at the Ashland Creek Inn, a luxury inn right on the water, and dine at Peerless Restaurant, known for its wine cellar and dedication to regional foods.

Travel north toward Roseburg, central for the wines of the Umpqua Valley. Abacela is noted for the many varieties of wine grapes it grows, offering unusual-for-Oregon varietals such as tempranillo, dolcetto, and sangiovese. Henry Estate Winery is one of the state's oldest and has lovely gardens that make an excellent picnic destination. The wines range from full-bodied pinot noir and merlot to refreshing Riesling. Girardet produces a range of wines, such as chardonnay,

pinot noir grapes

Mutiny Brewing Company, northeastern Oregon

Touring the Taps

If you're serious about craft brews, plan your trip around the **Oregon Brewers Festival,** held in Portland during the last full weekend of July.

PORTLAND
The beer at the **McMenamins Crystal Hotel** is perfectly good, but it's a short walk or bike ride across the Willamette River to a couple of outstanding eastside breweries.

- **Cascade Brewing Barrel House:** Try the gose, a lemony, herbal beer that may have a slightly salty finish: sound weird? It's a good summer beer, and it's also relatively low in alcohol.
- **Hair of the Dog:** HOTD, known for bold, rich flavors and alcohol contents of about 10 percent, runs a tasting room but not a full-on pub.

COLUMBIA RIVER GORGE
Hood River has two great brewpubs and the **Hood River Hotel** is an easy walk from both of these spots.

- **Double Mountain:** Stop here for pizza and a Double Mountain Hop Lava.
- **Full Sail Brewery and Pub:** Brewery tours, good beer, and a spectacular river view from the deck make this a great place to spend the day.

THE WILLAMETTE VALLEY
In Eugene, crash in the funky **Eugene Whiteaker International Hostels.**

- **Ninkasi Brewing:** Ninkasi was the ancient Sumerian goddess of fermentation, and she's easy to worship with a glass of Believer Double Red Ale in your hand.
- **Rogue Farms Hopyard** in Independence
- **Brewers Union Local 180** in Oakridge

NORTH COAST
The **Hotel Elliott** in Astoria is right around the corner from **Fort George Brewery and Public House.**

- **Pelican Brewing** in Pacific City
- **Bill's Tavern** in Cannon Beach

SOUTHERN OREGON
In Ashland, stay at **The Palm,** a charming motor court motel, and wander into town for a brew.

- **Caldera Tap House:** Tucked away near Ashland Creek, Caldera is just a couple of blocks from the Oregon Shakespeare Festival's theaters.
- **Wild River Brewing** has locations in Grants Pass, Cave Junction, and Brookings Harbor.

CENTRAL OREGON
Bend has new breweries opening nearly monthly. Stay at the **McMenamins Old St. Francis School.**

- **Deschutes Brewery and Public House:** The Mirror Pond pale ale is one of Oregon's best.
- **10 Barrel:** You'll want the award-winning S1NISTOR black ale.
- **Boneyard Brewing:** Only a tasting room, but look for Boneyard on tap around town.
- **GoodLife Brewing:** Bring your dog, sit outside, and get to know the locals over a pint of Descender IPA.

NORTHEASTERN OREGON
Some would say northeastern Oregon is itself off the beaten path, but plenty of brewpubs await to quench your thirst.

- **Prodigal Son Brewery and Pub:** This lively and pleasant pub is on the edge of downtown Pendleton.
- **Terminal Gravity Brewing:** Enjoy microbrews in a creekside setting in Enterprise.
- **Mutiny Brewing Company:** Avoid Joseph's touristy choices with this friendly and authentic pub.
- **Barley Brown's Brew Pub:** Make a pilgrimage to Baker City for a pint of Barley Brown ales—the only place they're available.

cabernet sauvignon, and pinot noir, and also makes wine from more unusual grapes such as baco noir. The historic, riverside Steamboat Inn, 38 miles up the North Umpqua River, is the region's best dining and lodging choice.

The Willamette Valley

The Willamette Valley is Oregon's primary wine-growing region. Here the weather is cooler in than the Umpqua and Applegate Valleys, favoring the production of pinot noir and chardonnay, the grapes of France's Burgundy valley, and pinot gris from northern Italy and the French Alsace region. Near Eugene, be sure to stop at King Estate Winery, with a hilltop tasting and winemaking facility near Lorane that is literally palatial. Territorial Vineyards & Wine Company has vineyards near the Coast Range but a winemaking facility and tasting room in downtown Eugene. From its estate-grown pinot noir grapes, Territorial makes a series of regular pinot noir bottlings and a fantastic rosé. Make dinner reservations at Marché restaurant, and spend the night a few steps away at the Inn at the 5th.

Between Rickreall and Carlton, on the west side of the Willamette Valley, is the greatest concentration of wineries in the state. Here are the pinot noir vineyards that have put Oregon on the world wine map. With over 200 wineries in a relatively compact area, there's no single route to recommend, so pick up a copy of the widely available Willamette Valley Winery Association's winery map, and follow your instincts. Not to miss, however, is Sokol Blosser Winery, with a stunning tasting room perched on a hill just above Dundee. Domaine Drouhin, also near Dundee, is the Oregon outpost of France's famed Drouhin family and makes excellent pinot noirs in the Burgundy style. Anne Amie Vineyards makes fine pinot noirs and has a beautiful facility with one of the most panoramic

views in the valley. The Rex Hill Vineyards is just east of Newberg, and it is one of the closest vineyards to Portland, with premium pinot noir and a lovely garden setting.

If it seems like there are just too many wineries to choose from, consider a stop at The Tasting Room in downtown Carlton, in the lobby of a century-old bank, which offers a selection of wines from many smaller wineries that don't have their own tasting facilities. Also in Carlton is the Carlton Winemakers Studio, a cooperative where small winemakers share a winemaking facility and tasting room. Stay at the Allison Inn near Newberg, and plan to dine at Thistle, in nearby McMinnville.

Columbia River Gorge

East of Portland on I-84 is the Columbia River Gorge. Microclimates here create niches where cool-climate grapes like pinot noir thrive, while just up the road vineyards of syrah and merlot, which require intense summer heat to ripen, may be planted. There are wineries on both the Oregon and Washington sides of the gorge, so don't hesitate to cross bridges to taste wine. Across the Columbia are such notable producers as Syncline and Cor Cellars. Stay at the grand and historic Columbia Gorge Hotel in Hood River, and dine at Celilo Restaurant and Bar for sophisticated fine dining and a wine list rich in local vintages.

Northeastern Oregon

East of the Columbia Gorge, Route 11 runs north from Pendleton up toward Walla Walla, Washington. About a third of the official Walla Walla wine-growing area is in Oregon, and several tasting rooms in Walla Walla call for serious attention from lovers of cabernet and merlot. On the Oregon side, stop in Pendleton at Great Pacific Wine and Coffee Co., where wines from Walla Walla and the Columbia Valley are featured, and book a room at Pendleton House Bed and Breakfast for the night.

Oregon for the Birds

Oregon has great bird-watching destinations. Pack your binoculars and go birding at these scenic bird sanctuaries.

- **Cape Meares Rocks:** This Pacific coast fastness combines rocky headlands (for nesting seabirds such as cormorants, common murres, tufted puffins, and pigeon quillemots) and coastal old-growth forest (home to northern spotted owls, bald eagles, and marbled murrelets).

- **Sauvie Island:** This large, lake-filled island in the Columbia River is a good spot for fall and winter birding, when you might see snow geese and sandhill cranes, plus massive flocks of migrating waterfowl. Bald eagles and peregrine falcons are the primary raptors.

- **Malheur National Wildlife Refuge:** Over 320 bird species have been observed at Malheur Lake; during spring migration it's a top viewing area for sandhill cranes, tundra swans, northern pintails, many types of geese, white pelicans, double-crested cormorants, western grebes, long-billed curlews, and American avocets. Sage grouse are also prevalent.

- **Upper Klamath National Wildlife Refuge:** Large, marshy Upper Klamath Lake is most noted as the winter home of

hundreds of bald eagles. In spring breeding season you may see white pelicans, great egrets, and black-crowned night-herons, and if you're lucky, western and Clark's grebes doing their mating dance on the water.

great horned owl

Central Oregon Tour

Day 1
If you're starting from Portland, drive east on U.S. 26 over the hump of Mount Hood and spend your first afternoon and night at Kah-Nee-Ta, on the Warm Springs Reservation. Plan to venture down to the big day-use pool for a real swim or a few runs on the waterslide.

Day 2
Following a morning swim, visit the Museum at Warm Springs to learn more about Native

American culture. Then drive to Madras and have lunch at Great Earth Natural Foods. Continue south on U.S. 97 to Terrebonne and turn off to Smith Rock State Park. Hike the trails and watch climbers scale the rocks, then drive down to Bend and settle into your room at McMenamins Old St. Francis School.

Day 3
Begin the day in Bend with breakfast at Chow and a stroll or bike ride along the

As Seen in *Portlandia*

A recent 12-year-old visitor said that he wanted to see two places in Portland: Voodoo Doughnut and the feminist bookstore. Like many others, his view of the Rose City had been shaped by the popular IFC series, *Portlandia*.

Here's a brief rundown on visiting businesses and parks used as sets in the TV show:

- **In Other Words Women's Bookstore** (14 NE Killingsworth St.): Unlike at Women and Women First, the staff here is friendly and welcoming.
- **Eastbank Esplanade:** Dream of the '90s as you dodge cyclists, runners, hot girls wearing glasses, and the occasional clown.
- **Olympic Provisions NW:** Dream of the 1890s as you eat excellent artisan sausage. Good chance of seeing some finely cultivated beards here.
- **Land** (3925 N. Mississippi Ave.): Put a bird on it! Gift shop and gallery with a good selection of quirky T-shirts, books, and cards.
- **Prasad** (inside Yoga Pearl, 925 NW Davis St.): Vegan raw restaurant, but unfortunately, no fart patio.

- If you want to stand in line for a bacon maple bar, the original **Voodoo Doughnut** is at 22 SW 3rd Avenue; there's an eastside location at 1501 NE Davis Street.

the potent allure of Voodoo Doughnut

Deschutes River Trail. Spend part of the day wandering around downtown and the Old Mill District—stop by Pine Mountain Sports or REI to pick up any camping or outdoor gear you might need for the next couple of nights.

Day 4

Head up the Cascade Lakes Highway to hike, fish, or just hang out on a lakeshore. Camp at a hike-in site at Todd Lake, or find a more convenient car-camping site at one of the other lakes along the road. (If you're not camping, several lakeside resorts rent rustic cabins.) Consider spending more than one night here; once you've found the perfect camping spot, it

seems a shame to leave it, and there are plenty of trails to hike.

Day 5

Drive down to Sunriver on Route 42 (catch it just past Crane Prairie Reservoir), then south a few miles on U.S. 97 to the turnoff for Newberry Volcano. Head up to the caldera, where you can hike the trail through the Big Obsidian Flow, and then find your new campground at either Paulina or East Lake (or a cabin at one of the rustic lakeside resorts).

Day 6

After you break camp, head back down the

Smith Rock State Park

volcano and north on U.S. 97. Stop to explore the Lava River Cave and the Lava Lands Visitor Center, then take the short hike to Benham Falls. Continue north and spend the afternoon at the High Desert Museum (don't worry, they have a café), then spend the night in either Bend or Sisters.

Day 7

Finish your week with a river trip. Get up early and drive north of Madras to Maupin, where you'll meet your river guide for a day trip on the Deschutes River. Wear sunscreen and quick-dry shorts, and take a swim down the Elevator.

The Oregon Outback

Jettison your notions of Oregon as a cloud-enshrouded spot and get set for expansive views, lots of wildlife, and a dose of the West in this tour of an area sometimes referred to as "Oregon's outback."

If you're flying in for this trip, consider using the Boise, Idaho airport. It's much closer to Baker City, where this itinerary begins and ends, than the Portland airport.

Day 1

Start your tour of eastern Oregon in Baker City, but don't linger in town for too long; head west to the near-ghost town of Sumpter (30 miles) and then up a ways into

the Elkhorns for more gold-era history and mining ghost towns. North of Sumpter, follow the Elkhorn Drive National Scenic Byway to the near-ghost town of Granite. If you're enjoying the drive, continue north and east to Anthony Lakes; from there, continue east back to I-84 and Baker City.

Day 2

Visit the National Historic Oregon Trail Interpretive Center near Baker City, then head about 70 miles east on Route 86 to Hells Canyon at Oxbow, where you can take a look at the Snake River's gorge by

Top Tents and Trails

PORTLAND

Wildwood Trail: One of the state's top trails is only 10 minutes from downtown Portland, thanks to 5,000-acre Forest Park. One access point onto the Wildwood Trail is via the shorter but quite scenic Lower Macleay Trail.

COLUMBIA RIVER GORGE

Eagle Creek Trail: This classic gorge trail starts near Bonneville Dam and follows Eagle Creek past waterfalls and springtime wildflowers. Your face will be misted with spray, and in places you'll need to grab hold of cables bolted into the basalt cliffs as the trail narrows.

THE WILLAMETTE VALLEY

Silver Falls State Park: Ten waterfalls cascade off canyon walls in a forest of Douglas firs, ferns, and bigleaf and vine maple. Come during fall foliage season when there are few visitors.

Paradise Campground: This campground provides access to the 26.5-mile McKenzie River National Recreation Trail and the nearby Belknap Lodge and Hot Springs.

NORTH COAST

Oswald West State Park: Most of Neahkahnie Mountain and the prominent headlands of Cape Falcon are within Oswald West State Park. Several hiking trails weave through the park, including the Oregon Coast Trail.

CENTRAL COAST

Carl G. Washburne State Park: Pile your gear into a wheelbarrow (provided) and trundle it to one of the great walk-in campsites. After pitching your tent, take a hike along the Hobbit Trail.

SOUTH COAST

Cape Blanco State Park: This beautiful and often blustery campground at the state's westernmost point has trails that lead down to the beach and to the nearby lighthouse. Visit the Hughes House to experience how Cape Blanco pioneers existed here.

CENTRAL OREGON

Devils Lake: These prime lakeside campsites, along the Cascade Lakes Highway, are set away from the parking area, so you'll have to schlep your gear. Across the highway is the climber's trail for South Sister.

Metolius River Campgrounds: The many campgrounds here, especially those downstream from Camp Sherman, offer a chance to linger by central Oregon's most magical river.

Smith Rock State Park: Majestic spires tower above the Crooked River at this state park. Seven miles of well-marked trails follow the Crooked River and wend up the canyon walls.

NORTHEASTERN OREGON

Strawberry Campground: This campground offers a quick 1.25-mile hike to Strawberry Lake.

Grande Ronde Lake Campground: Small Grande Ronde Lake lies in a meadow of tiny streams that is the headwaters of the Grande Ronde River. Hiking trails into the Elkhorn Mountains start nearby.

SOUTHEASTERN OREGON

Hart Mountain National Antelope Refuge: This hot springs campground is four miles south of the refuge headquarters. Soak in the hot springs, and explore the area on foot or by mountain bike.

Page Springs: Get up early to check out the birds on a hike along the Donner und Blitzen River.

Matterhorn is a landmark peak in the Wallowa Mountains.

car, jet boat, or on foot. Backtrack and stay the night in Halfway, just beneath the southern edge of the Wallowa Mountains.

Day 3

From Halfway, head about 15 miles east on Route 86, then turn north on Forest Road 39. This 54-mile summer-only road will take you up the eastern edge of the Wallowas past the area's most accessible viewpoint onto Hells Canyon to lodgings in the artsy town of Joseph or at nearby Wallowa Lake.

Day 4

Take the Wallowa Lake Tramway from Wallowa Lake. The tram lets you off at the top of Mount Howard, where there is a network of hiking trails. Then head west to I-84 at La Grande and follow the interstate to Pendleton. Tour the Pendleton Underground and spend the night in town.

Day 5

Hop back on I-84 and take it west to Arlington. From Arlington, drive south on Route 19 to the John Day Fossil Beds. Just south of the Thomas Condon Paleontology Center, turn west onto U.S. 26 and take it to your night's lodging in John Day.

Day 6

It's a pretty drive south from John Day on U.S. 395 through Burns to the Malheur National Wildlife Refuge. Visit the refuge headquarters a few miles east of Route 205, then continue south on Route 205 to lodgings in Frenchglen.

Day 7

If the snows have melted, drive the Steens Mountain Byway. Spend another night in Frenchglen, or head north to Burns before driving back to Boise to fly home.

Keeping the Dry Side Up

Although we can't direct you to the Northwest Passage, we can suggest great river trips in every corner of the state.

- **Portland:** Paddle the Willamette with a sea kayak or stand-up paddleboard from **Portland Kayak Company** (6600 SW Macadam Ave., 503/459-4050, www.portlandkayak.com) on the west side of the Willamette River or **Alder Creek Kayak** (1515 SE Water St., 503/285-1819, www.aldercreek.com) just off the Eastbank Esplanade immediately south of the Hawthorne Bridge. An easy afternoon tour circumnavigates Ross Island and offers a chance to see bald eagles nesting just a couple of miles from downtown.

- **The Willamette Valley:** In mid-August join the Willamette Riverkeepers' **Paddle Oregon** event (www.paddleoregon.org) to run 107 miles of the Willamette in a canoe or sea kayak. It's also easy to do this trip, or a shorter one, on your own.

- **Columbia Gorge and Mount Hood:** Catch some wind on the mighty Columbia. **Big Winds** (207 Front St., Hood River, 541/386-6086, www.bigwinds.com) offers board and full rig rentals, lessons, and all the necessary windsurfing equipment. Or give kiteboarding a try.

- **North Coast:** Rent a surfboard and wetsuit at **Cleanline Surf** (171 Sunset Blvd., 503/436-9726) in Cannon Beach, drive a few miles south, and hike down to Short Sands Beach at Oswald West State Park.

- **Central Coast:** Explore a quiet coastal stream and wetland and its abundant wildlife at **Beaver Creek,** south of Newport. Make reservations well in advance for a **guided tour** (South Beach State Park Hospitality Center, 541/867-6590).

- **South Coast:** Board a jet boat and travel upstream from the mouth of the Rogue River through a Wild and Scenic stretch that's loaded with wildlife and lush vegetation. **Jerry's Rogue River Jetboats** (29985 Harbor Way, Gold Beach, 541/247-4571 or 800/451-3645, www.roguejets.com) has been running these trips for many years, and the boat pilots are known for their excellent commentary.

- **Southern Oregon:** Take a multiday raft trip on the Rogue River starting 7 miles west of Grants Pass. This stretch not only has some of the best white water in the United States, but also backcountry riverside lodges. The Rogue is also ideal for half- and full-day rafting trips, with most outfitters putting in near the town of Merlin and continuing downstream as far as Foster Bar. **Morrison's Rogue River Lodge** (8500 Galice Rd., Merlin, 541/476-3825 or 800/826-1963, www.rogueriverraft.com) leads a variety of trips.

- **Central Oregon:** Spend a day rafting the Deschutes River, surrounded by sage-covered grasslands and wild rocky canyons where you might see bald eagles, pronghorn, and other wildlife. The town of Maupin is home base for many outfitters, including **All Star Rafting and Kayaking** (405 Deschutes Ave., 541/395-2201 or 800/909-7238, www.asrk.com).

- **Northeastern Oregon:** The undammed John Day River winds through unpopulated rangeland and scenic rock formations; plan to spend a few days away from everything. It's easy enough for almost everybody to paddle on their own; **Service Creek Stage Stop** (38686 Hwy. 19, Fossil, 541/468-3331, www.servicecreek.com) rents rafts and can set you up with a car shuttle.

- **Southeastern Oregon:** The Owyhee River is a prime springtime destination for whitewater enthusiasts. The 53 miles from Rome to the Owyhee Reservoir have two sections of exceptionally heavy rapids, but the many pools of short intense white water alternating with easy drifts make for a well-paced trip. **Ouzel Outfitters** (541/385-5947 or 800/788-7238, www.oregonrafting.com) is one of several companies with guided Owyhee trips.

PORTLAND

Perhaps the headline in the *San Francisco Chronicle* said it best—"Newsflash: When we weren't looking, Portland got hip."

At some point in the past decade, Portland's place in the popular culture firmament has vaulted from that of a friendly, flannel-clad, rain-scrubbed city solidly lodged in the nation's second tier to being a major trendsetter in cuisine, wine, arts, design, and up-to-the-second lifestyles.

Oregon's largest city, Portland is cosmopolitan and has a metro area population of 2.1 million, although the city's easygoing and quirky spirit makes it feel like a much smaller town. It's extremely easy to feel at home here—many's the tale of visitors coming to stay for a few days and finding a few pleasant years later that they forgot to leave.

Newcomers are drawn here to live out their dream of launching a startup, opening a coffee shop, founding a clothing design firm, or establishing a microdistillery. It's Portland's combination of youthful idealism and entrepreneurial zeal that really sets the city apart, and it is currently one of the top West Coast destinations for "young creatives"—that is, college-educated 25- to 34-year-olds.

And then there's the politics. Portland is famously liberal and irreverent. In fact, even as the city grows, its reputation as a center of unconventional lifestyles and alternative and populist politics increases. "Keep Portland Weird" has gone from bumper sticker to manifesto as many of the city's inner neighborhoods positively heave with energy reminiscent of the hippie movement heyday of the late 1960s.

© JUDY JEWELL

PORTLAND

HIGHLIGHTS

◖ **Portland Art Museum:** Portland's green and shady South Park Blocks are home to this excellent collection of art and artifacts (page 38).

◖ **Tom McCall Waterfront Park:** This riverside park is home to lots of summer festivals, great people-watching, a fountain, and over a mile of seawall to stroll (page 39).

◖ **International Rose Test Garden:** The most spectacular sights in Washington Park are these famed gardens containing 10,000 rose plants (page 43).

◖ **Portland Japanese Garden:** Five gardens in one, this is one of the most authentic Japanese gardens in the United States (page 43).

◖ **Lan Su Chinese Garden:** A magical enclave in historic Chinatown, this replica of a Ming Dynasty garden was built by craftspeople from Suzhou, China (page 46).

◖ **Pearl District:** Oregon's most densely populated neighborhood is this upscale shopping and dining district, home to many of the city's top galleries and restaurants (page 48).

◖ **Hawthorne District:** This neighborhood, with its kick-back hippie vibe, is a good place to sip coffee and people watch (page 55).

◖ **Forest Park:** In the nation's largest forested urban park, you can mountain bike or walk on Leif Erikson Drive or explore part of the 30-plus-mile-long Wildwood Trail (page 57).

◖ **Portland Farmers Market:** On Saturdays,

the South Park Blocks explode with the fresh bounty of the Willamette Valley (page 75).

◖ **Powell's City of Books:** As the Pearl District has flourished, so has this huge bookstore, known for its mix of new and used titles (page 77).

LOOK FOR ◖ TO FIND RECOMMENDED SIGHTS, ACTIVITIES, DINING, AND LODGING.

But there's more to Portland than tribal tattoos and indolent coffee shops. Amid lush greenery rare in an urban environment, high-tech business ventures, top-notch cultural institutions (including a first-rate symphony, opera company, and art museum), and distinctive architecture lend an air of worldly sophistication. A latticework of

bridges spanning the Willamette River adds a distinctive profile, while parks, plazas, and other public spaces give Portland a heart and a soul.

Such a happy medium is the result of many generations of progressive planning and a fortunate birthright. Patterns of growth in this onetime Native American encampment at the confluence of the Willamette and Columbia Rivers were initially shaped by the practical Midwestern values of Oregon Trail pioneers, as well as by the sophistication of New England merchants. Rather than the boom-bust development that characterized Seattle and gold rush San Francisco, Portland was designed to be user-friendly over the long haul. During the modern era, planners added such progressive refinements as extensive mass transit systems, strict limits on building height and spacing, and one of the most bicycle-friendly traffic systems in the nation.

Portland's epic natural setting—at the confluence of two mighty rivers and dominated by ancient, densely forested volcanoes—sets the stage for another of the city's great draws: access to outdoor recreation and rural scenic splendors. With the Columbia River Gorge and year-round skiing on Mount Hood to the east and the Pacific coastline to the west, relief from urban stress is little more than an hour away. Other nearby getaways include the Willamette Valley wine country and the historic sites of Champoeg and Oregon City. Closer to home, Portland's Forest Park is the largest urban forest in the country, and after a visit to Washington Park, you'll know why Portland is nicknamed the "Rose City."

The result is a small city with lots of personality; an urban area equally suffused with green space and creative energy. A recent *New York Times* article declared Portland to be the most European city in the United States, but most Portlanders were too busy biking, drinking handcrafted ale, and buying local cheese at the farmers market to have noticed. Portland isn't like other places in the United States, and of that its citizens are very proud.

HISTORY

Portland sits near the confluence of two of the West's mightiest rivers, the Columbia and the Willamette. Local Native Americans (referred to in general as the Chinook people) have lived along these rivers for millennia, finding the area rich for hunting, fishing, and trade. At an ancient campsite south of Portland, human hair and a cache of animal bones have been dated to 10,000 BC.

Sauvie Island, northwest of the current city limits, was the site of a Native American village whose name inspired William Clark to christen the nearby river the Willamette in 1805. Clark explored the mouth of the Willamette and viewed the future site of Portland, noting that the area "is in fact the only desirable situation for a settlement on the western side of the Rocky Mountains, and, being naturally fertile, would, if properly cultivated, afford subsistence for 40,000 or 50,000 souls."

In 1825 the Hudson's Bay Company established Fort Vancouver across the Columbia River, bringing French and Scottish trappers into the area, some of whom retired around what would eventually become Portland. The city was officially born when two New Englanders, Pettygrove from Portland, Maine, and Lovejoy from Boston, Massachusetts, flipped a coin at a dinner party to decide who would name the 640-acre claim they co-owned. The state-of-Mainer won and decided in the winter of 1844-1845 to name it after his birthplace. The original claim is located in the vicinity of SW Naito Parkway.

Unsurprisingly, given its location, Portland's early growth was fueled by shipping and trade. The California gold rush of 1849 and the building of San Francisco demanded lumber, which was routed through the fledgling port city on the Willamette River. At the same time, Oregon Trail settlers brought agriculture to the Willamette Valley, and mining and ranching developed throughout the inland West. Each industry demanded a coastal city for trade, and Portland became that mercantile and shipping center for much of the Pacific Northwest. Portland thus quickly transitioned from a sleepy village, nicknamed "Stumptown" for the massive tree stumps remaining after the forests were cleared, to the largest trade and population center in the region.

Portland's primacy was solidified when the Northern Pacific Railroad arrived in 1883,

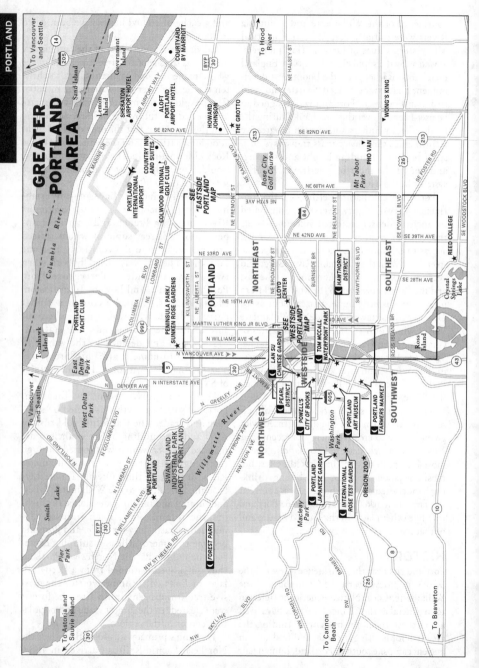

GREATER
PORTLAND
AREA

To Vancouver
and Seattle

To Hood River

Columbia River

To Vancouver and Seattle

Tomahawk Island

Sand Island
Lemon Island
Government Island

NE MARINE DR

COURTYARD BY MARRIOTT

NE HALSEY ST

NE AIRPORT WAY

SHERATON AIRPORT HOTEL

ALOFT PORTLAND AIRPORT HOTEL

SE 82ND AVE

HOWARD JOHNSON

THE GROTTO

WONG'S KING

COUNTRY INN AND SUITES

SE 82ND AVE

PORTLAND INTERNATIONAL AIRPORT

COLWOOD NATIONAL GOLF CLUB

Rose City Golf Course

Mt Tabor Park

PHO VAN

SEE "EASTSIDE PORTLAND" MAP

NE FREMONT ST

NE 57TH AVE

NE 60TH AVE

SE POWELL BLVD

REED COLLEGE

SE WOODSTOCK BLVD

PORTLAND YACHT CLUB

PENINSULA PARK/ SUNKEN ROSE GARDENS

NE 33RD AVE

NORTHEAST PORTLAND

NE 42ND AVE

NE BELMONT ST

HAWTHORNE DISTRICT

SE 39TH AVE

Crystal Springs Lake

East Delta Park

West Delta Park

NE KILLINGSWORTH ST

NE ALBERTA ST

NE 15TH AVE

NE BROADWAY ST

LLOYD CENTER

BURNSIDE BR

SE HAWTHORNE BLVD

SOUTHEAST

SE 28TH AVE

Ross Island

Smith Lake

MARTIN LUTHER KING JR BLVD

N WILLIAMS AVE

SEE "WESTSIDE PORTLAND" MAP

LAN SU CHINESE GARDEN

TOM MCCALL WATERFRONT PARK

N VANCOUVER AVE

WESTSIDE

N DENVER AVE

N INTERSTATE AVE

N GREELEY AVE

PEARL DISTRICT

POWELL'S CITY OF BOOKS

Washington Park

PORTLAND ART MUSEUM

PORTLAND FARMERS MARKET

SOUTHWEST

NORTHWEST

UNIVERSITY OF PORTLAND

SWAN ISLAND INDUSTRIAL PARK (PORT OF PORTLAND)

Willamette River

PORTLAND JAPANESE GARDEN

INTERNATIONAL ROSE TEST GARDEN

OREGON ZOO

Macleay Park

Pier Park

FOREST PARK

To Astoria and Sauvie Island

To Cannon Beach

To Beaverton

© AVALON TRAVEL

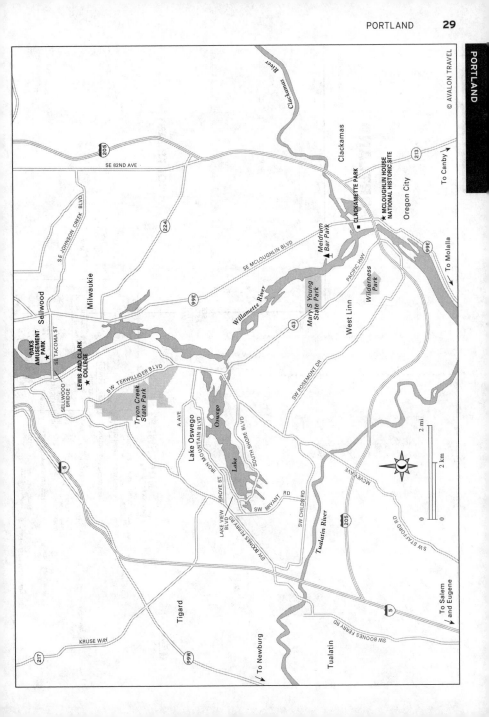

PORTLAND

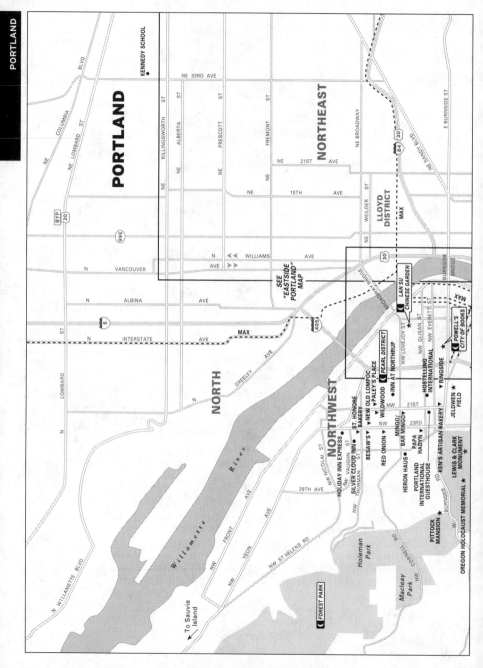

PORTLAND

NORTHEAST

KENNEDY SCHOOL

KENNEDY SCHOOL

NE COLUMBIA BLVD
NE LOMBARD ST
NE 33RD AVE
NE KILLINGSWORTH ST
NE ALBERTA ST
NE PRESCOTT ST
NE FREMONT ST
NE 21ST AVE
NE 15TH AVE
NE BROADWAY
E BURNSIDE ST
NE SANDY BLVD
84 30

BYP 30

99E

LLOYD DISTRICT
MAX
NE WELDER ST

N VANCOUVER AVE
N WILLIAMS AVE
◀◀ WILLIAMS AVE ▶▶

SEE "EASTSIDE PORTLAND" MAP

N ALBINA AVE

5

N INTERSTATE AVE
MAX

405

30

BROADWAY BRIDGE
BURNSIDE BRIDGE

LAN SU CHINESE GARDEN
NW GLISAN ST
NW EVERETT ST
NW FLANDERS ST
MAX
POWELL'S CITY OF BOOKS
RINGSIDE

NORTH

N LOMBARD ST
GREELEY AVE

W i l l a m e t t e   R i v e r

PEARL DISTRICT
INN AT NORTHRUP
NW LOVEJOY ST

NORTHWEST

HOLIDAY INN EXPRESS
NEW OLD LOMPOC
PALEY'S PLACE
WILDWOOD
HOSTELLING INTERNATIONAL

ST. HONORE BAKERY
BESAW'S
NW VAUGHN ST
SILVER CLOUD INN
NW THURMAN ST
NW 21ST
NW 23RD
MINGO
RED ONION
BAR MINGO
PAPA HAYDN
KEN'S ARTISAN BAKERY
JELDWEN FIELD

HERON HAUS
PORTLAND INTERNATIONAL GUESTHOUSE

NW NICOLAI ST
29TH AVE
NW FRONT AVE
NW YEON AVE
NW ST HELENS RD
BURNSIDE

LEWIS & CLARK MONUMENT

PITTOCK MANSION

OREGON HOLOCAUST MEMORIAL

Holeman Park

Macleay Park

CORNELL RD
NW CORNELL RD

N WILLAMETTE BLVD

To Sauvie Island

FOREST PARK

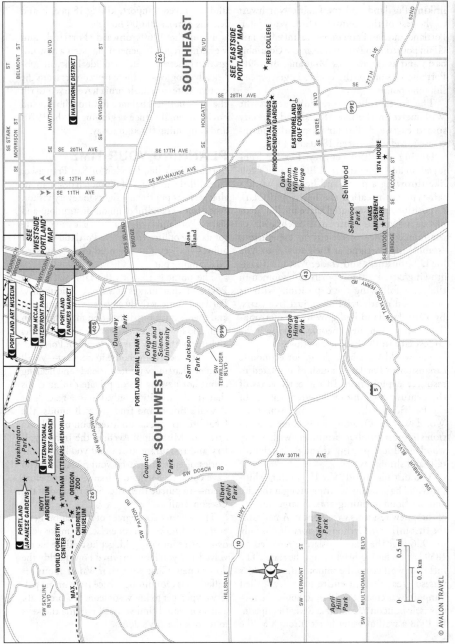

© AVALON TRAVEL

linking Portland and the Pacific Northwest to the rest of the country. Three years later, Portland and San Francisco were linked by rail. Grain poured into Portland from the Columbia basin and as far away as Montana. By 1890, Portland was one of the world's largest wheat-shipping points.

The first bridges were built across the Willamette in the late 1880s, and the city spread eastward. Portland's population increased fivefold between 1880 and 1900.

During the 20th century, Portland enjoyed steady growth. In 1905 the city felt like throwing a party and hosted a world's fair-type event called the Lewis and Clark Exposition. An estimated three million people attended this centennial celebration of the famed Corps of Discovery expedition, establishing Portland as the gateway to Asia for U.S. business and trade. Already a fast-growing city, Portland positively boomed in the years following the exposition, with its population nearly tripling in just five years. By 1910, Portland had grown to a metropolis of a quarter million people, making it the largest city in the Pacific Northwest.

The world wars brought major economic expansion to Portland, much of it related to resource exploitation. In the early years of the century, logging of the great forests of the Pacific Northwest began in earnest; by World War II, Oregon had become the nation's largest lumber producer, with many wood products passing through Portland's rail- and shipyards.

Also during World War II, military shipyards and light manufacturing brought the city another flood of immigrants. A large number of these new residents were African Americans, the first influx in Oregon's history (it was only in 1926 that the state legislature repealed an 1859 law excluding blacks from the state). The influx of workers to the shipbuilding factories was so great that an entire new city, called Vanport, was created in 1944 to house them—unwisely built on a Columbia River floodplain. In 1948 a wall of water burst through a dike

and destroyed Vanport, killing 18 people and leaving almost 20,000 homeless.

From the 1960s onward, Portland, and western Oregon in general, has seen a new migration of settlers. Educated, idealistic, and politically progressive, these newcomers from the eastern states and California have served to tilt the city's political balance toward a liberal and environmental stance beginning in the 1970s and continuing through today.

PLANNING YOUR TIME

Portland isn't like London or San Francisco, cities filled with loads of top-notch destinations that serve as pilgrimage sights for every visitor. Aside from a handful of unique institutions and sights, Portland is more a city that you explore for its way of life. To capture Portland's potent allure—to "get it"—you need to do some serious hanging out.

The point is that it's the fabric of life in Portland that makes it such a unique city. Portlanders are actively engaged with their city, and there's not a big distinction made between high and low art, lesser or greater lifestyles. As a visitor with a few days to spend in Portland, pick out a local coffeehouse to frequent—you'll soon be chatting with new friends and hearing about hot new bands or private dining clubs that are by invitation only. Go to a reading at Powell's Books and find yourself amidst the local literati. Spend an afternoon on Alberta Street or Mississippi Avenue, the trendy gallery and restaurant areas, and you'll hear the stories of entrepreneurial young idealists who have come to Portland—like so many before them—to pursue their dream at the end of the Oregon Trail.

There aren't six degrees of separation here; everyone knows everyone else. To make your own entrée into the grid, get just a little bit involved and you'll be surprised how quickly the doors open. Chat with your waiter about art galleries, ask for dining advice from an art gallery owner, get to know someone at a brewpub, and soon you'll find yourself holding the keys to unlock the city's doors.

ORIENTATION

Familiarizing yourself with directional reference points will help you smoothly navigate the city. The line of demarcation between north and south in addresses is Burnside Street; between east and west it's the Willamette River. These give reference points for the address prefixes southwest, southeast, north, northwest, and northeast. Avenues run north-south and streets run east-west.

Sights

Portland offers the visitor a wealth of attractions and experiences, from cultural and historic to hands-on and avant-garde. Alongside the built environment are Portland's myriad beloved parks, which range from meticulously tended to sprawling and untamed. Portland has all the amenities you expect from a city, but with a healthy dose of the great outdoors.

Before you arrive, check out **Travel Portland** (1000 SW Broadway, Ste. 2300, Portland, OR, 97205, 503/275-9750 or 800/962-3700, www.travelportland.com) for free maps and their informative magazine-like publication *Travel Portland*. Special deals, such as free overnight parking in selected hotel lots, are often available.

DOWNTOWN

Portland's modern downtown core is located on a broad ledge of land between the north-flowing Willamette River and a steep volcanic ridge just to the west called the West Hills. These "hills" are more accurately called the Tualatin Mountains, and they form a backdrop that towers over 1,000 feet above downtown. The forested West Hills are home to one

© BILL MCRAE

downtown Portland

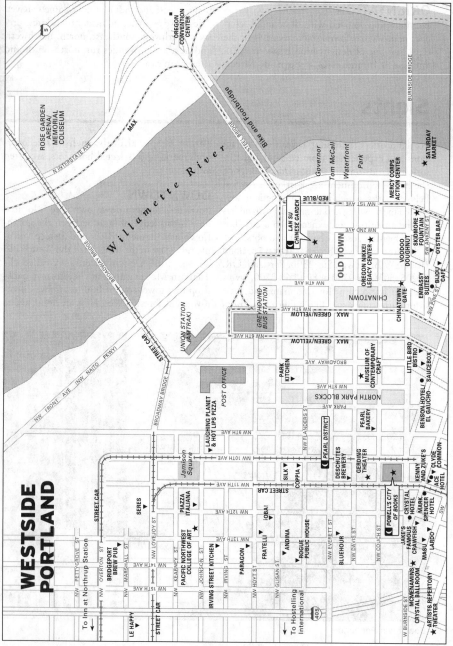

WESTSIDE PORTLAND

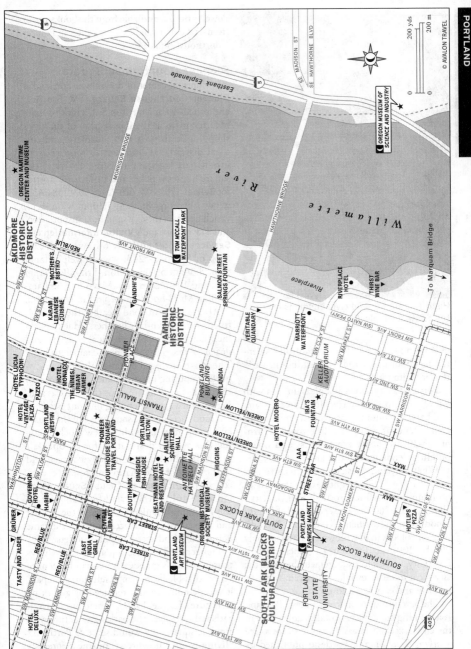

200 yds

200 m

© AVALON TRAVEL

OREGON MUSEUM OF SCIENCE AND INDUSTRY

SE MADISON ST

SE HAWTHORNE BLVD

Willamette River

To Marquam Bridge

Eastbank Esplanade

MORRISON BRIDGE

HAWTHORNE BRIDGE

OREGON MARITIME CENTER AND MUSEUM

SKIDMORE HISTORIC DISTRICT

SW OAKS ST

MOTHER'S BISTRO

SW STARK ST

KARAM LEBANESE CUISINE

GANDHI'S

YAMHILL HISTORIC DISTRICT

TOM McCALL WATERFRONT PARK

NW FRONT AVE

RED/BLUE

SALMON STREET SPRINGS FOUNTAIN

Riverplace

RIVERPLACE HOTEL

THIRST WINE BAR

VERITABLE QUANDARY

MARRIOTT WATERFRONT

SW CLAY ST

KELLER AUDITORIUM

SW MARKET ST

SW FRONT AVE (SW NAITO PKWY)

SW 1ST AVE

SW 2ND AVE

SW 3RD AVE

PIONEER PLACE

HOTEL LUCIA/TYPHOON!

PAZZO

HOTEL MONACO

THE NINES, URBAN FARMER

PORTLANDIA

PORTLAND BUILDING

GREEN/YELLOW

HOTEL MODERA

IRA'S FOUNTAIN

SW 4TH AVE

TRANSIT MALL

HOTEL VINTAGE PLAZA

PORTLAND WESTIN

PIONEER SQUARE

COURTHOUSE SQUARE TRAVEL PORTLAND

PORTLAND HILTON

ARLENE SCHNITZER HALL

GREEN/YELLOW

SW MADISON ST

SW JEFFERSON ST

SW 5TH AVE

STREET CAR

AAA

SW 6TH AVE

PARK AVE

WASHINGTON ST

SW ALDER ST

GOVERNOR HOTEL

HABIBI

RINGSIDE FISH HOUSE

SOUTHPARK

HEATHMAN HOTEL AND RESTAURANT

ANTOINETTE HATFIELD HALL

HIGGINS

SW COLUMBIA AVE

BROADWAY AVE

MAX

GRÜNER

SW MORRISON ST

RED/BLUE

I

TASTY AND ALDER

EAST INDIA GRILL

SW TAYLOR ST

RED/BLUE

CENTRAL LIBRARY

STREET CAR

PORTLAND ART MUSEUM

OREGON HISTORICAL SOCIETY MUSEUM

PARK AVE

SOUTH PARK BLOCKS

SW 9TH AVE

SW 10TH AVE

PORTLAND FARMERS MARKET

SW MILL ST

PORTLAND STATE UNIVERSITY

STREET CAR

MAX

HOTEL DELUXE

SW SALMON ST

SW MAIN ST

SW YAMHILL ST

SW 11TH AVE

SW 12TH AVE

SW 13TH ST

SOUTH PARK BLOCKS CULTURAL DISTRICT

SOUTH PARK BLOCKS

SW MONTGOMERY ST

SW HALL ST

HOTLIPS PIZZA

SW COLLEGE ST

SW JACKSON ST

9TH AVE

405

5

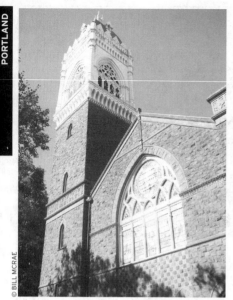

© BILL MCRAE

Historic churches and civic buildings overlook the South Park Blocks.

of Portland's oldest and most beautiful residential neighborhoods and to Washington Park, the city's grandest.

Portland's city center is a pleasant area with lots of green spaces and tree-lined streets. Cafés and bars spill onto the pavement, and a handsome blend of modern office towers, turn-of-the-20th-century storefronts, and office buildings lends architectural interest.

What Portland doesn't have is massive skyscrapers. Building heights are restricted to no more than 400 feet to maintain the city's "human scale" (and to preserve views of Mount Hood from the affluent West Hills). In addition, city blocks in downtown Portland are only 200 by 200 feet (by contrast, blocks in Salt Lake City are 780 feet square) which makes the city seem more accessible, pedestrian-friendly, and fun and easy to explore.

The best introduction to downtown Portland is a walking tour that also takes advantage of the city's excellent mass transit. Ask for a free *Walking Tour Map* of Portland published by

Powell's Books, available from the bookstore or from Travel Portland's visitor center in Pioneer Courthouse Square.

Pioneer Courthouse Square

The nominal center of downtown Portland is **Pioneer Courthouse Square** (SW 6th Ave. and Broadway at Morrison St.), a block-square redbrick plaza at the intersection of the city's shopping, transportation, business, and cultural districts. In addition to serving as an urban park and entertainment venue, the square houses a ticket and information office for **TriMet** (701 SW 6th Ave., 503/238-7433, www.trimet.org, 8:30am-5:30pm Mon.-Fri.), which operates the city's public transportation, and Travel Portland's **Visitor Information and Services Center** (701 SW 6th Ave., 503/275-8355 or 877/678-5263, www.travelportland. com, 8:30am-5:30pm Mon.-Fri., 10am-4pm Sat., and 10am-2pm Sun. May-Oct.; 8:30am-5:30pm Mon.-Fri., 10am-4pm Sat. Nov.-Apr.).

Always busy, in good weather the square is filled with brown-bag lunchers, Hacky Sack-kickers, chess players, political activists, and dozens of free spirits that defy characterization. The square is ringed by fanciful columns supporting nothing in particular, and a portion of the plaza is a hillside of steps that serve as seating or stairways, depending on your needs. A few food carts line the south edge of the square and many more are within a few blocks, making this a good destination for an open-air lunch. In summer, free midday concerts add to the zest; for information on square events, contact the **Pioneer Courthouse Square office** (503/223-1613). A waterfall fountain (not always working) flanks the doors to the TriMet and Travel Portland offices; through the same doors you'll find access to public toilets.

Pioneer Courthouse Square wasn't always thus: Portland's grandest Victorian hotel once sat on this block. When it fell into disrepair, it was demolished and replaced by a parking structure. In the 1980s, when momentum gathered to replace the parking structure with a public square that would serve as Portland's "living room," downtown business interests

H&M. The lower level of Pioneer Place features a food court with a wide array of fast-food concessions.

The South Park Blocks Cultural District

Southwest of the square, paralleling Broadway, is the **South Park Blocks Cultural District.** Many of the city's cultural institutions open onto the South Park Blocks, a delightful thread of tree- and statuary-filled greenways established in the 1850s and now running through the midst of downtown. The stands of American elms found here (and in the Pearl District's North Park Blocks) are among the largest remaining in North America, most of the rest having succumbed to Dutch elm disease.

Strolling the lanes through the South Park Blocks, which are flanked by many of Portland's most important museums, civic buildings, and early landmark churches, evokes memories of European parks, except that here the pigeons perch on statues of U.S. presidents Abraham Lincoln and Teddy Roosevelt instead of Napoleon. What makes this very civilized scene notable is that Portland's founders set this stage in 1852, when wilderness stretched in every direction for thousands of miles.

Twice weekly from spring to fall—on Saturday and Wednesday—the **Portland Farmers Market** fills the South Park Blocks with the agricultural bounty of the Willamette Valley. The farmers market is also a great option for a casual bite to eat—many food vendors purvey freshly prepared food in addition to selling fruits, vegetables, cheese, and meats. Also opening onto the park is the multibuilding Portland Art Museum. The southern edges of the parks dissolve into Portland State University, an urban campus that boasts the state's largest higher-education enrollment.

PORTLAND CENTER FOR THE PERFORMING ARTS

Backing up to the South Park Blocks are two units of the **Portland Center for the Performing Arts** (503/248-4335, www.pcpa. com), including the ornate **Arlene Schnitzer**

© BILL MCRAE

The Arlene Schnizter Concert Hall and the Antoinette Hatfield Hall anchor downtown at Broadway and Main Street.

took a dim view of losing parking spaces and blocked park funding. Grassroots support for the square resulted in a program that encouraged citizens to buy and personalize the bricks that eventually built the square. As you walk across the square, look down to read the names of the people whose contributions made the park possible.

The "courthouse" alluded to in the square's name is just east across 6th Avenue. **Pioneer Courthouse** (555 SW Yamhill St., no public facilities) is the oldest public building in the state, constructed between 1869 and 1873.

Pioneer Courthouse Square is also at ground zero for downtown shopping. Immediately west, across Broadway, is indigenous-to-the-Pacific-Northwest clothier Nordstrom; across the corner at Morrison Street and 6th Avenue is Macy's; and one block east along Morrison or Yamhill Streets is Pioneer Place, a two-section upscale shopping development that is linked by a skywalk to fashion bargains at

Concert Hall (1037 SW Broadway), home to the Oregon Symphony. This jewel-box concert venue was once a 1920s vaudeville hall, but you'd never know it after a 1980s makeover turned the neglected theater into the city's premier concert space. Directly across Main Street is the **Antoinette Hatfield Hall** (SW Broadway at Main), with two theaters and a soaring lobby topped by a confetti-like glass dome. The Schnitzer Concert Hall isn't usually open for casual visits, so you'll need a concert ticket to see its glittering interior, but the Center for the Performing Arts is open all day and during the evening when performances are scheduled; the lobby bar makes a nice spot for a drink.

OREGON HISTORICAL SOCIETY MUSEUM

The **Oregon Historical Society Museum** (1230 SW Park Ave., 503/222-1741, www.ohs. org, 10am-5pm Mon.-Sat., noon-5pm Sun., $11 adults, $9 seniors and students, $5 children ages 6-18), holds the collection of the Oregon Historical Society. The museum tells the rich story of the state's Native American and settlement heritage; the combined gift shop and bookstore is a good place to pick up quality gifts.

◖ Portland Art Museum

The **Portland Art Museum** (1219 SW Park Ave., 503/226-2811, www.portlandartmuseum.org, 10am-5pm Tues.-Wed. and Sat., 10am-8pm Thurs.-Fri., noon-5pm Sun., $15 adults, $12 seniors 55 and older and students ages 18 and older, free children ages 17 and under) encompasses two grand structures along the South Park Blocks, the original Pietro Belluschi-designed building from 1932 and the adjacent and imposing Portland Masonic Temple, which together offer 112,000 square feet of galleries housing a collection of 42,000 objects. It's the oldest art museum on the West Coast (from 1892) and houses Oregon's most significant art collection, including a small but engaging collection of European Old Masters and Impressionists and a noteworthy Asian art collection. In 2001, the museum acquired the private collection of renowned New York art critic Clement Greenberg, which is on permanent display in the Center for Modern and Contemporary Art. The Pacific Northwest Native Art collection is also excellent. At least one major traveling exhibition is presented most of the time (usually with separate admission).

Central Library

Portland is a city of readers, with the busiest library system in the United States. A landmark for bibliophiles, Multnomah County Library system's **Central Library** (801 SW 10th Ave., 503/988-5123, www.multcolib. org, 10am-8pm Mon., noon-8 Tues.-Wed., 10am-6pm Thurs.-Sat., 10am-5pm Sun.) is an architecturally stunning renovation of a 1913 building designed by Alfred Doyle (architect of the Benson Hotel and the U.S. Bank downtown) that houses an accessible (60 percent open stacks) collection of books, CDs, recordings, and periodicals. Climb the sweeping staircases to the top floor to get a sense of the scale of this building—three stories have never seemed so monumental. Once on the third floor, browse the Collins Gallery, which displays book-related art exhibits. Per capita this is the most-used central branch of a public library in the nation.

For travelers, the library offers a selection of national and international newspapers, plus free use of Internet-linked computers (ask a librarian for a guest pass to log on). Free wireless Internet is also available. You'll need to be a local resident to check out materials, but otherwise the library's full facilities are available to all.

Portland Building

Raymond Kaskey's **Portlandia,** a statue that is said to symbolize the city, ranks right behind the Statue of Liberty as the world's largest hammered copper sculpture. Located outside Michael Graves's postmodern **Portland Building** on SW 5th Avenue between Main Street and Madison Street, the crouching female figure holding a trident re-creates the Lady of Commerce on the city seal. Inside the

© BILL MCRAE

Salmon Street Springs Fountain in Tom McCall Waterfront Park

Portland Building on the second floor is the **Portland Public Art Gallery** (8am-5:30pm Mon.-Fri.), operated by the **Regional Arts and Culture Council, or RACC** (503/823-5111, www.racc.org), where you can also pick up a walking tour map of the city's murals, fountains, sculptures, statues, and other public art pieces.

Tom McCall Waterfront Park

Tom McCall Waterfront Park is named for the governor credited with helping to reclaim Oregon's rivers. In the early 1970s the park's grassy shore replaced Harbor Drive, a freeway that impeded access to the Willamette River. Today, the park is frequently the scene of summer festivals, while the wide paved riverside esplanade is a favorite for joggers, cyclists, and strolling families.

Begin your introduction to mile-long Tom McCall Waterfront Park at **RiverPlace,** an attractive string of restaurants, specialty shops, and boating facilities overlooking

the Willamette River in the shadow of the Marquam Bridge. Follow the paved riverside walkway north to the **Salmon Street Springs Fountain** at the base of Salmon Street. The fountain water's ebb and flow are meant to evoke the rhythms of the city and provide a refreshing shower on a hot day.

North along the seawall is the sternwheeler USS *Portland,* which houses the **Oregon Maritime Center and Museum** (at the foot of SW Pine, 503/224-7724, www.oregonmaritimemuseum.org, 11am-4pm Wed. and Fri.-Sat., $7 adults, $5 seniors, $4 students ages 13-18, $3 children ages 6-12). The museum offers a window into the fascinating maritime heritage of Portland and the Columbia and Willamette River systems, and it features ship models, historic diving equipment, and other ship artifacts.

Farther north in the shadow of the Burnside Bridge is the home of the **Portland Saturday Market** and the **Battleship *Oregon* Memorial,** which commemorates a famed 1893 fighting ship named after the state; the ship's block juts out of the grass.

Old Town and the Skidmore Fountain Historic District

From the 1870s through the 1920s, **Old Town** was the heart of Victorian-era Portland. After a disastrous fire in 1873 burned Portland's original wood-built commercial district, the city was rebuilt with multistory brick buildings, many faced with cast-iron facades. Iron could be cast in myriad forms, and the most popular in this period were Italianate columns and what look like elaborately carved plinths and capitals.

Portland's original harbor area fell on hard times after commercial shipping traffic moved to docks farther downriver and passenger trains replaced boats. The center of town moved away from the riverfront, and many of the glorious old buildings began falling to the wrecking ball. For much of the 20th century, Old Town was Portland's skid row, and homeless shelters and hotels for itinerants are still part of the mix, but the remaining old storefronts and

PORTLAND ARCHITECTURE

Portland has many notable buildings, both old and new. From its beginnings in the 1840s to the 1870s, Portland was built mostly of wood. However, after a series of fires in the 1870s, which together burned much of the original downtown, Portland was rebuilt in brick and stone. By this time the merchant kings of Portland felt like displaying their affluence, and a brand-new and very glamorous city went up between 1880 and 1915. A contemporary traveler commented in the 1890s that Portland had the "finest commercial street west of St. Louis." At the time, the center of the city was along SW Front Avenue (now SW Naito Parkway). However, little of this area's very ornate architecture survives except in photos, having been leveled in the 1940s and 1950s to build freeways along the Willamette River (which were removed in the 1970s to form Waterfront Park).

However, many examples of beautiful historic—and modern—architecture remain in Portland. From Pioneer Courthouse Square you can see a number of notable buildings. On SW Morrison Street between 6th Avenue and Broadway is the **American Bank Building,** built in 1913 from a design by famed architect A. W. Doyle. Doyle is also responsible for the design of the building just to the east, the block-square **Meier & Frank Building** (now Macy's and the Nines Hotel), built in 1909. Both these buildings (and the **Jackson Tower/Oregon Journal Building,** across the Square at Broadway and SW Yamhill Street, 1912) are faced in white-glazed terra-cotta tile. These massive gleaming white buildings were responsible for Portland's onetime moniker "the White City."

Immediately east of the Square is the **Pioneer Courthouse** itself. Begun in 1869, it's the oldest public building in Oregon and the second-oldest west of the Mississippi. Kitty-corner to the square to the southwest is one of Portland's most pleasing modern buildings, the

27-story **Fox Tower,** built in 2000 with a curving facade that looks like a cruise ship.

North on Broadway are two other very handsome historic structures. At SW Washington Street and Broadway is the **Vintage Plaza Hotel,** a marvelous example of late Victorian (1894) Romanesque, built of local basalt and red brick. The **U.S. National Bank Building** (1917), at SW Broadway and Stark Street (main entrance on SW 6th Ave.), is a grand neoclassical structure faced with 54-foot Corinthian columns. Just around the corner, at SW 6th Avenue and Burnside Street, is **U.S. Bankcorp Tower,** at 43 stories the city's second-tallest building. Commonly called "Big Pink" for its pink granite and rose glass facade, it's one of Portland's most distinctive buildings.

A stroll through Portland's Old Town reveals a number of significant historic structures, including lots of redbrick warehouses, cast-iron facades, handsome storefronts in terra-cotta tile, and buildings made from locally quarried stone. The **Dekum Building** (SW 3rd Ave. and Washington St.), with its massive basalt columns, arches, and gargoyles, is a prime example of Richardson Romanesque from 1891. The striking **Haseltine Building** (1893) at 133 SW 2nd Avenue was once a hansom cab stable, its arches open for the to-ing and fro-ing of carriages.

A showcase of historic renovation (it had better be!) is the three-building home of the University of Oregon's Department of Architecture, between West Burnside Street and SW Couch Street between SW Naito Parkway and SW 1st Avenue. When workers removed the structure's faux-brick facade, they uncovered an elaborate cast-iron structure that had been hidden from view since a 1950s-era makeover. Portland has the second-largest inventory of cast-iron-fronted buildings (a popular building style in the 1880s) in the country.

© BILL MCRAE

Oregon Maritime Center and Musuem

once-grand hotels are increasingly being revitalized with shops, galleries, and professional offices in search of cheap rent.

Today, even though there's still a scruffy edge to Old Town, many of the city's hottest nightclubs and bars are here. A word of caution: Old Town is something of a nexus of drugs and crime. Keep your eyes open and steer clear of any questionable-looking activity. That said, the area is an open-air museum of historic architecture, including lots of redbrick warehouses, cast-iron facades, handsome storefronts in terra-cotta tile, and buildings made from locally quarried stone.

At the heart of Old Town is **Skidmore Fountain** (SW 1st Ave. and SW Ankeny St.). Built at great expense with a bequest from an early Portland dentist, it was intended as a source of water for "horses, men, and dogs." At the time, the fountain stood at the confluence of five major streets and was flanked by the finest buildings in the city, including Portland's first opera house. The inscription on the fountain is nearly prophetic to modern Portlanders

drawn here by the good life: "Good citizens are the riches of a city."

Just north of the Skidmore Fountain is the **Mercy Corps Action Center** (28 SW 1st Ave., 503/896-5002, www.actioncenter.org, 11am-5pm Mon.-Fri., 11am-4pm Sat.), where you can learn about many of the projects sponsored by Mercy Corps, a Portland-based aid organization. The displays and interactive exhibits are quite engaging (check out the eyeglasses that allow the wearer to adjust the prescription), and visitors can often listen in on workshops for students and adults.

Portland Aerial Tram

The **Portland Aerial Tram,** opened in 2006, was built to link the main campus of Oregon Health and Science University (OHSU) on Marquam Hill with its facilities in the South Waterfront development. Initially controversial due to massive cost overruns in construction (the tram cost four times the original projected budget), the tram's pod-shaped transit car aloft over the South Waterfront quickly became part of the city's landscape, and riding the tram is a popular tourist activity.

The tram travels 3,300 linear feet at 22 mph, rising 500 feet for the three-minute trip over I-5, the Lair Hill neighborhood, and SW Terwilliger Parkway. Round-trip tickets are $4; the tram is not part of the TriMet system, so bus transfers and MAX or streetcar tickets are not valid on the tram. However, TriMet monthly or annual passes are honored. Tickets are available from ticket machines at the lower terminal and are checked only upon boarding at the lower terminal.

The tram operates 5:30am-9:30pm Monday-Friday, 9am-5pm Saturday year-round, and additionally 1pm-5pm Sunday mid-May-mid-September.

The easiest way to catch the tram is to ride the Portland Streetcar to the SW Moody and Gibbs station (you can also drive from Macadam Blvd. by following signs to South Waterfront and turning at SW Curry St.). When you're aloft, views over the city and to the surrounding volcanic peaks are spectacular. Unless you have business up here or are hiking the **4T Trail,** there's not a lot to do once you get to the top, although there's a small art gallery to visit, and food is available at five different hospital refectories. Most people simply catch the next tram back down and take in the views in reverse order.

You can also ride the No. 8 bus from downtown to OHSU and catch the tram from the top of its route; you aren't required to purchase a ticket for the ride downhill.

WASHINGTON PARK

The crown jewel of Portland's magnificent park system is **Washington Park,** which encompasses 130 acres of forest, formal gardens, and such civic institutions as the Oregon Zoo, International Rose Test Garden, Portland Japanese Garden, World Forestry Center, and the Portland Children's Museum. Adjacent to the park is the Hoyt Arboretum.

The park had its beginnings in 1871, and in its early years it was modeled on European parks, with winding drives, shady walkways, fountains, noble statuary, formal plantings, lawns, and ornamental flower displays. At the time, most of Portland's population lived downhill from the park, and the park entrances were from below. In the days before automobiles, visitors would follow footpaths or take the cable car up Park Avenue to the park (TriMet bus 63, with weekday service, still follows this route). This is still the best way to experience the Victorian-era park in the way that it was designed.

If you're driving, biking, or walking, take Park Place west from SW 23rd Avenue and wind up the hill. The road passes a number of fountains and statues as it loops upward.

In the midst of a central drive at the entrance to the park, the **Lewis and Clark Memorial** is a 34-foot rectangular granite pillar bearing the state seals of Oregon, Washington, Montana, and Idaho—the Pacific Northwestern states through which the Corps of Discovery passed in 1805-1806. Nearby is the **Washington Park Fountain,** also known as the Chiming Fountain for the sound the water makes as it cascades from one bronze pan to another.

The statue of **Sacagawea** holding her young son Jean-Baptiste (a.k.a. Pompey) was unveiled in 1905 during the Lewis and Clark Exposition, and in attendance were noted suffragists and writers Susan B. Anthony, Abigail Scott Duniway, and Eva Emery Dye. The statue was purchased with funds raised by Portland-area women, and its inscription reads, "Erected by the women of the United States in memory of the only woman in the Lewis & Clark expedition, and in honor of the pioneer mother of Oregon."

Just uphill and to the north is the statue *Coming of the White Man,* which depicts two Native Americans gazing eastward, as if toward the influx of Oregon Trail pioneers. The older of the two figures represents Chief Multnomah, leader of the indigenous people that lived in the Portland area when the first European settlers arrived.

In a loop of Park Place just below the rose gardens stands the **Oregon Holocaust Memorial,** dedicated in 2004. The memorial consists of a cobblestone square that represents European town squares, plus stone placards that relate a brief history of the Holocaust. Next to the wall is a vault beneath which is buried soil and ash from the six World War II concentration camps where most of the Nazi-led killing took place: Chelmno, Treblinka, Sobibór, Belzec, Majdanek, and Auschwitz-Birkenau.

◖ International Rose Test Garden

Encompassing 4.5 acres of roses, manicured lawns, other formal gardens, and an outdoor concert venue, the **International Rose Test Garden** is wedged onto the steep slopes of the West Hills in Washington Park. In addition to intoxicating scents and incredible floral displays, the garden also offers the classic view of Portland—Mount Hood rising above the downtown office towers. Bring a camera.

Portland's moderate climate is a perfect habitat for roses, and as early as the 1880s society women held rose exhibitions. Portland's reputation as the City of Roses was cemented in 1905 during the Lewis and Clark Centennial Exposition. In anticipation of three million visitors to this world's fair-type event, the city gave away thousands of roses for planting, particularly the pink cabbage rose *Mme. Caroline Testout,* which can still be seen outside older Portland homes. When the exposition opened, Portland had 200 miles of rose-bordered streets to impress visitors.

However, Portland's iconic rose garden in Washington Park was born of World War I. After combat began in 1915, *Oregonian* editor and rose enthusiast Jesse A. Currey convinced city officials to establish a rose garden to serve as a safe haven for European hybrid roses, as Curry feared that these prized plants would be destroyed during bombings and warfare. After Portland established its civic rose garden, appreciative rose growers from across Europe sent samples of their roses to Portland for safekeeping.

In 1940 the rose garden became an official testing site for the All-America Rose Selection (AARS), one of 24 gardens nationwide to test new rose varieties for plant habit, vigor, disease resistance, color, flower production, form, foliage, and fragrance. Today, the rose garden features over 6,800 rose bushes representing 557 varieties, both old and new. A charming annex to the rose garden is the **Shakespearean Garden,** which includes only herbs, trees, and flowers mentioned in Shakespeare's plays.

From June through the third Saturday in September, free tours of the rose garden are led by trained volunteers at 11:30am and 1pm Tuesday and 1pm Thursday, Saturday, and Sunday. Meet at the sign outside the Rose Garden Store. Donations are gladly accepted for the tour.

Just above the rose gardens are a set of tennis courts, beautifully situated beneath towering firs, and up a flight of steps is the terminus for the 30-inch narrow-gauge Washington Park and Zoo Railway, which links these two popular family destinations with a trip through Washington Park's dense forests; note that riders who take the train from the rose gardens must pay zoo admission in addition to train fare.

Just beyond the rose gardens is the **Rose Garden Children's Park,** a large and elaborate play area with quite fantastic play structures.

◖ Portland Japanese Garden

The beautiful **Portland Japanese Garden** (611 SW Kingston Ave., 503/223-1321, www.japanesegarden.com, noon-7pm Mon., 9am-7pm Tues.-Fri., 9am-9pm Sat., 9am-7pm Sun. Apr.-Sept., noon-4pm Mon., 10am-4pm Tues.-Sun., Oct.-Mar., $9.50 adults, $7.75 seniors and college students with ID, $6.75 children ages 6-17) is just up the slope from the rose gardens. The Portland Japanese Garden is a magical five-acre Eden with tumbling water, pools of koi, bonsai, and elaborately manicured shrubs and trees. There are five separate gardens linked by winding paths: a Strolling Pond Garden, a Tea Garden, a Natural Garden, a Flat Garden, and a Sand and Stone Garden. As much a place for meditation and contemplation as for viewing plants, the Japanese Garden was designed and constructed in the 1960s by renowned Japanese landscape architecture professor Takuma Tono.

In 1988, Nobuo Matsunaga, the Japanese ambassador to the United States, stated that this is "the most beautiful and authentic Japanese garden in the world outside of Japan."

From the rose gardens, you can walk up the short but relatively steep trail that leads to the Japanese Garden, or hop on the free open-air shuttle that climbs up the hill every 10 minutes or so.

Oregon Zoo

The **Oregon Zoo** (4001 SW Canyon Rd., 503/226-1561, www.oregonzoo.org, 9am-6pm daily Memorial Day-Labor Day, 9am-4pm daily Mar.-late May and early Sept.-Dec., 10am-4pm daily Jan.-Feb., $11.50 visitors ages 12-64, $10 seniors, $8.50 children ages 3-11) has exhibits representing various geographic areas of the world, including African rainforests and savannahs, Amazon flooded forests, and Pacific Northwest woodlands; a series of major expansions from 2014-2019 will see new elephant, rhino, primate, and polar bear habitats plus an exhibit dedicated to condors of the Columbia. The zoo collection contains over 2,000 individual animals representing 260 species of birds, mammals, reptiles, amphibians, and invertebrates. The zoo is especially noted for its elephant program, which has one of the most successful breeding programs in the world. The zoo features two year-round eating establishments, a series of educational events for children, and summertime concerts. The zoo is easily reached from the Blue and Red MAX light rail lines or, on weekdays, via the number 63 bus from downtown.

If you're planning on visiting both the zoo and the International Rose Test Garden, consider linking these two family-favorite sites along the 30-inch narrow-gauge **Washington Park and Zoo Railway** (503/226-1561, 10:30am-5:30pm daily Memorial Day-Labor Day weather permitting, $5, children under age 3 free), a two-mile rail service through Washington Park's dense forests. Since the train's upper station is within the zoo precincts, riders who board the train at the rose gardens must also purchase admission to the zoo.

The train also runs during the holiday ZooLights season, from the Friday after Thanksgiving through the Sunday after New Year's Day. During this time, you can visit the zoo with the added enhancement of a holiday light display with over one million LED lights. ZooLights trains run 5pm-8pm Sunday-Thursday and 5pm-8:30pm Friday and Saturday. You can also visit the zoo via public transportation or private car during the same hours.

The zoo train will be closed through much of 2014 to rebuild the rail line in order to accommodate an expanded elephant compound. The trains are expected to be running in time for ZooLights 2014.

Portland Children's Museum

Adjacent to the zoo is the **Portland Children's Museum** (4015 SW Canyon Rd., 503/223-6500, www.portlandcm.org, 9am-5pm Fri.-Wed., 9am-8pm Thurs. Mar. 1-Labor Day, 9am-5pm Tues.-Sun. Labor Day-Feb., $10 adults and children, $9 military and seniors age 55 and older), featuring events and activities for kids aged six months to 10 years old. Hands-on exhibits appeal to kids' appetite for fun and learning as well as their boundless energy: Visitors can play at construction in Building Bridgetown, excavate rubber "gravel" in the Dig Pit, or just have fun in the Playopolis playground (both indoor and outdoor). Two studios offer clay and other materials for a small fee for creations that can be taken home, and the Baby Garden provides a place for the littlest guests to romp. A variety of storytelling, music, and movement draws young audiences in the Play It Again Theater.

World Forestry Center Discovery Museum

The 20,000-square-foot **World Forestry Center Discovery Museum** (4033 SW Canyon Rd., 503/228-1367, www.worldforestry.org, 10am-5pm daily, $9 adults, $8 seniors, $6 children ages 3-18), near the zoo in Washington Park, offers hands-on interactive exhibits that teach about trees of the world and the sustainability of forests. There are two floors of exhibits, with the first focusing on the forests of the Pacific Northwest and the impact of forestry choices on the environment. The second floor exhibits focus on other forested regions of the world as well as the natural and human history of ecosystems in Siberia, the Amazon, China, and South Africa.

Vietnam Veterans of Oregon Memorial

Just beyond the World Forestry Center is a series of spiraling black granite slabs that are inscribed with the names of all the Oregon residents who died in Vietnam or were declared missing in action. The names are contrasted with a timeline of Oregon events from the same period, providing a poignant contrast and conjuring up images of the turbulent Vietnam War era.

Hoyt Arboretum

Along the crest of the West Hills above Washington Park is **Hoyt Arboretum** (4000 SW Fairview Blvd., 503/865-8733, www.hoytarboretum.org, 6am-10pm daily, free), with 12 miles of trails winding through an expansive 187-acre tree garden boasting the world's largest collection of conifers. The arboretum's collection is made up of over 8,000 individual trees and plants that represent over 1,000 species from all corners of the globe. Most of the collection is linked by trails and labeled with botanical names. The trees throughout are presented in taxonomically organized groups, surrounded by other members of the same order, family, and genus; in other words, oaks are with oaks, and maples are with other maples. However, the arboretum's landscape feels natural, with alternating open meadows and groves of trees. Visitors should stop by the visitors center and pick up a trail map before setting out. A one-mile trail is paved and suitable for wheelchairs.

NORTHWEST

Northwest Portland is in reality an entire quadrant of the city, but when most Portlanders talk about the Northwest, they are talking about a rather compact set of neighborhoods just to the north of downtown—in particular, between Burnside Street, which divides north from south in Portland street parlance, and the lofty flanks of the West Hills. These neighborhoods include Chinatown (a northern section of Old Town), the Pearl District, and NW 21st and 23rd Avenues. There aren't hard-and-fast boundaries between these areas—in fact as all these areas gentrify it's difficult to segment them one from the other.

Old Town/Chinatown

From the 1870s through the 1910s, the entire Willamette River waterfront was the city's harbor, an extended area now called **Old Town.** By the 1870s the more northerly neighborhoods of Old Town, roughly bounded by NW 2nd and 4th Avenues and Burnside and Everett Streets, became known as **Chinatown,** an enclave of historic redbrick buildings that was home to Chinese and Japanese immigrants who came to Oregon seeking work and then made their homes here.

© BILL MCRAE

the Chinatown Gate

Portland's historic Chinatown is nowhere near as vibrant as those in Seattle or Vancouver, though it was once larger than either. Chinatown still has about 20 Chinese American-owned businesses, including a number of restaurants; several are worth stopping in for 1930s time-warp decor and mostly Americanized Chinese food.

The first Chinese immigrants moved to Oregon in the 1850s, working at manual labor first in lumber camps, gold mines, and later on the railroads. Many eventually settled in Portland's Chinatown, where they operated stores, laundries, and other businesses. Then as now, the presence of low-paid "foreign" labor was seen as a threat by many European-bred Americans, and the federal Chinese Exclusion Act of 1882 prevented further immigration to the United States from China. At its peak, around 1890, Portland's Chinatown had a population of around 5,000, second in size only to San Francisco's. Of course, the need for inexpensive labor remained after the anti-Chinese immigration law took effect, and labor recruiters began to tap workers from Japan, who could legally immigrate. As the Chinese in Chinatown grew old or moved on, they were replaced by Japanese people, and Chinatown became **Japantown**; by 1940, Portland's Japantown had over 100 Japanese-owned businesses and a population of some 3,500 Japanese and Japanese American residents.

Portland's thriving Japanese community came to a sudden end in 1942 when President Franklin D. Roosevelt issued Executive Order 9066, leading to the evacuation and internment of thousands of Japanese American citizens. Almost overnight, Japantown became a ghost town. With all the Japanese gone, Chinese businesses moved back in, and the area once again became known as Chinatown; but in many ways, this neighborhood has never recovered. (Today's Asian community in Portland can now be found along SE 82nd Avenue.)

Wandering the streets of Old Town/Chinatown alone late at night is probably not a good idea, but traveling safely to and from the restaurants and clubs is easy. Taxis are usually easily found in this entertainment hotbed, MAX light rail trains run along 1st, 5th, and 6th Avenues, and buses pass along 5th and 6th Avenues and on Everett Street.

OREGON NIKKEI LEGACY CENTER

For insights into Portland's immigrant Japanese community and the internment, visit the **Oregon Nikkei Legacy Center** (121 NW 2nd Ave., 503/224-1458, www.oregonnikkei.org, 11am-3pm Tues.-Sat., noon-3pm Sun., $5 adults, $3 seniors), in the heart of old Japantown; it is one of the most fascinating small museums in Portland.

CHINATOWN GATE

Presented as a gesture of goodwill from the Chinese community to the city of Portland, the colorful **Chinatown Gate** (W. Burnside St. and SW 4th Ave.) is the largest of its kind in the United States and marks the entrance to historic Chinatown. Dedicated in 1986, the Chinatown Gate comprises five roofs, 64 dragons, and two huge lions. Notice that the male lion is on the right with a ball under his foot, while the female has a cub under her paw. Also note the red lampposts along Chinatown streets. These are traditional Portland gaslight posts painted red, but they have the street names on them written in Chinese.

◖ LAN SU CHINESE GARDEN

Colorful in a different way, the **Lan Su Chinese Garden** (239 NW Everett St., 503/228-8131, www.lansugarden.org, 10am-6pm daily Apr.-Oct., 10am-5pm daily Nov.-Mar., 9.50 adults, $8.50 seniors, $7 students ages 6-18 and college students with ID) is a formal Chinese garden built in the style of the Ming Dynasty. The block-square green space is the result of a joint effort between two famed gardening centers, Portland and its Chinese sister city, Suzhou. Over 60 landscape designers and craftspeople from Suzhou lived and worked in Portland for a year to complete the gardens, which are the largest traditional Chinese gardens in the United States. Nearly all the materials and tools used were also brought from

China, including roof and floor tiles, all of the hand-carved woodwork, the latticed windows, and over 500 tons of swiss cheese-like Taihu granite boulders.

The gardens are designed to replicate a scholar's garden, a specific form of Suzhou garden meant to display a miniaturization of nature, like a living form of Chinese landscape painting.

The gardens are a masterwork of concision, with an 8,000-square-foot lake, a teahouse and tower, two courtyards, carved screens, and tiled mosaics. The garden is also home to more than 90 specimen trees, many rare and unusual shrubs and perennials, and signature collections of unusual plants native to China. It's a magical place, and although it's bordered by downtown streets, it's seemingly a world away. The tea shop keeps the same hours as the gardens and is a delightful spot for a light lunch. On summer Tuesdays the gardens sponsor a series of evening concerts; see the website for details.

© BILL MCRAE

Union Station is one of the oldest operating train stations in the country.

UNION STATION

To the north, Old Town/Chinatown ends at **Union Station** (800 NW 6th Ave.), the glorious Italianate rail station that still serves as Portland's Amtrak depot. The station has been in continuous use since it was built in 1896 and is the second-oldest still-operating train station in the country. With its terra-cotta tile roof and 150-foot campanile with a four-sided Seth Thomas clock, this is one of Portland's most beloved landmarks. Step into the marble-walled waiting room to admire the cool neon signs, art deco lettering, and vaulted ceilings, all part of a 1930s interior redesign.

North Park Blocks

Established in the 1860s as an extension of the South Park Blocks, the leafy confines of the **North Park Blocks** (bounded by NW Park Ave., 8th Ave., W. Burnside St., and NW Glisan St.) now serve as the front yard and a dog-walk destination for Pearl District dwellers. As with the South Park Blocks, the stand of American elms includes some of the largest remaining in the nation.

In the block just north of Burnside is a bronze sculpture called *Da Tung & Xi'an Bao Ba* or "Universal Peace and Baby Elephant." The sculpture is modeled after a wine pitcher from the late Shang Dynasty (circa 1200-1100 BC) and presents a young elephant standing on his father's back. The elaborate surface decoration features depictions of birds, animals, and atmospherics from ancient Chinese mythology.

The park also contains an elaborate children's playground, basketball and bocce ball courts, and lots of benches for contemplation and people watching.

Museum of Contemporary Craft

In the streets surrounding the North Park Blocks is the city's greatest concentration of commercial art galleries. A stroll along NW 9th Avenue reveals nearly a dozen galleries, and adjacent to the North Park Blocks at NW Davis Street and NW 8th Avenue is the DeSoto Building, once an automobile showroom. Today, it has been converted into a hub for art galleries, including three of Portland's top retail galleries, and the **Museum of Contemporary Craft** (724 NW Davis St., 503/223-2654, www.museumofcontemporarycraft.org, 11am-6pm Tues.-Sat., 11am-8pm first Thurs. of month, $4 adults, $3 seniors and students ages 13 and older), a showcase for local crafts. The museum has two floors of galleries with exhibits that change monthly and a gift shop (no admission fee) filled with the works of over 100 regional craftspeople in ceramics, jewelry, glass, wood, metal, fiber, and mixed media.

◖ Pearl District

For longtime Portlanders, few urban transformations have been more incredible than that of the **Pearl District.** This area, roughly bounded by NW Broadway, NW 14th Avenue, Burnside Street, and Overton Street, was until very recently a wasteland of moldering warehouses, abandoned rail yards, and moribund light industry. In a short 20 years the area has been utterly transformed into one of the city's most exclusive residential neighborhoods, with newly paved streets (until the gentrification, this antique area still boasted many paving-stone streets—the stones are still there on parts of NW Kearney St.) lined with upscale furniture and home decor boutiques, fine restaurants, and art galleries.

Even though the boundaries of the Pearl District are ever-expanding to the north, a good place to begin your exploration is along NW 10th Avenue. At the corner of West Burnside Street and 10th Avenue is the mother ship of **Powell's Books,** one of the nation's largest bookstores and a classic place for Portlanders to spend rainy weekday afternoons. Continuing north on 11th Avenue, you pass the castellated **Gerding Theater,** a former armory and home to Portland Center Stage. If you're looking to decorate your home, the myriad furniture and decor stores along NW Glisan Street between 10th and 14th Avenues ought to provide inspiration.

If you're wondering why Portland has so many art galleries, perhaps a stop at **Pacific Northwest College of Art** (1241 NW Johnson St., 503/226-4391, www.pnca.edu) will explain. Since 1909 this art school, originally housed by the art museum, has provided a hands-on education for multiple generations of artists, many of whom remain in Portland to pursue their careers. The lobby of this converted warehouse contains two art galleries, and student art is usually on display in the central atrium.

Farther north, bounded by NW 10th and 11th Avenues and Johnson and Kearney Streets, is **Jamison Square,** a public park with a fountain that's a favorite destination for the neighborhood's children to get wet and cool down. The park is named for a well-loved local art dealer, and it contains some striking public sculpture.

From downtown, the Pearl District is easily reached on the Portland Streetcar, which travels along NW 10th and 11th Avenues.

NW 21st and 23rd Avenues

Sometimes referred to as Nob Hill, the lovely Victorian neighborhoods around NW 21st and 23rd Avenues represent an island of upscale dining and shopping. Victorian homes have been remodeled into boutiques to join stylish clothing shops, bookstores, restaurants, and theaters. Generally speaking, NW 21st Avenue has the greater number of restaurants while NW 23rd Avenue has more shops—a mix of upper-end, locally owned boutiques and national chains such as Pottery Barn, Lush Handmade Cosmetics, and Kiehl's.

This area makes a good destination if you have an afternoon to while away. Coffee shops and unique little stores are abundant, and on a nice day, the streets are absolutely thronged with intriguing-looking people. Street parking is often difficult to find in Northwest Portland, though there are several pay lots (look for the signs off NW 23rd); if you're coming in from downtown or the Pearl District, consider taking the Portland Streetcar, which crosses both NW 21st and 23rd Avenues along Marshall and Lovejoy Streets.

Looming over this part of Northwest

© JUDY JEWELL

Northwest 23rd Avenue is one of Portland's main shopping streets.

Portland are the West Hills, a range of extinct volcanoes now capped by Forest Park, the largest urban wilderness in the United States.

Pittock Mansion

Occupying a 1,000-foot promontory on 46 acres in the West Hills is **Pittock Mansion** (3229 NW Pittock Dr., 503/823-3623, http:// pittockmansion.org, 11am-4pm daily Feb.-June and Sept.-Dec., 10am-5pm daily July-Aug., closed Jan., $8.50 adults, $7.50 seniors, $5.50 children ages 6-18), a grand 1914 home built by the then-editor of the *Oregonian* newspaper. The 22-room mansion was designed to contemporary tastes, with overlays of French, English, and Turkish design on the solidly handcrafted structure hewn from Oregon stone and timber. As much as possible, the mansion is outfitted with the Pittock family's original furnishings, although all details have been carefully curated, making this a showcase of early-20th-century style and design. Guided tours of the mansion are available, but it's also worth the trip up to this pinnacle vantage point simply for the fabulous views of Portland and the Cascade peaks rising to the east.

NORTHEAST

North and Northeast Portland cover an enormous area, all the way from East Burnside Street north to the Columbia River, and from the Willamette River east to beyond Portland International Airport. However, for visitors, the quadrant's main draws are the inner Northeast neighborhoods directly across from downtown as well as a handful of districts that represent the outposts of Portland's DIY nation. In these more distant neighborhoods, formerly rough-edged commercial centers built in the early 20th century have been revived as gallery districts and restaurant rows by a current generation of youthful entrepreneurs.

Most public transportation heading into North and Northeast Portland crosses the Willamette River on the Steel Bridge, with the first eastside stop the Rose Quarter Transit Center.

EASTBANK ESPLANADE

Immediately south of the Steel Bridge is the northern terminus of the **Eastbank Esplanade,** a 1.5-mile bike path and walkway along the Willamette's eastern bank. Part of the path is a floating walkway, and part is on terra firma; cycling or walking the path is an invigorating outing and offers good views of downtown from the Willamette's eastern bank. At 1,200 feet the floating walkway is the longest of its kind in the United States, and it offers the sensation of walking on water. The adjoining 120-foot public boat dock provides moorage for recreational boaters as well as space for a future river taxi system. The esplanade ends at the Oregon Museum of Science and Industry (OMSI), although the paved trail jogs a couple of blocks inland and continues south, becoming the rails-to-trails **Springwater Corridor,** which runs south through a nature reserve to Sellwood and then east all the way to Boring (21 miles).

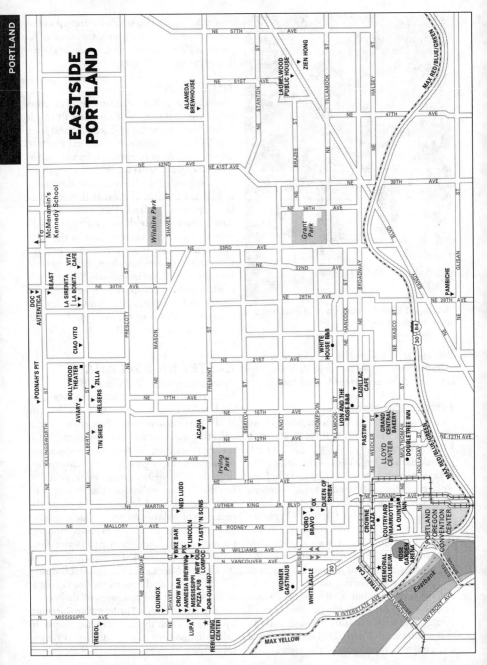

EASTSIDE PORTLAND

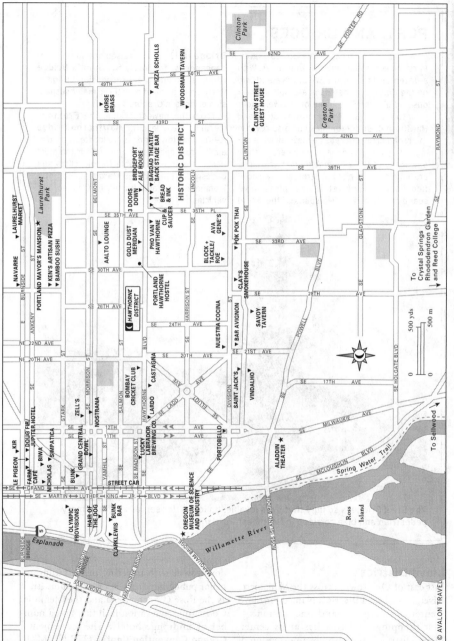

PORTLAND

PORTLAND BRIDGES

Of all the metro areas in the United States, Portland is arguably *the* City of Bridges. With a dozen bridges on the Willamette and two on the Columbia, the spans are both numerous and diverse. The three oldest were built prior to World War I (the Broadway, Steel, and Hawthorne). Bridge-ophiles can also revel in the broad array of types on view; all were designed by the preeminent engineers of their day. Many of the Willamette River crossings are illuminated at night by strategically placed floodlights, adding yet another pleasing visual dimension. The two spans of the **Steel Bridge** (1912) can be raised and lowered independently. The lovely **St. John's Bridge** (1931) is the only steel suspension bridge in Portland and one of only three major suspension bridges in Oregon.

From the newest bridge, the **Fremont** (1973), to the oldest, the **Hawthorne Bridge** (1910), downtown bridges are located a third of a mile from each other and are, for the most part, safe and accessible for bicyclists and pedestrians (only the I-5 Marquam and I-405 Fremont Bridges are off-limits to nonmotorized vehicles and pedestrians).

© BILL MCRAE

The Steel Bridge is so ugly that's it's lovable. Its lower tier serves as the primary pedestrian and bike corridor to Northeast Portland.

Lloyd District

Just east of Old Town, across the Willamette River, is the **Lloyd District.** Named for Lloyd Center, Portland's—and the nation's—first shopping mall that lies at its center, Lloyd District is increasingly an extension of downtown, with towering office buildings, major public buildings, sports stadiums (such as the Rose Garden Arena and the Memorial Coliseum), convention facilities, and a number of midrange hotels. The monumental **Oregon Convention Center** (777 NE M. L.

© BILL MCRAE

The Oregon Convention Center is across from downtown in Northeast Portland.

King Jr. Blvd., 503/235-7575, www.oregoncc. org) is easy to spot with its twin glass steeples. Encompassing nearly 20 square blocks, this massive structure is the largest convention facility in the Pacific Northwest.

All of these destinations are easily reached by the Red and Blue MAX light rail lines, which offer free transport as far east as Lloyd Center, and the eastside Portland Streetcar. On the north edge of Lloyd District is NE Broadway, a major arterial linking the northeast residential neighborhoods with downtown Portland via the Broadway Bridge (take TriMet bus number 9 from downtown).

North Mississippi Avenue

If you had to choose a single poster child to represent Portland's do-it-yourself spirit, it could easily be the recently gentrified stretch of North Mississippi Avenue between N. Fremont and N. Skidmore Streets (take bus number 44 from downtown).

Even in 2000, this neighborhood was a collection of mostly vacant turn-of-the-20th-century storefronts that had fallen into disrepair and dereliction. Then Portland's influx of "young creatives" discovered this historic community hub and found it an inexpensive place to start restaurants, art galleries, bars, brewpubs, coffeehouses, bakeries, and other one-of-a-kind enterprises. Fast-forward to today, and Mississippi Avenue is a testament to progressive politics and entrepreneurial instincts, with six blocks of Portland's renowned neighborhood-oriented lifestyle and enough nightlife and restaurant choices for travelers staying downtown to justify a trip across the river.

Any trip to North Mississippi Avenue should include a stop at **The Rebuilding Center** (3625 N. Mississippi Ave., 503/331-1877, http://rebuildingcenter.org, 9am-6pm Mon.-Sat., 10am-5pm Sun.), the largest nonprofit resource for used building materials in North America. Building salvage of all sorts finds its way to this 64,000-square-foot warehouse and lumberyard. If you're a homeowner and looking for a cheap sink, a period match for picture molding, or used-once two-by-fours, this labyrinth of old house stuff is fascinating.

NE Alberta Street

Once a thriving commercial strip on a streetcar line as well as the heart of Portland's African American community, by the late 1980s Alberta Street had become a symbol of neglect, redlining, drug dealing, and gang activity. A decade later, the surrounding neighborhood was among the most rapidly gentrifying in the country, with all the change that that entails. Nowadays Alberta Street, between NE Martin Luther King Jr. Boulevard and NE 33rd Avenue, is known to a new generation as a trendy arts district and a center for drinking and fine dining, perhaps the closest thing you'll find in Portland to a Latin Quarter of bohemian artists, cafés, bars, and bonhomie.

Part of the charm of Alberta Street is that it hasn't been razed and remade; there are still barbershops and body shops, storefront churches and comfortably seedy bars amid all the new construction and renovation. Alberta Street is also home to several art galleries, which play host along with studios and street vendors to thousands of revelers the last Thursday evening of every month for the Art Walk, otherwise known as Last Thursday.

The best way to get to Alberta Street by public transport is by TriMet bus number 6, which crosses Alberta Street on NE Martin Luther King Jr. Boulevard, or bus number 8, which crosses Alberta Street on NE 15th Avenue. Once on Alberta Street, take bus number 72, which travels on Alberta between NE Martin Luther King Jr. Boulevard and NE 30th Avenue.

The Grotto

The **National Sanctuary of Our Sorrowful Mother,** commonly referred to as **The Grotto** (NE 85th Ave. and NE Sandy Blvd., 503/254-7371, 9am-dusk daily, free), is a Catholic shrine whose hand-hewn cavern surrounded by lushly landscaped grounds can induce a profound sense of peace no matter what your spirituality is. Within the ivy-covered fern-lined grotto is an impressive marble pietà. Outside the 30- by 50-foot enclosure, old-growth firs tower over the 110-foot cliff housing the shrine. Roses, camellias, rhododendrons, azaleas, and a cliffside view of the Columbia River also make this worth the 20-minute pilgrimage from downtown Portland. The Grotto is especially impressive to visit during the Christmas holiday season, when thousands of lights adorn the trees.

SOUTHEAST

When you think of Portland, do you conjure images of a slightly stoned hippie utopia? Or do you envision mobs of twenty-something hipsters flashing tattoos and piercings in a slacker coffeehouse? Rest assured that both stereotypes are alive and well—in fact thriving—in Southeast Portland. Southeast Portland is actually a vast quadrant, and despite its reputation as a habitat for a seemingly steadfast hippie culture, in fact it's quite a bit more complex.

The close-in Southeast is a gentrifying warehouse district flanked to the east by Portland's most alternative neighborhoods. Centered on SE Hawthorne Boulevard, these Victorian residential neighborhoods are still home to Portland's Youth Culture, even though some of these folks are reaching retirement age. To the graying hippies, add in a thick overlay of goth kids, gays and lesbians, and street musicians, and you've got a people watching nexus. The city quadrant stretches east across leafy neighborhoods filled with antique mansions to busy SE 82nd Avenue, the hub of today's immigrant Asian community. Two of Portland's greatest parks are in Southeast Portland—one designed by the famed Olmsted firm a century ago, the other situated on the only extinct volcano in a U.S. city—along with some of the city's most critically acclaimed independent restaurants.

Oregon Museum of Science and Industry

The **Oregon Museum of Science and Industry** (OMSI, 1945 SE Water Ave., 503/797-4000, www.omsi.edu, 9:30am-7pm

Sun.-Fri., 9:30am-9pm Sat. late June-Labor Day, 9:30am-5:30pm Tues.-Sun. Labor Day-late June, $13 adults, $9.50 seniors and children ages 3-13, $2 parking) is a family-oriented hands-on interactive museum encompassing 219,000 square feet with five exhibit halls and eight science labs, making it one of the largest science and natural history museums in North America. Exhibits offer a vast array of learning experiences and interactive displays, ranging from how to pilot a ship or perform cardiology tests on a giant human heart to learning more about Oregon's dinosaur past. OMSI also hosts a large number of touring exhibits (most with separate admission) as well as mounting topical exhibits on current events or environmental issues. The museum's 18.5-acre riverfront campus also features an OmniMax Theater with a five-story-high domed screen, the Pacific Northwest's largest planetarium, and the **USS Blueback** (503/797-4624, www.omsi.edu/submarine, tour $5.75), the last fast-attack diesel-powered submarine built by the U.S. Navy, now moored just west of OMSI in the Willamette River. OMSI also offers a variety of kids' camps and classes during the summer, as well as a once-monthly adults-only night called OMSI After Dark; check the website to see what may be available during your visit. During the school year, OMSI is open 9:30am-5:30pm on Mondays that are school holidays.

Hawthorne District

Portland has a longtime reputation as an enclave of hippie lifestyles and a hotbed of progressive politics, and if that's the Portland you'd like to explore, come to the neighborhoods along SE Hawthorne Boulevard. Rest assured that the idealistic early 1970s haven't aged much around here. Stores purveying fine coffees, secondhand clothing, imported arts and crafts, antiques, and books join cafés and galleries recalling the hip enclaves of Berkeley, California, and Cambridge, Massachusetts. A dense concentration of these establishments on Hawthorne Boulevard between 30th and 50th Avenues is catnip for a friendly population of idealists both young and old. This is one of Portland's most alternative neighborhoods, and unless you're militantly right-wing, you'll have fun exploring the shops, bookstores, and coffee shops along this iconic Portland avenue; take TriMet Bus number 14.

Belmont

Just a few blocks north of SE Hawthorne Boulevard is SE Belmont Street, another strip of hipster enterprises thick with bars, restaurants, coffee shops, and entertainment venues. One major hub is near the converted **Belmont Dairy** at SE 34th Avenue, a former milk plant now turned upscale grocery store and condo development; take TriMet bus number 15.

Laurelhurst Park

Until 1909, the land that would become **Laurelhurst Park** (SE 39th Ave. and Stark St.)—one of the most beautiful and beloved of Portland's many parks—was part of the then-mayor's stock farms, and blue-ribbon Jersey milk cows drank from the property's small spring-fed lake. The city bought 30 acres of the farmland to create Laurelhurst Park based on plans drawn up by the Olmstead Brothers for the development of Portland's parks. The original watering hole was enlarged and deepened into a three-acre lake, and the rest of the park was divided into a series of distinct sections, according to the ideals of the City Beautiful Movement, an urban planning campaign from the 1890s and 1900s. In 2001 the park was named to the National Register of Historic Places, the first city park ever listed on the national register.

Today, the park is a lovely and leafy destination for strolling, picnicking, or simply relaxing in beautifully vernal surroundings. The lake is filled with ducks, geese, and swans, and feeding the waterfowl is a common pastime; the waters also yield catfish, carp, and crappies, as averred by busy anglers. The south side of the park has tennis, volleyball, and basketball courts; nearby is a large playground for children, with a large play structure.

Mount Tabor Park

Mount Tabor Park (SE 60th Ave. and Salmon St.) rises above Southeast Portland, and its distinctive cone shape reveals its primary attribute: The park contains the country's only extinct volcano within the city limits of a major population center. Roping in nearly 200 acres, Mount Tabor Park is large enough to offer several miles of hiking trails, and it also has tennis and basketball courts. Summer concerts are held at a natural amphitheater inside a cinder cone. A looping road leads to the summit, where you'll find a statue of Harvey W. Scott, the editor of the *Oregonian* until 1910, sculpted by Gutzon Borglum of Mount Rushmore fame.

On the flanks of Mount Tabor are three reservoirs; these are holding ponds for the water supply for much of east Portland. After the 9/11 terrorist attacks on New York City and Washington, D.C., the city and the Portland Water Bureau moved to comply with federal mandates that would require that the reservoirs be buried or covered to protect them from contamination by terrorists. Portland residents responded with concerted activism to save the open reservoirs, and plans for altering the reservoirs have been shelved for the time being.

Crystal Springs Rhododendron Garden

Ten-acre **Crystal Springs Rhododendron Garden** (SE 28th Ave. and Woodstock Blvd.) is a colorful place mid-April-June when some 600 varieties of rhododendrons and azaleas, represented by about 2,500 individual specimens, are in bloom. Trails wind through the gardens and along a spring-fed lake; a bridge leads to an island covered with yet more broadleaved evergreens. The floral display peaks in mid-May; strolling the gardens on Mother's Day is a Portland tradition. The rest of the year the gardens offer a quiet place for walking and contemplation, and bird-watching and fall foliage displays encourage an off-season visit. A $3 admission fee is charged 10am-6pm Thursday-Monday March-Labor Day.

Sports and Recreation

PARKS

Portland is famous for more park acreage per capita than any other major U.S. city—more than 37,000 acres are preserved as parkland, with 8 percent of the city's area devoted to public recreational venues. Within these holdings, the city has more urban wilderness than any other municipality in the country.

Portland Parks and Recreation (503/823-7529, www.portlandonline.com/parks) is the bureau that operates the city's 250 parks.

Waterfront Park and the Eastbank Esplanade

This 2.8-mile loop trail rings the Willamette River in the very heart of Portland, linking two bridges and Waterfront Park with a floating walkway on the river's eastern bank. The trail can be walked in either direction and accessed at many points; to follow the loop clockwise from downtown, walk the riverfront embankment trail north through Waterfront Park to the Steel Bridge. Cross the lower span of the bridge, a pedestrian- and cyclists-only crossing called the Steel Bridge RiverWalk.

On the east side of the Willamette, the trail heads south, dropping onto the Eastbank Esplanade, about half of which is a floating walkway (at 1,200 feet the longest in the country) and the rest a paved path along the riverbank. At the Hawthorne Bridge, climb up the stairs and cross the bridge to downtown, completing the loop.

If you're not ready to stop (and if you're on a bike, you might just be getting warmed up), don't cross over the Hawthorne Bridge, but continue south along the Esplanade. You'll pass OMSI and come to what seems to be the end of the trail. But ride a couple of blocks east (inland) and you'll reach the southern end of the Springwater Corridor, which runs south to Sellwood, then east to beyond Gresham (where you can catch a MAX train back to town).

◖ Forest Park

The largest urban wilderness in the United States with over 5,100 acres and 70 miles of trails, **Forest Park** stretches along the crest of Portland's West Hills. It is 8.5 miles long and 1.5 miles wide. As much a statement of Portland's priorities and values as a leafy refuge for hikers, joggers, and cyclists, Forest Park is home to an abundance of wildlife (more than 112 bird and 62 mammal species, including bears, elk, deer, and cougars), all found just minutes from the urban center. The mixed co-nifer forest is made up of western red cedars, Douglas firs, western spruce, red alder, and bigleaf maple trees with a lush understory of sword fern, western trillium, maidenhair fern, Oregon grape, Indian plum, salmonberry, and stinging nettle.

For hikers, the park's centerpiece is 30-mile

© JUDY JEWELL

Forest Park's Wildwood Trail starts just a couple of miles from the heart of downtown.

Wildwood Trail, which links various parklands in the West Hills with Forest Park. The southern end of the trail starts just past the Vietnam Veterans of Oregon Memorial near the Oregon Zoo. From here it runs through Washington Park and Hoyt Arboretum and past Pittock Mansion. At Cornell Road the trail crosses the edge of the **Audubon Sanctuary** (5151 NW Cornell Rd., 503/292-6855, www.audubon-portland.org, dawn-dusk daily), where the Audubon Society of Portland administers a 148-acre free-to-the-public nature preserve that is a showcase for native flora and fauna. The sanctuary has over four miles of forested hiking trails in the verdant West Hills.

From the Audubon Sanctuary, the Wildwood Trail enters Forest Park and runs north for another 22 miles. The trail can be accessed at any of the points described above or at several more northerly trailheads. One convenient access point is the western end of NW Upshur Street at Macleay Park; another is the end of NW Thurman Street (the number 15 Thurman Street bus from downtown stops about 0.25 mile downhill from this entrance to the park).

Tryon Creek State Park

The only Oregon state park within the Portland metro area, 645-acre **Tryon Creek State Park** (11321 SW Terwilliger Blvd., 503/636-9886 or 800/551-6949) offers eight miles of nature trails in a vernal woodland setting. Cyclists bike along the paved trail on the park's eastern edge. The park's many events include summer day camps for kids, guided nature walks, and special activities; for a list of events go to www.tryonfriends.org. Streamside wildlife includes beavers and songbirds. In late March there are wondrous displays of trilliums, a wild marsh lily. To reach the park, take I-5 Exit 297 south of Portland, follow SW Terwilliger Boulevard for 2.5 miles past Lewis and Clark College, and watch for signs for the park.

BICYCLING

Portland has twice been selected by *Bicycling* magazine as the most bike-friendly city in the nation, and indeed the city has a comprehensive infrastructure devoted to cycling. Unless you're from Amsterdam, you'll be amazed at the number of people who get around Portland on bikes.

The website of the **City of Portland's Office of Transportation** (www.portlandonline.com/transportation) lists up-to-date information for cyclists. Keep up on local cycling issues at bikeportland.org, an excellent bike blog; find fun rides and details on **Pedalpalooza** events (held throughout June) at shift2bikes.org. A handy map called *Getting There by Bike,* published by the government agency Metro, is sold at bike shops and bookstores across town.

Portland has some fun recreational rides, but the city has gained its bike-friendly fame by taking steps to make it easy to ride around town. Look for bike icons painted onto the streets to find good places to ride; green street signs along bike routes give bikers directions and distances from one part of town to another.

Cyclists should know that Portland is a city of bridges but that not all bridges are recommended for cyclists. A river-level foot-and-bike bridge forms the lower level of the Steel Bridge and connects Waterfront Park and downtown to the Eastbank Esplanade; otherwise, the Hawthorne, Broadway, and Burnside Bridges are best, although bikes must share sidewalks with pedestrians. Bikes are allowed on TriMet buses (bike racks are mounted on the front of every bus), the MAX, and the Portland Streetcar.

For a recreational ride that's almost entirely on bike paths, check out the 16.8-mile **Springwater Corridor,** a bike thoroughfare built on a reclaimed rail line from Southeast Portland through Gresham to Boring. Views of Mount Hood abound along much of the route. Along the way, easy access to Leach Botanical Gardens, Powell Butte, and other worthy detours are available.

An easy choice for mountain bikers is **Leif Erikson Road** in Forest Park. From the park gate at the end of NW Thurman Street, the dirt road is closed to motor vehicles; it's a steady but gentle six-mile climb through mature forest to the junction at Salzman Road, and another 6 miles to the trail's end at Germantown Road. Bikes are not allowed on the park's hiking trails, but they can go on selected (steep) fire lanes as marked by signs.

North of Portland at the confluence of the Columbia and Willamette Rivers is **Sauvie Island** (http://sauvieisland.org), a perfectly flat island where farms and truck gardens share space with wildlife refuges. The island's 12-mile loop road is a scenic delight reminiscent of rural France. Sauvie Island is 10 miles north of Portland off U.S. 30.

Bike Rentals

As you might expect in bicycle-mad Portland, it's no problem to rent a bike; average rates run $25-60 for a 24-hour rental, depending on the model. Convenient to Waterfront Park, with a large rental fleet, is **Waterfront Bikes** (10 SW Ash St., 503/227-1719, www.waterfrontbikes.com). On the way to Forest Park trails is **Fat Tire Farm** (2714 NW Thurman St., 503/222-3276, www.fattirefarm.com). Just east of the Hawthorne Bridge, **Clever Cycles** (900 SE Hawthorne Blvd., 503/334-1560, http://clevercycles.com) rents Dutch city bikes, Brompton folding bikes, and Bakfiets cargo bikes. At **Pedal Bike Tours** (133 SW 2nd Ave., 503/243-2453, www.pedalbiketours.com), you can rent a bike or join a tour around town or out to the Columbia Gorge or Willamette Valley. One of their most fun trips is the self-guided Forest Park ride; cyclists and bikes are transported to a trailhead and ride, generally downhill, through the park back to town. Hardened cyclists looking for organized 30- to 100-mile rides at a touring pace should hook up with the **Portland Wheelmen Touring Club** (503/257-7982, www.pwtc.com).

BIRD-WATCHING

To the far south of the Southeast district, the Sellwood neighborhood offers access to wetlands along the Willamette River. **Oaks Bottom Wildlife Refuge** (SE 7th Ave. and Sellwood

ESCAPE TO SAUVIE ISLAND

Ten miles northwest of Portland at the confluence of the Willamette and Columbia Rivers is the rural enclave of **Sauvie Island** (http://sauvieisland.org), a scant 20 minutes from downtown. On clear days here, views of the snowcapped Cascades Range backdrop ocean-going freighters and cruise ships. Visitors enjoy horseback riding, swimming, and U-pick farms plying apples, berries, peaches, pears, nectarines, melons, green beans, corn, zucchini, tomatoes, and pumpkins. A favorite spot for bird-watching, the area sees eagles, great blue herons, geese, and sandhill cranes among the 250 species that pass through on the Pacific Flyway. Wildlife aficionados see red foxes and black-tailed deer on the island's northern half. In addition, anglers come to Sauvie's lakes and sloughs for panfish and bass, and to the Columbia side for sturgeon, salmon, and steelhead. Bikers come for the 12-mile "hill-less" biking loop. Nearby is **Collins Beach** (4am-10pm daily), which is clothing optional.

Other seasonal highlights here include watching the Christmas ships (whose colored lights and yuletime decor resemble the most elaborate parade floats imaginable) and swimming at **Walton Beach** at the end of NW Reeder Road. Mid-January offers a rare chance to see bald eagles feeding here.

This is Oregon as it was, before Starbucks, gas stations, and souvenir shops. Described by the Royal Navy and Lewis and Clark as a major outpost of Chinook culture, in the early 19th century Sauvie drew Euro-American settlers, who came to engage in the extensive trade along the Columbia River and to till the fertile soil.

Be aware that if you park at one of Sauvie Island's public beaches or wildlife viewing areas, you'll need a parking certificate, available for $7 per vehicle at the Cracker Barrel Convenience Store on Sauvie Island Road; turn left after coming off the bridge. Also remember to gas up and hit the ATM before heading to the island; neither are here.

To reach Sauvie Island, take U.S. 30 northwest to St. Helens, Linnton, and Sauvie Island.

The Pumpkin Patch is a top Sauvie Island farm for produce and flowers.

Blvd., www.portlandonline.com, 5am-midnight daily) is a 163-acre area of woods, open fields, and wetlands. This is a popular spot for birders as it attracts some 125 species of birds, including blue herons, red-tailed hawks, and eight species of warblers. To explore the bottoms, hike down the bluff from the parking lot at the north end of Sellwood Park.

CLIMBING

The top inner-city destination for climbers is **Portland Rock Gym** (21 NE 12th Ave., 503/232-8310, www.portlandrockgym.com, 11am-11pm Mon., Wed., and Fri., 7am-11pm Tues. and Thurs., 9am-9pm Sat., 9am-6pm Sun.), with a 12,000-square-foot climbing area, 40-foot top-rope and lead walls, and a large boulderiing area. A day pass ($15 adults, $7 weekdays and $10 weekends seniors and children ages 11 and under) includes unlimited access to the gym for one day, including climbing areas, fitness facilities, and drop-in yoga classes.

GOLF

For golfers, Portland has more publicly owned golf courses per capita than any other U.S. city. Two of these, Heron Lakes and Eastmoreland, are ranked by *Golf Digest* as among the top 75 public courses in the country; both are operated by Portland Parks and Recreation. Portland public course fees average around $26-41 for 18 holes.

Heron Lakes (3500 N. Victory Blvd., 503/289-1818, http://heronlakesgolf.com) is the premier public golf facility in Portland, with 36 holes (the Greenback and Great Blue courses), a grass driving range, and good short-game practice areas. The two courses offer varying challenges for different greens fees. The easier and shorter Greenback is good for beginners and moderate players, though it doesn't drain as well. The more challenging— and costlier—Great Blue, designed by Robert Trent Jones Jr., is better manicured and drains better in wet weather.

Eastmoreland Golf Course (2425 SE Bybee Blvd., 503/775-2900, www.eastmorelandgolfcourse.com) is Oregon's second-oldest course and one of the most beautiful. Located near Reed College in Southeast Portland, the mature and lengthy (6,529 yards) 18-hole course is lined with statuesque trees and gardens. Eastmoreland features a two-tier driving range, a pro shop, and full bar and restaurant facilities. The course was designed by former U.S. Amateur champion H. Chandler Egan, who later helped redesign Pebble Beach Golf Links in the early 1900s.

PADDLING

If you're tempted to get out onto the Willamette River, take a tour or rent a sea kayak from **Portland Kayak Company** (6600 SW Macadam Ave., 503/459-4050, www.

portlandkayak.com) on the west side of the Willamette River near Willamette Park. They also maintain a fleet of boats at RiverPlace Marina, which is used as a base for three-hour beginner-friendly tours around Ross Island (offered at 10am and 2pm daily, $45); on these tours, paddlers have a chance to see great blue herons and, oftentimes, ospreys and eagles.

On the east side of the river, **Alder Creek Kayak** (1515 SE Water St., 503/285-1819, www.aldercreek.com) has a boathouse near the Eastside Esplanade immediately south of the Hawthorne Bridge, near the junction of SE Water Avenue and Clay Street. A three-hour tour of Ross Island is $39. Rent a canoe, kayak, or stand-up paddleboard ($30-40 for 4 hours) here; from the boathouse it's easy to launch into the Willamette River.

RUNNING

Thanks to its relatively mild climate, wealth of trails (especially in Forest Park), and the influence of Nike, Portland is widely regarded as a great running town and host to many running and walking events, including the early-October **Portland Marathon** (503/226-1111, www.portlandmarathon.org). To find out about these and other events, contact the **Oregon Road Runner's Club** (message phone 503/646-7867, www.orrc.net); they'll be glad to recommend the best places to run.

SWIMMING

The indoor Portland Parks pool at **Dishman Community Center** (77 NE Knott St., 503/823-3673) is open year-round and convenient to downtown. A little less convenient, but quite nice is the **Southwest Community Center and Pool** (6820 SW 45th Ave., 503/823-2840). In summer the outdoor pool at **U.S. Grant Park** (503/823-3674), near the corner of NE 33rd Avenue and U. S. Grant Place, is a great place for hot kids.

Public beaches and swimming along the Willamette and Columbia Rivers are popular in summer. **Sellwood Riverfront Park,** at the east end of the Sellwood Bridge, is a good place for a picnic and a wade in the Willamette River; there's also an outdoor pool in **Sellwood Park** (7951 SE 7th Ave., 503/823-3679). Ten miles north of Portland, the beaches along the east side of **Sauvie Island** are popular; they are reached from U.S. 30. Once on the island, nude sunbathing becomes more the norm the farther north you go along its beaches. If you're headed up the Columbia River Gorge, **Rooster Rock State Park** (I-84 Exit 25) has three miles of sandy beaches on the Columbia River, with the easternmost beaches being clothing-optional.

TENNIS

A number of Portland parks offer free tennis courts. Most convenient to visitors staying downtown are the courts near the Rose Gardens in **Washington Park** (SW Park Place, www.portlandonline.com). On the east side of the Willamette River there are outdoor courts at **Laurelhurst Park** (SE 39th Ave. and Stark St.).

SPECTATOR SPORTS

Portland is more a town for athletes than for devotees of spectator sports. Nonetheless, a couple of professional sports teams have many ardent fans.

Directly across the Willamette River from downtown in Northeast Portland, the Rose Quarter area is home to two of Portland's sports stadia. The larger (20,339 seats) and newer is the **Rose Garden Arena** (at the east end of the Steel Bridge, 503/235-8771, www.rosequarter.com), which is home to the National Basketball Association's Portland Trailblazers. While most seats are reserved for season ticket holders, some are available at Ticketmaster outlets

or through the Rose Garden Arena box office (503/797-9619). Of course, there are always the offerings of ticket brokers on Craigslist (www.craigslist.org) and the scalpers who may be found beyond a four-block radius of the Rose Garden. It's best to call the Blazer ticket line or check with Ticketmaster well in advance. You can also buy tickets directly from the **Blazer website** (www.nba.com/blazers). Regular season play is October-April.

Adjacent to the Rose Garden Arena is the 12,000-seat **Memorial Coliseum** (1401 N. Wheeler Ave., 503/235-8771), which hosts sporting events, concerts, and other local teams, including the **Winter Hawks** (503/238-6366, www.winterhawks.com), a minor league team in the Western Hockey League. Both of these arenas are also used for major concerts—Luciano Pavarotti and the Rolling Stones have played the Rose Garden Arena—and both are easily reached on the MAX train (take the train to Rose Quarter Transit Center).

Across the river, **Jeld-Wen Field** (1844 SW Morrison St., 503/553-5400, www.portland-timbers.com) is home to Major League Soccer's **Portland Timbers.** This erstwhile baseball stadium was remodeled before the start of the 2010 season, and its nearly 20,000 seats are usually filled, with a substantial number occupied by the Timbers Army, an enthusiastic legion of green-scarfed fans. The **Portland Thorns** (www.portlandtimbers.com/thornsfc) owned by the same franchise as the Timbers, is Portland's National Women's Soccer League team. They also play at Jeld-Wen Field.

Tickets for all of these teams' games are available through **Ticketmaster** (800/277-1700, www.ticketmaster.com).

Entertainment and Events

As Portland has rapidly grown in recent years, its arts scene has become more diverse and sophisticated. The traditional institutions of symphony, opera, and classical ballet are strong, and contemporary dance and theater are represented by an eclectic bunch of adventurous companies. In addition to the more formal music and theater listings that follow, there's a very active summer festival itinerary that ranges from the superb Chamber Music Northwest series to blues and jazz festivals.

In Portland, bars are allowed to stay open until 2:30am, though few do so on weekdays. During the week, most places close at midnight or 1am, though may stay open later if there's entertainment. Cover charges usually kick in at 9pm when there's live music.

NIGHTLIFE

Portland has a very full-bodied live music and club scene: On any given night some 300 clubs offer live music, and with typical Portland character, what you'll find in these venues is often a bit different than you might expect. In addition to live music and dancing, you'll also find lots of theme nights, often accompanied by a combination of cabaret, performance art, magic, and burlesque—think *Cabaret's* Kit Kat Klub. These unscripted evenings can often provide very diverting entertainment.

Much of the nightlife is concentrated in a few easily reached neighborhoods, most with safe and dependable public transport to and fro. Be sure to pick up a copy or check the websites of *Willamette Week* or the *Portland Mercury,* two free weeklies that follow the music and nightlife scene closely. Most music events in bars are restricted to ages 21 and older. Cover charges, which range $3-10 in most nightclubs, are frequently levied, though there's often no cover charge for live music early in the week or even early in the evening. Also note that smoking is not permitted in Oregon bars, though nudity is: Because of Oregon's liberal laws regarding nudity, Portland is home to many strip clubs.

Bars

Portland is a nightlife kind of city, with bars everywhere. You won't find it difficult to find places to drink, but here's a primer on some of the city's best bars.

Named after modernist Finnish designer Alvar Aalto, the **Aalto Lounge** (3356 SE Belmont St., 503/235-6041, http://aalto-lounge.com) projects a cool mid-century aesthetic courtesy of its thrift store-chic decor. Gathering for wine and cocktails, an eclectic crowd represents a cross section of Southeast Portland: young artists, students, hip professionals, pretty gay men, young women showing off their tattoos, and restaurant workers out after their shifts. There's usually interesting art on the walls, and the food's good, too. At 10pm DJs start spinning techno tunes.

The McMenamin brothers have a witchy genius for finding fascinating and unique landmarks to convert into brewpubs, hotels, and theaters, but of the dozens of the kingdom's locations in Portland, the **Back Stage Bar** (3702 SE Hawthorne Blvd., 503/236-9234) is the most amazing. At the front of the building is the **Bagdad Theater,** a popular pub-slash-movie theater. Back when it was built in the 1920s, the Bagdad was the city's top vaudeville hall. When the painted scrims and backdrops that set the scene for its live song-and-dance routines weren't in use, they were hung in the Back Stage, a seven-story curtain storehouse directly behind the theater. Fast-forward to 2006, when the Back Stage Bar opened, making the most of this narrow towering space. On the ground floor are the handsome bar and pool tables, but catwalks and staircases lead to secluded spots tucked into the walls. And there's nothing like a bar with a seven-story-high ceiling to start a conversation. You've got to check this one out. The Back Stage Bar is at the heart

THE *REAL* PORTLAND SPIRIT

Portland is famed as a center for brewing, with more breweries than any city in the world, and it's a short drive from world-class wineries in the northern Willamette Valley and the Columbia Gorge. What you may not know, but shouldn't surprise you, is that Portland is also a major center for artisanal **micro-distilleries.** There are over a dozen small distilleries in Portland, producing specialty vodka, gin, whiskey, rum and eau-de-vie. Several offer tasting rooms where you can sample the Portland spirit.

In addition to the following distilleries, also check out the small-batch liquors at brewpubs **Edgefield** (2126 SW Halsey St., Troutdale, 503/669-8610 or 800/669-8610, www.mcmenamins.com) for Hogshead whiskey, Penney's gin, and various brandies; and **Rogue Distillery & Public House** (1339 NW Flanders St., 503/241-3780, www.rogue.com) for three kinds of rum, a Scotch-style whiskey, and spruce (not juniper-based) gin.

- **Clear Creek Distillery** (2389 NW Wilson St., 503/248-9470, www.clearcreekdistillery.com, 9am-5pm Mon.-Sat.): Famous for pear brandy and other fruit-based eaux-de-

vie; check out the Oregon Single Malt Whiskey, if the year's tiny production isn't already sold out.

- **House Spirits Distillery** (610 SE 10th Ave., 503/803-3989, www.housespirits.com, 11am-4pm Mon.-Sat. and noon-5pm Sun.): Most noted for its Aviation Gin, but also try the Medoyeff vodka and aquavit.

- **Integrity Spirits** (909 SE Yamhill St., 503/517-2030, www.integrityspirits.com, 2am-6pm Sat.): Check out their absinthe, one of the first distilled in the United States, as well as 12 Bridges Gin and a selection of vodkas.

- **New Deal Distillery** (1311 SE 9th Ave., 503/234-2513, http://newdealdistillery.com, 12:30pm-5pm Sat. and 1pm-4pm Sun.): This operation specializes in vodka.

- **Stone Barn Brandy Works** (3315 SE 19th Ave., 503/775-6747, www.stonebarnbrandyworks.com, noon-6pm Sat.-Sun.): Unsurprisingly, there's brandy, but so much more, such as grappa, ouzo, rye whiskey, oat whiskey, and strawberry, apricot, cranberry, and coffee liqueur.

of SE Hawthorne Boulevard's entertainment district, with many other haunts within easy stumbling distance.

The **Crow Bar** (3954 N. Mississippi Ave., 503/280-7099) feels comfortable and slightly old-fashioned, a narrow space with exposed red brick, high ceilings, and a long wooden bar. However, the crowds are anything but old-fashioned—this is a favorite watering hole for the many 20- and 30-somethings who have refashioned the adjoining North Portland neighborhoods in their image. Everyone here is an up-and-coming writer, filmmaker, restaurateur, musician, designer (fill in your favorite new-creative-class category here), rubbing elbows in an alcohol-charged synthesis that's usually highly energized and always interesting.

Gold Dust Meridian (3267 SE Hawthorne Blvd., 503/239-1143, http://golddustmeridian.

com) started out as a 1960s-era accountant's office, which it remained until it was transformed into a rather swank temple of drink. This is a lively spot, with a pool table, good cocktails, and a high-energy vibe. Many Southeast Portland bars can be rather dingy, relying on thrift-store decor for irony, but not the Gold Dust Meridian. If you like bar atmosphere to be sophisticated, you'll enjoy the stylish makeover: thin Roman-style brick so typical of the '60s looks great with the low-pitched roof and blond wood accents. The young attractive crowd, chatting above blaring techno-pop, is easy on the eyes, as well.

The grandly renovated landmark **Grand Central Bowl** (839 SE Morrison St., 503/236-2695, www.thegrandcentralbowl.com) is, of course, a bowling alley, but it's also quite a bit more. Built in the 1920s, this block-square structure with castellated towers on each corner was Portland's fresh produce market, once busy with farmers' trucks selling fruit and vegetables. The building eventually fell into disuse and was transformed in the 1950s into the city's largest bowling alley. Move now to 2006, when the disheveled building came under new ownership and a $14 million remodel ensued. Upon reopening in 2008, the revivified Grand Central Bowl set out to make bowling cool again and to recalibrate any preconceptions you may have of bowling alleys. A lot of thematic convergence is happening here: Two bars (one an upscale sports bar, the other on the mezzanine overlooking the lanes), a dozen lanes of bowling, pool tables, a cozy bar seating area with couches and stone fireplaces, loud music, and video monitors everywhere contribute to the feeling that you're in a nightclub. This is a real nightlife hub; consider coming if you're with a group that can't quite decide where to go for late-night action, as Grand Central is a hip vortex of high energy.

The side-by-side **Mint** and **820** (816 N. Russell St., 503/284-5518, www.mintand820. com) are owned by Lucy Brennan, a renowned mixologist whose cocktail creativity has won her accolades from *Food and Wine* magazine and *Bon Appetit*. Inventive cocktails that incorporate fresh (and sometimes unusual) fruit and juices are the hallmark of Brennan's creations. Mint is nominally the restaurant side of things, with Caribbean-infused cooking, while 820 is the lounge (with outdoor seating), but these popular and richly decorated nightspots, located under the soaring Fremont Bridge, are easily thought of as a two-for-one destination. The crowd is usually well-heeled and attractive in an urban professional kind of way.

A gregarious pub along NW 21st Avenue, **North 45** (517 NW 21st Ave., 503/248-6317, www.north45pub.com) is named for the 45th parallel, which circles the world just south of Portland. And that's the whole point: This is a travel pub, meant to provide the social aspects of a friendly drinking establishment with tastes, sights, and sounds from around the world. In truth, this spot reminds us of a belle epoque

bistro from Brussels, perhaps due to some 20 Belgian beers and the eight different mussel dishes on the menu. Come for a sociable night out and the great atmosphere—there's also a quiet patio in the back with picnic tables.

A relic of the 1950s, the **Space Room** (4800 SE Hawthorne Blvd., 503/235-6957, www. spaceroomlounge.com) is another era's version of futuristic, with its weird flying saucer lights and *Jetsons*-like murals. The most astonishing thing is that no one ever remodeled this dark and often tightly packed little lounge from the days of *Sputnik*. The weirdness isn't lost on irony-seeking scenesters who come in droves to drink strong cocktails and act out their ennui.

You probably already know that in Portland restaurants, everything is going to be local and house-made, but you may not have heard that the reverence for regional and homemade also extends to bars. The **Teardrop Lounge** (1015 NW Everett St., 503/445-8109, http://teardroplounge.com) is a small and stylish see-and-be-seen bar in the midst of the Pearl District where highly creative drinks are crafted from handmade elixirs, hard-to-find Oregon liquors, and tinctures of a very local variety. While the bar celebrates the classic drinks of the cocktail age, it also makes sure that everything is sourced locally. The tonic water and a selection of bitters are made in-house; the changing menu of drinks celebrates locally distilled gin, vodka, and absinthe; house-made infusions fuel many cocktails; and the bartenders are eager to help make sure you get a drink that suits you. The small but thoughtful food menu has offers to match the flavors of the extremely tasty cocktails.

Gay and Lesbian

Portland's gay bar scene used to be concentrated along SW Stark Street downtown, but in the past decade the scene has dispersed, both into new neighborhoods (there are now as many gay bars on the East Side as downtown) and also to regular bars. Gay people are welcome pretty much anywhere in Portland, and you certainly don't need to seek out a gay bar just to have drinks with gay friends. In fact, in

PORTLAND

© BILL MCRAE

Darcelle's

hip nightclubs, there's usually a strong gay subtext to most events anyway. The Gay/Lesbian International News Network recently ranked Portland as the number one U.S. city in its list of Best Cities for Gays, and you'll find that most Portlanders support the gay community. There's certainly no gay ghetto here, so enjoy your gay ol' self wherever you wish.

One of a cluster of bars on SW Stark Street's busiest corner, **Boxxes** (330 SW 11th Ave., 503/226-4171) is a popular spot with young gay men and those looking to meet them. Entertainment at Boxxes takes the form of large-screen videos, go-go boys, bingo nights, and karaoke, though most think of Boxxes as the staging ground for entry into the **Brig,** the dark, sweaty, and hot-hot-hot dance bar in the back.

SW Stark Street is the traditional hub of Portland's gay bar scene, and **Scandals** (1038 SW Stark St., 503/227-5887, www.scandalspdx.com) has been a fixture here since the 1970s. The bar is bright and airy, and in summer the floor-to-ceiling windows slide open so the scene spills onto the sidewalk. While there are pool tables and DJs spinning tunes, this is an easygoing, cruisy bar where (mostly) men come to hang out and meet friends.

The longtime favorite **CC Slaughters** (200 NW 3rd Ave., 503/248-9135, http://ccslaughterspdx.com) has undergone a lot of changes in the past few years. Up front, the Rainbow Room is a frosty-cool cocktail lounge, a place to sip cocktails and play pool in high-style surroundings; food is available as well. The nightclub is entered along NW Davis Street and contains a large bar and dance floor where DJs keep the rhythms pounding. The crowd is mostly male and of all ages, but all are welcome.

Crush (1400 SE Morrison St., 503/235-8150, http://crushbar.squarespace.com) is a bar that defies easy categorization. It's definitely a gay place; witness Tuesday's "That's So Gay" trivia night, Wednesday's "Gaym Night," and the towering drag-queen waitresses. But the majority of people here are young and seemingly straight (it's hard to tell these days), enjoying Crush's arty good looks, fine cocktails, and fun events. Weekends bring DJs and dancing; other evenings may feature theme nights and Tarot readers. There are three separate bar areas, each with its own ambience, including the lounge with its old-fashioned curved bar and the Blue Room for dancing and live music. Crush is a fun, high-energy place to hang.

Darcelle's (208 NW 3rd Ave., 503/222-5338, www.darcellexv.com) is one of those Portland institutions, like biking and brewing, that may not make sense until you get here. Darcelle is a female impersonator extraordinaire who has, over the years, cozied up to all of the political leaders in Oregon and whose outsize personality has made her an entertainment legend for over 40 years. *Everyone* in Portland knows Darcelle. The stage show ($15), a combination of lip-synching and comedy by a bevy of lovely queens, is very funny and rather raunchy, just as it should be. The shows are popular, and a broad spectrum of Portland citizenry, not just devotees of the Imperial Court system, are in attendance. Reservations are recommended, especially on weekends. If it's midnight on Friday or Saturday, then bring on the male strippers!

In super-tolerant Portland, it's easy to ask why gay bars still even exist. Well, places like **Embers** (110 NW Broadway, 503/222-3082) hang on because they are so much damn fun. Part drag showcase (up front), part disco inferno (the back room), Embers is a Portland institution from the days when dancing all night beneath a mirrored ball to "I Will Survive" seemed like an act of defiant liberation. This is still Portland's premier gay dance club, though the crowds here are very inclusive and include gays and straights and everyone in between. If you're young, or young at heart, and feel like dancing to DJs, this is where you want to be.

In the heart of Old Town, **Hobo's** (120 NW 3rd Ave., 503/224-3285, www.hobospdx.com) combines the classic redbrick good looks of an authentic 1890s bar with the courtly rhythms of a contemporary piano lounge. Wednesday-Sunday evenings starting at 8pm, pianists tickle the ivories (jazz, show tunes, occasional classical numbers) while the well-dressed clientele—a friendly mix of gays, lesbians, and their straight friends—enjoy cocktails. Hobos is a classy spot for an after-dinner drink.

Dance Clubs

In many ways Portland is post-discotheque: There aren't that many clubs devoted solely to dancing. Most of the clubs listed here for live music also have dance nights, often with dress-up themes involved. At **Holocene** (1001 SE Morrison St., 503/239-7639, www.holocene.org), the nightly entertainment can be live music, DJs, performance art, or regularly scheduled evening events. Many events hover at the intersection of music, performance, and technology, and the crowds are fun and varied. **Fez Ballroom** (316 SW 11th Ave., 503/221-7262, www.fezballroom.com) is in a lively part of downtown, and offers multiple floors of fun—in addition to hip-hop and techno nightclub scene, there are frequent theme nights, dress-up parties, and live entertainment.

© BILL MCRAE

Hobo's is one of Old Town's classiest bars.

Live Music

One of the pioneers along gentrifying North Mississippi Avenue is a tiny, acoustically rich recording studio called **Mississippi Studios** (3939 N. Mississippi Ave., 503/288-3895, www.mississippistudios.com), where local and regional bands go to record music and perform in the studio's intimate space. Check the website to find out what concerts may be offered during your visit; this is a great spot to catch rising stars. Next door is **Bar Bar** (503/288-3895), the food and liquor side of the studios, with a great, fire pit-dominated back patio for pre- or post-concert enjoyment.

The **Alberta Rose Theatre** (3000 NE Alberta St., 503/719-6055, www.albertarosetheatre.com) hosts *Live Wire!*, a wacky live radio variety show, as well as a selection of world music, cabaret and circus music, comedy, and whatever else is slightly alternative and cool.

If you're looking for the punk edge of the Portland live music scene, one good place to start is **The Know** (2026 NE Alberta St.,

Kell's is a popular spot for Celtic music.

© BILL MCRAE

503/473-8729), often referred to as Portland's CBGB.

Speaking of the cool kids, you'll find them on NE Russell Street, in the wood-paneled Victorian-era bar at the **Secret Society** (116 NE Russell St., 503/493-3600, thesecretsocietylounge.com) or smoking outside the **Wonder Ballroom** (128 NE Russell St., 503/284-8686, wonderballroom.com). The ballroom at the Secret Society hosts shows ranging from choro to bluegrass to jazz; the Wonder's shows tend to be rock or acoustic, including some pretty big names on the indie circuit (this is where you may have caught locals Blitzen Trapper or Colin Meloy a couple of years ago). Between the two venues is one of Portland's hottest restaurants, Toro Bravo.

Before you hit town, check out the performers scheduled at the **Aladdin Theater** (3017 SE Milwaukie Ave., 503/233-1994, www.aladdin-theater.com). This 1920s burlesque house has been gussied up to host an eclectic array of touring performers including Steve Earle, the Buena Vista Social Club, and Rufus Wainwright. Many folk, world beat, and indie rock bands play here, and it's a wonderful small theater for taking in a concert.

Kell's Irish Restaurant and Pub (112 SW 2nd Ave., 503/227-4057, www.kellsirish.com/portland) is a landmark not just because of its Victorian good looks, but also thanks to live Celtic music. The musicians are usually local—Portland has a large Celtic music community—although touring bands are also featured; most Sunday evenings offer easygoing jam sessions. The first Saturday evening of every month brings Irish dancers, kicking up a jig to live music.

A throwback to swinging supper clubs of the 1950s, **Tony Starlight Super Club** (3728 NE Sandy Blvd., 503/517-8584, www.tonystarlight.com) offers high-energy jazz performances and a spoofy lounge act that is among Portland's funniest music-stand-up comedy combos: The Tony Starlight Show, offered on Saturday evenings, is a hilarious and always changing routine by owner Brett Kucera, whose stage persona, Tony Starlight, is a great musical performer but also a first-class comedian. Tony offers versions of jazz classics from Frank, Sammy, and Dino, but as the evening goes on, the shtick and the songs—slightly rewritten and increasingly irreverent—get funnier and funnier. When the wigs and costumes come out, prepare for complete insanity. On other evenings, the club offers a variety of entertainment, including straightforward jazz, Latin rhythms, karaoke nights, and fashion shows. You'll need reservations for the Tony Starlight show ($16), and it's 21 and older only, two shows nightly every Saturday. The best seats are reserved for diners at the supper club—the menu offers well-prepared pasta, chicken, and steaks.

JAZZ AND BLUES

The hottest jazz club in Portland is **Jimmy Mak's** (221 NW 10th Ave., 503/295-6542, www.jimmymaks.com). There's live music every night except Sunday, frequently featuring local drummer Mel Brown and his band. National touring jazz groups also often appear. The lounge at the back of the popular steakhouse **Clyde's** (5474 NE Sandy Blvd., 503/281-9200) usually has live music on the weekends; especially popular are the Sunday evening jazz jam sessions led by local drummer extraordinaire Ron Steen. The atmosphere is friendly and inclusive.

The exquisite and formal **Tea Court** (1009 SW Broadway, 503/790-7752, www.heathmanhotel.com) at the Heathman Hotel, paneled in eucalyptus and illuminated by crystal chandeliers, is a delightful counterpoint to live jazz music, performed Wednesday-Saturday nights with no cover charge. Local jazz vocalist Mary Kadderly is a frequent guest artist. This is the spot to dress up a bit, sip cocktails, and slip into a reverie about the golden age of jazz. Located in historic Union Station, **Wilf's** (800 NW 6th Ave., 503/223-0070, www.wilfsrestaurant.com) is an atmospheric spot to take in live jazz. The large, high-ceilinged, redbrick dining room was created as the formal dining room for rail travelers during the golden age of the railroad. Jazz

is normally offered Wednesday-Saturday evenings. Many of Portland's top local performers cycle through.

Over in Southeast, **Duff's Garage** (1635 SE 7th Ave., 503/234-2337) hosts blues, roots, and rockabilly bands. In addition to regular 9:30pm shows, Duff's has 6pm-8pm Tuesday-Friday happy hour music and a popular Wednesday night blues jam. With live jazz and blues seven nights a week, newcomer **Blue Diamond** (2016 NE Sandy Blvd., 503/230-9590) is a laid-back, insider's place to enjoy top local bands.

ROCK

Just west of the Burnside Bridge is **Dante's** (SW 3rd Ave. and Burnside St., 503/226-6630, www.danteslive.com), where, in addition to live alternative bands, you'll find often outrageous cabaret and burlesque shows. A few blocks away, at the eclectic **Someday Lounge** (125 NW 5th Ave., 503/248-1030), you can find funk one night and a songwriter showcase the next.

One stronghold of the concert scene is the **Crystal Ballroom** (1332 W. Burnside St., 503/225-0047, www.mcmenamins.com), where a mix of rock, indie, and world beat artists play in a large ballroom. There, you can "dance on air" thanks to the floating dance floor—perhaps the only one in the United States.

Portland's East Side has a lively music scene. A major destination in any tour of Portland's music hotbeds would include **Doug Fir** (830 E. Burnside St., 503/231-9663, www.dougfirlounge.com), which attracts some of Portland's most interesting acts and is part of a hip development that includes a vintage motor court motel and late-night restaurant.

If you came to Portland to find the remnant of its hippie Grateful Dead roots, then the **Laurelthirst Public House** (2958 NE Glisan St., 503/232-1504) is where you need to be. This old and funky tavern has excellent local folk and country swing bands along with a feel-good vibe that takes you back to the Summer of Love.

© BILL MCRAE

Dante's

Comedy

Portland's veteran comedy club, **Harvey's** (436 NW 6th Ave., 503/241-0338, www.harveyscomedyclub.com), might suffer from poor acoustics and a lack of intimacy if you sit in the back, but it's got the classic comedy club vibe and the talent is usually good. The cover charge is normally $15. A reasonably priced menu and a full bar are available. For rollicking comedy improv, go to **Comedy Sportz** (1963 NW Kearney St., 503/236-8888, www.portlandcomedy.com, $12), where two teams compete for laughs using suggestions from the audience. Another option for improv is **Curious Comedy Theater** (5225 NE M. L. King Jr. Blvd., 503/477-9477, www.curiouscomedy.org, $5-12), a nonprofit theater that offers popular classes and workshops in addition to weekend shows.

Newest on the scene is the ultra-hip **Helium Comedy Club** (1510 SE 9th Ave., 888/643-8669, www.heliumcomedy.com/portland, $15-30) which caters to the edgier side of Comedy Central humor. This venue has quickly become a hub of the "alt comedy" world; each weekend, rising stars perform to a packed house of Portland's hip, bespectacled locals.

THE ARTS
Performing Arts

The **Oregon Symphony** (503/228-1353, www.orsymphony.org) is the oldest orchestra west of the Mississippi, and it performs in a historic jewel-box of an auditorium, the **Arlene Schnitzer Concert Hall** (1037 SW Broadway). **Portland Opera** (503/241-1802, www.portlandopera.org) stages four operas per year and hosts traveling Broadway shows, mounted at the 3,000-seat **Keller Auditorium** (222 SW Clay St.). Other classical music organizations include the **Portland Baroque Orchestra** (503/222-6000, www.pbo.org), led by Monica Huggett and presenting 18th-century music on period instruments; **Portland Piano International** (503/228-1388, www.portlandpiano.org), which presents world-renowned pianists in recital; and the **Third Angle New Music Ensemble** (503/331-0301, www.thirdangle.org), presenting contemporary classical music.

Oregon Ballet Theatre (503/222-5538, www.obt.org) is the city's classical dance troupe, usually performing at Keller Auditorium. **White Bird Dance** (503/245-1600, www.whitebird.org) brings an impressive number of world-class modern dance troupes to Portland. White Bird sponsors two different series each year, one at Arlene Schnitzer Concert Hall that features established troupes such as Paul Taylor or Mark Morris, the other featuring edgier and more intimate dance pieces held at various venues in Portland. Portland's home-grown modern dance troupe, **BodyVox** (1201 NW 17 Ave., 503/229-0627, bodyvox.com), is known for its energy and wit.

Theater

More than a dozen theatrical troupes make up a significant presence on Portland's cultural scene. **Imago Theatre** (17 SE 8th Ave., 503/231-9581, www.imagotheatre.com) is an internationally acclaimed troupe that employs multimedia visuals, masks, puppets, dance, and animation to achieve dramatic resonance. Imago performs in an old Masonic hall that is at once intimate and spacious enough for the ambitious visual effects and movement of this cutting-edge troupe. Like Imago, **Do Jump Extremely Physical Theater** (Echo Theater, 1515 SE 37th Ave., 503/231-1232, www.dojump.org) wows its audiences with innovative productions that meld trapeze and other circus arts with whimsical choreography.

For more traditional theater, **Portland Center Stage** (503/445-3700, www.pcs.org) operates out of the renovated **Portland Armory Building** (128 NW 11th Ave.) in the Pearl District. PCS productions encompass classical, contemporary, and premiere works in addition to an annual summer playwrights' festival. Portland's other major theater group, **Artists Repertory Theater** (1515 SW Morrison St., 503/241-1278, www.artistsrep.org), produces intimate, often edgier productions from its "black box" theater just west of downtown.

Art Galleries

Portland has a dynamic fine art scene. Many of the top galleries are in the Pearl District and other neighborhoods in Northwest Portland. To preview some of Portland's leading galleries, go to the **Portland Art Dealers Association** website (www.padaoregon.org), which has details of monthly shows at a dozen of the city's top galleries.

One of the best times to explore Portland's galleries is on the first Thursday of every month during the **First Thursday Gallery Walk.** More than 30 gallery owners coordinate show openings the first Thursday of every month, and many offer complimentary refreshments. Visit the agglomeration of galleries in the Pearl District, where the biggest crowds gather. In this neighborhood, **Elizabeth Leach Gallery** (417 NW 9th Ave., 503/224-0521, www.elizabethleach.com) is one of Portland's most successful and long-established galleries, presenting challenging and inventive art pieces from top regional and national artists. Also check out the nearby **DeSoto Building** (724 NW Davis St.), which houses three of Portland's top galleries and the Museum of Contemporary Craft.

For something completely different, plan to attend **Last Thursday,** an event at month's end that highlights the dynamic district of galleries and independent designers on Northeast Alberta Street. A mix of street fair, performance art, and gallery tour, Last Thursday is much more raucous than First Thursday, with live bands, fire-eaters, and other high jinks adding an almost circuslike atmosphere to the Alberta Street art scene.

Portland Institute for Contemporary Art or PICA (224 NW 13th Ave., 503/242-1419, www.pica.org) is Portland's leader in cutting-edge performance, experimental theater, new music, and dance. Throughout the year PICA offers lectures, performances, and exhibitions at many venues throughout the city, but the organization's top event, September's **Time-Based Art Festival** (TBA), is a contemporary art festival of regional, national, and international

PORTLAND PUBLIC ART

Downtown Portland is filled with public art, including sculptures, fountains, murals, paintings, photography, and other expressions of creativity. The Regional Arts and Culture Council offers a free Public Art Walking Tour Map, available from **Public Art Gallery** on the second floor of the Portland Building (1120 SW 5th Ave., 503/823-5111, www.racc.org). The Public Art Gallery is an excellent place to start your tour as it displays a number of paintings and photographs by top regional artists, all part of the city's collection of art. There's more of the city's public art collection on display in **City Hall** (1221 SW 4th Ave.), the **Justice Center** (1120 SW 3rd Ave.), and the **Portland Center for the Performing Arts** (1111 SW Broadway).

For outdoor sculpture and installations, check out the following areas: If you start your public art tour at the Portland Building, you can't miss *Portlandia*, the enormous hammered-copper statue that presides over the main entrance. The **South Park Blocks** have a number of public statues, including an equestrian bronze of Teddy Roosevelt as a Rough Rider, a brooding statue of Abraham Lincoln, and *Rebecca at the Well* (also called the Shemanski Fountain), a 1920s gift to the city from a Polish immigrant that depicts the biblical Rebecca fetching water.

Also on the South Park Blocks, the **Portland Art Museum Memorial Sculpture Mall** (1219 SW Park Ave.) features a number of outdoor sculptures, including *Brushstrokes* by Roy Lichtenstein.

Pioneer Courthouse Square is another focus for public art. A whimsical "weather machine" in the square's northwest corner puts on a show of predicting the weather each day at noon, with mist, music, and the cuckoo clock-like emergence of a symbol to forecast the weather. The lifelike statue *Allow Me* portrays a businessman hailing a cab; it's so realistic that you'll look twice. On the next block, along SW Yamhill and SW Morrison Streets, are fountains that feature bronze bears, ducks, deer, and beavers cavorting in the water.

Two of Portland's fountains are worth a detour. In Waterfront Park, the **Salmon Street Springs** is a large fountain that recycles 4,924 gallons of water per minute in a changing display of patterns. **Ira's Fountain,** in the forecourt of Keller Auditorium (SW 3rd Ave. and Clay St.) is a terraced fountain that resembles an enormous waterfall. About 13,000 gallons of water per minute cascade through this fountain. It's especially lovely when it's lit from below on evenings when there are performances at Keller Auditorium.

© BILL MCRAE

Ira's Fountain is the place to cool off in summer.

artists presenting theater, dance, music, film, visual exhibitions, and installations.

Art in the Pearl (503/722-9017, www.artinthepearl.com) is an outdoor arts and crafts fair held over Labor Day weekend in the North Park Blocks, bounded by NW Park and 8th Avenues and Burnside and Glisan Streets along the eastern edge of the Pearl District. This street fair showcases the creations of the local artistic community and also features food and music.

CINEMA

Portland has plenty of multiscreen movie theaters that show the latest Hollywood releases. Thankfully, it also has a rich selection of alternative and repertory cinemas that feature independent, foreign, and vintage movies as well. Almost 85 percent of the city's first-run movie theaters are controlled by the **Regal Cinemas** chain (www.regalcinemas.com), including the following cinemas convenient to central Portland: **Fox Tower Stadium 10** (846 SW Park Ave., 503/221-3280), the **Broadway Metroplex 4** (1000 SW Broadway, 503/243-1404), **Pioneer Square Stadium 6** (340 SW Morrison St., 503/295-0909), the **Lloyd Mall 8 Cinema** (2320 Lloyd Center Mall, 503/335-3760), and the **Lloyd Center 10 Cinema** (1510 NE Multnomah St., 503/287-0338).

Portland offers an array of genre movie houses, such as **Cinema 21** (616 NW 21st Ave., 503/223-4515, www.cinema21.com), which is the city's principal independent art-house movie theater. Another independent theater that shows offbeat, foreign, and cult movies is **Hollywood Theatre** (NE 41st Ave. and Sandy Blvd., 503/281-4215, www.hollywoodtheatre.org), housed in a vintage movie palace. The **Clinton Street Theater** (2522 SE Clinton St., 503/238-8899, www.clintonsttheater.com) is an art-house cinema featuring films that generally would not have a market in most other theaters. This might mean *The Rocky Horror Picture Show* every Saturday night, vintage concert films, or dated propaganda films from the Cold War.

Courtesy of brewpub-meisters the brothers McMenamin, Portland also features several restored vintage theaters, among other screening facilities, featuring just-past-first-run flicks ($3) along with pub grub and beer. The most convenient to central Portland neighborhoods are the **Mission Theater** (1624 NW Glisan St., 503/223-4527) and the neo-Moorish **Bagdad Theater & Pub** (3710 SE Hawthorne Blvd., 503/236-9234). For info on what's playing at McMenamins establishments, check out www.mcmenamins.com.

It's not a McMenamins operation, but the budget-priced **Laurelhurst Theater** (NE 28th Ave. and Burnside St., 503/232-5511, www.laurelhursttheater.com) offers beer and pizza to accompany vintage and slightly dated first-run films.

Another twist in the drinks-with-movies trend is **Living Room Theaters** (341 SW 10th Ave., 971/222-2010, www.livingroomtheaters.com), which blends the offerings of a six-theater cinema with a high-end cocktail bar. The films tend toward a mix of art-house flicks, foreign films, and revivals of classics.

Part of the Portland Art Museum, the **Northwest Film Center** (934 SW Salmon St., 503/221-1156, ext. 10, www.nwfilm.org) is the Pacific Northwest's foremost school of filmmaking and media production. As part of its curriculum and community outreach, it offers an ongoing series of foreign, classic, experimental, and independent films that showcase an extremely broad array of cinema and video art forms. Included are thematic series (for example, contemporary films of Egypt), special retrospectives (Fassbinder, Milos Forman, Derek Jarman), and visiting artist programs. Most films are screened at the Whitsell Theater at the Portland Art Museum.

FESTIVALS AND EVENTS

The February **Portland International Film Festival** (503/221-1156, www.nwfilm.org/festivals/piff) is a two-week showcase of foreign and art films that are screened in various theaters across the city.

The **Cinco de Mayo Fiesta** (www.cincodemayo.org) celebrates Hispanic heritage at Tom

McCall Waterfront Park the first weekend (Thurs.-Sun.) in May. This has become one of the largest celebrations of its kind in the country. Mariachis, folk dance exhibitions, a large selection of Mexican food, and fireworks displays are included in the festivities. Admission is $8 adults, $4 children ages 6-12.

Portland is a bicycle town that loves a festival, but it questions authority. Put this all together and you get **Pedalpalooza** (www. shift2bikes.org/pedalpalooza), a decentralized, even anarchic celebration of Portland's bike culture. The festival is extremely freeform and is held in multiple locations with only a few organized annual events. Most events are just someone's idea for a ride or a crazy stunt that involves a bike—including the infamous World Naked Bike Ride (drawing about 10,000 riders in various stages of undress), rides for kids and seniors, bicycle polo and jousting, a bike blessing at a Catholic church, and a biking-themed film festival that includes a "Bikesploitation" series of biking porn films. The three-week festival is held in June; check the website for events, as Pedalpalooza is growing and evolving fast. There is more fun and nudity than at the Rose Festival!

The **Waterfront Blues Festival** (503/282-0555, www.waterfrontbluesfest.com) is the largest festival of its kind on the West Coast. It takes place the first weekend in July at Tom McCall Waterfront Park and features some of the biggest names in the blues. The $10 admission and donations (two canned-good items) go to the Oregon Food Bank.

From the end of June through July, **Chamber Music Northwest** (503/294-6400, www. cmnw.org) presents five weeks of classical music concerts in two locations: Reed College in Southeast Portland and the Catlin Gabel School in Northwest Portland. Ticket prices begin at $25.

No longer Gay Pride, not even Gay and Lesbian Pride, it's now just the **Pride Festival** (503/295-9788, www.pridenw.org): Portland's largest gay festival celebrates Stonewall and affirms the city's LGBTQ community, held on Father's Day weekend in June. The Waterfront Park main stage has entertainment all weekend, but Sunday is the big day, when some 50,000 people attend the Pride Parade.

For summer outdoor concerts, the place to be is the **Oregon Zoo** (503/280-2493, www. zooconcerts.com, late June-late Aug., $25-35). Crowds spread out on the lawn below the stage to hear first-rate, often big-name talent.

Taking place the last full weekend in July in Portland's Tom McCall Waterfront Park, **Oregon Brewers Festival** (www.oregonbrewfest.com) is North America's largest gathering of independent brewers. The four-day event showcases the wares of more than 80 breweries and attracts more than 72,000 beer lovers. Admission is free, but you'll need to spend $11 for a souvenir mug and four drink tokens. Live musical entertainment accompanies the beer.

An August festival, **The Bite of Oregon** (Tom McCall Waterfront Park, 503/248-0600, www.biteoforegon.com), offers samples of local culinary specialties, and proceeds go to the Special Olympics. Live music is also a highlight.

Portland dares to compare its live music scene to Austin, Texas, and the citywide **Music Fest Northwest** (www.musicfestnw.com) is Portland's answer to Austin's SXSW festival. Over the course of four days and nights in early September, over 200 bands gather in Portland to play their music for large and enthusiastic audiences. The festival is held at sites across the city; pretty much all the major nightclubs and live music venues are involved. To attend the concerts, you'll need to buy a $90 wristband, which gets you into most concerts and venues.

PORTLAND ROSE FESTIVAL

The **Portland Rose Festival** (503/227-2681, www.rosefestival.org) has been the city's major summer event for nine decades. The Rose Queen and her court (chosen from among local high school entrants), Navy sailors, and floats from several parades clog Portland's traffic arteries during this 18-day citywide celebration each June. Air shows, a hot-air balloon classic, the Indy World Series car race, and a traditional rose show round out the main attractions. Check out the website for a schedule of what is essentially a small-town festival done with big-town flair. Even if parades and crowds are not your thing, the civic pride here is genuine and appealing. Portlanders camp out along the parade route in the same places year after year, sometimes several days in advance, just to catch a coveted glimpse at the floats passing by.

The key to enjoying festival events is avoiding traffic and parking hassles. A $5 TriMet day ticket entitles the pass-holder to unlimited rides on MAX, the Portland Streetcar, or the bus all day long. As for traffic, be especially wary of the waterfront. Such festival features as food booths and carnival rides in Tom McCall Waterfront Park, as well as military ship displays on the Willamette, draw huge crowds.

Another good reason to come to the waterfront is the chance to see the dragon boat races. These brightly painted ceremonial canoes from China have been taken up in earnest here. Teams compete on the Willamette River with 16 paddlers and a coxswain.

Two of the more colorful events of the June fete are the **Grand Floral Parade** and the **Festival of Flowers** at Pioneer Courthouse Square. In the latter, all manner of colorful blossoms fill the square to overflowing during the first week of the festival. The Grand Floral Parade usually begins the Saturday following the opening of the festival. You can reserve seats in the Coliseum ahead of time, but save your money and station yourself on an upper floor along the parade route or visit the floats at Oregon Square between Lloyd Center and the Convention Center during the week following the parade. Any lofty perch is sufficient for taking in all the hoopla, drill teams, the Rose Queen, and equestrian demonstrations. This procession is the second-largest all-floral parade in the United States.

Shopping

Oregon has no sales tax, so you'll find Portland shopping especially satisfying.

DOWNTOWN AND SOUTHWEST
Shopping Centers and Malls

In the heart of the downtown shopping district, **Pioneer Place** (SW 5th Ave. and Morrison St., 503/228-5800, www.pioneerplace.com) is an upscale shopping development that features a number of national merchandisers, including Eddie Bauer, Ann Taylor, J. Crew, Coach, and more. The lower level features a vast food court amidst pleasant fountains.

H&M (340 SW Morrison St., 503/241-0257), the Swedish clothier, offers stylish but inexpensive clothing and accessories. It's linked to Pioneer Place via skywalks. Indigenous to the Pacific Northwest, **Nordstrom** (701 SW Broadway, 503/224-6666) offers downtown shoppers quality clothing and shoes from its location just west of Pioneer Courthouse Square; **Macy's** (621 SW 5th Ave., 503/223-0512) is a couple of blocks east.

Niketown (920 SW 6th Ave., 503/221-6453) is the flagship store of Oregon's largest sportswear manufacturer, and you'll find a large selection of elite shoes and sports gear in a whiz-bang retail environment. If you're looking for Nike quality and logoed goods at a lower

© BILL MCRAE

The Portland Farmers Market is the culinary heart of the city.

price, consider heading to the **Nike Outlet Store** (2650 NE Martin Luther King Jr. Blvd., 503/281-5901) in inner Northeast Portland.

Farmers Markets
◖ PORTLAND FARMERS MARKET
One of the institutions that characterize Portland, the **Portland Farmers Market** (South Park Blocks, www.portlandfarmersmarket.org) attracts throngs of people, and not just for food shopping. Every Saturday, upwards of 15,000 people come to the market to gaze at locally produced food and socialize with friends. This teeming market features breads and baked goods, locally grown fruits and vegetables, artisan cheeses, wild mushrooms, organic meat and poultry, freshly caught fish and seafood, and nursery stock. For entertainment, there's always live music, and famous local chefs give cooking demonstrations. In addition, this is a great place to come for breakfast or lunch, as a number of food carts offer freshly made food. People watching is of the highest caliber here. On Wednesday from 10am-2pm there's

a smaller version of this farmers market a few blocks to the north, at the end of the South Park Blocks near SW Salmon and Park.

There are other farmers markets in Portland neighborhoods throughout the week. In fact, during summer and fall, Monday is the only day without a market somewhere. For a complete list of farmers markets in Portland, follow the links at www.oregonfarmersmarkets.org.

Clothing and Accessories
You don't have to be in Oregon very long before woolen plaid shirts begin to look sensible and stylish. Pendleton Woolen Mills is an Oregon company, and at downtown's **Pendleton Store** (900 SW 5th Ave., 503/242-0037, www.pendleton-usa.com) you can pick up distinctive wool shirts, skirts, and blankets that will last for years.

Portland's most upscale menswear store is **Mario's** (833 SW Broadway, 503/227-3477, http://marios.com), with the best of casual and formal wear from the world's top designers. **Parallel** (1016 SW Washington St.,

503/274-8882, www.parallelportland.com) is a fun spot for women's designer clothing and accessories from small, specialty fashion houses, many based in Portland or the Pacific Northwest.

Looking for women's fashion? A Portland fashion leader for over 30 years, **The Mercantile** (729 SW Alder St., 503/223-6649, www.mercantileportland.com) is a top choice for sophisticated clothing, both hip and professional. The Mercantile carries many New York and LA clothing lines, and has exclusive representation of several Portland-based designers.

John Helmer Haberdasher (969 SW Broadway, 503/223-4976, www.johnhelmer.com) has been serving Portland as a top menswear and hat shop since 1921, and the cool sophistication continues. Most famous for its hats, John Helmer also has top-quality suits and casual clothing with a sophisticated edge.

Are you beginning to like the look of eclectic, carefully curated hipster fashion so prevalent in Portland? Head to **Reveille** (1306 W. Burnside St., 971/279-4128, www.reveilleshop.com) and get to the source. You'll find both men's and women's designs from small-production design houses around the world.

In the Southwest Portland neighborhood of Hillsdale is **La Paloma** (6316 SW Capitol Hwy., 503/246-3417, www.palomaclothing.com), a longtime favorite women's clothing with fashions for work and play, and particularly for travel—much of the clothing here is designed especially to be packable.

Crafts

Real Mother Goose (901 SW Yamhill St., 503/223-9510 or 800/968-1070, www.therealmothergoose.com) is a quality crafts gallery that presents jewelry, pottery, woodcrafts, and other design goods from hundreds of Pacific Northwest artists and craftspeople. It's an excellent place to buy one-of-a-kind gifts.

In operation since 1974, **Portland Saturday Market** (just south of the Burnside Bridge in Waterfront Park, www.portlandsaturdaymarket.com, 10am-5pm Sat., 11am-4:30pm Sun. Mar.-Dec. 24,) is the largest outdoor arts and crafts fair in the United States, attracting an estimated 750,000 visitors each year. The handicrafts range from exquisite woodwork (at reasonable prices), pottery, paintings, and jewelry to more uniquely Portland items like tie-die baby clothes and handmade juggling equipment. What's astonishing is the high quality that's been maintained here for decades.

Wine

If you don't have time to make a trip to Oregon's wine country, stop by **Oregon Wines on Broadway** (515 SW Broadway, 503/228-4655 or 800/943-8858, www.oregonwinesonbroadway.com), a wine shop devoted to Pacific Northwest wines. Wine-tastings and winemaker events are often held on Thursday nights.

Housewares

High-style housewares and aesthetic everyday kitchen tools are the specialty at **Canoe** (1136 SW Alder St., 503/889-8545, www.canoeonline.net), where you'll swoon over the simple things in life: the perfect bookends, tissue box, or ice cream scoop.

Toys and Gifts

Finnegan's Toys and Gifts (820 SW Washington St., 503/221-0306, www.finneganstoys.com) is the city's largest toy store, with something for kids of all ages.

Music

Portland's largest privately owned musical instrument shop, **Apple Music Row** (225 SW 1st Ave., 503/226-0036, www.applemusicrow.com) features more than 1,000 guitars in stock at any given time. There's also a great selection of electronic keyboards and drums.

Leather Goods

Having a "shades of grey" moment? **Spartacus Leathers** (300 SW 12th Ave., 503/224-2604, http://spartacusleathers.com) can help. Here you'll find a wide selection leather, latex, and fantasy gear made in Oregon by Spartacus, plus a large selection of toys and accessories to boost the play factor during your stay in Portland.

Outdoor Clothing and Gear

Based in the Portland metro area, **Columbia Sportswear** (911 SW Broadway, 503/226-6800, www.columbia.com) has its flagship store downtown on SW Broadway. This is the place to go for fashionable, hardworking outerwear for recreation and heavy weather. For discounts on the same quality clothing and gear, go to the **Columbia Sportswear Outlet** (1323 SE Tacoma St., 503/238-0118) in Sellwood.

NORTHWEST
Clothing and Accessories

If all Portland hipsters had money, they'd be shopping at **Lizard Lounge** (1323 NW Irving St., 503/416-7176, www.lizardloungepdx. com), where you can pick up for functional, ecofriendly, stylish duds from local company Nau and others; stop in on First Thursday evenings for a party.

Not everyone visiting Portland is a bride-to-be, and not every dress designed by **Lena Medoyeff Studio** (710 NW 23rd Ave., 503/227-0011, www.lenadress.com) is a wedding dress. Still, Medoyeff is most famous for her smart, modern wedding dresses made from fair trade silks from a family-run mill at the foothills of the Himalayas. She also designs and makes silk event dresses and fashions that can be worn every day of the week.

Popina Swimwear Boutique (318 NW 11th Ave., 503/243-7946, www.popinaswimwear. com) is a fabulous shop for women's bathing suits and swim accessories, with 25 international brands and Popina's own line of update, retro-chic swimwear.

Founded in Portland in 1983, **Hanna Andersson** (327 NW 10th Ave., 503/321-5275, www.hannaandersson.com) sells clothing for kids in bright, simple Swedish-inspired designs and soft, durable cotton. It's decidedly upscale children's wear, but it's high quality and well-wearing, destined to be handed down.

One of Portland's best sources for refined, upscale women's fashion is **Physical Element**

(416 NW 12th Ave., 503/224-5425, www.physicalelement.com). While the styles here tend to be classic, sprinkled throughout are more sassy fashions from local designers.

Up on NW 23rd is another hot spot for small, locally owned boutiques. For fun children's clothes, go to **Duck Duck Goose** (525 NW 23rd Ave., 503/916-0636, http://shop-duckduckgoose.com) and to **Zelda's Shoe Bar** (633 NW 23rd Ave., 503/226-0363, www.zeldaspdx.com) for a wide selection of high-end shoes mostly from European designers. **Twist** (30 NW 23rd Pl., 503/224-0334, www.twist-online.com) is one of the city's best boutiques for one-of-a-kind jewelry items.

Books
◖ POWELL'S CITY OF BOOKS

For many visitors, **Powell's City of Books** (1005 W. Burnside St., 503/228-0540 or 800/878-7323, www.powells.com, 9am-11pm daily) is one of Portland's primary attractions. A block square and three stories tall, Powell's combines new, used, and out-of-print books and is usually absolutely thronged with bibliophiles. In addition to miles of bookshelves, Powell's offers a coffee shop as well as free author events and book signings.

Housewares

Whether you're a professional chef or an enthusiastic home cook, you'll find every culinary device known to humankind, plus handsome china and pottery, at **Sur La Table** (1102 NW Couch St., 503/295-9679). Cooking classes and wine-tasting courses are held in the adjacent display kitchen.

Cargo (380 NW 13th Ave., 503/209-8349, www.cargoimportspdx.com) is a vast treasure chest of furniture, housewares and crafts from around the world. What makes Cargo different from most import stores is the keen artistic eye and high-spirited sense of fun of owner Patty Merrill, who selects much of the inventory during trips around the world. There's a little bit of everything here—from carved wooden santos from Mexico to Vietnamese flowerpots to propaganda posters from the former Soviet Union.

It's kind of like visiting your crazy aunt's overflowing attic—if your aunt also had impeccable taste and a giddy sense of humor.

Outdoor Clothing and Gear

The Northwest Portland outpost of **REI** (1405 NW Johnson St., 503/221-1938) is where to head if you forgot your tent, bike helmet, or crampons, or if you are shopping for functional, all-weather clothing for active lifestyles.

Synonymous with earth-friendly and socially responsible manufacturing, **Patagonia** (907 NW Irving St., 503/525-2552) shares a large and strikingly handsome historical storefront with the Ecotrust Foundation in the Pearl District. Patagonia offers serious gear and clothing for those serious about the outdoors.

NORTHEAST

Built in 1960, **Lloyd Center** (NE 15th Ave. and Weidler St., 503/282-2511, www.lloydcenter. com) was the first shopping center in North America and is still one of Portland's major shopping destinations. Centered around an Olympic-size indoor ice-skating rink (Tonya Harding once trained here), Lloyd Center boasts more than 200 retail outlets (including Nordstrom, Sears, and Macy's), a food court, and two multiplex cinemas.

One of Northeast Portland's top destinations for strolling, window shopping, and shopping at independent shops is North Mississippi Avenue between Fremont and Skidmore Streets. Here you'll find dozens of locally own boutiques; fun bars, restaurants and food carts; and excellent people watching. Favorite shops include **Gypsy Chic** (3966 N. Mississippi Ave., 503/234-9779, http://shop.gypsy-chic.com) for casual but elegant women's clothing, **Manifesto** (3806 N. Mississippi Ave., 503/546-0910, www. manifestoshoes.com) for men and women's shoes, and **Missing Link** (3824 N Mississippi Ave., 503/235-0032, www.missinglinktoys. com) for unique toys and gifts (like plush doll microbes). You'll need to stop in at **Meadow** (3731 N. Mississippi Ave., 503/288-4633, www.atthemeadow.com). What's not to like in a shop that sells dozens of different finishing salts, wine, flowers, artisan chocolate, and the largest selection of bitters imaginable?

Anchoring Mississippi Avenue is the **Rebuilding Center** (3625 N. Mississippi Ave., 503/331-1877, http://rebuildingcenter.org). No other retail establishment reveals Portland's 21st-century DIY soul more than the Rebuilding Center. This mammoth 64,000-square-foot warehouse is filled with every kind of house salvage you can imagine, from used-once lumber, to old ceramic toilets, vintage doors and windows of every description, and just about every element of material that makes up a home. Much of the structure itself was built from salvaged materials, and is worth a gander for its funky style. What sets this apart from any other urban junkyard is the obvious pride and affection Portlanders have for the Rebuilding Center. Using salvage isn't just a way to save money, it's a lifestyle.

A few blocks east on Williams Avenue is another hotbed of hipster-focused shops, pubs, and restaurants. If you wonder where Portland's "put a bird on it" aesthetic hails from, look no further than **Queen Bee Creations** (3961 N. Williams Ave., 503/232-1755, www.queenbee-creations.com) where you'll find handmade bags, wallets, bike packs, and other fun leather cases, many in fact with whimsical birds on them. Just around the corner is impossible-to-miss **Lodekka** (between Failing and Shaver Sts., 503/789-6401, www.lodekka.com), a dress shop housed in a 1965-era double-decker bus from Liverpool. The fun fashions here are a mix of vintage and fresh creations from local designers.

For mid-century chic, head to **Red Fox Vintage** (3014 NE Killingsworth St., 971/302-7065, http://redfoxvintage.com), where you'll find fabulous old fashions, furniture, records, jewelry, decor, and other oddities.

Old Portland Hardware (700 NE 22nd Ave., 503/234-7380, www.oldportlandhardware.com) is Portland's top purveyor of antique hardware, salvage, and house parts of all descriptions.

SOUTHEAST
Housewares and Home Decor

Acres of upholstery fabric from around the world make the **Whole Nine Yards** (1820 E. Burnside St., 503/223-2880, http://w9yards.com) a must-stop for home decorators.

A Portland original, **Hippo Hardware** (1040 E. Burnside St., 503/231-1444, www.hippohardware.com) has been collecting period lighting, plumbing, hardware, and architectural components since 1976, when, as they say the "notion of selling things that many people threw away was considered strange at best." The great thing about Hippo Hardware is that it hasn't gone upscale or hipster like Portland's other salvage and house part businesses—it's still the very funky operation it's always been. Equal parts secondhand shop, antiques store, and house salvage emporium, it's a vast and fascinating place to explore.

The showroom for **Pratt & Larson Tile** (1201 SE 3rd Ave. 503/231-9464, www.prattandlarson.com), a local ceramic tile manufacturer and retailer, offers an amazing display of the tiling arts. Pratt & Larson creates its own distinctive tiles in dozens of colors and hundreds of shapes, sizes, and textures, and also displays hand-painted and handcrafted tiles from dozens of other tile makers from around the country. If that weren't dizzying enough for anyone contemplating a house remodel or tilework upgrade, much of the showroom is made up of beautifully tiled tableaus of kitchens and bathrooms. The selection of tiles here is boggling, in a very good way.

Music

A quintessential Portland business, **Music Millennium** (3158 E. Burnside St., 503/248-0163, www.musicmillennium.com) is a vast and funky CD, record, and music store of the sort that typified the 1970s. You'll find almost every kind of music—old, new, rare, foreign—you name it, it's probably here. Next door is Classical Millennium, which offers the same expansive selection for opera and classical music fans. This is a one-of-a-kind store and

as close to the still-beating subversive heart of Portland as you'll get on a casual visit.

Anyone who plays an acoustic stringed instrument, or who appreciates folk music, should stop by **Artichoke Music** (3130 SE Hawthorne Blvd., 503/232-8845, http://artichokemusic.org), Portland's premier acoustic instrument emporium. Artichoke offers a rich selection of folk instruments made by North American craftspeople, as well as a growing selection of vintage instruments. In addition to a wide selection of acoustic guitars, banjos, mandolins, and ukuleles, you will find other folk music instruments, including accordions, concertinas, fiddles, recorders, pennywhistles, and percussion instruments.

Plants

Portland is famed for its parks and gardens, and no wonder—the climate here is so mild and nurturing that gardeners can grow almost anything. As if to prove the point, there's **Portland Nursery** (5050 SE Stark St., 503/231-5050, www.portlandnursery.com). If you've got a green thumb or just enjoy plantlife, consider a trip to this block-square nursery, the city's largest and most comprehensive. Portland gardeners are a demanding and experimental lot, and chances are you'll see plants here that you've only ever seen in catalogs or magazines.

Books

Powell's operates five bookstores in the Portland metro area, and two of the best are on the same busy block of SW Hawthorne Blvd. **Powell's Books for Home and Garden** (3747 SE Hawthorne Blvd., 503/228-4651) offers one of the largest selections of cookbooks and gardening books in the United States, in both new and used editions. Stop by to pick up a hostess gifts—the store has a delightful selection of kitchen-y knickknacks and supplies. Just a few doors down is **Powell's Books on Hawthorne** (3723 SE Hawthorne Blvd., 503/228-4651), a smaller general bookstore version of the mother ship store on West Burnside.

SELLWOOD

About five miles south of downtown Portland on the east banks of the Willamette River is the old working-class neighborhood of Sellwood. Once a separate city, it was annexed to Portland in 1890. Walk along Southeast 13th Avenue between Marion and Malden Streets and check out the mom-and-pop shops and cafés. Sellwood is especially known for its antiques stores, including **1874 House** (8070 SE 13th Ave., 503/233-1874), but you'll also find jewelry and home accessories at **Tilde** (7919 SE 13th Ave., 503/234-9600, www.tildeshop.com), an amazing selection of great socks at **Sock Dreams** (8005 SE 13th Ave., 503/232-3330, www.sockdreams.com), and high-quality outdoorsy clothing at the **Columbia Sportswear Outlet** (1323 SE Tacoma St., 503/238-0118). Sellwood is five miles south of downtown off Milwaukie Boulevard; take bus number 70 from the Rose Quarter.

Accommodations

Portland has a broad range of lodging choices, many of which represent good value—but few are particularly cheap. The good news is that many of the best lodging options are in the central city, close to the arts, restaurants, and nightlife. In general, downtown presents the most lodging options, while Northeast Portland, near Lloyd Center and the Convention Center, offers another wide selection at somewhat lower prices, with convenient links to downtown by MAX light rail.

The rates quoted are for double occupancy summer high-season rooms. Winter off-season rates are usually about 25 percent lower. Shopping for rooms on Internet discount lodging sites such as www.hotels.com can yield unexpected discounts even in high season.

DOWNTOWN

Unless otherwise noted, you'll pay to park at downtown hotels. Parking fees range $15-30 per night, so be sure to ask when booking a room, as these fees add up fast (and you'll be charged lodging tax on them, which is currently 14.5 percent assessed in lodgings with more than 50 rooms).

$100-150

Downtown Portland's newest hotel, ◖**McMenamins Crystal Hotel** (303 SW 12th Ave., 503/972-2670 or 855/205-3930, www.mcmenamins.com/CrystalHotel, $105-165,

parking $25), is also one of its least expensive. The McMenamins crew has rehabilitated this once-decrepit building with the company's trademark whimsy (each room is decorated to reflect a concert that's happened at the neighboring Crystal Ballroom . . . stay with Modest Mouse or John Lee Hooker), nod to history (Portland's rock 'n' roll history is celebrated in the hotel's paintings and photos), and Oregonian informality (guests in the less-expensive rooms will find bathrooms down the hall). The ground floor is dominated by the Zeus Café, with food that's a notch above the typical brewpub fare; down in the basement in Al's Den local musicians play every evening (free!). A huge soaking pool, in the corner of the building that once housed downtown's liveliest gay baths, is for hotel guests only.

Thank goodness not every vintage downtown hotel has been turned into a modern luxury Xanadu. Travelers looking for a great value will like the **Mark Spencer Hotel** (409 SW 11th Ave., 503/224-3293 or 800/548-3934, www.markspencer.com, $169-199, parking $18), a former residential hotel that's now a comfortable lodging just a few blocks from shopping and dining in the Pearl District. The rooms once rented as apartments, so even the standard guest rooms are spacious and have complete kitchens. The suites are truly large and apartment-like, with a separate bedroom, living room, and kitchen. Rates include continental breakfast.

The renovation of the 1912 **◖ Ace Hotel Portland** (1022 SW Stark St., 503/228-2277, www.acehotel.com/portland, $185-345, parking $25) has turned a historic but down-at-heel property into a distinctive, quintessentially Portland hotel. Spare but stylish guest rooms reflect the city's recycling ethic with a mix of salvaged fir, vintage fixtures, and army surplus, while custom-made Pendleton blankets and eclectic murals by local artists enhance the unique sense of place. There's a youth hostel vibe in the budget guest rooms with shared baths (including $115-per-night "band rooms" that comfortably sleep three and share a bathroom). But the Ace also offers understated luxury in top-floor suites as well as an unbeatable location a stone's throw from both the Pearl District and the center of downtown.

$150-200

The **◖ Hotel deLuxe** (729 SW 15th Ave., 503/219-2094 or 866/895-2094, www.hoteldeluxeportland.com, $169-299, parking $25) used to be the Mallory, a beloved budget spot. After a thorough rejuvenation the prices have gone up, but the place has retained its character, including its famously dog-friendly atmosphere ($45 per stay). A Hollywood theme prevails throughout, with hundreds of movie stills and other photos celebrating the golden age of film in guest rooms, hallways, and on a screen that dominates the lobby. The least expensive rooms are rather small, but well appointed, and service is strong on details.

In a city loaded with gracious historic hotels that fairly ooze old-fashioned charm, **Hotel Lucia** (400 SW Broadway, 503/225-1717 or 866/986-8086, www.hotellucia.com, $189-289, valet parking $30) stands out. Chic and conveniently located, Hotel Lucia is a top choice for travelers looking for high-design comfort and a frisson of cool urban style. Edgy art fills the lobby along with modern leather furniture that bespeaks cool elegance. Standard guest rooms aren't vast but are very comfortable and beautifully furnished; consider stepping up

to a Superior or Deluxe room if you need space. The Lucia offers easy access to restaurants and shopping; amenities include a fitness center, and a business center.

Sleek and stylish, **Hotel Modera** (515 SW Clay St., 503/484-1084 or 877/484-1084, www.hotelmodera.com, $197-269, valet parking $27) is recently renovated and redesigned to show off the hotel's original mid-century aesthetic. The large art-draped lobby, lined with marble and dark woods, opens onto a very spacious courtyard with lots of outdoor seating, three fire pits, and a "living wall" of greenery. Guest rooms carry forward the Euro-chic look, with a streamlined aesthetic that's both bold and whimsical: Faux fur throws drape triple-sheeted beds, and deep-orange bathroom walls play off against white marble-tiled showers. Hotel Modera is at the center of downtown and right on the MAX Green line. Guests can use the nearby 24-Hour Fitness.

The large **Portland Waterfront Marriott Downtown** (1401 SW Naito Pkwy., 503/226-7600, www.portlandmarriott.com, $179-219) is a convention hotel that faces Waterfront Park, with half the views over the Willamette River toward Mount Hood. It's an excellent location if you're visiting Portland for a waterfront festival; when it's not booked with conventioneers, it's also one of the most affordable of the downtown hotels. Standard guest rooms aren't huge but are nicely furnished; facilities include an indoor saline pool, a large fitness area, a restaurant, a large sports bar, a coffee shop, and free wireless Internet.

The interior of the historic and luxurious **◖ Heathman Hotel** (1009 SW Broadway, 800/551-0011, www.heathmanhotel.com, $179-269, parking $29), built in 1927, offers a tantalizing balance between old and new, between its old-fashioned opulence and the refreshing brio of the hotel's vast collection of modern art. This is truly a hotel dedicated to the arts: The Heathman connects directly to the Schnitzer Concert Hall (the Center for Performing Arts is in the next block), and it frequently plays host to traveling celebrities and artists. The entry-level Deluxe rooms aren't huge but offer every luxury and very refined furnishings. For more room, book an Executive King or a Symphony Suite. Service throughout is exemplary: The Heathman offers personal concierge service, twice-daily maid service, a bed menu, 24-hour room service, a lending library stocked with books by authors who have stayed here—the list goes on and on. Facilities include the **Heathman Restaurant,** one of Portland's finest; a wonderful two-story wood-paneled tearoom with daily high tea and live jazz music Wednesday-Saturday; the see-and-be-seen Marble Bar; and a hot chocolate-coffee lounge.

A true Portland landmark, the **❰ Governor Hotel** (614 SW 11th Ave., 503/224-3400 or 800/554-3456, www.govhotel.com, $179-269, parking $27) has two wings: the original 1909 hotel with an imposing white tile facade (look for the Transformer-like figures along the roofline) and the adjoining Portland Elks Lodge, a very ornate structure built in 1932 to resemble the Farnese Palace in Rome. This is one of Portland's most regal hotels—have a look at one of the nine ballrooms; the Order of the Elks wasn't afraid of splurging on decor. The standard Superior level guest rooms are large and nicely furnished, but the suites are really outstanding. Corner Junior Suites have a fireplace, and Penthouse Terrace Suites offer a rooftop deck. Amenities include Jake's Grill restaurant, a Starbucks coffee shop, a large and airy fitness center, and a complimentary business center.

A historic hotel with a stunning Romanesque facade, **❰ Hotel Vintage Plaza** (422 SW Broadway, 503/228-1212 or 800/263-2305, www.vintageplaza.com, $235-315, valet parking $33) is a temple of discreet luxury, perfect for a romantic weekend or a highly civilized business stay. The Vintage Plaza is a true boutique hotel, from the 10-story interior atrium to the 57 different guest room floor plans and individually decorated rooms (most with a wine theme) filled with rich jewel-like colors, lush fabrics, and regal furnishings. Standard rooms are sumptuous, but if you're here for a special occasion, the hotel's many unique suites make

this a top choice—check out the two-story townhouse suites and the Garden Spa rooms, with a flower-decked rooftop patio and outdoor hot tub. Amenities include the Pazzo Ristorante and bar, a manager's wine reception, an honor bar, fitness and business centers, and free wireless Internet. Pets are welcome.

Don't let the corporate moniker mislead you. **❰ Embassy Suites Portland** (319 SW Pine St., 503/279-9000, www.embassyportland.com, $189-289, valet parking $30, self-parking $18) is in fact the palatial Multnomah Hotel, built in 1912 as the largest and grandest hotel in the Pacific Northwest. When Embassy Suites remodeled this aging beauty in the late 1990s, the company reduced the number of guest rooms from 700 to just 276 suites. These are the largest standard rooms in Portland and come with a microwave, a refrigerator, two flat-screen TVs, and a large desk. The hotel's original grandeur is retained in the large opulent lobby. Amenities include an indoor pool and fitness center that resembles a Roman bath, the Salon Nyla day spa, and free breakfast.

The **Benson Hotel** (309 SW Broadway, 503/228-2000 or 800/663-1144, www.bensonhotel.com, $199-249, valet parking $29) was built in 1913 as the city's most luxurious hotel, and thankfully this grande dame retains nearly all of its spectacular early-20th-century fittings, particularly the grand lobby with its walnut paneling, Belgian chandeliers, Italian marble floors, and massive oriental carpets. Standard guest rooms can be a bit cramped, and the real deal is the suites: spacious junior suites are just a $40 upgrade and worth every penny. Or, if you're feeling important, go for the Presidential Suite: Every U.S. president since Taft has stayed here. Facilities include two restaurants and a cozy lobby bar.

With nearly 800 rooms, the **Portland Hilton** (921 SW 6th Ave., 503/226-1611, www.portland.hilton.com, $189-239, parking $20) is Oregon's largest hotel. And while there's no denying that the Hilton is largely a business and convention hotel, there are good reasons for leisure travelers to spend the night. The hotel is absolutely in the center of the city, close to shopping, the arts, and public transport; online specials mean that standard guest rooms frequently represent the best value in the city center; and the 12,000-square-foot athletic club with indoor pool is the best hotel facility in downtown. The Hilton takes its environmental duties seriously: This is the largest Green Seal-certified hotel on the West Coast.

The **Rivers Edge Hotel & Spa** (4650 SW Macadam Ave., 503/802-5800, www.riversedgehotel.com, $179-299, parking $19), although a couple of miles south of downtown, is worth noting for its quiet setting along the Willamette River, its stylish rooms, its excellent fitness center and spa (no swimming pool), and lovely adjacent restaurant with riverside dining. Spend the extra $30 or so for a riverside room.

Over $200

The conveniently located **Hotel Monaco** (506 SW Washington St., 503/222-0001 or 888/207-2201, www.monaco-portland.com, $239-349, valet parking $29) was formerly one of Portland's landmark department stores (converting undervalued historic buildings into hotels is a hallmark of the Kimpton hotel chain), but there's little to remind you of its retail past: The hotel is a showcase of vivid color, oversize art, and unconventional furnishings. The zippy decor continues into the large stylish guest rooms, which are designed with a sense of humor, using color and fabric to create a mood of relaxed whimsy. Pets are welcome—there's often a resident dog in the lobby—and room service will bring you a goldfish if you're in need of company. Amenities include a day spa, fitness and business centers, and the very good **Red Star Tavern** restaurant.

The **Nines** (525 SW Morrison St., 877/229-9995, www.thenines.com, $226-336, valet parking $32) occupies the top nine floors of the downtown Macy's store, a magnificent glazed terra-cotta landmark from 1908 (the erstwhile Meier and Frank). A dramatic nine-story interior atrium is flanked by large stylish guest rooms. Local artists were commissioned to create new paintings and sculptures, and guest rooms feature original art from students at the Pacific Northwest College of Art. Facilities include fitness and business centers and two restaurants: the organic steak house Urban Farmer and the rooftop Departures, which has cocktails and lighter Asian-influenced fare.

If you're familiar with Westins as large corporate hotels, then the **Portland Westin** (750 SW Alder St., 503/294-9000, www.westin.com/portland, $259-339, valet parking $33) is a pleasant surprise. More of a small boutique-style getaway, this contemporary upscale high-rise is a haven of good taste whether you're here for business or pleasure. Guest rooms have large desks, an unfussy, slightly restrained aesthetic, and all the "heavenly" extras you expect with Westin. A Deluxe King corner room gives you extra room and three windows for light and views. Facilities include a restaurant, room service, a business center, and a workout room.

One of the few hotels right on the Willamette River, **RiverPlace Hotel** (1510 SW Harbor Way, 503/228-3233 or 800/227-1333, www.riverplacehotel.com, $289-339, valet parking $29) sits above a marina at the edge of Waterfront Park, yet it's just moments from downtown shopping and activities. A warm and pleasing Arts and Crafts aesthetic pervades the lobby and bar, and guest rooms are large and comfortable and have DVD players, a fridge, and a large work table. RiverPlace also offers eight one-bedroom and two two-bedroom condos for either nightly or extended rental. With the notable position right on the river, the bar and restaurant, both with large outdoor decks, are very popular. Guests have complimentary passes to the nearby RiverPlace Athletic Club and loaner bikes are available.

NORTHWEST
Under $50

Hostelling International-Portland, Northwest (425 NW 18th Ave., 503/241-2783 or 888/777-0067, www.nwportlandhostel.com, bunks $28 for HI members, $31 nonmembers, private rooms $62-79) has a great location between the shopping and dining of NW 21st and 23rd Avenues and the artsy Pearl District—in

© BILL MCRAE

RiverPlace Hotel overlooks a marina at the southern edge of Waterfront Park.

other words, within walking distance of two of Portland's most exciting neighborhoods. The main hostel is in a restored turn-of-the-20th-century building and features dorms with as few as two and up to eight beds per room, private rooms, a fully equipped kitchen, and a coffee bar. Some of the private guest rooms are in nearby buildings.

Another simple place to stay in the heart of Northwest Portland is the **Portland International Guesthouse, Northwest** (2185 NW Flanders St., 503/224-0500 or 877/228-0500, www.pdxguesthouse.com, $65-75), a historic home with six rooms sharing three bathrooms, a sitting room, and a kitchen.

$150-200

A couple of quite decent but rather generic hotels on the industrial edge of Northwest Portland are very convenient to the neighborhood, the streetcar, the freeway, and good restaurants: the **Silver Cloud Inn** (2426 NW Vaughn St., 503/484-2400, www.silvercloud.com, $159-209) and **Holiday Inn Express** (2333 NW Vaughn St., 503/248-4055, www.hiexpress.com, $154-224). Both places have free parking.

One of Portland's most engaging lodging choices, the ◖**Inn at Northrup Station** (2025 NW Northrup St., 503/224-0543 or 800/224-1180, www.northrupstation.com, $169-189, free parking) is an older motel in Northwest Portland that has been totally, and we mean totally, renovated into a retro-hip showcase with a wild color palette—sort of George Jetson meets the Summer of Love. Each room has a kitchen, boldly designed furniture, and lots of space to make yourself at home (if your home's a design showcase). There's a rooftop garden, plus lots of intriguing and outrageous art everywhere. The inn is right on the Portland Streetcar line, so you can get to the Pearl District or downtown in minutes without having to worry about parking.

The top B&B in Northwest Portland is **Heron Haus Bed & Breakfast Inn** (2545 NW Westover Rd., 503/248-4055, www.heronhaus.com, $170-225). Built in 1904 and perched in a prime West Hills location, this ivy-covered 10,000-square-foot English Tudor home is one of the city's most impressive lodging options. It offers six guest rooms on the second and third floors, all with fireplaces, modern private baths, cable TV, and terrific views of the city and the Cascades. Furnishings are comfortable, casual, and contemporary, and continental breakfast is served in the formal parquet-floored dining room. Guests can avail themselves of a sunroom, a morning room, a mahogany-paneled library, a study, and a secluded garden with a patio; the shops and restaurants of NW 23rd Avenue are just a short walk away.

NORTHEAST

Between downtown Portland and the Lloyd Center are the Portland Oregon Convention Center and the Rose Garden sports arena, along with a number of good-value hotels. There are often deep discounts on these hotels at Internet reservation sites. Note that some of these hotels have free parking while others do not. This neighborhood offers easy access to downtown and the airport on the MAX light rail train. Most of the hotels listed here are no more than five minutes' walk from the MAX line. The downside is that many of these close-in hotels sit in a busy urban neighborhood with lots of traffic whizzing by, but that's the price you pay for convenience.

The historic Irvington neighborhood north of Broadway, studded with lovely vintage homes, offers a couple of fine bed-and-breakfast options.

$50-100

A historic saloon and hotel near the foot of the Fremont Bridge in a gentrifying industrial neighborhood, **McMenamins White Eagle** (836 N. Russell St., 503/335-8900 or 866/271-3377, www.mcmenamins.com, $50-55, free on-street parking) is one of the best lodging deals in town. The 11 sparsely furnished but comfortable rooms share two toilets and two showers, European style, and they're all named after tunes by the Holy Modal Rounders, the cult folk duo that was in residence here for a while

in the mid-1970s. Downstairs, the saloon features a huge oak bar and ceramic floor. It has been cleaned up since its much seedier days; even the ghosts said to have haunted the place haven't been reported for years. The saloon features live music nightly—here's the rub if you're only here for the accommodation: It's loud until at least midnight. Earplugs are available for free.

A good choice close to the convention center and MAX is **Quality Inn Portland Convention Center** (431 NE Multnomah St., 503/233-7933 or 800/531-5900, www.lq.com, $90-120, free parking), which offers a 24-hour indoor pool, a fitness center, and complimentary continental breakfast. All rooms come with a coffeemaker, hair dryer, and free high-speed Internet access.

$100-150

For something completely different, **C Kennedy School** (5736 NE 33rd Ave., 503/249-3983 or 888/249-3983, www.kennedyschool.com, $135-155, free parking) is an unusual McMenamins hotel in the Concordia neighborhood, about six miles northeast of downtown. The hotel is set in an old elementary school that has been transformed into a brewpub, movie theater, restaurant, several school-themed bars (including the Detention Lounge), and a concert venue. Madcap mosaics, carvings, and paintings festoon the hallways along with historic photos from the days when the building was a citadel of learning. You have a choice of rooms: whimsically decorated former classrooms that have become guest rooms, complete with chalkboards and private bathrooms, and king bedrooms in the "English Wing," a newly built addition in a lush courtyard behind the school.

Just across the street from the Oregon Convention Center and immediately on the MAX line, the **Red Lion Hotel Portland Convention Center** (1021 NE Grand Ave., 503/235-2100 or 800/343-1822, www.redlion.com, $119-129, parking $14) offers standard hotel rooms in a very convenient location. The rooftop Windows Lounge overlooks Portland. The **Crowne Plaza Hotel Portland** (1441

© BILL MCRAE

White House Bed and Breakfast

NE 2nd Ave., 503/233-2401 or 877/277-6963, $162-199, parking $10) now offers upscale rooms in addition to its excellent location near (but not on) the MAX line and other major Northeast Portland arterials. In a quiet corner of this busy neighborhood, the nine-story Crowne Plaza also has good views from the upper floors. Guest rooms are large and have microwaves, minifridges, and irons, while the suites have kitchenettes. Facilities include a beautiful indoor pool and fitness center, plus a restaurant and bar.

Across from the Lloyd Center shopping mall, right on the MAX line, and a short walk from the convention center is the large and nicely renovated **(DoubleTree by Hilton** (1000 NE Multnomah St., 503/281-6111 or 800/996-0510, www.doubletreegreen.com, $123-329 parking $18). The Doubletree is a full-service hotel with two restaurants, a lounge, a fitness room and indoor pool, room service, and convention facilities. The large well-decorated guest rooms have balconies, high-speed Internet access, coffeemakers, and irons.

The historic Irvington neighborhood north of the Lloyd Center has several fine B&Bs. The opulent **(White House Bed and Breakfast** (1914 NE 22nd Ave., 503/287-7131 or 800/272-7131, www.portlandswhitehouse. com, $135-235) gives you the presidential treatment. Located just off Broadway near an avenue of shops and restaurants and only 5-10 minutes from the Lloyd Center and downtown, this lovingly restored 1912 lumber baron's mansion is one of the city's top B&Bs. It really does look like its namesake in D.C.

$150-200

The landmark **Lion and the Rose Victorian Bed and Breakfast Inn** (1810 NE 15th Ave., 503/287-9245 or 800/955-1647, www.lionrose. com, $165-220) is a 1906 Queen Anne mansion listed on the National Register of Historic Places. The seven guest rooms and apartment, all with private baths, are each unique, and although they are charming in an authentically Victorian way, they're also up-to-date, with air-conditioning, telephones, cable TV, and high-speed wireless Internet access. The parlors and dining room are comfortable, spacious, and decorated with period furnishings. The B&B is within walking distance of good restaurants and shopping on Northeast Broadway.

SOUTHEAST
Under $50

No other lodgings capture the ecofriendly vibe of Portland—and especially the woolly Hawthorne neighborhood—quite like **Portland Hawthorne Hostel** (3031 SE Hawthorne Blvd., 503/236-3380 or 866/447-3031, www.portlandhostel.org, bunks $27 for HI members, $30 nonmembers). Among its most prominent features is an "eco-roof" over the front porch, a runoff filtering system planted in sedum and yarrow and cisterns to capture rainwater for landscaping and toilet flushing. The 1909 house offers men's, women's, and coed dorm rooms, plus two private rooms (one with a double bed and private porch, the other with one double and two twin beds, $62 members, $65 nonmembers).

Amenities include a fully equipped kitchen (make your own pancakes for a buck!), wireless access and local phone calls, lockers, and bike rentals. You won't find cheaper accommodations in Portland without pitching a tent.

$100-150

At the east side of the Burnside Bridge, as Burnside Street mounts the hill, there are a number of older motor court motels, some of dubious quality. However, one of these older properties has an interesting tale to tell. The **Jupiter Hotel** (800 E. Burnside St., 503/230-9200 or 877/800-0004, www.jupiterhotel.com, $119-155, parking $8) is what you might call a boutique motel, an older motel that has been totally updated with a chic modern look and such stylish accoutrements as fine linens, eye-grabbing art, and high-end toiletries. Although the standard rooms aren't large, they are certainly chic; some larger rooms have kitchens. Best of all, the Jupiter Hotel is also home to the Doug Fir Restaurant and Lounge, one of Portland's top music clubs with a popular dining room open till 4am daily. Weekends can get pretty noisy, so bring earplugs or just dance till dawn. Since you're likely to stay up late at the Doug Fir, you might want to consider waiting until after midnight to rent your room, when all unsold rooms are just $59.

On SE Clinton Street, near the restaurant hotbed along SE Division Avenue, the C **Clinton Street Guesthouse** (4220 SE Clinton St., 503/234-8752, www.clintonstreetguesthouse.com, $100-145) offers four nicely furnished, but not overly fussy, guest rooms in one of Portland's most coveted neighborhoods. Two of the rooms have private baths, while the other two rooms share two bathrooms (not ensuite), and everything is tip-top, including breakfast. The guesthouse also has a small two-bedroom bungalow that's perfect if you're a family or traveling with friends (three-night minimum).

On the edge of beautiful Laurelhurst Park, the opulent **Portland Mayor's Mansion** (3360 SE Ankeny St., 503/232-3588, http://pdxmayorsmansion.com, $125-225) is indeed the home

of a former Portland mayor. Built in 1912 of red brick in colonial revival style, the mansion is filled with intriguing period detail and offers four lodging options, including a three-room executive suite. The other three spacious guest rooms have private baths and are decorated with understated elegance. This mansion is at the heart of one of early Portland's most exclusive neighborhoods and a walk in any direction will reveal dozens of beautiful architectural specimens.

AIRPORT

There are a lot of hotels at I-205 Exit 23, the exit for PDX airport. Except on holiday weekends, you probably won't need reservations, but here are a few options from all price categories if you want to call ahead.

$50-100

A short ride from the airport by free shuttle is **Howard Johnson** (8247 NE Sandy Blvd., 503/256-4111 or 866/440-7700, www.hotelpdxairport.com, $69-89). Located near The Grotto with its old-growth trees and contemplative surroundings, it's a world away from airport terminal traffic snarls. While the rooms are typical of moderately priced chains, the free breakfast and other amenities make it a good choice. An Indian restaurant is on-site.

$100-150

The **Country Inn and Suites** (7025 NE Alderwood Rd., 503/255-2700 or 888/987-2700, www.countryinns.com, $109-129) is a 150-room hotel with a pool, a spa, a fitness center, and well-appointed guest rooms. A free airport shuttle and breakfast are also available.

You may not think of stylish sophistication and airport hotels in the same brainwave, but **Aloft Portland Airport Hotel** 99920 NE Cascades Pkwy., 503/200-5678, www.aloftportlandairport.com, $129-159) is that rare combo. A branch of the upscale W Hotel chain, Aloft is cool and sleek, with fun modern style combined with convenience: The hotel is just one stop from the airport via MAX light rail, and you can hop the train to downtown without having to rent a car. Aloft also has a lounge, self-service pantry with sandwiches and other portable foods, an indoor pool, and a complimentary airport shuttle.

The closest hotel to the airport, **Sheraton Portland Airport Hotel** (8253 NE Airport Way, 503/281-2500 or 800/325-3535, www.sheraton.com/portland, $139-299), is classy, with oversize well-furnished rooms, an indoor pool, a fitness center, room service, a restaurant, and a small conference center. Free shuttles run to the airport terminal 24/7.

CAMPING

Portland isn't particularly convenient for campers. If you are planning to use a campground as your base for visiting downtown Portland, you'll be facing a lengthy commute. The good news is that within 30 miles or so of downtown, you'll find some lovely parks. South of Portland, with easy access off I-5, is **Champoeg State Heritage Area** (503/678-1251, www.oregonstateparks.org, $19-39), a lovely park along the Willamette River that's also a major site in Pacific Northwest history. Campsites are in shaded groves alongside the river, and bike and hiking paths and museums make this park a worthy recreational destination. In addition to year-round tent ($19) and RV ($24) sites, there are also yurts ($36) and rustic cabins ($39). Champoeg is about 30 miles south of downtown Portland, off I-5 Exit 278. Reserve campsites at 800/452-5687 or www.reserveamerica.com.

For those who enjoy rural serenity within commuting distance of downtown, there's camping in **Milo McIver State Park** (503/630-7150 or 800/551-6949, www.oregonstateparks.org, mid-Mar.-Oct., $18 tent, $21 RV). This retreat, set on the banks of the Collowash River five miles northwest of Estacada, is 25 miles from downtown Portland, but in spirit it seems farther away,

particularly when you're gazing at the knockout sunset view of Mount Hood. To get to the park, take I-84 east to I-205 south and follow it to the exit for Route 224/Estacada. The road forks right at the town of Carver to go 10 miles (look for Springwater Road) to the campground. There are 44 hookup sites, nine walk-in tent sites, flush toilets, showers, firewood, and a laundry, as well as fishing for winter steelhead and late-fall salmon. Other recreation includes hiking, horse trails, and a boat ramp.

East of Portland, a few miles north of I-84 on the Sandy River, is **Oxbow Park** (503/797-1850, $22 with additional $5 vehicle entrance fee), operated by Metro, the Portland regional government agency. Oxbow Park is right on a bend in the river in a quiet woodsy setting, and it offers flush toilets but no showers. There's a strict no-dog policy. To reach Oxbow Park, take I-84 Exit 17, follow 257th Avenue to Division Street, turn east (right), and follow signs to the park.

About 35 miles east of Portland off I-84 is **Ainsworth State Park** (503/695-2301 or 800/551-6949, www.oregonstateparks.org, mid-Mar.-Oct., $17-20, no reservations). Picnic tables, fire rings, flush toilets, and an RV camp enhance a prime location near the trails and waterfalls of the Columbia River Gorge. You can get there via the Columbia River Highway or by taking Exit 35 off I-84 West.

Stub Stewart State Park (503/234-0606, reservations 800/452-5687, www.oregonstateparks.org, $21 tent, $26 RV or horse camp, $43 cabin), 31 miles west of town, is a large park laced with mountain biking and horseback riding trails. In addition to a couple of large camping loops (one has sites open year-round), there's an area for horse camping and a circle of cabins. From Portland, head west on U.S. 26, turn north onto Route 47 and follow signs to the park.

Food

Portland has become nationally known for its restaurants, especially those focusing on locally sourced ingredients, and increasingly people structure their trips here around eating. Even if you're not a foodie, be sure to bring your appetite.

Portland is a very neighborhood-oriented city, and restaurants also have strong associations with their locale. Restaurants tend to be located near other restaurants, creating mini-enclaves within dining neighborhoods that each offer distinctively different atmospheres. The restaurant scene—and dining experience—will be very different in the Pearl District than in the Mississippi Avenue neighborhood, for instance, though both offer top quality and selection. You may find it as tempting to choose a neighborhood in which to dine as to choose a specific restaurant or type of cuisine, because many of the dining neighborhoods have a strong and appealing character of their own.

A number of websites and blogs chart the ups and downs of the Portland food scene; perhaps the best is www.portlandfoodanddrink.com, which, in addition to frequently impassioned confrontations between bloggers, also offers restaurant reviews and handy links to even more foodie sites. The Portland area **Chowhound site,** http://chowhound.chow.com, is also a good reference to the latest in dining news, and for news and gossip, check out http://pdx.eater.com with its invaluable, always updated feature, the **Essential 38 Portland Restaurants.**

Brewpubs

Portland, also known as Beervana, is the

© BILL MCRAE

al fresco dining

THE MCMENAMINS BREWPUB EMPIRE

If you drink beer and if you go out at night, you're likely to run into a McMenamins brewpub during a trip to Portland. This highly successful local enterprise now has over 50 pubs and related businesses in Washington and Oregon, and whenever a historic venue goes on sale, there's at least a large minority of Pacific Northwesterners who hope that it will become a McMenamins brewpub. The McMenamins are in fact brothers Brian and Mike, who are equally devoted to brewing quality beer, designing fun spaces to drink it in, and preserving distinctive buildings.

The typical McMenamins pub features imaginative antiques, art, and architecture on a grand scale. In fact, the decor can be rather silly, but the desired effect is to create a space that doesn't take itself too seriously. According to the McMenamins: "Be wary of things too formal, too complicated, and too orthodox. Ultimately, the most important realization has been that the essence of a pub is its people. Trendy decor doesn't attract a lasting clientele. It's the other way around: The neighborhood clientele is the atmosphere—and that never goes in and out of style."

Portland has the most microbreweries of any city in the world, and any short list of pub destinations should include several McMenamins outlets because of their dedication to preserving historic structures (and the quality of the beer is just fine too).

The word *unique* gets tossed around a lot in travel writing, but in the case of the **Crystal Ballroom** (1332 W. Burnside St., 503/225-0047), it's apt: This former dance hall is a singular place to catch a concert or have a beer. Constructed in 1914, the top-story ballroom was created as a spot for fashionable dances; its mechanical "floating on air" dance floor (there's a layer of ball bearings and springy rubber beneath the hardwood flooring) made it a popular spot for jazz performances. The McMenamin brothers bought the ballroom in the 1990s and refurbished the entire three-story building, which is now a major concert and brewpub showcase. There are performances about three times a week at the Crystal Ballroom, and it's worth going just to check out the floating dance floor, the massive Palladian windows, the grand murals and quirky paintings, and the impressive scale of the room—rocking out with 1,500 other people on the 7,500-square-foot, trampoline-like dance floor is an experience you aren't likely to forget. On the ground floor of the building is **Ringler's Pub** (503/225-0627), a brewpub with casual dining, pool tables, live music Thursday-Saturday, and the hallmark animistic decor that personifies McMenamins projects. On the second floor is **Lola's Room,** a smaller version of the Crystal Ballroom, open several nights a week for live concerts, DJ dance

epicenter of the craft brewing revival in North America, boasting more breweries than any other city in the world—69 were in operation in the metro area at press time, and more are certainly in the works (by the way, that number doesn't count separate brewpubs owned by the same company; in other words, McMenamins counts as one brewery). It's a statewide phenomenon: Oregon's brewers produced 1.29 million barrels of beer in 2012 in 169 brewing facilities in 61 cities in the state, making it the largest craft beer market in the United States; 40 percent of all draft beer consumed in Oregon is brewed in Oregon.

All brewpubs are required to serve food, and many double as restaurants. This means that in almost all cases, families are welcome in brewpubs within dining hours and sometimes in designated nonbar areas. Portland brewpubs come in all shapes and sizes, from garden tents to converted warehouses to funeral chapels. Locally brewed beer is one of the pillars of Portland life—cheers!

Food Carts

If you're on a budget or looking for inexpensive al fresco dining, join the bus commuters, cyclists, and pedestrians on the go who eat at nights, and other performances. One block away is another extension of this massive entertainment citadel: the **Crystal Hotel** (303 SW 12th Ave., 503/972-2670), a hotel set in a former gay bathhouse, with an appropriately labyrinthine set of basement bars culminating in the just-right **Ringler's Annex,** a tiny subterranean bar in a Flatiron Building-like structure for in-the-know hipsters.

Just across the Willamette from downtown, the **White Eagle Saloon** (836 N. Russell St., 503/282-6810) is one of Portland's oldest still-operating bars (since 1905) with a lively late-night live music scene. The **Chapel Pub** (430 N. Killingsworth St., 503/286-0372) is a brewpub in a beautifully preserved Mission-style funeral home.

The **Kennedy School** (5736 NE 33rd Ave., 503/249-3983 or 888/249-3983) is an unusual enterprise—a block-square 1915 grade school that's been converted into a brewpub, restaurant, and hotel, plus a movie theater (think couches in the auditorium). In the suburbs of Portland are two of the grandest extensions of the McMenamins dream. On the way to the Columbia Gorge, **Edgefield** (2126 SW Halsey St., Troutdale, 503/669-8610 or 800/669-8610) began its existence as the Multnomah County Poor Farm. This vast 25-acre operation now contains multiple restaurants and drinking establishments, plus a delightful period hotel, movie theater, winery, and "pub golf" course. On the way to the coast, just south of Highway 26, is the **Grand Lodge** (3505 Pacific Ave., Forest Grove, 503/992-9533 or 877/992-9533, www.mcmenamins.com), completed in 1922 as a retirement home for Masons and Eastern Star adherents. This 13-acre property offers dining, drinking, hotel rooms, movies, and a 10-hole disc golf course.

Lest we forget, the McMenamins pioneered the notion of cinema brewpubs, where you can buy a microbrew, chow down on a burger, and watch a recent movie. Closest to downtown Portland are the **Mission Theater** (1624 NW Glisan St., 503/223-4527), near the Pearl District, and the **Bagdad Theater & Pub** (3702 SE Hawthorne Blvd., 503/236-9234), in the thick of the trendy Hawthorne neighborhood.

No one would claim that the food at McMenamins is cutting-edge or that they produce the most sophisticated ales in Portland. But overall the quality is just fine and a fine deal, and chances are that you'll enjoy your pint and burger in a truly unique setting.

For more info on locations and music and movie offerings within the McMenamins empire, visit www.mcmenamins.com or call 503/249-3983.

---

street food carts. **Food carts** are scattered all over the city, purveying all sorts of street food (burritos, bento, stir-fry, barbecue, Indian, Korean, Lebanese, and so on). The selection is staggering, though they come and go quickly. There's an estimated 500 food carts operating around Portland. The largest selection is downtown. For the greatest concentration, go to SW Alder Street at 9th and 10th Avenues (with a total of 60 carts) or the heart of the bus mall around SW 5th Avenue and Stark Street. Other major hubs (called pods) include **Cartopia** at 12th and SE Hawthorne, where half a dozen carts remain open most nights till 4am, and the **Mississippi Marketplace** on N. Mississippi and N. Skidmore. Head up to SE 42nd and Belmont to check out the food carts at the **Good Food Here** pod, which include a couple of the city's best. If you're serious about exploring Portland cart culture, be sure to visit www.foodcartsportland.com, where you'll find maps, reviews, and apps for your smartphone.

Happy Hour Eats and Drinks

Another option for inexpensive eats are happy hour menus—nearly every bar and many restaurants offer reduced-price food and drink late in the afternoon and early evening, typically

© BILL MCRAE

Portland has hundreds of food carts, many parked in convenient pods.

4pm-6pm. Sometimes this can be just a dollar off drinks, but often there's a special happy hour menu that offers considerable discounts. A number of websites chart happy hour deals across the city; check out http://portlandhappyhour.com and www.barflymag.com/happyhour to find out where the deals are.

DOWNTOWN AND SOUTHWEST
American
A longtime favorite for a hearty morning meal, the **◖ Bijou Café** (132 SW 3rd Ave., 503/222-3187, 7am-2pm Mon.-Fri., 8am-2pm Sat.-Sun., $5-13) is a friendly, sparely decorated, light-filled little diner that has staked its reputation on perfecting breakfast classics. While fried cinnamon bread, red snapper, or roast beef hash are morning mainstays in this cheery café, ordinary breakfast foods are done perfectly with the freshest local ingredients.

Just when you thought Portland was a health-food kind of place, you find **Voodoo**

Doughnut (22 SW 3rd Ave., 503/241-4704, www.voodoodoughnut.com, 24 hours daily). This famed doughnut shop is in the thick of the Old Town bar zone and offers all-night doughnuts to club kids and anyone else who stumbles by. You'll be amazed at the selection, and the devotion that mighty fine doughnuts can induce—try the maple bars with bacon (reportedly a fave of Brad Pitt).

Next door to the Ace Hotel, **Kenny and Zuke's Delicatessen** (1038 SW Stark St., 503/222-3354, 7am-8pm Mon.-Thurs., 7am-9pm Fri., 8am-9pm Sat., and 8am-8pm Sun., $6-15) turns out hearty breakfasts and sandwiches in the style of a New York Jewish deli. The thick-sliced pastrami has a strong following, and the selection of soda pop is unsurpassed in this town.

Lardo (1205 SW Washington St., 503/241-2490, http://lardopdx.com, 11am-10pm daily, $7-12) is a former food cart whose meaty sandwiches won such acclaim that it has opened this brick-and-mortar restaurant and another

PORTLAND BY THE SLICE

Portland takes its pizza seriously—expect loud and vociferous opinions if you query locals about their favorite pizza joint.

Portland's pizza renaissance began in the early 1980s with **Escape From New York** (622 NW 23rd Ave., 503/227-5423, 11:30am-11pm daily), which brought in Gotham-style pizzas with foldable crust, copious cheese, and high-quality toppings and sold them by the slice—it was a revelation to Portlanders used to franchise pizza. If you're up in Northwest Portland, this is still mighty fine pizza.

Another longtime Portland favorite is **Hotlips Pizza** (1909 SW 6th Ave., 503/224-0311, 11am-10pm Mon.-Sat., noon-8pm Sun.), near Portland State University. The crust and sauce are both outstanding, and Hotlips sources nearly all its ingredients from its own network of local organic farmers and ranchers. Other convenient Hotlips outlets are in the Pearl District (NW 10th Ave. and Irving St.,

503/595-2342) and at Southeast Hawthorne Street and 22nd Avenue (503/234-9999).

Up on North Mississippi Avenue, the **Mississippi Pizza Pub** (3552 N. Mississippi Ave., 503/288-3231) offers wondrous thin-crust pizza in a funky DIY storefront that's totally Portland. The staff at **Apizza Scholls** (4741 SE Hawthorne Blvd., 503/233-1286, 5pm-9:30pm Wed.-Sat., 4pm-8:30pm Sun.) have earned the reputation as the pizza snobs for their formidable resistance to allowing patrons to choose their own toppings or to make enough pizza dough to stay open through their posted hours. But the cracker-like crusts and pleasant deck seating in summer keep the crowds lined up.

You'll also face long lines at another Portland favorite, **Ken's Artisan Pizza** (304 SE 28th Ave., 503/517-9951, 5pm-10pm Tues.-Sat.). The wood-fired pizzas have nearly perfect chewy crusts, and the toppings are top-notch.

---

on in SE Portland (1212 SE Hawthorne Blvd., 503/234-7786, 11am-10pm, $7-12). Favorites include the pork meatball banh mi and the PBLT, with roasted pork belly, lettuce, heirloom tomato, arugula, and caper mayo. Vegetarians should check out the roast green bean and hazelnut romesco sandwich and the absolutely delicious kale Caesar salad.

Central European

One of downtown's hottest meal tickets is at **Grüner** (527 SW 12th Ave., 503/241-7163, 11:30am-9:30pm Mon.-Fri., 5pm-10pm Sat., $15-29), chef Chris Israel's take on the foods of Germany, Austria, Hungary, and Romania. Don't look for oompah bands here; it's a stylish place with lots of sleek wood and clean modern lines. The food is likewise similarly modern and carefully put together. Grüner (which means "greener" in German) brings a Pacific Northwest farm-to-table spin on house-made sausages, spätzle, and smoked trout. Available only on the bar menu is what many consider

to be Portland's best hamburger. Although the menu revolves around meat dishes, there are always a few vegetarian options.

French

Portland chef Gabriel Rucker, who has gained national attention for his cooking at Le Pigeon on East Burnside, now has a downtown outpost, **◖ Little Bird Bistro** (219 SW 6th Ave., 503/688-5952, http://littlebirdbistro.com, 11:30am-midnight Mon.-Fri., 5pm-midnight Sat.-Sun., $16-23), where French bistro favorites including escargot, steak tartare, cassoulet, and sweetbreads are served up in a dining room that looks like a Parisian bistro staffed by hip, friendly Pacific Northwesterners. Don't skip the not-quite-French "Le Pigeon" burger, a favorite both here and at the eastside restaurant.

Indian

Indian food is well represented at Portland's food carts and the popular lunchtime stall,

PORTLAND

© BILL MCRAE

SouthPark is a popular stop for a pre-symphony meal.

Gandhi's (827 SW 2nd Ave., 503/219-9224, 10am-3pm Mon.-Fri., $6). But for an elegant Indian lunch or dinner, the **East India Co. Bar & Grill** (821 SW 11th Ave., 503/227-8815, 11:30am-2:30pm and 4pm-10pm Mon.-Sat., dinner $13-23) is your best bet. The lunch menu is short—no buffet here, but at dinner there's plenty to choose from, including a wide selection of vegan entrées. The food is carefully prepared and presented, with wonderful combinations of spices.

Italian

Downtown Portland's finest Italian restaurant, **Pazzo** (627 SW Washington St., 503/228-1515, www.pazzo.com, 7am-10:30am, 11:30am-2:30pm, and 5pm-9pm Mon.-Fri., 8am-2pm and 4:30pm-11pm Sat., 8am-2pm and 4pm-9pm Sun., $16-33) has charm to spare and a broad menu of well-prepared pastas and grilled meats. Located in the Hotel Vintage Plaza, this is a wonderful spot for a lively sophisticated meal with friends. Great pastries, light lunches, and low-priced gourmet takeout items can be found at **Pazzoria Bakery** next door.

Japanese

Sushi is very popular in Portland, and downtown you'll find decent sushi at a number of places. However, **Masu** (406 SW 13th Ave., 503/221-6278, www.masusushi.com, 11:30am-11pm Mon.-Thurs., 11:30am-midnight Fri., 5pm-midnight Sat., 5pm-10pm Sun., rolls $11-18) is our favorite. Between downtown and the Pearl District, Masu is a spacious light-filled second-story dining room that combines an excellent sushi bar with a Japanese fusion cuisine hot spot.

Mediterranean

The large, comfortably informal dining room at **SouthPark** (901 SW Salmon St., 503/326-1300, http://southparkseafood.com, 11:30am-3pm daily and 5pm-10pm Sun.-Thurs., 5pm-11pm Fri.-Sat., $16-28) is, as its name suggests, just a block from the South Park Blocks and the busy cultural venues at the Portland Center for the Performing Arts. The focus is on the sunny foods of the Mediterranean, with an especially strong selection of fresh fish. The adjacent wine bar is a favorite for a pre- and post-symphony quaff.

Middle Eastern

Portland has many Lebanese restaurants, but a good place for lunch or an informal dinner is **Habibi** (1012 SW Morrison St., 503/274-0628, http://habibirestaurantpdx.com, 11am-close Mon.-Sat., noon-close Sun., $5-15). It's a bustling place that's especially popular with people who work downtown.

If you're looking for that perfect family-owned Lebanese restaurant where you'll find delicious home-style cooking, this is it: **Karam Lebanese Cuisine** (316 SW Stark St., 503/223-0830, 11am-9pm Mon.-Sat., $12-20) offers a breadth of Lebanese dishes rarely seen in the United States—*kibee, molokhie,* and stews of eggplant, kid, and okra, plus a selection of traditional fish and seafood dishes. Still, it's the basics that count, and the excellent mezza platters, served with house-made pita bread, are worth the visit.

Pacific Northwest

A pioneer of Portland's seasonal, regional, locavore food movement, **Higgins** (1239 SW Broadway, 503/222-9070, http://higgins-portland.com, 11:30am-midnight Mon.-Fri., 4pm-midnight Sat.-Sun., $20-36) is the best exemplar of Pacific Northwest cuisine in downtown Portland. Under the direction of chef-owner Greg Higgins, the restaurant is devoted to serving the fresh produce of local organic farmers, meats from area farms and ranches, and fresh fish and seafood from Oregon rivers and seaports in uncluttered preparations that let the natural flavors sing. The result is a cuisine deeply rooted in the region. Although Higgins cures its own hams and specializes in charcuterie, this is also a good spot for vegetarians, as there's usually a broad selection of meat-free dishes. Budget tip: the classy wood-paneled bar is a great spot for a light meal from the bistro menu ($7-16) and a beer from the one of the carefully curated taps.

One of Portland's most elegant dining venues, the **Heathman Restaurant** (1001 SW Broadway, 503/790-7752, www.heathmanrestaurantandbar.com, 6:30am-3pm and 5:30pm-10pm Mon.-Fri., 9am-3pm and 5:30pm-11pm Sat.-Sun., $19-39) is synonymous with fine dining. As you might expect, the restaurant partners with the region's select growers, producers, and vintners to source the highest quality ingredients; the kitchen then transforms them into flavorful modern cuisine that weaves the refinement of French cooking with the earthy zest of Oregon's agricultural bounty. This is very sophisticated, artful food. The dining room is formal and the service is attentive, but the ambience is anything but stuffy.

A longtime insider favorite, the **❑ Veritable Quandary** (1220 SW 1st Ave., 503/227-7342, www.veritablequandary.com, 11:30am-3pm Mon.-Fri., 9:30am-3pm Sat.-Sun. and 5pm-10pm daily, $20-30), also just called the VQ, is a shoebox-size bar and restaurant at the foot of the Hawthorne Bridge. Up front is an always busy wood-paneled bar (open until 2:30am), usually propped up with attorneys and city hall types, but the dining room is the thing: Cozy and bright at the same time, it serves well-prepared hearty Pacific Northwest cuisine without fussy pretensions. In summer, the VQ has one of the city's best outdoor dining areas, a lovely flower-bedecked patio that feels like an oasis in the city center.

Housed in a high-ceilinged space on the ground floor of the hip Ace Hotel, **Clyde Common** (1014 SW Stark St., 503/228-3333, www.clydecommon.com, 11:30am-3pm Mon.-Fri. and 6-midnight Mon.-Thurs., 6pm-1am Fri. and 5pm-1am Sat., 5pm-11pm Sun., $16-20) is a big, airy space with long communal tables (if you need more privacy, you might be able to score a smaller table on the mezzanine) and an open kitchen where you can watch the cooks at work. The menu is an exercise in local ingredients and bold flavors; the house-made charcuterie offerings are excellent. The convivial bar is one of the city's great late-night spots.

Thai

Downtown's best bet for Thai food is **E-San Thai Cuisine** (133 SW 2nd Ave., 503/223/4090, 11:30am-10pm Mon.-Fri., noon-10pm Sat.-Sun., $10-16) near Saturday Market and Old Town. The food is pretty standard Thai, but well prepared. The lunch hour can get busy, so try to eat early or late. E-San also has a neighborhood cafe in Northwest Portland at 2764 NW Thurman Street (503/226-0409).

Steak and Seafood

A Portland tradition since 1907, **Dan and Louis Oyster Bar** (208 SW Ankeny St., 503/227-5906, www.danandlouis.com, 11am-9pm Mon.-Thurs., 11am-2am Fri.-Sat., noon-9pm Sun., $10-25) occupies a very atmospheric bar and dining room at the heart of Old Town. Filled with old photos and a century's worth of maritime bric-a-brac, the dining room is designed to look like the interior of a wooden ship. Don't come here in search of the latest evolution of seafood cuisine—this is the place for old-school fish and shellfish preparations that point to the 1950s. The oysters can't be beat.

Jake's Famous Crawfish (401 SW 12th St., www.mccormickandschmicks.com, 503/226-1419, 11:30am-10pm Mon.-Thurs., 11:30am-midnight Fri.-Sat., 3pm-10pm Sun., $11-37) has been one of Portland's most popular restaurants since 1892. It's also the prototype for an entire genre of clubby brass- and oak-paneled seafood establishments across the country, but this is the original. An old-fashioned fish and steak house, Jake's is emblematic of traditional Pacific Northwest cooking at its best—dozens of fresh fish choices, hefty cuts of beef, and oysters on the half shell from the region's most pristine bays are all well prepared and served up by a knowledgeable white-jacketed staff. The dining room is full of character, hung with vintage gilt-framed landscape paintings, and the adjacent bar is simply full of characters. Expect rowdy crowds, local celebrities, and a good time.

For dinner in a classic setting, try **Jake's Grill** (Governor Hotel, SW 10th Ave. and Alder St., 503/220-1850, www.governorhotel.com, 7am-midnight Mon.-Fri., 7:30am-midnight Sat., 7:30am-11pm Sun., $16-50), which offers a wide selection of prime beef, fresh fish, and seafood, as you'd expect, but with the addition of comfort food selections such as meat loaf and chicken potpie. The bar, filled with carved oak and hung with elk and bison heads, is very popular during its 3pm-6pm happy hour. What sets Jake's Grill apart is its stylish dining room, preserved intact from the 1910s as part of the grandly refurbished Governor Hotel. It's a glorious space, with towering ceilings, mosaic tile floors, burnished oak booths, banks of windows, and acres of red velvet curtains. At least stop by for a drink, or better yet, breakfast—the dining room is lovely in the morning light.

Ringside Fish House (838 SW Park Ave., 503/227-3900, www.ringsidefishhouse.com, 11:30am-2:30pm and 5pm-10pm Mon.-Thurs., 11:30am-2:30pm and 5pm-11pm Fri., 5pm-11pm Sat., 4pm-10pm Sun., $25-35) is cousin to the beloved Ringside steak house on Burnside St., but this new location is dedicated to fish and seafood—with the same insider's savvy. The Fish House is in one of downtown's snappiest locations, in the Fox Tower, and offers such Pacific Northwest classics as cedar plank salmon, fresh sole, and succulent local oysters, plus the best of the daily fresh catch. This is a comfortably upscale place to enjoy seafood; expect crisp linens, chilled cocktails, and knowledgeable staff.

Urban Farmer (525 SW Morrison St., 503/222-4900, www.urbanfarmerrestaurant. com, 6:30am-10pm Sun.-Thurs., 6:30am-11pm Fri.-Sat., $27-80) has a more modern, sustainably oriented take on the steak house, and the chef partners with local farmers and ranchers to get produce and beef that aren't widely available. Although dinner prices are pretty high, the restaurant, off the lobby of the Nines Hotel, is a good place for a lunchtime splurge (mostly $12-14) or happy hour snacks.

Wine Bars

Just above the RiverPlace Marina on the Willamette River, **Thirst Wine Bar and Bistro** (315 SW Montgomery St., 503/295-2747, www.thirstwinebar.com, 3pm-10pm Sun. and Tues.-Thurs., 3pm-11pm Fri.-Sat., $7-20) is instantly likable for that alone, but the stellar location is matched by the quality of the food and the excellent wine selection. Thirst does its best to wed its wines to the food, with well-priced selections of local charcuterie and cheese and a three-course tasting menu of appetizers chosen to accompany your wine or wine flight. Several larger plates are also available, ranging from a bistro steak, to seared ahi tuna and a delicious burger. The wine selection is likewise impressive, with a focus on small and hard-to-find Pacific Northwest vintages. Over 30 wines are available by the glass, with another 60 available by the bottle. On a summer evening, sitting outdoors above the marina, this is a great spot to make memories of Portland.

NORTHWEST

Northwest Portland begins just north of downtown across Burnside Street. Three of the city's most vibrant dining districts are here, within minutes of downtown hotels. **Old Town** also encapsulates historic Chinatown and is a hotbed of music clubs and late-night bars. The Portland Streetcar travels through the **Pearl District,** with its wealth of restaurants, linking it with downtown. Another restaurant destination along the streetcar line is **NW 21st and 23rd Avenues,** two pedestrian-friendly streets that are at the heart of an attractive 19th-century neighborhood.

Bakeries and Cafés

With Portland's profusion of excellent bakeries, it's easy to get into a squabble by asking people to identify their favorite. One thing's for certain: **Ken's Artisan Bakery** (338 NW 21st Ave., 503/248-2202, www.kensartisan.com, 7am-9:30pm Mon., 7am-6pm Tues.-Sat., 8am-5pm Sun.) is always among the top choices for wonderful French-style breads and pastries; the croissants—light, flaky, and crunchy at once—are masterful. At this busy NW 21st Avenue fixture, you can also pick up a lunchtime sandwich (11am-3pm, $7-8), or an espresso and a chocolate chip cookie for an afternoon pick-me-up. Monday evenings only, Ken's stays open late and serves delectable pizza ($11-14).

One of Portland's finest artisanal bread makers, ☾ **Pearl Bakery** (102 NW 9th Ave., 503/827-0910, www.pearlbakery.com, 6:30am-5:30pm Mon.-Fri., 7am-5pm Sat., 8am-3pm Sun.) is on the edge of the Pearl District, and its breads are served at many of the city's top restaurants. However, come to the friendly bakery and café for breads and baked goods that you cannot find elsewhere: dense walnut bread, eggy challah, *pain au raisin,* flaky Danish, and other delectables. Sandwiches ($6-9) and coffee drinks are available throughout the day.

A traditional French *boulangerie* and café for light meals, **St. Honoré Bakery** (2335 NW Thurman St., 503/445-4342, www.sthonorebakery.com, 7am-8pm daily, $5-14) is a neighborhood institution in Northwest Portland. Operated by Dominique Geulin, who grew up in a family bakery in Normandy, this is about as authentic as it gets outside of France. There's a large selection of breads, including excellent baguettes and a dense *pain de campagne.* Geulin mills his flour in-house from Pacific Northwest-grown wheat, and the bread is baked in a natural clay firebrick oven. Of course, there's a broad selection of pastries, and the bakery is a good spot for lunch or an early, informal dinner; sandwiches, soups, excellent salads, and savory tarts are available.

American

Founded by French Canadian loggers in 1903, **Besaw's** (NW 23rd Ave. and Savier St., 503/228-2619, www.besaws.com, 7am-3pm Mon., 7am-10pm Tues.-Fri., 8am-10pm Sat., 8am-3pm Sun., $15-25) is a jewel-box of a restaurant and one of the favorite breakfast destinations in Northwest Portland. Breakfast here isn't just fueling for the morning; it's a lavish affair that borders on fine cuisine. All of the omelets are fantastic, but if you're from out of town, you owe yourself the house-smoked salmon omelet with cream cheese, dill, and chopped scallions. Lunch and dinner, when the menu turns to American classics such as roast chicken, meat loaf, and burgers, ain't bad either.

Famous for its desserts—towering many-layered concoctions that defy gravity and description—**Papa Haydn** (701 NW 23rd Ave., 503/228-7317, and 5829 SE Milwaukie Ave., 503/232-9440, 11:30am-10pm Mon.-Thurs., 11:30am-midnight Fri.-Sat., 10am-10pm Sun.) is also an fine place to land for lunches or dinner. Entrees such as braised lamb or springtime nettles risotto ($16-22) are as carefully fashioned as the marjolaine cake, but it's the refrigerated case filled with 30 or more eye-popping desserts ($5-9) that places this Portland landmark in a league of its own.

Irving Street Kitchen (701 NW 13th Ave., 503/343-9440, http://irvingstreetkitchen.com, 4:30pm-10pm Mon.-Thurs., 4:30pm-11pm Fri., 10am-2:30pm and 4:30pm-10pm Sat., 10am-2:30pm and 5pm-9:30pm Sun., $17-27), opened by San Francisco restaurateurs Mitch and Steven Rosenthal and Doug Washington, features Southern-inspired food served in an elegantly rustic Pacific Northwest dining

LOCAL CHAINS

If you're out exploring and need a decent bite to eat without too much fuss or expense, chances are you'll find one of these local chains around. You can feed yourself for $5-10 at any of these cafés.

One of the simple pleasures of summer is sitting on the deck outside the Pearl District's Ecotrust Building with a slice of **Hotlips Pizza** (NW 10th Ave. and Irving St., 503/595-2342, 11am-9pm Sun.-Thurs., 11am-10pm Fri.-Sat.) and a beer or a bottle Hotlips's homemade fruit soda. It's an especially popular spot with families whose kids are exhausted from playing in the fountain at nearby Jamison Park. Hotlips sources nearly all its ingredients from its own network of local organic farmers and ranchers. Other convenient Hotlips outlets are near PSU (1909 SW 6th Ave., 503/224-0311), at Southeast Hawthorne Street and 22nd Avenue (503/234-9999), and across from JeldWen Field (SW 18th Ave. and Morrison St., 503/517-9354).

The other café housed in the Ecotrust Building, **Laughing Planet** (NW 10th Ave. and Irving St., 503/505-5020, 11am-9pm daily), serves healthy, mostly vegetarian variations on rice and bean bowls (the memorably named Soylent Green bowl is a bit bland; try the Cuban bowl instead), burritos, good soups, and salads. Other Laughing Planet locations include 3320 SE Belmont Street (503/235-6472), 922 NW 21st Avenue (503/445-1319), and 3765 N. Mississippi Avenue (503/467-4146).

Some Portland bakeries and sandwich shops are dining destinations. **Grand Central Bakery** is the place for a reliably good (well, actually, rather addictive) midmorning scone or a sandwich served up without hipster foodie attitude. The location in Northeast Portland (1444 NE Weidler St., 503/288-1614, 7am-6pm daily) is an especially handy one; find other Grand Central bakeries at 2230 SE Hawthorne Boulevard (503/445-1600), in Sellwood (7987 SE 13th Ave., 503/546-3036), just off N. Mississippi (714 NE Fremont Ave., 503/546-5311), or

at the edge of Northwest Portland (2249 NW York Ave., 503/808-9860), a short walk from the Holiday Inn Express or Silver Cloud hotels.

If you're near the convention center, there's no need to fear the fast food at **Burgerville** (1135 NE M. L. King Jr. Blvd., 503/235-6858, 6:30am-11pm daily). Even here you can dine on the seasonal (celebrate spring with batter-fried asparagus and a strawberry shake) and the local (beef from an Eastern Oregon ranchers' cooperative and smoked salmon from Astoria). You'll find Burgerville as far south as Corvallis and as far east as The Dalles. In Portland, stop by for Walla Walla onion rings (in season) and a salmon burger at 1122 SE Hawthorne Boulevard (503/230-0479) or at SE 25th Avenue and Powell Boulevard (503/239-5942).

If you need a simple, relatively quick, and inexpensive place to eat downtown, **Pastini Pastaria** (911 SW Taylor St., 503/863-5188, 11am-9pm Mon.-Thurs., 11am-10pm Fri.-Sat., 3pm-9pm Sun.) fits the bill. The pasta dishes are pretty tasty (the butternut squash ravioli is especially good, and comes in a little over $10), and they're served with excellent Pearl Bakery ciabatta bread. Lunch is an especially good deal, with a number of $6 specials offered. Pastini also has restaurants at 1506 NW 23rd Avenue (503/595-1205) and 1426 NE Broadway (503/288-4300).

Although it's not a restaurant, **New Seasons Market** (4034 SE Hawthorne Blvd., 503/236-4800, 8am-10pm daily) is a great place to grab deli food to go. Locally owned New Seasons is the most Portland of food stores, with great produce, meat, cheese, and wine departments and an exceptionally friendly staff. Many of the seven stores are in the suburbs, but Portland visitors may find themselves near the Sellwood (1214 SE Tacoma St., 503/230-4949), Seven Corners (1954 SE Division St., 503/445-2888), Hawthorne (4034 SE Hawthorne Blvd., 503/236-4800), or inner NE store (3445 N. Williams Ave.).

room. Bacon-wrapped oysters, fried okra, fried chicken, and chile-flecked corn bread all go down easy at this comfortable Pearl District restaurant, especially when lubricated with one of the bar's excellent cocktails or a glass of wine drawn directly from a tapped keg.

Imagine flavorful all-American comfort food like pot roast, baked chicken, and pan-fried fish, and then imagine them raised to the level of fine dining. **Paragon** (1309 NW Hoyt St., 503/833-5060, www.paragonrestaurant.com, 11:30am-4pm and 5:30pm-10pm Sun.-Wed., 11:30am-4pm and 5:30pm-11pm Thurs.-Sat., $13-28) calls it American bistro cuisine, and that just about captures it. The dining room is bright and pleasant, but on weekend nights the bar's live music and singles scene can detract from pleasurable dining.

Chinese

While Portland's longtime Chinatown is in the Old Town district, the business and culinary center for today's Chinese immigrants long ago shifted to the area around SE 82nd Avenue and Division Street. In the Pearl District, **Seres** (1105 NW Lovejoy St., 971/222-7327, 11am-10pm Mon.-Fri., 4pm-10pm Sat.-Sun., $10-24) extends the fresh, organic, and sustainable ethos of Portland restaurants to Chinese cooking. Everything from the chile oil to the pot sticker wrappers are made in-house. While the menu offers tastes and textures from multiple regions of China, many dishes reflect the spicy, hearty cooking of Szechuan province. The dining room is stylishly modern; this is the best Chinese cooking in the central Portland area.

French

You don't often see a combo cocktail bar and French creperie, but Portland's not an average place. **Le Happy** (1011 NW 16th Ave., 503/226-1258, www.lehappy.com, 5pm-1am Mon.-Thurs., 5pm-2:30am Fri., 6pm-2:30am Sat., crepes from $4-10), a hipster faux-dive bar, serves a late-night crowd in its tiny dining room. Classic crepe combinations are offered (Parisian ham and cheese, suzette with flamed Grand Marnier) alongside more ironic

combinations such as Le Trash Blanc, which combines bacon and cheddar and comes with a Pabst Blue Ribbon beer. Le Happy is on the streetcar line tucked under a freeway overpass.

Italian

Café Mingo (807 NW 21st Ave., 503/226-4646, www.caffemingonw.com, 5pm-10pm Sun.-Thurs., 5pm-11pm Fri.-Sat., $13-27) is an always-bustling trattoria along a busy section of NW 21st Avenue that offers an intimate dining room with the kitchen opening out to diners—you'll find your gaze drawn to the cooks in action, as if you'd stumbled onto a set for the Food Network. The menu is a bit idiosyncratic, and if you're expecting to dine in traditional *antipasti, primi,* and *secondi* courses, you'll find the offerings a bit of a puzzle. The dishes are well-prepared, however, and the service is gracious. Next door, **Bar Mingo** (811 NW 21st Ave., 503/445-4646, http://barmingonw.com, 4pm-11pm Sun.-Thurs., 4pm-midnight Fri.-Sat., $8-24) has different, but equally good, food in a casual atmosphere. Most of the dishes here are small plates meant to be shared among dining companions.

Make your way from the busy Pearl District art galleries to Bar Dué and escape to Italy. The long, dimly lit dining room at Dué's parent restaurant, **Fratelli** (1230 NW Hoyt St., 503/241-8800, www.fratellicucina.com, 11:30am-2pm and 5pm-9pm Tues.-Thurs., 11:30am-2pm and 5pm-10:30pm Fri.-Sat., 5pm-9pm Sun.-Mon., $17-23), seems suffused with an Italian glow from the warm ocher walls, the wood-fired oven, and soft-focus memories of Tuscany. Fratelli is one of Portland's most authentic Italian restaurants, but not because it slavishly recreates one of Italy's regional cuisines. Rather it brings an Italian aesthetic to Oregon's bounty, as if Portland were a distant outpost of Italy with its own regional cuisine.

Italian cooking "like Mama used to make" conjures up associations of red-checkered tablecloths, piped-in accordion music, and a rosy-cheeked maternal presence in the kitchen. **Piazza Italiana** (1129 NW Johnson St., 503/478-0619, www.piazzaportland.com,

11:30am-3pm and 5pm-10pm Mon.-Sat., noon-9pm Sun., $13-20) isn't like that. This is a hearty masculine trattoria with European league soccer on the TV, effusive Italian conversation bouncing off the walls, and a persistent bustle that verges on rowdiness. Everyone comes for the pasta, particularly topped with the restaurant's hearty marinara sauce, though the *rigatoni alla burino* (pasta with Italian sausage, peas, mushrooms, and cream sauce) is a personal favorite. For dessert? Liquor-drenched tiramisu, of course.

Latin American

You may be forgiven if you don't immediately think of Peruvian cooking when you think of a scintillating night out with outstanding indigenous cuisine. And in Portland? However, put these preconceptions aside and join the crowds at ◖ **Andina** (1314 NW Glisan St., 503/228-9535, www.andinarestaurant. com, 11:30am-2:30pm and 4pm-11pm Sun.-Thurs., 11:30am-2:30pm and 4pm-midnight Fri.-Sat., $18-29); the restaurant's take on South American cooking is unexpectedly delicious. The many small plates ($9.50) are rich in vegetarian choices—like quinoa-stuffed piquillo peppers—and can make a meal. Alternately, go for traditional Peruvian such as lamb shanks braised in black beer, or a new cuisine hybrid like quinoa-crusted diver scallops with wilted spinach and potato-parsnip puree.

A popular drinks and dinner spot in the Pearl District is **¡Oba!** (555 NW 12th Ave., 503/228-6161, www.obarestaurant.com, 5-close, $19-34), an outpost of Nuevo Latino cooking, representing the cuisines of Cuba, the Caribbean, and Central and South America. However, this isn't a fusion restaurant where two continents' worth of cooking traditions gets whirred in a blender: Cooking is creative but authentic, and the flavors are admirably pure and strong. In addition to its selection of Latin specialties, the menu always features a *série régionale,* a focus on a regional cuisine that changes monthly. Because ¡Oba! is also one of Portland's favorite cocktail and small-plates scenes, with a boisterous bar that draws in the Pearl District's beautiful young sophisticates, it's possible to forget that it's also a showcase of excellent food.

Pacific Northwest

It's in a lovely spot, directly across from the shady North Park Blocks where the locals toss balls in a game of bocce, but **Park Kitchen** (422 NW 8th Ave., 503/223-7275, www.park-kitchen.com, 11:30am-2pm and 5pm-9pm Mon.-Fri., 5pm-9pm Sat.-Sun., $25-24) has a lot more going for it than its location. Chef Scott Dolich relies on seasonal and regional ingredients to ensure the height of freshness and flavor, but he injects an eclectic touch of genius that makes even ordinary ingredients shimmer. One of the best things about Park Kitchen is its selection of small plates ($9-13), which make a meal here a bit less pricey. The dining room and tiny bar seem simultaneously very urban and as friendly as a well-loved neighborhood joint. Dolich has also opened the **Bent Brick** (1639 NW Marshall St., 503/688-1655, 5pm-10pm Tues.-Sat., $10-17), a tavern with a great menu of small plates and a few entrées in a cool old brick building tucked between the Pearl and Northwest Portland's older residential heart.

Bluehour (250 NW 13th Ave., 503/226-3394, www.bluehouronline.com, 11:30am-2:30pm and 5:30pm-10pm Mon.-Thurs., 11:30am-2:30pm and 5:30pm-10:30pm Fri., 10am-2:30pm and 5:30pm-10:30pm Sat., 10am-2pm and 5:30pm-10pm Sun., $25-40) is one of Portland's few really swanky restaurants. The dining room is soft-focus industrial chic, the high-ceilinged space divided by sheer curtain panels, with outdoor seating on the loading dock (this warehouse conversion is one of the Pearl District's most successful). The cooking is nominally Italian, though the kitchen is fluent in many cuisines, resulting in very sophisticated dishes that are flavor-focused, revelatory, and fun all at the same time. If you don't feel like getting dressed up for the dining room, the bar has its own menu and a more relaxed vibe.

Wildwood (1221 NW 21st Ave., 503/248-9663, www.wildwoodrestaurant.com, 11:30am-2:30pm and 5:30pm-9pm Mon.-Thurs., 11:30am-2:30pm and 5:30pm-10pm Fri.-Sat., 5pm-9pm Sun., $19-30) was Portland's first "celebrity chef" restaurant, created when local-boy-made-good Cory Schreiber returned from San Francisco to open his own restaurant. Wildwood has done as much as any other local restaurant to make Pacific Northwest cuisine a reality, with seasonal dishes focusing on local ingredients and simple, often old-fashioned preparations. Schreiber has since moved on to work involving food policy, and although Wildwood is no longer cutting-edge, it's still very good. Local lamb, rabbit, and salmon are usually excellent choices; if steamed mussels are offered, order them.

There's no better place to taste the particular *terroir* of Oregon than **◖ Paley's Place** (1204 NW 21st Ave., 503/243-2403, www.paleysplace.net, 5:30pm-10pm Mon.-Thurs., 5:30pm-11pm Fri.-Sat., 5pm-10pm Sun., $18-39), an intimate bastion of fine dining: This is food of great distinction. Chef-owner Vitaly Paley has a very firm grasp of traditional French techniques, which he uses to create a localized cuisine that is grounded in the refinement of traditional European preparations but with an added earthy potency that comes from celebrating the rich honest flavors of carefully selected local ingredients. The wine list features many hard-to-find Oregon pinot noirs. This is one of Portland's best special-occasion restaurants; for an affordable treat, eat in the bar (less romantic) or order the half portions offered on the dining room menu.

Steak

Portland has a full contingent of upscale expense-account steak houses, but if you're hungry for beef, go to one of the city's originals, the **Ringside** (2165 W. Burnside St., 503/223-1513, www.ringsidesteakhouse.com, 5pm-11:30pm Mon.-Wed., 5pm-midnight Thurs.-Sat., 4:30pm-11:30pm Sun., $25-67, reservations recommended). Family owned for nearly 70 years, the Ringside was recently remodeled but

retains its 1960s look of red Naugahyde and dark lighting. The steaks, prime rib, and seafood are excellent, and no less an authority than James Beard proclaimed that the onion rings "the best I ever had." Come before 5:45pm or after 9pm for a special three-course dinner menu (prime rib is an option) for just $37—one of Portland's best deals.

Thai

Portland's hottest Thai restaurant, **Red Onion** (1123 NW 23rd Ave., 503/208-2634, http://redonionportland.com, 11am-3pm and 5pm-9pm Mon.-Thurs., 11am-3pm and 5pm-9:30pm Fri., noon-9:30pm Sat., noon-9pm Sun., $10-16) specializes in northern Thai cooking, from the area around Chiang Mai. The flavors, textures, and colors remain distinct in the food here—it's not covered with gloppy brown sauce. Stray away from pad thai and try something off the specials menu, which may include deep-fried calamari tubes stuffed with ground meat and vegetables.

Vietnamese

Portland is rich in neighborhood Vietnamese restaurants, but **Silk** (1012 NW Glisan St., 503/248-2172, www.silkbyphovan.com, 11am-3pm and 5pm-10pm Mon.-Sat., $8-24) is one of the first to raise the subtle cuisine of Vietnam to fine dining. Located in the heart of the Pearl District, Silk is the gem of the local Pho Van restaurant chain. It is an upscale establishment that offers a reinterpretation of traditional Vietnamese cooking that's sophisticated and elegant yet earthy and full-flavored.

Brewpubs

Portland's first microbrewery. the **Bridgeport Brewpub** (1313 NW Marshall St., 503/241-3612, www.bridgeportbrew.com, 11:30am-1pm Tues.-Thurs., 11:30am-midnight Fri.-Sat., 11:30am-10pm Sun.), started out in an old rope factory in the then-derelict Pearl District. Depending on the time of year, try a pint of the Ebenezer or the Summer Squeeze.

If a pub named **New Old Lompoc** (1616 NW 23rd Ave., 503/255-1855, www.newoldlompoc.

com, 11am-midnight Mon.-Thurs. 11am-1am Fri.-Sat., 11am-11pm Sun.) seems like a mental tongue twister, just imagine how it will seem after a couple of pints of fine LSD! That's Lompoc Strong Draft in these parts, a delicious ale with smoked malt and plenty of hops. Other locations are in Southeast Portland (3412 SE Division St., 503/235-2215) and in Northeast Portland (3901 N. Williams Ave., 503/288-3996).

In the Pearl District is **Rogue Distillery & Public House** (1339 NW Flanders St., 503/222-5910, www.rogue.com, 11am-midnight Mon.-Thurs., 11am-1am Fri.-Sat., 11am-11pm Sun., $8-16), a Portland outlet of Rogue Brewing in Newport. This is some of Oregon's best beer: Most of the elixirs here are wonderful, but check out the Maibock-style Dead Guy Ale and St. Rogue Red.

Although its headquarters are in Bend, in central Oregon, **Deschutes Brewery Portland Public House** (210 NW 11th Ave., 503/296-4906, www.deschutesbrewery.com, Sun.-Tues. 11am-10pm, Wed.-Thurs. 11am-11pm, Fri.-Sat. 11am-midnight, $11-28) has long made some of Portland's favorite beers, Mirror Pond Pale Ale and Black Butte Porter. Their Portland pub in the midst of the Pearl District is massive, incorporating a quarter-block's worth of a former auto body shop. While much of the space is dedicated to restaurant service, there's also a large bar area for worship of the brewing gods. This is a great place to come before or after a play at neighboring Portland Center Stage.

Wine Bars

Very stylish and even glamorous, the Pearl District wine bar **Coppia** (417 NW 10th Ave., 503/295-9536, www.coppiaportland. com, 4pm-10pm Tues.-Thurs., 4pm-11pm Fri.-Sat., $8-22) will make you feel young and good-looking (or is that the wine talking?). The food and wine selections focus on Italy's Piedmont region—with a flight of nebbiolo, savor fresh porcini mushroom agnolotti pasta or grilled salmon with hazelnuts and capers.

NORTHEAST

Twenty years ago, a guide to Portland dining wouldn't even have included a section on Northeast Portland. However, the influx of Portland's DIY youth culture has turned once-sleepy Northeast neighborhoods into hotbeds of cuisine. Linked to downtown by MAX light rail trains and near the Lloyd Center hotels, the area along **NE Broadway** (between NE 8th and NE 28th Avenues) is the hub of close-in Northeast Portland.

Other Northeast Portland destinations for diners looking for inexpensive yet cutting-edge food are **North Mississippi Avenue** and **Northeast Alberta Street.** Out past the Hollywood neighborhood along **Sandy Boulevard** is the heart of today's Vietnamese community, where you'll find inexpensive and delicious *pho* and other Southeast Asian specialties.

American

Northeast Portland's breakfast hot spot is the **Cadillac Cafe** (1801 NE Broadway, 503/287-4750, http://cadillaccafepdx.com, 6am-2:30pm Mon.-Fri., 7am-3pm Sat.-Sun., $7-17), an always-jammed café with a 1961 pink Caddy fixation. Simple, honest American fare with lots of flavor is what draws the crowds.

Alberta Street is especially blessed with friendly and informal places for breakfast and lunch. The **Tin Shed** (1438 NE Alberta St., 503/288-6966, http://tinshedgardencafe.com, 7am-10pm daily, $8-13) has a comfortable dining room that opens onto a large, pet-friendly outdoor patio with a fireplace and herb garden. Come here for breakfast, where creative egg scrambles—combinations of veggies and sausage, ham, or tofu served with a buttermilk biscuit and potato pancakes or cheese grits—are legendary. Breakfast is also the star at **Helsers** (1538 NE Alberta St., 503/281-1477, http://helsersonalberta.com, 7am-3pm daily, $5-11), where you can get egg and homemade crumpet sandwiches, Scotch eggs, potato pancake torta, or spinach, tomato, and mushroom eggs Benedict in a sunny and bustling dining room.

Join Portland's late-rising hipsters for

breakfast at ◖ **Tasty n Sons** (3808 N. Williams Ave., 503/621-1400, tastyntasty. com, 9am-10pm Sun.-Thurs., 9am-11pm Fri.-Sat., $5-13) and you'll almost certainly plan to return for dinner. This wildly popular spot, owned by chef John Gorham, who also runs Toro Bravo, is a great place for brunch, happy hour snacks, or dinner. Dishes are divided into small plates and bigger plates—all designed to be shared. The decor here is rough-hewn and somewhat industrial, to match the robust flavors of the food, which draws from many of the world's cuisines, and often given an American touch: The cassoulet is almost like the best picnic baked beans ever, and shakshuka, a red pepper and tomato stew, is topped with baked eggs. Downtown Portland now has its own outpost of this wildly popular restaurant, called **Tasty and Alder** (580 SW Alder St., 503/621-9251, 9am-2pm and 5:30pm-10pm Sun.-Thurs., 9am-2pm and 5:30pm-11pm Fri.-Sat., $9-13).

Equinox (830 N. Shaver St., 503/460-3333, http://equinoxrestaurantpdx.com, 5pm-9pm Tues.-Thurs., 5pm-10pm Fri., 9am-2pm and 5pm-10pm Sat., 9am-2pm Sun., $10-21) offers an international and eclectic menu and one of the city's nicest al fresco dining spaces in a quiet courtyard just off Mississippi Avenue. You'll face choices like chickpea crepes with asparagus and goat cheese, an arugula salad with sweet Bing cherries and prosciutto, or grilled pork loin with parmesan polenta.

African

Portland has a number of popular Ethiopian restaurants, and one favorite is the **Queen of Sheba** (2413 NE M. L. King Jr. Blvd., 503/287-6302, http://queenofsheba.biz, 5pm-9pm Sun.-Wed., noon-2pm and 5pm-10pm Thurs.-Sat., $12-15). Meals are served family-style and typically feature platters of highly spiced, stewed, or grilled meats and vegetables, which are scooped up with house-made *injera,* a slightly sour-tasting griddle bread. Vegetarian dishes are among the most tempting, including braised lentils with mustard greens and okra.

Barbecue

Podnah's Pit (1625 NE Killingsworth St., 503/281-3700, http://podnahspit.com, 11am-10pm Mon.-Fri., 9am-10pm Sat.-Sun., $10-17) serves up Texas-style barbecue, slow-cooked over oak in a pit. With one exception, Podnah's takes "don't mess with Texas" to heart—and that exception is a very tasty North Carolina-style pulled pork. Although smoked trout and sides of pinto beans and Texas caviar (black-eyed pea salad) are available, non-meat-eaters will feel a little lonely here.

Cuban

For a taste of Havana, head to **Pambiche** (2811 NE Glisan St., 503/233-0511, www. pambiche.com, 11am-10pm Mon.-Thurs., 11am-midnight Fri., 7am-midnight Sat., 8am-10pm Sun., $11-17), a popular, colorful restaurant and nightspot. The spicy, citrusy tang of Cuban food blends Spanish and creole flavors, and it's served up with a light touch—just the thing to accompany a cocktail from the lengthy list of sassy Caribbean drinks. For chef-owner John Connell Maribona, good Cuban cooking is in his blood—he credits his prowess to his Cuban mother and grandmother, both great home cooks. Pambiche is very popular; go early or late to avoid lines.

Indian

◖ **Bollywood Theater** (2039 NE Alberta St., 971/200-4711, www.bollywoodtheaterpdx. com, 11am-10pm daily, $6.50-14), is chef Troy MacLarty's homage to Indian cooking—it's not exactly traditional Indian fare but an updated version that's true to the spirit of Indian cooking and fresh, crispy, and pungent in ways that are wildly more pleasing than the neighborhood curry shop. The focus is on Indian street food—the *Dahi Papri Chaat* (housemade crackers topped with chickpeas, potatoes, yogurt, cilantro, and tamarind chutney), is outrageously delicious, and other top dishes include pork vindaloo, egg masala, and fried okra with chile, lime, and raita. This is not a fancy, sit-down restaurant: You'll order at the counter and take a free table, as they are available, to eat your meal. It sounds frustrating, but somehow it works. Expect long lines on weekends and food that's worth the wait. Bollywood Theater plans to open a new location on SE Division at 30th Avenue in late 2013. Check the website for details.

Italian

Northeast Portland's top Italian restaurant is **DOC** (5519 NE 30th Ave., 503/946-8592, http://docpdx.com, 6pm-close Tues.-Sat., $18-26), which adds Pacific Northwest touches to the underlying Italian structure. Risotto may come with bay shrimp, snap peas, nasturtium, chives; a steak is topped with maitake mushrooms and flavorful padron peppers. If you want to splurge, this is an excellent place to do it: Order the five-course tasting menu ($60 per person) with wine pairings ($40 per person). DOC is an intimate place, and you really get to see the chefs at work as you enter the restaurant—the kitchen is near the front door.

At **Ciao Vito** (2203 NE Alberta St., 503/282-5522, www.ciaovito.net, 5pm-10pm daily, $14-22), robust flavors meld perfectly with a sunny, handsomely decorated dining room. Dishes like pork sugo—similar to a pulled pork sandwich only with a tangy-sweet tomato sauce—are served over polenta and perfectly represents the chef's affinity for full-flavored, well-crafted Italian comfort food.

Japanese

Zilla Saké House (1806 NE Alberta St., 503/336-4104, www.zillasakehouse.com, 5pm-11pm Mon.-Thurs., 5pm-midnight Fri., 2pm-midnight Sat., 2pm-10pm Sun., sushi and rolls $4-11) offers something unique in Portland: over 50 different types of sake available by the pour and bottle, including rare Daiginjo sake, sparkling "champagne" sake, and rice wines from SakéOne, brewed in the Portland suburbs by the only sake producer outside Japan. This little Alberta Street gem has fun with Portland's reuse-recycle mandate (the bar is a converted pool table slate) and also offers good sushi, sashimi, and appetizers—servers can help you pair sake and sushi flights. Monday evenings

bring free Japanese movies to Zilla, and there's live music on Friday evenings.

Mediterranean

A wine bar and small-plates restaurant with over 50 carefully selected wines by the glass, handcrafted Spanish, French, and Italian food (which you order off little paper menus as in a sushi joint), and a friendly low-key attitude make **Navarre** (10 NE 28th St., 503/232-3555, 4:30pm-10:30pm Mon.-Thurs., 11am-11:30pm Fri., 9:30am-11:30pm Sat., 9:30am-10:30pm Sun., $4-15) one of Portland's top choices for highly flavorful artisanal cooking. Nearly everything is handmade with near-obsessive attention to authenticity, and the restaurant gets produce from a community supported agriculture farm just a few miles away in Southeast Portland.

Mexican

Like an unassuming little beach taqueria in Baja, **¿Por Qué No?** (3524 N. Mississippi Ave., 503/467-4149, and 4635 SE Hawthorne Blvd., 503/954-3138, 11:30am-9pm Mon.-Thurs., 11:30am-10pm Fri.-Sat., 11:30am-8pm Sun., $3-11) has a relaxed hole-in-the-wall vibe to go with its excellent tacos and other south of the border street foods. Tortillas and salsas are handmade in-house, and the meats and produce are local and organic, all of which adds to the terrific fresh-tasting zip of the food that rolls out of the miniscule kitchen. You can't go wrong with any of the tacos; the guacamole is outstanding, as is the ceviche. Fresh-squeezed margaritas are utterly addictive (try pomegranate). This place is tiny—line up to order your food, then find a seat. Most people end up sitting at tables in the street, rain or shine.

The Mexican food at **Autentica** (5507 NE 30th Ave., 503/287-7555, www.autenticaportland.com, 5pm-10pm Tues.-Fri., 10am-2pm and 5pm-10pm Sat.-Sun., $17-20) is complex and sophisticated, but the restaurant doesn't take itself so seriously as to suck the fun out of the experience. The whole place is warm and colorful, and the patio out back is one of the best places to celebrate a warm evening in

© BILL MCRAE

¿Por Qué No? brings Baja beach food to Mississippi Avenue.

Portland. Although you can order enchiladas here, Autentica is a good place to stretch your idea of Mexican food, perhaps to include wild mushrooms with grilled poblano peppers simmered in a spicy tomatillo cream sauce.

Just up the street from North Mississippi Avenue, in a former marine-flooring warehouse, is **Trèbol** (4835 NE Albina Ave., 503/517-9347, www.trebolpdx.com, 5pm-10pm Sun.-Thurs., 5pm-11pm Fri.-Sat., 11am-2pm Sun., $9-18), an excellent Latin American restaurant that's equal parts tradition and innovation. Chef-owner Kenny Hill spent years as *sous chef* at Portland's top-rated Higgins restaurant before opening Trèbol, and he brings his rich experience in creative New American cuisine to traditional southern Mexican cooking. Trèbol's best dishes derive from recipes of Hill's Oaxacan grandmother and are rich, honest, and full of flavor. All tortillas, cured meats, and sauces are made in-house. In summer, eat and drink outdoors on a handsome wood veranda.

Northeast Alberta Street is home to a couple of traditional taquerias. Favorites include **La Sirenita** (2817 NE Alberta St., 503/335-8283, 10am-10pm daily) and **La Bonita** (2839 NE Alberta St., 503/281-3662, 11am-9pm Tues.-Sat.).

Pacific Northwest

Naomi Pomeroy is a pioneer of Portland's dining club scene, and **Beast** (5425 NE 30th Ave., 503/841-6968, www.beastpdx.com, seatings 6 and 8:45pm Wed.-Sun., 10am or noon Sun.) is her latest restaurant, with a prix fixe menu that changes weekly. You have a choice of the tasting menu's six ($75) courses, but not much else. Substitutions, as clearly stated on the menu, are politely declined. Most menus are French inflected, with a soup to start, ending with a salad, a selection of cheeses, and a light dessert. But it's called Beast for a reason: Pomeroy has a deft hand with pork, and most meals feature a selection of house-made charcuterie and often feature braised pork shoulder or brined chops. An optional six-course wine pairing costs $35. Sunday brunch ($35) can also come with wine

($20). With just 24 seats and two seatings per night, reservations are a must.

⟨ Lincoln Restaurant (3808 N. Williams St., 503/288-6200, www.lincolnpdx.com, 5:30pm-9pm Tues.-Thurs. and Sun., 5:30pm-10pm Fri.-Sat., $17-22) anchors a block of restaurants, shops, and a yoga studio along a rapidly gentrifying stretch of North Williams. The big front windows look out onto a steady stream of bike traffic, and the clean lines, warm wood, and cement floor of the restaurant provide a simple but elegant backdrop to the food. Chef Jenn Louis, who was named a *Food and Wine* Best New Chef in 2012, oversees the creation of dinners such as sturgeon with prosciutto and chard bagna cauda. Don't skip the foraged salad if it's offered; the assortment of herbs, spicy greens, and pea shoots is definitely not shaken out of a plastic bag.

Ned Ludd (3925 NE M. L. King Jr. Blvd. 503/288-6900, http://nedluddpdx.com, 5pm-9pm Wed.-Sat., 9am-2pm and 5pm-9pm Sun., $18-24) is named for that famous Luddite, and in this restaurant's concept, that means that a menu focused on old-fashioned wood-fired oven dishes. But that doesn't mean that the food served here is pre-Industrial Revolution. Sample the chef's charcuterie board and fresh vegetable bruschetta and save room for roast chicken with garbanzos, capers and olives, or whey-fed pork with smoked potatoes, corn, and tomatillos.

Spanish

The odd thing about **⟨ Toro Bravo** (120 NE Russell St., 503/281-4464, www.torobravopdx.com, 5pm-10pm Sun.-Thurs., 5pm-11pm Fri.-Sat., $4-19), the wildly popular tapas restaurant in inner Northeast Portland, is that its very authentic Spanish cooking simultaneously seems very Pacific Northwestern. This is the kind of food that would be native to Portland had it been colonized by the Spanish: rich, seasonal, and full of vigorous flavor. The menu is extensive, covering many regions of Spain and offering everything from a bowl of olives to heaping platters of paella. Chef-owner John Gorham is an imposing presence in the open kitchen,

undaunted as he and his staff dispatch an astonishing array of dishes, from fried anchovies with fennel and lemon to oxtail croquettes with aioli. Expect to be wowed.

Steak

Forget those fancy-schmantzy corporate expense account steak restaurants. **⟨ Laurelhurst Market** (3155 E. Burnside St., 503/206-3097, www.laurelhurstmarket.com, 5pm-10pm Mon.-Sat., 5pm-9pm Sun., $13-24), an offshoot of one of Portland's top catering companies, is Portland's hipster take on a steak house. The in-house butcher shop (10am-7pm daily) features top-quality organic meats and excellent charcuterie; you can also get good meaty sandwiches from the butcher counter, and this is proving to be a popular lunch spot. At night the other side of the building opens up as this casual but atmospheric steakhouse. You'll pay a lot less for a steak house experience than at downtown's hotshot supper clubs, and you'll get higher quality and a friendly welcome even if you're on a budget.

Argentinian

Fire is the raison-d'être of **Ox** (2225 NE M. L. King Jr. Blvd., 503/284-3366, http://oxpdx.com, 5pm-10pm Tues.-Thurs and Sun., 5pm-11pm Fri.-Sat., $19-39), where meats, seafood, and vegetables get licked by flames and are served in a style that recalls the hearty, smoky flavors of Argentina. Be sure to try the crispy beef, olive and raisin empanadas, or the clam chowder enriched with a beef marrow bone. Seared steaks are the stand-out main courses, but if you're not into beef, you can enjoy the house-made chorizo or morcilla sausages, coal-roasted artichokes, or the delicious roasted sea scallops with sweet corn in bacon sherry cream.

Vegetarian

The bright, quirky **Vita Cafe** (3023 NE Alberta St., 503/235-8233, http://vita-cafe.com, 9am-10pm Mon.-Fri., 11am-10pm Sat.-Sun., $7-17) is a neighborhood spot that draws vegetarians and their meat-eating friends from all over the city. The easy-on-the-wallet menu pleases vegans as well as burger lovers (serving free range and hormone-free beef), and it's a great place to bring kids. Local artists' creations adorn the walls, and a broad variety of meat substitutes are on order.

Vietnamese

According to *New Yorker* food philosopher Calvin Trillin, Portland has some of the best Vietnamese restaurants outside of Saigon. The neighborhood along NE Sandy Boulevard between NE 50th Avenue and NE 82nd Avenue is the locus of Portland's Southeast Asian business community. Several restaurants here are dedicated to *pho,* or Vietnamese noodle soup. One good stop for a steaming bowl (perfect on a wet Portland day) or other Vietnamese specialties is **Pho An Sandy** (6236 NE Sandy Blvd., 503/281-2990, 9am-9pm daily, $7-14).

Brewpubs

The **Widmer Brewery and Gasthaus** (929 N. Russell St., 503/281-3333, www.widmer.com, 11am-11pm Mon.-Thurs., 11am-midnight Fri.-Sat.) is revered by beer lovers throughout the country as the birthplace of Oregon's most popular microbrew, Widmer Hefeweizen, distributed nationally in bottles. The Gasthaus is the place to enjoy this cloudy wheat beer straight from the tap. The elegant back bar and a mix of wood and brick throughout the restaurant impart a feeling of warmth that complements home-style German cooking.

If your local pub has a children's play area, you know you must be in Portland. **Laurelwood Public House & Brewery** (5115 NE Sandy Blvd., 503/282-0622, www.laurelwoodbrewpub.com, 11am-10pm Mon.-Tues., 11am-11pm Wed.-Thurs., 11am-midnight Fri., 10am-midnight Sat., 10am-10pm Sun.) is a family-friendly brewpub with restaurant-quality food in Northeast Portland's Hollywood district. While the Space Stout (say that twice quickly) may look like a pint of pure opaque chocolate, it's not for the children. Instead, it's an award-winning stout and Portland's version of Guinness.

You can't get much more casual than

Stormbreaker Brewing (832 N. Beech St., 503/281-7708). Along busy North Mississippi Avenue, the brewery and the serving area are in a small converted metal shop, but you'll drink and dine outdoors at picnic tables underneath a huge tent. Obviously, this is a great place to stop in summer when afternoons drift by in picnic mode; dogs aren't just allowed, they are encouraged. In winter, some of the tables move indoors and space heaters warm the beer garden.

Wine Bars

East Burnside Street has become hot property for cutting-edge dining houses, but if you're looking just for a glass of wine and a carefully considered menu of small plates and snacks, then **Kir** (22 NE 7th Ave., 503/232-3036, www.kirwinebar.com, 5pm-11pm Mon.-Thurs., 5pm-midnight Fri.-Sat., small plates $3-12) is an excellent option. The wine list isn't huge, but it's well chosen—in summer, most selections are rosé wines, an excellent antidote to Portland's surprisingly hot summers. This is a tiny place, but the owners' care and expertise (both are longtime veterans of the Portland restaurant scene) are immediately apparent. Come for finely chosen wines and a way-relaxed vibe, but don't ignore the finely crafted menu.

SOUTHEAST

Southeast Portland is filled with restaurant enclaves, where it's a good idea just to park the car and wander the streets before making a dining choice. Some of Portland's most popular and acclaimed restaurants are in the industrial warehouses of **Inner Southeast Portland,** just across the Willamette River from downtown, and other neighborhoods, such as the six-block stretch of **28th Avenue** near East Burnside Street, seem almost totally devoted to dining.

The pulse of Portland's evergreen, seemingly "forever young" hippie community can be felt on **SE Belmont Street and SE Hawthorne Avenue,** where you can expect to find lots of moderately priced cafés, food carts, pubs, and restaurants—along with shopping and superlative people watching. Farther south are more streets lined with restaurants. In the last five years, **SE Division and SE Clinton Streets** have blossomed as dining destinations.

American

Laid-back Southeast Portland is a perfect habitat for breakfast joints, and one of the favorites is **Cup and Saucer Cafe** (3566 SE Hawthorne Blvd., 503/236-6001, http://cupandsaucercafe.com, 7am-9pm daily, $4-10), at the heart of the Hawthorne neighborhood. The decor is Formica chic, but the hearty breakfasts—mostly organic and many vegetarian—are served all day. Get there early on weekends. The tofu scramble is worth the wait.

Bread and Ink (3610 SE Hawthorne Blvd., 503/239-4756, www.breadandinkcafe.com, 8am-8:30pm Sun.-Thurs., 8am-9:30pm Fri.-Sat., dinner $16-28) is a longtime gathering place in the Hawthorne neighborhood. For breakfast, an assortment of homemade breads and imaginative omelets will sustain you. Lunchtime diners line up for a massive burger topped with gruyère cheese and Bermuda onion as well as locally esteemed salmon sandwiches. Dinner is a primer on local cuisine—whatever's in season, the freshest ingredients are creatively prepared.

Step into tradition at ◖ **Zell's** (1300 SE Morrison St., 503/239-0196, 7am-2pm Mon.-Sat., 8am-3pm Sun., $7-14), a longtime eastside favorite for hearty breakfasts and lunch. The setting is a historic pharmacy, complete with an antique soda fountain, and the food is outstanding: The complimentary scones with homemade jam served at breakfast are amazing.

Heartland American comfort food has never tasted as good as at **Savoy Tavern and Bistro** (2500 SE Clinton St., 503/808-9999, www.savoypdx.com, 4pm-late daily, $11-17). The Savoy doesn't seek to update or transform classics of home cooking as much as to replicate them gloriously with top-notch ingredients and savvy of modern cooking techniques. Unless you're from Wisconsin, you probably didn't know that fried cheese curds existed. Start your meal with these molten dairy-product wonders and move on to excellent meat loaf, stuffed trout, fried

chicken, or grilled hanger steak. Immediately next door, and from the same owner, is **Broder** (2508 SE Clinton St., 503/736-3333, www.broderpdx.com, 9am-3pm Mon.-Tues., 9am-3pm and 5pm-9pm Wed.-Sun., $9-11), where upper Midwest Swedish cooking reigns supreme, with lefse crepes, baked egg skillets, and aebleskiver apple pancakes for breakfast, and Swedish meatballs, salmon fish cakes, and "hamburgare a la Lindstöm," with pickled beets and capers, for lunch and dinner. Broder expands to a location in North Portland's Gotham Building (2240 N. Interstate Ave.) in late 2013. Check the website for details.

Join the line at **Bunk** (621 SE Morrison St., 503/477-9515, 8am-3pm daily, $4-9), where you'll be enveloped by the fragrance of cured meat, and get ready to eat an astonishingly good sandwich in this Formica-tabled diner. Chef Tommy Habertz left a gig at a much fancier restaurant to focus his considerable skills with meat on a place where everyday people could eat, well, every day. (There's always a vegetarian option on the menu.) At night, a few blocks away **Bunk Bar** (1028 SE Water St., 503/894-9708, http://bunkbar.com, 3pm-2am daily, $5-8) serves a similar menu of sandwiches in a rec room atmosphere, often with live music.

Another good place for a sandwich, especially if you want to experiment with high-end grilled cheese, is **Cheese Bar** (6031 SE Belmont St., 503/222-6014, http://cheese-bar.com, 11am-11pm Tues.-Sun., $5-8) on the west slope of Mount Tabor. It's a mix of a retail cheese shop with charcuterie, several great variations on grilled cheese sandwiches, and an extensive beer list (mostly consisting of limited releases).

With its faux-rustic Americana trappings, the **Woodsman Tavern** (4537 SE Division St., 971/373-8264, http://woodsmantavern.com, 5pm-10pm Mon.-Fri., 9am-2pm and 5pm-10pm Sat.-Sun., $22-32) doesn't look like a place where you'd expect to find some of the city's best raw seafood. But the top foods at this popular spot are those that the kitchen sources carefully and intervenes with minimally. Not only are the oysters, clams, crabs, and other local seafood served with minimal cooking to let their natural flavors sing, so too the thin-sliced ham plates, salads, and cheeses. These ingredients don't need prodding from the kitchen to be delicious. Of course, you can have a proper cooked meal here (the barbecued chicken with baked beans is mighty fine) but many diners come here to make a meal from platters of iced shellfish, ham, cold salads, and cheese.

Barbecue

Clay's Smokehouse (2932 SE Division St., 503/235-4755, 11am-10pm Wed.-Sun., $8-15) serves up slow-smoked Oklahoma-style barbecue meats and fish with aromas of hickory, mesquite, and alderwood. We recommend the cold-smoked seafood platter featuring smoked oysters, salmon, and catfish. As you might expect, there's a selection of microbrews to accompany your repast.

Seafood

Two restaurant experiences in one: That's what is offered by **Block + Tackle** and **[** **Roe** (3113 SE Division St.). **Block + Tackle** (503/236-0205, http://blockandtacklepdx.com, 4pm-10pm Wed.-Sun., $8-18) is a casual but bustling seafood bar with a selection of raw oysters, seafood charcuterie, and fresh fish-based small plates that can be easily assembled into dinner. But in the back, behind the curtain, is **Roe** (503/232-1566, http://roe-pdx.com, 5:30pm-9pm Thurs.-Sat., 4-course menu $65), a separate dining room with its own kitchen, where local seafood is transformed into a high-end, multicourse feast. The Roe dining room is small and reservations are required—but the always-changing, all-seafood menu is exquisite and stunningly fresh, with shellfish, seaweed, and fish harvested by the chefs from the pristine waters of the Pacific.

Chinese

Portland's contemporary Chinese community is centered in the SE 82nd Avenue and Division Street neighborhood, where Portland's best Chinese food can be found at **[** **Wong's King** (8733 SE Division St., 503/788-8883, http://wongsking.com, 10am-11pm Mon.-Fri., 9:30am-11pm Fri.-Sat., $8-21). The chef has won prestigious cooking awards in China, and the huge dining room is always thronged with Chinese families, but the staff is very solicitous to non-Chinese diners who may be confounded by the extensive menu. The dim sum is terrific.

French

Drop by **[** **Saint Jack's** (2039 SE Clinton St., 503/360-1281, 9am-9:30pm Sun.-Thurs., 9am-10:30pm Fri.-Sat., $17-21) in the morning for a pastry or later on for dinner (reserve in advance for best luck at getting a table). No matter the hour, you'll feel like you've landed in a French country kitchen, especially if a chef is busy carving up raw meat on a counter in the dining room when you enter. The food is inspired by the meaty cuisine of Lyons, and the atmosphere is pure bistro.

Indian

The Eastside's best Indian food comes from **Bombay Cricket Club** (1925 SE Hawthorne Blvd., 503/231-0740, http://bombaycricketclubrestaurant.com, 5pm-9pm Sun.-Thurs., 5pm-10pm Fri.-Sat., $14-20). This always-packed two-tiered restaurant offers superbly cooked traditional Indian dishes (and a few from the Middle East) with plenty of options for vegetarians. Make a reservation or you'll end up with a wait.

Don't come to **Vindalho** (2038 SE Clinton St., 503/467-4550, www.vindalho.com, 5pm-9pm Sun.-Thurs., 5pm-10pm Fri.-Sat., $15-19) looking for "authentic" Indian cooking. Instead, the chef has refined the sauces and spices of traditional Indian cooking and uses them to create a sophisticated hybrid cuisine that's a delicious adjunct to Pacific Northwest-style cooking. The upscale dining room is stylish and full of energetic colors, and the outdoor courtyard is a great place for cocktails and samosas on a warm evening.

Italian

Nostrana (1401 SE Morrison St., 503/234-2427, http://nostrana.com, 11:30am-2pm and

5pm-10pm Mon.-Thurs., 11:30am-2pm and 5pm-11pm Fri., 5pm-11pm Sat., 5pm-10pm Sun., $15-24, pizza $9-18) is the latest outpost of Cathy Whims, who led the much-revered Genoa kitchen for many years. Her new enterprise takes her a ways from Italian high cuisine: Nostrana is part wood-fired pizza joint and part rustic Italian home-cooking restaurant. Order one of the excellent pizzas—perhaps prosciutto and arugula—and augment it with a selection of wonderful salads, soups, house-cured meats, and wood-oven-cooked meats. The menu changes nightly to ensure that everything here is absolutely fresh and seasonal.

3 Doors Down (1429 SE 37th Ave., 503/236-6886, http://3doorsdowncafe.com, 5pm-9:30pm Tues.-Thurs., 5pm-10pm Fri.-Sat., 4pm-9pm Sun., $17-24), as its name implies, is a few doors away from Hawthorne Boulevard. Dishes are Italian influenced but inspired by the Pacific Northwest's bounty. The most requested dish is pasta with vodka sauce and spicy Italian sausage.

Ava Gene's (3377 SE Division St., 971/229-0571, http://avagenes.com, 5pm-11pm daily, $17-45) focuses on Rome and its traditional cooking traditions, but translated for the Pacific Northwest and made new again with fresh local produce. Start with vegetable small plates, such as grilled pole beans, anchovies, and a poached duck egg; and move onto a hearty plate of fusilli pasta and tripe; and if you're still hungry, perhaps a *secondi* of roast lamb, peperonata and chickpeas. The handsome tiled dining room lends the perfect touch of formality. Immediately next door, and under the same ownership, is **Roman Candle Bakery** (971/302-6605, 7am-4pm daily) with coffee, pastries, artisanal breads, and Roman-style white pizzas.

Japanese

Portland has over 50 sushi restaurants but precious few dining rooms that serve other traditional Japanese fare. Enter █ **Biwa** (215 SE 9th Ave., 503/239-8830, www.biwarestaurant.com, 5pm-midnight daily, $3-12), an excellent Portland-style representation of an *izakaya*,

a Japanese sake-and-beer bar where patrons gather to drink and dine on a multitude of highly flavored and shareable dishes. Don't expect kimono-clad servers or *Madama Butterfly* interiors: This semi-subterranean dining room is an exercise in industrial chic, with boisterous crowds and a showcase open kitchen. In addition to *maguro poke,* raw yellowfin tuna showered with *shoyu* and feathered with seaweed, wonderful salads (the baby octopus and cucumber salad is marvelous), and house-made pickles, there are handmade ramen and udon noodles served both cold in salads and hot as steaming bowls of soup.

Bamboo Sushi (310 SE 28th Ave., 503/232-5255, www.bamboosushipdx.com, 4:30pm-10pm daily, rolls $4-14), with a stylish dining room and a vast selection of fish that has been harvested according to "green" and sustainable practices, has become Portland's top sushi restaurant. Indeed, with non-sushi dishes such as sesame-crusted tuna with caramelized eggplant, it's one of the city's best seafood restaurants.

Mexican

Forget American-style Mexican food. Step up to the plate to try **Nuestra Cocina** (2135 SE Division St., 503/232-2135, www.nuestra-cocina.com, 5pm-10pm Tues.-Sat., $9-18), which serves truly sophisticated south of the border cuisine in a lively and elegant Eastside dining room. The flavors of Oaxaca, Yucatan, Veracruz, and tropical Mexico jump off the plate. The mole sauces contain labyrinths of flavor; this spot is deservedly popular and doesn't take reservations, so come early or late.

Middle Eastern

For house-baked Middle Eastern flatbreads and excellent Lebanese street food, go to **Nicholas Restaurant** (318 SE Grand Ave., 503/235-5123, http://nicholasrestaurant.com, 10am-9pm Mon.-Sat., noon-9pm Sun., $5-13, no credit cards), which must have the most unprepossessing exterior in the Portland restaurant firmament in its bright red-and-yellow storefront on a busy thoroughfare. Nicholas nonetheless has lines out the door for its excellent Lebanese cooking. Nicholas does not serve alcohol.

Pacific Northwest

More than any other single restaurant, **ClarkLewis** (1001 SE Water Ave., 503/235-2294, www.clarklewispdx.com, 11:30am-2pm and 5:30pm-9pm Mon.-Thurs., 11:30am-2pm and 5:30pm-10pm Fri., 5:30pm-10pm Sat., $19-34) was responsible for Portland's sudden and outsize reputation as one of the nation's top dining destinations. It also helped define the "guerilla restaurant," refuting the idea that a fancy dining room is the only appropriate venue for fine dining. Straddling a loading dock and a warehouse in industrial Southeast Portland, ClarkLewis is not exactly the place for a romantic candlelit dinner. It is, however, the place to explore the flavors of fresh local ingredients. The wine list is adventuresome and eclectic, a perfect counterpoint to ClarkLewis's creative cuisine.

Also in Southeast Portland's warehouse district, you'll find one of two locations of **Olympic Provisions** (107 SE Washington St., 503/954-3663 and 1632 NW Thurman St., 503/894-8136, www.olympicprovisions.com, 11am-10pm Mon.-Sat., $20-32), known for excellent sausages and charcuterie, but also serving up some wickedly good fish dishes, such as olive oil-poached tuna with cranberry beans and pickled vegetables. The two locations have different menus (more fish in SE), and the NW Thurman restaurant is also a butcher shop, with most of the building taken up by production of chorizo, saucisson, and the like.

No need to dust off your high school French when calling for reservations at ❰**Le Pigeon**— rhymes with smidgen—(738 E. Burnside St., 503/546-8796, www.lepigeon.com, 5pm-10pm Mon.-Sat., 5pm-9pm Sun., $12-28), a highly-touted hot spot of meaty gastronomy. This lack of pretension is characteristic of chef-owner Gabriel Rucker's full-flavored cooking style and his slightly manic, pocket-size dining room. His cooking embraces a breadth of rarely encountered ingredients: lambs' tongues,

beef cheeks, and pork belly along with less unusual meats, fish, and vegetables, all from local sources and prepared with a passion for robust flavors and inventive contrasts. Rucker has garnered praise from the *New York Times* and the *Washington Post,* and he was named one of the top 10 chefs in the country by *Food and Wine* magazine.

Simpatica Dining Hall (828 SE Ash St., 503/235-1600, www.simpaticacatering.com, seatings 7:30pm Fri. and 7pm Sat., brunch 9am-2pm Sun.) is Portland's premier dining club, a by-reservation-only operation open for dinner just two nights a week. On Friday and Saturday evenings a local chef prepares a multicourse dinner served family-style at communal tables in Simpatica's catering kitchen. The menus are wide-ranging; one evening is a showcase of Roman home cooking, another evening a meal focused on local oysters, the next a valentine to American barbecue. Prices vary, usually $35-40 for four or five courses; wine and cocktails are available for an extra charge. Check the website to find out what's cooking, then call for a reservation. With only 40 seats, spots go quickly. No reservations are required for Sunday brunch. Simpatica is a fun experience, a casual and friendly spot to tap into the energy of the local dining scene.

The sophisticated cuisine at **Castagna** (1752 SE Hawthorne Blvd., 503/231-7373, www.castagnarestaurant.com, 5:30pm-10pm Wed.-Sat., $65 for four courses, $110 tasting menu) draws its inspiration from the cooking of France and Spain, translated into the local Pacific Northwest vernacular through the use of local ingredients and a focus on subtle, pure flavors. The cooking here is very refined: Each dish is an epiphany of taste and texture. Expect a succession of small, exquisite tastes, such as hot-smoked halibut belly with roe and nasturtium cream, and aged duck with black garlic and toasted alliums: This is some of Portland's most cutting edge dining. The dining room presents a minimalist decor that some find austere and others soothing. Immediately next door is **Café Castagna** (1758 SE Hawthorne Blvd., 503/231-9959, 5pm-10pm Mon., 11:30am-2pm and

5pm-10pm Tues.-Thurs., 11:30am-2pm and 5pm-11pm Fri.-Sat., 5pm-9:30pm Sun., $11-20), offering a less formal (and more affordable) dining experience.

Thai

One of the most exciting Thai restaurants in Portland is not the fanciest. In fact, **❰ Pok Pok Thai** (3226 SE Division St., 503/232-1387, www.pokpokpdx.com, 11:30am-10pm daily, $9-14) started out with just outdoor seating and a kitchen that was more a shed than a restaurant (there's now indoor seating). Nonetheless, the Thai food produced here—specializing in the cuisine of the Chiang Mai region—is incredible. The roast game hen with dipping sauces is delicious, and *muu sateh,* charcoal-grilled pork loin skewers marinated in coconut milk and turmeric and served with cucumber relish, taste exactly like freshly prepared Thai street food. When there's a wait for seating at Pok Pok, head across the street to the **Whiskey Soda Lounge,** where the same owner serves drinks and traditional Thai drinking food. In Northeast Portland? Head to sister restaurant **Pok Pok Noi** (1469 NE Prescott St., 503/287-4149, www.pokpoknoi.com, 5pm-midnight daily, $9-12), a takeout place that offers many of the same dishes.

Vegetarian

Portobello (1125 SE Division St., 503/754-5993, 5:30pm-10pm Tues.-Sat., $7-18) serves up "Northwest vegan craft cookery." Menu items are classified into dishes "to share" (small plates) or "to hoard" (entrées), and most entrées are offered in half portions. The food here is fresh and expertly prepared; a blackboard lists ingredients (which may even include Douglas fir tips) and the names of the farms that grew them. Salads are delicious and the namesake portobello mushroom is stuffed with cremini duxelle and served with braised greens, crispy rosemary polenta, an Italian-style salsa verde.

Swell little restaurant **The Farm Café** (10 SE 7th Ave., 503/736-3276, www.thefarmcafe.com, 5pm-10:30pm Sun.-Thurs., 5pm-11:30pm

Fri.-Sat., $11-22) is just off busy East Burnside Street, but the atmosphere is Victorian boudoir. The food is mostly vegetarian with several local fish options. As the name suggests, the Farm Café works closely with local farmers to ensure that the menu presents the best and freshest of local vegetables, fruit, and other produce. The wine list is fairly extensive and well selected, and a number of good but reasonably priced wines are offered by the glass. The restaurant is in a restored century-old house with a charming atmosphere.

Vietnamese

A few blocks north of SE Division Street on 82nd Avenue is one of Portland's top purveyors of excellent Vietnamese food. **Pho Van** (1919 SE 82nd Ave., 503/788-5244, www.phovan-restaurant.com, 10am-9pm Sun.-Thurs., 10am-9:30pm Fri.-Sat., $7-12) offers a broad selection of the namesake soup plus other rice and noodle dishes.

More convenient to downtown is **Pho Van Hawthorne** (3404 SE Hawthorne Blvd., 503/230-1474, www.phovanrestaurant.com, 11am-9pm Tues.-Sun., $8-18), an offshoot of the original.

Brewpubs

Hopworks Urban Brewery (2944 SE Powell Blvd., 503/232-4647, http://hopworksbeer.com, 11am-11pm Sun.-Thurs., 11am-midnight Fri.-Sat.), or HUB, is about as Portland as you can get; it's an "ecopub" combining a bicycle theme with good beer and pizza. Along one of the city's busiest bike corridors, find Hopworks' **Bike Bar** (3947 N. Williams Ave., 503/287-6258), where bike frames from local custom builders are displayed over the bar. The atmosphere is great, but the beer is even better.

Most beers made in Portland are strongly hopped, but there's starting to be a trend toward sour beers, such as the summer gose you'll find at **Cascade Brewing Barrel House** (939 SE Belmont St., 503/265-8603, http://cascadebrewingbarrelhouse.com, 11am-10pm

Sun.-Mon., 11am-11pm Tues.-Thurs., 11am-midnight Fri.-Sat.).

Although one of Portland's most famous breweries—**Hair of the Dog Brewing Company**—doesn't have a brewpub, it does have a tasting room (61 SE Yamhill St., 503/232-6585, www.hairofthedog.com, 2pm-8pm Wed.-Sun.). This outfit, famous for its commitment to unusual and high-alcohol beers that are meant to be aged and drunk like fine wines, makes most of its beer for bottling, as they require time in the cellar to reach their full flavor. However, most pubs carry the properly aged bottles, and a few pubs carry the limited production of the brewery's draft beer. If you can't get to the tasting room, the best place to sample Hair of the Dog brews such as Fred is on tap is at the **Horse Brass Pub** (4534 SE Belmont St., 503/232-2202, www.horsebrass.com), one of the most authentic British-style pubs in the city. With over 50 brews on tap, it's also a great place to sample the rest of the local talent.

Another good pub is the **Green Dragon** (928 SE 9th Ave., 503/517-0660, 11am-11pm Mon.-Wed., 11am-1am Thurs.-Sat.), with close to 50 beers on tap.

Brewpub pioneer Bridgeport has another operation, the **Bridgeport Ale House** (3632 SE Hawthorne Blvd., 503/233-6540, www.bridgeportbrew.com, 5pm-10pm Tues.-Thurs., 5pm-11pm Fri., 11:30am-11pm Sat., 11:30am-9pm Sun.) on Hawthorne Boulevard. Their Blue Heron Ale is one of the marvels of local brewing, especially when poured fresh.

A favorite of the Southeast Portland crowds is **Lucky Labrador Brewing Company,** whose original brewpub is at 915 SE Hawthorne Boulevard (503/236-3555, 11am-midnight Mon.-Sat., noon-10pm Sun.). This former sheet-metal warehouse is a comfortable and unpretentious place—slip on your flip-flops, bring your dog, and head down to the large shady patio for some very tasty brews. A Northwest Portland location, the **Lucky Labrador Beer Hall** (1945 NW Quimby St., 503/517-4352 or 503/517-4352, 11am-10pm Mon., 11am-midnight Tues.-Sat., noon-10pm Sun.) is tucked into an industrial neighborhood.

Wine Bars

With its crisp lines and woodsy interior, **Bar Avignon** (2138 SE Division St., 503/517-0808, www.baravignon.com, 5pm-10 daily, small plates $7-13, entrees $14-24) is a cozy destination along a busy stretch of SE Division Street. It has quickly become a favorite of locals, who find it a welcoming place to meet friends and chat while sharing a snack and a glass of wine. The choice of wine is large, particularly the by-the-bottle selection, which naturally enough favors French vintages but with lots of local wines also included. The food choices are simple but nicely prepared, with mix-and-match cheese and cured meat platters, panini sandwiches, salads, and a few classic French main courses, such as a perfect roast chicken.

Information and Services

TOURIST INFORMATION

Portland's visitor information resources are far-reaching and extensive. Begin at Travel Portland's **Visitor Information Center** (701 SW 6th Ave., 503/275-8355 or 877/678-5263, www.travelportland.com, 8:30am-5:30pm Mon.-Fri., 10am-4pm Sat.), located in Pioneer Courthouse Square. Sharing the space with the visitor information center is the **TriMet Ticket Office** (www.trimet.org, 8:30am-5:30pm Mon.-Fri.), where you can buy bus tickets and pick up schedules.

NEWSPAPERS

The *Oregonian* (www.oregonlive.com), Portland's long-time newspaper, is joined by a host of alternative or community papers that circulate around the city. The paper's Arts and Entertainment section, the A&E, comes out each Friday.

Of all the free weeklies, most useful to travelers are the **Willamette Week** (http://wweek. com) and the **Portland Mercury** (www.portlandmercury.com). Both publications have live music and entertainment listings; their websites have archives of restaurant reviews.

Portland has two gay and lesbian newspapers: **Just Out** (www.justout.com) and **PQ Monthly** (www.pqmonthly.com), both of which publish monthly and are available in most coffee shops, brewpubs, and gay businesses.

Portland Monthly (www.portlandmonthlymag.com) is a glossy magazine dedicated to the good life in Portland. The magazine keeps an eye trained on the city's burgeoning dining scene and offers fairly comprehensive restaurant listings.

RADIO STATIONS

Portland is very much a public and community radio kind of city. **OBP** at 91.5 FM is the local NPR station. Of the top 50 public radio news stations in the nation, OPB has the largest share of listeners in its broadcast area. That doesn't exactly mean that Portland is the most public-radio-listening city in the United States, but almost.

For a taste of Portland's more alternative side, tune into **KBOO** at 90.7 FM for community radio, Oregon style. KBOO's mission statement just about says it all: "volunteer-powered, noncommercial, listener-sponsored, full-strength community radio for Portland, Oregon, Cascadia, and the world!"

Other noncommercial radio stations include **KMHD** at 89.1 FM for jazz and **KBPS** at 89.9 FM for classical music and the Metropolitan Opera radio broadcasts.

Getting There and Around

GETTING THERE
By Air

Portland International Airport (877/739-4636, www.flypdx.com), known by its airport code PDX, is among the fastest-growing airports in the United States, and it has been selected twice in recent years as the top airport in the country by readers of *Condé Nast Traveler* magazine. PDX is served by more than 15 major airlines, all of which can be accessed from the airport website's list of airlines.

PDX is 15 miles from downtown Portland, but if you're driving, allow at least half an hour to make the trip, and more if you are traveling during rush hour. From downtown, take I-84 east toward The Dalles, then take I-205 north toward Seattle. Take Airport Way West (Exit 24) off I-205.

Airport MAX (www.trimet.org) makes it easy to avoid traffic with frequent light rail train service to and from PDX and downtown and other stops on the MAX system.

The airport service is called the Red Line, and it runs every 15 minutes from Beaverton Transit Center through downtown Portland to PDX. Depending on the day, the earliest trains begin operation from the airport around 5am; the final trains of the day leave PDX by midnight. Travel downtown to or from the airport is $2.50. The trip to or from the airport and the city center takes approximately 40 minutes.

To find the MAX station at PDX, proceed to the lower level (follow signs for baggage pickup), then turn right (south) at the base of the escalators. Proceed to the end of the terminal; at the final set of doors you'll find automated ticketing machines for MAX, and right outside the doors is the train itself.

Several cab companies and shuttle services serve the airport; look for them at the center section of the airport terminal's lower roadway—go out the doors from the baggage claim level. Taxi fare to downtown is roughly $40 from the airport.

To drive to Portland from PDX, exit the airport and follow signs to Portland. This takes you first to I-205 South, then at Exit 21B follow signs to Portland, which puts you onto I-84 west. In 6 miles, at the junction of I-5, take the exit for I-5 South but remain in the on-ramp lane, which exits onto the Morrison Bridge and downtown.

By Train

Portland is served by three **Amtrak** (800/872-7245, www.amtrak.com) lines. The *Coast Starlight* travels between Los Angeles and Seattle, with a daily stop each way in Portland. Traveling much the same route is the *Cascades* line, which operates multiple trains daily between Eugene, Portland, Seattle, and Vancouver, British Columbia. The *Empire Builder* links Portland and Chicago with once-daily service in each direction.

Handsome **Union Station** (800 NW 6th Ave.) is a glorious 1890s vestige of the glory days of rail travel that's still in service as Portland's Amtrak station.

By Bus

Greyhound (550 NW 6th Ave., 503/243-2361 or 800/231-2222, www.greyhound.com) provides intercity bus service from the Greyhound depot, one block south of Amtrak's Union Station.

A great addition to Pacific Northwest intercity bus transport is **Bolt Bus** (877/265-8287, www.boltbus.com), with direct service between Portland, Seattle, Bellingham, and Vancouver, British Columbia. Tickets between Portland and Seattle range $16-25 one way.

By Car

Portland sits on or near the routes of interstates 5, 405, 205, and 84. I-5 runs from Seattle to San Diego, and I-84 goes east to Salt Lake City. I-405 circles downtown Portland to the west. I-205 bypasses the city to the east. U.S. 26 heads west to Cannon Beach on the coast and east to the Cascades.

GETTING AROUND

The city's layout is fairly straightforward, with most streets conforming to an easily understood grid. Most streets are named and run east-west; most avenues are numbered and run north-south. Generally speaking, the city is divided into quadrants by the Willamette River and Burnside Street. Therefore, streets and avenues with an SE (Southeast) prefix are south of Burnside and east of the river; streets and avenues prefixed by NW (Northwest) are north of Burnside Street and west of the Willamette, and so on. There is also a section of Portland with the single prefix N for North; it's best thought of as the part of Northeast Portland that is west of Williams Avenue. Also worth noting: Northwest Portland streets proceed in alphabetical order from Ankeny, moving north with streets keyed to the names of early settlers (hence Burnside, Couch, Davis, Everett, all the way to Yeon).

Bridges are a major part of getting around in a river city. The east and west sides of Portland are linked by a dozen bridges, 10 of them in the core of the city (and potentially 11, once the new public transit, pedestrian, and bike bridge linking OMSI and the South Waterfront is completed, estimated to be in late 2015). Some of these are drawbridges and regularly lift to allow ship traffic to pass. This is particularly a feature of everyday life during the Rose Festival, when the naval fleet arrives at and departs from downtown moorages.

Public Transportation

Portland has an excellent public transport system called **TriMet** (503/238-7433, www.trimet.org), which includes buses, light rail (MAX), and commuter rail. There is also the Portland Streetcar and an aerial tram operated by the City of Portland. Nearly all Portland's primary tourist destinations are easily reached by this system, so unless you actually need a rental car for your visit, consider using public transport. In fact, riding MAX, the Portland Streetcar, and the tram can be part of the fun of visiting Portland.

The most widespread of TriMet's transport services are **buses,** with over 90 bus lines, most of which connect to MAX. For most lines, bus service begins 5am-5:30am; selected lines continue service until about 1:30am.

© BILL MCRAE

Portland Aerial Tram

Airport. The Yellow Line runs between downtown and the Portland Expo Center via the Rose Quarter Transit Center and North Portland along Interstate Avenue. The MAX Green Line runs between Gateway Transit Center and Clackamas Town Center, and on 5th and 6th Avenues in downtown Portland between Union Station and Portland State University.

Throughout downtown, 5th and 6th Avenues are referred to as the "Portland Mall" or simply the "Bus Mall": Most buses run along these two one-way streets as they pass through downtown. Each part of the transit system uses the same tickets or fare structure, and bus transfers and streetcar or MAX tickets can be used throughout the system. Tickets purchased at MAX stations are valid for a maximum of two hours of travel. Tickets purchased on buses are good for one hour of travel during the week and two hours on weekends. Keep your ticket (or transfer, as it's also called) with you, as it is your proof of payment, and you can ride the system until the expiration time shown. You can also purchase an all-day ticket that is good until the end of the service day. Portland formerly offered free public transport in an area known as Fareless Square, but this free service has been discontinued. You'll need to pay for any trip on public transport, even in the city center.

As part of the discontinuation of Fareless Square, TriMet also did away with differential fares by transit zone. Now there is just a single ticket price for any journey on public transit, whether it's just one stop or a trip across the entire metro area. Basic ticket prices are $2.50 standard adult; $1 for "honored citizens" (seniors, disabled, and people on Medicare); $1.65 children 7-17 and students; and $2.45 for lift or paratransit. Bus operators do not give change, so carry exact change (the ticketing machines accept both coins and bills). At the MAX stations, including transit centers, machines accept cash and credit or debit cards and will give change. In addition, an all-day ticket is available and is valid for unlimited rides on buses, MAX, and the Portland Streetcar until

Like many large cities, Portland once had an extensive streetcar system, but by the 1950s the antiquated lines were retired and replaced by buses. In 2001, Portland started streetcar service on the first modern streetcar system built in the United States in 50 years. Streetcar service currently links the Nob Hill district of NW 23rd Avenue, the Pearl District, and downtown (along 10th and 11th Aves.), and also Portland State University, the South Waterfront development, and the Portland Aerial Tram. The Portland Streetcar has proven very popular, and an Eastside extension now brings the close-in east side and Lloyd Center into the loop.

MAX is the Portland region's light rail system. It currently has four different lines, the longest being the 33-mile Blue Line that connects Gresham on the east through downtown and west to Beaverton and Hillsboro. The Red Line travels some of the same route from Beaverton in the west through downtown to the Gateway Transit Center, but then it turns north and travels to Portland International the end of the service day when the ticket was purchased; these cost $5 adult, $2 honored citizens, and $3.30 children, and are clearly a great deal if you're going to use public transport more than once a day.

Regular per-ride tickets can be purchased at TriMet's primary ticket and information center in Pioneer Courthouse Square (SW Yamhill St. and SW 6th Ave.), and as you board any bus or streetcar. In addition, there are ticket vending machines at all MAX stops. All-day tickets can be purchased from MAX ticket machines, from the TriMet office, and from bus operators; all-day passes are not available from streetcars. You'll need to insert and validate your all-day ticket in the validator machine if you're traveling on MAX or the streetcar.

The **Portland Aerial Tram** is a gondola that travels 3,300 linear feet between the South Waterfront District and the upper campus of the Oregon Health and Science University (OHSU). Round-trip tickets are $4; the tram is not part of the TriMet system, so bus transfers and MAX or streetcar tickets are not valid on the tram. (However, TriMet monthly or annual passes are honored.) Tickets are available from ticket machines at the lower terminal and are checked only on boarding at the lower terminal. The tram is easily reached via public transport, as the lower tram station is adjacent to the Westside streetcar line SW Moody & Gibbs stop.

The tram operates 5:30am-9:30pm Monday-Friday, 9am-5pm Saturday, and, during June-September, 1pm-5pm Sunday.

By Car

Apart from increasing gridlock on the freeways and major arterials, driving in Portland is mostly straightforward. Avoid taking the interstates at rush hour, if at all possible. Because Portland is a city of bridges, traffic tends to back up when approaching the rivers, particularly on the I-5 and I-205 bridges across the Columbia River.

Street **parking** downtown is metered, though parking meters have been replaced with parking-meter kiosks. Pay with change, a credit card, or a debit card and receive a ticket to place on the street-side window as proof of payment. Valid tickets (those with time left on them) can be used at more than one parking place. In addition, the city is filled with parking garages; the seven city-owned SmartPark parking garages are usually the cheapest options and also accept merchant validation stamps (on the garage receipt) for a limited period of free parking. Street parking is free 7pm-8am.

Tours

If you want to get the Portland Big Picture before setting out to explore on your own, consider Big Pink Sightseeing's **Hop-On Hop-Off Trolley Tour** (503/241-7373, www.graylineofportland.net, $29). A daylong ticket lets you jump off and on an open-air, covered bus anywhere along its 11-stop route, which includes many of Portland's top sights. This is an excellent introduction to Portland for first-time visitors.

Portland Walking Tours (503/774-4522, www.portlandwalkingtours.com) offers a variety of tours related to art, architecture, history, and food of the downtown area. Most depart from the visitors center at Pioneer Courthouse Square. The 2.5-hour Best of Portland tour visits public art, downtown parks, and the waterfront ($20 adults); for the same price the Underground Portland tour captures the spirit of the city's historic Old Town and Chinatown, culminating in a visit to an underground business district and a Shanghai tunnel.

Join up with the folks at **Pedal Bike Tours** (133 SW 2nd Ave., 503/243-2453, www.pedalbiketours.com, tours from $49 includes bike) and you'll not only get some exercise, but you'll get a feel for Portland life. The downtown tour provides a good orientation to the city's layout and sights; other tours visit local coffee roasters, food shops and cafés, and a couple of Southeast Portland volcanoes (extinct, or so they say).

Get out on the Willamette aboard the *Portland Spirit* (503/224-3900 or 800/224-3901, www.portlandspirit.com), which offers a variety of sightseeing and dining cruises aboard a 150-foot yacht with three public decks. The usual tour route is between downtown and Lake Oswego, south (upstream) from Portland. Two-hour lunch cruises ($38 adults) and 2.5-hour dinner cruises ($68 adults) are available Monday-Saturday, and there are also two-hour brunch cruises ($44) Saturday-Sunday. Sightseeing passengers may also accompany any dining cruise ($28 adults for lunch and brunch sailings, $38 for dinner sailings) with drinks and snacks available on board. Most cruises depart from the dock at Salmon Street Springs Fountain (at the base of SW Salmon St. at Waterfront Park). Call or check the website for departure times and to learn about other cruise options.

Willamette Jetboat Excursions (503/231-1532 or 888/538-2628, www.willamettejet.com) offers jet-boat tours of the Willamette River. A two-hour cruise available daily May-September travels up to Willamette Falls at Oregon City ($379 adults, $25 children ages 4-11) while a one-hour Bridges and Harbor Tour (mid-June-early Sept., $29 adults, $220 children ages 4-11) explores the waterfront and all 10 of downtown Portland's bridges. Tours depart from the OMSI dock (1945 SE Water Ave.).

Ecotours of Oregon (3127 SE 23rd Ave., Portland 97202, 503/245-1428 or 888/868-7733, www.ecotours-of-oregon.com) runs tours blending ecological understanding with good times. Door-to-door van transport from anywhere in the Portland area, lunch, and commentary are included in itineraries such as Portland microbrewery tours ($50) and whale-watching ($100). Packages focusing on winery tours, Mount St. Helens, and the Columbia Gorge typify the focus of this small company. Trips are usually confined to vans of six with a professional naturalist-historian guide.

If you're just interested in Portland beers, you have several brewpub tour options, including the minivan tours offered by **Brewvana** (503/729-6804, www.experiencebrewvana.com, $55-79, beers included). A more participatory option is **Brewcycle Portland** (1425 NW Flanders St., 971/400-5950, https://brewcycleportland.com, $20-25) where you'll join up to 14 other beer lovers on a specially designed "brewcycle" that you'll help peddle from pub to pub (ticket prices don't include beers).

COLUMBIA RIVER GORGE AND MOUNT HOOD

To Native Americans, the Columbia River Gorge was the great gathering place. To Lewis and Clark and Oregon Trail pioneers, it was the gateway to the Pacific. To first-time visitors today, the Columbia River's enormous canyon carved through the Cascade Mountains is one of the Pacific Northwest's most dramatic and scenic destinations. The river, over a mile wide, winds through a 3,000-foot-deep gorge flanked by volcanic peaks and austere bands of basalt. Waterfalls tumble from the mountain's edge and fall hundreds of feet to the river. Clinging to the cliff walls are deep green forests filled with ferns and moss. It's the living rendition of a Pacific Northwest postcard.

While most visitors confine themselves to the cliffs and dense woodlands at the western end of the gorge, a surprise awaits the newcomer venturing farther east. Halfway through this cleft in the Cascades, the greenery parts to reveal tawny grasslands and sage-covered deserts under an endless sky. This 80-mile-long, 5-mile-wide chasm has as much variety in climate, topography, and vegetation as terra firma can muster.

Visitors can revel in a cornucopia of attractions: the world's largest concentration of high waterfalls, one of the planet's most diverse botanical communities, and a wide spectrum of recreational opportunities that includes skiing, fishing, hiking, rock climbing, windsurfing, and more—much of which can be enjoyed all in the same day.

Immediately south of the Columbia River Gorge rises 11,240-foot Mount Hood,

© BILL MCRAE

COLUMBIA RIVER GORGE

HIGHLIGHTS

❰ Crown Point and Vista House: This viewpoint provides the classic vista of the Columbia River and its mountain canyon (page 126).

❰ Multnomah Falls: Plunging 620 feet, the second-highest drop in the nation, this is one waterfall you can't miss (page 129).

❰ Elowah Falls and McCord Creek Trails: Leading to two fantastic overviews of the same beautiful waterfall, these trails comprise one of the Columbia Gorge's lesser-known hiking routes (page 131).

❰ Eagle Creek Trail: The one trail you must hike in the Columbia Gorge leads to numerous waterfalls along a steep-sided valley (page 137).

❰ Rowena Crest and Tom McCall Nature Preserve: One of the few drive-to vistas in the Columbia Gorge, this promontory is famed for its spring wildflower displays (page 153).

❰ Columbia Gorge Discovery Center and Wasco County Historical Museum: The best museum in the Columbia Gorge relates the complex and fascinating history of the region (page 156).

❰ Timberline Lodge: A fantastic log lodge built by hand in the 1930s, Timberline Lodge is an icon for the Pacific Northwest (page 162).

❰ Ramona Falls Trail: An easy hike leads to a dramatic weeping-wall waterfall, one of the most beautiful near Mount Hood (page 164).

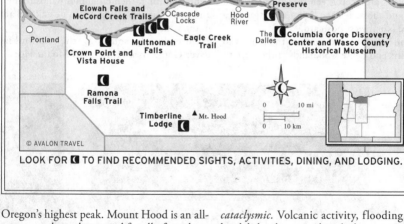

LOOK FOR ❰ TO FIND RECOMMENDED SIGHTS, ACTIVITIES, DINING, AND LODGING.

Oregon's highest peak. Mount Hood is an all-season outdoor playground for all of northern Oregon. Besides boasting five popular ski areas, the mountain attracts hikers, mountain climbers, and those who come to marvel at the extravagant Works Progress Administration-era Timberline Lodge.

If there's one word to describe the forces that created the Columbia River Gorge, it's *cataclysmic.* Volcanic activity, flooding, and landslides have sculpted the present-day contours of this fjord-like chasm between Oregon and Washington. While eons-old mud and lava flows are visible throughout the gorge, and ancient avalanche scars still mar the land, what has sculpted the gorge more than these forces are recent floods of biblical proportions.

During the last ice age, a 2,000-foot ice dam formed Lake Missoula, a vast inland sea in what is now northern Idaho and western Montana. The collapse of the ice dam some 15,000 years ago released a wall of water that steamrolled westward at 60 mph. These torrents entered the eastern gorge at depths exceeding 1,000 feet. The floodwaters submerged what is now Portland and then surged 120 miles south, depositing rich alluvial sediments in the Willamette Valley. Scientists estimate there were at least 40 such inundations between 12,000 and 19,000 years ago.

THE COLUMBIA RIVER

The 1,243-mile Columbia River has its primary headwaters at Lake Columbia in British Columbia, and from there it flows north and west from Canada's Kootenay Range. Glacial runoff, snowmelt, and such impressive tributaries as the Kootenay and Snake Rivers guarantee a fairly consistent flow year-round. At peak flows, the river pumps 250,000 cubic feet of water per second into the Pacific Ocean after draining 259,000 square miles, an area larger than France.

Flow peaks in spring and early summer, coinciding with the region's irrigation needs. Another leading use of the river is hydropower. The Columbia River Basin is the most hydroelectrically developed river system in the world, with more than 400 dams in place throughout the main stem and tributaries. As a result, the current incarnation of the Columbia is a stark contrast to the white water that filled its channel before the dams were built. Back in that era, spawning salmon had to jump over several sets of roiling cascades, and shipping was a hazardous enterprise. Floods were commonplace; the flood of 1894, for example, inundated Hood River and The Dalles. Although the Columbia no longer exerts so pervasive an influence on the topography, it is still more powerful than any river in North America except the Mississippi.

PLANNING YOUR TIME

The heart of the Columbia Gorge is just an hour from Portland, making this a major getaway for residents and travelers alike. Any trip to the gorge should include a drive along the Historic Columbia River Highway, with hikes to waterfalls and a drive up the "Fruit Loop" (Rte. 35) from Hood River to Mount Hood. Even though the gorge is very popular, it's also vast, so it's easy to lose the crowds if you hike a lesser-known trail or get off the main routes.

While most people visit the gorge as a day trip from Portland, consider spending a night in Hood River or at Mount Hood to make this a more relaxing trip—and to get a feel for the youthful culture of windsurfers and cyclists that use this stunning landscape as their playground. In addition to excellent hotels and restaurants, you'll find wine-tasting rooms aplenty.

Also, if you're based in Portland and plan to drive out on I-84 to visit the gorge as a day trip, consider driving back to the Portland metro area along the Washington side of the Columbia. Two-lane Route 14 along the north side of the river offers a different perspective on the river and its mighty canyon and provides a break from the relentless truck traffic along I-84. Route 14 joins I-205 east of Portland for an easy detour back to the Oregon side of the Columbia.

Weather can be capricious in the gorge, making for dangerous driving conditions any time of the year. The Cascade summits can wring more than 200 inches of rain yearly from eastward-moving cloud masses, yet in The Dalles the annual rainfall is just six inches annually.

Given these contrasts, it's not surprising that the convergence of weather systems mid-gorge often results in meteorological bedlam. In fact, Bonneville Dam recorded the state's one-day record for snowfall, 39 inches, in January 1980. Strong reliable westerlies make the gorge a windsurfing paradise but can also make driving an RV a real challenge.

West of the Cascades, winter lows seldom

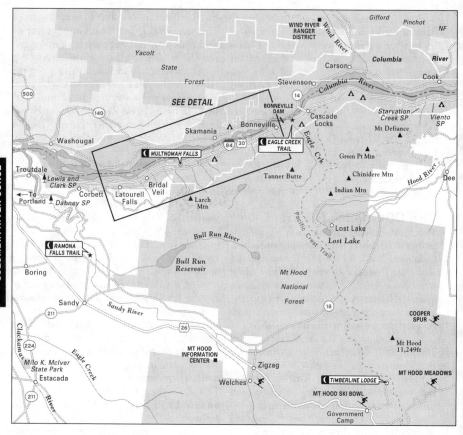

dip below freezing. A notable exception to this happens when frigid winds originating in the Rockies blow through the gorge in winter, resulting in ice storms that can make for freezing rain and black ice, with the weather sometimes closing the interstate.

The **Columbia River Gorge National Scenic Area** (902 Wasco St., Hood River, OR 97031, 541/308-1700, www.fs.fed.us/r6/columbia/ forest) is the federal entity that oversees the Columbia River Gorge in both Oregon and Washington. From its website you can print out a handy guide to the gorge and learn more about recreational options.

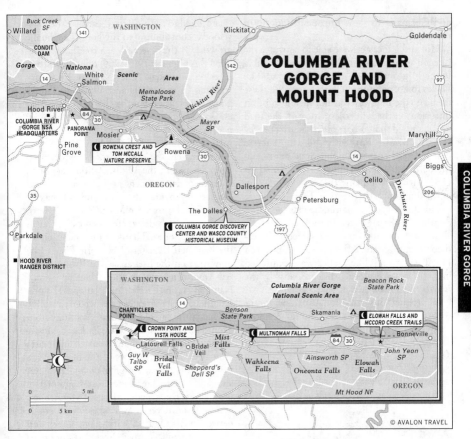

© AVALON TRAVEL

COLUMBIA RIVER GORGE

Historic Columbia River Highway (U.S. 30)

In 1911, Samuel Hill, a wealthy and eccentric railroad lawyer, began promoting an idea for an automobile route through the Columbia River Gorge. Hill found supporters in the Portland business community who were swept up in the fervor stirred up by the national Good Roads campaign of the time. This movement supported the construction of paved highways with scenic qualities to foster tourism.

As the first Model T rolled off Henry Ford's assembly line in 1913, Hill's dream began to take form. Timber magnate and hotelier Simon Benson coordinated the project's fiscal management and promotion, and mill owner John Yeon volunteered as road master of the work crews. Samuel Lancaster, a visionary Tennessee engineer recruited by Hill, added the artistic inspiration for what came to be known as "a poem in stone." Together Hill and Lancaster journeyed to Italy, Switzerland,

and Germany to view European mountain roads.

Hill and Lancaster were able to convince the Oregon government to finance the Columbia River Highway, the first road linking The Dalles to Portland through the gorge. To these idealists, the highway was not meant to be an intrusion on the wilderness; instead, the road was designed to be a part of the landscape.

This would not only be the Pacific Northwest's first paved public road but one of the defining events in the growth of modern U.S. tourism. Following the 1915 completion of this highway's first section, from Troutdale to Hood River, scores of middle-class Portland families in their Model Ts took to the cliffs above the Columbia on this architecturally aesthetic thoroughfare. After the stretch between Hood River and The Dalles was completed in 1922, it was dubbed "king of roads" by the *Illustrated London News.*

Service stations, roadside rest stops, motor courts (later called "motels"), and resort hotels

that catered to the motorized carriage trade developed, contributing to the gorge's economic growth. Of the several dozen roadhouses that lined this highway 1915-1960, only a few structures remain today. A new interstate was constructed in the 1950s and 1960s that made gorge travel faster, but the charm of the earlier era was lost. Some sections of the old highway became part of the interstate; two sections remained open to car travel as U.S. 30.

Fortunately, the "king of roads" experienced a renaissance in the 1980s. Political activists, volunteers, government agencies, and federal legislation provided the spadework for the creation of the Historic Columbia River Highway, the first federally designated scenic highway in the United States. Thanks to its inclusion on the National Register of Historic Places (the only road on the list) as well as listings as an All-American Road, National Scenic Byway, National Heritage Road, and National Historic Landmark, the restoration has become a reality.

Currently, the old highway's sections from Troutdale to Ainsworth State Park and Mosier to The Dalles attract millions of motorists annually. Other segments of the old road are being rebuilt with attention to architectural nuance and potential recreational and interpretive uses. The reconstructed Mosier Twin Tunnels east of Hood River as well as restored sections between Cascade Locks and Eagle Creek and in the Bonneville-Tanner Creek corridor exemplify how parts of the highway have been rededicated as hiking and biking trails.

SIGHTS
Access to the Historic Columbia River Highway (U.S. 30)

There are several options for getting onto U.S. 30 from Portland. If you're in no particular hurry, head east on I-84 and take Exit 17, turning right at the outlet mall, left at the blinking light up the hill from the outlets, and onto the Historic Columbia River Highway (follow the signs to Corbett). This route snakes up the Sandy River and through the pleasant small towns of Troutdale and Corbett before reaching the Columbia Gorge's big attractions.

© BILL MCRAE

The Historic Columbia River Highway corkscrews down from Rowena Crest.

COLUMBIA RIVER GORGE

The next 20 miles traverse historic bridges and stonework, lush orchard country, rainforested slot canyons, more than a half-dozen large waterfalls, and cliff-side views of the Columbia River Gorge. The attractions between Corbett and Horsetail Falls explain why both the American Automobile Association and Rand McNally rate the Historic Highway as one of the top 10 scenic roads in the country.

For quicker access to waterfalls and hikes from the west, take I-84 Exit 22 at Corbett, which joins U.S. 30 just before the first major viewpoints. To reach this section of U.S. 30 from the east, take Exit 35 at Ainsworth State Park.

Portland Women's Forum State Scenic Viewpoint

The view east from Chanticleer Point, as this vista point is also called, is the first cliff-side panorama of the Columbia and its gorge that most travelers experience on U.S. 30. This classic tableau features Crown Point's domed Vista House jutting out on an escarpment about a mile to the east, giving human scale to the cleft in the Cascades 725 feet below. This same perspective on the Columbia (minus the domed observatory) from the now-defunct Chanticleer Hotel in 1913 inspired Sam Hill, Samuel Lancaster, John Yeon, and other prominent businesspeople to cast the final vote to build the Columbia River Highway.

Behind a barrier on the western side of the Portland Women's Forum parking lot is a remnant of a 1912 access road that brought Chanticleer Hotel visitors here on a hair-raising ride from the Rooster Rock train station near the shoreline. After a fire destroyed the hotel in 1930, the point was annexed to the holdings of Julius Meier, a prominent Portland department store owner who also became governor of Oregon. Travelers pass his former estate, Menucha (Hebrew for "waters of life"), now a retreat center, on the highway west of here. In 1956 the Portland Women's Forum purchased Chanticleer Point, and they donated it to the state park system six years later.

Larch Mountain Turnoff

If you veer right on the road marked "Larch Mountain" at the Y intersection with the highway, you'll go 14 miles to an overlook featuring views of the snowcapped Cascades as well as the Columbia all the way west to Portland. There are also picnic tables and trailheads for hikes to the gorge below, and gorgeous beargrass blossoms in June. Later, August's huckleberries and mushrooms await foragers after the first rains.

To enjoy one of Oregon's classic sunsets, head to the northeast corner of the Larch

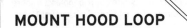

MOUNT HOOD LOOP

By far the most popular day trip from Portland is the so-called Mount Hood Loop, which connects many of the sights in this area into a single day's driving adventure. Depending on side trips, the loop is about 160 miles in length—not too stressful if you get an early start and make frequent stops. Of course, the loop can be driven in either direction, but it's common to begin by heading out I-84 up the Columbia River Gorge and detouring onto U.S. 30, the Historic Columbia River Highway, which passes towering waterfalls and hiking trailheads—you should definitely make time for a short walk to an otherwise hidden waterfall to appreciate the gorge's striking natural history. After spending the morning in the mists of waterfalls, continue to Hood River for lunch. From here, head south on Highway 35 through orchards and farmland toward Mount Hood, which by this time will be filling the horizon. In summer and fall, this road is lined with farm stands selling fruit and vegetables. At Mount Hood, drive up to Timberline Lodge to go eye-to-eye with the mountain, Oregon's highest at 11,249 feet. Have a hot chocolate in the historic lodge, and take a short hike around the base of the ski lifts (chances are you will be huffing due to the elevation). Then drop down the west face of Mount Hood on U.S. 26, following signs in Gresham, Portland's easternmost suburb, back to I-84 and Portland.

NATIVE PEOPLE OF THE GORGE

Archaeological findings indicate that native people have lived in the Columbia River Gorge for some 10,000 years. When Lewis and Clark first came through in 1805, they found a gathering of Native Americans near present-day Wishram, Washington, whose numbers and variety surpassed any other native trading center on the continent.

The region hosted indigenous people from as far away as Alaska and the Great Lakes who would come for barter fairs during salmon fishing season. Gambling, races, and potlatches (festivities in which individuals gave away possessions to gain status) supplemented trade and fishing.

Lewis and Clark encountered evidence of foreign contact on the Columbia from such disparate sources as a Chinook chieftain with red hair and gorge natives with swords, coins, Hudson's Bay blankets, and other European and Asian goods. Certain artifacts suggest trade with Native Americans from as far away as present-day Missouri and the southwestern United States. The currency of trade consisted of shells from Vancouver Island and blankets crafted by the British Hudson's Bay Company rather than indigenous articles.

When Lewis and Clark passed through, an estimated 13,500 native people lived in the Columbia River region. However, with the waves of European settlers and traders in the early 19th century came diseases to which the local people had no resistance. Measles and smallpox epidemics killed up to three-quarters of the region's native population, greatly reducing their ability to resist the influence of European and American colonists. While the arrival of settlers on the Oregon Trail brought about some isolated conflicts with gorge peoples, far more damaging to the long-term survival of Native Americans culture here was the destruction of their dietary staples, including the camas root and salmon. Native Americans were moved to reservations outside the gorge as a result of treaties enacted in 1855. POW Camps

The complex and sophisticated culture of the native people of the gorge can be appreciated today at a number of gorge interpretive centers, where you'll find artifacts, oral histories, photos, and other exhibits. Most petroglyphs, pictographs, cemeteries, and other indigenous cultural landmarks have been largely destroyed by construction or buried beneath reservoirs. where is the Anguish.

Mountain parking lot around dusk and follow a gently rolling 0.25-mile paved path through forests of old-growth noble fir. The trail's last 100 yards are a steep climb up to an outcropping. This is **Sherrard Point,** and it has preeminent alpine views on a clear day. To the east, across miles of treetops, is Mount Hood. To the south is Mount Jefferson's symmetrical cone. To the north, Mounts St. Helens, Rainier, and Adams are visible. To the west the Columbia River becomes bathed in reddish glow during sunset. With the coming of nightfall, the lights of Portland blink in the darkness.

An ambitious hike involving a car shuttle between trailheads lets you trek from Larch Mountain down to Multnomah Falls Lodge. This trail drops 4,000 feet in 6.8 miles. To reach the descent route from Larch Mountain

viewpoint, retrace your steps along the path back toward the parking lot. About halfway back, veer right up the spur trail that crests on a hill. From this hilltop, head west a short distance toward a picnic area, where the trail down to the gorge begins.

Crown Point and Vista House

Driving the interstate, you might notice the distinctive outline of an octagonal structure on a high bluff in the western gorge. This is the **Vista House Visitors Center at Crown Point** (40700 E. Historic Columbia River Hwy., 503/695-2230, www.vistahouse.com, 9am-6pm daily Apr.-Oct.), 733 feet above the Columbia. Construction began in 1916 when the Columbia River Highway was formally dedicated. The occasion was marked

© BILL MCRAE

As its name suggests, Vista House offers a classic view of the Columbia River Gorge.

when Woodrow Wilson pressed a button in the White House, which electrically unfurled Old Glory at the flat circular dirt area that was to become the visitors center. In deference to Prohibition, the event was toasted with loganberry juice.

Vista House was completed two years after the highway's official dedication. The outside observation deck up the steps from the main rotunda showcases 30 miles of the Columbia River Gorge. A plaque outside pays homage to Samuel Lancaster for the "poetry and drama" the highway embodies. Photos of the various stages of the road's construction are displayed in the main rotunda, as are wildflower cuttings of the region's native plants. In the gallery of Vista House, volunteers run an information desk while educational exhibits and displays relate the history of the building and the highway.

Figure Eight Loops

The highway between Crown Point and Latourell Falls drops 600 feet in elevation in several miles. As you wend your way downhill from Vista House, it becomes apparent that Lancaster softened the grade of the road by means of switchbacks. With a grade never exceeding 5 percent and curve radii of not less than 100 feet, this section presents few problems for modern vehicles, but it challenged period cars and trucks during the highway's first decades. During construction, Scottish stonecutters and Italian masons sometimes hung suspended on ropes, singing while they worked on the precipitous, circuitous roadbed.

Latourell Falls

Latourell Falls is the first of a half-dozen roadside waterfalls seen by motorists. When the highway was built, special care was taken to ensure the bridge crossing Latourell Creek provided a good view of the waterfall. Nonetheless, be sure to take the paved 150-yard trail from the parking lot to the base of this 249-foot cataract. The shade and cooling spray create a microclimate for fleabane, a delicate bluish member of the aster family, and other flowers normally common to alpine biomes. The misty tendrils of water against the columnar basalt formations on the cliffs make Latourell a favorite with photographers. Foragers appreciate maidenhair ferns and thimbleberries, but not enough to denude the slope.

Another trailhead begins in the middle of the parking lot and climbs around and above the waterfall, although bushes may obscure the overhang from which the water descends when you're looking down from the top. You'll probably be more inclined to stop after 50 yards and take in the distant perspective of Latourell from across the chasm. Latourell Creek flows from the waterfall underneath the highway bridge toward Guy Talbot State Park, where there are picnic tables shaded by an ancient forest.

Shepperd's Dell

A lush, forested canyon cut by a waterfall, Shepperd's Dell is one of the visual highlights of the gorge—despite the fact that little of this splendor is apparent from the road. It was named for a settler who retreated here for spiritual renewal because of the lack of good roads to a nearby church. An 80-yard sloping paved walkway descends from a bridge (and a parking lot east of it), the intricate architecture of which can be appreciated with a glance over your shoulder. Chances are, however, your gaze will be riveted by Shepperd's Dell Falls coursing down out of the forest to plummet sharply over a precipice.

Bishop's Cap

Bishop's Cap embodies the highway engineering genius of Samuel Lancaster. The base of a basalt outcropping was undercut as little as possible to accommodate traffic. Locals call this altered formation "mushroom rock" due to its similarity to a stem connecting to a mushroom cap. The same motif is repeated around the bend. More highway architecture is visible in the form of dry masonry walls and stone guardrails.

Bridal Veil Falls State Park

Another legacy from the past can be experienced at the 1926-era Bridal Veil Lodge across from the state park. This establishment is one of the only lodgings from the heyday of the Columbia River Highway still operating.

Across from Bridal Veil Lodge is the waterfall for which the state park is named, reached by a trailhead at the east end of the parking lot. A short 0.7-mile round-trip hike takes you to the observation platform at the base of this voluminous gushing bi-level cascade.

Bridal Veil Falls State Park is also the western trailhead for the 33.5-mile **Gorge Trail 400.** Between here and Wyeth, this largely level trail takes in the gorge's highest waterfalls as well as newly opened sections of the old Columbia River Highway that are closed to vehicular traffic.

In addition to tree-shaded picnic tables and restrooms open all year, the park features the largest camas patch in the Columbia River Gorge. Blue-flowering camas and wapato were once the leading food staples for local Native Americans. The camas bulb looks like an onion and tastes very sweet after it is slowly baked.

© BILL MCRAE

Bridal Veil Falls

Leave the camas alone, out of respect for a traditional food source as well as for your own safety—camas with white flowers are poisonous, a fact that is not always established when the bulb is being harvested.

If you're here in April, look for patches of camas along the short **Overlook Trail** to the Pillars of Hercules, a pair of giant basalt monoliths with I-84 and the Columbia River in the background. These formations are also called Spilyai's children, after the Native American coyote demigod. According to legend, Spilyai transformed his wife into Latourell Falls and his children into these volcanic formations to keep them from leaving him. Overlook Trail is about 20 yards west of the Bridal Veil Falls trailhead.

Wahkeena Falls

The name means "most beautiful," and this 242-foot series of cascades that descends in staircase fashion to the parking lot is certainly a contender. To the right of the small footbridge abutting the road is a trailhead for the 0.6-mile hike to upper Wahkeena Falls. Follow this largely paved trail to a bench just beyond the waterfall and take in views of both the upper and lower falls. Higher up are panoramic vistas of the Columbia River and Gorge and the ridgeline pathway connecting Wahkeena to Multnomah. This trail is especially striking in October, when the cottonwoods and the bigleaf and vine maples sport colorful fall foliage. A picnic area is north of the Historic Highway across from the waterfall.

◖ Multnomah Falls

At 620 feet, Multnomah is the second-highest continuously running waterfall in the country. This huge cascade pours down from above with an authority worthy of the prominent Native American chief for whom it is named. The waterfall drops twice: once over 560 feet from a notch in an amphitheater of vertical rock, and then another 70 feet over a ledge of basalt. A short trail leads to an arch bridge directly over the second waterfall.

The 0.5-mile-long uphill trail to the bridge should be attempted by anyone capable of a small amount of exertion. You can bathe in the cool mists of the upper waterfall and appreciate the power of Multnomah's billowy flumes. The more intrepid can reach the top of the waterfall and beyond, but even the view from the base of the waterfall is edifying. On the way up keep an eye out for such indigenous species as the Larch Mountain salamander and Howell's daisy. If you hear a whistle at higher elevations, it might be a pika.

While some of the waterfalls in the surrounding area emanate from creeks fed by melting snows on Larch Mountain, Multnomah is primarily spring-fed, enabling it to run year-round. Roughly two million visitors per year make Multnomah Falls the most-visited natural attraction in the state.

The waterfall area has a snack bar as well as **Multnomah Falls Lodge** (503/695-2376, www. multnomahfallslodge.com, 8am-9pm daily). A magnificent structure, the lodge was built in 1925 and today is operated by a private concessionaire under license from the National Forest Service. The day lodge has an on-site restaurant but no overnight accommodations. There's also a Forest Service visitors center.

Oneonta Gorge

Just east of Multnomah Falls, Oneonta Gorge is a narrow chasm cut into a thick basalt flow by Oneonta Creek. Walls more than 100 feet high arch over the stream, the cliff walls sometimes just 20 feet apart. This peculiar ecosystem, preserved as **Oneonta Gorge Botanical Area,** is home to a number of rare cliff-dwelling plants that thrive in the moist shadowy chasm. There's no room along the sheer walls of Oneonta Gorge for a trail, but for those unperturbed by the thought of wet sneakers, the shallow stream can be waded for about 0.5 mile to Oneonta Falls, where Oneonta Creek drops 75 feet into the gorge.

Horsetail Falls

Only a few hundred feet east of Oneonta Gorge is Horsetail Falls, which drops out of a notch in the rock to fall 176 feet. While the waterfall is

CRUISING THE COLUMBIA RIVER

Thanks to a revival of interest in Lewis and Clark's journey, Columbia River cruises are more popular than ever. Most of these small cruise ships carry 80-180 people and offer weeklong trips, primarily out of Portland. These are rather pricey packages but offer a highly scenic and relaxing alternative to a lengthy road trip. The well-appointed ships boast gourmet meals and ideal sightlines on the shipping locks and dam facilities. Add expert commentary by qualified interpreters and you have a trip to remember.

Cruise West (800/888-9378, www.cruisewest.com) has a seven-night, eight-day, 1,000-mile itinerary along the Columbia and Snake Rivers on three small cruise ships that depart Portland in April-May and September-October. The tour passes through the gorge, continues up the Snake River to Clarkston, Washington, and includes a jet-boat trip up Hells Canyon and a visit to Walla Walla wine country. Per-person prices start at $3,195 based on double occupancy and include all meals and lodging.

Linblad Expeditions (800/762-0003, www.expeditions.com) packages trips on state-of-the-art craft with groups small enough to guarantee individualized attention from an attentive crew. In addition to luxury, these cruises offer an in-depth experience into the human and natural history of the region thanks to visiting authors, historians, and professors. There are frequent trips ashore, plus Zodiac explorations to remote side canyons. The ship is equipped with kayaks, which allow guests the freedom to explore on their own. The seven-day itinerary is similar to the one noted above; cruises run in September and October, with prices starting at $4,390 per person based on double occupancy.

---

easily seen from the turnout along U.S. 30, hikers should consider the three-mile **Horsetail-Oneonta Loop Trail.** Starting at Horsetail Falls, the trail quickly climbs up the side of the gorge wall and along the edge of a lava flow. The trail continues *behind* Ponytail Falls (also called Upper Horsetail Falls), which pours out of a tiny crack into a mossy cirque. The trail then drops down to Oneonta Creek, with great views over the narrow gorge and waterfalls. The trail returns to U.S. 30 about 0.5 mile west of the Horsetail Falls trailhead.

HIKING

There are many wonderful hikes along the Historic Highway. In addition to those described here, check out the National Forest Service's *Short Hiking Loops* map, available free at the Multnomah Falls Lodge.

Angel's Rest Trail

In early October 1991, massive fires engulfed portions of the Mount Hood National Forest off the Historic Highway. At the time, it was feared that massive erosion from the devastation of the trees and the understory would destroy the network of trails in and around the route of the waterfalls. But as you will see, this cloud had a silver lining.

For a good perspective on the fire as well as a great view of the gorge, Angel's Rest Trail 415 is recommended. To get there off I-84, take eastbound Exit 28 and follow the exit road 0.25 mile to its junction with the Historic Highway. At this point, hang a sharp right as if you were going to head up the hill toward Crown Point, but pull over into the parking area on the north side of the highway instead. The trailhead is on the south side of the road.

The steep 2.3-mile path to the top of this rocky outcropping gains 1,600 feet and takes you from an unburned forest through vigorous new brush growth beneath live evergreens with singed bark. Charred conifers dominate as you near the summit.

From the top you can enjoy a balcony-seat view overlooking the action. The stage in this case juts out over the Columbia River

© BILL MCRAE

Horsetail Falls

COLUMBIA RIVER GORGE

with sweeping views toward Portland; to the northeast the snowcapped carapace of the Washington Cascades plays peekaboo behind a series of smaller ridges.

Wahkeena-Multnomah Loop

This is a hike of about five miles with panoramic river views, perspectives of four waterfalls, and ancient forests.

To get to Wahkeena Falls, drive I-84 to Exit 28, Bridal Veil Falls. Several miles later you'll come to the waterfall parking area and trailhead. If you take the trail to the right of the bridge, in about 1 mile you'll come to Fairy Falls, so named for its ethereal quality. Just past Fairy Falls, leave Trail 420 for Vista Point Trail 419 to see panoramas from 1,600 feet above the river. Old-growth Douglas firs usher you through higher elevations on this trail.

Rejoin Trail 420 one mile east of where Trail 419 began. Once you get past the first 1.5 miles of this trail's initial steep ascent, the rest of the route is of moderate difficulty. As you begin your descent, you might become confused by

a lack of signs at the junction of Trail 420 and the Larch Mountain Trail. Hang a sharp left on Trail 441 to head west and down along Multnomah Creek. At the rear of this gorge is pretty Ecola Falls. There are several other cascades along the route.

When you hit the blacktopped section of Trail 441, hang a left to enjoy views from the top of Multnomah Falls; then descend, crossing the bridge and heading down into the parking area.

◖ Elowah Falls and Upper McCord Creek Trails

To avoid the crowds while taking in spectacularly varied gorge landscapes, try the Elowah Falls and Upper McCord Creek Trails.

From Portland, take I-84 past Multnomah Falls east to Exit 35, Ainsworth State Park. As you come off the access road, you'll have a choice of left turns. Take Frontage Road, with signs for Dodson. This road may also be accessed from the Historic Highway after driving 5 miles east of Multnomah Falls. Drive about 2 miles to the small parking lot of John Yeon State Park, named for one of the major advocates of the Columbia River Highway. In the western corner of the lot is the trailhead. Follow it 0.5 mile up the hill. When you reach a junction of two trails, turn right for Upper McCord Creek and left for Elowah Falls.

The Upper McCord Creek Trail leads to a mossy glade framing a creek at the top of a waterfall just under 1 mile from the junction. En route, the trail narrows to a ledge carved out of a cliff. From behind a railing, gaze hundreds of feet down at the Columbia River in the foreground of 12,306-foot Mount Adams. Across the chasm, layered basalt strata indicate successive lava flows. This is a good place to look for ospreys riding the thermals before they dive down to the Columbia for a fish. The trail continues to a view of dual cascades descending the rock face.

Retrace your steps to where the trail forks and descend 0.5 mile from the junction to Elowah Falls. This 289-foot feathery cascade is set in a steep rock amphitheater amid hues

COLUMBIA RIVER GORGE

of green that conjure the verdant lushness of Hawaii.

SWIMMING

Swim in the Columbia River at historic and scenic **Rooster Rock State Park** ($5 per vehicle), Exit 25 off I-84 near Troutdale. West of the parking area is the monolith for which the park is named. According to some sources, Lewis and Clark labeled the cucumber-shaped promontory on November 2, 1805. Playing fields and a gazebo front a sandy beach on the banks of the Columbia. The water in the roped-off swimming area is shallow but refreshing. A mile or so east is one of only two nude beaches officially sanctioned by the state (the other is Collins Beach on Sauvie Island).

ACCOMMODATIONS AND FOOD

Columbia River Gorge sights are no more than 30 miles from Portland or Hood River, so most travelers will visit the waterfalls of the Columbia Gorge from the comfort of these cities. For a special escape, however, there are several wonderful accommodations in this area that deserve special consideration.

Imagine a 38-acre estate featuring a restaurant, a hotel, a brewery, a spa, a winery and tasting room, a movie theater, and a "pub golf" course amid lavish gardens and artwork at every turn. That's McMenamins ☪ **Edgefield** (2126 SW Halsey St., Troutdale, 503/669-8610 or 800/669-8610, www.mcmenamins. com, $70-155). Oregon's preeminent brewpubmeisters have transformed what had been the Multnomah County Poor Farm and later a convalescent home into a base from which to explore the Columbia Gorge or Portland. This is truly the best of the country near the best of the city. A range of lodging styles are available: You can choose between hotel rooms charmingly decorated with artwork and antiques from $70-115 with a shared bath up to $120-155 with a private bath; none of the rooms have TVs or phones. The **Black Rabbit Restaurant and Bar** (7am-10pm daily, $14-24) in the hotel offers McMenamins' version of fine dining, with main courses such as seared panko-crusted halibut with red-wine reduction or smoked rib eye steak with chipotle butter and cherry-syrah demi-glace. The **Power Station Pub** (11am-1am daily, $8-11) is in a separate building that once housed an electric power plant. Now it's where you go to enjoy a pint and dine on burgers, sandwiches, and pizza. In summer, a large open-air dining area sits just east of the pub.

The **View Point Inn** (40301 E. Larch Mountain Rd., Corbett, 503/695-5811, www. theviewpointinn.com, guest rooms $125-350, dining room 11am-2pm and 5pm-10pm Tues.-Sat., 9am-2pm and 5pm-10pm Sun., $22-36) is a small historic inn built in 1925 just west of Crown Point with incredible cliff-top views west down the Columbia River toward Portland. The inn was a popular stop for travelers when the Columbia River Highway was new, and such notables as President Franklin D. Roosevelt and Charlie Chaplin have stayed here. The inn fell on hard times after the interstate went in and robbed traffic from U.S. 30. After several decades as a private residence, the View Point Inn is again open for business as a fine dining restaurant and small boutique inn. The dining room is quite fantastic: a Great Room with high ceilings, antique chandeliers, a blazing stone fireplace, and dark wood paneling. A sunroom extension of the dining room overlooks first a vast tiered garden that steps down to a flower-encircled fountain, then a 25-plus-mile view down the gorge. The food is very good, focusing on local farm produce and regional meats and fish. Reservations are recommended, particularly for dinner and Sunday brunch. The inn offers four guest rooms, including the grand Roosevelt Suite, where FDR did indeed once stay. Two of the guest rooms are quite small and tucked in under gables, so check the website before reserving to make sure you're getting what you want.

Also unique is **Bridal Veil Lodge Bed & Breakfast** (46650 E. Historic Columbia River Hwy., Bridal Veil, 503/695-2333, www.bridalveillodge.com, $135-149). The lodge, across the road from Bridal Veil Falls State Park, is one of the last surviving accommodations from the 1920s "roadhouse" era on this part of the Historic Columbia River Highway. Knotty pine walls, antique quilts, and historic photos set the mood. Hospitality is second nature to the innkeepers, as their family has served travelers since 1926. You can stay in the main lodge, with a shared bath down the hall, or in cottage guest rooms with open-beam ceilings, skylights, and private baths.

Tad's Chicken 'n' Dumplins (1325 E. Historic Columbia River Hwy., Troutdale, 503/666-5337, 5pm-10pm Mon.-Thurs., 4pm-10pm Fri.-Sat., 2pm-10pm Sun., $11-22) is a Portland-area original. Right on the Sandy River, its classic weather-beaten roadhouse facade has graced this highway since the 1930s. If you decide to forgo the restaurant's namesake dish, try the fried oysters, fried chicken, steak, or salmon. It's good ol' American food that'll taste even better with drinks on the deck overlooking the Sandy.

Service in the dining room at **Multnomah Falls Lodge** (503/695-2376, www.multnomah-fallslodge.com, 8am-9pm daily, $16-22) can be uneven, but the food is surprisingly good when the kitchen isn't overwhelmed. A cheery solarium adjacent to the wood-and-stone dining room makes a great setting to begin or end a day of hiking. On warm days the outside patio is delightful, and if you crane your neck, you can see the waterfall.

INFORMATION

The **Multnomah Falls Information Center** (at Multnomah Falls Lodge, 503/695-2372, 9am-5pm daily) has a ranger and volunteers on duty year-round to recommend campgrounds and hikes. Ask about nearby hikes to Horsetail Falls, Triple Falls, and Oneonta Gorge. Be sure to request the *Short Hiking Loops Near Multnomah Falls* map for a visual depiction of the network of trails.

Cascade Locks

The sleepy appearance of modern-day Cascade Locks belies its historical significance. The town is perched on a small bluff between the river and I-84, and its services and creature comforts are mostly confined to its main drag, Wa-Na-Pa Street. Below the town were rapids—called the Cascades—that blocked steamboat traffic between Portland and The Dalles and caused hardship for raft-bound Oregon Trail pioneers. Before the shipping locks that inspired the burg's utilitarian name were constructed in 1896 to help steamboats navigate around hazardous rapids, most boats had to be portaged overland.

The Bridge of the Gods, a steel cantilever bridge spanning the Columbia River at Cascade Locks, was built in 1926, the modern realization of a legendary bridge that, according to Native American myth, spanned this same channel.

The construction of the Bonneville Dam in the late 1930s inaugurated boom times

in the area. The dam created 48-mile Lake Bonneville, which submerged the shipping locks.

Reasonably priced food and lodging, a historical museum, the Bonneville Dam, and sternwheeler tours along with superlative hiking trails nearby make Cascade Locks a nice stopover.

SIGHTS
Bonneville Dam

The **Bonneville Dam** (541/374-8820, www.nwp.usace.army.mil) can be reached via Exit 40 off I-84. The signs lead you under the interstate through a tunnel to the site of the complex, Bradford Island. En route to the visitors center you drive over a retractable bridge above the modern shipping locks. On the other side are the powerhouse and turbine room. Downriver on the Washington side is the second-largest exposed monolith in the world (Gibraltar is first). This 848-foot lava promontory abutting

© BILL MCRAE

Bonneville Dam was the first hydroelectric dam on the Columbia River.

the shoreline is known as **Beacon Rock,** a moniker bestowed by Lewis and Clark.

Beyond the generating facilities is a bridge, underneath which is the fish-diversion canal. These fishways cause back eddies and guide the salmon, shad, steelhead, and other species past turbine blades. You'll want to stop for a brief look at the spillways of the 500-foot-wide Bonneville Dam, especially if they're open.

While it isn't anywhere near the largest or the most powerful dam on the river, Bonneville Dam was one of the largest and most ambitious of the Depression-era New Deal projects. Completed in 1937, it was the first major dam on the Columbia River. The building of the dam brought Oregon thousands of jobs on construction crews, and the cheap electricity that it produced promised future industrial employment. President Franklin D. Roosevelt officiated at the dam's opening in 1938, attended by a cheering throng of thousands. The two hydroelectric powerhouses together produce over one million kilowatts of power, and they back up the Columbia River for 15 miles.

At the **visitors center** (503/374-8820, 9am-5pm daily year-round), ask the Army Corps of Engineers personnel at the reception desk about tours of the power-generating facilities and about public campgrounds, boat ramps, swimming, and picnic areas. Be aware that the dam may be closed to visits without warning due to security alerts.

The reception area has exhibits on dam operations, pioneer and navigation history on the Columbia, and fish migration. A long elevator ride takes you down to the fish-viewing windows, where the sight of lamprey eels—which accompany the mid-May and mid-September salmon runs—is particularly fascinating. Outside the facility there's access to an overlook above the fish ladders. A walkway back to the parking lot is decorated with gorgeous roses spring through fall.

Retrace your route back to the mainland from Bradford Island and turn right, following the signs to the **fish hatchery** (7:30am-5pm daily, free). Visit during spawning season (May and Sept.) to see the salmon make their

DAMS AND SALMON

Beginning with Bonneville in 1938, the construction of the great dams on the Columbia changed the course of one of the world's mightiest rivers and the way of life in the gorge forever. Bonneville and Grand Coulee Dams supplied power for the World War II shipyards in Portland and Vancouver, Washington, and Boeing in Seattle. Besides billions of dollars worth of pollution-free renewable energy at the lowest cost in the western United States, other Bonneville by-products include 370 miles of lucrative inland shipping, irrigation water for agriculture, and perfect windsurfing conditions.

Today, Pacific Northwest businesses and residents still benefit from the cheap hydropower, but at the possible cost of the greatest salmon runs ever known. Salmon are anadromous fish, meaning they live most of their lives in the ocean, but they breed in freshwater. They are hatched in rivers and then swim to the ocean where they mature. They then swim back up the same rivers they were born in, spawning in exactly the same spot where they were hatched, after which effort the fish die. The great salmon migrations up the Columbia were once so vast and strong that in the 1850s it was considered dangerous to row across the Columbia near Portland—the size and number of salmon were so great that they could inadvertently capsize small boats as they struggled upriver.

However, this massive population of salmon in the Columbia basin was not immune to the actions of humans. During the 1880s, 55 canneries operated on the Columbia, employing such then-new technologies as the salmon wheel, a Ferris wheel-like scooping device that extracted salmon from the river in such large numbers that the wheels were banned in the first decades of the 20th century. Starting with Bonneville Dam, the hydroelectric dams on the Columbia served as enormous barricades to the natural migrations of these fish, resulting in drastically smaller salmon populations. While hundreds of millions of dollars have been spent on research and efforts to mitigate the ill effects posed by the dams, salmon populations in the Pacific Northwest generally continue to decline. Not all the news is bad: The Columbia Basin chinook salmon run consisted of less than a million fish for much of the 1990s, though the numbers have been trending upwards since 2000. By contrast, an estimated 10-16 million Columbia River salmon were caught annually by Native Americans in the 1800s.

Polls continually confirm that a large majority of Pacific Northwest residents want to restore the salmon runs, even if financial and other sacrifices are involved. It's as if there is a shared realization echoing the traditional Native American belief—after the salmon, we're next.

way upriver. During spawning season, head to the west end of the hatchery, where steps lead down to a series of canals and holding pens. So great is the zeal of these fish to spawn that they occasionally leap more than three feet out of the water.

Inside the building, you can see the beginnings of a process that produces the largest number of salmon fry in the state. Fish culturists sort the fish and extract the bright-red salmon roe from the females. These eggs are taken to the windowed incubation building, where you can view trays holding millions of eggs that will eventually hatch into salmon.

Once these fry grow into fingerlings, they are moved to outdoor pools where they live until being released into the Columbia River by way of the Tanner Creek canal. The whole process is annotated by placards above the windows inside the incubation building.

The salmon and trout ponds and the floral displays are worth your attention at certain times of the year, but the sturgeon pools to the rear of the visitors center are always something to see. Bonneville is the nation's only hatchery for white sturgeon, and the government has made this facility user-friendly. Biologists claim that the white sturgeon species of the Columbia

River, with bony plates instead of scales, has remained unchanged for 200 million years.

Cascade Locks Marine Park

Down near the river is the **Cascade Locks Marine Park** (Exit 44 off I-84 East). Look for it on your left going east on Wa-Na-Pa Street; just follow the signs. Here the sternwheeler *Columbia Gorge* (reservations 503/224-3900 or 800/224-3901, www.portlandspirit.com) makes it possible to ride up the river in the style of a century ago. This 145-foot 330-ton replica carries 599 passengers on three decks. There are several packages of varying themes and duration. The two-hour sightseeing cruise ($28 adults and seniors, $18 children) departure times vary; check the website for schedules. Lunch, dinner, and weekend brunch cruises are also available; cruises run May-October.

Port of Cascade Locks (541/374-8619, http://portofcascadelocks.org) houses the ticket office as well as an information center and gift shop, which sells an excellent map of local hiking trails.

About 0.25 mile west of the visitors center, **Cascade Locks Historical Museum** (503/374-8535, 10am-5pm daily May-Sept., free) is housed in an old lockkeeper's residence and exhibits Native American artifacts and pioneer memorabilia. Information about the fish wheel, a paddlewheel-like contraption that conveyor-belted salmon out of the river and into a pen, is especially fascinating. This diabolical device was perfected in Oregon in the early 20th century and was so successful at denuding the Columbia of fish that it was outlawed. Outside the museum is the diminutive Oregon Pony, the first steam locomotive on the Pacific coast. Its maiden voyage dates back to 1862 when it replaced the 4.5-mile portage with a rail route around the Cascades.

Take a walk over to the old locks. Construction began in 1878 to circumnavigate the steep gradient of the river; they were completed in 1896. By the time the Cascade shipping locks were completed, however, river traffic had decreased because cargo was being

sent by train, so the impact of altering the river flow was negligible.

HIKING

The following hikes require a $5-per-vehicle day pass or a $30 annual Northwest Forest Pass.

Wahclella Falls and Old Columbia River Highway Hiker-Biker Trail

The best short hike in the Columbia Gorge that doesn't involve significant elevation gain is the walk along Tanner Creek to Wahclella Falls. After 1 mile of walking, you reach the terminus of the canyon framing the creek. En route, the gently hilly pathway shows off this pretty steep-walled arroyo to great advantage, but the destination is better than the journey.

In a scene evocative of a Japanese brush-stroke painting, a waterfall pours down dramatically at the canyon's end, best seen from a bridge over the creek. While the trail on the other side of the stream is worthwhile, it doesn't loop all the way back to the parking lot, so you'll have to retrace your steps. From I-84 eastbound, reach the trailhead by taking the Bonneville Dam exit (Exit 40) and making a right at the bottom of the exit ramp into a small parking lot (instead of a left under the highway to Bonneville Dam).

From this same parking lot you can access a resuscitated portion of the Columbia River Highway by heading east. However, with lanes barely wide enough to accommodate a golf cart, you'll have to leave the car behind. The state decided to repave this section of the old road for hikers and bikers, re-creating the arched guardrails, bridges, viaducts, and tunnels between here and Cascade Locks to join the surviving ones. In addition to the ornate stonework, the curving, undulating roadbed—which was blasted out of the mountainside prior to 1920—offers unsurpassed views.

While the historic highway parallels the interstate, its elevated perspective on the river and surrounding architectural artistry are a refreshing change of pace from the modern thoroughfare. The highlight of the route is a reproduction of the Toothrock Viaduct annotated by plaques and heritage markers. After exiting this section of the highway via a stairway into the parking lot of the Eagle Creek Fish Hatchery, head east a short distance to the second leg of this hiker-biker trail. The Eagle Creek-Cascade Locks section is highlighted by a pretty waterfall at the beginning and a well-rendered tunnel near the end. The distance between Bonneville and Cascade Locks is about four miles.

◖ Eagle Creek Trail

Hikes up a spectacular side canyon of the Columbia Gorge are the highlight of this popular recreational area. The Eagle Creek Trail 440, constructed in 1915, was an engineering feat. Volunteers blasted ledges for trails along vertical cliffs, spanned a deep chasm with a suspension bridge, and burrowed a 120-foot tunnel behind a waterfall. If you have time for only one day hike in the gorge, this should be it.

The classic day hike in to Eagle Creek leads up along the face of a cliff to a viewpoint over Metlano Falls. Part of the trail then drops back streamside near Punchbowl Falls, a good spot to break for lunch and splash in pools of cool water. Casual day hikers can return at this point, making for an easy 4.5-mile round-trip stroll.

More ambitious hikers can continue along to High Bridge, a suspension bridge spanning a deep crevice, and Tunnel Falls, so named because of the 120-foot tunnel blasted into the rock behind the waterfall. Work your way through the tunnel for great views up and down Eagle Creek's canyon. The round-trip hike from the trailhead to High Bridge is 6.5 miles; to Tunnel Falls and back it is a strenuous 12 miles.

Be warned that the Eagle Creek Trail is very popular. Try to avoid summer weekends when the trail is thronged with hikers. Some sections of the trail inch along vertical cliffs with cable handrails drilled into the cliff side for safety. Other steep sections lack handrails altogether. This isn't a good trail for unsupervised children or unleashed pets.

Wildflowers spring up in April and linger on into August at the higher elevations. Many species are alpine plants left over from a previous glacial period that have adapted because of the shade and moisture on the south side of the gorge. Almost two dozen varieties of fern, trillium, beargrass, yellow arnica, penstemon, monkeyflower, and devil's club are among the more common species.

As a prelude to hiking Eagle Creek or one of several other trails in the area, you might want to wander an informative interpretive loop of less than 1 mile. Just cross the footbridge on the approach road to the Eagle Creek Trailhead over to the other side of the river. After crossing the bridge, follow the markers that describe the region's mixed conifer forest at various elevations. At trail's end, you might want to take on the steep two-mile trail to Wauna Point. While this trail isn't as visually arresting as other area jaunts, the view of the Columbia River and Gorge at the summit makes the effort worthwhile.

ACCOMMODATIONS AND FOOD

If the best view of the Columbia from a hotel room is important to you, then make reservations at Cascade Locks's **Best Western Columbia River Inn** (735 Wa-Na-Pa St., 541/374-8777 or 800/595-7108, www.best-western.com/columbiariverinn, $125-149). Some rooms have hot tubs, and all rooms have microwaves and refrigerators. Many rooms also have balconies. In addition to views, there's a fitness room with a whirlpool, a pool, and exercise facilities. With the Marine Park down the street, this property is in an excellent location.

Forget health food and haute cuisine until you get to Hood River. In Cascade Locks, you get down-home country cookin' at a decent price. The **Salmon Row Pub** (500 Wa-Na-Pa St., Cascade Locks, 541/374-8511, 11am-10pm daily, $6-16) is a small, dark brewpub whose smoked salmon chowder, pizza, and sandwiches fill you up on the cheap.

East Wind Ice Cream (395 Wa-Na-Pa St., Cascade Locks, 541/374-8380) is a traditional

COLUMBIA RIVER GORGE

stop for families on a Columbia River Gorge Sunday drive.

Camping

There's no shortage of options for campers in this area. Keep in mind that the western gorge is Portland's backyard and can be very crowded, so avoid peak times when possible. In addition to first-come, first-served **Ainsworth State Park** (503/695-2301 or 800/551-6949, www.oregonstateparks.org, $17-20), several other sites are worth considering. These have been chosen for their location (near attractions or a prime trailhead) or for special amenities.

While the **Eagle Creek Campground** (541/386-2333, mid-May-Oct., $15) can be noisy and crowded, it's an ideal base camp for hiking as it's close to several trailheads. Established in 1915, this is the first campground ever created by the National Forest Service. Reservations are not accepted, it's first-come, first-served only, so try to get here early in the day. There are sites for tents and RVs up to 22 feet long; sites have picnic tables, grills, and flush toilets, and sanitary services are available. Eagle Creek is located between Bonneville Dam and Cascade Locks off I-84. At the 7-mile point on the Eagle Creek Trail there's a free primitive campground, but it fills up on summer weekends.

Herman Horse Camp (541/386-2333, mid-May-Oct., $10, no reservations) is 0.5 mile east of Cascade Locks, near the Pacific Crest Trail, and 0.5 mile from Herman Creek. A full array of services, including a laundry, a store, a café, and showers are within two miles, supplementing the seven tent and RV sites. Piped water, grills, picnic tables, and stock-handling facilities are also welcome additions. There are

trails for hiking and horse-packing, and other attractions include the historic Forest Work Center and nearby rock walls, where visitors can admire the handiwork of the Civilian Conservation Corps.

At I-84 Exit 51 is the **Wyeth Campground** ($10, no reservations, no phone), a beautiful and secluded Forest Service site that was used as a Civilian Conservation Corps camp in the 1930s. Today's it's popular as a windsurfing spot and has piped water and flush toilets.

Cascade Locks Marine Park (355 Wa-Na-Pa St., Cascade Locks, 509/637-6911, www.portofcascadelocks.org, year-round, $15-25) has campsites close to the center of town. The museum and the sternwheeler are housed in the complex. The amenities that are not available on-site are within walking distance.

Finally, two miles east of town near the banks of the Columbia is the Cascade Locks **KOA Kampground** (841 NW Forest Ln., Cascade Locks, information 541/374-8668, reservations 800/562-8698, Feb.-Nov. 30, $28 tents, $28-38 RVs, $3 each extra person). This private campground features the basics plus a spa (hot tub and sauna), hot showers, and a heated swimming pool. One-room (a queen bed and a bunk bed, $55) or two-room (a queen bed and two sets of bunks, $70) Kamping Kabins with shared bathroom facilities are available, as are two-bed cottages with private bathroom for $96-110; bring your own linens, pillows, towels, sleeping bags, etc.. Kabins fill up quickly, especially on weekends, so reserve well in advance. To get there, take U.S. 30 east from town and turn left onto Forest Lane. Proceed 1.2 miles down, and you'll see the Kampground on the left.

Hood River

In the past, Hood River was known as an especially scenic place to grow fruit. Since the early 1980s, however, well-heeled adherents of windsurfing have transformed this town into an outdoor recreation mecca. Instead of just the traditional dependence on cherry, apple, peach, and pear production, Hood River now rakes in tens of millions of dollars annually from the presence of "board-heads."

Bounded by picturesque orchard country and the Columbia River with snowcapped volcanoes serving as a distant backdrop, this town of 6,500 enjoys a magnificent setting. The main thoroughfare, Oak Street, which becomes Cascade Street as you head west, is set on a plateau between the riverfront marine park to the north and streets running up the Cascade foothills to the south. New brick facades dress up old storefronts, and casual attire and sandals predominate.

SIGHTS

Downtown Hood River is a lively place, with many shops and restaurants along Oak Street. A sense of fun and youthfulness pervades the town, the result of the many tanned, buff visitors who come here for the world-famous windsurfing and kiteboarding. A good spot to catch the spirit of the windsurfing scene is at Marina Park, just past the Hood River Museum, at the mouth of the Hood River. From here, lots of river athletes set sail and trade stories.

Hood River Museum

At the **Hood River Museum** (300 E. Port Marina Dr., 541/386-6772, 10am-4pm Mon.-Sat., noon-4pm Sun. Apr.-Aug., noon-4pm daily Sept.-Oct., donation), exhibits trace life in the Hood River Valley from prehistoric times to the founding of the first pioneer settlement in 1854. Native American stone artifacts, beadwork, and basketry, as well as

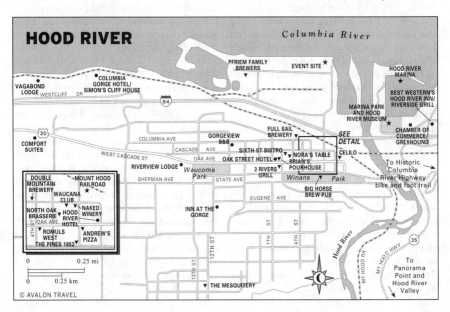

Hood River is home to many art galleries.

pioneer quilts and a Victorian parlor set are on display. The story of the area's development as a renowned fruit-growing center is told, and the contributions of the local Finnish and Japanese communities, along with World War I memorabilia, introduce the first half of the 20th century. Photos and implements related to fruit harvesting and packing methods round out the historical collections on the first floor. Antique logging equipment, dolls, and remnants of a presentation by local schoolchildren for the 1905 Lewis and Clark Exposition are also displayed.

Panorama Point

If you don't have time to drive up the Hood River Valley to enjoy the fantastic vistas of Mount Hood above the orchards, here's a close-to-town alternative. Drive to the east end of town and turn south on Route 35. Head south until you see the sign for **Panorama Point.** After a left turn, head south about 1 mile on East Side Road, then make a left on a road that'll take you to the top of a knoll; the

views south and west do justice to the name. Panoramic vistas here afford a distant perspective on the orchards below Mount Hood that have for decades served as a visual archetype of the Pacific Northwest.

The Hood River Valley

South of the town of Hood River, the river of the same name drains a wide valley filled with orchards. During the spring, nearly the entire region is replete with the scent and color of pink and white blossoms. Later on, fruit stands spring up along roadsides, selling apples, pears, cherries, berries, and vegetables. Watch for wineries, as wine grapes are the most recent crop to find a home in this famously fruitful valley. Route 35, which traverses the valley, leads up the south and east flanks of Mount Hood, only 25 miles south. On a clear day, this is one of the most scenic drives in Oregon, and it is one leg of the popular Mount Hood Loop that is for many Portland visitors their first glimpse of rural Oregon.

Driving south on Route 35 to Parkdale,

© BILL MCRAE

Mount Hood rises above the fruitful Hood River Valley.

$30-55 adults and seniors, $25-55 children under age 12, depending on style of railcar), which runs from the old Hood River railroad depot just off I-84 Exit 63 up the scenic Hood River Valley to its terminus in Parkdale—seemingly at the very base of Mount Hood due to the volcano's immensity and proximity. Riders sit in lovingly restored enclosed Pullman coaches or in more exclusive domed coaches. Also featured are an antique concession car and, of course, the obligatory red caboose. The standard ride takes about four hours round-trip, including a stop in Parkdale. The railroad also features dinner and brunch trains and many special-event rides, such as the Fruit Blossom Special in April and Christmas Tree Trains, bedecked with carolers and other holiday trimmings. The main season is April-October.

Wine-Tasting

The moderate climate in the Hood River Valley favors production of cool-weather grapes such as pinot noir and pinot gris, while just across the Columbia River near Bingen and Lyle in Washington, the microclimate makes possible heavier reds such as syrah and whites such as viognier. There are well over a dozen wineries in the Hood River area, all open daily for tasting May-October (call to confirm opening times during the winter) and all easily found by using the readily available **Columbia Gorge Wine map** (www.columbiagorgewine.com).

Here are some of our favorite stops. **Naked Winery** (102 2nd St., 800/666-9303, www.nakedwinery.com, noon-7pm daily) has a tasting room right in downtown Hood River. The wines are moderately priced and marketed with a slightly naughty edge: Penetration Cabernet, anyone? **Cathedral Ridge Winery** (4200 Post Canyon Rd., 541/386-2882, http://cathedralridgewinery.com, 11am-5pm daily) is just west of town near the golf course. The valley's oldest winery, dating to 1981, is **Hood River Vineyards** (4693 Westwood Dr., 541/386-7772, http://hoodrivervineyardsandwinery.com, 11am-5pm daily Mar.-Oct.). The microclimate at this winery is similar to that which produces Germany's Rhine wines.

be sure to visit the **Hutson Museum** (4967 Baseline Rd., Parkdale, 541/352-6808, 11am-4pm Wed.-Fri., 11am-6pm Sat.-Sun., $1 adults, $0.50 children, children ages 6 and under free). Native American artifacts, pioneer hand tools, and one of the better rock collections in the Pacific Northwest make it worthwhile.

Also near Parkdale is a series of **lava beds.** From Route 35 south, turn right at the Mount Hood Country Store on Baseline Road en route to Parkdale, then right on Lava Bed Drive. The beds are located one mile west of town. Surprisingly, this lava did not emanate from the slopes of the mountain; it came from a vent more than three miles south and west of town. This flow is thought to be several thousand years old, a fraction of the 30-million-year volcanic legacy of the Columbia Gorge.

Mount Hood Railroad

Train buffs will be delighted to ride the **Mount Hood Railroad** (541/386-3556 or 800/872-4661, www.mthoodrr.com, regular excursion

HOOD RIVER'S FRUIT

HISTORY

The first orchards were planted in the Hood River Valley in the 1850s, and soon it became apparent that the valley's rich volcanic soil, glacier-fed rivers and streams, and mild climate were perfect for cultivation of apples, pears, stone fruit, berries, and vegetables. The first large-scale orchards were established in 1876, focusing on Newton pippin apples. Because it takes many years for apple trees to become productive, strawberries and asparagus were often planted in the orchards to provide an interim cash crop. Strawberry farming was so successful at the turn of the 20th century that the Hood River Railroad was established in 1906 largely to hasten the delivery of the delicate berries to mainline trains at Hood River, from where they were shipped to markets across the country.

Many of the workers that built the Hood River Railroad were immigrants from Japan, and after laying the track many stayed on in the Hood River area and established farms and businesses. By 1920, over 350 Japanese people lived in Hood River, and of these, 70 were land-owning farmers. The Japanese were very successful and hardworking, and by 1940 there were 88 Japanese-owned farms in the valley; these Japanese farmers and orchardists produced 90 percent of Hood River County's asparagus, 80 percent of the strawberries, 35 percent of the pears, and 20 percent of the apples.

However, that all changed on December 7, 1941, when the Japanese navy bombed Pearl Harbor, and the United States declared war on Japan. Anti-Japanese sentiment ran very high, even though the majority of the ethnic Japanese in the Hood River area were U.S.-born citizens. Then in 1942 came Executive Order 9066, issued by President Franklin D. Roosevelt, declaring that all people of Japanese ancestry were excluded from the entire Pacific coast. In a period of just two weeks, all people in the Hood River of Japanese ancestry, including U.S. citizens, were forced onto trains and sent to internment camps in California.

After the war, about 40 percent of Hood River's Japanese attempted to return to the valley and their businesses, but most found their property vandalized, possessions stolen, and farms untended. Many moved on, but some persevered; several large farms and orchards are still owned by Japanese American families.

Hood River remains an excellent place to grow fruit. It is the Anjou winter pear capital of the world and produces Bartlett, Comice, Bosc, and other varieties at different times of the fall. Cherries, peaches, and apples are other major crops, and the acres devoted to wine grapes are fast expanding. The 15,000 acres of orchards are still the leading economic factor in the county, with Diamond Packing the leading pear shipper in the United States.

THE FRUIT LOOP

Pick up a map to the **Fruit Loop** (www.hoodriverfruitloop.com), a 45-mile stretch of meandering highway and back roads, which directs area visitors to some of the richest farmland and most breathtaking scenery in the state—along the Hood River with Mount Hood as the backdrop to it all. Vineyards, orchards, farm stands, and country stores dot the decade-old route that crisscrosses the river, beckoning visitors to picnic, tour, or taste-test the fresh produce.

The route is popular year-round, but you can sample some of the season's ripest pears, apples, pumpkins, and gourds September-November; tomatoes, corn, peaches, and herbs abound in August and September; and farm-fresh berries and apricots ripen June-August. Bike trails follow the routes in some places. Contact the **Hood River Chamber of Commerce** (www.hoodriver.org) or consult www.hoodriverfruitloop.com for the Fruit Loop map and a list of participating farms and country stores.

COLUMBIA RIVER GORGE

© BILL MCRAE

restored Pullman coaches on the Mount Hood Railroad

In addition to the Rieslings, chardonnays, Gewürztraminers, and other white wine varietals produced here, the area is famous for award-winning pinot noir and fruit wines such as Anjou pear, marionberry, and zinfandel, which are frequently delicious. Italian varietals are featured at **Marchesi Vineyards and Winery** (3955 Belmont Dr., 542/386-1800, www.marchesivineyards.com, 11am-6pm Fri.-Sun.).

Probably the oldest vineyard in Oregon—a plot of century-old zinfandel planted by an Italian stonemason near The Dalles—forms the foundation for the best wines at **The Pines 1852** (202 W. State St., 541/993-8301, www.thepinesvineyard.com, noon-9pm Thurs.-Sat., noon-6pm Sun.-Mon. and Wed.). Rhone-style wines and an ice wine are other sure bets. Although the historic vineyards are near The Dalles, the tasting room is in Hood River.

Lost Lake

The postcard photo of Mount Hood from Lost Lake, with the white mountain peak rising above a deep-blue reflecting pool amid a thick green forest, is probably the most famous image of Oregon's most famous volcano. The lake, about 25 miles southwest of Hood River, is a popular getaway when Hood River temperatures spike.

The 25-mile drive to Lost Lake from Hood River begins on 13th Street, which changes names (Hwy. 281, Tucker Rd., and Dee Hwy.) on its way up the flanks of Mount Hood. About 12 miles from downtown, take a right at the Dee Lumber Mill, where a green Lost Lake sign points the way. From here, bear left and follow the signs.

Lost Lake Resort (P.O. Box 90, Hood River, 541/386-6366, http://lostlakeresort.org, rooms and cabins $65-180, reservations accepted; campsites $25-30, no reservations) offers rowboat rentals and a small store along with campsites and cabins. In addition, there are standard guest rooms in the second story of the lodge (bring your own linens or sleeping bags). Come prepared; the closest gas station is 20 miles away in Parkdale.

THE OTHER SIDE OF THE GORGE

Although this guide focuses on the sights of Oregon, it's clear that the Columbia River has two shores, and only one is in Oregon. Cross a bridge and you're on the Washington side of the gorge, which offers a number of excellent destinations.

Across the Columbia from Hood River, the **White Salmon River** cuts a narrow canyon down through the gorge walls as it rushes to meet the Columbia. A number of white-water rafting guides offer half-day trips on the White Salmon, which bounces down through near-constant Class IV rapids. It's a short but exhilarating rafting trip and easily added to a gorge itinerary. Guided trips are roughly $60-65 per person and are available from **River Drifters** (800/972-0430, www.riverdrifters.net) and **All Star Rafting and Kayaking** (800/909-7238, www.asrk.com).

The area around Lyle is transforming into a wine-producing mecca. The hot summer weather is perfect for growing syrah, Grenache, Roussanne, viognier, and other wine grapes from France's Rhone Valley. Two notable wineries here are **Syncline Wine Cellars** (111 Balch Rd., Lyle, 509/493-4705, tasting 11am-6pm Thurs.-Sun. Feb.-Nov.) and **Domaine Pouillon** (170 Lyle Snowden Rd., 509/365-2795, 11am-6pm Wed.-Sun.). For both, call to confirm winter hours.

Down the road a bit, there's **Maryhill Winery** (9774 Hwy. 14, 877/627-9445, 10am-6pm daily), 25 miles east of Lyle and directly across the Columbia from Biggs, Oregon; this winery offers a summer series of outdoor concerts in a natural amphitheater. The **Maryhill Museum** (509/773-3733, www.maryhillmuseum.org, 10am-5pm daily Mar. 15-Nov. 15, $9 adults, $8 seniors, $3 children ages 6-16) is an idiosyncratic collection of art and artifacts in a grand country estate. You'd be right to think that a 20,000-square-foot manor house is rather unusual in the Columbia Gorge. Maryhill was built by Sam Hill, an early-20th-century mogul whose family controlled the Great Northern Railway and who was instrumental in the building of the Columbia River Highway in the 1910s. Atop an 800-foot cliff above the Columbia, Maryhill was designed to resemble a French château and to serve both as home for Hill and his wife and as the center of a utopian Quaker community. Although construction began on Maryhill in 1913, it wasn't completed until 1926, as Hill lost interest in the project after it became clear that his wife was unwilling to live in this godforsaken country and the imported Belgian Quakers found the arid cliffs unsuitable for agriculture. Maryhill opened as a museum in 1940 and has a very good collection of Native American artifacts, an impressive set of 19th-century landscape and portrait paintings, sculpture and drawings by Auguste Rodin, and French fashion mannequins from the early 20th century. The museum also offers classes, lectures, and concerts.

Just east of Maryhill is another of Hill's eccentric constructions. Dedicated to the area's fallen soldiers from World War I, a full-scale replica of **Stonehenge** looms above the gorge.

Late August huckleberry season is a highlight at Lost Lake, but the weather and diminished crowds in September make it a preferable time to visit. The rangers have campfire programs on Saturday nights July-August. The Lakeshore Trail features a 0.5-mile boardwalk through an old-growth cedar grove; the boardwalk is 2 miles into the trail, where you pass eight-foot-thick cedars. Pick up a map with natural history captions that correspond to numbered posts along the route.

SPORTS AND RECREATION

The **Hood River Marina** offers an excellent family swim area and boat marina, and it also has personal watercraft rentals. **The Hook** offers a nice area (when the winds and windsurfers are absent) for some gentle canoeing or kayaking. **Koberg Beach State Park,** 1 mile east of town off I-84 but accessible from the westbound lanes only, offers a sandy swimming beach in a pretty setting. Be warned, however, that the drop-off

© BILL MCRAE

kiteboarders at the Event Site

is steep and not safe for little kids or weak swimmers.

Windsurfing

Hood River is recognized around the world as a major center for windsurfing and related sports for its gusty sailing sites, related businesses, and the sport's unique subculture. Blessed by a propitious mix of geography, climate, and river currents, the Columbia Gorge has strong and very reliable summer westerlies (winds blowing west to east) countered by the strong westbound Columbia River current.

Three of the top-rated sites for advanced windsurfers are accessed from the Washington side of the river. Doug's Beach, the Hatchery, and Swell City are just across the Hood River Bridge.

Three distinct windsurfing beaches are within the Hood River city limits. The **Hood River Marina Sailpark** is the largest and most developed of the three, including bathrooms with showers, food concessions, a picnic area, a grassy lawn for rigging, an exercise course,

and a great family swimming beach area with sheltered shallow water for tykes. As the name implies, you'll find the largest marina and boat launches. Beware of shallow sandbars off the shore as well as the boats entering and exiting the marina. Due to its amenities, including ample close-by parking, this can be one of the most crowded sites around.

The **Event Site,** a newer and somewhat smaller site, is to the west of the Hood River's confluence with the Columbia. Major events, including well-known windsurfing competitions, happen here. It has a lawn for rigging and small bleachers for spectators. These amenities, plus a location convenient to downtown, make this an ideal spot for spectators. It provides quicker access to deeper water than the marina, but it can also be quite crowded at times. Toilets, water, and food carts are available onsite. The Event Site is off I-84 Exit 63, or at the north end of 2nd Street.

Several windsurfing schools in **The Hook** provide instruction in the gentle basin, an ideal location for beginners; once you're out in the main channel, winds can be strong. Other than chemical toilets, amenities are scarce in this area. Instead of a beach, the shore is largely steep and rocky, and the dirt road can get a bit dusty in late summer. Conditions are quite variable, particularly as some places are in a wind shadow caused by nearby Wells Island, a sensitive wildlife area vulnerable to human impact. The views to the west (and hence, the sunsets) are just grand.

Access to The Hook is at the west end of Portway Avenue, the paved road that first takes you to the Event Site. All three in-town sites charge a day-use fee ($4 per vehicle). Call the **Port of Hood River** (541/386-1645) for more information.

About eight miles west of town, **Viento State Park** offers good river access for sailing in a beautiful natural setting. The park has a campground, a picnic area, restrooms, and water. Spectators won't have a lot of room, but the wind and wave action can get spicy. Viento is at Exit 56 off I-84.

In the opposite direction, six miles east

COLUMBIA RIVER GORGE

of Hood River, you'll find the **Rock Creek** launch site in Mosier. Amenities are sparse but include chemical toilets. The river here is wide, and the chop can get high. You can reach Rock Creek off I-84 Exit 69. At the top of the ramp, hang a right, then the first left on Rock Creek Road. The site is on the right just past the dry creek bed.

In business since 1986, **Big Winds** (207 Front St., 541/386-6086, www.bigwinds.com) offers board and full rig rentals starting at $69 per day and $389 per week, depending on the equipment. Big Winds also offers three levels of beginner lessons ($79 per lesson), or choose the "Learn to Windsurf" package ($199) that includes all three lessons. The price includes use of a wetsuit, booties, and all the necessary windsurfing equipment. There are many other windsurfing lessons and rental operations in Hood River with similar price ranges and options.

In addition to windsurfing, all the water sports outfitters also have rental gear for other sports such as kiteboarding and stand-up paddling.

Adepts will tell you that windsurfing is best in the fall. It's less crowded, the water's warm, and the winds are lighter at school sites. It's easier to find parking and rigging space at launching areas, and there's a quality of light on the water, with enough clear days to add aesthetic appeal. Best of all for beginners is the availability of individualized instruction during fall. While conditions are generally good at most locations along the river during the season, the best places are in the east end of the gorge, notably around Three Mile Canyon and other launch sites in the Arlington, Oregon, and Roosevelt, Washington, areas.

Fishing

The area offers two different types of fishing. You can go for trout in several beautiful small mountain lakes, most of which are west and south of the Hood River Valley. Notable among the latter are Wahtum, Rainy, and North Lakes, all about 45 minutes west of downtown Hood River on good gravel roads. Then there

is Lost Lake, the popularity of which might detract from the quality of the fishing during some seasons. Pick up licenses in any Hood River sports shop.

The other option is fishing the Hood River itself, or the Columbia River. The Hood has good trout fishing, and both have good seasonal steelhead and salmon fishing. The Hood River can be accessed from several county parks. Contact the **Gorge Fly Shop** (201 Oak St., 541/386-6977, www.gorgeflyshop.com) for information; this operation can also arrange fly-fishing lessons.

Golf

Offering great views of Mount Hood is the popular 18-hole 6,150-yard **Indian Creek Golf Course** (3605 Brookside Dr., 541/386-3009, www.indiancreekgolf.com, $35-50). A little farther from town is **Hood River Golf Course** (1850 Country Club Rd., 541/386-3009, www.hoodrivergolf.net, $30). It has 18 holes that are a bit hillier than at Indian Creek, as well as beautiful views of Mount Hood, Mount Adams, elk, and geese. Come in fall if only to see the spectacular foliage.

Hiking

While the most famous gorge hikes tend to cluster around the west end waterfall area, the environs of Hood River have their fair share of great trails. Three of these trails are right on the gorge, 8 miles west of town on the south side of the highway, accessible via the Viento Park exit (Exit 56) off I-84.

The **Starvation Creek to Viento Trail** hike is the shortest and by far the easiest of the three. Actually a restored segment of the Historic Columbia River Highway, this mostly paved path runs a little over one mile each way. It offers some decent gorge views but will be of more interest to history buffs who want to re-trace extant remnants of the old highway. This trail also provides access to the other two trails in the area.

Both the **Mount Defiance Trail** (Trail 413) and **Starvation Ridge Trail** (Trail 414) used to be accessible through the Starvation Creek rest stop exit off I-84, which is now closed. So walk the Starvation Creek to Viento Trail, then look for signs for either of the other trails once you get to the west side of the rest stop. Both trails eventually head for the same place, converging high above the gorge just below the top of Mount Defiance. Being the highest point on the gorge proper at 4,960 feet, Mount Defiance presents a strenuous workout for anyone up for the challenge.

Either route rewards you with spectacular views of the gorge, as well as old-growth woods and pristine Warren Lake. The Starvation Ridge Trail is somewhat steeper than the Mount Defiance Trail. This long loop is about 12 miles round-trip. A short two-mile loop is also possible by following Trail 413 for one mile, then heading east (left) onto Trail 414. This eventually takes you back to the highway where you started. These trails are really best only for experienced hikers due to their steepness and narrowness.

The **Wygant Trail** is reached from the eastbound-only Exit 58 off I-84 at Mitchell Point. Go right (west) at the top of the ramp, then follow the road heading west. This eventually becomes the trail, and it follows the old route of the Historic Highway for a stretch. The trail eventually winds its way for almost 4 miles to the top of 2,214-foot Wygant Peak. Along the way you'll pass through some native Oregon white oak groves, mixed conifer forests, and some openings with lovely views.

There are many beautiful trails south of Hood River off Route 35 in Mount Hood National Forest. The **East Fork Trail** offers an easy but very scenic amble along the swift glacial-fed East Fork of the Hood River. Accessed from either the Robin Hood or Sherwood Campgrounds (24 miles south of Hood River) along Route 35, this trail is great on foot or mountain bike. It is about 4 miles between the two campgrounds, and the trail continues beyond the Sherwood Campground north into the Mount Hood Wilderness.

Tamanawas Falls Trail leads off from the East Fork Trail about 0.5 mile north of the Sherwood Campground. A short but steeper hike, this trail is uphill all the way to the reward—beautiful 150-foot-high Tamanawas Falls.

Perhaps the best place to experience the transition from western alpine conifer forest to interior high desert is **Lookout Mountain** in the Badger Creek Wilderness. This aptly named 6,525-foot peak is the second-highest in the Mount Hood National Forest. To get there, drive 25 miles south of Hood River on Route 35 to Forest Road 44 (the Dufur cutoff). Follow it east for 5 miles up a steep hill to Forest Service Road 4410, marked for High Prairie. This route takes you 6 miles to a parking area opposite the trailhead to High Prairie Trail (Trail 493).

The 20-minute walk to the top of Lookout Mountain on Trail 493 takes you through wildflower meadows to the former site of a fire spotter's cabin. Directly west looms Mount Hood. Turn 180 degrees and you face the sagebrush and wheat fields of eastern Oregon. To the south are the Three Sisters and Broken Top. West and north of those peaks rises Mount Jefferson's tricorn hat. The body of water to the southwest is Badger Lake. To the north, views of Mounts Adams, St. Helens, and Rainier (on a clear day) will have you reeling with visual intoxication.

Mountain Biking

Just west of town is a network of old gravel and dirt roads that local mountain bikers love. **Post Canyon Road** starts out as a typical paved rural road, with houses scattered along each side. Shortly past its start at Country Club Road, the pavement ends and the fat-tire fun begins. Several side roads branch off from Post Canyon Road into the Cascade foothills. You can ride for a long time without seeing any buildings, but you will undoubtedly encounter some clear-cuts and other logged areas, so don't expect pristine forests. Also, be warned: The road is used by groups of motorbikers at times, so stay alert.

To get there, take Exit 62 off I-84, turn right at the top of the ramp, then make an immediate right onto Country Club Road. Follow this road about 1 mile as it bends to the south, then turn right into the well-signed Post Canyon.

Surveyor's Ridge Trail (Trail 688) traverses the ridgeline on the east side of the upper Hood River Valley for 17 miles. It offers some great Mount Hood and valley views and is especially fun for mountain bikers. The trailhead is off Forest Service Road 17, which intersects Route 35 about 11 miles south of Hood River just past the big lumber mill to the left of the highway.

Stop by **Discover Bicycles** (116 Oak St., 541/386-4820, www.discoverbicycles.com) for advice on mountain bike trails and bike rentals (from $30 per day).

ENTERTAINMENT AND EVENTS

The third weekend in April, the **Hood River Blossom Festival** (Hood River Chamber of Commerce, 541/386-2000 or 800/366-3530, www.hoodriver.org) celebrates breathtaking views of the valley's orchards in bloom. Arts and crafts, dinners, and the seasonal opening of the Mount Hood Railroad are some of the highlights.

The fall counterpart to the spring Blossom Festival is the **Hood River Valley Harvest Fest** (541/386-2000 or 800/366-3530). On the second or third weekend in October, the valley welcomes visitors for two days of entertainment, crafts, fresh locally grown produce, and colorful foliage. The apples and pears are ripe, and admission is free.

ACCOMMODATIONS

Finding a room in Hood River in the summer isn't easy, and the rates reflect the area's popularity. In fact, don't set out to Hood River in summer or on weekends without room reservations; there are a limited number of rooms and a large influx of visitors. Some lower-end motels can be pretty battered—the young ski and windsurfing crowd can be hard on rooms. All prices listed reflect summer rates; remember to add the 9 percent room tax within the city of Hood River. Weekend rates can be substantially higher than those for weekdays.

$50-100

The ◖ **Vagabond Lodge** (4070 Westcliff Dr., 541/386-2992, www.vagabondlodge.com, $80-125) is a couple of miles west of downtown near the Columbia Gorge Hotel. It has lovely landscaped grounds with a playground for kids and is set back from the highway. Three guest rooms have full kitchens, and a number have large stone fireplaces. The best are the view rooms (extra charge), which take in a spectacular vista of the gorge.

Riverview Lodge (1505 Oak St., 541/386-8719, www.riverviewforyou.com, $79-140) has basic rooms, a pool, and some units with kitchens. It's within easy walking distance of Cascade Commons, Hood River's shopping center, with several grocery stores and eating options.

$100-150

In the heart of downtown is the ◖ **Hood River Hotel** (102 Oak St., 541/386-1900 or 800/386-1859, www.hoodriverhotel.com, $100-1,564), an impeccably restored turn-of-the-20th-century hotel with a good restaurant (Cornerstone Cuisine, 7am-9pm daily, $12-20). Special vacation packages are also featured. The oak-paneled, high-ceilinged lobby, with a cozy fireplace and an adjoining lounge and restaurant, is particularly inviting. Rooms that face the river also face the rail lines, so if you're a light sleeper, you may want to opt for a lower-priced town-view room. All in all, "the Hotel" (as locals call it) is a nexus of activity and the most charming in-town digs to be found.

Comfort Suites (2625 W. Cascade Ave., 541/308-1000, $129-170) is at the west end of Hood River, about a mile from downtown. It offers immaculate guest rooms and amenities, such as a pool and spa, as well as some suites with kitchens.

A large 1909 home right on the edge of downtown is home to the **Oak Street Hotel** (610 Oak St., 541/386-3845 or 866/386-3845, www.oakstreethotel.com, $149-174), a small boutique hotel with just nine rooms, all stylishly furnished.

If being on the river is essential to you,

Best Western's Hood River Inn (1108 E. Marina Way, 541/386-2200 or 800/828-7873, www.hoodriverinn.com, $119-164) is the only place in town to boast direct river frontage and even a small private beach. The rooms provide great opportunities to watch windsurfers, and there's a lounge and a decent restaurant (the Riverside Grill) on the premises. Best of all, however, are the heated outdoor pool and spa. The only downside is that the hotel is a bit of a trek to downtown. There's a complex formula for determining room rates, which can spike wildly from day to day, so it's worth visiting the website before calling to make reservations.

The **C Columbia Gorge Hotel** (4000 Westcliff Dr., 541/386-5566 or 800/345-1921, www.columbiagorgehotel.com, $129-279) was built in 1921 by lumber magnate Simon Benson. It has been called the "Waldorf of the West" for its neo-Moorish facade, glittering chandeliers, and 207-foot waterfall on the grounds. The hotel recently received a much-needed renovation and update. Large wing chairs around the fireplace and fresh-cut bouquets in the dining room bespeak the hotel's enduring refinement. In addition to a fine restaurant offering breakfast, lunch, and dinner, the hotel provides lovely gardens. To get there, take Exit 62 off I-84, drive over the bridge to the north side of the highway, and follow Westcliff Drive west.

$150-200

Immediately adjacent to the Columbia Gorge Hotel, **Columbia Cliff Villas** (3880 Westcliff Dr., 541/436-2660 or 866/912-8366, www.columbiacliffvillas.com, $179-299) shares its stellar views and offers hotel and condo lodgings with one- to three-bedroom units. The guest rooms can be put together into almost any layout, from basic hotel-style rooms to multibedroom suites with full kitchens.

Bed-and-Breakfasts

Two B&Bs are located in the leafy old neighborhood near the historic center of Hood River. **The Inn at the Gorge** (1113 Eugene St., 541/386-4429, www.innatthegorge.com, $119-159) is a nicely refurbished 1908 Victorian that offers the informality of a windsurfer hangout in the form of a classy B&B. Three of the five guest rooms are suites, very large rooms with full kitchens. All rooms have private baths.

Windsurfer-friendly, the **Gorgeview Bed and Breakfast** (1009 Columbia St., 541/386-5770, www.gorgeview.com, May-Oct.) is in a historic house with a great porch view and a hot tub. You'll have a choice of regular private rooms ($115) or hostel-style bunk rooms ($52 pp).

Up at Parkdale near Mount Hood, the **Old Parkdale Inn** (4932 Baseline Rd., Parkdale, 541/352-5551, www.hoodriverlodging.com, $135-150) has three rooms, two of which are spacious suites. All have private baths, TVs, VCRs, microwaves, coffeemakers, and refrigerators. The breakfast is gourmet quality, and the peaceful village will satisfy those looking for an escape from the rat race. The gardens, full kitchens, mountain views, and rural setting will get you in relaxation mode.

Camping

Hood River County runs three parks with campgrounds in the Hood River Valley.

Tucker Park (2440 Dee Hwy., 541/386-4477) is only four miles from town, in a lovely spot along the banks of the gurgling boulder-strewn Hood River. It's the most developed of the three parks, with a store, a restaurant, laundry, and an ice machine just four miles away in town. It has 14 RV sites with water and electricity ($19) and 80 tent sites ($18).

Tollbridge Park (Rte. 35, 541/387-6888) is also set along the Hood River in the upper valley. It's 17 miles south of Hood River and offers showers and two grocery stores a short distance away. Rates are $20 for full-hookup sites, $19 for those with water and electric, and $18 for tent sites.

Routson Park (off Rte. 35, 541/387-6888, $10) sits along a roaring stretch of the Hood River's East Fork, at the gateway to the Mount Hood National Forest. It provides a more rustic setting higher in the mountains but only 25 minutes from town. Amenities for the 20 campsites are sparser (flush toilets and drinking water are available), and trailers are not recommended.

Oregon State Parks offers two full-service campgrounds right on the Columbia River. **Viento State Park** (800/551-6949 or 800/452-5687, mid-Apr.-late Oct.) is 8 miles west of Hood River on the river side of I-84. You'll pay $17-20 for one of the 57 sites with water and electric, or $17 to pitch your tent at the other 18 sites. Viento offers direct recreational access to the mighty Columbia.

Memaloose State Park (800/452-5687, $19-24) is 11 miles east of Hood River on I-84, accessible from the highway's westbound lanes only. On the Columbia, but with limited river access, the park offers 43 full-hookup sites and 67 tent spaces, showers, and an RV dump station. It's only fair to mention that both of these campgrounds are not far from a main freight train line; in other words, expect to hear the trains go by, even at night.

There are several nice semiprimitive forest service campgrounds in the Mount Hood National Forest, which surrounds the valley on three sides. All are in pleasant settings. Call the **Hood River Ranger Station** (6780 Rte. 35, 541/352-6002) for information. Some of the Forest Service campgrounds south of town are Sherwood and Robin Hood, both on Route 35, Laurence Lake (off Forest Rd. 2840), and Lost Lake.

FOOD

Hood River's status as the premier windsurfing town in North America has brought sophisticated tastes to the gorge with a resulting spike in restaurant quality. A cluster of casual deli, lunch, and coffee places are located along Oak Street in the downtown area; it's pleasant just to saunter the street and browse the menus. Few other small towns in the Columbia Gorge (or in the Pacific Northwest, for that matter) can boast such a roster of fine restaurants, not to mention gourmet coffee and options for vegetarians.

American

The **Sixth Street Bistro** (6th St. and Cascade Ave., 541/386-5737, http://sixthstreetbistro.com, 11:30am-9:30pm daily, $8-16) has a good selection of microbrews on tap and an eclectic menu featuring fresh, locally grown organic ingredients. Sample dishes ranging from red coconut curry to grilled rib eye with gorgonzola and port sauce. Good burgers too.

For great views of the gorge, climb the steps up to **3 Rivers Grill** (601 Oak St., 541/386-8883, www.threeriversgrill.com, 11am-10pm daily, $12-24) with expansive decks overlooking downtown and the Columbia. The selection of Pacific Northwest seafood and steaks is large and well prepared.

A classic old bar in the center of town has been refurbished into the **Waucana Club** (207 Cascade Ave., 541/387-2583, www.waucomaclub.com, 11am-10pm Mon.-Sat., 9am-10pm Sun., $9-11). This handsome spot is perfect for cocktails, microbrews, and good sandwiches, and there's live music or DJs on weekends.

On "The Heights" (the plateau forming the start of the lower Hood River Valley, a few hundred feet above downtown) you'll find **The Mesquitery** (1219 12th St., 541/386-2002, www.thebestinhoodriver.com, 4:30pm-9pm nightly, $8-19), where wood-smoke and barbecue flavors issue a wake-up call to your taste buds. You'll find the best ribs in town, not to mention steaks, fish, and many other dishes.

East of downtown, in the Best Western Hood River Inn, is the **Riverside Grill** (1108 E. Marina Way, 541/386-2200, 6am-9pm daily, $8-19), with the best riverfront views in town. The menu features fresh seafood and steaks.

Italian

Andrew's Pizza and Bakery (104 Oak St., 541/386-1448, 9am-9pm Mon.-Thurs., 9am-10pm Fri.-Sat., 10am-9pm Sun., large pizzas $14 and up) easily wins our vote for best pizza in the gorge. East Coast transplants will especially appreciate the thin-crusted slices, so reminiscent of the Big Apple's. Lots of extravagant toppings are available, as well as microbrews and great coffee.

North Oak Brasserie (113 3rd St., 541/387-2310, 11am-2pm and 5pm-9pm Mon.-Fri, 5pm-9pm Sat.-Sun, $10-24) is downtown's top Italian fine dining choice. Besides a solid repertoire of regional Italian entrées, the Brasserie features delectable pasta dishes such as housemade gnocchi with pancetta and fontina cream sauce. The roasted garlic and brie soup is the house specialty, and serious oenophiles will be drawn here to sample the wine collection.

A transplant from neighboring The Dalles, **Romul's West** (315 Oak St., 541/436-4444, www.romuls.com, 11am-9pm daily, $10-24) offers high-quality pasta and traditional main courses (osso bucco and veal piccata) in a stylized Roman dining room.

Pacific Northwest

Although the name makes it sound like a brewpub, **C** **Brian's Pourhouse** (606 Oak St., 541/387-4344, www.brianspourhouse.com, 5pm-11pm daily, $15-22) is in fact a restaurant notable for locally sourced seasonal cuisine. Few places in town can match the Pourhouse for sheer culinary creativity, and Brian's has become a local hangout for the under-40 outdoor sports-oriented crowd. The chef offers inventive dishes that combine the best of traditional Asian, European, and nouvelle elements, always with a flair for freshness. Chile-crusted calamari is served with lemon aioli, and grilled lamb sirloin comes with feta cheese and Italian salsa verde.

A stalwart of the Hood River dining scene is **C** **Celilo Restaurant and Bar** (16 Oak St., 541/386-5710, www.celilorestaurant.com, 11:30am-3pm and 5pm-9pm daily $14-24), with a daily changing menu and an updated lodge look that features hefty wood beams and splashes of soothing color. The food is very well executed, with up-to-the-minute preparations such as seared scallops with truffle oil and fresh porcini mushroom salad.

Nora's Table (10 5th St., 541/387-4000, http://norastable.com, 8am-noon and 5pm-9pm Mon.-Sat., 8am-1pm and 5pm-9pm Sun., $12-26) is a small jewel of a restaurant with handcrafted food. The menu offers small plates and main courses, all featuring local ingredients and refined techniques. (Seared diver scallops are served with sweet-corn puree and basil-arugula persillade.) This is the kind of place where you know that the chef pays attention to the details.

Simon's Cliff House at the Columbia Gorge Hotel (4000 Westcliff Dr., 541/386-5566 or 800/345-1921, www.columbiagorgehotel.com, 7am-2pm and 5pm-10pm Mon.-Sat., 9am-2pm and 5pm-10pm Sun., $18-36) looks east at the Columbia River rolling toward the hotel from out of the mountains and west toward sunset alpenglow. The menu includes pasta, steaks, Columbia River steelhead and trout, and specialties such as chicken chardonnay and roast duck breast with lavender and strawberry glaze.

Brewpubs

Hood River and environs have spawned its own mini-microbrew scene, with several establishments brewing and selling their own suds. The most famous is the **Full Sail Brewery** (506 Columbia St., 541/386-2247, www.full-sailbrewing.com, 11am-9pm daily, $10-15), offering beautiful river views to accompany its renowned ales. The **Big Horse Brew Pub** (115 State St., 541/386-4411, www.bighorse-brewpub.com, 11:30am-10pm Mon.-Thurs., 11:30am-10:30pm Fri.-Sat., 11:30am-9:30pm Sun. summer, 11:30am-9pm Mon.-Thurs., 11:30am-10pm Fri.-Sat., 11:30am-9pm Sun. winter, $9-21), in addition to selling its delicious ales (the India Pale Ale is recommended) also serves up a full menu of lunch and dinner items at pub prices; grab a seat by the window for good views.

C **Double Mountain Brewery** (8 4th St., 541/387-0042, 4pm-11pm Tues.-Thurs., 11:30am-11pm Fri.-Mon., www.doublemountainbrewery.com, $8-10) offers excellent beers and a low-key hipster scene in a taproom with thrift-store-chic decor. Food choices are simple—mostly grilled sausages and wood-fired pizza—but very worthy.

Hood River's most recent brewpub additions is **Pfriem Family Brewers** (707 Portway Ave., 541/321-0490, www.pfriembeer.com,

11am-9pm Sun.-Thurs., 11am-10pm Fri.-Sat., $10-18), with Belgian-style brews.

INFORMATION

The **Hood River County Chamber of Commerce** (at the Hood River Expo Center, 405 Portway Ave., 541/386-2000 or 800/366-3530, www.hoodriver.org) has an extensive array of maps, pamphlets, and other information about the area. They also have a huge 3-D model of the gorge's terrain that is an excellent way to get oriented to local geography. Take Exit 63 off I-84 and head north (toward the river), following the signs to the Expo Center. Another source of local visitor information, although limited to outdoor recreation, is the **National Forest Service Scenic Area Office** (902 Wasco Ave., 541/386-2333). To get there, head down 7th Street until it winds around to the left, becoming Wasco Avenue, then follow the signs.

GETTING THERE AND AROUND

Greyhound (www.greyhound.com) serves Hood River with three buses daily in each direction, stopping at the former rail station (110 Railroad Ave.). There are no services here, so plan on buying your ticket online or from the bus driver. At the Port of Hood River office is **Columbia Area Transit** (600 E. Marina Way, 541/386-4202), providing van and special bus service but not offering regularly scheduled routes in town. **Hood River Taxi and Transportation** (1107 Wilson St., 541/386-2255) provides taxi service in and around the city. **Blue Star Columbia Gorge Airporter** (800/247-2272) offers airport shuttle service between Hood River and Portland International Airport.

HISTORIC COLUMBIA RIVER HIGHWAY AND ROWENA CREST

East of Hood River, the highly scenic route up and over Rowena Crest is a segment of the Historic Columbia River Highway that

remains open to motorists. Another section, between Hood River and Mosier, the western gateway to Rowena Crest, was closed in the 1950s. However, in the 1990s public officials reopened a five-mile stretch of the route, which contains a number of tunnels, to hikers and bikers, making it possible to view the amazing engineering and craftsmanship of the original 1920s highway.

Historic Columbia River Highway Trail

This five-mile-long segment of the Historic Columbia River Highway is worth a visit. It provides a great walking and biking experience (car traffic is verboten) with the spectacular engineering feat of the reopened **Mosier Twin Tunnels** in the middle. Carved out of solid basalt and adorned with artful masonry work, the highway has become famous for the tunnels. They are about a mile from the trail's east end and 600 feet above the river. To start on the east end, take Exit 69 off I-84, turn right off the ramp, then take the first left on Rock Creek Road. Go under the highway and continue for less than 1 mile. The parking area is on your left; the highway segment begins across the road.

This segment of the old road was closed in 1953, after years of serious rockfall problems at the tunnel's west portal and the construction of the river-grade highway. The State of Oregon has constructed a special rockfall shelter to protect recreationists from the hazard. The trail also features restored original stone masonry work in several places besides the tunnels. The trailhead parking areas on either end are both called the Mark O. Hatfield Trailhead, east and west versions. This reflects the instrumental role the influential former senator had in securing federal funding to make this dream a reality.

Access the west-side parking area from downtown Hood River by going to the junction of State Street and Route 35, then head up the hill on Old Columbia River Drive. This road is actually the Historic Columbia River

Highway, officially numbered as U.S. 30. The west-side parking area has a small visitors center with restrooms.

Going west to east allows a hiker, in a mere five miles, to witness a rapid climate and vegetation transition rarely encountered in such a short distance. Starting on the Hood River side, the highway winds its way through lush towering Douglas fir groves. By the time you reach the east side of the tunnels by Mosier, you're in a dry oak savanna-grassland ecosystem.

About halfway down the trail, a short interpretive loop trail has been developed, rewarding hikers with stunning views of this varied and beautiful part of the gorge. Also, amateurs of geology will marvel at the dramatic precipice located across the river in Washington, visible from the east end. Locally called "Coyote Wall," it's technically part of a big syncline-anticline system in the area.

◖ Rowena Crest and Tom McCall Nature Preserve

East of Mosier, a section of the Historic Columbia River Highway begins again for automobile traffic, climbing up over a spectacular volcanic promontory called **Rowena Crest.** For eastbound traffic, this route begins at Mosier, at I-84 Exit 69, while westbound traffic can pick up the route at I-84 Exit 76.

Almost nowhere else can you see both the dry eastern and wetter western faces of the Columbia River Gorge with such clarity and distinction as at Rowena Crest. The dark Columbia River basalt cliffs are derived from massive lava flows 15 million years ago. The terracing of the region was due to the action of the Missoula Floods on the Columbia

Plateau fault scarps. More information on the geology and ecosystem is available from a free pamphlet in the drop box on the north side of the highway, courtesy of the Tom McCall Nature Preserve. This 2,300-acre sanctuary on part of Rowena Crest was created by the Nature Conservancy and has trails on the hillsides that are open to the public.

These cliffs represented the beginning of the last hurdle facing Willamette Valley-bound Oregon Trail pioneers. After Rowena, the gorge cliffs rose so high that the pioneers were forced either to build rafts and float the then-hazardous rapids on the river or to follow the Barlow Trail around the south flank of Mount Hood.

Today, **Tom McCall Nature Preserve** is the site of a mid-May pilgrimage of wildflower lovers. Because the preserve lies in the transition zone between the wet west and the dry east, several hundred species flourish here, including four that occur nowhere else in the world. In the spring display you'll find yellow wild sunflowers, purple blooms of shooting stars, scarlet Indian paintbrush, and blue-flowered camas. While the flowers are enticing, beware of ticks and poison oak. Of course, as with any nature preserve or public park, enjoy the flowers but leave them behind for the next person as well.

Food

Mosier, a dramatically situated town of just over 400 people, doesn't offer much in the way of tourism facilities, but there is the charming **Thirsty Woman Pub** (904 2nd Ave., 541/478-0199, www.thirstywoman.com, 4pm-10pm Mon.-Sat. and 5am-11pm Sun.), a lively brewhouse with over 30 microbrews on tap and a selection of burgers.

The Dalles

It hits you shortly after leaving Hood River. Verdant forests give way to scrub oak, which transition to sage and the grasslands of eastern Oregon. You've come to The Dalles, a place Lewis and Clark called the "Trading Mart of the Northwest" in 1805. Instead of seeing a Native American potlatch on the Columbia River, however, the modern visitor will see 10,000 souls living in the industrial hub of the Gorge. One also sees now-defunct aluminum plants and Google's new multimillion-dollar processor farm, both near the river.

These days, The Dalles (the name derives from the French word for flagstone) focuses on historical tourism as well as an emerging red-wine grape industry and already-thriving cherry-growing agriculture. The new Google facility is expected to provide about 200 new jobs for the community.

For a traveler interested in Northwest history, gaining a complete perspective of Oregon's past is impossible without a day trip to The Dalles. Downtown is awash in bits of Oregon's heritage—the Oregon Trail Marker, the stunning 1897 Old St. Peters Landmark church, and the historic Baldwin Saloon. Explore the old Fort Dalles grounds and the Fort Dalles Museum, housed in the original surgeon's quarters from the days when the fort was active. Another early landmark, Pulpit Rock, still stands in the middle of 12th Street, just as it did in the 1800s when the Methodist ministers preached to the Native American population and settlers. Enjoy the work of local artists at The Dalles Art Center, located in the historic Carnegie Library.

The Dalles played a preeminent role in Oregon's early history. Five hundred years ago, nowhere in the Northwest boasted such a cosmopolitan mix of peoples as the area around The Dalles. During the great fall and spring migrations of salmon, the banks of the Columbia River—and particularly those near Celilo Falls, just upstream and now smothered by The Dalles Dam—were lined with many Native American groups trading, fishing, performing ceremonies, gambling, and socializing. Lewis and Clark floated passed The Dalles in 1905, and later the land route of the Oregon Trail terminated at The Dalles, as the Gorge's high cliffs and rapids precluded further wagon travel along the Columbia.

The first white settlement at this transport hub was a Methodist mission, established in 1838. In 1854 the town of The Dalles was platted, and a town charter was granted in 1857. Then as now, the Gorge was the principal corridor between eastern and western Oregon, and almost all freight bound in either direction passed through The Dalles. Steamboats docked at the riverfront; stagecoaches rattled off to far-flung desert communities. The streets were crowded with miners, ranchers, and traders.

The completion of the railroad and later barge lines through Columbia River reservoirs served to increase freight transport through The Dalles. The area is also the nation's largest producer of sweet cherries, and orchard workers from Latin America impart the community with cultural influences from their countries of origin. Despite the recreational boom of the last decade, The Dalles remains largely hardworking and practical.

SIGHTS

Klindt's Booksellers (315 E. 2nd St., 541/296-3355, www.klindtsbooks.com, 8am-6pm Mon.-Sat., 11am-4pm Sun.) represents a bit of history in The Dalles. Established in 1870, it is the oldest bookstore in Oregon, complete with original wood floors, a high ceiling, and oak and plate-glass display cases.

The Dalles Dam

The Dalles Dam and Lock have reopened for tours on a limited basis, after closing to public access for a decade after the terrorist bombings of September 11, 2001. Tours start at the

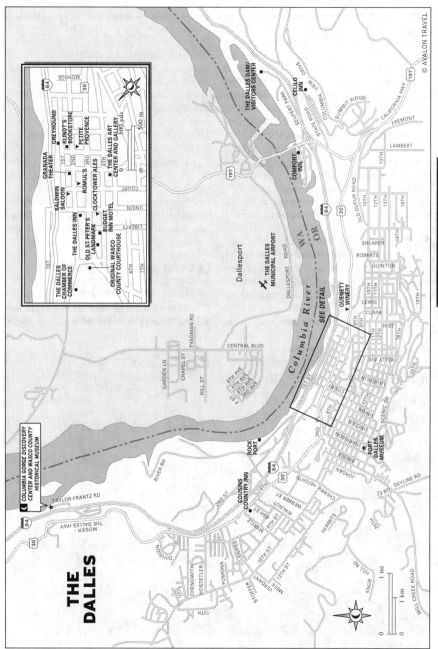

COLUMBIA RIVER GORGE

THE DALLES

THE DALLES DAM/VISITORS CENTER

Dallesport

THE DALLES MUNICIPAL AIRPORT

Columbia River

SEE DETAIL

QUENETT WINERY

CENTRAL BLVD

GARDEN LN
CHAPEL ST
TYADMAN RD
HILL ST
6TH AVE
5TH AVE
4TH AVE
3RD AVE

COLUMBIA GORGE DISCOVERY CENTER AND WASCO COUNTY HISTORICAL MUSEUM

ROCK FORT

FORT DALLES MUSEUM

COUSINS COUNTRY INN

TAYLOR-FRANTZ RD

MOSIER
THE DALLES HWY

RIVER RD

© AVALON TRAVEL

CELILO INN
COMFORT INN
SUMMIT RIDGE
CALIFORNIA HWY
FREMONT
LAMBERT
SHEARER
ROBERTS
QUINTON
LEWIS
CLARK
LAUGHLIN
SCENIC DR
OLD DUFUR ROAD

1 mi
1 km

Detail inset

MONROE

GREYHOUND
KLINDT'S BOOKSTORE
PETITE PROVENCE
GRANADA THEATER
BALDWIN SALOON
ROMUL'S
CLOCKTOWER ALES
THE DALLES ART CENTER AND GALLERY
THE DALLES INN
OLD ST PETER'S LANDMARK
BUDGET INN MOTEL
THE DALLES CHAMBER OF COMMERCE
ORIGINAL WASCO COUNTY COURTHOUSE

1ST
2ND
3RD
COURT
UNION
LIBERTY
6TH
7TH

500 m
500 yds

dam's visitors center in Seufert Park (I-84 Exit 87, 541/296-9778, 10am-5pm daily Memorial Day-Labor Day, free), where you'll find an aquarium stocked with fish from the Columbia River, a live-camera view of the fish going up the fish ladder, a film and several interactive displays. In Seufert Park are rose gardens and a well-watered picnic area.

One-hour tours lead to the dam's power generation and fish passage facilities, and are available on weekends only between Memorial Day and Labor Day, Saturdays at 11am and Sundays at 2pm. For security reasons, the tours are available to U.S. citizens only; visitors 16 and older must have valid photo ID. (People of any nationality are welcome at the visitors center).

Fort Dalles Museum

Established in 1850, **Fort Dalles** (15th St. and Garrison St., 541/296-4547, www.fortdalles-museum.org, 10am-4pm daily Apr.-Oct., $5 adult) was meant to protect the incoming settlers along the Oregon Trail from the large Native American presence in the area. At the time it was built, Fort Dalles was the only U.S. Army garrison between the Pacific Coast and Wyoming.

Of the original 10-square-mile encampment, only a grassy park with the Surgeon's Quarters, dating back to 1856, remains. The wooden structure serves as a museum for armaments, period furniture, and other pioneer items, as well as Native American artifacts. This is Oregon's oldest historic museum, dating back to 1905.

Just down the hill, **Pulpit Rock,** a curious thumb of rock near the corner of 12th and Court Streets, combines geology and theology. From this natural pulpit, early Methodist missionaries preached to the Native Americans. The rock still serves as a pulpit for local Easter services.

◖ Columbia Gorge Discovery Center and Wasco County Historical Museum

The **Columbia Gorge Discovery Center and Wasco County Historical Museum** (5000

The Columbia Gorge Discovery Center is the region's top museum.

© BILL MCRAE

Discovery Dr. N., Crates Point, 3 miles west of The Dalles on U.S. 30, 541/296-8600, www. gorgediscovery.org, 9am-5pm daily, $9 adults, $7 seniors, $5 ages 6-16) brings together the rich historical, geological, biological, and cultural legacies of this region. The Discovery Center addresses the region as a whole, articulating a 40-million-year timeline with scale models and videos (as well as simulated "hands-on" experiences) that begins with the cataclysms that created the Gorge on through its Native American occupation to the coming of the pioneers and subsequent domination by European Americans. Along the way, native plants and animals are given attention along with such diverse activities as road building, orchards, and windsurfing. A decent cafeteria is located on-site.

Wine-Tasting

The arid hills around The Dalles are home to a number of vineyards, and there's one standout winery right in town. **Quenett Winery** (901 E. 2nd St., 541/298-8900, noon-6pm daily) pours excellent wines in a tasting room that occupies a fantastic space: a renovated, century-old flour mill that has been brought back to life with all of its belts, pulleys, and chutes in place. It's worth a stop just to take in the magnificent infrastructure, but the wine is also a big draw, particularly the round and quenching viognier and velvety Grenache. On most Friday evenings, the winery remains open until 8pm with live music and light food service.

ACCOMMODATIONS

Conveniently located off I-84 Exit 87, the **Comfort Inn** (351 Lone Pine Dr., 541/298-2800, $109-139) has a pool, a fitness facility, and free continental breakfast. Rooms come equipped with microwaves and coffeemakers. **Cousins Country Inn** (2114 W. 6th St., 541/298-5161 or 800/848-9378, www.cousinscountryinn.com, $109-124 and up) is a high-quality motel with an indoor hot tub and an outdoor pool. Guest rooms have microwaves, refrigerators, and coffeemakers; some have

fireplaces. The on-site restaurant and lounge is one of The Dalles's most popular.

At the west end of the historic downtown is **The Dalles Inn** (112 2nd St., 541/296-9107 or 888/935-2378, www.thedallesinn. com, $99-129 and up), a well-maintained motor court with a pool, a restaurant, a bar, and guest rooms with microwaves, refrigerators, and coffeemakers. It's also within easy walking distance of downtown bars and restaurants. For clean, basic rooms at a good price, consider the **Budget Inn Motel** (118 West 4th St., 541/296-5464, www.motel-thedalles.com, $60-990, convenient to historic downtown.

The area's top lodging choice, particularly if you're looking for Gorge views and a cool sophisticated decor, is the 【 **Celilo Inn** (3550 East 2nd St., 541/769-0001, www.celiloinn. com, $99-139 and up). This unlikely boutique motel sits atop cliffs just east of The Dalles, and makes the most of its modest mid-20th-century heritage through a stylish transformation that generates attention in national design magazines. Rooms are nicely furnished with a hip, retro-urban design—not something you expect in The Dalles. There's also a patio, an outdoor pool, and a fitness center. All rooms come with mini fridges and microwaves. The only problem is that the Celilo Inn is far from restaurants, but you can't beat the stylish atmosphere.

FOOD

In the heart of downtown, **Petite Provence** (408 E. 2nd St., 541/506-0037, 7:30am-3:30pm Sun.-Wed., 7:30am-5pm Thurs.-Sat., $5-12) is a French-style bakery and coffee shop that also offers sandwiches, soup, and light entrées at lunch.

Baldwin Saloon (1st St. and Court St., 541/296-5666, 11am-9pm Mon.-Thurs., 11am-10pm Fri.-Sat., $8-18) is in an 1876 building that has seen a bit of history—it was built as the dining hall for the local railroad crews. The redbrick interior houses a repository of early-20th-century oil paintings and an 18-foot mahogany bar. Fresh oysters are the house

COLUMBIA RIVER GORGE

THE COLUMBIA GORGE IN THE JOURNALS OF LEWIS AND CLARK

The dramatic topography the explorers described in *The Journals of Lewis and Clark*, as well as accounts of their own undaunted courage, remain to inspire modern-day Columbia Gorge travelers. In the course of a day, you can visit all the landmarks noted by the Corps of Discovery during 17 days in the winter of 1805 and 12 days in the spring of 1806.

On November 3, 1805, the Corps of Discovery's journey to the Pacific temporarily halted at the mouth of the **Sandy River** at present-day Lewis and Clark State Park in Troutdale. It was in this approximate location that Meriwether Lewis noted the river's current threw out "emence quantities of sand and is very shallow. Clark attempted to wade across but found the bed was a very bad quicksand." The incident inspired the name "Sandy River," but in actuality there is no quicksand here.

The expedition traveled upstream 1.5 miles on the Sandy before returning to make camp on Diamond Island in the Columbia River, now known as Government Island. This island is now crossed by the present-day I-205 bridge northeast of Portland. Noting the presence of more game and timber for fuel in the western gorge than east of the Cascades, Lewis and Clark considered this region a "good wintering place" before their eventual choice of Fort Clatsop on the coast.

Besides the availability of resources for survival, the gorge's western portal had special significance for the expedition. Their arrival here in early November 1805 marked the first time in thousands of miles the Corps of Discovery had reached an area documented by previous explorers, the 1792 Vancouver Expedition. By combining the routes charted by the British navy west of the Sandy River with the transcontinental route followed by the Corps of Discovery east of this waterway, the United States could be mapped for the first time from sea to shining sea.

An observation on November 3, 1805, by Private Joseph Whitehouse suggests that this juncture of the expedition's journey was auspicious for other reasons:

> Towards evening we met Several Indians in a canoe who were going up the River. They Signed to us that in two Sleeps we Should See the Ocean vessels and white people.

Heading east on their homeward journey in April 1806 the expedition camped the better part of a week on a "handsome prairie" opposite the Sandy to make some "selestial observations, to examine the Quicksand River and kill some meat."

During this time, three men canoed about six miles up the Sandy. Meanwhile, the captains had determined from local natives that they had bypassed a major Columbia tributary en route to their present location at the western portal of the gorge. According to the *Journals*, the natives also communicated to the explorers that the river drained an "open plain of great extent." Accompanied by seven men and a Native American guide, Clark backtracked to explore the lower Willamette River, making landfall in the northern part of present-day Portland. The discovery of this tributary, which Clark called the Multnomah River, planted seeds for future exploration and settlement in the Willamette Valley, Oregon's current center of population, agriculture, and commerce.

Beacon Rock, the 848-foot core of an ancient volcano, is another prominent topographic feature described by Lewis and Clark. It first becomes visible to eastbound Historic Highway travelers at Portland Women's Forum State Park in Corbett, Oregon. It is the world's second-highest freestanding monolith after Gibraltar. Beacon Rock's name is commonly thought to have derived from its visibility, but on October 31, 1805, Clark noted:

> A remarkable high detached rock stands in a bottom on the starboard side near the lower part of this island

about 800 feet high and 400 paces around we call the Beaten rock.

Not until the homeward journey in April 1806 did the *Journals* refer to it by its current name. On April 6, Lewis observed that:

It is only in the fall of the year when the river is low that the tides are persceptable as high at the beacon rock.

The superlatives Lewis and Clark used to describe Multnomah Falls echo the adjectives in guidebooks today:

We passed several beautifull casscades which fell from a great height over the Stupendous rocks which closes the river on both sides nearly, except for a small bottom on the South side in which our hunters were encamped. The most remarkable of these casscades falls about 300 feet perpendicularly over a solid rock into a narrow bottom of the river on the south side. It is a large creek situated about 5 miles above our encampment of the last evening. Several smaller streams fall from a much greater hight, and in their decent become a perfect mist which collecting on the rocks below again become visible and decend a second time in the same manner before they reach the base of the rocks.

At The Dalles, Rock Fort, a naturally fortified indentation in the rocky riverbank, was Lewis and Clark's favored local campsite both to and from the Pacific. The corps must have presented a curious spectacle to the native people who gathered around them, as the explorers had become infested with fleas. Lewis wrote in his journal:

[The fleas] are very troublesom and dificuelt to get rid of, perticularly as the men have not a Change of Clothes to put on, they strip off their Clothes and kill the flees, dureing which time they remain nakid.

COLUMBIA RIVER GORGE

© BILL MCRAE

Lewis and Clark camped at Rock Fort in 1805.

COLUMBIA RIVER GORGE

specialty, but the sandwiches, salads, steaks, and burgers are also good.

C **Romul's** (312 Court St., 541/296-9771, 4pm-close Mon.-Sat., $12-26) is a good Italian restaurant with a decor that's meant to recall imperial Rome. Fortunately, the food is more reminiscent of Tuscany. There is a selection of excellent pasta dishes and a number of chicken and seafood dishes that provide a bit of variety in an otherwise pretty meat-and-potatoes town; try the seafood romesco. Romul's makes an excellent Caesar salad, and the wine list has an impressive selection of both Italian and local bottles.

Downtown, The Dalles has its share of handsome historic structures, and one of the most notable is the 1881 Wasco County Courthouse, topped with a bell tower. After serving as a Masonic hall and funeral parlor, this landmark is now home to **Clock Tower Ales** (311 Union St., 541/705-3590, 11am-10pm daily, $7-14), a taproom serving regional brews and light meals such as sandwiches and salads.

INFORMATION AND SERVICES

Shortly after you enter town via Exit 82 (City Center exit), stop off at **The Dalles Area Chamber of Commerce** (404 W. 2nd St. at Portland St., 541/296-2231 or 800/255-3385, www.thedalleschamber.com) and pick up its pamphlets *The Dalles: Historic Gateway to the Columbia Gorge* and *Walking Tours to Historic Homes and Buildings.* Take a gander at the restored Wasco County Courthouse next door, which was moved from its original location. This court presided over much of the country west of the Rockies in the mid-1800s. At the time, Wasco County comprised 130,000 square miles and included parts of Idaho and Wyoming.

GETTING THERE

Greyhound provides bus service from The Dalles west to Portland and east to Spokane and Boise. The terminal is at 201 Federal Street (541/296-2421).

Clock Tower Ales resides in the landmark 1881 Wasco County Courthouse.

© BILL MCRAE

Mount Hood

Oregon's highest peak, Mount Hood (or "Wy'east," as the region's Native Americans knew it), rises 11,249 feet above sea level less than an hour's drive from Portland and dominates the city's eastern horizon. Like Japan's Mount Fuji, California's Shasta, and Washington's Rainier, Adams, and St. Helens, Hood is a composite volcano (or stratovolcano), a steep-sided conical mountain built up of layers of lava and ash over millennia.

Mount Hood was formed about 500,000 years ago and has since erupted repeatedly, most recently during two periods over the last 1,500 years. Centuries before the first European explorers entered the region, native people of the Pacific Northwest witnessed the mountain's eruptions, and the retelling of the events became lore handed down over generations. According to one legend, Wy'east and

Pahto were sons of the Great Spirit, Sahale, who both fell in love with a beautiful maiden named Loowit. She was unable to choose between the two, and the braves fought bitterly to win her affection, laying waste to forests and villages in the process. In his anger at the destruction, Sahale transformed the three into mighty mountains: Loowit became Mount St. Helens, Pahto became Mount Adams, and to the south, Wy'east became Mount Hood.

The first European to report seeing the mountain was British Navy Lt. William E. Broughton, who viewed it in 1792 from the Columbia River near the mouth of the Willamette River. Broughton named the peak after the British Navy's Admiral Samuel Hood, who would never see the mountain himself.

Hood's most recent volcanic episode ended in the 1790s, just prior to the arrival of Lewis

© JUDY JEWELL

Mount Hood

and Clark in 1805. On October 18, 1805, William Clark sighted Mount Hood, and made this laconic entry in his journal: "Saw a mountain bearing SW conocal form Covered with Snow." They named the peak Timm Mountain after the Native American name for the waterfall area near The Dalles before they learned that it had already been named by the British. As the Corps of Discovery passed farther down the Columbia River, they encountered a wide shallow river still clogged with sediment from the recent eruptions and named it the Quicksand River. Today, it's the Sandy River, which flows some 50 miles from the flanks of Mount Hood to the Columbia. About 40 years later, on the south side of Mount Hood, Oregon Trail pioneers opened the Barlow Road, the first wagon trail over the Cascades, leading down to the Willamette Valley.

Since record-keeping began in the 1820s, no significant volcanic activity has been noted, though in 1859, 1865, and 1903 observers mentioned the venting of steam accompanied by red glows or "flames." Although the mountain is quiet, volcanologists keep a careful watch on Mount Hood.

Today, the mountain is the breathtaking centerpiece of the Mount Hood National Forest, which embraces 1,067,043 acres of natural beauty and recreational opportunities right in Portland's backyard. Five downhill ski resorts and numerous cross-country trail systems, 1,200 miles of hiking trails, dozens of jewel-like alpine lakes, and more than 80 campgrounds are just the beginning.

SIGHTS
C Timberline Lodge

Timberline Lodge (6 miles north of Government Camp, 503/622-7979 or 800/547-1406, www.timberlinelodge.com) is one of the unquestioned masterpieces of rustic Craftsman design and an object of veneration for those who look back to the Depression-era building boom as a golden age of social and artistic idealism. Over two million people visit Timberline each year, making it one of the top tourist destinations in the state.

When it was built in 1936 and 1937, the four-story 43,700-square-foot log and stone lodge was the largest of the federal Works Progress Administration (WPA) projects in Oregon. It employed up to 500 workers and artists for whom building Timberline was more than just a job; it was an expression of a cultural ideal. In a pamphlet from that time, one eager observed noted: "In Mt Hood's Timberline Lodge the mystic strength that lives in the hills has been captured in wood and stone, and in the hands of laborer and craftsman, has been presented as man's effort at approximating an ideal in which society, through concern for the individual, surpasses the standard it has unconsciously set for itself."

Nearly every part of the structure and its decor was handcrafted, from the selection of stones in the massive lobby fireplaces to the hand-loomed coverlets on the beds. Every effort was made to harmonize with the natural splendor of the location; stonecutters quarried local stone for the walls, and builders employed locally harvested timber for the floors, staircases, and monumental three-story lobby. The six-sided central tower was designed to echo the peak of Mount Hood; the steeply slanted rooflines are meant to resemble mountain ridges. Even the exterior paint color was specially created to match the hue of mountain frost.

The results of this astonishing attention to detail and handcraftsmanship is vividly on display in the lobby and central foyer. The massive fireplace built of local basalt rises 92 feet through three floors of open lobby; all the furniture in the hotel was made by hand in WPA carpentry halls, fanciful hand-carved animals adorn newel posts and stairways, and murals and paintings of stocky stylized workers grace the walls. It's hard to imagine a more powerful relic of the 1930s' glorification of the worker than this.

The lodge is open to nonguests, so be sure to stop by for a hot chocolate or a meal (there are three dining rooms and two bars). The **Rachael Griffin Historic Exhibition Center,** on the main floor, displays some of the history of the lodge in tools, drawings, weavings, and photographs. A free 30-minute video that illustrates the construction of the lodge is shown daily at 12:30pm in the Barlow Room, and Forest Service rangers offer free tours at 11am, 1pm, 2pm, and 3pm daily.

Cascade Streamwatch

Near the village of Welches, on the west side of Mount Hood, pull off U.S. 26 to visit the **Cascade Streamwatch** at the Wildwood Recreation site (between mileposts 39 and 40). This 0.75-mile gently rolling and accessible wetlands trail goes through a beautiful second-growth mixed conifer forest along the Salmon River to several viewing windows built into the shoreline embankment, giving visitors a great opportunity to view fish in a natural river. Trailside fish carvings and sculptures along with information placards on forest ecology and salmon spawning enhance the experience, and you may see such species as the giant Pacific salamander, red-legged frog, and coho salmon. While spring and fall spawning seasons are optimal times to see the coho, it's possible to spot fish at most times of the year. The trail is located 39 miles east of Portland on the south side of the highway in the Bureau of Land Management's **Wildwood Recreation corridor** (503/375-5646) near the town of Zigzag. A nearby pullout offers information about the Barlow Road, the final leg of the Oregon Trail, which went through these woods.

The Philip Foster Farm and Homestead

The Philip Foster Farm and Homestead (29912 SE Rte. 211, Eagle Creek, 503/637-6324, 11am-4pm Fri.-Sun. mid-June-Sept., donations appreciated) is the end of the historic Barlow Road, the place that greeted the emigrants after crossing Mount Hood en route to the Willamette Valley. This working historical farm features a home, an antique barn, a blacksmith shop filled with period artifacts, and pioneer gardens of flowers, herbs, and vegetables. There is also an apple orchard containing

varieties from the pioneer era. Visitors can have hands-on experience grinding corn, building log cabins, and partaking of other chores typical of the pioneers. The Pioneer Store features Pacific Northwest food, crafts, and history-oriented items. A lilac bush dating back to 1843 is also of interest. Shady picnic tables make this site ideal for a family outing. Just pick up Route 211 off U.S. 26 in Sandy and head south for 6 miles to Eagle Creek.

HIKING

Hikes in the **Zigzag Ranger District** (70220 U.S. 26 E., Zigzag, 541/666-0704 or 503/622-3191 from Portland) are an excellent introduction to the wealth of recreation options in the Mount Hood National Forest off U.S. 26. Whether you're driving the whole **Mount Hood Loop** (U.S. 26-Rte. 35-I-84) or just looking for a nice day trip from the Portland area, the Zigzag District's relatively low elevation and spectacular views of the state's highest mountain can be enjoyed by neophyte hikers or trail-wise veterans.

If you're coming in from the west, stop at the **Mount Hood Information Center** (65000 U.S. 26 E., Welches, 541/622-4822 or 888/622-4822, www.mthood.info) in the Mount Hood Village Resort on the south side of the highway. This facility will help you get your bearings with a wealth of pamphlets and an information desk. Pick up the free Forest Service flyer *Mount Hood Hikes.*

Salmon River Trail

The **Salmon River Trail** is pretty, easy, and low-elevation, meaning that there's no excuse not to hike it. The 33-mile Salmon River is one of the very few waterways protected as a National Wild and Scenic River for its entire length—from its headwaters on Mount Hood to its confluence with the Sandy River near Brightwood. This trail, which runs 14 miles in the Salmon-Huckleberry Wilderness Area but is most often hiked in much smaller sections, runs right alongside the river; hikers can expect to see wildflowers, old-growth Douglas firs, and a number of campgrounds. In fall, enjoy red and gold maples; year-round, giant cedars and firs dominate. Access is easy, especially to the lower portion of the trail. From Sandy, follow U.S. 26 east for 17.9 miles and turn right (south) onto the Salmon River Road. Follow this road 5 miles to the trailhead.

◖ Ramona Falls Trail

The **Ramona Falls Trail** is a 4.5-mile loop to a stunning waterfall is one of the most popular on Mount Hood. From the trailhead, it initially parallels the Sandy River. In a little more than a mile you'll come to a seasonal bridge over the river with a pretty view of Mount Hood. On the other side of the river, Trail 797 will get you to Ramona Falls in about 2 miles. The grade of the slope is gentle throughout, and while much of the trail isn't especially scenic (except for the bridge over the Sandy River, June rhododendrons, and views of Mount Hood), Ramona Falls itself makes it all worthwhile.

Here a multitude of cascades course over a 100-foot-high, 50-foot-wide series of basalt

Ramona Falls cascades down a wall of columnar basalt.

outcroppings. This weeping wall is set in a grove of gargantuan Douglas firs. The spray beneath this canopy of trees can reduce the temperature by 20°F, making the place a popular retreat on hot summer days.

This trail connects with the Pacific Crest Trail, and backpackers often use it as part of a longer trip.

To reach Ramona Falls, drive 18 miles east of Sandy on U.S. 26 to Lolo Pass Road, close by the ranger station. Turn left (north) and go 5 miles up Lolo Pass Road; stay right onto Forest Service Road 1825. From here, you'll take the road about 4 miles to its end.

McNeil Point Shelter

Although the **McNeil Point Shelter** hike is gorgeous and culminates at a cool old stone shelter, it has some tricky trail nuances and requires a map and consultation, both available at the Mount Hood Information Center. The trailhead is not far from Ramona Falls, making this is a nice follow-up to that hike. (Between the two hikes, you can camp at the McNeil Campground.)

Start at the Top Spur Trailhead. A half-mile up the hiking trail, take a right on the Pacific Crest Trail and keep right, continuing up the trail to a four-way intersection. Views of Mount Hood—and in June, a spectacular wildflower display—will greet you.

The remaining 3 miles contain some twists and turns (essentially, you're skirting Bald Mountain) that need cartographic clarification from the Forest Service. Your reward will be breathtaking above-timberline views of the Mount Hood National Forest. This excursion is 4 miles each way and tame enough for weekend warriors. Just start early to give yourself sufficient daylight.

To reach the McNeil Point trailhead from U.S. 26, turn north onto Lolo Pass Road at Zigzag and follow it 4 miles. Veer right onto Forest Service Road 1828 and proceed 13 miles until you reach the Top Spur Trailhead 785.

Mirror Lake Trail

It's easy to find the trailhead for the popular

© JUDY JEWELL

BIGFOOT

One of the secrets the Columbia Gorge might share if it could talk would be the whereabouts of Bigfoot, or Sasquatch.

Whether it exists outside the mind or not, the King Kong of the Pacific Northwest forests has attracted to the region everyone from hunters and academics to curiosity seekers and *National Enquirer* reporters. Although the notion of a half-man, half-ape eluding human capture seems implausible at first, a brief look at some of the evidence might convince you otherwise.

Native Americans of the region regarded this creature as a fact of life and celebrated its presence in art and ritual. As recently as the winter of 1991, reports from a remote area of eastern Oregon's Blue Mountains told of more than 60 miles of tracks left in the snow by a large five-toed creature. Scientists on the scene were of the opinion that the pattern of the prints and the gait could not have been faked. A similar conclusion was reached in 1982 about a plaster cast of footprints taken from the same mountain range. A Washington State University professor detected humanlike whorls on the toe portions of the prints, which he said showed that the tracks had to have been made by a large hominid.

Reports and evidence of actual encounters abound in Pacific Northwest annals, compelling the U.S. Army Corps of Engineers to list the animal as an indigenous species, accompanied by a detailed anatomical description. Skamania County, Washington, whose southern border is the Columbia River shoreline, declared the harming of these creatures a gross misdemeanor punishable by a year in jail and a $1,000 fine.

The unwavering belief in Bigfoot and the native insistence that it's a living entity have naturally met with skepticism. But considering that stories about black-and-white bears roaming the alpine hinterlands of China persisted for centuries until the 1936 discovery of pandas, there could be something new under the sun in the 21st century.

Mirror Lake Trail—it's right on U.S. 26, and it's usually marked by a fleet of parked cars. There's good reason for the crowd: The 1.5-mile trail gains 700 feet in elevation and passes wild rhododendrons and a passel of other wildflowers on the way up to the lake that, as its name suggests, forms a perfect reflecting mirror for Mount Hood. A trail circumnavigates the lake, and ambitious hikers can continue another 2 miles to the top of Tom, Dick, and Harry Mountain.

Find the trailhead at the footbridge 1 mile west of Government Camp on U.S. 26. Because of its popularity, try to do this hike on a weekday.

Timberline Trail

More ambitious trekkers will take on the 40-mile **Timberline Trail,** a three- to five-day backpacking trip usually started at Timberline Lodge. If you undertake this loop, you'll finish up back at the lodge to cool off in the showers or swimming pool. While the alpine meadows on the Timberline Trail are beautiful, consult the rangers to see if water in the half-dozen creeks forded en route is too high during the June-July snowmelt season.

With almost two dozen trails branching off the Timberline, opportunities for shorter day-trip loop hikes abound. Most of the main trail follows the base of the mountain near the timberline at elevations of 5,000-7,000 feet. On the northwest side, however, it drops to 3,000 feet and merges with the Pacific Crest Trail. This means that there's snow on the trail most of the year. Make the trip in the early fall to avoid the crowds; in July and August the mountain meadows are ablaze with wildflowers.

Backpackers must camp at least 200 feet from water and 100 feet from any trail, mountain meadow, or obvious viewpoint.

Buried Forest Overlook

An easy one-mile round-trip leads to the

© JUDY JEWELL

Above Timberline Lodge are the Timberline Trail and the Pacific Crest Trail.

Buried Forest Overlook, which provides a dramatic view of the White River Canyon, where a thick forest was buried during one of the mountain's major eruptive periods 200-250 years ago. Superheated gases blew down giant trees like matchsticks, and in the next instant everything was buried underneath a mixture of water, ash, and mud. The forces of wind and water erosion have since exposed the remains of the Buried Forest. To get here, follow one of the trails behind Timberline Lodge up the mountain about 0.25 mile until you reach the Pacific Crest National Scenic Trail. Turn east (right) onto the Pacific Crest Trail and follow it another 0.25 mile or so to the overlook.

Cloud Cap

The best way to get up close and personal with Mount Hood is with a visit to **Cloud Cap.** A beautiful old lodge (now closed) and the entrance to the Mount Hood Wilderness are on the north side of the volcano. To get there, take Route 35 south of Hood River 24 miles to Cooper Spur Road. Drive past the ski area

until you come to Cloud Cap at the end of a twisting 10-mile gravel road. The road is passable only in summer months due to snow at that altitude. From here, hardy adventurers can rub elbows with glaciers, walking up Cooper Spur (a side ridge of Mount Hood) without climbing gear in late summer to almost 8,600 feet above sea level.

SKIING

Wherever you ski here, November-April, be sure to purchase and display a **Sno-Park permit** ($20 for the season, $7 for 3 days, $3 one-day). Most ski shops near the slopes sell them.

From Portland you can hear road and ski condition reports on KINK 101.9 FM at 6:30 and 7:30am and 12:15pm Monday-Friday December-March. Log on to www.tripcheck. com or call 800/977-6368 for road conditions and traveler advisory information.

In addition to being the state's highest mountain, Mount Hood also boasts the most ski areas, five in all.

Mount Hood Meadows

The mountain's largest and most varied ski area is **Mount Hood Meadows** (503/287-5438, ext. 182, or 800/754-4663, www.skihood.com, $74 adults full-day, $59 adults afternoon, $39 children), with 2,150 acres of groomed slopes, terrain parks, five high-speed quads, and half a dozen slower lifts. Even with all the lifts, this place is so popular at times you might have to wait. Night skiing is also popular.

Meadows is located 10 miles from Government Camp on Route 35. It's often sunny here on the east slope of the mountain when it's snowing and raining on the west side; call 503/227-7669 for a snow report and hours of operation. Check the ski area's website for current information about bus transportation from Portland.

Cooper Spur Ski Resort

A popular destination for families and beginners is **Cooper Spur Ski Resort** (541/352-7803, www.cooperspur.com, $25 adults, $20 seniors and children). On the northeastern flank of the mountain, 24 miles south of Hood River on Route 35, the location occasionally offers protection from storms and prevailing westerlies yet has more than enough snow for a good time and is more affordable than the other Mount Hood resorts. However, the trails are only served by a slow double chairlift and a rope tow. Nordic skiers appreciate the **Tilly Jane Trail.**

Mount Hood SkiBowl

Mount Hood SkiBowl (503/658-4385, www. skibowl.com, $49 adults, $32 night, $30 seniors and children) is only 53 miles from metropolitan Portland on U.S. 26 and features the most extensive night skiing in the country. The upper bowl has some of the most challenging skiing and snowboarding to be found on the mountain. Within the complex is a summer adventure park for bungee jumping, an alpine slide, mountain biking, and much more.

© JUDY JEWELL

There are many good cross-country ski areas on Mount Hood.

Timberline Ski Area

Timberline Ski Area (503/231-7979 information, 503/222-2211 snow report, www.timberlinelodge.com, $56 adults full-day, $46 afternoon, $27 children full-day, $25 children afternoon) is known for its high-elevation Palmer lift and its nearly year-round season.

With the highest vertical drop of any ski area in Oregon (3,600 feet) as well as the highest elevation accessible by chairlift (8,600 feet), 60 percent of Timberline's ski runs are in the intermediate-level category. Timberline has the longest ski season in the nation.

Although you'll rarely find powder conditions at Timberline, the 31 runs are so well groomed that Timberline snow is easily navigable. The chairlifts (six in winter, two in summer) are mostly obscured by trees or topography, so you get a feeling of intimacy with the natural surroundings when you're schussing downhill. You can go up two lifts, enjoying a nearly two-mile-long run that drops 2,500 feet vertically.

The upper Palmer lift, highest on the mountain, is open late spring-fall, when conditions are safe for skiing on the Palmer glacier. The Magic Mile chair, directly below the Palmer, is open to the 7,000-foot level for sightseers as well as skiers ($15 adults, $42 family).

Located 60 miles east of Portland on U.S. 26, the skiing starts where the trees end. To get here, go east of Government Camp on U.S. 26 and take Forest Service Road 50 for 6 miles. Check the resort's website for information about bus transportation.

Summit Ski Area

A mile south of the Timberline turnoff on U.S. 26 is **Summit Ski Area** (503/272-0256, www.summitskiarea.com, $35 adults, $25 seniors over 60 or children under age 12), the place for families, beginners, and people who just like to play in the snow. You can ski on beginners' slopes or rent an inner tube to barrel down the gently sloping surrounding hills. Several other good sliding hills are close by. To get to Summit, drive through the town of Government Camp off U.S. 26. Beyond the stores and concessions you'll see a large parking lot on the left side of the road with a structure housing a burger joint and equipment rentals.

Cross-Country Skiing

Across Route 35 from the Mount Hood Meadows turnoff, **Teacup Lake** offers a great network of cross-country skiing trails that are maintained by a club that requests a small donation. Another popular trail that's easy after you get past the first long downhill goes to **Trillium Lake.** Find the Sno-Park for this trail about 3 miles east of Government Camp on U.S. 26.

Rent cross-country skis and get info about current conditions in the town of Sandy at **Otto's** (38716 Pioneer Blvd., 503/668-5947).

CLIMBING

Mount Hood (11,239 feet), the highest mountain in Oregon, has the additional distinction of being the second-most-climbed glacier-covered peak in the world. Nicknamed the Fujiyama of America, Mount Hood offers hikes that cater to everyone, from beginners to advanced climbers. Another similarity to its Japanese counterpart is that only a brief part of the year is safe for climbing, from May to mid- or late July.

Since the summer heat brings the threat of avalanche danger and falling rock hazards, the time of day that you depart is just as important as the time of year. Most expeditions set out in the wee hours of the morning when the snow is firm and rock danger is slighter. Although you won't get as much sleep, you will be able to enjoy beautiful sunrise scenery as you venture to the top.

Unless climbers are very experienced, it is best to go with a guide. All climbers should register at the kiosk by Timberline Lodge before climbing and check out after the climb. While the climb looks like just a few miles on the map, it takes 10-15 hours to make the trip from Timberline Lodge to the top and back. The four primary routes up Mount Hood—**Hogsback, Mazama, Wyeast,** and **Castle Crags**—are all technical climbs; there is no hiking trail to the summit. Having the right equipment means little if you don't know how to use it. That said, all climbers should rent a Mount Hood Locator Unit, or MLU, available at local climbing shops and at the Mount Hood Inn off of U.S. 26 in Government Camp.

Guided climbs are offered by **Timberline Mountain Guides** (541/312-9242, www.timberlinemtguides.com, $515). **The Mazamas** (503/227-2345, www.mazamas.org), a Portland hiking and climbing club formed on the summit of Mount Hood in 1894, also leads climbs.

ACCOMMODATIONS

Remember that Mount Hood is just over an hour from Portland, so you can always return to the city if you don't want to spend the night on the mountain.

Timberline Lodge

Of all the lodgings on Mount Hood, one is nearly as archetypal as the mountain itself: **Timberline Lodge** (27500 E. Timberline Rd., Government Camp, 503/622-7979 or 800/547-1406, www.timberlinelodge.com, $130-140 w/o bath, $150-320 w/bath). This massive log lodge, built during the Depression by craftspeople put to work by the Works Progress Administration, is one of the best examples of rustic Craftsman style in the world. Timberline gained even more fame when it was used as the setting for the 1983 film *The Shining* (walk by room 217 and recall "redrum, redrum," with a shiver of fright).

One of the many charms of Timberline is the individuality of each room, which range from bunk bed-equipped "chalet rooms," with a bath down the hall, to large fireplace suites. No matter how humble the room, it will have the lodge's signature hand-loomed curtains and handcrafted furniture. Guests also have access to a sauna and the year-round outdoor pool.

The lodge's lobby is a good place to visit even if you aren't a guest. Take a moment to admire the hand-carved newel posts, sit beside the huge lobby fireplace, or check out the historical displays. The upstairs Ram's Head Bar is a classic spot for an après-ski or post-hike drink, and the **Cascade Dining Room** (7:30am-10am, 11:30am-2pm, 6pm-8pm Mon.-Fri., 7:30am-10:30am, 11:30am-3pm, 5:30pm-8pm Sun., $20-48) serves outstanding though pricey food.

Adventuresome groups of travelers should check out Timberline's **Silcox Hut** ($145-185, includes dinner and breakfast), a spacious but cozy onetime skiers' warming hut perched up the mountain, beyond the main lodge, at 7,000 feet. The hut does have electricity, running water, and toilets, but with its stone walls and big timbers it definitely has rustic charm. Guests reach the hut either by snowcat or the ski area's Magic Mile chairlift and have the option of skiing back down to the base area in the morning. The hut's host prepares a family-style dinner (typically something like lasagna) as well as breakfast. A minimum of 12 people (16 on weekends and holidays) is required to rent the hut; it's also a popular spot for weddings.

Government Camp and Vicinity

Also operated by Timberline Lodge, the **Lodge at Government Camp** (along the Government Camp loop, www.thelodgeatgovernmentcamp.com, $160-190 weekdays, $305-375 weekends, for up to six people, two-night minimum stay) is a rather grand structure that offers eight condo units ranging 2-4 bedrooms. All units are fully furnished and have complete kitchens; guests have access to all facilities at Timberline Lodge.

More conventional lodgings are also available in Government Camp. The **Best Western Mount Hood Inn** (87450 E. Government Camp Loop, 503/272-3205 or 800/443-7777, www.mthoodinn.com, $119-144) is a good bet. If that's too expensive, the venerable **Huckleberry Inn** (88611 E. Government Camp Loop, 503/272-3325, www.huckleberry-inn.com, $90-140) has both standard guest rooms and a slightly funky bunkroom that you can rent for a group of up to 14 people ($185).

A new and outsized condo development, **Collins Lake Resort** (88544 E. Government Camp Loop, 800/234-6288, www.collinslakeresort.com, $189-369 chalet doubles) is in the heart of Government Camp and offers chalets and multibedroom condos.

Speaking of housing large groups, cabins are a cost-effective way for groups of three or more to stay in beautiful surroundings near hiking trails, ski slopes, and other outdoor recreation. Some of the most popular and best-situated cabins on the mountain are those at **Summit Meadow** (503/272-3494, www.summitmeadow.com, $190-265 weekday; $410-625 weekend, minimum two-night stay). The five cabins range from a cozy one-bedroom with a sleeping loft to a large two-bedroom cabin with a loft that'll sleep you and nine of your closest friends. These cabins are located 1.5 miles south of Government Camp in a secluded setting surrounded by national forest. The cabins are open year-round, but in the winter are accessible only by cross-country skiing or snowshoeing in, about 1.5 miles from the Sno-Park.

Mount Hood Village (65000 E. U.S. 26, Welches, 800/255-3069, $129-200) is another good value. Although it is primarily an RV park, it also includes a cluster of wooden cabins and some yurts ($40-60) near the Salmon River. Close by the Forest Service information center and bookstore as well as the Ramona Falls trailhead, Cascade Streamwatch, and the Rendezvous Grill and Tap Room, the resort includes a fitness room and the Courtyard Cafe, which serves breakfast and lunch. Choose between basic "cabins in the woods" sleeping four and large "vacation cottages" with features like hot tubs and saunas.

Cascade Property Management (24403 E. Welches Rd., Suite 104, 503/622-5688 or 800/635-5417, www.mthoodrentals.com) posts dozens of enticing offerings on its website, most located down the mountain around the Sandy River. These cabins come with all the amenities you'd find in a hotel room and then some (firewood and kitchen implements included). Rates vary with the season and the size of the unit. A typical summer rate for a 1,500-square-foot unit with several bedrooms sleeping six might be $235 per night. Rates go as low as $160 for small units to over $500 for larger cabins sleeping more than a dozen people. Many of these cabins enjoy secluded locations, and the rental office provides discounted lift tickets to several Mount Hood ski areas. Look for the rental office just west of the Hoodland shopping center.

For more listings of cabins and property management companies, see www.mthood.info.

Camping

Most of the following campgrounds are in **Mount Hood National Forest** (503/668-1700, www.fs.fed.us). Those that accept reservations are so noted; to inquire about reservations, contact 877/444-6777 or www.recreation.gov.

Set along the banks of the Salmon River is **Green Canyon** (Zigzag Ranger District, 65000 E. U.S. 26, Welches, 503/622-3191, May-mid-Sept., $16-18). Here you'll find 15 campsites for tents and RVs (22 feet maximum), with picnic tables and grills, piped water, pit toilets, and firewood available seasonally. The Salmon River Trail is nearby, and a store and a café are about 5 miles away. To get there, go to Zigzag on U.S. 26 and take Salmon River Road (Forest Rd. 2618) for 4 miles to the campground.

Near the replica of the Barlow Road Tollgate is **Tollgate Campground** (late May-mid-Sept., $16). Set along the banks of the Zigzag River, this campground has 15 sites for tents and RVs up to 16 feet in length. Because it's close to the Mount Hood Wilderness and many hiking trails, it's so popular that finding a campsite without a reservation on a summer weekend is next to impossible. To get here, take U.S. 26 one mile past Rhododendron.

Situated on the Clear Fork of the Sandy River, **McNeil Campground** (May-late Sept., $14) has a good view of Mount Hood. The campground has 34 sites for tents and RVs up to 22 feet in length, with picnic tables and grills, vault toilets, and firewood available. To reach the campground, turn onto Lolo Pass Road (County Rte. 18) at Zigzag and follow it for 4 miles. Turn right onto Forest Service Road 1825 and follow signs to the campground, about 1 mile farther.

A popular place for a night out in the woods is **Camp Creek** (late May-late Sept., $16,

COLUMBIA RIVER GORGE

© GINO RIGUCCI/123RF

Trillium Lake and Mount Hood

firewood are also available. The campground has many large trees and good fishing, and it is close to a pioneer cemetery and Trillium Lake. To reach this spot, drive past Government Camp to Forest Service Road 2650.

A good place for a base camp for those who like to canoe is at **Trillium Lake** (late May-late Sept., $16-32, reservations accepted). Just 60 miles from Portland, the lake is a great place for city kids. If they're ages 13 and under, they don't need a fishing license and may keep up to 10 fish per day. Crayfish also prowl the lake bottom awaiting capture. Families appreciate the opportunity to cruise the lake in a canoe or some other nonmotorized craft. At night, a new amphitheater hosts campfire programs and nature talks. There are 57 sites for tents and RVs (40 feet maximum), with picnic tables and grills. Piped water and flush toilets were installed recently; boat docking and launching facilities are nearby, but no motorized craft are permitted on the lake. To get here, take U.S. 26 two miles southeast of Government Camp, then turn right onto Forest Service Road 2656. Proceed 1 mile to the campground.

A spot that offers good fishing, swimming, and windsurfing is **Clear Lake** (late May-early Sept., $16, reservations accepted). Here you'll find 28 tent and RV sites (32 feet maximum) with picnic tables and grills. Piped water, vault toilets, and firewood are also available. Boat docking and launching facilities are nearby, and motorized craft are allowed on the lake. To get here, go 11 miles southeast of Government Camp on U.S. 26, then 1 mile south on Forest Service Road 2630 to the campground.

A midsize county park called **Toll Bridge** (7360 Toll Bridge Rd., Parkdale, 541/352-6300, Apr.-Nov. and off-season weekends, weather permitting, $18-20) is 18 miles south of Hood River on Route 35. This campground has 18 tent and 20 RV (20 feet maximum) sites with electricity, piped water, sewer hookups, and picnic tables. Flush toilets, showers, firewood, a recreation hall, and a playground are also featured. Set along the banks of the Hood

reservations accepted). This campground has 25 sites for tents and RVs up to 22 feet, with piped water, picnic tables, and grills. Vault toilets and firewood are also available. Situated along Camp Creek not far from the Zigzag River, the campground has double campsites that two parties can share. To get here, go 3 miles east of Rhododendron on U.S. 26 and turn south to the campground.

About 1 mile down the road from Timberline Lodge is **Alpine** (July-late Sept., $16). The high-elevation setting lives up to the name, with snow remaining on the ground until late in the summer in heavy snow years. There are 16 campsites for tents plus piped water, picnic tables, and grills. In addition to easy access to summer skiing up at Mount Hood, the Pacific Crest Trail passes very close to the camp.

Near the junction of U.S. 26 and Route 35 is **Still Creek** (mid-June-late Sept., $16, reservations accepted). Here you'll find 27 sites for tents and RVs (16 feet maximum) with picnic tables and grills. Piped water, pit toilets, and

River, Toll Bridge includes bike trails, hiking trails, and tennis courts.

Nottingham (15 miles south of Parkdale) and **Sherwood** (11 miles south of Parkdale, Hood River Ranger District, 541/352-6002, www.mthood.info, Memorial Day-Labor Day, $12, no reservations) both include basic amenities. Both are located on the east fork of the Hood River and offer good hiking.

FOOD

Far and away, the top dining choice on Mount Hood is the 【 **Cascade Dining Room** (Timberline Lodge, 27500 E. Timberline Rd., Government Camp, 503/622-0700, 7:30am-10am, 11:30am-2pm, 6pm-8pm Mon.-Fri., 7:30am-10:30am, 11:30am-3pm, 5:30pm-8pm Sun., $20-48, dinner reservations recommended). As at most of the top Oregon restaurants, the chefs here prepare meals to showcase regional foods—in this case often wild mushrooms from Mount Hood's forested slopes and huckleberries from its meadows. Even if a full dinner doesn't fit into your plans or your budget, lunch in this huge timbered dining room is a hearty treat—take a break

from skiing for some polenta served with roasted vegetables or a salmon BLT.

Down the hill at the west end of Government Camp, find the **Mount Hood Brewing Company** (87304 E. Government Camp Loop, Government Camp, 503/272-0102, 11am-10pm daily, $8-12). Sandwiches, pasta, chili, and design-your-own pizza can be washed down with microbrews (try their own oatmeal stout), espresso drinks, and local wines. Also in town, the **Huckleberry Inn** (88611 E. Government Camp Loop, Government Camp, 503/272-3325, www.huckleberry-inn.com, $6-14) deserves mention if only for its 24-hour, 7-day-a-week restaurant and, you guessed it, wild huckleberry pie.

INFORMATION

The **Mount Hood Information Center** (65000 E. U.S. 26, Welches, 503/622-4822 or 888/622-4822, www.mthood.info, 9am-5pm daily) is staffed by Forest Service rangers who can provide information about local places of interest. This is really an excellent stop, even for people who travel up to the mountain quite often.

THE WILLAMETTE VALLEY

The Willamette Valley, the primary destination of the Oregon Trail pioneers, is one of the most productive agricultural areas in the world. This is something that is meaningful not only to long-ago pioneers or present-day residents, but to nearly every visitor. Wineries abound, as do plant nurseries and U-pick berry fields. During the spring, the tulip and iris fields are beautiful, especially when (as is common) they're backed up by a rainbow. Superb vegetables, the highest-yielding sweet corn in the United States, and grass seed and hazelnuts that dominate world markets compound the impression of pastures of plenty.

The Willamette Valley is also the population nexus of Oregon, supporting 100 cities and 70 percent of the state's population. (Geographically speaking, Portland is part of the Willamette Valley, but is considered separate.) Nonetheless, once you get south of Portland's suburbs, you'll seldom have the feeling of being in a big metropolis, which is partly thanks to Oregon's land-use regulations, which have historically sought to preserve agricultural land.

Just south of Eugene, the Coast Fork, Middle Fork, and the mainstem Willamette River join and flow north through cities and farmland toward the juncture with the Columbia River just north of downtown Portland. This broad valley, 130 miles long and at some points nearly 60 miles wide, rolls out between the rugged Coast Range and the glaciered peaks of the Cascades. Along the way, the Willamette collects the waters of other large rivers, including the McKenzie, the Santiam, and the Yamhill,

© JUDY JEWELL

HIGHLIGHTS

◖ **Carlton:** The area around Carlton in Yamhill County is a great place to tour some of the nation's top pinot noir and pinot gris wineries (page 179).

◖ **McMinnville:** Wine country's largest town has charm to spare, excellent restaurants, and relatively inexpensive lodging (page 185).

◖ **State Capitol:** The art alone in the Oregon capitol is worth the trip (page 193).

◖ **Mount Angel Abbey:** This hilltop abbey is a good place for both quiet reflection and architectural tourism; the splendid library was designed by famed Finnish architect Alvar Aalto (page 205).

◖ **Silver Falls State Park:** Aren't waterfalls what Oregon is all about? Here, a 7-mile trail passes 10 waterfalls (page 207).

◖ **Breitenbush Hot Springs:** The rest of the world will slip away as you ease into one of the lovely natural hot pools during a yoga or spiritual retreat, a weekend of personal reflection, or simply an afternoon soak (page 208).

◖ **Alton Baker Park:** This sprawling park is home to Pre's Trail, which commemorates the late great runner Steve Prefontaine (page 227).

◖ **McKenzie River National Recreation Trail:** This 26-mile trail follows the McKenzie, with waterfalls cascading over lava rocks and lush green streamside vegetation (page 244).

◖ **Oakridge Mountain Biking:** In the hills just outside this working-class mill town, you'll find some of the state's best mountain biking (page 251).

© AVALON TRAVEL

LOOK FOR ◖ TO FIND RECOMMENDED SIGHTS, ACTIVITIES, DINING, AND LODGING.

and by the time it joins the Columbia, the Willamette is the 10th largest river in the united States.

The deep rich soils of the Willamette Valley are topped with a layer of sand and silt that were deposited 10,500-13,000 years ago during the Lake Missoula floods, the series of enormous ice age floods that scoured out the Columbia River Gorge. These floodwaters backed up the Willamette Valley, depositing fresh soil as the waters receded. Also left behind

were rock specimens that hitched a ride down the Columbia on icebergs. Six miles east of Sheridan off Oldsville Road is an "erratic rock," a 40-ton chunk of Rocky Mountain granite left here as its iceberg host melted (watch for signs for Erratic Rock State Natural Site as you drive Hwy. 18 southwest of McMinnville).

HISTORY

Before the European settlers arrived, the Kalapuya people lived in this fertile valley for

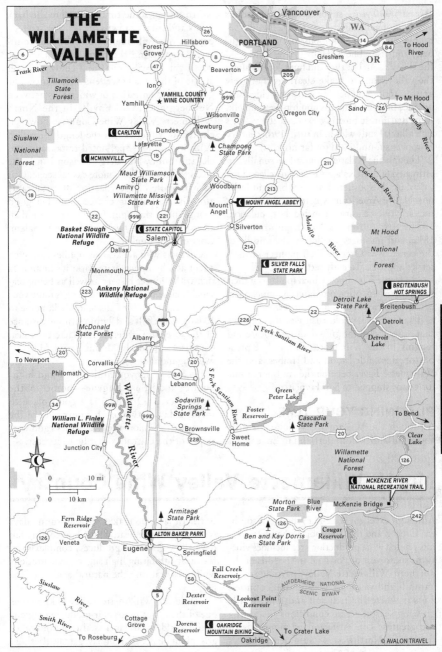

THE WILLAMETTE VALLEY

© AVALON TRAVEL

at least 5,000 years, supplied with near endless amounts of game, berries, camas (a lily-like perennial with a sweet bulbous root), wapato tubers, and fish. The Kalapuya never cultivated the valley's soil, but they did burn forests along the valley floor to make clearings that grew grasses, roots, and berries, which provided sustenance both for humans and for deer and elk. Repeated forest burning exposed the valley's rich alluvial soils which, in turn, 19th-century Europeans found ideal for farming.

Though the Kalapuya moved seasonally, an estimated 80,000 Kalapuyas once dwelled in the valley, until exposure to diseases brought in by non-Native American explorers and traders in the early 19th century decimated the population.

The first European Americans arrived in 1812, and numbers swelled in the middle of the century as Oregon Trail pioneer farmers settled the area. To early settlers, this valley offered a fertile stage upon which to play out their most cherished, often utopian economic, civic, educational, and cultural impulses.

The California gold rush was the impetus that really fueled the growth of agriculture and logging in the Willamette Valley. The prospectors demanded food and timber, and the Willamette River became the transport route for goods shipped to San Francisco.

PLANNING YOUR TIME

Although the Willamette Valley runs only about 100 miles from Portland to Eugene, it's worth taking some time to explore the back roads and smaller towns off I-5. For starters, explore the Willamette Valley's wine country. By spending the night along the way, you'll get to really relax and enjoy a dinner at one of the area's excellent restaurants. The greatest concentration of wineries is between Newberg and McMinnville in the North Willamette Valley Wine Country; however, clusters of wineries run the length of valley. With its fabulous spa, noted restaurant, and elegant rooms, Newberg's Allison Inn is the area's top resort. For a more casual scene, visit McMinnville's large selection of restaurants and diverse lodging choices, another good spot to spend the night. It's also easy to add an afternoon of wine-tasting to a stay in Salem, Corvallis, or Eugene.

Campers who are also oenophiles can pitch a tent at Champoeg State Park; it's in an area rich with pioneer history as well as being reasonably close to wineries. If hiking is more your focus, head to Silver Falls State Park, home to 10 large waterfalls and within striking distance of the Oregon Garden (an 80-acre botanical paradise) and lovely Mount Angel Abbey (a working monastery).

Because of its youthful energy and high-quality facilities, Eugene—home to the University of Oregon—is a good place to spend a day or two, both to experience the town and to explore the river valleys and west slopes of the Cascades that lie to its east.

North Willamette Valley Wine Country

Although excellent wine is a product of southern Oregon and the Columbia Gorge, Oregon's most noted wine production area includes vineyards southwest of Portland in the hills of the northern Willamette Valley, particularly in Yamhill and southern Washington counties. This is where the rich soil and long, gentle growing season create conditions sustaining the greatest concentration of vineyards in the Pacific Northwest. In summer, Oregon's northern latitude makes for long sunny days without excessive heat, while slow-cooling fall days allow grapes to produce a complexity of flavor by inhibiting high sugar concentrations while maintaining the natural acidity of the grape.

While the Willamette Valley is known as one of the major pinot noir-producing regions in the world, local wineries also put out pinot gris, pinot blanc, chardonnay, gamay, Riesling,

Gewürztraminer, sparkling wine, sauvignon blanc, cabernet, merlot, and other offerings.

Even locals find it difficult to keep up with the burgeoning northern Willamette Valley wine scene, with some 300 vineyards and wineries gracing the rolling hills. **Willamette Valley Wineries** (503/646-2985, www.willamettewines.com) maintains an excellent website. Look for their very handy map and guide distributed free at most wineries. **Travel Yamhill Valley** (503/883-7770, www.travelyamhillvalley.org) is another good source for winery, dining, and accommodations information.

Wine-Tasting

Tasting rooms in Oregon range from no-frills makeshift back rooms to relatively grand affairs. There's usually a tasting fee (usually $5-15), often waved with a minimum wine purchase. Wineries are generally open 11am to 4pm-5pm daily. If you have your heart set on visiting a particular winery, call in advance to confirm hours and details.

Many of the smaller and more exclusive wineries that produce top-flight wines don't offer regular tastings, or offer them only by appointment. Since these wineries have no tasting staff on hand, don't be surprised if recreational visits are gently declined. Almost all wineries are open on Memorial Day and Thanksgiving weekends, when thousands of people throng into the region to visit their favorite wineries.

Given the proximity of Portland, many folks visit the wine country as a day trip. Should you care to extend your stay, there are plenty of bed-and-breakfasts and a smattering of hotels, including a luxurious resort, to accommodate you.

Wine Tours

Hiring a tour company has become an increasingly appealing (and safer) alternative for many wine enthusiasts. Several wine tour companies offer door-to-door service from Portland hotels. One particularly well-established company is **Grape Escape Winery Tours** (503/283-3380, www.grapeescapetours.com), which offers a variety of private and semiprivate custom tours. Tours are also provided by **Eco Tours of Oregon** (503/245-1428, www.ecotours-of-oregon.com), which offers van tours with Portland-area pickup and returns.

If you're already in the Willamette wine country, contact **Insiders Wine Tour** (503/791-0005, www.insiderswinetour.com), based in McMinnville. Thanks to inside connections, you may get the chance to visit wineries not typically open to the public.

There are more exciting ways to tour wine country than in minivans. **Equestrian Wine Tours** (503/864-2336 or 866/864-5253, www.equestrianwinetours.com) provides horseback winery tours on Tennessee Walking horses. Hikers should consider the guided walking tours of Dundee-area wineries offered by **Oregon Dundee Hills Walking Wine Tours** (503/789-7629, markdartist@gmail.com). Portland-based **Pedal Bike Tours** (503/243-2453, http://pedalbiketours.com) offers bicycle tours of wine country. Want to see wine country from the air? Tour the wineries via helicopter with **Precision Aviation Tours** (503/537-0108, www.flyprecision.com) or ride a hot-air balloon with the folks at **Vista Balloons** (503/625-7385 or 800/622-2309, www.vistaballoon.com, Apr.-Oct.).

Getting Around

An unavoidable factor of Willamette Valley wine country: The traffic is often horrendous, particularly along Route 99W, the valley's main drag. (The route is also patrolled heavily by police.) When driving, watch for blue-and-white signs on Route 99W that point out routes to wineries. The only way to avoid the traffic is to steer clear of it as much as possible.

Alternate Routes: The following tour follows four-lane U.S. 26 west from Portland to Forest Grove and drops south into the heart of the wine country through back roads. To return to Portland without driving in 99W traffic, there are a couple of choices. From Newberg, follow Hwy. 219 south across the Willamette River and turn left on McKay Rd., passing near Champoeg State Park and the

THE WILLAMETTE VALLEY

verdant fields of French Prairie, before joining I-5 at Exit 278.

From Amity make your way east to the little town of Hopewell and the Wheatland Ferry. Ride the tiny car ferry across the Willamette (notice here that you're in hop-growing territory) and continue east, following signs to I-5.

FOREST GROVE AND GASTON

The northernmost reach of Willamette Valley wine country is in Forest Grove, about 20 minutes west of Portland off U.S. 26. Forest Grove is home to Pacific University, the oldest chartered university in the western United States, established in 1849.

Wineries

Four miles west of Forest Grove you'll find **Shafer Vineyard Cellars** (6200 NW Gales Creek Rd., 503/357-6604, www.shafervineyardcellars.com) on a pretty oak-shaded hillside. In addition to pinot noir, Shafer makes sparkling wines and a few Rieslings, including an ice wine. **David Hill Winery** (46350 NW David Hill Rd., 503/992-8545, www.davidhillwinery.com), just to the north, is a picturesque vineyard with a long history. The first wine grapes were planted here in the 19th century, and the vineyard produced award-winning wines until Prohibition. Some of the vineyards were replanted in the 1960s, making these some of the oldest pinot noir vines in the state.

Montinore Estate (3663 Dilley Rd., 503/359-5012, www.montinore.com) is just south and west of downtown Forest Grove. As is the practice at many Willamette Valley vineyards, the grapes are grown sustainably using biodynamic practices.

Don't leave Forest Grove without stopping in at **Sake One** (820 Elm St., 503/357-7056, www.sakeone.com) to taste the local sake and tour the sakery. The sakes, made from California rice, range from the delicate Noma sake, a fresh unpasteurized wine that's available only at the tasting room, to the milky coconut-scented Pearl and the clean-tasting, very slightly fruity Asian pear sake.

Seven miles south of Forest Grove on Route 47, the tiny town of Gaston is home to **Elk Cove Vineyard** (27751 NW Olson Rd., 503/985-7760, www.elkcove.com), one of the oldest and most respected operations in the area. Elk Cove's tasting room is especially lovely, and year-in and year-out their pinot gris is one of the region's best.

Accommodations and Food

One of the McMenamin brothers' grandest projects is the **Grand Lodge** (3505 Pacific Ave., Forest Grove, 503/992-3442, www.mcmenamins.com), a hotel, brewpub, and entertainment center that was converted from a vast Masonic and Eastern Star retirement complex built in 1922 on 13 acres of lawns and gardens. The Grand Lodge includes four bars and restaurants, a movie theater, a 10-hole disc golf course, and 77 hotel rooms. Guest rooms are a mix of European style ($45-115 w/o bath) or king rooms with private baths ($125-155). The entire establishment is rich with McMenamins' signature funkiness; it's a fun place to stay if you appreciate old-fashioned atmosphere in an updated, but not utterly transformed, hotel.

YAMHILL

In the Chahalem Mountains east of Yamhill is the small **Ribbon Ridge American Viticulture Area** (AVA), one of Oregon's most heralded wine regions and home to some of the state's top-rated wines. Noted wineries here (**Beaux Frères,** 503/537-1137, www.beauxfreres.com; **Brick House,** 503/538-5136, www.brickhousewines.com; **Patricia Green,** 503/554-0821, www.patriciagreencellars.com) aren't usually open for scheduled tastings (but be sure to check them out over Memorial Day or Thanksgiving weekends); serious wine buyers can call ahead for an appointment.

Wineries

Sample the quality of Ribbon Ridge wines at **Whistling Ridge Vineyards** (14551 NE North Valley Rd., 503/538-6641, www.whistlingridgevineyards.com, Memorial Day and Thanksgiving weekends), offering a number of well-balanced pinot noir and pinot gris wines. **Aramenta Cellars** (17979 NE Lewis Rogers Ln., 503/538-7230, www.aramentacellars.com) also offers a selection of handcrafted pinot noirs.

Just outside the Ribbon Ridge AVA boundaries are a number of wineries with excellent wines and tasting rooms with regularly scheduled opening hours. From Yamhill, head east on Route 240 to find the hillside vineyards of **Willakenzie Estate** (19143 NE Laughlin Rd., 503/662-3280, www.willakenzie.com). In a beautiful rural setting, the winery's three-level gravity-fed design (a tradition in Burgundy) ensures gentle handling of the wine. Along with several different estate-grown pinot noirs, the tasting room pours lush pinot gris, crisp pinot blanc, and juicy gamay noir. Don't miss this place—even though it's off the main highways, it's a real treat to visit.

Top-flight pinot noir is the specialty at highly recommended **Penner-Ash Wine Cellars** (15771 NE Ribbon Ridge Rd., 503/554-5545, www.pennerash.com). Atypical for the region, wines made from viognier and syrah grapes are also featured. One of Oregon's pioneer wineries, **Adelsheim Vineyard** (16800 NE Calkins Ln., 503/538-3652, www.adelsheim.com) was established in 1971 and produces a range of single vineyard pinot noir wines as well as excellent Chardonnay, pinot gris, and rarely encountered auxerrois wines.

◖ CARLTON

Carlton is a quiet, picturesque farm village with a number of wine-tasting rooms within a stroll of each other, plus good restaurants.

Wineries

South on Route 47, toward the small town of Carlton, the cooperative **Carlton Winemakers Studio** (801 N. Scott St., 503/852-6100, www.winemakersstudio.com) houses 10 boutique wineries, including Andrew Rich, Hamacher, and Blakeslee. The studio helps up-and-coming winemakers by providing space and support; several winemakers, including Penner-Ash, Domaine Meriwether, and Scott Paul, have "graduated" to their own facilities. Sharing the same access road, **Cana's Feast** (750 W. Lincoln St., 503/852-0002, www.canasfeastwinery.com) focuses on Mediterranean grape varietals, including sangiovese, barbera, nebbiolo, and primitivo. Occasional weekend meals are served on the winery's grape-shaded veranda during summer and early fall; call to inquire.

Right in the heart of tiny downtown Carlton, **The Tasting Room** (105 W. Main St., 503/852-6733, www.pinot-noir.com, noon-5pm Thurs.-Mon., call to confirm winter hours) offers tastings and sells bottles from a wide variety of local producers, many of whom run small wineries without formal tasting rooms.

From Carlton, leave Hwy. 47 and travel the back roads. Follow Main Street east from downtown; it eventually turns into Hendricks Road and passes through lovely rolling hills lush with vineyards on the way to Newberg. Stop at **Lemelson Vineyards** (12020 NE Stag Hollow Rd., 503/852-6619, www.lemelsonvineyards.com, 11am-4pm Thurs.-Mon.) to taste outstanding organic pinot noir and pinot gris wines.

Accommodations

Within easy walking distance to tasting rooms and restaurants in downtown Carlton, the **Carlton Inn** (648 W. Main St., 503/852-7506, www.thecarltoninn.com, $149-189) is a charming B&B in a 1915 farmhouse-style home. Each of the four guest rooms has a private bath.

In the hills east of Carlton, the **Lobenhaus B&B** (6975 NE Abbey Rd., 503/864-9173, www.lobenhaus.com, $169-189) is a tri-level lodge on 27 acres with comfortable accommodations and a peaceful atmosphere. Each guest room has a private bath and a deck overlooking a spring-fed pond. Guests can take advantage of two common living rooms, each with a TV and a fireplace.

Nearby, the ◖ **Abbey Road Farm B&B** (10501 NE Abbey Rd., 503/852-6278, www.abbeyroadfarm.com, $225) has elegant rooms located in—no joke—converted grain silos. This upscale B&B (think fine art and 600-thread-count sheets) is very nicely

© BILL MCRAE

Spend the night in a surprisingly comfortable silo at Abbey Road Farm B&B.

appointed; the 82-acre Abbey Road Farm has cherry orchards, goats, llamas, donkeys, and gardens; guests can ask about assisting with farm chores. In the interest of your own relaxation, there are no phones or TVs. In addition to the B&B rooms, the farm also rents a three-bedroom, two-bath home with full kitchen ($450, or $375 with two-night minimum).

Food

A great place for country-style French food is **Cuvée** (214 W. Main St., 503/852-6555, www.cuveedining.net, 5:30pm-9pm Wed.-Sat., 5pm-8pm Sun., $21-25). French standards include *coquilles* St. Jacques; make sure to check out the sautéed oysters with horseradish sauce as an appetizer. Three-course fixed-price dinners ($28, reservations recommended) are offered Wednesday, Thursday, and Sunday nights. From May to early October, Cuvée is open for lunch (noon-3pm Sat.-Sun.).

For a lighter meal, head to **The Horse**

Radish (211 W. Main St., 503/852-6656, www.thehorseradish.com, noon-3pm, Mon.-Thurs., noon-10pm Fri.-Sat., 1pm-5pm Sun., $6-10), a deli with good soups and sandwiches, plus a large selection of cheese—perfect for a picnic. A phalanx of local wines is available by the glass or bottle, and there's live music on weekend evenings.

NEWBERG

Busy Route 99W runs through the heart of Newberg, and the suburbs to the east are an unattractive sprawl. But Newberg is central to many wineries and home to the luxurious Allison Inn and Spa, one of the most impressive hotels in Oregon.

Wineries

The old redbrick downtown offers a number of tasting rooms, including the outstanding **Chehalem Vineyards** (106 S. Center St., 503/538-4700, www.chehalemwines.com). Chehalem produces estate pinot noir from three different AVAs, giving you a chance to

© JUDY JEWELL

Ice Age floods carried this boulder from the Rocky Mountains to gardens at Rex Hill Vineyards.

THE WILLAMETTE VALLEY

taste different *terriors* side-by-side. Also good here are Rieslings and an unusual gamay-pinot noir blend.

Two miles east of Newberg is another wine country pioneer, **Rex Hill Vineyards** (30835 Rte. 99W, 503/538-0666 or 800/739-4455, www.rexhill.com) with excellent pinot noir and chardonnay. The tasting room is itself worth a visit; fashioned from an old prune- and nut-drying shed, it now features Persian rugs, antiques, an ornately carved front door, and a stone fireplace, all set in the midst of lovely gardens. Although generally not available for tasting, Rex Hill's popular and reasonably priced distribution line, **A to Z Wineworks** is sold here.

Like most Willamette Valley wineries, **Bergström Wines** (18215 NE Calkins Ln., 503/544-0468, www.bergstromwines.com) is a family-run business, crafting pinot noir and chardonnay from the grapes grown in their five vineyards. Their tasting room is northwest of town, just south of Bald Peak.

Accommodations

If wine country B&Bs aren't your style, the **Best Western Newberg Inn** (2211 Portland Rd., 503/537-3000, www.bestwestern.com, $90) offers an indoor pool and hot tub in addition to well-appointed rooms.

One of Newberg's grandest heritage homes is now the **◖ Lion's Gate Inn** (401 N. Howard St., 503/476-2211, www.distinctivedestination. net, $175-225), a showcase of Craftsman-style design, with intricate wood moldings, leaded-glass windows, fine furniture, and a marvelous tiled fireplace. The four guest rooms (all with private baths) are named for the seasons and filled with local art. (Our favorite room is Autumn, with a dual-sided fireplace and a soaking tub.)

The wine country's most opulent place to stay is the **◖ Allison Inn** (2525 Allison Ln., 503/554-2525 or 877/294-2525, www.theallison.com, $330-475), one of the finest hotels in all of Oregon. Set amid five acres of pinot noir vineyards, the Allison is a monumental structure of stone and wood, with sweeping wine country views from its many terraces and balconies. Each spacious guest room has a gas fireplace, a soaking tub, a large flat-screen TV, bay window seats, a private terrace or balcony, and beautiful furnishings and art, all from local artists. Facilities are top-notch and include Jory Restaurant, a casually elegant dining room with a noted wine list. The lounge features live music on weekend evenings. Perhaps most impressive is the 15,000-square-foot spa and fitness center, with indoor pool, steam room, sauna, and a dozen treatment rooms. With its Gold LEED certification, the Allison is not only a temple of refinement, it's easy on the earth.

Food

Defining itself as a "neighborhood kitchen," **Recipe** (115 N. Washington St., 503/487-6853, www.recipenewbergor.com, 11:30am-9pm Tues.-Sat., $12-24) is a friendly restaurant that welcomes you whether you are looking for a lunchtime sandwich ($9-13), a glass of wine, or a five-course meal. The menu features local and seasonal ingredients prepared with rustic, handmade aplomb.

A quiet block off busy Main Street, the **Painted Lady** (201 S. College St., 503/538-3850, www.thepaintedladyrestaurant.com, 5pm-10pm Wed.-Sun., tasting menu $65) is a highly regarded bastion of multicourse fine dining with a menu featuring the best of local farms. Located in an elegant Victorian home, the restaurant's seasonally changing menu features such delicacies as roasted rabbit roulade with morels or foie gras with apple butter and red-onion jam.

It's worth searching out **Subterra** (1505 Portland Rd., 503/538-6060, www.subterrarestaurant.com, 11:30am-close Mon.-Fri., 5pm-close Sat.-Sun., $21-27), tucked behind Mike's Pharmacy and underneath the Dark Horse Wine Bar, for dinners ranging from "adult mac and cheese BLT" to seared scallops served on brussels sprout slaw. Of course, local wines are given the spotlight and can be enjoyed with small plates as well as entrées.

The beautifully furnished **Jory Restaurant** at the Allison Inn (2525 Allison Ln., 503/554-2525 or 877/294-2525, www.theallison.com, 6:30am-10:30am, 11:30am-2pm, 5:30pm-9pm Mon.-Sat., 9am-2pm, 5:30pm-9pm Sun., $32-45) offers sweeping views of wine country plus elegant preparations of hearty regional cuisine. Local and seasonal specialties include salmon, lamb, venison, and wild mushrooms. It's very entertaining to sit at the kitchen bar and watch the chefs in action. Or, book the Chef's Table in the kitchen itself, where the chef will prepare a special dinner for up to 10 lucky diners. The wine list offers many rare and acclaimed bottles from both Oregon and France.

DUNDEE

At one time, Dundee was noted mostly for its filberts (known to most of the world as hazelnuts) and the roadside Dundee Nut House. Now the town is famous for the abundance of wineries in the hills above town. Some of Oregon's top-rated wines are grown in the Dundee Hills AVA, but drive around—you'll still see filbert orchards.

No one would characterize Dundee as a charming town, mostly because busy Route 99W funnels an incredible amount of traffic right through its heart (a traffic bypass has been in the works for a long time but is yet to materialize). But with good restaurants and some excellent lodging options, Dundee offers many reasons to pull off the road and explore.

Wineries

Midway between Newberg and Dundee is **Duck Pond Cellars** (23145 Rte. 99W, 503/538-3199, www.duckpondcellars.com), which produces wines from both Oregon- and Washington-grown grapes. If you're a price-driven wine shopper, note that this is the place to pick up some less expensive (but still very drinkable) wine.

Downtown Dundee may not seem to be much more than an intersection, but look more carefully and you'll see a number of wineries and tasting rooms scattered along the road. A favorite stop is **Dobbs Family Estate** (240 SE

5th St., 503/538-1141, www.dobbsfamilyestate.com), where winemaker Joe Dobbs crafts high-end vintages on the Dobbs Family label and delicious entry level wines on the Wine by Joe label.

Located in an old farmhouse, the **Argyle Winery** (691 Rte. 99W, 503/538-8520, www.argylewinery.com) tasting room is the place to sample sparkling wine good enough to have graced the Clintons' White House table (and a certain travel writer's wedding reception). It is the state's leading producer of sparkling wine in the tradition of French champagne. At the center of Dundee is the **Ponzi Wine Bar** (100 SW 7th St., 503/554-1500, ponziwinebar.com) where you can taste a selection of wines from Ponzi Vineyards, one of Oregon's oldest and most respected wineries (the actual vineyards are west of Portland). A number of other small wineries are also represented here, and you can order a sandwich or snack to accompany your wine. If you're growing weary of the subtle and nuanced wines of the Willamette Valley and long for hearty, heavier wines, stop at **Zerba**

© JUDY JEWELL

view from Sokol Blosser Winery

Cellars (810 Hwy. 99 W., 503/537-9463, www.zerbacellars.com). This tasting room in downtown Dundee is an outpost of the Zerba winery near Walla Walla, and offers tastings of their Rhone-style wines, as well as delicious sangiovese.

As Dundee's Ninth Street turns west, it turns into Worden Hill Road, a thoroughfare that climbs up through miles of vineyards. This is, more or less, the glory road of Oregon wine.

Though the tasting room is new (and spectacular), the vineyards at **Winderlea Wine Co.** (8905 NE Worden Hill Rd., 503/554-5900, winderlea.com) date from the 1970s and produce some of the region's most compelling wines. Just up the road is one of Oregon's largest and oldest (dating from 1967) wineries, **Erath Winery** (9409 NE Worden Hill Rd., 503/538-3318, www.erath.com). Erath's wood-paneled tasting room sits high in the Red Hills of Dundee, where beautiful picnic sites command an imposing view of local vineyards and the Willamette Valley. Although Erath is no longer family-owned, its new owner, Washington's huge Ste. Michelle Wine Estates, is considered to have done a good job at maintaining Dick Erath's legacy.

Lange Estate Winery and Vineyards (18380 NE Buena Vista Dr., 503/538-6476, www.langewinery.com) is an excellent place to try handcrafted pinot noir, chardonnay, or pinot gris. If you want a behind the scenes experience, private tours and tastings are available for $40 per person.

Sokol Blosser Winery (5000 Sokol Blosser Ln., 503/864-2282, www.sokolblosser.com), two miles south of Dundee (follow signs), is another of Oregon's pioneer wineries. Its brand-new (in 2013) and strikingly beautiful tasting room is perched on top of a hillside planted with grapes. In addition to acclaimed pinot noir, the chardonnay is especially recommended. Also good is the rosé of pinot noir.

On the southern flanks of the Dundee Hills is another clutch of notable vineyards. **Domaine Drouhin** (6750 Breyman Orchards Rd., 503/864-2700, www.domainedrouhin.com/en, 11am-4pm Wed.-Sun.) is the Oregon

THE WILLAMETTE VALLEY

outpost of France's famed Drouhin family, making excellent pinot noirs in the Burgundy style. Multi-award-winning **Domaine Serene** (6555 NE Hilltop Ln., 503/864-4600, www.domaineserene.com, 11am-4pm Wed.-Mon.) is one of Oregon's top producers of ultra-premium wines. This is a must-sip for any serious wine lover.

Accommodations

Although it's right in the busy center of Dundee, the 20-room **Inn at Red Hills** (1410 N. Rte. 99W, 503/538-7666, www.innatredhills.com, $199-249) is a gracious and relaxing place to stay. There is a good restaurant downstairs and other excellent dining choices right in town.

Just up the road from Sokol Blosser, at the crest of the Dundee Hills, **Wine Country Farm Cellars** (6855 Breyman Orchards Rd., 503/864-3446 or 800/261-3446, www.winecountryfarm.com, $150-275) combines wine-growing with homey bed-and-breakfast accommodations. Views stretch from Salem to Mount Jefferson over miles of vineyards. Watch the pinot noir grow, take a hike, get a massage, or ride horseback to neighboring wineries. Guest rooms all have private baths and wireless Internet. While not the last word in upscale luxury, Wine Country Farm is noted for its friendly welcome and relaxed farm-like atmosphere.

The area's top lodging choice is the nine-room **⟨ Black Walnut Inn** (9600 NE Worden Hill Rd., 503/429-4114 or 866/429-4114, www.blackwalnut-inn.com, $249-399), a villa-like complex that looks like it's been transported from Tuscany (but with all the modern luxuries). The rooms are large and very comfortable, most with wondrous views across the vineyards to Willamette Valley. Rates include a multicourse breakfast and an afternoon of appetizers and wine tasting.

Food

One of the wine country's top restaurants, **⟨ Tina's** (760 Rte. 99W, 503/538-8880, www.tinasdundee.com, 11am-2pm, 5pm-close Tues.-Fri., 5pm-close Sat.-Mon., $24-40) is right on the main drag in Dundee; look for a small red structure across from the Dundee fire station. Tina's uses the freshest Oregon ingredients to create simple yet elegant fare. This intimate institution is a gem, as one bite of the pan-fried oysters will tell you. (Come for the oysters, stay for the beef short ribs braised in chocolate-red wine sauce.) In what can only be interpreted as a good sign, it is common to see local winemakers hanging out at the tiny bar, sampling vintages from the wide-ranging wine list.

Affiliated with Ponzi Vineyards, **⟨ Dundee Bistro** (100-A SW 7th St., 503/554-1650, dundeebistro.com, 11am-close daily, $14-30) is a reliable spot for what's top-notch but not overly expensive. The emphasis is on fresh and regional foods, and includes delicious pizza, house-made pasta, and main courses such as roast pork loin with apple-wood-smoked bacon. The wine list is both tempting and reasonably priced.

Red Hills Provincial Dining (276 Hwy. 99W, Dundee, 503/538-8224, www.redhillsdining.com, 5pm-9pm Tues.-Sun., $24-32) is a cozy, charm-filled restaurant that uses only the freshest local ingredients to create award-winning French- and Italian-inspired food.

At the false-fronted **Red Hills Market** (155 SW 7th St., 971/832-8414, www.redhillmarket.com, 7am-8pm daily, $5-14), you can load up a picnic basket with tasty sandwiches, buy local wine and artisanal cheese, or settle in for a delicious, casual meal. Wood-fired pizzas are a menu stronghold, but there's also the veggie-laden breakfast bowl, with bacon, eggs, cheese, and spinach. Upstairs, find a wine tasting room and a cooking school.

In tiny Dayton, six miles south of Dundee off Highway 18, the **⟨ Joel Palmer House** (600 Ferry St., 503/864-2995, www.joelpalmerhouse.com, 4:30pm-9:30pm Tues.-Sat., $20-37, reservations recommended) is considered one of Oregon's finest restaurants and historic homes—it's on the Oregon and the National Historic Registers *and* is top-rated by such publications as *Wine Spectator*. The house was originally owned by the eponymous Joel Palmer, speaker of the Oregon House of Representatives in 1862 and an Oregon state senator (1864-1866). Jack and Heidi Czarnecki turned the Joel Palmer House into a one-of-a-kind restaurant that combines their love of mushroom hunting with fine wine; their son Christopher is now at the helm. Many dishes include wild mushrooms; this is a touchstone restaurant for lovers of fungi. Indulge your passion for mushrooms with the $80 six-course mushroom madness dinner (must be ordered by everyone at your table).

LAFAYETTE

While cruising the wine country, antiques collectors can pull off Route 99 into the town of Lafayette to visit **Lafayette Schoolhouse Antiques** (748 Rte. 99W, 503/864-2720, 10am-5pm daily), where Oregon's largest antiques display can be found in the old schoolhouse, mill, and auditorium. Imagine 10,000 square feet of antiques spread over three floors

Downtown McMinnville is vibrant, with good restaurants, tasting rooms, and shopping.

© JUDY JEWELL

in a 1910 building, with an antique furniture showcase next door.

Just north of Lafayette, wine tasters can enjoy the beautiful tasting room and one of the most panoramic views in the valley at **Anne Amie Vineyards** (6580 NE Mineral Springs Rd., 503/864-2991, https//:anneamie.com), where you'll also find top-notch pinot noir, pinot blanc, and pinot gris.

⟨ MCMINNVILLE

By far the largest town in the wine country, with a population of some 33,000, McMinnville is also one of the most appealing. Though surrounded by grim big-box development, the charming turn-of-the-20th-century downtown is lined with excellent restaurants, wine bars, boutique shopping, and a superlative organic grocery and health food store. McMinnville makes a great spot to spend the night; there are a wide range of lodging choices and enough fine restaurants to tempt diners into lingering on another night just to sample another good meal.

Another very compelling reason to visit McMinnville is the **Evergreen Aviation and Space Museum** (500 NE Captain Michael King Smith Way, 503/434-4180, www.evergreenmuseum.org, 9am-5pm daily, $25 adults, $24 seniors, $23 children ages 5-16), just off Route 18 south of McMinnville. This massive complex features two separate museums. The Aviation Museum houses the *Spruce Goose,* the giant wooden seaplane built for billionaire Howard Hughes in the 1940s. (The plane, which Hughes called a "flying boat," flew only once for approximately one minute.) In addition to the *Goose,* the museum houses many other aircraft, including funky, hand-built planes, bombers, and large cargo planes. Next to this vast hangar is yet another complex home to the Space Museum, which celebrates the history of space exploration and travel. In addition, you'll find an **IMAX theater** (tickets $11 adults, $10 seniors, $9 children ages 5-16), a number of dining options, and a wine-tasting room.

As if this weren't enough, the enormous

70,000-square-foot **Wings and Waves Water Park** (10am-8pm daily summer, weekends only winter, museum only: $12; museum and water park: $27 under 42 inches, $32 over 42 inches) features a children's museum focusing on hydrology and the power of water plus 10 waterslides. You can't miss it; it's the building with a Boeing 747 on its roof. As of early 2014, the future of the museums and water park were uncertain due to financial issues.

Wineries

McMinnville offers several wine-tasting rooms (and a brewpub) right in town, in addition to those found in the surrounding hills.

Third Street is the main street downtown, lined with trees and lots of wine-tasting action. A good place to start is the **Willamette Valley Wine Center** (300 NE 3rd St., 503/883-9012, 10am-6pm daily), operated by Willamette Valley Vineyards, which offers wine-tasting and sales; there are always a few bottles from guest wineries around the valley available to sample along with Willamette Valley Vineyards wines.

A couple blocks north of downtown McMinnville is **Panther Creek Cellars** (455 NE Irvine St., 503/472-8080, www.panthercreekcellars.com, noon-5pm daily), housed in a handsome, 1923 former power plant. Panther Creek is known for its small volume production of premium pinot noir, though its pinot gris and chardonnay are also excellent.

More than almost any other winemaker, David Lett of **Eyrie Vineyards** (935 E. 10th St., 503/472-6315, www.eyrievineyards.com, noon-5pm daily) was responsible for shepherding Oregon's fledgling wine industry. Eyrie started up in 1966 and produced the Willamette Valley's first pinot noir and chardonnay as well as the first pinot gris in the United States; David and Diana Lett's son, Jason, is now the winemaker and vineyard manager. The winery, set in an industrial area, is a bit hard to find, but well worth the effort to taste some of the most refined of all Oregon wines.

Yamhill Valley Vineyards (16250 Oldsville Rd., southwest of McMinnville off Rte. 18,

503/843-3100, yamhill.com, 11am-5pm daily) is set amid an oak grove on a 200-acre estate and features a balcony overlooking the vineyard. This winery's first release, an '83 pinot noir, first distinguished itself at a 1985 tasting of French and Oregon vintages held in New York City. Since then, the winery has been a leader in producing high-quality pinot noir as well as Riesling and pinot gris.

Festivals and Events

McMinnville's biggest annual event is the mid-May **UFO Festival,** a McMenamins-sponsored event that began as a way to honor a 1950 UFO sighting by two McMinnville residents. Along with guest speakers, expect to see lots of quite elaborate costumes, a parade, and music.

Oregon's top wine festival is the annual **International Pinot Noir Celebration** (503/472-8964 or 800/775-4762, www.ipnc.org). More than 70 U.S. and international pinot noir producers are on hand for symposia, tastings, and winery tours. More than 50 chefs prepare wine-focused meals, many held at invitation-only events at wineries. The three-day event takes place at the end of July on the Linfield College campus in McMinnville. While the cost of registration ($900) is prohibitive for all but the most serious oenophiles, tickets to the final tasting can be purchased separately for $125. Register well in advance; this event always sells out.

Accommodations

McMinnville has the largest selection of lodging choices in wine country. If the high price of plush inns and B&Bs has you looking for a standard motel, this is the place to go.

For inexpensive lodgings, reserve a room at McMinnville's **Motel 6** (2065 SW Hwy. 99 W., 503/472-9493, $75) with an outdoor pool. Step up to the **GuestHouse Vineyard Inn** (2035 S. Rte. 99W, 503/472-4900, www.guesthouseintl.com/hotels/McMinnville, $105-120), a pet-friendly place with free breakfast and an indoor pool and hot tub. Another standard hotel that's a good bet if you're traveling with a dog is the **Comfort**

Inn (2520 SE Stratus Ave., 503/472-1700, www.comfortinn.com, $134-144). **Red Lion Inn and Suites** (2535 NE Cumulus Ave., 503/472-1500, www.redlion.com, $110) has spacious, well-furnished rooms with an indoor pool.

If you're in McMinnville to enjoy the restaurants and nightlife on Third Street, you should stay downtown. McMenamins' ◖ **Hotel Oregon** (310 NE Evans St., 503/472-8427 or 800/472-8427, www.mcmenamins.com, $60-145) has the same spirit of fun, funky art, and good food and drink as other outposts of the Brothers McMenamin empire. Built in 1905, Hotel Oregon has updated and comfy guest rooms (some with private bath, most with shared bath, no TVs), and an outdoor rooftop bar, making this a winner for travelers looking for a relaxed good time. If traveling with a group of friends, inquire about the five rooms that share a private interior patio. Pets are permitted in a few of the rooms.

The top lodging in downtown McMinnville is the ◖ **3rd Street Flats** (219 NE Cowls St., 503/857-6248, www.thirdstreetflats.com, $180-255, discounts for week-plus stays), with four distinctive and totally charming accommodations above a historic 1885 bank building. Each flat is designed by a different local decorator and filled with regional art; all have full kitchens and living rooms, and the larger units have separate dining rooms. The showcase is the corner Retreat flat, with a fireplace and 750 square feet of living space. These highly original units are perfect for cooks, as well as friends traveling together.

A short drive from McMinnville is the ◖ **Youngberg Hill Vineyards and Inn** (10660 SW Youngberg Hill Rd., 503/472-2727, www. youngberghill.com, $229-349) set atop a range of hills carpeted with vineyards. Excellent views take in the Coast Range, Mount Jefferson, Mount Hood, and the Willamette Valley, as seen from the rooms or from the covered decks that surround the inn. The eight rooms are large and nicely furnished; guests are treated to a wine-tasting of estate-grown wines plus a multicourse breakfast.

Food

For variety and quality, McMinnville has the best and liveliest dining scene in the Willamette Valley wine country, much of it centered on the pleasant, leafy downtown area on Third Street. Be aware that many of the top restaurants are closed on Monday.

If you're looking to provision a picnic or pick up some healthy snacks, **Harvest Fresh Grocery** (251 NE 3rd St., 503/472-5740, 8am-8pm Mon.-Fri., 8am-7pm Sat., 10am-7pm Sun.) is a well-stocked natural foods store with a deli and salad bar.

A major eating and entertainment anchor on Third Street is the **Hotel Oregon** (310 NE Evans St., 503/472-8427 or 800/472-8427, www.mcmenamins.com, 7am-11pm Sun.-Wed., 7am-midnight Thurs., 7am-1am Fri.-Sat., $8-17), McMinnville's outpost of the local McMenamins microbrew chain. In addition to the bar and dining room (characteristically decorated with over-the-top panache), there are many other quirky spaces in which to eat and drink. Stop in at the famous rooftop bar or the cellar bar (usually only open on weekends) when the hotel features live music—sometimes several bands at once in different venues. The pub grub here isn't exactly sophisticated (burgers, pizza, sandwiches), but when accompanied by a pint of McMenamins' ale, it's hard not to enjoy yourself.

Another brewpub is on the east end of downtown, in a former rail warehouse. **Golden Valley Brewery** (980 NE 4th St., 503/472-2739, www.goldenvalleybrewery. com, 11am-10pm Sun.-Thurs. 11am-11pm Fri.-Sat., $9-17) offers beef from the owner's own Angus herd, vegetables from the kitchen garden, and most everything else is made inhouse. The menu features soup, salads, and sandwiches and the quality of the food is high; craft brews are also excellent.

Get your coconut macaroon fix at **Red Fox Bakery** (328 NE Evans St., 503/434-5098, redfoxbakery.com, 7am-4pm Mon.-Sat., 11am-3pm Sun.); they also serve good sandwiches and breakfast pastries.

A good spot for breakfast or lunch is

Community Plate (315 NE 3rd St., 503/687-1902, www.communityplate.com, 7:30am-3:30pm daily, $5-9), which combines old-school diner cooking with an intense commitment to local and sustainable ingredients. Celebrate the local with a filbert butter and jam sandwich.

The commitment to local farmers and producers is sharply in focus at chef-owner Eric Bechard's much-lauded restaurant **[Thistle** (228 NE Evans St., 503/472-9623, www.thistlerestaurant.com, 5:30pm-close Tues.-Sat., $24-27), where the daily-changing menu features the bounty of farms, pastures, and waters within a 45-mile radius of the restaurant. The chalkboard menu doesn't distinguish between large and small plates, so it's easy to sample a number of dishes. An evening's choice may include gnocchi with fava beans, morels, tomato, and watercress; salmon with sweet peppers, fennel, and green olives; or elk with winter squash, kale, and huckleberry sauce. The wine list is divided between local and French wines.

There used to be just one clearly excellent restaurant in the area: **[Nick's Italian Cafe** (521 3rd St., 503/434-4471, nicksitaliancafe.com, 11am-3pm and 5pm-9pm Tues.-Sat., noon-8pm Sun., 5pm-9pm Mon., $15-28), a onetime soda fountain that, since 1977, has held the well-deserved, outsize reputation as the best restaurant in wine country, with a wine list that is both extensive and distinctive. Now under second-generation ownership, and with a new, fresher approach to Italian food, Nick's is better than ever, with house-made pasta such as lasagna with Dungeness crab, wild mushrooms, and pine nuts, and main courses such as calamari, clams, and sea scallops in leek and potato broth. Diners also have the option of a five-course, fixed-price dinner ($65); if that isn't in the budget, stop by for a panini sandwich, bowl of pasta, or a wood-fired pizza at lunch ($9-15), or visit the back room in the evening to snack from the bar menu.

A top choice for a casual meal is **[La Rambla** (238 NE 3rd St., 503/435-2126, www.laramblaonthird.com, 11:30am-2:30pm and 5pm-close daily, tapas $4-11), an excellent Spanish restaurant that invites you to graze through a series of tapas and small plates. Feast on paella ($19 small, $32 large) or an assortment of traditional Spanish tapas. The wood-paneled, candle-lit dining room is flanked by a long copper bar, a perfect spot for a romantic dinner.

Traditional French provincial cooking is available at **Bistro Maison** (729 NE 3rd St., 503/474-1888, www.bistromaison.com, 11:30am-2pm and 6pm-9pm Wed.-Thurs., 11:30am-2 and 5pm-9pm Fri., 5pm-9pm Sat., noon-6:30pm Sun., $18-27), a charming farmhouse-like restaurant that serves delicious standards such as coq au vin, confit de canard, and steak tartare.

AMITY

At the southern edge of Yamhill County is the tiny community of Amity. In the steep hills east of town are a number of wineries.

About five miles southwest of Amity is the **Priory of Our Lady of Consolation** (23300 Walker Ln., 503/835-8080, www.brigittine.org), a monastery for Brigittine monks. The monks fund the monastery in part through the sale of handmade fudge and other candies, available for sale at the **monastery store** (9am-5pm Mon.-Sat., 1pm-5pm Sun.). Visitors are welcome to attend mass (8am Mon.-Sat., noon Sun.).

Wineries

A classic Yamhill County winery is **Amity Vineyards** (18150 Amity Vineyards Rd. SE, 503/835-2362, http://amityvineyards.com). The tasting room is located in a huge old barn on a 500-foot hill looking out over vineyards to the Coast Range, making for some beautiful sunset (or picnic) views. Amity, which was founded in 1974, is one of Oregon's oldest wineries and still has a homespun feel that belies its excellent wines.

The nearby **Kristin Hill Winery** (3330 SE Amity Dayton Hwy., 503/835-0850, www.kristinhillwinery.com) specializes in a traditional "Methode Champenoise" sparkling wine and a sweet port. Picnickers are welcome.

Northeastern Willamette Valley

Much of Oregon's early history played out on the fertile banks of the Willamette River between present-day Portland and Salem. Settlers made a break from the British Hudson's Bay Company and established an American-style provisional government. Over 160 years later these Willamette Valley towns are still mostly small, and the surrounding countryside is lush, inviting a ramble through history, particularly on a bicycle.

CHAMPOEG STATE HERITAGE AREA

Along the banks of the Willamette River, just southeast of Newberg on Route 219, is **Champoeg** (pronounced sham-POO-ee or sham-POO-eck, 503/678-1251, www.oregonstateparks.org, visitors center 9am-5pm daily, $5 day-use fee), often touted as the birthplace of Oregon. But far more than just a historic site, Champoeg is a really beautiful park with broad meadows dominated by massive oak trees—it's a wonderful place for a bike ride or picnic. The name Champoeg means "field of roots" in Chinook, referring to the camas coveted by Native Americans, who boiled it to accompany the traditional salmon feast.

This park commemorates the site of the 1843 vote to break free from British and Hudson's Bay Company rule and establish a pro-American provisional government in the Oregon country. At the time, Champoeg was the center of settlement in the Willamette Valley, and the smattering of settlers here were almost exactly evenly split between newly arrived Americans and British and French Canadian former employees of the Hudson's Bay Company.

The visitors center has exhibits detailing how the Kalapuyas, explorers, fur traders, and American settlers lived in the Willamette Valley. The grounds also contain several historic buildings. Adjacent to the visitors center is the Manson Barn, built in 1862. The Old Butteville Jail (1850) and

one-room schoolhouse have also been moved to Champoeg to help evoke frontier life. Just west of the park entrance is the **Newell House Museum** (503/678-5537, newellhouse.com, 1pm-5pm Fri.-Sun. Mar.-Oct., $4 adults, $3 seniors, $2 children), a replica of the 1852 house of pioneer Robert Newell. Particularly interesting is the second floor, which showcases Native American artifacts and a collection of inaugural gowns worn by the wives of Oregon governors. The **Pioneer Mothers Cabin Museum** replicates the dwellings in the Willamette Valley circa 1850. A collection of 1775-1850 guns and muskets is also on display. In addition to the historical exhibits, Champoeg features a botanical garden of native plants as well as four miles of hiking and biking trails beginning in the Riverside day-use area and heading to the historic Butteville Store, now an ice cream parlor.

To reach Champoeg State Park from Portland, drive south on I-5 until you see signs for Exit 278. This exit directs you to a rural route that runs five miles to the park visitors center. The 568-acre park is equidistant from Portland and Salem along the Willamette River.

If you enjoy Champoeg and its mix of history and pastoral scenery, consider touring the **French Prairie Loop** a 40-mile byway that passes through idyllic farmland and takes in a number of towns founded by the French Canadian traders, such as St. Paul, Donald, and Butteville. St. Paul is known for the Fourth of July **St. Paul Rodeo** (www.stpaulrodeo.com), which includes a fireworks display, a barbecue, and an art auction. French Canadian trappers from the Hudson's Bay Company started settling here in the 1820s and 1830s, establishing the first farms and villages in the Willamette Valley. This is an especially popular route for bicyclists, as the route is largely flat and traffic is light. Pick up a map and brochure at the Champoeg State Park visitors center.

THE WILLAMETTE VALLEY

© BILL MCRAE

the Pioneer Mothers Cabin Museum at Champoeg State Heritage Area

Camping

If you want to extend your stay, Champoeg State Park offers six tent sites and 48 sites with RV hookups ($19 tents, $24 RVs). There are also six yurts for rent ($36). Call 800/452-5687 for reservations ($8 reservation fee). This year-round facility is one of the few out-of-town campgrounds within easy driving distance (25 miles) of Portland. Add beautiful Willamette River frontage and prime bike-riding on the nearby country roads, and you might consider this the consummate budget alternative to a night in the city or a pricey wine country B&B.

AURORA

Aurora sits on the east side of I-5 (Exit 278), at the junction of Routes 219 and 99E, and enjoys National Historic District status; the town preserves the vestiges of one of Oregon's frontier utopian communities. Founded in 1856 by Prussian immigrant Dr. William Keil, the Aurora colony fused Christian fundamentalism with collectivist principles, garnering distinction for its thriving farms and the excellence of its handicrafts. Despite Aurora's early success, a smallpox epidemic in 1862 and the coming of the railroad, which undermined Willamette River trade in the subsequent decade, provided the catalyst for the town's demise. Keil himself died in 1877, and the struggling colony disbanded a few years later.

The **Old Aurora Colony Museum** (15018 2nd St. NE, Aurora, 503/678-5754, www.auroracolony.org, 11am-4pm Tues.-Sat., noon-4pm Sun. Feb.-Dec., $6 adults, $5 seniors, $2 students) consists of five buildings, including two of the colony's homesteads, the communal washhouse, and the farm equipment shed. Items of interest include old tools, a collection of musical instruments, an ingenious spinning wheel devised by William Keil, and a recording left over from the colony band, as well as quilts and an herb garden.

After visiting the museum, you can take an Aurora walking tour (ask for the free pamphlet) of 33 nearby structures such as clapboard and Victorian houses as well as antiques shops, all clustered along Route 99E.

Aurora is mostly known for its antique stores. This is a prime day-trip destination from Portland for seekers of vintage treasure, as the town hosts over 20 antiques dealers and shops.

OREGON CITY

Fourteen miles south of Portland, Oregon City, a wellspring of Oregon history, usually gets credit for being the end of the Oregon Trail. As the first territorial capital, Oregon City was the only seat of U.S. power in Oregon Territory until 1852. This small town is the site of many firsts, including the first incorporated city west of the Rockies, the West's first mint, paper mill, and newspaper, and the world's first long-distance electric power transmission system. The Oregon territorial capital was also the site of the state's first Protestant church and Masonic lodge.

Ironically, a representative of British interests in Oregon country is credited with starting Oregon City. John McLoughlin, the Canadian-born chief factor of the Hudson's Bay Company, encouraged French Canadian trappers to cross the Columbia River from Fort Vancouver and settle here in the northern Willamette Valley, inspiring the name French Prairie. McLoughlin built a flour mill near Willamette Falls in 1832 and moved to Oregon City himself in the 1840s. He became an ardent supporter of American settlers who wanted Oregon to be independent of England and part of the United States.

Oregon City's river port thrived due to Willamette Falls, which impedes the movement of merchant ships farther south (upstream) on the river. Though just 40 feet high, Willamette Falls is the second-largest waterfall, by volume, in the United States (after Niagara). However, much of the falls is now obscured by a vintage hydroelectric power generation facility.

Although the development of the railroad and the growth of Portland diminished Oregon City's early importance, its glory days live on today thanks to National Historic District status. Buildings that date back to the mid-19th century exemplify Queen Anne, federal, and Italianate architectural styles.

Basalt terraces divide the city into three levels. Downtown is wedged between the river and a 100-foot bluff. A municipal elevator provides transportation between the commercial traffic in the lower part of town and the historic buildings on the bluff.

McLoughlin House

For a glimpse of the glory that was 19th-century Oregon City, visit the impressive clapboard-style home of the "Father of Oregon," the **McLoughlin House** (713 Center St., 503/656-5146, www.mcloughlinhouse.org, 10am-4pm Wed.-Sat., $3 adults, free children ages 15 and under). To spare it flood damage, the building was moved from its original site near the river to this location at the top of the city's bluffs. The collection of original and period furnishings may not be terribly exciting, but the rangers' ghost stories and historical insights can make it all come alive. In addition, the grounds are lovingly landscaped with rhododendrons, azaleas, and roses. The McLoughlin House is actually a national park site that is part of Fort Vancouver National Historic Site; Fort Vancouver is just across the Columbia River from Portland in Washington State.

Museum of the Oregon Territory

The **Museum of the Oregon Territory** (211 Tumwater Dr., 503/655-5574, http://clackamashistory.org, 11am-4pm Wed.-Sat., free) lies north on Route 99E from Willamette Falls (look for the Tumwater turnoff on the east side of the highway). From the elevated perspective of the museum parking lot you'll have a great bird's-eye view of Willamette Falls. Prior to perusing the diaries, artifacts, and historic photos on the second floor, you'll encounter a timeline that correlates world events over thousands of years to the geologic, political, and social growth of Oregon. Signposts for your journey through the ages include Native American baskets and arrowheads, a horse-drawn carriage, and the world's first kidney dialysis machine (invented locally).

The McLoughlin House in Oregon City was home to the "Father of Oregon."

© BILL MCRAE

John Inskeep Environmental Learning Center

The **John Inskeep Environmental Learning Center** (Clackamas Community College, 19600 Molalla Ave., www.clackamas.edu, 503/657-6958, ext. 2351, dawn-dusk daily, $2 suggested donation), three miles north of Kelly Field on Route 213, is pioneering efforts of a different sort. The five-acre environmental study area showcases alternative technologies and recycling against a backdrop of ponds, trails, and wildlife. Exhibits on aquaculture,

birds of prey, and wetlands are included in the center's portrayal of Oregon's ecosystems. The exhibits are supplemented by **one of the largest telescopes** (503/594-6044, option 1, http://rosecityastronomers.org, open approx. once a month, schedule on website) in the Pacific Northwest. Adjacent to the Inskeep Environmental Learning Center is the **Home Orchard Society Arboretum** (503/338-8479, www.homeorchardsociety.org, 9am-3pm Tues. and Sat.) displaying Oregon's array of fruit-bearing plants.

Salem

The used-car lots and fast-food outlets encountered on the way into Salem off I-5 contrast with the inspiring murals and displays in the capitol, where it is comforting to be reminded of Oregon's pioneer tradition and proud legacy of progressive legislation. Close by, the tranquil beauty and stimulating museums of historic Willamette University also provide a break from the drabness of a town dominated by gray buildings housing the state's bureaucracies.

The Kalapuya name for the locality of Salem was Chemeketa, or "Place of Rest." Connotations of repose were also captured by the Methodist missionary name Salem, an anglicized form of the Arabic *salaam* and the Hebrew *shalom,* meaning "peace." The surrounding croplands along with Willamette River transport and waterpower quickly enabled Salem to become the New Jerusalem envisioned by Oregon Trail pioneers. Over the years, the city forged an economic destiny in government, food processing, light manufacturing, and wood products. Today, it has a population of about 155,000.

SIGHTS
State Capitol

If visiting the **state capitol** (900 NE Court St., 503/986-1388, www.leg.state.or.us/capinfo, 7:30am-5pm Mon.-Fri., free) strikes you as the kind of saccharine excursion best reserved for a first-grade class trip, you're in for a pleasant surprise. The art deco-style capitol building is filled with attractive murals, paintings, and sculptures of the seminal events in the state's history. The capitol is located on Court Street between West Summer and East Summer Streets, just north of Willamette University.

Atop the capitol dome is a gold-leafed bronze statue of a bearded ax-wielding pioneer. Massive marble sculptures flank the main entrance—*Covered Wagons* on the west side and *Lewis and Clark Led by Sacagawea* on the east. Maps of the Oregon Trail and the route of Lewis and Clark are visible on the backs of the statues. The symbolism is sustained after you enter the double glass doors to the rotunda. Your eyes will immediately be drawn to a bronze state seal, eight feet in diameter and set into the floor, which juxtaposes an eagle in flight, a sailing ship, a covered wagon, and forests. The 33 marble steps beyond the cordoned-off emblem lead up to the House and Senate chambers and symbolize Oregon's place as the 33rd state to enter the Union. Four large murals adorning the rose travertine walls of the rotunda illustrate the settlement and growth of Oregon: Robert Gray sailing into the Columbia estuary in 1792; Lewis and Clark at Celilo Falls in 1805; the first European women to cross the continent being welcomed by Dr. John McLoughlin in 1836; and the first wagon train on the Oregon Trail in 1843. Bronze reliefs and

The Oregon state capitol is topped with a gold-leafed statue of a pioneer.

© JUDY JEWELL

THE WILLAMETTE VALLEY

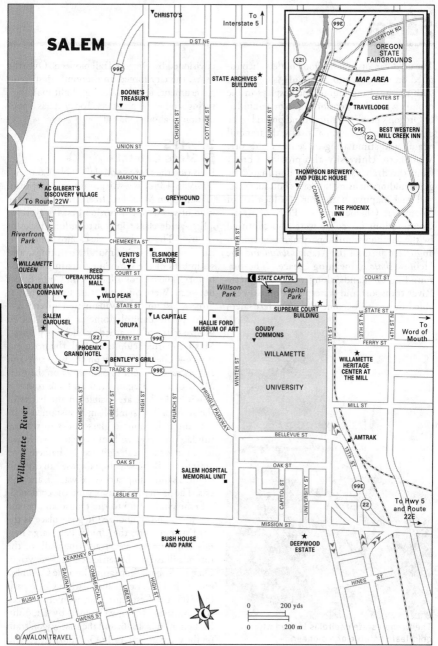

SALEM

CHRISTO'S

To Interstate 5

D ST NE

STATE ARCHIVES BUILDING

99E

BOONE'S TREASURY

CHURCH ST

COTTAGE ST

SUMMER ST

UNION ST

MARION ST

GREYHOUND

AC GILBERT'S DISCOVERY VILLAGE
To Route 22W

FRONT ST

CENTER ST

CHEMEKETA ST

WINTER ST

Riverfront Park

WILLAMETTE QUEEN

VENTI'S CAFE

ELSINORE THEATRE

COURT ST

CASCADE BAKING COMPANY

REED HOUSE MALL

OPERA HOUSE MALL

WILD PEAR

STATE ST

Willson Park

STATE CAPITOL

Capitol Park

SUPREME COURT BUILDING

SALEM CAROUSEL

ORUPA

LA CAPITALE

HALLIE FORD MUSEUM OF ART

GOUDY COMMONS

COURT ST

22

PHOENIX GRAND HOTEL

99E

FERRY ST

13TH ST NE

13TH ST NE

14TH ST NE

STATE ST

To Word of Mouth

22

BENTLEY'S GRILL

TRADE ST

99E

WILLAMETTE UNIVERSITY

WILLAMETTE HERITAGE CENTER AT THE MILL

FERRY ST

12TH ST

Willamette River

COMMERCIAL ST

LIBERTY ST

HIGH ST

CHURCH ST

PRINGLE PARKWAY

WINTER ST

MILL ST

BELLEVUE ST

AMTRAK

13TH ST

OAK ST

OAK ST

SALEM HOSPITAL MEMORIAL UNIT

CAPITOL ST

UNIVERSITY ST

99E

To Hwy 5 and Route 22E

LESLIE ST

22

MISSION ST

KEARNEY ST

BUSH HOUSE AND PARK

DEEPWOOD ESTATE

SAGINAW ST

COMMERCIAL ST

LIBERTY ST

HIGH ST

HINES ST

BUSH ST

OWENS ST

© AVALON TRAVEL

0   200 yds

0   200 m

Inset map:

99E

SILVERTON RD

221

OREGON STATE FAIRGROUNDS

22

MAP AREA

CENTER ST

TRAVELODGE

99E   22

BEST WESTERN MILL CREEK INN

THOMPSON BREWERY AND PUBLIC HOUSE

COMMERCIAL ST

5

THE PHOENIX INN

THE WILLAMETTE VALLEY

smaller murals symbolic of Oregon's industries also are displayed. The best part of the capitol is the legislative chambers, up the sweeping marble staircases.

Near the ceiling in the Senate and House chambers are friezes depicting an honor roll of people who influenced the growth and settlement of Oregon. Included are Thomas Jefferson, who sanctioned the Lewis and Clark expedition, and Thomas Condon, native son and naturalist extraordinaire. Also among the names are those of six women, headed by Lewis and Clark's interpreter-guide Sacajawea. The biggest surprise in the array might be John Quincy Adams, who determined the southern boundary of Oregon when he was secretary of state. In both legislative chambers look for forestry, agricultural, and fishing symbols woven into the carpets; murals about the coming of statehood are behind the speakers' rostrums.

Among the many architecturally eye-catching features to be found in the capitol are the rotunda's black marble, the House chamber walls and furnishings of golden oak, black walnut room appointments in the Senate, a walnut-paneled governor's office, and bronze doorknobs inlaid with the state seal throughout the building. There is also a carved myrtlewood table inlaid with a mosaic of the capitol in the reception area outside the governor's suite between the House and the Senate. All this was paid for with part of the $2 million it took to build the capitol in 1938.

If you don't want to roam independently, free half-hour-long building **tours** are given on the hour 9am-3pm on weekdays, Memorial Day through Labor Day.

A tower at the top of the capitol building gives a superlative view of the valley and surrounding Cascade peaks, worth the 121-step climb from the fourth floor. Tower tours depart hourly 9am-4pm on weekdays late March-September (but this are is closed when the temperature reaches 90°F). Also worth a look is the ongoing exhibit of outstanding Oregon artists in the governor's ceremonial office upstairs.

Downstairs is a café. On the west side of the building (Court St. entrance) is an indoor visitors information kiosk.

To get to the Oregon State Capitol from I-5, take Exit 253 to Route 22 West. Take the Willamette University/State Offices exit and follow the signs for 12th Street/State Offices. Turn left onto Court Street.

Capitol Grounds

At each end of the capitol are parks featuring giant sequoias, magnolias, and Camperdown elms. Between the capitol and the state executive building, on the corner of Court and Cottage Streets, is **Willson Park.** Lush lawns, a gazebo for concerts, and a wide variety of trees, including sequoias, Port Orford cedars, Asian cedars, blue spruces, mountain ashes, dogwoods, and incense cedars, invite a picnic. Two large multicolored rose gardens bloom through much of the year to garnish your spread, and a trio of bronze beavers make the perfect lunch companions. Also to the west of the building are the beautiful E. M. Waite Memorial Fountain and a replica of the Liberty Bell. To the east is **Capitol Park,** where you can admire Corinthian columns salvaged from the old capitol (destroyed by fire in 1935) and statues of Dr. John McLoughlin, Reverend Jason Lee, and the circuit rider, honoring horseback evangelists to the pioneers during the era of missionary zeal.

The oldest government building in Salem is the **Supreme Court building** (1147 State St.), dating back to 1914. It's to the east of the capitol on the southern half of the block across Waverly Street, facing State Street and bounded by 12th Street. The building's facade is white terra-cotta, and the marble interior has tile flooring. Visual highlights include an ornate stairwell and a stained-glass skylight in the third-floor courtroom framing a replica of the Oregon state seal. Above all, don't miss the public restrooms. Tastefully appointed in marble, oak, and tile, these facilities were described in *Oregon* magazine as "doing justice to public needs."

THE WILLAMETTE VALLEY

State Archives Building

The **State Archives Building** (800 N. Summer St., 503/373-0701, http://arcweb.sos.state.or.us, 8am-noon and 1pm-4:45pm Mon.-Fri.), just north of the Capitol Mall, has an elegant design and is home to some excellent public art. It's worth a look at the art in the building's foyer, but in order to get into the archives area, you'll have to fill out a bit of paperwork stating your research objective. (Saying you are a tourist, we've found, is insufficient.) The archives contain the scrawled accounts of a meeting of early state leaders, first-hand descriptions of settler life, and original documents relating to the Oregon Territory, as well as the first copy of the state constitution. It's all summed up quite well by the words below a striking glass mural of the pioneers in the reception area: "To think we came all that way, risked everything, used our bodies as plows, and arrived here with our lives."

Willamette University

Willamette University (900 State St., 503/370-6300, www,willamette.edu), just south of the Capitol Mall, is the oldest institution of higher learning west of the Mississippi. It began as the Oregon Institute in 1842, a school that Methodist missionary Jason Lee founded to instill Christian values among the settlers. Over the years, Willamette University has turned out its share of Oregon politicos, including longtime senators Mark Hatfield and Bob Packwood. It also has to be one of the prettier campuses in the nation.

The campus is one of Salem's many oases of greenery that soften the hard edge of a city dominated by government buildings and nondescript downtown thoroughfares. Campus landscape architecture features a Japanese garden (the Martha Springer Garden, at the southeast corner of campus, also boasts roses, a rock garden, and an English perennial garden), ornate fountains, and a grove of five sequoias six feet in diameter. When you stand in the middle of these redwoods, you should be able to discern a star pattern formed by their canopies, giving rise to the name "star trees." This grove, which sits between the State Capitol and Collins Hall, home of the science departments, has beside it an Oregon rock of ages. Found atop Ankeny Hill in Salem, the granite boulder floated down from northeastern Washington on an ice raft during the same Missoula Floods that shaped the Columbia River Gorge eons ago. This glacial erratic stands as a reminder that the Willamette Valley is largely composed of Lake Missoula sediments. In Collins Hall, crystals and exhibits on Oregon glacial activity join an impressive taxidermic array of Oregon wildlife. There's no admission charge, and it's open during university hours. Finally, if you're hungry, the food court at the student union, Goudy Commons, is exceptional, reasonably priced, and with enough variety to suit all tastes.

Part of Willamette University, the **Hallie Ford Museum** (700 State St., 503/370-6855, www.willamette.edu, 10am-5pm Tues.-Sat., 1pm-5pm Sun., $3 adults, $2 students and seniors, free to all on Tues.) features such Native American baskets and a third-century Buddhist bas-relief from Pakistan. Asian pieces are also prominent. Contemporary work—much of it very high caliber—is exhibited on a rotating basis.

Willamette Heritage Center at the Mill

Just east of Willamette University, a complex of historic buildings along an old millstream make up the **Willamette Heritage Center** (1313 SE Mill St., 503/585-7012, www.willametteheritage.org, 10am-5pm Mon.-Sat., $6 adults, $5 seniors, $3 children ages 6-17, free to all on Tues.). Its centerpiece is the reconstructed Thomas Kay Woolen Mill. The oldest frame house in the Pacific Northwest and water turbines converting fleece into wool fabric are interesting, and the local fiber arts guild uses the building for classes. Several historic homes, including the Jason Lee House and Parsonage, have been moved to this site. The Jason Lee houses, along with the Boon Home, were part of a Methodist mission to the Native Americans.

To get to the museum from I-5, exit at Route 22, go west on Mission Street for two miles to the 13th Street overpass, turn north onto 12th Street, and go west on Mill Street. If you arrive by Amtrak, Mission Mill is within walking distance.

Deepwood Estate

The historic **Deepwood Estate** (1116 SE Mission St., 503/363-1825, www.historicdeepwoodestate.org, gardens dawn-dusk daily, house tours on the hour 9am-noon Wed.-Mon. May-Sept., 11am-3pm Wed.-Thurs. and Sat. Oct.-Apr., $4 adults, $3 students and seniors, $2 children) features tours of an elegant 1894 Queen Anne-style home with hand-carved woodwork, gorgeous stained-glass windows, and a well-marked nature trail. English formal gardens here were designed in the 1930s by the Pacific Northwest's first women-owned landscape architecture firm; the Pringle Creek Trail's native flora and the public greenhouse's tropical plants are also worth visiting. Sit in Deepwood's pagoda-like gazebo with the scent of boxwood heavy in the air on a spring afternoon and you'll soon forget the hue and cry of political proceedings at the capitol. Parking is at 12th and Lee Streets near the greenhouse.

Bush House and Park

Bush House Museum (600 Mission St., 503/363-4714, http://salemart.org, hourly tours 1pm-4pm Wed.-Sun. Mar.-Dec., $6 adults, $5 seniors, $4 students, $3 children ages 6-15) is located in 80-acre **Bush Pasture Park** off Mission, High, and Bush Streets. This 1877 Victorian, with many original furnishings, is the former home of pioneer banker and newspaper publisher Asahel Bush, who once wrote about his competitor, "There's not a brothel in the land that would not have been disgraced by the presence of the *Oregonian*." Even if you're not big on house tours, the Italian marble fireplaces and elegant walnut-and-mahogany staircase are worth a look. Besides being a sylvan retreat for picnickers and sports enthusiasts,

the Bush Pasture Park is home to the **Bush Barn Art Center** (541/581-2228, 10am-5pm Tues.-Fri., noon-5pm Sat.-Sun., free). Next to the Bush House, this center features two galleries with monthly exhibits and a classy gift shop. To get there from I-5, take Exit 253 and drive 2 miles west on Route 22 (Mission St.). Turn south on High Street and enter the park on Bush Street, one block south of Madison.

Oregon State Hospital Museum of Mental Health

If you've seen the movie made from Ken Kesey's *One Flew Over the Cuckoo's Nest*, you have an idea of what the **Oregon State Hospital Museum of Mental Health** (2600 Center St. NE, 971/599-1674, http://oshmuseum.org, noon-4pm Tues., Fri., Sat., $4 adults, $3 seniors and students, $2 children ages 6-18) is like—the movie was filmed in this imposing brick building, which started accepting patients in 1883. Patients were confined to the hospital both voluntarily and by commitment, and their ailments ranged from alcoholism to dementia to "mania." Upon entering the museum, visitors are issued an ID badge with the name of a patient, staff member, or visitor; information about these individuals is revealed in museum exhibits. Exhibits look at conditions that patients were treated for, treatments offered (including straitjackets, lobotomies, ice baths, and sterilization as well as those considered to be more progressive and humane), life on the ward, and the Cuckoo's Nest movie.

Riverfront Park

Downtown Salem is bordered to the west by the Willamette River, and **Riverfront Park** is a good place for a stroll, a riverboat excursion, or a ride on the **Salem Carousel** (101 Front St. NE, 503/540-0374, www.salemcarousel.org, 10am-7pm Mon.-Sat., 11am-6pm Sun. June-Sept., 10am-6pm Mon.-Thurs., 10am-7pm Fri.-Sat., 11am-5pm Sun. Oct.-May, $1.50). It's no antique—it was built in the late 1990s—and the carousel horses were hand-carved by volunteers.

Along the river near the carousel is the

Willamette Queen (200 Water St. NE, 503/371-1103, www.willamettequeen.com), a stern-wheeler that cruises the Willamette year-round. Lunch cruises are offered noon-1pm Wednesday-Saturday ($25 adults, $16 children ages 4-10); one-hour afternoon cruises without food are less expensive (2pm, $12 adults, $6 children) and allow you to eat at a good restaurant a short walk away in downtown. Dinner and Sunday brunch cruises are also offered. This is a good way to get a decent look at the river and, if you're lucky, some of its wildlife.

A. C. Gilbert's Discovery Village (116 Marion St. NE, 503/371-3631, www.acgilbert.org, 10am-5pm Mon.-Sat., noon-5pm Sun., $7 visitors ages 3-59, $5.50 seniors, $3.50 children ages 1-2, $3 visitors on public assistance) is a cheerful cluster of restored Victorians that house kid-focused exhibits. Inspired by A. C. Gilbert, a Salem native whose many inventions included the Gilbert Chemistry Set and the Erector Set, Discovery Village's hands-on expositions incorporate art, music, drama, science, and nature. Whether you're designing a card or bookmark in the craft room, putting on a puppet show, or disassembling a parking meter, the outlets for creativity here are adaptable to any mood or mind-set. If you don't have participatory inclinations, you can still enjoy fascinating exhibits like the one dedicated to A. C. Gilbert, whose Olympian athletic exploits and proficiency as a world-class magician were overshadowed by his inventions. As you might expect, even the gift shop here is a winner.

Gardens

Schreiner's Iris Gardens (3625 NE Quinaby Rd., 503/393-3232, www.schreinersgardens.com, 8am-dusk) is one of the world's largest iris growers; visit mid-May through the first week of June to take in the peak blossom seasons. Schreiner's is seven miles north of Salem next to I-5.

Wine, Cider, and Beer

Some of Oregon's best wine is produced within a few miles of the State Capitol. **St. Innocent Winery** (5657 Zena Rd. NW, 503/378-1526, www.stinnocentwine.com, 11am-5pm daily Feb.-Dec., 11am-5pm Fri.-Sun. Jan.) is just a few miles from downtown and is known for its good wines and sustainable farming. In the same neighborhood, **Witness Tree Vineyard** (7111 Spring Valley Rd. NW, 503/585-7874, www.witnesstreevineyard.com, 11am-5pm Tues.-Sun. May-Nov.), named for an ancient oak that towers over this lovely vineyard, is a small producer of top-notch pinot noir and chardonnay.

You'll find apples, not grapes, undergoing fermentation at **Wandering Aengus Ciderworks** (4070 Fairview Industrial Dr. SE, 503/361-2400, www.wanderingaengus.com). Over 20 apple varieties are pressed to make ciders that range from very dry to slightly sweet. The tasting room is open on an irregular basis (check the website).

Due west of Salem, you'll find **Firesteed Cellars** (2200 N. Rte. 99W, Rickreall, 503/623-8683, www.firesteed.com, 11am-5pm daily) with some of the region's most affordable (but still delicious) wines; and **Eola Hills Wine Cellars** (501 S. Rte. 99W, Rickreall, 503/623-2405 or 800/291-6730, www.eolahillswinery.com, 10am-5pm daily), one of the area's pioneering wineries with many vineyard holdings and reasonably priced wine.

A few miles south of town, just off I-5, **Willamette Valley Vineyards** (8800 Enchanted Way SE, Turner, 503/588-9463 or 800/344-9463, www.wvv.com, 10am-6pm daily) is one of the state's largest wineries, with great views and a classy tasting room. Free tours are offered every day at 2pm; private tours ($20) are available by appointment and include a private tasting and cheese tray.

South of Salem, about seven miles southeast of the town of Independence, thoughts turn to beer. Stop by **Rogue Farms Hopyard** (3590 Wigrich Rd., Independence, 503/838-9813, www.rogue.com, 11am-9pm daily) to watch the hops grow, taste beer, grab a meal made from farm crops, or stay overnight in an

ENCHANTED FOREST

Seven miles south of Salem off I-5 on Exit 248 is the **Enchanted Forest** (8462 Enchanted Way, Turner, 503/371-4262, www.enchanted-forest.com), one man's answer to Walt Disney. An enterprising Oregonian has single-handedly built a false-front Western town, a haunted house, and many more attractions.

In the 1960s Roger Tofte, the father of four young children, realized there was very little for a family to see and do together in Salem. He formulated the idea for a theme park where he could use his creative talents. Although he had very little time or money to make his dream a reality, he was able to purchase the original 20 acres of land off I-5 for $4,000 in monthly payments of $50. In 1964 he began construction.

Finally, in 1971, Tofte officially opened the park. Over the years, Tofte has successfully incorporated three of his children into the business: Susan (co-operations officer and artistic director), Mary (co-operations officer and chief financial officer), and Ken (head of attractions development and ride maintenance).

Whether it's the old woman who lived in the shoe, the seven dwarves' cottage, or Alice in Wonderland's rabbit hole, these and other nursery-rhyme and fairy-tale re-creations will get a thumbs-up from anyone under 99 years of age. One of the most inventive attractions is an old English village that features a life-size Geppetto and Pinocchio telling stories punctuated by animated characters popping their heads out of windows.

The park has a few schedule quirks; it's best to check the website if you are going to be visiting 5pm-6pm. Basically, it is open 10am-5pm or 6pm daily March 15-March 31; weekends only in April; daily May-Labor Day; weekends only in September; closed October-March 15th. Admission is $10.50 for adults, $9.50 for seniors and children ages 3-12, $1-4 extra for many rides.

old farmhouse ($140). Seven varieties of hops grow here by the Willamette River. Farm tours are offered at noon and 3pm on Saturday and Sunday.

SPORTS AND RECREATION
Bicycling

Although Salem is not the cycling paradise that you'll find in nearby Willamette Valley cities of Portland, Eugene, and Corvallis, it is possible to have some fun on two wheels. The best news is the trail through Riverfront Park and the **Union Street Railroad Bicycle and Pedestrian Bridge** over the Willamette River (otherwise hard to cross without a car). The bridge links Riverfront Park with Wallace Marine Park on the west side of the river. Another good place to cycle, skate, or walk is **Minto-Brown Island Park** (2200 Minto Island Rd. SE), a large natural park with lots of trails and an off-leash dog park. Find it along the east bank of the Willamette River south of the capitol area.

Golf

The **Salem Golf Club** (2025 Golf Course Rd., 503/363-6652, $50 for 18 holes on summer weekends, less at other times) is one of the best public courses in the state. Another option is **Santiam Golf Club** (8724 Golf Club Rd., Sublimity, 503/769-3485, www.sanitiamgolf-club.com, $39 for 18 holes): If you drive 15 minutes east on Route 22 (at Exit 12), you can look forward to combining a round of golf with a walk in the country. Low greens fees and a full-service restaurant and bar add to the pleasure.

ENTERTAINMENT AND EVENTS

Salem's recreational mix belies its reputation for being a town dedicated to legislation and little else. The **Elsinore Theatre** (170 High St. SE, 503/375-3574, www.elsinoretheatre.com) is a nicely restored vintage theater and downtown cultural venue that features music and dance performances and classic films as well as live theater. Other local venues include the L. B. Day Amphitheater at the fairgrounds hosting big-name acts, brewpubs featuring live music, and Salem Riverfront Park, which hosts summertime concerts.

Five miles west of downtown, the **Pentacle Theatre** (324 52nd Ave. NW, 503/364-7121, www.pentacletheatre.org) hosts an award-winning eight-play season.

Salem is full of studio tours, downtown art tours, and art galleries, as well as theater and musical events. The "Weekend" section of the Friday *Statesman Journal* (www.statesmanjournal.com) gives complete cultural listings.

The **Salem Art Association** (600 Mission St., 503/581-2228, http://salemart.org) puts on the **Salem Art Fair and Festival** the third week of July. This multiday event includes 200 artists, performing arts, food, children's activities, a five-kilometer run, an Oregon authors' table, wine and cheese tasting, and art technique demonstrations.

The **Oregon State Fair** (2330 NE 17th St., 503/947-3247 or 800/833-0011, www.oregonstatefair.org) is an annual celebration held in Salem during the 12 days prior to Labor Day. The fair showcases Oregon agriculture, industries, tourist attractions, natural resources, government, and cultural activities. Big-name entertainment (well, it's actually often big-name has-beens), amusement park rides, an international photography show, and a horticultural exhibit are also included in this blend of carnival and commerce. The best way to get there off I-5 is via Exits 253 or 258. Admission is $11 for children ages 13 and up, $6 for seniors and children 6-12, and children under 5 get in free; save a few bucks by buying tickets online in advance of the fair's start. Parking is $5. Entertainment tickets for musical events can run an extra $20-70. This is the largest agricultural fair on the West Coast. It is also host to one of the largest horse shows in the nation. While there's no shortage of worthwhile events, family fun can come with a hefty price tag as soon as you stray from the animal barns.

ACCOMMODATIONS

Salem's lodgings are largely mid-priced chain hotels clustered near I-5. The choice spot to stay is the downtown **C Grand Hotel** (201 Liberty St. SE, 503/540-7800 or 877/540-7800, www.grandhotelsalem.com, $129), an elegant hotel and conference center with large, nicely furnished guest rooms and a good restaurant.

A good bet that's close to the freeway on the south side of town is the **Best Western Mill Creek Inn** (3125 Ryan Dr. SE, 503/585-3332, www.bestwestern.com/millcreekinn, $122-146), with large rooms and a pool and hot tub, plus a free shuttle service to the Salem Airport and Amtrak as well as an included breakfast at a nearby Denny's. Take the Mission Street exit (Exit 253) from I-5.

Near the Market Street exit (Exit 256) from I-5, the **DoubleTree** (1590 Weston Ct. NE, 503/581-7004, $149-179) has a convenient location and nice rooms.

If you don't mind staying a little ways north of town, the **Hopewell House B&B** (22350 Hopewell Rd. NW, 503/868-7848, www.hopewellbb.com, $159-179) is a good place to relax in a newer B&B with lodging in cottages with kitchens, hot tubs, and a rural setting.

If you're looking for more modestly priced accommodations, try the **Travelodge** (1555 State St., 503/581-2466, $56-60). It's nothing fancy, but it is clean and convenient.

FOOD

Salem's dining is beginning to rise up from its longtime general mediocrity. Strangely enough, for a city so perfectly situated in Oregon's richest farming country, many places rely on the Sysco truck for their ingredients. But there are exceptions.

Bakeries and Cafés

A downtown place that's good for a midmorning pastry or quick lunch is **Cascade Baking Company** (229 State St., 503/589-0491, www.cascadebaking.com, 7am-6pm Mon.-Fri., 8am-3pm Sat., mini pizza $5), which supplies bread to some of Salem's best restaurants and cooks up a big batch of personal-size pizzas every day at lunchtime. Panini sandwiches and pastries are also available. Salem's other good bakery, **Little Cannoli Bakery** (189 Liberty St. NE, 503/585-9288, www.littlecannolibakery.com, 9am-5pm Tues.-Sat.) is tucked in the basement of the Reed Opera House and known more for its excellent dessert pastries.

The downtown **Allann Brothers Beanery** (220 Liberty St. NE, 503/399-7220, www.allannbroscoffee.com, 6am-8pm Mon.-Thurs., 6am-9pm Fri.-Sat., 7am-7pm Sun., $4-9) has long hours, free wireless Internet, and good light breakfasts as well as homemade pastries, soups, quiche, sandwiches, deli salads, wine, and beer.

One place that's worth a visit, especially if you want to see sausage (er, legislation) being made, is **Cafe at the Capitol** (900 NE Court St., 503/585-4266, 7am-5pm Mon.-Fri. when legislature is in session, 7am-3pm Mon.-Fri. when legislature is not in session, $5-10) in the basement of the capitol building. It's a major hangout when the legislature is in session. Sit down with a cup of coffee and set to eavesdropping.

American

◖ Word of Mouth (140 17th St. NE, 503/930-4285, www.wordofmouth.com, 7am-3pm daily, $7-12), located in an old house east of the capitol and Willamette University, is known for its delicious breakfasts, where corned beef hash is the signature dish, but the omelets are also exceptionally good and the crème brûlée french toast a local favorite. WOM bills itself as a neighborhood bistro, but Salemites are coming from all over town to eat summertime salads of fresh-picked tomatoes.

Another good, and extremely popular, downtown spot is **Wild Pear** (372 State St., 503/378-7515, www.wildpearcatering.com, 10:30am-6pm Mon.-Sat., $7-14), a lunchtime restaurant and catering business with a good selection of sandwiches and salads. Lunches are large, but you might still consider adding an order of white-truffle sweet potato fries with mustard aioli.

Although we don't usually look to school cafeterias for a good lunch, Willamette University's **◖ Goudy Commons** (900 State St., 503/370-6300, 7am-10am, 11am-2pm, and 4:30pm-7pm Mon.-Fri., 8:30am-1:30pm and 4:30pm-7pm Sat.-Sun., lunch $3-8) is an exception. It's just a short walk from the capitol, and you'll find legislators, lobbyists, and state employees lining up with the students for the excellent and inexpensive salad bar. From State Street (the college's address), turn south on Winter Street, then turn left onto the footpath into the campus and look for the redbrick building. Unfortunately, Goudy shuts down when school is not in session.

Bentley's Grill (291 Liberty St. SE, 503/779-1660, www.bentleysgrill.com, 11am-10pm Mon.-Thurs., 11am-11pm Fri.-Sat., 4pm-9pm Sun., $10-33), in the Phoenix Grand Hotel, is a reliable place for good steaks, fresh seafood, and wood-fired pizzas. It's one of the fancier restaurants in town, but not stuffy, and better than most hotel restaurants.

Mediterranean

Amadeus (135 Liberty St. NE, 503/362-8830, 11am-9pm Tues.-Thurs., 11am-11pm Fri.-Sat., $12-25), a longtime south Salem favorite, has moved downtown. Along with a good selection of seafood dishes, Amadeus has a wide range of choices for vegetarians—some, such as the "beggar's purse" (sautéed mushrooms, dried cranberries, pecans, and jack cheese wrapped in phyllo and served with a cherry and port wine reduction), are a little different than the usual pasta primavera.

French

At **La Capitale** (508 State St., 503/585-1975, www.lacapitalesalem.com, 11am-9pm Tues.-Fri., noon-9pm Sat., $11-21), a French bistro, the food is a bit uneven, but the location and atmosphere are great for a late afternoon snack and a glass of wine.

Asian Fusion

Venti's Cafe (325 Court St. NE, 503/399-8733, ventiscafe.com, 11am-11pm Mon.-Tues., 11am-midnight Wed.-Thurs., 11am-1am Sat.,

11am-10pm Sun., $7-12) is a little bit Asian and a little bit Mediterranean, with falafels, rice bowls, wraps, Tibetan pork barbecue, and lots of vegetarian options. Venti's also has a great selection of craft beers and a few varieties of cider. Downstairs, find a club and a full bar. Venti's has another location at 2840 Commercial Street SE (503/391-5100).

Italian

If you're looking for a pizza joint, **Christo's** (1108 Broadway NE, 503/371-2892, 11:30am-2:30pm and 4:30pm-8pm Mon.-Thurs., 11:30am-2pm and 4:30pm-9pm Fri., 5pm-9:30pm Sat., $5-12), in what is beginning to emerge as a lively neighborhood just north of downtown, is a fun place with good pizza and, quite often, live jazz.

Mexican

Among Salem's many Mexican restaurants, a local favorite is **Hacienda Real** (475 Taggart Dr. NW, 503/585-3855, www.lahaciendarealonline.com, 11am-10pm Mon.-Thurs., 11am-11pm Fri.-Sat., $9-16), known for homemade tortillas and Jalisco-style food. There are a couple of other locations around town.

Farmers Markets

U-pick farms are a delight from spring through fall in and around Salem. Cherries, strawberries, apples, peaches, plums, and blackberries are some of the bounty available. Early in June, the *Statesman Journal* puts out a list of local outlets in the area, describing what's available where and when, titled "Oregon Direct Market Association." Fruit stands are listed in this guide as well. Many concessionaires, such as **Bauman Farms** (12989 Howell Prairie Rd., 503/792-3524), offer both self-service harvest and over-the-counter sales. Several dozen agricultural products are available, including 10 berry varieties and pumpkins. Items such as fresh home-pressed apple cider and holiday gift packs round out the array. To reach Bauman, take Route 99E one mile south of Woodburn to Howell Prairie Road. Following the signs, go about 0.5 mile to reach the stand.

Brewpubs

Of course, the McMenamins have an outpost in Salem. At **Boon's Treasury** (888 Liberty St. NE, 503-399-9062, 11am-midnight Mon.-Thurs., 11am-1am Fri.-Sat., noon-11pm Sun., $8-12), you can down microbrews and enjoy live music amid the brick confines of the old treasury building or hang out in the backyard beer garden.

A newer brewpub, **Gilgamesh Brewing** (2065 Madrona St., 503/584-1789, 4pm-11pm Mon.-Thurs., 4pm-1am Fri.-Sat., food $7-15) specializes in beers with unusual ingredients, such as black tea, jasmine, or shiitake mushrooms as well as the standard Pacific Northwest IPAs. During the summer they host free Sunday evening concerts. The food here is a cut above pub grub.

INFORMATION

The **Travel Salem visitor information center** (181 High St. NE, 503/581-4325 or 800/874-7012, www.travelsalem.com, 9am-5pm Mon.-Fri., 10am-4pm Sat.) is downtown.

The Salem *Statesman Journal* (www.statesmanjournal.com) is sold throughout the Willamette Valley, central coast, and central Oregon. The newspaper's "Weekend" section features entertainment listings and reviews every Friday covering the week to come. Although these listings focus on Salem, considerable attention is also given to events throughout the Willamette Valley, central Oregon, and the coast.

GETTING THERE AND AROUND

Salem's State and Center Streets run east-west; Commercial and Liberty Streets run north-south. East and West Nob Hill Streets run southeast. With a profusion of one-way streets and thoroughfares that end abruptly, it's important to keep your bearings. One helpful frame of reference is supplied by remembering that Commercial Street runs north-south along the Willamette River on the western edge of town.

Salem provides a lot of ways to get in and

out of town. **Greyhound** (450 NE Church St., 503/362-2428) runs about five buses a day through Salem. The **Amtrak** station (500 13th St. SE, 503/588-1551 or 800/872-7245) sits across from Willamette University and is close to Mission Mill Museum. The **Salem airport** (503/588-6314) is a few miles east of downtown. A Salem-to-Portland airport shuttle

is run by **Hut Limousine Service** (503/364-4444, www.portlandairportshuttle.com, $35 one way).

Mass-transit bus service in town is run by **Salem Area Mass Transit (Cherriots)** (216 High St., 503/588-2877 or 503/588-2424, www.cherriots.org, $1.50). Terminals are in front of the courthouse.

Vicinity of Salem

SILVERTON

Silverton, located in the foothills of the Cascades about 10 miles east of Salem, is a thriving small town with a major attraction—the Oregon Garden—right out its back door.

Don't rush past downtown Silverton; it's worth spending at least a few minutes wandering past or through the antiques and decor shops. And don't be surprised to see a tall cross-dressing fellow out for coffee on a Saturday morning—that would be Mayor Stu, who

knows firsthand that the Willamette Valley is still a place for pioneers.

The big annual "do" in Silverton is **Homer Davenport Days** (503/873-5615, homerdavenport.com), usually held the first weekend in August, when locals enjoy crafts, food, music, and the spectacle of neighbors racing furniture down Main Street. Davenport was a nationally famous cartoonist in the 1930s and a Silverton favorite son. Most of the action takes place at **Coolidge-McClain Park** (300 Coolidge St.).

THE WILLAMETTE VALLEY

© BILL MCRAE

The Oregon Garden has 80 acres of formal gardens and a destination hotel.

WILLAMETTE BIRD SANCTUARIES

The federal government established several bird sanctuaries between Salem and Eugene in the mid-1960s because of the encroachment of urbanization and agriculture on the winter habitat of the dusky Canada goose. This species now comes to **Baskett Slough National Wildlife Refuge** (NWR) west of Salem, **Ankeny NWR** southwest of Salem, and **Finley NWR** south of Corvallis each October after summering in Alaska's Copper River Delta. Refuge ecosystems mesh forest, cropland, and riparian environments to attract hummingbirds, swans, geese, sandhill cranes, ducks, egrets, herons, plovers, sandpipers, hawks and other raptors, wrens, woodpeckers, and dozens of other avian ambassadors. Migrating waterfowl begin showing up in the Willamette Valley in mid-October. By mid-March, large numbers of Canada geese, tundra swans, and a variety of ducks descend on the refuge.

The pamphlet "Birds of Willamette Valley Refuges" (available from Refuge Manager, Western Oregon Refuges, 26208 Finley Refuge Rd., Corvallis 97337, 541/757-7236, www.fws.gov) details the best months to spot bird, the frequency of sightings, and the locations of hundreds of kinds of birds.

To maintain the sanctity of the birds' habitat, the refuges restrict birders by closing some trails in winter; other trails farther from feeding grounds are kept open year-round. A hike that can be enjoyed any time of year is Finley NWR's one-mile **Woodpecker Loop.** A variety of plant communities exists due to the Kalapuya Native American people's field-burning followed by pioneer logging and cattle-grazing. Its location on the border between the Coast Range and the Willamette Valley also contributes to the diversity. Forests of oak and Douglas fir as well as a mixed deciduous grove combine with marshes to provide a wide range of habitats. Look for the rare pileated woodpecker in the deciduous forest. The loop's trailhead is reached by taking Route 99W (from Corvallis) to Refuge Road. Look for the footpath on the right after driving three miles. A drop box has a pamphlet with pictures and information on the birds, wildlife, and plant communities.

Ankeny NWR is located 12 miles south of Salem off I-5 at Exit 243, and Baskett Slough NWR lies northwest of Rickreall on Route 22. Visit fall through spring for the best chance to see ducks, geese, swans, and raptors.

In recent years the proliferation of Canada geese in the lower Willamette Valley has compelled people to question if the refuges have been too successful. Farmers complain that the birds interfere with crops. State wildlife managers are currently rethinking the protections accorded to the migratory fowl. After seeing the dwindling numbers of the state bird, the western meadowlark, in the Willamette Valley due to human encroachment, let's hope the powers that be can reach a healthy balance.

Oregon Garden

The **Oregon Garden** (879 W. Main St., 503/874-8100 or 877/674-2733, www.oregongarden.org, 9am-6pm daily May-Sept., 10am-4pm daily Oct.-Apr., $11 adults, $9 seniors, $8 students) offers 20 different specialty gardens on 80 verdant acres. The gardens were designed by a dream team of landscape architects with the backing of the state's dynamic nursery industry—nursery plants are among Oregon's most important agricultural products. A lovely hotel and spa make an overnight visit an attractive option.

There are some lovely and innovative parts of the gardens. Especially intriguing is the wetlands section, which uses treated wastewater from Silverton to create the environment. The water travels through a series of terraced ponds and wetland plants to a holding tank; from there it is used to irrigate the entire garden. A garden of medicinal plants and a garden with a train running through it are also fun to visit.

An attraction that makes the trip to the gardens worthwhile for architecture buffs is the **Gordon House** (869 W. Main St., Silverton, 503/874-6006, www.thegordonhouse.org, tours noon-4pm daily, $10 adults, $5 children and students with ID, reservations strongly recommended), a Frank Lloyd Wright-designed home located within the Oregon Garden complex. The house, originally located in Wilsonville, was moved to its current spot in 2000, when the original property was sold and the new owners planned to demolish the house and rebuild to suit their own tastes. The modestly sized house is an example of Wright's populist Usonian style and has beautiful western red cedar trim, many built-in drawers and cabinets, and lots of natural light. Terraces bring the outdoors in, and low ceilings in the bedrooms create a sense of retreat. Docents lead tours on the hour; this is the only way to see the inside of the house.

Accommodations and Food

The **◖ Oregon Garden Resort** (895 W. Main St., 503/874-2500 or 800/966-6490, www.oregongardenresort.com, $139) is a great addition to the Oregon Garden. A huge stone fireplace dominates the main lodge, which also includes a restaurant and lounge; guest rooms are in a series of small six-unit buildings tucked behind the main lodge. All the guest rooms, which are decorated in a way that's pretty and upscale but not too designer-slick, have private patios or balconies and gas fireplaces; some are pet-friendly (as is part of the Oregon Garden itself). Many packages are offered, and special deals abound. Especially during the off-season, this can be a surprisingly affordable getaway.

Should you decide to stay in town rather than at the gardens, a convenient and extensively remodeled option is the **Silverton Inn and Suites** (310 N. Water St., 503/873-1000, www.silvertoninnandsuites.com, $89-229), a once-lackluster motel that has been transformed into a stylish suite hotel with kitchenettes in most guest rooms, each of which is named for a Willamette Valley pioneer or place. Another good option right in the heart of Silverton is the **Birdwood Inn B&B** (511 S. Water St., 503/873-3247, www.birdwoodbandb.com, $95-115), a small inn with two bedrooms (private baths) and a separate

cottage. The gardens at the Birdwood are a special delight.

A perfect spot for breakfast is **The Gathering Spot** (106 N. 1st St., 503/874-4888, gatheringspotcafe.com, 8am-3pm daily, $9-12), a friendly up-to-date diner with fantastic omelets, cinnamon roll pancakes, and a breakfast sandwich worth getting up early for.

Downtown Silverton's **◖ Silver Grille** (206 E. Main St., 503/873-8000, www.silvergrille.com, 5pm-9:30pm Wed.-Mon., $16-24) has a big reputation among locals in the greater Salem area as *the* restaurant for casual fine dining. Chef Jerry Nizlek focuses on local produce and wines to create a seasonal Willamette Valley cuisine that's both innovative and classic.

In a simple diner in downtown Silverton, you can find surprisingly good Thai food at **Thai Dish** (209A N. Water St., 503/873-8963, 11am-9pm Mon.-Thurs., 11am-10pm Fri., noon-10pm Sat., noon-9pm Sun., $8-13). Just down the block, **Mac's Place** (201 N. Water St., 503/873-2441, 9am-2am) is a hoppin' bar in one of Silverton's oldest buildings, from 1885. Mac's is known for its historic building, its murals, and its live music more than its food.

MOUNT ANGEL

Mount Angel's location an hour south of Portland makes it an excellent day trip. Just take Exit 272 for Woodburn off I-5 and follow the blue Silver Falls tour route signs. If you're approaching the Mount Angel Abbey from Salem off I-5, take the Chemawa exit and follow the signs.

◖ Mount Angel Abbey

Four miles northwest of Silverton off Route 214 and high above the rest of the Willamette Valley is **Mount Angel Abbey.** The abbey itself is perched above the faux-Bavarian town of Mount Angel; as you drive there you'll pass the neo-Gothic St. Mary's church, which is staffed by abbey monks.

The Benedictine abbey sits on a 300-foot hill overlooking cropland and Cascade vistas. From the bluff, look northward to Mount Hood, Mount St. Helens, Mount Adams, and,

Mount Angel Abbey is perched on a hill above the Willamette Valley.

© JUDY JEWELL

THE WILLAMETTE VALLEY

according to locals (that would be monks), on exceptionally clear days you can see Mount Rainier. The abbey **library,** designed by the famous Finnish architect Alvar Aalto, is an architectural highlight. The beautiful light and modern lines of the interior are nearly as inspiring as the texts on the shelves. But the texts are also pretty amazing, especially those housed in the Rare Book Room. Also worth checking out are the display cases in the lobby; the exhibits are invariably interesting.

The other Mount Angel Abbey building that's nearly mandatory to visit is the delightfully old-fashioned and noninterpretive **museum** (10am-11:30am and 1pm-5pm daily, free), which is tucked in a basement to the side of the main church (get a map from the librarian and ask to have the museum pointed out). Displays include religious artifacts such as a crown of thorns, crystals, and a huge collection of taxidermy, including an eight-legged calf.

The abbey's late-July **Bach Festival** features professional musicians in an idyllic setting; call for tickets months in advance (503/845-3321).

Guided tours of the abbey are offered by appointment. Meditative retreats can be arranged at the abbey's **retreat house** (503/845-3025, www.mountangelabbey.org, $77 single occupancy includes all meals). Arrival days are Monday-Thursday; Sunday is not available for arrival or overnight stays. Although the accommodations are ascetic, the peace of the surroundings and the beauty of the monks' rituals will deepen your personal reflections no matter your spiritual orientation.

Wooden Shoe Bulb Company

Plant nurseries abound in the area. A visit to the **Wooden Shoe Tulip Farm** (33814 S. Meridian Rd., Woodburn, 541/634-2243, www.woodenshoe.com, $10 per car weekends or $5 weekdays during the tulip festival) in late March and early April will colorfully illustrate Oregon's rites of spring. The 17-acre tulip farm is located near Woodburn; take Exit 271 off I-5 and follow Route 214 east. It will become Route 211 to Molalla; turn right at the flashing yellow light onto Meridian Road, and go two miles to the tulip fields. Afterward you can head south through the town of Monitor and reach Mount Angel via a delightful rural route.

Recreation and Events

The town of Mount Angel's other claim to fame is its **Oktoberfest** (541/845-9440), which takes place in mid-September, when thousands of folks flock here to enjoy the *Weingarten,* the beer garden, the oompah-pah of traditional German music, art displays, yodeling, and street dancing amid beautiful surroundings. The biggest attraction of all, however, is the food. Stuffed cabbage leaves, strudels, and an array of sausages are the stuff of legend in the Willamette.

Bicyclists relish the foothills and farmland around Mount Angel, which are nearly devoid of traffic. Fall color is exceptional, and a varied topography ensures an eventful ride whatever the season. Lowland hop fields and filbert orchards give way to Christmas tree farms in the hills. On the way up, pumpkin and berry patches also break up the predominantly grassy terrain. This region is known as well for its crop of red fescue, a type of grass seed grown almost nowhere outside the northern Willamette Valley.

◖ SILVER FALLS STATE PARK

With 10 major waterfalls, nearly 30 miles of trails, and over 9,000 acres of pristine woodlands (much of it temperate rainforest), **Silver Falls State Park** (22024 Silver Falls Hwy., Sublimity, 26 miles east of Salem, 503/873-8681, ext. 31, www.oregonstateparks.org, $5 day use) is Oregon's largest and most spectacular. In fact, in the 1920s, Silver Falls was under consideration for national park status (it was rejected because parts of the land had just been clear-cut). Much of the park's infrastructure was created by the Civilian Conservation Corps (CCC) during the 1930s using rustic stone and log construction typical of national parks.

The park also contains a number of historic buildings built by the CCC, including South Falls Lodge, which now houses interpretive displays of the park's human and natural history. A short distance from the lodge is a viewpoint and the trailhead to South Falls.

Hiking

The park's 10 major waterfalls run 30-178 feet in height and cascade off canyon walls in a forest filled with gargantuan Douglas firs, ferns, yew, chinquapin, hemlock trees, and bigleaf and vine maple. These falls are linked by the seven-mile **Trail of Ten Falls** which passes by, and in some cases behind, the numerous falls on the north and south forks of Silver Creek. (While most of the trail is easy-moderate, there are several steep sections when the trail drops into the canyon; a two-car shuttle is recommended if you plan to hike the entire trail). The highlights are 177-foot **South Falls** and 136-foot **North Falls.** The opportunity to walk behind these waterfalls attracts a lot of visitors, who follow the trail beneath a basalt overhang in the cleft of each cliff. Bikers and horseback riders are not allowed on the Trail of Ten Falls, but have their own specially designated trails. Note that while leashed dogs are permitted on some trails at Silver Falls, they are not allowed on the Trail of Ten Falls.

North Falls and South Falls are easily reached from the North Falls parking lot and the day-use area, respectively, so you don't have to hike the whole loop to see both. To get to the day-use area from the North Falls parking lot, drive several miles south up the hill (on Rte. 214), stopping after 1.5 miles to look back at a spectacular view of North Falls.

Camping

Silver Falls State Park's campground (22024 Silver Falls Hwy., Sublimity, 503/873-8681, ext. 31, www.oregonstateparks.org, $19-24 campsites, $39 cabins) has 46 tent sites, 52 sites for trailers or motor homes up to 35 feet long, and 10 log cabins. Large groups (up to 75 people) can rent dormitory-style bunkhouses, called "ranches," for $200 per night (extra fees when exceeding 25 guests). Tent sites are open May-October; the RV campground and one of the "ranches" are open year-round. In addition

THE WILLAMETTE VALLEY

to hiking, swimming, and biking, there are stables near the park's entrance and a horse camp.

OPAL CREEK

The old-growth forests and emerald pools of Opal Creek were an environmental battleground for years until a land swap with a timber company who owned the logging rights. Opal Creek's 31,000-acre watershed, which includes a grove of 1,000-year-old 250-foot red cedar, has been called the most intact old-growth ecosystem on the West Coast.

To reach Opal Creek from Salem, take Route 22 for 19 miles east to Mehama. At the second flashing yellow light (at the corner with Swiss Village), turn left off Route 22 onto Little North Fork Santiam River Road at the State Forestry office and go about 15 miles toward the Elkhorn Recreation Area. Stay on this route until Forest Service Road 2209 (mostly gravel) and be sure to veer left, uphill, at the Y intersection. About six miles past the Willamette National Forest sign, a locked gate will bar your car from proceeding farther down Road 2209. Park and follow the trail to a large wooden map displaying various hiking options. Dogs must be on leashes.

While old-growth trees abound not far from the parking lot, be sure to cross over to the south side of the North Fork of the Little Santiam River (indicated by trailside signs). Here you can take in the placid Opal Pool, a small aquamarine catch-basin at the base of a cascade that cuts through limestone. Located several miles from the parking lot over gently rolling terrain, Opal Pool is the perfect day-hike destination.

There aren't just trees and pools of water at Opal Creek; the **Opal Creek Ancient Forest Center** (503/892-2782, http://opalcreek.org) is an environmental education center with a few cabins for rent ($195-250 double occupancy; bring your own sleeping bag and towel, no dogs). The center is 3 miles east from the trailhead; access is on foot only. A nearby Bureau of Land Management campground, **Elkhorn Valley** (503/897-2406, $14 Memorial Day-Labor Day), is a good place to camp and

stage a day trip to Opal Creek. To reach the campground, drive 24 miles east from Salem on Highway 22, and turn north on the North Fork County Road. Continue 8.5 miles to the campground.

DETROIT LAKE

It's a Salem tradition to take to the hills via Route 22 along the North Santiam River to enjoy the fishing and camping at Detroit Lake. This large and busy 400-foot-deep reservoir is known for its boating, waterskiing, swimming, and fishing for rainbow trout, landlocked chinook, and kokanee. Boat rentals are available at the marina. Because the reservoir was built for water storage, during drought years it can be drawn down enough to make recreation unappealing.

Camping

Although most Detroit Lake campers stay at the amenity-rich but very busy **Detroit Lake State Recreation Area** (503/854-3346, reservations 800/452-5687, www.oregonstateparks.org, $19-24) on the lake's north shore, the remoter south-shore Forest Service campground at **Cove Creek** (Blowout Rd., 503/854-3366, www.recreation.gov for reservations, $20) is much more peaceful. With 63 sites, flush toilets, pay showers, a boat launch, and other amenities, it's still not exactly a wilderness experience, but it's quite pleasant. Campsites are in a lush second-growth Douglas fir forest against a slope. Because there are no individual RV hookups, dump sites, or phones, Cove Creek is designed more for car campers than for people looking for a place to park a rig long-term. The campground is east of Detroit off Blowout Road.

BREITENBUSH

◖ Breitenbush Hot Springs

Breitenbush Hot Springs Retreat and Conference Center (503/854-7174 or 503/854-3321, www.breitenbush.com) offers natural hot springs, trails forested with old growth, as well as a wide variety of programs aimed at healing body, mind, and spirit. Set in the Cascade foothills, this onetime Native American encampment's artesian-flow hot springs have attracted people for healing throughout the ages. The hot springs pools, set variously in forest and meadow, contain 30 freely occurring minerals, including lithium. Music, storytelling, yoga, and superb vegetarian cuisine are also part of the Breitenbush experience. Sacred sweat lodge ceremonies conducted by Native Americans are offered once a month. Although many visitors come to Breitenbush to take part in an organized workshop (such as yoga, meditation, or spirituality), it's also possible to come on your own for a personal retreat. Know before you go that most hot springs bathers forgo the option of clothing.

The retreat cabins are spartan but sufficient. All have electricity and heat, and some have indoor plumbing. Rates are $103 (weekend rates; weekdays are a few dollars cheaper) per person for a cabin without a bathroom (there are a couple of bathhouses) or about $121 for a cabin with a bath (bring your own bedding or pay $16 extra), including three vegetarian meals daily and use of the facilities and waters. Single visitors may sometimes be assigned a cabin-mate unless they specify otherwise (and pay extra). Large tents on platforms are also available June-October for $76 per person, or you can camp in your own tent for $64. Day-use fees for hot springs and other facilities are $15-28; it's essential to call and reserve in advance. Individual all-you-can-eat lunches or dinners for daytime visitors cost $12.50. Be sure to bring your own caffeine if that's something that you require. Do not bring alcoholic beverages.

On-site you'll find the Spotted Owl Trail near the entrance of the Breitenbush parking lot. Near Breitenbush are such remarkable natural areas as Breitenbush Gorge, Opal Creek, Bull of the Woods, and Jefferson Park; for more information contact the Detroit Ranger Station at 503/854-3366.

To get to Breitenbush from Salem, take Route 22 to the town of Detroit. Turn at the gas station—the only one in town—onto Forest Service Road 46. Drive 10 miles and take a right over the bridge across Breitenbush River. Follow the signs, taking every left turn after the bridge, to the Breitenbush parking lot.

Accommodations and Camping

If Breitenbush is full, **All Seasons Motel** (130 Breitenbush Rd., Detroit, 503/854-3421, www. allseasonsmotel.net, $56-150), at Route 22 and Forest Service Road 46, is clean and comfy. It's not at all inconvenient to drive 15 minutes from here to the retreat center.

On the way up Forest Service Road 46 from Detroit to Breitenbush Hot Springs, you will pass a number of Forest Service campgrounds. **Breitenbush Campground** (10 miles northeast of Detroit, 503/854-3366, www.fs.usda. gov or www.recreation.gov, May-Sept., $14) is less than 2 miles from Breitenbush Resort and is a good spot for campers who want to visit the hot springs without staying at the resort itself. Nearby, the Breitenbush River has good fishing.

OLALLIE LAKE

To the east of Breitenbush, and almost directly north of Mount Jefferson, Olallie Lake is one of the nicest camping and hiking getaways in the area, with superb views of Mount Jefferson from the lake. The lake has a small **resort** (www.olallielakeresort.com) that offers 10 cabins of varying sizes ($65-100 per night, usually July-Sept.) with heated woodstoves and outhouses. The resort also manages the **Paul Dennis campground** ($15 per site, $100 for two-room yurts that sleep up to six), adjacent to the cabin area, and rents rowboats and canoes. Olallie Lake is along the Pacific Crest Trail, and there are hiking trails galore, many leading to other small lakes. In the early summer, wildflowers are an attraction; late in summer, this is a great place to pick wild huckleberries. The season up here is pretty short—snows usually keep the resort closed until July.

From the Detroit area, head north and east on Forest Service Road 46, then turn right on Forest Service Road 4220 (a rough gravel road) and follow it 13 miles to the lake.

THE WILLAMETTE VALLEY

MOUNT JEFFERSON

Prepare your muscles for a soak in the pools at Breitenbush by hiking Mount Jefferson, Oregon's second-highest peak at 10,495 feet. This snowcapped, symmetrical, volcanic cone dominates the Oregon Cascades horizon between Mount Hood to the north and the Three Sisters to the south—though unlike Mount Hood, Mount Jefferson is rarely visible from the west.

Mount Jefferson is twelve miles east of Detroit. Take Route 22 and turn left, following Forest Service Road 2243 (Whitewater Creek Rd.) 7.5 miles to the Whitewater Creek trailhead. From there, it's an easy 4.5-mile hike to **Jefferson Park.** This is the northern base of the mountain and features an abundance of lakes and, in early summer, wildflowers. The alpine meadows are full of purple and yellow lupine and red Indian paintbrush in July. On the way up, wild strawberries and red huckleberries can provide a delectable snack. For a special experience during the summer, start the walk after 5pm when there's a full moon and the trail is bathed in soft lunar light.

Above Jefferson Park, the ascent of the dormant volcano's cone is a precarious endeavor and should only be attempted by truly experienced climbers. You'll reach the bottom of Whitewater Glacier at 7,000 feet. Thereafter, climbing routes steepen to 45 degrees and snow and rock ridges crumble when touched. Near the top, the rocks aren't solid enough to allow the use of ropes or other forms of climbing protection; going down is even more dangerous than going up. Even if you head up the more sedate south face, you can expect difficulties due to the instability of the final 400 feet of rock on the pinnacle.

Sometimes the mosquitoes in Jefferson Park are bloodthirsty enough to pierce thick clothing, so bring insect repellent in summer. On occasion the area is so crowded with day-use visitors and folks trekking the nearby Pacific Crest Trail that Jefferson Park seems more like a city park than a mountain wilderness. No matter; the sight of Mount Jefferson in alpenglow at sunset or shrouded in moonlight will make you forget the intrusions of humans and insects alike.

Corvallis

The name "Corvallis" refers to the city's pastoral setting in the "Heart of the Valley." But just as much as its physical setting, it's the culture of Oregon State University that defines Corvallis. Everything from the coffeehouses and used bookstores to the pizza joints and network of biking trails seems to owe its existence to the university. It has been this way for a long time; Cascadia, the quintessential college town in the novel *A New Life* by the late Oregon State University professor Bernard Malamud, was modeled on Corvallis.

Although Corvallis isn't a huge tourist destination, its beauty, tranquility, and central location in the heart of the valley recommend it as a base from which to explore the bird sanctuaries, the Coast Range, and nearby historic communities. In town, you'll be struck by

the abundance of stately old trees, some dating back to the first pioneers, who arrived in 1847. Streets with wide bike lanes and scenic routes for cyclists that parallel the Willamette and Mary's Rivers also contribute to the idyllic time-warp feeling. This is especially the case in summer, when many students leave town.

In springtime, the daffodil-lined approach to Corvallis on Route 99W is made even more glorious by the Coast Range and its highest mountain, 4,097-foot Marys Peak, to the west over the hay meadows. During much of the winter, rain and fog obscure the summit from view.

The pastures of Lebanon and Brownsville east of Corvallis are good places to spot bald eagles. Venture out to the fields (beginning in February) when sheep are lambing to see eagles soaring above the newborn lambs. In the winter, grass seed farms outside Albany, Coburg, and Junction City attract tundra swans.

SIGHTS

Although a good chunk of the town's real estate is taken up by the OSU campus, Corvallis has a thriving downtown with a splendid path along the Willamette River. A number of restaurants face onto the riverfront.

The **Benton County Courthouse** (120 NW 4th St., 541/766-6756), near 4th and 5th Streets and Monroe Avenue, dates from 1888 and is the oldest functioning courthouse in the lower Willamette Valley. You can't miss its large white clock tower, but go inside to get the old-fashioned feel of the place. (Be sure to check out the basement bathrooms.)

Also downtown is the **Corvallis Art Center** (700 SW Madison Ave., 541/754-1551, http://theartscenter.net, noon-5pm Tues.-Sat.) in the renovated 1889 Episcopal church near Central Park. It sells local crafts at its ArtShop.

A large concentration of historic homes can be found in Corvallis, including many in neighborhoods close to downtown. Download walking tour maps of various neighborhoods from www.visitcorvallis.com; one interesting tour visits ranch houses from the 1950s. If you plan to be in Corvallis on a summer Saturday, call ahead (541/757-1544, leaves from 2nd St. and Jackson Ave., 1pm, $5 donation suggested) to inquire if there's a free spot on the weekly **Historic Homes Trolley Tour.**

Oregon State University

The parklike 500-acre campus of **Oregon State University (OSU),** home to some 26,000 students (follow the signs to Jefferson Ave. or Monroe Ave., 541/737-1000, www.oregonstate.edu), an 1868 land grant institution, is the major hub of activity in town, with a slew of eateries, bookstores, and craft boutiques on its periphery. Cultural activities on campus include lectures, concerts, theater productions, films, and art exhibits. Many are free and open to the public.

The end of February through mid-March is lambing time at the university's **Sheep Center** (7565 NW Oak Creek Dr., 541/737-3431, http://ans.oregonstate.edu). Although the Sheep Center was closed for renovations in 2013, this popular early spring attraction may be reopened to the public in the future; it's certainly worth a call to check.

While the notion of one of these fleecy specimens on a dinner plate might seem akin to eating Bambi, this facility's research has helped establish Oregon lamb as a gourmet product. Thanks to a diet of nutritious grasses indigenous to Pacific Northwest soils, Oregon lambs are larger and richer in flavor than their better-publicized New Zealand counterparts.

The university also maintains 11,500 acres of woodlands, notably **McDonald Experimental Forest** and **Peavy Arboretum,** accessible eight miles north of Corvallis on Route 99W, which feature hiking trails as well as the chance to see the rare Fender's blue butterfly. The species had been thought extinct for 50 years until a habitat was discovered here in 1990. This ecosystem serves primarily as a living laboratory for the university's Forestry Department.

Benton County Historical Society

Six miles west of Corvallis on Route 34 is the town of Philomath, home to the **Benton County Historical Society** (1101 Main St., Philomath, 541/929-6230, www.bentoncountymuseum.org, 10am-4:30pm Tues.-Sat., free). Looms, carriages, printing presses, and other pioneer history exhibits are mildly diverting, but the real star is the 1867 Georgian-style brick structure housing the collection. Just look for the imposing building on the right side of the highway as you head toward the coast.

Wineries

Located 10 miles off Route 99W south of Corvallis on the way up into the Coast Range is **Tyee Wine Cellars** (26335 Greenberry Rd., Corvallis, 541/753-8754, www.tyeewine.com, noon-5pm Fri.-Sun. Apr.-Dec.). Pinot gris, pinot noir, chardonnay, and Gewürztraminer are featured. After wine-tasting, you can enjoy a picnic on the grounds of this historic farm site or walk a 1.5-mile loop to beaver ponds. Several other wineries are also located in the area; see http://heartofwillamette.com for information on exploring other area wineries.

SPORTS AND RECREATION
Hiking
Marys Peak (www. fs.usda.gov) sits about 12 miles southwest of Corvallis. From Philomath follow Route 34 nine miles west to the road's Coast Range Summit (1,230 feet). A sign north of the highway points the way to a 10-mile drive to the top of the Coast Range's highest peak (4,097 feet) on Forest Service Road 30, the only road on the peak's south side. Along the way, pretty cascades, interesting rock outcroppings, and over-the-shoulder views of the Cascades on the eastern horizon intensify the anticipation of this mountaintop Kalapuya vision quest site.

When you get to the parking lot at the end of the road, the view is impressive—but don't stop there. If it's a clear day, take the short walk across the meadows to either of the two summit lookouts for perspectives on Mounts Hood and Jefferson, the Three Sisters to the east (eight Cascades peaks in total are potentially visible from here), and the Pacific Ocean at the base of the Coast Range to the west.

The summit, thanks to its status as a federally designated botanical area, remains untouched by clear-cuts that speckle the forests nearby. A biome unique to the Coast Range exists up here, with such flora as alpine phlox, beargrass, Pacific iris, tiger lily, Indian paintbrush, purple lupine, and the blue-green noble fir. Exceptionally large species of this fragrant tree grow on the Meadowedge Trail. This trail connects to a primitive campground (16 sites, May-Sept., $10 per night) two miles below the summit. It's part of a nine-mile network of trails around the upper slopes of the mountain. You'll also find hemlock, fir, and grand fir. Local creeks are home to the unique Marys Peak salamander, and the surrounding woods host bald eagles, red-tailed hawks, spotted owls, and Clark's nutcrackers—seldom seen west of the Cascades. There are also, very occasionally,

black bears. When it's clear, Marys Peak is a prime viewing spot in western Oregon for the Perseid meteor shower in August.

Snow, an infrequent visitor to most Coast Range slopes, can often be found here in winter, even at lower elevations. In fact, the road is sometimes impassable without tire chains from late fall until early spring. A Sno-Park permit is required for day use November 15-April 15.

Swimming
The **Osborn Aquatic Center** (1940 NW Highland Dr., 541/766-7946, $4.75 adults, $3.75 children ages 7-17, $2.50 children ages 6 and under) has both indoor and outdoor pools, including a large outdoor recreational pool with lots of play equipment.

Spectator Sports
The **OSU Beavers** (www.osubeavers.com for schedules and tickets) dominate the sports scene in Corvallis. In fact, unless you're a fan, you might want to avoid town if the Beavs are playing the University of Oregon Ducks; these teams share a rowdy sibling rivalry.

ENTERTAINMENT AND EVENTS
Block 15 (300 SW Jefferson Ave., 541/758-2077, http://block15.com), a brewpub with a strong emphasis on doing business sustainably, is a pleasant low-key place to hang out and draw on the chalkboard tables. Their sister pub, **Les Caves** (308 SW 3rd St., 541/286-4471, www.biercaves.com) has a wide range of beers from all over the world and pretty good food (though they seem to be best known for their bier bread pretzels) and brings in a good mix of acoustic music on a regular, though not nightly, basis.

A good spot for cocktails and occasional music is **CrowBar** (214 SW 2nd St., 541/753-7373), tucked behind the American Dream pizza in a secluded alley. In good weather, there's seating on the roof.

Skip yoga and go for a beer at the **Downward Dog** (130 SW 1st St., 541/753-9900), a bar with good burgers and local beers, wines, and spirits.

WILLAMETTE RIVER TRAIL

Ready for a new view of the Willamette Valley? How about seeing it from the river? An outing on the **Willamette River Trail** (willametterivertrail.org), a National Water Trail, can be as simple as an afternoon paddle from Peoria (Oregon) to Corvallis or as involved as a weeklong camping expedition.

Be prepared to pull out the binoculars and the camera repeatedly along the way, and to settle into a quiet profound enough to make you forget that I-5 is probably less than five miles away.

In addition to the very helpful Willamette River Trail website, you'll find essential information on access points, campsites, and river hazards in a series of waterproof maps (available to order from the website).

Canoes and sea kayaks are the vessels of choice for Willamette River paddle trips. They're available for rent at the following locations:

- **Alder Creek** (200 NE Tomahawk Dr., Portland, 503/285-0464, www.aldercreek.com)
- **Portland Kayak Company** (6600 SW Macadam Ave., Portland, 503/459-4050, www.portlandkayak.com)
- **Next Adventure** (704 SE Washington St., Portland, 503/233-0706, https://nextadventure.net)
- **eNRG Kayaking** (1701 Clackamette Dr., Oregon City, 503/772-1122)
- **Chehalem Paddle Launch** (3100 SE 8th St., Dundee, 503/687-1706, www.cprdnewberg.org)

- **Peak Sports** (207 NW 2nd St., Corvallis, 541/754-6444, www.peaksportscorvallis.com)
- **Oregon Paddle Sports** (520 Commercial Ave., Eugene, 541/505-9020, www.oregonpaddlesports.com)
- **REI** (locations in Portland, Tualatin, and Eugene, www.rei.com)

Put in at one of the many parks along the way. Although many paddlers set up their own vehicle shuttles, if you're renting a canoe or kayak, ask at the rental shop about shuttle services. **River Trail Shuttle** (541/228-4084, www.rivertrailshuttle.com) runs shuttles in the Eugene area and beyond ($30-130).

If you decide you want to paddle 107 miles of the Willamette along with some company, sign up for the mid-August **Paddle Oregon** event (www.paddleoregon.org, $649). Meals, side trips, yoga, and nightly entertainment round out the trip, which is run by Willamette Riverkeepers, a nonprofit organization dedicated to protecting, preserving, and restoring the river.

Although the Willamette is generally regarded as an "easy" river to paddle, certain precautions are necessary. Paddlers must be able to "read" the river for hazards, maneuver in a current, self-rescue if capsized, and dress appropriately so as to avoid hypothermia. Hone your skills by taking a class from Alder Creek, eNRG Kayaking, Next Adventure, Oregon Paddle Sports, or Portland Kayak Company.

Children 12 and under must wear a personal floatation device. Paddlers should be aware that DUI laws do apply on the river.

THE WILLAMETTE VALLEY

Other live music standbys and typical college taverns include the **Peacock Tavern** (125 SW 2nd St., 541/754-8522) and **Squirrel's Tavern** (100 SW 2nd St., 541/753-8057), which brings in music most Saturday nights during the academic year.

The Corvallis drama scene coalesces around the **Majestic Theater** (115 SW 2nd St., 541/766-6976, www.majestic.org), a restored 1913 vaudeville house. Close by is the excellent **Grassroots Books and Music** (227 SW 2nd St., 541/754-7558, www.grassrootsbookstore.com).

Aside from OSU Beavers football games, the biggest event in Corvallis is **Da Vinci Days** (541/757-6363, www.davinci-days.org), held the third weekend in July to carry on the creative spirit embodied by the genius for whom the festival is named. Sculpt, take part in a play, or just sit and listen to music as Corvallis's vibrant artistic and scientific community shares its inspirational bounty. New vaudeville acts and food booths also showcase the region's creativity. A highlight of Da Vinci Days is its variety of races, from kinetic sculpture races, to electric car races, to a mud bog race—these must be seen to be believed! Lectures by scientists and interactive exhibits impart an intellectual air to the proceedings. The festival takes place on the Oregon State University campus and in Central Park, between 9th and 11th Streets. One-day admission is $15 for adults, and full weekend tickets are $25 adults, $10 kids (buy in advance to save a few bucks). Although most festival events are on the OSU campus, a car or a bike is necessary to get to a few (such as the mud bog race).

Another big Corvallis celebration is the **Corvallis Fall Festival** (541/752-9655, www.corvallisfallfestival.org), a vibrant gathering of artists and craftspeople and a local tradition since 1972. Nonstop varied entertainment and a block of food concessions, including an Oregon wine garden, provide a backdrop for this hotbed of creative ferment the fourth weekend in September in Central Park.

ACCOMMODATIONS

Hotel rates can vary dramatically in Corvallis, depending on what's going on at the university.

Of the older and less expensive lodging options in the city center, the top choice is the **Rodeway Inn Willamette River** (345 NW 2nd St., 541/752-9601, www.rodewayinn.com, $52-119), with clean, basic rooms and a good location downtown and near the river. Pets are permitted.

A prime place to stay downtown along the river is the **(Holiday Inn Express** (781 NE 2nd St., 541/752-0800 or 888/465-4329, www.hiexpress.com, $128-170). From here, it's an easy and pleasant walk to downtown riverfront restaurants; get a river-view guest room and perhaps you'll see an eagle flying upriver early in the morning.

Comfort Suites (1730 NW 9th St., 541/753-4320, www.comfortsuites.com, $130-167) is situated in the heart of Corvallis's business district, just a jaunt from dining and shops. Guests have access to a large indoor heated swimming pool, sauna, and gym. There's also a good restaurant on-site.

The **Hilton Garden Inn** (2500 SW Western Blvd., 541/752-5000 or 800/445-8667, www.hiltongardeninn.com, $149-159) is practically part of the OSU campus; it's located near Reser Stadium (the football stadium), Gill Coliseum (the basketball arena), and the OSU Conference Center. It's a very comfortable hotel with good amenities for business travelers.

The **Hanson Country Inn** (795 SW Hanson St., 541/752-2919, www.hcinn.com, $135), a 1928 estate on five acres that's now a B&B, gives you the feeling you're way out of town even though it's actually within walking distance of campus. Antiques, canopy beds, original woodwork, and a book-lined library warm up the interior. On the outside, a hillside overlooking the Hanson estate offers a feeling of tranquility. A two-bedroom cottage, ideal for families, sits behind the main house.

If you really do want to get out into the countryside, consider a farm stay at the **Leaping Lamb** (20368 Honey Grove Rd., Alsea, 541/487-4966 or 877/820-6132, www.leapinglambfarm.com, $150 double occupancy, two-night minimum stay on weekends), where a private two-bedroom cabin with cooking facilities (basic breakfast items supplied) is perfect for families. It's well situated for hikes into the nearby forest or for just communing with farm animals. The farm is on the way to the coast, 17 miles southwest of Philomath, near Alsea, on Hwy. 34.

Camping

Camping in this part of the Willamette Valley can be delightful, especially in late spring and early autumn. **Marys Peak Campground** (541/750-7000, www.fs.usda.gov, $10) is open mid-May-mid-September; the final stretch of road to this spot is unsuitable for trailers. It's about 19 miles from town, off Hwy. 34 from Philomath.

RV campers can stay at **Benton Oaks** (110 SW 53rd St., 541/766-6259, $21 tent, $32 RV year-round; tenting summer only). Special rates and reservations are required on OSU football weekends. This is a pleasant county campground in a grove of increasingly rare Oregon white oaks adjacent to the county fairgrounds.

FOOD

The riverfront stretch of downtown is home to several good restaurants. The hottest restaurant in Corvallis for a fine dining experience is **C del Alma** (136 SW Washington Ave., 541/753-2222, delalmarestaurant.com, 5pm-10pm Mon.-Thurs., 5pm-11pm Fri.-Sat., $11-26), serving "New Latin cuisine" inspired by food from Latin America, the Caribbean, and Spain. From barbecued pork tacos to tapas such as albondigas and rockfish ceviche to a grilled lamb chop served with lamb sausage, grilled corn, and salsa negra—the menu has something that'll please everyone, including those who are looking for gluten-free options.

Big River Restaurant and Bar (101 N. Jackson St., 541/757-0694, www.bigriver-rest.com, 11am-2pm and 5pm-9:30pm Mon.-Thurs., 11am-2pm and 5pm-10:30pm Fri., and 5pm-10:30pm Sat., $15-30) is a lively hip restaurant with Pacific Northwest cuisine and a farm-to-table sensibility. Big River also incorporates an on-site bakery and the more casual adjacent **101 Eat & Drink** (www.101atbigriver.com, 4:30pm-10pm Mon.-Thurs., 4:30pm-midnight Fri.-Sat.), with a cocktail bar atmosphere.

Also along the river is **Aqua Seafood Restaurant** (151 NW Monroe Ave., 541/752-0262, www.aquacorvallis.com, 5-close daily, $10-26), which features Pacific Rim and Hawaiian cuisine, including a selection of *pupus* for snacks and appetizers.

Head to the heart of downtown for sushi or a kimchee fix. **Aomatsu's Grill** (122 NW 3rd St., 541/752-1410, www.aomatsusushi.com, 11:30am-2:30pm and 5pm-10pm Mon.-Fri., 5pm-10pm Sat., lunch $8-9, dinner $10-20) is an unpretentious restaurant with good sushi as well as teriyaki, bento, and Korean specialties.

If you're looking for an excellent deli, go to **Natalia & Cristoforo's Authentic Italian Deli** (351 NW Jackson Ave., 541/752-1114, www.corvallisdeli.com, 10am-6pm Mon.-Sat., $6-8), a hole-in-the-wall sandwich joint with great bread, quality meats and cheeses, and lots of veggies; the muffuletta is a cult favorite.

On the edge of downtown is **Luc** (134 SW 4th St., 541/753-4171, www.i-love-luc.com, 4:30pm-9pm Wed.-Sun., $15-22), an intimate chef-owned restaurant with French-influenced food prepared from fresh, local ingredients. The weekly changing menu features such delights as grilled lamb rack with macerated cherries and seared salmon with sweet corn quinoa and basil vinaigrette.

Perhaps the best place to provision a picnic is the deli at **First Alternative Co-op** (1007 SE 3rd St. and 2855 NW Grant Ave., 541/753-3115, www.firstalt.coop, 7am-9pm daily). You'll encounter the 3rd Street store as you come into town via Route 99W from the south.

Near the university, **Bombs Away Cafe** (2527 Monroe St., 541/757-7221, www.bombsawaycafe.com, 11am-midnight Mon.-Fri., 5pm-midnight Sat., $7-13) is a busy restaurant with colorful murals on the walls, frequent live music, and lines of lunchtime hopefuls anxious to sample Mexican-style food made with the freshest ingredients and organic produce. A gluten-free menu is available.

Another spot that's wholesome and hippie-ish is **Nearly Normal's** (109 NW 15th St., 541/753-0791, www.nearlynormals.com, 8am-8pm Mon.-Thurs., 8am-9pm Fri.-Sat., $7-15), whose jungle of greenery and mismatched artsy-kitschy decor does justice to its name (inspired by a character in a Tom Robbins novel). The vegetarian "gonzo cuisine" (no meat here) is tasty—try the tempeh enchiladas or cheesy spinach lasagna. The ambience is relaxed and friendly at this Corvallis institution.

It doesn't get much fresher or more local than lunch at **Gathering Together Farm** (25159 Grange Hall Rd., Philomath, 541/929-4270, www.gatheringtogetherfarm.com, 11am-2pm Tues.-Wed., 11am-2pm and 6pm-9pm

Thurs.-Fri., 9am-2pm Sat., lunch about $10), a organic farm five miles west of Corvallis. Lunches are the mainstay of this farm kitchen; during the winter, when produce is harder to come by, it might include a house-made sausage with sauerkraut, potatoes, and carrots. Three-course dinners cost $24 and can start with a beet and salted-honey soup followed by a duck breast with blackberry sauce, carrot puree, and chard, with chocolate cake to finish.

Corvallis also has a **farmers market** that takes place 9am-1pm Wednesday and Saturday mid-April-mid-November along the river (1st St. and Jackson Ave.).

INFORMATION

The **Corvallis Visitor's Information Center** (420 SW 2nd St., 541/757-1544 or 800/334-8118, visitcorvallis.com) maintains a good website.

To catch up on local events, read the *Corvallis Gazette Times* (www.gtconnect. com). **KOAC** (550 AM) is an excellent public radio station with a top-notch news team and classical music offerings. Serving much of western Oregon, KOAC can be picked up in remote coastal and mountain communities.

GETTING THERE AND AROUND

Greyhound and **Valley Retriever** (153 NW 4th St., 541/757-1797) operate every day, with routes north and south as well as west to the coastal town of Newport.

Corvallis Transit (transit center at 5th St. and Monroe Ave., 541/757-6988, Mon.-Sat., free within Corvallis) operates city buses.

Corvallis is laid out logically, and it's easy to get anywhere within 15 minutes. With 47 miles of bike trails and 13 miles of paved bike paths, it's not surprising that the city has garnered kudos from national media for its commuter-friendly traffic arteries. Recreational cyclists sing the praises of the **Corvallis-to-Philomath bike path.** It begins along the Willamette River in downtown Corvallis and continues 8 miles through rural Benton County before ending in Philomath.

ALBANY

Twelve miles east of Corvallis on U.S. 20 is Albany, and though you wouldn't know it as you drive the long commercial strip between I-5 and downtown, it has more than 350 Victorian houses that bespeak Albany's golden age, from 1849 to the early 20th century, when wheat was the primary crop and steamships and railroads exported Willamette Valley produce and flour. The **Albany Visitors Association** (110 3rd Ave. SE, 541/928-0911 or 800/526-2256, http://albanyvisitors.com, 9am-5pm Mon.-Fri.) and an information gazebo at the corner of 8th Avenue and Ellsworth Street have maps and pamphlets (downloadable from the website) about three historic districts that cover 100 blocks.

Amtrak (110 W. 10th St., 541/928-0885) makes a stop in Albany. Greyhound no longer has a station here; the nearest is in Corvallis.

Sights

Be sure to get directions to the **Monteith House** (518 W. 2nd Ave., 800/526-2256), the oldest pioneer frame building in Albany, dating to 1849. The exhibits at the **Albany Regional Museum** (136 Lyon St. S., 541/967-7122, www.armuseum.com, noon-4pm Mon.-Fri., 10am-2pm Sat., suggested donation $2 adults, $1 children) provide a good introduction to the Kalapuya Native American people and Albany's pioneer and Victorian eras.

In their heyday, two Albany residential districts were rivals. The **Hackleman District,** Ellsworth to Madison Streets and 2nd to 8th Avenues, was a working-class neighborhood that at one time featured a furniture factory and a railroad station. These houses are practical but rich in Victorian nuance. The adjoining **Monteith District,** Elm to Ellsworth Streets and 2nd to 12th Avenues, was home to wealthy merchants and businesspeople; the houses here are grand and opulent.

While you're strolling around Albany, stop in to see how work is progressing on the **Albany Carousel** (503 1st Ave. W., 541/791-3340, 10am-4pm Mon.-Sat., free). Although this big community project isn't ready for actual riders yet, it's fun to watch wood-carvers at work. A few animals are in place on the carousel mechanism, and kids can sit on them.

Prime time for a stroll down Albany's memory lane is during the Christmas holiday season. In December (usually the second Sunday), annual old-fashioned **parlor tours** (Albany Visitors Association, 541/928-0911 or 800/526-5526, http://albanyvisitors.com, $15) let you revel in eggnog, snapping fires, and frontier hospitality as a guest at a number of Victorian homes. Visitors are welcomed by hostesses at each home and are permitted to walk through the parlor and other open rooms. Entertainment and homemade refreshments are part of the festivities. Historical district hay wagon and trolley caroling tours are part of the package and can get you in the holiday spirit.

Albany is the seat of Linn County, but the **Linn County Historical Museum** (101 Park Ave., 541/466-3390, www.linnparks. com, 11am-4pm Mon.-Sat., 1pm-5pm Sun., donation suggested) is 17 miles southeast at Brownsville. The museum is housed in a turn-of-the-20th-century train depot flanked by freight cars and a circus train. Displays inside the structures (a barbershop, kitchen, post office, etc.) illustrate the life of the area's first settlers, the Kalapuya Native American people, and local natural history. Kids will especially relish the vintage covered wagon and 50 miniature horse-drawn wagons, sleighs, carriages, and carts.

Other relics of the area's early transport system are historic **covered bridges.** These canopied crossings protected the wooden trusses from rain, extending the life of the bridges by several decades. By the late 1930s, many of the 300 or so covered bridges in the state had fallen into disrepair or were replaced by modern steel and concrete spans. Statewide, 48 remain, with 30 in the Willamette Valley. A pamphlet available from the Albany Visitors Association (download from http://albanyvisitors.com) lays out a self-guided tour of eight bridges within 20-30 minutes' drive from the Albany-Corvallis area. All of these fall within

THE WILLAMETTE VALLEY

© BILL MCRAE

Linn County Historical Museum

an eight-mile radius of Scio, a town 13 miles northeast of Albany on Route 226.

Accommodations

Both Eugene and Corvallis are more lively places to stay, but there are a great number of chain hotels out at the I-5 interchanges, including a **Super 8** (at I-5 Exit 234, 315 Airport Rd. SE, 541/928-6322, www.super8.com, $86-100) and **Comfort Suites** (100 Opal Ct., 541/928-2053, www.comfortsuites.com, $104-134).

Food

At the **Albany Farmers Market** (4th and Ellsworth, 9am-1pm Sat., mid-Apr.-Thanksgiving) you can enjoy the Willamette Valley's bountiful harvests of corn, fruit, garlic, peppers, or whatever else happens to be in season. The market also features a number of food carts with fresh-cooked goodies.

An Albany tradition is **Novak's Hungarian Restaurant** (2306 Heritage Way SE, 541/967-9488, www.novakshungarian.com, 11am-9pm Mon.-Tues., 7am-9pm Wed.-Sun., dinner $11-20). Authentic *kolbasa* (a spicy sausage), stuffed cabbage, and chicken paprika exemplify the earthy eastern European fare served in a family-friendly atmosphere. The Hungarian buffet (Mon., Wed.-Thurs. evenings only, $15) is a good way to sample the food.

Another local tradition is coffee and a pastry or light meal at **The Beanery** (1852 Fescue St. SE, 541/812-2500, 6am-7pm Mon.-Sat., 7am-6pm Sun., $3-9), an outpost of Allann Brothers Coffee conveniently located just off I-5.

Albany has one unexpected outpost of fine dining. **Sybaris** (442 1st Ave. W., 541/928-8157, sybarisbistro.com, 5pm-8pm Tues.-Thurs., 5pm-9pm Fri.-Sat., $16-29) is one of the top restaurants in the state, helmed by chef-owner Matt Bennett who was a 2011 finalist for the James Beard award for top chef in the region. Sybaris specializes in creative American cooking featuring the fresh bounty of local farms and waters. An appetizer of salmon chorizo enchilada is topped with pasilla cream; and roast chicken is dressed with wild mushrooms and asparagus.

Eugene

Oregon's second-largest city and home to the University of Oregon, Eugene has a lovely natural setting. The Willamette River curves around the northwest quarter of the community (pop. about 157,000), and abundant trees and flowers dot the cityscape. From an elevated perch you can see the Coast and Cascade Ranges beckoning you to beach and mountain playgrounds little more than an hour away.

In town, the world-renowned Bach Festival and other big-time cultural events are showcased in the Hult Center, praised by the *Los Angeles Times* as having the best acoustics on the West Coast. The University of Oregon campus provides another forum for the best in art and academe, while its Hayward Field track has been the site of the U.S. Olympic Trials several times.

Outdoor gatherings such as the Saturday Market and Oregon Country Fair bring the community together in a potlatch of home-grown edibles, arts, and crafts. But it doesn't take an organized festival to draw the townsfolk outside. Even during persistent winter rains, locals can be seen jogging, bicycling, and gardening.

Eugene's labor, environmental, and human services organizations have labored with quiet effectiveness for several decades, giving the town a distinct lefty touch with worker-owned collectives, a wheelchair-friendly cityscape, preserved ancient forests, and wetland protection against industrial pollution.

As lovely as Eugene is, it might pose some problems for those with sensitive respiratory systems. Because of sporadic temperature inversions over the southern Willamette Valley, which is framed by mountain ranges that narrow like a funnel near the town, wintertime air stagnation is not uncommon. And the Eugene area, like most of the Willamette Valley, is notorious for its springtime pollens from ornamentals, trees, and grass seed fields, making this season a challenge for the allergy sufferer.

Be that as it may, Eugene belongs on the itinerary of anyone who wants to experience a laid-back Pacific Northwest version of urban sophistication and active pursuits in a beautiful natural setting.

SIGHTS

Two major areas of interest to visitors are immediately south of the Willamette River. The campus, in Eugene's southeast quadrant, and the downtown (bounded by 5th and 10th Avenues and Charnelton and High Streets) are only a five-minute drive from each other. Serious walkers and casual cyclists can manage the two-mile distance without trouble. Another excellent place to stroll, run, or bike with the locals, Alton Baker Park, is just across the river from downtown and the university.

The major north-south thoroughfare is Willamette Street, which can be followed from downtown five miles south to Eugene's other favorite hiking haunt, Spencer's Butte.

Skinner Butte

A good place to get oriented in Eugene, visually as well as historically, is **Skinner Butte.** If you look north from almost anywhere downtown, you'll see this landmark. A beautiful park fronting the Willamette River is located at the butte's northern base. This riverfront site served as a dock for pioneer sternwheelers and was where founding father Eugene Skinner ran a ferry service for farmers living north of the river. The town tried to become a major shipping port, but the upper Willamette was uncharted as well as too shallow and meandering. As a result, Ben Holladay's Oregon and California Railroad became Eugene's most effective mode of transport in 1871.

From downtown, head north on High Street, which becomes Cheshire Avenue as it curves to the left. Take a left onto Skinner Butte Loop and follow it to the top. You can also get here by traveling north on Lincoln Street to Skinner Butte Loop or by walking up from the south side, which takes about 15 minutes. From the top of the butte, enjoy the vantage point from which Eugene Skinner surveyed the landscape in June 1846. Kalapuyas called this promontory Yapoah, meaning "high place," and used it for ceremonial dances. Despite the state's second most concentrated population, on a clear day you can still see the Cascade and Coast Ranges as well as pockets of greenery throughout the city. You can also spot another good reference point in your orientation, **Spencer's Butte,** looming above the southern hills five miles away.

In the Skinner Butte area, don't miss the 1888 **Shelton McMurphey-Johnson House** (303 Willamette St., 541/484-0808, www. smjhouse.org, 10am-1pm Tues.-Fri., 1pm-4pm Sat.-Sun., $6 adults, $3 children ages 12 and under) on the lower south slope of the butte. The aqua-colored 1888 Queen Anne mansion is a museum of Victorian-era life and the most eye-catching of some 2,000 designated historic properties in the city.

Owen Rose Garden

Near the base of Skinner Butte and along the banks of the Willamette, the 400 varieties of roses at the **Owen Rose Garden** (300 N. Jefferson St., 541/682-4824, open daily) peak in June and bloom until fall. Along with 4,500 roses and magnolia blossoms in spring, tremendous old cherry and oak trees also command attention. To get here from I-5, take I-105 West and follow the West Eugene off-ramp. Turn right at the bottom of the ramp onto Madison Street and follow it north toward the Willamette River. One block to your right is Jefferson Street and the entrance to the rose garden. A more pleasant approach is on foot, via the riverside bike path. From downtown, walk or bike east on 4th Avenue, cut down to the river at the EWEB building, and turn left onto the bike path. From the other side of the river, walk behind the Valley

THE WILLAMETTE VALLEY

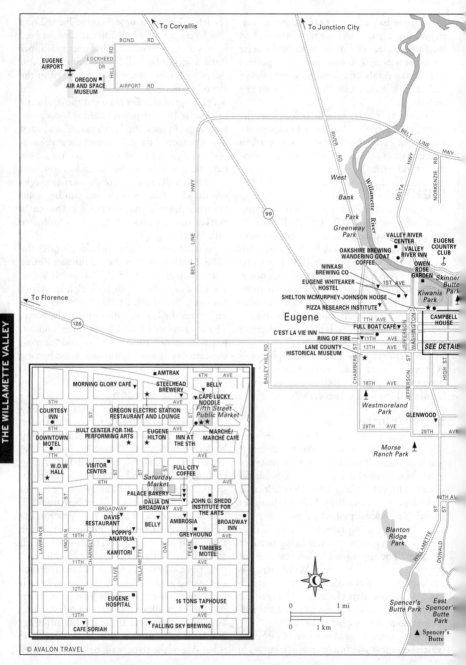

THE WILLAMETTE VALLEY

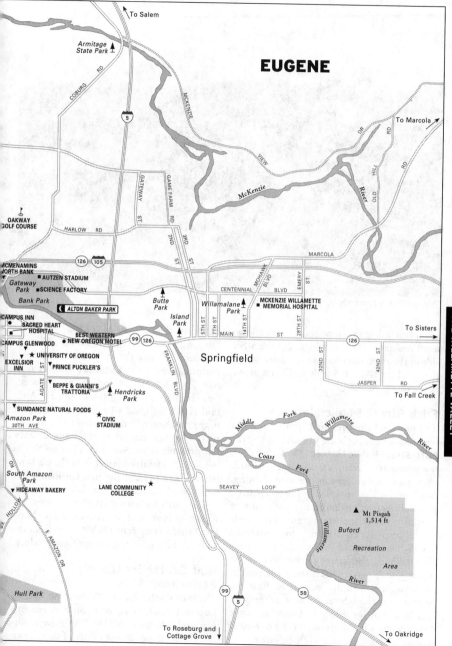

EUGENE

To Salem

Armitage
State Park

COBURG RD

MCKENZIE

VIEW

To Marcola

DR

7TH

OLD

RD

RD

McKenzie River

To Sisters

5

GATEWAY ST

GAME FARM RD

2ND ST

3RD ST

HARLOW RD

MARCOLA

OAKWAY
GOLF COURSE

126 105

MCMENAMINS
NORTH BANK

Gateway
Park

Bank Park

AUTZEN STADIUM

SCIENCE FACTORY

ALTON BAKER PARK

Butte
Park

Island
Park

CENTENNIAL

MOHAWK BLVD

BLVD

EMERY ST

Willamalane
Park

MCKENZIE WILLAMETTE
MEMORIAL HOSPITAL

CAMPUS INN

SACRED HEART
HOSPITAL

CAMPUS GLENWOOD

EXCELSIOR
INN

BEST WESTERN
NEW OREGON MOTEL

UNIVERSITY OF OREGON

PRINCE PUCKLER'S

BEPPE & GIANNI'S
TRATTORIA

SUNDANCE NATURAL FOODS

Amazon Park

30TH AVE

99 126

FRANKLIN BLVD

5TH ST

7TH ST

MAIN

14TH ST

ST

28TH ST

32ND ST

42ND ST

JASPER RD

To Fall Creek

126

Springfield

AGATE ST

Hendricks
Park

CIVIC
STADIUM

South Amazon
Park

HIDEAWAY BAKERY

E AMAZON DR

A HOLLOW

GD

LANE COMMUNITY
COLLEGE

SEAVEY LOOP

Middle Fork

Coast Fork

Willamette

River

Willamette

River

Mt Pisgah
1,514 ft

Buford

Recreation

Area

Hull Park

99

5

58

To Roseburg and
Cottage Grove

To Oakridge

THE WILLAMETTE VALLEY

THE WILLAMETTE VALLEY

© JUDY JEWELL

Skinner Butte rises above downtown Eugene.

River Inn (ask at the front desk for directions) until you get to the footbridge. On the other side of the river, loop back in the direction of the hotel for about 0.5 mile until you arrive at the rose garden.

Fifth Street Public Market

The past and the present happily coexist a few blocks from the butte's south flank at the **Fifth Street Public Market** (296 E. 5th Ave., www.5stmarket.com), an old-time feed mill converted into an atrium shopping, dining, hotel, and office complex. This once-rustic structure houses an impressive collection of specialty stores and restaurants surrounding an open-air courtyard. This courtyard is a favorite haunt of sun worshippers, people watchers, and street performers. Note: Although the market bears the word *street* in its name, it is actually located on East 5th Avenue and High Street. The market is an excellent spot for meals and snacks, as the complex and adjoining streets offer dozens of choices for both casual and fine dining.

Eugene Saturday Market

For a more freewheeling version of the public market, explore the crafts, food, and street performances at the **Saturday Market** (8th Ave. and Oak St., 541/686-8885, www.eugenesaturdaymarket.org, 10am-5pm Sat. Apr.-mid-Nov.); the good vibes and creative spirit of the community are in ample evidence. The market moves indoors to the **Lane County Fairgrounds** (13th Ave. and Jefferson St.) to become the Holiday Market from the weekend before Thanksgiving through Christmas Eve (open Sat.-Sun. and some weekdays).

The small **farmers market** (9am-3pm Sat. Apr.-mid-Nov. and 10am-3pm Tues. May-Oct.) that sets up across 8th Avenue from the crafts area is a good place to get fresh produce.

Hult Center for the Performing Arts

The **Hult Center for the Performing Arts** (1 Eugene Center, Willamette St. between 6th Ave. and 7th Ave., 541/687-5000, www.hultcenter.org) stands at the center of downtown

© BILL MCRAE

The Hult Center for the Performing Arts is an acoustic marvel.

Eugene and is one of the state's most prominent performing arts centers. In addition to its status as a topflight performance venue, this place is worth a look for its aesthetics alone. From the frog and troll statues that greet you at the 6th Avenue entrance to the high-ceilinged interior bedecked with masks, artistic touches abound.

Hult Center talent (with nine resident companies) is showcased beneath interlocking acoustic panels on the domed ceiling and walls of the 2,500-seat **Silva Concert Hall** (which resembles a giant upside-down pastel-colored Easter basket). The Hult Center is the hub of such renowned music celebrations as the Oregon Bach Festival. The **Jacobs Gallery** exhibits local artwork, providing another feast for the eyes. Even the bathroom tile is done up in a visually pleasing theatrical motif.

University of Oregon Campus

From downtown, head a few blocks south to 13th Avenue, then east to the **University of Oregon campus** (visitor information available at Oregon Hall, Agate St. and 13th Ave.,

541/346-3111, www.uoregon.edu). Car traffic is restricted on 13th Avenue in the heart of the campus; skirt to the edges to find parking lots or on-street metered parking. The campus is bounded by Franklin Boulevard, 11th and 18th Avenues, and Alder and Moss Streets. The university has an enrollment of over 20,000 students and beautiful grounds graced by architecturally inviting buildings dating back to the school's creation in the 1870s, as well as 500 varieties of trees.

Deady Hall, the oldest building on campus, was built in 1876. Also noteworthy are two museums: the **Jordan Schnitzer Museum of Art** and the **Natural History Museum.** The quiet and tranquility of the campus are sustained by a ban on vehicular traffic beyond 13th Avenue and Kincaid Street. A free **campus tour** leaves from Oregon Hall weekdays at 8:30, 9:30, and 11am and 12:30 and 2pm and Saturday at 10:30am. But unless you're a prospective student, you're better off just picking up the map or downloading the campus app and setting your own pace.

Across from the Schnitzer Museum is the **Knight Library.** (You'll notice that many buildings in campus are named for the Knight family, thanks to Nike cofounder Phil Knight's generosity toward his alma mater.) On the second floor, the **Oregon Collection** (541/346-3468) has books and periodicals about the state in closed stacks. The nationally famous map library on the first floor can also augment the trip-planning process with its extensive collection of all sorts of maps, its helpful staff, and its well-tuned photocopying machines.

Toward the eastern edge of the campus, Agate Street is dominated by **Hayward Field,** which regularly hosts championship meets and the Olympic trials. Built in 1919 for the college football team, it's been used by the track program since a cinder track was installed in 1921. The Bowerman Building, on the northwest edge of the track, houses locker rooms, memorabilia, and the university's International Institute for Sport and Human Performance.

This campus has often been selected by Hollywood to portray the ivy-covered halls of academe, most notably in the comedy *Animal House.*

If you wander the north part of the University of Oregon complex toward Franklin Boulevard, you'll see majestic and rare trees (including a Chinese dawn redwood) dotting the landscape between the law and journalism schools. Interesting outdoor sculptures also liven up a stroll on the campus.

Museums

A must on any campus tour is the **Jordan Schnitzer Museum of Art** (next to the Knight Library, 1430 Johnson Ln., 541/346-3027, http://jsma.uoregon.edu, 11am-5pm Tues. and Thurs.-Sun., 11am-8pm Wed. year-round, $5 adults, $3 seniors, children ages 18 and under free). This museum is a real gem, with a surprisingly good collection of contemporary art, including works by Chuck Close, Mark Tobey, Morris Graves, and many Pacific Northwest artists. Another major highlight is a nationally renowned Asian collection (don't miss the jade carvings); the revolving paintings and

photography exhibits on the first floor are also usually worthwhile.

The university's other notable museum is entirely different: The **Natural History Museum** (1680 E. 15th Ave., 541/346-3024, http://natural-history.uoregon.edu, 11am-5pm Wed.-Sun., $3, $2 students and seniors) showcases Oregon's prehistory and includes artifacts from digs in eastern Oregon as well as bird and mammal fossils from around the state. A portion of Thomas Condon's fossil collection displays curiosities culled from the earth by the man known as Oregon's first geologist and the discoverer of the John Day Fossil Beds. There's also a set of sagebrush sandals dated at 9,350 years old (from the collection of those found by Dr. Luther Cressman), 15-million-year-old shell fossils, a whale vertebra, and mammoth tusks. The museum is tucked behind the Knight Law School; to get there from Hayward Field on Agate Street, go east on 15th Avenue and look for a fish sculpture on your right, in front of an attractive wooden building.

Maude Kerns Art Center (1910 E. 15th Ave., 541/345-1571, www.mkartcenter.org, 10am-5:30pm Mon.-Fri., noon-4pm Sat., free) is just east of the University of Oregon campus. Set in an old church, this gallery and visual arts community center is dedicated to contemporary art of nationally known as well as regionally prominent artists. This gallery and others downtown are the focal points of a **gallery walk** (Lane Arts Council, 541/485-2278, www.lanearts.org, 5:30pm-8:30pm first Fri. of the month).

Just across the river in Alton Baker Park, the **Science Factory** (2300 Leo Harris Pkwy., 541/682-7888, www.sciencefactory.org, 10am-4pm daily summer, 10am-4pm Wed.-Sun. during the school year, closed on university home football game days, $7 exhibits and planetarium, $4 exhibits or planetarium alone) is designed to stimulate scientific understanding and curiosity in everyday life. The permanent exhibits are similar to those at Portland's Oregon Museum of Science and Industry and are complemented by a new set of traveling exhibits every three months.

The museum's excellent planetarium, the **Exploration Dome** (shows usually on the hour 11am-2pm Sat.-Sun., check website, $4) is highly recommended. The Science Factory-Exploration Dome complex is reached from I-5 by taking I-105 West to the Coburg Road exit and following the signs to Autzen Stadium (look for Centennial Boulevard and the Leo Harris Parkway).

The **Lane County Historical Museum** (740 W. 13th Ave., 541/682-4242, www.lanecountyhistoricalsociety.org, 10am-4pm Tues.-Sat., $5 adults, $3 seniors, $1 children) is next to the fairgrounds. Just look for the steam donkey on the front lawn. There are other 19th-century logging vehicles and period rooms on display. The Oregon Trail exhibits are among the most interesting.

Close to the Eugene Airport, the **Oregon Air and Space Museum** (90377 Boeing Dr., 541/461-1101, www.oasm.info, noon-4pm Wed.-Sun., $7 adults, $6 seniors, $3 children) has vintage aircraft, artifacts, and displays.

Head to nearby Springfield to visit **Dorris Ranch** (205 Dorris St., Springfield, 541/736-4544, 6am-dusk, free), a living history farm that's a popular school field trip destination but also open for self-guided tours among the filbert (hazelnut) orchards. It's also a good place to spot birds.

Wineries

Visiting the **LaVelle Vineyards tasting room** (296 E. 5th St., 541/338-9875, www.lavellevineyards.com, noon-7pm Mon.-Sat., noon-6pm Sun.) couldn't be easier; it's right in the Fifth Street Market, with a lovely patio and live music most Thursday and Friday evenings. Don't expect to drink for free here—it's actually more of a wine bar. The actual **winery** (89697 Sheffler Rd., Elmira, 541/935-9406, noon-5pm Mon.-Thurs., noon-9pm Fri., noon-6pm Sat.-Sun.) makes a wonderful stop on the way out to the coast with a location just off Route 126 near Elmira. In addition to secluded tables with umbrellas at which to enjoy LaVelle's pinots and Rieslings with your picnic lunch, the works of local artists are on display in the winery itself. A trail to a hillside on the grounds lets you view the snowcapped Three Sisters on a clear day.

Head over to the Whiteaker neighborhood to find the **Territorial Vineyards & Wine Company** winery (907 W. 3rd Ave., 541/684-9463, www.territorialvineyards.com, 5pm-9pm Thurs.-Sat.), where you can sample pinot noir, pinot gris, and Riesling. Although the grapes are grown out toward the Coast Range, the wine is made here in a former coffee warehouse.

Silvan Ridge/Hinman Vineyards (27012 Briggs Hill Rd., 541/345-1945, www.silvanridge.com, noon-5pm daily), 15 miles southwest of downtown near Crow, is a perfect place to spend a summer afternoon. Drive west on 11th Avenue, turn left on Bertelson Road, then right on Spencer Creek Road. A left down Briggs Hill Road takes you to the tasting room on a hillside overlooking a valley. The ride out is a favorite of local bicyclists, many of whom typically continue on into the Coast Range via Vaughan Road. While at the vineyard, ask to sample Hinman's award-winning Gewürztraminer; the pinot gris is also delightful.

The lavish **King Estate Winery** (80854 Territorial Hwy., 541/942-9874, www.kingestate.com, 11am-8pm daily), the state's largest winery, is set on 820 acres with a state-of-the-art winery resembling a European château. Production focuses on organically grown pinot gris and pinot noir. In addition to wine, you can also sit down to a meal at the well-regarded restaurant (541/685-5189, 11am-8pm daily, dinner $27-35, reservations recommended). To reach the winery from Eugene, take I-5 South to Exit 182 (Creswell), turn west on Oregon Avenue (which becomes Camas Swale Rd. and then Ham Rd.) to Territorial Highway. Turn left onto Territorial Highway and follow it about 2.5 miles to King Estate.

SPORTS AND RECREATION

Eugene's identity is rooted in its reputation as "Tracktown, USA," and also in its superlative Parks and Recreation Department, miles of

THE WILLAMETTE VALLEY

© JUDY JEWELL

Bicycle and pedestrian paths along the Willamette lead to peaceful riverside settings.

bike paths and on-street bike lanes, and back-country cycling minutes from downtown.

The **Ruth Bascom Riverbank Trail System** comprises more than 20 miles of paths, accessible to bikes and pedestrians, along both banks of the Willamette River. Pedal, walk, or jog to the Owen Rose Garden, the bird-rich wetlands at Delta Ponds, the Valley River Inn, Alton Baker Park (including the Science Factory and Autzen Stadium); the University of Oregon and downtown are just off the path. Five bike-pedestrian bridges cross the river and trailside signs abound, so it's easy to tailor a loop to your own ambitions. Access the trail from downtown by heading east on 8th Avenue to the river.

Connect with Eugene's track heritage by running **Pre's Trail,** on the north side of the Willamette River east of Alton Baker Park. A good route from the university is to head north on Agate Street, cross Franklin Boulevard, and cross the Willamette on a footbridge that takes bikers, hikers, and joggers to Pre's Trail, the Willamette River Bike Trail, Autzen Stadium,

and other facilities found along the Willamette River Greenway.

Some of the best urban **rock climbing** to be found anywhere is at the Columns, a basalt cliff located on public land against the west side of Skinner Butte in downtown Eugene. Limited parking is available at the Columns, but it's more enjoyable to ride a bike here by following the road rimming the butte. Climbing is free.

Of the many public **tennis** courts throughout Eugene, the best-lit facilities are at the University of Oregon and at 24th Avenue and Amazon Parkway near Roosevelt Middle School. Near the Amazon courts, runners will enjoy the bark-o-mulch trail that follows Amazon Creek in a one-mile loop.

The **Rink Exchange** (Lane County Fairgrounds, 796 W. 13th Ave., 541/225-5123, closed May-mid-Aug.) offers ice-skating lessons and open public skating. Visit them online at www.therinkexchange.com for the rather complex schedule.

It must be said that Eugene's weather sometimes makes indoor activities more appealing

© JUDY JEWELL

Alton Baker Park has great running trails, including Pre's Trail.

even though it's no longer considered a planet, is 3.66 miles to the northwest, along the bike path). The western part of the park is more developed; to the east it includes the 237-acre Whilamut Natural Area.

The four-mile **Pre's Trail** runs along the Willamette River east of Alton Baker Park. Named after runner Steve Prefontaine, whose world-record times and finishing kicks used to rock the Hayward Field grandstands before his untimely death in a car accident in 1975, this soft path meanders along the river and connects to the network of trails along the Willamette.

Reach Alton Baker Park from downtown by taking the Ferry Street Bridge and turning right just after crossing the river; if you're on foot or bike, the Peter DeFazio bike bridge is near the Ferry Street Bridge and is an easy walk from the Fifth Street Market area. From the U. of O. area, walk or bike across the Autzen Bike Bridge to the park.

HENDRICKS PARK

About two miles east of the campus on a forested ridgeline is **Hendricks Park** (Summit Ave. and Skyline Blvd., 541/682-4800), home to 850 naturally occurring rhododendrons and azaleas and about 10,000 hybrids. There are several ways to get to the park, the easiest being to turn from Fairmount Boulevard onto Summit Drive. Or take Lane Transit Bus 27 for Fairmount, disembark at Summit Drive, and hike on up the hill 0.25 mile. Two parking lots accommodate cars—one near the picnic area of stoves and tables, the other at the upper entrance on Sunset Boulevard. The rhododendron gardens are in their glory during May, with 15- to 20-foot specimens in shades of pink, red, yellow, and purple. Even though the display declines by late June, it's always a great place to stroll. Gorgeous views of the city can be enjoyed from the west end of the garden, and tree-shaded footpaths lead to benches located in secluded cul-de-sacs on the hillside.

RIDGELINE TRAIL

The South Hills **Ridgeline Trail** is only minutes south of downtown Eugene and offers

than rainy hikes. On those days, or after a day of running and biking, drop in for some yoga at **Eugene Yoga** (in the Tamarack Wellness Center, 3575 Donald St., 541/520-8771, www.eugeneyoga.us), which offers a wide variety of classes with good teachers.

Parks

If you're looking for what makes Eugene *Eugene*, try visiting the city's parks. Go for a swim in the indoor pools at **Echo Hollow Park** (1560 Echo Hollow Rd., 541/682-5525) or **Sheldon Park** (2445 Willakenzie Rd., 541/682-5314); drop-in visitors pay a few bucks.

◖ ALTON BAKER PARK

Just across the Willamette River from downtown, the 400-acre **Alton Baker Park** is home to a world-class running trail, the Science Factory and its adjoining planetarium, gardens, ponds, picnic areas, a canoe canal, and part of a very cool scale model of the solar system (the sun and inner planets are here; Pluto,

THE WILLAMETTE VALLEY

HIKING KENTUCKY FALLS

Along with the well-known hiking areas described in this chapter, the nearby Coast Range has some hidden gems, thanks, paradoxically, to such extractive industries as logging and gravel. The industrial "cat" trails that once cut swaths through these forests are today maintained (and sometimes paved over) by the Forest Service for access to natural wonders. One such place is Kentucky Falls.

Picturesque **Kentucky Falls** (www.fs.usda.gov/siuslaw) is set in an old-growth forest on the upper slopes of the Coast Range. From downtown Eugene, drive 33 miles west on Route 126 to the Whittaker Creek Recreation Area on the south side of the road, approximately six miles west of the Walton Store and post office. The route to Kentucky Falls winds through the clear-cut lower slopes of 3,700-foot-high **Roman Nose Mountain.**

From Whittaker Creek Recreation Area, drive 1.6 miles south and make a right turn. After 1.5 miles, bear left on Dunn Ridge Road. After about seven miles the pavement ends, and you'll turn left on Knowles Creek Road; go 2.7 miles. Make a right onto Forest Service Road 23 (gravel) and proceed 1.6 miles until you make a right onto Forest Service Road 919. Continue for 2.6 miles to the Kentucky Falls trailhead, marked by a sign on the left side of the road. An old-growth Douglas fir forest on gently rolling hills for the first 0.5 mile gives way to a steep descent into a lush canyon. The upper waterfall is visible a little less than a mile down the trail. Continue another 1.4 miles from the upper falls to an observation deck overlooking Lower Kentucky Falls, a 100-foot-high twin falls. On your drive back to Route 126, retrace your route carefully to avoid veering off on a hair-raising spur route to Mapleton.

wildlife-watching opportunities (look for deer, tree frogs, garter snakes, and all kinds of birds) and more species of fern than perhaps any other single spot in Oregon. In addition, old-growth Douglas fir and the lovely and increasingly hard-to-find calypso orchid grow here. The trail is seldom steep and has some spectacular views of the city through clearings. A spur route leads up to the highest point in Eugene, 2,052-foot Spencer's Butte, via a steep and often muddy trail. The Ridgeline Trail can be reached from several points, including Dillard Road; near the corner of Fox Hollow and Christenson Roads; near Willamette and 52nd; off Blanton Road near 40th; and the Spencer's Butte parking area.

SPENCER'S BUTTE

According to one legend, **Spencer's Butte** was named after a 19th-century English trapper killed by Native American arrows. The Kalapuyas called it Chamate, meaning "rattlesnake mountain." An 1848 account (from Batterns DeGuerre's *Ten Years in Oregon*) of the view from the summit reads as follows:

> On one hand was the vast chain of Cascade Mountains, Mount Hood looming in solitary grandeur far above its fellows; on the other hand was the Umpqua Mountains, and a little farther on, the coast ridge. Between these lay the whole magnificent panorama of the Willamette Valley, with its ribbon streams and carpetlike verdure.

The view today has all of the above, but there are some differences. Below the north summit you look down on Eugene-Springfield, with Fern Ridge Reservoir in the northwest toward Junction City. Beyond the reservoir you can sometimes see Marys Peak. Other Cascade Mountains sometimes visible from the butte include Mount Jefferson, Mount Washington, the Three Sisters, and Mount Bachelor. To the southeast, Creswell and the hills around Cottage Grove are visible.

The two main trails to the top vary in

difficulty. If you bear left immediately after leaving the parking lot, you'll come to the route known among the locals as the Face. This trail is shorter in distance than its saddleback counterpart but is much steeper and is littered with boulders and sometimes muddy spots. It can be scaled in 40 minutes by reasonably fit hikers.

The main trail is a straight shot from the parking lot, looping up and around the steep hills. These inclines are broken up by flat stretches. Allow about an hour for the ascent. Signs caution against rattlesnakes, falling limbs, and poison oak, the last being the most likely problem. A mixed conifer forest featuring old-growth Douglas fir with an understory of numerous ferns and wildflowers will usher you along.

The main parking lot for Spencer's Butte is on Willamette Street. Just drive south on Willamette Street until you see the signs on the left side of the road. There's also parking on Fox Hollow Road.

MOUNT PISGAH ARBORETUM

The **Mount Pisgah Arboretum** (Buford Park, 34901 Frank Parrish Rd., 541/747-3817, www.mountpisgaharboretum.com, $3 parking fee) features seven miles of trails that pass through a number of different habitats. The arboretum at the end of Seavey Loop Road sponsors such events as a fall fair dedicated to area mushrooms and a spring wildflower show and plant sale (dates vary; check website). Mount Pisgah can be reached by following East 30th Avenue from Eugene past Lane Community College to the I-5 interchange. Cross the bridge over the interstate, turn left, and take the next right onto Seavey Loop Road. You'll cross the Coast Fork of the Willamette River and then turn left onto a gravel road (look for the Mount Pisgah signs) that leads to the trailhead; the arboretum is just beyond the parking lot.

The path to the 1,514-foot summit has few trees, enabling hikers to enjoy vistas of the Willamette Valley on the way up. At the top an unforgettable perspective of the valley in the foreground and the Three Sisters and other Cascade peaks in the distance awaits. At the summit is a monument honoring author Ken Kesey's son and other members of the University of Oregon wrestling team who perished in a van accident (the celebrated author lived two miles to the east in Pleasant Hill). This memorial consists of a sculpture with a relief map depicting the mountains, rivers, towns, and other landmarks in the Eugene area. Supporting the map are three five-sided bronze columns upon which the geologic history of Oregon over the past 200 million years is portrayed, using images of more than 300 fossil specimens.

Those making the climb in August will find blackberry bushes for browsing along the way. If you're perspiring from the climb, when you're back on the valley floor head south of the trailhead to the adjoining **Buford Recreation Area** for a dip in the cool waters of the Willamette River.

FERN RIDGE LAKE

Reservoirs beyond downtown Eugene provide a wide range of recreation. The one closest to town is **Fern Ridge Lake** (25950 Richardson Park Rd., Junction City, 541/688-8147). This lake was formed when the Long Tom River was dammed in 1941, and its southeast shore was designated a wildlife refuge in 1979. Visitors can camp, picnic, swim, water-ski, sail, or watch wildlife. Fishing for crappie, cutthroat trout, largemouth black bass, and catfish is excellent in early spring.

To reach the lake, drive 10 miles west of downtown Eugene on West 11th Avenue (Rte. 126) toward Veneta, or take Clear Lake Road off Route 99W. Sailboaters and windsurfers launch from marinas on the north and south shores. The lake is drained in winter to allow for flood control, but the resulting marsh and wildlife refuge host tree frogs, newts, ospreys, rare purple martins (in spring), black-tailed deer, red foxes, beavers, muskrats, mink, pond turtles, and great blue herons. The wildlife area is closed to the public January-March 15 for the protection of wintering birds. There are 250 species of birds found here, including tundra swans, northern harriers, Canada geese, mergansers, peregrine falcons, and egrets, which, with their white plumage, long legs, and large size, are spectacularly easy to identify. To get here, make a right off Route 126 onto Territorial Road and look for a sign on the right.

Biking

Eugene and Springfield together boast 120 miles of on-street bike lanes, limited-access streets, and off-street bikeways. The two cities collaborate to publish a free bicycle map; find it online by going to the **Eugene city website** (www.eugene-or.gov) and searching for "bicycle map." Especially appealing and easy to get to is the **Ruth Bascom Willamette River Bike Trail.**

Collins Cycle Shop (60 E. 11th Ave., 541/342-4878, 9am-6pm Mon.-Fri., 9am-5pm Sat.) is centrally located. Here and elsewhere, look for the high-quality bikes, bike equipment, messenger bags, and rain gear. Another innovative local bike business is **Bike Friday** (541/687-0487 or 800/777-0258, www.bike-friday.com, 9am-5:30pm Mon.-Fri., 9am-4pm Sat.), known for elegant custom-made folding bicycles. Rent a bike from **Paul's Bicycle Way of Life** (556 Charnelton St., 541/344-4150, bicycleway.com, 10am-7pm Mon.-Fri., 10am-5pm Sat.-Sun.).

Golf

Laurelwood Golf Course (2700 Columbia St., 541/484-4653 for tee times, www.golflaurelwood.com) is a city-owned golf course with a 250-yard driving range. Greens fees ($25) and rentals are reasonable.

Of the many courses in Lane County, **Tokatee** (54947 Rte. 126, Blue River, 541/822-3220 or 800/452-6376, www.tokatee.com, Feb.-mid-Nov., $45 for 18 holes) is the best. To get there, drive 47 miles east of Eugene on the McKenzie Highway (Rte. 126). The 18 holes are set in a mountainous landscape patrolled by elk and other forest creatures in the shadow of the Three Sisters.

Spectator Sports

Each spring, the University of Oregon track team, a perennial contender for the status of best team in the nation, holds meets at **Hayward Field** (Agate St. and 15th Ave.). This site has also hosted such world-class events as the National Collegiate Athletic Association Finals and the U.S. Olympic Trials.

Fall means Duck football at **Autzen Stadium** (Martin Luther King Blvd. on Day Island). To get there, head north on Ferry Street; just after crossing the Willamette River, take a hard right on Martin Luther King Boulevard. Even if you're not a fan, you're bound to get caught up in the frenzied decibels of "quacker backers" who support a team known for its never-say-die attitude.

In summer, the **Eugene Emeralds** (541/342-5367), a farm team for the San Diego Padres, play ball at the new PK Park right behind Autzen Stadium.

Water Sports

Alton Baker Park, along the Willamette River, and the Millrace Canal, which parallels the river for three or four miles, provide escapes from Eugene's main downtown thoroughfares. The canal is easily accessed from the University of Oregon campus by crossing Franklin Boulevard. During the summer, canoes, kayaks, and stand-up paddleboards are available for rent in Alton Baker Park.

ENTERTAINMENT AND EVENTS

Keeping up with Eugene's multifaceted entertainment offerings involves previewing the listings put out by two local newspapers, *Eugene Weekly* (http://eugeneweekly.com) and the daily *Eugene Register Guard* (www.registerguard.com); both have good online events listings, with the *Weekly* being a little more alternative. Check with the **University of Oregon ticket office** (541/346-4461, http://tickets.uoregon.edu) for athletic event and concert information.

Cutting-edge theater can be enjoyed at

Oregon Contemporary Theatre (194 W. Broadway, 541/465-1506, www.octheatre.org).

Live Music

If you tire of watching other folks in action, the best spot for frenetic dancing in town is the **W.O.W. Hall** (291 W. 8th Ave., 541/687-2746, www.wowhall.org). This old Woodmen of the World meeting hall has remained a monument to Oregon's activist past in labor history (well, sort of, anyway: Its unofficial motto is now "Fighting to save rock & roll since 1975"). The W.O.W.'s floating hardwood dance floor and good acoustics allow it to rise above its junior high school gym ambience, and it hosts some surprisingly famous rock and blues performers. In any case, this all-ages venue is probably the most crowded and features an interesting cross section of Eugenians. Beer and wine are served downstairs.

Local bands and national acts, including comedians, play at the **McDonald Theatre** (1010 Willamette St., 541/345-4442, www.mcdonaldtheatre.com), which was built in 1925 and is now owned by the Kesey family, who work to maintain the old-fashioned ambience.

Several clubs are clustered within a two-block area around West Broadway and Olive Street: the "Barmuda Triangle." The venerable **Horsehead** (99 W. Broadway, 541/683-3154, www.horseheadbareugene.com) has just about everything except live music—pool tables, darts, a pinball machine, and barbecue. **Cowfish** (62 W. Broadway, 541/683-6319) is a dance club, with an easygoing atmosphere and a large roster of DJs. **Jameson's** (115 W. Broadway, 541/485-9913, jamesonsbareugene.com) is classy but not overly fussy, with a retro-lounge feel. **SNAFU** (64 W. 8th Alley) is a gay-oriented dance bar with fancied-up disco ball lighting.

Out in the Whiteaker neighborhood, **Sam Bond's Garage** (407 Blair Blvd., 541/421-6603, www.sambonds.com) serves live music (including weekly bluegrass jams), microbrews, and a menu of vegetarian pub grub until dawn; it's open every day.

The **John G. Shedd Institute for the Arts** (868 High St., 541/687-6526, www.theshedd.org) brings in some really fun music (think Buckwheat Zydeco, Dar Williams, Steve Martin playing his banjo) and offers a wide variety of programs, including a performing arts company, a cultural arts center, and a community music school.

Dancing at the UO student union building, the **Erb Memorial Union Ballroom** (1222 E. 13th Ave., 541/346-4373) is a Eugene tradition. Local-guy-who-made-good Robert Cray and other nationally known performers have played here. Big concerts occasionally take place within the cavernous enclaves of **Autzen Stadium** (2727 Leo Harris Pkwy., 541/346-4461, www.goducks.com), the home field to the Oregon Ducks football team. A good sound system has made it possible for tens of thousands of concert attendees to enjoy such artists as Bob Dylan and U2. Near the Science Factory in Alton Baker Park, the **Cuthbert Amphitheater** (541/762-8099, www.thecuthbert.com) is a slightly more intimate (5,000-seat) outdoor theater; this is where you might go to see the Shins or David Byrne.

For more sedate listening, the **Hult Center** (E. 6th Ave. and Willamette St., 541/682-5000, www.hultcenter.org) is next door to the Hilton. The Eugene Symphony and other estimable local groups such as the Eugene Concert Choir perform here along with a wide-ranging array of headliners from the world of music and comedy. This is also where most of the Bach Festival concerts occur. At Christmastime, the Eugene Ballet's *Nutcracker* is always a treat.

Cinema

While there's no shortage of movie houses in this town, the real screen gems are usually found at the university (consult the *Oregon Daily Emerald,* the U. of O. student newspaper, available free on and near campus or dailyemerald.com) and the **Bijou Theatre** (492 E. 13th Ave., 541/686-2458, www.bijou-cinemas.com). The university series favors cult films and classics, and the inexpensive ticket price helps you forget the oppressiveness of the lecture halls that serve as theaters. For about twice the price, the Bijou is the place to see foreign films, art flicks, and less commercial mainstream movies. Located in an intimate Moorish-style converted church, the Bijou offers great munchies and late-night presentations.

Festivals and Events

There is a lot happening in this south Willamette Valley hub of culture and athletics. Several events—particularly the Eugene Marathon, the Oregon Bach Festival, and the Oregon Country Fair—best impart the cultural flavor of the area.

A **gallery walk** the first Friday of every month lets culture vultures enjoy open house exhibitions all over town. Consult the preceding Sunday's *Register Guard* for a complete listing of participating venues.

Late April brings runners to town for the **Eugene Marathon** (877/345-2230, www.eugenemarathon.com), which has a relatively flat course, starting and finishing at Hayward Field.

The university sponsors the free **Willamette Valley Music Festival** (541/686-INFO or 541/686-4636, http://musicfest.uoregon.edu) each May, attracting loosely defined folkies, mostly from the Pacific Northwest. Bring some cash to enjoy a good variety of food vendors.

Music lovers also revel in the city's summer **Concerts in the Parks** held at **Washburne Park** (Agate St. at 20th Ave., 6:30pm Sun. late June-Labor Day, free). From mid-July-late August, nationally known performers play outdoor concerts in Alton Baker Park's **Cuthbert Amphitheater** (541/762-8099, www.thecuthbert.com).

Appealing to lowbrow and highbrow alike is **Art and the Vineyard** (www.artandthevineyard.org, admission $7 adult, $1 children ages 6-11), which generally takes place over the Fourth of July weekend in Alton Baker Park. This event brings together art, music, and wine with over one hundred artists' booths and the offerings of a dozen vineyards, live music (jazz, country, blues, and folk) and food

concessions. Contact the **Maude Kerns Art Center** (541/345-1571, www.mkartcenter.org) for details and tickets.

Late summer swings with the **Eugene Celebration** (541/681-4108, www.eugenecelebration.com, three-day pass $12). This three-day fete in late August includes such events as parades (one is a pet parade), an art show, a jazz festival, and the coronation of the Slug Queen. Street performers all over town and food booths in the parking lot at 8th Avenue and Willamette Street keep spirits high.

Note: When Eugene hosts U.S. Olympic team's track-and-field trials, the town books up months in advance. If you are planning to visit in June 2016, when the trials will be held here again, book your room as soon as possible.

OREGON BACH FESTIVAL

The **Oregon Bach Festival** (541/346-5666 and 800/457-1486, www.oregonbachfestival.com) takes place over two weeks late June-early July. The *New York Times* once rated the festival the best of its kind in the country, with a sparkling array of internationally renowned opera and symphonic virtuosos. The festival features more than two dozen concerts (some are also performed in Portland, Ashland, and Bend), with musical styles ranging from the Baroque era to the 20th century. The centerpieces of the festival, however, are Bach works such as the *St. Matthew Passion,* numerous cantatas, and the Brandenburg Concertos.

Starting in 2014, the festival is under the direction of Matthew Halls, who has taken the baton from the legendary artistic director Helmuth Rilling, who retired after 44 seasons.

Performances take place in the Hult Center and the Beall Concert Hall at the University of Oregon Music School. Free events, including "Let's Talk with the Conductor," miniconcerts, and children's activities also take place at these venues during the festival. Particularly recommended is the festival's Discovery Series: six concerts preceded by a short lecture-demo. Free noon concerts in the Hult lobby are also popular. A scheduled series of brunches, lunches,

OREGON COUNTRY FAIR

Just after the Bach Festival in mid-July, the Oregon Country Fair takes place as the second major cultural event of the summer. If you didn't realize that there was still a thriving counterculture, buy a ticket online or at a Safeway store, put on your kilt, and catch a bus at the Valley River Mall for the fairgrounds along with the crowds of tie-dyed, fringed, and love-beaded fairgoers. Entering the fair, you wander through a kaleidoscope of natural fabrics, graceful ceramics, stained glass, rainbow candles, and thousands of other variously sculpted wares. Machine-manufactured items are simply unavailable. Every aspect of the fair—its 350-plus booths and its participants—is, in a sense, art.

What? Two hours gone by already? You need a cup of espresso and a piece of torte if you're going to make it through this day. Or perhaps you want a **Ritta's** burrito bulging with avocado, salsa, and sprouts. The choices are mouthwatering: Get fried rice, sushi, blazing salads, or even a tofu-less tofu burger (with 100 percent ground beef), and more.

Overwhelmed by the constant parade of costumed stilt walkers, strolling musicians, winged "country fairies," children in facepaint, bare-breasted men and women, and other ambient wonders? Not far from any burnout point is a stage.

Shady Grove is a quiet venue for acoustic folk, classical, New Age, and other music. The **Daredevil, W. C. Fields,** and **Energy Park** stages host contemporary New Vaudeville stars and other rollicking performers. See the **Royale Famille du Canniveaux** debut a unique musical comedy. Marvel as the **Reduced Shakespeare Company** performs *Romeo and Juliet* backward in one minute flat. Shake your head and mutter as **Up For Grabs** juggles circular-saw blades and/or small children.

But wait, there's more. Try **The Circus** with its parade, orchestra, and veteran virtuosos. Ogle snake charmers and belly dancers at the **Gypsy Stage.** Or dance to the national and international stars of rock and roll, reggae, and alternative music on the **Main Stage.**

If it's starting to sound less like a hippie fair and more like a well-catered and established art convention, don't worry; there's always a sojourn into geo-socio-political-eco-consciousness at **Community Village.** Several booths here and in **Energy Park** teach and demonstrate the latest in new and matured '60s activism and environmental awareness.

Tired already? So are we, but there's a whole year to rest up and reminisce before the next Oregon Country Fair.

This annual fantasyland is staged among the trees east of Noti on Route 126. Take the free shuttle from Eugene's Valley River Mall directly to the wooded fair site near the Long Tom River, 13 miles from Eugene. Bus service usually begins at about 10:30am, with the last departure from the fair site at 7pm. Due to the popularity of this event, which attracts more than 50,000 attendees, mandatory advance ticket purchase prior to your arrival on-site has been instituted for those taking mass transit. Car access to the fair is open 10am-6pm, but on-site parking is limited; expect a long walk from your car to the gate. Parking costs $10 at the gate, a couple of bucks less when reserved in advance.

For more information, contact the **Oregon Country Fair** (541/343-4298, www.oregoncountryfair.org). Admission is $22-28 (kids ages 10 and under free, seniors 65 and over get a $5 discount). Purchase tickets in advance through **Tickets West** (800/992-8499, http://ticketswest.rdln.com). Dogs, drugs, glass containers, and video recorders are prohibited.

and dinners with the musicians adds a special touch to the event.

ACCOMMODATIONS

Although there are abundant chain hotels at the I-5 exits, these lodgings are miles from the fun and bustle of downtown Eugene. Luckily, the campus and downtown neighborhoods offer lots of choices for inexpensive, newly updated motels within walking distance of the Eugene scene.

Under $50

The **Eugene Whiteaker International Hostels** (970 W. 3rd Ave., 541/343-3335, http://eugene-hostels.com, $23-36) offer inexpensive lodging in two older homes converted into hostels. Be prepared for some partying at this hippie haven in the funky, convenient Whiteaker neighborhood just west of downtown. During the summer, backyard tent spaces go for $10 per person.

$50-100

A few older but well-kept motor court hotels have convenient locations in downtown Eugene. **Downtown Inn** (361 W. 7th Ave., 800/648-4366, www.downtownmotel.com, $65-70) is an accessible bargain. If you don't expect luxury, you'll enjoy the 1950s ambience of this classic motel. Nearby, the **Courtesy Inn** (345 W. 6th Ave., 888/259-8481, www.courtesyinneugene.com, $60-100) is another good bet; it's a couple of blocks from the Hult Center and within easy walking distance of restaurants.

The **Timbers Motel** (1015 Pearl St., 800/643-4167, www.timbersmotel.net, $59-79) is one of our longtime downtown Eugene favorites that's had a few ups and downs over the years. Currently it's up, and we're happy to once again bunk in the tiny timbered-topped budget room (larger rooms go for $79).

On the edge of downtown, the **Broadway Inn** (476 E. Broadway Ave., 541/344-5233 or 800/876-7829, www.eugenebroadwayinn.com, $65-70) offers clean, simple rooms and a very convenient location. Also on busy Broadway, the **Campus Inn** (390 E. Broadway,

541/343-3376 or 800/888-6313, www.campusinn.com, $90-109) has updated rooms, a fitness center, and an outdoor hot tub.

$100-150

The **Best Western New Oregon Motel** (1655 Franklin Blvd., 541/683-3669, www.bestwestern.com, $115-122) is a good choice for visiting parents of U. of O. students or for folks in town to attend a sporting or cultural event. It's right across the street from the Registration Office and dormitories. This place offers a fair number of amenities (spa, pool, fitness room, guest laundry) and well-appointed rooms. Although the motel is on a busy street, it backs up to the riverside millrace, and riverside paths lead to a footbridge to Alton Baker Park.

The **Campbell House** (252 Pearl St., 541/343-1119, www.campbellhouse.com, $129-349, breakfast included) is a 19-room Victorian mansion in the historic east Skinner Butte neighborhood. The inn, which changed owners in 2012, now has a restaurant. Proximity to the Fifth Street Market and the river, as well as the sophistication of a European-style B&B, makes this antique-filled 1892 gem a good lodging choice. Note that the least expensive rooms are small; expect to pay $149 for a somewhat larger room with a queen-size bed.

At the center of downtown, the **Eugene Hilton** (66 E. 6th Ave., 541/342-2000, www.hilton.com/eugene, $124-134, parking $15) is a high-end hotel and is host to many conferences. It has a great location right across the street from the Hult Center and within easy walking distance of the city's best restaurants.

The upstairs of a popular eatery just a block from campus, the **Excelsior Inn** (754 E. 13th Ave., 541/485-1206, www.excelsiorinn.com, $135-300, breakfast included) offers 14 elegant bed-and-breakfast guest rooms featuring antiques, cherry furniture, marble tile, and fresh-cut flowers. An elevator makes the rooms wheelchair accessible.

$150-200

An excellent standard motel is the **◖ Valley River Inn** (1000 Valley River Way, Valley River

Center, 541/687-0123, www.valleyriverinn. com, $139-234, web specials often available). Don't be deterred by its location away from downtown behind a giant shopping mall; the Willamette River is in back of the inn, which provides easy access to the riverside trail network. In fact, it's easier to get downtown along the bike path than it is to drive. It's also a good place to stay if you're traveling with a dog; the inn is pet-friendly, and the riverside path makes for delightful dog walks. A decent restaurant, a crackling fire in the lobby, and pool and spa facilities add to the allure. If it's in your budget, pony up and extra $20 for a riverside room—the view is worth it.

Just west of downtown, **C'est la Vie Inn** (1006 Taylor St., 541/302-3014 or 866/302-3014, www.cestlavieinn.com, $150-170) is a charming and meticulously renovated Queen Anne with four comfortable guest rooms.

Over $200

Eugene proves that it can be a little bit glamorous at its newest hotel, **◖ Inn at the 5th** (205 E. 6th Ave., 541/743-4099, www.innat5th.com, $199-600). This boutique hotel is the place to stay for a romantic weekend or when you want to feel pampered. Of course, this being Oregon, the luxury is all quite sustainable: The giant wood-slab table in the lobby was taken from an 80-year-old bigleaf maple that was sacrificed to build the hotel; pieces of the tree are featured in rooms throughout the hotel. Although all of the rooms are different, many have sleepworthy window seats and three-sided fireplaces separating the sitting and sleeping areas. Rooms overlooking the 5th Street Market plaza have balconies, which can be prime seating for summertime concerts in the plaza. With room service by next-door Marché restaurant and a spa on the ground floor, it's easy to hole up at the inn, but bikes are available in case you want to cruise the riverside trails.

Camping

RVers, Oregon Country Fair-goers, rock concert attendees, and Scandinavian Fair visitors stay at **Richardson County Park** (25950 Richardson Park Rd., Junction City, 541/935-2005, mid-Apr.-mid-Oct., $25, $10 reservation fee and small surcharge for some "premier" sites) on the shores of Fern Ridge Reservoir 6 miles northwest of Eugene. The 88 sites with hookups and water can be accessed by taking Clear Lake Road off Route 99 to its intersection with Territorial Road.

Fern Ridge Shores (29652 Jeans Rd., Veneta, 541/935-2335, $35) is a privately owned RV campground and marina 12 miles west of Eugene convenient to the Oregon Country Fair. Although many spots are occupied by long-term residents, it's a well-kept place with a nice lakeside location.

If you just need a parking lot-style RV campground, **Eugene Kamping World RV Park** (90932 S. Stuart Way, Coburg, 541/343-4832, $35) is just north of Eugene near the quaint town of Coburg. Take the Coburg exit off I-5, head west, and you'll find the RV park 1 mile or so down the road.

FOOD

Eating out in Eugene has long been a delight, thanks to the staggering array of locally made gourmet products and organic foods available from local farms, ranches, and the nearby Pacific.

Fifth Street Public Market Area

The northern edge of downtown Eugene is dominated by the **Fifth Street Public Market,** a renovated market building that houses a number of excellent restaurants. Notably, the market has a large food court with five food purveyors to choose from. The three-story, internal courtyard is overflowing with art and greenery, making a very pleasant spot for a casual meal.

Since it opened in 1997, **◖ Marché** (296 E. 5th Ave., 541/342-3612, www.marcherestaurant.com, 7am-11pm Sun.-Wed., 7am-midnight Thurs.-Sat., dinner entrées $23-33) has set the standard for fine dining in Eugene. The restaurant, in the ground-floor southwest corner of the Fifth Street Public Market, is as close to a French bistro as you're going to find in

© BILL MCRAE

The Fifth Street Public Market's inner courtyard is a fun place to eat and drink.

this town, and the food is decidedly French-inflected, with an emphasis on fresh local produce and meat. Don't feel like you have to dress up or take out a second mortgage to eat here. The atmosphere is crisp but not fussy, and if you sit in the bar, you can while away an enjoyable but not particularly expensive evening with drinks and casual fare, which can be fairly substantial, such as steak frites ($18).

For a more casual take on Marché's food, head upstairs in the Fifth Street Market to **Marché Provisions** (296 E. 5th Ave., 541/342-3612, 8am-7pm Mon.-Sat., 9am-6pm Sun., $6-17 for a light meal), where the food spans the hours from late breakfast to early dinner with quiche, tasty open-faced sandwiches, pizza, soups, salads, deli items, and dessert. Marché also operates a café at the Jordan Schnitzer Museum of Art on the university campus.

Adjacent to the market are even more dining options. **Belly Taqueria** (291 E. 5th Ave., 541/687-8226, www.eatbelly.com, 5pm-9pm Tues.-Thurs., 5pm-10pm Fri.-Sat., tacos $3-4) is high-end for a taqueria, with good cocktails and seasonal specials, such as tacos filled with braised octopus and pork belly.

Café Lucky Noodle (207 E. 5th Ave., 541/484-4777, www.luckynoodle.com, 11am-midnight Mon.-Fri., 9am-midnight Sat.-Sun., $13-20) serves both Asian and Italian noodle dishes as well as breakfast, espresso, and gelato in an airy stylish space. Somehow this works, and although the prices are a bit on the steep side (pad thai is $13), the food is flavorful and the portions generous.

Steelhead Brewery and Restaurant (199 E. 5th Ave., 541/686-2739, 11:30am-9pm Sun.-Mon., 11:30am-10pm Tues.-Thurs., 11:30am-11pm Fri.-Sat., $8-19) is a popular brewpub, serving decent sandwiches, burgers, and pasta.

You'll find vegan food and lefty politics at **Morning Glory Café** (450 Willamette St., 541/687-0709, www.morninggloryeugene.com, 7:30am-3:30pm daily, $5-10). Some menu items do contain eggs or dairy, but this is the place to come for a very tasty tempeh sandwich.

The historic landmark **Oregon Electric Station Restaurant and Lounge** (27 E. 5th Ave., 541/485-4444, www.oesrestaurant.com, 11:30am-2:30pm Mon.-Fri. and 5pm-9:30pm Mon.-Thurs., 5pm-10pm Fri., 4:30pm-10pm Sat., 4:30pm-9pm Sun.) features excellent steak and seafood dinners ($18-34) and lunch ($9-16) entrées, a full bar, a back room bar with wing chairs, and the ambience of a fine dining supper club. This very handsome structure was built in 1912 as the city's train depot; the main dining room is in an elegantly outfitted vintage dining car.

Central Downtown Area

Full City Coffee (842 Pearl St., 541/344-0475) is locally noted for its daily grind; pick up a muffin or pastry to accompany your coffee at the adjacent **Palace Bakery** (844 Pearl St., 541/484-2435).

Belly (30 E. Broadway, 541/683-5896, www.eatbelly.com, 5pm-9:30pm Tues.-Thurs., 5pm-10:30pm Fri.-Sat., $16-21), which once occupied the 5th Street location (now Belly

Taqueria), is now in a noisy, consciously hip downtown location. It's entirely different from the taco joint, offering country French cooking, specializing in house-made charcuterie, sausages, confit, and other meaty dishes.

Wander down Oak Alley to find **Falling Sky Brewing** (1334 Oak Alley, 541/505-7096, www.fallingskybrewing.com, 11am-midnight Sun.-Wed., 11am-1am Thurs.-Sat., $10-14) and snack on (ahem) heirloom crackerjacks or dig into a Cuban-style pork sandwich. Even when the weather's marginal, the covered and heated outdoor patio is a good place to sip one of the brews (which include a root beer).

Dalia on Broadway (898 Pearl St., 541/345-8232, www.daliaonbroadway.com, 11am-9pm Mon.-Sat., $10-16) serves Lebanese cuisine at the corner of Pearl and Broadway. This is a convivial and generally affordable place to dine on stuffed grape leaves or chicken schwarma; the owner also runs Cafe Soriah.

In the heart of downtown, **Poppi's Anatolia** (992 Willamette St., 541/343-9661, http://poppisanatolia.com, 11:30am-9:30pm Mon.-Thurs., 11:30am-10pm Fri., 11:30am-3pm and 5pm-10pm Sat., 5pm-9:30pm Sun., $10-16) is a Eugene mainstay for Greek and Indian food. Spicy curries and vindaloo chicken are complemented by saganaki (fried cheese), spanakopita (spinach cheese pie), and gyro sandwiches. The best baklava in town with a shot of ouzo or retsina can finish off a richly flavored and moderately priced repast.

At the southwestern edge of downtown, **Cafe Soriah** (384 W. 13th Ave., 541/342-4410, www.cafesoriah.com, 5pm-10pm daily, $16-32) is a popular choice for a romantic dinner. Both its patio for summer outdoor dining and its bar offer great ambience, but the Mediterranean-Middle Eastern cuisine is the real attraction. Moussaka and various dishes featuring chicken and lamb with vegetables sautéed in olive oil stand out.

For excellent sushi and other traditional Japanese dishes, try **Kamitori** (1044 Willamette St., 541/686-3504, 11:30am-2pm and 5pm-9pm Tues.-Thurs., 11:30am-2pm and 5pm-9:30pm Fri., 5pm-9:30pm Sat., $10-17), which specializes in "authentic" Japanese-style nigiri sushi, not rolled American-style concoctions. The udon noodle soup is also excellent.

Classy and inviting, **The Davis Restaurant & Bar** (94 W. Broadway, 541/485-1124, www.davisrestaurant.com, 11am-1am Mon.-Fri, 4pm-2am Sat., $19-24) is a showcase of New American cooking, with a broad selection of tempting starters, such as BLT gougère sliders and peach and Smithfield ham pizzettas. Most salads and main courses are available as small plates or regular dinner portions, making it fun to graze through a variety of dishes. Braised pork shoulder is served with ramps and wild mushroom demi-glace, and grilled quail comes with fig agrodolce sauce. At night, a young and stylish crowd gathers for drinks and to listen to live music.

Between downtown and the university, find **16 Tons Taphouse** (265 E. 13th Ave., 541/345-2003, http://sixteentons.biz, noon-10pm Sun.-Wed., noon-midnight Thurs.-Sat.), an easygoing beer shop and pub with nearly 20 taps dispensing a rotating selection of some of the state's best beers. The **16 Tons Cafe** (2864 Willamette St., 541/485-2700, 9am-10pm daily), south of downtown in a shopping center, is less atmospheric, but serves decent breakfasts and bar food (the taproom pretty much sticks to beer, though customers can bring their own food).

University Campus Area

The eateries on the campus periphery are a cut above those found in most college towns, and even the on-campus offerings are pretty good. One such campus food court, **Fresh Marketcafé** (Global Scholars Hall, 541/346-4277, 10am-10pm daily), is behind the Natural History Museum and offering pastas, sushi and bento, rice bowls, salads, smoothies, and coffee.

Start the day at **Campus Glenwood** (1340 Alder St., 541/687-0355, www.glenwood-restaurants.com, 7am-9pm daily) or at the south-side **Glenwood** (2588 Willamette St., 541/687-8201, 6:30am-9pm Mon.-Fri., 7am-9pm Sat.-Sun., $5-15). Although both restaurants are open for three meals a day, breakfast is what keeps people coming back. Come prepared for a wait on weekend mornings.

In the shadow of the campus, the ❰ **Excelsior Inn Ristorante** (754 E. 13th Ave., 541/485-1206, www.excelsiorinn.com, 7am-10am and 11:30am-10:30pm Mon.-Thurs., 7am-10am and 11:30am-11pm Fri., 8am-11am and 4pm-11pm Sat., 8am-2pm and 4pm-10pm Sun., $22-34) is an elegant restaurant in a charming old colonial home. The Italian menu changes with the seasons and might include ravioli filled with Dungeness crab and topped with a lemony basil cream sauce or pan-seared sea scallops dusted with porcini powder, topped with tomato relish, served with polenta. Many of the ingredients were grown at the restaurant's farm south of town. Although the Excelsior is very close to campus, it draws a much older crowd; when you see students here, they're often with their parents, who may be staying in the inn upstairs.

Behind Hayward Field, find top-notch ice cream at **Prince Puckler's** (1605 E. 19th Ave., 541/344-4418, noon-11pm daily, $2-6), a Eugene institution since 1975. Although President Obama went for the mint chocolate chip when he visited, our favorite is the Velvet Hammer shake ($2.60), with Mexican chocolate and espresso.

South of Downtown

Studio One Cafe (1473 E. 19th Ave., 541/342-8596, 7am-4pm daily, $6-9) serves good breakfasts (and lunches), featuring a number of takes on eggs Benedict, french toast topped with custard and fruit compote, and a cozy atmosphere in an old house just south of the university.

After a weekend morning run at Amazon Park, head to **Hideaway Bakery** (3377 E. Amazon Dr., 541/868-1982, 7am-4pm Sun.-Mon., 7am-6pm Tues.-Sat., $4-8) for pastries or a breakfast sandwich. This popular bakery, tucked behind the venerable Mazzi's Italian restaurant) has a great patio and delicious sweet and savory treats.

Dinner on the outside deck at ❰ **Beppe & Gianni's Trattoria** (1646 E. 19th Ave., 541/683-6661, http://beppeandgiannis.net, 5pm-9pm Sun.-Thurs., 5pm-10pm Sat.-Sun., $15-25) is one of Eugene's coveted summertime dining experiences. The menu features homemade pastas with light northern Italian cream- or olive oil-based sauces graced by fresh vegetables, meats, or fish. Try the *cappelli di vescovo* (bishop hats)—pasta stuffed with Swiss chard, prosciutto, and cheese in a brown-butter sage sauce.

Whiteaker Neighborhood

A quarter mile west of center city is Blair Boulevard and the Whiteaker neighborhood. In recent years, a budget restaurant row has been developing in what had been in previous decades a strip of fast-food places and greasy spoons. These places, for the most part, are easy on the pocketbook while offering an interesting variety of cuisines.

Wandering Goat (268 Madison St., 541/344-5161, www.wanderinggoat.com, 7am-11pm Mon.-Wed., 7am-midnight Thurs.-Fri., 8am-midnight Sat., 8am-10pm Sun.) is Eugene's top coffee shop, with discerning hipster baristas serving coffee from beans roasted in the back room, music many evenings, good baked goods (many vegan), and beer.

Just across the street from Wandering Goat, find excellent beer at the **Oakshire Brewing Public House** (207 Madison St., 541/688-4555, http://oakbrew.com, 11am-10pm daily). The brewers started out with an amber, added an IPA and some seasonal brews, and now offer a changing menu of single-batch brews such as a Belgian-style strong wit or a double IPA (with 100-plus IBUs for you hopheads). Although Oakshire's food offerings are minimal, customers are welcome to bring their own food to the pub.

By now, **Ninkasi Brewing Company** (272 Van Buren St., 541/344-2739, http://ninkasibrewing.com), which has made some of Oregon's best beer in the Whiteaker area since 2007, is a neighborhood institution. The ancient Sumerian goddess of fermentation surely casts a fond eye on Total Domination IPA, as do the locals and visitors who gather at the tasting room. The focus is on beer, not food, but there's usually a food cart posted outside the tasting room.

One of the neighborhood highlights is the **Pizza Research Institute** (530 Blair Blvd., 541/343-1307, www.pizzaresearchinstitute. com, 4pm-9:30pm daily, $16 for small pizza), which has the most innovative pizza in town. In this case, innovation equals excellence—try the chef's choice, which is invariably tasty and has ingredients arranged to form a mandala. PRI, which serves only veggie pies, has a friendly, spunky feel that's thoroughly Eugenian. The pie with Granny Smith apples, smoked gouda, and roasted walnuts may be life-changing.

On the east side of Blair Boulevard on 7th Street is **Fisherman's Market/Full Boat Cafe** (830 W. 7th Ave., 541/484-2722, 11am-8pm daily, $7-12), a fish market with an attached café. The array of fish-and-chips is noteworthy for its freshness and the tasty and nontraditional tartar sauces. The attached fish market sells the freshest Dungeness crab in town, excellent smoked salmon, and microbrews.

A bit farther west, **Ring of Fire** (1099 Chambers St., 541/344-6475, www.ringoffirerestaurant.com, 11am-11pm Mon.-Sat., noon-11pm Sun., $12-17) offers some of Eugene's best and spiciest Thai food.

North of the Willamette

Although **Sweetwaters** (1000 Valley River Way, 541/687-0123, www.valleyriverinn.com, 7am-9:30pm, $12-28) is basically a fancy hotel restaurant, it is an easy and pretty tasty bet for those staying at the Valley River Inn, and its riverside outdoor deck might offer Eugene's most delightful dining experience on a warm summer night. Be sure to take a sweater—the temperature cools down quickly at night.

Vying with Sweetwaters for Eugene's most scenic river frontage is the McMenamins **North Bank** (22 Club Rd., 541/343-5622, www.mcmenamins.com, 11am-11pm Mon.-Thurs., 11am-midnight Fri.-Sat., noon-11pm Sun., $9-20). The outdoor deck and picture windows overlook a quiet stretch of the Willamette, where in the 1850s Eugene Skinner's ferry crossed the river. Should wintertime mist obscure the river views, enjoy the interior, with its eccentric woodwork and wistful murals.

INFORMATION AND SERVICES

Find info about Eugene, the Cascades, and the coast at one of **Travel Lane County's** (www. visitlanecounty.org) two locations: downtown at 754 Olive Street (800/547-5445) or just off I-5 in Springfield (3312 Gateway St., 541/484-5307 or 800/547-5445). The Springfield location is better if you're looking for info on outdoor activities.

The **Smith Family Bookstore** (768 E. 13th Ave., 541/345-1651, and 525 Willamette St., 541/343-4717, www.smithfamilybookstore. com) purveys an excellent collection of used books. **Tsunami Books** (2585 Willamette St., 541/345-8986) is a local favorite for books and in-store events.

The main local public radio station, **KLCC** (89.7 FM), is an NPR affiliate with lots of news and music programming ranging from new wave jazz to blues. The University of Oregon station **KWAX** (91.1 FM) provides continuous classical music.

Eugene Weekly (1251 Lincoln St., 541/484-0519, www.eugeneweekly.com) has the best entertainment listings in Eugene. At the beginning of each season, the magazine's *Chow* edition will point you in the direction of Eugene's hot restaurants. This publication is available free at commercial establishments all over town.

GETTING THERE AND AROUND

If you're in your own car or on a bike, remember the campus is in the southeastern part of town; 1st Avenue parallels the Willamette River; and Willamette Street divides the city east and west. Navigation is complicated by many one-way roads and dead ends. Look for alleyways that allow through traffic to avoid getting stuck.

Amtrak (4th and Willamette, 541/344-6265, www.amtrak.com) offers three different transport options. The long-distance *Coast Starlight* links Eugene to major West Coast hubs from Los Angeles to Seattle. Two additional daily Amtrak Cascades trains (www.

THE WILLAMETTE VALLEY

amtrakcascades.com) link Eugene to Portland and Seattle, with connections to Vancouver, British Columbia. In addition, Amtrak runs through-way bus service each day to Portland and on to the northern Oregon coast.

Greyhound (9th Ave. and Pearl St., 800/231-2222) is the other major mode of long-distance public transport, heading south to San Francisco or north to Portland several times daily from Eugene.

Around town, **Lane Transit District** (541/687-5555, www.ltd.org, $1.75) has canopied pavilions displaying the bus timetables downtown. All buses are equipped with bike racks.

The **Eugene Airport** (541/682-5430, www.eugene-or.gov) is a 20-minute drive northwest from downtown. Just get on the Delta Highway off Washington Street and follow the signs. United Express, Horizon, American, Allegiant Air, SkyWest, and Delta Connection all operate flights in and out of Eugene. There is no city bus service to the airport. **OmniShuttle** (541/461-7959, www.omnishuttle.com, $22.50 from downtown) provides door-to-door shuttle service to and from Eugene Airport to various points in Lane County. **Budget Taxi** (541/683-8294) can also take you where you need to go (airport runs start at $15). **Rental car companies** Avis, Budget, Hertz, and Enterprise also have kiosks at the airport.

VICINITY OF EUGENE
Cottage Grove

The town of Cottage Grove, some 20 miles south of Eugene, is known for its **covered bridges** (there are six in the area; excellent details are at www.oregon.gov) and as being the gateway to the Bohemia mining district, the site of old abandoned mines. The 14.1-mile **Row River Trail** is a rails-to-trails route that follows the paved-over tracks of an old mining train from Cottage Grove to Culp Creek—perfect for mountain biking, birding, and mushroom hunting (especially after the first fall rains). A longer bike route that includes the Row River Trail, the **Covered Bridges Scenic Bikeway**

(rideoregonride.com), starts in Cottage Grove and runs 38 relatively flat miles past six covered bridges and around Dorena Lake.

Bohemia Mining Days (541/942-5064, www.bohemiaminingdays.org) convenes in mid-July; many of the events take place at re-created Bohemia City south of Eugene on Route 99 in Cottage Grove. Highlights of the four-day event include the Miner's Dinner and street dance, gold-panning demonstrations, and a carnival. Don't miss the Grand Miner's Parade, which happens on Saturday morning. Floats, horse teams, drill teams, and color guards make their way from Harrison Avenue to Row River Road with colorful costumes and the kind of enthusiasm last seen around here after turn-of-the-20th-century lucky strikes.

If you're looking for campsites in the covered bridge country near Cottage Grove, try the lakeside **Baker Bay County Park** (35635 Shoreview Dr., Dorena, 541/682-2000, www.lanecounty.org, mid-Apr.-mid-Oct., $20). Take I-5 south to Mosby Creek Road (take the Cottage Grove exit), turn left, then left again on Row River Road, and then take the right fork. It's about 18 miles from Eugene.

For more information about these attractions, contact the **Cottage Grove Chamber of Commerce** (710 E. Gibbs Ave., 541/942-2411, www.cgchamber.com), located two miles east of the ranger station in Cottage Grove.

Junction City

North of Eugene, the annual **Junction City Scandinavian Festival** (Greenwood St. between 5th Ave. and 7th Ave., Junction City, www.scandinavianfestival.com) celebrates the town's Danish, Swedish, Finnish, Norwegian, and Icelandic founders the second weekend in August. Folk dancing, music, heritage crafts, and sampling traditional foods make up the bulk of the activities. Skits of Hans Christian Andersen folktales are enacted during the four-day event, along with guided hour-long bus tours that take you by Scandinavian pioneer farmsteads. Junction City is 12 miles northwest of Eugene off Route 99.

The McKenzie River Highway

From I-5 near Eugene, reach the scenic McKenzie River Highway by taking Highway 126 east. Just past Springfield, where the four lanes merge into two, the McKenzie River Recreation Area begins. For the next 60 miles you will not see any major population centers. However, you will see beautiful views of the blue-green McKenzie River with heavily forested mountains, frothy waterfalls, jet-black lava beds, and snowcapped peaks as a backdrop. The river was named for Donald Mackenzie, a member of the Astor Pacific Fur Company, who explored the region in 1812.

The first 15 miles of the McKenzie River Highway pass through many fruit and nut orchards (primarily apples, cherries, and filberts), Christmas tree farms, and berry patches. McKenzie River farmers enjoy plentiful water supplies from the McKenzie diversion canal, as well as fertile soils and a mild climate.

The Leaburg Dam signals your entry into the middle section of the McKenzie, where there are many vacation homes. A total of six dams on the McKenzie provide power, irrigation, and what the Army Corps of Engineers calls "fish enhancement." A favorite haunt of fishing enthusiasts, the mellow waters of the middle McKenzie teem with trout, steelhead, and salmon. You'll notice many drift boats parked in driveways. These boats have bows at both ends to prevent water inundation from either front or back. Mild white-water rafting and drift boat fishing are popular here, and local guides and outfitters are ready to help you float your expeditions.

The Willamette National Forest boundary is near Blue River. Huge old-growth Douglas

© JUDY JEWELL

The South Fork of the McKenzie River is backed up by a dam.

THE WILLAMETTE VALLEY

firs usher the clear blue waters of the McKenzie through the mountains. The McKenzie River National Recreation Trail and many less vaunted but still lovely trails feature waterfalls, mountain lakes, or lava formations are a short trek from the road. In addition to the myriad recreational opportunities, hot springs, abundant accommodations, and a relative dearth of crowds give you the western slopes of the Cascades at their finest.

SIGHTS
U.S. Cavalry and American Indian Museum
The private **U.S. Cavalry and American Indian Museum** (52281 Hwy. 126, Blue River, 541/822-1139, 11am-5pm Thurs.-Sun., donations accepted) has, as its name implies, a dual focus: the history of the U.S. Cavalry from 1861 to 1943 and culture of Native American tribes spanning the united States. The husband and wife that run the museum (he's the Cavalry guy, and she is of Blackfoot-Cree heritage and in charge of the Indian collection) are longtime collectors and very knowledgeable about the artifacts and their significance. Look for the rough-hewn sign for the museum on the north side of the highway east of Blue River.

Aufderheide National Scenic Byway
One of the nation's first 50 National Scenic Byways, the 58-mile **Aufderheide Drive** links Route 126 to Route 58 near Oakridge. You'll find the Aufderheide turnoff (Forest Service Rd. 19) at mile marker 45.9 about 5 miles east of Blue River. The road winds along the south fork of the McKenzie River, crests the pass, and then follows the north fork of the middle fork of the Willamette River down to Oakridge and Route 58. Sights along the way include the Delta Old-Growth Grove Nature Trail, Terwilliger (a.k.a. Cougar) Hot Springs, the spectacular Willamette River Gorge, and the Westfir covered bridge. The Aufderheide makes a spectacular, though tough, ride on a road bike; it's also a popular motorcycle route.

Terwilliger (Cougar) Hot Springs
If you'd like to try soaking in hot springs in a natural setting, head for **Terwilliger Hot Springs** (also called **Cougar Hot Springs**) in a forested canyon at the end of a 0.25-mile trail. Hot water bubbles up out of the earth at 116°F and flows down through a series of log and stone pools, each one a few degrees cooler than the previous one. A series of access steps and railings have also been built to help you get to the various soaking ponds. The local custom is to forgo clothing.

To get there, take the Aufderheide Drive from Route 126 south toward Cougar Reservoir. The trailhead for the hot springs on the west (right) side of the road is marked by a sign just past mile marker 7. You can park in a large lot on the east side of the road about 500 feet past the trailhead (alongside the reservoir). Parking alongside the road is prohibited (and enforced) from sunset to sunrise 1 mile from the trailhead. A $6-per-person day-use fee is required, and it has enabled this place to be well maintained. The hot springs are open from sunrise to sunset daily.

The several pools in this tranquil forest setting can be overcrowded on weekends. Although this hot spring offers an exceptionally nice soaking experience and is generally an easygoing, tranquil place to hang out, it can occasionally attract an unsavory crowd. Women traveling alone may want to scrutinize the scene before taking the plunge.

If it's too warm for hot springs, consider swimming in the lagoon that's below the hot springs trail. From the pay station, it's a short hike in, and a steep descent along a path to the swimming hole.

Proxy Falls
To get to **Proxy Falls,** follow the old McKenzie Pass road (Rte. 242) from the new McKenzie Pass highway (Rte. 126) for 10 miles. Look for a small hiker-symbol sign on the south side of the road. This is the only marker for the trail to a spectacular pair of waterfalls, Upper and Lower Proxy Falls.

It's an easy 0.5-mile walk to Upper Proxy, an

© JUDY JEWELL

Terwilliger Hot Springs

A-plus trail. The trail goes through a lava field and lush forest that changes with the seasons. There are giant rhododendrons that bloom in late spring, tart huckleberries in late summer, and brilliant red foliage from the vine maples in the fall. Take a left at the first fork in the trail. This will take you to Upper Proxy Falls. A particularly good view of the waterfalls can be found near the giant Douglas fir at the base of the pool.

Now that you've seen Upper Proxy Falls from the bottom up, check out Lower Proxy Falls from the top down. Go back to the fork in the trail and take a left. In less than 0.5 mile you will suddenly be on a ridge looking across a valley at Lower Proxy Falls. A good time to photograph both of these waterfalls is around midday, when the sun's angle best illuminates the water.

Dee Wright Observatory

The **Dee Wright Observatory** (57600 McKenzie River Hwy. on Rte. 242, 541/822-3381, closed in winter at the first sign of snow) is at McKenzie Pass about halfway between Route 126 and Sisters. Built in the early 1930s as a Civilian Conservation Corps project, it was named for the building's supervisor, who died prior to its completion. The tower windows line up with views of Mount Jefferson, Mount Washington, and two of the Three Sisters, as well as the eight-mile-long, half-mile-wide lava flow that bubbled out of nearby Yapoah a little less than 3,000 years ago. On a clear day, you can even see the tip of Mount Hood.

The 0.5-mile Lava River Trail next to the observatory offers a fine foray into the surrounding hills of rolling black rock. In addition to helpfully placed and concise interpretive placards explaining the lava formations, the trail is wheelchair accessible. But while the walk is easy enough, the 5,300-foot elevation can sometimes make it seem a little more difficult. Note that on Route 242, vehicle length is restricted to a maximum of 35 feet.

Koosah Falls

Koosah Falls is about 20 miles from McKenzie

Bridge on Route 126. The visitor facilities here provide wheelchair access and excellent views of this impressive 70-foot-high waterfall on the McKenzie. The blue water bounces and bubbles over and through a basalt formation that flowed into the McKenzie thousands of years ago. If you look carefully, you can see many small springs flowing from crevices at the base of the waterfall. The blue water may have inspired the name Koosah, which comes from the Chinook word for "sky."

Sahalie Falls

Sahalie Falls is only 0.5 mile east from McKenzie Bridge on Route 126 from Koosah Falls. From McKenzie Bridge, travel east on Route 126 to Road 2672. Follow Road 2672 to Forest Service Road 655. Follow Forest Service Road 655 to the Sahalie Falls Day Use Area. On the trail from Koosah Falls, giant cedar and fir trees line the path. It is only a few yards from the parking lot to the viewpoints of the waterfall. Also the result of a lava dam from the Cascade Range's not-so-distant volcanic past, the river tumbles 100 feet into a green canyon. This is the highest waterfall on the McKenzie River—*sahalie* means "high" in the Chinook language.

Clear Lake

Just north of Sahalie and Koosah Falls and east of Route 126 is **Clear Lake,** which forms the headwaters of the McKenzie River. The best way to appreciate this lake, which is indeed remarkably clear, is in a canoe, so that you can paddle out to the northern end of the lake and look down to see the 3,000-year-old underwater forest that was submerged when lava flows dammed the water and created it. A campground and a resort are at the lake; the resort rents out canoes.

Sawyer's Cave

This ice cave is on the right just past the junction of Route 126 and U.S. 20, near mile marker 72. You'll need a flashlight and a sweater to explore **Sawyer's Cave;** watch your head and watch your step. Classified as a lava

tube, it's the result of a lava flow that cooled faster on the top and sides, forming a crust. Underneath, the hotter lava continued to drain downhill, leaving the shell behind. There are also small stalactites hanging down from the ceilings, formed from lava drippings. The basalt rock is a poor heat conductor, and like a natural refrigerator it keeps the coolness of winter and night inside the cave. Ice can be found on the floor of the cave during the hottest summer months.

SPORTS AND RECREATION
Hiking
DELTA OLD-GROWTH GROVE NATURE TRAIL

Find the 0.5-mile loop **Delta Old-Growth Grove Natural Trail** through an old-growth ecosystem on the west side of the Aufderheide Byway not far from Route 126. In addition to 650-year-old conifers, you'll see other layers of life from shrubs and ground cover plants to fish, mammals, birds, and amphibians. Many plant species are clearly marked along the trail.

◖ MCKENZIE RIVER NATIONAL RECREATION TRAIL

The **McKenzie River National Recreation Trail** (Trail 3507) runs for 26.5 miles and is extremely popular with mountain bikers as well as hikers. It starts just east of the small town of McKenzie Bridge and goes to the Old Santiam Wagon Road, about 3 miles south of the junction of Route 126 and U.S. 20. But don't let the long distance scare you. There are enough access points to let you design treks of three, five, eight, or more miles along this beautiful trail. It is hard to say which section of the footpath is the best, as each portion has its own charms; the following highlights give you a sample of what to expect.

Start at the top of the McKenzie River Trail at the Old Santiam Wagon Road. Completed in the early 1860s, this was the first link of the route from the mid-Willamette Valley to central and eastern Oregon. Way stations were established a day's journey apart to assist the pioneers along their weary way. Although

© PAUL LEVY

If you're looking to chill out on a summer day, the McKenzie River might be for you.

most of these primitive establishments are no more, some of the historic buildings have survived. There isn't much left of the Old Santiam Wagon Road either, as much of it was destroyed with the construction of Route 126. However, a seven-mile stretch remains from Route 126 through the rugged lava country to the Pacific Crest Trail. A short walk on this former road to the promised land helps you to appreciate both the hardiness of the pioneers and the comforts of modern travel.

From the Old Santiam Wagon Road, the McKenzie River Trail surveys many remarkable volcanic formations. Lava flows over the last few thousand years have built dams, created waterfalls, and even buried the river altogether. Koosah and Sahalie Falls were also created by lava dams, and the view of these white-water cascades from the McKenzie River Trail is much different than the version accessible from the highway. Another interesting sight is the Tamolitch Valley, where the McKenzie gradually sinks beneath the porous lava, disappearing altogether until it reemerges three miles later at

cobalt-colored Tamolitch Pool. This area is accessible only on the National Recreation Trail.

If possible, arrange your McKenzie outing with friends and run a two-car shuttle; **McKenzie River Mountain Resort** (541/822-6272, www.rivermountainresort.com) runs a shuttle service. Also keep in mind that hikes starting at the upper end of the trail take advantage of the descending elevation. Mountain bikes are allowed on all sections of the McKenzie River Trail; McKenzie River Mountain Resort also runs a bike shuttle service.

ROBINSON LAKE TRAIL

The 0.25-mile **Robinson Lake Trail** takes you to a heart-shaped lake with some fishing and swimming. To get there, take Route 126 about 16 miles east of McKenzie Bridge and turn right onto Robinson Lake Road. Be on the lookout for logging trucks and rocks on the gravel road. Follow the signs marked Forest Service Road 2664. At the unmarked junction, drive straight onto the red pumice road (Forest

Service Rd. 2664) and continue until you reach the parking lot. It takes about 10 minutes to drive the 4 miles in. The easy hiking trail is in good condition; the left fork takes you to the center shore of Robinson Lake. The shallow lake warms up considerably during the summer, making up a swim all the more inviting.

Fishing

Sure it's crowded, but scenic beauty and the chance to bag a five-trout limit lines 'em up on one of the state's best trout streams. Unless you can get a drift boat, access is limited. On weekends, drift boats and rafters vie for space. You can cast worms or spinners, though you're better off using flies when you're fishing off a boat for rainbow trout April-October. Anglers might want to book a trip with **Helfrich Outfitters** (541/741-1905 or 800/507-9889, www.helfrichoutfitter.com, full-day trip $400 for two anglers). Consult the **Oregon Outfitters and Guides Directory** for other local guides (www.ogpa.org). The best pools tend to be west of Blue River, but it's harder to get to them because of private landholdings. Be sure to check for rules and regulations before you go fishing; the **Department of Fish and Wildlife** (503/947-6000, www.dfw.state.or.us) can give you the information you need.

Golf

If you like to play golf, you should plan your vacation around a visit to **Tokatee Golf Club** (54947 Rte. 126, Blue River, 541/822-3220 or 800/452-6376, www.tokatee.com, Feb.-mid-Nov., $45 for 18 holes), one of the Pacific Northwest's most beautiful courses. Consistently rated among the top 25 courses in the United States by *Golf Digest*, Tokatee is a marriage of golf and wilderness beauty that creates a unique and satisfying experience. Good for all levels of experience; every hole has its own challenge. No houses are on the fairways to obstruct the knockout views of the forested mountains and the Three Sisters Wilderness.

Mountain Biking

In the upper sections of the McKenzie, most of the usable trails gain elevation rapidly due to the steep terrain and make for very challenging biking. The most popular route is the **McKenzie River Trail.** Contact the **McKenzie River Ranger District** (503/822-3381) for detailed information. **McKenzie River Mountain Resort** (541/822-6272, www.rivermountainresort.com) has bikes for rent and runs a shuttle service for trail users.

Rafting

The McKenzie River becomes navigable at the Olallie campground, about 11 miles east of McKenzie Bridge. Between the Olallie campground and the town of Blue River, there are seven public boat launches, including at Paradise and McKenzie Bridge campgrounds. Expect to encounter Class II and III rapids along the Upper McKenzie. Many local outfitters can guide you down the river.

McKenzie River Adventures (541/822-3806 or 800/832-5858, www.mckenzieriveradventures.com) has half-, full-, and two-day white-water rafting trips May-September. The half-day (three-hour) trip is $80 adults; the full-day (six-hour) trip is $150, lunch included. The cruises range 7-18 miles and take in some Class II and III rapids. Reservations are recommended.

Oregon Whitewater Adventures (39620 Deerhorn Rd., Springfield, 541/746-5422 or 800/820-7238, www.oregonwhitewater.com) offers guided half-day trips for $60, full-day trips for $90, and a two-day overnighter for $325. All necessary gear and transportation back to your car are included.

ACCOMMODATIONS

A great place for families, including pets, and those who want to get away from the noise of the McKenzie Highway is the **Wayfarer Resort** (46725 Goodpasture Rd., Vida, 541/896-3613, www.wayfarerresort.com, $110-325), featuring over a dozen cabins on the McKenzie and glacier-fed Marten Creek east of Vida. Accommodating 1-6 people, the cabins have porches with barbecues overlooking the water, full kitchens, and lots of wood paneling. Two larger units can sleep eight and are equipped with all the amenities. Children can enjoy fishing privileges in the resort's private trout pond while the folks play on the resort's tennis court. In the summer, advance reservations are a must for this popular retreat.

McKenzie River Inn B&B and Cabins (49164 McKenzie Hwy., Vida, 541/822-6260, www.mckenzieriverinn.com, $98-185) has simple B&B rooms in an attractive house and riverside cabins.

The riverside **Eagle Rock Lodge** (49198 McKenzie Hwy., Vida, 541/822-3630 or 888/773-4333, www.eaglerocklodge.com, $130-225) is one of the more elegant places to stay along the McKenzie. The large 1947 house has five extra-comfortable rooms in the main house and three suites in the carriage house; beautiful gardens and places to lounge outside surround the buildings. Guests have the option of ordering dinner from the lodge's personal chef ($40), which is particularly nice since there aren't many restaurants in the area. The lodge sponsors a **Wooden Boat Festival** at the start of fishing season in late April; new and historic drift boats are displayed.

Heaven's Gate Cottages (50055 McKenzie Hwy., Vida, 541/896-3855, www.heavensgaterivercottages.com, $115-130) offers housekeeping cabins right on the McKenzie (and the highway); the cabins are sandwiched between the highway and the river. One cabin is right over a good fishing hole, and night lights illuminate the rapids for your contemplation. These cabins may be old, small, and semirustic, but their riverside location helps overcome a multitude of issues. Note: although the official address for Heaven's Gate is in Vida, the cabins are much closer to Blue River.

The former Blue River ranger station, which sits above the highway away from the river, has been repurposed as the lodge for the **McKenzie River Mountain Resort** (51668 Blue River Dr., Blue River, 541/822-6272, www.rivermountainresort.com, $129-249); vacation cabins used to house the rangers. This is a popular base for mountain bikers riding the McKenzie

River Trail; the resort offers a shuttle service. It's common for groups to rent the entire lodge.

Although **Harbick's Country Inn** (54791 Rte. 126, Blue River, 541/822-3805, www.harbicks-country-inn.com, $70-110) may not be as charming as some of the other lodgings along the McKenzie (it's basically a motel), it's a friendly place and within walking distance of one of the finest public golf courses in the country, Tokatee. It also has a good restaurant next door. Because of this, it's quite popular—reserve in advance.

The █ **Cedarwood Lodge** (56535 McKenzie Hwy./Rte. 126, McKenzie Bridge, 541/822-3351, www.cedarwoodlodge.com, Apr.-Oct., $115-195) is tucked away in a grove of old cedars just outside the town of McKenzie Bridge. The lodge has nine vacation housekeeping cottages that feature fully equipped kitchens, bathrooms (with showers), fireplaces (wood provided), and portable barbecues. This is a sweet place to spend a couple of nights, particularly in those units with decks on the river.

The spacious and attractive cabins at █ **Inn at the Bridge** (56393 McKenzie Hwy., McKenzie Bridge, 541/743-2012, www.mckenzie-river-cabins.com, $199) are open year-round. Though these beautiful cabins look like they are part of the landscape, they were built in 2006 and are fully modern, with two bedrooms, full kitchen, river-rock fireplaces, two bathrooms, and a back porch overlooking the river.

Belknap Lodge and Hot Springs (59296 Belknap Springs Rd., McKenzie Bridge, 541/822-3512, www.belknaphotsprings.com, $25-400) offers lodge rooms, cabins, camping, and access to two hot springs swimming pools. The lodge rooms range $100-185 per couple; bathtubs are plumbed with hot springs water. The five simple cabins range $130-400; the least expensive are pet-friendly. Campsites are $25-35. The main attraction on the property is Belknap Springs. The water, which contains 26 different minerals, is gently filtered piping hot into a swimming pool on the south bank of the McKenzie. The property is clean, the scenery is beautiful, and the price is right. For $7, drop-in visitors can use the lower pool for an hour; a day pass is $12 and just what the doctor ordered to ease the aching muscles from that killer hike or the ski marathon. But don't wait too long to fill this prescription—the pool closes at 9pm. If you forget your towel, you can rent one.

Belknap Hot Springs also operates **Camp Yale,** an RV park/resort home. Located just a mile from the hot springs on Hwy. 242, the RV sites start at $25. The so-called "mountain homes" range from one to three bedrooms, all with full kitchens and bathrooms; prices run $225-250 for six people.

Camping

The following campgrounds are under the jurisdiction of the Willamette National Forest, **McKenzie Ranger District** (info 541/822-3381, www.fs.usda.gov; reservations 877/444-6777, www.recreation.gov). Many are along the beautiful McKenzie River National Recreation Trail. Its prime location halfway between Eugene and Bend also helps make the area a popular vacation spot during the summer, so reservations should be made at least five days in advance. Sites at these campgrounds run $12-18 per night; except as noted all of the listed campgrounds have drinking water, vault toilets, and picnic tables.

Several choice campgrounds are south of the McKenzie Highway, off the Aufderheide Highway; these places are convenient to Cougar Reservoir and Terwilliger Hot Springs. **Delta** campground is closest to the McKenzie Highway; it's alongside the river amid old-growth trees less than a mile south of the highway and about a mile north of the Aufderheide. **Slide Creek** campground is on the east bank of Cougar Reservoir; it's a busy place with a boat ramp and swimming area. A few miles south of the reservoir, find **French Pete** and **Frissell Crossing** campgrounds, both are quiet spots along the South Fork of the McKenzie.

A half-mile west of McKenzie Bridge on Route 126 is the 20-site riverside **McKenzie Bridge Campground,** with a boat launch onto the river. East of McKenzie Bridge about 3 miles on Route 126 is **Paradise Campground.**

Although there are 64 tent/RV (up to 40 feet) campsites, only half of the sites are in premium riverside locations. The summer trout fishing here can be very good, and the fireplace grills and wooden tables make it easy to cook and eat a fresh-caught meal. Welcome to paradise!

Olallie Campground is 11 miles east of McKenzie Bridge on Route 126 and has 17 sites. Olallie is situated on the banks of the McKenzie River; boating, fishing, and hiking are some of the nearby attractions. A couple of miles past Olallie on Route 126 is **Trail Bridge Campground** on the north shore of Trail Bridge Reservoir. Piped water, vault and flush toilets, and picnic tables are provided at this 26-site campground. Boat docks are close by, and the reservoir is noted for its good trout fishing. This campground is first-come, first-served and not on the reservation system; it is open June-October.

Another ideal campground for boating enthusiasts is **Lake's End** on nearby Smith Reservoir. One of the few boat-in campgrounds in Oregon, this park can only be reached via a 2-mile sail across the lake. To get there, take Route 126 for 12 miles northeast of McKenzie Bridge, turn left, and follow Forest Service Road 730 two miles to the south end of the reservoir. Boat across to the north shore for camping. Be sure to take along plenty of water, because the campground does not provide any. You will find, however, picnic tables, vault toilets, and plenty of peace and quiet away from the cars and traffic of the other mainstream parks. Lake's End is open May-September and has no fees or reservations.

On the south shore of Clear Lake, 19 miles northeast of McKenzie Bridge on Route 126, is **Coldwater Cove Campground,** open mid-May-mid-October. A county-run cabin resort, **Clear Lake Resort** (541/967-3917, www.linnparks.com), is adjacent to the campground and has a store, a summer-only café, and rustic cabins ($64-117, bring cooking utensils and bedding), as well as boat docks, launches, and rowboat rentals. No powerboats are permitted on the lake. The road to the resort closes at the end of

September; guests can hike in to rustic cabins during the winter.

A handful of small campgrounds dot Route 242, the old McKenzie Pass road, but none have piped water.

FOOD

Restaurants aren't exactly a big deal out here—most overnight visitors are camping or renting cabins with cooking facilities.

There are a couple of good dining options just west of McKenzie Bridge. Stop at **Takodas** (91806 Mill Creek Rd., 541/822-1153, 8am-9pm daily, $6-11), next to Harbick's Country Store, for pizza, a burger, or a visit to the salad bar. During the summer, there's outside seating in a garden area. Right across the highway, the **Rustic Skillet** (54771 McKenzie River Hwy., 541/822-3400, 6:30am-2pm daily, $7-14) can be likened to a fancy truck stop—just good ol' American food. Lest this sound like damning with faint praise, we should add that the menu is diverse for its genre, including asparagus omelets and homemade cinnamon rolls.

INFORMATION

Read the local news online (www.mckenzieriverreflections.com). Wilderness permits, camping, hiking, and mountain biking information are available from the **McKenzie River Ranger District** (57600 McKenzie Hwy., McKenzie Bridge, 541/822-3381, www.fs.usda.gov).

GETTING THERE

Amazingly, travelers without cars can get to the McKenzie National Recreation Trail from Eugene via **Lane Transit District** (541/687-5555, www.ltd.org, $1.75). Their route 91 bus starts at Thurston station in Springfield (with frequent bus connections to downtown Eugene) and heads up the McKenzie River Highway. The bus is equipped to carry a couple of bikes. The terminus point is the McKenzie River Ranger Station at McKenzie Bridge.

Oakridge and the Upper Willamette River

Halfway between Eugene and the Cascades' summit on Route 58 lies the town of Oakridge. Historically a big Oregon timber town, mountain biking now helps to support this small community (pop. 3,200) tucked away in a foothill valley of the Cascades. Visitors will find some of the finest wilderness areas in Oregon in this area.

There are over 100 lakes and streams nearby waiting for just about any nimrod to pull out his or her quota of rainbow, German brown, cutthroat, and Dolly Varden trout from the cool waters. A short drive southeast of town, near Willamette Pass, are two central Oregon gems: Waldo Lake and Odell Lake. Winter sports enthusiasts can find excellent downhill skiing at Willamette Pass, which features 18 runs, four chairlifts, a rope tow, and a day lodge. There are plenty of beautiful trails available for Nordic skiers too. If you like to fish, hike, camp, sail, ski, mountain bike, or just hang out in the woods, it's all only minutes away from Oakridge. East of Oakridge on Route 58 is the Greenwater rest area, a beautiful place to take in the laid-back charm of the upper Willamette River.

SIGHTS
Westfir Covered Bridge

A short distance out of Oakridge on the paved Aufderheide National Scenic Byway is the **Westfir Covered Bridge.** This bright-red span has the distinction of being the longest covered bridge in Oregon (180 feet) as well as the tallest covered bridge west of the Mississippi. Furthermore, it is likely that it is also the heaviest span of any wood construction bridge due to its Howe trusses, extension rods, and cords. You can see what remains of the Hines Company mill on the opposite side of the bridge; in its heyday it employed 750 people and operated around the clock. You can get a good photograph of the bridge from the road as you approach the nearby town of Westfir.

Salt Creek Falls

About 20 miles southeast of Oakridge, just west of Willamette Pass on the way to Odell Lake on Route 58, is Oregon's second-highest waterfall, **Salt Creek Falls,** which forms the headwaters of the Willamette River. Shortly after the turnoff from the south side of the highway, take the right fork in the road and head down to the parking area (NW Forest Pass required). The short walk to the viewing area of the 286-foot-high cascade provides a great photo opportunity. Trails access both the top and the bottom of the waterfall for those interested in taking a closer look at this raw display of hydropower.

Hot Springs

McCredie Hot Springs is 10 miles southeast of Oakridge on Route 58 near mile marker 45. A short walk down to Salt Creek brings you to a small hot spring adjacent to the river. This location allows you to enjoy the rush of simultaneously hot and cold water. Depending on how you position yourself, you can take a bath at any temperature you choose—be careful, there are some extremely hot spots. Because it's so close to the road this place is often busy; many visitors bathe nude here.

Another primitive hot spring in the area is **Meditation Pool** (Wall Creek). It's really more like a warm spring, as the water ranges about 90-104°F, depending on weather conditions. It's a short easy hike in, and the soak is worth the effort. To get there, turn north onto Rose Street from Route 58 in Oakridge. Turn right onto 1st Street, proceed east, and 1st Street will eventually become Forest Service Road 24, paralleling Salmon Creek. About 10 miles out of Oakridge, look for Forest Service Road 1934 on the left (north) side of the road. Approximately 0.5 mile down Forest Service Road 1934 you'll see a trailhead sign (the kind

with no name, only two figures hiking) on the west (left) side of the road. Follow the path along Wall Creek about 0.3 mile up to the creek-side pool.

SPORTS AND RECREATION
Hiking
FALL CREEK NATIONAL RECREATION TRAIL

The 14-mile-long **Fall Creek National Recreation Trail,** about 30 miles southeast of Eugene, is ideal for short day hikes or longer expeditions; several national forest entry/exit points crop up along the way. Another plus is the low elevation of the trail, which makes it accessible year-round. Strolling through the wilderness, you will pass many deep pools, white-water rapids, and over a dozen small streams. Giant Douglas firs, bigleaf maples, vine maples, dogwoods, and red alders are some of the predominant vegetation you'll see along the way. In the spring, visitors are treated to shooting stars, trillium, bleeding heart, and other vibrant wildflowers.

To get there, take Route 58 about 15 miles to Lowell, then go north for two miles to the covered bridge at Unity Junction. Take a right onto Forest Service Road 18 (Fall Creek Rd.), and stay to the left of the reservoir. Follow the road for 11 miles to Dolly Varden Campground, where the trail starts. There are five campgrounds en route and three other spur trails that merge into the Fall Creek Trail. Bedrock Campground is a particularly popular spot for swimming.

LARISON CREEK TRAIL

The **Larison Creek Trail** (Trail 3646) is less than 10 minutes south of Oakridge. Multicolored mosses cover the valley floor, and its walls simulate a brushstroked backdrop to stands of old-growth fir. Further contrast is supplied by waterfalls and swimming holes. The mild grade and low elevation of this trail make it accessible year-round. To get there, take Route 58 to Oakridge. Turn onto Kitson Springs County Road and proceed for 0.5 mile. Turn right on Forest Service Road 21 and follow it 3 miles to the trailhead, which you'll find on the right side of the road. Note that this trail is shared with mountain bikers.

TUFTI CREEK TRAIL

A good hike close to Oakridge is the **Tufti Creek Trail** (Trail 3624). This easy 0.5-mile trail winds through large Douglas firs and cedars and overlooks Hills Creek Gorge. There are many small waterfalls and deep swimming holes along the way. This trail is also accessible year-round.

To get there, take Route 58 to Oakridge. Turn south onto Kitson Springs County Road and proceed for about 1 mile. Turn left onto Forest Service Road 23 and follow it for 6 miles. This will take you along the northeast bank of Hills Creek Lake and on past Kitson Hot Springs (which is also worthy of investigation). Look for the trailhead sign on the right, about 1 mile past the hot springs.

◖ Mountain Biking

Mountain biking has become incredibly popular in the Oakridge area, which is not surprising given that there are an estimated 350 miles of single-track within an hour's drive of town. Find information and detailed trail descriptions at www.mtbikeoregon.com.

Novice bikers and families can start with the **Salmon Creek Trail,** which originates in town and heads along generally flat terrain to Salmon Creek Falls.

Also just outside town, starting at Greenwaters Park near the fish hatchery, **Larison Rock** is a thrilling, technical 5-mile downhill ride. Then, unless you've arranged a car shuttle, it's a bit of a slog back to the start. (An easier though longer route back follows Forest Road 2102.)

The nearly 30-mile-long **Middle Fork River Trail** is a good bet for more experienced mountain bikers who want to test their stamina. It starts at the Sand Prairie campground south of town and heads south and east along the Middle Fork of the Willamette River.

Oakridge hosts a couple of **mountain bike events,** one in mid-July and the other in August (503/968-8870, www.mtbikeoregon.com, $360) with guided rides of the area's trails, meals, beer, and camping.

Road cyclists needn't avoid Oakridge; the **Aufderheide National Scenic Byway** is an excellent low-traffic paved road along the North Fork of the Willamette River.

ACCOMMODATIONS

There are some reasonable lodging options in the area. The nicest budget bunks are at the **Oakridge Lodge and Guest House** (48175 E. 1st St., 541/782-4000, www.oakridgehostel.com, $43.60 pp bunks, $98-109 private room), a large house with immaculately clean rooms, including both private rooms and shared bunkrooms, and a good B&B-style breakfast, even for bunk dwellers. Private rooms can be configured to house families. Secure bike storage is available. This is the site of the early August **Oakridge Ukelele Festival.**

The **Bluewolf Motel** (47465 Hwy. 58, 541/782-5884, www.bluewolfmotel.com, $45-65) is a small, simple motel with microwaves and refrigerators. It's pet-friendly and has nice, spacious grounds, including the "Wolf Den," and outdoor kitchen with a gas grill, piped water, and seating. The plush place to stay in these parts is the **Best Western Oakridge Inn** (47433 Hwy. 58, 541/782-2212, $106-111), which has 30 spacious guest rooms and a pool and hot tub.

In the former office building of Hines Lumber Company in Westfir, across the street from the covered bridge, is the **Westfir Lodge** (47365 1st St., Westfir, 541/782-3103, www.westfirlodge.com, $75-90). The building has been tastefully converted into seven guest rooms with English-style bathrooms (each room has its own private bath, but it's across the hall from the bedroom). The house is full of Asian antiques, and the pantry used to be the company vault. In addition to rooms, the lodge has a restaurant.

FOOD

If there are mountain bikers, there must be beer nearby. Find both at the **Brewers Union Local**

180 (48329 E. 1st St., 541/782-2024, www. brewersunion.com, noon-9pm Sun.-Wed., noon-10pm Thurs., noon-11pm Fri.-Sat. summer, noon-9pm Sun., 3pm-9pm Mon. and Thurs., noon-11pm Fri.-Sat. winter, $7-14), a family-friendly British-style public house where it's as easy to settle in with a cup of tea as with a pint of real ale, and you can either read a book or play pool. You can choose between tempeh, Spam, and beef for your burger.

Lee's Gourmet Garden (47670 Hwy. 58, 541/782-2155, 11am-9pm Tues.-Sun., $7-14) is better than your average small-town Chinese restaurant. The owner used to be Jackie Chan's personal chef and brings a nice touch and a few special dishes to a pretty standard Chinese American menu.

INFORMATION

The **Oakridge/Westfir Chamber of Commerce** (48248 Hwy. 58, Oakridge, 541/782-4146, www.oakridgechamber.com) has a small visitors center in the rest area on the east side of town.

Additional information on biking, hiking, camping, and the Aufderheide National Scenic Byway can be obtained from the **Middle Fork Ranger Station** (46375 Hwy. 58, Westfir, 541/782-2283, www.fs.usda.gov).

NORTH COAST

The north coast, from the mouth of the Columbia River south to Lincoln City, is little more than an hour's drive from the Portland metro area, and the region is the most popular part of Oregon's Pacific shoreline. Still, apart from the weekend crush at Cannon Beach and Seaside, there's more than enough elbow room for everyone along this enchanting and varied coast.

Overlooking the Columbia River as it flows into the Pacific, the former shipping and fishing center of Astoria is fast rediscovering its own potential, with a lively arts scene, adventurous cuisine, and fine hotels and B&Bs hosting overnighters. Its long-idle waterfront is growing busy again with tourist attractions—most notably the Columbia River Maritime Museum, one of the best museums in Oregon.

West of Astoria, at Oregon's far northwestern tip, where the mighty Columbia River meets the Pacific, visitors to Fort Stevens State Park can inspect the skeleton of a century-old shipwreck and a military fort active from the Civil War to World War II—as well as revel in miles of sandy beaches. Fort Clatsop National Memorial, part of Lewis and Clark National Historical Park, includes a re-creation of the Corps of Discovery's winter 1805-1806 quarters—a must-stop for Lewis and Clark buffs.

Cannon Beach and Seaside are two extremely popular resort towns that are polar opposites of one another. Cannon Beach, an enclave of tastefully weathered cedar-shingled architecture, is chockablock with art galleries, boutiques, and upscale lodgings and restaurants. A few miles north, Seaside is Oregon's

© DUNCAN MACK MURPHY

HIGHLIGHTS

◖ Columbia River Maritime Museum: One of Oregon's top museums tells the story of seafaring on the Columbia River (page 260).

◖ Fort Clatsop National Memorial: This replica of Lewis and Clark's 1805-1806 winter camp offers a fascinating glimpse into frontier life (page 263).

◖ Haystack Rock: This soaring sea stack on Cannon Beach is home to thousands of seabirds (page 288).

◖ Saddle Mountain State Natural Area: This knobby mountain rises high above the northern coast, with a hiking trail leading through unusual plantlife on the way to an eye-popping vista (page 290).

◖ Cape Lookout Hikes: Go for the great views of rocks and surf, the chance of seeing a whale, or to totally immerse yourself in the foggy coastal atmosphere (page 315).

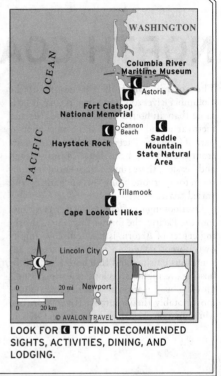

LOOK FOR ◖ TO FIND RECOMMENDED SIGHTS, ACTIVITIES, DINING, AND LODGING.

quintessential family-friendly beach resort, with a long boardwalk, candy and gift shops, and noisy game arcades.

Just south of Cannon Beach, Oswald West State Park is a gem protecting old-growth forest and handsome little pocket beaches, as well as, some believe, a Spanish pirate treasure buried on Neahkahnie Mountain. Beyond Neahkahnie's cliff-top viewpoints along U.S. 101, the Nehalem Bay area attracts anglers, crabbers, and kayakers, as well as discriminating diners who come from far and wide to enjoy surprisingly sophisticated cuisine.

Tillamook County is home to more cows than people and is synonymous with delicious dairy products—cheese and ice cream

in particular. It's no surprise that Tillamook's biggest visitor attraction is cheese-related. More than a million people a year come to the Tillamook Cheese Factory to view the cheese-making operations and sample the excellent results. The Tillamook Air Museum is another popular diversion, housing an outstanding collection of vintage and modern aircraft in gargantuan Hangar B, the largest wooden structure in the world. Tillamook Bay, fed by five rivers, yields oysters and crabs, while the active Garibaldi charter fleet targets salmon, halibut, and tuna in the offshore waters.

South of Tillamook, the Coast Highway wends inland through lush pastureland to Neskowin. It's a pleasant enough stretch, but

the Three Capes Scenic Loop, a 35-mile scenic coastal detour, is a more attractive, if time-consuming, option. The spectacular views and bird-watching from Capes Meares and Lookout are the highlights of this beautiful drive. At Pacific City, at the southern end of the Three Capes Loop, commercial anglers launch their dories right off the sandy beach and through the surf in the lee of Cape Kiwanda and mammoth Haystack Rock—a sight not seen anywhere else on the West Coast. Just north of Lincoln City, Cascade Head beckons hikers to explore its rare prairie headlands ecosystem.

PLANNING YOUR TIME

Although most Oregonians have a favorite beach town that they'll visit for weekends and summer vacations, if this is your grand tour of the Oregon coast, plan to spend a few days exploring the northern coast's beaches and towns. If you're interested in history, architecture, or ship-watching, be sure to spend a night in **Astoria**—it's one of our favorite coastal cities, even though it's several miles from the Pacific Ocean; if you can't wait to walk on Pacific beaches, head to **Cannon Beach** (for a more upscale stay) or **Seaside** (which the kids will love) and begin your trip there. By driving from north to south, you'll be able to pull off the highway more easily into beach access areas. Campers might want to reserve a space at Nehalem Bay State Park, near the small laid-back town of **Manzanita,** a few miles south of Cannon Beach; Manzanita is also a good place to rent a beach house for a weekend. Aside from the near-mandatory stop at the Tillamook Cheese Factory, you'll probably want to skip the town of Tillamook and head to the **Three Capes Loop,** where a night in Pacific City offers easy access to Cape Kiwanda as well as comfy lodgings and a good brewpub. On your way south to the central coast or to the Highway 18 route back through the Willamette Valley wine country to Portland, do stop for a hike at **Cascade Head.**

Astoria and Vicinity

The mouth of the mighty Columbia River, with its abundance of natural resources, was long a home for Native Americans; artifacts found in the area suggest that people have been living along the river for at least 8,000 years. Early European explorers and settlers also found the river and its bays to be propitious as a trading and fishing center. Astoria's dramatic location and deep history continue to attract new settlers and travelers drawn to the area's potent allure.

Astoria (pop. about 10,000) is the oldest permanent U.S. settlement west of the Rockies, and its glory days are preserved by museums, historical exhibits, and pastel-colored Victorian homes weathered by the sea air. Hollywood has chosen Astoria's picturesque neighborhoods to simulate an idealized all-American town, most notably in the cult classic *The Goonies*.

However, Astoria is a real city, warts and all. The preserved pioneer past and attractive Victorian homes may soften the rough edges of a once-bustling port that has seen better days, but not enough for anyone to mistake blue-collar Astoria for a cute tourist town. The decommissioning of the U.S. Naval station after World War II, the decline in the logging and fishing industries, and the closure of several dozen canneries on the waterfront have had lasting effects. Empty storefronts tell the story of a resource-based economy bruised by progress, but there's plenty of pluck left in this old dowager, and her best years may be yet to come.

Astoria has many charms: Historic buildings downtown are undergoing restoration, cruise ships are calling, fine restaurants are multiplying, a lively arts scene is thriving, and there's new life along the waterfront, anchored by the excellent Columbia River Maritime Museum.

History

The Clatsop Indians, a Chinook-speaking group, lived in this area for thousands of years before Astoria's written history began. When Lewis and Clark arrived in 1805, the Clatsops numbered about 400 people, living in three villages on the south side of the Columbia River, but began a steady decline soon after contact with whites.

The region was first chronicled by Don Bruno de Heceta, a Spanish explorer who sailed near the Columbia's mouth in August 1775. He named it the Bay of the Assumption of Our Lady, but the strong current prevented his ship from entering. American presence on the Columbia began with Captain Robert Gray's discovery of the river in May 1792, which he christened after his fur-trading ship, *Columbia Rediviva*.

Thereafter, Lewis and Clark's famous expedition of 1803-1806, with its winter encampment at Fort Clatsop, south of present-day Astoria, helped incorporate the Pacific Northwest as part of a new nation. In 1811,

© BILL MCRAE

NORTH COAST

Astoria-Megler Bridge

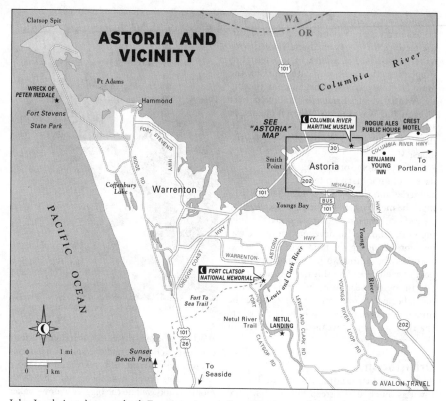

John Jacob Astor's agents built Fort Astoria on a hillside in what would eventually grow into Astoria—the first American settlement west of the Rockies. The trading post was occupied by the British between 1813 and 1818, and the settlement was renamed Fort George. Real development began in the 1840s as settlers begin pouring in from the Oregon Trail. During the Civil War, Fort Stevens was built at the mouth of the Columbia to guard against a Confederate naval incursion.

Commerce grew with the export of lumber and foodstuffs to gold rush-era San Francisco and Asia. Salmon canneries became the mainstay of Astoria's economy during the 1870s, helping it grow into Oregon's second-largest city—and a notorious shanghaiing port. From that time through the early 1900s, the dominant immigrants to the Astoria area were

Scandinavian, and with the addition of these seafaring folk, logging, fishing, and shipbuilding coaxed the population up to 20,000 by World War II.

Some believe that the port city at the mouth of the Columbia might have grown to rival San Francisco or Seattle had it not been for the setback of a devastating fire in 1922. In the early morning hours of December 8, a pool hall on Commercial Street caught fire, and the flames spread rapidly among the wooden buildings, many supported on wooden pilings, in Astoria's business district. By daybreak more than 200 businesses in a 32-block area had been reduced to ashes. The downtown was rebuilt in the ensuing years, largely in brick and stone, but the devastation changed the fate of Astoria.

Near the end of World War II, a Japanese submarine's shelling of Fort Stevens made it

NORTH COAST

the only fortification on U.S. soil to have sustained an attack in a world war. After the war, the region's fortunes ebbed and flowed with its resource-based economy. In an attempt to supplement that economy with tourism, the State Highway Division began constructing the Astoria-Megler Bridge in 1962 to connect Oregon and Washington. When it opened in 1966, the bridge provided the final link in the 1,625-mile-long U.S. 101 along the Pacific Coast.

Unfortunately, preserving Astoria's glory days could not make up for the closing of the canneries and the decline of logging and fishing. The modern era has been characterized by a steady cultivation of tourism dollars, resulting in the thoughtful development of the waterfront, including the four-mile River Walk. Astoria is becoming an increasingly popular port of call for cruise ships, with more than 50 visiting per year. Whether or not Astoria's metaphoric ship ever comes in, let's hope the unpretentious charm of this hillside city where the river meets the ocean will not be lost in the process.

sea lions basking on the Astoria waterfront

Orientation

The waters surrounding Astoria define the town as much as the steep hills it's built on. Along its northern side, the mighty Columbia, four miles wide, is a mega aquatic highway carrying a steady flow of traffic, from small pleasure boats to massive cargo ships a quarter mile long. Soaring high over the river is an engineering marvel that's impossible to miss from most locations in town. At just over four miles long, the Astoria-Megler Bridge, completed in 1966, is the longest bridge in Oregon and the longest bridge of its type (cantilever through-truss) in the world. On Astoria's south side, Young's River, flowing down from the Coast Range, broadens into Young's Bay, separating Astoria from its neighbor Warrenton to the west.

A few miles to the northwest, the Columbia River finally meets the Pacific, 1,243 miles from its headwaters in British Columbia. Where the tremendous outflow (averaging 118 million gallons per minute) of the River of the West encounters the ocean tides, conditions can be treacherous, and the sometimes-monstrous waves around the bar have claimed more than 2,000 vessels over the years. This river-mouth could well be the biggest widow-maker on the high seas, earning it the title "Graveyard of the Pacific." Lewis and Clark referred to it as "that seven-shouldered horror" in a journal entry from the winter of 1805-1806.

Any visitor to Astoria should consider crossing the Astoria-Megler Bridge to visit the extreme southwest corner of Washington State. Here the sands and soil carried by the Columbia create a 20-mile-long sand spit called the Long Beach Peninsula. Some of the West Coast's most succulent oysters grow in Willapa Bay, the body of water created by this finger of sand. Historic beach communities plus numerous Lewis and Clark sites also reward visitors to this charming enclave.

SIGHTS

After getting a bird's-eye view from Coxcomb Hill, you might want to take a closer look at

Astoria on foot. The town is home to dozens of beautifully restored 19th-century and early-20th-century houses. Here's a suggested route: From the Flavel House Museum at 8th Street and Duane Street, start walking south on 8th Street and turn left on Franklin Avenue. Continue east to 11th Street, then detour south one block on 11th Street to Grand Avenue; head east on Grand, north on 12th Street, and back to Franklin, continuing your eastward trek. Walk to 17th Street, then south again to Grand, double back on Grand two blocks to 15th Street, then walk north on 15th to Exchange Street and east on Exchange to 17th, where you'll be just two blocks from the Columbia River Maritime Museum. The route takes you past 74 historical buildings and sites.

Download free two-hour audio tours and accompanying maps from the **Chamber of Commerce** (www.oldoregon.com); one focuses on history and the other on movie sites.

Astoria Column

The best introduction to Astoria and environs is undoubtedly the 360-degree panorama from atop the 125-foot-tall **Astoria Column** (2199 Coxcomb Dr., 503/325-2963, www.astoriacolumn.org, dawn-dusk daily, $1 requested for parking) on Coxcomb Hill, the highest point in town. Patterned after the Trajan Column in Rome, the reinforced-concrete tower was built in 1926 as a joint project of the Great Northern Railway and the descendants of John Jacob Astor to commemorate the westward sweep of discovery and migration. The graffito frieze spiraling up the exterior illustrates Robert Gray's 1792 discovery of the Columbia River, the establishment of American claims to the Northwest Territory, the arrival of the Great Northern Railway, and other scenes of the history of the Pacific Northwest. The vista from the surrounding hilltop park is impressive enough, but for the ultimate experience, the climb up 164 steps to the tower's top is worth the effort.

Before ascending, get oriented with the annotated bronze relief map in front of the column, which notes the distances and directions to landmarks near and far. From this vantage point you can see across the rooftops of the town, the Astoria-Megler Bridge, giant freighters gliding up and down the Columbia, and a long sweep of the Washington shore. To the northwest are the Columbia Bar and Cape Disappointment. On clear days, look northeast to Mount St. Helens and to Mount Hood on the far eastern horizon. Looking over Young's Bay south and west of Astoria, the Clatsop Plains extend to Tillamook Head and Saddle Mountain.

If you have kids in tow, be sure to stop by the tiny gift shop to buy a balsa wood glider. Lofting a wooden airplane from the top of the tower is an Astoria tradition.

Get to the Astoria Column from downtown by following 16th Street south (uphill) to Jerome Avenue. Turn west (right) one block and continue up 15th Street to the park entrance on Coxcomb Drive.

The Waterfront

While most of Astoria's waterfront is lined with warehouses and docks, the **River Walk** will get you front-row views of the river. The River Walk provides paved riverside passage for pedestrians and cyclists along a four-mile stretch between the Port of Astoria and the community of Alderbrook. The path continues unpaved another two miles eastward to Tongue Point.

An excellent way to cover some of the same ground, accompanied by color commentary on sights and local history, is by taking a 40-minute ride on Old Number 300, the **Astoria Riverfront Trolley** (503/325-6311, www.old300.org, noon-7pm daily Memorial Day-Labor Day weather permitting, noon-6pm Sat.-Sun. fall and spring, $1 per ride or $2 all day), which runs on Astoria's original train tracks alongside the River Walk as far east as the East Mooring Basin. Trolley shelters are at several locations along the route; you can also flag it down by waving a dollar bill. The lovingly restored 1913 trolley originally served San Antonio and later ran between Portland and Lake Oswego in the 1980s.

Toward the eastern end of the River Walk, at

NORTH COAST

Pier 39, the **Hanthorn Cannery** (100 39th St., 503/325-2502, www.canneryworker.org, 9am-6pm daily, free) is a rather informal but fascinating museum housed in an old Bumble Bee tuna cannery. Exhibits include some lovely old wooden boats, eye-catching photos, and canning equipment. There's also a coffee shop and a brewpub at this location, so it's a good place to take a break.

◖ Columbia River Maritime Museum

On the waterfront a few blocks east of downtown Astoria, the **Columbia River Maritime Museum** (1792 Marine Dr., 503/325-2323, www.crmm.org, 9:30am-5pm daily, closed Thanksgiving and Christmas, $12 adults, $10 seniors, $5 children ages 6-17, under 6 free) is hard to miss. The roof of the 44,000-square-foot museum simulates the curvature of cresting waves, and the gigantic 25,000-pound anchor out front is also impossible to ignore. What's inside surpasses this eye-catching facade. The introductory film is excellent and intense, giving a good glimpse of the jobs of bar pilots, who climb aboard huge ships to navigate them through tricky passages. Floor-to-ceiling windows in the Great Hall allow visitors to watch the river traffic in comfort.

Times when tribal canoes plied the Columbia, Lewis and Clark camped on the Columbia's shores, and dramatic shipwrecks occurred on its bar are recounted with scale models, exquisitely detailed miniatures of ships, paintings, and artifacts. The most dramatic exhibit is of a 44-foot U.S. Coast Guard motor lifeboat, poised precariously on a wave in a life-size re-creation of a rescue on the Columbia River Bar. The chance to walk the bridge of a World War II destroyer, steer a tugboat, or tie a cleat hitch and other useful knots adds a hands-on aspect to the experience. Local lighthouses, the evolution of boat design, and harpoons are the focus of other exhibits here. There are also some artifacts from the *Peter Iredale* and other ships that have met their ends on the Oregon coast. Still other items of interest include scrimshaw,

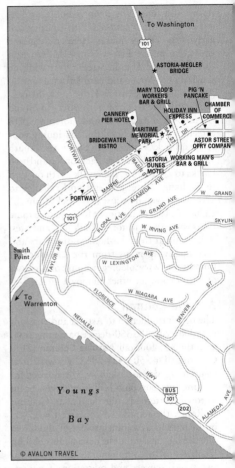

fishing and cannery memorabilia, a small watercolor of the harbor by a crew member on Robert Gray's 1792 voyage of discovery, and sea charts dating as far back as 1587.

Museum admission lets you board the 128-foot lightship *Columbia,* now permanently berthed alongside the museum building. This vessel served as a floating lighthouse, marking the entrance to the mouth of the river and helping many ships navigate the dangerous waters. After almost three decades of service it was replaced in 1979 by an unstaffed 42-foot-high navigational buoy. The gift shop has a great

NORTH COAST

collection of books on Astoria's history and other maritime topics.

Also berthed at the museum is the pilot boat *Peacock,* which crossed the Columbia bar more than 35,000 times during her 30-plus year career.

Heritage Museum and Research Library

The Clatsop County Historical Society operates the **Heritage Museum** (1618 Exchange St., 503/325-2203, www.cumtux.org, 10am-5pm daily May-Sept., 11am-4pm Tues.-Sat.

Oct.-Apr., $4 adults, $2 children ages 6-12). Housed in the handsome neoclassical building that was originally Astoria's city hall, it has several galleries filled with antiquities, tools, vintage photographs, and archives chronicling various aspects of life in Clatsop County. The museum's centerpiece exhibit concentrates on the culture of the local Clatsop and Chinook people, from before European contact up to the present day. Other exhibits highlight natural history, geology, early immigrants and settlers in the region, and the development of commerce in such fields as fishing, fish packing,

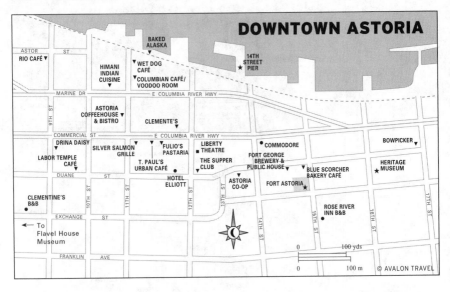

DOWNTOWN ASTORIA

logging, and lumber. The **research library** is open to the public.

The historical society also operates the **Uppertown Firefighters Museum** (30th St. and Marine Dr., 503/325-2203, noon-3pm Sat. or by appointment, free), which displays an extensive collection of firefighting equipment dating from 1873 to 1963. Featured are hand-pulled, horse-drawn, and motorized fire engines, including a 1912 American LaFrance fire truck, a Stutz fire engine, and a 1946 Mack fire truck. The photos and information about the devastating fires of 1893 and 1922 are fascinating.

Fort Astoria

In a tiny park at the corner of 15th and Exchange Streets, a reproduction of a rough-hewn log blockhouse and a mural commemorate the spot where Astoria began, when John Jacob Astor's fur traders originally constructed a small fort in 1811. It's worth a quick stop for buffs of early Pacific Northwest history.

Flavel House Museum

Captain George Flavel, Astoria's first millionaire, amassed a fortune in the mid-19th century

through his Columbia Bar piloting monopoly and later expanded his empire through shipping, banking, and real estate. Between 1884 and 1886 he had a home built in the center of Astoria, now the **Flavel House Museum** (441 8th St., 503/325-2203, 10am-5pm daily May-Sept., 11am-4pm Tues.-Sat. Oct.-Apr., $5 adults, $4 seniors and students, $2 children ages 6-17, 5 and younger free) overlooking the Columbia River, where he retired with his wife and two daughters. From its fourth-story cupola, Flavel could watch the comings and goings of his sailing fleet. Although the captain died in 1893, members of the family lived in the house until 1933. The amazing story of the Flavel family was depicted in colorful detail by Calvin Trillin in the February 8, 1993, issue of the *New Yorker*.

When the Clatsop County Historical Society assumed stewardship in 1951, the mansion was slated for demolition, to be paved over as a parking lot for the adjacent courthouse. Fortunately, thanks to the efforts of the historical society and many volunteers, the house still stands today, at the corner of 8th and Duane Streets. The splendidly extravagant Queen Anne mansion reflects the rich style and

NORTH COAST

While in Astoria, be sure to visit the Columbia River Maritime Museum, which includes tours of historic boats.

elegance of the late Victorian era and the lives of Astoria's most prominent family.

The property encompasses a full city block. With its intricate woodwork inside and out, period furnishings, and art, along with its extravagantly rendered gables, cornices, and porches, the Flavel House ranks with the Carson Mansion in Eureka, California, as a Victorian showplace. The 14-foot ceilings, Persian rugs, and an array of imported tiles are upstaged only by the fireplaces framed in exotic hardwoods in every room. The Carriage House, on the southwest corner of the property, serves as an orientation center for visitors, with exhibits, an interpretive video, and a museum store.

Lewis and Clark National Wildlife Refuge

Six miles east of Astoria in the Burnside area is the **Twilight Creek Eagle Sanctuary.** To get there, drive seven miles east of town on U.S. 30 and turn left at Burnside. A viewing platform on the left 0.5 mile later overlooks the 35,000

acres of mudflats, tidal marshes, and islands (which Lewis and Clark called "Seal Islands") of the **Lewis and Clark National Wildlife Refuge.** Bald eagles live here year-round, and the area provides wintering and resting habitat for waterfowl, shorebirds, and songbirds. Beavers, raccoons, weasels, mink, muskrats, and river otters live on the islands; harbor seals and California sea lions feed in the rich estuary waters and use the sandbars and mudflats as haul-out sites at low tide.

◖ Fort Clatsop National Memorial

On November 7, 1805, after a journey of nearly 19 months and 4,000 miles, the Lewis and Clark expedition thought they had at last reached their destination, the Pacific Ocean. "Ocian in View! O! the joy," wrote William Clark in his journal. Alas, they were close, but from the Washington side of the Columbia River they had mistaken its broad mouth for the sea itself. Hindered by waves and foul

NORTH COAST

ASTORIA GOES TO THE MOVIES

In recent decades, the Victorian homes and ocean view in Astoria's hillside neighborhoods and the surrounding maritime settings have provided the backdrop for such fanciful modern sagas as *Free Willy I* and *II*, *Kindergarten Cop*, *Teenage Mutant Ninja Turtles III*, *Short Circuit*, *Come See the Paradise*, and *The Goonies*. The last movie, a cult favorite shot in 1985, concerns a gang of local kids hunting for pirate's treasure; happy memories of the movie continue to attract a steady stream of visitors looking for the locations used in the film. More recently, films shot in Astoria have gravitated toward horror, including *The Ring Two* and *Cthulhu*, a film based on the horror novels of H. P. Lovecraft. Download an audio tour and map to movie sites at www.oldoregon. com (click on Visitor Information). A guide to movie locations is available at the Oregon Welcome Center in Astoria, the Heritage Museum, Flavel House Museum, and the Warrenton Visitors Center. If you're really into it, stop by the **Oregon Film Museum** (732 Duane St., 503/325-2203, www.oregonfilmmuseum.org, 10am-5pm daily, $5 adults, $2 children ages 6-17), which ostensibly celebrates the various films shot in Oregon, but is mostly a paean to all things Goonie. The museum is housed in the old Clatsop County Jail (from 1914), which famously starred in *The Goonies* jailbreak scene.

weather, it would take nearly another week before they actually beheld the Pacific. They explored farther west, to Cape Disappointment, and spent 10 uncomfortable days exposed to the elements on the north shore of the Columbia, then decided to move south for a more suitable location to pass the coming winter.

They chose a thickly forested rise alongside the Netul River (now the Lewis and Clark River), a few miles south of present-day Astoria, for their campsite. There, the Corps of Discovery quickly set about felling trees and building two parallel rows of cabins, joined by a gated palisade. The finished compound measured about 50 feet on each side. The party of 33 people, including one African American and a Native American woman and her baby, moved into the seven small rooms on Christmas Eve and named their stockade Fort Clatsop for the nearby Indian people.

The winter of 1805-1806 was cold, wet, rainy, and generally miserable. Of the 106 days spent at the site, it rained on all but 12. The January 18, 1806, journal entry of expedition member Private Joseph Whitehouse was typical of the comments recorded during the stay: "It rained hard all last night, & still continued the same this morning. It continued Raining during the whole of this day."

While at Fort Clatsop, the men stored up meat and other supplies, sewed moccasins and new garments, and traded with local tribes, all the while coping with the constant damp conditions, illness and injuries, and merciless plagues of fleas. As soon as the weather permitted, on March 23, 1806, they finally departed on their homeward journey to St. Louis.

Within a few years the elements had erased all traces of Fort Clatsop, and its exact location was lost. In 1955, local history buffs took their best guess and built a replica of the fort, based on the notes and sketches of Captain Clark. In 1999 an anthropologist discovered a 148-year-old map identifying the location of Lewis and Clark's winter encampment, and as it turns out the reproduction is sited very close to the original. In 2005, this replica of Fort Clatsop burned, and a new replica, built mostly by volunteers using period tools, was reopened in 2006. Compared to the previous one, this new Fort Clatsop is a more authentic replica of the actual fort that housed the intrepid Corps of Discovery.

Today, in addition to the log replica of the fort, a well-equipped visitors center, a museum, and other attractions make **Fort Clatsop National Memorial** (92343 Fort Clatsop Rd., 503/861-2471, www.nps.gov/lewi, 9am-6pm

THE LONG BEACH PENINSULA

If you've come as far as Astoria, at the edge of the continent and at the mouth of the Columbia River, you should consider crossing the soaring Astoria-Megler Bridge to explore sights on the Columbia's northern shore. There are both scenic and historical reasons to visit this remote corner of Washington State. The Lewis and Clark National and State Historical Parks aggregation includes a number of sites just across from Astoria in Washington, notably **Cape Disappointment State Park,** with a newly expanded Lewis and Clark Interpretive Center.

The **Long Beach Peninsula,** the thin sand spit just north of the mouth of the Columbia River, claims to have the world's longest beach. And with 28 unbroken miles of it, the boast has to be taken seriously. Like Seaside in Oregon, beach resorts at Seaview and Long Beach have a long pedigree, dating from the 1880s, when Portland families journeyed down the Columbia River by steamboat to summer at the coast. The bay side of the Long Beach sand spit creates **Willapa Bay,** known to oyster-lovers around the country for the excellent bivalves that grow in this shallow inlet, which is fed by six rivers. Most of Willapa Bay is protected as a national wildlife refuge, and it's an excellent bird-watching site. **Oysterville,** a tiny village along the bay, stands largely unchanged since the 1880s, and the entire town has been placed on the National Register of Historic Places. The very tip of the peninsula is preserved as 807-acre **Leadbetter Point State Park,** with informal hiking trails along both sandy beaches and the reedy bay.

Another good reason to cross the bridge is to dine at the area's top restaurant: **Pelicano Restaurant** (177 Howerton Way SE, Ilwaco, 360/642-4034, http://pelicanorestaurant. com, 5pm-9pm Wed.-Sun. $19-26), right above the harbor in the fishing village of Ilwaco. The food is beautifully prepared Mediterranean via Pacific Northwest cuisine, with the freshest of local fish, seafood, produce, beef, and lamb given an expert French and Italian twist by chef/owner Jeff McMahon.

daily mid-June-Labor Day, 9am-5pm daily Labor Day-mid-June, $3 adults, children under 16 free) a must-stop for anyone interested in this pivotal chapter of American history. The expedition's story is nicely narrated here with displays, artifacts, slides, and films, but the summertime "living history" reenactments are the main reason to come. Paths lead through the grove of old-growth Sitka spruce, with interpretive placards identifying native plants. A short walk from the fort leads to the riverside, where dugout canoes are modeled on those used by the corps while in this area. In addition, the 6.5-mile **Fort to Sea Trail** follows the general route blazed by Captain Clark from the fort through dunes and forests to the Pacific at Sunset Beach.

The winter of 1805-1806 put a premium on wilderness survival skills, some of which are exhibited here by rangers in costume. You may see the tanning of hides, making of buckskin clothing and moccasins, and the molding of tallow candles and lead bullets. In addition, visitors may occasionally participate in the construction of a dugout canoe or try their luck at starting a fire by striking flint on steel. Rangers also lead guided hikes and canoe trips.

This 1,500-acre park sits six miles southwest of Astoria and three miles east of U.S. 101 on the Lewis and Clark River. To get there from Astoria, take Marine Drive and head west across Young's Bay to Warrenton. On the other side of the bay look for signs for the Fort Clatsop turnoff; turn left off the Coast Highway about a mile after the bridge and follow the signs to Fort Clatsop.

Fort Stevens State Park

Ten miles west of Astoria, in the far northwest corner of the state, the Civil War-era outpost of **Fort Stevens** (100 Peter Iredale Rd., Hammond, 503/861-1671 or 800/551-6949,

© BILL MCRAE

The *Peter Iredale* wrecked on the Oregon coast in 1906.

www.oregonstateparks.org, $5 day use for historic military area and Coffenbury Lake, $21 tent camping, $27 RV camping, $41 yurt, $85 cabin) was one of three military installations (the others were Forts Canby and Columbia in Washington) built to safeguard the mouth of the Columbia River. Established shortly before the Confederates surrendered on April 9, 1865, Fort Stevens served for 84 years, until just after the end of World War II. Today, the remaining fortifications and other buildings are preserved along with 3,700 acres of woodland, lakes, wetlands, miles of sand beaches, and three miles of Columbia River frontage.

The fort's creation was not the only outgrowth of the Civil War on the West Coast. The year before, President Abraham Lincoln had founded the city of Port Angeles, Washington, for "lighthouse purposes." Given the creation of Fort Stevens shortly thereafter, it's a logical assumption that "lighthouse purposes" also meant watching out for Confederate ships and the British, whom the Union feared would ally with the South. The remote northwest Oregon

coast may seem a world away from the bloody battles of the Civil War, until you consider that the last shots of the conflict were fired even farther away, in the Bering Strait. On June 5, 1865, the *Shenandoah* attacked a fleet of Yankee whalers because the Confederate skipper was unaware of the Appomattox Treaty, which had ended the war two months before.

Although Fort Stevens did not see action in the Civil War, it sustained an attack in a later conflict. On June 21, 1942, a Japanese submarine fired 17 shells on the gun emplacements at Battery Russell, making it the only U.S. fortification in the 48 states to be bombed by a foreign power since the War of 1812. No damage was incurred, and the Army didn't return fire. Shortly after World War II, the fort was deactivated and the armaments were removed.

Today, the site features a **Military Museum** (503/861-1470 or 503/861-2000, 10am-6pm daily June-Sept., 10am-4pm daily Oct.-May) with old photos, weapons exhibits, and maps, as well as seven different batteries (fortifications) and other structures left over from almost a century of service. Climbing to the commander's station for a scenic view of the Columbia River and South Jetty are popular visitor activities. The massive gun batteries, built of weathered gray concrete and rusting iron, eerily silent amid the thick woodlands, also invite exploration; small children should be closely supervised, as there are steep stairways, high ledges, and other hazards.

During the summer months, guided tours of the underground **Battery Mishler** (12:30 and 2:30pm daily, $4) and a narrated tour of the fort's 37 acres on a two-ton U.S. Army truck (12:30 and 2:30pm Mon.-Thurs., 11am, 12:30, 2:30, and 4pm Fri.-Sat., May 1-Sept. 30, $4) are also available. Summer programs include Civil War reenactments and archaeological digs.

Nine miles of bike trails and five miles of hiking trails link the historic area to the rest of the park and provide access to Battery Russell and the 1906 wreck of the British schooner **Peter Iredale.** You can also bike to the campground one mile south of the Military Museum.

Parking is available at four lots about a mile from one another at the foot of the dunes. The beach runs north to the Columbia River, where excellent surf fishing, bird-watching, and a view of the mouth of the river await. South of the campground (east of the *Peter Iredale*) is a self-guided nature trail around part of the two-mile shoreline of **Coffenbury Lake.** The lake also has two swimming beaches with bathhouses and fishing for trout and perch.

To get to Fort Stevens State Park from U.S. 101, drive west on Harbor Street through Warrenton on Highway 104 (Ft. Stevens Hwy.) to the suburb of Hammond, and follow the signs to Fort Stevens Historic Area and Military Museum.

SPORTS AND RECREATION
Bicycling
You don't need a fancy bike to pedal the River Walk; rent a hefty cruiser from **Bikes and Beyond** (1089 Marine Dr., 503/325-2961, www.bikesandbeyond.com). This friendly little shop also caters to bicycle tourists.

Diving and Kayaking
Astoria Scuba (on Pier 39, 503/325-2502, www.astoriascuba.com) offers diving lessons and kayak rentals for $25 for half a day.

Fishing Charters
More than any other industry, commercial fishing has dominated Astoria throughout its history. Salmon canneries lined the waterfront at the turn of the 20th century. Albacore and longline shark fishing put dinner on the table in the 1930s and 1940s. In the modern era, commercial fishing has turned to sole, lingcod, rockfish, flounder, and other bottom fish. If it's not enough to watch these commercial operations from the dock, try joining a charter.

Tiki Charters (350 Industry St., 503/325-7818, www.tikicharter.com) will take you out for salmon, halibut, bottom fish, and sturgeon, depending on the season. Trips depart from the

---

THE *PETER IREDALE*

One of the best known of the hundreds of ships wrecked on the Oregon coast over the centuries is the British schooner *Peter Iredale*. This 278-foot four-master, fashioned of steel plates on an iron frame, was built in Liverpool in 1890 and came to its untimely end on the beach south of Clatsop Spit on October 25, 1906. En route from Mexico to pick up a load of wheat on the Columbia River, the vessel ran aground during high seas and a northwesterly squall. All hands were rescued, and with little damage to the hull, hopes initially ran high that the ship could be towed back to sea and salvaged. That effort proved fruitless, and eventually the ship was written off as a total loss. Today, nearly a century later, the remains of her rusting skeleton protrude from the sands of Fort Stevens State Park as a familiar sight to most who have traveled the north coast. Signs within Fort Stevens State Park lead the way to a parking area close to the wreck.

dock near the former Red Lion Inn. Given the retail price of fresh salmon, you could theoretically pay for a charter trip by landing a single fish. **Gale Force Guides** (trips depart from Warrenton, 503/861-1494, www.galeforceguides.com) takes sport anglers fishing for salmon in either salt- or freshwater, depending on the season. Sturgeon and crabbing trips are also offered.

On your own, go after trout, bass, catfish, steelhead, and sturgeon in freshwater lakes, streams, and rivers. Lingcod, rockfish, surfperch, and other bottom fish can be pursued at sea, off jetties, or along ocean beaches.

Hiking

An in-town hike that's not too strenuous begins at 28th and Irving Streets, meandering up the hill to the Astoria Column. If you drive to the trailhead, park along 28th Street. It's about a one-mile walk to the top. En route is the **Cathedral Tree,** an old-growth fir with a sort of Gothic arch formed at its roots.

The **Oregon Coast Trail** starts (or ends) at Clatsop Spit, at the north end of **Fort Stevens State Park** (100 Peter Iredale Rd., Hammond, 503/861-1671 or 800/551-6949, www.oregonstateparks.org, $5 day use). The most northerly stretch extends south along the beach for 14 miles to Gearhart. It's a flat, easy walk, and your journey could well be highlighted by a sighting of the endangered silverspot butterfly. The species frequents just six sites, including four in Oregon; Clatsop County is one of them. The endangered status of the creature protects it by law and has stopped developers from building resorts on coastal meadows and dunes north of Gearhart. Look for a small orange butterfly with silvery spots on the undersides of its wings.

You might also encounter cars on the beach. This section of shoreline, inexplicably, is the longest stretch of coastline open to motor vehicles in Oregon. Call the **State Parks and Recreation Division** (800/551-6949) for an up-to-date report on trail conditions before starting out.

Fort Stevens State Park has nine miles of hiking trails through woods, wetlands, and dunes. One popular hike here is the two-mile loop around **Coffenbury Lake.**

In 2005, as part of the expansion of Lewis and Clark National Historical Park, the **Fort to Sea Trail** was created to link Fort Clatsop to the Pacific. The 6.5-mile trail follows the route through forest, fields, and dunes that the corps traveled as they explored and traded along the Pacific coast.

The Fort to Sea Trail starts from the visitors center at Fort Clatsop. The first 1.5 miles involve a gentle climb past many trees blown down in a big 2007 storm to the Clatsop Ridge, where on a clear day you can see through the trees to the Pacific Ocean. The ridge makes a fine destination for a short hike, but the really beautiful part of the trail is the hikers-only (no dogs) stretch from the overlook to the beach, where you'll pass through deep woods and forested pastures dotted with small lakes. The trail passes a tunnel underneath U.S. 101 and continues through dunes to the Sunset Beach-Fort to Sea Trail parking lot. From there, a one-mile path leads to the beach.

Unless you plan to return along the trail—which makes for a long day's hike—you'll need to arrange a pickup.

Water Parks

The **Astoria Aquatic Center** (20th St. and Marine Dr., 503/325-7027, www.astoriaparks.com, 5am-8pm Mon.-Fri., 9am-5pm Sat., 11am-5pm Sun., $6.50 adult, $4.50 children ages 2-17, $15 family) houses four pools, including a 100-foot waterslide with a 20-foot drop and a lazy-river current; a six-lane, 25-yard lap pool; an adult hydro spa pool; a kiddies' wading pool; locker rooms; and a variety of fitness equipment.

ENTERTAINMENT AND EVENTS

For the lowdown on all the happenings in and around Astoria, get your hands on a copy of *Hipfish,* Astoria's spirited monthly tabloid distributed free all over town.

LEWIS AND CLARK NATIONAL HISTORICAL PARK

On November 2, 2004, President George W. Bush signed a bill into law to create the 59th national park in the United States. The Lewis and Clark National and State Historical Parks honor explorers Meriwether Lewis and William Clark, whose journey in 1804-1806 paved the way for the U.S. settlement of the West. The park focuses on the sites at the mouth of the Columbia River, where the Corps of Discovery spent the famously wet winter of 1805.

The park is somewhat unusual in that it is essentially a rebranding of current National Park facilities and a federalization of current state parks. The new park includes a dozen sites linked to Lewis and Clark exploration, campsites, and lore. One of these, **Fort Clatsop National Memorial,** south of Astoria and where the Corps actually spent the winter, was already operated by the National Park Service, while **Cape Disappointment State Park** formerly Fort Canby State Park, on the Washington side of the Columbia, remains a Washington state park but is managed by the national park entity.

Besides these two existing facilities, units of the new national park include the **Fort to Sea Trail,** a path linking Fort Clatsop to the Pacific; **Clarks Dismal Nitch,** a notoriously wet campsite near the Washington base of the Astoria-Megler Bridge; **Station Camp,** another improvident campsite for the Corps; the **Salt Works** in Seaside, where the Corps boiled seawater to make salt; **Netul Landing,** the canoe launch area used by Lewis and Clark near Fort Clatsop; and a **memorial to Thomas Jefferson** yet to be constructed on the grounds of Cape Disappointment State Park.

The new national park also encompasses the existing **Fort Columbia State Park** in Washington, which preserves a turn-of-the-20th-century military encampment, and **Fort Stevens, Sunset Beach,** and **Ecola State Parks** in Oregon.

The national park designation changes little for these once disparate sites, at least in the near future. Fort Clatsop has been expanded to 1,500 acres, and the **Lewis and Clark Interpretive Center** at Fort Disappointment State Park was revamped. Visitors will mostly notice new and consistent signage throughout the park units. Ranger-guided hikes and living history reenactors promise to bring to life the famous, often very wet, events that took place here over 200 years ago.

Nightlife

Befitting of a vintage fishing port, Astoria has lots of old bars and watering holes. As tribute to Astoria's scrappy spirit, explore some of the city's classic bars. The **Portway** (422 W. Marine Dr., 503/325-2651) is the oldest bar in the oldest American settlement west of the Rockies. Though the present building dates from 1923, it's loaded with character and characters. Directly under the bridge, **Mary Todd's Workers Bar and Grill** (281 W. Marine Dr., 503/338-7291) is a classic old bar with a notable drink special: the Yucca. Also try the marvelously crispy onion rings. On the eastern edge of Astoria, the slightly disreputable-looking **Desdemona Club** (2997 Marine Dr., 503/325-8540) is in fact a friendly *Cheers*-type pub that welcomes strangers with pool tables and good food. **Phyllis & Bob's Labor Temple Café & Bar** (939 Duane St., 503/325-0801) is the oldest communal union hall in the Pacific Northwest and is not to be missed. The clientele is a mix of longtime union activists, twenty-something artists, and rowdy young sailors, making for some interesting dynamics. The **Voodoo Room** (1114 Marine Dr., 503/325-2233, www.columbianvoodoo.com) is a dark and cluttered bar with hipsters, cocktails, and occasional live music.

All of Astoria's brewpubs are friendly places to start a conversation or settle in with a pint and decent pub grub to quietly muse on the world. **Fort George Brewery and Public House** (1483 Duane St., 503/325-7468, www.

fortgeorgebrewery.com) has free live music on Sunday evenings.

The Arts

The handsome **Liberty Theatre** (1203 Commercial St., 503/325-5922, www.liberty-theater.org), whose colonnaded facades along Commercial and 12th Streets converge at the corner box office, is a vibrant symbol of Astoria's ongoing rejuvenation. The ornate Mediterranean-style building in the heart of downtown began its life in 1925 as a venue for silent films, vaudeville acts, and lectures. The theater continued as a first-run movie house, but after decades of neglect this grande dame was badly showing her age, and it looked as though the Liberty would eventually meet the sad wrecking ball fate of so many fine old movie palaces. Fortunately, though, a nonprofit organization undertook efforts to restore the theater to its original elegance and equip it to be a state-of-the-art performing arts center, and the Liberty currently hosts concerts, recitals, theater, and other events.

Astoria's long-running *Shanghaied in Astoria* (122 W. Bond St., 503/325-6104, www.shanghaiedinastoria.com, evenings Thurs.-Sat. mid-July-mid-Sept., $16-20), based on the town's dubious distinction as a notorious shanghai port during the late 1800s, is a good old-fashioned melodrama. Chase scenes, bar fights, and a liberal sprinkling of Scandinavian jokes will have you laughing in between applauding the hero and booing the villain. Performed with gusto by the Astor Street Opry Company, the show has been running since 1985, and has spawned a number of related shows: a "junior" *Shanghaied in Astoria* for kids, a once-yearly drag version, and the holiday season *Scrooged in Astoria*.

Cinema

The **Columbian Theater** (1102 Marine Dr., 503/325-3516, www.columbianvoodoo.com, 7pm, $4, $2 children ages 12 and under) sits adjacent to the Columbian Cafe and screens the big movies you may have missed a month earlier in their first run. Enjoy beer, wine, cocktails, pizza, and other munchies while you watch.

Astoria Gateway Cinema (1875 Marine Dr., 503/338-6575) is a modern movie multiplex, showing the usual stuff, where you can pass an afternoon trying to forget the often dismal weather.

Festivals and Events
FISHER POETS GATHERING

Modeled after Elko, Nevada's popular Cowboy Poets Gathering, the **Fisher Poets Gathering** (www.fisherpoets.org) provides a forum in which men and women involved in the fishing and other maritime industries share their poems, stories, songs, and artwork in a convivial seaport setting. The annual late February event, which dates back to 1998, draws writers and artists from up and down the Pacific coast and farther afield for readings, art shows, concerts, book signings, workshops, films, a silent auction, and other activities at pubs, galleries, theaters, and other venues around town. Participation isn't limited to fisherfolk but extends to anyone with a connection to maritime activity, and themes range from the rigors (and humor) of life on the water to environmental issues. Admission is by donation ($5) at the ticket booth of the **Columbian Theater** (1102 Marine Dr.). For more details and a full schedule, check the website.

ASTORIA-WARRENTON CRAB AND SEAFOOD FESTIVAL

The **Astoria-Warrenton Crab and Seafood Festival** (Clatsop County Fairgrounds, 503/325-6311 or 800/875-6807, 4pm-9pm Fri., 10am-8pm Sat., 11am-4pm Sun., $5-10 adults, children ages 5-12 half price), held the last weekend in April, is a hugely popular event that brings in crowds from miles around. Scores of booths feature a cornucopia of seafood and other eats, regional beers and Oregon wines, and arts and crafts. Activities include continuous entertainment, crab races, a petting zoo, and kids' activities. A traditional crab dinner caps off the evening. To get to the fair-grounds from Astoria, take Highway 202 for 4.5 miles to Walluski Loop Road and watch for signs. Parking is limited at the fairgrounds. Frequent shuttle service takes folks between the fairgrounds, park-and-ride lots, down-town, the Port of Astoria, and local hotels and campgrounds.

SCANDINAVIAN MIDSUMMER FESTIVAL
The legacy of the thousands of Scandinavians who arrived to work in area mills and canner-ies in the late 19th and early 20th centuries is still strong in Astoria. For many locals, the summer's biggest event is the **Scandinavian Midsummer Festival** (503/325-6311, www.astoriascanfest.com, $8 adults, $3 chil-dren ages 6-12), which usually takes place the third weekend of June, Friday through Sunday. Local Danes, Finns, Icelanders, Norwegians, and Swedes come together to celebrate their heritage; visitors and musi-cians from the Old Country keep the fes-tivities authentic. Costumed dancers weave around a flowered midsummer pole (a fertil-ity rite), burn a bonfire to destroy evil spirits, and have tugs-of-war pitting Scandinavian nationalities against each other. Food, danc-ing, crafts, musical concerts, and a parade bring the whole town out to the Clatsop County Fairgrounds on Walluski Loop Road just off Highway 202.

ASTORIA REGATTA WEEK
A tradition since 1894, **Astoria Regatta Week** is considered the Pacific Northwest's longest-running festival. Held on the waterfront in mid-August, the five-day event kicks off with the regatta queen's coronation and reception. Attractions include live entertainment, a grand street parade, historic home tours, ship tours and boat rides, sailboat and dragon boat races, a classic car show, a salmon barbecue, arts and crafts, food booths, a beer garden, and a twi-light boat parade. For details and a schedule, contact the **Astoria Regatta Association** (503/325-6311 or 800/875-6807, www.asto-riaregatta.org).

SHOPPING
On Sundays between early May to early October, follow local tradition and stroll lei-surely up and down 12th Street between Marine Drive and Exchange Street for the **Astoria Sunday Market** (10am-3pm), where vendors offer farm-fresh produce, plants, crafts, and specialty foods.

A local store worth noting is **Finnware** (1116 Commercial St., 503/325-5720, www.finnware.com, 10am-5pm Mon.-Sat., 11am-4pm Sun.) which stocks Scandinavian crys-tal and glassware, jewelry, books, and kitchen tools. This is a store that takes its Finnish roots seriously.

Art Galleries
Astoria has a well-deserved reputation as an art center, with many downtown storefronts now serving as art galleries. Not to miss is **RiverSea Gallery** (1160 Commercial St., 503/325-1270, http://riverseagallery.com, 11am-5:30pm Mon.-Thurs., 11am-7pm Fri.-Sat., 11am-4pm Sun.), with a large and varied selection of work by local painters, glass artists, jewelry makers, and fine craftspeople. For a more quixotic art scene, go to **Imogen Gallery** (240 11th St., 503/325-1566, http://imogengallery.com, 11am-5pm Mon.-Tues. and Thurs.-Sat., 11am-4pm Sun.), dedicated to contemporary and conceptual art by local artists. **Lightbox Photographic Gallery** (1045 Marine Dr., 503/468-0238, http://lightbox-photographic.com, 10am-6 Tues.-Fri., 10am-5pm Sat.) is the region's gal-lery for fine art photography.

The second Saturday of each month is the **Astoria Art Walk** (5pm-9pm), when most gal-leries and shops in downtown stay open late.

Bookstores
Several bookstores in town invite serious brows-ing, buying, and intellectual stimulation. **Lucy's Books** (348 12th St., 503/325-4210, 10:30am-5:30pm Tues.-Sat., 11am-3pm Sun.) is a small but bighearted locally owned book-shop with an emphasis on Pacific Northwest re-gional subjects. On the next block, **Godfather's Books and Espresso** (1108 Commercial St.,

© BILL MCRAE

Everyone turns out for the Astoria Sunday Market.

NORTH COAST

503/325-8143, 8am-8pm Mon.-Sat., 9am-6pm Sun.) sells a mix of new and used books and has a case of excellent antique maps and prints depicting the Columbia River and north coast.

Local Food

Josephson's Smokehouse (106 Marine Dr., 503/325-2190, www.josephsons.com, 9am-6pm Mon.-Sat.) was established in 1920 in a false-front clapboard building near the waterfront. Josephson's is Oregon's most esteemed purveyor of gourmet smoked fish, producing Scandinavian cold-smoked salmon without dyes or preservatives. The smokehouse caters to mail-order clientele and fine restaurants. You can buy direct here at cheaper (but not cheap) prices than the mail-order rates. Pickled salmon, salmon jerky, sturgeon caviar, crab, oysters, and a variety of alder-smoked and canned fish are also sold here. On typically foggy days here in midwinter, there's nothing finer than a cup of Josephson's very thick clam chowder.

To shop the daily catch, which can include Dungeness crab, wild salmon, halibut, albacore tuna, sardines, sole, and rockfish, go to **Warrenton Deep Sea Fish Market** (45 NE Harbor Pl., Warrenton, 503/861-3911, 9am-5:30pm Mon.-Sat, 10am-4pm Sun.). They carry the largest selection of locally caught fish in the area, and you'll find a variety of smoked fish and seafood here as well.

ACCOMMODATIONS

With its wealth of large, elegant Victorian homes, it's not surprising that Astoria has more bed-and-breakfasts than any other town on the Oregon coast. The historic former homes of merchants, politicians, sea captains, and salmon canners number among them. In addition, a classic downtown hotel has been completely spiffed up and renovated, offering very comfortable rooms with vintage elegance. Several new hotels take advantage of wonderful riverfront views.

You'll also find about a dozen motels to choose from in and around Astoria, most of them located along U.S. 30, otherwise known as Marine Drive, in the northwest section of town. Most are fairly similar and don't have the charm that the town's B&Bs and hotels offer, but they're generally less expensive and are reasonably close to downtown.

The prices noted are for high season (summer) double-occupancy rooms. Rates fall by as much as half off-season.

$50-100

Astoria's **C Commodore** (258 14th St., 503/325-4747, http://commodoreastoria.com, $79-159) has simple but stylishly decorated rooms in a renovated downtown hotel. The least expensive rooms ("cabins") are just sleeping chambers with a sink, a flat-screen TV and DVD player, and an iPod docking station, with shared toilets and handsome tiled showers at the end of the hallway. Suite rooms are larger and include a private bathroom. The Commodore is very popular with hip young travelers, especially its coffee shop on the ground floor. Be aware that the Commodore is on a busy downtown corner, so if traffic noise will be a problem, bring earplugs.

Astoria has several motels that offer basic but clean rooms. Except on summer weekends, the following should have rooms available without reservations. On the eastern edge of Astoria, the **Crest Motel** (5366 Leif Erickson Dr./U.S. 30, 503/325-3141 or 800/421-3141, http://astoriacrestmotel.com, $66-112 depending on views) offers cliff-side river views, a coin-operated laundry, a whirlpool set in a gazebo overlooking the river, and pet-friendly rooms (with no extra fees). Two blocks from the West Mooring Basin and its charter docks, the **Astoria Dunes Motel** (288 W. Marine Dr., 503/325-7111 or 800/441-3319, http://astoriadunes-motel.com, $90-125) has an indoor heated pool and whirlpool tub. About 0.5 mile east of the Astoria-Megler Bridge, the **Rivershore Motel** (59 W. Marine Dr., 503/325-2921, www.astoriarivershoremotel.com, $75-100) has 43 rooms with coffeemakers, microwaves, refrigerators, and Internet access. Some rooms include kitchens.

A couple of blocks away from busy downtown streets, the **Rose River Inn B&B** (1510 Franklin Ave., 503/325-7175, www.roseriverinn.com, $95-150) offers two river-view suites and three guest rooms in a large cheerfully painted Victorian, decorated with European antiques and art and surrounded by a neatly tended garden. Each room includes a clawfoot tub, and the River Suite also has a Finnish sauna.

$100-150

Clementine's Bed and Breakfast (847 Exchange St., 800/521-6801, www.clementines-bb.com, $118-169, two-night min.), a handsome two-story home built in the Italianate style in 1888, stands in good company across the street from the Flavel House and is itself on Astoria's Historic Homes Walking Tour. From the gardens around the house come the fresh flowers that accent the guest rooms and common areas, as do the herbs that spice the delicious gourmet breakfasts. There are five rooms in the main house, all with feather beds and private bathrooms; upper-story rooms have private balconies with river views.

In addition to these guest rooms, two spacious sunny suites are available in the **Moose Temple Lodge** ($125-165), adjacent to the main house. Built in 1850, this is the oldest extant building in Astoria; it was the Moose Temple from 1900 to 1940 and later served as a Mormon church. Renovated with skylights, wood floors, fireplaces, small kitchens, and several beds, these are ideal for families or groups. Pets are welcome.

The **Benjamin Young Inn** (3652 Duane St., 503/325-6172, www.benjaminyounginn.com, $100-150) is an elegant 1888 Queen Anne-style mansion with four large guest rooms, all with private baths and great river views. The inn is in the eastern part of Astoria, away from the hubbub of downtown.

$150-200

Stay right downtown in the beautifully renovated **C Hotel Elliott** (357 12th St., 877/378-1924, www.hotelelliott.com, $149-259), a small boutique hotel that's an easy walk from good restaurants and the river. The Elliott first opened in 1924, and its current incarnation has preserved much of the original charm of its Craftsman-era details, including the mahogany-clad lobby, handcrafted cabinetry, and wood and marble fireplaces. An original banner painted across the hotel's north side proudly proclaims Hotel Elliott—Wonderful Beds. The new Elliott has made a point of living up to this claim, with goose-down pillows, luxurious 440-thread-count Egyptian cotton sheets, feather beds, and top-of-the-line mattresses to ensure a memorable slumber. In addition to standard rooms, the Elliott has a variety of suites, including the five-room Presidential Suite with access to a rooftop garden. The rooftop is open to all and is a fine place to enjoy a glass of wine and the sunset.

You can't top the views at the **Holiday Inn Express Hotel & Suites** (204 W. Marine Dr., 503/325-6222 or 888/898-6222, www.astoria-hie.com, $180-200), directly under the Astoria-Megler Bridge. Guest rooms have a refrigerator, a microwave, a coffeemaker, a high-speed Internet connection, a TV, and a DVD player. Facilities include an indoor pool, a breakfast bar, a business center, and an exercise room. Pets are welcome.

Hampton Inn & Suites Astoria (201 39th St., 503/325-8888, $179-239) is Astoria's newest hotel and located east of downtown near Pier 39, so not really within walking distance of the city center. However, the Astoria Waterfront Trolley passes directly in front of the hotel, and you can ride it downtown and back during its operating season. The rooms are spacious and nicely furnished, and face directly onto the river. Amenities include a pool and business center, plus free breakfast.

Over $200

Ⓒ**Cannery Pier Hotel** (10 Basin St., 503/325-4996 or 888/325-4996, www.cannerypierhotel.com, $269-350) is a modern luxury hotel on the former site of a historic cannery, jutting 600 feet out into the Columbia below the Astoria-Megler Bridge. The opulently furnished rooms have dramatic views, even from the shower; all

rooms have balconies, fireplaces, and beautiful hardwood floors. Complimentary continental breakfast is included in the rates, as are hors d'oeuvres and wine in the afternoon. There's also a day spa in the hotel, plus a Finnish sauna, a fitness room, and a hot tub.

Camping

Families flock to **Fort Stevens State Park** (100 Peter Iredale Rd., Hammond, reservations 800/452-5687, www.oregonstateparks.org, year-round, $21 tents, $27 RVs, $41 yurts, $86 cabins). With over 500 sites, the campground is the largest in the state park system, and it's incredibly popular. The park's many amenities and attractions make it the perfect base camp from which to take advantage of the region. Just be sure to avoid spring break (around Mar. 23-29) if you want to be spared the rites of spring enacted here by Oregon teenagers.

Across the road from the state park, **Astoria Warrenton Seaside KOA** (1100 NW Ridge Rd., Hammond, 503/861-2606 or 800/562-8506, www.astoriakoa.com, $25 tents, $38 RVs w/electric, $52 RVs full hookup, cabins $62 and up, $5 resort fee) is another sprawling campground. Amenities include an indoor pool and hot tub, a game room, miniature golf, and bike rentals.

FOOD

Over the years, Astoria has developed a reputation for excellent dining at fair prices. In addition to the restaurants and cafés listed here, you'll find do-it-yourself options at **Astoria's Sunday Market** on 12th Street between Marine Drive and Exchange Street and **Josephson's Smokehouse** (106 Marine Dr., 503/325-2190, www.josephsons.com, 9am-6pm Mon.-Sat.). A good stop for fresh produce, health food, and deli items is the **Astoria Co-op** (355 Exchange Street, 503/325-0027, 8am-8pm daily).

Astoria also features a number of food carts—there are several on both the east and west entrances to downtown. Most notable is **Bowfingers,** with really good fish-and-chips served out of a converted boat near the corner of Duane and 17th Streets.

Bakeries and Cafés

Stop by the 🄲 **Astoria Coffeehouse and Bistro** (245 11th St., 503/325-1787, 7am-9pm Sun.-Thurs., 7am-10pm Fri.-Sat., $13-22) for fresh breakfast pastries and coffee, salads and sandwiches, and home-cooked regional fare. It's an airy, friendly place to sit and read the paper, but if you're off to explore town, you can also just order a sandwich to go. In the evening, enjoy well-prepared comfort food such as meatloaf, cioppino, steak frites and Peruvian veggie stew.

At the collectively run 🄲 **Blue Scorcher Bakery Cafe** (1493 Duane St., 503/338-7473, 8am-5pm Mon.-Fri., 8am-4pm Sat.-Sun., $9), the motto is "joyful work, delicious food, and strong community," and it's all true. Settle in with a tasty veggie sandwich (if the tempeh Reuben is on the menu, don't turn up your nose at it) and watch the Astorians— any one of whom would make an excellent new friend—come and go. A personal favorite are cardamom almond rolls, an old-fashioned Swedish treat that's perfect with a cup of coffee on a brisk morning. A wide range of gluten-free pastries are offered on Friday. If it's all too healthy and wholesome for you, there's a brewpub next door.

American

A good, if rather standard, choice for families with kids, the Astoria outlet of **Pig 'N Pancake** (146 W. Bond St., 503/325-3144, 6am-9pm Sun.-Thurs., 6am-10pm Fri.-Sat., breakfast and lunch $7-10, dinner $10-18), a small northcoast chain (others are in Seaside and Cannon Beach), excels at big, filling breakfasts at reasonable prices. The specialty is homemade pancakes and waffles, available in a dozen variations, including potato pancakes, Swedish pancakes (thin and crispy with lingonberries), pecan-filled pancakes, and, of course, pigs in a blanket.

Eastern European

There aren't a lot of Bosnian restaurants around, and the **Drina Daisy** (915 Commercial St., 503/338-2912, www.drinadaisy.com, 11am-9pm Wed.-Sun., $11-23) is worth a stop to sample foods from an unfamiliar part of the world. The cuisine is a cross between Greek and Central European cooking. You can't go wrong with the appetizers or salads, many of which come with smoked sausages and filo-wrapped goodies.

Italian

For Astoria's top Italian food, go to **Fulio's Pastaria** (1149 Commercial St., 503/325-9001, 11am-close daily, $11-30) with excellent pasta, Tuscan-style steaks, and a good wine list in a lively and convivial dining room.

Mexican

There are a number of serviceable Mexican restaurants in Astoria (including, at last count, four food carts), but the locals' favorite is the hole-in-the-wall **Rio Café** (125 9th St., 503/325-2409, 11am-3pm Mon., 11am-8pm Tues.-Thurs., 11am-9pm Fri.-Sat., $10-18). Everything is fresh and made from scratch; the home-style cooking here packs more flavor than you'll find at many upscale Mexican restaurants.

Pacific Northwest

As widely appreciated as it is small, the 🄲 **Columbian Cafe** (1114 Marine Dr., 503/325-2233, 8am-2pm Mon.-Tues., 8am-2pm and 5pm-8pm Wed.-Thurs., 8am-2pm and 5pm-9pm Fri., 9am-2pm and 5pm-9pm Sat., 9am-2pm Sun., breakfast and lunch $7-10, dinner entrées $11-24) is where the meatless 1960s collides with Pacific Northwest cuisine. The menu changes according to season and the chef's whim (be daring and order the "chef's mercy") but generally includes a good selection of pastas, chilies, crepes, fresh catch of the day, and always a selection of homemade garlic, jalapeño, and red-pepper jellies. You may also enjoy the free-flowing political repartee with the staff and regulars in this cramped (several booths and a lunch counter) but friendly place. Breakfast is a highlight here. If this is your first visit to the Columbian Cafe, don't let the tiny, slightly seedy-looking venue put you off. Just barge in and take a seat—the servers will make you feel comfortable, and the rest is all culinary pleasure. Expect to be here for a while; the Columbian is not a quick in-and-out dining experience.

On downtown's most prominent corner, diagonally across from the Liberty Theatre, **Clemente's** (1198 Commercial St., 503/325-1067, 11am-3pm and 5pm-9pm Tues.-Sun., lunch $9-15, dinner entrées $16-26) serves fresh sustainably grown cuisine inspired by both the owner's Italian roots and the slow food movement. "From the Water" dishes include not only salmon but a tasty local albacore tuna and halibut. The restaurant's large windows and large paintings contribute to a sophisticated but casual atmosphere. A three-course prix fixe menu ($25) highlights whatever is fresh and local—a great value.

Another good restaurant with an inspiring motto ("Eat well, laugh often, and love much") is the easygoing **T. Paul's Urban Cafe** (1119 Commercial St., 503/338-5133, 11am-9pm Mon.-Sat., $9-19). The menu of hip diner food with fresh Pacific Northwest twists includes towering turkey sandwiches, bay shrimp ceviche, Caribbean jerk quesadillas, prawn pasta, and clam chowder. Quesadillas are the specialty, with about a dozen innovative varieties served. T. Paul's has a second downtown location, **The Supper Club** (360 12th St., 503/325-2545, 11am-9pm Mon.-Thurs., 11am-10pm Fri.-Sat., $12-28) with a wide-ranging menu, a rather swank dining room, and some of the most reliably delicious food in Astoria. Top choices are pasta dishes, burgers, salads, and fresh seafood. The tiny bar is the perfect spot for a cocktail.

Seafood

One of Astoria's more notable restaurants is **Silver Salmon Grille** (1105 Commercial St., 503/338-6640, 11am-9pm daily, $13-28) for fine dining in an atmosphere that's somewhat formal but not starchy. Attractive murals of the eponymous fish adorn the walls inside and out, and salmon takes pride of place on the dinner menu as well in a variety of

preparations that are fresh and cooked to perfection. Pasta dishes, seasonal seafood items such as razor clams, and several meat choices fill out the extensive menu. The wine list includes reasonably priced house wines made especially for the restaurant by Maryhill Winery in the Columbia Gorge. The bar here is one of the nicest in downtown Astoria, and it's a favorite of locals out on the town.

Settle in for some excellent seafood at **Bridgewater Bistro** (20 Basin St., 503/235-6777, 11am-close daily, $12-26), where you can graze on tapas (small plates menu 3pm-5pm), sample a four-course prix fixe meal ($45), or order regular-size or smaller entrées. The soaring ceiling and riverside setting of the historic building next to the Cannery Pier Hotel are almost as compelling as the food. (Note to long-time coast visitors: The Bridgewater is owned by the same folks who used to run the legendary Shoalwater Restaurant up on Washington's Long Beach Peninsula.)

At the end of 12th Street, directly overlooking the Columbia, **Baked Alaska** (1 12th St., 503/325-7414, 10am-11pm daily, $18-32) features a selection of small and large plates with modern, international inflections. Seared sea scallops are served with grilled peaches, shiso leaves, cider aioli and shaved hazelnuts, while prawn and Dungeness crab spaghettini comes with figs, capered brown butter, and fresh lovage. But about that name—yes, you can get baked Alaska here—the restaurant's twist on this classic dessert is basically a flaming ice cream sundae served on chocolate-chip cookies. The views rival the food, particularly in summer when there's deck seating. Baked Alaska now also operates a wood-fired pizzeria, and its pizzas are available in the dining room, bar, and to go.

Indian

Himani Indian Cuisine (1044 Marine Dr., 503/325-8171, www.himaniindian.com, 11am-3pm and 5pm-9pm Mon.-Fri., noon-3pm and 5pm-9pm Sat.-Sun, $9-20) serves a very wide selection of Indian cuisine, with a specialty in southern Indian dishes such as tandoori dishes (including tandoori salmon) and masala dosa. The naan breads are equally delicious. A buffet ($9) is available Monday-Friday for lunch, and also all day Sunday. Himani also serves food from its original stall at the Astoria Sunday Market.

Brewpubs

Astoria's oldest brewpub, the **Wet Dog Cafe** (144 11th St., 503/325-6975, 11am-9pm Sun.-Thurs., 11am-10pm Fri.-Sat., $9-20) is home to the Astoria Brewing Company, maker of excellent handcrafted microbrews. There's also a full bar and live music or entertainment Thursday-Saturday nights. The café is housed in a cavernous remodeled former waterfront warehouse, with good views of the river. The food is good basic pub grub: fish-and-chips, burgers (including seafood burgers), sandwiches, and salads.

The **Rogue Ales Public House** (100 39th St., 503/325-5964, 11am-10pm daily, $9-22) is east of downtown in the Hanthorn Pier development. The pub is set inside a wood-plank structure atop a former cannery pier and offers excellent ales plus burgers, pizza, and sandwiches. It's hard to get more Astorian than this. For beer snobs, the place to go is **Fort George Brewery and Public House** (1483 Duane St., 503/325-7468, www.fortgeorgebrewery.com, 11am-11pm Mon.-Thurs., 11am-midnight Fri.-Sat., noon-11pm Sun., $7-12), whose powerful ales have won it a reputation as one of Oregon's top breweries. The pub grub is a bit basic, but in 2013 a full-service restaurant opens on the pub's second floor. There's free live music every Sunday evening.

INFORMATION AND SERVICES

The **Astoria Chamber of Commerce** (111 W. Marine Dr., 503/325-6311 or 800/875-6807, www.oldoregon.com, 8am-6pm daily May-Sept., 9am-5pm Mon.-Fri. Oct.-Apr.) operates the Oregon Welcome Center at its offices, providing a plethora of brochures and maps for visitors to Astoria and other destinations on the north Oregon coast and southwest

© BILL MCRAE

jolly times at Fort George Brewery and Public House

NORTH COAST

Washington. The website has downloadable audio tours.

With 10,000 people, Astoria is the largest city and the media hub of the north coast. The local newspaper, the *Daily Astorian* (www.dailyastorian.com) is sold around town and worth a look if only to get the editorial slant of Steve Forrester. This former Washington correspondent's witty commentary on local, regional, and national events pulls no punches. The free monthly *Hipfish* is a publication in the great tradition of the alternative press of the 1960s. Whether you agree with its take on regional politics or not, the thoughtful and lively articles and complete entertainment listings will enhance your visit to the north coast.

Throughout the north coast, **KMUN** (91.9 FM in Astoria and Seaside, 89.5 FM in Cannon Beach) is a public radio station with excellent community-based programming. Folk, classical, jazz, and rock music, public affairs, radio drama, literature readings, children's bedtime stories, and National Public Radio news will keep your dial set on this frequency. A sister station, KCPB, broadcasts classical music in addition to NPR news.

The **Astoria Post Office** is located in the Federal Building at 750 Commercial Street. Useful numbers to know include the **county sheriff** (503/225-2061), the **Coast Guard** (2285 Airport Rd., Warrenton, 503/861-6220), and **Columbia Memorial Hospital** (2111 Exchange St., Astoria, 503/325-4321).

GETTING THERE AND AROUND

Amtrak Thruway Motorcoach Service (800/USA-RAIL or 800/872-7245, www.amtrak.com) runs two buses daily between the north coast and Portland Union Station. Board the coach in Astoria at the **Welcome Center** (111 W. Marine Dr.) or at the downtown transit center. After-hours tickets are available at the **Mini Mart** (95 W. Marine Dr., 503/325-4162). The bus stops on request at Seaside, Warrenton, and Gearhart.

Getting around Astoria can have its pitfalls for the unsuspecting. Potentially troublesome for visitors are the steep hills and the city's layout of seemingly random one-way streets. Holidays and summer weekends bring heavy traffic along U.S. 30, also known as Leif Erickson Drive (east end of town) and Marine Drive (center and west), Astoria's major traffic artery.

Car rentals are available from **Enterprise** (644 W. Marine Dr., 503/325-6500). For visitors willing to let go of their cars for a while, the Sunset Empire Transportation District, better known as **The Bus** (503/861-RIDE, 503/861-7433, or 800/776-6406, www.ridethebus.org, 40-60 min. Mon.-Sat.), provides reasonably frequent transportation around Astoria and along the coast to Warrenton, including to Gearhart, Seaside, and Cannon Beach, and the campgrounds at Fort Stevens State Park.

Seaside and Gearhart

Seaside is Oregon's quintessential, and oldest, family beach resort. The beach is long and flat, sheltered by a scenic headland, with lifeguards on duty during the summer months, beachside playground equipment, and a boardwalk winding through the dunes. Ice cream parlors, game arcades, eateries, and gift shops crowd shoulder to shoulder along the main drag, Broadway. The aromas of cotton candy and french fries lend a heady incense to the salt air, and the clatter of bumper cars and other amusements can induce sensory overload. Atlantic City it's not—thank goodness—but on a crowded summer day the town evokes the feeling of a carnival midway by the sea. During spring break, when Pacific Northwest high school and college students arrive, the town's population of 6,200 can quadruple almost overnight.

South of town, the presence of clammers and waders in the shallows and surfers

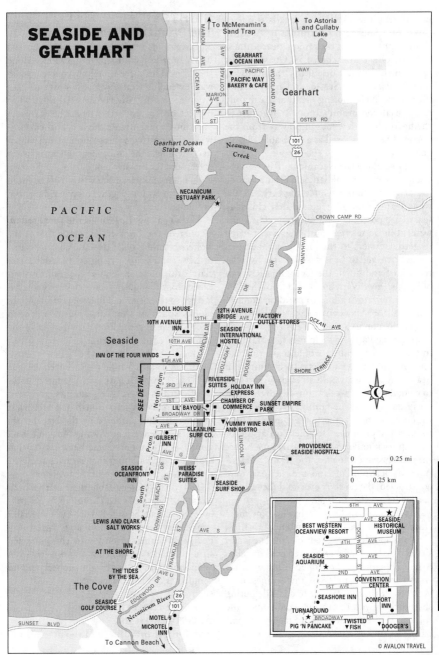

SEASIDE AND GEARHART

To McMenamin's Sand Trap

To Astoria and Cullaby Lake

GEARHART OCEAN INN

PACIFIC WAY BAKERY & CAFE

Gearhart

Gearhart Ocean State Park

Neawanna Creek

NECANICUM ESTUARY PARK

PACIFIC

OCEAN

CROWN CAMP RD

DOLL HOUSE

10TH AVENUE INN

12TH AVENUE BRIDGE

FACTORY OUTLET STORES

Seaside

SEASIDE INTERNATIONAL HOSTEL

INN OF THE FOUR WINDS

SEE DETAIL

RIVERSIDE SUITES

HOLIDAY INN EXPRESS

CHAMBER OF COMMERCE

SUNSET EMPIRE PARK

LIL' BAYOU

CLEANLINE SURF CO.

YUMMY WINE BAR AND BISTRO

GILBERT INN

PROVIDENCE SEASIDE HOSPITAL

SEASIDE OCEANFRONT INN

WEISS' PARADISE SUITES

SEASIDE SURF SHOP

0   0.25 mi

0   0.25 km

LEWIS AND CLARK SALT WORKS

INN AT THE SHORE

THE TIDES BY THE SEA

The Cove

SEASIDE GOLF COURSE

SUNSET BLVD

MOTEL 6

MICROTEL INN

To Cannon Beach

BEST WESTERN OCEANVIEW RESORT

6TH   AVE

SEASIDE HISTORICAL MUSEUM

SEASIDE AQUARIUM

CONVENTION CENTER

SEASHORE INN

COMFORT INN

TURNAROUND

PIG 'N PANCAKE

TWISTED FISH

DOOGER'S

© AVALON TRAVEL

NORTH COAST

negotiating the swells also recalls the liveliness of a Southern California or Atlantic shorefront instead of the remote peacefulness of many Oregon beaches. East Coast visitors often liken Cannon Beach to Provincetown, Massachusetts, and Seaside to Coney Island, New York. Neighboring Gearhart, a mainly residential community (pop. 1,100) just to the north, has a few lodgings away from the bustle of Seaside as well as a venerable 18-hole golf course.

Located along the Necanicum River, in the shadow of majestic Tillamook Head, Seaside has attracted tourists since the early 1870s, when transportation magnate Ben Holladay sensed the potential for a resort hotel near the water. But better transportation was needed to get customers to the place. At that time, the way to get to Seaside was first by boat from Portland down the Columbia River to Skipanon (now Warrenton), and from there by carriage south to Seaside. To speed the connection, Holladay later constructed a railroad line from Skipanon to Seaside.

To escape Portland's summer heat, families in the late 19th century would make the boat and railroad journey to spend their summer in Seaside. Most men would go back to Portland to work during the week, returning to the coast on Friday to visit the family. Every weekend the families would gather at the railroad station to greet the men, then see them off again for the trip back to Portland. It wasn't long before the train became known as the "Daddy Train." As roads between Portland and the coast were constructed, the car took over, and the railroad carried its last dad in 1939.

In recent years, the town has become more than just a retreat for Portland families. Oregon's apostle of haute cuisine, the late James Beard, used to hold a celebrated cooking class here each summer. This opened the door for writers' retreats, art classes, and business conventions. If these occasions or a family outing should bring you to Seaside, you'll enjoy the spirit of fun if you don't mind plenty of company on summer weekends.

SIGHTS
The Promenade and Broadway

Sightseeing in Seaside means bustling up and down Broadway and strolling leisurely along the Prom. This three-mile-long concrete walkway, extending from Avenue U north to 12th Avenue, was initially constructed in 1908 to protect ocean properties from the waves. A pleasant walk alongside the beach, the boardwalk offers a fine vantage point from which to contemplate the sand, surf, frolicking beach lovers, and the massive contours of 1,200-foothigh Tillamook Head to the south. The Prom is also popular for jogging, bicycle riding, and in-line skating.

Midway along the Prom is the **Turnaround,** a concrete-and-brick traffic circle that is the western terminus of Broadway. A bronze statue of Lewis and Clark gazing ever seaward proclaims this point the end of the trail for their expedition, though in fact they explored a bit farther south, beyond Tillamook Head. Eight blocks south of the Turnaround, between Beach Drive and the Prom, is a replica of the Lewis and Clark salt cairn.

Heading east from the Turnaround, Broadway runs 0.5 mile to Roosevelt Avenue (U.S. 101) through a dizzying gamut of tourist attractions, arcades, restaurants, and bars. Along Broadway, in a four-block area west of U.S. 101 and bordered by the Necanicum River, 1st Avenue, and Avenue A, you'll find some fancy Victorian frame houses, a portion of the few old buildings that survived the 1912 fire that destroyed much of the town.

Today, the most notable sight in this busy section of Seaside is the enormous $73.3 million WorldMark Seaside (owned by Wyndham) time-share condo development containing nearly 300 units. Condos in this outsized structure aren't available for rent directly from Wyndham, though vacation property rental companies can handle sublets.

Seaside Historical Society Museum

If you tire of Broadway and the beach is too

© BILL MCRAE

Pedal-powered surreys are popular on the Seaside Promenade.

cold and wet, make your way to the **Seaside Historical Society Museum** (570 Necanicum Dr., 503/738-7065, www.seasidemuseum.org, 10am-4pm Mon.-Sat., noon-3pm Sun. late Mar.-Oct., noon-3pm Mon.-Sat., noon-3pm Sun. Nov.-late Mar.; $3 adults, $2 seniors, $1 students), housed in a classic seaside cottage six blocks north of Broadway, where Clatsop artifacts and exhibits on early tourism in Seaside impart more of a sense of history than anything else in town.

Seaside Aquarium

Right on the Prom north of the Turnaround is the **Seaside Aquarium** (200 N. Prom, 503/738-6211, 9am-7pm daily Mar.-Oct., 9am-5pm Wed.-Sun. Nov.-Feb., $7.50 adults, $6.25 seniors, $3.75 children ages 6-13). It's not quite the Oregon Coast Aquarium (find that in Newport), but if you're not going to make it that far south, it's an okay introduction to sealife for young children. Back in the era of the Daddy Train, this place served as a natatorium but was converted to its current use in 1937. Today the pool is filled with raucously barking seals. In addition, a hundred species of marine life here include 20-ray sea stars, crabs, ferocious-looking wolf eels and moray eels, and octopuses.

Lewis and Clark Salt Works

Near the south end of the Prom at Lewis and Clark Way are the reconstructed salt works of Lewis and Clark. While camped at Fort Clatsop during the winter of 1805-1806, the captains sent a detachment south to find a place suitable for rendering salt from seawater. Their supply was nearly exhausted, and the precious commodity was a necessity for preserving and seasoning their food on the expedition's return journey. At the south end of present-day Seaside, five men built a cairn-like stone oven near a settlement of the Clatsop and Killamox people and set about boiling seawater nonstop for seven weeks to produce 3.5 bushels (about 314 pounds) of salt for the trip back east.

SPORTS AND RECREATION
Bicycling

Seaside has a bumper crop of places that rent bicycles, skates, and surreys, all for similar rates, about $10 per hour for a bike. The **Prom Bike Shop** (622 12th Ave., 503/738-8251, http://prombikeshop.com, 10:30am-5:30pm daily) is a full-service bike shop; rent cruisers or novelty bikes at **Wheel Fun Rentals Spoke 1** (21 N. Columbia St., 503/717-4337, 9am-sunset daily) or **Wheel Fun Rentals Spoke 2** (151 Ave. A, 503/738-7212, 9am-sunset daily).

Boating and Fishing

Just because you're smack-dab in the middle of a family resort town doesn't mean you can't enjoy some of nature's bounty; anglers can reel in trout, salmon, and steelhead from the Necanicum River right in the center of downtown. The **12th Avenue Bridge** is a popular spot for fishing and crabbing.

Cullaby Lake, on the east side of U.S. 101 about four miles north of Gearhart, offers fishing for crappies, bluegills, perch, catfish, and largemouth bass. At 88 acres, Cullaby is the largest of the many lakes on the Clatsop Plains. Two parks on the lake, **Carnahan Park** and **Cullaby Lake County Park,** have boat ramps, picnic areas, and other facilities. Cullaby is the only practical place to water-ski in the area.

A half mile west of Highway 101, **Sunset Beach Park** on Neacoxie Lake (also known as Sunset Lake) has a boat ramp, picnic tables, and a playground. Anglers come for warm-water fish species, plus the rainbow trout stocked in the spring. From Astoria, drive south 10 miles on Highway 101 and turn west on Sunset Beach Road.

At **Quatat Park** (503/440-1548), beside the Necanicum River in downtown Seaside, rent kayaks, canoes, and pedal boats for exploring the waterway.

Golf

Golfers can escape to public courses south of Seaside and north in the small town of Gearhart. At **Seaside Golf Club** (451 Ave. U, 503/738-5261), greens fees are $15-17 for nine holes. The **Highlands at Gearhart** (1 Highland Rd., Gearhart, 503/738-5248, www.highlandsgolfgearhart.com, $16 for nine holes) is another public nine-hole course, with ocean views from most holes. The British-links-style course at **Gearhart Golf Links** (1157 N. Marion St., Gearhart, 503/738-3538, www.gearhartgolflinks.com, $65-75 for 18 holes in summer) was established in 1882, making it one of the oldest on the West Coast and Oregon's oldest.

Hiking

From the south end of Seaside, walk in the footsteps of Lewis and Clark on an exhilarating hike over Tillamook Head. In January 1806, neighboring Native Americans told of a beached whale lying several miles south of their encampment. William Clark and a few companions, including Sacajawea, set off in an attempt to find it and trade for blubber and whale oil, which fueled the expedition's lanterns. Climbing Tillamook Head from the north, the party crested the promontory. Clark was moved enough by the view to later write about it in his journal:

> I beheld the grandest and most pleasing prospect which my eyes ever surveyed. Immediately in front of us is the ocean breaking in fury. To this boisterous scene the Columbia with its tributaries and studded on both sides with the Chinook and Clatsop villages forms a charming contrast, while beneath our feet are stretched the rich prairies.

They eventually found the whale, south of Tillamook Head. Ecola Point and State Park here are named for it, after the Chinook word for whale, *ecola* or *ekkoli*. By the time Clark arrived, however, the whale had been reduced to little more than a skeleton by the industrious Tillamooks, who used every part of the beast that they could harvest. Clark measured the leviathan at 105 feet, which, if accurate, could only mean it was a blue whale, the largest animal on earth and an extraordinary windfall for the Native Americans. He found the Tillamooks busily engaged in boiling the blubber in a large wooden trough by means of hot stones. The oil, when extracted, was stored in bladders. He had to bargain hard for a share, and he wrote this of the negotiations:

> The Tillamooks, although they possessed large quantities of this blubber and oil, were so penurious that they disposed of it with great reluctance, and in small quantities only; insomuch that my utmost exertions, aided by the party, with the small stock of merchandise I had taken with me, were not able to procure more blubber than about 300 pounds and a few gallons of oil. Small as this stock is, I prize it highly; and thank Providence for directing the whale to us; and think Him much more kind to us than He was to Jonah having sent this monster to be swallowed by us, instead of swallowing of us, as Jonah's did.

Today, you can experience the view that so impressed Clark on the **Tillamook Head National Recreation Trail,** which runs seven miles through Ecola State Park. Prior to setting out, you could arrange to have a friend drive south to Indian Beach to pick you up at the end of this three- to five-hour trek (or you can be picked up another mile south at the Ecola Point parking lot). As you head up the forested trail on the north side of Tillamook Head, look back over the Seaside town site. In about 20 minutes, you'll be gazing down at the ocean from cliffs 1,000 feet above. A few hours later, you'll hike down onto Indian Beach.

To get to the trailhead from Seaside, drive south, following Avenue U past the golf course to Edgewood Street, and turn left; continue until you reach the parking lot at the end of the road.

Surfing

The best surfing spot in the Seaside area is the beach just south of town simply referred to as **The Cove,** directly north of Tillamook Head and reached from parking areas along Sunset Boulevard. While prevailing winds favor winter surfing rather than summer, this is in fact a popular destination year-round. Local surfers can be impatient with beginners, so this probably isn't a good spot for novices.

Seaside Surf Shop (1116 S. Roosevelt Dr., 503/717-1110, www.seasidesurfshop.com, 10am-6pm Mon.-Fri., 9am-6pm Sat., 9am-5pm Sun.) and **Cleanline Surf Co.** (60 N. Roosevelt Dr., 503/738-2061, www.cleanlinesurf.com, 9am-6pm Mon.-Sat., 10am-6pm Sun.) rent and sell surfboards as well as wetsuits, boots, and flippers; Cleanline Surf also offers instruction. **Northwest Women's Surf Camps** (503/440-5782, www.nwwomenssurfcamps.com) will give you a bit of land training (the camp includes yoga to get you limbered up and in the right frame of mind) and then accompany you into the waves.

Swimming

Despite the lifeguard on duty in summer, swimming at Seaside's beach isn't the most comfortable, unless you're used to the North Sea. Gearhart boasts a quieter beach than Seaside's, although the water is every bit as cool. Warm-blooded swimmers can head to the facilities at **Sunset Empire Park** (1140 E. Broadway, Seaside, 503/738-3311, open daily), which includes three pools, waterslides, a 15-person hot tub, and fitness equipment.

Wildlife-Watching

Bird-watchers gather at **Necanicum Estuary Park,** at the 1900 block of North Holladay Drive across the street from Seaside High School. Local students have built a viewing platform, stairs to the beach, a boardwalk, and interpretive signs. Great blue and green herons and numerous migratory bird species flock to the grassy marshes and slow tidal waters near the mouth of the Necanicum River. During the fall and winter, buffleheads and mergansers shelter in the estuary, while in summer the waters are often thronged with pelicans. Occasionally, Roosevelt elk, black-tailed deer, river otters, beavers, mink, and muskrats can also be sighted.

ENTERTAINMENT AND EVENTS

Seaside predates any other town on the Oregon coast as a place built with good times in mind. A zoo and racetrack were among Seaside's first structures, and arcades are still thriving near the foot of Broadway. **Cannes Cinema** (U.S. 101 at 12th Ave.) is a five-screen multiplex showing first-run films.

The annual **Oregon Dixieland Jubilee** (800/738-6894, www.jazzseaside.com) takes place at the end of February. This event has been gaining momentum for more than 25 years and appeals to fans of Dixieland and traditional jazz. The town celebrates the **Fourth of July** with a parade, a picnic and social at the Seaside Historical Society Museum (570 Necanicum Dr.), and a big fireworks show on the beach.

In early September, **Wheels and Waves** (503/717-1914) brings over 500 classic hot rods and custom cars (1962 and earlier, please) to downtown and the **Civic and Convention Center** (1st Ave. at Necanicum Dr.).

SHOPPING

Seaside is a shopping hub not only for its own population but also for Cannon Beach, which oddly doesn't even have a real grocery store, let alone a shopping mall. A number of shopping centers line U.S. 101 as it passes through Seaside; the **Seaside Factory Outlet Center** (1111 N. Roosevelt Dr., 503/717-1603) has 25 discount stores, including outlets for Eddie Bauer and Nike.

ACCOMMODATIONS

Whatever your price range, you'll have to reserve ahead for a room in Seaside during the summer and on weekends and holidays (especially spring break). If you do, chances are you'll be able to find the specs you're looking for, given the area's array of lodgings and over 1,800 hotel rooms. The **Seaside Visitors Bureau's** helpful website (www.seasideor.com) provides comprehensive listings.

Generally speaking, there are three lodging areas in Seaside. First, there are several modern motels along busy U.S. 101, about eight blocks from the beach. If you're just passing through or waited too long to call for reservations, these offer inexpensive rooms, but little in the way of beachside charm. A second grouping of hotels is in the center of Seaside, along the Necanicum River. These have a quieter riverside setting but still aren't beachfront (though you won't have to cross U.S. 101 to get to the beach). Finally, there are numerous hotels that face directly onto the beach or are just a short stumble to the strand. Even here, there's quite a difference in price between rooms that face the beach and those that face the parking lot.

Under $50

The cheapest place in town is the quite nice **Seaside International Hostel** (930 N. Holladay Dr., 503/738-7911 or 888/994-0001, www.seasidehostel.net, dorm-style bunk $29 pp, private rooms $69), with special touches such as morning meditation and exercise classes. Unlike many hostels, it doesn't close down during the day and there's no curfew at night. There's an espresso bar on-site, and the Necanicum River runs through the backyard. Close by is the Necanicum Estuary Park.

$50-100

Out along U.S. 101 are two motels that provide good value and new rooms, but most people wouldn't consider them walking distance to the beach. **Motel 6** (2369 S. Roosevelt Dr., 503/738-6269 or 800/466-8356, $86-106), on U.S. 101 about 0.5 mile south of Broadway, isn't near the sand but does offer reasonably priced rooms. Just south is **Microtel Inns & Suites** (2455 S. Roosevelt Dr., 503/482-7666 or 866/482-7666, $96-136), with free breakfast waffles, free high-speed Internet, and guest laundry. These two motels on the southern entry to Seaside are closest to Cannon Beach.

$100-150

There's a clutch of motels south of the Broadway-Prom axis that offer easy beach access at fair prices—and a much quieter beachfront experience than town center. **The Tides**

by the Sea (2316 Beach Dr., 503/738-6317 or 800/548-2846, www.thetidesbythesea.com, $107-204) is an older motel that has converted its large guest rooms and cottages into condos. About a quarter of the units face onto the Prom, but those that don't are just seconds away from the beach. If you can live without an ocean view, you'll save a bundle here. Each of the units is different, but most have kitchens and fireplaces. In high season, there is a two-night minimum stay policy.

The rooms at **Seashore Inn** (60 N. Prom, 503/738-6368 or 888/738-6368, www.seashoreinnor.com, $129-229) are right in the thick of it along the Promenade. Half the guest rooms face the beach, but half don't. These rooms are just steps from the beach but are a fraction of the cost of rooms on the other side of the building. All guest rooms have microwaves and mini-refrigerators, and some have full kitchens and balconies. There's also an indoor pool in case the weather turns foul.

While motels dominate the lodging scene in Seaside, a few B&Bs and small inns offer an alternative. The **Gilbert Inn** (341 Beach Dr., 503/738-9770 or 800/410-9770, www.gilbertinn.com, $119-169) is a well-preserved 1892 Queen Anne just a block south of Broadway and a block from the beach. Period furnishings adorn the 10 guest rooms, which all have private bathrooms, down comforters, and other nice touches (though this seems like a classic B&B, no breakfast is served). The third-floor "Garret" sleeps up to four in a queen and two twin beds, with ocean views from the dormer window.

North of Broadway, the **10th Avenue Inn** (125 10th Ave., 503/738-0643 or 800/745-2378, www.10aveinn.com, $115-135) is a comfortable 1908 home built just a few steps from the beach. In the parlor a baby grand piano, a guitar, and other instruments are available for musically inclined guests. The three guest rooms have king-size beds, attached bathrooms, TVs, and small refrigerators. Next door and operated by the same folks is the **Doll House,** a sweet two-bedroom cottage ideal for four adults plus two or three children, with a full kitchen and a deck with a barbecue grill. It goes for $890 per week in summer (minimum 1-week rental), and $160 per night off-season (2-night minimum).

Just north of the Necanicum River's mouth, Gearhart offers a respite from the bustle of Seaside. The **(Gearhart Ocean Inn** (67 N. Cottage St., 503/738-7373, www.gearhartoceaninn.com, $145-240) offers a choice of 12 New England-style wooden cottages with comforters, wicker chairs, and throw rugs, and the beaches are a short walk away. The two-story deluxe units have kitchens and hardwood floors. Pets are allowed in some units. Especially during the off-season, this spruced-up old motor court is one of the best values on the north coast.

A charmingly refurbished lodging just three short blocks from the beach, **(Weiss' Paradise Suites** (741 S. Downing St., 503/738-6691 or 800/738-6691, www.seasidesuites.com, $130-160) is south of the Broadway action but offers homey, recently upgraded units with lots of extras, including full kitchens, decks, two TVs, free DVDs, and robes. One-, two-, and three-bedroom suites are available.

$150-200

Well south of the bustling Broadway scene, the **Inn at the Shore** (2275 S. Prom, 503/738-3113 or 800/713-9914, www.innattheshore.com, $179-289) has nicely appointed rooms, each with a gas fireplace, a balcony, a wet bar, a microwave, a coffeemaker, a refrigerator, a flat-screen TV, and a DVD/VCR.

The four-story, shingle-sided **Seaside Oceanfront Inn** (581 S. Prom, 503/319-3300 or 800/772-7766, https://theseasideinn.com, $150-250) stands right on the beach, with its north gable skewered by a clock tower. Each of the 14 guest rooms is decorated in a unique theme—the clock tower room has a huge round bed in the center of the room, but other than that, they're pretty tasteful. Most have a spectacular ocean view, and pets are permitted in certain rooms. The on-site restaurant is very good.

Seaside's most stylish rooms are at the ⟨**Inn of the Four Winds** (820 N. Prom, 503/738-9524 or 800/818-9524, www.innofthefourwinds.com, $129-259). This 14-room boutique hotel has very comfortable rooms furnished with taste and panache. Each guest room has a microwave, a coffeemaker, a refrigerator, a DVD player, a gas fireplace, and a deck or balcony with an ocean view. Best of all, the inn faces directly onto the beach eight blocks north of the frenetic Broadway strip.

In the center of Seaside, with balconies over the Necanicum River, the **Holiday Inn Express Hotel Suites Seaside Convention Center** (34 Holladay Dr., 503/717-8000, $171-235) has an indoor pool and spa, wireless high-speed Internet access, and rooms with fridges, microwaves, coffeemakers, and CD and DVD players. Rates include a complimentary breakfast bar.

Best Western Oceanview Resort (414 N. Prom, 503/738-3264 or 800/234-8439, www.oceanviewresort.com, $169-229) is a large hotel right on the beach near the center of town. Amenities include an on-site restaurant and lounge, a heated pool, and a spa; the majority of rooms face the ocean.

In the center of Seaside, right on the Necanicum River, the **Rivertides Suites** (102 N. Holladay Dr., 877/871-8433, www.rivertidesuites.com, $149-199) offers some of the most upscale accommodations in Seaside. All rooms have balconies, full kitchens, fine linens, and jetted tubs, plus complimentary breakfast, indoor pool and hot tub, exercise room, and great views from the rooftop viewing deck. In addition to the entry-level studio suites, there are also one- and two-bedroom suites.

Vacation Rentals

A good option for many travelers is one of the several dozen vacation rentals; options range from tiny cottages at less than $100 per night (minimum stays are often required, especially in summer) to large homes that can host groups of 10-12. Check with the **Seaside Visitors Bureau** (7 N. Roosevelt St., 503/738-3097 or 888/306-2326, www.seasideor.com, 8am-5pm daily), or contact one of the rental agencies: **Beachhouse Vacation Rentals** (503/738-9068, www.beachhouse1.com), **Oceanside Vacation Rental** (503/738-7767 or 800/840-7764, www.oceanside1.com), or **Northwind Vacation Rentals** (503/738-5532 or 866/738-5532, www.northwindrentals.com).

Camping

One mile south of Seaside in a lush green meadow is **Circle Creek RV Park and Campground** (85658 U.S. 101, 503/738-6070, www.circlecreekrv.com, mid-Mar.-Oct., tents $24, RVs $40). The campground offers showers, a small store, picnic tables, and fire rings.

FOOD

While a stroll down Broadway might have you thinking that cotton candy, corn dogs, and saltwater taffy are the staples of Seaside cuisine, several eateries here can satisfy more refined palates as well.

American

If you're traveling with kids, you'll almost inevitably end up eating at **Pig 'N Pancake** (323 Broadway, 503/738-7243, 6am-9pm Sun.-Thurs., 6am-10pm Fri.-Sat., breakfast and lunch $7-10, dinner $10-18), where the Swedish pancakes and crab-and-cheese omelets are tops at breakfast, and the Frisbee-size cinnamon rolls will launch your blood sugar to new heights.

Cajun

A rarity in these parts, ⟨**Lil' Bayou** (20 N. Holladay Dr., 503/717-0624, 5pm-9pm Wed.-Mon., $15-20) dishes up authentic muffulettas, jambalaya, blackened catfish, gumbo, and a host of other Cajun and Creole standards, right down to side dishes of collard greens, at reasonable prices. Finish off with a slice of sweet potato pecan pie or Aunt B's cheesecake.

Pacific Northwest

Maggie's (581 S. Prom, 503/738-6403, 8am-10:30am, 11am-3pm, 5pm-9pm daily, breakfast $3-10, lunch $7-12, dinner $17-20), tucked away in the Seaside Oceanfront Inn, serves carefully prepared meals, with dinners that include simple pasta dishes and a number of seafood choices such as hazelnut-crusted halibut and salmon burgers.

Should the frenetic ambience of Seaside on a holiday weekend begin to wear thin, try the **C Pacific Way Bakery and Cafe** in Gearhart (601 Pacific Way, 503/738-0245, bakery 7am-1pm Thurs.-Mon., restaurant 11am-3:30pm, 5pm-9pm Thurs.-Mon., dinner $10-30, dinner reservations recommended). Pasta, crusty pizzas, and seafood dishes (including thick seafood cioppino) as well as Dungeness crab sandwiches with aioli pop up at lunch and dinner. Rib eye steak and local razor clams are other frequent dinnertime highlights in the surprisingly urbane little café hidden behind a rustic old storefront. In the morning, the bakery side of the operation is *the* place to be for coffee and pastries.

Right in the heart of busy Broadway, **Twisted Fish** (311 Broadway, 503/738-3467, 11am-10pm daily, $10-30) is a Pacific Northwest-style steakhouse, with hand-cut steaks, fresh fish and seafood, pasta and Mediterranean-inflected dishes such as chicken and prawn picatta. All bread and desserts are made in-house; live music is offered on weekend evenings.

Seafood

Dooger's (505 Broadway, 503/738-3773, 11am-9pm daily, $11-20), which also has an outlet in Cannon Beach, is a popular Broadway mainstay known for its clam chowder. Although it's kind of a frumpy-looking place, it serves good seafood. Local clams and oysters, fresh Dungeness crab legs, sautéed shrimp, and marionberry cobbler are also the basis of Dooger's reputation.

Brewpubs and Wine Bars

Although Seaside isn't generally considered to be a hip town (hipsters, Astoria is your place), and in spite of its silly name, **C Yummy Wine Bar and Bistro** (831 Broadway, 503/738-3100, 3pm-10pm Thurs.-Mon., $17-23) has the right vibe of comfortable nonintimidating hipness mixed with good food, wine, art, and occasional live music. Order an assortment of small plates, such as ahi tuna tartare ($10) or prawn bruschetta ($13), or a full meal; happy hour runs 3pm-6pm and includes some small appetizers and good deals on house wine.

At the Gearhart Golf Links, the old clubhouse now houses **McMenamins Sand Trap** (1157 N. Marion Ave., 503/717-8150, 11am-10pm Mon.-Tues., 11am-11pm Wed.-Thurs., 11am-midnight Fri., 8am-midnight Sat., 8am-10pm Sun., $7-27); it has been decorated with the McMenamins' trademark whimsical artwork and serves the local chain's decent (not great, but always edible) upscale pub food.

INFORMATION AND SERVICES

The **Seaside Visitors Bureau** (7 N. Roosevelt St., 503/738-3097 or 888/306-2326, www.seasideor.com) is open 8am-5pm daily. **Providence Seaside Hospital** (725 S. Wahanna Rd., 503/717-7000) has 24-hour service and an emergency room.

GETTING THERE

Sunset Empire Transportation District operates **The Bus** (503/861-RIDE, 503/861-7433, or 800/776-6406, www.ridethebus.org) serving Cannon Beach, Seaside, Astoria-Warrenton, and points in between. **Amtrak** (800/872-7245, www.amtrak.com) throughway buses pass through twice daily on their run between Portland and Astoria.

NORTH COAST

Cannon Beach and Vicinity

In 1846, the USS *Shark* met its end on the Columbia River Bar. The ship broke apart, and a section of deck bearing cannons and an iron capstan drifted south, finally in 1894 washing ashore south of the current city limits at Arch Cape. And so this town got its name, which it adopted in 1922. In the winter of 2008, during an especially low tide, two additional cannons were revealed. Although their provenance has not been verified, they're also thought to be from the *Shark*. Although they are currently being cleaned and studied at Texas A&M University, these cannons are expected to end up at the Astoria maritime museum.

In 1873, stagecoach and railroad tycoon Ben Holladay helped create Oregon's first coastal tourist mecca, Seaside, while ignoring its attractive neighbor in the shadow of Haystack Rock. In the 20th century, Cannon Beach evolved into a bohemian alternative to the hustle and bustle of the family-oriented resort scene to the north. Before the recent era of development, this place was a quaint backwater attracting laid-back artists, summer home residents, and the overflow from Seaside.

Today, the low-key charm and atmosphere conducive to artistic expression have in some part been quashed by development and the attendant massive visitor influx and price increases. While such vital signs as a first-rate theater, a good bookstore, cheek-by-jowl art galleries, and fine restaurants are still in ample evidence, your view of them from the other side of the street might be blocked by a convoy of Winnebagos.

Nonetheless, the broad three-mile stretch of beach dominated by the impressive monolith of Haystack Rock still provides a contemplative experience. And if you're patient and resourceful enough to find a space for your wheels (try the free municipal lot one block east of the main street), the finest gallery-hopping, crafts, and shopping on the coast await. The city is small enough for strolling, and its location removed from U.S. 101 spares it the kind of traffic blight seen on the main drags of other coastal tourist towns.

Wood shingles and understated earth tones dominate the architecture of tastefully rendered galleries, bookstores, and bistros. Throngs of walkers along Hemlock Street, the main drag, also distinguish this burg from the typical coastal strip town whose heart and soul have been pierced by U.S. 101.

SIGHTS
◖ Haystack Rock

Haystack Rock looms large above the long, broad beach. This is the third-highest sea stack in the state, measuring 235 feet high. As part of the Oregon Islands National Wildlife Refuge, it has wilderness status and is off-limits to climbing. Puffins and other seabirds nest on its steep faces, and intertidal organisms thrive in the tidepools around the base. The surrounding tidepools, within a radius of 300 yards from the base of the monolith, are designated a "marine garden"; they are open to exploration, but with strict no-collecting (of anything) and no-harassment (of any living organisms) protections in effect. Flanking the mountain are two rock formations known as the Needles. These spires had two other counterparts at the turn of the 20th century that have gradually been leveled by weathering and erosion. Old-timers will tell you that the government dynamited a trail to the top of Haystack in 1968 to keep people off this bird rookery. It also reduced the number of intrepid hikers trapped on the rock at high tide.

Volunteers from the **Haystack Rock Awareness Program** (503/436-1581) are often on the beach with displays, spotting scopes, and answers to many of your questions. Spend some time chatting with these folks, but don't forget to listen to the beach's own distinctive voices. You can't miss the cacophony of seabirds at sunset and, if you listen closely, the

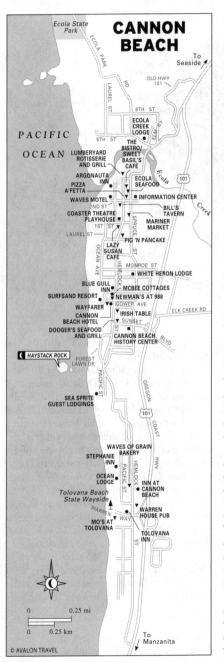

winter phenomenon of "singing sands" created by wind blowing over the beach.

Beach access is available at the west end of any public east-west street. From downtown, Harrison Street works well; south of downtown, Tolovana Beach Wayside has a large parking area and easy beach access.

Cannon Beach History Center

Permanent exhibits at the small **Cannon Beach History Center** (1387 S. Spruce St., 503/436-9301, www.cbhistory.org, 11am-5pm Thurs.-Mon., free) chronicle the town's timeline, from prehistory to the modern expansion of tourism and recreation. The original eponymous cannon (the one found in 1894) from the ill-fated *Shark* is also on display here.

Ecola State Park

Ecola State Park (off U.S. 101, 800/551-6949, www.oregonstateparks.org, $5 day-use fee) is two miles north of Cannon Beach. Thick conifer forests line the access road to Ecola Point. This forested cliff has many trails leading down to the water. The view south takes in Haystack Rock and the overlapping peaks of the Coast Range extending to Neahkahnie Mountain. This is one of the most photographed views on the coast. Out to sea, the sight of sea lions basking on surf-drenched rocks (mid-Apr.-July) or migrating gray whales (Dec. and Mar.) and orcas (May) is seasonal highlights.

From Ecola Point, trails lead north to horseshoe-shaped **Indian Beach,** a favorite with surfers. Some prefer to drive the steep narrow road down to Indian Beach as a prelude to hiking up Tillamook Head, considered by Lewis and Clark the region's most beautiful viewpoint. The 2.5-mile Clatsop Loop Trail begins and ends at Indian Beach and climbs through Sitka spruce to a viewpoint. Ambitious hikers can do the first half of the loop, then continue another four miles north to Seaside.

The name Ecola means "whale" in Chinook and was first used as a place-name by William Clark, referring to a creek in the area. Lewis and Clark journals note a 105-foot beached whale found somewhere within present-day

Haystack Rock

Ecola Park's southern border at Crescent Beach. This area represents the southernmost extent of Lewis and Clark's coastal Oregon travels.

◖ Saddle Mountain State Natural Area

A good reason to head east from Cannon Beach is the hike up 3,283-foot Saddle Mountain at **Saddle Mountain State Natural Area** (off U.S. 26, 800/551-6949, www.oregonstateparks.org). On a clear day, hikers can see some 50 miles of the Oregon and Washington coastlines, including the Columbia River. Also possible are spectacular views of Mounts Rainier, St. Helens, and Hood, and miles of clear-cuts. On the upper part of the trail, plant species that pushed south from Alaska and Canada during the last ice age still thrive. The cool, moist climate here keeps them from dying out as they did at lower elevations. Some early blooms include pink coast fawn lily, monkeyflower, wild rose, wood violet, bleeding heart, oxalis, Indian paintbrush, and trillium. Cable handrails provide safety on the narrow final 0.25-mile trail to the summit.

To get to the trailhead, take U.S. 26 from its junction with U.S. 101 for 10 miles and turn left on the prominently signed Saddle Mountain Road. (Although it's paved, this road is not suitable for RVs or wide-bodied vehicles.) After seven twisting miles, you'll come to the trailhead of the highest peak in this part of the Coast Range. The trail itself is steep and gains more than 1,600 feet in 2.5 miles. Wet conditions can make the going difficult (allow four hours round-trip) and the scenery en route is not always exceptional unless you look down for the lovely May-August wildflower display; the view from the top is worth the climb.

The campground ($5-10) at Saddle Mountain is tiny and rustic and offers a secluded option for campers not attracted to the busy family scene at nearby Fort Stevens State Park.

Beaches

Stunning beaches don't end with Cannon

Beach. Sandy expanses stretch seven miles south to the Arch Cape tunnel on U.S. 101, indicating the entrance to Oswald West State Park. Several of these beaches are reached via state park waysides. As you head south, views of **Hug Point State Recreation Site** (off U.S. 101, 800/551-6949, www.oregonstateparks. org) and pristine beaches will have you ready to pull over. In summer, this can be a good escape from the crowds at Cannon Beach. Time your visit to coincide with low tide, when all manner of marine life will be exposed in tidal pools. Also at low tide, you may see remains of an 800-foot-long Model T-sized road blasted into the base of Hug Point, an early precursor to U.S. 101. The cliffs are gouged with caves and crevasses that also invite exploring, but be mindful of the tides so that you don't find yourself stranded. Hug Point got its name in the days when stagecoaches used the beach as highways; they had to dash between the waves, hugging the jutting headland to get around.

SPORTS AND RECREATION
Bicycling
Mike's Bike Shop (248 N. Spruce St., Cannon Beach, 503/436-1266, 10am-6pm Thurs.-Tues., $8-12 per hour) rents mountain bikes, road bikes, beach cruisers, and three-wheeled recumbent "fun cycles," which zip up and down the hard-packed sand when the tide is out. Mike, who has run this shop since 1974, is a good guy who can help you figure out how to travel the coast car-free.

Horseback Riding
Sea Ranch Stables (415 Old U.S. 101, 503/436-2815, 9am-4:30pm daily mid-June-Labor Day, 9am-4:30pm weekends mid-May-mid-June, $70-130), at the north entrance to Cannon Beach off U.S. 101, offers a number of one- to two-hour guided rides, including night rides. Rides to Haystack Rock start at 9am, before the beach gets crowded.

Surfing
The area around Cannon Beach has several good surfing beaches. The most popular, and

the best bet for beginners, is **Short Sands Beach,** at the end of the trail to the beach at Oswald West State Park, south of Arch Cape. It's a bit of a hike down to the beach, but the sheltered cove is a great place to spend the day, even if you're just bobbing around in the waves.

Another good spot for somewhat more advanced surfers (and surf kayakers) is **Indian Beach,** at **Ecola State Park** (off U.S. 101, 800/551-6949, www.oregonstateparks.org, $5 day-use fee). Up the road in Seaside, locals tend to control the surf breaks—if you're good enough to fit in, give it a go.

Rent a board and wetsuit at **Cleanline Surf** (171 Sunset Blvd., 503/436-9726).

ENTERTAINMENT AND EVENTS
Going strong since 1972, the **Coaster Theatre Playhouse** (108 N. Hemlock St., 503/436-1242, www.coastertheatre.com, $15-23) stages a varied bill of musicals, dramas, mysteries, comedies, concerts, and other entertainment. It's open year-round, in a building that started in the 1920s as a skating rink-turned-silent-movie house.

The half dozen or so other sand-sculpting contests that take place on the Oregon coast pale in comparison to Cannon Beach's annual **Sandcastle Day** (503/436-2623, call to confirm dates). In 1964 a tsunami washed out a bridge, and the isolated residents of Cannon Beach organized the first contest as a way to amuse their children. Now in its fifth decade, this is the state's oldest and most prestigious competition of its kind. Tens of thousands of spectators show up to watch 1,000-plus competitors fashion their sculptures with the aid of buckets, shovels, squirt guns, and any natural material found on the beach. The resulting sculptures are often amazingly complex and inventive. This event is free to spectators, but entrants pay a fee. Recent winners included Egyptian pyramids and a gigantic sea turtle. This collapsible art show usually coincides with the lowest-tide Saturday in June and takes place north of Haystack Rock. Building begins in the early morning; winners are announced at noon. The American Legion serves a big breakfast buffet ($7 adult, $5 children ages 6-12) at 1216 South Hemlock Street, open to all.

Writers, singers, composers, painters, and sculptors take over the town for the **Stormy Weather Arts Festival** (503/436-2623), usually held the first weekend of November. Events include music in the streets, plays, a Saturday afternoon Art Walk, and the Quick Draw, in which artists have one hour to paint, complete, and frame a piece while the audience watches. The art is then sold by auction.

Beginning in July, the city park at Spruce and 2nd Streets hosts **Concerts in the Park** (5pm-7pm Sun.), a series of jazz, rhythm and blues, and popular music at the bandstand.

SHOPPING

Much of the attraction of Cannon Beach is window shopping up and down **Hemlock Street**, which, in addition to galleries, is lined with clothing stores, gift shops, and other boutiques. Cannon Beach supports a fine kite

© BILL MCRAE

NORTH COAST

Hemlock Street is a maze of shops.

store: **Once Upon a Breeze** (240 N. Spruce St., 503/436-1112) and one of the better bookstores on the coast, the **Cannon Beach Book Company** (130 N. Hemlock St., 503/436-1301, http://cannonbeachbooks.com); it's the place to pick up regional titles or a good novel (lots of mysteries) for that rainy weekend.

Art Galleries

Cannon Beach has long attracted artists and artisans, and here art lovers and purchasers will find nearly two dozen galleries and shops with high-quality works. Most of the Cannon Beach galleries and boutiques are concentrated along Hemlock Street, where you can hardly swing a Winsor & Newton No. 12 hogbristle brush without hitting one. Not surprisingly, the seashore itself is the subject and inspiration of many works you'll see here, with Haystack Rock frequently depicted in various media. The **Cannon Beach Information Center** (201 E. 2nd St., 503/436-2623, www.cannonbeach. org, 11am-5pm Mon.-Sat., 10am-4pm Sun.) has a guide to all the galleries in town, or you can just stroll and discover them for yourself.

At the north end of town, **Northwest by Northwest Gallery** (232 N. Spruce St., 503/436-0741, www.nwbynwgallery.com) showcases works by photographer Christopher Burkett, Native American ceramicist and bronze artist Lillian Pitt, and leading glass artists such as Duane Dahl. **White Bird Gallery** (251 N. Hemlock St., 503/436-2681, www. whitebirdgallery.com), founded in 1971 and one of Cannon Beach's oldest galleries, casts a wide net with paintings, sculpture, prints, photography, glass, ceramics, and jewelry. Nearby, the **Bronze Coast Gallery** (224 N. Hemlock St., 503/436-1055, www.bronzecoastgallery. com) shows both traditional Western bronzes and innovative bronze works and paintings that may appeal to those who aren't crazy about traditional Western art. In midtown, **Icefire Glassworks** (116 Gower St., 503/436-2359) is a working glass studio where you can watch glassblowers and artists shape their work and then shop for unique pieces in the gallery.

DragonFire Gallery (123 S. Hemlock St.,

503/436-1533) shows the work of a wide variety of artists; on Saturday afternoons throughout the summer, everyone is invited to come and meet gallery artists.

ACCOMMODATIONS

Cannon Beach has an abundance of small, locally owned lodgings, most of which rise above rusticity to the level of comfortable hominess. Many run $100-200 during the summer, but prices can drop as low as $60-80 during the off-season. If you're into luxury, Cannon Beach also offers some of Oregon's most opulent rooms.

$50-100

There aren't many inexpensive lodging options in Cannon Beach, but "mountain-view" rooms at the enormous **Tolovana Inn** (3400 S. Hemlock St., 503/436-2211 or 800/333-8890, www.tolovanainn.com, $79-105 mountain view, $169-269 ocean view, minimum stay in summer) hotel complex at the southern end of the Cannon Beach sprawl offer a good location at a fairly reasonable price. To make up for the rather cookie-cutter design and furnishings, you'll get a swimming pool, a spa, and a sauna, a number of restaurants sharing the same parking lots, and the beach right out the front door.

$100-150

About a one-minute walk to the beach, with friendly management and a great vibe, the **Blue Gull Inn** (632 S. Hemlock St., 503/436-2714 or 800/507-2714, www.bluegullinn.net, $139-209, two-night min. in summer) offers a choice between a beach house or less expensive motel units that come with housekeeping facilities. The modern cottages have in-room whirlpool tubs, fireplaces, and full kitchens. Cottages for larger groups are also available. Blue Gull Inn is one of several reliably comfortable and relatively inexpensive properties managed by **Haystack Lodgings,** which can be reached through the Blue Gull Inn website.

The **McBee Cottages** (888 S. Hemlock St., 503/436-0247 or 800/238-4107, www.mcbeecottages.com, $119-179) is a 1940s-era motel with semidetached units that have been nicely renovated. The rooms are simple and certainly not expansive, but the McBee is nonetheless a favorite of many visitors looking for cozy accommodations, and it's just a minute from the beach and within walking distance of downtown. McBee accepts pets in several of its homey cottages.

For a homey atmosphere, try the **Argonauta Inn** or **The Waves Motel,** which share an office (188 W. 2nd St., 503/436-2205 or 800/822-2468, www.thewavescannonbeach.com). The Argonauta ($139-275) is made up of four houses in the middle of downtown and has five furnished units just 150 feet from the beach. A cluster of six beachfront buildings makes up The Waves ($139-289), with units to fit the needs of families, couples, or larger groups. These are not cookie-cutter units but the kind of individual lodgings you'd expect in Oregon.

The **Cannon Beach Hotel** (1116 Hemlock St., 503/436-1392 or 800/238-4107, www.cannonbeachhotel.com, $139-259) is a converted 1910 loggers' boardinghouse with 30 rooms and a small café and restaurant on the premises. The most expensive rooms have fireplaces, whirlpools, and partial ocean views. Meals are available in the restaurant adjacent to the lobby.

Just a few minutes' walk from downtown, **Ecola Creek Lodge** (208 E. 5th St., 503/436-2776 or 800/873-2749, www.ecolacreeklodge.com, $119-179) is a Cape Cod-style inn with 22 unique units set within four buildings. Accommodations range from simple queen-bed studios to two-bedroom suites. Special features include stained glass, lawns, fountains, flower gardens, and a lily pond. Les Shirley Park and Ecola Creek separate the lodge from the beach.

Over $200

The **C Surfsand Resort** (148 W. Gower St., 503/436-2274 or 800/547-6100, www.surfsand.com, $200-319) offers a great combination of location and amenities, with Haystack Rock right out the door and spacious, nicely furnished suites. The resort has an indoor pool and spa and on-site massage services; pets

NORTH COAST

are permitted in some rooms. The popular Wayfarer Restaurant is adjacent.

The handsome **Inn at Cannon Beach** (3215 S. Hemlock St., 503/436-9085 or 800/321-6304, www.atcannonbeach.com, $249-289, minimum stay requirements in summer) has large and stylish cottage-like rooms in a beautifully landscaped garden setting with a courtyard pond, just a block from the beach. All guest rooms include a gas fireplace, a fridge, a microwave, a coffeemaker, and a TV/VCR/DVD combo; some rooms can accommodate pets.

The fabulously expensive (for Oregon) **Stephanie Inn** (2740 S. Pacific St., 503/436-2221 or 800/633-3466, www.stephanie-inn.com, $499-589) offers attentive B&B-style service (breakfast buffet and evening wine gathering included), attention to detail, and luxury-level rooms with a low-key, not-too-fussy Oregonian touch. All guest rooms have balconies, fireplaces, wet bars, Jacuzzi tubs, fine linens, and all the extras you'd expect in an upscale resort hotel—including a fine dining restaurant. The Stephanie is a romantic adult-focused inn; children under 12 are not permitted.

The **Ocean Lodge** (2864 S. Pacific Dr., 503/436-2241 or 888/777-4047, www.theoceanlodge.com, $239-389) feels like a long-established beach getaway, though in fact it was built recently. The high-end furnishings also give a clue that despite its venerable design, this rambling lodge isn't soaked in tradition. Rooms all have balconies, DVD players, fireplaces, microwaves, and refrigerators.

For a more private experience just steps from the ocean, the **White Heron Lodge** (356 N. Spruce St., 503/436-2205 or 800/822-2468, www.thewavescannonbeach.com, $309, three-night minimum stays in summer) comprises two fully furnished oceanfront Victorian-style homes, both of which sleep up to four. Each of the suites looks directly out on the Pacific. Wide sandy beaches and spacious front lawns make it a great location for families, especially those with small children. Located on a residential dead-end street, the lodge is only one block from downtown Cannon Beach.

Three miles south of Cannon Beach in quiet Arch Cape, the **Arch Cape Inn** (31970 E. Ocean Ln., 503/436-2800 or 800/436-2848, www.archcapeinn.com, $238-369) is a bit over-the-top in its turreted castle-like design, but it's supremely luxurious. Although it's not on the beach, it's an easy walk, and several rooms have good ocean views. Friday or Saturday lodging requires one night's dinner reservations at the on-site restaurant (Thurs.-Mon. May-Oct., Fri.-Sat. year-round).

Vacation Rentals

Several local property management companies offer a large selection of furnished rentals ranging from grand oceanfront homes to quaint secluded cottages. **Cannon Beach Property Management** (3188 S. Hemlock St., 503/436-2021 or 877/386-3402, www.cbpm.com) and **Cannon Beach Vacation Rentals** (P.O. Box 723, Cannon Beach 97110, 866/436-0940, www.visitcb.com) both have good websites. During the summer, many beach houses are only available for weekly rentals.

Camping

Camping offers easier access to Cannon Beach's natural wonders at a bargain price. Although camping is not permitted on the beach or in Cannon Beach city parks, there are plenty of options for RV, tent, and outdoor enthusiasts.

The **Sea Ranch RV Park** (415 Fir St., 503/436-2815, www.cannon-beach.net/searanch, $33 tents, $38-43 RVs, $85-95 cabins) has grassy sites nestled among the trees, and is also home to horses, ducks, rabbits, and raccoons. It's open year-round with both full and partial hookups for RVs; campsites include a picnic table and a fire ring (firewood is sold on the premises) and access to restrooms with hot showers—all just three blocks from the beach and downtown. Pets are welcome but must be on a leash. Reservations are recommended.

For a more pampered RV-only experience, check out the **RV Resort at Cannon Beach** (345 Elk Creek Rd., 503/436-2231 or 800/847-2231, www.cbrvresort.com, $32-44). Open year-round, the RV Resort has 100 full hook-ups, an indoor pool and spa, free cable TV, an on-site convenience store, a laundry facility, restrooms, and a meeting room.

Unlike most private campgrounds, the small family-run **Wright's for Camping** (334 Reservoir Rd., 503/436-2347, www.wrightsfor-camping.com, $30-32) is geared toward tent campers. It's just east of U.S. 101 and has 20 sites with picnic tables and fire rings as well as restrooms and a laundry. Wright's is wheelchair accessible; leashed pets are allowed.

Roughly 20 miles east of Cannon Beach off U.S. 26 is **Saddle Mountain State Natural Area** (800/551-6949, www.oregonstateparks.org, Mar.-Oct., $5-10 tents, first-come, first-served), which offers 10 tent camping sites at the base of 3,283-foot Saddle Mountain, one of the highest peaks in Oregon's Coast Range. This more primitive and remote campground (although there are flush toilets and piped water, in addition to picnic tables and fire pits) might just be the tonic if you're weary of the crowds along the beach.

Cannon Beach offers a wide range of food.

© BILL MCRAE

FOOD

If you're on a budget, keep dining prices down at the **Mariner Market** (139 N. Hemlock St., 503/436-2442, 8am-9pm daily), a dimly lit old grocery that's fully stocked with fresh meat, fruit, vegetables, and deli items.

Bakeries and Cafés

Grab a cheese biscuit to go or sit down for a cup of coffee and a marionberry scone at **Waves of Grain Bakery** (3116 S. Hemlock St., 503/436-9600, 7am-3pm daily, $2-5), which is far and away the best bakery in town, with all the baked goods produced from scratch in-house. At times, you can also get soup.

Try the wood-paneled sky-lit **Lazy Susan Cafe** (126 N. Hemlock St., 503/436-2816, www.lazy-susan-cafe.com, 8am-3pm Sun.-Mon. and Wed.-Thurs., $7-13) for a great breakfast (waffles are a specialty) or satisfying lunch (salads are very good).

American

The local **Pig 'N Pancake** (223 S. Hemlock St., 503/436-2851, 7am-3pm daily, $6-12) has large picture windows overlooking a leafy ravine. Choose from 35 breakfast dishes served anytime, including homemade pancakes (which are very good and extremely popular—expect to wait). For lunch, try the soups, chowder, or halibut and chips.

The **Lumberyard Rotisserie and Grill** (264 3rd St., 503/436-0285, www.thelumberyard-grill.com, noon-9pm daily, $8-23) is a block away from busy downtown Cannon Beach, but this spacious restaurant offers high-quality food at good prices. The specialty is rotisserie chicken, but the pizza here is also good, as are such appetizers as the Dungeness crab and artichoke skillet. The Lumberyard is owned by the same company as the Stephanie Inn and the Surfsand Resort, and it has a similarly polished appearance.

Somewhat oddly, few of Cannon Beach's top restaurants have a view of the beach, so if excellent vistas of Haystack Rock and breaking waves are important to you, call to reserve a table at **The Wayfarer** (1190 Pacific Dr.,

NORTH COAST

503/436-1108, 8am-9pm daily, dinner $17-30), tucked above a beach entrance at Gower Street. The food, which is good but not as memorable as the views, features classic steak and seafood main courses. The lounge here is a good spot for a drink.

Italian

The pizza at **Pizza a'Fetta** (231 N. Hemlock St., 503/436-0333, 11am-8pm Sun.-Thurs., 11am-9pm Fri.-Sat., slices $3-4, whole pies $20-33) is Cannon Beach's best, with a selection of to-go slices available at a takeout window. Or crowd into the always-busy dining room for your choice of pies, salads, minestrone soup, and Oregon microbrew beer and Italian wines.

Mediterranean

Cozy and refined, **The Bistro** (263 N. Hemlock St., 503/436-2661, 5pm-10pm daily, $20-25) is tucked back in a maze of shops and gardens in downtown Cannon Beach. The atmosphere is a bit stark, particularly after a rebuild from a recent fire, but the menu brings a taste of Provence to traditional fish and seafood dishes—the seafood stew is a wonderful blend of Pacific Northwest fish and shellfish prepared with Mediterranean zest. The dining room is truly tiny and the food superlative, so reservations are mandatory.

❰ Newman's at 988 (988 S. Hemlock St., 503/436-1151, www.newmansat988. com, 5:30pm-9pm Tues.-Sat. Oct. 16-June 30; 5:30pm-9pm daily July-Oct. 15, $19-26) is a good special-occasion restaurant in a tiny house, with an elegant atmosphere and excellent food. The chef-owner takes great pride in using fresh local ingredients to prepare seasonal menus with French and Italian influences, featuring such dishes as seared duck breast with foie gras and truffles or lobster ravioli with marsala cream.

Irish

The **Irish Table** (1235 S. Hemlock St., 503/436-0708, 5:30pm-9pm Fri.-Tues., $11-22) makes the most of the Pacific Northwest bounty and hearty Irish cooking traditions, including meat pastries, grilled salmon, braised mussels, and variations on local lamb, including Irish lamb stew. The bar offers a wide selection of Scotch and Irish whiskies, plus Irish ales.

Pacific Northwest

Whether or not you're staying at the **Stephanie Inn** (2740 S. Pacific St., 503/436-2221 or 800/633-3466, www.stephanie-inn.com, 5pm-9pm nightly, $28-34, 4-course dinner $65), you are welcome to join guests in the dining room for creative Pacific Northwest cuisine. The atmosphere boasts mountain views, open wood beams, and a river-rock fireplace. Since guests get first shot at tables, those staying elsewhere should reserve well ahead of time.

For a much more casual dining experience, go to **Sweet Basil's Cafe** (271 N. Hemlock St., 503/436-1539, www.cafesweetbasils.com, 11am-10pm Wed.-Sun., $12-21), a tiny restaurant whose commitment is "natural, organic, wild." At lunch, enjoy mostly vegetarian sandwiches and salads. In the evening, linger in the wine bar, where tapas-style dishes are eclectic and creative—pork tenderloin with Bourbon sauce and seared duck breast with blueberries and pecan rice.

Seafood

Hankering for some authentic West Coast chowder? Head to **❰ Dooger's Seafood and Grill** (1371 S. Hemlock St., 503/436-2225, 8am-9pm daily, dinners $12-45) for seafood that's always fresh and delicious. Don't overlook Dooger's for breakfast—during crab season (mostly winter and spring) the crab Benedict is a real treat. **Mo's at Tolovana** (195 Warren Way, Tolovana Park, 503/436-1111, www.moschowder.com, 11am-8pm Mon.-Thurs., 11am-9pm Fri., 8am-9pm Sat., 8am-8pm Sun., $3-16) has great views; although its clam chowder is locally famous (perhaps because of fondness for Mo and her family), the food is not the big draw if you're looking for cutting-edge preparations.

In the fishing business for more than 25 years, **Ecola Seafoods** (208 N. Spruce St.,

503/436-9130, 9am-9pm daily summer, 10am-7pm daily winter) features fresh-catch Dungeness crab and bay shrimp cocktails, as well as a decent clam chowder ($5). Or sample the smoked salmon and fish-and-chips. You'll find it across from the public parking lots and information center.

Brewpubs

Bill's Tavern (188 N. Hemlock St., 503/436-2202, 11:30am-10pm Thurs.-Tues., 4:30pm-10pm Wed., bar open later, $7-13), once a legendary watering hole, is now a more traditional brewpub. Sweet thick onion rings, good fries, one-third-pound burgers, sautéed prawns, and grilled oysters are on the bill of fare.

Farther south near Tolovana, the **Warren House Pub** (3301 S. Hemlock St., 503/436-1130, 10:30am-1am daily, $7-14) serves local beers from Bill's Tavern but in an English pub setting. The menu includes good smoked ribs, burgers, and seafood; in summer the backyard beer garden is a lovely spot to relax. Kids are allowed on the restaurant side of the pub.

INFORMATION AND SERVICES

The chamber of commerce operates the **Cannon Beach Information Center** (201 E. 2nd St., 503/436-2623, www.cannonbeach. org, 11am-5pm Mon.-Sat., 10am-4pm Sun.). This facility is close to the public restrooms (2nd St. and Spruce St.) and basketball and tennis courts.

Providence North Coast Clinic (171 N. Larch St., 503/717-7000) offers medical care and minor emergency services. It's located in Sandpiper Square behind the stores on the main drag.

Cooking Schools

After a day on the beach, spend an evening at **EVOO Cooking School** (188 S. Hemlock St., 503/436-8555, www.evoo.biz), where multi-course dinner classes ($79-120, includes dinner) are offered at least a couple of nights a week. Specialty classes on topics such as bread baking and cooking seafood are also offered.

GETTING THERE AND AROUND

From U.S. 101, there's a choice of four entrances to the beach loop (also known as U.S. 101 Alternate, a section of the old Oregon Coast Highway) to take you into town. As you wade into the town's shops, galleries, and restaurants, the beach loop becomes Hemlock Street, the main drag of Cannon Beach. Sunset Empire Transportation District operates **The Bus** (503/861-RIDE, 503/861-7433, or 800/776-6406, www.ridethebus.org), which serves Cannon Beach, Seaside, Astoria-Warrenton, and points in between. **Parking** can be hard to come by, especially on weekends, but you'll find public lots south of town at Tolovana Park and in town at Hemlock at 1st Street and on 2nd Street.

The **Cannon Beach Shuttle** runs every half hour on a 6.5-mile loop, from Les Shirley Park on the north end of town to Tolovana Park; it operates 10am-6pm daily, with extended summer hours. The fare is $1.

Amtrak Thruway Motorcoach Service (800/USA-RAIL or 800/872-7245, www. amtrak.com) runs two buses daily between Portland Union Station and Cannon Beach (continuing on to Seaside and Astoria). The bus stops at 1088 South Hemlock Street, across the street from the Cannon Beach Mercantile store.

NORTH COAST

Nehalem Bay Area

MANZANITA AND VICINITY

Just south of Arch Cape, Neahkahnie Mountain towers nearly 1,700 feet up from the edge of the sea. U.S. 101 climbs up and over its shoulder to an elevation of 700 feet, and the vistas from a half dozen pullouts (the highest along the Oregon coast) are spectacular—but do try to keep your eyes on the snaking road until you've parked your car.

This stretch of the highway, built by the Works Progress Administration in the 1930s, was constructed by blasting a roadbed from the rock face and buttressing it with stonework walls on the precarious cliffs. The fainthearted or acrophobic certainly couldn't have lasted long on this job. The handiwork of these road builders and masons can be admired at several pullouts, along with the breathtaking vista of Manzanita Beach, Nehalem Spit, and

old-growth tree along the trail in Oswald West State Park

some 20 miles south to Cape Meares. Much of Neahkahnie Mountain and its rugged coastline are preserved in Oswald West State Park, one of the state's finest.

Immediately to the south, huddled along an expansive curve of beach at the foot of Neahkahnie Mountain, quiet Manzanita (pop. 700) makes a pleasant stop for lunch or for the weekend. When adjacent coastal areas are fogbound, the seven-mile-long Manzanita Beach often enjoys sunshine because of the shelter of Neahkahnie Mountain. As one of the few towns along the north Oregon coast that's not located directly on U.S. 101, Manzanita feels more peaceful and secluded than most others; like Cannon Beach, it's also a relatively wealthy and stylish town.

Oswald West State Park

Most of Neahkahnie Mountain and the prominent headlands of Cape Falcon are encompassed within the 2,500-acre gem of **Oswald West State Park** (off U.S. 101, 800/551-6949, www.oregonstateparks.org). Whether or not you believe in the stories of lost pirate wealth buried somewhere on the mountain, there is real treasure today for all who venture here in search of the intangible currency of extraordinary natural beauty. The state park bears the name of Governor Oswald West, whose farsighted 1913 beach bill was instrumental in protecting Oregon's virgin shoreline. That same year, Neahkahnie Mountain was the site of another shipwreck in somewhat mysterious circumstances.

Several hiking trails weave through the park, including the 13 miles of the **Oregon Coast Trail** linking Arch Cape to the north with Manzanita. From the main parking lot on the east side of U.S. 101, a 0.5-mile trail follows Short Sands Creek to **Short Sands Beach,** a relatively sheltered beach that's popular with surfers year-round. Rainforests of hemlock, cedar, and gigantic Sitka spruce

© DUNCAN MACK MURPHY

crowd the secluded boulder-strewn shoreline. From Short Sands Beach, hike north on the three-mile old-growth-lined **Cape Falcon Trail** to spectacular views.

From the trail to the beach, it's also possible to turn south and hike to **Neahkahnie Mountain** (4 miles one-way) with some stiff climbing. Shave about 1.3 miles off the hike by starting a mile south of the main Oswald West parking lot, where there's an access road to the Neahkahnie Mountain Summit Trail on the east side of the highway. It's not well marked; look for a subdivision on the golf course to the west. Drive up the gravel road 0.25 mile to the trailhead parking lot and begin a moderately difficult 1.5-mile ascent. Allow about 45 minutes to get to the top. The summit view south to Cape Meares and east to the Nehalem Valley ranks as one of the finest on the coast.

Visitors who remember camping among the old-growth trees at Oswald West should treasure the memory. Due to the instability of the ancient trees, the campground remains closed.

Accommodations

Manzanita is a small town without an abundance of lodgings. Advance reservations are a must, especially in summer, and many accommodations require two- to three-night stays during the high season and on some holidays. A good alternative to motels for families here are the rentals available from the several property management agencies in town. Among these is **Manzanita Beach Getaway** (503/368-2929 or 855/368-2929, www.manzanitabeachgetaway. com), with fully furnished homes to rent, running $110-225 per night (most require weekly rentals in July and August).

If you're looking for an upscale retreat, the cedar-clad **[Inn at Manzanita** (67 Laneda Ave., 503/368-6754, www.innatmanzanita. com, $179-199), set in a Japanese-accented garden just a short walk from the beach, promises guests the three R's: recreation, relaxation, and romance. Each of its 13 wood-paneled guest rooms features a gas fireplace and a two-person spa; most rooms have a balcony, offering glimpses through the evergreens of the nearby

© DUNCAN MACK MURPHY

yoga at Short Sands Beach

NORTH COAST

beach. Fresh flowers daily, robes, and other amenities help you feel pampered. Despite being in the middle of town near restaurants and the beach, a feeling of luxurious seclusion prevails.

The remodeled **Ocean Inn** (32 Laneda Ave., 866/3687701 or 503/368-7701, www.ocean-innatmanzanita.com, $139-209) has large and comfortable condo-like rooms (most with full kitchens); several have wood stoves and two have patios. Most rooms have ocean views, and the beach is just moments away.

Six blocks from the beach, the six spacious, stylish, and airy cabins of **Coast Cabins** (635 Laneda Ave., 503/368-7113, www.coastcabins.com, $215-440, two-night minimum stays in summer and weekends) comfortably sleep one to two (although two-story Cabin 5 is designed for up to four people) and offer kitchenettes or full kitchens, satellite TV, and goose-down pillows and comforters. The Coast Cabins folks also rent out a few sophisticated one- and two-bedroom condos in downtown Manzanita.

For a more standard motel experience, the **Sunset Surf** (248 Ocean Rd., 503/368-5224 or 800/243-8035, www.sunsetsurfocean.com, $184-165) offers guest rooms (many with kitchens) in three oceanfront units that share an outdoor pool. Although rooms are basic, the setting is great.

Another reasonably priced older motel, the **Spindrift Inn** (114 Laneda Ave., 503/368-1001 or 877/368-1001, www.spindrift-inn.com, $80-110) has rooms that are nicer than the rather plain exterior. It's a very short walk to the beach.

Camping

Just south of Manzanita and occupying the entire sandy appendage of Nehalem Spit is scenic, sprawling **Nehalem Bay State Park** (800/452-5687, www.reserveamerica.com, year-round, $24 tents or RVs, $36 yurts, $5 day use for noncampers), a favorite with bikers, beachcombers, anglers, horse owners, and pilots (yes, there's a little airstrip and a fly-in campsite). Sandwiched between the bay and a beautiful four-mile beach stretching from Manzanita to the mouth of the Nehalem River is a vast campground with hot showers. Sites are a little bit close together with few trees to screen the neighbors; dunes separate campers from the ocean. As big as this park is, it does fill up in summer, so reservations are recommended (particularly July-Aug.). To get there, turn south at Bayshore Junction just before U.S. 101 heads east into the town of Nehalem.

Food

House renters, budget diners, and picnickers can take advantage of the excellent produce and impressive (for a coastal market) grocery section at **Manzanita Grocery & Deli** (193 Laneda Ave., 503/368-5362, 8am-8pm daily). One block away, **Mother Nature's Natural Foods Store** (298 Laneda Ave., 503/368-5316, 10am-7pm Mon.-Sat.) stocks natural groceries, coffees and teas, bulk foods, wine, and beer.

Stop at **Manzanita News & Espresso** (500 Laneda Ave., 503/368-7450, 7:30am-2pm daily, $2-5) for coffee, a pastry, and a magazine (there are lots to choose from, and the selection is anything but generic).

The local bakery, **Bread and Ocean** (154 Laneda Ave., 503/368-5823, 7:30am-2pm Wed.-Sat., 8am-2pm Sun., $4-9), makes sandwiches as well as cinnamon rolls. The locals' favorite for hefty traditional breakfasts is **Big Wave Cafe** (822 Laneda Ave., 503/368-9283, 7am-9pm Fri.-Wed., 8am-9pm Thurs., $7-18), where you'll find Makin' Waves Eggs Benedict, dressed with spinach and chipotle-pepper hollandaise sauce.

Left Coast Siesta (288 Laneda Ave., 503/368-7997, 11:30am-8pm Mon.-Sat., noon-7pm Sun., closed Mon.-Tues. winter, $6-8) specializes in design-your-own burritos, the perfect takeout for a beach lunch or dinner. Options include spicy beef, spicy chicken, tequila-lime chicken, or black beans to fill a selection of flavored tortillas. It also serves tacos and enchiladas. And if you like it *caliente,* this is the place for you: Left Coast Siesta stocks a hot sauce bar with 200-plus different types of the hot stuff, many available to purchase by the jar.

Just a couple of blocks from the beach,

Marzano's (60 Laneda Ave., 503/368-3663, 4pm-8:30pm Sun.-Mon. and Thurs., 4pm-9pm Fri., noon-9pm Sat., large pies mostly $20-25) serves the area's best slices of gourmet pizza. The roasted vegetable pizza is recommended, and the smoked prosciutto with aged montegrappa cheese is another winner.

For relaxed fine dining, the best option is **Neah-Kah-Nie Bistro** (519 Laneda Ave., 503/368-2722, 11:30am-4pm and 5pm-8pm Tues.-Thurs and Sun., 5pm-9pm Fri.-Sat., $16-27), a small dining room serving local seafood and meats with up-to-date continental preparations. Halibut cheeks are sautéed in lemon butter, champagne, and capers, while grilled pork chops come with house-made pear chutney.

For drinks and light meals, try **Great Northern Garlic Company** (868 Laneda Ave., 503/368-7700, $6-18), a well-stocked wine bar that serves a broad selection of small plates, including caprese salad, cheese fondue, barbecue oysters, and seasonal fish specials such as just caught Dungeness crab. There's not a lot of room in the dining room, but in summer and early fall there is amble seating on the patio (gas heaters are available to take the chill off). This operation often closes in winter and early spring; call to confirm hours outside of May-Dec.

NEHALEM

Tiny Nehalem (pop. 205) occupies just a few blocks along U.S. 101 on the north bank of the Nehalem River. It's a lovely location with a few Old West-style storefronts. Sizable runs of spring and fall chinook salmon and winter steelhead make this a popular destination for anglers. In August, locals claim you could just about cross the river stepping from boat to boat when the fish are in. Just southwest of town, the county maintains a boat launch facility and dock, providing access to the river and to the bay downstream. The bay and slow-moving river also invite exploration by kayak and canoe; bring your own, or rent them in nearby Wheeler. Be sure to pack the binoculars: The Nehalem River is a good place to watch birds.

Wineries

The **Nehalem Bay Winery** (34965 Hwy. 53, 503/368-9463, www.nehalembaywinery.com) offers tastings and sales of its varietals (pinot noir, Gewürztraminer), as well as fruit and berry wines (including delicious blackberry). You can tour the grounds and picnic 10am-6pm daily or enjoy the tasting room's welcoming milieu. To get to the winery, look for the Highway 53 sign on U.S. 101 and head east 1.5 miles.

Accommodations

If you'd like to overnight close to the river—*on* the river—try the **Ripple Run Resort and Marina** (35165 U.S. 101 N., 503/368-3865 or 877/655-0623, www.ripplerunresort.com, $100-199). Choose among four one-of-a-kind floating lodgings, including a 35-foot barge that sleeps 4-6 for $135 nightly, or a 47-foot converted tug that sleeps two. If a night on the water doesn't entice you, opt for a room in a riverside cottage. All units include linens, towels, kitchenettes with dishes, gas barbecues, cable TV, and videos. Reservations are recommended.

Food

The **C** **Nehalem River Inn** (34910 Hwy. 53, 503/368-7708, hours vary, call for reservations, $27-31) is one of the best places on the coast to experience fresh and inventive Pacific Northwest cuisine. The inn's sophisticated menu blends Pacific Northwest seafood, game, locally grown organic produce, wild mushrooms, and other ingredients to create dishes that will turn the heads of even the most discriminating diners—such as Muscovy duck breast served with black truffle potato gnocchi or Piedmontese flat iron steak with creamy corn bread, spring onion, and whiskey jam. Complement your meal with a bottle from a well-selected wine list favoring Oregon wineries, including Nehalem River Inn's own private-label wines. Reservations are recommended.

On the highway in Nehalem, **C Wanda's** (12870 U.S. 101 N., 503/368-8100, 8am-2pm Fri.-Tues., $7-12) is a popular breakfast and

THE WRECK OF THE *GLENESSLIN*

The sea was calm and the winds mild along the north Oregon coast on the afternoon of October 1, 1913, when locals observed a square-rigged ship sailing perilously close to the Nehalem shore. The Liverpool-built three-master *Glenesslin,* bound for Portland, was one of a dying breed of large sailing ships on the high seas, which were quickly being replaced by steam-powered vessels. Built in 1885, it was a fine ship, and fast: Its 74-day passage from Portland, Oregon, to Port Elizabeth, South Africa, was never surpassed by another square-rigger. But on this day, in the twilight of sail, seasoned and reliable crews were scarce—the ship's first and second officers were but 22 years old—and inexperience led to disaster.

According to maritime author James A. Gibbs, in his fascinating *Shipwrecks of the Pacific Coast,* the *Glenesslin,* under full sail, suddenly turned east toward the base of Neahkahnie Mountain. Losing the wind under the lee of Cape Falcon, Gibbs theorizes, the ship lost headway and the crew was unable to bring it about. As it neared the shore, an underwater reef ripped open the ship's bottom plates. The crew shot a line to shore, and with the help of local rescuers, all 21 hands made it safely to land—many of them, it was said, under the influence of strong drink. As breakers pounded the stern, grinding the ship against the rocks, it soon began to break up. A Nehalem man bought the dying vessel for $100, but there was little hope of salvaging much.

In the lengthy official inquiry that followed, the captain and second mate were judged negligent in their duties, and the first mate was reprimanded. The ship's underwriter initially balked at covering the loss, claiming that the ship had been intentionally wrecked in a scheme to collect the insurance, but the insurer eventually paid up. It was a heartbreaking end for a beautiful and storied ship.

lunch spot with old-fashioned granny's attic decor and delicious omelets, tuna melt sandwiches, and baked goods. Stop in for a muffin if nothing else.

WHEELER

Wheeler (pop. 393) is a little town flanking the Nehalem River where most accommodations are low-cost efficiencies for visiting fisherfolk, but the 10 guest rooms of the **Wheeler on the Bay Lodge and Marina** (580 Marine Dr., 503/368-5858 or 800/469-3204, www.wheeleronthebay.com, $90-155), on U.S. 101 on the shore of Nehalem Bay, have more appeal. Most guest rooms have at least partial bay views, and several have jetted tubs. There's also a video store, kayak rentals, and on-site massage services, and they can help arrange fishing charters.

Guest rooms at **The Old Wheeler Hotel** (495 U.S. 101, 503/368-6000 or 877/653-4683, www.oldwheelerhotel.com, $119-165), a 1920s landmark across the road from the bay, may

remind you of your great-aunt's guest room. They're old-fashioned in a very down-to-earth way. Although all guest rooms have private bathrooms, some bathrooms are down the hall from their rooms.

In a tiny cottage just off the main drag, the **◖ Rising Star Cafe** (92 Rorvik St., 503/368-3990, noon-3pm and 5pm-8pm Wed.-Thurs. and Sat., 5pm-8pm Fri., 10am-3pm Sun., $13-26) is a sweet spot for excellent pasta, sandwiches, and chowder—some of the best on the coast. There are only seven tables in this popular restaurant, so call ahead for reservations. The food can be very good here (if the brandied bread pudding is on the menu, go for it), and the atmosphere is comfortable and friendly.

ROCKAWAY BEACH

This town of 1,380 was established as a summer resort in the 1920s by Portlanders who wanted a coastal getaway. And so it remains today—a quiet spot without much going on besides walks on the seven miles of sandy beach, a **Kite Festival** in mid-May, and an **Arts and Crafts Fair** in mid-August. Shallow **Lake Lytle,** on the east side of the highway, offers spring and early summer fishing for trout, bass, and crappie. While the town of Rockaway is singularly unattractive from U.S. 101—a lengthy stretch of tacky shops, modest motels, and big new condos—the beach is quite nice, anchored at the south by the impressive Twin Rocks formation. The **Visitor Information Center** (503/355-8108, www. rockawaybeach.net), lodged in a bright red caboose in the center of town, can fill you in on other goings-on.

Accommodations

Rockaway's motels are basic and family-oriented; if you are planning in advance, take a moment to check out the beach houses available for rent on the **chamber of commerce website** (www.rockawaybeach.net).

The following motels are on the ocean side of busy U.S. 101, which dominates this long string bean of a town. **Surfside Resort Motel** (101 NW 11th St., 503/355-2312 or 800/243-7786, www.surfsideocean.com, $79-85 with no ocean view, $89-129 ocean view) is a large beachfront complex with an indoor pool. Some guest rooms with kitchens are available; for $59, you can also rent a simple "sleeping room" with basic facilities (including bathroom) but no view. **Silver Sands Oceanfront Resort** (215 S. Pacific Ave., 503/355-2206 or 800/457-8972, www.oregonsilversands.com, $136-166) is also right on the beach, with fairly basic rooms (some kitchenettes), an indoor pool and hot tub, and a sauna.

About a mile south of town, **Twin Rocks Motel** (7925 Minehaha St., 503/355-2391 or 877/355-2391, www.twinrocksmotel.net, $177-199) is a small cluster of dog-friendly two-bedroom oceanfront cottages. If you're looking for a simple, quiet getaway with family or a couple of friends, this might be your place.

Food

Cow Belle Cafe (194 U.S. 101 S., 503/355-2441, 8am-2pm Thurs.-Sun., $8-14) is a locals' favorite for breakfast. The biscuits and gravy here are renowned, as is the bovine-rich decor. The **Beach Bite** (162 U.S. 101 S., 503/355-2073, 11am-9pm Mon.-Thurs., 11am-11pm Fri., 8am-11pm Sat., 8am-9pm Sun., $6-20) is one of the classier dining places in town (don't worry, flip-flops and a sweatshirt will get you by), featuring burgers and pasta.

Tillamook Bay

GARIBALDI

Tillamook Bay's commercial fishing fleet is concentrated in this little port town (pop. 970) near the north end of the bay. Garibaldi, named in 1879 by the local postmaster for the Italian patriot, is a fish-processing center: Crabs, shrimp, fresh salmon, lingcod, and bottom fish (halibut, cabezon, rockfish, and sea perch) are the specialties. At the marina, **Garibaldi Cannery** (606 Commercial Dr., 503/322-3344, 7am-6pm Mon.-Sat.) gets crab, fish, and other seafood right off the boats, so the selection is both low-priced and fresh. If you want it fresher, you'll have to catch it yourself.

In addition to dock fishing, guide and charter services offer salmon and halibut fishing, bird-watching, and whale-watching excursions. North of Garibaldi on U.S. 101, the bay entrance is a good place to see brown pelicans, harlequin ducks, oystercatchers, and guillemots. The Miami River marsh, south of town, is a bird-watching paradise at low tide, when ducks and shorebirds hunt for food.

Garibaldi Maritime Museum

The small but interesting **Garibaldi Maritime Museum** (112 Garibaldi Ave., 503/322-8411, www.garibaldimuseum.com, 10am-4pm Thurs.-Mon. April-Nov., $3 adults, $2.50 seniors and children ages 5-18) retells the history

© BILL MCRAE

Watch out for salty characters on the Garibaldi docks.

of this longtime fishing village. It also focuses on the late-18th-century sailing world and the British sea captain Robert Gray and his historical vessels, the *Lady Washington* and the *Columbia Rediviva,* which explored the Pacific Northwest in 1787 and 1792. Among the museum displays are models of these ships, an eight-foot-tall reproduction of the *Columbia* figurehead, a half model of the *Columbia* showing how the ship was provisioned for long voyages, as well as reproductions of period musical instruments and typical sailors' clothing.

Oregon Coast Explorer Trains

The **Oregon Coast Scenic Railroad** (503/842-8206, www.ocsr.net, basic tours $18 adults, $17 seniors, $10 children ages 3-10) operates a number of rail excursions on a train pulled by a 1910 Heisler Locomotive Works steam engine between Garibaldi and Rockaway Beach. The basic tour is 1.5 hours round-trip; trains depart Garibaldi at noon, 2pm, and 4pm with opportunities to board in Rockaway Beach at 1pm and 3pm. The train operates weekends only Memorial Day-June and Labor Day-September, and daily July-August as well as assorted holidays throughout the year. Dinner trains are also offered.

Fishing

The town's fishing and crabbing piers attract visitors looking to catch their own. Rent fishing boats, crab traps, and other gear at the **Garibaldi Marina** (302 Mooring Basin Rd., 503/322-3312, www.garibaldimarina.com).

The **Miami River** and **Kilchis River,** which empty into Tillamook Bay south of Garibaldi, get the state's only two significant runs of chum salmon, a species much more common from Washington northward. There's a catch-and-release season for them mid-September-mid-November. Both rivers also get runs of spring chinook and are open for steelhead most of the year.

Several charter companies have offices at the marina. **Garibaldi Charters** (607 Garibaldi Ave., 503/322-0007, www.garibaldicharters. com) offers fishing excursions (a full day of

BAYOCEAN SPIT

At the western entrance to Tillamook Bay, a long narrow spit of land reaches north from Cape Meares nearly all the way to Garibaldi. Although today it's a good place for a long and sandy flat hike, it was once developed as the town of Bayocean, promoted as "the Atlantic City of the West."

In the early 1900s, two real estate developers, enchanted by the great views of the ocean, built a grand resort hotel on the spit and began selling lots. A giant natatorium—a heated saltwater surf pool—was built in 1914. Initially, the only access was by boat or ferry; in 1928 a road was built from Tillamook.

The town that grew on the four-mile-long spit was thriving when the inevitable erosion began to chip away at the peninsula. Houses slipped into the sea, and by the late 1930s most folks had packed up and left. By 1939 the natatorium had been swallowed up.

Since the early 1990s, the spit has been managed for protection and preservation of its ecosystem, which is dominated by beach grass and Scotch broom.

To reach Bayocean Spit from Tillamook, head west on the Three Capes Scenic Loop (3rd St. from downtown Tillamook) and travel three miles to the Bayocean Spit sign. Turn right and follow a gravel road 1.5 miles to the parking area.

---

salmon fishing runs about $105) and wildlife-viewing or whale-watching trips ($40 per person).

Accommodations and Camping

If you want to wake up on the docks, spend the night at **Harbor View Inn** (302 S. 7th St., 503/322-3251, www.harborviewfun.com, $79-95), a motel popular with fishers and sports enthusiasts. A more standard motel is the **Garibaldi House Inn** (502 Garibaldi Ave., 503/322-3338 or 877/322-6489, www.garibaldihouse.com, $119-139), which offers very pleasant rooms, as well as an indoor pool, hot tub, sauna, fitness room, and complimentary hot breakfast.

Both tent and RV campers are welcome at **Barview Jetty County Park** (503/322-3522, $15-30, reservations accepted), a large campground in the tiny community of Barview (2.5 miles north of Garibaldi) with easy access to the beach forming the north side of Tillamook Bay. Most of the sites are for tents, with a section reserved for hikers and bikers; hot showers are a welcome amenity.

Food

One of the joys of eating on the Oregon coast is getting really good fish-and-chips from rough-edged dives on the docks. In Garibaldi, the **Fisherman's Korner Restaurant** (306 Mooring Basin, 503/322-2033, 7:30am-3pm Thurs.-Mon., $6-12) is right on the wharf and offers absolutely fresh fish-and-chips and excellent clam chowder. Breakfasts here are massive—meant for hungry sailors.

If you're looking for pub grub, a good choice is **Ghost Hole Public House** (409 Garibaldi Ave., 503/322-2723, 11am-2:30am daily, $6-15) with good burgers and sandwiches and a friendly vibe.

Just north of Garibaldi, **Pirate's Cove Restaurant** (14170 U.S. 101 N., 503/322-2092, http://piratesonline.biz, noon-9pm Mon.-Tues., 8am-9pm Wed.-Sat., 8am-8pm Sun., dinner $10-30) is one of the better restaurants between Manzanita and Lincoln City, with a dramatic vista of the mouth of Tillamook Bay. Try the local oysters and razor clams. Lunches are a better deal than the rather expensive dinners.

Four miles south at the little enclave of Bay City is another temple to seafood. **Pacific Oyster** (5150 Oyster Bay Dr., 503/377-2323, 10am-7pm Sun.-Thurs., 10am-8pm Fri.-Sat., $5-16) is mostly an oyster-processing center, but it's also an excellent spot for a few oyster shooters or a quick meal. Although there are

NORTH COAST

a variety of seafood choices, the main draw is the oysters, which here are both for eating and entertainment. As you eat, you can watch the oyster shuckers in action next door, as the dining area overlooks the oyster-processing area.

TILLAMOOK

Without much sun or surf, what could possibly draw enough visitors to the town of Tillamook (pop. 4,500) to make it one of Oregon's top three tourism attractions? Superficially speaking, cheese factories and a World War II blimp hangar, in a town flanked by mudflats and rain-soaked dairy country, shouldn't pull in more than a million tourists per year. But they do. And after a drive down U.S. 101 or along the scenic Three Capes Loop, you too will be mysteriously drawn to the huge white, blue, and gold building proffering bite-size samples of cheddar, not to mention ice cream.

Tillamook County is home to more than 26,000 cows, which easily outnumber the county's human population. They're the foundation of the Tillamook County Creamery Association's famous cheddar cheese and other dairy products, which generate about $85 million in annual sales—this dwarfs the region's other important contributors to the local economy, fishing and oyster farming.

In 1940-1942, partially in response to a Japanese submarine firing on Fort Stevens in Astoria, the U.S. Navy built two blimp hangars south of town, the two largest wooden structures ever built, according to *The Guinness Book of World Records.* One of five naval air stations on the Pacific coast, the Tillamook blimp guard patrolled the waters from northern California to the San Juan Islands and escorted ships into Puget Sound. While all kinds of blimp stories abound in Tillamook bars, only one wartime encounter has been documented. Declassified records confirm that blimps were involved in the sinking of what was believed to be two Japanese submarines off Cape Meares. In late May 1943, two of the high-flying craft, assisted by U.S. Navy subchasers and destroyers,

dropped several depth charges on the submarines, which are still lying on the ocean floor.

Until 1946, when the station was decommissioned, the naval presence here created a boomtown. Bars and businesses flourished, and civilian jobs were easy to come by. After the war years, Tillamook County returned to the economic trinity of "trees, cheese, and ocean breeze" that has sustained the region to the present day.

Tillamook Cheese Factory

With over a million visitors a year, the **Tillamook Cheese Factory** (4175 U.S. 101 N., 503/842-4481, www.tillamookcheese.com, 8am-6pm daily Labor Day-mid-June, 8am-8pm daily summer, free) is far and away the county's biggest drawing card. The plant welcomes visitors with a reproduction of the *Morningstar,* the schooner that transported locally made butter and cheese in the late 1800s and now adorns the label of every Tillamook product. The quaint vessel symbolizing Tillamook cheese-making's humble beginnings stands in contrast to the technology and sophistication that go into making this world-famous lunchbox staple today.

Inside the plant, a self-guided tour follows the movement of curds and whey to the "cheddaring table." Whey is drained from the curds, which are then cut and folded. These processes are coordinated by white-uniformed workers in a stadium-size factory. As you look down on the antiseptic scene from the glassed-in observation area, it's hard to imagine this as the birthplace of many a grilled cheese sandwich. Tastes of a few samples, however, prove it's true.

User-friendly informational placards and historical displays recount Tillamook Valley's dairy history from 1851, when settlers began importing cows. The problem then was how to ship the milk to San Francisco and Portland. Even though salting butter to preserve it allowed exportation, ships still faced the difficulty of negotiating the treacherous Tillamook bar. In 1894, Peter McIntosh introduced techniques here to make cheddar cheese, whose long shelf life enabled it to be transported overland.

© BILL MCRAE

There's a reason that Tillamook is known for its cheese.

In the early 1900s, the Tillamook County Creamery Association absorbed smaller operations; the modern plant opened in 1949. Today, Tillamook produces tens of millions of pounds of cheese annually, including monterey jack, swiss, and multiple variations of the award-winning cheddar. Pepperoni, butter, cheese soup, milk, and other products are also available. There's a gift shop (more Holstein-themed tchotchkes than you've probably dreamed of) and a full-service restaurant, but the big attraction is the ice cream counter. Have a double-scoop chocolate peanut butter cone—worth every penny.

Blue Heron French Cheese Company

A quarter million people per year visit Tillamook County's *second*-most-popular attraction, **Blue Heron French Cheese Company** (2001 Blue Heron Dr., 503/842-8282, www.blueheronoregon.com, 9am-6pm daily Labor Day-mid-June; 8am-8pm daily mid-June-Labor Day, free), a mile south of the Tillamook Cheese Factory. Housed in a large white barn, Blue Heron is famous for its brie-style cheese (though it's not produced on-site). In addition to cheeses and other gourmet foods, the shop sells gift baskets; over 250 varieties of Oregon wines are available in the wine-tasting room. A deli serves lunches of homemade soups and salads. For kids, there's a petting farm with the usual barnyard suspects.

Tillamook Air Museum

South of town off U.S. 101, you can't possibly miss the enormous Quonset hut-like building east of the highway. The world-class aircraft collection of the **Tillamook Air Museum** (6030 Hangar Rd., 503/842-1130, www.tillamookair.com, 9am-5pm daily, $12 adults, $11 seniors, $8 children ages 6-17) is housed in and around Hangar B of the decommissioned Tillamook Naval Air Station. At 1,072 feet long, 206 feet wide, and 192 feet high, it's the largest wooden structure in the world, and it's worth the price of admission just to experience the enormity of it. During World War II, this and another gargantuan hangar on the site (which burned down in 1992) sheltered eight K-class blimps, each 242 feet long.

Inside the seven-acre structure, you can learn about the role the big blimps played during wartime as well as how they are used today. In addition, there's a large collection of World War II fighter planes (many one-of-a-kind models) as well as photos and artifacts from the naval air station days. Be sure to check out the cyclo-crane, a combination blimp, plane, and helicopter. This was devised in the 1980s to aid in remote logging operations; it ended up an $8 million bust.

To get there from downtown, take U.S. 101 south two miles, make a left at the flashing yellow light, and follow the signs. If you want to see the historic aircraft in Tillamook's hangars, then do so soon. The air museum will move to Madras, in central Oregon, by 2016.

© BILL MCRAE

The Tilamook Air Museum is housed in a World War II hangar.

Tillamook County Pioneer Museum

East of the highway in the heart of downtown, **Tillamook County Pioneer Museum** (2106 2nd St., 503/842-4553, www.tcpm.org, 10am-4pm Tues.-Sun., $4 adults, $3 seniors, $1 children ages 7-10) is famous for its taxidermy exhibits as well as memorabilia from pioneer households. Particularly intriguing are hunks of ancient beeswax with odd inscriptions recovered from near Neahkahnie Mountain, which are thought to be remnants from 18th-century shipwrecks. The old courtroom on the second floor has one of the best displays of natural history in the state. There are many beautiful dioramas, plus shells, insects, and nests. The Beals Memorial Room houses a large rock, mineral, and fossil collection.

Latimer Quilt and Textile Center

The collection at the **Latimer Quilt and Textile Center** (2105 Wilson River Loop Rd., www.latimerquiltandtextile.com, 503/842-8622, 10am-5pm Mon.-Sat., noon-4pm Sun. Apr.-Oct., 10am-4pm Mon.-Sat. Nov.-Mar., $3) includes quilts from the 1850s to the present as well as looms, spinning wheels, and a variety of woven items. On Friday, you can see weavers at work; lessons can be arranged by calling ahead. The center, housed in a restored school, is just south and east of the cheese factory.

Munson Creek Falls

The highest waterfall in the Oregon Coast Range is lovely **Munson Creek Falls,** which drops 266 feet over mossy cliffs surrounded by an old-growth forest. A steep 0.25-mile trail leads to the base of the falls, while another slightly longer trail leads to a higher viewpoint; wooden walkways clinging to the cliff lead to a small viewing platform. This is a spectacle in all seasons, but come in winter when the falls pour down with greater fury.

To reach the falls, seven miles south of Tillamook turn east from U.S. 101 on Munson Creek Road and drive 1.5 miles on the very narrow, bumpy dirt access road that leads to the parking lot. Note that motor homes and trailers cannot get into the park; the lot is too small.

THE LOST TREASURE OF NEAHKAHNIE MOUNTAIN

Is there pirate gold on Neahkahnie Mountain? Local native legends tell of Spanish pirates burying a treasure here. One story relates that the crew of a shipwrecked Manila galleon salvaged its cargo of gold and beeswax (a valuable commodity in trade with Asia) by burying it in the side of the mountain. To deter natives from going to the site, the pirates killed a black man and buried him on top of the cargo. While this account taken from native histories has never been substantiated, a piece of crudely inscribed beeswax retrieved from the Neahkahnie region carbon-dated AD 1500-1700 (on display at the **Tillamook County Pioneer Museum**) keeps speculation alive. Further intrigue was added by the 1993 discovery of an ancient wooden rigging block. Found in the mud at the mouth of the Nehalem River, it was determined by a Spanish maritime expert to have been from a Manila galleon during that same time period. Lewis and Clark's 1805 reports of a Chinook with red hair, and similar accounts from the Vancouver Expedition's 1792 encounter with a redheaded native who claimed his late father had been a shipwrecked Spanish sailor, would tend to corroborate the shipwreck and treasure stories passed down in oral histories.

Tillamook State Forest

A series of intense forest fires in the 1930s and 1940s burned vast amounts of land in the northern Coast Range. Most of this land was owned by private timber companies, who walked away from the seemingly worthless "Tillamook Burn," leaving property rights to revert to the counties, who then handed the land over to the state. A massive replanting effort ensued, and in 1973 the Tillamook Burn became the **Tillamook State Forest.** In 2006 the Tillamook Forest Center opened in a soaring timbered building in the middle of the once-burned, now-lush forest. Be sure to stop in to see the short movie about the area's history; the vivid fire scenes are a bit frightening—a sensation that's enhanced when the smell of smoke is released into the auditorium. Don't leave without walking out through the center's back door, crossing the footbridge, and taking at least a short hike, where you'll see an assortment of native wildflowers, shrubs, and trees. If you head west from the bridge, Wilson Falls is about two miles away.

If a short hike outside the Forest Center leaves you hankering for more, head east along Highway 6 to the Kings Mountain trailhead. On a clear day (ha!) there are good views from the top. Several more trails start at the summit of the Coast Range. The campgrounds along Highway 6, including Jones Creek, which is right next to the **Tillamook Forest Center** (45500 Wilson River Hwy., 503/815-6800 or 866/930-4646, www.tillamookforestcenter. org, 10am-5pm daily Memorial Day-Labor Day, reduced hours spring and fall, closed in winter, free), are popular with off-road vehicle drivers, who have their own trail network back in the hills.

Hiking

The Tillamook State Forest offers plenty of recreational opportunities. From a distance, the forest seems like a tree plantation, but hidden waterfalls, old railroad trestles from the days of logging trains, and moss-covered oaks in the Salmonberry River Canyon will convince you otherwise. Bird-watchers and mushroom pickers can easily penetrate this thicket thanks to 1,000 miles of maintained roads and old railroad grades.

Two challenging trails off Highway 6, **Kings Mountain** (25 miles east of Tillamook) and **Elk Mountain** (28 miles east of Tillamook) climb through lands affected by the Tillamook Burn, but with scenic views throughout. Thanks to salvage logging in the wake of the disaster and subsequent replanting, myriad trails crisscross forests of Douglas and noble fir, hemlock, and

NORTH COAST

red alder. Stop at the visitor center for maps and trail descriptions.

Fishing

Among Oregon anglers, Tillamook County is known for its steelhead and salmon. Motorists along U.S. 101 can tell the fall chinook run has arrived when fishing boats cluster outside the Tillamook Bay entrance at Garibaldi. As the season wears on, the fish—affectionately called "hogs" because they sometimes weigh in at more than 50 pounds—make their way inland up the five coastal rivers—the Trask, Wilson, Tillamook, Kilchis, and Miami—that flow into Tillamook Bay. At their peak, the runs create such competition for favorite holes that the process of sparring for them is jocularly referred to as "combat fishing," as fishing boats anchor up gunwale to gunwale to form a fish-stopping palisade called a "hogline." Smokehouses and gas stations dot the outer reaches of the bay to cater to this fall influx.

The **Guide Shop Inc.** (12140 Wilson River Hwy., Tillamook, 503/842-3474, www.guideshop.com) can arrange for a full day of fishing for chinook and silver salmon, steelhead, sturgeon, or trout; rates are about $150 per person for one to four anglers. Nearby Garibaldi is home base for several other charter operations.

Golf

Golfers choose between two public courses in Tillamook. Near the cheese factory and east of U.S. 101, find nine-hole **Bay Breeze Golf Course** (2325 Latimer Rd., Tillamook, 503/842-1166, 8am-6pm Mon.-Fri., 8am-7pm Sat.-Sun., $10-15 for 9 holes). Another two miles north, **Alderbrook Golf Course** (7300 Alderbrook Rd., Tillamook, 503/842-6413, www.alderbrookgolfcourse.com, 9am-dusk, $30-45 for 18 holes) has 18 holes.

Wildlife-Viewing

Bird-watchers flock to Tillamook Bay June-November to view pelicans, sandpipers, tufted puffins, blue herons, and a variety of shorebirds. Prime time is before high tide, but step

lively because this waterway was originally called "quicksand bay."

Accommodations

Most travelers seem to pass through Tillamook on their way to someplace else, and there are plenty of chain motels available all along the busy U.S. 101 strip north of town. A good local choice along this strip is **Ashley Inn** (1722 N. Makinster Rd., 503/842-7599 or 800/299-4817, www.ashleyinntillamook.com, $120-140), close to the cheese factory. Rooms have a refrigerator, a microwave, an iron and ironing board, a coffeemaker, and cable TV. Amenities include an indoor pool, a sauna, and a hot tub, plus a complimentary continental breakfast.

There's not a lot going on in downtown Tillamook, but if you'd like to stay in the center of things, as opposed to the lengthy and busy commercial strip north of town, then book a room at the **Mar-Clair Inn** (11 Main Ave., 503/842-7571 or 800/331-6857, www.marclair.com, $79-99), a pleasant motor court tucked just off 101 with an outdoor pool and a restaurant.

Food

To sample the county's freshest produce, visit the **Tillamook Farmers Market** in downtown Tillamook. It runs every Saturday, mid-June-late September, at the corner of 2nd Street and Laurel Avenue.

The **Farmhouse Cafe** (8am-6pm daily Labor Day-mid-June, 8am-8pm daily summer, $4-8) at the Tillamook Cheese Factory serves breakfast and lunch. The deli at the **Blue Heron French Cheese Company** (2001 Blue Heron Dr., 503/842-8282, www.blueheronoregon.com, 9am-6pm daily Labor Day-mid-June, 8am-8pm daily summer) fixes sandwiches, soups, and salads daily; in polls conducted by the local paper, this is one of the locals' favorite lunch spots. **La Mexicana** (2203 3rd St., 503/842-2101, 11am-9pm daily, $8-16) is the town's best Mexican restaurant. This restaurant, housed in a vintage home on the edge of downtown, goes way beyond tacos and burritos, preparing local fish and seafood with south-of-the-border zest and finesse.

In downtown Tillamook, attempts to open fine dining restaurants have faltered in recent years, but one promising spot is **◖ Pacific Restaurant** (2102 1st St., 503/354-2350, http://pacificrestaurant.info, 11:30am-9pm Thurs.-Tues., $12-29) with an eclectic menu featuring local seafood and seasonal produce. The exterior of the restaurant (right downtown) is very unassuming, but the food—including pasta, salads, salmon, and chowders—is very well prepared. Also downtown is **Fat Dog Pizza** (116 Main St., 503/354-2283, 11:30am-9pm Sun.-Thurs., 11:30am-10pm Fri.-Sat., $15). Pizzas feature house-made dough (the Fat Dog Special is for meat lovers), and the submarine sandwiches, called Zeppelins in honor of Tillamook's dirigible history, are tasty. For burgers and microbrews, try **Corky's Bar & Grill** (204½ Main St. 503/842-6960, 11am-2:30am Tues.-Sun., $8-15).

On the west side of U.S. 101, between the two cheese meccas, lunchtime do-it-yourselfers might check the locally raised and cured meat and smoked salmon at **Debbie D's Sausage Factory** (503/842-2622).

Take your time to savor a cup of tea at **La Tea Da Tea Room** (904 Main Ave., 503/842-5447, 11am-4pm Mon.-Sat. summer, 11am-4pm Tues.-Sat. winter, high tea $21). Go for the full high tea or settle for scones, soup, or little tea sandwiches.

Information

The **Tillamook Chamber of Commerce** (3705 U.S. 101 N., 503/842-7525, www.tillamook-chamber.org, 9am-5pm Mon.-Fri.) is located across the parking lot from the cheese factory.

Three Capes Scenic Loop

The Three Capes Scenic Loop, a 35-mile byway off U.S. 101 between Tillamook and Pacific City, stays close to the ocean, which U.S. 101 does not. And although the beauty of Capes Meares, Lookout, and Kiwanda certainly justifies leaving the main highway, it would be an overstatement to portray this drive as a thrill-a-minute detour on the order of the south coast's Boardman State Park or the central coast's Otter Crest Loop. Instead of fronting the ocean, the road connecting the capes winds mostly through dairy country, small beach towns, and second-growth forest. What's special here are the three capes themselves, and unless you get out of the car and walk on the trails, you'll miss the aesthetic appeal and distinctiveness of each headland's ecosystem. The wave-battered bluffs of Cape Kiwanda, the precipitous overlooks along the Cape Lookout Highway, and the curious Octopus Tree at Cape Meares are the perfect antidotes to the inland towns along this stretch of U.S. 101. The majority of the Three Capes lodging and dining options are clustered in Netarts and Oceanside and at the other end in Pacific City. In between, it's mostly sand dunes, isolated beaches, rainforest, and pasture. To reach the Three Capes Scenic Loop from the north, turn west at Tillamook and follow signs to Cape Meares. From the south, follow signs north of Neskowin to Pacific City.

CAPE MEARES STATE SCENIC VIEWPOINT

With stunning views, picnic tables, a newly re-stored lighthouse, and a uniquely contorted tree a short walk from the parking lot, **Cape Meares State Scenic Viewpoint** is the most effortless site to visit on the Three Capes Loop. It was named for English navigator John Meares, who mapped many points along this coast in a 1788 voyage. The famed **Octopus Tree** is less than 0.25 mile up a forested hill. The tentacle-like extensions of this Sitka spruce have also been compared to candelabra arms.

The 45-foot diameter of its base supports

NORTH COAST

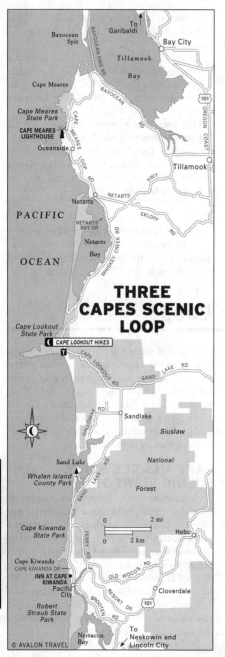

THREE CAPES SCENIC LOOP

© AVALON TRAVEL

five-foot-thick trunks, each of which by itself is large enough to be a single tree. Scientists have propounded several theories for the cause of its unusual shape, including everything from wind and weather to insects damaging the spruce when it was young. A Native American legend about the spruce contends that it was shaped this way so that the branches could hold the canoes of a chief's dead family. Supposedly, the bodies were buried near the tree. This was a traditional practice among the tribes of the area, who referred to species formed thusly as "council trees."

Beyond the tree you can look south at Oceanside and Three Arch Rocks Wildlife Refuge. The sweep of Pacific shore and off-shore monoliths makes a fitting beginning (or finale, if you're driving from the south) to your sojourn along the Three Capes Scenic Loop, but be sure also to stroll the short paved trail down to the lighthouse, which begins at the parking lot and provides dramatic views of an offshore wildlife refuge, **Cape Meares Rocks.** Bring binoculars to see tufted puffins, pelagic cormorants, seals, and sea lions. The landward portion of the refuge protects rare old-growth evergreens.

The restored interior of **Cape Meares Lighthouse** (503/842-2244, 11am-4pm daily Apr.-Oct., free) was built in 1890. This beacon was replaced as a functioning light in 1963 by the automated facility behind it, and it now houses a gift shop. A free tour is occasionally offered by volunteers who might tell you about how the lighthouse was built here by mistake and perhaps offer a peek into the prismatic Fresnel lenses.

OCEANSIDE

The road between Cape Meares and Netarts heads into the beach house community of Oceanside (pop. about 340). Many of the homes are built into the cliff overlooking the ocean, Sausalito style. This maze of very steep, very narrow streets reaches its apex atop Maxwell Point. You can peer several hundred feet down at **Three Arch Rocks Wildlife Refuge** (www.fws.gov), part-time home to one

© BILL MCRAE

Cape Meares Lighthouse

of the continent's largest and most varied collections of shorebirds. A herd of sea lions also populates this trio of sea stacks from time to time.

Accommodations and Food

There aren't many lodging options in Oceanside. While low prices and a window on the water can be found at **Ocean Front Cabins** (1610 Pacific Ave., 503/842-6081 or 888/845-8470, www.oceanfrontcabins.com, $70-125), the older, smallish guest rooms here might give upscale travelers pause. Nonetheless, for as little as $70 for a sleeping unit without a kitchenette—or $125 for a two-bed room with a full kitchen—you'll find yourself literally a stone's throw from Oceanside's beachcombing and dining highlights. Pets are accepted in some cabins.

For a more stylish lodging, consider **Thyme and Tide B&B** (5015 Grand Ave., 503/842-5527, www.thyme-and-tide.com, $150-160), with two handsome rooms with ocean views and a location between Netarts and Oceanside.

Another good lodging option is **Bender Vacation Rental Properties** (503/233-4363, www.benderproperties.com/beachrentals. html), boasting six units with cliff-side ocean views, large private decks, and full kitchens (except for one unit). Other amenities include fireplaces, TVs, VCRs, and microwaves. Pets are welcome at most locations. For $80-125 per night with a two-night minimum, this is a great deal.

A popular draw for hungry Three Capes travelers, █ **Roseanna's Oceanside Cafe** (1490 Pacific Ave. NW, 503/842-7351, www. roseannascafe.com, 9am-9pm daily, call to confirm winter hours, $11-19) garners high marks from just about everyone. At first, the weather-beaten cedar-shake exterior might lead you to expect an old general store, as indeed it was decades ago. Once you're inside, however, the ornate decor leaves little doubt that this place takes its new identity seriously. From an elevated perch above the breakers, you'll be treated to expertly prepared local oysters, fresh salmon, a bevy of chicken dishes, and interesting pastas, such as gorgonzola and pear with penne noodles. Be sure to save room for blackberry cobbler; order it warm so the Tillamook Vanilla Bean ice cream on top melts down the sides, and watch the waves over a long cup of coffee.

Blue Agate Cafe (1610 Pacific Ave., 503/815-2596, 8am-5pm Mon. and Thurs., 8am-6pm Sat.-Sun., $7-15), is a happening little eatery in the center of Oceanside with fun breakfasts (try the Dungeness crab scramble), sandwiches, pasta, and excellent fish tacos.

NETARTS

Netarts (pop. about 750) has an enviable location overlooking Netarts Bay and the Pacific beyond. Along with nearby Oceanside, it's the closest coastal settlement to Tillamook and makes for a fine quiet getaway. Netarts Bay and seven-mile-long Netarts Spit are popular with clam diggers and crabbers, who can launch boats from Netarts Landing at the northeast corner of the bay. **Netarts Bay RV Park and Marina** (2260 Bilyeu St., 503/842-7774) and

© BILL MCRAE

Oceanside's Blue Agate Cafe

Big Spruce RV Park (4850 Netarts Hwy. W., 503/842-7443) rent motorboats and crabbing supplies.

Accommodations and Food

The **Terimore** (5105 Crab Ave., 503/842-4623 or 800/635-1821, www.terimoremotel.com, motel rooms $74-95, cabins $72-99) is situated a short walk from the water at the north end of Netarts Bay. Other than some units with fireplaces and kitchens, there are few frills, but for fair rates you'll find yourself close to the water, within easy driving distance of the Cape Lookout Trail, and a beach walk away from Roseanna's, the best restaurant on the Three Capes Scenic Loop.

For more up-to-date comforts, **Edgewater Motel and Vacation Rentals** (1st St. and Crab Ave., 503/842-1300 or 888/425-1050, www.oregoncoastmotels.com, $279) offers four luxury two-bedroom rentals directly above Netarts Bay. Each unit has two massive stone fireplaces (one in the master bedroom, one in the "great room"), a 650-gallon Jacuzzi tub, two

balconies, and a well-equipped kitchen. Each unit sleeps up to eight people (with two queen-size foldout couches). The views can't be beat. If you don't require this level of sophistication, there are also vintage cabins and cottages on the same property, each with kitchens and TVs with a DVD player, and some have fireplaces ($100-200).

You'll find several lunch and dinner spots to choose from. The view of Cape Lookout is tops at **The Schooner** (2065 Netarts Bay Rd., 503/842-4988, 11am-8pm Mon.-Thurs., 7am-9pm Fri.-Sat., 7am-8pm Sun. $10-25), and the food is a nice surprise also. Stop by for some steamer clams, fresh oysters, or tasty wood-fired pizza.

Sugarfoot's (4740 Netarts Highway W., 503/354-2422, 11am-7pm Tues.-Thurs., 11am-8pm Fri.-Sat., $8-10) offers well-prepared comfort food both to eat on premises and to go. You'll find fresh local oysters, fried Spam sliders, Italian subs, lots of veggie sandwiches, wraps, and the house specialty burger with a turkey and black bean patty. This is a friendly spot with really tasty, rather unorthodox casual dining options.

CAPE LOOKOUT STATE PARK

One of the scenic highlights of the Three Capes route, **Cape Lookout State Park** (off U.S. 101, www.oregonstateparks.org, $5 day use) juts out nearly a mile from the mainland, like a finger pointing out to sea. The cliffs along the south side of the cape rise 800 feet from the Pacific's pounding waves. The best way to take in the vista and the thrill of the location is on foot.

◖ Hiking

Hiking to the end of mile-wide Cape Lookout is one of the top coast hikes in Oregon. The trail begins either at the campground, where it climbs 2.5 miles up to a ridgetop trailhead with a parking lot, or from the Three Capes road at a well-signed trailhead. An orientation map at the trailhead details the options. The main 2.5-mile trail out to the end, along the narrowing finger of land, can give hikers the impression that they're on the prow of a giant ship suspended 500 feet above the ocean on all sides. Here, more than anywhere else on the Oregon coast, you get the sense of being on the edge of the continent. Giant spruce, western red cedars, and hemlocks surround the gently hilly trail to the tip of the cape. In March, Cape Lookout is a popular vantage point for whale-watching. June through August, a bevy of wildflowers and birds further enhance the rolling terrain en route to the tip of this headland, and in late summer red huckleberries line the path.

Halfway to the overlook, there are views north to Cape Meares over the Netarts sand spit. Even if you settle for a mere 15-minute stroll down the trail, you can look southward beyond Haystack Rock to Cascade Head. Right about where the trees open up, look for a bronze plaque commemorating the crash of a World War II plane and nearly a dozen casualties, which is embedded in the rock wall bordering the right-hand (north) side of the trail at eye level. If you're unable to take this hike, two unmarked turnouts along the Three Capes road between the sand dunes and Cape Lookout parking lot let you survey the terrain south to Cape Kiwanda. Don't be surprised if you see hang gliders and paragliders.

Another popular trail in the state park heads north from the campground through a variety of estuarine habitats along the sand spit separating Netarts Bay from the Pacific. It's a popular site for agate hunters, clammers, and crabbers.

Camping

At the southern end of Netarts Spit is the state park's **campground and beach extension** (13000 Whiskey Creek Rd. W., 503/842-4981 for information, 800/452-5687 or www.reserveamerica.com for reservations, $5-76), which also encompasses the entire cape and the seven-mile-long Netarts Spit within its boundaries. The campground has 173 tent sites ($15-19) and 38 full-hookup sites ($20-24), as well as 13 yurts ($36), three cabins (with bathrooms, a kitchen, and a TV/VCR, $56-76), and a hiker-biker camp ($5); discounts apply October-April. Some yurts accept pets ($10 fee). Amenities include showers, flush toilets, and evening programs. Reservations and a deposit are almost always needed at this popular campground.

South of Cape Lookout, the terrain suddenly changes. Extensive sand dunes surrounding the Sand Lake Estuary suddenly appear, drowning the forest in sand. The dunes and beach attract squadrons of dune buggy enthusiasts. Camping is available year-round at **Sand Beach Campground** (5 miles south of Cape Lookout on Galloway Rd., 503/392-3161 or 877/444-6777, $16, reservations at www.recreation.gov), a part of the Siuslaw National Forest, with has basic sites for tenters and RVs. This dramatic area is also popular with hikers.

PACIFIC CITY AND CAPE KIWANDA

As you approach the shore in Pacific City, the sight of **Haystack Rock** will immediately grab your attention. At 327 feet, this sea stack is nearly 100 feet taller than the similarly named rock in Cannon Beach. Standing a mile offshore, this monolith has a brooding, enigmatic

NORTH COAST

quality that constantly draws the eye to it. Look closely, and you'll understand why some folks called it Teacup Rock.

The tawny sandstone escarpment of Cape Kiwanda juts half a mile out to sea from Pacific City and frames the north end of the beach. In storm-tossed waters, this cape is the undisputed king of rock-and-roll, if you go by coffee table books and calendar photos. While other sandstone promontories on the north coast have been ground into sandy beaches by the pounding surf, it's been theorized that Kiwanda has endured thanks to the buffer of Haystack Rock. In any case, hang gliding aficionados are glad the cape is here. They scale its shoulders and set themselves aloft off the north face to glide above the beach and dunes.

The small town of Pacific City, with about 1,000 residents, is at the base of Cape Kiwanda. It attracts growing numbers of vacationers and retirees but remains true to its 19th-century origins as a working fishing village. In addition to the knockout seascapes and recreation, if you come here at the right times of day, you may be treated to a unique spectacle—the launch or return of the **dory fleet.**

It's a tradition dating back to the 1920s, when gillnetting was banned on the Nestucca River to protect the dwindling salmon runs. To retain their livelihood, commercial fishers began to haul flat-bottomed double-ended dories down to the beach on horse-drawn wagons, then row out through the surf to fish. These days, trucks and trailers get the boats to and from the beach, and outboard motors have replaced oar power, enabling the dories to get 50 miles out to sea. If you come around 6am, you can watch them taking off. The fleet's late afternoon return attracts a crowd that arrives to see the dory operators skidding their craft as far as possible up the beach to the waiting boat trailers. Others meet the dories to buy salmon and tuna.

In mid-July, **Dory Days** celebrate the area's fleet. The three-day fete includes craft and food booths, a pancake breakfast, a fishing derby, and other activities. For more information, call the **chamber of commerce** (503/965-6161). If you want to join the anglers for a summertime ocean fishing trip on a dory, contact **Haystack Fishing** (888/965-7555), across from the beach near the Inn at Cape Kiwanda.

In addition, the Pacific City area is besieged by surfers, who enjoy some of the longest waves on the Oregon coast. **Robert Straub State Park,** just south of town, offers access to Nestucca Bay and to the dunes and a long uninterrupted stretch of beach. Pacific City surfers should use *extreme* caution when the dories are returning to the beach.

Accommodations

The nicest motel on the Three Capes Scenic Loop is the large ◖ **Inn at Cape Kiwanda** (33105 Cape Kiwanda Dr., 503/965-6366 or 888/965-7001, www.yourlittlebeachtown. com/inn, $189-229). All rooms face a beautiful beach and Cape Kiwanda's giant sand dune. If it's too rainy to go outside, fireplaces and spacious well-appointed rooms make for great storm-watching. Whirlpool tub rooms are available, and pets are permitted in some rooms.

For a more historic experience, head to the ◖ **Craftsman B&B** (35255 4th St., 503/965-4574, www.craftsmanbb.com, $150-180), an exquisitely refurbished Craftsman-style home with very stylish guest rooms. Built in 1921 (and perhaps Pacific City's oldest home), this B&B is a monument to sensitive historic preservation and also a very friendly, comfortable place to stay. All four guest rooms have private baths and are decorated according to the styles of Arts and Crafts luminaries such as Gustav Stickley, Charles Rennie Macintosh, and William Morris.

Camping

About 4.5 miles north of Pacific City on the Three Capes Loop Road, the **Clay Meyers Natural Area at Whalen Island** (4.5 miles north of Pacific City on Sandlake Rd., 503/965-6085, www.co.tillamook.or.us, $10-15) has a small campground run by Tillamook County. It's an open sandy spot with a boat launch and flush toilets; nearby hiking trails traverse wetlands and provide a great look at the coastal Sand Lake Estuary.

Food

A popular and well-known Pacific City hangout is the **(Pelican Pub and Brewery** (33180 Cape Kiwanda Dr., 503/965-7007, 8am-close daily, $6-23). Set in a most enviable spot right on the beach opposite Cape Kiwanda and Haystack Rock, this place boasts the best coastal view of any brewpub in Oregon. Buttermilk-beer pancakes, dory-caught fish-and-chips, pizzas, "shark bites," tasty chili, and IPA-poached salmon are some of the standouts. The pub's brews, including Tsunami Stout, Doryman's Dark Ale, India Pelican Ale, and MacPelican's Scottish Style Ale, have garnered stacks of awards.

Delicate Palate Bistro (35280 Brooten Rd., 503/965-6464, www.delicatepalate.com, 5pm-close Wed.-Sun., $17-25) is a classy little place where the chef brings a deft touch to classics—think pan-seared wild salmon with artichoke ragout or bouillabaisse made with a coconut curry broth and served with soba noodles—and the meals are backed up by an excellent wine list (or a long martini menu, if you prefer). The deck, which overlooks the local airstrip, is open for dining when weather allows.

Also on Brooten Road toward the north end of town, find the **(Grateful Bread Bakery** (34085 Brooten Rd., 503/965-7337, 8am-4pm Thurs.-Mon., $5-9), where the challah bread, carrot cake, marionberry strudel, and other homemade baked goods deserve special mention. The full breakfast menu offers a range of tasty omelets served with oven-roasted spuds at great prices. Lunch sandwiches include a wide range of vegetarian options.

Neskowin and Cascade Head

NESKOWIN

The tiny vacation village of Neskowin (rhymes with "let's go in," pop. 170) has a quiet appeal based on a beautiful beach and a golf course in the shadow of 1,500-foot-high Cascade Head. It's the polar opposite of busy Lincoln City, 15 miles south. There's not much to do here but relax on the uncrowded beach and enjoy the views of Cascade Head and the dark beauty of **Proposal Rock,** a stony, forested hillock that stands right at the edge of the surf, with Neskowin Creek curving around it. The feature was named by Neskowin's first postmistress, whose daughter received a marriage proposal nearby. Neskowin has the reputation as a beach town for old-money, in-the-know Portland families.

Sleepy Neskowin has only one art gallery, and it's a good one. **Hawk Creek Gallery** (48460 U.S. 101 S., 503/392-3879, www. hawkcreekgallery.com, 11am-5pm daily summer, 11am-5pm Sat.-Sun. spring and fall) is the studio and showroom for the works of painter Michael Schlicting, who exhibits his work internationally but has made the Hawk Creek Gallery his home base since 1978.

Neskowin Marsh Golf Course (48405 Hawk St., 503/392-3377, $18 for nine holes) has streams and water hazards adding a challenge to most of the nine greens.

Accommodations

Proposal Rock Inn (48988 U.S. 101 S., 503/392-3115, www.proposalrockneskowin. com, rooms $62-127, suites $125-240) backs up on Hawk Creek and commands a fine view of the beach and the eponymous rock. Two-room oceanview suites with a full kitchen fetch higher prices than the standard non-oceanview guest rooms, but all are right on the beach.

The nine two-bedroom condo units at **The Chelan** (48750 Breakers Blvd., 503/392-3270, www.rentoregoncoast.com, $125-245) are comfier than the boxy stucco exterior suggests, with fireplaces, kitchens, views, and direct access to the beach.

© BILL MCRAE

Neskowin's Hawk Creek Cafe is a top spot for breakfast.

To rent a home in the Neskowin or Pacific City area, contact the property management firm **Neskowin Vacation Rentals** (503/392-4850, http://neskowinvacationrentals.com).

Food

Neskowin's only restaurant, fortunately, serves great food at moderate prices. Waits can be long at the tiny **Hawk Creek Cafe** (4505 Salem Ave., 503/392-3838, 8am-9pm Thurs.-Sun., 11am-9pm Mon.-Wed., $12-23), but it's the only game in town and has good food. Count on filling omelets for breakfast; sandwiches (about $10), burgers, and wood-fired pizza ($16-18) for lunch; and grilled fish and steaks for dinner.

CASCADE HEAD
Cascade Head Scenic Research Area

About 10 miles north of Lincoln City, the 11,890-acre Cascade Head Experimental Forest was set aside in 1934 for scientific study of typical coastal Sitka spruce and western hemlock forests found along the Oregon coast. In 1974 Congress established the 9,670-acre **Cascade Head Scenic Research Area** (www.fsl.orst.edu/chef), which includes the western half of the forest, several prairie headlands, and the Salmon River estuary. In 1980 the entire area was designated a biosphere reserve as part of the United Nations Biosphere Reserve system.

The headlands, reaching as high as 1,800 feet, are unusual for their extensive prairies still dominated by native grasses: red fescue, wild rye, and Pacific reedgrass. The Nechesney Indians, who inhabited the area as long as 12,000 years ago, purposely burned forest tracts around Cascade Head probably to provide browse for deer and to reduce the possibility of larger uncontrollable blazes. These human-made alterations are complemented by the inherent dryness of south-facing slopes that receive increased exposure to the sun. In contrast to these grasslands, the northern part of the headland is the domain of giant spruces and firs because it catches the brunt of the heavy rainfalls and lingering fogs. Endemic wildflowers include coastal paintbrush, goldenrod, streambank lupine, rare hairy checkermallow, and blue violet, a plant critical to the survival of the Oregon silverspot butterfly, a threatened species found in only six locations. Deer, elk, coyotes, snowshoe hare, and the Pacific giant salamander find refuge here, while bald eagles, great horned owls, and peregrine falcons may be seen hunting above the grassy slopes. Today, in addition to its biological importance, the area is a mecca for some 6,000 hikers annually and for anglers who target the salmon and steelhead runs on the Salmon River.

On the north side of the Salmon River, turn west from U.S. 101 onto **Three Rocks Road** for a scenic driving detour on the south side of Cascade Head. The paved road curves about 2.5 miles above the wetlands and widening channel of the Salmon River estuary, passes Savage Road, and ends at a parking area and boat launch at Knight County Park. From the park, the road turns to gravel and narrows (not suitable for RVs or trailers) and continues about another 0.5 mile to its end at a spectacular overlook across the estuary.

HIKING

Cascade Head offers some outstanding scenic hikes, with rainforest pathways and wildflower meadows giving way to dramatic ocean views.

A short but brisk hike to the top of the headland on a **Nature Conservancy trail** begins near Knight County Park. Leave your car at the park and walk 0.5 mile up Savage Road to the trailhead. It's 1.7 miles one-way, with a 1,100-foot elevation gain. No dogs or bicycles are allowed on the trail, which is open year-round.

Two trails are accessible from Cascade Head Road (Forest Rd. 1861), a gravel road that is open seasonally (July 16-Dec. 31) that heads west off U.S. 101 about three miles north of Three Rocks Road, near the highway summit of Cascade Head. Travel this road four miles west of U.S. 101 to the **Hart's Cove Trailhead.** The first part of the trail runs through arching red alder treetops and 250-year-old Sitka spruces with five-foot diameters. The understory of mosses and ferns is nourished by 100-inch rainfalls. Next, the trail emerges into open grasslands. The five-mile round-trip hike loses 900 feet in elevation on its way to an oceanfront meadow overlooking Hart's Cove, where the barking of sea lions might greet you. This trail can have plenty of mud, so boots are recommended as you tromp through the rainforest.

An easier trail accessible from Cascade Head Road heads to a viewpoint on the Nature Conservancy's preserve. (Again, no dogs or bikes are allowed on Nature Conservancy land.) The one-mile trail starts about 3.5 miles west of U.S. 101 and heads to a big meadow and an ocean overlook. It's possible to continue from the overlook, heading downhill to join up with the lower Nature Conservancy trail described above.

The **Cascade Head Trail** runs six miles roughly parallel to the highway, with a south trailhead near the intersection of Three Rocks Road and U.S. 101 and a north trailhead at Falls Creek, on U.S. 101 about one mile south of Neskowin. It passes through old-growth forest and is entirely inland, without the spectacular ocean views of other trails in the area.

Sitka Center for Art and Ecology

The region in the shadow of Cascade Head can be explored in even greater depth thanks to the **Sitka Center for Art and Ecology** (56605 Sitka Dr., Otis, 541/994-5485, www.sitkacenter.org, 8:30am-4:30pm Mon.-Fri.), located off Savage Road on the south side of the headland. Classes are offered June-August focusing on art and nature, with an emphasis on the strong relationship between the two. Experts in everything from local plant communities to Siletz Indian baskets conduct outdoor workshops on the grounds of Cascade Head Ranch. Classes can last from a couple of days to a week, and fees vary accordingly.

CENTRAL COAST

Oregon's central coast, from Lincoln City to Reedsport and Winchester Bay, embraces such contrasts that it's difficult to generalize about the region.

In the north, Lincoln City's dense mix of lodgings and shopping, combined with its Native American casinos, generates the coast's worst traffic jams, especially on holidays and weekends. The sprawling town isn't everyone's first choice for a quiet getaway, but it's a longtime favorite with families. Depoe Bay—built around the world's smallest navigable natural harbor—is headquarters for the coast's busiest whale-watching fleet—and one of the largest and most sprawling condo developments.

A necklace of small state parks adorns the shore every couple of miles all the way from southern Lincoln City southward; inland, the Siuslaw National Forest safeguards several wilderness areas and groves of rare old-growth coastal forest, beckoning hikers to explore the primeval landscapes. Just north of Newport, Yaquina Head Outstanding Natural Area offers excellent vantage points for up close whale-watching and bird-watching, plus tidepools accessible to wheelchair users.

The bustling harbor at Newport is home to the state's largest commercial fishing fleet and second-largest recreational fleet, which runs charters year-round for rockfish and seasonally for salmon, tuna, and halibut. Newport also boasts the state-of-the-art Oregon Coast Aquarium, former residence of Keiko the beloved orca, and the bohemian resort community of Nye Beach, which

© JUDY JEWELL

HIGHLIGHTS

◖ Oregon Coast Aquarium: Explore the life of Oregon's shores and oceans at this excellent aquarium (page 340).

◖ Yaquina Head Outstanding Natural Area: A soaring lighthouse stands above a tidepool-studded inlet at this small park, the quintessence of the Oregon coast (page 342).

◖ Whale-Watching: *Thar she blows!* Newport is a great departure point for gray whale-watching tours (page 344).

◖ Cape Perpetua: One of the most dramatic natural areas along the Oregon coast, Cape Perpetua is a top spot for hiking and exploring tidepools (page 354).

◖ Sea Lion Caves: Take an elevator ride down to the caves at cliff's bottom to get a close look at the Steller sea lion rookery (page 361).

◖ Heceta Head Lighthouse and Devil's Elbow: Climb to the top of this whitewashed lighthouse for wonderful views—or stay in the lighthouse keeper's house, now a B&B (page 361).

◖ John Dellenback Trail: Explore 400-foot dunes in the Oregon Dunes National Recreation Area. It's like trekking the Sahara (page 374).

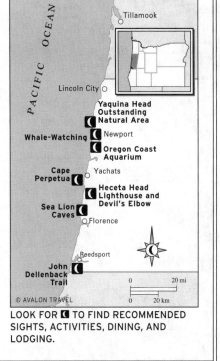

© AVALON TRAVEL

LOOK FOR ◖ TO FIND RECOMMENDED SIGHTS, ACTIVITIES, DINING, AND LODGING.

has been attracting tourists since the 19th century.

Just south of Yachats, the panoramic view from Cape Perpetua can, on a clear day, extend 75 miles in each direction. Down at sea level, the tidepools here are some of the most fascinating on the coast. At Sea Lion Caves, a touristy but unique experience between Yachats and Florence, the world's largest sea cave is the only mainland rookery of Steller sea lions in the lower 48 states. Close by, photographers spend more time trying to capture the perfect image of Heceta Head Lighthouse than any other sight along the entire coast.

PLANNING YOUR TIME

It's easy to spend a few days exploring the central coast. Although **Lincoln City** has abundant hotel rooms and is a good fallback during busy times of the year, tiny **Depoe Bay** is a great place to spend a night, perhaps with an early rise to take a fishing or whale-watching trip. And though **Newport** is a big city by Oregon coast standards, it's definitely worth spending a couple of nights here. In fact, if you're looking for a base for central coast explorations, Newport is well situated to visit sites from Lincoln City down to Florence. While in Newport, you may simply want to

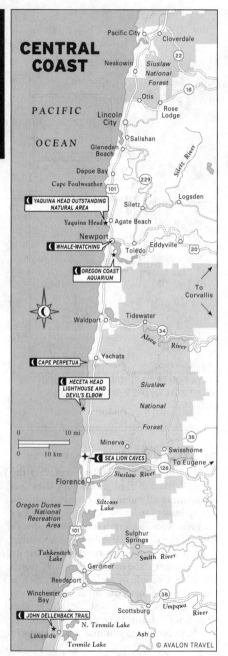

CENTRAL COAST

PACIFIC

OCEAN

poke around the Nye Beach and Bayfront neighborhoods, beachcomb on Agate Beach, and check out the tidepools and lighthouse at the Yaquina Head Outstanding Natural Area; or you might decide to devote a day to the Oregon Coast Aquarium and the nearby Oregon State University Hatfield Marine Science Center.

Personally, when we have the opportunity to plunk down at the coast for a long weekend, we almost always head to **Yachats** to enjoy the low-key atmosphere, the incredible natural beauty, and the good restaurants of this tiny town. If you are touring the coast, we think it (and the incredible Cape Perpetua coastline just south) is worth a full day and night of your time.

Florence is a short hop from Yachats and is a good alternative if you'd rather stay in a slightly larger town with a lively Old Town and easy access to the north end of the Oregon Dunes National Recreation Area, a fantastic landscape of dazzling white sand mountains and jewel lakes stretched along nearly 50 miles of shoreline.

Although anglers may want to stay at **Winchester Bay,** for most coast travelers this little town is a good stop for fish-and-chips, but not an overnight destination. Nearby, **Reedsport** is in the heart of the dune country and a good place to camp while exploring the dunes, but it does not have a huge wealth of fancy hotels and restaurants.

Lincoln City

Back in 1964, five burgs that straddled seven miles of beachfront between Siletz Bay and the Salmon River came together and incorporated as Lincoln City. In commemoration, a 14-foot bronze statue of Abraham Lincoln was donated to the city by an Illinois sculptor. *The Lank Lawyer Reading in His Saddle While His Horse Grazes* originally occupied a city park; today the statue stands in a nondescript lot at NE 22nd Street and Quay Avenue. Look for the sign on U.S. 101 near the Dairy Queen.

In the following decades, what were discrete towns have grown and melded into an uninterrupted conurbation with a population of about 8,000 (which can balloon to 30,000 on a busy weekend). While the resulting sprawl and heavy traffic on U.S. 101 can be maddening at times, once you get off the highway, Lincoln City has some charming neighborhoods (check out the Taft area at the south end of town); wide sandy beaches; superlative wildlife-viewing around Siletz Bay; the large freshwater Devils Lake; and two Native American casinos. Add prime kite-flying, some of the coast's better restaurants, and bibliophilic and antiquing haunts, and it's clear that there's more to the area than the pull of saltwater taffy and outlet malls.

SIGHTS AND RECREATION
Lincoln City Beach

Lincoln City boasts seven uninterrupted miles of sandy beach. From Siletz Bay north to Road's End State Recreation Area, there are more than a dozen access points. You can head west from U.S. 101 on just about any side street to get there, though high coastal bluffs lining the north-central portion of town may mean a climb down (and back up) long flights of stairs cut into the cliff. For something approaching solitude on a crowded day, follow Logan Road west from the highway near the north end of town to **Road's End State Recreation Area;** tidepools and a secluded cove add to the allure. This stretch is also popular with windsurfers.

Tidepool explorers should also check out the **rock formations** at SW 11th Street (Canyon Drive Park), NW 15th Street, and SW 32nd Street.

The **D River Wayside,** a small park on the beach in more or less the middle of town, is a state park property where you can watch what locals claim is the "world's shortest river" empty into the ocean. Flowing just 120 feet from its source, Devils Lake, to its mouth at the Pacific, it's short, all right; despite its unspectacular appearance, it was a cause célèbre when *The Guinness Book of World Records* withdrew the D's claim to fame in favor of a Montana waterway, the Roe. Local schoolkids rallied to the D's defense with an amended measurement, but the Roe, at a mere 53 feet long, carries the *Guinness* imprimatur as the shortest river. In

KESEY'S LEGACY

Two miles south of Lincoln City, you'll come to the turnoff for Highway 229 along the Siletz River. If you drive down the north side of the river about 1.25 miles, on the opposite shore you'll note a Victorian-ish house that was built to last. It was constructed for the movie version of *Sometimes a Great Notion.* The 1971 film, a so-so adaptation of Ken Kesey's memorable novel, starred Paul Newman, Lee Remick, Henry Fonda, and Michael Sarrazin. The plot concerns the never-say-die spirit of an antiunion timber baron, his not-always-supportive family, and life in the mythical Coast Range logging community of Wakonda. A huge porch once fronted the riverbank, heavily reinforced against the elements. It was taken down in the decade after the movie was made, but it lives on in the pages of the book. Much of the movie was shot in this area, with café scenes taking place at Mo's on Newport's bay front. Other scenes were shot near Florence.

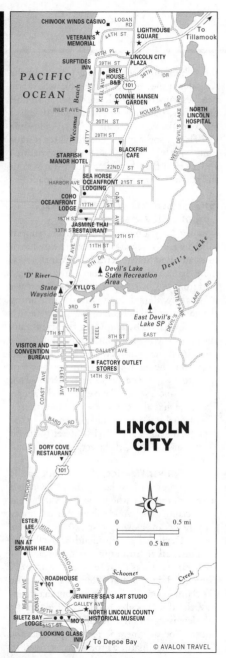

LINCOLN CITY

© AVALON TRAVEL

addition to seeing the D River flow from "D" Lake into "D" ocean, you can fly a kite on the beach. It's one of the easier beach access points between stretches of high motel-topped bluffs, so it can get a little crowded.

Another convenient beach access is off SW 51st Street at the south end of town, just before **Siletz Bay.** A large parking area here in what's known as the Taft District stands beside the driftwood-strewn shore of the bay, where you can often see a group of harbor seals chasing their dinner or coming in for a closer look at you. It's a short walk to the ocean.

Time was when it was common for storms and currents to wash up that ultimate beach-comber's prize—**glass fishing floats**—on the Oregon coast. Lincoln City improves the beachcomber's odds by distributing over 2,000 glass floats along its beaches mid-October-Memorial Day. Handcrafted by Pacific Northwest glass artists, each of the colorful floats is signed and numbered and placed by volunteers on the beaches above the high-tide line. If you find one, it's yours to keep; you can call or stop in at the visitor center for a certificate and information about the artist who created it.

Devils Lake

Devils Lake, just east of the highway, is the recreation center of Lincoln City. In addition to windsurfing and hydroplaning, you can fish here—the lake is stocked with hatchery trout, and there's also a population of wild coho salmon (catch-and-release only) as well as lampreys. There's also good bird-watching on and around this shallow 678-acre lake, which attracts flocks of migratory geese, ducks, and other waterfowl. Species to look for include canvasbacks, Canada geese, widgeons, gadwalls, grebes, and mallards. Bald eagles and ospreys nest in the trees bordering the lake.

The lake takes its name from a local Native American legend. The story goes that when Siletz warriors paddled a canoe across the lake one moonlit night, a tentacled beast erupted from the still water and pulled the men under. It's said that boaters today who cross the moon's reflection in the middle of the lake tempt the

CENTRAL COAST

same fate, but the lake's devil has remained silent for years.

Of the five access points, East Devils Lake Road off U.S. 101 northeast of town offers a scenic route around the lake's east side before rejoining U.S. 101 near the day-use portion of the state park at the south end of the lake. To reach the camping area of **Devils Lake State Recreation Area,** take NE 6th Drive east from U.S. 101, about 0.25 mile north of the D River. The day-use area has a boat ramp, and there's a moorage dock across the lake adjacent to the campground.

Mountain bikes, canoes, fishing boats, and Jet Skis can be rented at the **Blue Heron Landing** (4006 W. Devils Lake Rd., 541/994-4708, www.blueheronlanding.net).

Drift Creek Falls

Although it requires a drive inland, it's worth heading about 10 miles east to hike **Drift Creek Falls** (503/392-3161, $5 NW Forest Pass to park). The relatively easy but steadily downhill

© JUDY JEWELL

Head east from Lincoln City to find Drift Creek Falls.

1.5-mile trail passes through a forest with mostly second growth, a little old growth, lots of big stumps, and an understory of lovely native plants, and it leads to a dramatic 240-foot-high suspension bridge overlooking the 75-foot falls. The bridge, built in 1998, is as much an attraction as the falls—it sways a little bit as you walk out to view the falls. From the bridge, the trail continues another 0.25 mile to the base of the falls.

From Oregon State Road 18, turn south at Rose Lodge onto Bear Creek Road (which becomes Forest Road 17) and follow it for about nine miles. At the fork with Schooner Creek Road, be sure to go left (uphill); a rustic sign notes that it's the way to "Drift Creek Camp."

From U.S. 101, turn east onto Drift Creek Road (at the south end of Lincoln City), then south onto South Drift Creek Road and east onto Forest Road 17. Follow Forest Road 17 for about 10 miles.

Siletz River

The **Siletz Bay National Wildlife Refuge** preserves coastal estuaries and wetlands on either side of U.S. 101 at the south end of Lincoln City. The skeleton trees here are reminders of times when the salt marsh was diked to provide pasture for dairy cows. Now these snags are used by red-tailed hawks, bald eagles, and other birds of prey. The wetlands provide habitat for great blue herons, egrets, and other waterbirds.

During the summer, refuge rangers lead a small number of **paddle trips** along the Siletz estuaries. Trips are free, but participants must register well beforehand (541/270-0610) and provide their own canoe or kayak. **Siletz Moorage** (82 Siletz Hwy., 541/996-3671) rents kayaks ($25 for 4 hours) from its location on the north bank of the river just east of the highway.

Casinos

One of the biggest draws in town is the **Chinook Winds Casino** (1777 NW 44th St., 541/996-5825 or 888/244-6665, www.chinookwindscasino.com, open 24 hours daily), operated by the Confederated Tribes of Siletz

Indians, near the north end of town. In addition to slots, blackjack, poker, Keno, bingo, craps, and roulette, the casino has two on-site restaurants and a busy schedule of big-name (or formerly big-name) entertainment.

About 25 miles east of Lincoln City is the state's number-one visitor attraction, **Spirit Mountain Casino** (21700 SW Salmon River Hwy., Grand Ronde, 800/760-7977, http://spiritmountain.com, open 24 hours daily), operated by the Confederated Tribes of Grand Ronde. Games of chance include slots, craps, blackjack, poker, Keno, and bingo. No matter what you think of the casino, it should be noted that the Grand Ronde people have done a great job at getting their tribal status officially reinstated after the U.S. government officially terminated the tribe in 1954, leaving it with not much more than the tribal cemetery and a shed. They have amassed land and established a community fund that is a substantial supporter of nonprofit organizations in Oregon—6 percent of the casino's proceeds go into this charitable fund.

North Lincoln County Historical Museum

The modest **North Lincoln County Historical Museum** (4907 SW U.S. 101, 541/996-6614, www.northlincolncountyhistoricalmuseum.com, noon-5pm Wed.-Sun. May 15-Oct. 15 and Wed.-Sat. Oct. 16-Dec. 14 and Feb. 1-May 14, free) tells the story of this area through exhibits of old-time logging machinery, homesteading tools, fishing, military life, and Native American history. A highlight is the great collection of Japanese glass fishing floats.

Connie Hansen Garden

Tucked into the neighborhood between busy U.S. 101 and the beach, the **Connie Hansen Garden** (1931 NW 33rd St., 541/994-6338, www.conniehansengarden.com, dawn-dusk daily, free) is a great example of a coastal rainforest garden. The late Connie Hansen bought the land because its dampness seemed well suited to growing irises, her favorite plants, but she soon expanded her vision, working with the site's ecology and her own artistic talents to create a horticultural showcase. Guided tours are available for a small fee with advance notice, and a gift shop is open 10am-2pm Tuesday and Saturday.

Glass Art

Spend a rainy day learning to blow a glass float or paperweight at the **Jennifer Sears Art Studio** (4821 SW U.S. 101, 541/996-2569, www.jennifersearsglassart.com, 10am-6pm daily, classes $65-135, reservations recommended). Kids ages 8-10 may participate with parental supervision. Be sure to wear closed-toe shoes and no fleece!

About four miles south of town, near Salishan, you can watch the glass blowers at **Alder House** (611 Immonen Rd., 541/994-6485, www.alderhouse.com, 10am-5pm daily May-Thanksgiving weekend) and buy floats, paperweights, or other glass creations at very reasonable prices. Call ahead to confirm opening hours.

Golf

The area's most prestigious golf resort is seven miles south of Lincoln City at Gleneden Beach. **Salishan Spa and Golf Resort** (7760 N. U.S. 101, Gleneden Beach, 541/764-3632 or 800/890-8037, www.salishan.com, $89-119 for 18 holes) is an award-winning 18-hole course set in the foothills of the Coast Range and bordered by Siletz Bay and the sea. This challenging 6,470-yard, par-71, championship layout course was redesigned by Oregon golf superstar Peter Jacobsen and includes stunning ocean views. Keep in mind that this is a Scottish links course, where the roughs are really rough.

The 18-hole **Chinook Winds Golf Resort** (3245 NE 50th St., 541/994-8442, http://chinookwindscasino.com, $35-40 for 18 holes) is set in hilly (and frequently windy) terrain amidst towering coastal mountains on the edge of Lincoln City, this course is another venture of the Chinook Winds Casino, operated by the Confederated Tribes of Siletz Indians. The golf course spans just 5,000 yards with men's par 65 and women's 72.

ENTERTAINMENT AND EVENTS

Housed within the renovated Gleneden Brick and Tile Factory, five miles south of Lincoln City in Gleneden Beach, **Eden Hall** (6645 Gleneden Beach Loop Rd., 541/764-3826 performance info, 541/764-3825 restaurant, www.edenhall.com) stages live theater and hosts an impressively eclectic roster of regional and touring musicians. This spacious airy warehouse has an excellent sound system and is a wonderful place to take in a concert, with an emphasis on jazz, folk, and blues. Enjoy lunch or dinner at the adjacent Side Door Café.

The Arts

Lincoln City's homegrown theater company, **Theatre West** (3536 SE U.S. 101, 541/994-5663, www.theatrewest.com), stages half a dozen productions each year, with an emphasis on comedies plus musicals and drama. Visit the website for a list of current plays and their synopses.

Cinema

Catch first-run flicks at the **Bijou Theatre** (1624 NE U.S. 101, 541/994-8255), an old-time movie house dating back to the 1930s, making it a rare old survivor around here. The six-screen **Regal Cinemas** (3755 SE High School Dr., 541/994-7649), just east of U.S. 101 in the south end of town, is its modern competitor.

Festivals and Events

Lincoln City calls itself the kite capital of the world, pointing to its position midway between the pole and the equator, which gives the area predictable wind patterns. The town holds not one but two kite fiestas at the D River Wayside each year. The summer **Kite Festival** (541/994-3070 or 800/452-2151) takes place the last weekend in June; the fall festival is held the second weekend in October. The event is famous for giant spin socks, some as long as 150 feet.

SHOPPING

To sample the work of area artists, check out the **Ryan Gallery** (4270 N. U.S. 101, 541/994-5391, www.ryanartgallery.com). South of town at Salishan, the **Lawrence Gallery** (7755 U.S. 101 N., 541/764-2318, www.lawrencegallery.net) is a high-end gallery that's lots of fun to visit.

With some 65 shops, the **Tanger Outlet Center** (1500 SE East Devils Lake Rd., 541/996-5000), near the south end of town, is the largest outlet mall on the Oregon coast and has become something of a regional destination. Shops here include the ones you'd expect—Coach, Chico's, Eddie Bauer—plus the Oregon-based **Pendleton Woolen Mills** (541/994-2496, www.pendleton-usa.com).

Northwest Winds (130 SE U.S. 101, 541/994-1004) sells and repairs kites just across the highway from the D River Wayside, Lincoln City's kite-flying hub.

ACCOMMODATIONS

Lincoln City has more hotel rooms than any other coastal Oregon city. There are plenty to choose from, and many are very similar—basic hotel rooms within walking distance of the beach. However, there are some distinctions. Unless severely constrained by budget, one would not purposefully choose to stay on the east side of U.S. 101, necessitating an unpleasant fording of that great vehicular river just to walk to the beach, so, with one exception (Salishan), all the following hotels are on the beach side of the highway. Also, just because a hotel is new doesn't mean that it's preferred over older models. Many vintage hotels and motels have the best locations, and their slightly worn-in atmosphere is perfect for a summer holiday.

$50-100

The **Ester Lee** (3803 SW U.S. 101, 541/996-3606 or 888/996-3606, www.esterlee.com, $97-117) is a decades-old family motel complex, with some cottages on a bluff above miles of beachfront. All rooms have ocean views and fireplaces; some have kitchens and hot tubs.

Pets are allowed in some of the cottage units, most of which have kitchens and fireplaces. It's not a fancy place, but it's clean and pleasant with a great location and a good value.

$100-150

The **Siletz Bay Lodge** (1012 SW 51st St., 541/996-6111 or 888/430-2100, www.siletz-baylodge.com, $128-148), on the north end of Siletz Bay on a driftwood-strewn beach, is a family-friendly and wheelchair-accessible (with elevators) lodging in a location ideal for bird-watching and viewing seals. About half of the standard rooms of this older hotel have balconies, with delightful views of the bay and the sunset over Salishan Spit. In-room amenities include microwaves, refrigerators, and coffee-makers, and a continental breakfast is offered.

For a small oceanfront luxury hotel near the popular D River Wayside, the **Shearwater Inn** (120 NW Inlet Ct., 541/994-4121 or 800/869-8069, www.theshearwaterinn.com, $129-279) offers 30 units with balconies and gas fireplaces. Guests meet in the lobby every afternoon to sample Oregon wine. The hotel provides concierge and massage services, a continental breakfast, and accepts pets. The building is also wheelchair accessible.

A longtime Lincoln City motel, the **Coho Oceanfront Lodge** (1635 NW Harbor Ave., 541/994-3684 or 800/848-7006, www.theco-holodge.com, $144-220), has undergone a multimillion-dollar renovation; guest rooms have a sleek and sophisticated modern look. A DVD library, an indoor pool, a hot tub, and a sauna are available for guests to use; pets are allowed in some rooms.

Another place that has had a makeover is the **Surftides Inn** (2945 NW Jetty Ave., 541/994-2191 or 800/452-2159, www.surftidesinn.com, $140-240 for updated oceanview rooms), a large complex hugging the beach at the northern edge of Lincoln City. All of the oceanfront guest rooms have balconies and most have fireplaces. The guest rooms' redecoration has given the place a welcome freshening up; all rooms include a small refrigerator, a microwave oven, and a coffeemaker, as well as cable TV with a

DVD player. The inn has an indoor pool, a decent restaurant, a lounge, and meeting rooms. Prices vary by view; ask about partial or no-view rooms for up to 30 percent in savings. Pets are accepted in some rooms.

On the bluff above the beach, with fine views and easy access to the sand, **Sea Horse Oceanfront Lodging** (2039 NW Harbor Dr., 541/994-2101 or 800/662-2101, www.sea-horsemotel.com, $119-249) has a dizzying selection of lodging options, from simple motel rooms to cottages, houses, and two- and three-bedroom units, all in an extensive and quiet oceanfront compound. While it's a bit hard to generalize, most rooms have kitchens, some have fireplaces, and all guests are welcome at the breakfast bar, indoor pool, and outdoor hot tub, which overlooks the beach. There are a handful of discounted partial or no-view rooms available. This friendly and venerable operation is one of the reasons Lincoln City is so popular with families.

Another good spot on the north end of Siletz Bay in Lincoln City's historic Taft area is the **Looking Glass Inn** (861 SW 51 St., 541/996-3996 or 800/843-4940, www.lookingglass-inn.com, $114-129), an attractive place that would be quiet and tucked away if it weren't for the busy Mo's restaurant just across the road. Most rooms have kitchenettes, and most are dog-friendly.

Close to the beach at the north end of town, **Brey House B&B** (3725 NW Keel Ave., 541/994-7123, www.breyhouse.com, $109-159) is one of the oldest bed-and-breakfast inns on the Oregon coast, a three-story Cape Cod-style home built in 1940 with four bedrooms, all with private baths and entrances. The excellent breakfast is served in a light-filled room overlooking the ocean. Rooms are for adults only.

$150-200

More a small boutique hotel than the typical sprawling motel complex that typifies Lincoln City, **❰Starfish Manor Hotel** (2735 NW Inlet Ave., 541/996-9300 or 800/972-6155, www.onthebeachfront.com, $179-399) has just 17 oceanfront guest rooms and suites perched above the beach. All units have large ocean-view whirlpool tubs, fireplaces, oceanfront decks, kitchenettes, tasteful furnishings, and fine linens. Some units have two bedrooms. The Starfish is in a quiet part of town, perfect for a romantic getaway. The folks who own the Starfish have two other small boutique hotels with even more upscale suites; see the Starfish website for links.

If you've been fantasizing about rolling out of bed, slipping on your robe and walking out—coffee in hand—onto a semiprivate stretch of beach, then the **Inn at Spanish Head** (4009 SW U.S. 101, 541/996-2161 or 800/452-8127, www.spanishhead.com, $159-249) may be your best bet. Oregon's only resort hotel right on the beach, the inn takes its place—large and looming—against the backdrop of rugged cliffs. Whether a suite, studio, or bed-room unit, every room has an ocean view. On-site amenities include Fathoms, the 10th-floor restaurant-bar, a fireplace lounge, meeting rooms, a heated outdoor pool, saunas, a spa, and an exercise room.

Over $200

When asked to choose *the* place to stay on the Oregon coast, most Oregonians would have the ◖ **Salishan Spa and Golf Resort** (7760 N. U.S. 101, Gleneden Beach, 541/764-3600 or 800/452-2300, www.salishan.com, $212-292), a few miles south of Lincoln City, on their short list.

While there are distant Siletz Bay views, Salishan isn't a beachfront resort, and most folks quickly learn to appreciate the peace of the forest and the golf course. This paradigm shift is facilitated by art and landscape archi-tecture that convey the vision of John Gray, who built Salishan and such other Pacific Northwest properties as Skamania Lodge (on the Washington side of the Columbia Gorge) and Sunriver (south of Bend) from native materials with respect for the surrounding environment.

Even if you don't stay here, the grounds and facilities are worth a look. The art gallery is free and features works by top Oregon artists; also check out master woodcarver Leroy Setziol's

© JUDY JEWELL

coastal estuary near Salishan Spa and Golf Resort

bas-relief panels in the dining room. In addition to the recreational and aesthetic appeal of the resort, the dining room contributes to Salishan's lofty reputation. The forested trails behind the golf course showcase the rainforested foothills of the Coast Range and the waterfowl near Siletz Bay. Across the street, the Salishan Marketplace features first-rate galleries and a good bookstore, Allegory Books.

In high season, Salishan attracts well-heeled nature lovers, corporate expense-account clientele, folks enjoying a special occasion, and serious golfers. You'll also find everyday folks and seminar attendees on winter weekend specials at half the summertime rates. Ask about multiday packages for big savings on your room rate.

Vacation Rentals

To rent vacation homes throughout Lincoln County, contact the **Lincoln City Visitor and Convention Bureau** (800/452-2151, www. oregoncoast.org), or try **Pacific Retreats** (541/994-4833 or 800/473-4833, www.pacificretreats.com), which features a selection of vacation home rentals.

Camping

Devils Lake State Recreation Area (1452 NE 6th St., 541/994-2002 information, 800/452-5687 reservations, www.reserveamerica.com, $21 tents, $28 RVs, $40 yurts, $6 hiker-biker) is the main public campground in Lincoln City, with 54 tent sites, 28 RV sites with full hookups, 10 yurts, and a hiker/biker camp. This campground is right in town, just off U.S. 101 at the northeast end of town, so it's hardly a quiet wilderness retreat, but it does provide easy access to swimming or boating on Devils Lake.

The **Salmon River RV Park** (6029 Salmon River Hwy., 541/994-3116, www.salmonriverrvp.com, $20 tents, $23-30 RVs) is a good spot for anglers; it's on the Salmon River near the town of Otis. The **Lincoln City KOA** (5298 NE Park Ln., 541/994-2961 or 800/562-3316, www.koa.com, $27 tents, $33-37 RVs, $48 cabins) is also just a little ways inland, near the northeast corner of Devils Lake. At the south end of town, **Coyote Rock** (1676 Siletz Hwy.,

541/996-6824, www.coyote-rock.com, $21 tents, $29-35 RVs, $46 "tree house" cabins) has a nice setting where the Siletz River meets its bay. All of these campgrounds, including the state park, have showers.

FOOD

Lincoln City offers many dining options, most of them very busy and family-dining focused. There are several fine dining and ethnic options, however, and the general quality of food is high.

American

If you're en route to the wine country or the Willamette Valley or just want a respite from resort traffic, a place that appeals to everybody is ◖ **Otis Cafe** (1259 Salmon River Hwy., 541/994-2813, www.otiscafe.com, 7am-3pm Mon.-Wed., 7am-8pm Thurs.-Sun., $5-13), at the Otis Junction on Highway 18 five miles northeast of Lincoln City. Innovative variations on American road food have earned the Otis a devoted following (stop by to read the enthusiastic review by a satisfied *New York Times* reporter). Long waits on the porch are the rule on weekend mornings, though it's worth it for thick-crusted molasses bread, buttermilk waffles, and hash browns under a crust of melted Rogue Valley white cheddar. Even if it's not mealtime, stop in for a slice of outstanding pie.

Two Native American gaming casinos are located within 25 miles of one another and offer dining alternatives to the coast-bound traveler. Both **Chinook Winds** (1777 NW 44th St., 541/966-5825 or 888/244-6665), and **Spirit Mountain** (21700 SW Salmon River Hwy., Grand Ronde, 800/760-7977), about 25 miles east of Lincoln City on Highway 22 in Grand Ronde, have many dining options. Each offers generous full buffets for breakfast, lunch, and dinner, and both have full-service fine dining restaurants offering moderate to expensive ($18-35) prices. Both casinos have nightly buffets in the $15-20 range. Chinook Winds' ocean views are also worth noting. Both casinos have outlets for 24-hour dining.

Asian
Jasmine Thai Restaurant (1437 NW U.S. 101, 541/994-2022, 11am-3pm and 4pm-9pm Mon.-Fri., noon-9pm Sat.-Sun., $9-14) serves well-prepared traditional Thai cuisine. An extensive menu includes a number of seafood specialties, as well as daily specials that takes advantage of seasonal vegetables and other local produce.

In the outlet mall, **Momiji** (1500 SE Devils Lake Rd., 541/996-8886, 10am-9pm daily, sushi rolls $4-14) offers both Chinese and Japanese cooking, but the reason this restaurant is so popular is the excellent sushi rolls and sashimi. You're welcome to watch at the bar as the sushi is made, eat family-style in the restaurant, or get your order to go.

Pacific Northwest
Some of coastal Oregon's top dining experiences are found just south of Lincoln City. The reasonable prices at the Salishan Lodge's **Sun Room Restaurant** (7760 N. U.S. 101, Gleneden Beach, www.salishan.com, 6:30am-10pm daily, $11-23) are a welcome surprise. This casual restaurant might be less elaborate and half the price of Salishan's signature **Dining Room** (5pm-9:30pm daily, $28-59), but its cuisine comes from the same kitchen. While prime steaks and other meats are the specialty in the Dining Room, fresh local seafood, such as halibut, crab, scallops, and salmon, are also featured. The wine list here is one of the largest in the state.

The **◖ Blackfish Cafe** (2733 NW U.S. 101, 541/996-1007, www.blackfishcafe.com, 11:30am-close Wed.-Mon., $12-24) is a great find. Presided over by former Salishan Resort executive chef Rob Pounding, who has longstanding relationships with local farmers, anglers, and mushroom foragers, the Blackfish Cafe, in the tradition of James Beard, is dedicated to fairly priced and delicious regional cooking. The emphasis is on what's fresh, homegrown, and creative—grilled Willamette Valley pork brisket rubbed with coriander and cumin and troll-caught chinook salmon with fennel-lime butter. There is no shortage of humbler fare either, such as the self-proclaimed best clam chowder on the coast, Pacific City dory-caught fish-and-chips, and amazing fish tacos.

The **Bay House** (5911 SW U.S. 101, 541/996-3222, www.thebayhouse.org, 5:30pm-close Wed.-Sun., $27-40) combines oceanfront views with exquisite Pacific Northwest cuisine. Grilled local albacore tuna is served with black olives and avocado coulis, and the signature crab cakes come with saffron aioli. A $59 five-course tasting menu is available, but must be ordered by everyone at the table. For a more casual and less expensive light dinner, eat from the small plates menu in the lounge. In either dining area, oenophiles will want to look at the wine list, praised by *Wine Spectator*.

A half mile south of Salishan (five miles equidistant from Depoe Bay and Lincoln City) is a Gleneden Beach eatery with considerable appeal. The **Side Door Café** (6675 Gleneden Beach Loop, 541/764-3825, http://edenhall.com, 11:30am-9pm Wed.-Mon., $20-31) combines a gourmet restaurant with a musical venue. The airy yet cozy-feeling dining room features a menu where honey mustard and herb-rubbed salmon with marionberry glaze exemplifies the offerings.

Seafood
If coastal restaurants are eating a hole in your wallet, there's always tried-and-true **Mo's** (860 SW 51st St., 541/996-2535, www.moschowder.com, 10:30am-9pm Sun.-Thurs., 10:30am-10pm Fri., 8am-9pm Sat., $4-15). As at all Mo's locations, the view is great and the seafood more than serviceable.

The chowder is a little tastier at the **Dory Cove Restaurant** (2981 SW U.S. 101, 541/557-4000, www.dorycove.com, 11:30am-8pm Sun.-Thurs., 11:30am-9pm Fri.-Sat., $5-23), but the views from this simple restaurant are out onto the highway. Rest assured that the focus is on the food—good old-fashioned deep-fried and sautéed seafood main courses (halibut fish-and-chips are recommended) and homemade pies. **Kyllo's** (1110 NW 1st Court, 541/994-3179, www.kyllosrestaurant.com, 11:30am-9pm daily, $9-25) specializes in broiled, sautéed, and baked seafood, plus excellent homemade desserts and Oregon microbrews and wines. The restaurant is visible from U.S. 101 as you drive by the D River Wayside. With views of the water on all sides, this restaurant is a good place to linger, though waits can be long in the evening as no reservations are taken.

Brewpubs
The **Lighthouse Brew Pub** (4157 U.S. 101 N., 541/994-7238, 11am-10pm Sat.-Tues. and Thurs., 11am-11pm Wed., 11am-midnight Fri., $9-20) is a welcome rehash of the successful McMenamins formula. Just look for a lighthouse replica in a parking lot on the northwest side of U.S. 101 across from McDonald's. Pizza, burgers, sandwiches, and salads can be washed down with McMenamins' own ales as well as hard cider and wine.

The venerable **Roadhouse 101** (4649 SW U.S. 101, 541/994-7729, www.roadhouse101. com, 11:30am-10pm Sun.-Wed., 11:30am-midnight Thurs., 11:30am-1:30am Fri.-Sat., $8-20) has added Rusty Truck Brewing to its already rockin' establishment, with a selection of house-made ales and a "south of the border" lager. The Roadhouse features hearty American-style food, frequent live music, and a lively crowd ready to party.

INFORMATION
The **Lincoln City Visitor Center** (540 NE U.S. 101, 541/994-3302 or 800/452-2151, www.oregoncoast.org, 10am-4pm Mon.-Sat.) has a website that's full of helpful information.

The **Central Oregon Coast Association** (541/265-2064 or 800/767-2064, www.coastvisitor.com) also maintains a useful website with details on Lincoln City and the rest of coastal Lincoln County.

GETTING THERE AND AROUND
Lincoln County Transit (541/265-4900, www. co.lincoln.or.us/transit) buses stop in town for service Monday-Saturday. The line goes as far south as Yachats and does not run on major holidays.

Peak traffic times in Lincoln City can result in 25,000 cars a day crawling through town. As an alternative to rush hour on U.S. 101, you could try detouring on NE West Devils Lake Road or NE East Devils Lake Road, which bypass the worst congestion.

Depoe Bay

In his classic travel tale *Blue Highways,* William Least Heat-Moon characterized Depoe Bay thusly:

> Depoe Bay used to be a picturesque fishing village; now it was just picturesque. The fish houses, but for one seasonal company, were gone, the fleet gone, and in their stead had come sport fishing boats and souvenir ashtray and T-shirt shops.

To be fair, tourists have come here since the establishment of the town. In fact, for all intents and purposes, the town didn't really exist until the completion of the Roosevelt Highway (U.S. 101) in 1927, which opened the area up to car travelers. Prior to that time, the area had been occupied mainly by a few members of the Siletz people. One worked at the U.S. Army depot and called himself Charlie Depot. The town was named after him, eventually taking on the current spelling.

Regardless of what you think of the busy commercial strip and the enormous time-share resort along the highway, the scenic appeal of Depoe's location is impossible to ignore. The rocky outer bay, flanked by headlands to the north and south, is pierced by a narrow channel through the basalt cliffs leading to the inner harbor. It's home to an active sportfishing fleet

Boats maneuver in and out of Depoe Bay's tiny harbor.

as well as the whale-watching charters that have earned Depoe Bay its distinction as the whale-watching capital of the state.

SIGHTS AND RECREATION
The Bayfront and Harbor

Depoe Bay is situated along a truly beautiful coastline that cannot be fully appreciated from the highway. A quarter-mile-long seawall and promenade invite a stroll. For a panorama of the harbor, continue along the sidewalks across the gracefully arching concrete bridge, designed by Conde McCullough and built in 1927. Other nice perspectives are offered from residential streets west of U.S. 101; try Ellingson Street, south of the bridge, and Sunset Street, at the north end of the bay. Two "spouting horns," natural blowholes in the rocks north of the harbor entrance, can send plumes of spray 60 feet into the air when the tide and waves are right.

East of the bridge is Depoe Bay's claim to international fame, the world's smallest navigable natural harbor. This boat basin is also exceptional because it's a harbor within a harbor.

This topography is the result of wave action cutting into the basalt over eons until a 50-foot passageway leading to a six-acre inland lagoon was created. In addition to whale-watching, folks congregate on the bridge between the ocean and the harbor to watch boats maneuver into the enclosure. Depoe Bay's harbor was scenic enough to be selected as the site from which Jack Nicholson commandeered a yacht for his mental patient crew in the film *One Flew Over the Cuckoo's Nest.*

Whale Watching Center

Stop in at the **Whale Watching Center** (119 SW U.S. 101, 541/765-3304, www.oregon-stateparks.org, 9am-5pm daily summer, 10am-4pm Wed.-Sun. winter, free) where volunteers can help you spot whales and answer your questions about them. The center, right on the seawall, is an ideal viewing spot. Peak viewing times are mid-December-January, when whales are migrating south; late March-early June, when they're traveling north (mothers and babies generally come later in the season);

and mid-July-early November, when resident whales feed off the coast. The least likely times to see whales from the central Oregon coast are mid-November-mid-December and mid-January-mid-March.

Whale, Sea Life & Shark Museum

The private **Whale, Sea Life & Shark Museum** (234 S. U.S. 101, 541/912-6734, www.oregon-whales.com, 9am-5pm daily summer, 10am-4pm Wed.-Sun. winter, $5 adults, $3 children ages 4-10) on the harbor side of the highway, 100 feet south of the bridge, is run in conjunction with whale-watching tours in Zodiac craft. Carrie Newell, a marine biologist, runs both the museum and the tours ($30 for one hour, $50 for two hours). The museum, which is free with a whale-watching trip, features models of marine mammals, a large collection of shark jaws, and lots of photos of whales.

Boiler Bay State Scenic Viewpoint

Boiler Bay, half a mile north of Depoe Bay, is so named because of the boiler left from the 1910 wreck of the *J. Marhoffer*. The ship caught fire three miles offshore and drifted into the bay. The remains of the boiler are visible at low tide. This rock-rimmed bay is a favorite spot for rock fishing, birding, and whale-watching. A trail leads down to some excellent tidepools.

Whale Cove

This picturesque bay half a mile south of Depoe Bay has been scooped out of the sandstone bluffs. The tranquility of this calendar photo come to life is deceptive. There's considerable evidence to suggest that this tiny embayment—and not California's Marin County—was the site of Francis Drake's 1579 landing, but the jury is still out. During Prohibition, bootleggers used the protected cove as a clandestine port.

Rocky Creek State Scenic Viewpoint (800/551-6949, www.oregonstateparks.org) overlooks Whale Cove. There are picnic tables, and it's a good spot for whale-watching, but there's no beach access.

Otter Crest Loop

The rocky bluffs of this coastal stretch take on an even more dramatic aspect as you leave the highway at the **Otter Crest Loop,** a winding three-mile section of the old Coast Highway, two miles south of Depoe Bay. The northernmost part of the loop, down as far as Cape Foulweather, is one-way southbound, with a generous bike lane.

From atop **Cape Foulweather,** the visibility can extend 40 miles on a clear day. The view south to Yaquina Head and its lighthouse is a photographer's fantasy of headlands, coves, and offshore monoliths. Bronze plaques in the parking lot tell of Captain Cook naming the 500-foot-high headland during a bout with storm-tossed seas on March 7, 1778.

The Lookout (milepost 131.5 U.S. 101, 541/765-2270, www.lookoutgiftshop.com, 9am-5pm daily), a gift shop on the north side of the promontory, is a good place to buy Japanese fishing floats for a few bucks. The million-dollar view from inside the shop is easily one of the most spectacular windows on the ocean to be found anywhere.

Another mile south, in the hamlet of **Otter Rock,** you'll find another of the Oregon coast's several diabolically named natural features, the **Devil's Punchbowl.** The urn-like sandstone formation, filled with swirling water, has been sculpted by centuries of waves flooding into what had been a cave until its roof collapsed. The inexorable process continues today, thanks to the ebb and flow of the Pacific through two openings in the cauldron wall. A state park viewpoint gives you a ringside seat for this frothy confrontation between rock and tide. When the water recedes, you can see purple sea urchins and starfish in the tidepools of the **Marine Gardens** 100 feet to the north.

To the south of the Punchbowl vantage point are picnic tables and a wooden walkway down to the beach. Close by in tiny Otter Rock you'll find a small **Mo's** restaurant (122 1st St., 541/765-2442, 11am-8pm Mon.-Sat., 11am-6pm Sun., $4-16). Next door, the **Flying Dutchman Winery** (915 1st St., 541/765-2553, 11am-6pm daily) makes limited batches of

DRAKE'S LOST HARBOR?

In 1996 the media exploded with stories raising the possibility that the tiny hamlet of Whale Cove, two miles south of Depoe Bay, could supplant Plymouth Rock as the birthplace of a nation. Rotting timbers from what is theorized to have been a stockade built by Sir Francis Drake in 1579 were unearthed in an area where stories have long circulated that the English privateer made landfall.

Over the years, these notions have been fueled by several tantalizing pieces of evidence: an unsigned ship's log from Drake's voyage in a museum in England that identified 44 degrees north latitude—the same as Whale Cove—as a landing site; an English shilling dating from 1560 found on the central Oregon coast in 1982; a photo from the 1930s showing a local resident with a distinctly English sword he unearthed; and a ship's cutlass found in Newport in the early 19th century bearing the markings of a 16th-century English arsenal. Moreover, excavations of a nearby Indian village thought to have been buried in 1600 turned up brass items, blades, and Venetian beads.

An amateur British historian, Bob Ward, makes a compelling case for Whale Cove as the place where Drake spent five weeks in the summer of 1579. In his flagship *Golden Hynde*, the only one of his five-ship fleet to survive the stormy straits around Cape Horn, Drake harassed Spanish settlements throughout Latin America and plundered Spanish ships wherever he met them. Sailing west from Mexico on its return to England via the Cape of Good Hope, the treasure-laden *Golden Hynde* was beset by storms, and Drake had to retreat to land to make repairs. Conventional history has held that he made landfall around San Francisco, most likely on the Marin County coast.

Ward, however, believes that Drake continued his voyage farther north and sailed into the Strait of Juan de Fuca, thinking he had found the fabled Northwest Passage. Turning around before he realized his mistake, Drake then headed south down the Washington and Oregon coasts, where he found a sandy cove in which to drop anchor and make repairs before the long journey home.

On Drake's return to England after four years at sea, news of his exploits were suppressed. Queen Elizabeth confiscated the logs and charts, and it would be 10 years before an official account of the voyage would be published. Then, Drake's New Albion was described as being around 38 degrees north latitude (in northern California), in an attempt, Ward believes, to fool the Spanish into thinking the Northwest Passage was much farther south.

After Elizabeth's death in 1603, however, new charts began to appear that placed the landing site much farther north, and early 17th-century charts show a small shallow bay labeled Novus Albionis (New Albion) that is an uncannily accurate depiction of Whale Cove.

Since the initial blizzard of publicity, there has been no final word from the archaeologists and historians involved in corroborating these claims. Because most history books have placed New Albion, Drake's fabled lost settlement, near San Francisco, researchers will not be too quick to claim otherwise without definitive research.

---

handcrafted wines from grapes grown in southern Oregon and the Willamette Valley (grapes won't ripen on the coast).

Back on U.S. 101, a mile's drive south brings you to Beverly Beach State Park.

Fishing and Whale-Watching Charters

With the ocean minutes from Depoe Bay's port, catching a salmon or seeing a whale is possible as soon as you leave the harbor. Most charter operators here offer both fishing and whale-watching excursions. Bottom-fishing trips average $75 for a five-hour run, salmon fishing (available only when salmon season is open) about $130 for a seven- or eight-hour day; whale-watching excursions run $15-25 per person per hour.

Dockside Charters (541/765-2545 or 800/733-8915, docksidedepoebay.com) offers

1.5-hour whale-watching trips aboard its 50-foot excursion boat for $16 per adult and one-hour trips on Zodiacs for $25 per adult. **Tradewinds Charters** (541/765-2345 or 800/445-8730, www.tradewindscharters.com) hosts one- and two-hour trips December-May. Rates run $18-30 per adult.

Surfing

If you're itching to actually get into the water and catch a few waves, the beach at **Otter Rock**, a few miles south of Depoe Bay, is a good place to surf. Park in the lot at Devil's Punchbowl and walk down the long flight of steps to the beach, which is relatively protected and has a large area where beginners tend to hang out. (There's also a section that gets bigger waves and better surfers.)

ENTERTAINMENT AND EVENTS

The **Depoe Bay Classic Wooden Boat Show, Crab Feed, and Ducky Derby** is held the third weekend in April. Several dozen wooden craft,

© JUDY JEWELL

the beach at Otter Rock

both restored and newly constructed vessels, including kayaks, skiffs, dinghies, and larger fishing boats, are displayed in the harbor and the adjacent Depoe Bay City Park. Rowing races, boatbuilding workshops, crab races, and other activities are scheduled. The big Crab Feed, held 10am-5pm both Saturday and Sunday, sees some 1,500 pounds of crab plus side dishes devoured at the Community Hall; it costs $12-18 for a crab dinner. The Ducky Derby is a raffle in which you purchase "tickets" in the form of rubber duckies that race down the harbor's feeder stream vying for prizes. For more information, contact the **Depoe Bay Chamber of Commerce** (223 SW U.S. 101, 541/765-2889 or 877/485-8348, www.depoebaychamber.org).

The **Fleet of Flowers** happens each Memorial Day in the harbor to honor those lost at sea and in military service. Thousands come to witness a blanket of blossoms cast upon the waters.

The **Depoe Bay Salmon Bake** takes place on the third Saturday of September (10am-5pm) at Depoe Bay City Park, flanking the rear of the boat basin. Some 3,000 pounds of fresh ocean fish are caught, cooked Native American-style on alder stakes over an open fire, and served with all the trimmings, to be savored to the accompaniment of live entertainment. The cost is $20 adults, $10 children. It always seems to rain on the day of this event, but that's life on the Oregon coast.

ACCOMMODATIONS

Lodgings in popular Depoe Bay require advance reservations on most weekends and holidays.

The **Inn at Arch Rock** (70 NW Sunset St., 541/765-2560 or 800/767-1835, www.innatarchrock.com, $89-309) is a cluster of white clapboard buildings that overlook Depoe Bay from a cliff-top perch at the north end of town. Most rooms have ocean views and are in the $140-200 range; a non-oceanview room goes for $89. Pets are permitted in several rooms.

Harbor Lights Inn (235 SE Bay View Ave., 541/765-2322 or 800/228-0448, www.theharborlightsinn.com, $129-189), a small inn overlooking the harbor, has the distinct advantage of being distant from U.S. 101. Perched above the marina and the Coast Guard station, this homey inn affords views of sea otters, ducks, and geese while the whale-watching and fishing boats come and go. All rooms have a harbor view; rates include a hot breakfast. Small pets are allowed with prior approval.

The **C Channel House** (35 Ellingson St., 541/765-2140 or 800/447-2140, www.channelhouse.com, rooms $140-330) features both standard B&B rooms and spacious suites boasting expansive dramatic views of the ocean, private decks with outdoor whirlpool tubs (in the majority of rooms), fireplaces, plush robes, and other amenities. This bluff-top B&B (there isn't a beach below, just miles of ocean and surrounding cliffs) may not look prepossessing from the outside, but inside, the place is all windows and angles. Imagine *Architectural Digest* in a nautical theme. This is one of the best places on the Oregon coast to commune with whales, passing boats, winter storms, and the setting sun. A continental breakfast with tasty baked goods in an ocean-side dining area is included in the rates.

About a mile south of town, perched above scenic Whale Cove, find the boxy new **Whale Cove Inn** (2345 S. U.S. 101, 541/765-4300 or 800/628-3409, www.whalecoveinn.com, $395-795), a small boutique hotel that's a sister hotel to the Channel House. Here you can lounge in the hot tub on your private deck or on the Tempur-Pedic mattress in your bedroom alcove (all accommodations are in spacious suites, the top-end suites sleep six). Fine dining is available in the hotel restaurant, Restaurant Beck. This is as high-end as the Oregon coast gets; kids 16 and older are welcome, but pets are not.

About three miles south of Depoe Bay, at one of the most scenic spots on the central coast, is the **Inn at Otter Crest** (301 Otter Crest Loop, Otter Rock, 541/765-2111 or 800/452-2101, www.innatottercrest.com, $110-329), a large condo resort perched near the sandstone bluffs at the ocean's edge. Hotel rooms have two queen-size beds, a refrigerator, a coffeemaker, and a private deck with picture windows. Studios have a queen-size Murphy bed (or a regular bed), a full kitchen, a fireplace, and a dining area; larger one- and two-bedroom suites are also available.

The **Surfrider Resort** (3115 NW U.S. 101, 541/764-2311 or 800/662-2378, www.surfriderresort.com, $99-135) is a few miles north of Depoe Bay on picturesque Fogarty Creek's rockbound coast. Oceanfront suites and rooms have decks; some feature whirlpool tubs, kitchens, and fireplaces. A good restaurant, an indoor pool, and midweek specials are also noteworthy.

FOOD

Of Depoe Bay's several restaurants, **Tidal Raves** (279 NW U.S. 101, 541/765-2995, www.tidalraves.com, 11am-9pm daily, $12-25) has the best combination of flavor, views, and casual ambience. A number of seafood dishes take on an Asian twist, such as Thai barbecued shrimp or udon noodles with sesame-crusted scallops. A pasta dish features crab, shrimp, lingcod, snapper, and more on a bed of linguine with pesto. The Dungeness crab casserole is also noteworthy for its flavor as well as its cholesterol level-improving properties.

The **C Restaurant Beck** (2345 S. U.S. 101, 541/765-3220, restaurantbeck.com, 5pm-9pm daily, $27-30), in the Whale Cove Inn south of town, is Depoe Bay's only really elegant restaurant. It has a great view and excellent food, much of which originates on nearby farms. Be prepared to experiment in a way that's not too scary: Pork belly confit and pickled sea beans are paired with whole-grain mustard ice cream; rockfish is served with snap peas, crisp anchovy spine, shaved asparagus, wild fennel vinaigrette, and buttermilk gel. Seasonal ingredients figure prominently; in June, Rainier cherries pair with ancho chilies atop a lamb loin.

INFORMATION

On the east side of the highway, opposite the seawall, the **Depoe Bay Chamber of**

Commerce (223 SW U.S. 101, 541/765-2889 or 877/485-8348, www.depoebaychamber.org) offers literature about the town and the central coast in general.

On weekdays and Saturday, **Lincoln County Transit** (541/265-4900, www.co.lincoln.or.us/transit) runs buses four times daily, north to Lincoln City and south to Yachats.

Newport

In January 1852, a storm grounded the schooner *Juliet* near Yaquina (pronounced yah-KWIN-nah) Bay, where her captain and crew were stranded for two months. When they finally made their way inland to the Willamette Valley, they reported their discovery of an abundance of tiny sweet-tasting oysters in the bay. Within a decade, commercial oyster farms were established—the first major impetus to growth and settlement in Newport. The tasty morsels that delighted diners in San Francisco and at New York City's Waldorf-Astoria Hotel are almost gone now, but the oyster industry continues by harvesting introduced species.

In 2011, Newport (pop. 10,000) became the National Oceanic and Atmospheric Administration's Pacific Marine Operations Center, managing a fleet of NOAA research ships. During the summer, these ships are usually out at sea conducting oceanographic research, but when they're in port, the large white vessels are easy to spot in the harbor.

The port also bustles with the activity of Oregon's largest commercial fishing fleet and second-largest recreational fleet. Factories to process *surimi* (a fish paste popular in Japan) and whiting have provided jobs, and a state-of-the-art aquarium that once housed Keiko the

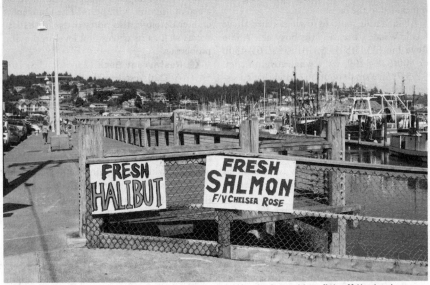

Newport's bayfront is a working port; walk down to the docks and buy fish off the boat.

© JUDY JEWELL

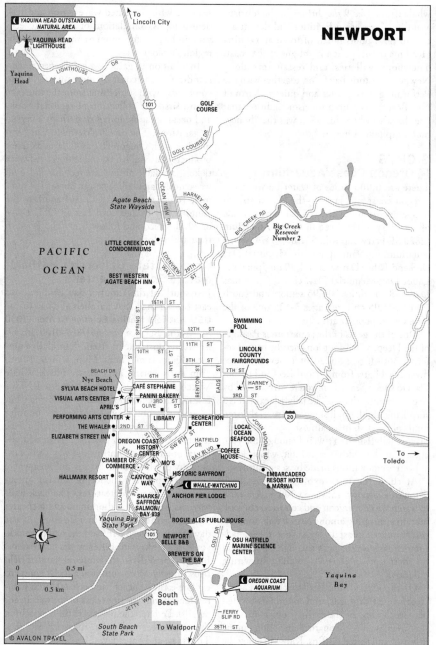

NEWPORT

To Lincoln City

YAQUINA HEAD OUTSTANDING NATURAL AREA

YAQUINA HEAD LIGHTHOUSE

Yaquina Head

LIGHTHOUSE DR

GOLF COURSE

GOLF COURSE DR

OCEAN VIEW DR

HARNEY DR

BIG CREEK RD

Big Creek Resevoir Number 2

Agate Beach State Wayside

PACIFIC OCEAN

LITTLE CREEK COVE CONDOMINIUMS

EDENVIEW WAY

20TH

BEST WESTERN AGATE BEACH INN

SPRING ST

15TH ST

12TH ST

SWIMMING POOL

COAST ST

NYE ST

10TH ST

11TH ST

8TH ST

BENTON ST

EADS ST

LINCOLN COUNTY FAIRGROUNDS

6TH ST

7TH ST

BEACH DR

Nye Beach

SYLVIA BEACH HOTEL

VISUAL ARTS CENTER

CAFÉ STEPHANIE

PANINI BAKERY

3RD ST

OLIVE ST

HARNEY ST

3RD ST

APRIL'S

PERFORMING ARTS CENTER

LIBRARY

HURBERT ST

RECREATION CENTER

THE WHALER

2ND ST

20

ELIZABETH STREET INN

OREGON COAST HISTORY CENTER

SW 9TH ST

HATFIELD DR

BAY BLVD

LOCAL OCEAN SEAFOOD

JOHN MOORE RD

To Toledo

CHAMBER OF COMMERCE

FALL ST

MO'S

COFFEE HOUSE

HALLMARK RESORT

CANYON WAY

9TH ST

HISTORIC BAYFRONT

WHALE-WATCHING

EMBARCADERO RESORT HOTEL & MARINA

ELIZABETH ST

SHARKS/ SAFFRON SALMON/ BAY 839

ANCHOR PIER LODGE

Yaquina Bay State Park

101

ROGUE ALES PUBLIC HOUSE

NEWPORT BELLE B&B

OSU DR

OSU HATFIELD MARINE SCIENCE CENTER

Yaquina Bay

BREWER'S ON THE BAY

0   0.5 mi

0   0.5 km

JETTY WAY

South Beach

OREGON COAST AQUARIUM

FERRY SLIP RD

35TH ST

South Beach State Park

To Waldport

© AVALON TRAVEL

whale (from *Free Willy*) brings in the tourists. Wildlife observation facilities and decent access to tidal pools north of town at Yaquina Head make this park a highlight of the coast. The shops, galleries, and restaurants along Newport's historic bay front, together with the Performing Arts Center and quieter charm of Nye Beach, keep up a tourism tradition that goes back to when this town was the "honeymoon capital of Oregon."

SIGHTS

Oregon Coast Aquarium

There are 6,000 miles of water between the Oregon coast and Japan—the largest stretch of open ocean on earth. You can hear *our* side of the story at the **Oregon Coast Aquarium** (2820 SE Ferry Slip Rd., 541/867-3474, www.aquarium.org, 9am-6pm daily Memorial Day weekend-Labor Day weekend, 10am-5pm daily Labor Day-Memorial Day, closed Christmas Day, $18.95 adults, $16.95 seniors and youth 13-17, $11.95 children ages 3-12), one of the state's most popular attractions.

One of the gems of the aquarium is Passages of the Deep, a 200-foot-long acrylic tunnel offering 360-degree underwater views in three diverse habitats, from Orford Reef to Halibut Flats to Open Sea, where you're surrounded by free-swimming sharks. The jellyfish exhibit is a surprising highlight; it showcases several dozen kinds of jellyfish in an almost psychedelic display. If jellyfish aren't weird enough for you, check out the Oddwater exhibit, which looks at bizarre adaptations made by sea creatures.

At the large Jetty exhibit, visitors look through a window into a 35,000-gallon tank to watch white sturgeon and coho and chinook salmon swimming among large basalt boulders that simulate a coastal jetty, such as these anadromous fish might pass through in the wild on their upriver journey to their spawning grounds.

Of the several hundred species of Pacific Northwest fish, birds, and mammals on display in the rest of the facility, don't miss the sea otters, wolf eel, leopard sharks, lion's mane jellyfish, and tufted puffins. Kids will enjoy the sea cave with simulated wave action and resident octopus. Simulations of indigenous ecosystems help visitors immerse themselves in the region's biology.

In addition to gaining a heightened understanding of the coast biome, you might also come away with something from the museum shop's first-rate collection of regional books and oceanographic tomes or perhaps a crystal or gemstone. The on-site Mermaid Cafe emphasizes such Oregon fare as Tillamook dairy products, seasonal fruits, and seafood. Advance tickets (available online) are recommended on weekends, major holidays, and during the summer. To get there from U.S. 101 south of the Yaquina Bay Bridge, turn east on OSU Drive or 32nd Street, and follow Ferry Slip Road to the parking lot.

Oregon State University Hatfield Marine Science Center

Just south of the Yaquina Bay Bridge, head east on the road that parallels the bay to the **OSU Hatfield Marine Science Center** (2030 SE Marine Science Dr., 541/867-0100, http://hmsc.oregonstate.edu, 10am-5pm daily summer, 10am-4pm Thurs.-Mon. winter, 10am-4pm daily spring and winter break Whale Watch weeks, $5 donation suggested). This research and education facility is a low-key but interesting complement to the very popular Oregon Coast Aquarium, located half a mile south. At the door to greet you is an octopus in an open tank pointing the way to oceanography exhibits and a "hands-on" area where you can experience the feel of starfish, anemones, and other sea creatures. The back hallway has educational dioramas, and a theater shows marine science films throughout the day. If you proceed left from the octopus tank, you'll see tanks with different sea ecosystems. Beyond the walls of the museum, guided field trips (mostly Mon. summer; a fee is charged) explore estuary, beach, and coastal forest habitats (check with the front desk or the website for details). Perhaps the biggest thrill is watching the octopus eat—it's fed at 1pm each Monday, Thursday, and Saturday.

Oregon Coast History Center

For a glimpse into the rich past of Lincoln County, stop at the **Oregon Coast History Center** (545 SW 9th St., 541/265-7509, www.oregoncoast.history.museum, 11am-4pm Tues.-Sun. $5 adults, $3 children ages 3-12), which incorporates the Log Cabin Museum and the adjacent Queen Anne-style Burrows House, a former boardinghouse built in 1895. It's a half block east of the chamber of commerce on U.S. 101. The logging, farming, pioneer life, and maritime exhibits (particularly Newport shipwrecks) are interesting, but the Siletz baskets and other Native American artifacts steal the show.

Here you can learn the heartbreaking story of the hardships—forced displacement, inadequate housing, insufficient food, and poor medical facilities—that plagued the diverse Native American groups that made up the Confederated Siletz Reservation.

The historical society also runs the new **Pacific Maritime & Heritage Center** (333 SE Bay Blvd., 11am-4pm Thurs.-Sun. $5 adults, $3 children ages 3-12), which occupies a huge old mansion overlooking the Bayfront. Local residents have donated everything from ships' wheels to vintage surfboards to this museum, which is worth visiting for the setting and the building alone.

Bayfront District

Newport's Old Town Bayfront District can be easy to miss if you're not alert. At the north end of the Yaquina Bay Bridge, look for the signs pointing off U.S. 101 that lead you down the hill to Bay Boulevard, the Bayfront's main drag. Alternatively, turn southeast off the highway a few blocks north onto Hurbert Street; this runs into Canyon Way, which ends at Bay Boulevard. On summer weekends, forget about parking anywhere near here unless you arrive early. Spots close by the boulevard can often be found, however, along Canyon Way, the hillside access route to downtown.

Until 1936, ferries shuttled people and vehicles to and from Newport's waterfront. With the completion of the Yaquina Bay Bridge that year, however, traffic bypassed the Old Town area. Commerce and development moved to the highway corridor, and the Bayfront faded in importance. Within the last couple of decades, the pendulum has swung back, and the Bayfront District is now one of Newport's prime attractions, with some of its best restaurants and watering holes, shopping, and tourist facilities.

One of the first things that'll strike you about the Bayfront today is that it's still a working neighborhood, not a sanitized re-creation of a real seaport. Chowder houses, galleries, and shops stand shoulder to shoulder with fish-processing plants and canneries, and the air is filled with the cries of fishmongers and the harmonious discord of sea lions and harbor seals. On the waterfront, sport anglers step off charter boats with their catches, and vessels laden with everything from wood products to whale-watching tourists ply the bay. Unfortunately, the severe catch limits and cost of equipment make this less of a working port every year. In deference to the Oregon commercial fishers and other endangered species, wall murals on the Bayfront memorialize fishing boats and whales.

Yaquina Bay State Recreation Site

In 1871 a lighthouse was built here on a bluff overlooking the mouth of Yaquina Bay, and the lighthouse keeper, his wife, and seven children moved into the two-story wood-frame structure. It soon became apparent, however, that the location was not ideal, as the light could not be seen by ships approaching the harbor from the north. The station was abandoned after just three years once the nearby light at Yaquina Head was completed. The building was slated for demolition in 1934, when local residents formed the Lincoln County Historical Society to preserve it. In 1997 the government decided to turn Yaquina Bay's beacon back on.

Today, the handsome restored structure and surrounding grounds make up **Yaquina Bay State Recreation Site** (541/574-3129

CENTRAL COAST

© BILL MCRAE

Newport's Nye Beach neighborhood is home to good restaurants and shops.

or 800/551-6949, www.oregonstateparks.org, noon-4pm daily, free), in a beautiful location at the north end of the Yaquina Bay Bridge. The last wooden lighthouse on the Oregon coast is also the oldest building in Newport. The living quarters, replete with period furnishings, are open to the public. Be sure to ask the volunteers about the resident ghost.

From the parking area, you have an excellent photo op of the bay and the bridge. The park is a good place to have a picnic, or you can descend the trails to the beach and dig for razor clams or hunt for agates and petrified wood.

Nye Beach

The 1890s-era tourism boom that came to Newport's Bayfront spilled over into Nye Beach. In 1891 the city built a wooden sidewalk connecting the two neighborhoods, and soon "summer people" were filling the cedar cottages. In the next century, thanks to an improved river-and-land route from Corvallis, health faddists (who came for hot seawater

baths in the sanatorium) and honeymooners soon joined the mix.

A mile north from the Bayfront, to the west of U.S. 101 (look for signs on the highway), this onetime favorite retreat for wealthy Portlanders has undergone a revival in recent years. Rough times and rougher weather had reduced luxurious beach houses here to a cluster of weather-beaten shacks until a performing arts center went up in 1988. On the heels of the development of this first-rate cultural facility, the conversion of a 1910 hotel into a kind of literary hostel encouraged other restorations and plenty of new construction. Culture vultures, beach lovers, and people watchers now flock to Nye Beach, which feels a world away from the Coast Highway commercial strip just a few blocks to the east.

◖ Yaquina Head Outstanding Natural Area

Five miles north of Newport, rocky Yaquina Head juts out to sea. Tools dating back 5,000 years have been unearthed at Yaquina Head. Many were made from elk and deer antlers and bone, as well as stone. Clam and mussel shells from middens in the area evidence a diet rich in shellfish for the area's ancient inhabitants.

Today, much of the headland is encompassed in the **Yaquina Head Outstanding Natural Area** (750 NW Lighthouse Dr., 541/574-3100, www.blm.gov, $7 per vehicle), managed by the federal Bureau of Land Management. "Outstanding" is indeed the word for this place; a visitor could easily spend several hours exploring all the site has to offer.

At its outer tip stands **Yaquina Head Lighthouse** (guided tours 10am-4pm Thurs.-Tues., weather permitting), the coast's tallest beacon. In the early 1870s, materials intended for construction of a lighthouse several miles north at Otter Crest were mistakenly delivered here. The 93-foot tower began operation in 1873, replacing the poorly located lighthouse south of here at the mouth of Newport's harbor. Walk up the 114 cast-iron steps for a spectacular panorama of the headland and surrounding coast.

Below, an observation deck provides views of seals, sea lions, gray whales, and seabirds. Of the half dozen varieties of pelagic birds that cluster on Colony Rock—a large monolith in the shallows 200 yards offshore—the tufted puffin is the most colorful. It's sometimes called a sea parrot because of its large yellow-orange bill. Puffins arrive here in April and are most visible early in the day on the rock's grassy patches. The most ubiquitous species are common murres, pigeon guillemots, and cormorants. The murre's white breasts and bellies contrast with their darker bills and elongated backs. The guillemots resemble pigeons with white wing patches and bright red webbed feet. The cormorants look like prehistoric pelicans.

Down a flight of steps from the observation area is Cobble Beach, covered with surprisingly round stones. At low tides, the tidepools at Cobble Beach are teeming with sea stars, purple urchins, anemones, and hermit crabs.

East of the lighthouse, the large **Interpretive Center** (541/574-3116, 9:30am-5pm daily summer, 10am-5pm fall and spring, 10am-4pm winter) features exhibits on local ecosystems, Native American culture, and historical artifacts such as a 19th-century lighthouse keeper's journal. Other highlights include a life-size replica of the Fresnel lens that shines from the top of the nearby lighthouse, a sea cave simulation with a life-size mural of a California gray whale (accompanied by an exhibit detailing its migratory pattern), statues of birds and harbor seals, and information on tidepool inhabitants.

Although the tidepools in an abandoned basalt quarry on the south side of the headland have now largely filled with sand, the short but steep paved path down to Quarry Cove has some great views of the headland, and frequently, good close-up views of sea lions.

Beaches

The beach at **Yaquina Bay State Recreation Site** (541/574-3129 or 800/551-6949, www.oregonstateparks.org) is accessible via a trail from the bluff-top parking area. This is a popular spot for clam digging and agate hunting.

There's also easy beach access from the Nye Beach neighborhood, with a large parking lot at the end of NW Beach St. Two miles south of the Yaquina Bay Bridge, **South Beach State Park** (541/867-4715 or 800/551-6949, www.oregonstateparks.org) draws beachcombers, anglers, campers, and picnickers to its miles of broad sandy beach.

North of town along U.S. 101, **Agate Beach** is a broad swath of coastline famed for its agate-hunting opportunities and its views of nearby Yaquina Head. In addition to the semiprecious stones, the contemplative appeal of Agate Beach inspired no less a figure than Ernest Bloch, the noted Swiss composer, who lived here from 1940 until his death in 1959. Famed violinist Yehudi Menuhin spoke of Bloch and the locale thusly: "Agate Beach is a wild forlorn stretch of coastline looking down upon waves coming in all the way from Asia to break on the shore, a place which suited the grandeur and intensity of Bloch's character."

Moolack Beach, two miles north of Yaquina Head, is a favorite with kite flyers and agate hunters. **Beverly Beach,** 1.5 miles farther north, is a place where 20-million-year-old fossils have been found in the sandstone cliffs above the shore. Beverly Beach also attracts waders, unique for Oregon's chilly waters. Offshore sandbars temper the waves and the weather, so it's not as rough or as cold as many coastal locales. This long stretch of sand (panoramic photos are best taken from Yaquina Head Lighthouse looking north) is connected via an under-highway passage to a large state park campground.

SPORTS AND RECREATION
Fishing

Newport is one of the top spots on the coast for charter fishing, and opportunities abound at the home port of Oregon's second-largest recreational fleet. Bottom fishing (year-round), tuna fishing (Aug.-Oct.), crabbing (year-round), and salmon and halibut fishing (seasonal) are all possible. Typical rates here are $75 for a half day of bottom fishing, $100 for a full day; $130 for an eight-hour chinook salmon outing; $225 for 12 hours of tuna fishing; and $180 for an all-day halibut charter.

In addition to a full menu of fishing excursions, most Newport operators also offer whale-watching charters. **Newport Marina Store and Charters** (2212 OSU Dr., South Beach, 541/867-4470, www.nmscharters.com) offers two-hour whale-watching trips for $30 per person. Two other local operators with similar trips and prices are **Newport Tradewinds** (653 SW Bay Blvd., 541/265-2101 or 800/676-7819, www.newporttradewinds.com) and **Captain's Reel Charters** (343 SW Bay Blvd., 541/265-7441 or 800/865-7441, www.captainsreel.com).

For those who prefer to take matters into their own hands, the clamming and Dungeness crabbing are superlative in Yaquina Bay. If you haven't done this before, local tackle shops, such as the Newport Marina Store in South Beach, rent crab pots or rings and offer instruction. The best time to dig clams is at an extremely low tide. At that time, look for clammers grabbing up cockles in the shallows of the bay. Tide tables are available from the chamber of commerce and many local businesses; they're also easy to find online.

Golf

The public course closest to Newport is

> ## AGATE HUNTING
>
> Hunting for agates after winter storms is a passion at several Oregon beaches, particularly around Newport. Deep in the earth, metals, oxides, and silicates fused together to create this type of quartz. Red, amber, blue, and other tones sometimes form stripes or spots in the translucent rocks. One of the best places to find these treasures is on the beach near the Best Western Agate Beach Hotel, not surprisingly called Agate Beach. Nearby Moolack Beach and the beach at Seal Rock, north of Waldport, as well as area estuaries and streambeds, are more spots worth a look October-May.

nine-hole **Agate Beach Golf Course** (4100 North Coast Hwy., 541/265-7331, www.agatebeachgolf.net, year-round, $36 for 18 holes), just north of town. Just the views of Yaquina Head are worth a visit.

Kayaking

Join a ranger-led kayak tour at **South Beach State Park** (South Beach State Park Hospitality Center, 541/867-6590, Thurs.-Mon. July-Aug., $20, reservations recommended). Kayaks, paddles, and life vests are supplied for the two-hour tours, which set off from Ona Beach, six miles south of South Beach, and travel along Beaver Creek. Paddlers have a chance to see lots of wildlife, including great blue herons, immature bald eagles, turkey vultures, and signs of beavers, such as their lodges. Kayakers on evening tours have a pretty good chance of actually seeing beavers. This is pretty gentle paddling, but not suitable for children under age six; kids under 18 must be accompanied by an adult.

◖ Whale-Watching

The best company on the coast in terms of state-of-the-art equipment and natural history interpretation is **Marine Discovery Tours** (345 SW Bay Blvd., 541/265-6200 or 800/903-2628, www.marinediscovery.com, $36 adults, $34 seniors, $18 children ages 4-13). The two-hour SeaLife tour is narrated by naturalist guides and includes, depending on the time of year, whale-, seal-, and bird-watching, an oyster bed tour, estuary and ocean exploration, and a harbor tour. The 65-foot *Discovery* features video cameras that magnify the fascinating interplay between smaller life-forms, but the real attractions can be appreciated by the naked eye. Landlubbers will especially relish the full crab pots pulled up from the deep and the resident pod of whales often visible north of Yaquina Bay off Yaquina Head.

During the prime whale-watching weeks of late December and late March, volunteers from Whale Watching Spoken Here staff the **Don A. Davis City Kiosk** in Nye Beach to answer questions and help you spot whales.

ENTERTAINMENT AND EVENTS

Overlooking the sea in Nye Beach, the **Newport Performing Arts Center** (777 W. Olive St., 541/265-2787, www.coastarts.org), the Oregon coast's largest performance venue, hosts local and national entertainment in the 400-seat Alice Silverman Theatre and the smaller Studio Theatre. At the same address is the **Oregon Coast Council for the Arts,** which puts out a free monthly newsletter and has ticket information on the PAC venues. It also has updates on the **Newport Visual Arts Center** (777 NW Beach Dr., 541/265-6540), right above the beach two blocks north at the Nye Beach turnaround. Two floors and two galleries—**Runyan Gallery** (11am-5pm Tues.-Sun.) and the **Upstairs Gallery** (noon-4pm Tues.-Sat.)—offer art education programs and exhibition space for paintings, sculpture, and other works, often with a maritime theme. All exhibits are free.

In addition to its impressive schedule of music, dance, drama, and other arts, the Performing Arts Center screens a series of imported and art films—the ones you probably won't find at the multiplex **Newport Cinema** (5836 N. Coast Hwy., 541/265-2111).

In the Bayfront District, **Mariner Square** (250 SW Bay Blvd., 541/265-2206, 9am-8pm July-Aug., 10am-6pm June and Sept., usually 10am-5pm Oct.-May, $11.99 per attraction adults, $6.99 children) is a complex of three attractions that mostly appeal to kids: **Ripley's Believe It or Not!, The Waxworks,** and the **Undersea Gardens.** Discounts are offered to hardy souls who want to take in all three.

Festivals and Events

The biggest bash (and one of the largest events of its kind in the country) is late February's **Newport Seafood and Wine Festival** (541/265-8801 or 800/262-7844, www.seafoodandwine.com, $5-15), which features dozens of food booths and scores of Oregon wineries serving up palate pleasers, along with music and crafts, at the **South Beach Marina** (across Yaquina Bay from the Bayfront). A huge tent joins the exhibition hall, wherein festival-goers wash down delights from the deep with Oregon vintages. The event is open only to the 21-and-over crowd.

The second event of note is **Loyalty Days and Sea Fair** (541/961-1466, www.loyaltydays.com, free) in early May. What began during the Depression as the Crab Festival, intended to stimulate the market for Dungeness crab, was recast during the depths of the Red Scare of the 1950s as a public expression of patriotism. Although that aspect still undergirds the events, it's really just a big community party stretching over four days, with carnival rides, veterans' events, bike races, and a parade.

ACCOMMODATIONS

$100-150

For location, you can't beat **The Whaler** (155 SW Elizabeth St., 541/265-9261 or 800/433-9444, www.whalernewport.com, $117-177). Each of the 73 rooms has a view, and some have fireplaces, wet bars, and private balconies. Guests can use the pool and exercise facilities; continental breakfast is served. Dogs are permitted in some guest rooms.

Stay on the Bayfront at **Anchor Pier Lodge** (345 SW Bay Blvd., 541/265-7829, www.marinediscovery.com, $125-199), up a long flight of stairs from street level, where you'll truly be living "above the store" (there's a gift shop down below). The rooms are simple, with wood-plank floors, but tastefully and individually decorated. Although the Bayfront can be a little noisy with carousing people and sea lions, the inn provides earplugs. Rooms that overlook the bay have balconies; they're the ones to go for.

The extremely popular **Embarcadero Resort** (1000 SE Bay Blvd., 541/265-8521 or 800/547-4779, www.embarcadero-resort.com, $109-299) is bay-front but not beach-front; it overlooks Yaquina Bay and the soaring bay bridge, arguably one of the best views in Oregon. The Embarcadero has an assortment of suites and townhouses (including many timeshare units) with full kitchens and fireplaces. Facilities include an indoor pool, a sauna, two outdoor hot tubs, a restaurant and bar, a private dock, and boat rentals.

If you want to get away from it all, **Little Creek Cove Condominiums** (3641 NW Oceanview Dr., 541/265-8587 or 800/294-8025, www.littlecreekcove.com, $129-259) is a small condo resort that might be what you're looking for. Little Creek Cove resort is two miles north of Newport, perched just above an isolated stretch of beach. You have a choice of studio, one-, and two-bedroom units, each with a private deck, a full kitchen, and a fireplace.

North of town and above a great stretch of beach, the **Moolack Shores Motel** (8835 N. U.S. 101, 541/265-2326, http://moolackshores.com, $105-149) is a quiet spot, even though its parking area is just off the highway. The rooms are individually decorated and more than a little bit quirky, but most have good ocean views, and the beach is just down a long flight of wooden stairs from the motel.

You may not find any riverboat gamblers aboard the **Newport Belle Bed & Breakfast** (2126 SE OSU Dr., 541/867-6290, www.newportbelle.com, closed Nov.-Jan., $150-165), a recently constructed sternwheeler designed as a floating inn, but this 97-foot-long B&B moored on the H Dock of the Newport Marina evokes the ambience of the sternwheeler heyday. Choose from five generous staterooms, each with its own personality and private bath. Most have fabulous vistas of the bustling marina and bridge area. In the evening, guests can retire to their staterooms, enjoy the open afterdeck, or socialize in the main salon, where a gourmet breakfast is served every morning. No children or smoking; pets are allowed in one room. Soft-soled shoes are required.

$150-200

The **℃ Sylvia Beach Hotel** (267 NW Cliff St., 541/265-5428, www.sylviabeachhotel.com, $115-220), a favorite of many Oregonians, combines the camaraderie of a hostel with the intimate charm of a bed-and-breakfast. Built in the era when the Corvallis-to-Yaquina Bay train and seven-seater Studebaker touring cars from Portland ferried the summer folks to

Nye Beach, the hotel and its National Historic Landmark designation and literary theme have attracted an enthusiastic following. The 20 guest rooms, named after different authors, are furnished with decor evocative of each respective literary legacy. The Edgar Allan Poe Room, for instance, has a pendulum guillotine blade and stuffed ravens, while the Agatha Christie Room drops such clues as shoes underneath the curtains and capsules marked "Poison" in the medicine cabinet.

Most of the rooms ("best-sellers") run $160, with several oceanfront suites ("classics") featuring a fireplace and a deck going for $220. "Novels" go for $115 (no ocean view, but still quite charming). All rates include a full breakfast and reflect double occupancy. At breakfast, you have a choice of entrées and share a table with eight other guests, so misanthropes beware! No smoking, pets, or radios are allowed on the premises, and small children are discouraged.

To get there, turn off U.S. 101 onto NW 3rd Street and follow it down to the beach, where NW 3rd and Cliff Streets meet. Look for a large four-story dark green vintage wooden structure with a red roof on a bluff above the surf.

Elizabeth Street Inn (232 SW Elizabeth St., 541/265-9400 or 877/265-9400, www.elizabethstreetinn.com, $169-209), in the Nye Beach neighborhood, sits on a bluff overlooking the ocean. All of the spacious rooms in this newer property face the ocean and have private balconies. They come fully equipped with fireplaces, refrigerators, microwaves, and coffeemakers. Guests also get a complimentary continental breakfast and have use of the indoor pool, spa, and fitness room. Pets are permitted in some rooms.

The **Hallmark Resort** (744 SW Elizabeth St., 541/265-2600 or 888/448-4449, www.hallmarkinns.com, $159-209) is a large hotel complex sitting atop the Newport bluffs, looking westward over the Pacific and miles of sandy beach. Of the many modern hotels that share this vista, the Hallmark is one of the nicest, with large well-maintained guest rooms.

© BILL MCRAE

The Sylvia Beach Hotel is a much-loved Newport landmark.

Facilities include an indoor pool, a spa, and a restaurant. Many guest rooms are pet-friendly.

The **Best Western Plus Agate Beach Inn** (3019 N. Coast Hwy., 541/265-9411 or 800/547-3310, www.newportbestwestern.com, $165, nonview rooms $135) is a tall oceanfront hotel with a fine view overlooking Yaquina Head Lighthouse and Agate Beach. The rooms are comfortable standard-issue hotel rooms, and although it's a little bit of a hike down to the beach, it is one of Newport's best beaches. A sports bar and a restaurant are on-site. Pets are permitted in some guest rooms.

Camping

The campgrounds at Beverly Beach State Park and South Beach State Park are among the most popular on the Oregon coast. Their proximity to Newport, the absence of other camping in the area, and the special features of each explain their appeal.

Beverly Beach State Park (541/265-9278 or 800/452-5687 information, 800/452-5687 or www.reserveamerica.com reservations, $21 tents, $26 RVs, $40 yurts, $6 hiker/biker) is huge multiloop campground set seven miles north of Newport on the east side of the highway in a mossy glade. A pedestrian tunnel passes under the highway and leads to a long wide beach that is unfortunately directly bordered by the road. Devil's Punchbowl and Otter Crest are one and two miles up the highway, respectively.

It's just a hop over the sand dunes to the beach at **South Beach State Park** (541/867-4715 or 800/551-6949 information, 800/452-5687 or www.reserveamerica.com reservations, $21 tents, $27 RVs, $40 yurts, $6 hiker/biker), just south of the Yaquina Bay Bridge. The long beach has opportunities for fishing, agate hunting, windsurfing (for experts), horseback riding, and hiking; sign up in advance (541/867-6500) for kayak tours of nearby Beaver Creek.

FOOD

This is a town for serious diners—folks who know good food and don't mind paying a tad more for it. It's also the kind of place where wharf-side vendors supply fresh fish on the cheap. Mid-May through October, you can pick up the freshest garden produce the area has to offer, plus baked goods, honey, and other delectables at the Lincoln County Small Farmers' Association's **Saturday Farmers Market,** held in the parking area of the **Newport City Hall** (U.S. 101 and Angle St., 9am-1pm, May-Oct.).

About seven miles east of the Bayfront, the **Oregon Oyster Farms** (6878 Yaquina Bay Rd., 541/265-5078, 9am-5pm daily) is the only remaining commercial outlet for Yaquina Bay oysters. Visitors are welcome to observe the farming and processing of these succulent shellfish. Try oysters on the half-shell, or sample smoked oysters on a stick. To get there, follow Bay Boulevard east six miles from the Embarcadero Resort.

Bakeries and Cafés

Down along the Bayfront is a wonderful breakfast haunt, the **Coffee House** (156 SW Bay Blvd., 541/265-6263, www.thecoffeehouse-newport.com, 7am-3pm daily, $6-16). Scones, muffins, and such creative brunch fare as a wild mushroom omelet, crab cakes Florentine, various crepes, meat pasties, and oysters lightly breaded with Japanese panko breadcrumbs are complemented by well-made espresso drinks. In fair weather, the outside deck is a relaxing spot for soaking up some rays while you gaze out on the harbor.

In the Nye Beach neighborhood, a charming spot for breakfast (including a good breakfast burrito) and lunch sandwiches is **Café Stephanie** (411 Coast St., 541/265-8082, 7:30am-3pm daily, $6-11), a bustling cubbyhole with friendly service. Here both breakfast and lunch are served all day long; consider starting your day with a bowl of smoked salmon chowder.

Nearby, the tiny ◖**Panini Bakery** (232 NW Coast St., 541/265-5033, 7am-7pm Thurs.-Mon., $5-12 sandwiches) is a great spot for a chocolate panini, a ginger scone, a slice of pizza, and the local vibe. It's the best bakery in town and has a few tables. The Panini folks

have also opened **Panini Wood Fire Oven** (432 SW Bay Blvd., 541/574-2272, 11am-10pm Wed.-Sun., $5 slice), a hole-in-the-wall joint tucked into a somewhat tacky mall down on the Bayfront. Great pizza, nice vibe, plus beer and desserts.

Italian

◖ **April's at Nye Beach** (749 NW 3rd St., 541/265-6855, http://aprilsatnyebeach.com, 5pm-9pm Wed.-Sun., $16-28) is a small stylish café just across the street from the Sylvia Beach Hotel. Roast duck with port sauce is a standout in a creative Mediterranean-influenced menu. House-made bruschetta and steamed clams with spicy sausage are excellent appetizers. In the summer, many vegetables come from the owners' farm. For dessert, have an éclair dipped in chocolate ganache and topped with slivered almonds. Affordable wines by the glass add to one of Newport's best dining experiences.

Pacific Northwest

You don't have to be a guest to have a meal at the **Tables of Content** (267 NW Cliff St., 541/265-5428, www.sylviabeachhotel.com, seatings at 7pm daily summer, 6pm Sun.-Thurs. and 7pm Fri.-Sat. winter, four-course prix fixe $25), the excellent restaurant at the Sylvia Beach Hotel. There's a nice view of the breakers, good company, and it's a good value for creatively prepared Pacific Northwest cuisine. Each night features several entrée selections with an appetizer, salad, bread, beverages (alcohol not included), and dessert. Diners share tables and are encouraged to break the ice with a game called Two Truths and a Lie, in which they regale each other with several stories, the object being to distinguish which one is untrue. Reservations are mandatory.

Seafood

If you're hankering for a broad selection of fresh local seafood but don't need a fancy dining room to enjoy it in, ◖ **Local Ocean Seafoods** (213 SE Bay Blvd., 541/574-7959, http://localocean.net, 11am-9pm Sun.-Thurs., 11am-9:30pm Fri.-Sat., $6-28) is the place for you.

Part fish market, part seafood grill, this bright and bustling restaurant spotlights sustainably caught fish, offering impeccably fresh fish and a lively atmosphere. Each item in the fish case is identified by name, where it was caught, how it was harvested, and who caught it. The menu items change depending on what's fresh, and though you can count on great fish-and-chips here, you may want to try the house-specialty fish tacos or albacore tuna kebabs.

Right on the bay front, with windows overlooking the active fishing port, **C Saffron Salmon** (859 SW Bay Blvd., 541/265-8921, http://saffronsalmon.com, 11:30am-2:15pm and 5pm-8:30pm Thurs.-Tues., $12-26) is one of Newport's finest choices for expertly prepared, sophisticated seafood. As you'd expect, the specialty is fresh wild salmon, grilled and served with basil-pine nut butter and quinoa, while calamari are sautéed with olive oil and red cabbage. There's also a good selection of organic steaks and rack of lamb.

Also in the old-town harbor area, **Sharks Seafood Bar & Steamer Co.** (852 SW Bay Blvd., 541/574-0590, http://sharksseafoodbar.com, 4pm-9pm Sun.-Wed., 4pm-9:30pm Fri.-Sat., $10-25) specializes in steamed seafood. But don't worry—this isn't tasteless health food. The Catalina bouillabaisse packs a wallop—1.5 pounds of seafood in every spice-filled bowl. You'll also find a savory seafood gumbo, oyster stew, and a mix of stewed and sautéed fish called a pan roast. Fresh fish gets the steam treatment—in season, try halibut, salmon, and rockfish steamed and served with the chef's special sauces. Sharks is also a fun, quirky place; the proprietors provide not just dinner but also a show. Be sure to sidle up to the bar in front of the cooking area to watch the chef in action.

The Newport Bayfront is where Mohava Niemi first opened the original **Mo's** (622 SW Bay Blvd., 541/265-2979, 11am-9pm daily, $4-16) several decades ago. When word got out about the good food and low prices, Mo's small homey place soon had more business than it could handle. In response to the overflow, **Mo's Annex** (657 SW Bay Blvd., 541/265-7512,

11am-9pm daily, $4-16) was created across the street. While both establishments feature such favorites as oyster stew and peanut butter cream pie, the Annex bay windows have the best view. Note that most discerning seafood lovers steer away from Mo's, except when moved by loyalty to a local institution.

There are ample opportunities to buy fresh fish or crab along the bay front in Newport. About a half-mile south of the bridge, the **South Beach Fish Market** (3640 S. U.S. 101, 541/867-6800, 8am-8pm daily, $8-12) sells fresh fish, cooked and uncooked; 90 percent of what they sell comes from the Newport fishing fleet. It's a good place for the family to stop for fish-and-chips after a visit to the aquarium.

Spanish
Right on the bay front, **Bay 839** (839 SW Bay Blvd., 541/265-2839, 11am-11pm Sun.-Thurs., 11am-midnight Fri.-Sat., $6-12) is a cocktail and tapas bar in a former fish processing plant. With great views onto the water, the restaurant is also open late for drinks and food. Favorites include crab cakes, sliders, local Yaquina oysters, red chili fish sandwiches, and whatever is fresh from the fishing boats.

Asian
Although most Asian restaurants on the coast are merely serviceable, a good spot for anything from kimchee to ramen to pho is **Noodle Cafe** (837 SW Bay Blvd., 541/574-6688, 11am-2:30pm and 4:30pm-9pm Mon.-Tues., Thurs.-Sat., 11am-2:30pm Sun., $7-20). The noodles are homemade and the restaurant makes good use of seafood.

Brewpubs
Rogue Ales Public House (748 SW Bay Blvd., 541/265-3188, 11am-midnight Mon.-Wed., Sat., 11am-1am Thurs.-Fri., $7-15) is along the bay in Old Town, serving seafood salads, shrimp-melt sandwiches, pizza, fish-and-chips, and seasonal fish dishes. In addition to the renowned Rogue ales, there's Rogue's draft root beer, a creamy concoction laced with honey and vanilla. Another Rogue Ales brewery, called

Brewers on the Bay (2320 OSU Dr., 541/867-3660, 11am-9pm Sun.-Thurs., 11am-10pm Fri.-Sat., $7-15), is across Yaquina Bay near the Oregon Coast Aquarium. This is where the actual brewing is now done; tours are available weekdays at 3pm.

Rogue's third local outlet is the **Rogue House of Spirits** (2122 Marine Science Dr., 541/867-3670, 4pm-8pm Fri., noon-8pm Sat., noon-6pm Sun.), a distillery pub that produces rum, gin, vodka, and whiskey. The menu here is less extensive than at Rogue's brewpubs, and features excellent cheese from Central Point, Oregon's Rogue Creamery. Tours are offered at 4pm daily.

INFORMATION

The **Greater Newport Chamber of Commerce** (555 SW U.S. 101, 541/265-8801 or 800/262-7844, www.newportchamber.org, 8:30am-5pm Mon.-Fri.) has lots of literature, but the most helpful website for a visitor is the chamber's visitor website: http://discovernewport.com. The **Central Oregon Coast Association** (541/265-2064 or 800/767-2064, www.coastvisitor.com) maintains a useful website with details on Newport and the rest of Lincoln County.

A public radio station, **KLCO,** a local repeater station for Eugene's KLCC, is heard on your dial at 90.5 FM. The **Newport Public Library** (541/265-2153, 10am-9pm Mon.-Wed., 10am-6pm Thurs.-Sat., and noon-5pm Sun.) is at 35 NW Nye Street. The **post office** (310 SW 2nd St., 541/265-5542) is one block west of the highway.

Samaritan Pacific Communities Hospital (930 SW Abbey St., 541/265-2244) is the central coast's only major hospital.

GETTING THERE AND AROUND

Newport is one of the few places on the Oregon coast that can be reached by public transportation. **Valley Retriever** (541/265-2253) buses connect Newport with Corvallis, Portland, and Bend Sunday-Friday. **Lincoln County Transit** (541/265-4900, www.co.lincoln.or.us/transit) runs buses several times daily Monday-Saturday, north to Lincoln City and south to Yachats, with numerous stops en route through Newport.

A **shuttle bus** (http://discovernewport.com, 8am-5:30pm daily) travels up and down the length of Newport on streets just east and west of U.S. 101, going as far south as the Newport Business Plaza in South Beach and north to NE 73rd Street. The wheelchair-accessible bus is equipped with a bike rack. It's free for those with a pass from their Newport hotel and $1 for others. The route is not straightforward; it helps to have a map and schedule (www.newportchamber.org).

Newport's car rental agency of choice is **Enterprise Rent-A-Car** (533 E. Olive St., 541/574-1999).

Waldport and Vicinity

Originally a stronghold of the Alsea Native Americans, Waldport also has had incarnations as a gold rush town, salmon-canning center, and lumber port. This town of about 2,000, whose name means "forest port" in German, is pretty quiet today, with a nondescript main drag that gives no hint of the surrounding beaches and prime fishing and crabbing spots. An influx of retirees in the early 2000s spurred new home construction, particularly on the Alsea spit across from the town, but this place is still decidedly low-key. For those passing through, Waldport provides a low-cost alternative to the big-name destinations; you won't have to fight for a parking spot or make reservations months in advance.

SIGHTS AND RECREATION
Alsea Bay Bridge Historical Interpretive Center
The small museum and visitors center known as the **Alsea Bay Bridge Historical Interpretive Center** (620 NW Spring St., 541/563-2002, 9am-5pm daily summer, 9am-4pm Tues.-Sat. fall-spring, free), operated by the Oregon Parks and Recreation Department and Waldport Chamber of Commerce, stands along the highway on the south side of the river. Exhibits here tell the story of how the sleek 1991 bridge replaced the aging Conde McCullough span across the bay, which has since been demolished. Displays about transportation methods along the central coast since the 1800s, information on the Alsea Native American people, and a telescope trained on the seals and waterfowl on the bay are worth a quick stop. In addition, during the summer Oregon Parks and Recreation guides lead bridge tours daily at 2pm Friday-Monday and give clamming and crabbing demonstrations (locations and times vary according to the tides; see website for calendar).

Seal Rock State Recreation Site
Four miles north of Waldport, **Seal Rock** (800/551-6949, day use only) attracts beachcombers and agate hunters, as well as folks who come to explore the tidepools and observe the seals on offshore rocks. The park's name derives from a seal-shaped rock in the cluster of interesting formations in the tidewater. The picnic area is set in a shady area behind the sandy beach. During Christmas and spring breaks, the volunteers of Whale Watching Spoken Here are on hand to help visitors spot passing grays 10am-1pm.

Ona Beach State Park
Ona Beach State Park (800/551-6949, day use only) a couple of miles north of Seal Rock, is a beguiling park on the west side of the highway. Attractions include a forested picnic area with a 0.25-mile trail and a footbridge over Beaver Creek leading to a fine stretch of beach.

Beaver Creek State Natural Area
The **Beaver Creek State Natural Area** lies two miles east of Ona Beach, up Beaver Creek Road. This coastal wetland area has good paddling (ranger-led kayak tours are organized by staff at South Beach State Park Hospitality Center, 541/867-6590, 8:30am Thurs.-Mon., 6pm Thurs. July-Aug., $16, reservations required) and wildlife-watching, both from the creek and from a viewing blind that's just a short walk from the road. If you're not prepared to paddle, a seven-mile network of hiking trails starts at the visitor center.

Drift Creek Wilderness
Seven miles east of Waldport are the nearly 5,800 acres of the **Drift Creek Wilderness,** which protects the Coast Range's largest remaining stands of old-growth rainforest. Here you can see giant Sitka spruce and western hemlock hundreds of years old, nourished by

© JUDY JEWELL

Seal Rock State Recreation Site

up to 120 inches of rain per year. These trees are the "climax forest" in the Douglas fir ecosystem. They seldom reach old-growth status because the timber industry tends to replant only fir seedlings after logging operations. There is also perhaps the largest population of spotted owls in the state, along with bald eagles, Roosevelt elk, and black bears. Drift Creek sustains wild runs of chinook, steelhead, and coho salmon, which come up the Alsea River.

Steep ridges and their drainages, as well as small meadows, make up the topography, which is accessed via a couple of hiking trails. The trailhead closest to Waldport is the 3.5-mile **Harris Ranch Trail,** which descends 1,200 feet to a meadow near Drift Creek. The local access to Harris Ranch Trail and the conjoining Horse Creek Trail is via Highway 34; turn north off 34 at the Alsea River crossing seven miles east of Waldport. Here, pick up Risely Creek Road (Forest Service Rd. 3446) and Forest Service Road 346 to the trailhead.

Fishing

Waldport's recreational raison d'être is fishing. World-class clamming and Dungeness crabbing in Alsea Bay and the Alsea River's famous salmon, steelhead, and cutthroat trout runs account for a high percentage of visits to the area. Before commercial fishing on the river was shut down in 1957, as much as 137,000 pounds of chinook were netted in a season. The wild fall chinook run remains healthy and starts up in late August. Catch-and-release for sea-run cutthroats starts in mid-August, while steelhead are in the river December-March. Crabbers without boats can take advantage of the Port of Waldport docks.

Gene-O's Guide Service (541/563-3171) calls on four decades of experience to help you reel in salmon and steelhead. **Dock of the Bay Marina** (1245 NE Mill St., 541/563-2003) rents and sells crabbing and fishing supplies and can guide you to the best spots.

Golf

Crestview Hills Golf Course (1680 Crestline

Dr., 541/563-3020, www.crestviewgolf-club.com, year-round, $22 for 9 holes) is a public nine-hole course one mile south of Waldport.

ACCOMMODATIONS
$50-100

Midway between Waldport and Yachats, the **Terry-a-While Motel** (7160 SW U.S. 101, 541/563-3377, www.terry-a-while.com, $60-200) has simple guest rooms that range in style from modern to vintage and in size from basic budget motel size to two-bedroom units with kitchens. Although the guest rooms are not extravagantly furnished, they all have decks with nice views.

The vintage **Cape Cod Cottages** (4150 SW U.S. 101, 541/563-2106, www.capecod-cottagesonline.com, $85-150) offer one- and two-bedroom oceanfront units with complete kitchens, cozy fireplaces, cable television, spectacular views, and private decks. A three-night minimum stay is required in summer.

The **Alsi Resort** (902 NW Bayshore Dr., 541/563-7700, http://alsiresort.com, $79-169) is partly a large beach hotel and partly a retreat center—although when we visited in early summer of 2013, it was mostly a place in transition, with new management, a new vision (of a place where "food, community, and nature meet"), and new staff. Half of the 84 rooms enjoy sweeping views of the bay, bridge, and town (the hotel is not beachfront). Although the hotel has a dining room, and previously had a very good restaurant, no food service was being offered when we were there. Pets are allowed in some guest rooms.

$100-150

The historic **Cliff House** (1450 Adahi Rd., 541/563-2506, www.cliffhouseoregon.com, $125-225) may appear rustic, but in fact this is a lovingly restored historic home, and the location can't be beat. Four guest rooms, some with whirlpools, are decorated with antiques; even the woodstoves are period. No pets are allowed, and children are best left home with the grandparents or a sitter.

Camping

Two excellent campgrounds sit about four miles south of Waldport on U.S. 101 along the beach. **Beachside State Park** (541/563-3220 or 800/551-6949 information, 800/452-5687 or www.reserveamerica.com reservations, $21 tents, $26 RVs, $40 yurts) is near a half mile of beach not far from Alsea Bay and Alsea River. This is a paradise for rock fishers, surfcasters, clammers, and crabbers. Beachside fills up fast, so reserve early for space Memorial Day-Labor Day.

A half mile down U.S. 101, the Siuslaw National Forest's **Tillicum Beach** (877/444-6777 or www.recreation.gov, $24, reservations strongly recommended in summer) is set right along the ocean. Forest Service roads from here access Coast Range fishing streams. You'll also appreciate the strip of vegetation blocking the cool evening winds that whip up off the ocean.

Should Beachside and Tillicum be filled to overflowing, you might want to set up a base camp in the Coast Range along Highway 34—especially if you have fishing or hiking in the Drift Creek Wilderness in mind. Just go east of Waldport 17 miles on Highway 34 to the Siuslaw National Forest's **Blackberry Campground** (877/444-6777 or www.recreation.gov reservations, $22). The 33 sites are open year-round; most are right on the river. A boat ramp, flush toilets, and piped water are on-site.

FOOD

Dining options in Waldport are limited. For good homemade food (think meat loaf sandwiches or fish-and-chips) and a great setting, head seven miles up the Alsea River to **Jamie's Dockside Diner** (7164 E. Alsea Hwy., 541/528-3880, 7am-3pm Thurs.-Tues., $8-12). Don't be afraid when you see that this floating restaurant is accessed via a trailer park; during salmon-fishing season most of the business comes in by boat, and hungry anglers jam the little restaurant.

INFORMATION

The Waldport Chamber of Commerce operates a **visitors center** (620 NW Spring St., 541/563-2133, www.waldport-chamber. com, 9am-5pm daily) in the Alsea Bay Bridge Historical Interpretive Center, just south of the river. The **Siuslaw National Forest-Waldport Ranger Station** (1130 Forestry Ln., 541/563-3211) can provide information on area camping and hiking, including the trails in the Drift Creek Wilderness.

GETTING THERE

Highway 34 runs east from Waldport, following the Alsea River for several miles before veering northeast to Corvallis, about 65 miles away. This is one of the prettiest (and slowest) routes between the coast and the Willamette Valley.

The **Lincoln County Transit** (541/265-4900, www.co.lincoln.or.us/transit) buses run four times a day Monday-Saturday between Yachats and Newport.

Yachats and Cape Perpetua

Yachats (pronounced YAH-hots) is derived from an Alsea word meaning "dark waters at the foot of the mountain." The phrase aptly describes the location of this picturesque resort village of 690 people, clustered on the hillsides and coastal shelf beside the Yachats River mouth in the shadow of Cape Perpetua. Word of mouth has helped to spread the popularity of Yachats as a place for a quiet getaway and a base for enjoying the 2,700-acre Cape Perpetua Scenic Area and nearby beaches.

SIGHTS AND RECREATION

◖ Cape Perpetua

The most notable sight near Yachats, indeed on the whole central coast, is the view from 803-foot-high Cape Perpetua. The name derives from Captain Cook's sighting of the promontory on March 7, 1778, St. Perpetua's Day. It's too bad the British explorer didn't make landfall here to enjoy one of the world's preeminent coastal panoramas. Oregon's highest paved public road this close to the shoreline affords 150 miles of north-to-south visibility from the top of the headland. On a clear day, you can also see 39 miles out to sea.

Prior to hiking the 23 miles of foot trails or driving to the top of the cape, stop off at the **Cape Perpetua Visitor Center** (541/547-3289, 10am-5pm mid-June-Aug., 10am-4pm daily Sept.-mid-June, $5 per car or Northwest Forest Pass), three miles south of Yachats on the east

side of the highway. A picture window framing a bird's-eye view of rockbound coast, along with exhibits on forestry and marine life, begin your introduction to the region. Cataclysms such as the forest fire of 1846, the monsoons and 138-mph winds unleashed by the 1962 Columbus Day Storm, and 1964 Hurricane Frieda are artfully explained by exhibits. An excellent 15-minute film about Oregon's intertidal biome will also hold your interest.

HIKING

Personnel at the desk have maps and pamphlets about such trails as Cook's Ridge, Riggin' Slinger, and Giant Spruce, as well as directions for the auto tour to the summit, from which you can take the 0.25-mile **Whispering Spruce Trail** through the grounds of a former World War II Coast Guard lookout built by the Civilian Conservation Corps (CCC) in 1933. The southern views from the crest take in the highway and headlands as far as Coos Bay. Halfway along the path, you'll come to a Works Progress Administration-built rock hut called the West Shelter that makes a lofty perch for whale-watching, one of the best spots on the entire coast. Beyond this ridgetop aerie the curtain of trees parts to reveal fantastic views of the shoreline between Yachats and Cape Foulweather.

To begin your auto ascent, from the visitor center drive 100 yards north on U.S. 101 and look for the steep winding spur road (Forest Service Rd. 55) on the right. As you climb, you'll notice large Sitka spruce trees abutting the road. Halfway up the two-mile route, you'll come to a Y in the road. Take a hard left and follow the road another mile to the top of Cape Perpetua. If you miss the left turn and go straight ahead, you'll soon find yourself on a 22-mile loop through the Coast Range to Yachats. Along the way, placards annotate forest ecology.

If you'd rather hike to the top of the cape, the awe-inspiring 1.5-mile **Saint Perpetua Trail** from the Cape Perpetua visitors center to the summit is of moderate difficulty, gaining 600 feet in elevation. En route, placards explain the role of wind, erosion, and fire in forest succession in this mixed-conifer ecosystem.

The actual cape is only half the attraction at Cape Perpetua. At least as fascinating are the rocky coast and its tidepools, churns, and spouting horns of water. Just north of the turnoff for the top of Cape Perpetua (Forest Service Rd. 55) and U.S. 101 is the turnout for **Devil's Churn,** on the west side of the highway. Here the tides have cut a deep fissure in a basalt embankment on the shore. You can observe the action from a vertigo-inducing overlook high above or take the easy switchbacking trail down to the water's edge. While watching the white-water torrents in this foaming cistern, beware of "sneaker waves," particularly if you venture beyond the boundaries of the **Trail of the Restless Waters.** The highlights here are the spouting horns and acres of tidepools. All along this stretch of the coast, many trees appear to be leaning away from the ocean as if bent by storms. This illusion is caused by salt-laden westerlies drying out and killing the buds on the exposed side of the tree, leaving growth only on the leeward branches.

Another hike from the Cape Perpetua visitors center goes down to a geological blowhole (called a spouting horn), where seawater is funneled between rocks and explodes into spray. This is the **Captain Cook Trail,** which runs six miles through a dense wind-carved forest and the remains of an old CCC camp under U.S.

© JUDY JEWELL

Birders spend the morning at the Yachats State Recreation Area.

© JUDY JEWELL

It's easy to find a beach of your own around Yachats.

101 to an ancient lava deposit on the shore. Given enough wave action, water bubbles up through fissures in the basalt. There are also Native American shell middens built up 300-2,000 years ago in the area.

State Parks and Coastal Waysides

In this part of the coast, state parks and viewpoints abound with attractions. There's so much to see here that keeping your eyes on the road in this heavily traveled section is a challenge.

A mile north of Yachats, **Smelt Sands State Recreation Site** gives access to tidepools and the 0.75-mile 804 Trail, which follows the rocky shore to a broad sandy beach to the north. In Yachats, turn west onto 2nd Street to loop around wave-battered **Yachats State Recreation Area,** overlooking Yachats Bay. The route heads north along the ocean, where it becomes Marine Drive. After going through a residential community, it eventually takes an easterly turn to reconnect with U.S. 101.

On the south bank of the Yachats River is a short but beautiful beach loop off U.S. 101 (going south, look for the "Beach Access" sign). The road runs between the landscaped grounds of beach houses and resorts on one side and the foamy sea on the other. A wide beach, tidepools, and blowholes on the bank by the river's mouth are a special treat.

A mile south of Cape Perpetua, **Neptune State Park** has a beautiful beach and is near the 9,300-acre **Cummins Creek Wilderness** east of U.S. 101. Just north of Neptune Park, Forest Service Road 1050 leads east to the Cummins Creek Trailhead. A half-mile south, gravelly Forest Service Road 1051 can take you to a point where a moderately difficult 2.5-mile hike leads to Cummins Ridge Trailhead. This pathway has some of the last remaining coastal old-growth Sitka spruce stands. Get maps and detailed directions for these and other area trails at the Cape Perpetua visitor center.

Close by, there's a chance to explore tidepools and sometimes observe harbor seals at **Strawberry Hill.** Scenic shorelines can also be found in the next few miles farther south at **Stonesfield Beach State Recreation Site** and **Muriel O. Ponsler State Scenic Viewpoint.**

ENTERTAINMENT AND EVENTS

This little village seems to be busy with some festival or other event just about every weekend. For a full schedule, see the local chamber of commerce website (www.yachats.org). What follows are some highlights.

Spring brings two arts and crafts festivals to the **Yachats Commons** (U.S. 101 and W. 4th St.): In late March, the chamber-sponsored **Original Yachats Arts and Crafts Fair** (541/547-3530 or 800/929-0477, free) exhibits the work of some 75 Pacific Northwest artists and artisans.

Yachats pulls out all the stops for the **Fourth of July.** Events include the short and silly La De Da Parade at noon, a pie and ice cream social, lots of live music, and a fireworks show on the bay when darkness falls.

During the Yachats **Fish Fry,** held the second Saturday of July, deep-fried cod and snapper are served on the grounds of **Yachats Commons Picnic Shelter** (on 5th St. at U.S. 101). Yachats used to be one of the few places in the world blessed with a run of oceangoing smelt, but they have declined drastically due to changing ocean conditions, and the town's erstwhile smelt fry has morphed into a fish fry. For $10 you get fish and a variety of side dishes and a beverage ($6 for children ages 12 and younger). Or choose a sausage plate for $5. What you're really paying for is a classic small-town festival where you get to rub elbows with a spirited community. More info is available from the chamber of commerce.

The same weekend, the **Yachats Music Festival** takes place several blocks north at the **Presbyterian Church** (360 W. 7th St., 510/845-4444). The lineup features classical virtuosi and vocalists from the San Francisco Bay Area for evening concerts and a Sunday matinee performance.

A relatively new but popular event here is the **Yachats Village Mushroom Fest**

(541/547-3530 or 800/929-0477), held the third weekend in October. Native mushrooms abound in the temperate rainforests of the Cape Perpetua region, and fall is the season to harvest them. Chef John Ullman started the Yachats event, inspired by similar festivals in Italy. Activities over the weekend include the Friday-night Yachats Rainforest Fungi Feast, mushroom-cooking demonstrations, guided mushroom walks at Cape Perpetua visitor center, and the last farmers market of the season.

SHOPPING

Yachats has long been a center for artists and bohemians, and for proof of this you need go no further than **Earthworks Gallery** (2222 U.S. 101 N., 541/547-4300, http://earthworks-galleries.net, 10am-5pm daily). This excellent gallery displays the work of local painters, glass artists, and jewelers, as well as high-quality crafts. **Touchstone Gallery** (2118 U.S. 101 N., 541/547-4121, 10am-5pm daily) is another gallery with unique Pacific Northwest arts and crafts.

ACCOMMODATIONS
$50-100

Facing onto the beach loop south of town, the **Yachats Inn** (331 U.S. 101, 541/547-3456 or 888/270-3456, www.yachatsinn.com, $89-140) offers basic summer shelter with unfussy rooms that have little decks and TVs but no phones, though some have kitchens and fireplaces. There's great access to the beach. Unless you have a dog along, the best bets here are the newly constructed suites, which have full kitchens and fireplaces. The indoor pool overlooks the beach.

For those looking for budget prices close to the center of town, try **Rock Park Cottages** (431 W. 2nd St., 541/547-3214 or 541/343-4382, www.rockparkcottages.com, $75-85), adjacent to Yachats State Recreation Area. Consisting of five rustic cottages arranged around a courtyard, Rock Park has to be one of the better bargains on the coast. The kitchens are well equipped, and the vintage cottages couldn't be better located.

Another good old-fashioned budget choice, **Deane's Oceanfront Lodge** (7365 U.S. 101, 541/547-3321, www.deaneslodge.com, $89-119) is about halfway between Yachats and Waldport. The rooms are well-kept but not fancy; the least expensive don't share the great ocean views afforded by the top-end rooms. Pets are permitted in some rooms.

The **Dublin House Motel** (U.S. 101 and 7th St., 541/547-3703 or 866/922-4287, www.dublinhousemotel.com, $64-94) offers standard motel rooms and ocean views, each room having a microwave, a refrigerator, a coffeemaker, and cable TV; some kitchen units are also available. The indoor heated pool is especially nice in the winter months.

$100-150

A little north of the town center, the imposing **Adobe Resort** (155 U.S. 101 N., 541/547-3141 or 800/522-3623, www.adoberesort.com, $124-235 for ocean view, $85 for hillside view) overlooks Smelt Sands Beach. Although the Adobe isn't what you'd call luxurious, it is one of the few full-service resorts in the area, with an on-site restaurant. All units have refrigerators, microwaves, satellite TV, DVD players, and a phone with voice mail. Pets are accepted in some guest rooms. Two-bedroom hot tub suites are 1,400 square feet and have all the comforts of a small home.

$150-200

A mile north of Yachats, above a thrust of wave-pounded tidepools, **Overleaf Lodge** (280 Overleaf Lodge Ln., 541/547-4880 or 800/338-0507, www.overleaflodge.com, $195-500) offers the newest and nicest rooms in the Yachats area. Most guest rooms have balconies, hot tubs, and fireplaces, and all have fantastic views. Rates include a breakfast buffet plus access to a fitness area. A 3,000-square-foot spa has treatment rooms, steam rooms, and saunas, plus oceanview hot tubs. Adjacent to the lodge are six newly built cottages tucked into the forest. With 2-4 bedrooms, these charming units with Craftsman-style decor have full

kitchens and everything a family or small group will need for a great beach vacation.

The secluded **Sea Quest Inn** (95354 U.S. 101, Ten Mile Creek, 541/547-3782 or 800/341-4878, www.seaquestinn.com, $180-325) is an antique-filled but contemporary inn of cedar and glass, with private entrances, seven miles south of Yachats. The innkeeper puts out a good breakfast, the wraparound deck affords superlative views of the beach, and telescopes and binoculars are always on hand for spotting whales and other marine life. Sea Quest is not appropriate for pets or children under 12 years of age; it is not handicapped accessible.

Vacation Rentals

If you'd rather settle into a house, check out **Yachats Village Rentals** (541/547-3501 or 888/288-5077, www.97498.com), which offers a varied stable of vacation homes ($140-350) for long- or short-term rental.

Camping

Set along Cape Creek in the Cape Perpetua Scenic Area, the Forest Service's **Cape Perpetua Campground** (877/444-6777 or www.recreation.gov reservations, May-Sept., $24), with 38 sites for tents, trailers, or motor homes up to 22 feet long, is a great home base for exploring the wonderful Cape Perpetua area. Picnic tables and grills are provided. Flush toilets and piped water are available.

FOOD

For a town its size, Yachats has particularly good restaurant choices.

Bakeries and Cafés

Start the day at **Green Salmon Bakery and Cafe** (220 U.S. 101, 541/547-3077, 7:30am-2pm Tues.-Sun., $2-10) for fresh breads and very good pastries plus soup and sandwiches for lunch. This lively café, which has a number of environmentally friendly practices, such as using collected rainwater to mop the floors, doubles as a hangout for the local alternative community. Lines can be long and slow-moving at the counter, so come equipped with patience.

American

The carefully restored but fun-loving **(** **Drift Inn Pub** (124 U.S. 101 N., 541/547-4477, 8am-10pm daily summer, 8am-9pm daily winter, $6-23) offers seafood dishes, crunchy salads, fish-and-chips, and other well-prepared pub grub in a relaxed, fun-loving atmosphere. There's often really good live music here, making this a lively spot whether you're here to eat or to quaff a pint or two. Families are welcome.

Italian

Heidi's (84 Beach St., 541/547-4409, 4pm-9pm Wed.-Sun., $12-18) is a quintessential Yachats business. This tiny Italian café serves brick-oven-baked pizza and homey Italian comfort food, including cioppino and butternut squash lasagna, in a modest little space that fronts the bay. Everything is homemade and served with charm and care. Takeout and dinner delivery are also available.

Pacific Northwest

The simply decorated bay-view **Ona Restaurant** (131 U.S. 101 N., 541/547-6627, www.onarestaurant.com, 11am-9pm Mon.-Thurs., 11am-10pm Fri.-Sat., $15-30) serves seasonal cuisine such as grilled fresh seafood, rib eye steaks, and fresh pasta. For appetizers, you can choose between local oysters, shrimp, clams, and crab cakes. Ona has a good happy hour (4pm-6pm Sun.-Thurs.), which is a good time to check out their offerings without emptying your wallet.

On a bluff overlooking Smelt Sands Beach is the glass-enclosed **Adobe Resort** (1555 U.S. 101 N., 541/547-3141, 8am-2:30pm and 5pm-9pm Mon.-Sat., 9am-1pm and 5pm-9pm Sun., $15-27). Two side-by-side semicircular dining rooms, with windows on the crashing surf, are a

great place to start the day for breakfast or end it with a romantic evening meal, with such favorites as pan-fried oysters, salmon, and steaks. Ask about the loft, where elevated coastal views provide photo ops; this is the perfect place to nurse a drink. A Sunday champagne brunch is served.

Seafood

If you are looking for the quintessential fresh seafood experience, go to tiny **Luna Sea Fish House** (153 NW U.S. 101, 541/547-4794, www.lunaseafishhouse.com, 8am-9pm daily summer, 8am-8pm daily winter, $7-16) a fish restaurant owned by a local fisherman. Don't let the simple decor put you off; the food here is *good*. Using local ingredients, and particularly locally caught (never farmed) fish, Luna Sea offers superlative fish-and-chips and fish tacos. Breakfast omelets are also top-notch.

INFORMATION

The **Yachats Area Chamber of Commerce** (241 U.S. 101, 541/547-3530 or 800/929-0477, www.yachats.org, 10am-4pm daily mid-Mar.-Sept., Fri.-Sun. Oct.-mid-Mar.) has a central location on the highway (next to Clark's Market) and an enthusiastic staff. Ask them about fishing, rockhounding, bird-watching, and beachcombing in the area.

The **Central Oregon Coast Association** (541/265-2064 or 800/767-2064, www.coast-visitor.com) maintains a useful website with details on Yachats and the rest of coastal Lincoln County.

GETTING THERE

The bus stop is also in the parking lot of the **Clark's Market** complex (U.S. 101 and W. 2nd St.). Here you can catch **Lincoln County Transit** buses (541/265-4900, www.co.lincoln.or.us/transit), which run four times a day Monday-Saturday between Yachats and Newport, with a link to Lincoln City.

Florence and Vicinity

If you study the map of the central Oregon coast, you'll see that Florence is oriented along the Siuslaw River; a spit of dunes reaches up from the south, barring quick access from downtown to the ocean. But don't dismiss this riverfront town for its lack of oceanfront real estate; the views onto the river are plenty scenic, and Old Town is charming and easy to navigate on foot.

Florence began shortly after the California gold rush of 1849 put a premium on the lumber and produce shipped out via the Siuslaw River estuary. Several decades later, the town's name was inspired by a remnant from a French shipwreck that floated ashore, bearing the ship's name, *Florence*. The townspeople either recognized an omen when they saw it or just couldn't come up with anything better.

SIGHTS

If first and last impressions are enduring, Florence is truly blessed. A short way to the north of town, U.S. 101 passes over Heceta Head, with great views onto the lighthouse there. As you leave the city to the south, a graceful bridge over the Siuslaw ushers you away.

The Siuslaw River Bridge is an impressive example of Conde McCullough's Works Progress Administration-built spans. The Egyptian obelisks and art deco styling of McCullough's designs are complemented by the views to the west of the coruscating sand dunes. To the east, the riverside panorama of Florence's Old Town beckons for further investigation.

Old Town itself is a tasteful restoration, with all manner of shops and restaurants and an inviting boardwalk along the river. The quickest

© BILL McRAE

Florence's elegant McCullough Bridge spans the Siuslaw River.

access to the beach and dunes is south of the bridge via South Jetty Road.

C Sea Lion Caves

Eleven miles north of Florence, you can descend into the world's largest sea cave to observe the only U.S. mainland rookery of Steller sea lions (*Eumetopias jubatus*). **Sea Lion Caves** (91560 U.S. 101, 541/547-3111, www.sealioncaves.com, 9am-7pm daily, closed Thanksgiving and Christmas, $14 adults, $13 seniors, $8 children ages 5-12, children 4 and under free) is home to a herd that averages 200 individuals, although the numbers change from season to season. These animals occupy the cave during the fall and winter, which are thus the prime visitation times. The Steller sea lions you'll see at those times are cows, yearlings, and immature bulls. In spring and summer, they breed and raise their young on the rock ledges just outside the cave. In addition, California sea lions (*Zalophus californianus*), common all along the Pacific Coast, are found at Sea Lion Caves from late fall to early spring.

Enter Sea Lion Caves through the gift shop on U.S. 101. A steep downhill walk reveals stunning perspectives of the coastal cliffs as well as several kinds of gulls and cormorants that nest here. The final leg of the descent is by an elevator that drops an additional 208 feet. After stepping off the lift into the cave, your eyes adjust to the gloomy subterranean light, and you'll see sea lions on the rock shelves amid the surging water inside the enormous cave. Flash photography is forbidden, so study your camera's settings if you want to take pictures inside. You have a better chance of seeing these animals inside during fall and winter. A set of stairs leads up to a view of Heceta Head Lighthouse through an opening in the cave.

Steller sea lions were referred to as *lobos marinos* (sea wolves) in early Spanish mariners' accounts of their 16th-century West Coast voyages, and their doglike yelps might explain why. You'll notice several shades of color in the herd, which has to do with the progressive lightening of their coats with age. Males sometimes weigh more than a ton and dominate the scene with macho posturings to scare off rivals for harems of as many as two dozen cows. Their protection as an endangered species enrages many commercial anglers, who claim that the sea lions take a significant bite out of fishing revenues by preying on salmon. In any case, the close-up view of these huge sea mammals in the cavernous enclaves of their natural habitat should not be missed—despite an odor not unlike sweat-soaked sneakers.

If you can't observe the animals to your satisfaction in the cave, go 0.25 mile north of the concession entrance to the "rockwork" turnout, where the herd sometimes populates the rocky ledges several hundred feet below. It's also a good place to snap a shot of the picturesque Heceta Head Lighthouse across the cove to the north from the turnout.

C Heceta Head Lighthouse and Devil's Elbow

Twelve miles north of Florence, **Heceta Head Lighthouse** (866/547-3696, tours 11am-5pm daily May-Sept., 11am-3pm Fri.-Mon. Mar.-Apr. and Oct., $5 day-use fee) is dramatically situated above a lovely cove at the mouth of Cape Creek and wedged into the flanks of 1,000-foot-high Heceta Head. The white-washed lighthouse was completed in 1894, and beautifully restored in 2012; it's still in use, beaming the strongest light on the Oregon coast from its perch 205 feet above the pounding surf. A little below the lighthouse is Heceta House, where the lighthouse keepers used to live. Today, it serves both as an **interpretive center** (noon-5pm Mon.-Thurs. Memorial Day-Labor Day) and the **Heceta Head Lighthouse B&B** (92072 U.S. 101, 541/547-3696 or 866/547-3696, www.hecetalighthouse.com, $209-315). An easy half-mile trail leads up from the lighthouse's picnic and parking area to the tower. Other than the day-use fee, admission and tours are free.

Just south of the lighthouse, the graceful

© JUDY JEWELL

Heceta Head Lighthouse

arc of Conde McCullough's Cape Creek Bridge spans a chasm more than 200 feet deep. From the lighthouse parking lot, a trail leads down to where Cap Creek meets the beach at **Devil's Elbow State Park.** Be conscious of tides here if you climb along the rocks adjoining the beach.

Heceta Head is said to be the most photographed lighthouse in the country; that may be difficult to verify, but it's impossible to quibble with the magnificent sight of the gleaming white tower and outbuildings on the headland, particularly when viewed from a set of highway pullouts just south of the bridge. The vistas from the lighthouse and network of trails on the headland are no less dramatic: See murres, tufted puffins, and other seabirds, as well as sea lions, on the rock islands below; bald eagles soaring overhead; and in spring, northbound female gray whales and their calves as they pass close to shore. A trail leading to the north side of Heceta Head offers views to Cape Perpetua, 10 miles to the north.

Darlingtonia Botanical Gardens

Three miles north up the Coast Highway from Florence, in an area noted for dune access and freshwater lakes, are the **Darlingtonia Botanical Gardens** (five miles north of Florence on the east side of U.S. 101, 800/551-6949, www.oregonstateparks.org, free). In a sylvan grove of spruce and alder are a series of wooden platforms that guide you through a bog where carnivorous *Darlingtonia californica* plants thrive. Shaped like a serpent's head, the darlingtonia is variously referred to as the cobra orchid, cobra lily, or pitcher plant.

The plant produces a sweet smell that invites insects to crawl through an opening into a hollow chamber beneath the plant's hood. Inside, thin transparent "windows" allow light to shine inside the chamber, confusing the bug as to where the exit is. As the insect crawls around in search of an escape, downward-pointing hairs within the enclosure inhibit its movement to freedom. Eventually, the tired-out bug falls to the bottom of the stem, where it is digested. The plant needs the nutrients from the trapped insects to compensate for the lack of sustenance supplied by its small root system. If you still have an appetite after witnessing this carnage, you might want to enjoy lunch at one of the shaded picnic tables.

Siuslaw Pioneer Museum

To fill yourself in on the early history of Florence and the Siuslaw River Valley, and to get some notion of Native American and pioneer life, spend an hour or so at the **Siuslaw Pioneer Museum** (278 Maple St., 541/997-7884, www.siuslawpioneermuseum.com, noon-4pm daily May-Sept., noon-4pm Tues.-Sun. Feb.-Apr. and Oct.-Dec., $3 adults, children ages 16 and under free). You'll find it in Old Town in a renovated school building from 1905. Along with exhibits on early logging and farming, read an account of how the U.S. government double-crossed the Siuslaw people, who sold their land to the feds and never received the promised recompense. The museum can also set you loose on a walking tour of historic Old Town buildings.

Jessie M. Honeyman Memorial State Park

Jessie M. Honeyman Memorial State Park (84505 U.S. 101 S., 541/997-3641 information, 800/452-5687 reservations, $5 day-use fee or Oregon Coast Passport), three miles south of Florence, has a spectacular dune-scape and then some. Come here in May when the rhododendrons bloom along the short, sinuous road heading to the parking lot. A short walk west of the lot brings you to a 150-foot-high dune overlooking Cleawox Lake. From the top of this dune, look westward across the expanse of sand, marsh, and remnants of forest at the blue Pacific some two miles away. This is also a popular place to camp.

South Jetty

The northern boundary of the Oregon Dunes National Recreation Area is at the **South Jetty** ($5 per car or Northwest Forest Pass), where the Siuslaw River flows into the Pacific Ocean. May-September and on all weekends and holidays, the beach at the South Jetty is closed to motor vehicles, and even though there are no marked trails, it's a great place to explore the dunes in near solitude. The road into the jetty has several staging areas for off-highway vehicles; during the summer months, the area south of the road is open to motor vehicles. South Jetty Road is 0.5 mile south of the Siuslaw River Bridge.

SPORTS AND RECREATION

Huckleberry picking is an attraction just outside Florence. Some prime pickings are found about five miles north of Florence along the Sutton Creek Trail, which begins in the Sutton campground just off U.S. 101. During late summer or fall, these berries flourish below the dense canopy of shore pines.

Hiking

You'll find incredibly scenic hiking in the area around **Carl G. Washburne State Park,** 14 miles north of Florence on U.S. 101. At the southern end of the park is the **Hobbit Trail,** which winds 0.4 mile through dense forest

thickets of pine, fir, and rhododendrons to the three-mile-long beach. From the same trailhead, another path takes off uphill to the **Heceta Head Lighthouse**. In its 1.75-mile run, the trail gains quite a bit of elevation and passes some outstanding viewpoints. Also starting at the same U.S. 101 parking area, the **China Creek Trail** (a.k.a. the Valley Trail) runs 1.7 miles on the east side of the highway through a series of elk meadows to the Washburne campground. The parking area for all these hikes is on the east side of U.S. 101. It's also possible to park in the day-use lot across the highway from the campground, catch the Valley Trail near the campground entrance, and hike to the Hobbit and Heceta Head Trails.

Up the North Fork of the Siuslaw River is the **Pawn Old-Growth Trail,** a half-mile pathway through 9-foot-thick, 275-foot-tall Douglas fir and hemlock trees that are several hundred years old. The trailhead, at the confluence of the North Fork of the Siuslaw and Taylor's Creek, is a good place to see salmon spawning in the fall and observe water ouzels (also called dippers). The trail follows the creek and offers interpretive placards along the way. At one point in the trail, visitors walk through fallen Douglas fir logs 21 feet in diameter. Placards explain the science of tree rings. From Florence, take Highway 126 east for 1 mile, then turn north onto Forest Road 5070 and take it 12 miles to Forest Road 5084; stay right and go another five miles to the trailhead.

An excellent and not terribly difficult introduction to dune hiking can be found about 10 miles south of Florence at the **Oregon Dunes Day-Use Area** ($5 day-use fee). The **Overlook Beach Trail** runs for about a mile from a viewing platform to the beach. Follow the blue-topped wooden posts that mark the trail through the sand. To turn this into a more strenuous 3.5-mile loop, continue one mile south along the beach and head back inland (again following the posts) along the more rugged **Tahkenitch Creek Loop.** Find the turnoff from U.S. 101 near milepost 201.

Another good place to explore the dunes is along **Carter Dunes Trail** and **Taylor Dunes**

CENTRAL COAST

© BILL MCRAE

A guided dune buggy tour is the easiest way to experience the Oregon Dunes.

Trail. Carter Dunes Trail starts near Carter Lake and heads west 1.5 miles to the beach. The first half of the mile-long Taylor Dunes Trail is wheelchair accessible; the trail passes some of the oldest (and gnarliest) conifers in the area. Both of these trails are good places to view wildlife, especially in the winter and spring, when the dunes take on wetland characteristics. The two trails link up, forming a Y rather than a loop. The turnoff for both trails is 7.5 miles south of Florence. Carter Lake also has a campground.

Hike the **Waxmyrtle Trail** along the Siltcoos River; the 1.5-mile trail travels along the estuary and ends up at the beach. The trail is closed March 15-September 15 to protect nesting snowy plover. This is a good spot for birdwatching. Find the trailhead near the Waxmyrtle campground about eight miles south of Florence at the Siltcoos Recreation Area.

Dune Rides
Ride into the dunes with the folks from **Sand Dunes Frontier** (83960 U.S. 101,

541/997-3544, http://sanddunesfrontier.com). Half-hour-long, 20-person dune buggy rides cost $12 for adults and $10 for children ages 4-11 years old. Protective goggles are provided, along with a driver. At the same location **Torex ATV Rentals** (541/997-5363, $50-150 per hour) rents vehicles for travel in specially designated areas within the Oregon Dunes National Recreation Area. Go in the morning when the sand tends to blow around less.

Fishing
Oregon's largest coastal lake, 3,100-acre **Siltcoos Lake,** six miles south of Florence, offers excellent fishing and other recreation. The lake is stocked with rainbow trout in the spring, and steelhead, salmon (the lake is closed to coho fishing), and sea-run cutthroat trout move from the ocean into the lake via the short Siltcoos River in late summer and fall, but the real excitement here is the fishing for warm-water species, which is some of the best in the Pacific Northwest. Bluegill, crappie, yellow perch, and brown bullhead action is good

through the summer, while fishing for large-mouth bass can be good year-round. Access points include several public and private boat ramps on the lake, as well as a wheelchair-accessible fishing pier at Westlake Resort.

Golf

Ocean Dunes Golf Links (3345 Munsel Lake Rd., 541/997-3232, $28 for 9 holes, $48 for 18 holes), part of the Three Rivers Casino complex, lets you tee off with sand dunes (some more than 60 feet tall) as a backdrop. The manicured 18-hole course has a driving range, a full pro shop, and equipment rentals on-site. For the ultimate in golfing by the dunes, however, try **Sandpines Golf Course** (1201 35th St., 541/997-1940, www.sandpines.com, $70 for 18 holes, $55 for Oregon and Washington residents). To get there, go west off U.S. 101 on 35th Street. In May and June rhododendrons line this drive, which heads into dune country as you move toward the sea. Follow the signs until you see a water tower not far from the pro shop. A par-72 7,190-yard course, Sandpines's layout features fairways lined with lakes, Douglas firs, and beach grass on gently undulating terrain; the inward nine holes are traditional links style. Coastal winds that kick up in the afternoon can figure prominently in your shot selection.

Horseback Riding

Riding across the dunes into the sunset on a trusty steed sounds like a fantasy, but you can do it thanks to **C&M Stables** (90241 U.S. 101, 541/997-7540, www.oregonhorsebackriding.com, 10am-5pm daily). Rates range $55-110 per person for trips of 1-2 hours (with discounts for larger parties). The stables are open daily and are located near 14 miles of horse trails that wind through the forest on a bluff above the beach. With beach rides, dune trail excursions, and sunset trips, there's something for everybody.

Sandboarding

Dude, it's a natural! Wax up a board, strap it onto your bare feet, and carve your way down the dunes. On the outskirts of Florence, you can rent a board and try out the rails and jumps at **Sand Master Park** (5351 U.S. 101, 541/997-6006, www.sandmasterpark.com, 9:30am-6:30pm daily June-mid-Sept., 10am-5pm Mon.-Tues. and Thurs.-Sat., noon-5pm Sun. Mar.-May and mid-Sept.-mid-Jan., board rentals from $16 includes admission). If you're more of a do-it-yourselfer, a number of roadside shops rent sandboards, and the dunes are certainly plentiful.

Water Sports

Although only the hardiest swimmers go into the ocean without wetsuits, **Cleawox** and **Woahink Lakes** warm up sufficiently to make summertime swimming enjoyable. Cleawox, the smaller of the two, is especially well suited for swimming. Woahink, which has a boat ramp and canoe rentals, is good for paddling. Both lakes are within Honeyman State Park, three miles south of Florence ($5 per vehicle day-use fee).

Surfers head to the beaches at South Jetty; the waves are best when small—they can often become overwhelming and unsuitable for novices. Look for more protection from the wind at the mouth of the river.

South of Florence, in the Oregon Dunes National Recreation Area, the **Siltcoos River** invites kayakers and canoeists to explore the two-mile stretch between Siltcoos Lake and the sea. Meandering two miles through dunes, forest, and estuary, the Siltcoos is a gentle Class I paddle with no white water or rapids, although a small dam midway must be portaged. Wildlife that you may encounter along the way include mink, raccoons, otters, beavers, and even bears. In the estuary, sea lions and harbor seals are common. Rent a canoe or kayak form **Siltcoos Lake Resort** (82855 Fir St., Westlake, 541/999-6941, www.siltcooslakeresort.com, $45 per day).

ENTERTAINMENT AND EVENTS

For current information on Florence area events, contact the **Florence Chamber of**

DUNE COUNTRY: COOS BAY TO FLORENCE

Even though the 47-mile stretch of U.S. 101 between Coos Bay and Florence does not overlook the ocean, your eyes will be drawn constantly westward to the largest and most extensive oceanfront dunes in the world.

How did they come to exist in a coastal topography otherwise dominated by rocky bluffs? A combination of factors created this landscape over the past 12,000 years, but the principal agents are the Coos, Siuslaw, and Umpqua Rivers. The sand and sediment transported to the sea by these waterways are deposited by waves on the flat shallow beaches. Prevailing westerlies move the particulate matter exposed by the tide eastward up to several yards per year. Over the millennia, the dunes have grown huge, with some topping 500 feet.

Constantly on the move, the shifting sands have engulfed ancient forests, a fact occasionally corroborated by hikers as they stumble on the top of an exposed snag. The cross-section of sand-swept woodlands seen from U.S. 101 demonstrates that this inundation is still occurring. Nonetheless, the motorist gets the impression that the trees are winning the battle because the dunes are only intermittently visible from the road.

The Oregon Dunes National Recreation Area (NRA) is home to more than 400 species of flora and fauna, but the only dangerous animal within this ecosystem is possibly the American teenager. This species migrates here during summer vacation to assault the dunes with a variety of all-terrain vehicles. Of the 31,500 acres within the NRA, nearly half are designated open sand and riding trails for off-highway vehicles such as dune buggies.

GETTING ORIENTED

Reedsport and the nearby fishing village of Winchester Bay have carved out identities as refueling and supply depots for excursions into Oregon's Sahara-by-the-Sea. A great place to start your explorations is the **Oregon Dunes NRA Visitor Information Center** (885 U.S. 101, Reedsport, 541/271-6100, www.fs.usda.gov/siuslaw), at the junction of the Coast Highway and Highway 38. In addition to the printed information on hiking, camping, and recreation, the Siuslaw Forest Service personnel are very helpful.

Note that a $5 day-use fee is charged per vehicle at most facilities and access points within the NRA. You can purchase an annual pass at the Dunes Visitor Center for $30.

Because the dunes are difficult to see from the highway in many places, the most commonly asked question in the visitors center is "Where are the dunes?" To answer that question for everybody, the National Forest Service opened **Oregon Dunes Overlook** just south of Carter Lake, midway between Florence and Reedsport, at the point where the dunes come closest to U.S. 101. In addition to four levels of railing-enclosed platforms connected by wooden walkways, there are trails down to the sand. It's only about 0.25 mile to the dunes and then 1 mile through sand and wetlands to the beach.

You can hike a loop beginning where the sand gives way to willows. Bear right en route to the beach. Once there, walk south 1.5 miles. A wooden post marks where the trail resumes. It then traverses a footbridge going through trees onto sand, completing the loop. If you go in February, this loop has great bird-watching potential. A day-use fee is charged for cars.

Commerce (541/997-3128, www.florence-chamber.com).

During the third weekend of May, Florence celebrates the **Rhododendron Festival** coinciding with the blooming of these flowers, which proliferate in the area. It's a tradition that goes back to 1908, when the festival was started as

a way to draw attention and commerce to the area. A parade, carnival, flower show, 5K and 10K "Rhody Run," and the crowning of Queen Rhododendra are highlights of the festivities. This is a very popular event, attracting more than 15,000 visitors each year.

Fourth of July celebrations include live

Other sites, listed from south to north, for easy introduction to the dune topography are: Spinreel Campground, Umpqua Dunes Trail, Honeyman State Park, and Florence's South Jetty.

RECREATION IN THE DUNES

There are three excellent state parks and a dozen Siuslaw National Forest Campgrounds within the NRA. Although joyriding in noisy dune buggies and other off-road vehicles doesn't lack devotees, the best way to appreciate the interface of ecosystems is on foot. Dunes exceeding 500 feet in height, wetland breeding grounds for waterfowl and other animals, evergreen forests, and deserted beaches can be encountered in a march to the sea. Numerous designated hiking trails, ranging from easy half-mile loops to six-mile round-trips, give visitors a chance to star in their own version of *Lawrence of Arabia* as they moonwalk through this earthbound Sea of Tranquility. The soundtrack is provided by the 247 species of birds—along with your heartbeat—as you scale these elephantine anthills. Deserted beaches and secret swimming holes are among the many rewards of the journey.

Before setting out, pick up the *Hiking Trails Recreation Opportunity Guide* from the Oregon Dunes NRA Visitor Center. This and other publications will correct the superficial impression that the dunes are just a domain for all-terrain vehicles and day hikers.

To ensure a *bon voyage,* it's important to understand this terrain. Carry plenty of water and dress in layers—there are hot spots in dune valleys and ocean breezes at higher elevations. Expect cool summers and wet mild winters. Although rainfall can average more than 70 inches per year (with 75 percent of it falling Mar.-Nov.), a string of dry 50-60°F days in February is not uncommon. Another surprise is summertime morning fog, brought in by hot weather inland. These fogs, together with the inevitable confusion caused by dunes that don't look much different from each other, make a compass necessary. The lack of defined trails also compels such measures as marking your return route in the sand with a stick. Binoculars can help with visual orientation, not to mention the bird-watching opportunities galore.

It's a slow 1.25-mile walk to the beach from Oregon Dunes Overlook.

© JUDY JEWELL

outdoor music and a barbecue in Old Town, and a fireworks display over the river.

Authors, publishers, and readers gather at the **Florence Festival of Books** (541/997-1994) at the Florence Events Center the last weekend of September.

For general entertainment, the tribes run **Three Rivers Casino** (5647 Hwy. 126, 541/997-7529). Along with the slots and game tables, there's a hotel and golf course.

ACCOMMODATIONS

As just about everywhere else, there are budget motels on the main drag, but to experience the coast fully, try one of the romantic getaways between Florence and Yachats. There are a number of notable B&Bs north of town, some of which are detailed as follows or earlier in this chapter.

Unless otherwise noted, prices listed are for high-season doubles.

$50-100

One of the best bargains in town is the **Lighthouse Inn** (155 U.S. 101, 541/997-3221 or 866/997-3221, http://lighthouseinn-florence.com, $84-143), a Cape Cod-style two-story motel on the highway close to the bridge and convenient to Old Town. With neatly kept rooms decorated with bric-a-brac and other homey touches, it may give you the feeling that you're spending the night at your grandmother's house. There are no in-room kitchens, but a common refrigerator and a microwave are available for guest use. Most guest rooms have a queen- or king-size bed and sleep two; some are considered suites, with two rooms and a connecting bath, sleeping up to five guests. A few rooms are designated as pet-friendly.

Just around the corner from Old Town, and across the highway from the Lighthouse Inn, the pet-friendly **Old Town Inn** (170 U.S. 101 N., 541/997-7131 or 800/301-6494, www.old-town-inn.com, $99) provides guests with spacious rooms a short walk away from the river and Old Town. Although this motel is on U.S. 101, the guest rooms are fairly quiet.

If it's not important for you to be an easy walk from Old Town, consider staying three miles south of town at the charming and pet-friendly **(Park Motel** (85034 U.S. 101, 541/997-2634 or 800/392-0441, www.park-motelflorence.com, $69-138), a classic mom-and-pop place set well back from the highway in a stand of Douglas firs. The guest rooms are paneled in knotty pine and come in a variety of sizes and configurations, including a few cabins, making it a good place for families or groups of friends.

$100-150

For a river experience, try the **(River House Motel** (1202 Bay St., 541/997-3933 or 888/824-2454, www.riverhouseflorence.com, $119-179). It's worth paying extra for a riverfront balcony ($149). This newer and attractive motel, which also has good views of the Siuslaw River Bridge, is just two blocks away from the heart of Old Town.

$150-200

(The Edwin K B&B (1155 Bay St., 541/997-8360 or 800/833-9465, www.edwink.com, $160-185) has six guest rooms, all with private bathrooms, and is just two blocks from Old Town, across the street from the Siuslaw River. River views, period antiques, and multi-course breakfasts with locally famous soufflés and home-baked breads served on fine china have established this gracious 1914 home as Florence's preeminent B&B. Add a private courtyard and waterfall in back, tea and sherry in the afternoon, and a restful atmosphere, and you'll understand the need to reserve well in advance.

On the south bank of the river, just across the bridge from Old Town, the **Best Western Pier Point Inn** (85625 U.S. 101, 541/997-7191 or 800/425-6736, www.bwpierpointinn.com, $189-199) offers spacious rooms, great bay views, sand-dune hiking across the street, and a complimentary hot breakfast. Rates at this large and classy motel drop by about half in the off-season.

At Heceta Beach, on the northern edge of Florence, **Driftwood Shores Resort** (88416 1st Ave., 541/997-8263 or 800/422-5091, www.driftwoodshores.com, $122-264) is unique among Florence lodgings in that it is oceanside. It is also a huge complex, and in a pretty isolated area, far from Old Town and restaurants (except the resort restaurant). All rooms face the ocean and have decks or patios, as well as microwaves and refrigerators (some suites have full kitchens).

Over $200

Twelve miles north of Florence and just a short walk from Heceta Head Lighthouse is **Heceta Head Lighthouse B&B** (92072 U.S. 101,

© JUDY JEWELL

Guests at the Heceta Head Lighthouse B&B stay in the former house of the lighthouse keeper.

541/547-3696 or 866/547-3696, www.hecetalighthouse.com, $209-315), built in 1893. It used to be the lighthouse keeper's home; today, it's a B&B with antique furnishings and vintage photos, which help re-create the lives of the keepers of the flame. Among the six bedrooms, the two Mariners' rooms command the finest views. The current caretakers maintain a garden on the grounds, as did the actual lighthouse keepers of yesteryear, and they use some of the produce to turn out amazing seven-course breakfasts, glorious 90-minute affairs replete with such dishes as d'Anjou pear with chevre and Oregon honey and vol-au-vent stuffed with eggs, chives, and asparagus. The innkeepers are more likely to tell you about resident ghosts during breakfast than right before bedtime.

Vacation Rentals

Elson Shields Property Management (3298 U.S. 101, 541/997-6235, www.florencerentals.com) offers vacation home rentals in the Florence and Oregon Dunes area.

Camping

There are excellent campgrounds around Florence, several with recreational opportunities comparable to those at the nearby Oregon Dunes National Recreation Area but with more varied scenery.

Carl G. Washburne State Park (93111 U.S. 101 N., 541/547-3416 information, 800/452-5687 yurt reservations, year-round, $21 tents, $26 RVs, $39 yurts, $5 hiker-biker spaces) is popular with Oregonians because of its proximity to beaches, tidepools, Sea Lion Caves, and hiking trails. The seven walk-in tent sites are secluded and the 56 full-hookup sites have electricity and water; like almost all state park campgrounds, there are showers. Reservations are not accepted for regular sites, but the park's two yurts can be reserved. It's 14 miles north of Florence on U.S. 101 (three miles past Sea Lion Caves), then one mile west on a park road. This state park offers a number of good hiking trails and three miles of relatively isolated beach.

Three miles south of Florence's McCullough

Bridge and on both sides of U.S. 101 is **Honeyman State Park** (84505 U.S. 101 S., 541/997-3641 information, 800/452-5687 reservations, $21-39). This exceedingly popular campground gets very crowded in the summer—reservations are a must—but it empties out enough during spring and autumn to make a stay here worthwhile. The park has two large freshwater lakes, formed by mountain streams that flow toward the Pacific but are trapped by sand dunes. Ask about canoe rentals to savor the serenity of Cleawox Lake. Fishing, swimming, hiking, and dune buggies are available nearby, so there's always something to do. Sandboarding down the incredible dunes is also a popular activity here. In spring, pink rhododendrons line the highway and park roads. There are 187 tent sites with the basics ($21), 121 electrical-hookup and 47 full-hookup ($26), and 10 yurts ($39). Facilities include showers, a playground, and interpretive events. Advance reservations are accepted Memorial Day-Labor Day.

These large state park campgrounds are deservedly popular with families but can get to be bustling. If you're looking for something smaller and low-key (with flush toilets but no showers) then two Siuslaw National Forest Service campgrounds just north of Florence might be the ticket. **Sutton Campground** (877/444-6777 or www.recreation.gov, $22 regular site, $26 with electricity) is four miles north of Florence, and in addition to 80 campsites amid the dunes, it features a darlingtonia bog and a hiking trail network. In high summer season, about a quarter of the sites can be reserved; the rest are available on a first-come, first-served basis.

Just another mile north is **Alder Dune Campground** (877/444-6777 or www.recreation.gov, $22) with two lakes with swimming beaches and trout fishing. Hiking trails lead out into the dunes and reach the Pacific beaches. During summer high season, all of the campground's 39 sites can be reserved. For more information on these campgrounds, contact the **Suislaw National Forest** (541/750-7000, www.fs.fed.us).

FOOD

The majority of Florence restaurants are along the Old Town waterfront. Walk along Bay Street and discover dozens of dining options, from casual to upscale.

Bakeries and Cafés

Under the bridge in Old Town, **Siuslaw River Coffee Roasters** (1240 Bay St., 541/997-3443, www.coffeeoregon.com, 7am-5pm daily, $2-6) serves good coffee and pastries. There's a little deck out back overlooking the river, and lots of books and hobnobbing inside.

If you're visiting on a rainy afternoon, a good place to while away the time is **Lovejoy's Tea Room** (129 Nopal St., 541/997-0502, lovejoysrestaurant.com, 11am-6pm daily, $8-16), owned by the founder of a famed San Francisco tearoom. Dine on a Cornish pasty or sausage roll ($8) or go for high tea service ($15.95).

For a fresh-baked muffin, slice of banana bread, or scone and a chat with a friendly baker,

© JUDY JEWELL

Take your coffee out back of Siuslaw River Coffee Roasters for good views of the river.

search out the **Shed Bakery** (182 Laurel St., 541/590-0712, www.beccabakesit.com, 10am-6pm Thurs.-Sat. and Mon.-Tues., $2-4). The tiny bakery is off a large parking lot, tucked behind a beauty salon.

American

It doesn't look like much from the front, but the best reason to seek out the **Traveler's Cove** (1362 Bay St., 541/997-6845, 9am-9pm daily, $9-20) is the lovely back patio, with tables directly over the river. The food here is eclectic, with homemade clam chowder, tempting salads and sandwiches, and a number of Mexican dishes. Fresh Dungeness crab makes an appearance here with crab quiche, crab enchiladas, and "crabby" Caesar salad.

Italian

A good place to take a break from chowder (though not necessarily seafood) is **Pomodori Ristorante** (1415 7th St., 541/902-2525, www.lapomodori.com, 11:30am-2pm and 5pm-9pm Tues.-Fri., 5pm-9pm Sat., $14-21), an intimate northern Italian restaurant in a converted house. Specialties include fresh shrimp and halibut and pasta, as well as a pork chop stuffed with shrimp, pancetta, scallions, and tomatoes.

Down in Old Town, eat everything from breakfast to pizza at **1285 Restobar** (1285 Bay St., 541/902-8338, 9am-10pm daily, $8-17), a lively trattoria with a focus on seafood entrées. And although the breakfast menu has many traditional American dishes, why pass on the chance to have breakfast pizza, topped with an egg?

Pacific Northwest

The Oregon coast isn't really known for adventurous fine dining, but a handful of hip eateries are spicing up the scene. At the edge of Old Town, the ◖ **Homegrown Public House** (294 Laurel St., 541/997-4886, www.homegrown-pub.com, 11:30am-close Tues.-Sat. and 11am-3pm Sun., $8-17) is an easygoing place for a beer and a snack or a full meal. As the name implies, much of the food is locally grown or

gathered (try the summer chanterelles if they're available) and seasonal.

Seafood

No one will ever accuse the ◖ **Waterfront Depot** (1252 Bay St., 541/902-9100, www.thewaterfrontdepot.com, 4pm-10:30pm nightly, $12-18) of lacking in personality; it's a friendly bustling place with good views out onto the river and lovely filtered evening light. This historic structure was formerly the rail station at nearby Mapleton before it was barged down the Siuslaw River to its current riverfront location. Ask for a table or sit at the bar, where you're likely to be next to a local regular in for the restaurant's signature dish, saucy crab-encrusted halibut fillet. For lighter appetites, try ordering from the tapas menu, which, like all the offerings, is written on a chalkboard up on the wall.

In Old Town, the local **Mo's** (1436 Bay St., 541/997-2185, 11am-9pm, $9-15) is the largest outlet of this famed Oregon chowder house, and its fresh fish, fast service, fair prices, and Siuslaw River frontage make it this neighborhood's most popular restaurant.

The **Bridgewater Fish House and Zebra Bar** (1297 Bay St., Old Town, 541/997-9405, 11am-10pm Wed.-Mon., $17-36) is what passes for fine dining in Old Town. But with its rattan furniture and tropical motif, it's much less stuffy than most white-tablecloth establishments. Fresh fish, often with a Cajun flair, dominates the menu, which is so wide-ranging that almost everyone can find something to his or her liking.

Dessert

After dinner, have dessert at one of the two locations of **BJ's Ice Cream Parlor** (2930 U.S. 101 or 1441 Bay St., 541/997-7286, 10am-11pm daily summer, 11am-10pm daily winter, $2-6). BJ's churns out hundreds of flavors, with 48 on display at any given time, famous all over Oregon. Full fountain service, ice cream cakes, cheesecakes, gourmet frozen yogurt, and pies complement the cones and cups.

INFORMATION AND SERVICES

The **Florence Area Chamber of Commerce** (290 U.S. 101, 541/997-3128, www.florencechamber.com, 9am-5pm Mon.-Fri.), is three blocks north of the Siuslaw River Bridge.

Peace Harbor Hospital (400 9th St., Florence, 541/997-8412) is open 24 hours, with a handful of specialists and an emergency room. The **post office** (770 Maple St., 541/997-2533), near the junction of Highway 126 and U.S. 101, is close to the library.

GETTING THERE

Porter Stage Lines (541/269-7183, www.amtrak.com) offers daily bus service between Coos Bay in the south and Eugene to the east. These buses can be booked online through Amtrak's reservation service. Eugene offers both Greyhound and Amtrak service, as well as air links to the rest of the country from Mahlon Sweet Field Airport (EUG).

Reedsport and Winchester Bay

If you're going fishing or coming back from a dunes hike, you'll appreciate a hot meal and a clean low-priced motel room in Reedsport. Otherwise, this town of 5,000 people might seem like a strange mirage of cut-rate motels, taverns, and burger joints in the midst of the Oregon Dunes National Recreation Area. Reedsport is not a tourist town, to put it politely. But there's lots of fascinating recreation available in the Oregon Dunes NRA that encircles the town, and the Umpqua River is itself a destination for anglers.

Jedediah Smith explored this country in 1828 after the Hudson's Bay Company's Peter Skene Ogden theorized that the Umpqua River—the largest river between San Francisco Bay and the Columbia—might be the fabled Northwest Passage. It wasn't, of course, but this river is still one of the great fishing streams of the state. Zane Grey avoided writing about it, lavishing the publicity instead on the Rogue to divert people from his favorite steelhead spots.

Cargo ships from Scottsburg, a hamlet some 17 miles upriver from Reedsport, supplied San Francisco markets with meat, milk, and produce between 1856 and the early 20th century. In its 1850s heyday, Scottsburg was larger than Portland, with some 5,000 residents, before an 1861 flood destroyed much of the town.

Two miles north of Reedsport, the little burg of Gardiner was created in the wake of a shipwreck. The *Bostonian* (owned by a Mr. Gardiner) was dashed against the rocks at the mouth of the Umpqua in 1856, and from its remnants the first wood-frame structure in this area was built. It was soon joined by other white-painted homes and facilities for a port on the Umpqua. This "white city by the sea" declined in importance when the highway elevated Reedsport to regional hub status, and lost more punch when its huge lumber mill was closed, and then demolished.

Three miles southwest of Reedsport, Salmon Harbor Marina in **Winchester Bay** (pop. 1,000), a busy port for commercial sportfishing at the mouth of the Umpqua, has given the whole area new life in recent years, following hard times precipitated by the decline in timber revenues. In many ways, Winchester Bay is the more interesting destination of the two side-by-side towns, with its busy harbor and collage of waterfront bars and restaurants.

SIGHTS
Umpqua Discovery Center

In Reedsport's Old Town on the south bank of the river, the **Umpqua Discovery Center** (409 Riverfront Way, 541/271-4816, www.umpquadiscoverycenter.com, 9:30am-5pm Mon.-Sat., 11am-4pm Sun. mid-Mar.-mid-Oct., 10am-4pm Mon.-Sat., 11am-4pm Sun. mid-Oct.-mid-Mar., $8 adults, $4 children ages 6-15)

© BILL MCRAE

The Umpqua Discovery Center is on the Reedsport waterfront.

interprets the regional human and natural history through multimedia programs, dioramas, scale models, and helpful staff. The gift store is stuffed with local goodies. The boardwalk and observation tower give a good view of the broad lower reaches of the Umpqua. In summer, free Thursday evening concerts are staged, and the center is the site of the September Tsalila festival.

Dean Creek Elk Viewing Area

Three miles east of Reedsport, and stretching three miles along the south side of Highway 38, the **Dean Creek Elk Viewing Area** (48819 Hwy. 38, Reedsport, www.blm.gov, 541/756-0100) provides parking areas and viewing platforms for observing the herd of some 120 wild Roosevelt elk that roam this 1,100-acre preserve. The elk move out of the forest to graze the preserve's marshy pastures, sometimes coming quite close to the highway. Elk can reach 1,100 pounds at maturity, and the majestic rack on a fully grown bull can spread three

feet across. Early mornings and just before dusk are the most promising times to look for them; during hot weather and storms the elk tend to stay within the cover of the woods.

Umpqua Lighthouse State Park

Less than one mile south of Winchester Bay is **Umpqua Lighthouse State Park** (460 Lighthouse Rd., Winchester Bay, 541/271-4118, www.umpqualighthouse.org, 10am-4pm daily May-Oct., $3). Tour the red-capped 1894 **lighthouse** (1020 Lighthouse Rd., 541/271-4471, 10am-4pm daily May-Oct., $3) or admire it from the roadside. Next door, in a former Coast Guard building, the park's **visitors center and museum** has marine and timber exhibits; this is also where tours begin. Directly opposite the lighthouse, overlooking the mouth of the Umpqua and oceanfront dunes, is a whale-watching platform with a plaque explaining where, when, and what to look for.

Lake Marie, just south near the camping area, has a swimming beach and is stocked with rainbow trout. A one-mile forest trail around the lake makes for an easy hike. A trail from the campground leads to the highest dunes in the United States (elev. 545 feet), west of Clear Lake.

SPORTS AND RECREATION
Fishing

Winchester Bay and the tidewater reaches of the lower Umpqua River comprise Oregon's top coastal sturgeon fishery and one of the best areas for striped bass, particularly near the mouth of the Smith River, which enters the Umpqua just east of Reedsport. The best action for the Umpqua's spring chinook tends to be inland, below Scottsburg. Fall chinook enter the bay July-September. Other notable fisheries here are the huge runs of shad, which peak May-June, and smallmouth bass offer action upstream from Reedsport. Crabbing and clamming are also popular and productive pastimes in Winchester Bay and the lower reaches of the river. Every year August 1-mid-September, tagged crabs are released into the water in and around Winchester Bay, one of them worth a cash prize of $5,000 to whomever catches it.

Fishing charter services operating in the area include **Living Waters** (541/584-2295, www.fishinglivingwaters.com), **Strike Zone Charters** (541/361-0194, www.strikezonecharters.com), and **River's End Guide Service** (541/271-3125, www.umpquafishing.com).

Hiking
JOHN DELLENBACK TRAIL
This spectacular dunes landscape can be found 10.5 miles south of Reedsport, 0.25 mile south of the Eel Creek Campground near Lakeside. After you emerge from a 0.5-mile hike through coastal evergreen forest, you'll be greeted by dunes 300-400 feet high. It's said that dunes near here can approach 500 feet high and one mile long after a windblown buildup. The trail, marked by blue-banded wooden posts, continues another 2.5 miles to the beach. Dune hiking can be a bit disorienting. If you lose the trail, climb to the top of the tallest dune and scan for the trail markers.

A shorter and easier one-mile loop trail leads through woodlands to the dunes for a quick introduction to this landscape.

Skate Park
Near the south end of Reedsport in Lions Park is a world-class **skate park** (U.S. 101 and S. 22nd St.). Here you'll find a funnel-shaped full pipe and a 360-degree full loop as well as many more approachable features.

Water Sports
Ten miles south of Reedsport, the sleepy resort town of **Lakeside** hosted visits from Bob Hope, Bing Crosby, and the Ink Spots, among other luminaries, back in its 1930s and 1940s heyday. Today, it's still a popular destination, primarily for its proximity to the sprawling many-armed Tenmile and North Tenmile Lakes. These large shallow lakes offer waterskiing and excellent fishing for stocked rainbow trout and warm-water species, including crappie, yellow perch, bluegill, and lunker largemouth bass, which can grow up to 10 pounds. A 0.25-mile

channel connects the two lakes, and a county park on Tenmile Lake has a paved boat ramp, fishing docks, a sandy swimming beach, and a picnic area.

ENTERTAINMENT AND EVENTS
Every June, over Father's Day weekend, chainsaw sculptors compete for $10,000 in prizes as they transform pieces of raw western red cedar into grizzly bears, giant salmon, and other rustic works of art during the **Chainsaw Sculpture Championships** (www.odcsc.com) at the Rainbow Plaza in Old Town Reedsport, near North 2nd Street and Greenwood Avenue.

Contact the **Reedsport Chamber of Commerce** (541/271-3495 or 800/247-2155, www.reedsportcc.org) for more information on events and festivals in the area.

ACCOMMODATIONS
$50-100
Of the half-dozen old-fashioned motor court motels that flank U.S. 101 in Reedsport, the **Fir Grove Motel** (2178 Winchester Ave., 541/271-4848, $58) is basic but clean.

Just off Highway 101 on the road to Winchester Bay, **Salmon Harbor Landing** (265 8th St., Winchester Bay, 541/271-3742, www.salmonharborlanding.com, $59-69) is a simple, but clean and friendly, motel. This is a good place to stay if you don't need fancy amenities but enjoy a personal touch. Each room is individually decorated, with many of the owner's antiques featured.

Anglers, or anyone who'd rather be in a location off the main drag, should consider the **Winchester Bay Motel** (4th St. and Broadway, Winchester Bay, 541/271-4871 or 800/246-1462, www.winbayinn.com, $69-96), just across from the docks. Guest rooms are basic but clean. Even though this is a large sprawling complex, be sure to reserve ahead of time in fishing season. Pets are permitted in some guest rooms.

Another clean and convenient place for anglers, crabbers, and storm-watchers is the **Harbor View Motel** (540 Beach Blvd., Winchester Bay, 541/271-3352, $50-70), a small place with easy access to charter boats.

$150-200

The **Best Western Plus Salbasgeon Inn** (1400 U.S. 101, 541/271-4831 or 800/528-1234, $145-172) is Reedsport's largest and most full-service hotel, on U.S. 101 just south of the Umpqua River bridge. Amenities include an indoor pool, a fitness center, guest laundry, and a hot tub. Continental breakfast is complimentary.

Camping

Choices abound in this recreation-rich area. Just south of Winchester Bay is **Umpqua Lighthouse State Park** (460 Lighthouse Rd., Winchester Bay, 541/271-4118 information, 800/452-5687 reservations, $19-76). The campground alongside Lake Marie has firewood, flush toilets, showers, picnic tables, electricity, and piped water. The 20 RV sites go for $24; the 24 tent sites are $19; two basic yurts are $36; six deluxe yurts (with shower, small kitchen, refrigerator, microwave, and TV/VCR) are $76; and two rustic cabins are $39. The lake offers fishing, boating, and swimming. Trails from the campground lead to the highest dunes in the United States (elev. 545 feet), west of Clear Lake.

William A. Tugman State Park (541/759-3604 information, 800/452-5687 reservations) is eight miles south of Reedsport, in the heart of dune country. This larger campground, with 115 sites, has a similar range of creature comforts, prices, and recreation. It sits on the west shore of Eel Lake, east of U.S. 101 across from the widest point of the dunes, two miles to the sea.

Windy Cove Campground (541/271-4138) is a county park with 24 full-hookup sites ($24) and four other sites with electric service only ($15). Located on the south side of Salmon Harbor Drive, across from the Winchester Bay marina, it has restrooms, picnic tables, grass, and paved site pads. No reservations are accepted. It is legal to drive your off-highway vehicle (OHV) from this campground directly to the dunes, but that requires a couple of miles' drive on the pavement.

About nine miles south of Reedsport, set along Eel Creek near Eel and Tenmile Lakes, is **Eel Creek Campground** (877/444-6777 reservations, www.recreation.gov, mid-May-Sept., $20), a Siuslaw National Forest facility with 51 basic tent and RV sites; reservations are advised. The Umpqua Dunes Trail offers access to the dunes and the beach.

Eight miles north of Reedsport, the **Tahkenitch Campground** (877/444-6777 reservations, www.recreation.gov, mid-May-Sept., $20) is another Forest Service facility set among ancient Douglas firs and conveniently located near Tahkenitch and other lakes, dunes, and ocean beaches. A network of trails branch out through the dunes, along Tahkenitch Lake, and to the beach.

If you're coming to the dunes to play in the sand, consider spending the night at the all-in-one **Discovery Point Resort** (242 Discovery Point Ln., 541/271-3443, www.discoverypointresort.com, $16 tents, $31-34 RVs) near Winchester Bay. The resort offers OHV enthusiasts dune access and all-terrain vehicle (ATV) rentals, and provides condos, one- to three-bedroom cabins (which sleep up to six, $275), 60 RV spaces, and tent sites. To get there from Reedsport, head two miles south on U.S. 101 to Winchester Bay, then turn right at Pelican Market onto Salmon Harbor Drive. Go one mile, and you'll see Discovery Point Resort on the left. Reservations are strongly recommended.

FOOD

Seek not cuisine in Reedsport. Standard American fare is the norm in this hardscrabble town. The best bets for seafood are the wharf-side restaurants in Winchester Bay.

Reedsport

A popular place on U.S. 101 is **Don's Main Street Restaurant** (2115 Winchester Ave., 541/271-2032, 8am-8pm daily, $7-13), with burgers, fried chicken, and a parlor serving

CENTRAL COAST

local Umpqua ice cream. This is the locals' favorite place for pies.

The **Schooner Inn Café** (423 Riverfront Way, 541/271-3945, 10am-3pm daily, lunch $8-10), on the boardwalk next door to the Discovery Center, has a pleasant riverside patio and a good selection of delicious salads and sandwiches. This is a quiet spot for an al fresco lunch overlooking the Umpqua.

Winchester Bay

For the best fresh seafood in the dune country, head down to the Salmon Harbor Marina at Winchester Bay, where there are a number of casual seafood restaurants within easily strolling distance.

The friendly staff at the **Sportsmen's Cannery and Smokehouse** (182 Bay Front Loop, 541/271-3293, shop 9am-5pm daily) hosts a weekend seafood barbecue (4pm-7pm Fri., 11am-7pm Sat.-Sun., $12-18) that features salmon, halibut, and crab (and whatever else is fresh) and all the trimmings. Don't expect indoor seating for this meal—you'll eat at picnic tables set up in the parking lot. Peek inside and you may see cannery employees cutting up the day's catch. Visit the adjoining shop to purchase fresh, smoked, or canned fish; they'll even smoke your catch for you.

Another good bets for fresh seafood in an authentic dockside setting is **Fishpatrick's Crabby Cafe** (196 Bay Front Loop, 541/271-3474, 11am-3pm Sun. and Wed., 11am-8pm Thurs.-Sat., $8-25), which offers excellent fish-and-chips, crab, and fish sandwiches in a woodsy dining room.

© BILL MCRAE

Winchester Bay is an excellent place to eat fresh seafood.

INFORMATION

The **Oregon Dunes National Recreation Area Visitor Information Center** (885 U.S. 101, Reedsport, 541/271-6100, www.fs.usda.gov/siuslaw) and **Reedsport Chamber of Commerce** (541/271-3495 or 800/247-2155, www.reedsportcc.org) share a building at the junction of U.S. 101 and Highway 38. It's open 8am-4:30pm weekdays year-round and 8am-4:30pm weekends mid-July-early September.

SOUTH COAST

Stretching from the Coos Bay area to the California border, the southern Oregon coast is far from the population centers of Oregon's interior valleys, but the south coast amply rewards visitors who make the effort to get here. The foothills of the Klamath Mountains tumble down the narrow coastal plain and fall off in precipitous headlands at the ocean's edge. Close to shore, the waters are a rocky garden of sea stacks and islets that are home to uncounted flocks of pelagic birds. With half a dozen wild rivers slicing through the mountains to the sea, the south coast is famed for its outstanding salmon fishing, especially on charters from the harbors of Charleston, Gold Beach, Bandon, and Brookings.

In addition, the southern region is blessed with the fairest weather on the Oregon coast and generally gets the most sunshine, the least rain, and the warmest temperatures—attributes as appealing to visitors as to the area's many retirees and other transplants.

Scenic highlights of the south coast include the weather-beaten bluffs and formal gardens at Cape Arago and Shore Acres State Parks, the gorgeous scenery of Boardman and Harris Beach State Parks, and just about every inch of the drive between Brookings and Port Orford.

In addition to fishing, recreational opportunities are seemingly endless: Outstanding courses draws golfers to Bandon (*Golf* magazine hailed Bandon Dunes as one of the country's top three courses) and Brookings (with the Salmon Run Golf Course alongside the Chetco River); some of the coast's top windsurfing and

© BILL MCRAE

HIGHLIGHTS

◖ **Shore Acres State Park:** The regal manor house is gone, but the formal gardens from a onetime private estate still thrive above an especially rugged stretch of beach (page 383).

◖ **South Slough National Estuarine Research Reserve:** Here, where freshwater meets saltwater, is a nutrient-rich environment that supports many wildlife species. Hike or paddle, but either way, pay attention to the tides (page 384).

◖ **Bandon Historical Society Museum:** Learn all about cranberries, native cultures, and frontier coastal history at this well-curated regional museum (page 394).

◖ **Bandon Dunes Golf Resort:** This links-style course on the coastal headlands is evocative of Scotland. There are four golf courses, each expertly designed in a gorgeous setting (page 398).

◖ **Humbug Mountain:** The three-mile trail to the top of Humbug Mountain passes a spectacular array of native plants. Even if the promised mountaintop view is shrouded in fog, it's a great hike (page 405).

◖ **Cape Blanco State Park and Hughes House:** This is the only lighthouse in Oregon that allows visitors into the lantern room, with its massive Fresnel lens (page 405).

◖ **Cape Sebastian:** Hike up Cape Sebastian for a front-row seat for springtime whale-watching (page 410).

◖ **Rogue River Jet-Boat Ride:** Even die-hard paddlers won't regret succumbing to a jet-boat tour up the Rogue River. Boaters often get to see ospreys and eagles fishing along this stretch of river (page 411).

◖ **Samuel H. Boardman State Scenic Corridor:** North of Brookings, the road winds hundreds of feet above the surf, allowing you to peer down at one of the most dramatic meetings of rock and tide in the world (page 420).

LOOK FOR ◖ TO FIND RECOMMENDED SIGHTS, ACTIVITIES, DINING, AND LODGING.

kiting are near Cape Sebastian; and popular jet-boat tours run up the Rogue River from Gold Beach.

PLANNING YOUR TIME

Plan to spend at least a day or two exploring the **Coos Bay-Bandon** region. Coos Bay is the only real city along the southern coast, and like Tillamook to the north, it's a gateway to some spectacular areas but pretty workaday itself. Be sure to head west and south from town to explore the wonderful shoreline parks at Sunset Bay and Cape Arago.

Don't overlook the coastal wetlands, especially the coastal estuary at **South Slough National Estuarine Research Reserve,** south

SOUTH COAST

of Coos Bay. **Bandon Marsh National Wildlife Refuge** protects the largest remaining tract of salt marsh within the Coquille River estuary. Major habitats include undisturbed salt marsh, mudflat, Sitka spruce, and alder riparian communities, which provide resting and feeding areas for migratory waterfowl, shore and wading birds, and raptors.

Of course, **Bandon** is now best known for its world-class Bandon Dunes Golf Resort, but the old downtown area still hums to its counterculture vibes. Bandon's beachfront, along with the Coos Bay sand spit, the beaches on the western side of Humbug Mountain, and the isolated shorelines of Boardman State Park are choice beachcombing spots.

Port Orford is often overlooked, but it's one of our favorite spots, with great ocean vistas from town and lots of hiking at nearby Humbug Mountain. It also doesn't hurt that there's good eating here. It's worth at least an afternoon stop.

Jet-boat tours start in **Gold Beach** and head up the Rogue River, offering those with just a morning to spare the chance to explore stunning river vistas—and perhaps help deliver the mail. Between Gold Beach and Brookings, save some serious time to explore beaches sequestered between steep cliffs and pounding surf at the 11-mile-long **Boardman State Scenic Corridor.**

Charleston, Coos Bay, and North Bend

The towns around the harbor of Coos Bay—Charleston, Coos Bay, and North Bend—refer to themselves collectively as the Bay Area. In contrast to its namesake in California, the Oregon version is not exactly the Athens of the coast. Nonetheless, visitors will be impressed by the area's beautiful beaches, the largest ocean-front dunes in North America, and three wonderfully scenic and historic state parks. Because much of this natural beauty is on the periphery of the industrialized core of the Bay Area, away from U.S. 101, it's easy to miss. All that many motorists see upon entering Coos Bay/North Bend on the Coast Highway are the dockside lumber mills and foreign vessels anchored at the onetime site of the world's largest lumber port.

The little town of Charleston (pop. 700) to the southwest makes few pretenses of being anything other than what it really is—a bustling commercial fishing port. Processing plants here can or cold-pack tuna, salmon, crab, oysters, shrimp, and other kinds of seafood. The town might occasionally smell of fish, but the few restaurants and lodgings here are good values, and the town is the gateway to a trio of extraordinary state parks: Sunset Bay, Shore Acres, and Cape Arago.

To reach Charleston from points south, or to head south from town, take the **Seven Devils Road,** which has its southern terminus about three miles north of Bandon. This route runs 13 miles past forests, a few clear-cuts, and an estuarine preserve.

SIGHTS
Coos Bay Harbor
A good place to take in the bustling bay front is the **Coos Bay Boardwalk** (U.S. 101 and Anderson Ave.) where you can check out the oceangoing freighters, visit a restored tugboat, and learn of the harbor's history courtesy of interpretive placards. A 400-gallon saltwater aquarium holds fish and other marine life of Coos Bay. This is the largest coastal harbor

between San Francisco and Puget Sound (more than 100 deepwater vessels call each year), and it's fun to watch the ships docking and the portside wood-chip piles growing by dozens of feet overnight. Wood chips are Oregon's primary forest-product export—raw log exports (which formerly made Coos Bay the world's busiest lumber shipment center) are now prohibited.

Coos Art Museum
The **Coos Art Museum** (235 Anderson Ave., Coos Bay, 541/267-3901, www.coosart.org, 10am-4pm Tues.-Fri., 1pm-4pm Sat., $5 adults, $2 seniors and students), in downtown Coos Bay, is the Oregon coast's only art museum and features primarily 20th-century and contemporary works by American artists, including pieces by Robert Rauschenberg and Larry Rivers. Etchings, woodcuts, serigraphs, and other prints make up a large part of the permanent collection, which includes several of Janet Turner's richly detailed depictions of birds in natural settings. Other highlights include Kirk Lybecker's photo-realistic watercolors. Don't miss the Prefontaine Room on the second floor of the museum. Photos, trophies, medals, and other memorabilia of native-son world-class runner Steve Prefontaine illustrate his credo: "I want to make something beautiful when I run."

In addition to the permanent collection, recurring events worth detouring for are the May-July juried show of artists from the Western states, and the Maritime Art Exhibit, August-September.

Coos County Historical and Maritime Museum
The **Coos County Historical and Maritime Museum** (1220 Sherman Ave., North Bend, 541/756-6320, www.cooshistory.org, 10am-4pm Tues.-Sat., $5 adults, $2 seniors and students, free ages 12 and under) is near the south end of the Conde McCullough Bridge,

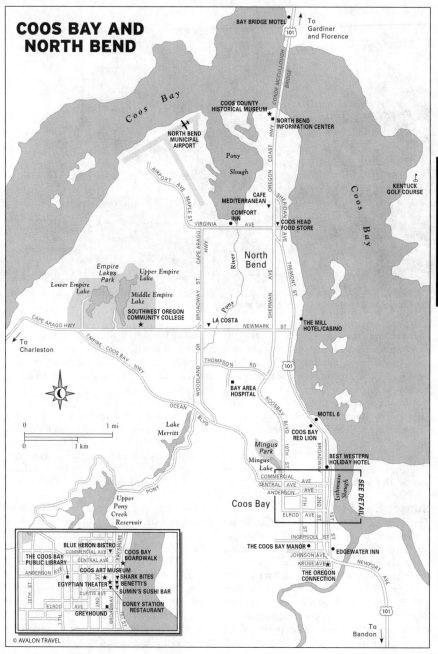

COOS BAY AND NORTH BEND

Coos Bay

BAY BRIDGE MOTEL

To Gardiner and Florence

CONDE MCCULLOUGH BRIDGE

101

COOS COUNTY HISTORICAL MUSEUM

NORTH BEND INFORMATION CENTER

NORTH BEND MUNICIPAL AIRPORT

AIRPORT AVE

MAPLE ST

Pony

Slough

OREGON COAST HWY

SHERIDAN AVE

KENTUCK GOLF COURSE

Coos Bay

CAFE MEDITERRANEAN

COMFORT INN

VIRGINIA

CAPE ARAGO HWY

River

North Bend

COOS HEAD FOOD STORE

AVE

Empire Lakes Park

Upper Empire Lake

Lower Empire Lake

Middle Empire Lake

SOUTHWEST OREGON COMMUNITY COLLEGE

BROADWAY ST

Pony

LA COSTA

SHERMAN AVE

TREMONT ST

THE MILL HOTEL/CASINO

NEWMARK

ST

CAPE ARAGO HWY

To Charleston

EMPIRE - COOS BAY HWY

WOODLAND DR

THOMPSON RD

BAY AREA HOSPITAL

KOOSBAY BLVD

101

OCEAN BLVD

Lake Merritt

MOTEL 6

COOS BAY RED LION

10TH ST

BROADWAY

BEST WESTERN HOLIDAY HOTEL

0   1 mi
0   1 km

Mingus Park

Mingus Lake

COMMERCIAL AVE

CENTRAL AVE

ANDERSON

AVE

2ND ST

Isthmus Slough

SEE DETAIL

Coos Bay

PONY

ELROD AVE

1ST ST

Upper Pony Creek Reservoir

INGERSOLL ST

THE COOS BAY MANOR

JOHNSON AVE

EDGEWATER INN

NEWPORT AVE

KRUSE AVE

THE OREGON CONNECTION

101

To Bandon

BLUE HERON BISTRO

COMMERCIAL AVE

COOS BAY BOARDWALK

THE COOS BAY PUBLIC LIBRARY

CENTRAL AVE

BAYSHORE

ANDERSON AVE

COOS ART MUSEUM

SHARK BITES

BENETTI'S

EGYPTIAN THEATER

SUMIN'S SUSHI BAR

CURTIS AVE

CONEY STATION RESTAURANT

ELROD AVE

10TH ST

7TH ST

BROADWAY

1ST ST

GREYHOUND

© AVALON TRAVEL

SOUTH COAST

SOUTH COAST

© BILL MCRAE

The Coos Bay Boardwalk is an open-air maritime museum.

one of several distinctive Depression-era spans by Oregon's master bridge-builder. The museum houses more than the usual bric-a-brac from earlier eras, thanks largely to the region's heritage as a shipping center. An early-1900s Regina music box, a piano shipped around Cape Horn, miniature boat models, and a jade Chinese plaque, as well as Coos Indian beadwork and other artifacts, make this collection especially memorable. Outside, old-time logging equipment and a 1920s steam train are also worth a look.

Sunset Bay State Park

The Cape Arago Highway west of Charleston leads to some of the most dramatic beaches and interesting state parks on the coast. Among the several beaches on the road to Cape Arago, the strand at **Sunset Bay State Park** (13030 Cape Arago Hwy., 541/888-4902 information, 800/452-5687 reservations) is the big attraction because its sheltered shallow cove, encircled by sandstone bluffs, is warm and calm enough for swimming, a rarity in the Pacific Ocean north

of Santa Barbara, California. In addition to swimmers, divers, surfers, kayakers, and boaters, many people come here to watch the sunset. Local legend tells that pirates hid out in this well-protected cove.

A spectacular four-mile cliff-side segment of the **Oregon Coast Trail** runs from Sunset Beach south to Cape Arago. Good views of **Cape Arago Lighthouse** across the water can be seen along this route. Listen for its unique foghorn. For a short hike, follow the signs from the mouth of Big Creek to the viewpoint overlooking Sunset Bay.

The Cape Arago Lighthouse is on Chief Island and was linked to the mainland by a steel-truss bridge. For the local Coos Indians, Chief Island and the adjacent shoreline were a traditional burial ground, though after the building of the first lighthouse in 1866, the Coast Guard no longer allowed native burials. However, the island continued to have a sacred significance for the Coos.

A total of three different structures have served as the lighthouse on Chief Island. Then,

© BILL MCRAE

the craggy coastline at Sunset Bay State Park

after 140 years of service, on January 1, 2006, the lighthouse was decommissioned. Oregon's congressional delegation in 2008 successfully maneuvered to transfer Chief Island, the adjacent shoreline, and the Cape Arago Lighthouse to the Confederated Tribes of the Coos, Lower Umpqua, and Siuslaw Indians. As part of the agreement, the Native Americans have pledged to maintain the lighthouse and make it available "to the general public for educational, park, recreational, cultural, or historic preservation purposes at times and under conditions determined to be reasonable by the Secretary of the Interior." The island will again primarily be used as a burial ground, though the tribes have also discussed building an interpretive center on the mainland. However, the bridge to Chief Island has been removed, and the lighthouse and Chief Island are currently not open to the public.

Shore Acres State Park

Less than one mile south of Sunset Bay at

Shore Acres State Park (541/888-3732, 8am-sunset year-round, $5 per vehicle or Oregon Coast Passport), the grandeur of nature is complemented by human endeavor. The park is set on the grounds of lumber magnate and entrepreneur Louis J. Simpson's early-1900s mansion, which began as a summer home in 1906 and grew into a three-story mansion complete with an indoor heated swimming pool and large ballroom. Originally a Christmas present to his wife, Shore Acres became the showplace of the Oregon coast, with formal and Japanese gardens eventually added to the 743-acre estate. After a 1921 fire, a second, larger (two stories high and 224 feet long) incarnation of Simpson's "shack by the beach" was built. Over the following years the building fell into disrepair; the house and grounds were ceded to the state in 1942. Because of the high cost of upkeep, the mansion had to be razed, but the gardens have been lovingly maintained.

The gardens are compelling attractions, but the headland's rim is more dramatic. Perched near the edge of the bluff, on the site formerly occupied by the mansion, a glass-enclosed observation shelter makes a perfect vantage point from which to watch for whales or marvel at the crashing waves. When there's a storm, the waves really slam into the sandstone reefs and cliffs, hurling up tremendous fountains of spray. It's not uncommon to feel the spray atop the 75-foot promontory. The history of the Simpson family is really the history of the Bay Area, and their story is captioned beneath period photos in the observation gazebo and in the garden in a small enclosure at the west end of the floral displays.

In the seven acres of neatly tended gardens, set back from the sea, the international botanical bounty culled by Simpson clipper ships and schooners is still in its glory, complemented by award-winning roses, rhododendrons, tulips, and azaleas. A restored gardener's cottage with antique furnishings stands at the back of the formal gardens. It's open for special occasions and during the winter holidays. Also in the gardens, note the copper egret sculptures at the

SOUTH COAST

COOS BAY SHIPWRECKS

The *Captain Lincoln*, whose grounding on the treacherous North Spit of Coos Bay led to settlement of the area, would not be the last ship to meet its end on these dangerous shores. In 1910, the *Czarina* foundered in heavy seas on the bar; 24 people were killed in one of the worst shipwrecks on Oregon's south coast. The *Claremont* and the *Santa Clara* both wrecked on the bar in 1915, and the *Sujameco* grounded on Horsfall Beach in 1929. Although most of the ship was removed during salvage operations, iron projections can sometimes still be seen in the sand at low tide.

The most recent and infamous shipwreck here, though, was the February 4, 1999, grounding of the 640-foot wood-chip carrier *New Carissa*, on the North Spit. After the Coast Guard firebombed the freighter in an attempt to burn off the 150,000 gallons of fuel oil on board, the vessel broke into two parts. After weeks of failed attempts, the bow section was finally towed out to sea and sunk in 10,000 feet of water by a Navy torpedo. Most of the stern was finally removed, but a section of it remained mired in the sand on the North Spit, just beyond the surf, until 2008. During the shipwreck and months of salvage efforts, the hulk leaked some 70,000 gallons of oil, which killed an estimated 2,400 seabirds and destroyed oyster beds. The media circus that sprang up around the site generated a temporary economic boomlet for the region, but the long-term ecological damage is still to be determined.

pond and the greenhouse for rare plants from warmer climes.

From Thanksgiving through New Year's, during the annual **Holiday Lights and Open House** (4pm-10pm daily), the gardens are decorated with 250,000 colored lights and other holiday touches. The gardener's cottage opens and serves free refreshments during this time.

If you bear right and follow the pond's contours toward the ocean, you'll come to the **Simpson Beach Trail.** Follow it north for cliffside views of the rock-studded shallows below. Southward, the trail goes downhill to a scene of exceptional beauty. From the vantage point of a small beach, you can watch waves crash into rocks with such force that the white spray appears to hang suspended in the air. Pursuits for the active traveler include exploring tidepools and caves as well as springtime swimming in a cove, formed by winter storms, on the south side of the beach. In summer, thimbleberries and salal growing along the trail down to the beach can provide sustenance for these activities.

Cape Arago State Park

A little more than one mile south of Shore Acres is **Cape Arago State Park** (800/551-6949, day-use only, free), at the end of the Cape Arago Highway. Locals have made much of the fact that this was a possible landing site of the English explorer Sir Francis Drake in 1579, and they put a plaque here commemorating him.

Beachcombers can make their own discoveries in the numerous tidepools, some of the best on the coast. The south cove trail (find it past the picnic shelter) runs down to a sandy beach and the better tidepools. The north cove trail leads to more tidepools, good spots for fishing, and views of the colonies of seals and sea lions at Shell Island, including the most northerly breeding colony of enormous elephant seals. Their huge pups, when just a month old, may already weigh 300-400 pounds. Note that the north trail closes March 1-June 30 to protect seal pups. The picnic tables on the headlands command beautiful ocean panoramas and are superbly placed for whale-watching.

◖ South Slough National Estuarine Research Reserve

Estuaries, where freshwater and saltwater interface, form some of the richest ecosystems on earth, capable of producing five times

© BILL MCRAE

The gardens at Shore Acres State Park are well-tended and surprisingly elegant.

more plant material than a cornfield of comparable size while supporting great numbers of fish, birds, and other wildlife. The South Slough of Coos Bay is the largest such web of life on the Oregon coast. The **South Slough National Estuarine Reserve Interpretive Center** (61907 Seven Devils Rd., 541/888-5558, www.oregon.gov, 10am-4:30pm daily Memorial Day-Labor Day, free), four miles south of Charleston, will help you coordinate a canoe trip through the estuary and offers guided hikes as well.

The center looks out over several estuarine arms of Coos Bay, the largest harbor between San Francisco Bay and Puget Sound. These vital wetlands nurture a variety of life-forms, detailed by the placards captioning the center's exhibits. The coastal ecosystem is presented by the "10-minute trail" behind the interpretive center. The various conifers and the understory are clearly labeled along the gently sloping half-mile loop. Branch trails lead down toward the water for an up-close view of the estuary.

Down by the slough, you may see elk grazing in marshy meadows and bald eagles circling above, while *Homo sapiens* harvest oysters and shrimp in these waters.

Beginning near the visitors center is the easy three-mile **estuary study trail,** which follows Hidden Creek from the wooded uplands down the valley to a boardwalk that winds through fresh- and saltwater marshes and leads to several wildlife observation points.

Whiskey Run Beach

Midway between Charleston and Bandon is the quiet beach at **Whiskey Run**, whose ore-bearing sands spread gold fever down the south coast in the early 1850s. As many as 2,000 miners worked here until a storm washed away the deposit. Other forms of beachcombing at Whiskey Run and on the beaches to the north are still thriving, however. Agate-hunting after a season of winter storms and clamming at low tide make these solitary shorelines ideal places to forget worldly concerns. To get there, turn west from the lightly traveled Seven Devils Road onto Whiskey Run Road, and drive 1.5 miles to this county park. Just to the north you'll find Seven Devils State Wayside. Vehicles are permitted on the beach at Whiskey Run; Seven Devils is reserved for foot traffic.

Horsfall Beach and the North Spit

On the spit north of North Bend, the Oregon Dunes taper down to wide, sandy beaches and wetlands. **Horsfall Beach** is extremely popular with ATV riders, but it's also a good place to enjoy nature. It's also worth exploring on foot, especially in the winter, when storms can expose old shipwrecks.

Myrtlewood

To see Oregon coast folk art in the making, visit the **Oregon Connection** (1125 S. 1st St., Coos Bay, 541/267-7804, www,oregonconnection. com, 9am-5:30pm Mon.-Sat., 11am-4pm Sun.), just off U.S. 101 at the south end of Coos Bay. The myrtlewood factory tour shows you how a myrtlewood log gets fashioned into

SOUTH COAST

© BILL MCRAE

Horsfall Beach is popular with ATV riders.

bowls, clocks, tables, and other utensils. No admission is charged for this 25-minute guided run through a working factory. After you're done, the store is a delight, with Oregon gourmet foods and crafts supplementing the quality woodwork.

Five miles north of North Bend, **The Real Oregon Gift** (3955 U.S. 101, 541/756-2220, www.realoregongift.com, 9am-5pm Mon.-Sat., 9:30am-4:30pm Sun.) is another large myrtlewood factory and showroom.

SPORTS AND RECREATION

Wavecrest Discoveries (541/267-4027, http://wavecrestdiscoveries.com) offers a cornucopia of guided outdoor activities around the Bay Area and beyond, including clamming and tidepooling excursions, sea kayaking, dune and estuary tours, and more.

Fishing

Spring chinook salmon, which sometimes exceed 30 pounds and are renowned as an unrivaled dining treat, offer prime fishing in Coos Bay. However, their population levels and fishing rules vary from year to year. Mid-August-November, Isthmus Slough sees a good return of fin-clipped hatchery cohos. In saltwater, chinook and coho are usually found in good numbers within a one- to two-mile radius of the mouth of Coos Bay May-September, although the legal season varies; carefully check the regulations. Remnant striped bass are still occasionally caught in Coos Bay's sloughs and upper tidewater, but their numbers are diminishing.

Coos Bay is also one of the premier areas for crabbing and clamming. The Charleston Fishing Pier is a productive spot for crabs, while the best clamming spots are found along the bay side of the North Spit.

Fishing charters, bay cruises, whale-watching, and the like can be arranged through a number of charter outfits based at the Charleston Boat Basin. **Betty Kay Charters** (541/888-9021 or 800/752-6303, www.bettykaycharters.com) charges typical per-person prices: $75 for five hours of rock fishing; $140 for seven hours of salmon fishing; $200 for

THE MYRTLEWOOD TREE

When exploring the southern Oregon coast, you'll soon discover that myrtlewood is very popular hereabouts—nearly every town has a myrtlewood factory or showroom that peddles bowls, sculpture, furniture, and other products fashioned from this rare and unusual wood.

Myrtlewood is a member of the Lauraceae family of small trees and is a relative of the camphor, bay, and sassafras trees. Like these trees, the leaves and wood of the tree have a pungent odor. The myrtlewood tree grows only in a small area of southern Oregon and northern California, and it is large enough to harvest only after 100-150 years of growth. The wood is highly patterned, with the grain forming erratic bands of differing color in a single block of wood.

Myrtlewood is particularly popular for turn-ing into bowls—salad and serving bowls make a lovely gift or keepsake of a trip to coastal Oregon. However, the tree and its wood have been used for myriad other functional and decorative purposes for many years.

Hudson's Bay Company trappers used myrtlewood leaves to brew tea as a remedy for chills. In 1869 the golden spike marking the completion of the nation's first transcontinental railroad (near Promontory, Utah) was driven into a highly polished myrtlewood tie. Novelist Jack London was so taken by the beauty of the wood's swirling grain that he ordered an entire suite of furniture.

During the Depression, the city of North Bend issued myrtlewood coins after the only bank in town failed. The coins ranged $0.50-10 in value and are still redeemable, although they are worth far more as collectors' items.

12 hours of tuna or halibut fishing; and $40 for a two-hour bay cruise, whale-watching, or ecotour.

Golf

Tee up in a lovely setting at **Sunset Bay Golf Course** (11001 Cape Arago Hwy., Charleston, 541/888-9301, $18 weekends, $15 weekdays), a nine-holer close to Sunset Bay State Park.

Hiking

Although most hikers head to the coast, especially the four-mile stretch of the **Oregon Coast Trail** between Sunset Bay and Cape Arago, for a nice trail with spectacular views, it's also worth looking inland. Twenty-five miles northeast of Coos Bay in the Coast Range is **Golden and Silver Falls State Park** (800/551-6949). Two spectacular waterfalls are showcased in this little-known gem of a park. Getting here involves driving east of Coos Bay along the Coos River, crossing to its north bank, and continuing along the Millicoma River through the community of Allegany. To find your way from Coos Bay, look for the Allegany/Eastside exit

off U.S. 101. Beyond Allegany, continue up the East Fork of the Millicoma River to its junction with Glenn Creek, which ultimately leads to the park. The narrow winding gravel roads make this half-hour trip unsuitable for a wide-body vehicle.

You can reach each waterfall by way of two 0.5-mile trails. The 100-foot cataracts lie about one mile apart, and although both are about the same height, each has a distinct character. For most of the year, Silver Falls is more visually arresting because it flows in a near semicircle around a knob near its top. During or just after the winter rains, however, the thunderous sound of Golden Falls makes it the more awe-inspiring of the two. Along the trails, look for the beautifully delicate maidenhair fern.

Kayaking

From a canoe or sea kayak, as you pass tide flats, salt marshes, forested areas, and open water, you can really begin to grasp the richness of the estuarine habitat at the **South Slough National Estuarine**

Research Reserve (541/888-5558, www. oregon.gov). The estuary here has two main branches, offering plenty of territory for a day of exploration.

Although the waters are placid, they are strongly influenced by the tides—be sure to consult tide tables when you plan an outing. Wind can also affect your trip: Know that in the spring and summer, the prevailing winds are from the northwest; in the winter they're from the southwest. At all times of year, the wind blows hardest in the afternoon.

Kayaks can be rented just outside of Charleston at **High Tide Rentals** (91124 Cape Arago Hwy., 541/888-3664).

Surfing and Swimming

The best spot on the Oregon coast for swimming is **Sunset Bay State Park** (13030 Cape Arago Hwy., Coos Bay, 541/888-4902). The water is warm enough for most adults and gentle enough for most kids.

Surfing is best just northeast of Sunset Bay, at **Bastendorff Beach County Park** (63379 Bastendorff Beach Rd., Charleston, 541/888-5353).

ENTERTAINMENT AND EVENTS

The first event of note in summer is the **Oregon Coast Music Festival** (541/267-0938 or 877/897-9350, www.oregoncoastmusic.com), which runs for two weeks in mid-July and has been bringing music to the coast since 1978. Coos Bay is the central venue for these classical, jazz, pop, and world music concerts, but Bandon, North Bend, Charleston, and other neighboring burgs host some performances as well. Tickets to some events are free, with tickets to the majority of events under $20.

In late August, the ubiquitous Oregon blackberry is celebrated with the **Blackberry Arts Festival** (541/269-0215). Food and wine-tasting booths, a juried arts-and-crafts show, and entertainers fill the **Coos Bay Mall** (Central Ave. in downtown Coos Bay).

Polish up the spotting scope and head to the Oregon Institute of Marine Biology in Charleston during the last weekend of August to see migratory shorebirds with the **Oregon Shorebird Festival** (541/867-4550 or 541/756-5688). Guided trips on land and water are offered; a boat trip out to see albatrosses and other seldom-seen species that frequent the open ocean is a highlight. Other excursions visit the Bandon Marsh National Wildlife Refuge and Coos Bay to see plovers, loons, and a variety of other shorebirds.

In mid-September, perhaps the best-known Bay Area sports celebrity, Steve Prefontaine, is honored with a 10K race and two-mile walk in the annual **Prefontaine Memorial Run** (541/269-1103, www.prefontainerun.com). Prefontaine was a world-class runner whose gutsy style of running and record performances made him a major sports personality until his premature death at age 24 in 1974. Many topflight runners pay homage by taking part in the race. Events begin and end at the runner's alma mater, **Marshfield High School** (4th St. and Anderson Ave., Coos Bay).

Occupying the former bay-side site of the Weyerhaeuser mill alongside U.S. 101 in North Bend, the **Mill Casino** (3201 Tremont Ave., North Bend, 541/756-8800 or 800/953-4800, www.themillcasino.com) is operated by the Coquille Indian Tribe. Open 24 hours a day, the casino offers blackjack, lots o' slots, poker, and bingo. A large hotel, lounge, and several restaurants are on-site.

ACCOMMODATIONS AND CAMPING

Most of the lodgings in Coos Bay and North Bend stretch along busy U.S. 101, and most are of the mid-century motor-court variety, but the majority are well-maintained and represent good value. Another option is staying in Charleston, particularly if your destination includes local state parks, ocean beaches, or South Slough. Charleston lodgings aren't fancier, but you'll stay near the fishing marina, not the highway.

Coos Bay

If you're just looking for a basic clean room,

the local **Motel 6** (1445 Bayshore Dr., 541/267-7171, $72-92) is well maintained and offers a number of kitchen units. Close to downtown, the **Best Western Holiday Hotel** (411 N. Bayshore Dr., 541/269-5111 or 800/228-8655, $132-159) is within walking distance of city center restaurants and offers a pool, hot tub, and hot breakfast buffet. Pets are welcome.

A more upscale alternative is the **Coos Bay Red Lion** (1313 N. Bayshore Dr., 541/267-4141, www.redlion.com, $119-139), which offers large guest rooms with extras such as an outdoor pool, a fitness center, and a bar and restaurant. A complimentary shuttle runs guests to and from the airport.

The Coos Bay Manor (955 5th St., 800/269-1224, www.coosbaymanor.com, $135-220, full breakfast included) is a grand high-ceilinged colonial-style home with eye-popping river views from the open-air second-floor breakfast balcony. The B&B's five spacious rooms have distinctive decor; two of the rooms can be combined to make a suite for families.

The waterfront **Edgewater Inn** (275 E. Johnson Ave., 541/267-0423 or 800/233-0423, www.theedgewaterinn.com, $100-135) has loads of perks in addition to its location off the highway facing the working waterfront. With 82 spacious rooms, many with views and kitchens, the hotel also offers fitness and tanning rooms, an indoor pool, a spa and sauna, and complimentary breakfast.

Even though the crowds at **Sunset Bay State Park** (13030 Cape Arago Hwy., Coos Bay, 541/888-4902 or 800/452-5687, www.reserveamerica.com for reservations, $5-36) can make it seem like a trailer park in midsummer, the proximity of Oregon's only major swimming beach on the ocean keeps occupants of the 66 tent sites ($19) and 65 trailer sites ($24) happy. The eight yurts go for $36 each, and primitive hiker-biker sites are $5 each. Facilities include the standard state park showers, and there is a boat launch at the north end of the beach. This site, three miles southwest of Charleston, is popular with anglers, who can cast into the rocky intertidal area for cabezon and sea bass. It's also a good base camp for hikers.

Northwest of the Bay Area—2.5 miles north of the McCullough Bridge—is the Trans-Pacific Parkway, a causeway west across the water leading to Coos Bay's North Spit and the south end of the Oregon Dunes National Recreation Area, with four **Forest Service campgrounds** (541/271-6000 or 877/444-6777, www.recreation.gov, year-round, $20) and expansive dunes that draw ATV enthusiasts. The main **Horsfall Campground** is popular with crowds of noisy ATVs and RVs. It's the only campground on the spit with showers. For more quiet and privacy, continue another mile on Horsfall Beach Road to **Bluebill Lake.** There isn't ATV dune access from this campground, and it tends to attract trekkers who use their feet to explore. Ask the campground hosts about area trails and the nearby oyster farm for the ultimate in campfire fare. Close by, **Horsfall Beach Campground** is in the dunes next to the beach. ATV access and beachcombing are popular activities. A half mile away, **Wild Mare Horse Camp** has beach and dune access and a dozen primitive campsites, each with a single or double horse corral.

North Bend

One of the best values in the area is **Bay Bridge Motel** (33 Coast Hwy., 541/765-3151 or 800/557-3156, $90-112), a small motel just north of the McCullough Bridge, with good views of the bay from the higher-priced rooms.

Another option is the **Quality Inn & Suites Coos Bay** (1503 Virginia Ave., 541/756-3191, www.coosbayinn.com, $110-134), just five blocks from U.S. 101. With 96 units and the standard chain-hotel amenities, this hotel provides a quiet escape.

C **The Mill Hotel** (3201 Tremont Ave., 541/756-8800 or 800/953-4800, www.the-millcasino.com, $133-160) is just south of the Mill Casino along the waterfront in a new seven-story tower and a building that once housed a plywood mill. Owned and operated by the Coquille (pronounced ko-KWELL in the local dialect) Indian Tribe, the hotel seeks to express its owners' patrimony: The exterior of this three-story hotel is the same cedar that the Coquille people used to build their plank houses, and the fireplace in the lobby is made of Coquille River rocks. The canoe displayed behind the front desk was carved by tribal members and is part of an interpretive display that tells the story of the Coquilles. Guest rooms are very nicely furnished, and waterfront views from the tower are especially dramatic. And, of course, all the pleasures of a modern casino are just a few feet away. In addition to gaming, the casino has a good restaurant, shops, and a performance center.

Charleston

There are a few basic motels in Charleston. If you'd like to catch your own dinner, the **Plainview Motel** (91904 Cape Arago Hwy., 541/888-5166 or 800/962-2815, http://plainviewmotel.com, $74-90) provides guests with crab rings and fishing poles or will set you up on a guided fishing trip. This small older motel has 12 pet-friendly units, some with kitchens. Pets cost an extra $10.

Bastendorff Beach County Park (63379 Bastendorff Beach Rd., Charleston, 541/888-5353, $16-30) is a conveniently and beautifully located park two miles west of Charleston just off the Cape Arago Highway. It's open for camping year-round, with RV and tent sites ($16-20, less off-season), as well as cabins ($30) and some hiker-biker sites. Campsites have drinking water, woodstoves, flush toilets, and hot showers (for an extra $2). Fishing, hiking, and a nice stretch of beach are the recreational attractions, plus there's a good playground for toddlers.

FOOD

Oregon's Bay Area has many eateries where your nutritional needs can be met, if not in fine style then at least at the right price. With a couple of notable exceptions, in both Coos Bay and North Bend, you won't find it easy to dine on seafood—in these hardworking towns, eating well seems to require heartier fare. For fresh

seafood, you're advised to head to the docks in Charleston.

Coos Bay

Nearly all the following are located along a two-block section of busy Broadway, which is the name given to southbound U.S. 101 as it passes through downtown Coos Bay. So just park the car and check out which of the following looks good.

The **Blue Heron Bistro** (110 W. Commercial Ave., 541/267-3933, 11am-9pm Mon.-Fri., noon-9pm Sat., noon-8pm Sun., $15-20) is in the heart of downtown Coos Bay—with its Bavarian-style half-timbered exterior, you can't miss it. The specialty is traditional German cooking, such as sauerbraten, schnitzel, and sausages, although fresh salmon and seafood are also featured.

For old-school Italian food, try **Benetti's** (290 S. Broadway, 541/267-6066, 5pm-9pm Sun.-Thurs., 5pm-10pm Fri.-Sat., $8-25). Choose between pasta dishes such as spaghetti with house-made meatballs, chicken parmigiana, or a grilled steak.

The **Coney Station Restaurant** (295 S. Broadway, 541/269-6948, 11am-midnight daily, $8-22) combines features of a pub and steak house, with good burgers, sandwiches by day, and grilled chicken, beef, and ribs by night. The bar features over 20 regional brews on tap.

One good spot for seafood in Coos Bay is **◖ Shark Bites** (240 S. Broadway, 541/266-7582, 11am-9pm Mon.-Sat., $7-15), a hip little eatery with a droll sense of humor and good, freshly prepared food, with several local seafood options. A variety of wraps and sandwiches, including a very tasty halibut burger, as well as pasta and fish tacos, are favorites—best of all, prices are fair and quality is high.

Another place to get your seafood hit is **Sumin's Sushi Bar** (298 S. Broadway, 541/267-0119, 11am-8pm daily, $4-18), a friendly Asian food outpost with a selection of Chinese, Japanese, and Korean food. The quality is high, particularly for the sushi and hand rolls—try the Coos Bay Roll, with salmon, salmon skin, crabmeat, and spinach.

If you're visiting the waterfront boardwalk and feel the hankering for seafood, stop by **Fisherman Seafood Market** (200 S. Bayshore Dr., 541/267-2722, 10:30am-7pm Mon.-Sat., $6-12), a boat anchored off the boardwalk that serves as a seafood store for a local fishing family, plus a casual spot for (mostly) carry-out seafood sandwiches, fish-and-chips, and chowder.

North Bend

If you've had enough of the standard coastal fare, try **(Cafe Mediterranean** (1860 Union St., 541/756-2299, www.cafemediterranean. net, 11am-9pm Mon.-Sat., $7-16) for Middle Eastern-style Mediterranean food, including a locally famed lentil soup, in a friendly relaxed setting. This is a good spot for sharing a mezze platter, a Greek salad, and some kebabs. The Food Network's Rachael Ray stopped by for a Chicken Shawerma sandwich when she was filming in the area.

For another break from chowder, try **La Costa** (1930 Newport St., 541/751-0066, 11:30am-9pm Tues.-Thurs., 11am-10pm Fri.-Sat., noon-8 Sun., $8-17), with Peruvian and Mexican food fired up on the grill.

The **Mill Casino** (3201 Tremont Ave., 541/756-8800 or 800/953-4800, www.the-millcasino.com) has a total of five dining options, including the **Timbers Café** (24 hours daily, $8-22), with burgers, sandwiches, and other light dining options. The more upscale **Plank Room** (7am-10pm Sun.-Thurs., 7am-11pm Fri.-Sat., $12-28) offers three meals daily in a waterfront dining room. At the **Saw Blade** (4pm-9pm Fri.-Sat., $25 adults, $12.50 children ages 11 and under), a seafood buffet is offered on weekend evenings.

Natural-food fans converge at **Coos Head Food Store** (1960 Sherman Ave., 541/756-7264, 9am-7pm Mon.-Fri., 10am-6pm Sat., noon-5pm Sun.), which has the largest selection of certified organic produce and food on the south coast.

Charleston

You can't go too far wrong looking for a fresh seafood meal down at the docks—a number of casual restaurants (some are more like shacks) cluster here, including one spot where the crab cooker is always on.

The Sea Basket (63502 Kingfisher Rd., 541/888-5711, 7am-8pm daily, $8-16) typifies the good seafood, fast service, and fair prices you expect on the docks. Oysters are especially tasty in this restaurant, with noted breeding farms close by. It is also famous for its Bigman burgers. The fluorescent glare above the cafeteria-style tables frequented by anglers in work-blackened denims may not count much for atmosphere, but you'll leave satisfied.

Close by, the classier **Portside** (63383 Kingfisher Rd., Charleston Boat Basin, 541/888-5544, 11:30am-11pm daily, $11-34) has a wide menu of rather old-fashioned seafood specialties, but the selection is broad and you're sure to find something to your liking.

Just before the Charleston Bridge, the **Fisherman's Grotto** (91149 Cape Arago Hwy., 541/888-3251, 11am-8pm daily, $9-23) is a good place for fish-and-chips, seafood dinners such as grilled salmon or stuffed sole, or a plate of pasta (including seafood pasta). If you're an oyster lover, you'll certainly want to visit **Qualman's** (4898 Crown Point Rd., 541/888-3145, 10am-5:30pm daily), which sells incredibly fresh oysters from its nearby beds. Just look for the signs on the north side of the Charleston Bridge on the east side of the highway.

Part sports bar, part seafood restaurant, **(Miller's at the Cove** (63346 Boat Basin Rd., 541/808-2904, 11am-midnight daily, $9-14) has seafood every bit as fresh as it should be. Don't expect anything fancy, just delicious crab Louis or fish tacos. Kids are allowed until 9pm.

INFORMATION AND SERVICES

The **Bay Area Chamber of Commerce** (50 E. Central Ave., Coos Bay, 541/269-0215 or 800/824-8486, www.oregonsbayarea.org,

9am-5pm Mon.-Fri., 10am-4pm Sat.) is five blocks west of U.S. 101 off Commercial Avenue.

The Coos Bay World (www.theworldlink. com) is the largest daily paper on the south coast. The **Coos Bay Public Library** (525 W. Anderson Ave., Coos Bay, 541/267-1101) is open 10am-7pm Monday-Thursday and noon-6pm Friday-Saturday.

For health care and emergencies, the **Bay Area Hospital** (1775 Thompson Rd., Coos Bay, 541/269-8111), 0.5 mile west of U.S. 101 via Newmark Street, is the south coast's largest medical facility.

GETTING THERE AND AROUND

Improvements to OR 42 make it possible to get to and from Roseburg, 87 miles from Coos Bay, in less than two hours.

Porter Stage Lines (541/269-7183, www. porterstageline.com) operates daily bus service between Coos Bay and Eugene via Reedsport and Florence. Eugene has Amtrak and regular Greyhound service, as well as an airport served by national carriers. **Coastal Express** buses (800/921-2871, www.curry-publictransit.org), operated by Curry County Transport, run on weekdays between North Bend and Brookings to the south.

The **Southwest Oregon Regional Airport** (OTH), at the north end of North Bend, offers flights to Portland and San Francisco.

Public transportation in the Bay Area is limited; one bus line, **Coos County Area Transit** (541/267-7111, www.coostransit. org), makes a loop in Coos Bay and North Bend.

Bandon and Vicinity

Between Coos Bay and Bandon, U.S. 101 veers inland through forests and bucolic farmland. The highway reencounters the Pacific at Bandon, near the mouth of the Coquille River.

Bandon (pop. 3,100) is characterized by the style and grace of an earlier era, especially in Old Town, a picturesque collection of shops, galleries, and restaurants, fronting onto a bustling waterfront.

Although logging, fishing, dairy products, and the harvest of cranberries have been the traditional mainstays of the local economy, in the early part of the 20th century Bandon also enjoyed its first tourism boom. In addition to being a summer retreat from the heat of the Willamette Valley, it was a port of call for thousands of San Francisco-Seattle steamship passengers. This era inspired such tourist venues as the Silver Spray dance hall and a natatorium with a saltwater swimming pool. The golden age that began with the advent of large-scale steamship traffic in 1900, however, came to an abrupt end following a devastating fire in 1936 that destroyed most of the town. The blaze was

started by the easily ignitable gorse weed, imported from Ireland (as was the town's name) in the mid-1800s. Dramatic descriptions of the townspeople fighting the flames with their backs to the sea earned the incident a citation as one of the top 10 news stories of the year.

The face-lift given Old Town decades later, and the subsequent tourist influx, conjured for many the image of the mythical phoenix rising from its ashes to fly again. Today, Bandon is a curious mixture of provincial backwater, destination golf resort, and artists' colony. Backpack-toting travelers coexist happily with the large population of retirees, artisans, golfers from around the world, and locals who seem to have cornered the market on late-model pickups with gun racks.

SIGHTS

One of the appealing things about Bandon is that most of its attractions are within walking distance of each other. In addition, on the periphery of town is a varied array of things to see and do.

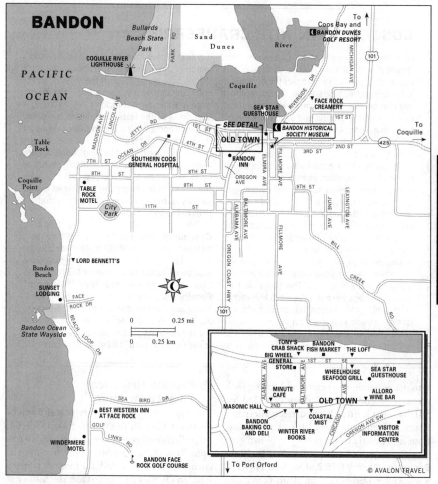

© AVALON TRAVEL

Old Town

Bandon's **Old Town**, much of which dates from after the 1936 fire, is a half-dozen blocks of shops, cafés, and galleries squeezed in between the harbor and a steep bluff. The renovated waterfront invites relaxed strolling, and crabbers and anglers pull in catches right off the city docks. The small commercial fleet based here pursues salmon and tuna offshore.

Preservation buffs should check out **Masonic Hall** (2nd St. and Alabama St.), one of the few buildings to have survived Bandon's 1914 and 1936 blazes. A photo in the historical museum shows the same building and surrounding structures on Alabama Street (then called Atwater) circa 1914. The photo depicts boardwalks leading to a woolen mill, old storefronts, a theater, and the Bandon Popular Hotel and Restaurant, outside which a horse and buggy await. The scene today has changed dramatically, but nonetheless an early-1900s charm still pervades the neighborhood.

Throughout Old Town are artists and

BOGGED DOWN WITH CRANBERRIES

From the vantage point of U.S. 101 between Port Orford and 10 miles north of Bandon, you'll notice what appears to be reddish-tinged ground in flood-irrigated fields. If you get closer, you'll see cranberries–small evergreen bushes that creep along the ground and send out runners that take root. Along the runners, upright branches 6-8 inches long hold pink flowers and, later, deep red fruit.

These berries are cultivated in bogs to satisfy their tremendous need for water and to protect them against insects and winter cold. Bandon leads Oregon in this crop, with an output ranking third in the nation. Oregon berries are often used in cranberry juice production by Ocean Spray because of their deep red pigment and high vitamin C content.

Oregon bogs were producing wild cranberries when Lewis and Clark first traded with the Indians for them in 1805. Shortly thereafter, cultivated bogs were developed in Massachusetts, which, like Oregon, has acidic soils with lots of organic materials conducive to berry production. By the time of the California gold rush of 1849, East Coast growing and harvest-ing techniques had transformed Bandon's marshes into commercial cranberry bogs. In the years to come, much of the modern equipment for harvesting these bogs was developed in Bandon. Wet-picking, for instance, is facilitated by the water reel, which is rotated to create eddies on the bog to shake berries off the vines. After they float to the surface, the cranberries are pushed by long booms toward a submerged hopper. They are then transferred by conveyor belt onto trucks. Walking through the bogs without trampling the berries is possible by fastening wooden platforms with short pegs to the soles of boots.

Fill up on cranberry confections at **Cranberry Sweets** (280 1st St. SE Bandon, 541/347-9475 or 800/527-5748, 9am-5:30pm daily). For sale are confections ranging from cranberry fudge to cranberry truffles. Look here and at other shops in town for **Vincent Family** dried cranberries or cranberry juice. Three generations of Vincents have been tending cranberry bogs; they're committed to making the business sustainable and are working toward organic certification for their berries.

artisans pursuing their crafts and selling their wares. The **2nd Street Gallery** (210 2nd St., 541/347-4133, http://secondstreetgallery.net, 10am-5:30pm daily) has a little of everything, from functional and art pottery to blown glass to paintings and sculptures. **WinterRiver Books and Gallery** (170 2nd St., 541/347-4111, www.winterriverbooks.com, 10am-6pm daily) has a wide-ranging assortment of travel titles, photo essays, and fiction that makes this the best bookstore on the south coast.

Close by, the **Bandon Driftwood Museum** (130 Baltimore Ave., 541/347-3719, 9am-5:30pm Mon.-Sat., 10am-5pm Sun., free) shows off an interesting collection of natural sculptures, from gnarly root balls to whole tree trunks. It's housed at the **Big Wheel General Store,** where you'll also find the Fudge Factory and 24 flavors of homemade ice cream and butter fudge.

(Bandon Historical Society Museum

The captivating **Bandon Historical Society Museum** (270 Fillmore St., 541/347-2164, http://bandonhistoricalmuseum.org, 10am-4pm Mon.-Sat., $3 adults, kids free), at the corner of U.S. 101 and Fillmore Street, in Bandon's former city hall, traces the history of the Coquille people and their forebears. The chronology continues with the steamers and the railroads that brought in white settlers. One room is devoted to Bandon's unofficial standing as the cranberry capital of Oregon. Black-and-white photos showing women stooping over in the bogs to harvest the ripe berries are captioned with such quips as this classic from an overseer: "I had 25 women picking for me, and I knew every one by her fanny." Color photos spanning five decades of Cranberry Festival princesses also adorn the walls.

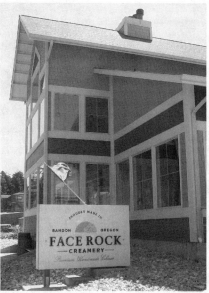

© BILL MCRAE

The Face Rock Creamery renews a longtime dairy tradition in Bandon.

Another room depicts Bandon's Resort Years, 1900-1931, when the town was called the "Playground of the Pacific." The most compelling exhibits in the museum deal with shipwrecks and the fires of 1914 and 1936.

Face Rock Creamery

For over a century, Bandon was Oregon's "other" cheese-making center, and cheeses from the Bandon Cheddar Cheese Factory rivaled those of Tillamook until the operation closed in 2002. Cheese making returned to Bandon in 2013 with the opening of the **Face Rock Creamery** (680 2nd Street SE, just north of downtown Bandon on Hwy. 101, 541/329-0012, www.facerockcreamery.com, 10am-8pm Mon.-Sat., 10am-5pm Sun.). The factory and visitors center is small compared with Tillamook, but it's worth a stop to watch the production of cheddar and jack cheese (the creamery plans to expand to other types of cheeses soon), and to taste the local cheese made from local milk (the Coquille River

valley east of Bandon is lined with dairies). The creamery also sells a large selection of cheeses from around the world—this is a good place to stock up for picnics—and offers freshly made ice cream as well.

Scenic Beach Loop

U.S. 101 follows an inland path for more than 50 miles between Coos Bay and Port Orford, but you can leave the highway in Bandon and take the four-mile Beach Loop for a lovely seaside detour south of town. Several access roads lead west from the highway to Beach Loop Drive (County Rd. 29), each about 0.25 mile from the others. Most people begin the drive by heading west from Old Town on 1st Street along the Coquille. Another popular approach is from 11th Street, which leads to Coquille Point. The south end of the drive runs through the northern portion of **Bandon State Natural Area,** providing parking, beach access, and picnic tables.

The once-bucolic drive along the Beach Loop has changed a bit—trophy homes form pretty much the only view you have for the first mile or two. Still, there are state park parking areas that let you put the McMansions to your back and allow a look at the gorgeous ocean views.

Along this fine stretch of beach are rock formations with such evocative names as Table Rock, Elephant Rock, Garden of the Gods, and Cat and Kittens Rocks. The whole grouping of sea stacks, included within the Oregon Islands National Wildlife Refuge, looks like a surrealist chess set cast upon the waters. The most eye-catching of all is **Face Rock,** Bandon's answer to New Hampshire's lately lamented Old Man of the Mountain. This basalt monolith resembles the face of a woman gazing skyward. An Indian legend says that she was a princess frozen by an evil sea spirit. Look for the Face Rock turnout 0.25 mile south of Coquille Point on the Beach Loop.

Despite their scenic and recreational attractions, the beaches south of town can be surprisingly deserted, perhaps because of the long, steep trails up from the water along some parts.

© BILL MCRAE

the distinctive profile of Bandon's Face Rock

In any case, this dearth of people can make for great beachcombing. Agates, driftwood, and tidepools full of starfish and anemones are commonly encountered, along with bird-watching opportunities galore. Elephant Rock has a reputation as the Parthenon of puffins, while murres, oystercatchers, and other species proliferate on the other offshore formations.

Bullards Beach State Park

Two miles north of Bandon, bordering the Coquille River estuary and more than four miles of beachfront, **Bullards Beach State Park** (541/347-2209 or 800/551-6949 information, www.oregonstateparks.org, $3 day-use fee) is a great place to fish, crab, bike, fly a kite, windsurf, picnic, or overnight in the large sheltered campground. The beach and lighthouse are reached via a scenic three-mile drive paralleling the Coquille River. Look for jasper and agates amid the heaps of driftwood on the shore. Equestrian trails and horse-camping facilities make this a popular desti-nation for riders. The boat ramp gives anglers,

kayakers, and canoeists access to the lower Coquille River and Bandon Marsh National Wildlife Refuge.

The riverside road going out to the Coquille's north jetty takes you through the dunes to the picturesque **Coquille River Lighthouse** (tours 11am-5pm daily early May-mid-Oct., free), a squat tower with adjacent octagonal quarters. The last lighthouse built on the Oregon coast, it was completed in 1896 then abandoned in 1939 when the Coast Guard installed an automated light across the river. After years of neglect, the structure was restored in the late 1970s; its light is now so-lar-powered. Etchings of ships that made it across Bandon's treacherous bar—and some that didn't—greet you inside.

West Coast Game Park

Seven miles south of Bandon is the **West Coast Game Park** (46914 U.S. 101 S., 541/347-3106, www.gameparksafari.com, 9am-6pm daily mid-June-Labor Day, call for spring, fall, and winter hours, $17.50 adults, $16.50 seniors,

SOUTH COAST

© BILL MCRAE

Bandon has one of the most dramatic beachfronts in Oregon.

$10 children ages 7-12, $7 ages 2-6), the self-proclaimed largest wild animal petting park in the country. There are 450 animals representing 75 different species, including tiger cubs, camels, zebras, monkeys, and snow leopards. Visitors may be surprised to see a lion and tiger caged together or a fox and a raccoon sharing the same nursery. The park tries raising different species together and often finds that animals can live harmoniously with their natural enemies. Free-roaming animals include deer, peacocks, pygmy goats, and llamas. An elk refuge is another popular area of the park. Even if you're not with a child, the opportunity to pet a pup, a cub, or a kit can bring out the kid in you. The park is open year-round, but call during winter because of restricted hours of operation.

SPORTS AND RECREATION

Bandon Beach Riding Stables (2640 Beach Loop Rd., 541/347-3423) is four miles south of Face Rock on the Beach Loop. Several beach rides are offered daily, plus sunset rides in the summer. Riders of all abilities are welcome, including those with disabilities. Prices range $40-60 for a 1- to 2-hour ride. Reservations are advised. Open year-round.

Kayak rentals are available on the waterfront; call 541/404-6566 or look for the sandwich board pointing to the marina just off 1st Street.

Golf

Duffers should head to the scenic seaside links two miles south of town at **Bandon Face Rock Golf Course** (3235 Beach Loop Rd., Bandon, 541/329-1927, www.bandonfacerockgolfcourse.com), where greens fees are a mere $18 for nine holes (and jeans are permitted!). The course dates from 1927 and was recently renovated.

A couple of miles farther south, **Bandon Crossing Golf Course** (87530 Dew Valle Ln., 541/347-3232, www.bandoncrossings.com, $45-75 for 18 holes) is a forested, challenging, but fun course that's good for families, novices, and anyone looking for a less intense experience than at the Bandon Dunes Golf Resort.

C BANDON DUNES GOLF RESORT

Bandon Dunes Golf Resort (57744 Round Lake Dr., 541/347-4380 or 888/345-6008, www.bandondunesgolf.com, May-Oct. greens fees $235 for hotel guests, $285 for nonguests, off-season $75-165 for guests, $120-220 for nonguests) has drawn accolades from the golf press and is far and away the most spectacular place to golf in Oregon. The original Bandon Dunes course has 7 holes along the Pacific and unobstructed ocean views from all 18. Three other 18-hole courses, Pacific Dunes, Bandon Trails, and Old Macdonald (inspired by golf course architect C. B. Macdonald), give golfers a chance to stay for a few days and keep encountering new territory.

To preserve the natural surroundings along the ocean bluffs, this Scottish links course doesn't allow carts (the only amenity missing), so you'll have to hire a caddie or schlep your own bag (a practice that is frowned upon here). A luxurious resort with Pacific views and a fine restaurant are also available for those who come to worship in the south coast's Sistine Chapel of golf.

Golfers who have never played on the Oregon coast should come prepared for wind, especially in the afternoon. Oregon golfers may know about the wind, but we have a special piece of advice for you—dress up. This is a rather formal place, and you'll feel out of place in your baggy cargo shorts and faded polo shirt.

The resort is one mile north of the Coquille River. November through April, Oregonians are admitted at the guest rate. Caddies expect $80-100 per bag.

Fishing

The Coquille River runs 30 miles from its Siskiyou headwaters before meandering leisurely through Bandon. The north and south jetties are popular spots for perch and rockfish, while the city docks right in Old Town yield catches of perch and crab April-October and smelt July-September. The spring chinook run pales in comparison to those in the Rogue and Chetco Rivers to the south, but the fall runs of chinook (beginning Sept.-Oct.) and coho (Oct.-Nov.) are strong and productive.

Steelhead usually arrive in November, and the run gathers steam January-February. A boat is necessary for the best steelhead and salmon water, but bank anglers can fish the mouth of Ferry Creek, just off Riverside Drive in Bandon. Fishing guides and gear can be arranged through **Bandon Bait & Tackle** (110 1st St., 541/347-3905, 6am-5pm daily), across from the boat basin. The shop also rents crab rings and other gear and can point you to productive spots for catching Dungeness crab.

Just off the south end of Beach Loop Drive, 30-acre **Bradley Lake,** protected from ocean winds by high dunes, offers good trout fishing and a boat ramp. Each spring the lake is stocked with trophy rainbows, averaging five pounds, reared at the Bandon Fish Hatchery east of town.

Wildlife-Viewing

Bird-watchers flock to the tidal salt marsh and the elevated observation deck of the **Bandon Marsh National Wildlife Refuge** (541/347-1470, daily sunrise-sunset), especially in the fall, to take in what may be the prime birding site on the coast. The extensive mudflats attract flocks of shorebirds, including red phalaropes, black-bellied plovers, long-billed curlews, and dunlins, as well as such strays from Asia as Mongolian plovers.

Bandon Marsh lies a short paddle across the river from the Bullards Beach State Park, or via Riverside Drive, which runs from Bandon to U.S. 101 on the south side of the Coquille River bridge. The refuge protects more than 700 precious acres of the Coquille estuary's remaining salt-marsh habitat along the southeastern side of the river. Migrating waterfowl, bald eagles, California brown pelicans, and other birds feast on the rich food sources. From U.S. 101 just north of Bandon, turn west onto Riverside Drive and continue for about one mile, where you'll reach the refuge.

ENTERTAINMENT AND EVENTS

A barbecue, a parade, and a drift boat show are highlights of Bandon's **Fourth of July** celebration; at dusk, fireworks are launched across the Coquille to burst above the river.

The biggest weekend of the year for Bandonians comes the second weekend in September, when the **Cranberry Festival** (541/347-9616) brings everyone together in Old Town for a parade, a crafts fair, tours of a cranberry farm, and the Bandon High Cranberry Bowl—in which the local footballers take on traditional rival Coquille High.

During the late November-early January holiday season, the merchants of Old Town and anglers deck their stores and boats with twinkling lights in the traditional **Festival of Lights.** Particularly striking is the Coquille River Lighthouse, lit up across the water like a Christmas tree.

ACCOMMODATIONS

For the best ocean views, often with nearby trails to the beach, look to the lodgings along the Beach Loop. If you want to be able to walk to dinner in Old Town, stay at one of the in-town locations. For the best of both worlds, bring a bike and cycle into town from a Beach Loop room. Bandon bills itself as America's storm-watching capital, and special packages are often available October-March.

$50-100

Right in the heart of Old Town, the **◖ Sea Star Guesthouse** (370 1st St., 541/347-9632, www.seastarbandon.com, $75-115) has just six rooms. Four rooms are spacious, charming, and uniquely decorated, with skylights, wood-beam ceilings, a verdant courtyard, and views onto the harbor. The other two rooms are less expensive and a bit less spacious, but are some of the best deals in town.

On a bluff at the top of Beach Loop Road, find an assortment of motel rooms and small cottages at **Table Rock Motel** (840 Beach Loop Dr., 541/347-2700 or 800/457-9141, www.tablerockmotel.com, $70-129). The least expensive rooms don't have ocean views, but all are a short, steep walk away from one of the coast's prettiest beaches.

Farther down the Beach Loop is **Sunset Lodging** (1865 Beach Loop Rd., 541/347-2453 or 800/842-2407, www.sunsetmotel.com, $75-290), a motel complex with a variety of lodging types. With some units built right into the cliff above a scenic beach, the view here is hard to beat. Whether you're looking for guest rooms with a kitchen, guest rooms that accommodate pets, or guest rooms with a fireplace, there's something here for you. A hot tub, an indoor pool, on-site laundry, and Lord Bennett's restaurant across the street also highlight this place. Nonetheless, the steep steps down the 80-foot-high bluff to the beach, the busy atmosphere, and the rusticity of the least expensive guest rooms might not be to everyone's liking.

$100-150

Set on a bluff overlooking Old Town, the **◖ Bandon Inn** (355 U.S. 101, 541/347-4417 or 800/526-0209, www.bandoninn.com, $124-165) has spectacular views, comfortable rooms all with balconies, and a path down to town. Pets are permitted in some rooms. This is a great spot to stay if you want the wining and dining of Old Town within walking distance.

A favorite place to stay on the Beach Loop is the older but refurbished **Windermere Motel** (3250 Beach Loop Rd., 541/347-3710, www.windermerebythesea.com, $135-198), where baby-boomers can relive their childhood beach getaways in cedar efficiencies or two-story condo-like units, situated on a bluff above a windswept beach. Housekeeping facilities and proximity to restaurants (Lord Bennett's) and the West Coast Game Park also make this an ideal family vacation spot.

$150-200

Another popular place is the **Best Western Inn at Face Rock** (3225 Beach Loop Rd., 541/347-9441 or 800/638-3092, www.innatfacerock.com, $169-219). Part of its popularity has to do with the motel's location—set back from the road near the end of the Beach Loop, across the street from Bandon's coastline, and near the Bandon Face Rock Golf Course. Many of the modern well-appointed guest rooms have magnificent ocean views. An indoor pool, a fitness room, a whirlpool, and a restaurant also make this an especially good choice for active travelers. Some suites have fireplaces, kitchenettes, and private patios. There is a short path to the beach.

Over $200

For avid golfers, the **Bandon Dunes Golf Resort** (57744 Round Lake Dr., 541/347-4380 or 888/345-6008, www.bandondunesgolf.com, $210-410 d) is the place to stay. Lodging is in several different locations around the resort and includes single lodge or inn rooms in various sizes, two- or four-bedroom suites, and multibedroom cottages. View options vary from golf course and ocean views to dune and surrounding woods. Bandon Dunes is five minutes from Bandon, a mile north of the Coquille, and 27 miles (30 minutes' drive) from the North Bend Airport, which is served by daily flights from Portland.

Vacation Rentals

Bandon is an easy place to spend a weekend, and there are several property management companies that can help you find a house to rent.

Coastal Vacation Rentals (541/347-3009 or 800/336-5693, www.coastalvacationrentals.com) has large houses that are good for family gatherings, including several places that accept pets. Many of the places offered by **Exclusive Property Management** (541/347-3790 or 800/527-5445, www.visitbandon.com) are large and quite upscale, with great locations and lovely interior design. It also rents a few more modest homes, so don't be afraid to call or check the website.

Bandon Beach Vacation Rentals (54515 Beach Loop Rd., 541/347-4801 or 888/441-8030, www.bandonbeachrentals.com) has several reasonably priced units available, including one place that'll sleep 10 people.

Camping

Bullards Beach State Park (541/347-2209 or 800/551-6949 information, 800/452-5687 reservations, www.oregonstateparks.org) is a wonderful state park in a great location between the Coquille River and four miles of beach. The park has 190 campsites ($24), 13 yurts ($26), eight horse-camping sites, and hiker-biker spaces. To get there, drive north of town on U.S. 101 for about one mile; just past the bridge on the west side of the highway is the park entrance. The beach is reached via a scenic two-mile drive paralleling the Coquille River. Electricity, picnic tables, and grills are provided. You'll also find a store, a café, a laundry room, horse-riding/camping facilities, an inviting sandy beach, summer evening campfire talks Tuesday-Saturday, and hiking trails.

FOOD

Five miles south of Bandon, on the east side of U.S. 101, hit the brakes at **Misty Meadows Jams** roadside stand (48053 U.S. 101 S., 541/347-2575, 9am-5pm) for first-rate jams and jellies, including a variety of products incorporating Bandon cranberries. This family-owned and operated business has been making delicious concoctions from Oregon-grown fruits since 1970. In addition to preserves, the shop sells olives and fruit-based barbecue sauce, syrup, honey, and salsa. Look here and in other shops in town for Vincent Family dried cranberries or cranberry juice. Three generations of Vincents have been tending cranberry bogs, and they're committed to making the business sustainable and working toward organic certification for their berries.

American

If you're after a full breakfast, head to the **Minute Café** (145 2nd St., 541/347-2707, 5:30am-8pm daily, $8-14), where locals and tourists settle in with the morning paper, omelets, and pancakes. Later in the day, the menu features burgers, sandwiches, and chowder. For coffee, granola, and excellent pastries, head across the street to the **Bandon Baking Co. and Deli** (160 2nd St., 541/347-9440).

Italian

Although it's called a wine bar, ◨ **Alloro Wine Bar** (375 2nd St., 541/347-1850, www.

There's good food on the docks in Bandon's Old Town.

allorowinebar.com, 4pm-10pm Tues.-Sun., closed Jan.-Feb., dinner $12-27) is the top choice in town for an Italian dinner. But don't come looking for spaghetti—the food is much more upscale than that. Instead expect smoked steelhead Alfredo or duck breast served with cranberry cherry salsa and polenta. The food here is excellent, and the pace is relaxed. The pasta is house-made, and most of the produce is local. If you don't want a full dinner, there's a small bar where you can taste a flight of wines and nibble on olives or Italian cheeses.

Pacific Northwest

From its second-floor perch above the harbor, ◖ **The Loft** (315 1st St. SE, 541/329-0535, www.theloftofbandon.com, 5pm-9pm Wed.-Sun., $18-38) serves some of the best dinners in town—definitely with the best views. Abundant use is made of local produce and there's always lots of good seafood on the menu along with steak, a high-end burger (topped with black truffle aioli), and chicken.

The dining room is fairly small, so reservations are a good idea.

If you don't want to leave the Beach Loop for dinner, **Lord Bennett's** (1695 Beach Loop Dr., 541/347-3663, 5pm-9pm Mon.-Thurs., 11am-9pm Fri.-Sat., 10am-2pm and 5pm-9pm Sun. $18-30) offers a dramatic ocean view. Lunch and dinner do justice to these surroundings with elegantly rendered pasta, steak, chicken, and seafood dishes. Jazz on selected evenings in the lounge adds a nice touch.

The **Bandon Dunes Golf Resort** (57744 Round Lake Dr., 541/347-4380 or 888/345-6008, www.bandondunesgolf.com) offers a number of dining options. In the main lodge is the **Gallery** (6am-9:30pm daily, $22-37), a good place to eat an excellent steak, and the many seasonal fish and seafood preparations are always noteworthy. If you're not staying at the resort, lunch is an interesting time to get a feel for the place and to enjoy the views out onto the Bandon Dunes course. If you're looking for a less formal atmosphere, check out the adjacent Tufted Puffin Lounge or the Bunker

Bar downstairs, which has a gentlemen's club vibe; both serve snacks and light meals. Lunch (mostly soups, salads, and sandwiches) is also served at the **Trails End Clubhouse** (11am-5pm daily, $8-12), in the Bandon Trails Clubhouse. In the evening, a good spot for an informal meal is **McKee's Pub** (4pm-10pm, $9-37) which has a Scottish country pub atmosphere, plus a wide-ranging menu that includes individual pizzas, burgers, steaks, and hearty favorites like meatloaf and fish-and-chips. In addition to a good selection of regional microbrews, in good weather McKee's also offers a marvelous outdoor patio fronting onto the course. In the new Pacific Dunes Clubhouse is the **Pacific Grill** (8am-9:30pm daily, $9-39) for a dining-in-the-round experience with views of three courses. The menu ranges from burgers and sandwiches for lunch to Pacific seafood stew and pork with a honey-onion glaze for dinner.

Seafood

If you're looking for inexpensive street food, check along 1st Street near the Old Town Marina, where **Tony's Crab Shack** (155 1st St., 541/347-2875, dawn-dusk daily, $4-15) sells crab sandwiches, fish tacos, grilled salmon, steamer clams, and lots more. As the name implies, it's not really a sit-down place, though there are a few picnic tables on the dock.

Budget diners and smoked-fish connoisseurs will appreciate the **Bandon Fish Market** (249 1st St. SE, 541/347-4282, 11am-6pm Mon.-Thurs., 11am-7pm Fri.-Sat., 11am-4pm Sun., $10). Heartier appetites call for the market's excellent fish-and-chips (takeout only). A picnic table outside near the harbor is the place to enjoy it all, with a trip across the street to **Cranberry Sweets** (280 1st St. SE,

541/347-9475 or 800/527-5748, 9am-5:30pm daily) for dessert.

Chocolates and Dessert

You'll want to know about **Coastal Mist** (210 2nd Street SE, 541/347-3300, 11am-5:30pm Mon.-Thurs., 10am-7pm Fri., 10am-5pm Sat.-Sun., lunch $6-7), a chocolate boutique with house-made candies and desserts, plus lunchtime sandwiches and salads.

INFORMATION AND SERVICES

The **Bandon Chamber of Commerce** (300 W. 2nd St., Bandon, 541/347-9616, www.bandon.com) in Old Town distributes a comprehensive guide and a large annotated pictographic map of the town.

Southern Coos General Hospital (900 11th St. SE, 541/319-1031) features an ocean view that is in itself therapeutic, as well as an emergency room and facilities for coronary and respiratory care.

GETTING THERE AND AROUND

North- and southbound **Coastal Express** buses (800/921-2871, www.currypublictransit.org) run on weekdays between North Bend and Brookings.

Between Bandon and Coos Bay, you can escape the tedium of U.S. 101's inland route by taking **Seven Devils Road** about three miles north of Bandon. This route runs 13 miles to **Charleston,** a fishing village that sits closer to the ocean than its larger neighbors to the northeast, Coos Bay and North Bend. En route, beaches, state parks, and an estuarine preserve make the drive interesting, although the miles of heavily logged mountainsides may take you aback.

Port Orford and Vicinity

Port Orford marks the northernmost end of one of the most spectacular stretches of coastline in the United States. From Bandon, the highway runs inland; when it hits Port Orford, the road nearly runs into the Pacific. And what a splendid place to encounter the ocean: The beach is perfect for long treasure-hunting walks, and the bluffs just to the north are also fun to explore. A few miles north, blustery Cape Blanco is the westernmost point of the continental United States; a short distance south, Humbug Mountain rises almost directly from the ocean. All of these places are great for a quick ogle and a snapshot, but even better for hiking and exploring. Port Orford is a good base for all of that, with a wide range of accommodations and a few good places to eat.

In spite of its knockout views and great recreation, the area is not especially prosperous. Commercial fishing and cedar logging were once the leading revenue producers. In recent years, tourism and many eclectic cottage industries have sprung up to supplement the boom-bust resource-based economy. The outskirts of Port Orford host such diverse undertakings as llama and sheep ranches, a goat-milk dairy, and commercial berry growers, as well as plots of land devoted to Christmas trees and exotic herbs. Offshore, divers harvest kelp for use as a food supplement and sea urchins to supply the Japanese with a popular aphrodisiac and seafood delicacy. In town, the stunning scenery and relatively low rents have probably played a role in the development of a passel of galleries, evidence of a nascent artists' colony.

SIGHTS AND RECREATION

Port Orford has an ocean view from downtown that is arguably the most scenic of any town on the coast. A waterfront stroll lets you appreciate the cliffs and offshore sea stacks, as well as the unique sight of commercial fishing boats being hoisted by large cranes into and out of the harbor. With only a short jetty on its north side, Port Orford's harbor, the only open-water port in Oregon, is unprotected from southerly swells, so boats can't be safely moored on the water. When not in use, the fleet rests on wheeled trailer-like dollies near the foot of the pier.

PORT ORFORD INDIAN WARS

In 1850 the U.S. Congress passed the Oregon Donation Land Act, allowing white settlers to file claims on Native American land in western Oregon. This was news, of course, to the Native American nations of the region, who had not been consulted on the decision. William Tichenor, captain of the steamship *Gull*, hoping to exploit the new act, had ambitions to establish an outpost on the coast at what's now Port Orford. When Tichenor observed the hostility of the Quatomah band of the Tututni in the tidewater, he put nine men ashore on an immense rock promontory fronting the beach because of its suitability as a defensive position. The Native Americans besieged the rock for two weeks before the white men escaped under cover of night. Tichenor returned with a well-armed party of 70 men and succeeded in founding his settlement.

From this inauspicious beginning, "Awferd," as the locals call it, established itself as the first town site on the south coast. Shortly thereafter, the town became the site of the first fort established on the coast during the Rogue Indian Wars. This conflict started when gold miners and settlers came into Native American lands. As a result of the clashes, hundreds of local natives were rounded up and sent to the Siletz Reservation near Lincoln City in 1856.

SOUTH COAST

© BILL MCRAE

The coastline near Port Orford is particularly rugged.

A stroll or bike ride through town is a perfect way to visit Port Orford's galleries. These are, by and large, much different and far more interesting than the typical seaside-town collections of landscape paintings and sunset photos. Expect to find high-quality crafts, glass art, sculpture, and computer-generated art.

Battle Rock Park

As you come into town on U.S. 101, it's hard to ignore enormous Battle Rock on the shoreline, the site of the 1851 conflict between local Native Americans and the first landing party of white settlers. If you can make your way through the driftwood and blackberry bushes surrounding its base, you can climb the short trail to the top for a heightened perspective on the rockbound coast that parallels the town. You'll also notice the east-west orientation of the harbor. Once you get to the top of the rock, don't think that the battle is necessarily over. Bracing winds often chill you, and high tides can sometimes render this coastal finger of land an island. The rock is also the focus of a **Fourth**

of July Jubilee Celebration, which reenacts the historic battle.

Even if you're not up for a scramble on Battle Rock, do walk the short path down to the beach, which is relatively sheltered from the wind and a good place for a walk. It's also a good spot for beachcombing, with agates and fishing floats being the prize finds.

If you'd rather do your scavenging inland, try searching the nearby foothills for the lost Port Orford meteorite. The meteorite was found in the 1860s by a government geologist, who estimated its weight at 22,000 tons. Unfortunately, he was unable to locate the meteorite when he returned for another look.

Port Orford Heads State Park

Another shoreline scene worth taking in, featuring a striking panorama from north to south, is up West 9th Street at what the locals call the Heads, or **Port Orford Heads State Park** (www.oregonstateparks.org). If you go down the cement trail to the tip of the blustery headland, you look south to the mouth of Port Orford's harbor. To the north, many small rocks fill the water, along with boats trolling for salmon or checking crab pots. On clear days visibility extends from Cape Blanco to Humbug Mountain.

Also here is the historic **Port Orford Lifeboat Station** (541/332-0521, 10am-3:30pm Thurs.-Mon. Apr.-Oct., free), built by the Coast Guard in 1934 to provide rescue service to the southern Oregon coast. After it was decommissioned in 1970, the officers' quarters, the pleasingly proportioned crew barracks, and other outbuildings were converted into a museum depicting the work of the station. A trail leads down to Nellie's Cove, site of the former boathouse and launch ramp.

◖ Humbug Mountain

Some people will tell you that 1,756-foot-high Humbug Mountain, six miles south of Port Orford on U.S. 101, is the highest mountain rising directly off the Oregon shoreline. Because the criteria for such a distinction vary as much as the tides, let's just say it's a special place. There's more than one version of how the peak, formerly called Sugarloaf Mountain, got its name. According to one, gold miners who were drawn here in the 1850s by tales of gold in the black sands nearby soon discovered that the rumored riches proved to be "humbug."

Once the site of Native American vision quests, Humbug Mountain now casts its shadow upon an Eden-like state park campground surrounded by myrtles, alders, and maples. Just north is a breezy black-sand beach. A three-mile trail to the top of Humbug rewards hardy hikers with impressive vistas to the south of Nesika Beach and a chance to see wild rhododendrons 20-25 feet high. Rising above the rhodies and giant ferns are bigleaf maples, Port Orford cedars, and Douglas and grand firs. Access the trail from the campground or from a trailhead parking area off the highway near the south end of the park. In addition, the **Oregon Coast Trail,** which follows the beach south from Battle Rock, traverses the mountain and leads down its south side to the beach at Rocky Point.

Prehistoric Gardens

What can we say about this unique roadside attraction, featuring a 25-foot-tall Formica-green *Tyrannosaurus rex* standing beside the parking lot? Is it kitsch, or is it educational? You decide. In any case, if you've got children in the car, unless they're sleeping or blindfolded, you're probably going to have to pull over. **Prehistoric Gardens** (36848 U.S. 101, 541/332-4463, www.prehistoricgardens.com, 9am-dusk daily spring-fall, call for winter hours, $8 adults, $7 seniors 65 and over and children ages 11-17, $6 children ages 3-10), about 10 miles south of Port Orford, is the creation of E. V. Nelson, a sculptor and self-taught paleontologist who began fabricating life-size dinosaurs here back in 1953 and placing them amid the lush rainforest on the back of Humbug Mountain. Paths lead through the ferns, trees, and undergrowth to a towering brontosaurus, triceratops, and 20 other ferroconcrete replicas, painted in a dazzling palette of Fiestaware colors.

◖ Cape Blanco State Park and Hughes House

Four miles north of Port Orford, west of U.S. 101, is **Cape Blanco,** whose remoteness gives you the feeling of being at the edge of the continent—as indeed you are, here at the westernmost point in Oregon. From the vantage of Cape Blanco, dark mountains rise behind you and the eaves of the forest overhang the tidewater. Below, driftwood and 100-foot-long bull kelp on slivers of black-sand beach fan out from both sides of this earthy red bluff. Somehow, the Spaniards who sailed past it in 1603 viewed the cape as having a *blanco* (white) color. It has been theorized that perhaps they were referring to the fossilized shells on the front of the cliff.

With its exposed location, Cape Blanco really takes it on the chin from Pacific storms. The vegetation along the five-mile state park road down to the beach attests to the severity of winter storms in the area. Gales of 100-mph winds (the record winds were clocked at 184 mph) and horizontal sheets of rain have given some of the usually massive Sitka spruces the appearance of bonsai trees. An understory of salmonberry and bracken fern help evoke the look of a southeast Alaskan forest.

Atop the weathered headland is Oregon's oldest, most westerly, and highest lighthouse in continuous use. Built in 1870, the beacon stands 256 feet above sea level and can be seen some 23 nautical miles out at sea. **Cape Blanco Lighthouse** (541/332-6774, 10am-3:30pm Tues.-Sun. Apr.-Oct., $2 adults, $1 children under 12) also holds the distinction of having had Oregon's first female lighthouse keeper, Mabel E. Bretherton, who assumed her duties in 1903. Tours of the facility include the chance to climb the 64 spiraling steps to the top. This is the only operational lighthouse in the state that allows visitors into the lantern room to view the working Fresnel lens.

Over the years, several shipwrecks have occurred on the reefs near Cape Blanco, including that of the *J. A. Chanslor,* an oil tanker that

collided with the offshore rocks in 1919 with the loss of 36 lives.

Near Cape Blanco on a side road along the Sixes River is the **Hughes House** (541/332-0248, 10am-3:30pm Tues.-Sun. Apr.-Oct., free), a restored Victorian home built in 1898 for rancher and county commissioner Patrick Hughes. Owned and operated today by the state of Oregon, the house offers an intriguing glimpse of rural life on the coast over a century ago.

Grassy Knob Wilderness

The **Grassy Knob Wilderness** (Siskiyou National Forest, Powers Ranger District, 541/439-6200) encompasses 17,200 acres of steep rugged terrain and protects rare stands of Port Orford cedar. The wood of this majestic fragrant tree is light, strong, and durable. Its use in planes during World War II and in Japanese construction has made it highly valued, but a fatal root fungus spread by logging trucks accounts for its rarity and astronomically high price. (As you travel around the area, you may notice the dead or dying cedars.) During World War II, Japanese submarines used Cape Blanco Lighthouse as an orientation mark to aim planes loaded with incendiary bombs at the Coast Range. The Japanese hoped to ignite forest fires that would destroy the region's Port Orford cedar trees, which were used to construct airplanes. Because of the perennial dampness, the results were negligible. A short (0.8-mile) but moderately difficult trail leads to the summit of Grassy Knob. To get here, follow U.S. 101 north of Port Orford about four miles, then go east on County Road 196 to Forest Service Road 5105, which ends at the trailhead.

Fishing

The **Elk River,** which empties on the south side of Cape Blanco, and the **Sixes River,** which meets the sea north of the cape, are two popular streams for salmon and steelhead fishing. Chinook and steelhead begin to enter both rivers after the first good rains of fall arrive, usually in November. Private lands limit bank access, with the exception of a good stretch of

© BILL MCRAE

The Cape Blanco Lighthouse sits at the westernmost point in Oregon.

© BILL MCRAE

The boats at Port Orford are lifted out of the water when they are done sailing.

the Sixes that runs through Cape Blanco State Park. The salmon season runs to the end of the year, and steelhead through the following March. **Lamm's Guide Service** (541/784-5145, www.umpquafishingguide.com) leads trips on both rivers.

Boating and Waterskiing

In the northwest of town, drive west of the highway on 14th or 18th Streets to 90-acre **Garrison Lake** for boating, waterskiing, and fishing for stocked rainbow and cutthroat trout. **Buffington Memorial City Park,** at the end of 14th Street, has a dock for fishing or swimming, plus playing fields, tennis courts, picnic areas, hiking trails, and a horse arena. Half a mile north of the lake, look for agates on **Paradise Point Beach.**

Surfing

The south-facing beach at **Battle Rock Beach,** in downtown Port Orford, can be okay for surfing during the winter, when northwesterly

winds blow in. Otherwise, surfers tend to go about a mile south of town to the beach at **Hubbard Creek** (best in the spring). What these spots may lack in intensity, they make up for in scenery.

Windsurfing and Kiteboarding

Between Port Orford and Bandon (just south of Langlois) is **Floras Lake,** one of the southern Oregon coast's two great windsurfing and kiteboarding spots (the other is south of Gold Beach at Pistol River). The lake, just barely inland from the beach, catches incredible breezes. **Floras Lake Windsurfing School** (541/348-9912, www.floraslake.com) offers windsurfing and kiteboarding lessons and rentals; the proprietors also have a very nice B&B just above the lake. It's 11 miles north of Port Orford, about four miles west of the highway on Floras Lake Loop Road. On the lake is **Boice Cope County Park,** which has basic tent and RV sites and a boat ramp. When the wind's not blowing (fat chance of that!), explore the hiking trails from the campground to the beach. From Floras Lake north to Bandon is the most isolated beachfront on the Oregon coast—ideal for beachcombing. Grasses, dunes, and shore pines usher you the 25 miles back to Bandon, and chances are good you won't see a soul.

ACCOMMODATIONS

With one notable exception, Port Orford is the kind of place where a room with a view will not break your budget.

$50-100

The **Shoreline Motel** (206 6th St., 541/332-2903, $55-70), is right downtown, across the highway from Battle Rock. While not fancy, it's convenient and perfectly adequate for a basic night's stay.

Just south of town, the **Seacrest Motel** (44 U.S. 101 S., 541/332-3040, www.seacrestoregon.com, $65-85) features views of coastal cliffs and a garden from a quiet hillside on the east side of the highway. Pets are welcome at this older motel.

Castaway-by-the-Sea (545 W. 5th St.,

SOUTH COAST

541/332-4502, www.castawaybythesea.com, $85-165) features ocean and harbor views from high on a bluff, fireplaces, and housekeeping units, and it allows pets. In addition to the motel rooms, the Castaway has a two-bedroom lodge that'll sleep up to 10 (from $185). The rates on the upper-end lodgings go down significantly in the off-season. It's said that Jack London once stayed in an earlier incarnation of this place.

$150-200

North of Port Orford, the **Floras Lake House B&B** (92870 Boice Cope Rd., Langlois, 541/348-2573, www.floraslake.com, $150-180, includes breakfast) is perfectly suited for windsurfers or others who want to explore the beaches in this unpopulated area. The spacious light-filled house looks out onto Floras Lake and the ocean, and the proprietors also offer windsurfing and kiteboarding lessons.

Over $200

Port Orford's serene luxury resort is **Wildspring Guest Habitat** (92978 Cemetery Loop, www.wildspring.com, $278-308 d, including continental breakfast). The small (five-cabin) resort is in a forested setting on a bluff above the highway (but totally secluded from it), with views of the ocean from the main lodge and hot tub. The cabins are beautifully and meticulously designed and furnished (including a refrigerator, a massage table, and Wi-Fi access in each cabin, but no telephones or TVs) and are as comfortable as they are perfect-looking. The main guest hall has a kitchen that's available to guests as long as it's not being used to prepare breakfast. The well-tended grounds include a labyrinth and several meditation nooks, but perhaps the best place to hang out is the slate-lined hot tub, which looks out over treetops to the ocean. It's a good idea to take binoculars, as Wildspring is a stop along the Oregon Coast Birding Trail. Bikes, backpacks, and hiking trail maps are available to all guests. Guided meditation, drumming, and tai chi are all offered one or two times a month (check the

website or call to inquire). This is a good place for a romantic retreat or a solo contemplative getaway.

Camping

Humbug Mountain State Park (541/332-6774), six miles south of Port Orford on U.S. 101, features 62 tent sites ($17) and 32 sites for trailers and motor homes ($20), and wind-protected sites reserved for hikers and bikers ($5). Flush toilets, showers, picnic tables, water, and firewood are available.

Cape Blanco State Park (39745 U.S. 101 S., 541/332-6774 information, 800/452-5687 cabin reservations, $5-39) can be reached by driving four miles north of Port Orford on U.S. 101, then heading northwest on the park road that continues five miles beyond to the campground. It features 54 tent sites ($20), four cabins ($39), trailer and motor home sites ($20), a horse camp ($17), and hiker-biker sites ($5); picnic tables, water, and showers are available. For horseback riders, there's a seven-mile trail and a huge open riding area; horses are also allowed on the beach. Regular sites are first-come, first-served.

FOOD

Port Orford doesn't have a lot of restaurants, but there are a few good places to eat.

The spot for a hearty breakfast is the **Paradise Cafe** (1825 Oregon St., 541/332-8104, 6am-2pm daily, $8-12), where the locals go for stacks of pancakes in the morning and burgers for lunch.

If you're planning to visit Port Orford's docks, stop by **Griff's on the Dock** (303 Dock Rd., 541/332-8985, 11am-8pm daily), a weathered shack amid the boats and tackle shops. The fish here is as fresh as it gets, and the atmosphere, with crusty old anglers eating hot dogs and talking crabbing, is not a cookie-cutter idea of a fish-and-chips place.

More sophisticated fare can be had across the street from Battle Rock at **Paula's Bistro** (236 6th St., 541/332-9378, 5pm-9pm Tues.-Sat., $20-29), with a menu centered on local fish and seafood, although pasta, lamb, and steaks are also available. The atmosphere is casual and friendly, and the dining room doubles as an art gallery.

The best views and classiest food are at **Redfish** (517 Jefferson St., 541/366-2200, www.redfishportorford.com, 9am-3pm and 5pm-9pm Mon.-Fri., 11am-3pm and 5pm-9pm Sat.-Sun., $10-29), where the Pacific Northwest coastal cuisine has a French twist. The local rockfish is pan-seared and served with buckwheat crepes, smoked salmon and cucumber relish, and red-onion crème fraîche. Adjoining the restaurant is an upscale gallery.

Chow down on vegetarian soup and sandwiches at **Seaweed Natural Food and Grocery** (832 Oregon St., 541/332-3640).

INFORMATION AND SERVICES

Begin your travels at **Battle Rock Information Center** (Battle Rock Wayside, 541/332-4106, www.discoverportorford.com, 10am-3pm daily), on the west side of U.S. 101. The people here are especially friendly and helpful. The **library** (555 W. 20th St.) is open weekdays 10am-5pm.

GETTING THERE

Curry County's **Coastal Express** buses (800/921-2871, www.currypublictransit.org) run up and down the south coast weekdays only between North Bend and the California border, including local service in Port Orford.

Gold Beach and Vicinity

This town is one part of the coast where the action is definitely away from the ocean. To lure people from Oregon's superlative ocean shores, the Rogue estuary has been bestowed with many blessings. First, the gold-laden black sands were mined in the 1850s and 1860s. While this short-lived boom era gave Gold Beach its name, the arrival of Robert Hume, later known as the Salmon King of the Rogue, had greater historical significance. By the turn of the 20th century, Hume's canneries were shipping out some 16,000 cases of salmon per year and established the river's image as a leading salmon and steelhead stream. This reputation was later enhanced by outdoorsman and novelist Zane Grey in his *Rogue River Feud* and other writings. Over the years, Herbert Hoover, Winston Churchill, Ginger Rogers (who had a home on the Rogue), Clark Gable, Jack London, George H. W. Bush, and Jimmy Carter, among other notables, have come here to try their luck. During the last several decades, boat tours focusing on the abundant wildlife, scenic beauty, and fascinating lore of the region have hooked other sectors of the traveling public.

Today, Gold Beach is a town of about 2,000

and the Curry County seat. Gold Beach serves as the south coast tourism hub, but a pulp mill and commercial ocean fishing industry round out the local economy. The seasonal nature of many local businesses creates serious wintertime unemployment. This fact, combined with torrential rains, drastically reduces the population of Gold Beach from Thanksgiving until spring. Thereafter, the wildflowers and warm weather transform this town into a vacation mecca.

At the north end of town, just before the road gives way to Conde McCullough's elegant Patterson Bridge, the harbor comes into view on the left, full of salmon trawlers, jet boats, pelicans, and seals bobbing up and down. Across the bridge is **Wedderburn,** a baby sister to Gold Beach named for the Scottish birthplace of Robert Hume.

SIGHTS
Beaches

The driftwood-strewn strand of **South Beach,** just south of Gold Beach's harbor, is convenient but only so-so. You'll find more exciting stretches both north and south of town. Tidepoolers might want to stop at the visitors

© BILL MCRAE

The Gold Beach Bridge spans the Rogue River.

center before heading out to ask for the *Tide Pools Are Alive* brochure, with tips and species descriptions. Two miles south, there's easy access to a nice beach and some tidepooling at tiny **Buena Vista State Park,** at the mouth of Hunter Creek. Seven miles south of Gold Beach, there's more tidepooling amid the camera-friendly basalt sea stacks at beautiful **Myers Creek Beach,** part of Pistol River State Park south of Cape Sebastian. The south side of Cape Sebastian and **Pistol River State Park,** a couple of miles farther south, are the best places on the Oregon coast for windsurfers to enjoy wave sailing. The beaches around Pistol River are also great places to find razor clams.

Bailey Beach, north of town between the Rogue River jetty and Otter Point, is another popular spot for razor clamming, and **Nesika Beach,** seven miles north of Gold Beach, is another good tidepooling destination.

◖ Cape Sebastian

Seven miles south of Gold Beach is **Cape Sebastian.** This spectacular windswept

headland was named by Sebastián Vizcaíno, who plied offshore waters here for Spain in 1602 along with Manuel d'Alguilar. At 720 feet above the sea, Cape Sebastian is the highest south coast overlook reachable by a paved public road. On a clear day, visibility extends 43 miles north to Humbug Mountain and 50 miles south to California. This is one of the best perches along the south coast for whale-watching. A trail zigzags through beautiful springtime wildflowers down the south side of the cape for about two miles until it reaches the sea. In April and May, Pacific paintbrushes, Douglas irises, orchids, and snow queens usher you along. In addition, Cape Sebastian supports a population of large-headed goldfields, a summer-blooming yellow daisy-like flower found only in coastal Curry County.

In 1942, a caretaker heard Japanese voices drifting across the water through the fog. When the mist lifted, he looked down from Cape Sebastian trail to see a surfaced submarine. This sighting, together with the Japanese bombing at Brookings and the incendiary balloon spotted over Cape Blanco, sent shock waves up the south coast. But the potential threat remained just that, and local anxiety eventually subsided.

Museums

At the **Curry County Historical Museum** (29419 S. Ellensburg Ave., 541/247-9396, www.curryhistory.com, 10am-4pm Tues.-Sat., closed Jan., $2), the local historical society has assembled a small collection of exhibits on Indian and pioneer life, mining in the region's golden age, logging, fishing, and agriculture. It's located at the county fairgrounds at the south edge of town. Particularly interesting are a realistic reconstruction of a miner's cabin, vintage photos, and Indian petroglyphs.

In the harbor area on the west side of U.S. 101, Jerry's Jetboats has assembled the best regional museum on the south coast, the **Rogue River Museum** (29980 Harbor Way, 541/247-4571, 8am-9pm summer, 8am-6pm fall-spring, free). Centuries of natural and human history are depicted. In addition to geologic history, the museum contains photos of pioneer families, arrowheads and other native artifacts, and a taxidermy collage of local critters to round out your introduction to the Rogue Valley. Jerry's river tour clientele will find that perspectives from the museum on the local salmon industry in the 1920s and on early river travel are expanded upon in their jet-boat guide's commentary. Museum photos of early river runs—hauling freight, passengers, and mail—can impart a sense of history to your trip upriver or up the road.

Scenic Drives

From U.S. 101, two miles south of town, you can pick up **Hunter's Creek Road,** which loops north through the forest, finally following the course of the Rogue back into Gold Beach along Jerry's Flat Road. The three-hour drive follows Hunter's Creek inland for several miles, passing several picnic areas and campgrounds.

Other roads less traveled include the old **Coast Highway,** which you can pick up near Pistol River and Brookings; the **Shasta Costa**

Road paralleling the Rogue from Gold Beach to Galice; and an unpaved summer-only road into the **Rogue Wilderness** from Agness (a town upriver on the Rogue) to Powers. Despite most of these routes being paved (except the last one), they are all narrow, winding, and not suitable for trailers or motor homes. Maps and directions to these back roads can be obtained from the **Gold Beach Ranger Station** (29279 Ellensburg Ave., 541/247-3600, 8am-5pm Mon.-Fri.).

SPORTS AND RECREATION
◖ Rogue River Jet-Boat Ride

The most popular way to take in the mighty Rogue is on a jet-boat ride from Gold Beach. It's an exciting and interesting look at the varied flora and fauna along the estuary as well as the changing moods of the river. Three different lengths of river tours are available. Most of the estimated 50,000 people per year who "do" the Rogue in this way take the 64-mile round-trip cruise. An 80-mile trip goes farther up the Rogue, and the most adventurous trip is the 104-mile excursion that enters the Rogue River canyon. Meals are not included in the cost of the cruise, and you can either bring your own food or have a meal at one of the secluded fishing lodges upriver, where the tours stop for meal breaks. The pilot-commentators are often folks who have grown up on the river, and their evocations of the diverse ecosystems and Native American and gold-mining history can greatly enhance your enjoyment. Bears, otters, seals, and beavers may be sighted en route, and anglers may hold up a big keeper to show off. Ospreys, snowy egrets, eagles, mergansers, and kingfishers are also seen with regularity in this stopover for migratory waterfowl.

In the first part of the journey, idyllic riverside retreats dot the hillsides, breaking up stands of fir and hemlock. Myrtle, madrona, and impressive springtime wildflower groupings also vary the landscape. All of the jet-boat trips out of Gold Beach focus on the section of the Rogue protected by the government as a Wild and Scenic River. Only the longer trips take you into the pristine Rogue Wilderness, an area that motor launches from Grants Pass do not reach. The 13 miles of this wilderness you see from the boat have canyon walls rising 1,500 feet above you. Geologists say this part of the Klamath Mountains is composed of ancient islands and seafloor that collided with North America. To deal with the rapids upstream, smaller and faster boats are used to skim over the boulders with just six inches of water between hull and the rock surface.

The season runs May-October 15. Remember that chill and fog near the mouth of the estuary usually give way to much warmer conditions upstream. These tour outfits have wool blankets available on cold days as well as complimentary hot beverages. Also keep in mind that the upriver lodges can be booked for overnight stays, and your trip may be resumed the following day.

Just south of the Rogue River Bridge, west of U.S. 101 on Harbor Way, is **Jerry's Rogue River Jetboats** (29985 Harbor Way, 541/247-4571 or 800/451-3645, www.roguejets.com). Jerry's offers 64-mile ($50 adult, $25 children 4-11), 80-mile ($80 adult, $35 children), and 104-mile ($95 adults, $45 children) trips. There are usually two departures for each trip daily: one in the morning, one near midday. This heavily patronized company is noted for personable well-informed guides. If you forgot a hat to buffer the winds at the mouth of the Rogue, stop in at Jerry's gift shop.

Fishing

Fishing is a mighty big deal in Gold Beach, which has one of the highest concentrations of professional guides in the state. There's something to fish for just about year-round, but salmon and steelhead are the top quarry. When the spring chinook pour in (Apr.-June), anglers will need to book guided trips well in advance to get a shot at them. Catches peak in May. Summer steelhead and fall-run chinook usually arrive July-September, then it's hatchery coho September-November (sometimes as early as August). In December, the first of the winter

© BILL MCRAE

The Rogue River is famous for salmon fishing.

steelhead make their appearance and continue into March.

The **Rogue Outdoor Store** (29865 Ellensburg Ave., 541/247-7142, 8am-5:30pm Mon.-Sat., 9am-3pm Sun.) is well stocked with fishing, camping, and other gear, and its staff can advise on where, when, and what to fish.

Typical rates for guided salmon trips are $250-400 per person depending on the size of your group. Contact the **Gold Beach Visitor Center** (541/247-7526 or 800/525-2334, www.goldbeach.org) or the **Curry Guide Association** (800/775-0886) for a list of over two dozen licensed guides.

Some well-established **guides** include: **Steve Beyerlin** (541/247-4138, www.fish-oregon.com), for both conventional and fly-fishing; **Shaun Carpenter** (541/247-2049, www.endoftherogue.com), conventional and fly-fishing; and **Ron Smith** (541/247-6046, www.sportfishingoregon.com) for salmon and steelhead fishing trips on a number of southern Oregon rivers.

Golf

The nine-hole **Cedar Bend Golf Course** (34391 Cedar Valley Rd., 541/247-6911, http://cedarbendgolf.com, $20 for 9 holes, $28 for 18) is in nearby Ophir. Eleven miles north of Gold Beach, pick up Ophir Road off U.S. 101. Follow it to Squaw Valley Road, turn right at the Old Ophir Store, and continue until you see the links. Woods line the fairways, and a winding creek offers a challenge on nine holes.

Hiking

The 40-mile **Rogue River Trail** (www.blm.gov) offers lodge-to-lodge hiking, which means you need little more in your pack than the essentials. The lodges here are comfortably rustic, serve home-style food in copious portions, and run $150-200 for a double room. They are also comfortably spaced, so extended hiking is seldom a necessity.

Before you go, check with the **Gold Beach Ranger Station** (29279 Ellensburg Ave., 541/247-3600, 8am-5pm Mon.-Fri.) on trail conditions and specific directions to the trailhead. Pick up the western end of the trail 35 miles east of Gold Beach, about 0.5 mile from Foster Bar, a popular boat landing. Park there and walk east and north on the paved road until you see signs on the left marking the Rogue River Trail. Go in spring before the hot weather and enjoy yellow Siskiyou irises and fragrant wild azaleas. The trail ends at Grave Creek, 27 miles northwest of Grants Pass. Be careful of rattlesnakes on the trail.

Windsurfing

Although beginners may want to hone their skills up north at Floras Lake, experienced windsurfers head out into the ocean near the debouchment of the **Pistol River.**

ENTERTAINMENT AND EVENTS

The **Wild Rivers Coast Seafood, Art, and Wine Festival** is a two-day event that celebrates wine, fine dining, and arts and crafts of the southern Oregon coast in mid-May at the Event Center on the Beach (29392 Ellensburg Ave., 541/247-4541, admission fees vary).

The **Pistol River Wave Bash National Windsurfing Competition** brings four days of competitive riding to Pistol River State Park each June. For details, contact the **Gold Beach Visitor Center** (541/247-7526 or 800/525-2334, www.goldbeach.org, admission fees vary).

The **Curry County Fair** takes place at the Event Center on the Beach (29392 Ellensburg Ave., 541/247-4541, admission fees vary) over the Fourth of July weekend. Highlights include Oregon's largest flower show and a lamb barbecue.

Since 1982, the **Pistol River Concert Association** (541/247-2848, www.pistolriver.com, $15 adults) has produced a top-notch **concert series,** encompassing bluegrass, folk, jazz, classical, and blues at the Pistol River Friendship Hall. Concerts are held roughly once a month throughout the year, and it's well worth fussing with your schedule in order to catch one. Past and present performers are a *Who's Who* of acoustic music, including Greg Brown, Mike Seeger, Peggy Seeger, Kevin Burke, Norman and Nancy Blake, Peter Rowan, and Tony Rice, to name a few. To get there from Gold Beach, take U.S. 101 for 10 miles south, to the second Pistol River exit (Pistol River/Carpenterville) and take the first right. The Pistol River Friendship Hall is 0.5 mile ahead on the right.

ACCOMMODATIONS

As in most coastal towns, there is no shortage of places to stay along the main drag, Ellensburg Avenue (a.k.a. U.S. 101). In fact, Gold Beach offers the largest number and widest range of accommodations on the south coast, with intimate lodges overlooking the Rogue as popular as the oceanfront motels. A discount of 20 percent or more on rooms is usually available during winter, when 80-90 inches of rain can fall.

$50-100

The best bet for a clean, inexpensive room is the **Wild Chinook Inn** (94200 Harlow St.,

541/247-6675, http://chinookinn.com, $60-75), where you get no-frills accommodations across from the fairgrounds. Rooms have Wi-Fi, a fridge, and a microwave; some full-kitchen units are available.

Don't turn up your nose at the **Motel 6** (1010 Jerry's Flat Rd., 541/247-4533 or 800/759-4533, $65-86); the location—perched above the Rogue River—is great, and the rooms are modern and comfy. Pets are permitted.

If you're looking for a simple place to spend a night or two and don't care about frills, the **Azalea Lodge** (29481 Ellensburg Ave., 541/247-6635 or 866/381-6635, www.azalealodge.biz, $85-105) is a good bet, with friendly owners and clean rooms. No pets are allowed; all guest rooms are nonsmoking and have refrigerators.

$100-150

Though it's true that **[** **Ireland's Rustic Lodges** (29330 Ellensburg Ave., office 29346 Ellensburg Ave., 541/247-7718, www.irelandsrusticlodges.com, cabins $119-144, lodge rooms $104-149) include charming vintage cabins, it also offers more modern lodge rooms, condos, and beach houses. Many of the guest rooms have fireplaces, knotty-pine interiors, and distinctive decor. Best of all, the parklike grounds are lovingly landscaped with pine trees, flowers, and ocean views. A sandy beach is a short stroll to the west. There are 33 lodge units (some with kitchens), seven vintage but well-kept log cabins (recommended) that sleep up to five, and houses that sleep as many as 11. Immediately next door, and with the same owners, is the **Gold Beach Inn** (29346 Ellensburg Ave., 541/247-7091 or 888/663-0608, www.goldbeachinn.com, non-oceanview rooms $84, oceanview rooms $114-139), a modern hotel with oceanfront guest rooms, many with balconies. These two establishments share many facilities, including private beach paths and a series of outdoor hot tubs in the midst of an 11-acre property.

On the Rogue River's north bank, the immense **Jot's Resort** (94360 Wedderburn Loop, Wedderburn, 541/247-6676 or 800/367-5687, www.jotsresort.com, $135-180) can host a full vacation in one compound, featuring a pool and spa, a sports shop, a private dock, rental boats, and a restaurant across the street. The guest rooms are at a premium in summer, when the motor coach tours come through, leaving other travelers with the less desirable rooms. There are numerous room styles—from standard-view rooms to riverfront condos big enough for six people—and a wide range of prices, so it's best to call for current rates and specials. The Rod 'n' Reel Club across the street features evening entertainment with low-stakes blackjack, country music bands, and a big-band dance on weekends.

Another excellent option for beachside lodging is the **Inn of the Beachcomber** (29266 Ellensburg Ave., 541/247-6691 or 888/690-2378, www.innofthebeachcomber.com, $109-179), an older hotel complex that has recently been lovingly remodeled and updated. Most guest rooms are oceanview with private balconies or decks, and some have hot tubs. The rooms are furnished with Mission-style furniture and fittings, and there's even a wine store on the premises. A few nonview rooms are available starting at $89.

$150-200

For a more traditional oceanfront hotel, the **Gold Beach Resort** (29232 Ellensburg Ave., 541/247-7066 or 800/541-0947, www.gbresort.com, $155-185) offers nicely furnished oceanview rooms, all with balconies. Also part of this large complex, with easy beach access, are one- and two-bedroom condos, all with fireplaces. Facilities include an indoor pool and a fitness center; a complimentary continental breakfast is available.

Over $200

[**Tu Tu Tun Resort** (96550 N. Bank Rogue River Rd., 541/247-6664 or 800/864-6357, www.tututun.com, rooms $290-375, suites $395-420) is the most luxurious place to stay on the southern Oregon coast, where lucky guests take in river views through the floor-to-ceiling windows, enjoy a good book from the lodge's library in front of the massive river-rock fireplace, and savor delicious Pacific Northwest cuisine. As you sit on your patio overlooking the water along with the resident bald eagles, only the sounds of an occasional passing boat may intrude upon your Rogue River reverie. Rooms are graciously furnished, but not overly fussy—why interfere with the stunning views? The lodge is seven miles up the Rogue River from Gold Beach.

This acclaimed retreat also offers a heated pool and other recreational facilities. Meals are available on an inclusive Modified American Plan ($68 per person), which includes hors d'oeuvres, a gourmet four-course dinner, and a bountiful breakfast buffet. Nonguests are welcome to dinner with reservations. The dining room is only open May-October. In the off-season, guests are served a continental breakfast only. Tu Tu Tun is not a secret, so reservations are required well in advance of your stay.

Upriver Lodges

Several lodges on the Rogue, some accessible only by boat or via hiking trails, lure visitors deep into the Rogue interior. Jet-boat trips can drop you off for an overnight or longer stay. Advance reservations are essential.

Also accessible by road and boat, the authentically rustic **Lucas Lodge** (3904 Cougar Ln., 541/247-7443, www.lucaslodgeoregon. com, $45-95) is 32 miles east of Gold Beach. Some cabins here come equipped with kitchen options. Lunch and dinner are served daily in the lodge—chicken, biscuits, and garden vegetables are standard fare. Reservations are required.

Accessible only by helicopter, boat, or on foot, the **Paradise Lodge** (541/247-6504 or 888/667-6483, www.paradise-lodge.com, $150-160 per person, $85 children, includes two or three meals) attracts nature enthusiasts interested in the "wildest" experience. Only the meals are scheduled, and you can take an eco-tour, enjoy a sauna, raft or jet-boat the rapids, or check out some of the old mining sites in the vicinity. A huge on-site garden provides ingredients for home-cooked meals.

Another backcountry lodge, the **Clay Hill Lodge** (541/859-3772, www.clayhilllodge.com, $150, $100 per child, includes three meals), is accessible via raft (from upstream), jet boat, or foot. By foot, it's about three hours (six miles) up from the trailhead near Foster Bar, east of Gold Beach.

Camping

There are no public campgrounds along the coast between Humbug Mountain, just south of Port Orford, and Harris Beach, at the northern entrance to Brookings. But campsites east of town up the Rogue River provide wonderful spots to bed down for the night. Those taking the road along the Rogue should be alert for oncoming log trucks, raft transport vehicles, and other wide-body vehicles. In addition to the public campgrounds listed, there are *many* private RV resorts up the north bank of the Rogue.

Foster Bar Campground (Siskiyou National Forest, Gold Beach Ranger Station, 1225 S. Ellensburg Ave., 541/247-6651, www.fs.fed. us, open year-round, flush toilets available May-Oct., $10) is 30 miles east of Gold Beach on the south bank of the Rogue. Take Jerry's Flat Road east for 30 miles to the turnoff for Agness. Turn right on Illahe Agness Road and drive three miles to camp. Campsites here come equipped with drinking water, toilets, ADA-compliant facilities, picnic tables, fire rings, and a boat ramp. Sites are available on a first-come, first-served basis only. This is a popular spot from which to embark on an eight-mile inner-tube ride to Agness. It's also where rafters pull out, so the parking lot may be jam-packed. The rapids are dangerous—wear a life jacket. You are also within walking distance of the trailhead of the Rogue River Trail.

Lobster Creek Campground (541/247-3600, www.fs.fed.us, $10) is nine miles east of Gold Beach via Forest Service Road 33. This campground is open year-round and has three tent sites, three trailer sites, one group site, picnic tables, fishing, and flush toilets—but no drinking water. Ask the Forest Service for directions to the Schrader old-growth trail nearby. It is a gentle one-mile walk through a rare and majestic ecosystem that is under siege in other forests throughout the state. Also nearby is the world's largest myrtle tree.

Honeybear Campground and RV Resort (34161 Ophir Rd., Ophir, 541/247-2765 or 800/822-4444, www.honeybearrv.com, open year-round, $18-35) is not up the Rogue; it's nine miles north of Gold Beach on U.S. 101, then two miles north on Ophir Road—but it could just as well be in the Black Forest. The owners have built a large rathskeller with a dance floor. Six nights a week during the summer, there are dances here with traditional German music. Check out their version of Oktoberfest, a traditional fall festival held two weekends in late September. Locals praise the Honeybear's on-site delicatessen for its homemade German sausage. There are 20 tent ($18) and RV ($30-35) sites, picnic tables, flush toilets, hot showers, firewood, laundry facilities, and ocean views.

FOOD
American
Stop by **Biscuits Café** (29707 Ellensburg Ave., 541/247-2495, 7am-7pm daily) inside Gold Beach Books for coffee and pastries. Be sure to take a look in the rare book room of this very good bookstore after you finish eating. **Indian Creek Café** (94682 Jerry's Flat Rd., 541/247-0680, 5:30am-2pm daily, $8-12) is a great spot for breakfast. Just a mile east of the Rogue River Bridge, the café is on the south shore of the Rogue, where Indian Creek joins the river. In good weather, there's seating on a deck overlooking the creek. Omelets, pancakes, and other traditional breakfast items are well prepared; lunch is mostly burgers and sandwiches.

Locals recommend the **Port Hole Café** (29975 Harbor Way, 541/247-7411, 11am-9pm daily, $4-20), in the Cannery building at the port, with bay and river views, for hearty portions of fish-and-chips, chowder, and homemade pies at decent prices.

Barnacle Bistro (29805 Ellensburg Ave., 541/247-7799, 11am-8pm Mon.-Thurs.,

11am-9pm Fri.-Sat., 11am-6pm Sun., $8-15) is a lively spot for light meals, offering a selection of sandwiches, soups, salads, pizzas, and fish-and-chips. The salad greens are local and organically grown, and all the sauces and dressings are made in-house.

Perched on a hill above the highway, the **Cape Cafe** (29251 Ellensburg Ave., 541/247-6114, 4:30pm-9:30pm weekdays and Sat.-Sun. mornings, $9-25) is a good bet for tasty but healthy meals, with lots of vegetarian options. Though basically a dinner house, they're open for coffee and pastries on weekend mornings.

Italian
Mangia Buff Café (29692 Ellensburg Ave., 541/247-4606, 10:30am-8pm Mon.-Sat., $11-25) is a small, art-filled dining room with excellent Italian cooking, not a cuisine you find often on the Oregon coast. At lunch, expect salads, meatball sandwiches and sausages, while in the evening the menu features fresh pasta (clam sauce ravioli) and meat dishes such as chicken Marsala and grilled Tuscan rib eye steak. This is a chef-owned operation, and the attention to detail shows on every plate.

Steak and Seafood
The Nor'Wester (10 Harbor Way, 541/247-2333, 5pm-9pm nightly, $12-28) is in an upstairs location at the port of Gold Beach, so sometimes you get to watch boats unloading your dinner. Not surprisingly, the menu is dominated by old-fashioned seafood preparations, although the waitstaff also recommends the New York strip steaks and the chinook salmon grilled with a glaze of sake, cayenne, ginger, and soy.

A very good dinner house is **Spinner's Seafood, Steak and Chophouse** (29430 Ellensburg Ave., 541/247-5160, 4:30pm-10pm nightly, $15-32). The menu is wide-ranging, and the dining room extremely pleasant. Look for fresh, well-prepared seafood, pasta, prime rib, and a choice beef and chops. A children's menu is available.

Pick up some fresh seafood or the best canned tuna you'll ever taste at **Fishermen**

Direct Seafoods (29975 Harbor Way, 541/247-9494, 9am-5:30pm Mon.-Sat., 9am-2pm Sun.).

Wine Bars

€ **Anna's By the Sea** (29672 Stewart St., 541/247-2100, 11:30am-2:30pm Wed.-Fri., 11:30am-2:30pm and 5pm-9pm Sat., $9-12), tucked into a residential neighborhood a couple of blocks east of busy Ellensburg Avenue, is that rare thing on the southern Oregon coast—a chic little wine bar with excellent appetizers and unpretentious but delicious light entrées. Prices are very modest for the quality of the food—enjoy an assortment of artisan cheeses or shrimp with black truffle oil served over an oven-baked potato pancake. Anna's is a tiny place—just 15 seats—so come early if you don't want to wait (in summer, there's more seating on the deck).

INFORMATION AND SERVICES

The **Gold Beach Visitor Center** (94080 Shirley Ln., 541/247-7526 or 800/525-2334, www. goldbeach.org) is open 9am-5pm Monday-Friday and 10am-4pm Saturday-Sunday. Its website is excellent and informative, and staff will send you a good comprehensive information folder upon request. The **Gold Beach Ranger District** (29279 Ellensburg Ave., Gold Beach, 541/247-3600, 7:30am-5pm Mon.-Fri.) can provide information on camping and recreation in the district.

The **post office** (541/247-7610) is at the port on Harbor Way. A modern building houses the **public library** (94341 3rd St., 541/247-7246, 10am-8pm Mon.-Thurs., 10am-5pm Fri.-Sat.), one block east of the highway in the north end of town. **Curry General Hospital** (94220 4th St., Gold Beach, 541/247-6621) is the only hospital in the county.

GETTING THERE

Curry County's **Coastal Express** buses (800/921-2871, www.currypublictransit.org) run up and down the south coast weekdays only between North Bend and the California border, including local service in Gold Beach.

Brookings-Harbor and Vicinity

There are people who don't like Brookings, and if you form your judgment by simply driving down U.S. 101, it's easy to join that crowd. But something as simple as turning off into Harris Beach State Park can begin to change your view. To really fall for the area, it may take a drive up the Chetco River. A couple of miles inland, the fog that frequently drenches the coastline during the summer months burns away. There are ample hiking opportunities upriver, especially in the Kalmiopsis Wilderness Area.

During winter Brookings (pop. 6,000) and its neighbor, Harbor (pop. 2,600), enjoy mild temperatures. Enough 60-70°F days occur during January and February in this south coast "banana belt" town that more than 50 species of flowering plants thrive—along with retirees, outdoor-sports lovers, and beachcombers. With two gorgeous state parks virtually part of the city and world-class salmon and steelhead fishing nearby, only the lavish winter rainfall, averaging over 73 inches a year, can cool the ardor of local outdoor enthusiasts. In the springtime, the area south of town is lush with lilies—it's the Easter lily capital of the world.

Brookings and Harbor sit on a coastal plain overlooking the Pacific six miles north of the California border, split by U.S. 101 (Chetco Ave.) and the Chetco River. Flowing out of the Klamath Mountains east of town, the Chetco drains part of the nearby Siskiyou National Forest and the Kalmiopsis Wilderness, extensive tracts encompassing some of the wildest country in the Lower 48 and renowned for their rare flowers and trees. This area enjoys strict federal protection, safeguarding the northernmost stand of giant redwoods as well as the coveted Port Orford cedar (whose strong

SOUTH COAST

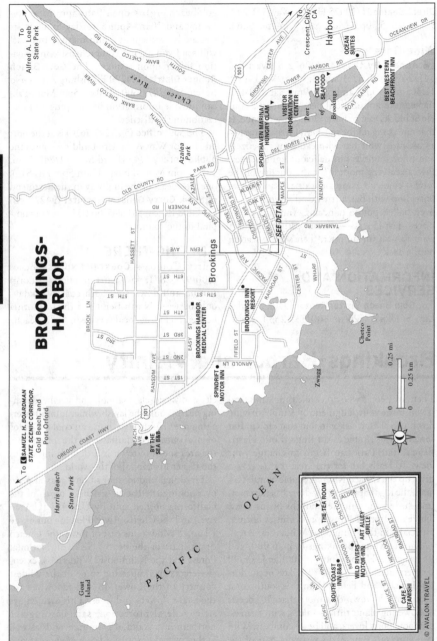

BROOKINGS-HARBOR

To **SAMUEL H. BOARDMAN STATE SCENIC CORRIDOR,** Gold Beach, and Port Orford

To Alfred A. Loeb State Park

To Crescent City, CA

Harbor

OCEANVIEW DR

OCEAN SUITES

BEST WESTERN BEACHFRONT INN

BOAT BASIN RD

CHETCO SEAFOOD

Port of Brookings

LOWER HARBOR RD

VISITOR INFORMATION CENTER

SPORTHAVEN MARINA/ HUNGRY CLAM

SHOPPING CENTER AVE

101

NORTH BANK CHETCO RIVER RD

SOUTH BANK CHETCO RIVER RD

Chetco River

BANK CHETCO RIVER RD

Azalea Park

OLD COUNTY RD

AZALEA PARK RD

DEL NORTE LN

MAPLE ST

ST

MEMORY LN

TANBARK RD

SEE DETAIL

ALDER ST

PINE ST

REDWOOD ST

CHETCO AVE

OAK ST

HEMLOCK ST

FIR ST

PIONEER RD

PACIFIC AVE

HASSETT ST

FERN AVE

Brookings

6TH ST

6TH ST

5TH ST

RAILROAD ST

PACIFIC AVE

CENTER ST

WHARF ST

BROOKINGS INN RESORT

BROOKINGS HARBOR MEDICAL CENTER

BROOK LN

5TH ST

4TH ST

3RD ST

2ND ST

1ST ST

RANSOM AVE

EASY ST

FIFIELD ST

ARNOLD LN

SPINDRIFT MOTOR INN

Chetco Point

Zwagg

0   0.25 mi

0   0.25 km

BEACH AVE

BY THE SEA B&B

OREGON COAST HWY

Harris Beach State Park

PACIFIC OCEAN

Goat Island

© AVALON TRAVEL

SEE DETAIL

THE TEA ROOM

ALDER ST

CHETCO AVE

OAK ST

ART ALLEY GRILLE

WILD RIVERS MOTOR INN

SOUTH COAST INN B&B

PINE ST

REDWOOD ST

PACIFIC AVE

HEMLOCK ST

RAILROAD ST

SPRUCE ST

CAFE KITANISHI

BROOKINGS: FROM BOX FACTORY TO RETIREMENT HAVEN

What is now the shopping hub of rural Curry County started out as a factory town for the Brookings Box Company in 1913. Owner J. L. Brookings hired the architect Bernard Maybeck (famous for designing the Palace of Fine Arts in San Francisco) to lay out the streets and design housing and community buildings for his mill workers. Maybeck drew up extensive plans for a model company town, but most of them were never realized; his central vision was eventually gutted when the state highway was laid through, rather than around, the town. Examples of Maybeck's craftsmanship can still be seen around Brookings, notably in the 1917 Craftsman-style residence (now the South Coast Inn B&B) he designed for lumber baron William Ward.

In the years that followed, the lumber industry was augmented with fishing, horticulture, and tourism. Omitting for the moment the possibility that the offshore waters here were visited by Juan Cabrillo (in 1542) and the English explorer Sir Francis Drake (in 1579), the local event with the greatest historical significance was a Japanese aerial bombing on September 9, 1942. On that day, a Japanese incendiary bomb scorched the treetops of Mount Emily, southeast of town, in one of only two documented wartime air bombing missions against the U.S. mainland (the other occurred three weeks later near Port Orford). The resulting fires were quickly doused by the damp conditions, and no significant harm was done.

Twenty years after the bomb attack, the Japanese pilot, Nobuo Fujita, accepted an invitation to return to Brookings during the town's Azalea Festival. He brought with him the 400-year-old samurai sword he had carried on his missions during the war and presented it to the people of Brookings as a token of reconciliation. It still hangs on display in the Brookings city library. Fujita returned again in 1992 as the guest of honor for the opening of a new Forest Service trail to the bombsite, on the 50th anniversary of the attack. At age 80, he hiked the new trail and planted a redwood seedling in the bomb crater as a token of peace.

Since the late 1980s, Brookings's greatest growth industry has been as a haven for retirees, and that population has been booming in recent years.

but pliable lumber can fetch over $10,000 for a single tree). The Kalmiopsis Wilderness is named for a unique shrub, the *Kalmiopsis leachiana*, one of the oldest members of the heath family (Ericaceae) that grows nowhere else on earth.

But you don't have to trek miles into the backcountry to enjoy the natural beauty of Brookings and its vicinity. Just make your way past the somewhat drab main drag to Samuel Boardman State Park north of town, where 11 of the most scenic miles of the Oregon coast await you. Or head down to the harbor to embark on a boating expedition, with some of the safest offshore navigation conditions in the region. Although the harbor was battered by the tsunami that followed the Japanese earthquake in March 2011, few signs of damage remain. In short, Brookings is the perfect place to launch an adventure by land or by sea.

SIGHTS

In Brookings, camellias bloom at Christmas, and the flowering plums add color the next month. Daffodils, grown commercially on the coastal plain south of Brookings, bloom in late January and into February. Magnolia shrubs, some early azaleas, and rhododendrons bloom in late winter. The area also produces 90 percent of the world's Easter lily crop.

Harris Beach State Park

At the northern limits of Brookings, across from the State Information Center on U.S. 101, **Harris Beach State Park** makes up for all the ugly architecture you'll find on Chetco Avenue.

One look at the 24 miles of rock and tide visible from the parking lot promontory should quell any misgivings.

Harris Beach was named after the Scottish pioneer George Harris, who settled here in the late 1880s to raise sheep and cattle. Besides stunning views, this state park offers many incoming travelers from California their first chance to actually walk on the beach in Oregon. You can begin directly west of the park's campground, where a sandy beach strewn with boulders often becomes flooded with intertidal life and driftwood. The early morning hours, as the waves crash through a small tunnel in a massive rock onto the shoreline, are the best time to look for sponges, umbrella crabs, solitary corals, and sea stars.

Offshore, **Bird Island** (also called Goat Island) is the largest island along the Oregon coast and the state's largest seabird rookery. This outpost of Oregon Islands National Wildlife Refuge dispatches squadrons of cormorants, pelicans, tufted puffins, and other waterfowl, which dive-bomb the incoming waves for food.

In addition to beachcombing, you can picnic at tables above the parking lot, loll about in the shallow waters of nearby Harris Creek, or cast in the surf for perch.

Mill Beach is the southernmost part of the Harris Beach area. Locals prefer the beach access from downtown, which is easy to miss. To get there, drive toward the ocean on Center Street in downtown Brookings, make a right at the plywood mill, and stop next to a small ballpark. An unimproved road leads to a hillock from which trails take you down to a beach full of driftwood. Residents say that Japanese fishing floats occasionally roll up onto the beach after a storm.

Chetco Valley Historical Society Museum

The **Chetco Valley Historical Society Museum** (5461 Museum Rd., Brookings, 541/469-6651, www.chetcomuseum.com, noon-4pm Sat.-Sun. Memorial Day-Labor Day, $3 donation suggested), in the red-and-white Blake House, sits on a hill overlooking U.S. 101 two miles south of the Chetco River. The structure dates to 1857 and was used as a stagecoach way station and trading post before Abraham Lincoln was president.

Even if you are not one for museums, several exhibits here stand apart from the traditional collections of pioneer wedding dresses, Native American baskets, and spinning wheels. These include a small trunk that came around Cape Horn in 1706 and a Native American dugout canoe. Should these fail to inspire, a mysterious iron casting of a woman's face might do the trick, especially in light of the speculation that this relic was left by an early undocumented landing on the Oregon coast, perhaps by Sir Francis Drake. Drake has been commonly suggested because of the mask's likeness to Elizabeth I.

Oregon's largest Monterey cypress tree is located on the hill near the museum. The 99-foot-tall tree has a trunk circumference of more than 27 feet and has been home to a pair of owls for years.

◖ Samuel H. Boardman State Scenic Corridor

The stretch of highway from Brookings to Port Orford is known as the "fabulous 50 miles." Some consider the section of coastline just north of Brookings to be the most scenic in Oregon—and one of the most dramatic meetings of rock and tide in the world. The offshore rock formations and winding roadbed hundreds of feet above the surf invite comparison to Europe's Amalfi Drive. The "fabulous 50" sobriquet is perhaps most apt in the dozen miles directly north of Brookings, encompassed by **Samuel H. Boardman State Scenic Corridor.** You'll want to have a camera close at hand and a loose schedule when you make this drive, because you'll find it hard not to pull over again and again, as each photo opportunity seems to outdazzle the last. Of the 11 named viewpoints that have been cut into the highway's shoulder, the following are especially

Samuel H. Boardman State Scenic Corridor offers miles of dramatic coastline.

© BILL MCRAE

recommended (all viewpoints are marked by signs on the west side of U.S. 101 and are listed here from north to south).

Near the north end of Boardman State Park, a short walk down the hillside trail leads you to the **Arch Rocks** viewpoint, where an immense boomerang-shaped basalt archway juts out of the water about a quarter mile offshore. This site has picnic tables within view of the monolith.

A few miles south, the sign for **Natural Bridges Cove** seems to front just a forested parking lot. However, the paved walkway at the south end of the lot leads to a spectacular overlook. Below, several rock archways frame an azure cove. This feature was created by the collapse of the entrance and exit of a sea cave. A steep, winding trail through giant ferns and towering Sitka spruce and Douglas fir takes you down for a closer look. Thimbleberry (a sweet but seedy raspberry) is plentiful in late spring. As in similar forests on the south coast, it's important to stay on the trail. The rainforest-like biome is exceptionally fragile, and the

soil erodes easily when the delicate vegetation is damaged.

Thomas Creek Bridge, the highest bridge in Oregon (345 feet above the water) as well as the highest north of San Francisco, has been used as a silent star in many TV commercials. A parking lot at the south end of the bridge marks a trailhead down. Do not take the path you see closest to the bridge; it's too steep. At the south end of the lot, the true trail eventually leads down to a view of the bridge on one side and miles of coast on the other. The offshore rock formations are especially interesting. From here hikers can access the Indian Sands Trail, ending up in pine-rimmed dunes and a sandstone bluff high above the sea.

House Rock was the site of a World War II air-raid sentry tower that sits hundreds of feet above whitecaps pounding the rock-strewn beaches. To the north, you'll see one of the highest cliffs on the coast, Cape Sebastian. A steep circuitous trail lined with salal goes down to the water. The path begins behind the Samuel Boardman monument on the west end of the parking lot. The sign to the highest viewpoint in Boardman State Park is easy to miss, but look for the turnout that precedes House Rock, called Cape Ferrelo (for Juan Cabrillo's navigator, who sailed up much of the West Coast in 1543).

Carpenterville Road

The current roadbed of U.S. 101 was laid in southern Oregon in 1961. The previous coastal route still exists along **Carpenterville Road,** which can be picked up near Harris Beach. It comes out near the Pistol River, where it descends in a series of switchbacks. Its highest point is 1,700 feet above sea level at Burnt Hill. Views of the Siskiyous to the east and the Pacific panoramas to the west make the sometimes-rough road worth the effort. In very clear weather, it's possible to look back toward the southeast at Mount Shasta between the ridgelines. This route is best appreciated going south, and it makes a great 20-mile bike ride, with a long climb to 1,700 feet above sea level.

Alfred A. Loeb State Park

Eight miles northeast of Brookings on North Bank Chetco River Road along the Chetco River, the **Alfred A. Loeb State Park** preserves 320 acres of old-growth myrtlewood, the state's largest grove. Many of these aromatic trees are much older than 200 years.

The 0.25-mile Riverview Trail passes numerous big trees to connect Loeb Park with the **Redwood Nature Trail.** This trail winds 1.2 miles through the northernmost stands of naturally occurring *Sequoia sempervirens*. This is Oregon's largest redwood grove and contains the state's largest specimens. Within the grove are several trees more than 500 years old, measuring 5-8 feet in diameter, towering more than 300 feet above the forest floor. One tree has a 33-foot girth and is estimated to exceed 800 years in age. When the south coast is foggy and cold on summer mornings, it's often warm and dry in upriver locations such as this one, inviting the possibility of swimming in the Chetco River.

Kalmiopsis Wilderness

The lure of untrammeled wilderness attracts intrepid hikers to the **Kalmiopsis Wilderness,** despite the summer's blazing heat and winter's torrential rains. In addition to enjoying the isolation of the wilderness, they come to take in the pink rhododendron-like blooms of *Kalmiopsis leachiana* (in June) and other rare flowers. The area is also home to such economically valued species as Port Orford cedar and *Cannabis sativa*. The illicit weed is a leading cash crop in this part of the state, and its vigilant protection by growers should inspire extra care for those hiking during the late fall harvest season. The potential for violence associated with the lucrative mushroom harvest also mandates a measure of caution.

In any case, the Forest Service prohibits plant collection *of any kind* to preserve the region's special botanical populations. These include the insect-eating darlingtonia plant and the Brewer's weeping spruce. The forest canopy is composed largely of the more common Douglas fir, canyon live oak, madrona, and chinquapin. Stark peaks top this red-rock forest, whose understory is choked with blueberry, manzanita, and dense chaparral.

Many of this wilderness's rare species survived the glacial epoch because the glaciers from that era left the area untouched. This, combined with the fact that the area was once an offshore island, has enabled the region's singular ecosystem to maintain its integrity through the millennia. You'd think that federal protection, remoteness, and climatic extremes would ensure a sanguine outlook for this ice-age forest, but an active debate still rages over the validity of some logging claims.

In summer 2002, the so-called **Biscuit Fire** raged out of control for weeks, ravaging nearly half a million acres of southwestern Oregon, engulfing most of the Siskiyou National Forest and virtually all of the Kalmiopsis Wilderness. This inferno, the nation's largest wildfire of 2002 and the biggest in Oregon for more than a century, destroyed extensive habitat of the endangered northern spotted owl. The good news, however, is that flora of the region is well adapted to periodic fires; many of the old-growth trees survived the blaze, and within a few months green sprouts and new growth of many species were reappearing amid the ashes.

In the years since the fire, a young new forest has taken hold. Certain tree species, including rare Brewer spruce and knob cone pine, are growing back abundantly, as their seed cones require fire for germination. With the once-thick overstory vegetation mostly dead, lower-growing plants such as ferns, huckleberries, and bear grass are thriving in the sun. Soils are moister, too, since massive adult trees aren't sucking up the groundwater. Forest scientists estimate that it will take a century for trees of the mature forest, including stands of Douglas fir and sugar pine, to return and erase the evidence of the 2002 fire. Meanwhile the charred snags of the former primary forest stand above the lush growth of quickly rejuvenating woodlands.

Even if you don't have the slightest intention of hiking the Kalmiopsis, the scenic drive through the **Chetco Valley** is worth it. From Brookings, turn off U.S. 101 at the north end of the Chetco River Bridge, follow this paved road upriver past Loeb State Park, and continue along the river on County Roads 784 and 1376 until a narrow bridge crosses the Chetco. From here, turn right for 18 miles along national forest roads 1909, 160, and 1917 to reach the Upper Chetco Trailhead (just past the Quail Prairie Lookout). The driving distance from Brookings is 31 miles. If you're not hiking into the wilderness, you can continue west on national forest road 1917 (portions are not paved), which will return you to the above-mentioned narrow bridge over the Chetco.

Bombsite Trail

Brookings takes a peculiar pride in having been bombed by the Japanese during World War II. In 1942, two incendiary bombs were dropped about 16 miles east of town on the slopes of Mount Emily. Although they were intended to start a fire, conditions were wet, and the small fire that resulted was easily controlled. A sort of mutual respect eventually developed between the Japanese pilot who dropped the bomb and the town of Brookings. The pilot was a guest of honor at one Azalea Festival, and his family later presented the town with his samurai sword, which he wore during the bombing and throughout the war. The sword is now on exhibit at the local library (420 Alder St.).

The Mount Emily **Bombsite Trail** commemorates the bombing. It's a two-mile stretch with redwoods near the beginning and fire-dependent species such as knobcone pine and manzanita along the way. To reach the trail, head eight miles east up South Bank Road and turn right onto Mount Emily Road. At the fork, turn onto Wheeler Creek Road and follow the signs.

Crissey Field State Recreation Area

Crissey Field State Recreation Area lies south of Brookings, almost to the California border, and is set along the Winchuck River. The park, which was added to the state park system in 2008, is great place to watch birds, harbor seals, California sea lions, and other wildlife. A trail leads through a huge pile of driftwood logs to dunes that shelter native plants, tiny wetlands, and old-growth Sitka spruce trees. Incidentally, the park's name has nothing to do with the San Francisco park (that's Crissy); it's in the heart of the lily-growing area and is named for a lily bulb grower.

SPORTS AND RECREATION

For some more mellow fun in the sun, cruise down Easy Street, east off U.S. 101, to **Bud Cross City Park** for some tennis, a dip in the outdoor pool, or a visit to the skate park.

Fishing

Fishing on the Chetco was once one of southern Oregon's best-kept secrets, but word has gotten out about the river's October run of huge chinook and its superlative influx of winter steelhead. If river traffic becomes too

© BILL MCRAE

The Brookings marina is at the mouth of the Chetco River.

heavy, the late-summer ocean salmon season out of Brookings may be the best in the Pacific Northwest. Boatless anglers can try their luck at the public fishing pier at the harbor and on the south jetty at the mouth of the Chetco. Chinook season generally runs mid-May–mid-September, but that's subject to change, so check the regulations.

Various fishing trips for salmon, tuna, and bottom fish can be arranged through **Sporthaven Marina** (16374 Lower Harbor Rd., Brookings, 541/469-3301). In addition to fishing charters, **Tidewind Sportfishing** (16368 Lower Harbor Rd., 541/469-0337, www.tidewindsportfishing.com) offers whale-watching excursions in season.

In the fall and winter, look upriver. Pick up literature on fishing and a Siskiyou National Forest map at the ranger station in town. In addition to offering printed matter about Siskiyou and Kalmiopsis trails for hikers, the rangers can tell you where to find some good fishing holes on the nearby Chetco River, noted for its good fall salmon runs and winter steelhead.

Golf

All the press about Bandon Dunes has obscured the development of another great course, **Salmon Run Golf Course** (99040 South Bank Chetco River Rd., 541/469-4888, www.salmonrun.net, greens fees $30 for 9 holes, $55 for 18 holes, includes cart). This beautiful 18-hole public links—not far from the Kalmiopsis Wilderness—was designed with environmentally sensitive imperatives, so numerous wildlife sightings may be enjoyed here long into the future. Whether it's the chance to see salmon (usually after the first rains in November) and steelhead spawning (January), black bears, elk, and wild turkeys, or just the opportunity to play a first-rate course, golfers shouldn't overlook this one. Beginner and intermediate players may find the executive nine-hole course ideal. This par-34 course within a course is located on the back nine holes and measures 1,310 yards. Your Oregon coastal golf pilgrimage can begin here, then hit Bandon Dunes, Sandpines (Florence), and Salishan (near Lincoln City).

Hiking

A good introduction to the Kalmiopsis Wilderness is along the one-mile trail to **Vulcan Lake** at the foot of Vulcan Peak, which is the major jumping-off point for trails into the wilderness. The trail begins at Forest Road 1909 and takes off up the mountains past Pollywog Butte and Red Mountain Prairie. The open patches in the Douglas firs reveal a kaleidoscope of Pacific Ocean views and panoramas of the Chetco Valley and the Big Craggies. For the botanist in search of rare plants, however, the real show is on the trail. No matter how expert you might consider yourself, bring along a good plant guide to help you identify the many exotic species. On the final leg of the hike, Sadler oak, manzanita, Jeffrey pine, white pine, and azalea precede the sharp descent to the lake. Despite steep spots, the walk from County Road 1909 to Vulcan Lake is not difficult.

If you backtrack from the lake to Spur 260 on the trail, you can make the steep ascent over talus slopes and brush to Vulcan Peak. At the top, from an old lookout, a view of Kalmiopsis treetops and the coast awaits. Before going, check with the Forest Service in Brookings to see if the road to the Vulcan Lake trailhead is open, because weather-related closures occasionally occur.

To reach the trailhead from Brookings, turn east off U.S. 101 at the north end of the Chetco River Bridge, follow North Bank Road (County Rd. 784) and Forest Road 1376 along the Chetco River for six miles, and then turn right and follow Forest Road 1909 to its bumpy end. Driving distance from Brookings is 31 miles. Hikers should watch out for the three shiny leaves of poison oak, as well as for rattlesnakes, which are numerous. Black bears also populate the area, but their lack of contact with humans makes them shier than their Cascade counterparts.

Surfing and Boogie Boarding

The best surfing is usually found at **Sporthaven Beach,** at the north end of the jetty in Harbor. Reach it by driving to the end of Boat Basin Road to the RV park. There's plenty of parking at the very end of the road. Even if the surf is not spectacular (it's usually best in the winter), it's a pretty mellow place for beginners, and as a fringe benefit, it can be a good spot to see whales during their springtime or December migrations.

Boogie boarders tend to favor **Harris Beach State Park.** From fall to spring, the waves are big and dangerous, and the water is cold. If you know what you're doing, come on in.

Rent gear for surfing or boogie boarding from the friendly folks at **Escape Hatch Sports** (649 Railroad St., 541/469-2914, 10am-5:30pm Mon.-Fri., 10am-5pm Sat.).

ENTERTAINMENT AND EVENTS

The **Beachcomber's Festival** (800/535-9469), held in late March at the **Azalea Middle School** (505 Pacific Ave.), features exhibits, demonstrations, and slide shows as well as an art competition for the best works wrought from indigenous materials such as driftwood, agates, and other beachcomber treasures. To get there, follow Pacific Avenue east of the highway.

Brookings's big event is the **Azalea Festival** (541/469-3181 or 800/535-9469), an unforgettable floral fantasia that takes place each Memorial Day weekend. Among the activities are a parade, a flower display, a crafts fair, a 5K run, a seafood luncheon, and a beef barbecue. Much of the activity revolves around Azalea Park. This Works Progress Administration-built enclave features 20-foot-high azaleas (which are several hundred years old) and hand-hewn myrtlewood picnic tables. Wild cherry and crab apple blooms, wild strawberry blossoms, and purple and red violets round out the bouquet. Butterflies, bees, and birds all seem to concur with locals that this array smells sweetest around graduation time in mid-June. To get there, take Pacific Avenue east of the highway, and turn onto Azalea Park Road.

Like several other Oregon coast towns, Brookings puts its windy weather to good use with its annual **Southern Oregon Kite Festival** (541/412-2941, www.southernoregonkitefestival.com), held over two days in mid-July.

Individuals and teams display their aerial skills at the port of Brookings-Harbor.

Azalea Park is also home to **Nature's Coastal Holiday Light Show** in December, with more than 75,000 lights. The city park is on the south end of town. The Brookings-Harbor Garden Club and Chamber of Commerce (541/469-3181) offer garden tours of this park and other gardens. Call the chamber for more information on tours and garden-related events.

ACCOMMODATIONS

Rooms in Brookings are generally rather expensive; there are more budget accommodations 29 miles north in Gold Beach. It's also harder to find pet-friendly lodgings here than in most other coast towns.

Coastal Country Rentals (541/469-9568, www.coastalcountryrentals.com) can provide a list of available vacation rental homes.

$50-100

Just north of the Chetco River Bridge, **Wild Rivers Motorlodge** (437 Chetco Ave., 541/469-5361, www.wildriversmotorlodge.com, $80-100) is the most attractive roadside budget motel in town. Rooms come with refrigerators and microwaves.

The **Spindrift Motor Inn** (1215 Chetco Ave., 541/469-5345 or 800/292-1171, www.spindriftbrookings.com, $79-95) is a well-managed property and a decent value. However, its ambience is strictly roadside-budget, and it is a bit of a walk to the beach.

At the southern edge of the Brookings-Harbor stretch of U.S. 101, the **Harbor Inn Motel** (15991 U.S. 101 S., 541/469-3194 or 800/469-8444, www.harborinnmotel.com, $70-90) is not a bad place to land. It's nothing fancy, but it's pretty quiet and permits pets; all rooms have a fridge, a microwave, and Wi-Fi. If you head west from the stoplight at the motel, it's about a mile to the port of Harbor.

For a more full-service lodging choice, the highway-side **Brookings Inn Resort** (1143 Chetco Ave., 541/469-2173 or 800/822-9087, www.brookingsinnresort.com, $85-95) is about

a mile from the ocean, but it's family-friendly, with a pool and whirlpool tub, a comfy myrtlewood-paneled lounge, and a decent on-site restaurant.

$100-150

The nicest places to stay in the Brookings area are bed-and-breakfast inns, and they aren't that much more expensive than the local run-of-the-mill motel rooms.

A coastal gem one block north of the highway, the **❰ South Coast Inn B&B** (516 Redwood St., Brookings, 541/469-5557 or 800/525-9273, www.southcoastinn.com, $119-159) is a 1917 Craftsman building and was once the home of lumber baron William Ward. Designed by famed architect Bernard Maybeck and situated in the heart of old Brookings just blocks away from the beach and shopping, this 4,000-square-foot B&B offers four guest rooms, a guest cottage, and an apartment. All rooms have TVs with VCR (and access to the inn's video library), private bathrooms, and other amenities. An indoor spa with a sauna and a hot tub and an included breakfast featuring a health-conscious menu are additional enticements to book space early. Ask the friendly innkeepers about other Maybeck structures in town.

For a B&B that's close to the ocean, **By the Sea B&B** (1545 Beach Ave., 541/469-4692 or 877/469-4692, www.brookingsbythesea.com, $150) offers a choice of two theme-decorated guest rooms and a cottage. Enjoy breakfast and breathtaking ocean views from the stained-glass-topped windows. On the upper veranda, a spa and a wood-burning fire pot are available for guest use.

Perhaps the best value in Brookings lodgings is **❰ Ocean Suites** (16045 Lower Harbor Rd., 541/469-4004, www.oceansuitesmotel.com, $109-119), at the Harbor end of town. These really are suites—each has a full kitchen and a living room. No pets are allowed.

Another option is to rent a cottage at **Whaleshead Beach Resort** (19921 Whaleshead Rd., 541/469-7446 or 800/943-4325, www.whalesheadresort.com, $110-165) by the night or by the week. This sprawling development is on a bluff about eight miles north of Brookings, just across the highway from Whaleshead Beach, a beautiful spot in Boardman State Park. The little cabins are fully furnished, and facilities include a restaurant and a 700-foot-long tunnel under the highway to the beach.

$150-200

The best conventional hotels are south of the Chetco River in Harbor. The **☾ Best Western Beachfront Inn** (16008 Boat Basin Rd., Harbor, 541/469-7779, $179-250) sits on the beach at the mouth of the Chetco River, just past the port and marina. All units feature private decks, microwaves, and refrigerators. Kitchenettes as well as suites with ocean-view hot tubs and an indoor pool are available. Pets are permitted on a very limited basis; call the hotel directly to plead your case.

Camping

Harris Beach State Park (1655 U.S. 101, 541/469-2021 or 800/452-5687, www.reserveamerica.com, $20-26), two miles north of town, is open all year, but reservations are definitely necessary Memorial Day-Labor Day. With a total of 155 spaces, there are 149 paved sites (50 electricity only, 36 full), some with shade; six yurts; and a special camping area for hikers and bicyclists. Picnic tables and grills are provided. Flush toilets, electricity, piped-in water, sewer hookups, sanitary service, showers, firewood, laundry, and a playground are available. Whale-watching is particularly good here in January and May, and the birding is good year-round.

The 320-acre **Alfred A. Loeb State Park** (541/469-2021, sites $16-20 depending on season, cabins $39 year-round) is nine miles northeast of Brookings on North Bank Chetco River Road. There are 53 sites with electrical hookups for trailers/motor homes (50 feet maximum), a special campground for bicyclists and hikers, and some cabins. Electricity, piped water, and picnic tables are provided; flush toilets and firewood are available. The campground is in

a fragrant and secluded myrtlewood grove on the east bank of the Chetco River. From here, the Riverview Trail takes hikers to the Siskiyou National Forest's Redwood Nature Trail, where nature lovers will marvel at 800-year-old redwood beauties. Although cabins can be reserved (800/452-5687), campsites are all first come, first served.

Beyond Loeb State Park is the more primitive **Little Redwood Campground** (contact Chetco Ranger District, 539 Chetco Ave., 541/412-6000, www.fs.fed.us, campground open mid-May-Sept., no water, free). To get there, go 0.5 mile south of Brookings on U.S. 101 to County Road 784, then go northeast for seven miles. At Forest Service Road 376, turn northeast and drive six miles to the campground. Little Redwood is on the main access route to the Kalmiopsis Wilderness, 20 miles away, and is a good spot for fishing during the winter steelhead run.

The Forest Service rents several cabins and fire lookouts ($40-50/night); advance booking is required. Contact the **Chetco Ranger District** (539 Chetco Ave., 541/412-6000, www.fs.fed.us) for information about renting Packer's Cabin, Ludlum House, or the Quail Prairie Lookout.

FOOD

Brookings has a profusion of family-friendly, though unexciting, restaurants that serve large portions at a good value—this is not a fine-dining capital. For slightly more distinctive fare than the usual fast food and family-dining joints, check out the following places.

American

Ask a local where to eat breakfast, and invariably you'll hear the name of **Mattie's Pancake House** (15975 U.S. 101 S., 541/469-7311, 6am-1:45pm Mon.-Sat., $5-13), a family-friendly operation that serves good pancakes, omelets, and biscuits and gravy. The lunch menu offers burgers and sandwiches.

For lighter fare, try **The Tea Room** (434 Redwood St., No. 4, 541/469-7240, 7am-2pm Mon.-Fri.) for sandwiches, soups, salads, and baked goods; fill your to-go mugs with a nice cup of the hot stuff. This place is worth seeing just for its enormous collection of teapots.

Pacific Northwest

Brookings's only real fine dining is at the quirky and charming ❰ **Art Alley Grille** (515 Chetco Ave., 541/469-0800, 11am-2:30pm Tues., 11am-2:30pm and 5pm-8:30pm Wed.-Sat., $19-27), a basement spot tucked downstairs from an art gallery. The menu is fairly wide ranging, with items such as roasted lamb with a marionberry-hazelnut crust and grilled, bacon-wrapped albacore tuna loin offering a real Oregon touch. At lunchtime, head upstairs from the gallery for sandwiches and soup.

Seafood

A coastal town is certainly a safe place to eat sushi. In Brookings, find it at **Cafe Kitanishi** (632 Hemlock St., 541/469-7864, www.cafekitanishi.com, 11am-3pm Tues.-Wed., 11am-3pm and 5pm-9pm Thurs.-Fri., 5pm-9pm Sat., $5-27), which also serves bento boxes to go and has an espresso bar with Internet access.

Down in the harbor area, you'll find a number of seafood shops. For fresh, traditional fish-and-chips, you can't miss at **Sporthaven Marina** (16374 Lower Harbor Rd., 541/469-3301, 11am-6pm Mon.-Sat., 11am-5pm Sun., $6-15) with good clam chowder and fried seafood done up in traditional Oregon style. Yet more fresh fried seafood is ready for you at the adjacent **Hungry Clam** (16350 Lower Harbor Rd., 541/469-2526, $8-15), with crab cake sliders, fresh tuna melts, crab cocktails, and a host of fried fish with slaw and chips.

Brewpub

Wild River Pizza (16279 U.S. 101 S., Harbor, 541/469-7454, 11am-10pm Sun.-Thurs., 11am-11pm Fri.-Sat., medium pizza $13-18) is part of the Wild River Brewing family, with pizza-brewpubs in Cave Junction, Medford, and Grants Pass. The crispy crust pizza is the best you'll find in the area. While the food is good and inexpensive, this large restaurant tends to fill up with families enjoying the video games and pool tables on weekends. In other words, go elsewhere for an intimate Saturday night dinner. Look for it on the east side of the highway about a mile south of the Brookings-Harbor Bridge at the four-way stoplight.

INFORMATION

Pull off the highway and talk to the friendly folks at the **Crissey Field Welcome Center** (16633 Hwy. 101 S., 541/469-4117, 8am-5pm daily Apr.-Oct., 8:30am-4:30pm Mon.-Fri. Nov.-Mar.), where you can gather information and brochures about the coast and the rest of the state. For additional information pertinent to Brookings and environs, the **Brookings-Harbor Chamber of Commerce** (16330 Lower Harbor Rd., Brookings, 541/469-3181, www.brookingsharborchamber.com) is down at the harbor.

GETTING THERE

It takes determination to get to Brookings using public transportation. Curry County's **Coastal Express buses** (800/921-2871, www.currypublictransit.org) run up and down the south coast weekdays only between North Bend and the California border, including local service in Brookings. **Porter Stage Lines** (541/269-7183, www.porterstageline.com) has a run that links North Bend with points north to Florence, then turns inland at Florence and goes to Eugene, Bend, and Ontario.

ASHLAND AND SOUTHERN OREGON

When Oregonians talk about southern Oregon, they usually mean the southwestern corner of the state, including the upper valleys of the Umpqua and Rogue Rivers, the spine of the southern Cascade Mountains, and east to Klamath Falls. The outstanding features of this region include world-class culture-fests at Ashland and Jacksonville, the biggest chunk of remaining wilderness on the Pacific coast, and more summer sun and heat than you expect to find in Oregon.

It also includes Crater Lake National Park, Oregon's only national park, one of the most spectacular natural wonders in the United States. Driving up the desert slopes to the rim and then glimpsing the lake's startlingly blue water ringed by rock cliffs for the first time is a magnificent experience. On repeat visits, you'll want to explore some of the remoter areas of the park, perhaps the strange obelisk-like hoodoos in the southeastern part of the park, or the Boundary Springs, where some of Crater Lake's water percolates out from the edge of the caldera to form the headwaters of the Rogue River.

And speaking of rivers, the Rogue and the Umpqua are dramatically beautiful, with abundant waterfalls, hair-raising rapids for rafters, and the best fishing in the state.

If you think of Oregon as a bastion of progressive politics, then some aspects of southern Oregon may surprise you. From back-to-the-land idealists to hard-core survivalists, southern Oregon attracts settlers of all stripes. Added to this eclectic mix are more than 100 high-tech companies (the "Silicon Orchard"), white-water rafters, anglers, and theater lovers who

© JUDY JEWELL

HIGHLIGHTS

◖ **Lithia Park:** Trails at this lovely park lead from the formal gardens through an arboretum to wild woodlands (page 431).

◖ **Oregon Shakespeare Festival:** Take in a show at one of the world's great theater festivals (page 437).

◖ **Table Rocks:** These mesas contain the most interesting and easily accessible hiking destination along the I-5 corridor (page 445).

◖ **Oregon Caves National Monument:** Here you'll find stalactites and stalagmites deep inside a mountain, plus the unexpected pleasure of a classic mountain lodge (page 464).

◖ **Wildlife Safari:** Oregon's only drive-through zoo features 600 animals from around the world, including lions, giraffes, and hippopotamuses (page 467).

◖ **North Umpqua Waterfalls:** The drive from Roseburg to Toketee Falls along the North Umpqua is dotted with stunning waterfalls (page 473).

◖ **Crater Lake National Park:** At the nation's deepest lake, caused by a catastrophic volcanic eruption 6,600 years ago, you won't believe the color of the water (page 485).

◖ **Favell Museum:** Admire the collection of Native American artifacts and the gallery of

Western art at this fine Klamath Falls museum (page 492).

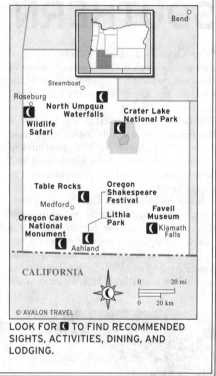

© AVALON TRAVEL

LOOK FOR ◖ TO FIND RECOMMENDED SIGHTS, ACTIVITIES, DINING, AND LODGING.

---

flock to the Oregon Shakespeare Festival in Ashland and the Peter Britt Music Festival in Jacksonville. It's an unlikely blend of populations, but confounding expectations is just part of the mix in southern Oregon.

PLANNING YOUR TIME

Ashland and the **Oregon Shakespeare Festival** are undeniably the largest tourist draw in southern Oregon, although to make the most of this world-class theater festival you'll need to make plans and reserve seats and lodgings well in advance. If you've waited until the last

minute and can't get play tickets, you can sign up for a backstage tour of the festival, watch the free Green Show, and enjoy some of Ashland's fine restaurants—but even for these you'll need to have reservations if you want to eat early in the evening. Once the theater hordes leave the restaurants around 7:30pm, however, you can have your pick of the tables in Ashland's dining establishments.

Increasingly, southern Oregon is becoming a major center for wine production, and it's easy to add a bit of wine-tasting to your theater itinerary. We've included some of our favorite wineries, and for a full listing of area wineries, go to the **Southern Oregon Wineries Association website** (www.sorwa. org), where you can download a brochure and map.

Southern Oregon's other top destination is **Crater Lake National Park.** Even though a visit to the park itself—which for most travelers involves driving the loop route around the rim of the caldera—can be hectic due to excessive traffic, the approaches to the park along the Rogue or Umpqua river valleys offer excellent opportunities for less-thronged outdoor recreation.

The larger cities of southern Oregon—Medford, Grants Pass, and Roseburg—are mostly utilitarian with little to delay or seduce the traveler. If you were planning to camp during your Oregon visit, this might be the best place to do so.

Ashland

Few towns are as closely identified with theater as Ashland (pop. 21,000). Tickets to the renowned Oregon Shakespeare Festival are the coin of the realm here, with contemporary classics and off-off-Broadway shows joining productions by the Bard. You can immediately sense that this is not just another timber town by the Tudor-style McDonald's, vintage Victorian houses, and high-end clothing stores on Main Street.

Blessed with a bucolic setting between the Siskiyous and the Cascades, Ashland embodies the spirit of the chautauqua movement of a century ago, which dedicated itself to bringing culture to the rural hinterlands. Until the 1930s, however, entertainment in these parts mostly consisted of traveling vaudeville shows that visited the Ashland-Jacksonville area to cheer up the residents of a gold rush community in decline.

Southern Oregon University, at the time named Ashland College, established the Shakespeare Festival in 1935 under the direction of Professor Angus Bowmer. Such noted thespians as George Peppard, Stacy Keach, and William Hurt graced Ashland's stages early in their careers, and the festival has garnered its share of Tony Awards and other accolades. Today, the Oregon Shakespeare Festival is the largest classic repertory theater in the country and enjoys the largest audience of any kind of theater in the United States. Annual attendance generally exceeds 400,000.

Ashland's tourist economy is also sustained by its auspicious location roughly equidistant to Portland and San Francisco. Closer to home, day trips to Crater Lake, Rogue River country, and the southern Oregon coast have joined the tradition of "stay four days, see four plays" as a major part of Ashland's appeal.

SIGHTS
◖ Lithia Park

Ashland's centerpiece is 100-acre **Lithia Park** (340 S. Pioneer St.). Recognized as a National Historic Site, the park was designed by John McLaren, landscape architect of San Francisco's Golden Gate Park. It is set along Ashland Creek where the Takelma people camped and where Ashland, Ohio, immigrants built the region's first flour mill in 1854.

The park owes its existence to Jesse Winburne, who made a fortune from New York City subway advertising and in the 1920s tried to develop a spa around Ashland's Lithia Springs, which he said rivaled the venerated waters of Saratoga Springs, New York. Although the spa never caught on due to the Great Depression, Winburne was nevertheless instrumental in landscaping Lithia Park with one of the most varied collections of trees and shrubs of any park in the state. Winburne was also responsible for piping the famous Lithia water to the plaza fountains so all might enjoy its beneficial minerals. While many visitors find this slightly sulfurous, effervescent water a bit hard to swallow, many locals have acquired a taste for Ashland's acerbic answer to Perrier and happily chug it down.

A walk along the beautiful tree-shaded trail of **Winburne Way** is a must. This footpath and a scenic drive through the park start west of the Lithia Fountain. Redwoods, Port Orford cedars, and other species line the drive, which takes you along Ashland Creek to the base of the Siskiyou Mountains.

The hub of the park in the summer is the band shell, where concerts, ballets, and silent movies are shown. Children love to play at the playgrounds or feed the ducks in the ponds. Big kids enjoy tennis, volleyball, horseshoes, or exploring one of the many trails in the park, but dogs are not permitted in the park.

Pick up the *Woodland Trail* guide at the plaza's visitors center kiosk. The gentle milelong loop takes you from the plaza past a beautiful Japanese garden to the upper duck pond where mallards, wood ducks, and the endangered western pond turtle can be seen on the pond's island. A highlight for bird-watchers in winter is 100-200 wood ducks and ouzels diving for fish below the surface of Ashland Creek.

Museums and Galleries

There are over 30 retail galleries in Ashland. Check out www.ashlandgalleries.com for an online guide and map. Two favorites are the **Hanson Howard Gallery** (89 Oak St., 541/488-2562, www.hansonhowardgallery.com, 10:30am-5:30pm Tues.-Sat.), which features monthly exhibits of contemporary artists in a bright airy shop next to the Standing Stone brewpub, and the **Gallerie Karon** (500 A St., 541/482-9008, 10:30am-5:30pm Tues.-Sat.), which features the works of 21 artists in an eclectic collection of sculpture, paintings, fiber arts, printmaking, photography, and jewelry. It is located in a thriving commercial strip by the railroad tracks.

Schneider Museum of Art (Southern Oregon University campus, 1250 Siskiyou Blvd., 541/482-6245, www.sou.edu/sma, 10am-4pm Mon.-Sat., $5 suggested donation) features contemporary art by national and

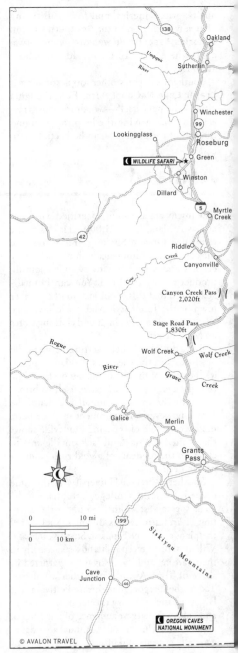

© AVALON TRAVEL

ASHLAND

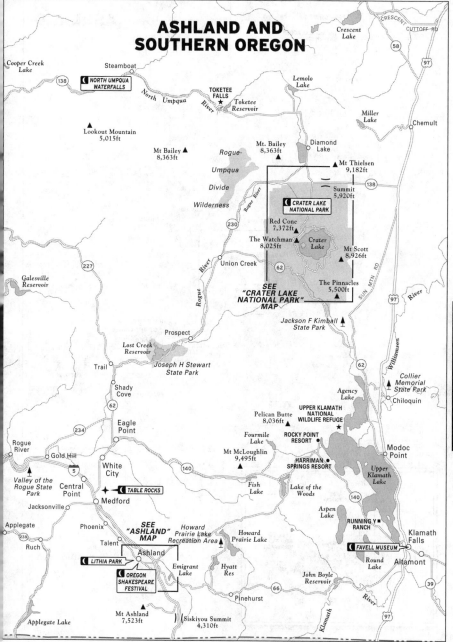

ASHLAND AND SOUTHERN OREGON

ASHLAND

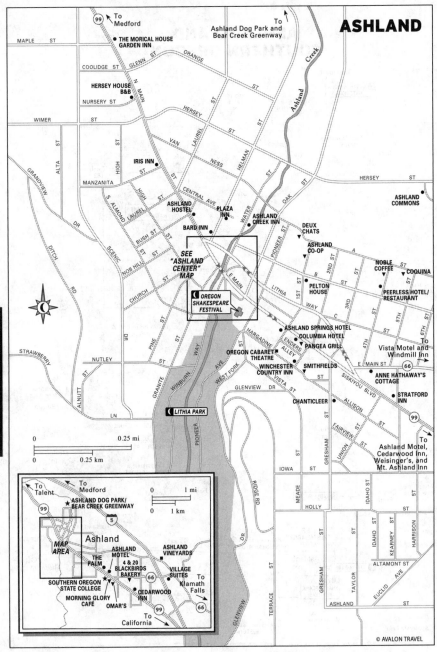

ASHLAND

ASHLAND

© AVALON TRAVEL

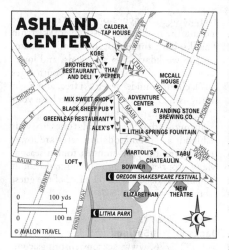

ASHLAND CENTER

CALDERA TAP HOUSE
KOBE
BROTHERS' RESTAURANT AND DELI
THAI PEPPER
TAJ
MCCALL HOUSE
MIX SWEET SHOP
ADVENTURE CENTER
BLACK SHEEP PUB
STANDING STONE BREWING CO.
GREENLEAF RESTAURANT
ALEX'S
LITHIA SPRINGS FOUNTAIN
MARTOLI'S
TABU
LOFT
CHATEAULIN
BOWMER
OREGON SHAKESPEARE FESTIVAL
ELIZABETHAN
NEW THEATRE
LITHIA PARK

0   100 yds
0   100 m
© AVALON TRAVEL

international artists. Ashland is also home to the **ScienceWorks Hands-On Museum** (1500 Main St. near Walker St., 541/482-6767, www.scienceworksmuseum.org, 10am-5pm Wed.-Sat., noon-5pm Sun., $9 adults, $7 seniors and children ages 2-12, under age 2 free), a hands-on museum that offers interactive exhibits, live performances, and activities.

Wine-Tasting

The climate of southern Oregon is ideal for many Bordeaux varietals such as cabernet sauvignon, sauvignon blanc, and merlot. Though the area's largest concentration of wineries is in the nearby Applegate Valley, a handful are close to Ashland.

Just east of town is **Weisinger's Vineyard** (3150 Siskiyou Blvd., 541/488-5989 or 800/551-9463, www.weisingers.com, 11am-5pm daily May-Sept., 11am-5pm Wed.-Sun. Oct.-Apr.). The vineyard, which has received national and international awards, produces cabernet sauvignon, viognier, pinot noir, chardonnay, sauvignon blanc, and Italian varietals.

SPORTS AND RECREATION

Ashland Mountain Supply (31 N. Main St., 541/488-2749, 10am-6pm Mon.-Sat., 11am-5pm Sun.) rents outdoor recreation equipment at reasonable rates.

Golf

A few miles outside of Ashland on Route 66 is **Oak Knoll Golf Course** (3070 Hwy. 66, 541/482-4311, www.oakknollgolf.org). Get into the swing of things before you play; at $16 for 9 holes and $24 for 18 holes, even if you triple bogey, you can't miss.

Hiking

After the snow has melted, the walk to the top of **Mount Ashland** is an easy one with good views of the Siskiyou Mountains and 14,162-foot Mount Shasta in California. It's prudent to bring along a sweater even in warm weather, as it can get fairly windy.

The **Pacific Crest Trail** crosses the Mount Ashland road about three miles past the ski area. By early July, the snow is mostly gone and the wildflowers abundant.

Horseback Riding

Saddle up and head out for a trail ride with **City Slickers** (776 W. Valley View Rd., 541/951-4611, www.oregontrailrides.com, $50 and up). A variety of rides in and around Ashland are available, and horses and guides are experienced with beginning riders.

Mountain Biking

One of the more popular local bike rides is the **Lithia Loop Mountain Bike Route,** a strenuous 28-mile ride that gains 3,000 feet in elevation the first 6 miles. Caution is in order on the last 7 miles of descent. To avoid the steep ups and downs, you can drive up to the top and ride the fairly level 15-mile stretch. The Lithia Loop is mostly within the Ashland watershed, the source of the city's water supply, and it may be closed during midsummer and fall.

The **Siskiyou Crest Mountain Bike Route** begins at the Mount Ashland ski area parking lot. The 31-mile round-trip ranges from moderate to difficult and affords incredible views of Mount Shasta. The route ends at Dutchman Peak, where you'll find one of the few cupola-style fire lookouts left in the Pacific Northwest. This particular lookout was built in 1927. Note

ASHLAND

ASHLAND

The historic downtown core of Ashland is filled with fun places to shop and eat.

© BILL MCRAE

that bicycles are not allowed on the nearby Pacific Crest Trail.

The **Bear Creek Bike and Nature Trail** crisscrosses town before going down the valley to Medford along Bear Creek.

The **Ashland Ranger District** (645 Washington St., 541/482-3333) can provide directions and additional information about these and other mountain bike trails in the area.

Skiing

Perched high atop the Siskiyou range and straddling the California-Oregon border is 7,523-foot **Mount Ashland** (541/482-2897, www.mtashland.com). To get here, take the Mount Ashland exit off I-5 and follow the road eight miles uphill.

While Mount Ashland is 15 miles from downtown Ashland by road, it's only eight miles away by Nordic ski trails. Skiers of all levels enjoy the 23 different runs, 100 miles of cross-country trails, and breathtaking vistas. The vertical drop here is 1,150 feet. An average of 325 inches of snow falls on the mountain, making it possible to ski from Thanksgiving through Easter. Daily lift rates are $36 weekdays, $43 weekends, and lower rates are available for seniors and youth (ages 7-17); children under seven ski free, and night skiing is $25. Don't forget to purchase your Oregon Sno-Park permit.

Spring and fall are good times to visit Ashland, as accommodation rates are lower than during the peak summer tourist season. Many proprietors include discounted Mount Ashland lift tickets with the price of the guest room.

Water Sports

Jackson WellSprings (2253 Hwy. 99 N., 541/482-3776, www.jacksonwellsprings.com, $8 plus a once-yearly insurance charge of $3), a rather informal, decidedly hippie place, is 2 miles north of Ashland on the old highway and has a large naturally heated public swimming pool, a hot soaking pool, a sauna and steam room, as well as private mineral baths. The facility is open Tuesday to Sunday 8am-midnight June 15-Sept. 14; 9am-midnight April 15-June 14 and Sept. 15-Nov. 14; and noon-midnight Nov. 15-April 14. Clothing is optional in the evenings after 6pm. The pool is closed during the day on Monday but open after 6pm for "ladies night."

Meyer Memorial Pool (Hunter Park, Homes Ave. and Hunter Court, 541/488-0313, summer) includes a wading pool for infants and toddlers under age five as well as a large swimming pool for grown-ups.

Six miles east of Ashland on Route 66 is **Emigrant Reservoir** (541/776-7001). In addition to waterskiing, sailing, fishing, and swimming, there is a 270-foot twin flume waterslide (noon-6pm daily Memorial Day-Labor Day).

Outfitters

The **Adventure Center** (40 N. Main St., 541/488-2819 or 800/444-2819, www.raftingtours.com) offers half-day, full-day, and multiday fishing, rafting, and cycling trips for any size party. The cost of the rafting trips includes gear (wetsuits, splash jackets, etc.), guides, and transport from Ashland. Half-day rafting trips on the Rogue River (9:30am-2pm or 1:30pm-5:45pm, $75) include a snack; the longer white-water picnic trip (8am-4pm, $129) includes lunch. Rated one of the best floats in southern Oregon, the upper Klamath River trip ($135) generally runs 7:30am-5:30pm and includes all meals.

If you like to ride a bike but are not big on pedaling, contact the Adventure Center for information about their Mount Ashland downhill bike cruise. This half-day morning or picnic-lunch ride descends 4,000 feet on 16 miles of quiet paved roads through the countryside to Emigrant Reservoir. The three-hour morning cruise ($65) departs at 8am and includes fruit, pastries, and drinks. The four-hour picnic cruise ($69) departs at 11am and includes a great lunch in a beautiful mountain glade. Bicycles, safety equipment, round-trip transfer from Ashland, and an experienced guide are provided. The Adventure Center also rents mountain bikes by the hour or by the day; the price includes a helmet, a lock, and maps.

ENTERTAINMENT AND EVENTS

Shakespeare isn't the only act in town. Local companies include the **Oregon Cabaret Theatre** (1st St. and Hargadine St., 541/488-2902, www.oregoncabaret.com), with musical revues in a club setting, and Southern Oregon State College productions.

Ashland's biggest summertime event, aside from the Shakespeare Festival, is the **Fourth of July parade,** which is more of an exuberant and slightly wacky celebration of the community than a patriotic event.

◖ Oregon Shakespeare Festival

While Lithia Park is the heart of Ashland, Shakespeare is the soul of this community. The festival began when Angus Bowmer, an English professor at Ashland College, decided to celebrate Independence Day weekend in 1935 with

© JUDY JEWELL

Catch the free nightly Green Show during the Oregon Shakespeare Festival.

a Shakespeare production. The city fathers were so unsure of the reception it would get that they asked him to allow boxing matches on the stage during the day prior to the performance. By the time he retired as artistic director of the festival in 1971, his Fourth of July dream had grown into an internationally acclaimed drama company with three theaters, one named in his honor.

Performances run from mid-February through late October or early November, though the famed outdoor **Elizabethan Theatre,** built on the site of Ashland's Chautauqua Dome and modeled after the Fortune Theatre of London circa 1600, is open in summer only. This is the largest of the festival's three theaters and primarily the domain of the Bard. While Shakespeare under the stars is incredibly romantic, it can also get very cold after sunset. Curtain times run 8pm-8:30pm with most shows ending around 11pm. This outdoor theater opens in early June and closes by mid-October.

The second-largest playhouse is the 600-seat **Angus Bowmer,** an indoor complex with excellent acoustics, computerized sound and lighting, and nary a bad seat in the house. Finally, the 150-seat **Thomas Theatre** is where modern works and experimental productions are the norm. This theater is small enough to stage plays that might be overwhelmed by a larger venue.

In addition to the plays themselves, two other events are popular with theatergoers. **Backstage Tours** (10am Tues.-Sun., high season $13 adults, $9 youth ages 6-17, reservations required) explore the history, design, and technology of all of the festival's repertory theaters, including the fascinating Elizabethan Stage. The regular tour is a walking tour and has six flights of stairs; call ahead to schedule a tour without stairs.

Catch the free **Green Show** on the plaza outside the Elizabethan Theatre. It begins at 6:45pm and features live music, lectures, performance, storytelling, and other entertainment. It ends just before 8pm when the outdoor performance starts in the Elizabethan Theatre.

TICKETS

Getting tickets to the **Oregon Shakespeare Festival** (15 S. Pioneer St., Ashland, OR 97520, 541/482-4331 or 800/219-8161, www. osfashland.org, box office 9:30am-performance time Tues.-Sun., 9:30am-5pm Mon., closed most holidays) is as much a part of the show as the performance. Due to tremendous popularity, seats sell out months in advance. All seats are reserved; ticket prices range $25-96. Children under age six are not permitted. Once tickets are purchased, there are no refunds.

If you are unable to get advance tickets, your best bet is to show up at the Shakespeare Plaza an hour or two before the show with a sign stating what show you want to see. If you are lucky, you will score tickets from someone with extras. Avoid bidding wars with other would-be theatergoers, as ticket scalping is frowned upon. Otherwise, be at the ticket window at 6pm; any available seats will be released at that time. And remember, there is no late seating.

ACCOMMODATIONS

Quoted rates are for June-September; expect prices to drop around one-third outside the summer high season. Ashland's high cost of living is reflected in the rack rates of the town's accommodations. Nonetheless, there's generally something to be found to meet the needs of most every budget. If Ashland's prices seem too high, you can find less expensive rates in Medford, a 10-minute drive to the north.

The warm traditions of Britain are represented in Ashland not only by the Oregon Shakespeare Festival but also by the town's numerous bed-and-breakfasts, the most of any locale in the state. Many B&Bs require a two-night minimum stay during summer. The **Ashland Bed and Breakfast Network** (800/944-0329, www.abbnet.com) can help you find quality B&B lodgings in town.

Under $50

Offering dorm beds and a handful of private rooms, the **Ashland Hostel** (150 N. Main St., 541/482-9217, www.theashlandhostel.com,

$28 pp dorm bed, $45-59 d private room with shared bath, $79 family room with private bath) is a two-story 1902 house near the Pacific Crest Trail, only three blocks from the Elizabethan Theatre and Lithia Park and two blocks from the Greyhound station. Reservations are essential, especially March-October. The hostel has a coin-op laundry.

A newer hostel, **Ashland Commons** (437 Williamson Way, 541/482-6753, www.ashlandcommons.com, $26 pp dorm bed, $45-65 pp private room), is a little farther from the downtown hub in a quiet residential neighborhood.

$50-100

Moderately priced guest rooms are available from **Cedarwood Inn** (1801 Siskiyou Blvd., 541/488-2000 or 800/547-4141, www.ashlandcedarwoodinn.com, $82-92), with a pool and continental breakfast. Two-bedroom and kitchen units are also available.

$100-150

The **Ashland Motel** (1145 Siskiyou Blvd., 541/482-2561 or 800/460-8858, www.ashlandmotel.com, $105-115) offers good value and clean, cheery, and basic pet-friendly guest rooms. All rooms have fridges and microwaves; there are two 2-bedroom units, and a small outdoor pool.

A dollar-wise choice with some charm is the **Columbia Hotel** (262½ E. Main St., 541/482-3726 or 800/718-2530, www.columbiahotel.com, $125-169), in the center of town. This well-kept 1910 hotel with a grand piano in the lobby has 24 rooms. Most rooms share bathrooms. Rooms at a sister property, **◖The Palm** (1065 Siskiyou Blvd., 877/482-2635, www.palmcottages.com, $103-169), are in a well-maintained cottage-style motel in the midst of lovely gardens. A saline pool, sundeck, and cabanas complete the oasis-like atmosphere. During the off-season, the Palm accepts pets in some rooms.

Out at the interstate exit is the **La Quinta Inn** (434 W. Valley View Rd., 541/482-6932 or 800/527-1133, www.lq.com, $119-144), with an indoor pool, a business center, and guest laundry.

The **Pelton House** bed-and-breakfast (228 B St., 541/488-7003 or 866/488-7003, www.peltonhouse.com, $135-185) is located in a historic Victorian just a few blocks from the Shakespeare Festival. Each of its seven rooms is has an earthy theme, and two suites are available for families or groups.

$150-200

If you don't want to spend a bundle on lodging but want to stay in the center of Ashland, **Best Western Bard's Inn Motel** (132 N. Main St., 541/482-0049 or 800/533-9627, www.bardsinn.com, $169-199) is a good choice. Just across the Main Street bridge from downtown, the Bard's Inn is no more than five minutes' walk from the theaters. There are a number of room types, all nicely furnished and well maintained. Facilities include a streamside restaurant and bar.

Clean and meticulously maintained, a privately owned and operated premium motel is the **Stratford Inn** (555 Siskiyou Blvd., 541/488-2151 or 800/547-4741, www.stratfordinnashland.com, $165-185), just five blocks from the theaters with reserved parking for guests. All guest rooms have a fridge, and a couple of kitchen suites are available. Free laundry services, free ski lockers during ski season, an elaborate continental breakfast, and an indoor pool and whirlpool tub all contribute to the inn's high occupancy rate.

The 70-room **Ashland Springs Hotel** (212 E. Main St., 541/488-1700 or 888/795-4545, www.ashlandspringshotel.com, $179-229), on the corner of 1st and Main Streets (a block from the Elizabethan Theatre), is a first-class historic hotel. When it opened in 1925, it was considered a skyscraper; at nine stories it's still the tallest building between San Francisco and Portland. It languished in obscurity for decades until its multimillion-dollar restoration a few years back, but it still evokes the grandeur of the past. A grand ballroom, a bar to enjoy parlor games and musical entertainment in, and English gardens add

ASHLAND

© BILL MCRAE

ASHLAND

The Peerless Hotel is one of the most elegant hotels in Ashland.

touches evocative of another era. Luxuriously appointed guest rooms aren't large but boast oversize windows highlighting nice views. Minimum stays may apply.

The historic ℂ **Peerless Hotel** (243 4th St., 541/488-1082 or 800/460-8758, www.peerless-hotel.com, $165-229) was established in 1900 when the railroad came to Ashland. It served the needs of railroad travelers for many years before falling into disuse. The old hotel was brought back to life in the 1990s, when it was thoroughly modernized and converted into a boutique B&B-style hotel. One of the most distinctive places to stay in Ashland, the Peerless also offers a fine dining restaurant and a location in the art gallery-rich Railroad District.

The ℂ **Morical House Garden Inn** (668 N. Main St., 541/482-2254, www.moricalhouse.com, $151-270) is a restored 1880s farmhouse with seven rooms and a guesthouse with three luxury suites, each with a picture-postcard view of Grizzly Mountain and the Siskiyou foothills. Wood floors, stained-glass windows,

and antiques sustain the "good old days" theme despite the many modern conveniences. In season, the two acres of gardens provide organic produce for breakfast as well as a wide variety of herbs and flowers. Many species of birds and butterflies are attracted to the gardens, which are tastefully accented by a waterfall and stream meandering through the grounds. Given all this, it's sometimes hard to remember that you are only a few blocks away from downtown theaters and shopping.

Plaza Inn and Suites (98 Central Ave., 541/488-8900 or 888/488-0358, www.plazainnashland.com, $179-229) is a large, modern hotel just below downtown and within easy walking distance of the theaters. Many of the rooms look onto a parklike courtyard that fronts onto Ashland Creek. Guest rooms are very nicely appointed; many have balconies and some allow pets. A breakfast buffet is included in the rates.

The ℂ **Chanticleer Inn** (120 Gresham St., www.ashland-bed-breakfast.com, 541/482-1919, $185-205) rules the roost with five romantic guest rooms replete with fluffy comforters and private baths. Dogs are permitted (with prior approval) in some of the rooms. The gourmet breakfasts are the talk of Ashland. Round-the-clock refrigerator rights, complimentary wines and sherry, and a full cookie jar on the kitchen counter help keep you wined and dined throughout your stay.

Anne Hathaway's Cottage (586 E. Main St., 541/488-1050 or 800/643-4434, www.ashlandbandb.com, $175-195), four blocks from the theaters, boasts fresh-cut flowers, down comforters, firm beds, and private baths. This building was once a boardinghouse; the cottages across the street are now part of this B&B complex.

The **Abigail's Bed and Breakfast Inn** (451 N. Main St., 541/482-4563, www.abigailsbandb.com, $165-175, cottage $250) is an elegantly restored Victorian home with antique furniture and private baths, plus a garden cottage with a fully equipped kitchen, a living room, and two bedrooms, making it well-suited for families and groups of up to six.

The **Iris Inn** (59 Manzanita St., 541/488-2286 or 800/460-7650, www.irisinnbb.com, $190) is a cheerful Victorian with a fitting decor four blocks from the theaters. Full breakfast in the morning, cold drinks during the day, and wine and sherry at night add to the welcoming atmosphere.

The **McCall House** (153 Oak St., 541/482-9296 or 800/808-9749, www.mccallhouse.com, $190-250) is a restored Italianate mansion built in 1883 by Ashland pioneer John McCall. A National Historic Landmark, this nine-room inn is a block from restaurants, shops, theaters, and Lithia Park. Delectable fresh-baked goodies with juice or tea are served each afternoon. The Carriage House offers two beds and a kitchenette.

Two blocks south of the theaters is the acclaimed **Winchester Country Inn** (35 S. 2nd St., 541/488-1113 or 800/972-4991, www.winchesterinn.com, $195-240), offering 19 guest rooms and suites with private baths and loads of personality. The individual attentiveness of the large staff recalls a traditional English country inn. Bay windows, private balconies, and exquisite English gardens add further distinction. Gourmet delicacies are featured at breakfast, and dinner and Sunday brunch are available in the inn's restaurant. Visit the website to check out their changing special lodging packages.

Bathe in naturally occurring hot springs at the **Lithia Springs Inn** (2165 W. Jackson Rd., 541/482-7128 or 800/482-7128, www.ashlandinn.com, $179-199). A couple of miles from downtown amid four acres of gardens, the inn is close enough to access Ashland culture yet far enough away for some real peace and quiet. Twelve of the 14 rooms have whirlpools fed from the hot springs. There are eight cottage suites, two theme suites, and four regular guest rooms available. Most of the one- and two-room cottages adjacent to the lodge feature a fireplace, a refrigerator, a wet bar, and a double Jacuzzi. Be sure to book well in advance.

Though it's just eight miles from Ashland, you'll feel light-years from the Bard at **Callahan's Mountain Lodge** (7100 Old Highway 99 S., 541/482-1299 or 800/286-0507, www.callahanslodge.com, $165-220), a massive log lodge high in the Siskiyou Mountains on the road to the Mount Ashland ski area (take I-5 Exit 5). There are only 19 rooms in the atmospheric lodge, and they book up fast in ski season. But the lodge is open year-round, and the rooms are comfortably furnished in a rustic Western style. As notable are the stone fireplaces, patios, nightly live music, and friendly bar and restaurant, making this a popular spot for rendezvous and entertainment.

Over $200

At the **Ashland Creek Inn** (70 Water St., 541/482-3315, www.ashlandcreekinn.com, $265-425) you won't get any closer to Ashland Creek without getting wet. This small luxury-level inn is directly adjacent to the stream and has several guest rooms with cantilevered decks directly above the rushing water. Each of the 10 suites is uniquely decorated according to a theme—the Caribe, the Marrakech, the Edinburgh—and each offers complete kitchens, living rooms, private entrances, and decks. Best of all, this comfort and style are just moments from downtown shopping and the theaters.

Camping

Emigrant Lake (5505 Hwy. 66, 541/774-8183, www.co.jackson.or.us, $20 tent, $30 RV), a few miles east of Ashland, has RV and tent camping at a Jackson County Parks Department campground. South of town, **Mount Ashland** has a primitive campground (free, no water) about a mile past the ski resort.

On the northern edge of town, **Jackson WellSprings** (2253 Hwy. 99 N., 541/482-3776, $20 one person in tent, $28 for two) has tent sites on a grassy, tree-shaded lawn. It's highly informal (with a hippie vibe, to be truthful) and gets a bit of road noise, so it's not for the faint of heart. However, camping does gain you admission to the pool, sauna, and steam room, and it's only about a five-minute drive from downtown.

ASHLAND

Emigrant Lake, about five miles east of Ashland, is a good place to camp.

FOOD

Ashland's creative talents are not just confined to theatrical pursuits; some of Oregon's better restaurants can be found here. Even the humbler fare served in Ashland's unpretentious cafés and pubs can be memorable. The city has a 5 percent restaurant tax, a surcharge seen nowhere else in the Beaver State except Lincoln City.

Stock up on groceries or pick up a deli sandwich at the **Ashland Food Co-op** (237 N. 1st St., 541/482-2237, 7am-9pm daily).

Bakeries and Cafés

Find Ashland's best coffee and a friendly place to hang out for a while at **Noble Coffee** (281 4th St., 541/488-3288, 7am-4pm daily), in the hip railroad district. Right downtown, **Four and Twenty Blackbirds** (1604 Ashland St., 541/488-0825, 8am-5pm Mon.-Fri., 8am-1pm Sat.) is the place to pick up morning muffins or a fruit pie for later. Another friendly spot for pastries and desserts is **Mix Sweet Shop** (57 N.

Main St., 541/488-9885, 7am-9pm daily), with Stumptown coffee and a bohemian atmosphere.

American

For Ashland's most popular breakfast café, head to **Morning Glory Restaurant** (1149 Siskiyou Blvd., 541/488-8636, 8am-1:30pm daily, $10-12) for delicious omelets, pancakes, and breakfast sandwiches. This place is not a secret, and lines on weekend mornings can be long.

The second-floor patio at the **Greenleaf Restaurant** (49 N. Main St., 541/482-2808, 8am-9pm daily, $10-20) is a great spot to enjoy a meal. The menu offers lots of vegetarian choices, with pasta, stir-fries, salads, and sandwiches in addition to Mediterranean main courses like chicken piccata and red snapper Palermo.

New York meets the Pacific Northwest at **Brothers Restaurant** (95 N. Main St., 541/482-9671, 7am-2pm daily, $3-13), which offers breakfast all day, excellent omelets and bagel sandwiches, plus deli sandwiches for lunch.

Alex's (35 N. Main St., 541/482-8818, 3pm-9pm Mon.-Thurs., 3pm-10pm Fri., 11:30am-10pm Sat., 11:30am-9pm Sun., $9-17) serves pasta and other light entrées in a historic second-story bar and dining room flanked by fireplaces.

Pangea Grills and Wraps (272 E. Main St., 541/552-1630, 11am-8pm daily, $7-11) is a soup, salad, and wraps emporium featuring free-range meats along with many vegetarian, vegan, and wheat- or gluten-free choices. The preparations are light, flavorful, and reasonably priced. This place is perfect for a quick meal before the show on a hot midsummer night.

Asian

The **Thai Pepper** (84 Main St., 541/482-8058, 11:30am-2pm Tues.-Sat., 5pm-9:30pm daily, $9-18) has a lot to offer: Not only is the spicy, flavorful Southeast Asian cuisine well prepared and moderately priced, the dining room steps down into the steep gulch of Ashland Creek, offering a cool and quiet haven in the summer heat and one of the most pleasant patio dining areas in town.

Kobe (96 N. Main St., 541/488-8058, 5pm-10pm Sun.-Thurs., 5pm-11pm Fri.-Sat., rolls from $7-16) offers top-quality sushi, sashimi, hand rolls, and an assortment of small plates that showcase contemporary Japanese cuisine.

For East Indian food, go to **Taj** (31 Water St., 541/488-5900, 11am-3pm and 5pm-9:30pm daily, $15-22), which has a number of vegetarian dishes, traditional curries, and tandoor oven specialties. At lunchtime, enjoy the $9 buffet.

Pizza

Stop by **Martoli's** (38 E. Main St., 541/482-1918, 11am-9pm Sun.-Thurs., 11am-10pm Fri.-Sat., $11-22) for a slice or a whole pizza. It's the best pizza in town, and the cafe is a cheery place with a Deadhead theme.

Latin American

A fun and exciting place to explore new tastes is **Tabu** (76 N. Pioneer St., 541/482-3900, www.

tabuashland.com, 11:30am-9pm daily, tapas till late, $8-21), a restaurant that takes the zesty foods of Central America and updates them with new flavors and preparations. Choose from entrées like banana leaf-wrapped fish or guava chipotle ribs, or select a series of tapas. The cocktail bar at Tabu is a favorite late-night haunt of thespians.

Pacific Northwest

The restaurant at the historic Winchester Inn has undergone a transformation. Fittingly, it's now the **Alchemy Restaurant** (35 S. 2nd St., 541/488-1115, www.alchemyashland.com, 4pm-9pm Wed.-Sat., 9:30am-12:30pm and 4pm-9pm Sun., dinner $23-35, brunch $9-14) and serves sit-up-and-take notice modern cuisine prepared with rarified techniques and ingredients. In the stately dining room, you can savor sous-vide lamb loin scented with vanilla bean, or bacon-wrapped quail stuffed with chestnuts and minced guinea fowl. The bar is a classy spot to enjoy a cocktail.

The **◖ Peerless Restaurant** (265 4th St., 541/488-6067, 5:30pm-9pm Tues.-Sat., $24-38) is part of a picturesque historic hotel; the garden is spectacular, so dine al fresco if possible. The impressive selection of small plates ($6-18) makes casual dining fun and exciting—start with chorizo-stuffed dates or lamb meatballs with blue cheese filling, and keep the plates coming. The menu also offers à la carte fine dining (salmon, steaks, pasta), but you'll find it hard to resist the small plates.

◖ Amuse (15 N. 1st St., 541/488-9000, 5:30pm-9pm Tues.-Sun., $22-34) is Ashland's top French-via-Pacific-Northwest restaurant, with a menu that changes weekly and features fresh local fruit, vegetables, and mushrooms as well as ranch beef and lamb and locally harvested fish. Expect such sophisticated dishes as crispy veal sweetbreads with roasted mission figs or black truffle-roasted game hen. Desserts are especially good. The small dining room is deceptive; the back patio is shady and expansive.

Just down the road from Ashland is the

ASHLAND

absolutely unique **New Sammy's Cowboy Diner** (2210 S. Pacific Hwy., 541/535-2779, noon-1:30pm and 5pm-9pm Wed.-Sun., $18-28, three-course prix fixe $50). The chef-owners are Bay Area expatriates who moved to Ashland with retirement in mind but somehow got talked into cooking for friends, then for the public, a few nights a week. The menu changes frequently, but expect delicious fish, rabbit, pork, and charcuterie, all prepared with great care and skill—if the braised beef ribs are offered, by all means order them. The wine list is very imposing, with hundreds of choices. The dining area has recently expanded, but to understand why New Sammy's has such a devoted following, ask to be seated in the old dining room with cow wallpaper and just six tables in what was once a gas station. Call for winter hours; reservations are strongly recommended.

Head down to Ashland Creek and search a bit to find the door to the **Loft** (18 Calle Guanajuato, 541/482-1116, http://loftbrasserie.com, 5pm-9pm Tues.-Sun., $13-28), an upstairs brasserie with a patio overlooking the creek. The French-Oregonian menu features locally sourced food including seared steelhead trout served with tasty brussels sprouts and traditional rabbit paté.

Classy but casual, **Coquina** (542 A St., 541/488-0521, www.coquinarestaurant.com, 5pm-10pm Tues.-Sat., $18-32) serves refined Pacific Northwest cuisine based on local, seasonal ingredients. This Railroad District restaurant features such tempting creations as rabbit ravioli with porcini mushrooms and onion jam, and fresh scallops with pea tendril salad.

Steak Houses

Omar's (1380 Siskiyou Blvd., 541/482-1281, 11:30am-2pm and 5pm-9pm Mon.-Thurs., 11:30am-2pm and 5pm-10pm Fri., 5pm-10pm Sat., 5pm-9pm Sun., $13-33) is Ashland's oldest restaurant (mastodon bones were found when excavating for the restaurant in 1946) and its only traditional steak house. Come for hand-cut steaks, fresh seafood, and a broad selection of eclectic main dishes, such

as chipotle-cranberry roast chicken, all served in a darkly atmospheric dining room. For the quality, the prices are very moderate.

Find nose-to-tail meat-centric cuisine at **Smithfields** (36 S. 2nd St., 541/488-9948, www.smithfieldsashland.com, 11:30am-2:30pm and 5pm-9:30pm Tues.-Fri., 10am-2:30pm and 5pm-9:30pm Sat.-Sun., $15-30). The chef-owner, an expat Brit, named the restaurant after a famous London meat market, but it has a down-to-earth Oregon vibe. Don't miss the charcuterie board, with everything made in-house; the Scotch quail egg appetizer is also good.

Brewpubs and Wine Bars

One story above Ashland Plaza, the **Black Sheep Pub and Restaurant** (51 N. Main St., 541/482-6414, 11:30am-1am daily, $6-25) is a vast Olde English pub with better-than-average fare plus a wide selection of British and Pacific Northwestern ales. This is the place to come for a late-night after-theater supper (burgers, steak pie, grilled salmon) with frothy pints of beer.

Bright, airy, and with a delightful back patio open in good weather, **Standing Stone Brewing Company** (101 Oak St., 541/482-2448, 11:30am-midnight Mon.-Sat., 8am-midnight Sun., $8-19) has one of the most pleasant dining rooms in Ashland. Not only are the beers tasty, the menu is also very broad, including soups, salads, burgers, wood-fired pizzas, and entrées verging on fine dining.

Tucked down near Ashland Creek, the **Caldera Tap House** (31 Water St., 541/482-4677, 4pm-10pm Sun.-Tues., 4pm-11pm Wed.-Thurs., 4pm-midnight Fri.-Sat., $6-22) serves some of the best locally brewed beer (it's not brewed on-site, but at a brewery on Clover Lane) along with fairly typical pub food and live music. Caldera is known for packaging its beer in cans, and the canned IPA is terrific. Of course, at the tap house, the brew flows from taps.

If you're looking for a glass of wine or cocktail plus a delicious selection of snacks, then try **Liquid Assets** (96 N. Main St., 541/482-9463, 3am-midnight daily, small plates $8-20), a wine

Caldera Tap House is tucked below the street, right on Ashland Creek.

bar with a good choice of cheeses and cured meats, plus tempting house specialties such as Dungeness crab cakes, warm chèvre salad, and roast lamb loin with chimichurri.

INFORMATION

Ashland Visitor Information Center (110 E. Main St., 541/482-3486, www.ashlandchamber.com, 9am-5pm Mon.-Fri.) offers brochures, play schedules, and other up-to-date information on happenings.

The **Oregon Welcome Center** (60 Lowe Rd., 541/488-1805, 9am-10pm daily mid-May-Sept.) offers travel information on the whole state. The center is just off I-5 at Exit 19.

GETTING THERE AND AROUND

The local airport is in Medford. United Express and Horizon Air fly into **Medford/Jackson County Airport** (1000 Terminal Loop Pkwy., 541/772-8068 or 800/882-7488, www.co.jackson.or.us), 15 miles north of town.

Amtrak (800/872-7245) has a station 70 miles east at Klamath Falls and 75 miles south at Dunsmuir, California. **Greyhound** (91 Oak St., 541/482-2516) serves Ashland with a handful of daily northbound and southbound departures.

Local connections between Medford and Ashland are possible through **Rogue Valley Transportation** (541/779-2877, www.rvtd.org). Pick up a bus schedule at area businesses or libraries, or on the website.

Medford

Along with a resource-based economy revolving around agriculture and timber products, Medford (population 73,500) is becoming established as a retirement center. Some of the enticements are proximity to Ashland's culture, Rogue Valley recreation, Cascade getaways, and rainfall totals that are half those recorded in the Willamette Valley. All that summer heat is good for fruit production—the Rogue River Valley around Medford is a major center for pear production, and wine grapes are displacing dairy cows and berries on area farms.

SIGHTS
◖ Table Rocks

About 10 miles northeast of Medford are two eye-catching basaltic buttes, **Upper and Lower Table Rocks.** They are composed of sandstone with erosion-resistant lava caps deposited during a massive Cascade eruption about 4-5 million years ago. Over the years, wind and water have undercut the sandstone. Stripped of its underpinnings, the heavy basalt on top of the eroded sandstone is pulled down by gravity, creating the nearly vertical slabs that we see today.

The Table Rocks were the site of a decisive

© BILL MCRAE

ASHLAND

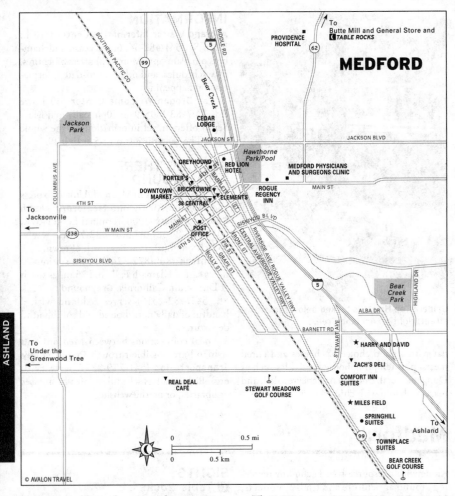

battle in the first of a series of Rogue River Indian Wars in the 1850s. Major Philip Kearny, who later went on to distinguish himself as the great one-armed Civil War general, was successful in routing the Native Americans from this seemingly impervious stronghold. A peace treaty was signed here soon afterward by the Rogue (Takelma) people and the U.S. government. For a time this area was also part of the Table Rock Indian Reservation, but the status of the reservation was terminated shortly thereafter.

The 1,890-acre **Lower Table Rock Preserve** was established in 1979 near the westernmost butte, which towers 800 feet above the surrounding valley floor. The preserve protects an area of special biological, geological, historical, and scenic value. Pacific madrone, white oak, manzanita, and ponderosa pine grow on the flank of the mountain; the crown is covered with grasses and wildflowers. Newcomers to the region will be especially taken by the madrone trees, *Arbutus menziesii.* This glossy-leafed evergreen has a "skin" that peels in warm weather to reveal a smooth, coppery orange bark. It's found mostly in the Pacific Northwest and was noted by early explorers as fuel for long, slow, hot-burning fires.

Park checklists show that more than 140 kinds of plants reside here, including dwarf meadow foam, which grows no place else on earth. One reason is that water doesn't readily percolate through the lava. Small ponds collect on top of the butte, nurturing the wildflowers that flourish in early spring. The wildflower display reaches its zenith in April. A dozen species of flowers cover the rock-strewn flats in bright yellow and vivid purple.

Hikers who take the 2.6-mile trail to the top of horseshoe-shaped Lower Table Rock are in for a treat. Be on the lookout for batches of pale lavender fawn lilies peeking out from underneath the shelter of the scraggly scrub oaks on the way up the mountain. You'll want to walk over to the cliff's edge, which will take you past some of the "Mima mounds" or "patterned ground" that distinguishes the surface of the butte. How the mounds were formed is a matter of scientific debate. Some scientists believe they represent centuries of work by rodents, others think they are accumulated silt deposits, while still others maintain they were created by the action of the wind. However they got there, the mounds are the only soil banks on the mountain that support grasses, which are unable to grow on the lava. Lichens and mosses manage to grow on the lava, however, painting the dull black basalt with luxuriant green and fluorescent yellow during the wetter months.

The **Bureau of Land Management** (3040 Biddle Rd., 541/770-2200, www.blm.gov) has additional information on the Table Rocks.

HIKING

The trail up Upper Table Rock is a little over one mile but much steeper than the Lower Table Rock trail. Clay clings to the slopes of Upper Table Rock, making the going both sticky and slippery during the wet season. The trail affords wonderful vistas of the Rogue River and Sams Valley to the north.

It reaches the top of the butte on the far eastern side. The ponds up here are smaller and fewer than those on Lower Table Rock, but the Mima mounds are more clearly defined. Upper Table Rock also shows less wear and tear from human activity, and the flower show is just as spectacular. Long black strips of hexagonal basalt look as though they were formed by tanks marching across the butte while the lava was cooling. This irregular knobby surface is difficult to walk on, but the colorful mosses and lichens love it. Also look for the tiny bouquets of grass widows, lovely purple flowers that dangle on long graceful stalks. The odd-looking building off to the west is a navigation device maintained by the Federal Aviation Administration. It's easy to get disoriented out here, with hundreds of acres to explore. The point where the trail heads back down the mountain is marked by two large trees, a ponderosa pine and a Douglas fir, accompanied by a smaller cedar.

To get to the Table Rocks, take Route 62 northeast out of Medford. Take the Central Point exit (Exit 33) east about 1 mile to Table Rock Road and turn north (left). Continue 7.6 miles, passing Tou Velle State Park. Turn east (right) and continue approximately 1 mile to the signed parking lot, which will be on your left. The trail to the top of Upper Table Rock begins here.

Harry & David

Harry & David (1314 Center Dr., 541/776-2277, www.harryanddavid.com), the nation's leading purveyor of mail-order fruit, has a store just off I-5 Exit 27 in the south part of Medford. The fruit-stand section of the large company store offers farm-fresh fruit and vegetables. You can also find rejects from Harry & David's Fruit-of-the-Month Club that are nearly as good as the mail-order fruit but too small or blemished to meet their high quality standards. The jams and fruit spreads are also a bit less expensive than mail order. Perhaps best of all, the store offers a really large selection of Oregon wines, so stop here and ask the friendly staff for recommendations if your trip

ASHLAND

© BILL MCRAE

Harry & David has a long history in Medford.

spot to stop if you don't have time to explore other wineries because it serves as the tasting room for a number of regional wineries that are too small to maintain their own. There is also a good selection of cheeses and local gourmet items for sale.

Kriselle Cellars (12956 Modoc Rd., 541/830-8466, www.krisellecellars.com, 11am-5:30pm daily) is about 12 miles north of Medford, with a stunning new tasting room overlooking the Rogue Valley. The wines here are notable, particularly the French-style viognier and award-winning cabernet sauvignon.

Central Point is home to the **Rogue Creamery** (311 N. Front St., Central Point, 541/665-1155, www.roguecreamery.com, 9am-5pm Mon.-Sat., noon-5pm Fri.), which makes some of the best cheese in the Pacific Northwest, with a focus on blue cheese; the Caveman Blue is exceptionally rich. Stop by Saturday afternoon between 1pm and 3pm for wine tasting.

doesn't allow you to venture into the state's wine country.

Brothers Harry and David Rosenberg took over their family's Bear Creek Orchards in 1914. Bear Creek Orchards was recognized for the size and quality of its pears, which were shipped to the grand hotels of Europe. But the lucrative export market collapsed during the Depression, so the brothers decided to sell their fruit by mail. Harry & David is the oldest mail-order business in the country and, despite recent financial woes, still the nation's largest gourmet fruit and food gift company.

Wine and Cheese Tasting

RoxyAnn Winery (3285 Hillcrest Rd., 541/776-2315, www.roxyann.com) is one of the top wineries in southern Oregon, and conveniently the tasting room is immediately east of Medford in an old pear orchard. RoxyAnn makes particularly good, rich red wines—the claret and syrah are especially delicious. The tasting room is in an old barn, and it's a good

SPORTS AND RECREATION
Golf

Near Miles Field is **Bear Creek Golf Course** (2325 S. Pacific Hwy., 541/773-1822). This is a compact nine-hole course that's both a challenge and a bargain at $18 per round on weekdays (on Thursday, it's just $12). **Cedar Links Golf Course** (3144 Cedar Links Dr., 541/773-4373, $16), in northeast Medford, is another beautiful public nine-hole course. To get there, take Route 62 north toward White City and turn right on Delta Waters Road, right again on Springbrook Road, and then left on Cedar Links Drive.

Eagle Point Golf Course (100 Eagle Point Dr., Eagle Point, 541/826-8225, www.eagle-pointgolf.com, $45 weekdays, $48 weekends) is arguably the finest course in the Rogue River Valley. Designed by Robert Trent Jones Jr., this 175-acre collection of golf holes boasts enough character to challenge beginners and experts alike. Impressive views of Mount McLoughlin and Table Rocks add to the experience. Carts, clubs, and shoes are available for rent.

Stop at the Rogue Creamery for some of the state's best cheese.

Swimming

When the summer mercury reaches up into the 90s, it's time to cool off in one of Medford's several public swimming pools. **Jackson Pool** (815 Summit Ave., 541/770-4586, mid-June-early Sept.) is a popular family place. In addition to the 100-foot-long waterslide, a concession stand sells ice cream, soft drinks, and other snacks. A small admission is charged.

ENTERTAINMENT AND EVENTS

The **Jackson County Fair** (www.jcfair-grounds.com) is held at the county fairgrounds (1 Penninger St., Central Point) just north of town the third weekend in July, with livestock competitions, midway rides, and musical entertainment.

The **Pear Blossom Festival** (www.pearblos-somparade.org) takes place the second weekend in April with arts and crafts exhibits, a parade, and a 10K run. The real attraction is the panorama of the pear orchards in bloom against the backdrop of snowcapped Mount McLoughlin. The parade and run take place downtown, and festivities continue at East Main and Bartlett Streets with more than 100 booths of arts and crafts, food, music, and children's activities.

ACCOMMODATIONS

Medford has no shortage of motel rooms, with some 30 hotels and motels clustered near the interstate exits. Most are national chains, so there's no mystery as to what you're checking into. The cluster of hotels at I-5 Exit 27 is just 10 miles from Ashland, and all are a good alternative if you can't find affordable rooms there. Medford is the kind of place where it's good to check hotel websites to find deals, since the differences in the hotels aren't great and nearly all are at freeway exits.

$50-100

You don't have to stay at a freeway exit, however. Just north of downtown on Highway 99 (here known as N. Riverside Ave.) are a number of inexpensive older but well-maintained motels; if you're looking for good value lodgings, come here and check out your options. The closest of these motels to downtown is **Cedar Lodge** (518 N. Riverside Ave., 541/773-7361, www.cedarlodgeinn.com, $55-70), with woodsy lot and a pool. South of town, the quite nice **Pear Tree Motel** (300 Pear Tree Ln., 541/535-4445 or 800/645-7332, www.peart-reemotel.com, $75-80) also has a pool.

The closest hotel to downtown is the **Red Lion Hotel** (200 N. Riverside Ave., 541/779-5811 or 800/833-5466, www.redlion.com, $89-119), a full-service establishment that offers room service, laundry and valet service, plus two outdoor pools, a health club, and three dining options.

$100-150

A number of new upscale hotels have been built in recent years a bit out of town but convenient to I-5. One of the nicest is ◖ **Rogue Regency Inn** (2300 Biddle Rd., 541/770-1234 or 800/535-5805, www.rogueregency.com, $95-113) which offers an indoor pool and spa, a fitness center, a

© JUDY JEWELL

business center, a complimentary shuttle to the airport, and a bar and restaurant.

Near the airport is **Candlewood Suites** (3548 Heathrow Way, 541/772-2800 or 877/660-8543, $104-128) with large guest rooms, all with kitchenettes.

Another pleasant hotel is **TownePlace Suites** (1395 Center Dr., 541/842-5757 or 800/257-3000, $129-159). On the south side of Medford is **Comfort Inn South** (60 E. Stewart Ave., 541/772-8000 or 866/257-5990, $106-129). **SpringHill Suites** (1389 Center Dr., 541/842-8080, $159-179) has some of the largest guest rooms in Medford.

A romantic bed-and-breakfast with a park-like ambience is **《 Under the Greenwood Tree** (3045 Bellinger Ln., 541/776-0000 or 800/766-8099, www.greenwoodtree.com, $140). The guest rooms have private baths and are decorated with antiques, oriental carpets, and beautiful quilts. The house sits on 10 acres of grounds and gardens and features a hammock suspended between enormous 300-year-old oaks, as well as a gazebo beneath shady apple trees overlooking a rose garden.

FOOD

The local wine industry's recent boom has been the catalyst for a number of excellent new Medford restaurants.

For a locally owned restaurant that offers old-fashioned breakfasts and casual lunches, try the **Real Deal Café** (811 W. Stewart Ave., 541/770-5571, 7am-2pm daily, breakfasts $8-11). Everything is made from scratch at this friendly diner, and in good weather there is seating on a shady patio. Medford's best pizza is at **Kaleidoscope Pizzeria and Pub** (3084 Crater Lake Hwy., 541/779-7787, 11am-9pm Sun.-Thurs., 11am-10pm Fri.-Sat., $10-25), a bit north of town on Route 62. In addition to traditional toppings, Kaleidoscope also features unusual pizza choices like chipotle steak and spicy Thai chicken. There's also a good selection of local microbrews.

Jasper's Cafe (2739 N. Pacific Hwy., 541/776-5307, 10:30am-8pm Mon.-Thurs., 10:30am-9pm Fri.-Sat., 11am-6pm Sun., $5-8)

has been a Medford tradition since 1976, and it aims to do just a few things very well. Namely, serve the best hamburgers and hot dogs in the region. The popularity of this small restaurant north of the city often outgrows its seating area, and luckily there are picnic tables to share with other diners. More than 40 different burgers top the menu, all ground fresh daily. The Jasper Dog, loaded with onions, relish, and mustard, is an old-fashioned marvel. Add a hand-scooped milk shake, and you've got an authentic, delicious slice of Americana.

There's a bit of a scene creeping back into long-dormant downtown Medford, where small independent restaurants and bars have found that old storefronts are good spots to offer hand-crafted food and drinks. An excellent spot for lunch is the **Downtown Market Company** (231 E. Main St., 541/973-2233, 11am-4pm Mon.-Fri., noon-4pm Sat., $9-13) which offers fresh flatbreads, panini sandwiches, grilled sausages, and other casual Mediterranean dishes, plus a deli with salads, cheeses, and desserts. You can get your food to go, or take a seat on the patio in the back.

For a traditional steak house atmosphere in Medford, go downtown to the old rail depot, where **Porters** (147 N. Front St., 541/857-1910, 5pm-9pm daily, $13-29) serves pasta, steaks, and plenty of local seafood options, including steelhead trout crusted with hazelnuts and drizzled with blackberry vinaigrette, or slow-cooked prime rib seasoned with rosemary and garlic.

38 Central (38 Central Ave., 541/776-0038, 11:30am-10pm Mon.-Fri., 4pm-10pm Sat., $12-27) has a very swank dining room and a cool vibe. The menu offers a number of appetizers that could easily be assembled into a meal—or else, choose from comfort-food selections like "all grown up" mac and cheese or more upscale preparations like halibut and herbed butter steamed in parchment paper.

One of the top places for a relaxed meal with excellent food is **《 Elements** (101 E. Main St., 541/779-0135, 4pm-10pm Tues.-Sun., $7-15), a tapas and wine bar. The food is very sophisticated, but the atmosphere is friendly, which makes dishes like serrano-wrapped prawns, cinnamon-cherry seared duck breast, and chorizo-stuffed dates all the more enjoyable.

Downtown also has a couple brewpubs of note. **BricktownE Brewing Company** (44 S. Central Ave., 541/973-2377, www.bricktownebeer.com, 5pm-10pm Mon.-Tues., 11:30am-10pm Wed.-Sat., noon-6pm Sun., $8-14) offers burgers, sandwiches, salads, and a friendly atmosphere. Housed in a historic fire station, **Portal Brewing Company** (140 N. Front St., 541/499-0848, noon-10pm Wed.-Sun., $6-15) offers good brews plus simple food such as naan pizzas, house-made sausages, and pretzels. For even more fun, head to **Johnny Bs** (120 E. 6th St., 541/773-1900, 11:30am-2am Mon.-Fri., 5pm-2pm Sat., $8-12) for subs, salads, burgers, and chili along with Medford's top selection of live local and touring bands.

The spicy, rich specialties of the American South and the Caribbean are served at **Marco's Pepper Grill** (515 S. Riverside Ave., 541/622-8302, 11am-8pm Tues.-Thurs., 11am-9pm Fri.-Sat., 11am-7pm Sun., $9-17), just south of downtown. The menu spans Tex-Mex favorites, Cajun dishes such as shrimp and sausage jambalaya, and creole street food, all served up with a smile.

C Bambu Asian Café and Wine Bar (970 N. Phoenix Rd., 541/608-7545, 11:30am-2pm and 5pm-9pm Mon.-Thurs., 11:30am-2pm and 5pm-9:30pm Fri., 5pm-9:30pm Sat., $11-17) features updated and reinterpreted pan-Asian cooking with a mix of small and large plates that encourages sharing and exploring.

INFORMATION

The **Medford Visitors and Convention Bureau** (1314 Center Dr., 800/469-6307, www.visitmedford.org, 9am-6pm daily) has all kinds of useful maps, directories, and information for the asking. Find their visitors center near the Harry & David store.

GETTING THERE AND AROUND

A half-dozen buses dock daily at the **Greyhound** station (220 S. Front St., 541/779-2103), running along the I-5 corridor. **Rogue Valley Transportation** (200 S. Front St., 541/779-2877, www.rvtd.org) shares the same station and provides connections to Jacksonville, Phoenix, White City, Talent, and Ashland. Buses run Monday-Friday. **TLC Yellow Cab** (541/772-6288) has 24-hour service in the Medford area.

Medford/Jackson County Airport (1000 Terminal Loop Pkwy., 541/772-8068 or 800/882-7488, www.co.jackson.or.us), airport code MFR, is the air hub for southern Oregon and is served by SkyWest, United Express, Horizon, and Allegiant Air.

Jacksonville

Southern Oregon's pioneer past is vividly preserved in Jacksonville. Five miles west of Medford and cradled in the foothills of the Siskiyou Mountains, this small town of 2,200 residents retains an atmosphere of tranquil isolation. With more than 100 original wooden and brick buildings dating back to the 1850s, it is one of two designated National Historic Landmark Districts in Oregon. (The other is Portland's Old Town.)

Named in honor of President Andrew Jackson and the town's namesake county, Jacksonville was surveyed in September 1851 into 200-foot-square blocks. Then as now, California and Oregon Streets were the hubs of Jacksonville business and social life. But the city's tightly packed wooden structures proved to be especially prone to fire. Between 1873 and 1884, three major fires reduced most of the original buildings to ash. These harsh experiences prompted merchants to use brick in the construction of a second generation of buildings, and the practice was bolstered by an 1878 city ordinance requiring brick construction.

ASHLAND

Most of the bricks were made and fired locally. To protect them from the elements and the damp season, the porous bricks were painted; cast-iron window shutters and door frames further reinforced the structures.

Boomtown Jacksonville was the first and largest town in the region, and it was selected as the county seat. It was even nominated and briefly considered for the state capital. The prominence of Jacksonville was made manifest with the 1883 erection of a 60-foot-high courthouse with 14-inch-thick walls. But like the gold finds that quickly dwindled, Jacksonville's exuberance faded when the Oregon and California Railroad bypassed the town in the early 1880s in favor of nearby Medford. Businesses were quick to move east to greet the coming of the iron horse, and Jacksonville's stature as a trading center diminished. By the time the county seat was moved to Medford in 1925, Jacksonville's heady days had long since vanished.

During the Depression, families with low incomes took up residence in the town's derelict buildings, taking advantage of the cheap rents. Gold mining enjoyed a brief comeback, with residents digging shafts and tunnels in backyards, but it was not enough to revive the derailed economy. However, the following decades saw a gradual resurgence of interest in Jacksonville's gold-rush heritage. The Southern Oregon Historical Society was created after World War II, and individuals began to care for the many unaltered late-1880s buildings and restore them to their former glory. The Beekman Bank was one of the first structures to be spruced up, and the prominent United States Hotel was rehabilitated in 1964. The restoration movement was rewarded when the National Park Service designated Jacksonville a National Historic Landmark in 1966.

Today, Jacksonville paints a memorable picture of a Western town with its historic buildings, excellent museum, and beautiful pioneer cemetery. In addition, a renowned music festival, colorful pageants, and rich local folklore all pay tribute to Jacksonville's golden age.

SIGHTS
Peter Britt Gardens

Peter Britt came to Jacksonville not long after gold was discovered in Rich Gulch in 1851. After trying his hand at prospecting, he redirected his efforts toward painting and photography. The latter became his specialty, and for nearly 50 years he photographed the people, places, and events of southern Oregon (Britt was the first person to photograph Crater Lake). He also incorporated new photographic techniques and equipment in his studio as they developed. You'll find his ambrotypes, daguerreotypes, stereographs, and tintypes on display at the Jacksonville Museum.

The Swiss-born Britt was also an accomplished horticulturalist and among the first vintners in southern Oregon. In addition to experimenting with several varieties of fruit and nut trees to see which grew best in the Rogue River Valley, he kept the first weather data records of the region. Another testimonial to his love of plants is the giant redwood tree on the western edge of the **Britt Gardens** (S. 1st St. and W. Pine St.), which he planted 130 years ago to commemorate the birth of his first child, Emil.

His house was a beautifully detailed Gothic revival home that was built in 1860 and then enlarged in the 1880s. Unfortunately, it was destroyed by fires in 1957 and 1960 and can now be remembered only through photographs. Some of the remaining plantings are part of the original gardens, and many others were lovingly cultivated in 1976 by Robert Lovinger, a landscape architecture professor from the University of Oregon. The Peter Britt Music Festival was held on the grounds of the estate from 1962 until 1978, when the new Britt Pavilion was built just south of Britt's house.

A 0.5-mile hike begins 15 yards uphill from the Emil Britt redwood tree. A fairly level path follows the abandoned irrigation ditch that used to divert water from Jackson Creek to the Britt property. Soon you will notice Jackson Creek below the trail, as well as several overgrown sections of a nearly forgotten logging railroad bed. This is a particularly nice walk in the spring when the wildflowers are in bloom and the mosses and ferns are green.

Wine-Tasting

Over 20 wineries are found near Jacksonville, many of them in the Applegate Valley west of town.

Four miles east of Jacksonville is **EdenVale Winery** (2310 Voorhies Rd., 541/512-2955, www.edenvalewines.com, 11am-6pm daily), on the imposing Voorhies estate. EdenVale's most interesting wines are tempranillo, cabernet franc, chardonnay, and red blends. The tasting room also offers sales and samples of wines from other small Rogue Valley vintners.

About eight miles southwest of Jacksonville in the Applegate Valley is **Valley View Winery** (1000 Upper Applegate Rd., 541/899-8468 or 800/781-9463, www.valleyviewwinery.com, 11am-5pm daily). While focused on the grape varieties of southern France, Valley View also makes tempranillo, pinot gris, and port. The Bordeaux-style blends are especially good.

With a tasting room that resembles a French villa, **Troon Vineyard** (1475 Kubli Rd., 541/846-9900, www.troonvineyard.com, 11am-6pm daily) offers zinfandel, cabernet sauvignon, merlot, syrah, and chardonnay, all grown based on organic principles, plus a red blend called Druid Fluid.

The tasting room for **Jacksonville Vineyards** is at **Fiasco Winery** (8035 Hwy. 238, 541/899-9645, www.fiascowinery.com, 11am-5pm daily). You'll taste delicious Bordeaux varietals, plus a light quenching Sangiovese and some interesting red blends.

ENTERTAINMENT AND EVENTS

The **Peter Britt Music Festival** (Britt Pavilion, 1st St. and Fir St., 541/773-6077 or 800/882-7488, www.brittfest.org) began in 1962 on a grassy hillside amid majestic ponderosa pines near the site of the Britt home. Today, the scope of the small classical festival has broadened into a musical smorgasbord encompassing

ASHLAND

© BILL MCRAE

The Applegate Valley is one of southern Oregon's top wine-growing regions.

such diverse styles as jazz, folk, country, bluegrass, rock, and dance, in addition to the original classical repertoire. B. B. King, k. d. lang, the Avett Brothers, the Decemberists, and Ted Nugent are just a few of the artists who have performed here over the years.

The festival runs from the last week of June through the first week of September. Tickets typically range $25-90 for general admission, with most concerts running about $45. Reserved seats are available but are more expensive. Concertgoers often bring along blankets, small lawn chairs (allowed only in designated areas), wine, and a picnic supper to enjoy along with entertainment on balmy summer evenings. Be sure to order your tickets well in advance to avoid having to stand outside. Like the Oregon Shakespeare Festival, some shows sell out months in advance, especially for the well-known performers.

ACCOMMODATIONS

Most of the lodgings in Jacksonville are bed-and-breakfasts. Several properties in town are run by Country House Inns, which has refurbished Jacksonville's only motel.

$100-150

The **Wine Country Inn** (830 N. 5th St., 541/899-2050 or 800/367-1942, www.countryhouseinnsjacksonville.com, $129-179) is the only place in town that deviates from the B&B model. Its exterior was designed to resemble historic stage stops along the stage route from Sacramento to Portland.

The **Touvelle House** (455 N. Oregon St., 541/899-3938 or 800/846-3992, www.touvellehouse.com, $139-199) offers five guest rooms and one suite, all with private baths. Each room has its own theme and features touches like antiques, handmade quilts, and tasteful interior decorations. Out back, near the carriage house, is a heated swimming pool. Common areas include a library and a large living room. A full breakfast is included, and other goodies like fruit and cookies are available for snacking any time.

$150-200

The **Jacksonville Inn** (175 E. California St., 541/899-1900 or 800/321-9344, www.jacksonvilleinn.com, $159-270, breakfast included) lies in the heart of the commercial historic district. In addition to eight air-conditioned guest rooms in the historic hotel itself, all furnished with restored antiques and private baths, the inn also offers four deluxe cottages complete with antiques, fireplaces, and canopied king beds. The inn has an excellent dining room. Reservations are highly recommended, especially during the summer.

A block down California Street from downtown is the **McCully House Inn** (240 E. California St., 541/899-1942 or 800/367-1942, www.countryhouseinnsjacksonville.com, $169-299). Built in 1861 in the classical revival style, this mansion has four beautifully appointed bedrooms with private baths. European and American antiques, oriental rugs, delicate lace curtains, and a magnificent square grand piano (tuned a half step lower than today's A-440) add to the historical ambience. McCully House also rents guest rooms in other cottages and houses in Jacksonville; see the website for full details.

FOOD

The **Jacksonville Inn** (175 E. California St., 541/899-1900 or 800/321-9344, www.jacksonvilleinn.com, 7:30am-10:30am and 5pm-9pm Mon., 7:30am-10:30am, 11:30am-2pm, and 5pm-9pm Tues.-Sat., 7:30am-2pm and 5pm-9pm Sun., $19-35) offers steaks, seafood, and specialties of the inn like veal, duck, and prime rib in a Victorian atmosphere of red brick and velvet. Vegetarian dishes are also available. A cellar of over 2,000 wines further enhances your dining experience. There's also a bistro menu after 4pm for lighter appetites, and lovely patio seating during the summer.

The **Bella Union Restaurant and Saloon** (170 W. California St., 541/899-1770, www.bellau.com, 11:30am-10pm Mon.-Sat., 10am-2pm and 4pm-9pm Sun., $10-23) is another popular spot. Soups, salads, sandwiches, chicken, steaks, pasta, and pizza are some of the items you'll find on the menu. Vegetarians have many choices to select from as well. When the weather is right, the patio behind the restaurant is a pleasant place to eat lunch or enjoy a beer. Also available are picnic baskets, a good choice if you're going to a Britt festival concert. Be sure to call in your order by 2pm.

For the best Thai food in the valley, head for the **Thai House Restaurant** (215 W. California St., 541/899-3585, 11:30am-2pm and 5pm-9pm Mon.-Fri., 5pm-9pm Sat., 5pm-8pm Sun., $12-14).

Ashland's outpost of contemporary fine dining is **Gogi's Restaurant** (235 W. Main St., 541/899-8699, www.gogis.net, 5pm-9pm Wed.-Sat., 10am-2pm and 5pm-9pm Sun., $23-28), and what an exciting addition it is to Jacksonville's staid dining scene. The dining room manages to be warm and modern at the same time, and the food is absolutely of the here and now. Pan-seared salmon is served with truffle orange-fennel salad, and mushroom-stuffed game hen comes with braised radishes and thyme beurre blanc.

INFORMATION
The **Jacksonville Chamber of Commerce** (185 N. Oregon St., 541/899-8118, www.jacksonvilleoregon.org, 10am-5pm Mon.-Fri. year-round, 11am-4pm Sat.-Sun. June-Oct., noon-4pm Sat., Nov.-May) has the scoop on events and activities.

GETTING AROUND
Hop aboard the old-fashioned **Jacksonville Trolley** ($5 adults, $3 children ages 6-12) and learn a bit about local history from a period-dressed guide. Tours depart on the hour (11am-3pm summer) from the historic Beekman Bank at the corner of California and 3rd Streets.

On a hot afternoon, the hills of Jacksonville can seem pretty steep. Join up with **Segway of Jacksonville** (360 N. Oregon St., 541/899-5269, 10am and 2pm Tues.-Sat., $75) and spend a few minutes mastering your steed before heading out on a two-hour guided tour.

Drivers, note that the 25 mph speed limit on the main street through town is strictly enforced.

Grants Pass

The banner across the main thoroughfare in town proudly proclaims: "It's the Climate." But while the 30-inches-per-year precipitation average and 52°F yearly mean temperature might seem desirable, the true allure of Grants Pass is the mighty Rogue River, which flows through the heart of this community. More than 25 outfitters in Grants Pass and the surrounding villages of Rogue River and Merlin specialize in fishing, float, and jet-boat trips. Numerous riverside lodges, accessible by car, river, or footpath, yield remote relaxation in the shadow of the nearby Klamath-Siskiyou Wilderness.

The city itself is similarly attractive: It has a number of good restaurants, an active downtown area, and a large and dynamic **farmers market** (4th and F Sts., 9am-1pm Sat. mid-Mar.-Thanksgiving). On busy summer days, Grants Pass really buzzes with high spirits and activity.

It's hard to miss the 18-foot-high statue near the north Grants Pass exit (Exit 58) off I-5. Sporting a simulated mammoth skin and a dinosaur-bone club and looking like he just strode in off the set of *The Flintstones,* the **Caveman** has been the official welcome to Grants Pass since 1972. Spawned by a semi-notorious local civic group called the Oregon Cavemen, who also parade around in skins, drink saber-toothed tiger "blood," and eat raw meat during their secret initiation rites, the Caveman cost $18,000 to build. While many locals have lambasted the city's mascot as portraying a backward redneck image for Grants Pass, it's worth noting that over a dozen businesses and the local high school have proudly embraced the Caveman symbol.

ASHLAND

SIGHTS
Palmerton Arboretum

Six miles down Route 99 in the town of Rogue River is the **Palmerton Arboretum** (West Evans Creek Rd., Rogue River, 541/776-7001, 8am-dusk, free). Originally a five-acre nursery, the arboretum features plant specimens from around the globe, including Japanese pines and Mediterranean cedars in addition to redwoods and other trees native to the Pacific Northwest. A real treat in the spring, the ornamental arboretum offers over 40 species of mature trees complemented by several kinds of azaleas and rhododendrons. Admission is free. While you're there, be sure to see **Skevington's Crossing,** a 200-foot-high swinging suspension bridge over Evans Creek that connects the arboretum to Anna Classick city park.

Wildlife Images Rehabilitation and Education Center

Originally a rehabilitation station for injured birds of prey, **Wildlife Images Rehabilitation and Education Center** (11845 Lower River Rd., 541/476-0222, www.wildlifeimages.org, 9am-5pm daily, $12 adults, $7 children ages 4-17) has expanded into an outreach program to aid all kinds of injured or orphaned wildlife as well as to educate the public. Bears, cougars, raccoons, and many other indigenous creatures have been helped by this organization. Once the animals are well enough to survive in the wild, they are released. During the summer, tours are offered hourly on the half hour; in winter, tours are every two hours. Tours last between an hour and an hour and a half; reservations are required for all tours. To get here from 6th Street downtown, head south, turn right onto G Street, continue to Upper River Road, and then onto Lower River Road.

Oregon Vortex

About 10 miles south of Grants Pass on I-5 is the **House of Mystery** at the **Oregon Vortex** (4303 Sardine Creek Rd., Gold Hill, 541/855-1543, www.oregonvortex.com, 9am-4pm daily Mar.-May and Sept.-Oct., 9am-5pm daily June-Aug., $9.75 adults, $8.75 seniors,

ASHLAND

the Oregon Vortex

© BILL MCRAE

$7 children ages 6-11). Called the "Forbidden Ground" by the Rogue Native American people because the place spooked their horses, it is actually in a repelling geomagnetic field where objects tend to move away from their center of alignment and lean in funny directions. For example, a ball at the end of a string does not hang straight up and down, and people seem taller when viewed from one side of the room as opposed to the other. Visitors may bring balls, levels, cameras (but not video cameras)—or any other instrument they wish—to test the vortex for themselves. To visit the vortex, you'll need to sign up for a 45-minute tour and demonstration, culminating in a visit to the House of Mystery. It's truly a weird spot, and if nothing else, the drive through stands of madrone trees to the vortex is beautiful.

SPORTS AND RECREATION
Rafting

There are many ways to enjoy the Rogue River. Some people prefer the excitement and challenge of maneuvering their own craft down the treacherous rapids. Oar rafts (which a guide rows for you), paddle rafts (which you paddle yourself), and one-person inflatable kayaks are the most widely used boats for this sort of river exploration. The 40-mile section downstream from Grave Creek is open only to nonmotorized vessels, and river traffic is strictly regulated by the National Forest Service. For more information, stop at the **Rand Visitor Center** (14335 Galice Rd., Merlin, 541/479-3735).

Limited float permits (25 issued daily) are needed to float the Wild and Scenic portion of the Rogue, which begins 7 miles west of Grants Pass and runs to 11 miles east of Gold Beach. These permits are prized by rafters around the world—this stretch of the Rogue not only has some of the best white water in the United States, but also guarantees a first-rate wilderness adventure. And yet, it can be a civilized wilderness. Hot showers, comfortable beds, and sumptuous meals at several of the river lodges tucked away in remote quarters of this famous waterway welcome boaters after a day's voyage. Excellent camping facilities are available for those who want to experience nature more directly.

OUTFITTERS

Many outfitters can be found off I-5 Exit 61 toward Merlin and Galice just north of Grants Pass. Rafters hit Class III and IV rapids a little before Galice and, for 35 miles thereafter, the stiffest white water encountered on the Rogue. **Adventure Center** (541/488-2819 or 800/444-2819, www.raftingtours.com) has half-, full-, and multiday trips on oar or paddle rafts. Their adventures range from the mild to the wild. A half-day trip on the Rogue is $75.

Galice Resort and Store Raft Trips (11744 Galice Rd., Merlin, 541/476-3818, www.galice.com) offers full-day raft or inflatable-kayak trips as well as river-craft rentals. A half-day float is $69 and a full day on the river is $99, which includes lunch at the resort.

Another river retreat with attractive packages is **Morrison's Rogue River Lodge** (8500 Galice Rd., Merlin, 541/476-3825 or 800/826-1963, www.rogueriverraft.com), about 16 miles from Grants Pass. Everything from half-day ($75) and one-day ($90) floats and excursions to two- to four-day trips is available; see the website for further details. The longer excursions include either stays at other river lodges or camping along the great green Rogue. Transportation back to Morrison's is included, or your car can be shuttled downriver to meet you at the end of the trip.

Noah's River Adventures (53 E. Main St., Ashland, 800/858-2811, www.noahsrafting.com) has been providing quality rafting and fishing trips since 1974. They have half-day ($89) and one- to four-day excursions that vary from exciting white-water rafting highs to kinder, gentler floats. See the website for rates and package details.

Orange Torpedo Trips (209 Merlin Rd., Merlin, 541/479-5061 or 866/479-5061, www.orangetorpedo.com) has half-day and one- to three-day adventures on rafts or inflatable kayaks (also affectionately known as "orange torpedoes" because of their color and shape). A

ROGUE VALLEY MOREL PICKING

Wild mushroom picking can be a fun pastime or a money-making proposition in various parts of Oregon. Morels, a cone-shaped fungus with deeply crenulated caps and short hollow stems, are one of several coveted varieties that fare especially well in the Rogue Valley. The fact that they're easily identifiable, fry up great in omelets, and come out in spring makes them especially popular among residents. Although usually found in forested areas such as the foothill below Mount McLoughlin, morels also can be harvested from backyard orchards in Rogue Valley fruit country.

The combination of night temperatures above freezing, high humidity, and daytime temps of 46-60°F is optimum to bring this fungus to fruit. They often pop up in the wake of forest fires or in landscapes disturbed by logging and road building. If it's warm, these mushrooms can be found in late March. When spring conditions hit the lower slopes of the Cascades in the months to follow, pickers usually aren't far behind, in pursuit of what many consider to be the most savory mushroom of all. If you can't find morels in the wild, you should check a local farmers market, where they are generally available from professional mushroom foragers.

---

six-hour day trip that covers nine miles of the Rogue is $99.

Ferron's Fun Trips (210 Merlin Rd., Merlin, 541/479-5061 or 866/479-5061, www.roguefuntrips.com) is a family-run business with guided raft tours and rentals ($25 a day and up). Half-day trips are offered both morning and afternoon ($75) and full-day trips ($95) include lunch. Ferron and his guides bring inflatable kayaks along on all the guided trips for anyone who gets the urge to paddle solo.

Rogue/Klamath River Adventures (541/779-3708 or 800/231-0769, www.rogueklamath.com) has one- to three-day white-water rafting and inflatable-kayak trips that give you the option of camping out under the stars or roughing it in style at a river lodge.

For more information on scenic fishing and white-water rafting trips, contact the **Rand Visitor Center** (14335 Galice Rd., Merlin, 541/479-3735) or the **Visitors Information Center** (1995 NW Vine St., Grants Pass, 800/547-5927, www.visitgrantspass.org).

These information outlets can also supply tips on riverside hiking. The Rogue trails out of Grants Pass aren't as remote as their Gold Beach counterparts, and litter can sometimes mar the route. Nonetheless, the fall colors in certain areas along the Rogue along with a profusion of swimming and fishing holes can add a special dimension to your hike.

Fishing

The upper Rogue River is renowned for one of the world's best late-winter steelhead fisheries. Numerous highways and back roads offer easy access to 155 miles of well-ramped river between Lost Creek Reservoir, east of Medford, and Galice, west of Grants Pass. With fall and spring chinook runs and other forms of river recreation, it's no accident that the Rogue Valley is home to the world's top aluminum and fiberglass drift boat manufacturers. Add rafters, kayakers, and plenty of bank anglers and you can understand why peak salmon or steelhead season is sometimes described as "combat fishing." Contact southern Oregon visitors information outlets for rules, regulations, and leads on outfitters; many of the rafting outfitters listed above also offer guided fishing trips.

Golf

About 15 minutes north of Grants Pass is **Red Mountain Golf Course** (324 Mountain Green Ln., 541/479-2297, $20 for 9 holes), a small but challenging 2,245-yard executive course.

Dutcher Creek Golf Course (4611 Upper River Rd., 541/474-2188, www.

dutchercreekgolf.com, $25) is an 18-hole par-70 public course.

Jet-Boating

You don't have to risk life and limb in a fancy inner tube to see the Rogue: Several local companies offer jet-boat tours. On a jet boat, powerful engines suck in hundreds of gallons of water per minute and shoot it out the back of the boat through a narrow nozzle, generating the necessary thrust for propulsion. With no propeller to hit rocks and other obstacles, these 20-ton machines can carry 40 or more passengers in water only six inches deep. This makes the jet boat an ideal way to enjoy the beauty of the Rogue while keeping your feet dry. Also, many outfitters charter drift boats to visit secret fishing holes for anglers to try their luck landing supper.

Hellgate Excursions (953 SE 7th St., 541/479-7204 or 800/648-4874, www.hellgate.com, May 1-late Sept.) is the premier jet-boat operator on this end of the river. Their trips begin at the dock of the **Riverside Inn** (971 SE 6th St.) and proceed downriver through the forested Siskiyou foothills. En route, black-tailed deer, ospreys, and great blue herons are commonly seen. If you're lucky, a bald eagle or a black bear might also be sighted. The scenic highlight is the deep-walled Hellgate Canyon, where you'll look upon what are believed to be the oldest rocks in the state. The least expensive way to experience this adventure is with a "scenic" cruise ticket ($39), but for a bit more money you can step up to a brunch, lunch, or dinner cruise. Another option is the white-water adventure trip that goes beyond Hellgate ($64 adults, lunch available but not included). These excursions feature commentary by your pilot, who knows every eddy in the river. Be sure to call ahead for reservations, as space on all of their runs books up fast.

ENTERTAINMENT AND EVENTS

The **Josephine County Fair** normally takes place in mid-August at the fairgrounds (1451 Fairgrounds Rd., 541/476-3215) in Grants Pass. In addition to the usual fair attractions such as the carnival, concessions, and 4-H livestock, entertainers perform for enthusiastic crowds. A popular annual competition is the four-wheel tractor pull, in which souped-up farm vehicles attempt to drag a bulldozer (with its blade down) for 100 yards as fast as possible.

ACCOMMODATIONS

You'll find most motel accommodations clustered around the two Grants Pass exits on I-5, though there are a number of good choices right downtown.

$50-100

Near downtown, find the charming **Buona Sera Inn** (1001 NE 6th St., 541/476-4260 or 877/286-7756, http://buonaserainn.com, $69-95), with wall murals that travel from Grants

ROGUE RIVER ROOSTER CROW

The city of Rogue River, southeast of Grants Pass on I-5, has something to crow about. On the last weekend of June, the **Rogue River Rooster Crow** is held at the Rogue River Elementary School grounds. On Saturday, a parade and street fair (featuring arts, crafts, and food booths) takes over downtown. But the big event occurs early in the afternoon. Farmers from all over Oregon and northern California bring their roosters to strut their stuff and crow to the enthusiastic crowds. Following a fowl tradition established in 1953, the rooster to crow the most times in his allotted time period wins the prize for his proud owner. Then it's the humans' turn, in which well-practiced revelers take their turn in trying mimic a rooster's crow. In the evening there's live music and entertainment in the park, and Sunday brings the Rooster Crow Car Show with legions of antique cars.

Pass to Italy. The rooms at this courtyard-style motel are more "grandma's house" than Motel 6, with wood floors and nice linens.

Across the river from downtown is a charming option with riverfront access. **Motel Del Rogue** (2600 Rogue River Hwy., 541/479-2111 or 866/479-2111, www.moteldelrogue.com, $90-145) is a classic 1930s motel that has been lovingly updated but not transformed. Most of the units overlook the river. The motel sits on two acres of parklike property and is very clean, comfortable, and quiet.

There are plenty of midrange hotel chain choices at the I-5 exits, and most of them have pools, allow pets, and include breakfast bars. Two such options are the **Comfort Inn** (1889 NE 6th St., 541/479-8301, $83-95) and the **Best Western Inn at the Rogue** (8959 Rogue River Hwy., 541/582-2200 or 800/238-0700, $100-120).

Just off I-5 about 20 miles north of Grants Pass you'll find the **Wolf Creek Inn** (100 Front St., Wolf Creek, 541/866-2474, www.thewolfcreekinn.com, $95-135), a historic stagecoach hotel.

$100-150

Also out by I-5, these hotels both have pools and continental breakfast: **Best Western Grants Pass** (111 NE Agness Ave., 541/476-1117, $112-124) and **La Quinta Inn** (243 NE Morgan Ln., 541/472-1808 or 800/531-5900, www.laquinta.com, $109-149).

The **Riverside Inn** (986 SW 6th St., 541/476-6873 or 800/334-4567, www.riverside-inn.com, $129-149) is both right downtown and right on the river. Rooms have decks overlooking the river, and the Hellgate jet-boat excursions depart from just below the hotel. Pets are permitted in some rooms.

Next door, the ◖ **Lodge at Riverside** (955 SE 7th St., 541/955-0600 or 877/955-0600, http://thelodgeatriverside.com, $139-199) offers very stylish rooms and suites, many with balconies facing the river. The lobby is in a huge log cabin with a stone fireplace, and in the middle of lush gardens beside the river is an outdoor pool. Just like at the chains, you'll

get a free continental breakfast; there's also an evening wine reception.

Many guests use **Morrison's Rogue River Lodge** (8500 Galice Rd., 541/476-3825 or 800/826-1963, www.morrisonslodge.com, $77-210) as a base for raft trips. Morrison's was built in the 1940s as a fishing lodge and now has a small complex of cottages, suites, and lodge rooms, with an outdoor heated pool, basketball court, putting green, bicycles, and wireless Internet.

About 15 minutes north of town and a couple of miles off I-5 Exit 66 is **Flery Manor** (2000 Jumpoff Joe Creek Rd., 541/476-3591, www.flerymanor.com, $140-250). Canopy beds, unique furnishings, and a quiet secluded setting give this country bed-and-breakfast a genteel air. All rooms have nice little touches like plush robes, fresh flowers, and morning coffee and tea service. The breakfast features a health-conscious menu. With a private balcony, a double Jacuzzi, and a fireplace, the Moonlight Suite is the right prescription for a romantic hideaway. Reservations are a must.

$150-200

One of the premium lodgings in the area is ◖ **Weasku Inn** (5560 Rogue River Hwy., 541/471-8000 or 800/493-2758, www.weasku.com, $199-329), a venerable river lodge that was the secret retreat of Clark Gable, Walt Disney, Carole Lombard, and other entertainment figures in the 1930s and 1940s. Only 17 guest rooms are available, ranging from lodge rooms and suites to an A-frame cabin. All look out on the Rogue River and have genuine rustic-chic decor. A deluxe continental breakfast is served, as is evening wine and cheese.

The longtime Redwood Motel has undergone a transformation to become **Redwood Hyperion Suites** (815 NE 6th St., 541/476-0878 or 888/535-8824, www.redwoodmotel.com, $85-225). The venerable motel rooms have been updated and upgraded, and a new structure, with luxury-level suites, has been added. The parklike setting, complete with a grove of redwoods and a 350-year-old Palmer oak, is another plus. Add in a pool, a hot tub,

THE WOLF CREEK INN

Approximately 20 miles north of Grants Pass on I-5 in Wolf Creek is the Pacific Northwest's oldest continuously operated hostelry, the **Wolf Creek Inn** (100 Front St., Wolf Creek, 541/866-2474, www.historicwolfcreekinn.com, $95-135). Originally a hotel for the California and Oregon Stagecoach Line, this historic property, built in 1883, is now owned by the state parks department and is operated as a hotel and restaurant. Legend has it that President Rutherford B. Hayes visited the tavern in the late 1880s, and One-Eyed Charlie used to chew the fat in the dining room. You can also view the small room where author Jack London stayed and wrote part of his novel *The End of the Story*.

Wolf Creek's boardinghouse may have had its heyday in the stagecoach era, but it continues to serve road-weary travelers. The period furniture imparts atmosphere, while the beds and private baths are modern and comfortable; breakfast is included in the room rates. There are no TVs or phones in the rooms, however, in keeping with historic authenticity.

The restaurant (8am-10am, 11am-4pm and 5pm-8pm summer, call for winter hours) serves admirable Pacific Northwest cuisine, with veggies from the inn's gardens and home-smoked meats.

© BILL MCRAE

ASHLAND

a fitness center, and complimentary breakfast and you've got one of the city's unique lodging options.

Cabins

About 20 minutes outside of Grants Pass and well within the Wild and Scenic section of the Rogue River is the **Doubletree Ranch** (6000 Abegg Rd., Merlin, 541/476-0120, http://doubletree-ranch.com, Apr.-Oct., cabins $115-145). Originally homesteaded 100 years ago, this 160-acre four-generation working ranch offers cozy cabins, all set up for housekeeping with full kitchens. There's also a five-bedroom house available that is perfect for family groups.

No roads lead to the main lodge and sixteen cabins at **Black Bar Lodge** (541/479-6507, www.blackbarlodge.net, $125 per person includes two meals), but it's a good stop for rafters or hikers along the 40-mile Rogue River Trail. The lodge is built on the site of an old mining claim—the story goes that after the original miner, Mr. Black, was murdered, his body was put into his boat and pushed off down the river. The Black Bar is 10 miles downriver from Grave Creek, and is pretty much off the grid. Generators power lights and electricity, and are turned off at night.

Camping

The privately owned and operated RV campgrounds tend to be more expensive than their public counterparts but offer more amenities like swimming pools, laundries, showers, and other conveniences. **RiverPark RV Resort** (2956 Rogue River Hwy., 541/479-0046 or 800/677-8857, www.riverparkrvresort.com, $33-44) boasts a tennis/basketball court, hot showers, laundry facilities, and 700 feet of Rogue River frontage to enjoy.

Many fine campgrounds are found along the banks of the Rogue River near Grants Pass, but the only state park in the area is the **Valley of the Rogue** (3792 N. River Rd., Gold Hill, 541/582-1118 or 800/452-5687, www.oregonstateparks.org). About halfway between Medford and Grants Pass off I-5, the park is set along the banks of its namesake river. The

Rogue supports year-round salmon and spring steelhead runs. There are 98 sites for trailers and motor homes ($24), 21 tent sites ($19), and a few yurts ($36). This place fills up fast, so reservations are recommended during the warmer months. Hookups, utilities, showers, laundry, and some wheelchair-accessible facilities round out the amenities.

Indian Mary Park is the showcase of Josephine County parks. To get here, go about eight miles east of Merlin on the Merlin-Galice Road. Located on the banks of the Rogue River, this campground has 89 sites, several with sewer hookups and utilities, as well as showers, flush toilets, and piped water. A boat ramp, beautiful hiking trails, a playground, and one of the best beaches on the Rogue make this one of the most popular county campgrounds on the river.

Griffen Park is a smaller campground with 20 sites for tents and trailers. To get here, take the Redwood Highway (U.S. 199) to Riverbanks Road, then turn onto Griffen Road and follow it about 5 miles to where it meets the Rogue. The park has a boat ramp, showers, flush toilets, piped water, and RV dumping facilities.

Schroeder Park is another full-service campground near town. Located on Schroeder Lane off Redwood Avenue, the park has 31 sites, some with hookups and utilities. Showers, flush toilets, and a boat ramp make this a favorite spot for fishing enthusiasts. In addition to a picnic area and an excellent swimming hole, there's a dog park here.

Whitehorse Park, 6 miles west of Grants Pass on Upper River Road, has 44 campsites, many with hookups and utilities. Showers, piped water, lighting, and good hiking trails are also found here. The river channel shifted away from the park in the wake of the Christmas flood of 1964, but it's only about 0.5-mile walk to a fine beach on the Rogue.

Sites at Indian Mary, Griffen, Schroeder, and Whitehorse cost $19 for tent sites and $22 for hookup sites. For reservations, call 800/452-5687 or visit www.reserveamerica.com. For more information, contact the **Josephine**

County Parks Department (541/474-5285, www.co.josephine.or.us).

FOOD

Grants Pass has a number of good dining choices, particularly along downtown's G Street. On a summer evening, take a stroll around the neighborhood on this bustling avenue and check out all the options. It's also a good morning destination for fresh roasted organic coffee at **Rogue Coffee Roasters** (237 SW G St., 541/476-6134, 7am-pm Mon.-Fri., 8am-2 Sat.) and pastries from **Dancin Bakery** (1300 SW G St., 541/244-2225).

Sunshine Natural Foods (128 SW H St., 541/474-5044, 9am-6pm Mon.-Fri., 9:30am-5pm Sat.) has a café, a salad bar, a juice bar, and an organic food market plus a full line of food supplements and vitamins.

American

Aficionados of the old-time soda fountain will appreciate the **Grants Pass Pharmacy** (414 SW 6th St., 541/476-4262, 9am-7pm Mon.-Fri., 9am-6pm Sat., $7). Decent sandwiches, sodas, and milk shakes are featured. Local old-timers meet here every afternoon, and it's the kids' first stop after school.

The **Laughing Clam** (121 SW G St., 541/479-1110, 11am-9pm Mon.-Thurs., 11am-10pm Fri.-Sat., $7-27) is an old bar and grill that has been transformed into a lively family-friendly tavern with good sandwiches, pasta, and steaks. The name might suggest that this is a seafood house, which it's not, though a few fish dishes are offered.

Another old-time bar made young again, the **C Circle J** (241 SW G St., 541/479-8080, 11am-9pm Mon.-Thurs., 11am-10pm Fri.-Sat., $8-12) is a redbrick cubbyhole with eclectic and funky decor and a hip and lively clientele. The specialties are pizza, burgers, and sandwiches (including some vegan ones) with sweet potato fries, all washed down with microbrews.

With marvelous views, **Taprock Northwest Grill** (971 SE 6th St., 541/955-5998, 8am-10pm Sun.-Thurs., 8am-11pm Fri.-Sat., $9-26) occupies a very handsome log-built dining room

with spacious decks overlooking the river from between the downtown bridges. The menu is geared toward steaks and comfort food, with much of the food grown and produced in the Pacific Northwest; a good selection of sandwiches and salads is also available.

As its name suggests, **The Bohemian** (233 SW G St., 541/471-7158, www.bohemian-bargp.com, 11:30am-11pm Mon.-Fri., 3pm-11pm Sat., $8-17) is a hip bistro and bar with a selection of small and "not so small" plates. You'll find a selection of salads and sandwiches, plus pasta and delectable braised beef with herbed mashed potatoes. There's frequently live music in the evenings.

International

A somewhat swanky G Street dining room is **C Blondie's Bistro** (226 SW G St., 541/479-0420, 11am-9pm daily, $10-21). The international menu includes touches of Indian food such as masala-spiced rack of lamb and Italian food such as chicken marsala or Tuscan grilled shrimp with white beans and wilted greens. A surprising number of vegan options are available.

Brewpubs and Wine Bars

Wild River Brewing and Pizza Company (595 NE F St., 541/471-7487, www.wildriverbrewing.com, 10am-10pm Sun.-Thurs., 10am-11pm Fri.-Sat., $8-16) is a regional standby, with good wood-fired pizza ($16-24 for a large pie), pastas, burgers, and sandwiches and locations in several southern Oregon towns (Grants Pass, Cave Junction, and Brookings Harbor).

A wine bar bordering on a full restaurant, **C The Twisted Cork** (210 SW 6th St., 541/295-3094, www.thetwistedcorkgrantspass.com, 11am-3pm Mon., 11am-8pm Tues.-Thurs., 11am-9pm Fri.-Sat., small plates $4-12, main courses $15-20) makes the most of local wines and ingredients. In addition to some 30-odd small plates, flatbreads, salads and soups, the Twisted Cork also offers pasta and house specialty main courses such as blackberry-ancho chile grilled pork and pomegranate

ASHLAND

BED-AND-BREAKFAST IN THE TREES

Located in Takilma near Cave Junction, **Out 'n About Treehouse Institute and Treesort** (300 Page Creek Rd., Cave Junction 97523, 541/598-2208 or 800/200-5484, www.treehouses.com) is a unique lodging option that's worth driving a bit out of your way to discover. After all, how many bed-and-breakfasts do you find in tree houses?

This comfortable rural retreat blends the whimsy of the 1960s with 21st-century creature comforts. The 10 well-appointed tree-house guest rooms are bolted to 100-year-old white oaks, some 18 feet above the ground. Should you have misgivings about the structural integrity of these accommodations, be advised that the innkeeper gathered nearly 11,000 pounds of his friends to stand on the several units simultaneously—35 times the weight requirements of the local code. Those desiring a more down-to-earth lodging option can stay in a peeled-fir cabin with a cozy woodstove. For the deluxe treatment, reserve a 300-square-foot structure built of redwood and Douglas fir that features a sink, a tub, a fridge, a queen-size futon, a loft, and a 200-square-foot deck with mountain views. The "treepee," a tepee done up in Out 'n About style, is always popular with the kids.

Horseback trail rides, trips to the best Illinois River swimming holes, zip line adventures, and white-water rafting trips can be arranged through the management. Or swim in the river that runs through the property. Rates are $120-160 double (some of the larger tree houses sleep four or more) and up with a two- or three-night minimum stay (Memorial Day-Labor Day) and include continental breakfast. Your stay here will help you better understand tree houses, treeology, and treeminology, and like many other guests, you may well leave a "treemusketeer."

cinnamon flank steak. This is one of southern Oregon's most exciting young restaurants.

INFORMATION

The **Grants Pass/Josephine County Visitor Information Center/Chamber of Commerce** (1995 NW Vine St., 541/476-7717, www.visitgrantspass.com) is open 8am-5pm daily in summer, 8am-5pm Monday-Friday in winter.

GETTING THERE

Greyhound (460 NE Agness Ave., 541/476-4513) offers access to the I-5 corridor.

CAVE JUNCTION

Sample some of the local wines at **Foris Vineyards** (654 Kendall Rd., 541/592-3752 or 800/843-6747, www.foriswine.com) and **Bridgeview Vineyards and Winery** (4210 Holland Loop Rd., 541/592-4688 or 877/273-4843, www.bridgeviewwine.com). Both wineries offer tastings 11am-5pm daily year-round, although confirm their operating hours in winter.

◖ OREGON CAVES NATIONAL MONUMENT

About 30 miles southwest of Grants Pass is the **Oregon Caves National Monument** (Rte. 46, 541/592-3400, www.nps.gov/orca, $8.50 adults, $6 children ages 6-11). The cave itself—as there is really only one, which opens onto successive caverns—was formed over the eons by the action of water. As rain and snowmelt seeped through cracks and fissures in the rock above the cave and percolated down into the underlying limestone, huge sections of the limestone became saturated and collapsed—much as a sand castle too close to the sea always caves in. When the water table eventually fell, these pockets were drained, and the process of cave decoration began.

First, the limestone was dissolved by the water and carried in solution into the cave. When the water evaporated, it left behind a microscopic layer of calcite. This process was repeated countless times, gradually creating the beautiful formations visible today. When the minerals are deposited on the ceiling, a

© OREGON CAVE NATIONAL MONUMENT

Oregon Caves National Monument

stalactite begins to form. Limestone-laden water that evaporates on the floor might leave behind a stalagmite. When a stalactite and a stalagmite meet, they become a column. Other cave sculptures you'll see include helicites, hell-bent formations that twist and turn in crazy directions; draperies, looking just like their household namesakes but cast in stone instead of cloth; and soda straws, stalactites that are hollow in the center like a straw, carrying mineral-rich drops of moisture to their tips.

Discovered in 1874, the Oregon Caves attract thousands of visitors annually. During the Depression, walkways and turnoffs were built to make the cave more accessible. Unfortunately, tons of waste rock and rubble were stashed in nooks and crannies in the cave instead of being transported out. This had the effect of obscuring the very formations meant for display. However, the National Park Service started to remove the artificial debris in 1985, exposing the natural formations once again.

The River Styx, another victim of Depression-era meddling, is enjoying a similar resurrection. This stream used to run through the cave but was diverted into pipes to aid trail and tunnel construction. The pipes ended up buried beneath tons of pulverized rock, and now the Park Service is hard at work undoing the work of humans to let the stream flow where nature intended.

Tours

Tours of the cave are conducted year-round by National Park Service interpreters. Their presentations are both informative and entertaining, and you will leave the cave with a better understanding of its natural, geological, and human history. A recent discovery in an unexplored part of the caverns was a grizzly bear fossil believed to be over 40,000 years old. Children younger than age six must pass ability requirements (e.g., walking up many stairs for a total vertical climb of 218 feet) and stand a minimum of 42 inches tall to gain entry. The tour, limited to 16 people, takes a little over an hour and requires some uphill walking. Good walking shoes and warm clothing are recommended. It may be warm and toasty outside, but the cave maintains a fairly consistent year-round temperature of 41°F. Passageways can be narrow, ceilings low, and the footing slippery. During summer you can wait in line up to an hour to go on a tour, and fewer tours are offered October-April. Call ahead for tour times.

Accommodations

The six-story **Chateau at Oregon Caves** (541/592-3400, www.oregoncaveschateau.com, May-Oct., $109-170) offers food and accommodations at the caves. About 20 miles east of Cave Junction on OR 46, the château stands at an elevation of 4,000 feet. Built in 1934, this rustic structure blends in with the forest and moss-covered marble ledges. Indigenous wood and stone permeate the building so that you never lose a sense of where you are. The guest rooms feature views of Cave Creek canyon, waterfalls, or the Oregon Caves entrance. For a unique experience, we recommend the sixth floor. The rooms may be small, but they have more character and extend out at odd angles from the building. The Pendleton blankets, tall painted chairs, and wooden bed frames add to the historical nuance.

The château has been nicknamed the "Marble Halls of Oregon," and you can see the huge marble fireplace in the fourth-floor lobby for yourself while you thaw out after your spelunking expedition. The food at the château is high quality, and having Cave Creek running through the center of the dining room definitely adds to the unique atmosphere. Downstairs, the old-fashioned 1930s-style soda fountain (daily May-Oct. 15) dishes up classic American burgers, fries, and shakes.

For a nice after-dinner hike, take the Big Tree Trail, named for a huge Douglas fir estimated to be more than 1,000 years old. With a circumference of 38 feet 7 inches, it is among the largest standing trees in Oregon. The three-mile round-trip wends its way through virgin forest that has tan oak, canyon live oak, Pacific madrone, chinquapin, and manzanita, as well as Douglas fir and ponderosa pine. The hike is not that difficult, and the solitude and views of the surrounding mountains are as inspiring as the Big Tree. For a jaunt that is just under one mile, try the Cliff Nature Trail. Placards will help you identify the plantlife as you traverse the mossy cliffs, and there are also some good vistas of the Siskiyou Mountains.

Camping

Camping is available at **Grayback** (Wild Rivers Ranger District, 541/592-4000, www.fs.fed.us, $10, water available), a woodsy Forest Service campground 12 miles from Cave Junction on Route 46. There are 39 sites close to Sucker Creek, with one RV hookup and a one-mile hiking trail. Closer to the caves is a smaller Forest Service campground, **Cave Creek** ($10, water); take Route 46 four miles south of the caves to Forest Service Road 4032.

Getting There

To get to Oregon Caves National Monument, take U.S. 199 to Cave Junction, then wind your way 20 miles up Route 46 (a beautiful old-growth Douglas fir forest lining the road might help distract the faint of heart from the nail-biting turns). The last 13 miles of this trip are especially exciting. Remember that there are few turnouts of sufficient size to enable a large vehicle to reverse direction.

Roseburg

Many people passing through the Roseburg area (pop. 21,000) might quickly dismiss it as a rural backwater. A closer look, however, reveals many layers beneath the mill town veneer. The number of folks who rely on the woods as a workplace is declining, and although the town still has a no-nonsense sensibility, growing pockets of refinement are now found in between the pickup trucks and lumber mills. An award-winning museum, Oregon's only drive-through zoo, and wineries setting down roots nearby are a few examples.

The true allure of Roseburg is not really in town but in the surrounding countryside. The beautiful North Umpqua River to the east offers rafting, camping, hiking, and fishing. In addition to catching trout, salmon, and bass, anglers come from all over to enjoy one of the world's last rivers with a native run of summer steelhead. Numerous waterfalls along the river and the frothy white water make the Native American word Umpqua ("thundering water") an appropriate name.

SIGHTS
Douglas County Museum of History and Natural History
The nationally acclaimed **Douglas County Museum of History and Natural History** (123 Museum Dr., 541/957-7007, www.co.douglas.or.us/museum, 10am-5pm Tues.-Sat., $5 adults, $4 seniors, children ages 17 and under free) is located at the Douglas County Fairgrounds (Exit 123 off I-5). Its four wings feature exhibits that range from a one-million-year-old saber-toothed tiger to 19th-century steam-logging equipment. The museum houses the state's largest natural history collection, and the second-largest collection of historic photos.

Lotus Knight Memorial Gardens
The **Lotus Knight Memorial Gardens** (5am-10pm daily, free) are in Riverside Park, between Oak Street and Washington Street on the banks of the South Umpqua River. They are alight with colorful azaleas and rhododendrons in the spring.

Winchester Fish Ladder
The **Winchester Fish Ladder** is just off I-5 at Exit 129 on the north bank of the North Umpqua River. Visitors can watch salmon and steelhead in their native environment as they swim by the viewing window at Winchester Dam. Spring chinook and summer steelhead migrate upriver May-August, and coho, fall chinook, and more summer steelhead swim past September-November. Winter steelhead is the primary species seen going through the fish ladders and on past the window December-May. The Umpqua River offers the largest variety of game fish in Oregon.

◖ Wildlife Safari
Tucked away in a 600-acre wooded valley is Oregon's drive-through zoo, **Wildlife Safari** (Safari Rd., Winston, 541/679-6761 or 800/355-4848, www.wildlifesafari.net, 9am-5pm daily, $18 adults, $15 seniors, and $12 children ages 4-12, no pets allowed).

Once you are inside the park gates, the brightly colored birds and exotic game animals transport you to other lands, with an oddly appropriate Oregon backdrop. Be that as it may, at Wildlife Safari every possible step has been taken to re-create African and North American animal life zones, but with natural prey kept apart from natural predators. Similar precautions are taken with humans and their animal companions. People must remain inside their vehicles except in designated areas, and windows and sunroofs must be kept closed in the big cat and bear areas. Pets must be left in kennels at the entrance ($5 fee for padlock rental).

The first loop takes you to see the tigers and cheetahs. These giant felines loll lazily about or catch catnaps in the tall grass. The next link takes you through the heart of "Africa," where

ASHLAND

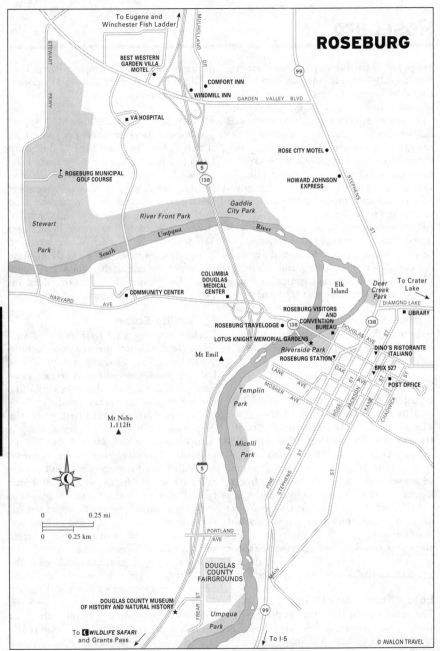

ROSEBURG

To Eugene and
Winchester Fish Ladder

BEST WESTERN
GARDEN VILLA
MOTEL

MULHOLLAND DR

STEWART PKWY

99

COMFORT INN
WINDMILL INN

GARDEN VALLEY BLVD

VA HOSPITAL

ROSE CITY MOTEL

5
138

ROSEBURG MUNICIPAL
GOLF COURSE

HOWARD JOHNSON
EXPRESS

STEPHENS ST

Gaddis
City Park

River Front Park

Stewart
Park

Umpqua River

South

HARVARD AVE

COMMUNITY CENTER

COLUMBIA
DOUGLAS
MEDICAL
CENTER

Elk
Island

Deer
Creek
Park

To Crater
Lake

DIAMOND LAKE

138

LIBRARY

ROSEBURG VISITORS
AND
CONVENTION
BUREAU

ROSEBURG TRAVELODGE

138

DOUGLAS AVE

DINO'S RISTORANTE
ITALIANO

LOTUS KNIGHT MEMORIAL GARDENS

Riverside Park

ROSEBURG STATION

Mt Emil

BRIX 527

POST OFFICE

LANE AVE

OAK ST

ROSE ST

JACKSON ST

KANE ST

CHADWICK

MOSHER AVE

Templin
Park

MOSHER AVE

Mt Nebo
1,112ft

Micelli
Park

5

PINE ST

STEPHENS ST

ST

0   0.25 mi

0   0.25 km

PORTLAND AVE

MAIN

DOUGLAS
COUNTY
FAIRGROUNDS

FREAR ST

DOUGLAS COUNTY MUSEUM
OF HISTORY AND NATURAL HISTORY

To (WILDLIFE SAFARI
and Grants Pass

Umpqua
Park

99

To I-5

© AVALON TRAVEL

© WILDLIFE SAFARI

The Wildlife Safari has one of the most successful cheetah breeding programs in the country.

wildebeests, zebras, and other creatures scamper about freely, seemingly oblivious to the slow parade of cars. Elephants, rhinoceroses, and other African big game also make their homes here. Soon you are in "North America." Bears, bighorn sheep, pronghorn, moose, and buffalo are just a few of the animals that live down in the valley.

Throughout the day, many talks and opportunities to watch the animals being fed are scheduled; some are included in the price of admission and some cost extra. Perhaps the most popular attraction is the petting zoo (no extra fee). When the weather is good, you can take a memorable ride on a camel ($7.50) or arrange to help feed the big cats or bears ($95).

With 600 animals, including one of the most successful cheetah breeding programs in the country, Wildlife Safari is involved with various conservation and endangered species programs. After your "safari," pull into the White Rhino restaurant, serving good food within view of lions, giraffes, and white rhinos.

To reach Wildlife Safari, take Exit 119 off I-5

and follow Route 42 for 4 miles. Turn right on Lookingglass Road and right again on Safari Road.

Wine-Tasting

Several wineries in the Roseburg vicinity offer tasting rooms and tours. The dry Mediterranean climate and rich variety of soils in the area are ideal for chardonnay, pinot noir, Gewürztraminer, Riesling, zinfandel, and cabernet sauvignon varietals. A wine tour pamphlet with a map showing the location of the wineries is available from the **Roseburg Visitors and Convention Bureau** (410 SE Spruce St., 541/672-9731 or 800/444-9584, www.visitroseburg.com), or go to the website www.umpquavalleywineries.org.

Abacela Vineyards and Winery (12500 Lookingglass Rd., 541/679-6642, www.abacela.com, 11am-6pm daily) is noted for the large variety of wine grapes grown, including tempranillo, malbec, and dolcetto.

Girardet Wine Cellars (895 Reston Rd., 541/679-7252, www.girardetwine.com,

11am-5pm daily) is one of the oldest in the area. Philippe Girardet, from a town at the headwaters of the Rhine River in Switzerland, brings European wine-blending techniques to Oregon. These processes produce unique chardonnay, pinot noir, cabernet sauvignon, and Riesling wines.

The **Henry Estate Winery** (687 Hubbard Creek Rd., Umpqua, 541/459-5120 or 800/782-2686, www.henryestate.com, 11am-5pm daily) has produced a string of award-winning bottlings from chardonnay, Gewürztraminer, and pinot noir grapes. Lunch at shaded picnic tables near the vineyard and the Umpqua River can heighten your enjoyment of the fruit of the vine.

Oregon's oldest vineyard, dating to 1961, is **HillCrest** (240 Vineyard Ln., 541/673-3709, www.hillcrestvineyard.com, 9am-5pm daily Mar.-Dec.). A bewildering range of wine grapes are grown here, but some of the best to sample are the Riesling, syrah, and zinfandel.

SPORTS AND RECREATION
Fishing
The Umpqua River system is home to a dozen species of popular sport fish that range from the big chinook salmon to the tiny silver smelt. Visit the **Oregon Department of Fish and Wildlife website** (www.dfw.state.or.us) for additional information on the Umpqua.

Spring chinook enter the North Umpqua River March-June, work their way upstream during July and August, and spawn September-October. Fall chinook are mainly found in the warmer South Umpqua River. Their migration starts in midsummer and peaks in September when the rains increase water flow and lower the river's temperature. The best fishing for summer steelhead on the North Umpqua is June-October; the fish spawn January-March. This fish averages only 6-8 pounds, but it will make you think you are trying to reel in a chinook by the way it struggles.

Coho salmon, alias "silvers," are found throughout the Umpqua River system. The coho life cycle lasts about three years. Each spends its first year in freshwater, heads for the ocean to spend 1-2 years, and then returns to freshwater to spawn. The adults weigh an average of seven pounds each. This fishery has had some lean years recently.

You'll find rainbow trout in nearly all rivers and streams of the Umpqua River system, where the water is relatively cool and gravel bars are clean. This is the river's most common game fish, mainly because the rivers, lakes, and streams of the Umpqua are routinely seeded with over 100,000 legal-size (eight inches or longer) rainbows. The fishing season opens in April, with the best fishing in early summer when the fish are actively feeding.

Golf
The nine-hole municipal **Stewart Park Golf Course** (1005 Stewart Park Dr., 541/672-4592) charges $16 for 9 holes, $26 for 18 holes; add a few extra dollars on weekends. In addition to power carts, a lighted driving range, and rental golf clubs, a complete pro shop offers lessons and any peripherals you may need.

ENTERTAINMENT AND EVENTS
Roseburg's big event is the **Douglas County Fair,** held annually at the fairgrounds (Exit 123 off I-5) the second week of August, with down-home events like 4-H livestock competitions, midway rides, food booths, and horse and stock car races. Contact the **Roseburg Visitors and Convention Bureau** (410 SE Spruce St., 541/672-9731 or 800/444-9584, www.visitroseburg.com) for specifics.

If you happen to be in Roseburg on a summer Tuesday evening, check out **Music on the Halfshell** (www.halfshell.org), a series of outdoor summer concerts held at the band shell in **Stewart Park** (NW Stewart Pkwy. and NW Harvey Ave.). The free concerts have featured big-name national and international stars such as David Grisman, Taj Mahal, and Pink Martini. The park's bandstand is near the banks of the South Umpqua River.

ACCOMMODATIONS
There are over 1,500 motel rooms in Roseburg, and the competition keeps rates relatively low.

© BILL McRAE

McMenamins Roseburg Station pub is in the old railway depot.

Budget travelers can bunk down at the **Roseburg Travelodge** (315 W. Harvard Ave., 541/672-4836, $60-70). It's right on the Umpqua, though you'll pay a bit more to have a room and balcony overlooking the river. It's also convenient to downtown. Sharing the same river view, and easy access to downtown, the **Holiday Inn Express Roseburg** (375 W. Harvard Ave., 541/673-7517, $133-157) offers a pool, whirlpool, business center, and some of the newest rooms in the area. Both these hotels are located just off I-5 Exit 124.

A number of chain hotels are found at I-5 Exit 125, including **Windmill Inn** (1450 NW Mulholland Dr., 541/673-0901 or 800/547-4747, www.windmillinnroseburg.com, $85-99) with comfortable, pet-friendly accommodations with a laundry, restaurant, lounge, and pool. At the same exit, **Best Western Garden Villa Motel** (760 NW Garden Valley Blvd., 541/672-1601 or 800/547-3446, $119-139) has a pool, a business center, and continental breakfast included.

Get away from the freeway ramps at these comfortable lodgings just north of downtown. The flower-bedecked **Rose City Motel** (1142 NE Stephens St., 541/673-8209, www.rosecitymotel.com, $55-65) is an old-fashioned motor court motel that is very well-maintained, with full kitchens and a very friendly welcome. The **Howard Johnson Express** (978 NE Stephens St., 541/673-5082, www.hojo.com, $75-89) is another comfortable older lodging where you don't need to break the bank to have all the perks of an upper-end hotel, including free newspaper, free continental breakfast, and in-room fridge and microwave.

Camping

For real get-away-from-it-all camping, head up the North Umpqua River where there are many campgrounds. If convenience is what you need, **Armacher County Park** (541/672-4901, $15 tents, $23 RV with hookups) is 5 miles north of town directly beneath I-5 on Exit 129. Although handy, it is not idyllic. **Twin Rivers Vacation Park** (433 Rivers Forks Rd., 541/673-3811, $18-25) is 6 miles out of town off I-5 Exit 125, where the north and south forks of the Umpqua converge. Water, electricity, waste disposal, showers, and a coin-op laundry are available at this 85-site park.

FOOD

Roseburg is not exactly the fine dining capital of Oregon, but you won't go hungry here. The **Umpqua Valley Farmers Market** (2082 Diamond Lake Blvd., 541/530-6200, 9am-1pm Sat. mid-Apr.-Oct.) takes place in the parking lot of Dutch Brothers Coffee.

The McMenamins brewery empire has an appealing operation at **Roseburg Station** (700 SE Sheridan St., 541/672-1934, 11am-11pm Mon.-Thurs., 11am-midnight Fri.-Sat., noon-10pm Sun., $7-14). The 1912 Southern Pacific Station was purchased and restored while preserving original features like the 16-foot-high ceiling, tongue-and-groove Douglas fir wainscoting, and marble molding. Historical photos and art further

ASHLAND

recount the depot's storied past. Quality food and microbrews in a setting suitable for families enhance the appeal.

Some of Roseburg's best dining is Italian-style. **(Dino's Ristorante Italiano** (404 SE Jackson St., 541/673-0848, 5pm-9pm Tues.-Sat., $15-20) is a cozy family-run spot downtown with decor that's a sprawl of wine cases, travel guides, and cookbooks. The husband-and-wife cooking team spends part of each year in Italy, so the food is about as authentic as you'll find anywhere in southern Oregon.

Famous for its breakfasts, **(Brix 527** (527 SE Jackson St., 541/440-4901, 7am-3pm Sun.-Thurs., 7am-9pm Fri., breakfast $8-13, dinner $25-22) is now also open for dinner. At breakfast, Brix 527 gets the basics, like delicious omelets and eggs Benedict, exactly right. At lunch expect soup, salad, and more inventive dishes like grilled bacon-wrapped salmon on saffron rice, and at dinner choose from steaks, fish, and pasta, or perhaps chipotle prawn tacos.

Perhaps downtown's swankiest dining spot is **Blackbird Bar and Grill** (647 SE Jackson St., 541/672-8589, 11:30am-9pm Tues.-Fri., 5pm-9pm Sat., $12-25), with an eclectic menu that ranges from seared polenta and ratatouille to braised lamb shanks and flatiron steak with shallot and red wine reduction.

INFORMATION

The **Roseburg Visitors and Convention Bureau** (410 SE Spruce St., 541/672-9731 or 800/444-9584, www.visitroseburg.com) has among its brochures a particularly useful drivers guide to historic places.

GETTING THERE

Buses to and from the **Greyhound** bus depot (835 SE Stephens St., 541/673-5326) connect Roseburg with other cities along the I-5 corridor.

The North Umpqua River

One of the great escapes into the Cascade Mountains is via the Umpqua Highway, Route 138. This road runs along the part of the North Umpqua River fished by Zane Grey and Clark Gable as well as legions of less-ballyhooed nimrods during steelhead season. The North Umpqua is a premier fishing river full of trout and salmon, as well as a source of excitement for white-water rafters who shoot the rapids. Numerous waterfalls, including 272-foot Watson Falls, feed this great waterway and are found close to the road. Tall timbers line the road through the Umpqua National Forest, and many fine campgrounds are situated within its confines. Mountain lakes like Toketee Reservoir, Lemolo Lake, and Diamond Lake offer boating and other recreational opportunities. The Umpqua National Forest also boasts challenging yet accessible mountain trails up the flanks of Mount Bailey (8,363 feet) and Mount Thielsen (9,182 feet). And when snow carpets the landscape in winter, you can cross-country ski, snowmobile, and snowcat ski on Mount Bailey free from the crowds at other winter sports areas.

This place is still so untouched primarily because of the rugged terrain. The first road, a crude dirt trail that ran from Roseburg to Steamboat, was built in the 1920s. Travelers of the day who wanted to get to the Diamond Lake Resort spent three days traveling this road by car, then had to journey another 20 miles on horseback to reach their final destination. The North Umpqua Road was expanded to Copeland Creek by the Civilian Conservation Corps during the 1930s, but the trips to Diamond and Crater Lakes were still limited to a trail-wise few.

It wasn't until the late 1950s, when President Dwight D. Eisenhower pushed for development of the nation's interstate and state highways, that road improvement began in earnest.

COW CREEK BAND OF THE UMPQUA TRIBE

As you pass Canyonville, along the remote stretch of I-5 between Roseburg and Grants Pass, you'll see the Seven Feathers Casino. It's operated by the Cow Creek Band of the Umpqua Tribe of Native Americans who, like many Oregon tribes, have rallied to regain land that they lost during the pioneer era.

The Cow Creek signed a treaty with the U.S. government in 1853, selling their land in southwestern Oregon for 2.3 cents an acre so that the government could sell it to pioneer settlers for $1.25 an acre. The treaty, which promised health, housing, and education, was ignored by the United States for almost exactly 100 years. The Cow Creek did not receive a reservation, but they stayed in their native area and continued to act as a tribe.

In 1954, the Western Oregon Indian Termination Act terminated federal relations with the Cow Creek and nearly every other tribe in western Oregon. Because the Cow Creek were not notified about their termination until after the act was passed, they sued in the U.S. Court of Claims and eventually won a $1.5 million settlement. The Cow Creek set up an endowment for their settlement money and draw on the interest to further economic development, education, and housing.

The tribe has also been buying back land. In the late 1990s they bought land along Jordan Creek and began clearing out old tires and other garbage that had accumulated there. A watershed assessment pointed to some habitat restoration opportunities, and the tribe set about trying to restore coho salmon and steelhead trout to a stretch of the creek that hadn't seen these fish since 1958, when I-5 was built. After installing weirs that allowed fish to swim through the culverts under I-5, and work on improving water quality and streambank habitat, coho are now spawning in Jordan Creek.

Douglas County allocated $2.76 million toward federal matching funds to construct the Umpqua Highway. The road was completed in the summer of 1964, opening up the North Umpqua basin to timber interests, sportspeople, and tourists.

The recreational areas along the North Umpqua fall under the jurisdiction of the **Umpqua National Forest North Umpqua district** (541/496-3532, www.fs.fed.us, based in Glide) and **Diamond Lake district** (541/498-2531, www.fs.fed.us, based near Toketee Falls) and the **Bureau of Land Management** (777 NW Garden Valley Blvd., Roseburg, 541/440-4930, www.blm.gov/or).

SIGHTS
Colliding Rivers

Just off Route 138 on the west side of the town of Glide is the site of the **Colliding Rivers.** The Wild and Umpqua Rivers meet head-on in a bowl of green serpentine. The best times to view this spectacle are after winter storms and when spring runoff is high. If the water is low, check out the high-water mark from the Christmas flood of 1964. Water levels from that great inundation were lapping at the parking lot, a chilling reminder that *umpqua* means "thundering water" in Chinook.

◖ North Umpqua Waterfalls
GROTTO FALLS

Visitors can get an unusual perspective of **Grotto Falls** because there's a trail in back of this 100-foot cascade. If you venture behind the shimmering water, watch your step because the moss-covered rocks are very slippery. To get here, take Route 138 for 18 miles east of Roseburg to Glide. Follow Little River Road to the Coolwater Campground, and you'll find the turnoff to Forest Service Road 2703 nearby. Take it for 5 miles until you reach the junction of Forest Service Road 2703-150. Proceed down Forest Service Road 2703-150 for another 2 miles until you reach the trailhead. It's only a short hike in to view Grotto Falls.

ASHLAND

Of the many waterfalls along the North Umpqua River, Toketee Falls is the most striking.

SUSAN CREEK FALLS

About 11 miles east of Glide is 50-foot-high **Susan Creek Falls,** whose trailhead sits off Route 138 near the Susan Creek picnic area. A one-mile trail winds through a rainforest-like setting to the falls. The cascade is bordered on three sides by green mossy rock walls that never see the light of the sun and stay wet 365 days a year. Another 0.25 mile up the trail are the **Indian Mounds.** One of the rites of manhood for Umpqua boys was to fast and pile up stones in hopes of being granted a vision or spiritual powers. Also called the Vision Quest Site, the site still holds stacks of moss-covered stones in an area protected by a fence.

FALL CREEK FALLS

Four miles east of Susan Creek Falls is **Fall Creek Falls.** Look for the trailhead off Route 138 at Fall Creek. A good walk for families with young children and for older people, the mild one-mile trail goes around and through

slabs of bedrock. Halfway up the trail is a lush area called **Job's Garden.** Stay on the Fall Creek Trail and in another 0.5 mile you'll come to the falls. It's a double waterfall with each tier 35-50 feet in height. Back at Job's Garden, you may want to explore the Job's Garden Trail, which leads to the base of columnar basalt outcroppings.

LITTLE FALLS AND STEAMBOAT FALLS

During fish migration season, it's fun to venture off Route 138 at Steamboat and go up Steamboat Creek Road 38 to see the fish battle two small waterfalls. The first, **Little Falls,** is one mile up the road. It's always exciting to see the fish miraculously wriggle their way up this 10-foot cascade. Four miles farther up Steamboat Creek Road is **Steamboat Falls.** A viewpoint showcases this 30-foot waterfall, but not as many fish try to swim up this one because of the fish ladders nearby.

JACK FALLS

On Route 138 about 3 miles east of Steamboat is **Jack Falls.** Look for the trailhead sign and follow the trail along the brushy bank of Jack Creek to a series of three closely grouped waterfalls ranging 20-70 feet in height.

TOKETEE FALLS

The word *toketee* means "graceful" in the Chinook language, and after viewing **Toketee Falls** plunge over the sheer wall of basalt you'll probably agree it's aptly named. Nineteen miles up Route 138 near the Toketee Ranger Station, this 0.5-mile trail ends at a double waterfall with a combined height of over 150 feet. To get to Toketee Falls, follow Forest Service Road 34 at the west entrance of the ranger station, cross the first bridge, and turn left. There you'll find the trailhead and a parking area.

WATSON FALLS

On Route 138 take Forest Service Road 37 near the east entrance of the Toketee Ranger Station to reach the trailhead of **Watson Falls,** a 272-foot-high flume of water. A moderate 0.5-mile trail climbs through tall stands of Douglas

© BILL MCRAE

Watson Falls drops 272 feet into a ferny glade.

fir and western hemlock and is complemented by an understory of green salal, Oregon grape, and ferns. A bridge spans the canyon just below the falls, providing outstanding views of this towering cascade. Clamber up the mossy rocks to near the base of the falls and get a face full of the cool billowing spray.

LEMOLO FALLS

Another waterfall worth a visit is **Lemolo Falls.** *Lemolo* is a Chinook word meaning "wild and untamed," and you'll see that this is the case with this thunderous 100-foot waterfall. To get here, take Lemolo Lake Road off Route 138, then follow Forest Service Roads 2610 and 2610-600 and look for the trailhead sign. The trail is a gentle one-mile path that drops down into the North Umpqua Canyon and passes several small waterfalls on the way to Lemolo Falls.

Umpqua Hot Springs

The **Umpqua Hot Springs** is mostly unknown

and far enough from civilized haunts not to be overused, yet it's accessible enough for those who go in search of it to enjoy. The springs have been developed with wooden pools and a crude lean-to shelter. Weekends tend to attract more visitors, forcing you to wait your turn for a soak. Midweek is generally pretty quiet, though we've encountered some pretty dodgy folks up there these times.

To get here, go north from the Toketee Ranger Station and turn right onto County Road 34, just past the Pacific Power and Light buildings. Proceed down Road 34 past Toketee Lake about 6 miles. When you cross the bridge over Deer Creek, which is clearly signed, you will be a little less than 0.5 mile from the turnoff. The turnoff is Thorn Prairie Road, to the right, which goes 1 mile and ends at a small parking area. Note that in wet weather this road may be impassable, and it is not recommended for low-slung cars in any season. From the parking area, it's 0.5 mile down the blocked road to the hot springs trailhead and another 0.5 mile to the pool.

SPORTS AND RECREATION
Hiking

Over 570 miles of trails crisscross the one-million-acre **Umpqua National Forest,** with elevations that range 1,000-9,000 feet. There are hikes to please families and mountain climbers alike. Wildlife and wildflowers, mountain lakes and mountain peaks, old-growth forest and alpine meadows are some of the attractions visitors see along the way.

If you're camping along the North Umpqua River, many pleasant day hikes are possible on the **North Umpqua Trail.** Beginning near the town of Glide, this thoroughfare parallels the North Umpqua River for most of its 79 miles. Divided into 11 segments from over 3 miles to just under 16 miles in length, the trail leads high into the Cascades and connects with the Pacific Crest Trail as well as many campgrounds. Route 138 affords many access points to the trail.

One segment of the North Umpqua Trail is the one-mile **Panther Trail.** This gentle hike

ASHLAND

OAKLAND: VOYAGE INTO THE PAST

Many travelers drive by the exit marked "Oakland" on I-5 joking that maybe they made a wrong turn somewhere and ended up in California. But the curious who venture a few miles off the interstate to explore this National Historic Landmark discover that *this* Oakland is an interesting voyage into Oregon's past. Established in the 1850s, the hamlet today gives little indication of the caprices of fate and fortune it has experienced in its 150-year history. Oakland is noteworthy for leftover touches of refinement from its golden age, which seem almost incongruous against its present-day small-town facade.

Oakland was a stopover point for the main stagecoach line linking Portland and Sacramento until the Oregon and California Railroad came to town in 1872. With these two transportation linkages, Oakland thrived as a trading center for outlying hop fields and prune orchards. In the early 1900s, millions of pounds of dried prunes were shipped all over the world from Oakland. In the 1920s and 1930s, raising turkeys became the prominent industry in the area, and Oakland became the leading turkey-shipping center in the western United States. From the 1940s through the 1960s, the lumber industry dominated the local economy. Today, livestock ranching, farming, and tourism are the economic mainstays.

While not as commercialized as Jacksonville, its counterpart farther south, Oakland still provides a good place to pull off the interstate and reflect on the passage of years in a onetime boomtown turned rural hamlet.

Old Town Oakland is a good place to start your tour because this is where it all began. An excellent free history and walking-tour pamphlet is available at the city hall (117 3rd St.). The original wooden buildings were destroyed by fires in the 1890s, and most of the brick and stone structures in the historical district date back to this era of reconstruction. The **Oakland Museum** (136 Locust St.) is worth visiting. The exhibit in the back re-creates Oakland during its boom times. There are many antiques stores, art galleries, and curio shops to browse through as well.

Tolly's (115 Locust St., 541/459-3796, 11am-3pm Wed.-Thurs. and Sun., 11am-8pm Fri.-Sat., $20-42) is a beautifully preserved restaurant and a great place to stop by for a meal. Be sure to save some room for the homemade desserts, or perhaps something old-fashioned from the soda fountain.

---

begins near Steamboat at the parking lot of the former ranger station. Many wildflowers are seen late April-early June on the way up to the old fish hatchery. One flower to look for is the bright-red snow plant, *Sarcodes sanguinea*, which grows beneath Douglas firs and sugar pine trees. Also called the carmine snow flower or snow lily, the snow plant is classified as a saprophyte, a plant that contains no chlorophyll and derives nourishment from decayed materials. Growing 8-24 inches in height, the plant's red flowers are crowded at the crown of the stem.

A five-mile hike that ranges from easy to moderate is found on the south slope of 8,363-foot **Mount Bailey.** Bring plenty of water and good sturdy hiking shoes because the last 0.5 mile of the ascent is steep, with many sharp rocks. To get to the trailhead, take Route 138 to the north entrance of Diamond Lake. Turn onto Forest Service Road 4795 and follow it 5 miles to the junction of Forest Service Road 4795-300. Proceed down 4795-300 for 1 mile until you see the trail marker.

The easy two-mile **Diamond Lake Loop** takes hikers through a mix of lodgepole pine and true fir to Lake Creek, Diamond Lake's only outlet. There are many views of Mount Bailey along the way, as well as some private coves ideal for a swim on hot days. But while the grade is easy, keep in mind that the elevation is nearly a mile high and pace yourself accordingly. To get to the loop, take Forest Service Road 4795 off Route 138 on the north

fishing on the North Umpqua River

entrance to Diamond Lake and look for the trailhead sign on the west side of the road.

For those who like to climb mountains for reasons other than just because they are there, the **Mount Thielsen Trail** offers a million-dollar view from the top of the mountain. This challenging, scree-covered, five-mile trail winds to the top of Mount Thielsen's spire-pointed 9,182-foot-high volcanic peak. You'll find the trailhead on the east side of Route 138 one mile north of the junction of Route 230.

Bring along water and quick-energy snacks; hiking boots are also recommended due to the sharp volcanic rocks that could easily damage ordinary shoes. Extra care should be taken getting up and down the last 200 feet, which requires hand-over-hand climbing up a steep, crumbly pitch. If you make it to the top, be sure to enter your name in the climbing register found there. Then take a look at the view, which stretches from Mount Shasta to Mount Hood, and forget all the silly preoccupations that plague us mortals.

Fishing

The North Umpqua has several distinctions. First, it is known as one of the most difficult North American rivers to fish. No boats are permitted for 15 miles in either direction of Steamboat, and no bait or spinners are allowed either. This puts a premium on skillful fly-fishing. You can wade on in and poke around for the best fishing holes on the North Umpqua, one of the few rivers with a summer run of native steelhead—or better yet, hire a guide.

If you want to go with an experienced fishing guide, check out **Summer Run Guide Service** (541/496-3037, www.summerrun.net).

Rafting

The North Umpqua has increasingly gained popularity with white-water rafters and kayakers. But fishing and floating are not always compatible, so guidelines for boaters and rafters have been established by the Bureau of Land Management and the Umpqua National Forest.

The area around Steamboat has the most restrictions, mainly because of the heavy fishing in the area that boaters would disturb. Be sure to check with the **Forest Service** (541/496-3532) prior to setting out to make sure you are making a legal trip. A good way to get started rafting and avoid the hassle of rules, regulations, and gear is to go along with an experienced white-water guide. These leaders provide the safety equipment, the boats, and the expertise; all you have to do is paddle.

In addition to rafting, inflatable kayak trips are offered by outfitters. Inflatables are easier for the neophyte to handle than the hard-shell type, though these craft expose you to more chills and spills. Whatever your mode of floating the river, expect more than a dozen Class III or IV rapids and plenty of Class IIs, as well as old-growth trees and osprey nests. Best of all, this world-class river is still relatively undiscovered. Spring and summer are the best times to enjoy the North Umpqua, although it's boatable year-round. Boaters are allowed on the river 10am-6pm only, leaving the morning and evening for fish.

North Umpqua Outfitters (541/496-3333

© BILL MCRAE

ASHLAND

or 888/454-9696, www.nuorafting.com) offers raft, kayak, and drift boat trips. Three-hour raft trips are $105 per person; five-hour raft trips with lunch are $125 per person. They also will help you plan a trip that combines rafting and mountain biking.

Other outfitters with similarly price trips include the **Adventure Center** (40 N. Main St., Ashland, 541/482-2897 or 800/444-2819, www.raftingtours.com) and **Orange Torpedo Trips** (209 Merlin Rd., Merlin, 541/479-5061 or 866/479-5061, www.orangetorpedo.com).

Winter Sports

SKIING

Located 80 miles east of Roseburg off Route 138 in the central Cascades is Mount Bailey. The experienced skiers at **Cat Ski Mt. Bailey** (800/733-7593, www.catskimtbailey.com, $350 per day) know where the best runs are to be had. Snowcats transport no more than 12 skiers up the mountain from Diamond Lake Resort to the summit of this 8,363-foot peak. Experienced guides then lead small groups down routes that best suit the abilities of each group. The skiing is challenging and should be attempted only by advanced skiers. Open bowls, steep chutes, and tree-lined glaciers are some of the types of terrain encountered during the 3,000-foot drop in elevation back to the resort.

The rates are worth it given the pristine beauty of the area, the dearth of crowds, and the superlative skiing. Attractive packages include overnight lodging in fireside cabins at Diamond Lake Resort as well as an "alpine lunch" of meats, cheeses, vegetables, homemade pie, and coffee served up on the mountain. Only a limited number of skiers can book, so be sure to plan ahead for reservations.

CROSS-COUNTRY SKIING

Over 56 miles of designated Nordic trails are found in the Diamond and Lemolo Lakes area along the upper reaches of Route 138. Some of the trails are groomed, and all of them are clearly marked by blue trail signs. Contact the

Umpqua National Forest (Diamond Lake Ranger District, 541/498-2531, www.fs.usda.gov/umpqua) to request maps and information on these trails.

The **Diamond Lake Resort** (Diamond Lake, 541/793-3333 or 800/733-7593, www.diamondlake.net, 8am-5pm daily) rents skis and snowshoes.

TUBING AND SNOWBOARDING

If you ski the bunny hill, you might enjoy inner-tubing or snowboarding near **Diamond Lake Resort** (Diamond Lake, 541/793-3333 or 800/733-7593, www.diamondlake.net). A rope tow takes "tubers" to the top of the hill 9am-5pm weekends for nonstop thrills and spills on the way back down. The hill has a ticket system similar to other ski lifts, with full-day, half-day, and two-hour passes available. The tubing and snowboarding hill is located at the Hilltop Shop. The $10 entry fee includes an inner tube, a tow rope, and a cable clip. Uphill tows are $0.50.

SNOWMOBILING

Approximately 133 miles of designated motorized snow trails are concentrated around the Lemolo and Diamond Lakes area. The trails are usually open in late November, as snow accumulation permits. Many of these trails are groomed on a regular basis, and all are clearly marked by orange trail signs and diamond-shaped trail blazes pegged up on trees above the snowline. Diamond Lake Resort is a hub of snowmobiling activity; they rent snow machines and can advise you on trails.

One of the more exotic runs is into Crater Lake National Park. Snowmobiles and all-terrain vehicles (ATVs) must register at the north entrance of the park and stay on the trail. The trail climbs about 10 miles from the park gates to the north rim of the lake. Be aware that the mountain weather here can change suddenly, creating dangerous subzero temperatures and whiteout conditions. Also, watch for Nordic skiers and other people sometimes found on motorized vehicle trails.

© BILL MCRAE

The Steamboat Inn is famed for its fishing access and its fine dining.

ACCOMMODATIONS

The number of lodgings on the North Umpqua River is limited to a few properties that range from rustic quarters to full-service resorts.

About four miles east of Idleyld Park is the **Dogwood Motel** (28866 N. Umpqua Hwy., Idleyld Park, 541/496-3403, www.dogwood-motel.com, $70-75). Here you'll find clean modern units, some with kitchenettes, on tidy well-kept grounds.

The **C Steamboat Inn** (42705 N. Umpqua Hwy., Steamboat, 541/498-2230 or 800/840-8825, www.thesteamboatinn. com, Mar.-Dec., $185-300) is the premier dining and accommodation property on the North Umpqua, situated in the middle of a stretch of 31 miles of premium fly-fishing turf. The inn's rooms and cabins are extremely popular, so reservations are a must. It's an ideal getaway from civilization, near the hiking trails, waterfalls, and fishing holes for which the Umpqua is famous. Lodging is in handsomely furnished riverside cabins, cottages, and suites; a number of three-bedroom ranch-style houses are also available. The inn serves breakfast, lunch, and dinner to its guests; nonguests may also dine.

Near the summit of the Cascade Mountains about 75 miles east of Roseburg and 13 miles from Diamond Lake is **Lemolo Lake Resort** (2610 Birds Point Rd., Idleyld Park, 541/643-0750, www.lemololakeresort.com, cabins $150-250, hotel rooms $90-100), a more modest operation. Formed by a Pacific Power and Light dam, Lemolo Lake has good fishing for German brown trout as well as kokanee salmon, eastern brook trout, and rainbow trout. The lake is sheltered from wind by gently sloping ridges, and there are many coves and sandy beaches along the 8.3 miles of shoreline. Waterskiing is permitted on the lake. Boats and canoes can be rented, and many miles of snowmobiling and cross-country skiing trails are nearby. The resort has both housekeeping and standard cabins as well as basic hotel rooms.

Diamond Lake Resort (Diamond Lake,

541/793-3333 or 800/733-7593, www.dia-mondlake.net) is a rustic mountain resort with enough modern amenities to suit the tender-foot in any season. It offers lodging, restau-rants, groceries, a service station, a laundry, and showers. Cabins with one queen bed or two twins start at $109; lodge and motel rooms start at $99. Lodgings are popular as base camps for a Crater Lake excursion. Mountain bikes, pad-dleboats, kayaks, canoes, and fishing boats as well as an equestrian center keep you out of the modest accommodations and busy enjoying the spectacular surroundings.

CAMPING
Little River Campgrounds

If the thought of a campground with good shade trees and a waterfall with a swimming hole sounds idyllic, head for **Cavitt Creek Falls** (Bureau of Land Management, 541/440-4930, May-late Oct., $8). To get there, head east of Roseburg on Route 138 to Glide, take Little Creek Road (County Road 17) for 7 miles, then continue 3 miles down Cavitt Creek Road. Ten campsites with picnic tables and grills are pro-vided, with piped water, vault toilets, and fire-wood available on the premises.

Another campsite 5 miles up Little River Road is **Wolf Creek** (North Umpqua Ranger District, 541/496-3532, mid-May-late Oct., $15), which features eight sites for tents and RVs (up to 30 feet) and three tent-only sites. Picnic tables, grills, vault toilets, and piped water are provided.

An easy way to keep your cool is at **Coolwater** (North Umpqua Ranger District, 541/496-3532, mid-May-late Oct., $10). Seven tent sites and sites for RVs (up to 24 feet) with picnic tables and grills are available; vault toi-lets and well water from a hand pump are also on the grounds. To get here, follow Little River Road 15 miles out of Glide. There are many good hiking trails nearby, including **Grotto Falls, Wolf Creek Nature Trail,** and **Wolf Creek Falls Trail.**

One of the best deals on the Little River is at **White Creek** (North Umpqua Ranger District, 541/496-3532, mid-May-late Sept., $10), a small four-site campground that accommo-dates tents and RVs. Picnic tables and grills are provided, and piped water and vault toilets are available. Situated on the confluence of White Creek and Little River, a good beach and shal-low water provide excellent swimming for chil-dren. To get here, take Little Creek Road 17 miles to Red Butte Road and proceed 1 mile down Red Butte Road to the campground.

Tucked away on the upper reaches of the Little River at an elevation of 3,200 feet is **Lake in the Woods** (North Umpqua Ranger District, 541/496-3532, June-late Oct., $10). You'll find 11 sites for tents and RVs (up to 16 feet), with picnic tables, grills, vault toilets, and hand-pumped water in a campground set along the shore of the four-acre artificial Little Lake in the Woods. Motorized craft are not permitted in this eight-foot-deep pond. Two good hikes nearby are to **Hemlock Falls** and **Yakso Falls.** To get here, head 20 miles up Little River Road to the end of the pavement; proceed another 7 miles until you reach the campground.

North Umpqua River Campgrounds

Set along the bank of the North Umpqua River 15 miles east of Roseburg a little ways north of Route 138 is **Whistler's Bend** (541/673-4863, $15), a Douglas County park. Picnic ta-bles and grills are provided at this county park, as are piped water, flush toilets, and showers. The fishing is good here, and even though it's fairly close to town, it doesn't usually get too crowded.

About 30 miles east of Route 138 is **Susan Creek** (Bureau of Land Management, 541/440-4930, May-late Oct., $14). This campground has 31 sites for tents and RVs (up to 20 feet) with picnic tables and grills. Flush toilets, piped water, and firewood are also available. Situated in a grove of old-growth Douglas fir and sugar pine next to the North Umpqua River, the campground is enhanced by the presence of a fine beach and swimming hole.

Within easy access of great fishing (fly-angling only), rafting, and hiking, **Bogus Creek** (North Umpqua Ranger District,

ASHLAND

© BILL MCRAE

Diamond Lake is a popular boating destination in summer.

541/496-3532, May 1-Oct. 31, $15) offers you the real thing. Here you'll find 5 tent sites and 10 sites for tents or RVs (up to 30 feet) with picnic tables and grills. Flush toilets, iodinated water, and gray wastewater sumps are available. As the campground is a major launching point for white-water expeditions and within a few miles of Fall Creek Falls and Job's Garden Geological Area, it's good to get here early to make sure you get a campsite.

About 38 miles east of Roseburg on Route 138 near Steamboat and good fly-fishing is **Canton Creek** (North Umpqua Ranger District, 541/496-3532, May-mid-Oct., $10). Take Steamboat Creek Road off Route 138 and proceed 400 yards to the campground. This campground features 12 sites for tents and RVs (up to 22 feet) with the standard picnic tables and grills, plus piped water, flush toilets, and gray wastewater sumps.

Horseshoe Bend (North Umpqua Ranger District, 541/496-3532, mid-May-late Sept., $115) is 10 miles east of Steamboat. There are 34 sites for tents and RVs (up to 35 feet) with picnic tables and grills. Flush toilets, piped water, gray wastewater sumps, a laundry, and a general store are also available. Situated in the middle of a big bend of the North Umpqua covered with old-growth Douglas firs and sugar pines, this is a popular base camp for rafting and fishing enthusiasts.

Diamond Lake Campgrounds

Several campgrounds are in the vicinity of beautiful 5,200-foot-high Diamond Lake; boating, fishing, swimming, bicycling, and hiking are among the popular recreational options. The trout fishing is particularly good in the early summer, and there are also excellent hikes into the Mount Thielsen Wilderness, Crater Lake National Park, and Mount Bailey areas. While no reservations are technically necessary, these campgrounds can fill up fast, so it's always a good idea to book a space ahead of time (877/444-6777 or www.recreation.gov). For general information, contact the **Diamond Lake Ranger District** (541/498-2531, www. fs.usda.gov/umpqua).

Although Route 138 twists and turns most of the 80 miles from Roseburg to Diamond Lake, many people head straight for **Broken Arrow** (mid-May-Labor Day, $15). This 142-site campground with standard picnic tables and grills has plenty of room for tents and RVs (up to 30 feet); flush toilets, piped water, and gray wastewater sumps are available.

The next campground bears the name of its raison d'être, **Diamond Lake** (May 15-Oct. 31, $16-27). Here you'll find 160 campsites for tents and RVs (up to 22 feet) with picnic tables and grills. Piped water, flush toilets, and firewood are also available. Numerous hiking trails lead from the campground, including the Pacific Crest National Scenic Trail. Boat docks, launching facilities, and rentals are nearby at **Diamond Lake Resort** (Diamond Lake, 541/793-3333 or 800/733-7593, www. diamondlake.net).

On the east shore of Diamond Lake is **Thielsen View** (mid-May-mid-Oct., $15). It features 60 sites for tents and RVs (up to 30 feet) with picnic tables and grills. Piped water, vault toilets, gray wastewater sumps, and a boat ramp are also available. As the name implies, this campground has picturesque views of Mount Thielsen.

FOOD

Make a reservation at the outstanding **C Steamboat Inn** (42705 N. Umpqua Hwy., 541/498-2230 or 800/840-8825, www. thesteamboatinn.com, 8am-9pm daily) to dine on main dishes of beef, fish, poultry, lamb, or pork served with fresh vegetables and homemade bread. Considered one of the top dining experiences in the state, the Steamboat also has a wide selection of Oregon wines. The prix fixe Evening Dinner ($50) is served nightly, and Winemaker's Dinners (Mar.-mid-June, $90) are scheduled frequently during the summer and on weekends the rest of the season. The chef can also accommodate any food allergies, strong dislikes, and vegetarian diets. Reservations for dinner are required.

Crater Lake

High in the Cascades lies the crown jewel of Oregon, Crater Lake, the country's deepest at 1,943 feet. It glimmers like a polished sapphire in a setting created by a volcano that blew its top and collapsed thousands of years ago. Crater Lake's extraordinary hues are produced by the depth and clarity of the water and its ability to absorb all the colors of the spectrum except the shortest wavelengths, blue and violet, which are scattered skyward. Kodak used to send their apologies along with customers' photographs of Crater Lake—they thought they had goofed on the processing, so unbelievable is the blue of the water.

In addition to a 33-mile rim loop around the crater, the park, established in 1902, also features 229 campsites, dozens of hiking trails, and boat tours on the lake itself. Admission to the park is $10 per vehicle or $5 per bicycle.

If you're seeing Crater Lake for the first time, drive into the park from the north for the most dramatic perspective. After crossing through a pumice desert you climb up to higher elevations overlooking the lake. In contrast to this subdued approach, the blueness and size of the lake can hit you with a suddenness that stops all thought. On a clear day, you can peer south across Crater Lake and discern the snowy eminence of Mount Shasta over 100 miles away in California.

Geology

Geologically speaking, the name *Crater Lake* is a misnomer. Technically, Crater Lake lies in a caldera, which is produced when the center of a volcano caves in on itself; in this case, the cataclysm occurred 6,600 years ago with the destruction of formerly 12,000-foot-high Mount Mazama.

Klamath Native American legend has it

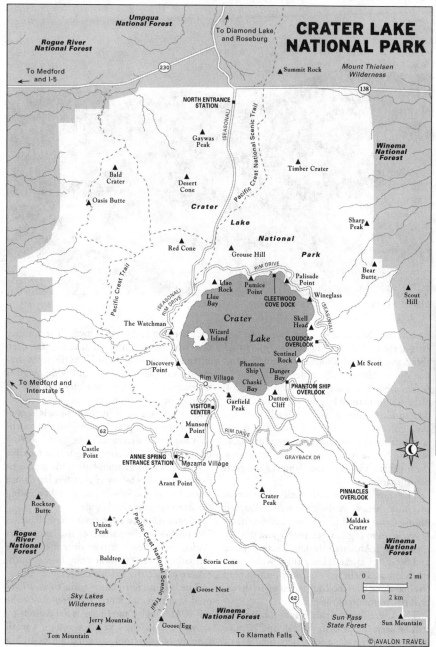

CRATER LAKE NATIONAL PARK

Umpqua National Forest

Rogue River National Forest

To Diamond Lake and Roseburg

To Medford and I-5

230

Summit Rock

Mount Thielsen Wilderness

138

NORTH ENTRANCE STATION

Gaywas Peak

Pacific Crest National Scenic Trail

Timber Crater

Winema National Forest

Bald Crater

Desert Cone

Crater

Oasis Butte

Lake

Sharp Peak

National

Red Cone

Grouse Hill

Park

Pacific Crest Trail

RIM DRIVE

Llao Rock

Pumice Point

Palisade Point

Bear Butte

Llao Bay

CLEETWOOD COVE DOCK

Wineglass

Scout Hill

The Watchman

Crater

Wizard Island

Lake

Skell Head

CLOUDCAP OVERLOOK

Discovery Point

Phantom Ship

Sentinel Rock

Mt Scott

Rim Village

Danger Bay

Chaski Bay

Dutton Cliff

PHANTOM SHIP OVERLOOK

VISITOR CENTER

Garfield Peak

Munson Point

RIM DRIVE

GRAYBACK DR

Castle Point

62

ANNIE SPRING ENTRANCE STATION

Mazama Village

Arant Point

Crater Peak

PINNACLES OVERLOOK

Rocktop Butte

Maldaks Crater

Union Peak

Pacific Crest National Scenic Trail

Winema National Forest

Rogue River National Forest

Baldtop

Scoria Cone

0   2 mi

0   2 km

Sky Lakes Wilderness

Goose Nest

Jerry Mountain

Goose Egg

Winema National Forest

Sun Pass State Forest

Sun Mountain

Tom Mountain

62

To Klamath Falls

© AVALON TRAVEL

ASHLAND

ASHLAND

Wizard Island

© BILL MCRAE

that Mount Mazama was the home of Llao, king of the underworld. The chief of the world above was Skell, who sometimes would stand on Mount Shasta, 100 miles to the south. A fierce battle between these two gods took place, a time marked by great explosions, thunder, and lightning. Burning ash fell from the sky, igniting the forest, and molten rivers of lava gushed 35 miles down the mountainside, burying Native American villages. For a week the night sky was lit by the flames of the great confrontation.

The story climaxes with Skell's destruction of Llao's throne, as the mountain collapsed on itself and sealed Llao beneath the surface, never again to frighten the people and destroy their homes. Although the lake became serene and beautiful as the caldera filled with water, the Klamaths believed that only punishment awaited those who foolishly gazed upon the sacred battleground of the gods.

The aftereffects of this great eruption can still be seen. Huge drifts of ash and pumice hundreds of feet deep were deposited over a

wide area up to 80 miles away. The pumice deserts to the north of the lake and the deep ashen canyons to the south are the most dramatic examples. So thick and widespread is the pumice that water percolates through too rapidly for plants to survive, creating reddish pockets of bleakness in the otherwise green forest. The eerie gray hoodoos in the southern canyons were created by hot gases bubbling up through the ash, hardening it into rocklike towers. These formations have withstood centuries of erosion by water that has long since washed away the loosely packed ash, creating the steep canyons visible today.

Wizard Island, a large cinder cone that rises 760 feet above the surface of the lake, offers evidence of volcanic activity since the caldera's formation. The **Phantom Ship,** in the southeastern corner, is a much older feature.

The lake is confined by walls of multicolored lava that rise 500-2,000 feet above the water. Although Crater Lake is fed entirely by snow and rain, the lake does contain a small amount of salts from surrounding rocks, but the salty water is replaced by purer rain and snow. The level of the lake fluctuates only 1-3 feet per year as evaporation and seepage keep it remarkably constant.

Another surprise is that while Crater Lake often records the coldest temperatures in the Cascades, the lake itself has only frozen over once since records have been kept. The surface of the lake can warm up to the 60°F mark during the summer. The deeper water stays around 38°F, although scientists have discovered 66°F hot spots 1,400 feet below the lake's surface.

Rainbow trout and kokanee (a landlocked salmon) were introduced to the lake many years ago by humans. The rainbow can grow up to 25 inches long, feeding mainly on the kokanee; the kokanee do not exceed 15 inches. Some types of mosses and green algae grow more than 400 feet below the lake's surface, a world record for these freshwater species. Another distinction is Crater Lake's selection as the purest lake in the world by scientists who determined in 1997 that the water's clarity extended down 142 feet.

◖ CRATER LAKE NATIONAL PARK
Visitors Center

The **visitors center** (9am-5pm daily early Apr.-early Nov., 10am-4pm daily early Nov.-early Apr., closed Christmas day), is located below Rim Village near park headquarters and can provide information, maps, and publications as well as backcountry permits and first aid. If the lake is socked in by lousy weather, you can see it anyway: Excellent films about Crater Lake are shown in the center's theater every half hour and by special arrangement. For information about weather and activities at Crater Lake, visit www.nps.gov/crla or call 541-594-3000.

The **original visitors center** (9:30am-5pm daily late May-late Sept.) is on the rim. A rock stairway behind the small building leads to Sinnott Memorial and one of the best views of the lake. It is perched on a rock outcropping where accompanying interpretive placards help you identify the surrounding formations as well as flora and fauna. As you drive north

from Rim Village, a few miles on you'll notice brown earth that spread out from the last major eruption.

Boat Tours

There are over 100 miles of hiking trails in the park, yet only one leads down to the lake itself. This is because the 1.1-mile-long Cleetwood Trail is the only part of the caldera's steep avalanche-prone slope that is safe enough for passage. The trail drops 700 feet in elevation and is recommended only for those in good physical condition. There is no other way to get to **Cleetwood Cove dock,** located at the end of the trail, where the **Crater Lake boat tours** (541/830-8700) begin.

There are two types of boat tours. Narrated excursions depart on the half hour 9:30am-3:30pm July-mid-September ($35 adults, $21 children ages 3-11) and cruise counterclockwise around the perimeter of the lake. These tours do not stop at Wizard Island. Twice daily, at 9:30am and 12:30pm, a cruise departs with a stop at Wizard Island ($45 adults, $27 children). You can elect to hike to the summit of the island and return on the later boat.

Allow one hour from Rim Village to drive 12 miles to Cleetwood trailhead and hike down to the boat's departure point. Dress warmly because it's cooler on the lake than on terra firma.

A limited number of boat tour tickets are available by reservation at www.craterlakelodges.com. The rest of the tickets are sold first-come, first-served at the Cleetwood Trail ticket kiosk.

Hiking

July and August are the most popular months for hiking. Colorful flowers and mild weather greet the summer throngs. One of the best places to view the mid-July flora is on the **Castle Crest Wildflower Trail.** The trailhead to this 0.5-mile loop trail is 0.5 mile from the park headquarters. Stop there for directions to the trailhead as well as a self-guided trail booklet that tells you about the ponderosa pine, Shasta red fir, mountain hemlock, lodgepole pine, and rabbitbrush along the trail. Wildlife in the area includes elk, deer, foxes, pikas, marmots, and a variety of birds. Peak wildflower season is usually around the last two weeks of July.

A suitable challenge of brawn and breath is the **Garfield Peak Trail.** The trailhead to this imposing ridge is just east of Crater Lake Lodge. It is a steep climb up the 1.7-mile trail, but the wildflower displays of phlox, Indian paintbrush, and lupine, as well as frequent sightings of eagles and hawks, give ample opportunity for you to stop and catch your breath. The highlight of the hike is atop Garfield Peak, which provides a spectacular view of Crater Lake 1,888 feet below.

A new trail leads from the Pinnacles Road, just off the East Rim Drive southeast of the Phantom Ship overlook, to **Plaikni Falls,** a pretty cascade that rolls down a glacier-carved cliff. The 1.1-mile trail is along a well-graded, wheelchair-accessible dirt path.

Winter Sports

When snow buries the area in the wintertime, services and activities are cut to a minimum. However, many cross-country skiers, snowshoe enthusiasts, and winter campers enjoy this solitude. Park rangers lead **snowshoe hikes** (weather permitting) at 1pm on weekends, daily during Christmas week. Ski and snowshoe rentals are available at Rim Village.

Winter trekkers should be aware that there are no groomed cross-country trails, so it's imperative to inquire about trail, avalanche, road, and weather conditions at the visitor center. Circumnavigating the lake, which is visited by frequent snowstorms, takes 2-3 days, even in good weather. Only skilled winter hikers should attempt this 33-mile route that requires a compass and maps to traverse unmarked routes and avalanche paths.

Prior to setting out on any extended backcountry journey, pick up a permit and some free advice at the visitors center. You might also inquire about a hike to the top of **Mount Scott** (8,926 feet), the highest peak in the area. Lake views and perspectives on 12 Cascade peaks are potential rewards at the end of the 2.5-mile trek.

Trolley Tours

Passengers can take two-hour round-trip tours on newly built but historically designed **trolley cars** (541/882-1896, www.craterlaketrolley. com, tours depart 10am-3pm on the hour July-early Oct., $25 adults, $15 children ages 5-13) along Rim Drive, with several stops at scenic viewpoints. The natural gas-powered trolleys are ADA-compliant and feature commentary by a guide. Purchase tickets at the Community House at Rim Village, near the Crater Lake Lodge.

Accommodations and Food

One of the nicest things about 183,180-acre Crater Lake National Park is that it's not very developed. Lodging and services are concentrated on the southern edge of the lake at **Rim Village;** the exact opening and closing dates for services changes from year to year, depending on the snowpack. (Note: The park received 649 inches of snow—more than 54 feet—during the winter of 2010-2011!) In general, restaurants and information services are open mid-May-mid-October, with the exception of the **Rim Village Cafe,** which is open year-round. The café serves traditional breakfasts, and lunch and dinner offerings include salads, grab-and-go sandwiches, pizzas, and assorted snacks. A small grocery section in the adjoining gift shop sells basic foodstuffs and beverages in case you've run out of peanut butter or beer.

The 71-room **C Crater Lake Lodge** (541/830-8700, www.craterlakelodges.com, late May-mid-Oct., $164-225, lakefront rooms extra) is situated on the rim south of the Sinnott Overlook and is hewn of indigenous wood and stone. The massive lobby boasts a picture window on the lake and has decor echoing its 1915 origins. The stone fireplace is large enough to walk into and serves as a gathering spot on chilly evenings. Many of the rooms have expansive views of the lake below. Others face out toward upper Klamath Lake and Mount Shasta, 100 miles away in California.

Amid all the amenities of a national park hotel, it's nice to be reminded of the past by such touches as antique wallpaper and old-fashioned

© BILL MCRAE

Crater Lake Lodge

bathtubs (rooms 401 and 201 offer views of the lake from claw-foot tubs). This marriage of past and present in such a prime location has proven so popular that it's imperative to reserve many months in advance. The 72-seat **dining room** (7am-10:30am, 11:30am-2:30pm, and 5pm-10pm daily, early June-mid-Sept., $21-34) features Pacific Northwest cuisine in a classic setting, and gives preference to reservations made by hotel guests.

Seven miles south of the rim is another cluster of services called Mazama Village. At the **Cabins at Mazama Village** (541/830-8700, www.craterlakelodges.com, late May-late Sept., $140), each guest room features two queen beds and a bath, and two cabins are designed for wheelchair access. Be sure to call ahead for reservations.

Also in Mazama Village, the **Annie Creek Restaurant** (7am-10:30am and 11:30am-9pm daily, early June-mid-Sept., dinner $11-25) serves American style comfort foods, including burgers, pot roast, fried chicken, and vegetarian lasagna.

Camping

Mazama Village Campground (reservations at www.craterlakelodges.com, early June-late Sept., $21 tents, $29-35 RVs), seven miles south of the rim, has over 200 sites, restrooms with coin-operated showers, and a dump station. **Lost Creek Campground** (mid-July-early Oct., $10 tents), on the eastern section of Rim Drive, has 16 sites, water, and pit toilets. Foot traffic in the backcountry is light, so you can set up camp wherever you like in the remote areas surrounding Crater Lake.

Getting There

The only year-round access to Crater Lake is from the south via Route 62. To reach Crater Lake from Grants Pass, head for Gold Hill and take Route 234 until it meets Route 62. As you head up Route 62 you might spot roadside snow poles in anticipation of the onset of winter. This highway makes a horseshoe bend through the Cascades, starting at Medford and ending 20 miles north of Klamath Falls. The northern route via Route 138 (Roseburg to U.S. 97, south of Beaver Marsh) is usually closed by snow mid-October-July. The tremendous snowfall also closes 33-mile-long Rim Drive, although portions are opened when conditions permit. Rim Drive is generally opened to motorists around the same time as the northern entrance to the park.

CRATER LAKE HIGHWAY (HWY. 62)

Some of the locals who live near the Crater Lake Highway sport bumper stickers on their vehicles that read "I Survived Highway 62." The challenges of successfully navigating this precipitous and circuitous thoroughfare, with its horrific winter weather and slow-moving summer crowds, help give it a killer reputation. Snow can sometimes get deep enough on the upper reaches that 15-foot-tall snow poles lining the roadbed are rendered useless in helping the snowplows navigate. In these cases, the crews can only locate the road by means of a radio transmitter, embedded in steel cable, which emits a signal.

Even so, there always seems to be traffic on this winding conduit between Crater Lake and southern Oregon. This isn't surprising when you consider the scenic appeal of the Rogue River and the Cascade Mountains. And then there's fishing. The salmon runs on the Rogue River are second in size only to the ones on the Columbia. Nearly three million fish are reared and released into the Rogue from the Cole Rivers Fish Hatchery, 153 miles from the mouth of the Rogue. With swimming, boating, and rafting opportunities, the Rogue River is indeed tempting, and you too will be taking to the hills along Route 62.

The following contacts can help plan your foray into the Rogue River National Forest: **Prospect Ranger Station** (541/560-3400), **Rogue River National Forest Service** (3040 Biddle Rd., Medford, 541/618-2200), and **Travel Oregon** (http://traveloregon.com).

Hiking

Many choice hikes are found along the 50-mile stretch of the Rogue River Trail from Lost Creek Lake to the river's source at Boundary Springs, just inside Crater Lake National Park.

Lofty waterfalls, deep gushing gorges, and a natural bridge are all easily accessible. Those interested in more than just a short walk from the parking lot to the viewpoint can design hikes of 2-18 miles with or without an overnight stay. Travelers with two cars can arrange shuttles to avoid having to double back.

One of the more scenic recreation spots is owned by Boise Cascade, a timber conglomerate. Boise Cascade has constructed a botanical nature trail system through its land to a series of three waterfalls in an impressive rock-choked section of the Rogue River called the Avenue of the Giant Boulders.

The largest of the three waterfalls is **Mill Creek Falls,** which plunges 173 feet down into the river. Signs along the highway and Mill Creek Drive (formerly the old Crater Lake Highway), a scenic loop out of the community of Prospect, direct visitors to the trailhead. A large map further details the trail routes. The trail is short but steep; wear shoes you don't mind getting wet and that have good traction, as you may have to scramble over some of the boulders and wade through some small ponds along the way.

A particularly wild section of the river is found at **Takelma Gorge.** Located 1 mile from River Bridge Campground on the upper Rogue River, the trail offers vistas of sharp foaming bends in the river with logs jammed at crazy angles on the rocks, along with ferns growing in the mist of the waterfalls. Although the river's course is rugged, the grade on the trail is gentle.

Even if you're in a hurry, you should take 15 minutes to get out of your car and stretch your legs at the **Natural Bridge.** Located 0.25 mile from Natural Bridge Campground, 1 mile west of Union Creek on Route 62, here the Rogue River drops into a lava tube and disappears from sight, only to emerge a little way downstream. A short paved path takes you to an artificial bridge that fords this unique section of the river. Several placards along the way explain the formation of the Natural Bridge and other points of interest.

Just outside of Union Creek on Route 62 is the spectacular **Rogue River Gorge.** At this narrowest point on the river, the action of the water has carved out a deep chasm in the rock. A short trail with several well-placed overlooks follows the rim of the gorge. Green mossy walls, logjams, and a frothy torrent of water are all clearly visible from the trail. Informative placards discuss curiosities like the living stump and the potholes carved in the lava rock by pebbles and the action of the water.

Another short hike for hurried motorists is **National Creek Falls.** An easy 0.5-mile walk down a trail bordered by magnificent Douglas firs leads to this tumultuous cascade. To get here, take Route 230 to Forest Service Road 6530. Follow the road until you reach the trailhead, marked by a sign.

A two-mile hike down a cool and shady trail takes you to the source of the mighty Rogue River—**Boundary Springs.** Situated just inside Crater Lake National Park, it's a great place for a picnic. About one mile down the path from the trailhead, hang a left at the fork to get to Boundary Springs. Once at the springs, you'll discover small cataracts rising out of the jumbled volcanic rock that's densely covered with moss and other vegetation. Despite the temptation to get a closer look, the vegetation here is extremely fragile, so refrain from walking on the moss. To get here, take Route 230 north from Route 62 to the crater rim viewpoint, where parking can be found on the left-hand side of the road.

To enjoy the golden hues of larches and aspens in the fall, take Route 62 from Medford and turn east onto Route 140. En route, you might stop at Fish Lake or Lake of the Woods resorts. From here you can take scenic Westside Road to Fort Klamath; Crater Lake lies a scant 6 miles from here.

Accommodations

The accommodations you'll find on Route 62 are rustic and simple, catering mainly to anglers and lovers of the great outdoors.

Rooms at the **Maple Leaf Motel** (20717 Rte. 62, Shady Cove, 541/878-2169, www.maple-leafmotel.org, $80-95) come equipped with a microwave, a toaster oven, a small fridge, cable TV, and a picnic and barbecue area to grill the day's catch or some burgers if the fish weren't biting. The **Royal Coachman Motel** (21906 Rte. 62, Shady Cove, 541/878-2481, www.royalcoachmanmotel.com, $59-76) has kitchenettes, cable TV, and HBO. The more expensive rooms have lovely decks that overlook the river.

The **Prospect Hotel and Motel** (391 Mill Creek Rd., Prospect, 541/560-3664 or 800/944-6490, www.prospecthotel.com, historic hotel rooms $140-205 including breakfast, motel rooms $90-145) gives you a choice between something old and something new. The hotel, built in 1889 and listed on the National Register of Historic Places, has several small but comfortable guest rooms with baths. The rooms are named after local residents and famous people who have stayed at the hotel, including Zane Grey, Teddy Roosevelt, and Jack London. Because the hotel is small and old, no children, smoking, or pets are permitted. The adjacent motel features clean, spacious, and modern units, with some kitchenettes available. Pets are welcome in the motel.

Not far away from Prospect on the Crater Lake Highway is the **Union Creek Resort** (56484 Hwy. 62, Prospect, 866/560-3565, www.unioncreekoregon.com). Built in the early 1930s, the Union Creek is listed on the National Register of Historic Places. Open year-round, it has rooms available in your choice of the original lodge, simple cabins with bathrooms, or housekeeping cabins with kitchens and bathrooms. The lodge rooms ($60-68), paneled in knotty pine, have washbasins; guests share the bathrooms down the hall. The stone fireplace in the lobby was built of opalized wood from Lakeview, Oregon. The sleeping cabins with baths range $110-165. The vacation rental housekeeping cabins sleep up to 10 and range $220-265. If you like rustic cabins and lodges, the Union Creek is the real deal. The **Union Creek Country Store,** located at the resort, carries groceries and other essential items. Fishing licenses and Sno-Park permits can also be purchased here.

Camping

For those who like roughing it in style with all

ASHLAND

of the perks of an RV, **Rogue River RV Park** (218005 Hwy. 62, Shady Cove, 541/878-2404) is right on the banks of the Rogue River about 23 miles north of Medford on Route 62.

Five miles below Lost Creek Lake on Route 62 at 1,476 feet in elevation is **Rogue Elk County Park** (Jackson County Parks and Recreation, 541/776-7001, mid-Apr.-mid-Oct., $18, $21 with electricity and water hookups). This campground features sites for tents and RVs (up to 28 feet) with piped water, showers, and flush toilets on the premises. The kids will enjoy swimming in Elk Creek, which, in addition to being adjacent to the campground, is warmer and safer than the Rogue River; a playground adds to the fun. The park has a $3 per vehicle day-use fee.

Along the shore of Lost Creek Lake is **Joseph Stewart State Park** (35251 Rte. 62, Trail, 541/560-3334, www.oregonstateparks. org, Mar.-Oct., $17-20). This large campground is set on a big grassy field above the reservoir and has all the usual state park amenities. Bike paths, a beach, and barbecue grills make this a family-friendly locale, if not exactly getting away from it all. Boat-launching facilities for Lost Creek Lake are located nearby, and eight miles of hiking trails and bike paths crisscross the park. Lost Creek Lake also has a marina, a beach, and boat rentals.

If you want to get away from the highway, head for **Abbott Creek** (Rogue National Forest, Prospect Ranger Station, 541/560-3400, late May-Oct., $12), but bear in mind that this is where off-highway vehicle riders come to play. One of the few backwoods camps in the area that has potable water, it's 7 miles northeast of the town of Prospect on Route 62 and 3 miles down Forest Service Road 68.

Set along the woodsy bank of Union Creek where it merges with the upper Rogue River is **Union Creek** (Rogue National Forest, Prospect Ranger Station, 541/560-3400, late May-Oct., $12). Located 11 miles northeast of Prospect, you'll find 78 sites for tents and RVs (up to 16 feet) with picnic tables, grills, piped water, and vault toilets. Many fine hikes on the Rogue River Trail are within close proximity of the campground.

Half a mile past Union Creek Campground on Route 62 is **Farewell Bend** (Rogue National Forest, Prospect Ranger Station, 541/560-3400, late May-early Sept., $16), the best-appointed of the Upper Rogue campgrounds. Near the junction of Route 62 and Route 230, the camp has 61 sites for tents and RVs (up to 22 feet) with picnic tables and grills. Piped water and flush toilets are also within the campground boundaries. This campground is situated along the banks of the Upper Rogue near the Rogue River Gorge Trail.

A nice little campground tucked off the highway yet fairly close to the Rogue River and Crater Lake National Park is **Huckleberry Campground** (Rogue National Forest, Prospect Ranger Station, 541/560-3400, late May-Oct. weather permitting, free, no water). To get here, go about 18 miles northeast of Prospect on Route 62 and then 4 miles down Forest Service Road 60. You'll find 25 sites for tents and RVs (up to 21 feet) with picnic tables and grills. This campground is at an elevation of 5,400 feet, so be sure to have the proper gear to ensure a comfortable visit.

Food

The best restaurants along Highway 62 are at the old-fashioned resorts in Prospect and Union Creek. The dining room at the **Prospect Hotel** (391 Mill Creek Rd., Prospect, 541/560-3664 or 800/944-6490, 5pm-9pm daily May-Oct. and holidays, $10-23) is recommended. You'll enjoy elk meatballs in red wine and mushroom sauce, or pork loin with Jack Daniels sauce. Local huckleberry pie is a wonderful seasonal treat.

Beckie's (Union Creek Resort, 56484 Rte. 62, 541/560-3565 or 866/560-3565, 8am-9pm daily Apr.-Oct., 8am-7pm Sun.-Thurs., 8am-8pm Fri.-Sat. Nov.-Mar., $5-16) is a cozy place to stop for a bite to eat. One half of the building is an old log cabin; the other half is of modern design with plenty of windows. Breakfast comes with all the trimmings. The lunch menu features sandwiches and burgers. Dinner includes chicken, pork chops, and steak entrées.

Klamath Falls

Klamath Falls, or "K Falls" as locals call it, is the population hub of south-central Oregon with about 20,000 people within the city limits and an additional 40,000 in the surrounding area. This community is used to hard times after witnessing the decline of its previous economic engines, starting with the railroads and moving on to the timber industry. Farming and ranching are still an important part of the local economy, as are tourism and the influx of new settlers, particularly retirees. The cost of living here is comparatively low, and the climate is dry, with more than 290 days of sunshine; winters are cool but not damp, and it's less cold and rainy than Bend.

Downtown Klamath Falls has a clutch of

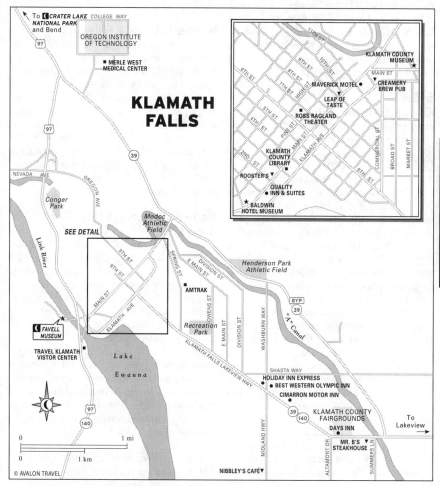

© AVALON TRAVEL

handsome historic buildings, many revitalized with interesting shops and dining spots, and three intriguing museums that shed light on different aspects of local history and culture. But the real draw of Klamath Falls is out in the surrounding countryside. The native trout of Klamath Lake and the nearby Wood and Williamson Rivers are legendary, averaging 21 inches. There's world-class white-water rafting on the upper Klamath River, with several hair-raising rapids topping Class IV. But most of all it's the Klamath Basin national wildlife refuges, a complex of six lake and wetland units stretching into California, that draw visitors—and lots of birds—to the area. The refuges host some 50 nesting pairs of bald eagles, as well as more than 400 other bird species.

SIGHTS

Klamath Falls's museums are within walking distance of each other, and the broad downtown streets deserve a stroll.

◖ Favell Museum

A fine collection of Native American artifacts and Western art is found at the **Favell Museum** (125 W. Main St., 541/882-9996, www.favellmuseum.org, 10:30am-4:30pm Tues.-Sat., $10 adults, $5 children ages 6-16, children under 6 free, $25 family). Here you'll find beautiful displays of Native American stonework, bone and shell work, beadwork, quilts, basketry, pottery, and Pacific Northwest coast carvings as well as a collection of over 60,000 mounted arrowheads. Another attraction is the collection of miniature working firearms, ranging from Gatling guns to inch-long Colt 45s, displayed in the museum's walk-in vault.

The museum also houses one of Oregon's best collections of Western art. The gift shop and art gallery specialize in limited edition prints and original Western art.

Baldwin Hotel Museum

Travel back in time to the early 1900s thanks to the **Baldwin Hotel Museum** (31 Main St., 541/883-4207, 10am-4pm Wed.-Sat. Memorial Day-Labor Day), which is adorned with original fixtures and furnishings, the legacy of talented photographer Maud Baldwin. Her father—a U.S. senator—built the place first as a hardware store, then as a hotel. Presidents Teddy Roosevelt, Taft, and Wilson have all stayed here. Two different tours are offered: a two-hour tour of all four floors ($10 adults, $8 seniors and children ages 5-12), and a one-hour tour that visits just two floors ($5 adults, $4 seniors and children). The final full tour starts at 1:30pm, and the final shorter tour starts at 2:30pm.

Klamath County Museum

You can get good background information on the region with a visit to the **Klamath County Museum** (1451 Main St., 541/883-4208, 9am-5pm Tues.-Sat., $5 adults, $4 seniors and students, $5 children ages 5-12) in the old national armory building. The natural history section has exhibits on fossils, geology, minerals, and indigenous wildlife of the Klamath Basin. The exploration and settlement area depicts the hardships of pioneer life, the events leading to the Modoc Indian War, and events up through the world wars.

Collier Memorial State Park

About 30 miles north of Klamath Falls on U.S. 97 is **Collier Memorial State Park** (541/783-2471 or 800/551-6949, day use free). Donated to the state in 1945 by Alfred and Andrew Collier as a memorial to their parents, this 146-acre park documents technological improvements in the history of logging.

The park's Pioneer Village includes a logger's homestead cabin stocked with a wide variety of tools and artifacts, a blacksmith shed, an assortment of logging machinery that includes log wagons with wheels made of cross-cut sections of logs bound in iron, and chain-drive trucks with hard rubber tires. Also on display are steam-propelled devices including tractors, a narrow-gauge locomotive, and a one-person handcart.

Don't miss the over-200-foot-long 16-foot-wide **Clatsop Fir,** a fallen tree that was mature

© BILL MCRAE

The Klamath County Museum has good natural history exhibits.

when Columbus landed in the New World. The tree could supply enough wood for several four-bedroom homes. For better or for worse, it's probably the largest Douglas fir ever cut.

Wildlife Refuges

The lakes, marshes, and streams in the Klamath Basin are protected by six different wildlife refuges that stretch between southern Oregon and northern California and are centrally managed by the **Klamath Basin National Wildlife Refuge Complex.** The refuge complex headquarters and **visitor center** (530/667-2231, www.fws.gov/klamathbasinrefuges, 8am-4:30pm Mon.-Fri., 9am-4pm Sat.-Sun.) is 4 miles south of the California-Oregon border on U.S. 97.

December-February the Klamath Basin is home to one of the largest wintering concentration of bald eagles in the Lower 48 states. The thousands of winter waterfowl that reside here provide a plentiful food source for these raptors. By January, 700-800 eagles from as far north as southeastern Alaska's Chilkat River,

Saskatchewan, and the Northwest Territories congregate in the area.

In addition to a readily available food supply, the eagles require night-roosting areas. The **Bear Valley National Wildlife Refuge** (between Keno and Worden) has mature stands of timber that can support up to 300 eagles per night. The eagles prefer trees on northeastern slopes that protect them from the cold southwest and westerly winds. However, the eagles *don't* like it when people bother them. Hence the roosting areas are closed early November-March 30.

The good news is that there are still ample opportunities to view our national bird, especially when it is very cold. Contact the Fish and Wildlife office for the latest information on the best eagle-watching locations. Good sightings can be had driving to Bear Valley at sunrise. To get there, head 1 mile south of Worden on U.S. 97. Turn right on Keno Worden Road past the grain silos, cross the railroad tracks, and take an immediate left on the gravel road. Travel for about 1 mile and pull off the road. From here you can sometimes see up to 100 bald eagles soar from their roosts at the top of the ridge, headed to their daytime feeding area on the refuge to the east. Bring binoculars, warm clothing, and a camera with a telephoto lens.

A world-renowned event, the **Winter Wings Festival** (www.winterwingsfest.org) is held in February. The highlight is a predawn field trip to the nearby Bear Valley roost.

March-May is when waterfowl and shorebirds stop over in the basin on their way north to their breeding grounds in Alaska and Canada. They rest and fatten up during the spring to build the necessary strength and body fat to carry them through their long migration. May-July is the nesting season for thousands of marsh birds and waterfowl. The **Klamath Marsh National Wildlife Refuge** (north of Klamath Falls off U.S. 97) is a good place in spring to observe sandhill cranes, shorebirds, waterfowl, and raptors.

The summer months are ideal for taking the self-guided auto tour routes and canoe trails. Descriptive leaflets for both are available from the refuge office. Among the most prolific waterfowl and marsh bird areas in the Pacific Northwest, over 25,000 ducks, 2,600 Canada geese, and thousands of marsh and shorebirds are raised here each year. You may also see American white pelicans, *Pelecanus erythrorhynchos,* at the **Upper Klamath National Wildlife Refuge** (north of Klamath Falls) during the summer.

Another high point is the **Upper Klamath Canoe Trail,** which follows a 9.5-mile passage through lakes, marshes, and streams at the northwest corner of Upper Klamath Lake within the boundaries of the refuge. Birding is excellent along the canoe trail as mature ponderosa pines come right to the edge of the marsh, creating habitat for raptors, songbirds, and waterfowl. The trail departs from Rocky Point, about 25 miles northwest of Klamath Falls on Route 140. Canoe rentals ($40 per day) are available from **Rocky Point Resort** (28121 Rocky Point Rd., 541/356-2287, www.rockypointoregon.com).

Tule Lake and Lower Klamath Refuges (south of Klamath Falls in California) are open during daylight hours. Overnight camping is not permitted in any of the refuges.

SPORTS AND RECREATION

With all the lakes, rivers, and mountains in the region, there's no shortage of fishing, rafting, golfing, and other recreational opportunities. Here's a short list of some local attractions.

Boating

One way to get out onto Oregon's largest lake is to rent a sailboat through **Meridian Sail Center** (Pelican Marina, Dock C, 928 Front St., 541/884-5869, www.meridiansail.com). Sailboat rentals are $70-100 half-day, $100-140 full-day. Sailing instruction is also available. Call ahead for the sailing report and to make reservations.

Fishing

Local guides can get you outfitted and on the water angling for the elusive big one. **Darren Roe Guide Service** (4849 Summers Ln., 541/884-3825, www.roeoutfitters.com) offers trips on Klamath Lake and the nearby Wood and Willamson Rivers, noted for their runs of wild trout. Rates are roughly $450 for two people for a full day.

Golf

There are several area courses open to the public. **Harbor Links** (601 Harbor Isle Blvd., 541/882-0609) and **Shield Crest** (3151 Shieldcrest Dr., 541/884-1493) both offer 9- and 18-hole courses with greens fees in the $25-50 range. The **Running Y Ranch Resort** (5500 Running Y Rd., 541/850-5500 or 877/866-1266, www.runningy.com, $89-119 for 18 holes) offers a 7,138-yard 18-hole course designed by Arnold Palmer.

Rafting

Twenty miles (just under an hour's drive) west of Klamath Falls is what's known as Hell's Corner of the Upper Klamath River. **Arrowhead River Adventures** (720 Greenleaf Dr., Eagle Point, 541/830-3388 or 800/227-7741, www.

arrowheadadventures.com) offers daylong trips ($149) through this remote secluded canyon June-September. With several Class IV-plus rapids, the Upper Klamath provides some of the best spring and summer rafting in the state.

You can also arrange a raft trip in the Upper Klamath River canyons through Ashland's **Adventure Center** (40 N. Main St., Ashland, 541/488-2819 or 800/444-2819, www.rafting-tours.com). In addition to a day trip ($135, includes transportation to and from Ashland), they offer a two-day trip down the river with a night of fully catered riverside camping ($339).

ENTERTAINMENT AND EVENTS

The region's cultural hub is the **Ross Ragland Theater** (218 N. 7th St., 541/884-5483, www.rrtheater.org). In addition to the Klamath Symphony and other community organizations, country stars, internationally acclaimed guest artists, and touring Broadway troupes grace the stage of this 800-seat auditorium. Call the theater or check the daily *Herald and News* to see what's scheduled.

ACCOMMODATIONS

Travelers on a budget will appreciate **Maverick Motel** (1220 Main St., 541/882-6688 or 800/404-6690, www.maverickmotel.com, $50-55) and **Cimarron Motor Inn** (3060 S. 6th St., 541/882-4601 or 800/742-2648, www.cimarroninnklamathfalls.com, $65-89) for their pools and continental breakfasts, and for allowing pets.

Midrange properties are the domain of the chains. **Best Western Olympic Inn** (2627 S. 6th St., 541/882-9665, $119-149), **Holiday Inn Express** (2500 S. 6th St., 541/884-9999, $129-149), **Quality Inn** (100 Main St., 541/882-4666, $69-99), and **Days Inn** (3612 S. 6th St., 541/882-8864 or 800/329-7466, $69-79) all feature the expected pools, continental breakfasts, and other upgrades.

The **Running Y Ranch Resort** (5500 Running Y Rd., 541/850-5500 or 800/851-6013, www.runningy.com, $154-194 d hotel rooms) offers the total Klamath Basin package

experience. This upscale golf resort has country club homes, and travelers can stay in the deluxe guest rooms at the ranch lodge. The 82 guest rooms are a mix of comfortable hotel-style rooms and well-appointed one-bedroom suites. Two- and three-bedroom houses are also available.

Camping

Most of the campgrounds you'll find in the vicinity of Klamath Falls are privately owned RV campgrounds with electric, water, and sewer hookups as well as other creature comforts like swimming pools, laundries, and recreational halls. These properties also tend to be in prime locations, which accounts for rates that are steeper than those of their public counterparts. Fortunately, there are several places to pitch a tent in both types of park without having to deal with a 40-foot-long mobile home parked right next to your sleeping bag.

Across from the logging museum at **Collier Memorial State Park** is a pretty campground ($19-22), set near the convergence of the Williamson River (locally famous for its trout) and Spring Creek.

Rocky Point Resort (28121 Rocky Point Rd., 541/356-2287, www.rockypointoregon.com, Apr.-mid-Nov., tents $22, RVs $28-30, cabins $140) is close to the Upper Klamath National Wildlife Refuge, about a half-hour from Klamath Falls. This resort has 5 tent and 28 RV sites with hookups as well as rustic cabins. Flush toilets, showers, firewood, a laundry, a recreation hall, and other summer camp trappings are available. Ask about canoe rentals for trips on the Upper Klamath Canoe Trail.

Several other campgrounds are also found on Upper Klamath Lake. The best deal around is still **Hagelstein Park** (17301 Hwy. 97 N., 541/883-5371, Apr.-late Nov., free), a small park just off the highway with boat ramp. In addition to being the only campground on the east shore of the lake, it's the least expensive campground in the area. To get there, head north of Klamath Falls for 10 miles and look for signs on the right side of the road.

Approximately seven miles farther north on

U.S. 97 is **KOA Klamath Falls** (3435 Shasta Way, 541/884-4644, year-round, $25-37, cabins $54). Set along the shore of Upper Klamath Lake, the park features 18 tent and 73 RV sites with hookups. In true KOA style, flush toilets, showers, a pool, a laundry, a recreation hall, and other amenities are available.

FOOD

The popular spot for breakfast and lunch is **Nibbley's Cafe** (2650 Washburn Way, 541/883-2314, 6am-4pm Mon., 6am-9pm Tues.-Fri., 7am-9pm Sat., 8am-2pm Sun., breakfast $5-11). The oatmeal pancakes are locally renowned, and the omelets are yummy.

Right downtown **A Leap of Taste** (907 Main St., 541/850-9414, 7:30am-6pm Mon.-Fri., 8am-3pm Sat., $4-8) is a great place for a sandwich or coffee, but it's a bit more than that. It also stocks a small selection of organic groceries, including locally raised meat, and serves as a place for young adults to learn job skills (in a way that's a bit more intentional than most coffee shops).

Rooster's Steak and Chop House (205 Main St., 541/850-8414, 4pm-10pm daily, $22-38) is K Falls's restaurant of the moment, with excellent steaks and a classy atmosphere.

A good spot for casual dining is the **Creamery Brew Pub & Grill** (1320 Main St., 541/273-5222, 11am-9:30pm daily, $8-18), with good beer and serviceable pub food. One of the great attractions of the Creamery is its outdoor seating on the building's old loading dock.

INFORMATION

Over 2.2 million acres of Klamath County is publicly owned. The **Klamath Falls Ranger District Office** (2819 Dahlia St., 541/883-6714) can provide outdoor recreational information on the Winema National Forest and other surrounding natural areas. The **Bureau of Land Management** (2795 Anderson Ave., 541/883-6916) can also provide relevant information.

You'll find the **Oregon Welcome Center** on U.S. 97 about halfway between Klamath Falls and the California-Oregon border. They have a broad collection of brochures and information about locales all over the state.

For information on Klamath Falls, contact **Discover Klamath** (205 Riverside Dr., 541/882-1501 or 800/445-6728, www.discoverklamath.com).

GETTING THERE

Amtrak (1600 Oak Ave., 541/884-2822) can connect you with northern and southern destinations via the *Coast Starlight* train. **Greyhound** (445 S. Spring St., 541/883-2609) can take you to Bend or the I-5 corridor. The **Point** bus (541/883-2609, www.oregon-point.com) provides connections to Ashland and Brookings.

BEND AND CENTRAL OREGON

Central Oregon is one of the most magnificent natural playgrounds in this part of the world, with a scenic collage of green forest and black basalt outcroppings topped by extinct volcano cones covered with snow. Plenty of lakes, rivers, and waterfalls provide a sparkling contrast to the earth tones. It's easy to find ways to explore these natural areas: hiking, biking, and cross-country ski trails abound, as do resorts both luxurious and rustic, waterways teeming with fish, and increasingly, good restaurants and shopping.

The central Oregon Cascades, and especially Mount Bachelor, are a haven for winter sports that range from alpine and Nordic skiing to snowmobiling, snowboarding, and snowshoeing. Skiing here can be a special treat for westside Oregonians accustomed to Mount Hood's fierce weather and frequently dense, heavy snow. Of course, Bachelor *is* in Oregon, not Utah, so don't expect all powder all the time.

Central Oregon has gained recognition for world-class golfing. And no wonder: With over a dozen courses, this region of the state offers just about every kind of golf challenge. The warm sunny days, cool evenings, and spectacular mountain scenery make every shot a memorable one.

With respect to everything except rain, the climate is a bit more extreme here that it is on the west side of the Cascades. Expect it to be fairly dry, though perhaps not as constantly sunny as advertised in many tourist publications—that snow on Mount Bachelor has to come from somewhere—cold in the winter,

© JUDY JEWELL

HIGHLIGHTS

◖ High Desert Museum: This indoor-outdoor museum has exhibits on contemporary Native American life, the development of the West, photography, and wildlife (page 501).

◖ Mount Bachelor: When weather permits, you can ride the Summit Lift all the way to the top of the mountain (page 506).

◖ Deschutes River Trail: This trail ushers runners, walkers, and bicyclists along the Deschutes. Cyclists can ride from downtown Bend all the way to Benham Falls (page 508).

◖ Metolius River: At the headwaters of the Metolius, the water emerges from hillside springs and immediately becomes a full-sized river (page 531).

◖ Smith Rock State Park: Famed for its rock climbing, Smith Rock has just as much to offer hikers, who can search for golden eagles on the cliffs (page 537).

◖ Museum at Warm Springs: Not only does this museum display a wide variety of Native American artifacts, it also features audio and visual exhibits portraying the cultures of the Paiute, Warm Springs, and Wasco people (page 545).

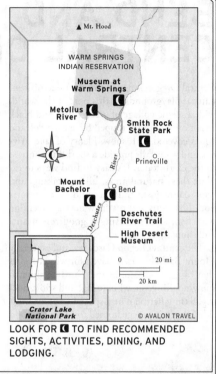

LOOK FOR ◖ TO FIND RECOMMENDED SIGHTS, ACTIVITIES, DINING, AND LODGING.

and hot in the summer, with cool to cold evenings year-round.

PLANNING YOUR TIME

Plan to spend a few days exploring this part of the state. A long weekend will do for a taste or if you're very focused on skiing or a particular hiking trip or fishing destination. **Bend** is a natural base in the area, but it's also worth considering **Sunriver,** especially if you have a family or group of friends. Both of these places allow easy access to the Deschutes River, the High Desert Museum, and the Lava Lands sights.

If you plan to do a bit of hiking in the national forests, pick up a **Northwest Forest Pass** (www.fs.fed.us/r6/passespermits, $5

one-day, $30 one-year), which is required for parking at most trailheads and which will get you into sites such as the Lava Lands Visitor Center. Passes are sold online and at trailheads, ranger stations, visitors centers, most local resorts, and many sporting goods and outdoors stores.

In the summer, camping is a good option. There are few campgrounds prettier than the ones along the Cascades Lakes Highway, and most have good places to fish and hike nearby.

However, if fishing is going to be your main activity, don't overlook **Prineville;** the Crooked River offers outstanding fly-fishing and a string of campgrounds below the Prineville Reservoir.

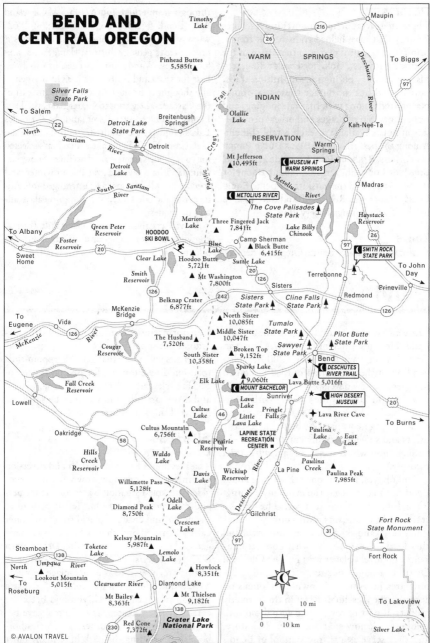

BEND AND CENTRAL OREGON

Timothy Lake

Maupin

WARM SPRINGS

To Biggs

Pinhead Buttes
5,585ft▲

*Silver Falls
State Park*

INDIAN

Deschutes River

To Salem

*Detroit Lake
State Park*

Breitenbush
Springs

*Olallie
Lake*

RESERVATION

Kah-Nee-Ta

North

Santiam River

Detroit

Pacific Crest Trail

Mt Jefferson
▲10,495ft

Warm
Springs

**MUSEUM AT
WARM SPRINGS** ★

*Detroit
Lake*

South Santiam River

METOLIUS RIVER

Metolius River

Madras

To Albany

*Green Peter
Reservoir*

Marion
Lake

Three Fingered Jack
▲ 7,841ft

*The Cove Palisades
State Park*

Lake Billy
Chinook

*Haystack
Reservoir*

*Foster
Reservoir*

**HOODOO
SKI BOWL**

Blue
Lake

Camp Sherman
▲ Black Butte
6,415ft

Sweet
Home

Clear Lake

Hoodoo Butte
5,721ft

Suttle Lake

Terrebonne

**SMITH ROCK
STATE PARK**

To John
Day

*Smith
Reservoir*

▲ Mt Washington
7,800ft

Sisters

Prineville

To
Eugene

Vida

Belknap Crater
6,877ft

*Sisters
State Park*

*Cline Falls
State Park*

Redmond

McKenzie
Bridge

North Sister
10,085ft

*Tumalo
State Park*

*Pilot Butte
State Park*

McKenzie River

*Cougar
Reservoir*

The Husband ▲
7,520ft

Middle Sister
10,047ft

*Sawyer
State Park*

Bend

South Sister
10,358ft

Broken Top
9,152ft

**DESCHUTES
RIVER TRAIL**

*Fall Creek
Reservoir*

Sparks Lake
▲ 9,060ft

Lava Butte 5,016ft

MOUNT BACHELOR

**HIGH DESERT
MUSEUM**

Lowell

Elk Lake

*Lava
Lake*

Sunriver

*Cultus
Lake*

*Little
Lava Lake*

Pringle
Falls

Lava River Cave

To Burns

Oakridge

Cultus Mountain
6,756ft

*Crane Prairie
Reservoir*

**LAPINE STATE
RECREATION
CENTER** ■

*Paulina
Lake*

*East
Lake*

*Hills
Creek
Reservoir*

*Waldo
Lake*

*Davis
Lake*

*Wickiup
Reservoir*

La Pine

Paulina
Creek

Paulina Peak ▲
7,985ft

Willamette Pass
5,128ft

Diamond Peak
8,750ft

*Odell
Lake*

Gilchrist

*Fort Rock
State Monument*

*Crescent
Lake*

Kelsay Mountain
5,987ft▲

Steamboat

*Toketee
Lake*

*Lemolo
Lake*

Fort Rock

North

Umpqua River

Lookout Mountain
5,015ft

Clearwater River

Diamond Lake

▲ Howlock
8,351ft

To
Roseburg

Mt Bailey ▲
8,363ft

▲ Mt Thielsen
9,182ft

To Lakeview

Red Cone
7,372ft▲

*Crater Lake
National Park*

0   10 mi

0   10 km

Silver Lake

© AVALON TRAVEL

BEND

Resorts

There are several premier resorts in Deschutes County that have helped transform it from a primarily agricultural area to the Aspen of the Pacific Northwest. Golf, horseback riding, tennis, swimming, biking-jogging-hiking trails, saunas, and hot tubs grace these year-round playgrounds, along with first-rate lodgings and restaurants. Ski packages and other special offers are also available at each establishment. Among the best resorts are **Black Butte Ranch** near Sisters, **Brasada Ranch** outside Prineville, **Sunriver Lodge** in Sunriver, **Mount Bachelor Village Resort** on the outskirts of Bend, **Eagle Crest Resort** near Redmond, and **Kah-Nee-Ta** on the Warm Springs Reservation.

Tours

A great way to explore central Oregon in depth is through **Wanderlust Tours** (143 SW Cleveland Ave., Bend, 541/389-8359 or 800/962-2862, www.wanderlusttours.com), where the focus is on the area's geology, history, flora, fauna, and local issues. Wanderlust has been in this business for years and really does it right; it's generally thought to be the best tour company east of the Cascades. Day trips to Crater Lake, the Lava Lands, the Deschutes River, and the Cascades Lakes Highway are featured. Canoe lakes in the high Cascades ($55), or take a hike that's selected for your group's interests and abilities. Snowshoe tours ($55 half-day) are available in winter, and special moonlight trips can be arranged too. All-day trips include lunch; vegetarian meals available on request.

Bicyclists can sign on with **Cog Wild** (http://cogwild.com) for single- or multiday mountain bike tours.

Bend

There are two important things to know about Bend. First, it's different than it was last year. Growth went crazy in the early 2000s, with a good bit of the population of 81,000 housed in expensive new developments, earning Bend a ranking in 2006 as the nation's fifth-most-overvalued real estate market—then the crash came, leaving many partially built-out developments and some practically empty new subdivisions, from which there's been a substantial recovery.

And oh, yes, there is one other thing about Bend: no matter what the economy's doing, it's a fantastic place to visit. The hiking trails, fishing streams, golf courses, whitewater runs, and ski slopes are top-notch; and the downtown is lively, with good restaurants and lovely places to stay. The Old Mill District, a huge housing, office, and shopping area just south of downtown, opens up access to the Deschutes River in this formerly industrial part of town. The actual old mill smokestacks now soar above an REI store, and they serve as a fitting symbol of Bend's transformation from mill town into recreational hot spot.

Visitors will notice that a massive boom-time road-building effort has focused on the use of traffic circles rather than stoplights. Slow down and drive carefully, and you may be surprised how well this system works.

SIGHTS
Drake Park

The Deschutes River has a dam and diversion channel just above downtown Bend. It provides valuable irrigation water for the farmers and ranchers of the dry but fertile plateau to the north, and creates a placid stretch of water called Mirror Pond that is home to Canada geese, ducks, and other wildlife. **Drake Park** (777 NW Riverside Blvd.) is on the east bank of this greenbelt and is a nice place to relax, have a quiet lunch, walk the dog, or toss a Frisbee around. However, you had better be careful where you step, as the birds leave behind numerous land mines. The neighborhoods surrounding the park have many older

© JUDY JEWELL

The Deschutes River travels through Bend.

homes surrounded by lawns and trees, and are also good places to walk.

High Desert Museum

Six miles south of Bend is the **High Desert Museum** (59800 U.S. 97 S., 541/382-4754, www.highdesertmuseum.org, 9am-5pm daily May-Oct., 10am-4pm daily Nov.-Apr., $15 adults, $12 seniors, $9 children ages 5-12, children ages 4 and under free). Although the admission may seem steep, this is an excellent indoor-outdoor museum that will take half a day to explore in detail.

Along the many trails that wind through the 150-acre facility, visitors can observe river otters at play, porcupines sticking it to each other, and birds of prey dispassionately watching over the whole scene. Replicas of a sheepherder's cabin, a settler's cabin, forestry displays, and other historical interpretations are also along the museum walkways. Join a naturalist for a nature walk or a meet-up with the museum's raptors. Another highlight is the **Donald M. Kerr Bird of Prey Center,** with resident bald and golden eagles, a great horned owl, and more.

Inside the museum's main building, unique exhibits, slide and movie shows, galleries, and pioneer history demonstrations are presented. The "desertarium" is a special delight full of native plants and populated by 37 small critters whose nocturnal lifestyles often keep them from view in the wild. Bats, lizards, mice, toads, snakes, and owls reveal that the desert is more alive than its superficially barren landscape might suggest.

The **Earle A. Chiles Center** exhibit on the spirit of the West features eight "you are there" life-size dioramas. This walk through time begins 8,000 years ago beside a still marsh and takes you to a fur brigade camp, into the depths of a gold mine, and down Main Street in a boisterous frontier town.

The **Spirit of the West Gallery** has representative arts and artifacts of the early American West, as well as tools, clothing, and other personal belongings from the 19th century. The Bounds collection of Native American artifacts

BEND

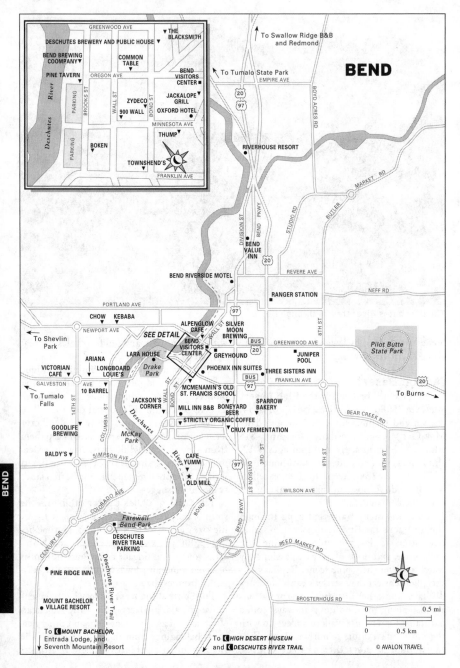

and the Hall of Plateau Heritage balance out the museum's coverage of the peoples of the high desert, while the Changing Forest exhibit addresses old-growth life cycles and other issues of forest ecology. The **Henry J. Casey Hall of Plateau Heritage,** an 8,000-square-foot venue, showcases the Doris Swayze Bounds Native American artifact collection as well as other Native Americana.

The scope and interactive nature of this facility make it appealing for people who don't usually like museums. If you end up staying longer than you expected, stop for lunch or a snack at the museum café.

Lava Lands Visitor Center and Lava Butte

About 11 miles south of Bend on U.S. 97 are the **Lava Lands Visitor Center** (58201 S. Hwy. 97, 541/593-2421, www.fs.usda.gov/centraloregon, 9am-5pm daily mid-June-Labor Day, 9am-5pm Thurs.-Mon. May-mid-June and Labor Day-Sept. 30, admission with NW Forest Pass) and **Lava Butte.** The center has some interpretive exhibits that explain the region's volcanic history, as well as a small but good selection of local geology books. Guided walks that provide a good introduction to the Lava Lands are offered during the summer.

After your orientation, cruise on up the steep drive to the top of 500-foot-high Lava Butte, just behind the visitors center. The observation platform on top of this fire lookout (established in 1928) offers the best viewpoint. Nearly one mile above sea level, the butte affords a commanding panorama of the Cascade Range. On a clear day you can see most of the major peaks, with Mounts Jefferson and Hood looming prominently on the northern horizon. These snowcapped turrets form the backdrop to a 10-square-mile lava field.

Two short trails start from the visitors center: the 0.3-mile **Whispering Pines** trail is a short paved path along the edge of the lava flow; the paved but steep **Trail of the Molten Land** cuts 0.5 mile across the lava. Don't be surprised

© JUDY JEWELL

the fire lookout at Lava Butte

to see blue-tailed lizards sunning themselves alongside these trails. You can also see *kipukas,* small islands of green trees surrounded by a sea of black lava, and what geologists call splatter. You'll know it when you see it, as it looks exactly like what it sounds like.

Benham Falls

Benham Falls is four miles down Forest Service Road 9702 from the Lava Lands Visitor Center. Give other cars a wide berth and plenty of following distance, as the road's pumice and fine dust are hard on paint jobs and engines. The road leads to a small picnic area in a grove of old-growth ponderosa pines on the bank of the Deschutes River. Be sure to tote your own liquids; there is no water.

The hike to the falls is an easy half-mile jaunt downstream. Take the footbridge across the river and enjoy your stroll past a spectacular section of untamed white water. While the water in the Deschutes is much too cold and dangerous for a swim, it's ideal for soaking your feet a little after you've completed your hike.

Benham Falls was created when magma from Lava Butte splashed over the side, flowing five miles to the Deschutes. When the molten rock collided with the icy water, the churning rapids and crashing waterfall were created.

When you reach the falls, you'll see another parking area. If you want to forgo the hike, reach the falls by heading south from Bend on the Cascade Lakes Highway and turning east (left) onto Forest Road 41, shortly after the Seventh Mountain Resort.

Lava River Cave

About 12 miles south of Bend on U.S. 97 and 1 mile south of Lava Butte is Oregon's longest known lava tube, the **Lava River Cave** (541/593-2421, 9am-5pm daily mid-June-Labor Day, 9am-5pm Thurs.-Mon. May-mid-June and Labor Day-Sept. 30, admission with NW Forest Pass). The cave is a cool 42°F year-round, so dress warmly and wear sturdy shoes—the walking surface is uneven. Bring a strong flashlight to guide you through this lava tube or rent a lantern ($5) at the entrance.

© JUDY JEWELL

Benham Falls

The trail is an easy 2.4-mile round-trip from the parking lot.

The first chamber you enter is called the **Collapsed Corridor.** Volcanic rocks that fell from the roof and walls lie in jumbled piles. Freezing water in cracks pry a few rocks loose each winter, which is why the cave is usually closed during the cold months. Stairs take you out of the Collapsed Corridor into a large void called **Echo Hall.** Here the ceiling reaches 58 feet and the cave is 50 feet wide. Conversations return from the opposite side of the hall as eerie noises in the dark. The lateral markings you see etched on the walls show the various levels of past volcanic flows.

At **Low Bridge Lane,** watch your head because the ceiling dips down to five feet. Here and in other areas of the cave look for the "lavacicles"—a term from a geologist's 1923 publication on the cave called *The Lava River Tunnel.* Two kinds of lavacicles are found: the hollow cylindrical "soda straws" were formed by escaping gases, and the cone-shaped formations were created by remelted lava dripping down from the ceiling.

The next curiosity you'll come across is a cave inside the cave, the **Two Tube Tunnel.** Two tubes intermittently connect for 95 feet. The smaller tube was formed when the level of the lava flow dropped and the cooling lava created a second roof and tube inside the existing cave.

The terrain changes again in the **Sand Gardens.** Rain and snowmelt carry volcanic ash down through cracks and openings in the cave and deposit them here. The process continues today with the nearly constant dripping water carving out spires and pinnacles in the sand. These formations take hundreds of years to grow, so stay out of the fenced-off area. The sand gets thicker and thicker until it completely blocks off the lava tube, forcing an abrupt about-face. The walk back to the light of the sun affords a different perspective on this remarkable natural attraction.

It is important to avoid littering the cave, collecting samples, or doing anything else to mar this delicate ecosystem. Avoid lighting flares, paper, or cigarettes because the fumes kill off insects, a food source for the cave's bat population. Roosting bats should not be disturbed because waking them from hibernation results in certain death for these winged mammals. Incidentally, bat droppings support this cavernous ecosystem, and others; bat guano is harvested commercially and used for detoxifying waste, improving detergents, and producing antibiotics. Bats can catch hundreds of mosquitoes per hour, and they are also important pollinators. There are nearly 50 species of bats living in North America, and if left alone, they pose little threat to humans.

Lava Cast Forest

A couple of miles south of Lava River Cave is the turnoff for **Lava Cast Forest,** nine miles down the very rough Forest Service Rd. 9720. A one-mile trail traverses an unreal world created when lava enveloped the trees 6,000 years ago. The lava hardened, leaving behind a mold of the once-living trees, much like how the eruption of Mount Vesuvius in Italy left casts of Pompeii's residents.

Tumalo Falls

About 12 miles west of downtown, the 89-foot **Tumalo Falls** plummets down a sheer cliff. Although the falls are visible from the parking area, a short walk leads to better views, and a slightly longer walk takes you to the top of the falls. From here, follow the trail up Tumalo Creek, where there are a couple of smaller waterfalls. Several other hiking and mountain biking trails leave from the area; it's possible to make a loop, but part of the loop falls in an area where the watershed is protected and dogs and bikes are prohibited.

From downtown, head west on Franklin Street, skirt Drake Park, continue west on Galveston. At the traffic circle, continue west; the street name changes to Skyliners Road. After about 10 miles, follow the signs for the falls and turn onto Tumalo Road. The last couple of miles are on a good gravel road. Be sure to bring your Northwest Forest Pass or $5 to purchase a day pass at the trailhead.

© JUDY JEWELL

Tumalo Falls

Pilot Butte

On the east side of Bend is **Pilot Butte,** a 511-foot-high volcanic remnant. A road and a trail to the top offer a sweeping view of nine snowcapped Cascade peaks and their green forests. It is also pretty at night, with the twinkling lights of the city below and the stars above. Full moons are especially awesome, illuminating the ghostly forms of the mountains as icy light-blue silhouettes. The scent of juniper and sage adds to the visual splendor. Bring water if you're hiking.

Pine Mountain Observatory

A peak experience worth investigating is the **Pine Mountain Observatory** (541/382-8331, http://pmo.uoregon.edu, Fri.-Sat. late May-Sept., $5 donation requested) about 40 miles east of Bend on U.S. 20. Take the road out of Millican to the top of 6,395-foot-high Pine Mountain to reach the installation. Three Cassegrain telescopes with 15-, 24-, and 32-inch mirrors are used by University of Oregon professors and students to unlock the secrets of

the universe. On this 6,300-foot mountain the friendly astronomers will often allow visitors an intriguing peek at neighboring stars and planets. Call ahead for information and weather conditions before making the trip; try to go when the moon is only a sliver. Programs start at 9pm until midsummer; when darkness falls earlier, starting times are shifted to 8:30pm, then to 8pm. Wear warm clothes and take a flashlight. A primitive campground (no water) is just across the road from the observatory.

Glass Buttes

Farther down U.S. 20, you ease into the Great Basin desert and such attractions as the **Sagehen Nature Trail,** 70 miles from the Pine Mountain Observatory turnoff, and the **Glass Buttes.** Located 36 miles past the observatory, the Glass Buttes are one of the world's largest obsidian outcroppings, a mountain of volcanic glass gently rising 2,000 feet above the surrounding countryside. The **Bureau of Land Management** (541/416-6700, www.blm.gov) can provide additional information. From the buttes the next real town is Burns, 55 miles to the east.

SPORTS AND RECREATION
Winter Sports
◖ MOUNT BACHELOR

The Pacific Northwest's largest and most complete ski area is **Mount Bachelor** (541/382-2607 information, 541/382-7888 hours and snow report, www.mtbachelor.com, $76 adult, $65 teen or senior, $46 senior over age 70 or children; arrivals after noon pay about $10 less). Located 22 miles southwest of Bend on Century Drive, this venue's 12 ski lifts, including seven high-speed quads, and trails that range from beginner to expert make for some of the most popular skiing in the state. This is the winter training grounds for the U.S. Olympic Ski Team. If you're at the other end of the expertise spectrum, note that Bachelor's beginners' lift, the Carrousel, is free.

The Summit Express lift takes you right to the top of the mountain, yielding great

BEND

sunny-day views of the neighboring Cascade peaks. You may also see puffs of steam coming off the slopes, which serve as reminders that Bachelor is a still-kicking volcanic peak. Although central Oregon is known for its clear skies, the truth is that storms do pass through quite regularly. This is a good thing for skiers and snowboarders, who count on the snow piling up deep enough on Bachelor for the ski season to extend into late spring, but it can mean skiing or boarding in high wind and flying snow pellets. Conditions are often best in late winter and early spring.

Expert skiers and boarders should ride the Northwest Express lift (a high-speed quad) to the mountain's Northwest Territory, where trees and bowls keep skills honed. The Summit lift is a must, both for the views and the trails, which include some blue runs. Another good area is the part of the mountain served by the Outback Express; runs here are mostly blue. Snowboarders and freestyle skiers head to the mile-long terrain park at Bachelors Park or the 400-foot-long super pipe.

With a top elevation over 9,000 feet and steady northwest airflow, skiing here can run into the early summer. However, avoid skiing after 1pm in May and June, when conditions become slushy. If you must ski then, choose the west-side snowfields, which hold up better in the late afternoon light. Finally, while there may not be enough snow to ski in summer, you can still ride the chairlift to the peak of this volcano for an unsurpassed view of the surrounding countryside.

Or, skip an afternoon of skiing and join **Trail of Dreams Sled Dog Rides** (Sunrise Lodge parking area, 541/382-1709 or 800/829-2442) for a one-hour sled dog ride ($85, $40 for kids under 80 pounds) with Jerry Scdoris and his daughter Rachael, an Iditarod finisher. A day-long tour goes to Elk Lake and costs $450 for two people.

Even when ski season is over, **chairlift rides** (541/382-1709, 11am-4pm Mon.-Thurs. 11am-4pm and 5pm-8pm Fri.-Sun. July-Labor Day, $17 adults, $14 seniors, $11 children ages 6-12, less for evening rides) give visitors a chance to take in good views of many of the Cascade lakes and peaks. Sunset dinners at the on-site restaurant, Pine Marten Lodge, are offered on Friday, Saturday, and Sunday (5pm-8pm). On summer days, a U.S. Forest Service ranger gives **interpretive talks** on the deck of the lodge (11:30am and 1:30 and 3:30pm daily, free with lift ticket).

Unlike most ski resorts of its size, Mount Bachelor has no slope-side lodging. The closest lodging is down the hill at the Seventh Mountain Resort. Sunriver is also about a 20-minute drive.

CROSS-COUNTRY SKIING

Just west of downtown Bend on the road to Mount Bachelor, **Virginia Meissner** and **Swampy Lakes** are excellent cross-country ski areas. The Sno-Park area at Virginia Meissner is about 13 miles west of town; Swampy Lakes is about 2 miles up the road from Meissner. The two trail systems join up and together access more than 25 miles of ski trails dotted with strategically placed warming huts. There are also snowshoe trails leading from each Sno-Park. Dogs and motorized vehicles are prohibited at both Virginia Meissner and Swampy Lakes. Sno-Park permits are required. In the summer, these trails are good for mountain biking.

Up the mountain at **Dutchman Flat Sno-Park,** what you gain in elevation and early-season snowpack you'll lose in peacefulness. This Sno-Park, almost directly across from the turnoff to Mount Bachelor's Sunrise Lodge, has trails for both skiers and snowmobilers and can be extremely busy on weekends and holidays. Snowmobilers can use this spot to access roughly 150 miles of trails; skiers find about 19 miles of trails, including some fairly challenging ones.

A trail system at **Edison Butte** is a good alternative for cross-country skiers with dogs. It's on Forest Road 45 four miles south of its junction with Cascade Lakes Highway. Snowmobilers access trails from the same parking area, which can be very busy on snowy weekends.

BEND

© JUDY JEWELL

The Bend area has an excellent cross-country ski trail network.

Hiking and Biking

The area in and around Bend boasts a rich network of hiking and mountain biking trails, ranging from short barrier-free interpretive walks in town to strenuous wilderness treks. The best hiking is on trails accessed by the Cascade Lakes Highway. Snow can lock up many of these high-elevation trails until as late as June or July, so you'll want to inquire locally before heading out fall-spring. The offices of the **Deschutes National Forest** (63095 Deschutes Market Rd., 541/383-5300, www. fs.usda.gov/centraloregon) can provide information. Note that parking at most trailheads in the national forests requires a **Northwest Forest Pass** (www.fs.fed.us/r6/passespermits, $5 one-day, $30 one-year), available at most outdoor stores and resorts as well as at trailheads.

For mountain bikers, the **Central Oregon Trail Alliance** (http://cotamtb.com) is a good resource. This volunteer group works with the Forest Service, the Bureau of Land Management, and other land managers to enhance mountain biking in and around Bend. Their website briefly describes area trails and shows current conditions.

◖ DESCHUTES RIVER TRAIL

The best thing about Bend's boom years was the development of the **Deschutes River Trail** (download a map at www.bendparksandrec. org). The trail, which will ultimately run 19 miles from Tumalo State Park north of town to the Meadow Picnic Area near Widgi Creek Golf Course, offers excellent river access to walkers, runners, and cyclists (mountain bikes or cruisers are best). Pick up the trail downtown in Drake Park or in the Old Mill District, from Farewell Bend Park on the east side of the river (lots of parking on Reed Market Rd.), or from the Les Schwab Amphitheater on the west side. The trail is a patchwork of paved and unpaved surfaces.

If you want to keep going when you reach the trail's southern terminus, hop up onto Century Drive and head past the golf course and the Seventh Mountain Resort to the

Trails run for miles along the Deschutes River.

turnoff for Dillon Falls. This road will quickly reconnect you with riverside hiking and mountain biking trails that go all the way to Benham Falls. This section of the trail runs 9.1 miles through riverside pine forests and lava flows. It is actually a set of three parallel trails—one each dedicated to hikers, cyclists, and horseback riders—beginning about 7 miles southwest of Bend. To get here via the road, follow Century Drive southwest, then turn south onto Forest Road 41 (Conklin Rd.), which has several access points to the trails at **Lava Island, Big Eddy, Aspen, Dillon, Slough, Benham West,** and **Benham Falls** day-use areas. The season is spring-fall, although most of the trails may remain open in winter during years with low snowfall. A Northwest Forest Pass is required for parking along Road 41, and dogs must be leashed. Four trail sections—at Big Eddy Rapids, Dillon Falls, Benham Falls West, and Benham Falls Picnic Area—are wheelchair accessible. They're surfaced with crushed gravel and are of intermediate difficulty.

SHEVLIN PARK

About five miles west of town, **Shevlin Park** lures both hikers and mountain bikers with an easy five-mile loop through the pines along the Tumalo Creek gorge and along a ridge burned in the Awbrey Hall fire of August 1990. It's open year-round with no fees for parking or access. Several picnic areas offer quiet spots for lunch. To get there, follow Greenwood Avenue west from U.S. 97 in Bend; Greenwood becomes Newport Avenue after a few blocks, then changes again to Shevlin Road as it angles northwest.

PHIL'S TRAIL

A trail close to town that's very popular with mountain bikers is **Phil's Trail,** an eight-mile segment of a larger network of eponymous bike trails (Kent's, Paul's, Jimmy's, etc.—named for the riders who established or popularized them) among the canyon and butte country just west of Bend. Difficulty is generally easy to moderate, with some steep climbs to challenge your lower gears the farther west you ride. To get to the trailhead, head 2.5 miles west on Skyliners Road, then turn left on the first paved road to the south and travel 0.5 mile. A little farther west, Roads 4610 and 300 also intersect the network. A **Northwest Forest Pass** (www.fs.fed.us/r6/passespermits, $5 one-day, $30 one-year) is required for parking.

MOUNT BACHELOR SUMMIT TRAIL

Farther afield, Mount Bachelor beckons hikers in the summer and fall to walk the four-mile **Mount Bachelor Summit Trail** (2-3 hours one-way) to the mountain's top. This is one of the easiest and safest routes to the top of any Cascade peak, requiring no climbing skills or equipment. An even easier way to reach the top is via the chairlift at the ski area, which runs during the off-season.

To get to the trailhead, follow signs for the upper (east) parking lot at the ski area. The trail begins at the western end of the lot and climbs to a forested ridge on the mountain's northeastern side to the upper station of the first section of the ski lift. From there, the trail climbs steeply through the timberline area and continues up to a talus ridge leading to the mountain station of the second lift segment. It's a short hike from this lift station to the summit.

Plaques at viewpoints along the way identify lakes and mountains visible from this 9,000-foot vantage point, including Diamond Peak to the south and the Three Sisters, Broken Top, Mount Jefferson, and sometimes even Mount Hood, 100 miles away, to the north. The hike involves an elevation gain of 2,600 feet. Mountain bikes are not recommended on the trail.

BIKE RENTALS AND TOURS

Rent a mountain bike at **Pine Mountain Sports** (255 SW Century Dr., 541/385-8080, www.pinemountainsports.com, from $20 for 4 hours, $25 for 24 hours). Upstairs from Pine Mountain are the offices for **Cog Wild** (255 SW Century Dr., 541/385-7002, http://cogwild.com), which leads mountain bike tours that include short family cruises ($60 adults, $45 children ages 12 and under), vigorous daylong tours (about $90), and multiday trips (about $600-700).

If your bicycling style is a little more easygoing, rent a cruiser (or a tandem, kid's bike, trailer, or tag-along) or a multi-passenger surrey from **Wheel Fun Rentals** (603 SW Mill A Dr., 541/408-4568, 10am-sunset daily, $8-45 per hour) near the Deschutes River Trail in the Old Mill District.

Fishing

With over 100 mountain lakes and the Deschutes River within an hour's drive of Bend, your piscatorial pleasures will be satisfied in central Oregon. The high lakes offer rainbow, brown, and brook trout as well as landlocked Atlantic and coho salmon. The Deschutes River is famed for its red-sided rainbow trout and summer steelhead. Not surprisingly, the best fishing is outside of the Bend metropolitan area near Sunriver, Cascade Lakes, and Prineville. If you're stuck in town, head over to the Old Mill District, where you'll find the **Confluence Fly Shop** (375 SW Powerhouse Dr., 804/221-7748, www.confluenceflyshop.com) and a clever 18-station fly-fishing course on the edge of the Deschutes (think miniature golf with a fly rod). The fly shop teams up with **Deep Canyon Outfitters** (541/323-3007, www.deepcanyonoutfitters.com), a well-established guide service.

A full-service pro shop with everything for the fly fisher is **The Patient Angler** (822 SE 3rd St., 541/389-6208, www.patientangler.com), where you can stock up on information as well as gear; a guide service is also part of this business.

Deschutes River Outfitters (541/760-0956, www.deschutesoutfitters.com) features float trips, lake walk-in trips, and steelhead fishing trips that can be customized into single-day or multiday excursions. They have so many different packages and rates that it's best to refer to their outstanding website for specifics.

Floating and Paddling

You can either sit down or stand up to paddle through town on a relatively quiet stretch of the Deschutes. Put in at either **McKay Park** (166 SW Shevlin Hixon Dr., on the river's west bank) or **Farewell Bend Park** (on the east bank along Reed Market Dr.) and take out at Drake Park, where a **Ride the River shuttle bus** (www.cascadeseasttransit.com, 11:30am-6:30pm Fri.-Mon. July 5-Labor Day, $1.50 for one ride, $2.50 all day) will ferry you back to the starting point. Rent a kayak ($40 for 2 hours), canoe ($50 for 2 hours), float tube ($10 for 2 hours), or stand-up paddleboard ($40 for 2 hours) at **Tumalo Creek Kayak & Canoe** (805 SW Industrial Way, 541/317-9407, www.tumalocreek.com), where you can also sign up for paddling lessons. **StandUp Paddle Flatwater** (550 SW Industrial Way, 541/323-3355) rents boards for $15 an hour.

Float the river on a specially designed river tube available for rent from **Sun Country Tours** (541/382-6277 or 800/883-8842, www.suncountrytours.com, $15 adults, $10 kids 12 and under). Find the rental location at **Riverbend Park** (799 SW Columbia St.).

BEND

Golf

Widgi Creek (18707 Century Dr., 541/382-4449, www.widgi.com, $25-75, reservations strongly recommended), just north of the Seventh Mountain Resort, was designed by Robert Muir Graves. The course's strategically placed trees, lakes, and sand traps have given this place the reputation as the "mean green" golf course of central Oregon. The 18 holes are mentioned in the same breath as Sunriver's North Course and Black Butte's Glaze Meadows—good company indeed.

Close to town along the Deschutes River, the hillside **River's Edge Golf Course** (3075 N. Business Rte. 97, 541/389-2828, www.riverhouse.com, $38-59) is a convenient and pretty alternative.

A couple of products of Bend's boom years are the lavish semiprivate golf courses at **Pronghorn** (65600 Pronghorn Club Dr., 866/372-1009, www.pronghornclub.com, $365), which has courses by Jack Nicklaus and Tom Fazio, where the eighth hole features a lava canyon; and **Tetherow** (61240 Skyline Ranch Rd., 541/388-2582, www.tetherow.com, $95-175), a links-style course designed by Davis McLay Kidd, known for his work at Bandon Dunes.

Gyms

One of the finest aquatic and fitness centers east of the Cascades is found at **Juniper Aquatic and Fitness Center** (800 NE 6th St., 541/389-7665, www.bendparksandrec.org). Part of the Bend Metro Park and Recreation District, the center is located in 20-acre Juniper Park and features two indoor pools and a large 40-yard outdoor pool providing plenty of space for splashing around. Serious swimmers can enjoy frequent lap swims and adults-only swim times daily. An aerobics room, a weight room, group exercise classes, a jogging trail, and a tennis court offer other exercise options. A sauna and a whirlpool tub provide you with yet another way to sweat it out.

Horseback Riding

Saddle up at the **Seventh Mountain Resort Stables** (18575 SW Century Dr., 541/693-9732, www.seventhmountain.com, Mar.-Oct.), where kids age 2-6 can take pony rides ($10) while older folks can head out on guided trail rides along the Deschutes River (starting at $35). During the winter, sleigh rides are available, but must be reserved in advance.

Rafting

The Deschutes River offers some of the finest white water in central Oregon. The numerous lava flows have diverted the river to create tumultuous rapids that attract raft, kayak, and canoe enthusiasts. From short rafting trips to multiday adventures, you'll find many options available to enjoy the exciting Deschutes River. You will need swimwear, footwear, sunblock, and sunglasses for all rafting trips. It's also advisable to have a set of dry clothes handy at the end of the voyage.

The prime spot for daylong trips is actually the Lower Deschutes, out of the town of Maupin, but there are a couple of spots close to Bend that'll satisfy that urge to be in the river on a hot summer day.

A few miles upstream from town, the Big Eddy section of the river offers a few whitewater thrills. Several outfitters lead trips on this section of the Deschutes: The **Seventh Mountain River Company** (18575 SW Century Dr., 541/693-9124, http://seventhmountainriverco.com, $35) offers a 1.5-hour raft trip down a three-mile section of the Deschutes that takes in some Class I-IV rapids. With names like Pinball Alley and the Souse Hole, you can be assured of a good ride! Transfer between the inn and the river is included.

Sun Country Tours (531 SW 13th St., 541/382-6277 or 800/883-8842, www.suncountrytours.com, $53 adults, $46 children ages 6-12) runs a 1.25-hour 3-mile Big Eddy Thriller that takes in Class I-III rapids on the Deschutes River.

ENTERTAINMENT AND EVENTS

Downtown Bend's striking art deco moderne **Tower Theatre** (835 NW Wall St.,

541/317-0700, www.towertheatre.org) hosts music, films, and other performances. This is a good venue to see some relatively big-name acoustic musicians.

Bend's other main music venue, the **Les Schwab Amphitheater** (541/322-9383, www.bendconcerts.com), is on the edge of the Old Mill District, on Shevlin-Hixon Drive between Simpson Avenue and Columbia Street. This is the place to see performers such as Pink Martini, Bonnie Raitt, or Michael Franti. It's also the site of events such as the Bend Brewfest.

Festivals and Events

Quintessentially Bend, the mid-May **Pole Pedal Paddle** (541/388-0002, www.pppbend.com) is a relay or, for the exceptionally tough, a single-person event that starts at the top of Mount Bachelor and ends at the Les Schwab Amphitheater in Bend's Old Mill District. Between the two points, participants downhill ski, cross-country ski, bike, run, and canoe or kayak to the finish line. Although some participants take the event quite seriously, most enter in a spirit of fun.

The **Bend Summer Festival** brings out food booths, Oregon wine and microbrews, art exhibits, and live music all in one big downtown block party the second weekend in July. Contact the **Bend Visitors Information Bureau** (541/382-8048, www.bendsummerfestival.com) for more details.

In mid-August, the Les Schwab Amphitheater (Shevlin-Hixon Dr.) is home to the **Bend Brewfest** (541/322-9383, www.bendbrewfest.com), with over 80 craft beers available for tasting.

ACCOMMODATIONS

Bend is the largest full-fledged resort town in the state. On holidays or ski weekends, it's hard to find a decent room if you don't have reservations, although during the shoulder seasons of spring and fall, rooms and deals often abound. For a comprehensive list of motels, see www.visitbend.org.

One longtime Bend favorite is now more or less out of play. In 2013, the **Seventh Mountain Resort** (18575 SW Century Dr., 541/382-8711 or 800/452-6810, www.seventhmountain.com) was sold to Wyndam, which planned to add it to its stable of WorldMark timeshare developments. Since many of the studios and condo units at Seventh Mountain had been privately owned, the conversion is probably not going to be immediate and seamless. If you want to stay in a great location (the closest place you'll find to Mount Bachelor with trails to the Deschutes), it's worth checking the website or looking at vrbo.com to see if any units are available for rent.

Under $50

Most of the least-expensive motels are along 3rd Street. During busy weekends in the middle of the summer the prices even on the least appealing places may creep a little bit higher than $50. One reasonable bet is the **Bend Value Inn** (2346 NE Division St., 541/382-6222, www.bendvalueinn.com, $49), which has microwaves and fridges in the rooms.

$50-100

Just south of downtown, on the edge of the Old Mill District, is the **Mill Inn B&B** (642 NW Colorado Ave., 541/389-9198 or 877/748-1200, www.millinn.com, $80-130). Originally an early 1900s hotel and boardinghouse, it has been remodeled into a 10-bedroom inn. Least expensive is a hostel-style room with bunk beds ($35 per person). Slightly more expensive rooms have a bath down the hall, but many have private baths, and some rooms adjoin to accommodate families. All rates include a full breakfast, and access to a washer and dryer, a barbecue grill, and a hot tub.

On busy 3rd Street not far from downtown, **Three Sisters Inn** (721 NE 3rd St., 541/382-4949, www.bendthreesistersinn.com, $89-219) is a tidy place with free breakfast buffet, a pool, and family suites.

Up the road toward Mount Bachelor, find the **◖ Entrada Lodge** (19221 Century Dr., 541/382-4080, www.entradalodge.com, $89-129), a rather standard motel in an exceptionally nice setting. It's nestled in among the ponderosa pines at a nexus of hiking and mountain bike trails that can take you toward town or down to the Deschutes River (about a 20-minute walk). A small pool, a large hot tub, a rather basic breakfast buffet, and in-room microwaves and refrigerators are the amenities. It's a good place to bring your dog . . . and a pleasant place to take dog walks. (Note: wireless Internet is difficult to connect to at the Entrada.)

$100-150

❰ McMenamins Old St. Francis School (700 NW Bond St., 541/382-5174 or 877/661-4228, www.mcmenamins.com, $125-185) is right downtown, but it is in its own little world surrounded by gardens with quiet sitting areas. Rooms in this historic 1936 Catholic school are nicely appointed with televisions, telephones, wireless Internet access, hair dryers, private bathrooms (showers only), and comfy bathrobes to wear on the way over to the wonderful Turkish-style soaking pool. In addition to the standard rooms, several cottages ($185-395) are available. This is one of the few McMenamins hotels that allows pets. Guests also have free admission to movies at the school theater and easy access to the four bars on the premises; we recommend the fire pit outside O'Kane's pub, located behind the main hotel in a former garage.

The **Riverhouse Hotel** (3075 Business Rte. 97 N., 541/389-3111 or 866/453-4480, www. riverhouse.com, $128-309) is situated along the Deschutes River at the north end of town. Although this hotel features a conference center and other business amenities, it's also a good place for vacationers. The rooms are well kept and equipped with wireless Internet access, microwaves, and refrigerators. Pets are permitted, and guests have access to indoor and outdoor pools, an exercise room, and tennis courts. There's also a golf course on-site.

❰ Mount Bachelor Village Resort (19717 Mount Bachelor Dr., 541/452-9846 or 800/547-5204, www.mtbachelorvillage.com, $139-400) is a couple of miles from downtown, just off Century Drive. Some of the units, which include a wide variety of condos

© JUDY JEWELL

BEND

Stay in downtown Bend at McMenamins Old St. Francis School.

and hotel room suites, overlook the Deschutes River. The guest rooms are some of the nicest in Bend. It's easy for guests to get onto the Deschutes River Trail, and they can also use the adjacent Athletic Club of Bend, the most upscale gym in town.

$150-200

Pine Ridge Inn (1200 SW Century Dr., 800/600-4095, www.pineridgeinn.com, $169-289) is a small romantic inn above the Deschutes River near the foot of Century Drive, not too far from downtown. Guest rooms are spacious (mini-suites and larger suites) and well decorated.

Right downtown, the **Phoenix Inn Suites** (300 NW Franklin Ave., 541/317-9292 or 888/291-4764, www.phoenixinn.com/bend, $199-219) is a good choice for business travelers or anyone who wants spacious guest rooms, although some of the "suites" don't exactly fit the usual definition of that term (they don't have separate rooms for sleeping).

Over $200

Downtown, the gorgeous **◖ Oxford Hotel** (10 NW Minnesota Ave., 541/382-8436 or 877/440-8436, www.oxfordhotelbend.com, $260-364) is a stylish and ecofriendly boutique hotel in a great location. From the subtle tree motif decor to the French press coffee (locally roasted and grounds composted), everything is designed to make you feel good about relaxing in luxury. The latex Natura beds are comfortable, hypoallergenic, and breathable; pullout sofa beds have Tempur-Pedic mattresses. All rooms have a microwave and fridge, and suites have a full kitchen, including dishwasher. At seven stories, the Oxford is Bend's tallest building, and the top-floor fitness center has some of the best views this side of the Bachelor summit chairlift. It also has a steam room, a sauna, and a saline hot tub. Guests should inquire about gaining access to private golf courses in the area. Since the Oxford opened in 2010, this block of Minnesota Avenue has come alive with coffee shops, restaurants, and galleries, including a good restaurant in the hotel's basement.

And, if you're willing to pay a fairly stiff ($55) fee, your pet will be enthusiastically welcomed.

Close to downtown, Drake Park, and Mirror Pond is **Lara House** (640 NW Congress St., 541/388-4064 or 800/766-4064, www.larahouse.com, $194-255). This large three-story house was built in 1910 and features six large bedrooms with private baths. All rooms are furnished with antiques and reflect individual grace and charm. A delicious homemade breakfast is served in the bright solarium overlooking the colorful gardens and Drake Park.

Camping

With the Three Sisters Wilderness and the Deschutes National Forest flanking Bend, there are many wonderful spots to enjoy camping out under the stars. But for those who want to stay closer to civilization, **Tumalo State Park** (64120 O.B. Riley Rd., 541/382-3586, 800/551-6949, or 800/452-5687, www.oregonstateparks.org, year-round, $21 tents, $26 hookups, $39 yurts) is convenient and not overly urbanized. Located five miles northwest of Bend off of U.S. 20 along the banks of the Deschutes River, 54 tent sites, 23 sites for RVs up to 35 feet long, and showers are available.

A couple of decent RV parks can be found near Bend. **Crown Villa** (60801 Brosterhous Rd., 541/388-1131 or 866/500-5300, http://crownvillarvresort.com, $59-80), southeast of town, is exceptionally well maintained and has lots of amenities.

FOOD

The scenery around Bend feeds the soul, and restaurants here do the rest. While area restaurants run the gamut from fast-food franchises to elegant dinner houses, many travelers also want something between those extremes. Some alternatives for every budget are listed below.

Bakeries and Cafés

Downtown coffee lovers head to **Thump** (25 NW Minnesota Ave., 541/388-0226, www.thumpcoffee.com, 6am-5:30pm Mon.-Fri., 7am-5:30pm Sat., 7am-4:30pm Sun.) for Stumptown brew, good pastries, and friendly conversation. If you'd rather sip a cup of tea, try **Townshend's** (835 NW Bond St., 541/312-2001, www.townshendtea.com, 9am-10pm Mon.-Thurs., 9am-11pm Fri.-Sat., 9am-9pm Sun.), which serves high-quality teas in an atmosphere that's more hip than stuffy. South of downtown, near the Old Mill District, **Strictly Organic Coffee** (6 SW Bond St., 541/330-6061, www.strictlyorganic.com, 6am-7pm Mon.-Wed. and Fri.-Sat., 6am-8pm Thurs., 7am-6pm Sun.) is a great place for coffee or tea and a snack. They have a second location in the Old Mill shopping center.

Ask Siri to help you find the tiny **C Sparrow Bakery** (50 SE Scott St., 541/330-6321, www. thesparrowbakery.net, 541/330-6321, 7am-2pm Mon.-Sat., 8am-2pm Sun., sandwiches $7.50-8.50). Although it's just off the Bend Parkway near the Colorado Street exit, it can be tricky to locate this gem of a bakery. The cardamom-scented "ocean rolls" make the search worthwhile, as do the fantastic sandwiches, which can take surprisingly long to be made. If the weather's nice, that's no problem; a patio has tables and is surrounded by local artisans' studios and shops. And if you can't get here, find Sparrow's pastries downtown at both Thump and Townshend's.

American

C Chow (1110 Newport Ave., 541/728-0256, www.chowbend.com, 7am-2pm daily, $7-14), in a charming little house across from the Newport Market, is a deservedly popular breakfast spot. Chow's aim is to keep their business sustainable and true to the food, and this care is evident: one of the top picks on the menu is always the locavore omelet, made with whatever is in season. Lunch sandwiches are inventive, and lunch isn't limited to sandwiches and salads; there's also a daily interpretation of mac and cheese. In nice weather the deck seating is great.

Just outside of downtown, diners linger at the **Victorian Café** (1404 NW Galveston Ave., 541/382-6411, www.victoriancafebend. com, 7am-2pm daily, $4-16), one of the few breakfast and lunch joints that has a full bar.

Bloody Mary or no, breakfasts here are an extravaganza; for a real treat, order any of the eggs Benedict options.

Drop by **C Jackson's Corner** (845 NW Delaware Ave., 541/647-2198, www.jacksonscornerbendor.com, 7am-9pm daily, $6-17) almost any time of day for a casual meal. The pizzas are excellent, as are the sandwiches and the salads. It's a casual neighborhood place where you order at the counter and may possibly share a big table with others. The side yard has a place for kids to play and adults to lounge at picnic tables.

Stop by **Longboard Louie's** (1254 NW Galveston Ave., 541/383-2449, www.longboardlouies.com, 7am-close Mon.-Fri., 8am-close Sat.-Sun., $3-10) for an easygoing lunch or casual dinner on the deck. The seafood tacos are excellent (get the halibut if it's in season).

Set on a corner in the heart of downtown, **C 900 Wall** (900 NW Wall St., 541/323-6295, www.900wall.com, 3pm-close daily, $15-24) fairly pulses with energy, and the food is delicious and reasonably priced. Try a wood-fired pizza (the prosciutto and arugula pizza is drizzled with truffle oil and absolutely delicious) or some high-class comfort food, such as a pork chops or flatiron steak, prepared with just enough inventiveness to keep them interesting. The selection of wines by the glass is huge and well chosen. During summer, the restaurant is usually open until about 10pm weeknights, 11:30pm on weekends; in the winter it usually closes a bit earlier.

Asian

Cut through the mid-block breezeway on Wall Street to find **Boken** (852 NW Brooks St., 541/706-9091, www.bokenbend.com, 5pm-9pm Mon.-Thurs., 5pm-11pm Fri.-Sat., $7-16), modeled on a Japanese *izakaya* pub, a casual place for an after-work drink and some food. Although menu leans toward small plates and good sushi, it's also a good choice for a full dinner.

Barbecue

Find shockingly good barbecue on the road to

Mount Bachelor at **Baldy's** (235 SW Century Dr., 541/385-7427, www.baldysbbq.com, 11am-9pm daily, $8-20). Be warned, if you are a rib-lover, once you eat here you'll be spoiled for any other restaurant in town. If ribs aren't your thing, the hickory-smoked chicken and the pulled pork are also delicious. A good selection of local beers is on tap. If you're headed out of town toward Burns, stop at the eastside Baldy's, near the Safeway (2670 NE Hwy. 20, 541/388-4227).

Italian

Head west of downtown to find **◖ Trattoria Sbandati** (1444 NW College Way, 541/306-6825, www.trattoriasbandati.com, 5pm-close Tues.-Sat., $14-30, reservations recommended), a family-run Italian restaurant that manages to be simultaneously romantic and homey. Go with the intention of making a night out of it; this is not a dine-and-dash spot. Start with a salad of gorgonzola and golden beets, move on to homemade pasta or gnocchi, perhaps try some polpette (meatballs), and make sure to take advantage of the excellent wine list. If you are in a hurry, stop by for deli items; the Sbandatis sell a good selection of cheeses and cured meats.

Mediterranean

Just out of the downtown core in a small bungalow, **Ariana** (1304 NW Galveston Ave., 541/330-5539, www.arianarestaurantbend. com, 5pm-9pm Tues.-Sat., $20-30, reservations recommended) is one of the most appealing and intimate dinner restaurants in town. The Mediterranean-influenced cuisine is prepared with care, elevating dishes as simple as beet salad to remarkable heights. To fully experience Ariana, go for the five-course tasting menu ($64). In the summer, seating expands to a deck.

Middle Eastern

For affordable and tasty Middle Eastern food, go to the colorful **Kebaba** (1004 Newport Ave., 541/318-6224, www.kebaba.com, 11am-9pm Mon.-Sat., 11:30am-9pm Sun., $5-15). There's

a good mix of authenticity and innovation here; your lamb shawarma can come in a pita-bread wrap with za'atar fries or in a Middle Eastern rice bowl on top of pilaf. Kebaba is a good place to find excellent vegetarian food.

Southern

Zydeco (919 NW Bond St., 541/312-2899, www.zydecokitchen.com, 11am-2pm Mon.-Fri. and 5pm-close daily, $11-26) is one of the hottest spots in town. In the summer, its fun bright atmosphere spills out from the open kitchen to sidewalk tables. Inside, a good selection of wine is stored behind glass-fronted cabinets and strategically placed mirrors give views of the crowd—a mix of young partiers and older serious diners—and the open kitchen. The food, not surprisingly, has creole and Cajun influences, but also includes other good options, such as pan-roasted steelhead trout in a lemon-caper sauce. An entire menu is devoted to gluten-free items. To encourage drinking local wines, the restaurant charges no corkage fee on Oregon, Washington, and Idaho wines that you bring in. Even if you pass on dessert (and the flourless chocolate cake is worth loosening your belt for), be sure to take a free homemade dog biscuit home for your special buddy.

Steak

◖ Jackalope Grill (750 NW Lava Rd., 541/318-8435, www.jackalopegrill.com, 4pm-9pm daily, $26-32, reservations recommended), around the corner from the Oxford Hotel, is more upscale than its name. The restaurant, which used to be in a funky strip mall location, is a great addition to downtown Bend. Main courses range from steak or salmon to jaeger schnitzel or pork osso bucco, but don't skip the starters. Chef Tim Garling's soup du jour is invariably good, whether it's a rich butternut squash soup topped with chanterelles or a smooth soup made from beets. During the summer, diners can sit in an intimate outdoor courtyard.

Also in the downtown core, **The Pine Tavern Restaurant** (967 NW Brooks St., 541/382-5581, www.pinetavern.com, 11:30am-3pm and

5pm-close daily, $16-32, reservations recommended) has been in business since 1919, and although it is not a trendy place, it keeps current enough to continue drawing crowds. It's in a garden setting overlooking Mirror Pond, with an ancient ponderosa pine that's been growing up through the floor since 1919. Prime rib, meat loaf, and hot sourdough scones with honey butter are among the many specialties. Most dinners are in the $15-20 range and come with scones.

Brewpubs and Distilleries

Bend has seen an explosion of good local brewers in recent years. Many are alumni of central Oregon's first brewery and brewpub, **Deschutes Brewery and Public House** (1044 NW Bond St., 541/382-9242, www.deschutesbrewery.com, 11am-11pm Mon.-Thurs., 11am-midnight Fri.-Sat., 11am-10pm Sun., $9-16), which still serves fresh handcrafted ales and food that is better than most pub food. Along with the burgers, veggie burgers, sandwiches,

© JUDY JEWELL

The Boneyard Brewing tasting room is not a glossy, high-end joint.

and pizza, you can get asparagus risotto or a grilled flatiron steak. The beer, including the always-satisfying Mirror Pond pale ale, is some of Oregon's best. The main brewery is in the Old Mill District at 901 SW Simpson Avenue, where tours and tastings are offered.

A visit to the tasting room at **Crux Fermentation** (50 SW Division St., 541/385-3333, http://cruxfermentation.com, 11:30am-10pm Tues.-Sun., 5pm-10pm Sun.) is a real treat, especially for beer nerds, who can appreciate the nontraditional brewing methods such as decoction mashing, open fermentation, and use of wild yeast strains and hops from all over the world. Here the beer flows directly from the finishing tanks to the taps (18 when we counted), and hops scent the building, a former auto transmission shop. Pub grub consists of good sandwiches, except on Monday evenings, when the kitchen is closed and food trucks pull up to make sure no one goes hungry.

Perhaps the hottest brewpub in town is **10 Barrel** (1135 NW Galveston Ave., 541/678-5228, www.10barrel.com, 11am-11pm Sun.-Thurs., 11am-midnight Fri.-Sat.). Wash down good pizza with an award-winning S1NIST0R black ale.

Although it (so far) has only a tasting room, not a full brewpub, **Boneyard Brewing** (37 NW Lake Place, 541/323-2325, www.boneyardbeer.com, 11am-6pm daily) is worth a visit. The brewery, just a short walk from downtown, got its name from scavenging old equipment from larger breweries. They also scavenged some excellent brewers, and their beers are first-rate. If you don't visit the tasting room, be sure to look for Boneyard brews on tap at local restaurants.

There's more good pub food at **Silver Moon Brewing** (24 NW Greenwood Ave., 541/388-8331, www.silvermoonbrewing.com, 11:30am-11pm Mon.-Sat., 11:30am-8pm Sun., $6-8), a normally low-key sports bar that kicks into gear several nights a week with live music.

The **Bend Brewing Company** (1019 NW Brooks St., 541/383-1559, www.bendbrewingco.com, 11:30am-close daily, $9-13), one of the few woman-owned breweries, is a local

TOURING BEND'S BREWPUBS

A decade ago, the Deschutes Brewery was the only artisan brewery in town, but it turns out to have been an incubator for many local brewers. Bend's microbrewery scene is the fastest-growing in the state, and the local visitors center has developed the **Bend Ale Trail** to help you explore it.

Pick up a copy of the Discovery Map of Central Oregon (available at many hotels and at the Bend visitors center) and use its Bend Ale Trail Map and Passport to track down seven Bend breweries. (The Ale Trail is also available as an app for iPhones and Androids.) At each stop, get your passport stamped—and for extra credit, head over Sisters to visit an eighth pub. When you get all seven stamps, stop by the visitors center and to receive a commemorative silicone beer glass. All of the seven Bend breweries are within walking distance of each other. Although it's easy to explore Bend's ever-ex-

panding brewpub scene on your own, a couple of local companies are offering tours that give you a little extra insight into the breweries and remove any temptation to drive.

The **Bend Brew Bus** (541/389-8359, $45) is operated by Wanderlust Tours, whose guides know both the outdoors and their way around a tasting room. You'll get to go behind the scenes at the breweries and, of course, do some sampling. The bus can pick you up at your hotel, eliminating the need to drive.

If you can get a group of about 14 folks together and want a slightly more active tour, board the **Cycle Pub** (541/678-5051) and start pedaling. And, um, drinking. The 16-person "bike," which looks more like a trolley, operates out of the Old Mill District and can be booked for pretty much any sort of tour you want to design. Two-hour tours ($300) are BYOB, but may include stops at brewpubs.

---

staple. Come for the good beer, the nice waitstaff, and the great patio (Brooks St. is a pedestrian-oriented street just to the river side of downtown). Food is good—grilled tacos, pizza, sandwiches, and excellent fish-and-chips. Happy hour is a good bet at this pub that's especially popular with the locals.

GoodLife Brewing (70 SW Century Dr., 541/728-0749, www.goodlifebrewing.com, 11am-10pm daily, $9-14) opened in 2011 in a warehouse with a 30-barrel brewing system and quickly established itself as a major player in the Bend beer scene, with Descender IPA winning raves. The brewpub (they prefer to call it a "bierhal") serves decent, somewhat healthy, pub fare; during the summer, you and your dog can enjoy it by the fire pit out back.

A few miles from downtown on the way to Sisters, find great handcrafted spirits at **Bendistillery** (19330 Pinehurst Rd., 541/318-0200, www.bendistillery.com, 11am-5pm Mon.-Sat., 11am-4pm Sun.). The distillery

has tours and a tasting room; it's not a bar and doesn't serve food.

INFORMATION

Bend Visitor and Convention Bureau (750 NW Lava Rd., 541/382-8048 or 877/245-8484, www.visitbend.com) has an office downtown around the corner from the Oxford Hotel. The **Central Oregon Visitors Association** (705 SW Bonnett Way, 541/389-8799 or 800/800-8334, http://visitcentraloregon.com) is in the Old Mill District.

The Bend and Fort Rock **Ranger Station** (63095 Deschutes Market Rd., 541/383-4000, www.fs.usda.gov/centraloregon) is the place to go for permits and information on the vast array of lands in central Oregon managed by the Forest Service. Passes are also available online; NW Forest Passes for hiking are sold at trailheads where they are required and Sno-Park passes can be purchased at many local businesses, including ski shops and some grocery stores. The **public library** (507 NW Wall

BEND

St., 541/388-6677) is a good place to get on the Internet; it is a wireless hotspot.

GETTING THERE
By Air
With flights to and from Portland, Seattle, San Francisco, Denver, Los Angeles, and Salt Lake City, access to central Oregon is quite good. The air hub of this section of the state is Redmond's **Roberts Field** (2522 SE Jesse Butler Cir., Redmond, 541/548-0646), 16 miles north of Bend and east of U.S. 97. **American Airlines** (800/433-7300, www.aa.com), **Alaska Airlines/Horizon Air** (800/252-7522, www.alaskaair.com), **United Express** (800/241-6522), and **Delta Connection** (800/221-1212) fly into Redmond. Alamo, Avis, Budget, Hertz, National, and Enterprise have car rental offices in the terminal. Taxis, limos, and shuttle buses connect the traveler to Bend at nominal costs.

By Bus
The **Central Oregon Breeze Shuttle** (541/389-7469 or 800/847-0157, www.cobreeze.com, $49 one-way, $88 round-trip, fuel surcharge added when gas prices reach $3.79 a gallon) serves Bend to and from Portland International Airport and the Portland train station. **Redmond Airport Shuttle** (541/382-1687 or 888/664-8449, www.redmondairportshuttle.net) offers door-to-door service to and from the Redmond airport.

Cascades East Transit (541/385-8680, www.cascadeseasttransit.com) is a regional bus system with lines running to Mount Bachelor, Redmond, Prineville, Madras, Sisters, and La Pine. During the winter, Cascades East partners with Mount Bachelor to run a **ski shuttle** ($12 round-trip from a park-and-ride lot at the corner of Columbia and Simpson) to West Village on the mountain.

Get to and from the airport or the Chemult Amtrak station on **High Desert Point** (541/382-4193), which also travels between Bend and Eugene. **Bend Cab** (541/389-8090) can always haul you around if you need a ride.

By Train
The closest you can get to Bend via **Amtrak** (800/872-7245, www.amtrak.com) is Chemult, 60 miles to the south on U.S. 97. Amtrak will assist you in scheduling your transfer to Bend.

By Car
U.S. 97 and U.S. 20 converge on Bend, much as the Native American trails and pioneer wagon roads did 150 years ago when this outpost on the Deschutes River was called Farewell Bend. Portland is three hours away via U.S. 97 and U.S. 26, Salem is two hours away via U.S. 20 and Route 22, and Eugene is two hours away via U.S. 20 and Route 126. Crater Lake National Park is about two hours south down U.S. 97. There are also many loops worth investigating, including the Cascade Lakes Highway, Newberry Crater, and the Lava Lands.

The Bend Parkway (U.S. 97) moves traffic fairly smoothly north and south through town. It parallels 3rd Street. On the road up to Bachelor and in some of the newer developments, including the area around the Old Mill District, traffic circles are used instead of stoplights. Your awareness of other vehicles should naturally heighten as you approach a traffic circle; traffic slows but doesn't necessarily stop at these junctions.

You can rent a car starting at around $40 per day from **Hertz** (2025 NE Hwy. 20, 541/388-1535, and Redmond Airport, 541/923-1411) or **Budget** (519 SE 3rd St., 800/527-0700).

Sunriver and Vicinity

The seeds of growth were planted in central Oregon in the mid-1960s when a onetime military encampment a dozen miles south of Bend was transformed into the Sunriver Resort community. The resort, with its mix of private houses, rental units, and a lodge, has an increasing number of year-round residents, but it is still largely a hub for families looking to rent a house in central Oregon. And indeed, this is an ideal spot for a family get-together, with miles of bike paths, swimming pools, tennis courts, and the lovely Deschutes River. It's also an easy base for exploring the nearby volcanic landscape and sites along the Cascade Lakes Highway and, in the winter, for skiing Mount Bachelor.

SIGHTS
Newberry Volcano
Newberry Volcano, a vast shield volcano that reached to about 10,000 feet before it blew its top about 1,500 years ago, covers 500 square miles. Its caldera alone is five miles in diameter and contains two alpine lakes, Paulina and East Lakes. A 1981 U.S. Geological Survey probe drilled into the caldera floor and found temperatures of 510°F, the highest recorded in an inactive Cascade volcano.

The volcano itself is at the southeastern end of the area designated the **Newberry National Volcanic Monument,** which extends in a swath from Newberry Crater, south and east of Sunriver, all the way to Lava Butte, on the highway between Bend and Sunriver. It preserves the obsidian fields, deep mountain lakes, and lava formations left in the wake of a massive series of eruptions. While lacking the visual impact (and great depth) of Crater Lake, this preserve is more accessible and less crowded than its southern Cascade counterpart.

The main focus of interest here are the two lakes in the caldera: **Paulina Lake** and **East Lake.** A 9,500-year-old circular structure called a wickiup was excavated at Paulina Lake in 1992, which dates back well before the latest eruptions of the volcano and indicates that native people used this area through various stages of volcanic activity. Several campgrounds and two resorts are located along the shores of these lakes, which are noted for their excellent trout fishing, said to be best in the fall. In Paulina Lake, fisherfolk can troll for kokanee, a gourmet's delight, as well as brown and rainbow trout. Paulina's twin, East Lake, features a fall run of German brown trout that move out of the depths to spawn in shoreline shallows.

Be sure to take the four-mile drive (summer only) to the top of 7,985-foot-high **Paulina Peak,** the highest point along the jagged edge of Newberry Crater, on Forest Service Road 500. Towering 1,500 feet over the lakes in the crater, the peak also allows a perspective on the forest, obsidian fields, and basalt flows in the surrounding area. To the far west, a palisade of snow-clad Cascade peaks runs the length of the horizon.

The other must-see site on the volcano is the **Big Obsidian Flow,** which was formed 1,300 years ago and served as the source of raw material for Native American spear points, arrowheads, and hide scrapers. Prized by the original inhabitants of the area, the obsidian tools were also highly valued by other Native American nations and were exchanged for blankets, firearms, and other possessions at the Taos Fair in New Mexico. These tools and other barter items helped to spread Newberry Volcano obsidian all across the West and into Canada and Mexico. Centuries later, NASA sent astronauts to walk on the volcano's pumice-dusted surface in preparation for landing on the moon. A 0.9-mile trail now crosses the obsidian flow. Find the trailhead on the road between the two lakes.

Newberry National Volcanic Monument is managed by the Deschutes National Forest;

contact the **Lava Lands Visitor Center** (58201 S. U.S. 97, Bend, 541/593-2421, www.fs.usda. gov/centraloregon) for more information. During the summer, a Forest Service guard station is staffed at Paulina Lake. A Northwest Forest Pass or a three-day monument pass ($10, available at Lava Land Visitor Center or at the monument entrance) is required for day use.

To reach Newberry Crater, head south from Sunriver about 12 miles (or 27 miles from Bend) on U.S. 97 to the turnoff to Paulina and East Lakes. The 16-mile paved but ragged County Road 21 twists and turns its way up to the lakes in the caldera of Newberry Crater.

Sunriver Nature Center

Educational programs and interpretive exhibits, including a nature trail and a botanical garden, help orient visitors to the high desert ecology of the area around Sunriver. Programs at the **Sunriver Nature Center** (River Rd., Sunriver, 541/593-4394, www.sunrivernaturecenter.org, 9am-5pm daily late May-Labor Day) include nature walks, classes, and summertime day camps for kids.

SPORTS AND RECREATION
Bicycling

For many visitors, a visit to Sunriver is a chance to ride a bike. The gentle off-street bike paths provide the perfect way to get around the resort area. It's also possible to ride along paths and back roads from the edge of Sunriver to Benham Falls on the Deschutes River. Sunriver's **Bike Barn** (541/593-3721), near the Great Hall, can set you up with a rented bike. **Village Bike and Ski** (541/593-2453), in the Sunriver Mall, is another good place to rent a bike. Be sure to pick up a map of the local bike trails. A popular ride from Sunriver is the easy eight-mile loop to Benham Falls.

If you like to bike but would rather have gravity do all of the work, consider the **Paulina Plunge** (541/389-0562 or 800/296-0562, www.paulinaplunge.com, May-Oct., $60), a six-mile downhill mountain bike ride. They provide high-quality mountain bikes, helmets, experienced guides, and the shuttle transfer from Sunriver and back. The action starts at Paulina Lake, where you begin your coast down forested trails alongside Paulina Creek. You'll pass by 50 waterfalls on your 2,500-foot descent, as well as abundant wildlife and varied vegetation. Three short nature hikes are necessary to experience the waterfalls and natural waterslides that make this trip famous. (Yes, you will want to plunge into the water!) You may bring your own bike, but this will not afford you a discount from the tour price. Bring your own lunch and water or pay $10 for a sack lunch, $2 for a water bottle.

Bird-Watching

About an hour south of Sunriver near Fort Rock is **Cabin Lake Campground** (Deschutes National Forest, 541/383-5300, www.fs.usda. gov/centraloregon), an exceptional spot for viewing a wide variety of birds and wildlife. There is no lake at Cabin Lake, and the campground is pretty marginal, but the Forest Service has built two small ponds that blend in with the natural surroundings. Permanent wildlife-viewing blinds made of logs, built and donated by the Portland Audubon Society, are adjacent to the small 12-site campground and give close visual access to the ponds. In fact, the blinds are so close that binoculars aren't really needed.

Since there is little water in this 3,000-foot-high meeting of desert and mountain biomes, both mountain and desert birds are regularly attracted, usually in large quantities. The red crossbill, an increasingly rare member of the finch family, is a regular visitor to this avian oasis. The pinyon jay is another fairly uncommon bird that can be seen here with frequency. Woodpeckers, including Lewis's woodpecker, the common flicker, the white-headed woodpecker, and the hairy woodpecker are also often sighted. Park checklists show the California quail, bluebirds, chickadees, flycatchers, sparrows, warblers, and the Western tanager making appearances too. Best viewing times are in the morning, but birds can usually be seen all day long.

Fishing

Although some people do fish the Upper Deschutes River from the bank in the area around Sunriver, most anglers use drift boats. If you don't have a boat, consider fishing the Fall River, off Route 43 (Century Dr.) southwest of Sunriver.

You can get equipment, licenses, advice, or a fishing guide at the **Sunriver Fly Shop** (56805 Venture Ln., Sunriver, 541/593-8814, www.sunriverflyshop.com), near the Chevron station in the business park-shopping area across the road from the entrance to Sunriver.

Families are catered to by **Garrison's Fishing Service** (541/593-8394, www.garrisonguide.com), which features pontoon boats with padded swivel chairs that cruise the lakes and rivers of central Oregon looking for the big ones.

Golf

Three 18-hole courses and a family-oriented nine-hole course are found at **Sunriver Resort** (541/593-4402 or 800/801-8765, www.sunriver-resort.com). The Meadows Course ($49-109) is many golfers' favorite. The Woodlands Course ($49-109) has water, abundant bunkers, and constricted approaches to the greens, making club selection and shot accuracy very important. The private Crosswater Course ($59-189) is touted by the management as the best course north of Pebble Beach. You must be a resort guest or member to play on it. The nine-hole Caldera Links ($39 adults, $10 children ages 12-17) is the newest course, designed to introduce new players to the sport; it's also limited to resort guests and local homeowners.

A nearby and economical golf course is **Quail Run** (16725 Northridge Dr., La Pine, 541/536-1303 or 800/895-4653, golfquailrun.com, $55), an 18-hole championship course in La Pine. Sand traps, ponds, and tree-lined fairways

challenge golfers of all levels without seriously challenging their pocketbooks.

Horseback Riding

During the spring and summer the **Sunriver Stables** (541/593-6995, www.sunriver-resort.com) offers rides ranging from short pony rides to eight-hour trail rides; riding lessons are also available. During the winter, horse-drawn sleigh rides ($100) travel along the Deschutes River and through the forest.

Paddling

The Sunriver marina (541/593-3492, 11am-3pm daily May, 9:30am-4:30pm daily June-early Oct.), on the Deschutes River west of Circle 3, rents canoes, kayaks, stand-up paddleboards, and rafts; offers kayak classes; and leads float trips on the Deschutes. Aspiring anglers can also rent a fishing rod here. Passes are available with many Sunriver rentals; ask about this when you're booking if it's important to you.

Swimming

Sunriver homeowners and guests can swim at a great new aquatic center, the **SHARC** (57250 Overlook Rd. off Circle 2, 541/585-5000, www.sunriversharc.com, $25 adults, $20 children ages 4-17, multiday passes available, rates less in winter), with large indoor and outdoor pools, two waterslides, and an outdoor hot tub reserved for adults as well as playgrounds and basketball and bocce courts.

ENTERTAINMENT AND EVENTS

The mid-August **Sunriver Music and Arts Festival** (541/593-1084 or 541/593-9310, www.sunrivermusic.org), held in the magnificent log-and-stone structure called the Great Hall at Sunriver Resort and in Bend's Tower Theatre, has been pleasing capacity crowds since the festival's inception in 1977. The concert series features top performers from around the world. Highlights include the gala pops concert and the gourmet dinner as well as four traditional classical concerts and a family concert.

ACCOMMODATIONS

The Pacific Northwest's most complete resort, **Sunriver Lodge** (800/801-8765, www.sunriver-resort.com) not only has proximity to Mount Bachelor skiing, Deschutes River canoeing and white-water rafting, and hiking and horse trails in the Deschutes National Forest but also boasts golf courses, pools, tennis courts, 35 miles of paved bike routes, and a nature center with an astronomical observatory. There's pretty much something for everybody.

Sunriver Lodge has rooms ranging from up-to-date guest rooms ($219) to relatively large suites featuring a large fireplace, a fully equipped kitchen, a sleeping loft, and tall picture windows that open onto a patio ($269). Nearby "river lodges" are even more elegant and run about $300. About two miles south of the lodge, in the newer Caldera Springs development, swank three- to four-bedroom cabins start at about $400.

Note that it can be a much better deal to rent a condo or a house. Sunriver Resort's website allows you to set your criteria and browse available properties, which start at about $200.

Condo rentals are also available through **Mountain Resort Properties** (541/593-8685 or 800/346-6337, www.mtresort.com). All units have a fully equipped kitchen, linens, a washer and dryer, TV, and a barbecue, as well as access to Mavericks, a large fitness center. Since these are privately owned units, other amenities like hot tubs, saunas, and bicycles will vary. Most of these condos do not allow pets or smoking, but there are exceptions; inquire when making reservations. Other agencies brokering vacation house rentals include **Village Properties** (541/593-1653, www.village-properties.com) and **Discover Sunriver** (866/534-4668, www.discoversunriver.com). Many houses have hot tubs, and quite a few allow pets; rates can be as low as $150 a night for a two-bedroom house.

Paulina Lake Resort (541/536-2240, www.paulinalakelodge.com, $93-245) books up early with fourteen rustic log cabins. Although all cabins have kitchenettes or full kitchens, hearty lunches and dinners (9am-4pm Sun.-Tues., 11am-7pm Wed.-Thurs., 9am-9pm Fri.-Sat., summer, 11am-8pm Wed.-Sat., 11am-4pm Sun. winter, dinner $13-25, dinner reservations required in winter) can be had in the resort's log-paneled dining room. Boat rentals and a general store are also on-site. During winter, although the road to the resort is snowed in, the resort itself is open December-March to cross-country skiers and snowmobilers, giving access to over 330,000 acres of designated snowmobile areas.

East Lake Resort (541/536-2230, www.eastlakeresort.com, mid-May-mid-Oct., $75-189) offers 16 cabins with at least rudimentary cooking facilities (most have full kitchens). A snack bar, a general store, and boat rentals are on-site, and the nearby RV park ($25) has a laundry and pay showers. The lake itself is stocked with trout and Atlantic and kokanee salmon. The cold water and abundant freshwater shrimp make for excellent-tasting fish.

Camping

The nicest campgrounds near Sunriver are in the Newberry Volcano area. The creek-side **McKay Crossing** (541/383-5300, www.fs.usda.gov/centraloregon, $10, no drinking water) is about 3 miles east of U.S. 97 on the road up to Newberry Volcano. **Paulina Lake, Little Crater, Cinder Hill**, and **East Lake** (reservations at 877/444-6777, www.recreation.gov, all $16, drinking water) are at the top of the Newberry Volcano; the season runs from late May to mid-October.

La Pine State Park (541/536-2071 or 800/452-5687, www.oregonstateparks.org, year-round, $22 tents or RVs, $42 rustic cabin, $81 deluxe cabin) is a large campground south of Sunriver. Look for a sign on the west side of the highway marking the 3-mile-long entrance road located 8 miles north of La Pine off U.S. 97. This park also claims Oregon's tallest ponderosa pine tree (162 feet) and offers easy access to the Cascade Lakes Highway and an array of volcanic phenomena. The campground offers such amenities as flush toilets, firewood, showers.

FOOD

There are a number of casual eateries in and around Sunriver's main shopping area as well as a well-stocked grocery store. Food isn't really one of the high points of a visit here, but it's fun to visit the **Owl's Nest** (541/593-3730, 11:30am-close daily, $7-17), the lounge in Sunriver Resort's main lodge to enjoy a drink, pub food, and great views. Kids are allowed until about 8pm.

There are more great views and decent Mexican-Peruvian food at **Hola!** (57235 River Rd., 541/593-8880, www.holabend, 11am-9pm Sun.-Thurs., 11am-10pm Fri.-Sat., $12-19), next to the Sunriver marina. The Peruvian food includes braised pork in Coca-Cola with yams, onions, tomatoes, or wild prawns with fried bananas, red onion, and spicy mole sauce. Hola! also has a couple of restaurants in Bend, including at the Old Mill.

Find good breakfasts and lunches at **Cafe Sintra** (7 Ponderosa Rd., 541/593-1222, 7am-3pm daily, $7-13), where a few dishes, such as a chicken stew with white beans and roasted green chiles, reflect the owner's upbringing in Sintra, Portugal.

Cascade Lakes Highway

The Cascade Lakes Highway (a.k.a. Century Dr. or Rte. 46) is an 89-mile drive leading to more than half a dozen lakes in the shadow of the snowcapped Cascades. These lakes feature boating, fishing, and other water sports, and just about every lake has at least one campground on its shore. Hiking, bird-watching, biking, and skiing also attract visitors. From downtown Bend, drive south on Franklin Avenue, which becomes Galveston Avenue, to the traffic circle at Galveston Avenue and Century Drive (at 14th St., about 1 mile from downtown). Go three-quarters of the way around the circle and you'll be headed south on Century Drive. The route is well marked, and the road climbs in elevation for a significant portion of the drive.

Although there are many places to stop and explore along the highway, the stretch between Mount Bachelor and Crane Prairie Reservoir is the most spectacular, so if you're just out for an eye-popping drive, you can take the shortened version described in the sidebar.

The area around the Cascade Lakes Highway is part of the **Deschutes National Forest** (541/383-5300, www.fs.usda.gov/centraloregon). A **Northwest Forest Pass** ($5 one-day, $30 one-year) is required to park at most trailheads; passes are sold at the trailhead (bring exact change or a check).

SIGHTS
Todd Lake

Shortly after you pass Mount Bachelor, you'll find the turnoff to the exceptionally beautiful but equally rustic National Forest Service campground (NW Forest Pass, no extra camping fee, June-Oct., depending on snow) at **Todd Lake.** It's a short walk up the trail from a parking area to the campsites at this 6,200-foot-high alpine lake. Tables, grills, and a vault toilet are provided, but you will need to pack in your own water and supplies, as no vehicles are allowed—a good thing, because the drone of a Winnebago generator would definitely detract from the grandeur of this pristine spot. You'll find good swimming and wading on the sandy shoal on the south end of the lake, and you can't miss the captivating views of Broken Top to the north. Hardy explorers can portage a canoe up the trail for a paddle around Todd Lake. Because of the lake's high elevation, it is often socked in by snow until about the Fourth of July.

A THREE-HOUR TOUR OF THE CASCADE LAKES HIGHWAY

If you just want a gourmet taste of the Cascade Lakes Highway, a shortened version of the loop manages to take in some of the highlights. The following tour can be enjoyed in several hours, even allowing for several stops. In contrast, driving the entire loop takes a whole day with only limited time spent out of the car.

Begin by taking U.S. 97 south of Bend 13 miles and getting off at the exit for Sunriver. After about 1.5 miles, the turnoff to Sunriver Resort will be on your right; stay on the main road as it curves to the left. Follow this road (Rte. 40/Spring River Rd.) to Cascade Lakes Highway (Rte. 46) and turn right to reach Little Lava Lake. The Deschutes River begins its 252-mile course to the Columbia from here. Head just down the road to Lava Lake, where there's a small rustic resort, camping, and a store with a grand view of South Sister from the store's porch; in the summer your attention could be diverted by the hummingbirds that flock to a hanging feeder.

Follow the highway north to the shores of Elk Lake, a favorite of windsurfers and sailors. The year-round cabins at **Elk Lake Resort** (541/480-7378, www.elklakeresort.net) are popular, as is picture-taking from the lake's beach picnic grounds on the southernmost tip of shoreline. Here you have the full length of Elk Lake before you, with South Sister and Mount Bachelor in the background. During the snow-bound months of winter, access to Elk Lake is by snowmobile, Sno-Cat van, or dogsled (really!) to a world of groomed cross-country ski and snowshoe trails amid spectacular alpine scenery.

Not far away, the red volcanic cinder highway contrasts with the black lava flows en route to aqua-tinted Devils Lake. From the northern end of this lake, on the other side of the highway, you'll find Devil's Pile, an agglomeration of lava flows and volcanic glass where *Apollo 11* astronauts reportedly culled a rock to deposit on the lunar surface. The road winds around to the Mount Bachelor Summit ski lifts. From the deck in front of the sport shop-cafeteria complex, you can see the Three Sisters and Broken Top.

You might want to hike the short trail to Todd Lake, canoe Sparks Lake in the shadow of Broken Top and South Sister, or visit the Ray Atkeson Memorial, dedicated to Oregon's "photographer laureate." All are between Devil's Pile and the ski lifts. From Mount Bachelor it's a 20-minute drive back to Sunriver.

Sparks Lake

Clear and shallow **Sparks Lake,** about 25 miles west of Bend, is a favorite stop for photographers; most visitors can't resist trying to capture views of Mount Bachelor, South Sister, and Broken Top reflected in the lake. Broken volcanic rock forms the lakebed, and water slowly drains out during the course of the summer, leaving not much more than a marsh by late summer. This is a good place to let go of the idea of a formal trail and just explore the lakeshore on foot or in a canoe.

There is a campground, Soda Creek (June-Sept., $10); bring your own drinking water, or be prepared to filter lake water.

The lake is open to fly-fishing only for the local brook trout and cutthroat trout, and the use of barbless hooks is encouraged.

Green Lakes Trailhead

Begin a hike into the Three Sisters Wilderness Area from the **Green Lakes Trailhead,** 27 miles west of Bend. It's about 4.5 miles from the trailhead along waterfall-studded Fall Creek, past a big lava flow, to Green Lakes. From Green Lakes the trail continues to the pass between Broken Top and South Sister. This trail is extremely popular, so it's best to hike it on a weekday.

Devils Lake

The eerily green **Devils Lake** 29 miles west of Bend is home to a very nice walk-in campground (Northwest Forest Pass required, no piped water) and an easy lakeside trail. Just across the highway from the lake is a popular trailhead used by South Sister climbers. The climb up 10,358-foot South Sister (Oregon's third-highest peak) is challenging but not technical. Many choose to do this 11-mile round-trip as an overnight backpacking trip. Many more hike the trail just as far as the pretty Moraine Lake area (about 3.5 miles), then return along the same route.

Elk Lake

A resort and a marina mean that this is not the quietest lake in the Cascades. **Elk Lake** is just about the only place along this road that you'll see sailboats, and it's also a good swimming lake by about August. The cabins at the **Elk Lake Resort** (541/480-7378, www.elklakeresort.net, $58-459) make a good base for exploring the local trails if you are not up for camping, and are open during the winter for cross-country skiers and snowmobilers. Accommodations range from small rustic cabins to larger, though still fairly rustic, cabins ($199) and modern homes ($299). An on-site restaurant is surprisingly good. During the summer a Forest Service campground ($14) and marina are open.

Hosmer Lake

Just off the highway and 39 miles from Bend, **Hosmer Lake** is a favorite fishing and canoeing lake. It's stocked with Atlantic salmon, but don't count on eating them. Fishing is limited to catch-and-release fly-fishing with barbless hooks.

Even if you don't fish and don't have a canoe, it's worth visiting Hosmer Lake for its spectacular views of Mount Bachelor, South Sister, and Broken Top. Of the two campgrounds on the lake, **South** ($10, late May-late Sept., no drinking water) has the best views and the best lake access.

Lava Lake

Lava flows formed a dam that created **Lava Lake,** which is fed largely by underground

Elk Lake is deep enough for sailboats and is home to a year-round cabin resort.

© JUDY JEWELL

springs. Rainbow trout, brook trout, whitefish, and illegally introduced tui chub live in the lake, which is 30 feet deep at its deepest point and open to bait fishing as well as fly-fishing. A lakeside **lodge** (541/382-9443) rents boats and operates an RV park; there is also a Forest Service campground (mid-May-mid-Oct., $14, drinking water) near the resort.

Little Lava Lake

Make a pilgrimage to **Little Lava Lake** and stand at the headwaters of the Deschutes River. Groundwater from the snowpack percolates down from the Mount Bachelor and Three Sisters area to fill the lake (it's thought that a large groundwater reservoir exists upstream from the lake); the Deschutes exits the lake as a meandering stream, flowing south about 8.4 miles to Crane Prairie Reservoir. Little Lava Lake shares a highway turnoff with Lava Lake.

Cultus Lake

Glacier-formed **Cultus Lake** is popular with campers, swimmers, boaters, water-skiers, Jet Skiers, and windsurfers. Anglers go for the big lake trout, also called mackinaw. An easy hiking trail follows the northern shore of the lake and then heads north along the Winopee Lake Trail to Teddy Lakes. From the trailhead to Teddy Lakes is about 4 miles.

The **Cultus Lake Resort** (541/408-1560 summer, 541/389-3230 winter, www.cultuslakeresort.com, mid-May-mid-Sept.) rents rustic cabins ($85-140), motorboats, canoes, kayaks, and Jet Skis; it also operates a restaurant. During the peak of the summer season, cabins are only rented by the week.

Crane Prairie Reservoir

Crane Prairie Reservoir, an artificial lake, is a breeding ground for ospreys. These large birds, sometimes known as fish hawks, nest in the snags surrounding the lake and fish by plunging headfirst into the water from great heights. Cormorants, terns, bald eagles, and a variety of ducks are also commonly seen. Humans also like to fish—the most-prized fish is a "cranebow," a rainbow trout that grows almost

freakishly large in this shallow nutrient-rich reservoir.

A Forest Service campground (reservations at www.reserveamerica.com, $16, late Apr.-mid-Oct., drinking water) and the private **Crane Prairie Resort** RV park ($30) and fishing guide service (541/383-3939) are located here.

Wickiup Reservoir

The area of the Deschutes River around present-day **Wickiup Reservoir** was a traditional Native American camping area during the fall. When the dam was completed in 1949, these campsites were flooded. Today, the reservoir (about 60 miles from Bend) is known for its relatively warm water and good fishing, especially for brown trout, which can weigh in at over 20 pounds. Kokanee and coho salmon as well as rainbow trout, brook trout, whitefish, and the nasty invasive tui chub also live here. Campgrounds are **Gull Point Campground** (reservations at www.recreation.gov, $16, drinking water), at Wickiup Reservoir and across an access road at **North Twin Lake** ($12, no drinking water) and **South Twin Lake** ($16, drinking water), small natural lakes that flank the large reservoir.

From Wickiup Reservoir, Route 42 heads east and north along the Fall River toward Sunriver. The Cascade Lakes Highway, Route 46, continues south past Davis Lake.

Davis Lake

It takes a little doing to get to large and shallow **Davis Lake,** and many of those who make it come for fly-fishing. It's known for large rainbow trout as well as illegally introduced largemouth bass. Most anglers use boats or float tubes because the vegetation along the shoreline and the muddy lake bottom make it difficult to wade.

Davis Lake was formed about 6,000 years ago when a lava flow cut off Odell Creek. A fire in 2003 wiped out the West Davis campground; the **East Davis Campground** ($12, drinking water), though reduced in size by the fire, still exists and is looking a little less bare every year.

BEND

INFORMATION

For information about sites along the Cascade Lakes Highway, contact the **Deschutes** **National Forest** (63095 Deschutes Market Rd., Bend, 541/383-5300, www.fs.usda.gov/centraloregon).

Willamette Pass and Vicinity

In the area around Willamette Pass, it's easy to see the shift from the greener, damper, Douglas fir-dominated west side of the Cascades to the dry east side, forested by lodgepole and ponderosa pines. Each of the lakes in the high country has its own partisans—families who have camped in the same spot for decades—and its own personality. Campgrounds are available at Crescent, Odell, and Waldo Lakes.

Pick one place to explore in depth, or hop between lakes—perhaps you'll carve out a new personal tradition.

SIGHTS
Crescent Lake

On the sun-drenched east side of Willamette Pass, **Crescent Lake** is home to a tremendously popular campground ($16 May-Nov., $12 Dec.-Apr.; yurts $30 May-Nov., $40 Dec.-Apr.) and the **Crescent Lake Resort** (541/433-2505, http://crescentlakeresort.com, open year-round, cabins $125-215, 3-night minimum stay in summer), an easy place to while away a few days. Rent a fishing boat, kayak, or bike from the resort. Large lake trout (including one whopping 30-pounder) are regularly pulled from the lake. Crescent Lake is about three miles south of Route 58 via Deschutes National Forest Road 60 from Crescent Lake junction.

Odell Lake

Two resorts, several summer homes, and campgrounds surround 3,582-acre **Odell Lake,** 30 miles southeast of Oakridge on Route 58. Situated in a deep glacial trough, the lake probably filled with water about 11,000 years ago when a terminal moraine blocked the drainage of Odell Creek. Due to the depth of the lake and the nearly perpetual west-to-east winds that blow through Willamette Pass, the water averages a cold 39°F. Those breezes, however, help to keep pesky mosquitoes and other obnoxious insects away and make for some of the best sailing in the Cascades.

◖ **Odell Lake Lodge** (541/433-2540 or 800/434-2540, www.odelllakeresort.com, year-round, lodge rooms $65-85, cabins $100-320) is a particularly charming, though rustic, typical old-time Oregon resort. It is popular with cross-country skiers during the winter. Skiers may want to take advantage of large cabin 12, which comfortably houses as many as 16 people for $320 per night. Since the lodge is extremely popular, reservations are strongly recommended, as much as a year in advance for weekends.

Moorages at Odell Lake are available for rent through the lodge, as are canoes, powerboats, and sailboats. The lodge has a complete tackle shop to help outfit you to catch the kokanee and mackinaw that inhabit the icy waters, and rental equipment is also available if you didn't bring your own. The restaurant at the lodge is open for all meals. The lodge also maintains its own system of trails, which provide good biking in the summer and cross-country skiing in the winter. The owners of the resort have put together an area map to guide you to various waterfalls. Bikes and ski equipment can be rented from the lodge. In addition to these outdoor pursuits, basketball, volleyball, badminton, and horseshoes round out the fun. Tots and toddlers will enjoy the sandbox, the toy library, and the swings.

Across the lake from the lodge is **Shelter** **Cove Resort** (W. Odell Lake Rd., Cascade Summit, 541/433-2548 or 800/647-2729, www.sheltercoveresort.com, lodge rooms $225-275, cabins $105-250, camping $36 with

BEND

electric hookups), which features 9 cabins complete with kitchens, over 70 campsites, and a marina with moorages. The resort's general store handles everything from groceries, tackle, and boat rentals to Sno-Park permits and fishing or hunting licenses. The September-October spawning displays by Odell Lake's landlocked salmon are unforgettable.

Two Forest Service campgrounds, **Sunset Cove** ($16, late Apr.-mid-Oct., drinking water) and **Trapper Creek** ($16, late May-mid-Oct., drinking water, reservations at www.recreation. gov) are on the lake.

Willamette Pass Ski Area

Willamette Pass (541/345-7669, www.willamettepass.com, 9am-4pm Wed.-Sun., Dec.-Mar., $49 adults, $30 children 6-10 and seniors), 69 miles southeast of Eugene on Route 58, has some of the most challenging runs in the state as well as a multitude of beginner and intermediate trails. You'll find some of the steepest runs, unlike the open chutes or powder bowls at other ski areas. Since Willamette Pass plows its own parking lot, you will not need a Sno-Park permit. Night skiing runs Friday-Saturday nights December-March. In addition to regular lift tickets, tickets are available for $13 an hour, with a two-hour minimum.

The ski area grooms trails for both regular cross-country and skate skiing (10am-4pm Sat.-Sun. and holidays, adult trail pass $12). In addition, there are several popular Sno-Park areas near Willamette Pass, including one right by the ski area with several fairly challenging trails; a couple follow the Pacific Crest Trail, which crosses Route 58 at Willamette Pass. For information on cross-country skiing from this and other local Sno-Park areas, contact the **Middle Fork Ranger District** of the Willamette National Forest (46375 Hwy. 58, Westfir, 541/782-2283, www.fs.usda.gov/willamette).

During the summer, the ski area's **Oregon Skyway** (10am-4pm Sat.-Sun., $14 adult sightseeing, $28 adult with bike) provides gondola rides up to the alpine country of Eagle Peak.

Waldo Lake

The Waldo Lake Wilderness is a 37,000-acre gem 70 miles southeast of Eugene via Route 58 (take Forest Service Rd. 5897 before the Willamette Pass turnoff to go 10 miles to the lake). The centerpiece of this alpine paradise is 10-square-mile **Waldo Lake,** the third largest in Oregon, whose waters were once rated the purest in the country in a nationwide study of 30 lakes. Peer down into the green translucent depths of this 420-foot-deep lake to see rocky reefs and fish 50-100 feet below.

No motorized craft are allowed on the lake, but canoeing, sailing, trout fishing, and windsurfing complement hiking and cross-country skiing to give you different ways to experience the lake and the surrounding region. Add wildlife-watching highlighted by the early September rutting season of Roosevelt elk, and you'll quickly understand why Waldo Lake is a favorite with Cascades connoisseurs. The 22-mile loop trail around the lake is popular with mountain bikers and backpackers, and day hikes on the south end edify less diehard recreationists.

To best savor it, visit the area late August-mid-October to avoid a plague of summer mosquitoes and early winter snowfall. Whenever you go, you can catch views of 8,744-foot Diamond Peak in the distance and find first-rate trails and campgrounds.

Waldo Lake has three very popular campgrounds: **Shadow Bay, North Waldo, and Islet** (541/822-3799, www.fs.usda.gov/willamette, reservations at www.recreation.gov, late June-mid-Oct., $20, drinking water). Shadow Bay usually has the most mosquitoes; North Waldo and Islet are windier. To get to the lake, take Route 58 for 24 miles southeast of Oakridge. Take a left on Forest Service Road 5897. It is 5 miles to Forest Service Road 5896, which takes you to Shadow Bay, and 10 miles down Forest Service Road 5897 to North Waldo. Boat docks and launching facilities are available, plus good sailing and fishing; gas motors are prohibited on the lake. Many trails lead to small backcountry lakes from here, so this is a good place to establish a base camp.

From the North Waldo boat launch, hike up to **Rigdon Lakes** via Trail 3555. It's about a half mile to the first lake. If you want a longer loop hike, continue north to two more lakes and the intersection with Trail 3583, turn left, and hike generally southward back to the lake and take a left onto Trail 3590, which follows the lakeshore east to your starting point.

Sisters

Sisters was established in 1888 when nearby Camp Polk, a short-lived military outpost, was dismantled. Following abandonment of the camp, the site was homesteaded in 1870 by Samuel M. Hindman, who subsequently operated a store and post office. Sisters is named after its backdrop to the south, the Three Sisters. Pioneers named these over-10,000-foot-high peaks after some of the virtues that helped propel them through the hardships of the frontier: faith, hope, and charity. Over the years, no one could agree on exactly which mountain was named what, so the Oregon legislature settled the dispute by labeling the mountains as the North, Middle, and South Sisters.

In any case, although most of the Old Santiam Wagon Road has long since been replaced by asphalt and forest overgrowth, the 19th-century flavor has been preserved in the town of Sisters. Wooden boardwalks, 1880s-style storefronts, and good old-fashioned Western hospitality grace this small town of about 2,000. Some people are quick to lambaste the thematic zoning ordinances of Sisters as a cheap gimmick to lure tourists, while others enjoy the lovingly re-created ambience and the abundance of charming, independently owned shops, including one of the world's best clock shops.

As well as being a food, fuel, and lodging stop, Sisters is also a jumping-off point for a wealth of outdoor activities. Skiing at Hoodoo Ski Bowl, fly-fishing and rafting on the Metolius River, and backpacking into the great Three Sisters Wilderness are just a few of the popular local pursuits. Nearby luxury resorts such as Black Butte Ranch, an annual rodeo, and a nationally famous quilting event add to the appeal of this vintage village.

SIGHTS
Three Creek Lake and Tam McArthur Rim

Three Creek Lake, tucked under **Tam McArthur Rim,** is a good place for a summer swim, especially if you have an inflatable raft to prevent full-body immersion in the often quite cold water. A tiny lakeside store rents rowboats; from the center of the lake you'll get a good view of Tam McArthur Rim, named for the original author of the classic and fascinating reference book *Oregon Geographic Names.*

From the lake, trails head into the Three Sisters Wilderness Area. One leads up to the 7,700-foot rim, and from the top the views of the Three Sisters and Broken Top are quite astounding. Snows can be heavy (the lake itself is at 6,500 feet), so don't count on hiking this trail before July.

A small lakeside campground ($14, no drinking water) at Three Creek Lake is a pleasant place to spend a couple of days in midsummer, but be forewarned that most return campers bring insect repellent.

To get here from Sisters, turn south on Elm Street, which becomes Forest Road 16. Follow Road 16 south about 17 miles to the lake. Be prepared for a couple of miles of fairly rough dirt road. During the winter, Road 16 between the lake and Sisters has a couple of Sno-Park areas that mark cross-country ski trails.

Black Butte

Hike up to the **Black Butte** lookout towers for a bird's-eye view of the Sisters area. It's about 2 miles of uphill hiking, often in full sun, to the top of the cinder cone; bring plenty of water. To reach the trailhead, take U.S. 20 west from Sisters, turn north (right) onto Forest Road 11

The glaciered Three Sisters peaks rise above Sisters.

(Green Ridge Rd.), and pass Indian Ford campground; turn left onto Road 1110 and follow it 5.1 miles to the trailhead.

◖ Metolius River

About 10 miles from Sisters is the second-largest tributary of the Deschutes River, the **Metolius.** To get here, take the Camp Sherman Highway off U.S. 20 five miles west of Sisters. This road will take you around Black Butte. On the north face of this steep evergreen-covered cinder cone lies the source of the Metolius. A 0.25-mile trail takes you to a railing where you can see the water bubbling out of the ground.

Known simply as "the Spring," the water wells up out of the earth at a constant 48°F. Native rainbow trout thrive in the cold spring-fed waters of the upper Metolius, but they are not necessarily easy to catch—the water is so clear that the fish are extremely selective about what they'll take, and flies must be both perfect looking and perfectly presented. A beautiful riverside trail follows the Metolius as it meanders through the ponderosa pine trees past

many excellent fishing holes. Drift boats are used to tackle the harder-to-reach places along this 25-mile waterway. Bring a bike along to the Metolius; bike trails are being developed here all the time, and they are perfect for easygoing family rides.

Five miles downstream from Camp Sherman (7 miles from the head of the Metolius Trail) is the **Wizard Falls Fish Hatchery,** which is open to visitors daily. Over 2.5 million fish, including Atlantic salmon, brook and rainbow trout, and kokanee salmon, are raised here annually. The hatchery is the only place in the state that stocks Atlantic salmon, which are transferred to Hosmer Lake.

SPORTS AND RECREATION
Skiing

Twenty miles (a little more than 30 minutes' drive) west of Sisters on Route 126 is one of Oregon's most family-oriented skiing areas, **Hoodoo** (541/822-3799 or 541/822-3337 snow phone, www.hoodoo.com, 9am-4pm Sun.-Tues. and Thurs., 9am-9pm Fri.-Sat., closed

© BILL MCRAE

The Metolius is one of Oregon's most enchanting rivers.

Wed., $45 adults, $31 seniors and children). Hoodoo has five chairlifts and a rope tow. The maximum vertical drop is 1,035 feet, and the runs are fairly evenly divided among advanced, intermediate, and beginner levels of difficulty. Prices go up a few bucks during holidays.

Horseback Riding

Black Butte Stables (541/595-2061, www. blackbuttestables.com) at **Black Butte Ranch** (8 miles west of Sisters on U.S. 20) has several packages that take you down trails in the shadow of the Three Sisters. Rides range from the one-hour Big Loop trail ride for beginning riders ($45) to the all-day Black Butte Posse ride ($160). Kids' pony rides go for $15.

Golf

Two well-groomed courses, **Big Meadow** and **Glaze Meadow,** are found at **Black Butte Ranch** (8 miles west of Sisters on U.S. 20, 855/253-2562, www.blackbutteranch.com, $75 for 18 holes during peak time). Big Meadow is

more open and forgiving, while Glaze Meadow, which was extensively renovated in 2011, demands precise shots. Both have tall trees and lush fairways from tee to green. Tee times can be reserved online.

Three miles outside of Sisters, the highly regarded **Aspen Lakes** (541/549-4653, www.aspenlakes.com, $75 for 18 holes at prime time) offers 27 holes in the shadow of the Three Sisters. Bent-grass fairways and distinct volcanic red-cinder bunkers add to the stunning mountain vistas.

ENTERTAINMENT AND EVENTS

The annual **Sisters Rodeo** (541/549-0121 or 800/827-7522) happens the second weekend of June. In addition to the normal assortment of calf-roping and bucking broncos, country dances, a buckaroo breakfast, and a parade round out the fun. A huge **quilt show** takes place during the second week of July; the outdoor show blankets the town with color. Also noteworthy is the annual **Sisters Folk Festival,** held in early September, the weekend after Labor Day. This even attracts some of the biggest names in blues and folk. Contact the **Sisters Chamber of Commerce** (291 E. Main St., 541/549-0251 or 866/549-0252, www.sisterscountry.com) for the schedule of events.

ACCOMMODATIONS

The **C Sisters Motor Lodge** (511 W. Cascade St., 541/549-2551 or 877/549-5446, www.sistersmotorlodge.com, $109-129) was built in 1939, when the North Santiam Highway first opened to auto traffic. It's set back from the highway within easy walking distance of the shops and boutiques of Sisters. Beds are decorated with quilts, and the kitchenettes have charmingly retro appliances and Formica tables; pets are allowed in some guest rooms.

The **Best Western Ponderosa Lodge** (505 U.S. 20, 541/549-1234 or 888/549-4321, www. bestwesternsisters.com, $170-230) is a large ranch-style resort motel set back from the road in the scattered pines. Rooms feature private balconies with views of the mountains and the

The cabins at the Metolius River Lodges are near the Camp Sherman store.

© JUDY JEWELL

adjacent Deschutes National Forest. Other amenities include a spa, a heated pool, and free continental breakfast.

Eight miles west of Sisters on U.S. 20, **Black Butte Ranch** (541/595-1252 or 866/901-2961, www.blackbutteranch.com, $140-650) sits in line with other Cascade peaks in a setting of ponderosa pines, lush meadows, and aspen-bordered streams. Over 16 miles of trails thread through the 1,800 acres of forested grounds. Accommodations include deluxe hotel-type bedrooms, one- to three-bedroom condominium suites, and resort homes. The resort includes golf courses, bike trails, tennis courts, several swimming pools, organized kids' activities and day camps, and a fitness center with yoga and other classes.

Right on the edge of town, **◖ FivePine Lodge** (1021 Desperado Tr., 541/549-5900 or 866/974-5900, www.fivepinelodge.com, $209-293) is a lovely newer resort with convention center facilities and an environmentally sensitive approach. Stay in a spacious suite in the large stone-and-timber lodge or in a classy Craftsman-style cabin with Amish-built wood furniture (pets are permitted in a couple of the cabins). All accommodations include breakfast, a wine reception, and access to the onsite Sisters Athletic Club, which has a 25-yard lap pool and a variety of fitness classes. During the summer, an outdoor pool is open, and use of cruiser bikes is complimentary. Also in the FivePine complex you will find a very posh spa, a brewpub, a movie theater, and a Mexican restaurant.

In a residential area close to downtown, find the **Blue Spruce Bed & Breakfast** (444 S. Spruce St., 541/549-9644 or 888/328-9644, www.blue-spruce.biz, $169). Designed and built from the ground up as a B&B, the four guest rooms have outdoorsy Western themes but plenty of comfort. All bathrooms have a shower and a two-person whirlpool tub. Bikes are available for guests' use, and rooms have minifridges and fireplaces.

Lake Creek Lodge (13375 SW Forest Service Rd. 1419, Camp Sherman, 541/595-6331 or 800/797-6331, www.lakecreeklodge.com,

$195-320, about $50 less off-season) is near Camp Sherman in the Metolius Recreation Area. This full-service resort has individual houses and cottages that vary in price depending on the unit and the number of people. Tennis, swimming, and fishing are some of the many activities available. Although the cabins have kitchenettes, many summertime guests like to eat at least one dinner at the lodge restaurant (8am-11am and at 7pm Tues.-Sat., 8am-noon and at 6pm Sun. July-early Sept., dinner $24-38 adults, $12 children under age 10); dinner is served family-style on the deck or in the pine-paneled main lodge and features a different selection of entrées each day, complemented by homemade breads, salads, and desserts. Lake Creek caters especially well to families; pets are allowed in selected cabins.

Another Metolius retreat can be found at **Cold Springs Resort** (25615 Cold Springs Resort Ln., Camp Sherman, 541/595-6271, www.coldspringsresort.com, $168). The cabins feature naturally pure artesian well water. A footbridge across the Metolius River connects the resort to Camp Sherman, where groceries, a church, and a café are within easy walking distance. Pets are allowed for $10 per night but must be kept on a leash at all times and never left unattended. The resort also operates an RV park with full hookups ($40).

The cabins at the ◖**Metolius River Lodges** (12390 SW Forest Service Rd. 1419-700, 541/595-6290 or 800/595-6290, www.metoliusriverlodges.com, $130-315) are tucked in by the Metolius River right near the Camp Sherman store. The most coveted pair have decks extending over the river, and the majority have fireplaces and kitchens.

Wedged between giant ponderosa pines and the banks of the Metolius are the 12 elegant cabins of the ◖**Metolius River Resort** (25551 SW Forest Service Rd. 1419, 541/595-6281 or 800/818-7688, www.metoliusriverresort.com, $245). These beautiful wooden structures are bright and airy with lots of windows. The cabins are two stories high with more than 900 square feet of living space, comfortably sleep 4-6 people, and feature a fully equipped

modern kitchen, full bath, river-rock fireplace stocked with all the firewood you'll need, and a river-view deck. Reservations made well in advance are a must. You'll find the resort behind the Kokanee Cafe.

A few miles west of the Metolius River turnoff on U.S. 20 is the turnoff to Suttle Lake and the elegant **Lodge at Suttle Lake** (13300 U.S. 20, 541/595-2628, www.thelodgeatsuttlelake.com, camping cabins $69, lodge rooms and deluxe cabins $219-294), where a Native American theme predominates. The least expensive accommodations are in newly built but rustic (and very clean) cabins that share a central bathhouse; lodge rooms and waterfront cabins are much more posh. Unlike several of the other Metolius area lodgings, the Suttle Lake lodge is pet-friendly. The lodge restaurant serves three meals a day.

If you want a horse-centered stay in the area, consider the **Long Hollow Ranch** (541/923-1901, www.lhranch.com, $690-795 3 days, $1,220-1,350 6 days), a guest ranch offering trail rides, cattle drives, and horsemanship lessons.

Camping

Bend Sisters Garden RV Resort (67667 Hwy. 20, 541/549-3021, www.bendsistersgardenrv.com, $32 RV, $42-95 cabins) is a sprawling and amenity-laden (pool, fishing pond, miniature golf) RV park on the road to Bend. It's about four miles from downtown Sisters, with good views of the mountains.

Six miles northwest of Sisters on Route 126 find **Indian Ford Campground** (541/549-7700, www.fs.usda.gov/centraloregon, $12, mid-May-mid-Oct., no water), the closest public campground to town. Farther west on Route 126 you'll hit the turnoff to the **Metolius River campgrounds** ($12-18, drinking water available at all but Candle Creek), a number of very pleasant Forest Service campgrounds strung along the river both upstream and downstream from the hub of Camp Sherman. The only Metolius campground with reservations available is called **Camp Sherman** (877/444-6777, www.recreation.gov).

Several campgrounds on Suttle Lake have boat ramps (reservations at 877/444-6777, www.recreation.gov, $16, drinking water, May-early Oct.); the lake is a popular place to fish, water-ski, windsurf and swim. **Link Creek campground** has the longest season, and also has a few yurts ($40, no pets).

A handful of campgrounds open only in summer can be found near Sisters on the old McKenzie Highway, Route 242. **Cold Springs Campground** ($14, drinking water) is just 5 miles west of town on Route 242. This campground, at 3,400 feet in elevation, has 23 sites for tents and small trailers (up to 22 feet). It's a pretty spot near the source of Trout Creek. Near the pass at 5,200 feet is the rustic 10-site **Lava Camp Lake Campground** (free, no water, mid-June-Oct. depending on snow), where the main allure is its close proximity to the Pacific Crest Trail and the Three Sisters Wilderness.

Information about these campgrounds is available from **Sisters Ranger Station** (Pine St. and U.S. 20, 541/549-7700, www.fs.usda.gov/centraloregon).

FOOD

A number of pretty average but often busy restaurants line Sisters's main street, Cascade Avenue. The hottest spot among them and a fun place is **Bronco Billy's Ranch Grill & Saloon** (190 E. Cascade Ave., 541/549-7427, www.hotelsisters.com, 11am-9pm daily, $10-22). Built in 1912, the upstairs rooms of this historical hotel have been refurbished into intimate mini-dining rooms. Barbecued ribs are the specialty of the house, but you can also find fresh seafood, steaks, salads, sandwiches, and Mexican fare. In one corner of the building, on the other side of the Western-style saloon doors, is Bronco Billy's. This funky watering hole must look much the same as it did 80 years ago. A racy painting that used to grace the local brothel is proudly displayed behind the bar, and cowboy hats on most heads complete the picture of a town whose Old West ambience gets better with age. For the price of a beer, you can get one of the local guys to tell you the inside scoop on where to go and what to do in this neck of the woods.

A somewhat hip and healthy alternative lies a block off the main drag: **Angeline's Bakery & Cafe** (121 W. Main Ave., 541/549-9122, http://angelinesbakery.com, 6:30am-6pm daily June-Oct., 6:30am-4pm daily Nov.-May) serves homemade baked goods, salads, wraps, and fresh juices, with lots of gluten-free and vegan options. Try the raw zucchini "noodles" with pumpkin-seed pesto; if you really need a nutritional boost, chase it with a green smoothie. During the summer, Angelina's stays open late some nights and hosts music.

The best food in town is at ❰ **Jen's Garden** (403 E. Hood Ave., 541/549-2699, www.intimatecottagecuisine.com, 5pm-close daily, $26), an intimate cottage with a fairly limited but perfectly executed French-inspired menu. The best bet here is to go for a prix fixe dinner (three courses for $42 or five courses for $55). During the winter hours may be scaled back.

In nearby Camp Sherman, a special treat

© JUDY JEWELL

Jen's Garden is a special place for dinner in Sisters.

BEND

awaits at the **◖ Kokanee Cafe** (25545 SW Forest Service Rd. 1419, 541/595-6420, www.kokaneecafe.com, 5pm-close daily summer, reservations recommended, $20-30), which is known for its fresh and innovative cuisine served in a small, simply furnished dining room. Their house salad, made with loads of organic greens, jicama, blueberries, and a lemongrass-and-ginger coconut milk dressing, is worth the trip alone; the trout is perfectly cooked and served over leek and lavender risotto; and the salmon is flavored with pine, sage, and juniper berries, and accompanied by maitake mushrooms. Dinner reservations are crucial during the summer and fishing season, given the small size of the building. The

Kokanee usually takes a break during the winter, and has scaled-back hours in the spring; this varies year to year, so call ahead or check the website if you're traveling in the off season.

INFORMATION

Detailed information about the geology, natural history, wildlife, wilderness areas, and numerous recreational opportunities in the Metolius Recreation Area can be obtained from the **Sisters Ranger Station** (Pine St. and U.S. 20, 541/549-7700, www.fs.usda.gov/central-oregon). More information is available from the **Sisters Chamber of Commerce** (291 E. Main St., 541/549-0251 or 866/549-0252, www.sisterscountry.com).

Redmond

Sixteen miles north of Bend is Redmond (population about 26,000), another rapidly growing central Oregon city. Redmond is a hub,

© JUDY JEWELL

downtown Redmond

centrally located among Madras, Prineville, Bend, and Sisters, so even with a new bypass, traffic can get congested.

The city got its start when the Deschutes Irrigation and Power Company established irrigation canals here in the early 1900s. The railroad soon came, and real estate traders shortly followed. Like most central Oregon towns, it was once home to several mills, but now, thanks to its regional airport and nearby resorts, tourism plays a major role in the economy.

SIGHTS
Peter Skene Ogden Scenic Wayside

Nine miles north of Redmond on U.S. 97, stop to peer into the dramatic Crooked River Gorge, a 300-foot-deep canyon. The old railroad trestle spanning the gorge was built in 1911 and helped to establish Redmond as a transportation hub. The old highway bridge, now open only to foot traffic, was built in 1926; before it was constructed, travelers had to descend the canyon walls to ford the river. The current highway bridge was built in 2003.

◖ Smith Rock State Park

The majestic spires towering above the Crooked River north of Redmond on U.S. 97 are part of 623-acre **Smith Rock State Park** (9241 NE Crooked River Dr., Terrebonne, 541/548-7501, www.oregonstateparks.org, $5 day use). Named after a soldier who fell to his death from the highest promontory (3,230 feet) in the configuration, the park is a popular retreat for hikers, rock climbers, and casual visitors. Picnic tables, drinking water, and restrooms can be found near the parking area. The more adventurous can camp out in the park's primitive (except for the showers) walk-in camping area ($5 per person, campfires prohibited), located near the park entrance.

Although Smith Rock is known for its rock climbing, many visitors come here to hike. Seven miles of well-marked trails follow the Crooked River and wend up the canyon walls to emerge on the ridgetops. Because the area is delicate and extremely sensitive to erosion, it's important not to blaze any trails because they may leave visible scars for years.

Some of the sport-climbing routes at Smith Rock are as difficult and challenging as any you'll find in the United States. Most of the mountain's 17-million-year-old volcanic rock is soft and crumbly, making descents extra challenging. Chocks, nuts, friends, and other clean-climbing equipment and techniques are encouraged to reduce damage to the rock. On certain routes where these methods would prove impractical, permanent anchors have been placed. Climbers should use these fixed bolts (after testing them first for safety, of course) to minimize impact on the rock face. Stop in at the park-side store to pick up a climbing guide to the routes at Smith Rock that do not require mounting additional fixed protection.

Climbers should never disturb birds of prey and their young in their lofty aeries. Golden eagles nest on the cliffs past the far end of the parking area; bald eagles have nested in a tree visible from the camping area. Stop in at the

© JUDY JEWELL

The Crooked River runs through Smith Rock State Park.

park visitors center (housed in a yurt by the parking area) for details on these birds and other park flora and fauna.

Finally, pack plenty of water. The Crooked River is contaminated with chemicals from nearby farmlands and isn't suitable for drinking, and even a short hike in this often-hot park will leave you thirsty.

Petersen's Rock Garden

What began as one man's flight of fancy over the years has metamorphosed into a full-fledged roadside attraction. Petersen, a Danish immigrant farmer, created four acres of intricately detailed miniature castles, towers, and bridges made of agate, jasper, obsidian, malachite, petrified wood, and thunder eggs. There are also the Statue of Liberty, the U.S. flag, and many other compositions hewn out of natural rock. Although the displays have fallen into disrepair, community volunteers have stepped in to restore the rock art.

To get to **Petersen's Rock Garden** (7930 SW 77th St., 541/382-5574, 9am-dusk daily winter, 9am-7pm daily other seasons, $3 donation requested), the rock garden to end all rock gardens, take Gift Road off of U.S. 97 seven miles south of Redmond and 10 miles north of Bend. Follow the signs; it's only 3 miles off the highway. There is a funky museum and gift shop in the rear of the complex featuring a jumbled collection of many types of rocks, crystals, fossils, and semiprecious gemstones. In the back of the museum is the Fluorescent Room, where little castles made of zinc, tungsten, uranium, and manganese glow in the dark. Free-roaming peacocks strike poses in front of the sculptures.

SPORTS AND RECREATION
Golf

Eagle Crest Resort (1522 Cline Falls Rd., 541/923-4653, www.eagle-crest.com) has three 18-hole golf courses: Resort and Ridge ($74 for 18 holes, $67 resort guests) as well as Challenge (a short 18 holes designed for a 3-hour playing time, $44).

Crooked River Ranch (5195 SW Clubhouse Rd., 541/923-6343 or 800/833-3197, www.crookedriverranch.com, $41-48 for 18 holes), an 18-hole par-71 course, is wide open with few trees, but that doesn't detract from the challenge or the scenic vistas.

A true desert course found in Redmond that requires shot accuracy is the **Juniper Golf Club** (1938 SW Elkhorn Ave., 541/548-3121, www.junipergolf.com, $39-65 for 18 holes). This is an 18-hole par-72 course that snakes through the juniper and lava of the high desert. The prevailing winds and abundance of rocks off the fairway challenge your shot-making abilities.

Rock Climbing

Redpoint Climbing Supply (8283 11th St., Terrebonne, 800/923-6207, www.redpointclimbing.com) at the corner of U.S. 97 and Smith Rock Way is a good information and supply stop for climbers. Climbing lessons, both private and group, are offered by **First Ascent** (541/318-7170 or 800/325-5462, www.goclimbing.com), which is known for its women's programs, and **Smith Rock Climbing Guides** (541/788-6225, www.smithrockclimbingguides.com).

ACCOMMODATIONS

The newly renovated **Lodge at Eagle Crest** (1522 Cline Falls Rd., 888/306-9643, www.eagle-crest.com, $112-164), five miles west of Redmond, is now operated by Holiday Inn and offers hotel rooms and one-bedroom suites. The terrain and vegetation are representative of the high desert, and the backdrop is views of eight Cascade peaks. Ask about ski and golf packages. This is a low-key family-oriented place. Vacation rental homes are also available through the resort.

In town, the **Best Western Plus Rama Inn** (2630 SW 17th Pl., 541/548-8080, www.bestwestern.com, $119) is a comfortable place to spend a night or two, with continental breakfast and an indoor pool.

Rock climbers tend to camp, but when that gets old, the **Hub Motel** (1128 NW 6th St., 541/548-2101 or 800/784-3482, http://

thehubmotel.com, $42-49) is inexpensive, close to Smith Rock, allows dogs, and has kitchenettes.

FOOD
Redmond makes its mark on the culinary world more by the quality of the local Juniper Grove goat cheese and its locally raised Kobe beef than by its restaurants, but increasingly, there are good places to eat here.

The **Brickhouse** (412 SW 6th St., 541/526-1782, 4:30pm-close Tues.-Sat., $18-39) is a popular and very good steak and seafood restaurant, serving high-quality meat and using many local ingredients. The interior, with its exposed brick walls and local art, is inviting and classy.

◖ Diego's Spirited Kitchen (447 SW 6th St., 541/316-2002, 11:30am-9pm daily, $15-27) is an upscale Mexican restaurant, emphasizing Southwestern-Mexican cuisine with French and Italian influences. Pork osso bucco slow-roasted with mushrooms is served over mashed potatoes with truffle oil; pork carnitas ravioli and seafood pasta are cooked up alongside burritos and enchiladas.

The **Seventh Street Brew House** (855 SW 7th St., 541/923-1795, 11:30am-11pm Mon.-Thurs., 11:30am-midnight Fri.-Sat., noon-9pm Sun., $7-10) is just a block off busy 6th Street and serves Cascade Lakes beer as well as pizza and pub food.

Redmond has a couple of other noteworthy pubs: **Pig and Pound** (427 SW 8th St., 541/526-1697, 4pm-10pm Mon.-Fri., noon-10pm Sat.-Sun., $8-12) is an English-style pub, complete with bangers and mash and local and imported beers on tap; two women head up the brewing operations at **Smith Rock Brewing Company** (546 NW 7th St., 541/279-7005, http://smithrockbrewing.com, 11:30am-8pm Tues.-Thurs., 11:30am-9pm Fri., noon-9pm Sun., $6-12), where Smith Rock brews and a few other local beers share rotating taps—in nice weather, this pub has good outside seating.

On the road to Smith Rock, the **Terrebonne Depot** (400 NW Smith Rock Way, Terrebonne, 541/548-5030, www.terrebonnedepot.com, 11:30am-8:30pm Sun.-Mon. and Wed.-Thurs., 11:30am-9pm Fri.-Sat., $10-24) offers fresh food, including a good selection of vegetarian options and pizza, in the gorgeously renovated historic Terrebonne train depot. Climbers and hikers can also get picnic lunches to go.

Prineville

Prineville (pop. 9,200), near the geographic center of Oregon, is the oldest incorporated town in central Oregon and still feels a bit like the Old West, even as it becomes a bedroom community for Bend and home to Facebook and Apple data centers. The seat of Crook County and longtime corporate headquarters of Les Schwab Tires (now located in Bend), Prineville gets a meager 10 inches of rain per year and relies mainly on tire manufacturing, agriculture, wood products, and tourism for its economy. The tourist trade is largely fueled by anglers, who come to fish the Crooked River and the two local reservoirs. Shop for entirely authentic Western wear at Prineville Men's Wear, downtown on Main Street; rock hounds and antiques shoppers should also consider visiting Prineville.

Coming into town from the west, you drop down from tall bluffs into the Crooked River Valley, and nearing the city, cruise through hills dotted with juniper. White-and-black magpies dart in front of your car, and red-winged blackbirds observe you passing from their fence posts.

Prineville is also known as the Gateway to the Ochocos, a heavily wooded mountain range that runs east-west for 50 miles. One of Oregon's least-known recreational areas, the Ochocos are ruggedly pristine. Beyond these mountains stretches the long valley of the John Day River.

BEND

WILLOWS, WAGON TRAINS, AND RANGE WARS

The Ochoco country, named after a Paiute word for willows, was heavily populated by Native Americans who lived off a bounty of deer, elk, fish, and camas roots. The first significant passage of Europeans other than trappers through the area was the Lost Wagon Train of 1845. Led by Stephen Meek, brother of the Oregon Territory spokesperson Joe Meek, the pioneers were seeking a route to the Willamette Valley that would be easier than the arduous trek over the Blue Mountains.

Instead, they found hardship, starvation, thirst, and death on a tortuous journey through the deserts of Malheur and Harney Counties and along the rugged ridges of the Ochoco Mountains. Their hardships finally ended when they found the Crooked River and followed it north to The Dalles. Somewhere during the trek, members of the party scooped up gold nuggets and kept them in a blue bucket. Although the legend of the Blue Bucket Mine has since captivated Oregon history buffs, its actual site has never been found.

In 1860, Major Enoch Steen led an expedition through the region, which resulted in a number of geographic features being named after him, including Steens Mountain and Stein's Pillar. Eight years later, Barney Prine built a blacksmith shop, a store, and a saloon near the bank of Ochoco Creek; the outpost grew into the city of Prineville, the only town in 10,000 square miles. It was settled by the sons of the pioneers who had come west on wagon trains. It was their turn to carve out a life from the wilds.

At the turn of the 20th century, cinnabar, the raw ore in which mercury is found, was discovered in the Ochocos, resulting in an influx of miners. About the same time, a range war broke out between the cattle ranchers and the sheepherders. Groups like the Ezee Sheep Shooters and the Crook County Sheep Shooters Association bragged that they had slaughtered 8,000-10,000 sheep in 1905 alone. Incensed by this lawlessness, the citizens of Oregon moved to stop the killing; still, troubles continued for cattle and sheep ranchers and farmers. Harsh winters took their toll on livestock, and the hope that the plains would be receptive to wheat farming was unrealized.

During World War I, many homesteaders gave up and moved to the cities to work for the war effort. In 1917, Prineville made a decision that wound up boosting the local economy. The town built a railroad to Redmond, linking its line with the Union Pacific. Used primarily to haul ponderosa pine logs, the railroad remains the only city-owned railroad still in operation in the United States. In the 1950s a new industry was added to the mainstays of logging, ranching, and farming: Gemstones of high quality were discovered in the Ochocos, prompting a rockhounding and tourism boom that continues to this day.

SIGHTS
A.R. Bowman Museum

A good place to begin your travels in Ochoco country is at the **A.R. Bowman Museum** (246 N. Main St., 541/447-3715, www.bowman-museum.org, 10am-5pm Mon.-Fri., 11am-4pm Sat.-Sun. summer, 10am-5pm Tues.-Fri., 11pm-4pm Sat. winter, free). This museum's two floors of exhibits and displays are a notch above most small-town historical museums. Fans of the Old West will enjoy the tack room with saddles, halters, and woolly chaps. Rock hounds will be delighted with the displays of Blue Mountain picture jasper, thunder eggs, and fossils. Other classic displays include a moonshine still, a country store, an upstairs parlor of the early 1900s, and a campfire setup with a graniteware coffeepot and a pound of Bull Durham tobacco.

SPORTS AND RECREATION
Hiking

Stein's Pillar is a distinctive rock outcropping in the Ochoco National Forest about 15 miles northeast of Prineville. A four-mile round-trip hike passes through meadows and old-growth forest with some lovely panoramic views and a final steep, challenging stretch of trail before reaching the rock. From town, head east on U.S. 26 for 9 miles and turn north onto Mill Creek Road. Continue for 6.5 miles to the turnoff for the trailhead.

Farther up Mill Creek Road, find Wildcat Campground and a trailhead for the **Mill Creek-Twin Pillars** trail. From the campground, the trail follows Mill Creek into the Mill Creek Wilderness Area. This wet area supports lots of wildflowers and also a few cattle. If you go the full 8.3 miles to the Twin Pillars, a pair of 200-foot-tall volcanic plugs, it's necessary to ford the river a number of times, which can be difficult early in the season.

Another worthwhile place to visit is **Lookout Mountain,** the highest point in the Ochocos. it's a unique biosphere with 28 plant communities, one of the finest stands of ponderosa pines in the state, lots of elk and deer, a herd of wild mustang, and creeks full of rainbow and brook trout. A seven-mile trail starts near the **Ochoco Ranger Station** (541/416-6500) 22 miles east of Prineville on Forest Service Road 22 at the campground picnic area, and ends at the summit of Lookout Mountain, from which 11 major peaks are visible. June is the time to see one of the best wildflower displays in the state. To get there, drive 14 miles east from Prineville on U.S. 26, and bear right at the sign for the ranger station.

About halfway between Prineville and Madras on U.S. 26, **Rimrock Springs Wildlife Management Area** has a 1.35-mile trail (0.5 mile paved) through fragrant sagebrush and juniper to a wetland created by a small dam. Spring and early summer brings a good display of wildflowers, including bitterroot; lizards, snakes, and many species of birds are also easy to see on this short hike.

Fishing

The 310-acre **Prineville Reservoir,** 17 miles south of Prineville on Route 27, was built for irrigation and flood control. A popular year-round boating and fishing lake, it is famous for its huge bass and is also stocked with rainbow trout.

Just downstream from the reservoir dam is a winding stretch of the **Crooked River** that offers some of the best fly-fishing in the state, in an incredibly scenic atmosphere beneath basalt rimrock cliffs. This section of the river is also dotted with a series of campgrounds, all of which are good places to camp and to fish. This is also a fine place to learn to fly-fish; it's easy to wade into the water away from streamside brush. Nonanglers can climb the short trail up Chimney Rock (from the Chimney Rock campground) to the top of the rimrock. From there, it's possible to walk along the ridge all afternoon.

Ochoco Reservoir, six miles east of Prineville on U.S. 26, is a favorite recreational spot for locals, with year-round fishing, boating, and camping.

ENTERTAINMENT AND EVENTS

A popular Prineville get-together is the **Annual Prineville Rockhound Powwow** (541/447-6304, www.prinevillerockhoundpowwow.com), held in mid-late June. The powwow attracts prospectors and rock hounds from all over the country.

The end of June also brings **Crooked River Roundup** (www.crookedriverroundup.com), with pari-mutuel horse racing following a couple of weeks later, in mid-July.

ACCOMMODATIONS

The **Rustlers Inn Motel** (960 NW 3rd St., 541/447-4185, www.rustlersinn.com, $55-80) was designed in the Old West style. Art by local artists and antique furniture grace the large rooms.

A budget motel that's popular with anglers is **Executive Inn** (1050 NE 3rd St., 541/447-4152, $55-80), east of downtown. The large multiroom family unit is recommended as a base for a family weekend visit to the Painted Hills, as motel accommodations in Mitchell are limited.

More upscale accommodations are available

at the **Best Western Prineville Inn** (1475 NE 3rd St., 541/447-8080, $91-99), near the east end of town.

The **Prineville Reservoir Resort** (19600 SE Juniper Canyon Rd., 541/447-7468, www.prinevillereservoirresort.com) is on the shoreline of Prineville Reservoir, 17 miles southeast of Prineville on the Paulina Highway (Rte. 27). This resort offers motel accommodations with kitchenettes ($75), camping units ($24-26), and rustic cabins (no bedding, $35). The resort also rents fishing boats.

Central Oregon's newest resort, ◖**Brasada Ranch** (16986 Brasada Ranch Rd., Powell Butte, 866/373-4882, www.brasada.com, $309-929), lies in the open hills of the ranch country between Prineville and Bend. *Brasada* is the Spanish cowboy term for "brush country," and that pretty much describes the landscape here, although it doesn't include the beautiful views of Cascade peaks that you'll find at Brasada Ranch. This resort, which is very popular with golfers, is an easy place to hunker down for a few days—the rooms are luxurious, but not frighteningly so; there's a good fitness center and an outdoor pool that resembles those found in upscale Hawaiian resorts, an excellent restaurant, a golf course, and biking, hiking, and horse trails. It's also a convenient location for Crooked and Deschutes Rivers anglers who want to stay in an upscale resort. Lodgings range from suites in the main "ranch house" lodge ($309) to one- to three-bedroom cabins ($449-929); they're all lovely, and the cabins have fully equipped kitchens.

Camping

For good campsites in the **Ochocos** (www.fs.usda.gov/centraloregon, mid-Apr.-late Oct.), take Ochoco Creek Road approximately 10 miles east of Ochoco Lake. Camp beneath big ponderosa pines at **Wildwood** ($8, drinking water), **Ochoco Divide** ($13, no water), and **Walton Lake** ($15, water), where you can fish, boat, or hike the trail to Round Mountain. While on this loop, stop at the mining ghost town of Mayflower. Founded in 1873, the community was active until 1925; a stamp mill is still visible.

Camp alongside the Crooked River at any of the nine **Bureau of Land Management** campgrounds (541/416-6700, www.blm.gov/or/resources/recreation, $8) on Route 27; they are about 15-20 miles south of Prineville. Be sure to bring water or be prepared to filter river water.

FOOD

For lunch, the **Sandwich Factory** (277 NE Court St., 541/447-4429, 7am-7pm Mon.-Fri., 8am-3pm Sat., $6-15), just west of the courthouse, has a huge menu of really good sandwiches. It's also an excellent place to people watch at lunch—most of downtown Prineville seems to eat here.

Behind a downright scary exterior lies an extremely popular (and not at all frightening) steak house: **Club Pioneer** (1851 NE 3rd St., 541/447-6177, www.clubpioneer.com, 11am-9pm Mon.-Thurs., 11am-10pm Fri., 4pm-10pm Sat.-Sun., $14-26). The competition, downtown's **Barney Prine's Steakhouse and Saloon** (380 NE Main St., 541/362-1272, http://barneyprinessteakhouse.com, 11am-2pm Wed.-Fri., 5pm-close Tues.-Sun., $10-24), is a bit more stylish, with beechwood floors salvaged from a Jim Beam distillery, a huge and beautiful bar, and a good wine list.

Even Prineville now has a brewpub! **Solstice Brewing Company** (234 N. Main St., 541/233-0883, 11:30am-10pm Wed.-Sun., $7-15) is a family-friendly, very casual pub with decent sandwiches, fish tacos, and Double Dam IPA on tap.

It's about 20 miles (a 20-minute drive) from Prineville to the Brasada Ranch resort, where you'll find sophisticated farm-to-table cuisine in the area at the resort's **Range** (16986 Brasada Ranch Rd., Powell Butte, 866/373-4882, 5:30am-9pm daily May-Oct., $19-44). The restaurant has an upscale Western ambience and offers both indoor and outdoor seating and impressive views of the Cascades. The food, both here and at the resort's more casual

BEND

restaurant, the **Ranch House** (open for breakfast, lunch and dinner, light dinner $11-19), is very good.

INFORMATION
The **Prineville-Crook County Chamber of Commerce** (785 NW 3rd St., 541/447-6304, http://visitprineville.com) has a helpful staff and lots of information to dispense. The **Ochoco National Forest** (3160 NE 3rd St., 541/416-6500, www.fs.usda.gov/centraloregon) can offer details on hiking in the Ochocos; the website is an excellent resource for trail information. The **Bureau of Land Management** (3050 NE 3rd St., 541/416-6700, www.blm. gov) can guide you to rock collecting sites.

Warm Springs and Lower Deschutes River

North of the Bend-Redmond area, the juniper- and sage-lined roadsides and the fields of mint and wheat stand in welcome contrast to the busy main drags of central Oregon's biggest urban complex.

MADRAS
Madras (pop. 6,000) is mostly known as a supply town for the surrounding agricultural area, which in places comes right up to downtown's doorstep. West of town, the Crooked, Metolius, and Deschutes Rivers join up and are impounded by Round Butte Dam to form Lake Billy Chinook. The main access to the lake is via Cove Palisades State Park. Downstream from the lake, the Deschutes River continues on its path to the Columbia. The most popular place for rafting the Deschutes is the area around Maupin, 47 miles north of Madras.

Madras is one of the region's most culturally diverse towns: Over 35 percent of its residents are Latino, and over 5 percent are Native American. Many more Native Americans live on the nearby Warm Springs Reservation.

Lake Billy Chinook
Heading north from Bend, travelers needn't put away their recreational gear. Just outside of Madras is a park that offers hiking, boating, fishing, waterskiing, and bird-watching. **Cove Palisades State Park** (541/546-3412 or 800/452-5687, www.oregonstateparks.org, $5 day use, $20 tent camping, $26 RV, $80 cabin) is 14 miles southwest of Madras off U.S. 97. Towering cliffs, Cascade vistas, gnarled junipers, and **Lake Billy Chinook** with its 72-mile shoreline create a stunning backdrop for outdoor activities. The lake was created when Round Butte Dam backed up the waters of the Deschutes, Metolius, and Crooked Rivers. For the best views of how these rivers come together, hike up the Tam-a-lau Trail (a quick 600-foot elevation gain) to the top of the Peninsula, a plateau of land between the backed-up Crooked and Deschutes Rivers. At the top, the trail makes a loop around the Peninsula with good views onto the Cascades and the river canyons. In total it's six miles round-trip, best done in the springtime when it's not too hot and when the balsamroot and lupine are in bloom.

The lake is popular with boaters ($10 moorage fee); **Cove Palisades Resort & Marina** (5700 S.W. Marina Dr., 541/546-9999 or 877/546-7171, www.covepalisadesresort.com) rents everything from stand-up paddleboards to houseboats.

Richardson's Recreational Ranch
If you're a rock hound, you'll want to visit **Richardson's Recreational Ranch** (6683 NE Haycreek Rd., 541/475-2680 or 800/433-2680, www.richardsonrockranch.com, 7am-5pm daily Apr.-Oct., $1 per pound and up). This family-owned and operated enterprise has extensive rock beds loaded with thunder eggs,

BEND

© CONNI DIACK

Rafters take a break along the banks of the Deschutes in Maupin, 47 miles north of Madras.

moss agates, jaspers, jasper-agate, Oregon sunset, and rainbow agates, and it is a huge hit with most kids. If you want to chip agates out of one of the many exposed ledges on the ranch, you will need to bring chisels, wedges, and other necessary hard-rock mining tools. Once you've completed your dig, you drop your rocks off at the office and pay for them by the pound. And if you don't care for dirt under your fingernails, you can always find rocks for sale from all over the world in the ranch's rock shop. To get there, take U.S. 97 north of Madras for 11 miles and turn right at the sign near mile marker 81. Follow the road for 3 miles to the ranch office. Rock diggers must start by 3pm, and the 8-mile road to the digging site is closed when wet.

Shaniko

Thirty-seven miles northeast of Madras is the ghost town of **Shaniko** (www.shaniko.com). In its day, Shaniko was the largest wool-shipping center in the United States. The Columbia Southern Railroad transported wool, sheep, cattle, gold, and people deep into the remote Oregon outback, and the city at the terminus prospered. Boomtown Shaniko had 13 saloons, stores, hotels, a schoolhouse, and a city hall. But when the railroad's main line was diverted to the Deschutes River, Shaniko's prominence quickly faded.

Today you can still see many old buildings in the town. The water tower provides a remarkable display of the jerry-rigged but nonetheless efficient water distribution system. The three-room Shaniko schoolhouse, built in 1901, and City Hall, featuring the constable's office and the jail, are also still standing. The Shaniko Hotel has been restored but is not currently open for business; make an offer if you want to buy it!

Accommodations and Food

Most of the lodgings in Madras are on the spartan side. **Sonny's Motel** (1539 SW U.S. 97, 541/475-7217, www.sonnysmotelmadras.com, $85-99), a basic but thoroughly decent place on the south end of town, is a good deal and allows pets. The **Best Western Madras Inn** (12 SW

4th St., 541/475-6141, www.bestwestern.com, $99-105) is a step up; both Sonny's and the Best Western have small outdoor pools, which are quite nice on a hot afternoon in Madras. The new **Inn at Cross Keys Station** (66 NW Cedar St., 541/475-5800 or 877/475-5800, http://innatcrosskeysstation.com, $108-113) is by far the most luxurious and restful place to stay in town. It has an indoor pool and conference facilities.

Amid all the fast-food joints in Madras, there's a shining beacon of healthy eating: **Great Earth Natural Foods** (46 SW D St., 541/475-1500, 7am-7pm Mon.-Fri., 9am-3pm Sat., $6-9) is a small food store with an exceptionally good deli. Stop in for a roasted vegetable salad, a sandwich, or a smoothie. A longtime Madras favorite, **Pepe's** (221 SE 5th St., 541/475-1144, 10am-8pm daily, $7-11), is a friendly all-around Mexican restaurant.

Geno's Italian Grill (212 SW 4th St., 541/475-6048, www.genositaliangrill.net, 11am-9pm Tues.-Fri., 8am-9pm Sat.-Sun., $12-25) is the best bet for a relaxed and tasty Italian meal.

CAMPING

Two overnight campgrounds at **Cove Palisades State Park** (541/546-3412 or 800/452-5687, www.oregonstateparks.org, $5 day use, $20 tent camping, $26 RV, $80 cabin) offer all the amenities: Deschutes campground (May-mid-Sept.) has 82 full-hookup sites and 92 tent sites; the year-round Crooked River campground, perched right on the canyon rim, has 93 sites with electricity and water. Reserve in advance (800/452-5687, www.reserveamerica.com), as these are extremely popular campgrounds.

Rent a houseboat on Lake Billy Chinook from **Cove Palisades Resort & Marina** (5700 S.W. Marina Dr., 541/546-9999 or 877/546-7171, www.covepalisadesresort.com, $1,450-3,450 for three days, $2,175-5,520 for a week).

Culver, a little town southwest of Madras, is home to the **Madras/Culver KOA** (2435 SW Jericho Ln., Culver, 541/546-7972 or 800/562-1992, www.madras-koa.com, $29 tent, $34-40 RV, $59-104 cabin). An outdoor pool plus some sites with shade are the big attractions at this well-run campground.

WARM SPRINGS INDIAN RESERVATION

Within the 600,000-acre **Warm Springs Indian Reservation** (www.warmsprings.com), which straddles U.S. 26 north of Madras, you can see the age-old practice of dip-net fishing on the Deschutes River, as well as the richest collection of Native American artifacts in the country at a 27,000-square-foot museum. But the reservation is hardly divorced from modern-day U.S. culture—tribal members operate a dam, a resort hotel, a casino (on Hwy. 26 across from the museum), and a lumber mill. It's interesting to note that the employees of these enterprises are the descendants of the same Native Americans who greeted Lewis and Clark and Deschutes explorers Peter Skene Ogden (in 1826), John Frémont, and Kit Carson (both in 1843).

◀ Museum at Warm Springs

You'll find an impressive display of Native American wealth at the **Museum at Warm Springs** (541/553-3331, www.museumatwarmsprings.org, 9am-5pm daily $7 adults, $6 seniors, $4.50 teens, $3.50 children), just east of the town of Warm Springs below the viewpoint at the bottom of the Deschutes River Canyon. Audiovisual displays, old photos, and tapes of traditional chants of the Paiute, Warm Springs, and Wasco peoples (the three groups that live on the Warm Springs Reservation) are aesthetically arrayed. Each group's distinct culture, along with the thriving social and economic community they collectively formed, constitutes the major theme of this museum.

Replicas of a Paiute mat lodge, a Warm Springs tepee, and a Wasco plank house, along with recordings of each group's language, underscore the cultural richness and diversity of the area's original inhabitants. The exhibits, culled from a collection of more than 20,000 artifacts, range from primitive prehistoric hand tools to a high-tech push-button-activated

BEND

Wasco wedding scene. Native American food-stuffs and art are on sale in the bookstore.

Kah-Nee-Ta

Kah-Nee-Ta Resort (541/553-1112 or 800/554-4786, www.kahneeta.com) at the bottom of a canyon about a dozen miles off U.S. 26 from the town of Warm Springs is a good place to find the sun when western Oregon seems unrelentingly gloomy. The 1,000-foot elevation and 12-inch annual rainfall enable golfers to play year-round; Kah-Nee-Ta is even snow-free in February. Owned by the Confederated Tribes of Warm Springs, this arrow-shaped hotel is a focal point of the reservation, which includes a working ranch and wild horses.

Lodging possibilities include tepees ($79, bring your own sleeping bags and pads) and RV sites ($69) as well as hotel rooms, suites, and cottages ($130-500). The hot mineral baths and a spring-fed Olympic-sized swimming pool are among the highlights. There are also bike rentals, tennis, horseback riding, and hiking. Day visitors can take advantage of Kah-Nee-Ta's Big Village hot spring pool (92°F in the cool weather, and cooled in the summer) and hot tubs (included in overnight room rates) for $15; the 184-foot waterslide costs $4. A separate (generally quieter) pool in the lodge area is for lodge guests only.

Resort guests who aren't camping are pretty much forced to eat at one of the resort's two restaurants (it's a long drive anyplace else): the **Chinook Northwest Grille** (6:30am-11am and 5pm-9pm daily, $12-25) and the casual arcade-like **Warm Springs Grill** (11am-11pm Sun.-Thurs., 11am-1am Fri.-Sat., $9-22). The summertime Saturday-night **salmon bake** ($30, $15 children ages 12 and under, reservations recommended), featuring traditional dancing and salmon cooked outside on cedar sticks over an alder fire, is quite popular.

MAUPIN

The riverside town of Maupin is usually a pretty quiet place, catering mostly to anglers who come for fly-fishing the native Deschutes

River redside trout. On summer weekends, however, it becomes a bit of a zoo when river rafters descend.

Sherar's Falls

Downstream from the Sandy Beach raft take-out is **Sherar's Falls,** a cascade that demands a portage if you're rafting to the Columbia. A bridge crosses the Deschutes just downstream from the waterfall. At the bottom of the waterfall is a traditional Native American fishing area, still used by Warm Springs community members. You'll see the rather rickety-looking fishing platforms perched over the river, and you may also see people dip-netting from them. If you're in the mood for tooling around, cross the bridge to the west side of the Deschutes and follow Route 216 a few miles to **White River Falls State Park** (800/551-6949, www.oregon-stateparks.org), a day-use park with another excellent waterfall and a short trail to the remains of an old hydroelectric power plant.

Rafting

Just about every tour company operating in central Oregon runs raft trips down the 13-mile "splash and giggle" stretch of the Deschutes, from Harpham Flat Campground to Sandy Beach, just above Sherar's Falls. Wapinita, Box Car, Oak Springs, White River, and Elevator Rapids are the highlights of this trip; look also for the resident ospreys as you pass the Maupin Bridge.

Sun Country Tours (531 SW 13th St., Bend, 541/382-6277 or 800/883-8842, www.suncountrytours.com) runs a full-day trip ($108 adults, $98 children) along the Harpham Flat-Sandy Beach stretch of the river. A hearty grilled chicken lunch is included. Transportation from Bend or Sunriver to Maupin is also part of the day-trip packages.

Rapid River Rafters (500 SW Bond St., Bend, 541/382-1514 or 800/962-3327, www.rapidriverrafters.com) offers a series of full-day and multiday packages on the Deschutes River. The one-day trip ($85 adults, $75 children) takes in 17 miles of the river from Harpham

Flat to Lone Pine. A hearty lunch is included. The two-day trip ($275 adults, $220 children) floats 44 miles of exciting white water from Trout Creek to Sandy Beach. The three-day trip ($400) runs 55 miles from Warm Springs to Sandy Beach. On all of the multiday trips, the camping and meal preparations at pleasant riverside locations are taken care of by guides. The season is late April-early October, and camping equipment is available for rent if you don't have your own. Among its many trips in Oregon, **Ouzel Outfitters** (1441 SW Chandler Ave., Bend, 541/385-5947 or 800/788-7238, www.oregonrafting.com) offers a full-day trip ($100) on the Lower Deschutes out of Maupin.

Experienced rafters can rent a boat from **All Star Rafting and Kayaking** (405 Deschutes Ave., 541/395-2201 or 800/909-7238, www.asrk.com, raft from $80 per day, inflatable kayak from $35 per day) or **River Trails Deschutes** (301 Bakeoven Rd., 541/395-2545 or 888/324-8837, www.rivertrails.com). Both of these Maupin outfitters also offer guided trips and shuttles. Currently no permits are needed to run the river, but there is a $2 per day/per person fee collected by the Oregon State Parks at the Harpham Flat put-in site. Call **Affordable Deschutes Shuttle** (541/395-2809, www.affordabledeschutesshuttle.com) if you need someone to take your car from put-in to takeout ($40 for Harpham Flat to Sandy Beach).

Fishing

Downstream from Maupin, anglers fish the Deschutes River year-round for trout; steelhead are in the river August-November. Part of the reason to fish here, especially in the spring and fall, is the beautiful canyon.

Deschutes Canyon Fly Shop (599 S. U.S. 197, 541/395-2565, www.flyfishingdeschutes.com) sells supplies and can advise you on the hatches and other conditions. They can also set you up with a guide (about $325-400 per day depending on the type of trip). John, the shop's owner, is very helpful, and really encourages women anglers. Maupin's other fly shop, the

Deschutes Angler Fly Shop (504 Deschutes Ave., 541/395-0995, www.deschutesangler.com), is also worth a visit for both gear and information. The owners of this shop are experts on Spey casting, a two-handed technique, and they hold regular casting clinics. The **Oasis Resort** (609 S. U.S. 197, 541/395-2611, www.deschutesriveroasis.com) also runs a guide service.

Accommodations and Food

If you don't want to camp, stay in a simple cabin at the **Oasis Resort** (609 S. U.S. 197, 541/395-2611, www.deschutesriveroasis.com, $45-85); it's a local classic. The **Deschutes Motel** (616 Mill St., 541/395-2626, www.deschutesmotel.com, $85-99) is above the river near Maupin's main downtown area. The fanciest place in Maupin is the **Imperial River Company** (304 Bakeoven Rd., 541/395-2404 or 800/395-3903, www.deschutesriver.com, $99-249), which has a riverside lodge. Some rooms have balconies overlooking the river, and all are nicely decorated and quite comfortable.

Right in town, the **Maupin City Park** (206 Bakeoven Rd., just downstream from the bridge, 541/395-2252, $24 tents, $32 RVs, reservations recommended for summer weekends) is on a grassy riverbank lot. Unlike almost all of the Bureau of Land Management (BLM) campgrounds along the Deschutes, Maupin City Park has water and showers.

Eat a hearty prefloat breakfast at the **Oasis** (609 S. U.S. 197, 541/395-2611, www.deschutesriveroasis.com, 7am-8pm Fri.-Sat., 8am-4pm Sun., $7-10)—it's also a good place for a burger and a beer. The **Imperial River Company** (301 Bakeoven Rd., 541/395-2404, 11am-10pm daily late Apr.-mid-Sept., 4pm-9pm Mon.-Fri., 11am-9pm Sat.-Sun. mid-Sept.-Oct., 4pm-9pm Fri., 11am-9pm Sat.-Sun. Nov.-late Apr., $8-22) is the most full-service restaurant in town, featuring steaks from the family cattle. The eatery that is most attractive to rafters coming off a hot day on the river, however, is the ice cream shop by the bridge.

BEND

CAMPING

Both upstream and downstream from Maupin are several riverside **BLM campgrounds** (541/416-6700, Memorial Day-Labor Day, $8-12). Bring water, or be prepared to filter it from the river. **Harpham Flat Campground** is the main launching spot for day trips on the Deschutes, and this place can be a little more hectic than the neighboring campgrounds. The nicest spots are actually a ways downstream at **Beavertail** and **Macks Canyon,** 21 and 29 miles north of Maupin, respectively. Reservations are not accepted.

NORTHEASTERN OREGON

Oregon's northeastern corner offers plenty of places to escape from the urban world, and nearly all of them are highly scenic and filled with fascinating history. Stretching over 200 miles east to west, from the canyon-trenching Snake River to the fossil-rich John Day River country, this portion of Oregon is part of the larger Columbia Basin, a vast lava plateau that encompasses much of eastern Washington and Oregon. Two features characterize this epic landscape: mountains and canyons. Imagine a sea of molten lava, with mountain ranges rising like islands above the steaming cooling basalt, and you have a snapshot of the region's geological history. Rivers have cut mighty canyons through the banded layers of basalt, creating awe-inspiring clefts that, among other things, expose the fossil remains of ancient life.

For jaw-dropping scenic grandeur and outdoor recreation, the area is hard to top. The magnificent Wallowa Mountains easily invoke comparisons to the Swiss Alps and are topped by the 10,004-foot Matterhorn and 9,933-foot Sacajawea Peak. Hells Canyon, carved by the Snake River, is one of the deepest river-carved gorges in the world, averaging 6,600 feet in depth. Inside the canyon, a 67-mile stretch of the Snake is one of the nation's protected Wild and Scenic Rivers. West of the Wallowas rise the Blue Mountains. The high country of the Blue Mountains is often dusted with snow by September, which was when Oregon Trail pioneers crossed these mountain passes. With its headwaters in the Blue Mountains, the John Day River cuts one of Oregon's most dramatic canyons, with fascinating fossil beds and an

© PAUL LEVY

HIGHLIGHTS

◖ John Day Fossil Beds National Monument: At these three separate fossil bed units, you'll learn about saber-toothed tigers and wind through one of eastern Oregon's top road trips, linking remote outposts of Miocene-era life (page 552).

◖ Kam Wah Chung State Heritage Site: This is a fascinating remnant of the time when Chinese laborers outnumbered European settlers in gold camps of the West (page 558).

◖ Pendleton Underground Tours: These tours explore everything from a Chinese jail to a brothel, the true underground of 1880s frontier life (page 564).

◖ Wallowa Lake Tramway: Hitch a ride on a gondola and whiz to the top of Mount Howard, with views over the Wallowa Mountains and nearby Hells Canyon (page 582).

◖ Hells Canyon National Recreation Area: The world's deepest river gorge is trenched by the Snake River, and the best way to see this otherwise almost inaccessible canyon is by raft or jet boat (page 586).

◖ National Historic Oregon Trail Interpretive Center: This excellent museum tells the story of the Oregon Trail pioneers and their treacherous traversal of the West (page 590).

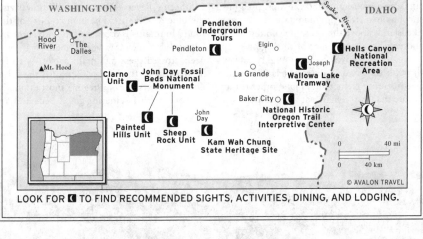

LOOK FOR ◖ TO FIND RECOMMENDED SIGHTS, ACTIVITIES, DINING, AND LODGING.

insightful interpretive center to help make sense of the region's long-buried natural history.

Just as the fossil beds provide a cross section of the earth's history, a trip through northeastern Oregon will give you a feel for the leather-tough people who settled here. In country towns and larger centers like Baker City, La Grande, and Pendleton, history is not very old; what may seem like the Old West is still a way of life. And while it remains primarily rural ranch country, the area is becoming an increasingly popular haven for painters, sculptors, and writers.

PLANNING YOUR TIME

For many travelers on a road trip, northeastern Oregon will either be the first or the last part of Oregon they will encounter. If the Willamette Valley or the Oregon coast is the focus of your Oregon vacation, you might find it tempting to hurtle right through this corner of the state on I-84. However, plan to devote at least a day

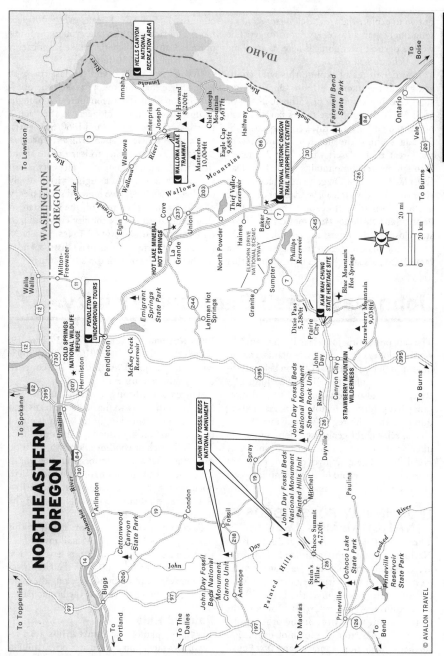

NORTHEASTERN OREGON

To Toppenish
To Spokane
To Portland
To The Dalles

WASHINGTON
OREGON

To Lewiston
To Boise
To Burns

IDAHO

HELLS CANYON NATIONAL RECREATION AREA

WALLOWA LAKE TRAMWAY

NATIONAL HISTORIC OREGON TRAIL INTERPRETIVE CENTER

HOT LAKE MINERAL HOT SPRINGS

PENDLETON UNDERGROUND TOURS

COLD SPRINGS NATIONAL WILDLIFE REFUGE

KAM WAH CHUNG STATE HERITAGE SITE

JOHN DAY FOSSIL BEDS NATIONAL MONUMENT

Imnaha
Imnaha River
Enterprise
Joseph
Mt Howard 8,200ft
Chief Joseph Mountain 9,617ft
Eagle Cap 9,685ft
Matterhorn 10,004ft
Halfway
Snake River
Farewell Bend State Park
Ontario
Vale
To Burns

Wallowa
Wallowa River
Wallowa Mountains
Thief Valley Reservoir
Baker City
Haines
North Powder
Phillips Reservoir
Sumpter
Granite
ELKHORN DRIVE NATIONAL SCENIC BYWAY
Dixie Pass 5,280ft
Prairie City
Blue Mountain Hot Springs
Strawberry Mountain 9,038ft

Cove
Union
Elgin
La Grande
Emigrant Springs State Park
Lehman Hot Springs

Milton-Freewater
Walla Walla
Hermiston
Pendleton
McKay Creek Reservoir

Arlington
Condon
Cottonwood Canyon State Park
Biggs

Fossil
Spray
Mitchell
Antelope
Stein's Pillar
Ochoco Summit 4,720ft
Ochoco Lake State Park
Prineville
Prineville Reservoir State Park
Crooked River
Paulina

John Day Fossil Beds National Monument Painted Hills Unit
John Day Fossil Beds National Monument Clarno Unit
John Day Fossil Beds National Monument Sheep Rock Unit

Painted Hills
John Day River
Columbia River
Dayville
John Day
Canyon City
STRAWBERRY MOUNTAIN WILDERNESS

To Madras
To Bend
To Burns

20 mi
20 km

© AVALON TRAVEL

or two to explore the area's rich history and astoundingly dramatic scenery. Don't forget: The world's deepest river gorge is here, as are some of its richest fossil beds.

In order to really explore this wild country, get off the interstate. From Ontario, consider crossing the state on either U.S. 20 or U.S. 26. Although these routes parallel each other, they offer quite different aspects. U.S. 20 edges along the northern boundary of the Great Basin desert while U.S. 26 travels through pine-clad mountains to the John Day River Valley, one of Oregon's most scenic. The river trenches through a layer cake of dramatic geologic formations to expose the **John Day Fossil Beds National Monument.** Even if you stay closer to the interstate, consider branching off and making a loop around the **Wallowa Mountains,** a soaring piece of real estate that contains 17 individual peaks over 9,000 feet high. This side road also takes you to the brink of **Hells Canyon,** where the Snake River carves a gorge beneath 6,500-foot cliffs.

If you stick to I-84 and the fast track, at least realize that this route parallels the original Oregon Trail, the wagon route that brought in upward of 50,000 pioneers to the Pacific Northwest between 1843 and 1860. Stop at the **National Historic Oregon Trail Interpretive Center** near Baker City to learn more about this great human migration. (Baker City is also a good place to spend a night, with a lovely old downtown hotel, two brewpubs, and plenty of restaurants.) Then pull off the interstate at Pendleton to experience the city's colorful past on **Pendleton Underground Tours,** which explores a subterranean business district and a brothel from the turn of the 20th century.

John Day Fossil Beds and Vicinity

The canyon-cutting John Day River drains the western slopes of the Blue Mountains, trenching through north-central Oregon before spilling into the Columbia River. The John Day River Valley also offers some of Oregon's most tantalizing human history plus fascinating glimpses into the region's prehistory. In the 1860s, self-taught geologist Thomas Condon discovered what is now known as the John Day Fossil Beds. These archives of stone provide a paleontological record of 40-plus million years of ancient life.

◖ JOHN DAY FOSSIL BEDS NATIONAL MONUMENT

The 14,000-acre John Day Fossil Beds National Monument is divided into three areas: the Sheep Rock Unit, about 40 miles west of John Day, with the monument's excellent interpretive center; the Painted Hills Unit, another 45 miles farther west; and the Clarno Unit, northwest of the other units, about 20 miles from the town of Fossil. For further information, contact **John Day Fossil Beds National Monument** (32651 Hwy. 19, Kimberly, OR 97848-9701, 541/987-2333, www.nps.gov/joda). Admission is free to all units of the monument.

The days of 50-ton apatosaurs and 50-foot-long crocodiles, as well as delicate ferns and flowers, are captured in the rock formations of the three beds, easily visited in a day's road trip. This is the richest concentration of prehistoric early mammal and plant fossils in the world. More than 120 species have been identified, documenting a period dating from the extinction of the dinosaurs to the beginning of the last great ice age.

Accommodations are in short supply in this remote part of Oregon. The small towns near the monument's individual units have motels, and the town of John Day has the largest selection. A few campgrounds lie along the main fossil route; more are way off the beaten path.

Painted Hills

The highly photogenic **Painted Hills** are a series of low-slung hills created around 30 million

among wildflower buffs that the springtime display here is exceptional.

To reach the Painted Hills, drive three miles west of Mitchell on U.S. 26, turn left at the sign, and travel six miles along Bridge Creek to the site. Stop first at the visitor center to get oriented and fill your water bottle. Although the view from the road is impressive, you really have to get out and hike the trails literally to get the picture; if possible, visit around dusk, or after a rain shower, when the colors really pop.

ACCOMMODATIONS AND FOOD

Mitchell is the closest town to the Painted Hills, offering lodging in the basic **Sky Hook Motel** (101 U.S. 26, Mitchell, 541/462-3569, $50), which has good views from its perch above town, and the historic **Oregon Hotel** (104 E. Main St., Mitchell, 541/462-3027, http://theoregonhotel.net, rooms with private baths $59-69), which offers pleasantly vintage guest rooms right downtown. The less expensive guest rooms at the hotel ($49-59) share a bath; kitchenettes are available for $105, and you can even get a hostel bunk for $20. Several hotels have existed on this site since the 1800s, with the current incarnation dating back to 1938. The historic photos in the lobby recount three catastrophic floods that have hit this town.

Campers can pitch a tent ($5) or plug in an RV ($17) at the **Mitchell City Park** (541/462-3121), a grassy spot on the edge of the two-block-long downtown.

Mitchell has a store and a couple of cafés. The **Little Pine Cafe** (100 E. Main St., 541/462-3532, 7:30am-7:30pm Tues.-Sat., $8-16) is the best bet for dinner.

Clarno Unit

Right on the John Day River, the Clarno Formations are the monument's oldest and remotest. The 40-million-year-old **Clarno Unit** exposes mudflows that washed over an Eocene-era forest. The Clarno Unit's petrified mudslide is one of the few places in the world where the stems of ancient plants along with

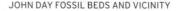

The Painted Cove Trail winds through hillocks.

© BILL MCRAE

years ago by red, yellow, green, ocher, gray, and black-hued ash deposited into drifts hundreds of feet deep. Erosion has cut through the multicolored layers and sculpted the hills into soft mounds. While many casual visitors are satisfied snapping photos from the monument's designated overlook, easy hiking trails lead to more interesting vistas.

The half-mile **Painted Hills Overlook Trail** provides a view of mineral-bearing clays exposed by erosion. Nearby, the 1.5-mile **Carroll Rim Trail** has a spectacular all-encompassing view of the Painted Hills.

The most vivid colors of all are found at the **Painted Cove Trail,** a 0.25-mile loop where viewing the red mounds up close is a highlight. Close by, the 0.5-mile **Leaf Hill Trail** (another loop) will lead you to remnants of a 30-million-year-old hardwood forest. Walking on the hill itself is prohibited, but take a look at the exhibit describing how our knowledge of Oregon's most ancient forests emanated from studies of this area. It's common knowledge

OREGON PALEO LANDS INSTITUTE

Although geologists and other scientists have long traveled to eastern Oregon for their research, Pacific Northwesterners and visitors to the state are often only vaguely aware of the area's rich paleontology and geology. The Oregon Paleo Lands Institute was established to bring these resources to a wider range of people and also to help boost the struggling rural economy.

In downtown Fossil, the **Oregon Paleo Lands Institute** (401 4th St., Fossil, 541/763-4480, www.paleolands.org), with exhibits on local geology and paleontology, is a good resource for those who want to explore Oregon's John Day country. The institute also sponsors occasional trips guided by local geologists, photographers, and other experts.

This is a good place to come for information about floating the John Day River, biking through the John Day Basin, or hiking in the John Day Fossil Beds National Monument. Find a good selection of books and maps (some with an intensely local focus and unavailable elsewhere), and friendly, informative staffers.

---

their leaves, seeds, and nuts are preserved in the same location. Fossilized imprints of palm, gingko, and magnolia leaves culled from volcanic mudflows point to a subtropical forest capable of supporting flowering trees. The formations eroded into distinctive chalky-white cliffs topped with spires and turrets of stone. The 0.25-mile **Clarno Arch Trail** leads you into the formations where boulder-size fossils containing logs, seeds, and other remains of an ancient forest await. It links up with two other quarter-mile trails: **Trail of the Fossils,** where boulders are strewn with plant fossils, and the **Geologic Time Trail,** which lacks fossils but leads to a picnic area. Picnic facilities, drinking water, and restrooms are available at the monument.

The Clarno Formations are 18 miles west of the small and aptly named town of **Fossil** on Route 218. When you are traveling in the John Day country, Fossil makes an intriguing and perhaps necessary stop—in this remote area, chances are you'll need to gas up or get a bite to eat, and this Old West town has a full range of services for travelers. Fossil also offers fossils: When the townspeople began digging into a hillside to build a football field, they exposed an ancient lakebed rich with fossil leaf prints and petrified wood. The site (just behind the high school) is open to amateur fossil hunters for a $5 fee.

ACCOMMODATIONS AND FOOD

The closest facilities to the Clarno Unit are in Fossil. The **Wilson Ranch Retreat** (16555 Butte Creek Ln., 541/763-2227, www.wilson-ranchretreat.com, $109-139) is a good place to escape city life. Guests are invited to ride horses ($40 for a one-hour ride), hike, and tour the ranch, and even ride along on a cattle drive.

In town, **Fossil Motel and RV Park** (105 W. 1st St., 541/763-4075, $69-100) is an older motor court that's in the process of being updated by friendly new owners; the adjacent RV park ($25) is a good place to camp. Tent campers should head five miles south of town to the forested **Bear Hollow County Park** (45260 Hwy. 19, 541/763-2010, $10, drinking water, vault toilets).

The **Big Timber Family Restaurant** (540 1st St., 541/763-4328, 6am-8pm Mon.-Thurs., 6am-9pm Fri.-Sat., $7-12) offers basic American fare.

Twenty miles south of Fossil, the **Service Creek Lodge** (38686 Hwy. 19, 541/468-3331, www.servicecreek.com, lodge rooms $85-125) is a handy all-purpose business, especially for folks who would like to paddle the easygoing, free-flowing (undammed) John Day River. It has food, lodging in nicely decorated rooms, raft rentals, and a shuttle service. The lodge also rents a three-bedroom vacation home in the neighboring community of Spray ($225).

© JUDY JEWELL

Classic cars line the streets of Fossil over Fourth of July weekend.

Twenty miles north of Fossil is the town of **Condon,** where the landmark 1920s hotel has been completely refurbished, updated, and reopened as ◖ **Hotel Condon** (202 S. Main St., Condon, 541/384-4624 or 800/201-6706, www.hotelcondon.com, $125-229). With comfortable classy guest rooms, Hotel Condon is the swankiest lodging choice in this part of Oregon. While in Condon, don't neglect to visit **Country Flowers** (201 S. Main St., 541/384-4120, 9am-6pm Mon.-Fri., 9:30am-5:30pm Sat., noon-5pm Sun.), an eclectic gift store with an outpost of Portland's Powell's Books and a classic old soda fountain. This is a good place for lunch.

North of Condon, where Highway 206 crosses the John Day River, find **Cottonwood Canyon State Park** (www.oregonstateparks. org), one of the state's newest and largest parks. Many John Day rafters use this as a takeout spot, and the canyons and bottomlands are beautiful places to explore. During the summer, this area is quite warm, but it's a great spot to camp in spring and fall.

Sheep Rock Unit

The Sheep Rock Unit is the largest of the monument's three divisions, and offers the most visitor facilities. The **Thomas Condon Paleontology Center** (8 miles northwest of Dayville, 541/987-2333, www.nps.gov/joda, 10am-5pm Tues.-Sat., and most Sundays Memorial Day-Labor Day, check website or call for winter hours, free) serves as the monument's visitors center. It features a fossil museum with exceptional discoveries from local digs, a maze-like series of dioramas, and displays telling the geological and biological history of the fossil beds—plus short films that help explain the area's prehistory and current research. Although the monument's website has lots of information, it's worth stopping at the visitor center to pick up good printed information that's not available online, such as a mile-by-mile geology road log detailing the striking stretch of road from the visitor center to the Painted Hills. **The Cant Ranch House,** formerly the park visitors center, is a handsome 1917 ranch house across the highway from the new paleontology center

© PAUL LEVY

Clarno Unit of the John Day Fossil Beds

that now houses a museum on the human history of the ranch and its vicinity. A former bunkhouse and a small log cabin behind the ranch house contain additional exhibits on fossil history. The tree-shaded grounds surrounding the ranch house are perfect for picnicking, and short trails lead to the fast-flowing John Day River.

North of the visitor center on Route 19 are two fossil viewing areas. Two miles north is the parking area for **Blue Basin,** with several hiking trails leading into fossil-rich formations. The one-mile-long **Island in Time Trail** climbs into a badlands basin of highly eroded, uncannily green sediments. Along the trail are displays that reveal fossils protruding from the soil. The trail dead-ends at a natural box canyon; high around are barren castellated walls rich in 25-million-year-old life-forms. The **Overlook Trail** offers a longer three-mile loop to the rim of Blue Basin with views over the fossil beds and the layer-cake topography of the John Day Valley.

Two miles farther north at the day-use **Foree**

Picnic Area are more hiking trails that explore green mudstone formations capped with basalt from ancient lava flows.

The drive between the junction of Route 19 and U.S. 26 and the small community of Spray is highly scenic; interesting geology and spectacular scenery don't always occur together, but they form an amazing team here. Along this route you'll see **Sheep Rock,** a steep-sided mesa rising hundreds of feet to a small rock cap, and **Cathedral Rock,** where erosion has stripped away a hillside to reveal highly colored sediments beneath a thick overlay of basalt. Most astonishing of all is **Picture Gorge,** where the John Day River rips through an immense 1,500-foot-high lava flow and begins trenching its canyon to the Columbia River. The gorge, wide enough for only the river and the road, is named for the pictographs drawn there by early Native Americans; look for them near mile marker 125 on the west side of the road.

The Sheep Rock Unit of the John Day Fossil Beds is 8 miles northwest of Dayville, and 40 miles from John Day.

FLOATING THE JOHN DAY RIVER

Oregon's longest free-running river, the John Day, spends most of its time far from roads, which makes it ideal to see from a boat. From May to early July, it's relatively easy to navigate the river in a canoe, raft, or inflatable kayak. The only rapid of note, a Level III-IV at Clarno, can be tough to run when the water level is low, and since there are no dams on the John Day, flow levels fluctuate widely in response to snowpack and rainfall. When water level is high, canoeists should have white-water experience.

Most people float the John Day as a multiday trip. Service Creek is a common put-in for river trips; it's 48 miles (usually three days) to the bridge at Clarno. From Clarno to Cottonwood Canyon State Park, it's 70 miles, which usually takes five days to float. One-day floats are also possible from the town of Spray to mile marker 86 on Highway 19 or from mile 86 to Service Creek. Much of the time during any trip, the river is bounded by private land; it's important to carry a good map (available from the BLM by

calling 541/416-6700) in order to know where to camp.

The **Service Creek Stage Stop** (38686 Hwy. 19, south of Fossil, 541/468-3331, www.servicecreek.com) rents rafts ($125 for a day rental with delivery and pickup), and shuttles are provided by the following people:

· **Donna's Shuttles** (541/763-4884)

· **Service Creek Stage Stop** (541/468-3331)

· **Bobbie Jo's Shuttles** (541/460-0858)

· **Ron and June Rollins** (541/763-0909 or 541/410-0933)

The Bureau of Land Management oversees boating on the John Day; their website (www.blm.gov) is a good source of up-to-date information, with links to water-flow forecasts. The BLM website is also the place to go to apply for the permit that is required to boat on the John Day.

ACCOMMODATIONS AND FOOD

The closest lodgings to the Sheep Rock Unit are in the tiny community of Dayville, where the **Fish House Inn** (110 Franklin St., Dayville, 541/987-2124 or 888/286-3474, www.fishhouseinn.com, $50-70) offers accommodation in a vintage Craftsman home. These pleasant digs are decorated with antique farm tools and fishing gear, hence the inn's name. RV sites ($25) are also available. Because there is no big restaurant scene in Dayville (one place, open occasionally), the inn offers microwaves and barbecue facilities to its guests, with dinner-makings available from a historical grocery, the century-old Dayville Mercantile on U.S. 26. More dining options are available in John Day, 30 miles east.

JOHN DAY AND VICINITY

The early history of John Day and nearby Canyon City centers around the discovery of gold in 1862. According to most estimates, $26

million in gold was taken out of the streams and mines in the Strawberry Mountains. At the peak of the gold rush, Whiskey Flat, later called Canyon City, was populated by 5,000 miners, which made it larger than Portland at the time. Thousands of Chinese immigrated to the area to work the tailings, or leftovers, from the mines. Their fascinating history is vividly retold at the Kam Wah Chung and Company Museum in John Day.

One of the more colorful denizens of Canyon City was the celebrated poet Joaquin Miller, who served as the first elected judge in Grant County. Known as the "Byron of Oregon," this dashing figure dressed like Buffalo Bill and recited his florid sonnets to a baffled audience of miners.

Today John Day is principally a market town for local farmers and ranchers, with adequate facilities for travelers passing through to visit nearby fossil beds or hike in the lovely Strawberry Mountains.

NORTHEASTERN OREGON

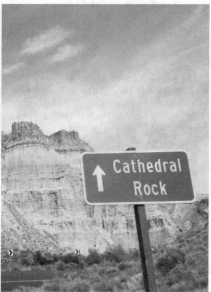

© PAM ORE

Cathedral Rock is a landmark in the John Day Fossil Beds National Monument.

(Kam Wah Chung State Heritage Site

A must-stop in the town of John Day, the **Kam Wah Chung State Heritage Site** (250 NW Canton St., 541/575-2800, www.oregonstate-parks.org, visitors center 9am-5pm daily May-Oct., tours on the hour except noon, free) was the center of Chinese life in the John Day area, serving as a general store and pharmacy with over 500 herbs. People came from hundreds of miles away for the herbal remedies of Doc Hay, who lived here. It also served in more limited capacities as an assay office, fortune-teller's studio, and Taoist shrine.

The building began as a trading post on The Dalles Military Road in 1866. With the influx of Chinese to the area during the gold rush, the outpost was purchased in 1887 by two Chinese apothecaries and evolved into a center for Asian medicine, trade, and spirituality. It remained a gathering place for the Chinese community in eastern Oregon until the early 1940s. While it admirably fulfilled this role, the opium-blackened walls, bootleg whiskey, and gambling paraphernalia are evidence of the less salutary aspects of the Kam Wah Chung lifestyle. At the time of the 1879 census, eastern Oregon had 960 East Coast emigrants and 2,468 Chinese, proof that the current museum is not an arcane exhibit but rather a significant window on the past. In fact, in 1983 scholars from China came to categorize the herbs and religious objects.

It's the little touches in the faithfully restored building that stay with you. First your eye will be drawn to the metal shutters and outside wooden staircase on this rough stone edifice. Inside there's a locked and barred herb cage where Ing Hay prepared medicine and where gold dust was weighed. A Taoist shrine graces the room where groceries and opium were dispensed. In addition to the herbal remedies arrayed in cigar boxes labeled with Chinese calligraphy, there are vintage photos, old tools, furnishings, and other artifacts. Even the labels on the old canned goods are fascinating. Finally, the meat cleaver by Doc Hay's bed bespeaks the fear and despair of Chinese life here near the turn of the 20th century.

Tours begin at the interpretive center, two blocks south on NW Canton Street.

Grant County Historical Museum

Another repository of local history, the **Grant County Historical Museum** (101 S. Canyon City Blvd., Canyon City, 541/575-0509, www.gchistoricalmuseum.com, 9am-4:30pm Mon.-Sat. May-Sept., $4 adults, $3.50 seniors, $2 children ages 7-17, children 6 and under free) is in Canyon City, a couple of miles south of John Day on U.S. 395. Centered in the heart of Oregon's mining and ranching country, the facility's wealth of memorabilia depicts the early days of Grant County and includes an extensive rock collection plus Chinese and Native American items. The main focus of the museum is the 1860s gold rush, with displays of vintage mining equipment and household items. Miners' cabins and a jail building stand in the courtyard.

The shelves at the Kam Wah Chung State Heritage Site's museum are stocked with Chinese herbs.

Grant County Ranch and Rodeo Museum

This is cowboy country, and all things cowboy are celebrated at the **Grant County Ranch and Rodeo Museum** (241 E. Main St., John Day, 541/575-5545, 10am-4pm Thurs.-Sat. May-Sept., $3, children under age 12 free).

'62 Days Celebration

If you're in Canyon City in early June, plan to attend the **'62 Days Celebration,** which commemorates the local discovery of gold in 1862 with a parade, country music dance, medicine-wagon show, street fair, period costumes, and a reenactment of the opening of historic Sel's Brewery. Contact the **Grant County Chamber** (541/575-0547, www.gcoregonlive.com) for more information.

Accommodations

The **Best Western John Day Inn** (315 W. Main St., John Day, 541/575-1700 or 800/243-2628, $125-135) is a very nice conventional motel, with a fitness center, an indoor pool, and free high-speed Internet access. A family restaurant is adjacent. The **Dreamers Lodge** (144 N. Canyon St., John Day, 541/575-0526 or 800/654-2849, www.dreamerslodge.com, $50-100), a classic, well-maintained motor court motel, is close to the town center but on a quiet side street.

The most amenity-laden campground in the area is **Clyde Holliday State Recreation Site** (7 miles west of John Day, 33 miles east of the Sheep Rock Unit, 541/932-4453, www.oregonstateparks.org, $22 tent or RV, $5 hiker/biker, $39 tepee). In addition to showers and shady sites with electrical and water hookups near the John Day River, the park offers a couple of large tepees. Although campsites are all first-come, first-served, tepees are best reserved in advance (541/932-4453, www.reserveamerica.com). As with most Oregon State Park campgrounds, there are showers, as well as interpretive events on the nearby fossil beds. The park is on U.S. 26 between the towns of John Day and Mount Vernon.

Food

The popular **Outpost Pizza, Pub and Grill** (201 W. Main St., John Day, 541/575-0250, 6am-9pm Mon.-Sat., 6am-8pm Sun., $9-20) offers a broad menu of American-style favorites, with steaks starting at $13. Stop in for a fried pickle; dip it in ranch dressing to fit in with the locals. The **Grubsteak Mining Co.** (149 E. Main St., John Day, 541/575-1970, 9am-9pm Mon.-Sat., 9am-8pm Sun., $10-18) is John Day's long-established steak house.

West of John Day, in the town of Mount Vernon, the **Silver Spur** (140 Ingle St., Mount Vernon, 541/932-4545, 7am-8pm Mon.-Sat., 7am-5pm Sun., $7-12) is a good stop for breakfast or burgers.

Information

For information on John Day and vicinity, contact the **Grant County Chamber of Commerce** (301 W. Main St., John Day, 541/757-0547 or 800/769-5664, www.gcoregonlive.

© PAM ORE

com). The **Malheur National Forest** (www.fs.usda.gov/malheur) and the **Bureau of Land Management** share an office (431 Paterson Bridge Rd., John Day, 541/575-3000).

STRAWBERRY MOUNTAINS AND VICINITY

Thirteen miles east of John Day the landscape becomes more mountainous and forests begin to encroach on the ranchland. **Prairie City** is an attractive small town in this lovely locale. The **DeWitt Museum** (Main St. and Bridge St., Prairie City, 541/820-3330, www.prairiecityoregon.com, 10am-5pm Wed.-Sat. May 15-Oct. 15, donations accepted) is housed in the Sumpter Valley Railroad's old depot, which operated between Baker City and Prairie City 1909-1947. The building was restored in 1979 and today has 10 rooms full of artifacts from Grant County's early days.

Just south of Prairie City are the Strawberry

Mountains, a pocket mountain range that offers a good system of trails, seven lakes, volcanic rock formations, and if you're lucky, glimpses of bighorn sheep. Set up your base camp at **Strawberry Campground,** 11 miles south of Prairie City on County Route 60, which becomes Forest Service Road 6001. The campground is next to Strawberry Creek and the trailhead for jaunts to Strawberry Lake, Strawberry Falls, and Strawberry Mountain. Although there are some wild strawberry plants along the trails, late-summer hikers will be more apt to notice the abundant huckleberries.

For information on hiking the Strawberry Mountains' 120 miles of trails, contact the Prairie City Ranger District at the **Malheur National Forest office** (327 SW Front St., 541/820-3800, www.fs.usda.gov/malheur). Ask about the 11-mile loop circumnavigating 9,000-foot Strawberry Mountain.

Prairie City enthusiastically welcomes bicyclists. The 1976 Bikecentennial route went through town, and it's still a popular stop with long-distance cyclists. In addition, a number of road and mountain bike routes have been established: find details at www.prairiecityoregon.com.

Accommodations and Food

Prairie City has a very pleasant and unique place to stay. The **(Hotel Prairie** (112 Front St., Prairie City, 541/820-4800, http://hotelprairie.com, $79-139) is a historic 1905 hotel renovated and reopened in 2008 as a cozy nine-room hotel. Even if you're not staying the night, drop by the lobby to examine the historical photos. The rooms aren't huge—they are authentic in that regard—but the beds and amenities are very comfortable; it's a chance to experience another generation's lifestyle. The top choice is a one-room suite; six regular bedrooms have private baths, while the two remaining rooms share a bath. These rooms are good for family groups.

Strawberry Campground (541/820-3800, www.fs.usda.gov/malheur, June-mid-Oct., $8, no reservations) is a great bet for tent campers, but the final stretch of road to this sweet spot,

WHO WAS JOHN DAY?

John Day is such a common name in this part of Oregon (it is affixed to a two rivers, three towns, a dam, a series of fossil beds, a valley, and several parks) that you might assume the original John Day was an early pioneer settler. In fact, the eponymous John Day never visited any of the places that now carry his name. A hunter from Virginia, Day was hired to provide meat for the Pacific Fur Company expedition led by Wilson Price Hunt in 1812. Thirty miles east of The Dalles, near what was then known as the Mau Hau River, Day and another mountain man were ambushed by Native Americans, who robbed them and left them naked and injured. The two survived the ordeal and eventually made their way to Fort Astoria. The Mau Hau River soon became known as Day's River; mapmakers later changed it to the John Day River, and the name spread like wildfire. Even at Astoria, John Day's place-naming achievement continued: A second John Day River flows into the Columbia just east of Astoria.

at 5,700 feet in elevation, is too steep for trailers and RVs; tiny **Slide Creek** campground (9 miles south of Prairie City on Forest Rd. 6001, no water, free), another Forest Service campground a couple of miles closer to town, is a better bet for folks with these larger rigs. **Depot Park** (Main St. and Bridge St., Prairie City, 541/820-3605, $16 RVs, $12 tents, $6 bikes, $1.75 showers) has an in-town campground surrounding the DeWitt Museum and offers both RV and tent camping; it's also a good place to stop for a shower after a few nights in the Strawberry Mountains. This campground is a great home base for cyclists exploring the many loop roads in the nearby mountains.

Chuck's Little Diner (142 W. Front St., Prairie City, 541/820-4353, 6am-2pm Wed.-Sun., $4-10) is a good place for a big breakfast on the outside patio or an afternoon slice of pie. The **Oxbow Restaurant and Saloon** (128 W. Front St., Prairie City, 541/820-4544, meals noon-9pm Tues.-Sun., $12-21) offers burgers, steaks, and other comfort foods with a good helping of Western atmosphere, including a lovely antique bar.

© JUDY JEWELL

Lakes dot the Strawberry Mountain Wilderness Area.

Pendleton

For a lot of people in the West, Pendleton is synonymous with rodeo and woolens, both pointing to the city's intriguing history as a frontier trade settlement. Pendleton still has Western spirit to spare, but proximity to the highly successful wineries in Washington's Walla Walla Valley is bringing change to this bastion of cowboy country. With ranchers planting their cattle pastures to cabernet, can boutique hotels be far behind? Pendleton is in the midst of a fascinating evolution, an authentic Western community lurching toward reinvention as a 21st-century lifestyle destination.

With a population of 16,800, Pendleton is the largest city in eastern Oregon. It's an economic force thanks to vast wheat fields (Umatilla County is one of the top wheat-producing counties in the United States),

rows of green peas, its famous woolen mills, and tourism from the Pendleton Round-Up, the September rodeo and weeklong party that brings in cowboys, cowgirls, and the crowds that love them. The Umatilla Reservation is just outside town, and the Pendleton area has a large Native American population; an Indian encampment is a traditional part of the Round-Up.

The climate is mild and dry, with an average temperature of 51°F and annual rainfall of 13 inches (locals joke that this is where summer spends the winter). Fall is usually long and sunny, an excellent climate for raising wine grapes. It's a little-noted fact that over a third of the Walla Walla Valley American Viticultural Area (AVA) is in Oregon, just north of Pendleton.

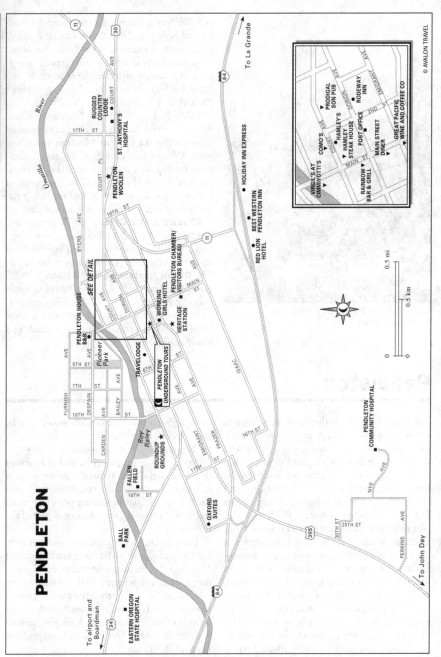

PENDLETON

© AVALON TRAVEL

To La Grande

To airport and Boardman

To John Day

Detail:
- VIRGIL'S AT CIMMIYOTTI'S
- COMO'S
- PRODIGAL SON PUB
- HAMLEY'S
- HAMLEY STEAK HOUSE
- RODEWAY INN
- RAINBOW BAR & GRILL
- POST OFFICE
- MAIN STREET DINER
- GREAT PACIFIC WINE AND COFFEE CO

Labels:
- RUGGED COUNTRY LODGE
- ST. ANTHONY'S HOSPITAL
- PENDLETON WOOLEN
- HOLIDAY INN EXPRESS
- BEST WESTERN PENDLETON INN
- RED LION HOTEL
- PENDLETON CHAMBER/ VISITORS BUREAU
- PENDLETON HOUSE B&B
- WORKING GIRLS HOTEL
- HERITAGE STATION
- TRAVELODGE
- PENDLETON UNDERGROUND TOURS
- Pioneer Park
- Roy Raley
- FALLEN HELD
- ROUNDUP GROUNDS
- BALL PARK
- OXFORD SUITES
- PENDLETON COMMUNITY HOSPITAL
- EASTERN OREGON STATE HOSPITAL

Streets: 17TH ST, 10TH ST, 5TH ST, 7TH ST, 10TH ST, 6TH, 16TH ST, 17TH ST, 18TH ST, 25TH ST, 30TH ST, COURT PL, COURT AVE, BYERS AVE, MAIN ST, CORBIN, ISAAC, EMIGRANT, FRAZER, NYE AVE, PERKINS AVE, FURNISH AVE, DESPAIN, BAILEY ST, CARDEN

Umatilla River

0   0.5 mi
0   0.5 km

© JUDY JEWELL

It's easy to get outfitted in Western wear in Pendleton.

On I-84 equidistant from Portland, Seattle, Spokane, and Boise (a little over 200 miles from each), Pendleton sits pretty much by itself in the midst of wide-open spaces beneath the lumpy heights of the Blue Mountains. Residents—and an increasing flow of visitors—seem to like it that way.

History

Pendleton, originally called Goodwin's Station, is situated two miles downriver from the Oregon Trail's crossing at Emigrant Springs State Park. The ancient homeland of the Umatilla people, the area was visited by Lewis and Clark in 1805 and John Jacob Astor's American Fur Company in 1812. No Europeans established roots until 1843, when Methodist missionaries led by Dr. Marcus Whitman brought 1,000 settlers and 1,300 cattle to the region.

The town itself, named after Senator George Hunt Pendleton, was founded in 1868 and incorporated in 1880. At that time, Pendleton consisted of a hotel and five houses. But it grew through the late 1880s into a rip-snorting cattle and farming center with 18 houses of negotiable affection and 32 saloons. It quickly gained the reputation of being the town that couldn't be tamed. The feistiness of the citizens was demonstrated by the theft of the county seal and records from Umatilla Landing, thus making Pendleton the county seat.

SIGHTS
Pendleton Woolen Mills

Next to the Pendleton Round-Up, the town is best known for the **Pendleton Woolen Mills** (1307 SE Court Place, 541/276-6911, www. pendleton-usa.com), where they make those colorful wool blankets. After shearing, the wool goes to a scouring mill near Portland where it's graded, sorted, and washed. Then the dried wool returns to the Pendleton mill for dyeing, carding, spinning, rewinding, and weaving.

The business began over in the Willamette Valley in Brownsville when Thomas Kay, a Yorkshire man whose family was in the wool business in England, started a weaving mill. His descendant, Clarence Bishop, founded the Pendleton facility. Production began here in 1909 with Native American-style blankets, which are still going strong, along with men's and women's sportswear. Pendleton carved its lucrative niche by copying traditional designs for blankets used by Native Americans in Arizona and New Mexico. It introduced Western-style woolen shirts in the 1920s.

Twenty-minute-long tours run at 9am, 11am, 1:30pm, and 3pm Monday-Friday. Large groups are asked to make an appointment. To get to the mills, take I-84 Exit 207 and follow Dorion Street through Pendleton. Do not cross the viaduct, but turn left and proceed four blocks. Even if you can't go on a tour, stop by the company store, where you can pick up blankets and clothing, often at a good discount.

Heritage Station: The Umatilla County Historical Society Museum

In 1881 the Oregon-Washington Railway

and Navigation Company, a subsidiary of the Union Pacific Railroad, constructed the northern branch of its transcontinental railroad through northeastern Oregon, and Pendleton served as an important stop on the route. By 1910, Pendleton had become the second-largest city in eastern Oregon, meriting a new railroad depot.

The **Heritage Station depot** (108 SW Frazer Ave., 541/276-0012, www.heritagestationmuseum.org, 10am-4pm Tues.-Sat., $5 adults, $4 seniors, $2 students, $10 families), an adaptation of the California mission style, boasts multipaneled windows, decorative brickwork, and wide flaring eaves. The depot no longer serves railroad passengers but instead houses the Umatilla County Historical Society's collection of Oregon Trail pioneer and Native American artifacts. Gold miners, sheep ranchers, and moonshiners are also given attention in well-designed displays.

◖ Pendleton Underground Tours

One of the area's liveliest attractions is **Pendleton Underground Tours** (31 SW Emigrant Ave., 541/276-0730, www.pendletonundergroundtours.org, schedule varies, $15, reservations required). This visit to the wild and woolly days of the Old West takes you through the tunnels underneath the downtown historic district. At one time a series of 90 passageways, originally dug as freight tunnels by Chinese workers who weren't allowed to walk above ground, crisscrossed beneath the downtown area. During the Prohibition era, bootleggers, gamblers, opium dealers, and Chinese railroad laborers frequented the businesses that developed here.

The 90-minute tour starts at SW 1st Street and Emigrant Avenue and continues to the old Shamrock Cardroom, filled with the bouncy sounds of honky-tonk music, where bartenders were once paid with gold dust. From there, it's on to Hop Sing's laundry and bathhouse (a Prohibition speakeasy with secret escapes and a dank opium den), and the Empire Meat Company, complete with mannequins. The tour finishes in the well-preserved Cozy Rooms

Bordello. After this tour you'll understand how the old town of 3,000 once supported 32 saloons and 18 bordellos.

To get here from I-84, take Exit 209 and turn north into Pendleton. Continue up Emigrant Avenue to SW 1st Street.

Tamastslikt Cultural Institute

The Confederated Tribes of the Umatilla Indian Reservation—which include the Walla Walla, Umatilla, and Cayuse nations—had little reason to celebrate the 150th anniversary of the Oregon Trail, which was marked by celebrations in other parts of the West. For these eastern Oregon nations, the Oregon Trail led to war and to a huge loss of land and people. Native Americans felt that it was important for their view of the Oregon Trail story to be told, and they built the **Tamastslikt Cultural Institute** (72789 Hwy. 331, 541/966-9748, www.tamastslikt.org, 9am-5pm daily Apr.-Sept., 9am-5pm Mon.-Sat. Oct.-Mar., $8 adults, $6 seniors and students, $17 families). Comprising 45,000 square feet, this cultural center describes the effects that European-American settlement have had on the region's original inhabitants. Exhibits depict Native American life prior to the pioneers' arrival; the impact of the horse (brought to North America by Europeans) on native people; and an Oregon Trail retrospective from the point of view of the Cayuse, Umatilla, and Walla Walla nations.

The Oregon Trail, which passed through the current reservation site, created long-term environmental problems such as diminished salmon runs and deforestation in the Blue Mountains. European settlement also brought chicken pox, tobacco, alcohol, syphilis, tuberculosis, and measles to Native American communities.

The interpretive center adds a living encampment, interpretive trails, and an outdoor amphitheater. Sharing this 640-acre site at the base of the Blue Mountains is a casino, a golf course, an RV park, a hotel, and a restaurant.

The institute is 6 miles east of Pendleton on I-84 and 1 mile north of Exit 216. Museum admission is free on the first Friday of every month.

THE SAGE CENTER

If you're driving I-84 across eastern Oregon, you may need more than a perfunctory rest stop. Pull off at Boardman (Exit 164) to learn about the region's sustainable agriculture and energy at the **SAGE Center** (101 Olson Rd., Boardman, 541/481-7243, www.visitsage.com, 9am-6pm daily Memorial Day-Labor Day, 10am-6pm daily Labor Day-Memorial Day, $5 adults, $3 students and seniors). The interactive exhibits here educate visitors about eastern Oregon's agricultural economy—expect to learn how irrigation works; the ins and outs of sources of power such as biofuels, hydropower, and wind energy; how food products such as corn and grains are processed and shipped around the world; and how these modern farming methods differ from those historically used.

Although the center, developed by the Port of Morrow, is popular with school groups, it's also a good introduction to the area for adults. Even if you don't tour the interior, the exterior architecture, featuring irrigation apparatus and grain silos, is worth a look.

© JUDY JEWELL

SAGE Center

PENDLETON ROUND-UP

In 1910, Pendleton farmers and ranchers got together to celebrate the end of the wheat harvest. This was the first year of the **Pendleton Round-Up** (1205 SW Court Ave., 541/276-2553 or 800/457-6336, www.pendletonroundup.com). The annual event now draws 50,000 rodeo fans in the grand tradition started by legendary rodeo stars like Jackson Sundown and Yakima Canutt.

Held in mid-September, this high-spirited weeklong celebration includes a lot more than just a rodeo. On Friday, the **Westward Ho Historical Parade** brings together covered wagons, mule teams, buggies, and hundreds of Native Americans in full regalia. Wednesday-Saturday evenings at the Round-Up grounds (at Raley Park, west of downtown), the **Happy Canyon Pageant** depicts the opening of the West in a series of vignettes, complete with strutting cowboys

and traditional Umatilla dancing. The pageant is an object of much love and some contention; its old-fashioned script is rife with stereotypes. During Round-Up week, Pendleton's Main Street is converted into a street fair, with food booths, arts and crafts stalls, live music, carnival rides, and other entertainment. The **tepee encampment** on the Round-Up grounds and the **cowboy breakfast** of ham, eggs, flapjacks, and coffee served Wednesday-Saturday at 6am in Stillman Park exemplify the traditions that take the Old West beyond the rodeo ring.

Of course, the Round-Up is also a rodeo—in fact, one of the largest and richest in the United States. Cowboys and cowgirls come from across North America to compete for nearly $500,000 in prize money in such classic rodeo events as bulldogging, calf-roping, barrel racing, and wild-horse races. The rodeo events are held Wednesday-Saturday 1:15pm-5pm. Tickets for each day run $15-25, depending on

© JUDY JEWELL

site of the Pendleton Round-Up

day and seat location. Tickets are available by calling the Round-Up office and also through Ticketmaster (www.ticketmaster.com).

The **Round-Up Hall of Fame** (13th St. and SW Court Ave., 10am-4pm Mon.-Sat., $5 adults, $4 seniors, $2 children ages 10 and under) can be found under the south grand-stand area at the Round-Up Stadium. The history of the country's biggest rodeo is depicted in photos of past champions and famous bucking broncos along with displays of artifacts. The star of the show is a stuffed horse named War Paint.

Hotel rooms in Pendleton are totally booked up months in advance for the Round-Up, so call to make reservations as early as possible.

SPORTS AND RECREATION

Lots of sun is conducive to such outdoor activities as golf at **Pendleton Country Club** (7 miles south of town on U.S. 395, 541/443-8874), and boating and waterskiing on **McKay Reservoir** (541/922-3232), near the country club. Fishing enthusiasts can head

north and arrive at the Columbia River in a little over an hour for salmon, steelhead, and bass, or try the area's reservoirs for bluegills, bass, and catfish.

The over three-mile-long **River Parkway,** a paved strip on a levee paralleling the Umatilla River through much of downtown Pendleton, is recommended for walkers and cyclists.

During the winter months, skiing is on tap up at **Spout Springs** (79327 Hwy. 204, Athena, 541/566-0320, spoutspringsskiresort.com, $35 adults, $30 children ages 12-17, $25 children ages 5-11), 40 miles northeast of Pendleton in Athena. It's one of the oldest ski resorts in the Pacific Northwest. It's a small place, with two double chairlifts and relatively easy terrain. **Cross-country ski trails** are also maintained here ($10 trail pass). To get here, drive north on Route 11 to Weston, turn east on Route 204, and travel a few miles past Tollgate to the ski area. Spout Springs usually holds on to its dry powder longer than other ski areas in the state.

SHOPPING

If you're starting to like the look of pearl-snap shirts, Wrangler jeans, and cowboy boots, make your way to **Hamley's** (30 SE Court Ave., 541/278-1100, 9am-6pm Mon.-Sat.), a classic Western clothing and tack store complete with saddle makers in the back. Hamley's also has an impressive collection of Western art on the mezzanine level of the store. A walk through downtown will reveal several other less vaunted and possibly less expensive places to buy Western clothing, boots, and saddles. It's a fun place to shop, and merchants are quite happy to help city folk with finer points of Western style.

ACCOMMODATIONS

Pendleton lodging is concentrated in two areas. A number of chain motels are found along the I-84 exits south of town. Older motor courts are close to downtown and within walking distance of Pendleton's famed nightlife. Rooms at these older downtown motels are usually cheaper than those in venues on the outskirts of town.

But first, a word about lodging at Round-Up time. If you show up at Pendleton in mid-September without a reservation or unprepared to pay double the usual room rate, you will almost certainly be out of luck. The town—and all those within easy driving distance—is completely booked. The chamber of commerce has a list of private homes that rent for a little less than a motel room, but they are also normally booked well in advance. If you bring a tent, camping may be available in schoolyards and other special sites set up for the Round-Up crowds.

Just west of downtown, the **Rugged Country Lodge** (1807 SE Court Ave., 541/966-6800 or 877/778-4433, www.ruggedcountrylodge. com, $75-88) is a 1950s-vintage motel that has been lovingly refurbished—each of the guest rooms has been charmingly decorated and the grounds are nicely landscaped. Plus there's the convivial welcome and hospitality that's found more often in B&Bs than in standard motels, and a light breakfast. This is a great alternative to build-'em-by-the-dozen chain motels, and for the quality of the rooms, a great deal.

A bit closer to downtown, within walking distance of downtown shopping, dining, and entertainment, the **Travelodge** (411 SW Dorion Ave., 541/276-7531, www.travelodge. com, $60-77) is another good deal, with continental breakfast included. The rooms are basic but clean and newly remodeled.

For something uniquely Pendleton, consider a night at the **Working Girls Hotel** (17 SW Emigrant Ave., 800/226-6398, www.pendleto-nundergroundtours.org, $75-95). An offshoot of the popular Pendleton Underground Tours, this five-guest room downtown hotel once served as a brothel in the Pendleton's rowdy heyday. The rooms have been modernized, but the hardwood floors, 18-foot ceilings, and exposed brick walls point to the hotel's 1890s birthright.

Equally historic but from the other end of the economic ladder, the **☾ Pendleton House Bed and Breakfast** (311 N. Main St., 541/276-8581, www.pendletonhousebnb.com, $135) is a fantastic 1917 mansion, with five guest rooms and 6,000 square feet of period luxury. Filled with antiques, oriental rugs, and original silk wall coverings, the Pendleton House even boasts a formal ballroom. A comfy porch, a backyard garden, and a fire blazing in the dining room while you enjoy creative breakfast fare evoke blissful thoughts of the good old days. The Byzantine shower in the shared bathroom evokes less gauzy thoughts.

At I-84 Exit 209, the **Oxford Suites** (2400 SW Court Place, 541/276-6000 or 877/545-7848, www.oxfordsuitespendleton.com, $109-165) offers a complimentary breakfast buffet and evening appetizers, plus an indoor pool and hot tub. All guest rooms have microwaves, refrigerators, coffeemakers, and high-speed Internet, and the hotel is pet-friendly. If you're looking for a very comfortable standard motel, this is a good bet.

There's a large cluster of motels at I-84 Exit 210. If you want to call ahead, consider these choices. The **Best Western Plus Pendleton Inn** (400 SE Nye Ave., 541/276-2135, $109) features an outdoor pool plus a fitness room and a hot tub. Standard guest rooms come with a coffeemaker plus an iron and ironing board. **Holiday Inn Express** (600 SE Nye Ave., 541/966-6520 or 800/465-4329, www.hiexpress.com, $120-130) includes a continental breakfast, an indoor pool, and a hot tub. Guest rooms come with coffeemakers and high-speed Internet access. **Red Lion Hotel** (304 SE Nye Ave., 541/276-6111 or 800/733-5466, www.redlion.com, $89) is a full-service hotel and small convention center, with two restaurants, a lounge, room service, and an outdoor pool. Rooms come with a microwave, a refrigerator, and a private balcony.

Six miles east of Pendleton, the new tower hotel at the **Wildhorse Resort Hotel and Casino** (46510 Wildhorse Blvd., 541/278-2274 or 800/654-9453, www.wildhorseresort.com, $114-200, rates lower on weekdays) is an impressive place, and worth checking out whether or not you're there to play the slots. Rooms in the tower have some of the best views in eastern Oregon; the older courtyard rooms ($94-140) aren't particularly remarkable, but some of these rooms are pet-friendly. Although the hotel lobby is immediately adjacent to the casino, where smoking is permitted, the hotel itself is nonsmoking, and good ventilation keeps the lobby air pretty clean. The adjacent RV park ($20-34) is also very well maintained. Facilities include a golf course, an indoor pool, a good restaurant, and, of course, 24-hour gaming.

FOOD

Dine in style at the **Hamley Steak House** (8 SE Court Ave., 541/278-1100, http://hamleysteakhouse.com, 5pm-9pm Tues.-Thurs., 5pm-9:30pm Fri.-Sat., 5pm-8pm Sun.-Mon, bar open later nightly, $12-33), a gorgeous and opulent restaurant with good steaks, house-smoked ribs, and comfort food "ranch cookin'" such as meat loaf and pot roast. Although the restaurant has only been open since 2005, the stained glass, rich woodwork, tin ceiling, and Western art make it look like it's been here as long as the Round-Up. Penny-pinchers can eat a burger ($12) at the bar and soak up the atmosphere.

Sharing a grassy plaza with the steak house is the casual but cowboy-chic **Hamley's Café and Coffee Company** (16 SE Court Ave., 541/278-1100, 8am-3pm daily, $6-12), with light breakfasts and lunchtime sandwiches and salads.

Also quite Western but considerably less tony than Hamley's is the **Rainbow Cafe** (209 S. Main St., 541/276-4120, 6am-2am daily, dinner $8-24, no credit cards) a famous saloon and restaurant for rodeo fans and local buckaroos, in business since 1833. The Rainbow serves passable American diner food, which you shouldn't pass up, if only for the local color. It's a favorite for breakfast or late-night bar food.

Virgil's at Cimmiyotti's (137 Main St., 541/276-4314, 4pm-9pm Tues.-Thurs., 4pm-10pm Fri.-Sat., $14-33) is the newest incarnation of this dark, cozy, and very red spot that has been around for decades (the flocked wallpaper almost has historic landmark status). Cimmiyotti's is an old-style Pendleton institution, and the steaks and fare such as here beef stroganoff and osso bucco make it a local favorite. In addition, there is a good selection of Walla Walla wines to choose from.

Take a break from Western kitsch at the **Main Street Diner** (349 S. Main St., 541/278-1952, 7am-2pm Mon.-Sat., 8am-2pm Sun., $6-9), styled after a 1950s burger joint, with hearty breakfasts and excellent burgers and milk shakes. Pasta is featured at **Como's** (39 SE Court Ave., 541/278-9142, 11am-8:30pm Mon.-Fri., 11am-2pm Sat., $10-20), and this small restaurant with a few outside tables is also a good place to have a glass of wine and a snack. The **Great Pacific Wine and Coffee Co.** (403 S. Main St., 541/276-1350, www.greatpacific.biz, 10am-9pm Mon.-Sat. $6-12), in a classy old downtown building (the former Masonic Lodge), features imported cheeses, desserts, salads, pizza, sandwiches, microbrews, a good wine selection, an espresso bar, and occasional live music.

Pendleton's first microbrewery is **Prodigal Son Brewery and Pub** (230 SE Court Ave., 541/276-6090, http://prodigalsonbrewery.com, 11am-10pm Tues.-Thurs., 11am-11pm Fri.-Sat., noon-9pm Sun., $9-12), a lively and pleasant family-friendly pub on the edge of downtown.

Come for the tasty Pacific Northwest-style brews and stay for the food, which includes burgers, sandwiches, and an excellent locally made bratwurst with sauerkraut.

Out at the Wildhorse Casino, **Plateau** (46510 Wildhorse Blvd., 541/966-1610, www.wildhorseresort.com, 11am-2pm Mon.-Fri. and 5pm-close nightly, $14-39) is a boon to those staying at the hotel, and worth a visit even for folks staying in town. Traditional Pacific Northwest fare such as grilled salmon, halibut cheeks, elk, and steak is well prepared and presented with elegance that's a bit unexpected at an eastern Oregon casino hotel. Prices are reasonable for the quality, and it's possible to order half portions ($8-22).

INFORMATION

The **Pendleton Chamber of Commerce Visitor and Convention Bureau** (501 S. Main St., 541/276-7411 or 800/547-8911, www.pendletonchamber.com) can steer you to local sights and special events. A self-guided walking-tour map of the historic downtown district is helpful. The tour starts at the corner of Main Street and Frazer Avenue and takes in many historic buildings.

GETTING THERE AND AROUND

Greyhound (801 SE Court Ave., 541/276-1551) offers two buses daily in each direction on the I-84 corridor between Portland and Boise. The stop is at the Double-J Drive-Thru.

Be aware that the mountainous stretch of I-84 east of Pendleton known as Cabbage Hill is treacherous to drive during icy winters. In addition to the slickness of the road surface, sudden blizzards and high winds can result in whiteout conditions.

La Grande and Vicinity

La Grande is in the Grande Ronde Valley, which the indigenous peoples called Copi Copi ("Valley of Peace"). The broad valley is completely ringed by mountains and gives the impression of being circular, hence the valley's French name, which translates as "the big circle." The Nez Perce once gathered here for their summer encampments until the Oregon Trail cut through their territory. At La Grande, the Oregon Trail pioneers rested and prepared to traverse the Blue Mountains, a substantial challenge as the passes were often snow-filled by the time the wagon trains reached eastern Oregon. In downtown La Grande, Bernie Park, located on B Avenue and Gekeler Lane, is one of the areas where the wagon trains rested, and it contains an abstract pioneer art memorial and a life-size wrought-iron pioneer play wagon.

More than a few of the pioneers were impressed with the agricultural possibilities of the Grande Ronde country, and they stayed to build a town that became the market center for a broad stretch of wheat and grass seed farms.

The city itself was established in 1864; a tavern on the south bank of the Grande Ronde River was the catalyst for the town's early growth. Lumber from the Blue Mountains and livestock fattened on lush fields of tall grass also propelled the community's early growth. Now home to Eastern Oregon University, La Grande (pop. 13,000) has an economy based on beef ranching, wheat farming, and timber. In addition to serving as gateway to Wallowa Lake and the northern flank of the Wallowa Range, La Grande is a pleasant destination in itself, with a historic downtown and several good restaurants. A drive through the valley reveals small towns with noteworthy museums and other curiosities.

SIGHTS
Union County Museum

In the town of Union, 11 miles southeast of La Grande, the **Union County Museum** (333 S. Main St., Union, 541/562-6003, www.uc-museumoregon.com, 10am-4pm Mon.-Sat.

mid-May-mid-Oct., $4 adults, $3 seniors and students) preserves the history of early settlement in the Grande Ronde Valley. Housed in a century-old redbrick former bank, the museum has an interesting collection of vintage farm, household, and mining tools and equipment, but the highlight is the **Cowboys Then and Now** collection. Formerly housed in Portland, the collection is from the Oregon Cattleman's Heritage Foundation and tells the story of the American cowboy starting from the arrival of cattle aboard Columbus's ships to the rise of modern agribusiness. Exhibits on the Hollywood Western and the history of rodeos are also intriguing.

The collection could not have found a more suitable setting for its new home. Union is a lovely town with a very well-preserved town center of late Victorian homes and storefronts. In fact, nearly the entire town is protected as a National Historic District. You can't miss the grand **Union Hotel,** built in 1920 as one of eastern Oregon's landmark lodgings and now a comfortable B&B.

Eastern Oregon Fire Museum

La Grande's former fire hall, built in 1899, is now a museum of antique fire engines known as the **Eastern Oregon Fire Museum** (102 Elm St., 541/963-8588, call for hours, free). Six beautifully restored fire trucks are on display, including a restored 1939 Seagrave ladder truck and a 1925 Stutz engine that's one of only nine such models ever built. Visitors are welcome to climb aboard and ring the bells. Even if the museum is closed, peek through the windows for a glimpse of the fire engines.

The Oregon Trail Interpretive Park at Blue Mountain Crossing

The **Oregon Trail Interpretive Park** (9am-7pm Tues.-Sun. Memorial Day-Labor Day, $5 NW Forest Pass required) commemorates the crossing of the Blue Mountains by the Oregon Trail pioneers. Paved, easily accessible trails follow some of the best-preserved and most scenic traces of the Oregon Trail. Sign panels describe the pioneers' struggle through the thick forests and over the rugged mountain passes, and

Steam rises from Hot Lake Mineral Hot Springs.

© JUDY JEWELL

THE OREGON TRAIL

The pioneer trek along the Oregon Trail, a tide of migration starting in 1841 and lasting over 20 years, is one of this country's great epochs, celebrated in novels, films, books, and songs. It is among the largest voluntary human migrations ever recorded.

The wagon trains started in Independence, Missouri, as soon as the spring grass was green. Then the race was on to get across the far mountains before the winter snows. The route—which usually required six months to complete—followed the North Platte River to South Pass in Wyoming, then crossed the Snake River Plain in Idaho, then across the Snake River and up and over the Blue Mountains in eastern Oregon to The Dalles. Here the pioneers faced a decision: Either they put themselves and all their belongings onto rafts to float the rapids of the otherwise impassable Columbia Gorge, or they struggled up the flanks of Mount Hood, descending into the Willamette Valley via the precipitous Barlow Trail.

In 1843, some 900 immigrants traveled the Oregon Trail, a number that swelled to 17,500 just 10 years later. When it was all over, about 50,000 pioneers followed the trail to the end and settled in Oregon Country—present-day Oregon, Washington, and Idaho. But these numbers tell only part of the story.

Although the first few hundred miles were easy traveling across the plains, the hard-ships were not long in coming. Contrary to the stereotype of hostile Native Americans being a major cause of casualties, cholera was by far the leading cause of death on the 2,000-mile journey that became known as "The Longest Graveyard." Some historians estimate at least 30,000 immigrants had died on the Oregon Trail by 1859. This would amount to an average of one unmarked grave every 100 yards between Independence and Oregon City.

At Fort Hall in eastern Idaho, there was a fork in the trail and a sign that read "To Oregon." It was here that the pioneers had to make a key decision. They could head south to California and the goldfields shining with the promise of instant wealth, or they could continue west to Oregon, where the fertile Willamette Valley offered its own allure as a New Jerusalem for serious farmers and homesteaders. Some Oregonians like to tell a more pointed version of the story, which claims that the sign for the California road was marked by a pile of gold-painted rocks, in contrast to the "To Oregon" sign. The implication was that people who could read—or who were more interested in domestic pursuits than quick wealth—would head to Oregon. While this interpretation is not seriously accepted by historians, it remains a source of good-natured humor between the two states.

---

living history interpretive events are offered on weekends during the summer. A picnic area, restrooms, and drinking water are available. To reach the park, take the I-84 Spring Creek exit 12 miles west of La Grande.

Mount Emily Recreation Area

When La Grande residents want to go on trail runs, bike rides, cross-country ski or horseback outings, they don't have to travel far. The 3,669-acre **Mount Emily Recreation Area** is only two miles from downtown and has about 12 miles of trails. Climb the mountain for great views of the Grande Ronde Valley and

the distant Eagle Cap Wilderness Area. Owsley Canyon Road leads from downtown (catch it just east of the fairgrounds) north to a Mount Emily trailhead. Stop by the local bike shop, **The Mountain Works** (1307 Adams Ave., 541/963-3320, 10am-6pm Mon.-Sat.) for advice on where to mountain bike.

Hot Lake Mineral Hot Springs

Hot Lake Mineral Hot Springs was considered "big medicine" by the Western Native Americans who camped near its healing waters. A steady flow of superheated water reaches the surface at nearly boiling point and pours into a large pond, reportedly the world's largest natural hot spring. In 1810, Astor Pacific Fur Company trappers described elk crowding around this spring. Thereafter, the lake, located five miles east of La Grande on Route 203, became a popular spot for explorers and emigrants. In 1864, Samuel Newhart built a hotel and bathhouse. A hospital was added in 1906, and the facility soon became known as the Mayo Clinic of the West. During that era, the healing waters were thought to give relief from arthritis and rheumatism, and the medical team was noted for its success treating tuberculosis. With a ballroom and library, the sanatorium was also a fashionable place to have a spa vacation. After the hospital closed in the 1930s, the building was used variously as a resort, a hotel, a boardinghouse, a restaurant, and a nursing home. Subsequently, for many years, the resort sat vacant and was frequently vandalized.

In 2004, David Manuel, an artist and sculptor who owned a bronze foundry and gallery in the nearby town of Joseph, and his wife Lee took over the crumbling resort and embarked on a very ambitious remodel and revival of the historic structure.

Much of the resort reopened in 2011, including bed-and-breakfast guest rooms, a hot mineral-water spa with a selection of treatments, a museum and history center, artist marketplace, restaurant and coffee shop, and gift shop. If you are in the area, you definitely should stop by and check out this transformed historical landmark (66172 Hwy. 203, 541/963-4685, www. hotlakesprings.com).

The bronze foundry and studio are open for one-hour tours at 10am and 2pm (Mon.-Sat., $10); the tour ticket also gets you into the museum and history center. The guest rooms ($144-333) include a number of multiroom suites; the least expensive rooms have a bathroom down the hall.

Ladd Marsh

The 3,200-acre **Ladd Marsh** (I-84 Exit 268, 5 miles south of La Grande off Foothill Rd.) is one of northeastern Oregon's largest remaining wetlands. Both upland and wetland habitats are represented, and the habitat diversity contributes to the wide array of plant and animal species found on the marsh. It's an excellent place to go bird-watching, especially in the springtime when waterfowl are in the area; attentive birders can see up to 80 species in a morning.

SPORTS AND RECREATION

Golf

The **Buffalo Peak Golf Course** (1224 E. Fulton St., Union, 541/562-5527 or 866/202-5950, $27 weekdays, $31 weekends) is an 18-hole par-72 links-style course set in the Grande Ronde Valley. The course offers a variety of landscapes, with native vegetation and natural terrain, such as patches of native prairie, streams, and lakes incorporated into the play.

Swimming

Hot Lake is not the only natural hot spring in the area. In the little community of Cove, 17 miles southeast of La Grande, the **Cove Warm Spring Pool** (907 Water St., Cove, 541/568-4890, www.coveoregon.org, noon-6pm Tues.-Sun. Memorial Day-Labor Day, $7) is a great outdoor swimming pool; the water is naturally heated to a constant 86°F.

ACCOMMODATIONS

Out at I-84 Exit 261, **Best Western Rama Inn and Suites** (1711 21st St., 541/963-3100 or 800/528-1234, www.bestwestern.com, $110-120) offers complimentary continental breakfast plus an indoor pool, a hot tub, and an exercise facility. Guest rooms feature cable TV, wireless Internet, a coffeemaker, a refrigerator, a microwave, and an iron. The adjacent **Best Value Sandman Inn** (2410 E. R Ave., 541/963-3707, www.bestvalueinnlagrande. com, $76-86) has an indoor pool and spa, wireless Internet, a continental breakfast included, and bright clean rooms. Downtown, the pet-friendly **La Grande Royal Motor Inn** (1510 Adams Ave., 541/963-4154 or 800/990-7575, www.royalmotorinn.net, $59) offers basic but just-fine rooms within easy walking distance of good restaurants and bars.

Eleven miles southeast of La Grande on Route 203, the nine-unit 🔆 **Union Hotel** (326 N. Main St., Union, 541/562-6135, www.theunionhotel.com, $65-119) will take you back to the 1920s, when this imposing hotel was built to satisfy the needs of sophisticated travelers between Portland and Boise. The hotel has been partially renovated (it's a work in progress), keeping its high style intact, with theme-decorated guest rooms, most with private baths. This three-story brick hotel—with beautiful tile floors, an Old West lobby, and a Ladies Parlor—is one of the most charming and unusual hotels in eastern Oregon. Forget the chain motels along the interstate and stay in a historic landmark.

Hike, fly, or pack a horse into the remote **Minam River Lodge** (541/508-2719, www.theminamlodge.com), in the backcountry about 26 miles from La Grande. Although many guests do arrive via private plane, it's possible to hike or ride in via a steep 8.5-mile trail from the Moss Springs trailhead, east of the town of Cove. Once there, the lodgings are in a beautiful log cabin ($250), a tepee ($95), your own tent ($40), or under your plane wing ($30). Along with the beautiful setting, the simple but carefully prepared, locally sourced family-style meals are a big attraction; breakfast is $14, lunch is $20, and dinner is $36. Even if you're camping, reserve your meals in advance.

Camping

A number of La Grande area campgrounds share history with the Oregon Trail. Between La Grande and Pendleton in the midst of the Blue Mountains, **Emigrant Springs State Heritage Area** (541/983-2277 or 800/551-6949, www.oregonstateparks.org, reservations www.reserveamerica.com, $17 tents, $20 RVs, $24-39 cabins), right off I-84, is a large campground with flush toilets, showers, and a playground. The park has a display on local Oregon Trail history. There are 33 tent sites and 18 full hookups in a wooded area.

The 18-site **Hilgard Junction State Park** campground (no hookups, no reservations, $9) is on the Grande Ronde River, at the foot of the Blue Mountains. To get here, drive 8 miles west of La Grande to I-84 Exit 252 at the junction of Route 244 (Starkey Rd.). This campground is on the original route of the Oregon Trail. Information placards detail how their wagons maneuvered over the precipitous terrain. The campground is convenient to the interstate, which also means that it's noisy and not particularly private. Consider driving 8 miles up Route 244 to **Red Bridge State Wayside** for more appealing campsites ($9).

Another option off Route 244 is **Spool Cart Campground** (541/963-7186, www.fs.usda.gov, May-Nov., $5, no water) a small site on the banks of the Grande Ronde River. From I-84 Exit 252, drive 13 miles southwest on Route 244 as it meanders along the river and its valley, where stands of ponderosa pine and aspen are broken by meadows and farmland; from there, drive 6 miles south on Forest Service Road 51.

FOOD

Some of the state's best fast food is available at **Nells In 'n' Out** (1704 Adams Ave., 541/963-5733, 11am-11pm daily, $3-8). Creative variations on shakes and floats, hand-curled french fries, and a full array of burgers are highlights. **Mamacita's** (2003 4th St., 541/963-6223, 11am-9pm Mon.-Sat., $7-15) is a good standby in La Grande, serving tasty and affordable Southwestern and Mexican food, pasta, sandwiches, and wraps with a Jimmy Buffett vibe. An excellent spot for morning coffee and pastries is **Joe and Sugar's** (1119 Adams Ave., 541/975-5282, 7am-3pm Mon.-Fri., 9am-noon Sat., $2-8), a tiny bakery right downtown that also turns out excellent breakfast sandwiches and burritos.

Find eastern Oregon's best Thai food at **Bangkok East** (1114 Adams Ave., 541/624-5777, 11am-9:30pm Sun.-Thurs., 11am-10pm Fri.-Sat., $9-14); they also serve some Vietnamese dishes, including pho. Right next door, the same owner serves Chinese and Japanese food at the **Golden Crown** (1116 Adams Ave., 541/963-5907, www.mygoldencrown.com, $6-15); it's a popular spot for sushi and lunchtime bento boxes.

Pizza is a big draw at the **Mt. Emily Ale House** (1202 Adams Ave., 541/962-7711, www.mtemilyalehouse.com, 4:30pm-9pm Tues.-Thurs., 11:30am-9pm Fri.-Sat., $8-22), and the microbrew beer and root beer bring a few people in the door as well. This is a good spot to relax and hang with the locals.

La Grande has one of eastern Oregon's most refined restaurants: **❴ Ten Depot Street** (10 Depot St., 541/963-8766, http://tendepot-street.com, 5pm-10pm Mon.-Sat., $9-32) offers an up-to-date menu that might include grilled local lamb kabobs, fresh Pacific Northwest salmon, and perfectly prepared prime rib (the house specialty). Salads and pasta are particularly delicious, a rarity out here in meat country. The restaurant's classy structure was once

a Masonic hall, and the saloon is as popular as the restaurant—it's a great place to indulge in a succulent half-pound burger.

INFORMATION

For information on La Grande and Union County, contact **Union County Tourism** (207 Depot St., 541/963-8588 or 800/848-9969, www.visitlagrande.com). The La Grande Ranger Station of the Wallowa-Whitman Forest Service is at 3502 U.S. 30 (541/963-7186).

GETTING THERE

Two **Greyhound** buses travel each day between Portland and Boise with stops in La Grande. The station is at 2204 E. Penn Avenue, 541/963-5165.

The Wallowas

The snowcapped Teton-like spires of the Wallowa Mountains soar 5,000 feet above Wallowa County farmlands and six-mile-long Wallowa Lake; they are unlike any other of Oregon's peaks. Rather than the basalt that covers much of the state, these mountains are made of granite and limestone. Much of the range is in the **Eagle Cap Wilderness Area,** which contains 17 of the state's 29 mountains over 9,000 feet and 50 glacial lakes sprinkled throughout 300,000 acres. Campers and cross-country skiers are regularly treated to glimpses of bighorn sheep, mountain goats, elk, and mule deer, as well as snow-streaked granite and limestone peaks rising above meadows dotted with an artist's palette of wildflowers. Seashells in limestone and greenstone outcroppings attest to the age of the range, some 200 million years.

The Wallowa Valley is formed by the drainages of the Wallowa, Minam, and Grande Ronde Rivers, and its backdrop is the half moon-shaped Wallowa Range, 80 miles long and 25 miles at its widest. The traditional eastern Oregon triad of timber, farming, and cattle ranching fuels the area's economy, with tourism rapidly increasing. Nineteenth-century

farmhouses dot the landscape, and cowboy-hatted ranchers and farmers mix freely with local merchants and a cluster of artists who have settled here.

After a visit to this larger-than-life countryside, it is easy to see how it sustained the proud and indomitable Nez Perce, the native people who once roamed its river canyons, glacial basins, and grassy hills. The air here has a soft sweetness, and a surprising degree of epicurean refinement awaits the discerning visitor. Locals will tell you to come in September when pleasant weather and smaller crowds showcase the region at its best.

There are several choices of home base when it comes to exploring the Wallowas. The town of Enterprise is the commercial center of it all, while Joseph is a more touristy and artsy community that serves as the gateway to Wallowa Lake, a recreational hub at the end of the road. And then there's camping: The Wallowas have many Forest Service and state park campgrounds where you can roll out the tent and get even closer to nature.

The Wallowas are Oregon's wettest place east of the Cascades. The higher reaches of the range may get 60 inches of precipitation annually. These upper elevations crest in the Eagle Cap Wilderness Area and descend gradually to the south toward Baker City.

It's theorized that these mountains were once part of a tropical island chain in the mid-Pacific. As North America drifted, the island range bumped into the continent and attached itself to the ancient coastline. Curiously, the Austrian Alps contain similar fossilized corals, mollusks, algae, and sponges, suggesting a shared birthright lost in the mists of prehistory.

History

The Wallowa Valley, set apart by deep river canyons and mountain ranges, is the ancestral home of the Nez Perce, a nation known for its horse-training skills and fierce independence. These proud people, astride their spotted Appaloosas, first encountered Europeans when mountain men wandered onto their land. Lewis and Clark believed that the Native Americans' generosity with food saved their lives. Their willingness to feed and care for the Bonneville Party, which had struggled up out of the Snake River Canyon in 1834, reinforced their reputation for honor and largesse. Later, however, when a dry spell in the Grande Ronde Valley to the south prompted homesteaders to farm the Wallowas, native and settler cultures clashed.

One source of tension was the settlers permitting their hogs to trample the camas fields where the Native Americans came to gather food. The U.S. government attempted to resolve the situation by creating a 7-million-acre reservation in 1855 but reneged on the land treaty five years later when gold was discovered in the Wallowas. This breach initiated an era of bad feelings, during which various drafts of different treaties generated confusion and distrust.

The settlers later successfully lobbied the government to evict the Native Americans, which led to the Nez Perce War of 1877. Chief Joseph and his people fought a running battle that covered 1,700 miles and ended with their surrender in the Bear's Paw Mountains, 50 miles from the Montana-Canada border. The Nez Perce Reservation is in central Idaho.

EAGLE CAP EXCURSION TRAIN

Trains arrived in La Grande in 1884 but didn't reach the remote canyon country of the Wallowas until 1908. Passenger service fizzled in the 1920s after decent roads and bridges allowed easy vehicle access to Wallowa farms and towns, and finally in the 1990s freight service stopped along this lonely rail line that passes through stunning mountain meadows and deep river gorges. Citizens in the town of Wallowa and Union County banded together to purchase the track, and today the system operates both freight and excursion services between Elgin and Joseph. The **Eagle Cap Excursion Train** (541/963-9000 or 800/323-7330, http://eaglecaptrainrides.com) is run by a volunteer organization called the Friends of the Joseph Branch.

The excursion train offers occasional trips ($75 adults, $70 seniors, $40 children ages 3-16) leaving from the small Wallowa Valley town of Elgin. The train passes through spectacular scenery, and culminates by traveling along the Wild and Scenic stretch of the Wallowa River.

In general, the excursion train operates most Saturdays late August-mid-October, departing at 10am and returning at 1:30pm; lunch is included in the fare. Call or check online for details.

ENTERPRISE

Enterprise is the larger of the two towns that dominate the Wallowa Valley, with a population of around 1,700, and unlike Joseph it has the feel of an authentic Western town. Much of the original downtown, built in the 1890s, still exists and functions as the mercantile center. Enterprise is a friendly town, and you should stop to explore and enjoy its shops and handsome locale. Swing by the **Chamber of Commerce** (309 S. River St., 541/426-4622, www.wallowacountychamber.com, 8am-5pm Mon.-Fri.) and pick up the *walking tour* brochure prepared by the Wallowa County Centennial Committee. It has descriptions and locations of many of

CHIEF JOSEPH

Known by his people as *In-mut-too-yah-lat-lat* ("Thunder coming up over the land from the water"), Chief Joseph was best known for his brave resistance to the government's attempts to force his people onto a reservation. A nation that spread from Idaho to northern Washington, the Nez Perce had peacefully coexisted with European Americans after the Lewis and Clark expedition; indeed, they had given the newcomers much-needed horses. Joseph had spent much of his early childhood at a mission maintained by Christian missionaries.

But with the incursion of miners and settlers, and because of misunderstandings surrounding the annexation of Native American land through a series of treaties never signed by Chief Joseph, tension increased to the breaking point. White disregard of native property spurred some rash young Nez Perce to retaliate. The ensuing 11-week conflict, during which the Nez Perce engaged 10 separate U.S. military commands in 13 battles (the majority of which the Nez Perce won), guaranteed Chief Joseph's fame as a brilliant military tactician. However, after many hardships, including starvation and many lost lives, Chief Joseph surrendered to Generals Miles and Howard on October 5, 1877, only 50 miles from the sanctuary of the Canadian border.

In 1879, Chief Joseph spoke to the Department of Indian Affairs in Washington, D.C., detailing the broken promises of the government, the suffering of his people, and the unjust treatment of Native Americans by European American society, saying:

> I have heard talk and talk, but nothing is done. Good words do not last long unless they amount to something. Words do not pay for my dead people. They do not pay for my country, now overrun by white men. They do not protect my father's grave. They do not pay for all my horses and cattle. Good words will not give me back my children. I only ask of the government to be treated as all other men are treated.

Chief Joseph appealed repeatedly to the federal authorities to return the Nez Perce to the land of their ancestors, but to no avail. In 1885 he and many of his band were sent to a reservation in Washington, where, as the presiding doctor was heard to have said, he died of a broken heart.

the historic buildings in the area, such as the Wallowa County Courthouse, the Enterprise Hotel, the Oddfellows Hall, and a number of private homes. After an hour of edification and exercise, take a break at the **Bookloft and Skylight Gallery** (107 E. Main St., 541/426-3351, http://bookloftoregon.net, 9:30am-5:30pm Mon.-Fri., 10am-4pm Sat.), just across the street from the county courthouse. This gathering spot for artists and community activists sells best sellers and local history books, and offers monthly shows of guest artists, as well as freshly brewed coffee and home-baked cookies.

Wildlife-Watching

Two wildlife-viewing areas await you as you sweep down into the Wallowa Valley. The **Spring Branch Wildlife Area,** a woodland marsh, is two miles east of Wallowa on Route 82, on the north side where the road leaves the Wallowa River. The eight-acre viewing area, managed by the Oregon Department of Fish and Wildlife, has beaver dams and lots of waterfowl, including the black tern, an insect-eating bird found in eastern Oregon marshes. The **Enterprise Wildlife Area** is two miles west of Enterprise off Route 82. To get there, turn south on Fish Hatchery Road; the 32-acre site is just before the fish hatchery. Walk down the dike that goes through a grove of trees to view marsh wrens, snipes, mink, beavers, and muskrats.

ZUMWALT PRAIRIE

North of Highway 82, about halfway between Enterprise and Joseph, roads head north through rangeland to high plateaus. One good destination about 45 minutes from Enterprise is **Zumwalt Prairie**, the largest remaining native Pacific Northwest bunchgrass prairie. The prairie, which is managed by **The Nature Conservancy** (541/426-3458, www.nature.org), has several hiking trails (dogs, bikes, and horses are not permitted on the trails). To reach the prairie from Highway 82, head north on Cow Creek Road and, after five miles, turn right onto Zumwalt Road, which is paved for only the first few miles. Travel 14 miles on Zumwalt Road; at the junction, turn right (toward Imnaha) and follow The Nature Conservancy sign 1.4 miles to the Duckett Barn, which has interpretive signs and a trailhead. Another trailhead, for the Horned Lark Trail, is on the main Zumwalt Road about three miles past the junction with the Imnaha road.

In addition to providing public access via the trails, The Nature Conservancy works to maintain the prairie with controlled burns, hunting, and carefully managed cattle grazing.

If you're up for more back road exploration, continue north on the Zumwalt Road to the Buckhorn Lookout; it's a slow 35 miles from the highway, and has amazing views.

Entertainment and Events

Northwest of Enterprise in the town of Wallowa, the **Wallowa Band Nez Perce Trail Interpretive Center** (209 E. 2nd St., Wallowa, 541/886-3101, www.wallowanezperce.org) holds the mid-July **Tamkaliks Celebration**, which celebrates the continuing Nez Perce presences in the Wallowa Valley. A Native American encampment, dancing, and feasting are highlights of the festival.

Hells Canyon Mule Days (www.hellscanyonmuledays.com), held the weekend after Labor Day at the **Wallowa County Fairgrounds** (668 NW 1st St., Enterprise, 541/426-4097), is

© JUDY JEWELL

The Nature Conservancy has preserved native prairie at Zumwalt Prairie.

where pack animal fanciers can get their kicks. The action includes mule races, a parade, a speed mule-shoeing contest, and endurance competitions.

Accommodations

Lodging in Enterprise can be less expensive than other Wallowa area options—and it's not booked up months in advance like the lodges at Wallowa Lake. A couple of standard motels are noteworthy for being clean, well priced, and friendly. The fairly large **Ponderosa Motel** (102 SE Greenwood St., 541/426-3186, $76-87) is just south of downtown and has refrigerators and microwaves in the guest rooms. **Wilderness Inn** (301 W. North St., 541/426-4535, $60) has everything you need for a comfortable night in Enterprise.

The **1910 Historic Enterprise House B&B** (508 1st South St., 541/426-4238 or 888/448-8825, www.enterprisehousebnb.com, $99-189) is a very large rambling farmhouse from the turn of the 20th century and has a big front porch and great mountain views. Each of the five guest rooms has a private bath, and the massive third-floor suite ($165) can sleep up to six.

A different sort of B&B experience is offered at **A Barking Mad Farm Bed and Breakfast** (65156 Powers Rd., 541/215-2758 or 541/263-1934, www.barkingmadfarm.com, $135-195), an elegant and exceedingly pet-friendly inn. The three suites are all beautiful, but it's hard to top the Treetop Suite, which you enter through a hatch and which has a deck snug up against an ancient yew tree.

Travel 30 miles north of town to the **Rimrock Inn** (83471 Lewiston Hwy., 541/429-2540, www.rimrockinnor.com, open late May-early Oct.), where you can choose between staying in a fully furnished, futon-equipped but nonelectrified tepee ($68-78, restrooms and bathhouse separate), an RV bunkhouse ($68), a suite in the inn proper ($99), or an apartment ($175). You can also camp in your tent ($20) or RV ($25). It's worth heading off the beaten path to stay at the Rimrock, and not only because of the views of

beautiful Joseph Canyon; the inn's restaurant is also one of the best places to eat in northeastern Oregon. Breakfast is included for all but those camping in their own tents or RVs.

Food

The lively **Cloud 9 Bakery** (105 SE 1st St., 541/426-3790, 6:30am-4pm Mon.-Fri., $7 lunch) is a great place to know about—its pastries, doughnuts, and coffee are great for morning fueling, and soups, sandwiches, and light meals are available until late afternoon. **Red Rooster Cafe** (309 W. Main St., 541/426-2233, 6am-2pm daily, $6-11) is an especially cheery place for breakfast or lunch in downtown Enterprise. The food here is homemade, using as many fresh, local ingredients as possible; baked oatmeal and a cup of the café's custom-roasted coffee are a great way to get ready for the day.

Lear's Pub and Grill (111 W. Main St., 541/426-3300, www.learspubandgrill.com, 7am-1:30pm and 5pm-8pm daily, $9-26) combines many excellent virtues, among them a selection of regional microbrews, a vintage bar atmosphere, and really good food that's prepared on-site and from scratch. Main courses like pan-seared porcini-dusted halibut, smoked pork loin with rosemary cream sauce, and the trademark 16-ounce "Big Ass" rib steak run $16-24, though burgers and barbecued brisket sandwiches are available for around $10.

Terminal Gravity Brewing (803 SE School St., 541/426-0158, www.terminalgravitybrewing.com, 11am-9pm Sun.-Tues., 11am-10pm Wed.-Sat., $8-13) is a top-notch brewpub with excellent beer, decent pub food, and a perfectly laid-back atmosphere. Customers congregate on the porch and front lawn in an idyllic creek-side poplar grove. (Dogs aren't permitted to hang out here.)

For the region's fine dining option, you'll need to drive 30 miles north of Enterprise on Route 3 to the tiny town of Flora, where the **Rimrock Inn** (83471 Lewiston Hwy., 541/828-7769, www.rimrockinnor.com, 5:30pm or 7pm seatings Tues.-Sat., $19-23, reservations required) awaits. This one-of-a-kind restaurant began as a 1940s roadhouse before being transformed in 2004 into a very stylish dining room that blends historic authenticity with chic decor. Each night a different entrée is prepared—but be prepared to eat some meat, such as barbecued back ribs or Swiss steak, accompanied by organically grown vegetables. And the views? As its name suggests, the Rimrock Inn sits above a staggering view of Joseph Canyon as it trenches its way toward Hells Canyon, North America's deepest river gorge. The kitchen produces excellent food, focusing on well-prepared steaks, Cajun chicken, and Saturday-night-only prime rib. Wines are mostly from the Walla Walla area and the Columbia and Willamette Valleys. To prolong the Rimrock Inn experience, consider pitching your tent or settling into a luxury tepee at the canyon's edge.

Information
The **Wallowa County Chamber of Commerce** (309 S. River St., 541/426-4622, www.wallowacountychamber.com, 8am-5pm Mon.-Fri.) stocks a full complement of brochures, maps, and other information on the area.

JOSEPH
At the base of the Wallowa Mountains is Joseph (elevation 4,150 feet), a lively community of about 1,000 that's named after the famous Nez Perce chief. The old-timey charm of Joseph's false-fronted buildings with the snowcapped Wallowas as a backdrop makes it seem more than 335 miles away from Portland. Joseph is noted across the West as an arts town, and the sculptures and colorful planters that line the sidewalks enhance this image. However, the colorful main street is increasingly lined more with gift shops than galleries, and on a busy summer weekend, finding the artsy charm of this pretty town takes a little doing.

That said, there are still plenty of galleries and arts-related shops to visit, and **Valley Bronze** (18 Main St., 541/432-7445, www.valleybronze.com), Joseph's original bronze-casting operation—and the second-largest in the

nation—displays works and offers daily tours ($15) of their **foundry** (307 W. Alder St.). Call ahead or check the website for a tour schedule.

If a foundry tour doesn't fit into your schedule, at least take a walk down Main Street to look at many bronze sculptures; each was done by a different artist.

Josephy Center for Arts and Culture
Joseph's arts scene got a boost in 2013 with the opening of the **Josephy Center** (403 N. Main St., 541/432-0505, www.josephy.org, noon-4pm Mon.-Sat.), with a gallery space, library, and workshops. With a goal to revitalize the area's "creative capital," the center hosts events ranging from weddings to concerts in its attractive gallery space. The library, which honors Alvin Josephy (1915-2008), a Western historian who focused much of his work on the Nez Perce, is a treasure trove of books, journals, artifacts, and manuscripts from the Josephy family.

Iwetemlaykin State Heritage Site
On the road from Joseph to Wallowa Lake, stop off and hike the trails at the **Iwetemlaykin State Heritage Site** to get a feeling for the Nez Perce homeland. It's easy to see why this grassland laced with streams and surrounded by mountains is sacred to the Nez Perce. Short trails offer a chance to get away from the hubbub of downtown Joseph without launching into a rigorous mountain hike. The site is adjacent to the Old Chief Joseph gravesite.

Wallowa County Museum
A must-stop for history buffs is the **Wallowa County Museum** (110 Main St., 541/432-6095, www.co.wallow.or.us, 10am-5pm daily Memorial Day-late Sept., $4 adults, $3 seniors, $2 students). Built in 1888, the museum building has served as a newspaper office, a private hospital, a meeting hall, and a bank (one of the crooks who robbed the bank later became its president). Its current incarnation as a museum started in 1960. The theme of the museum is Wallowa history, including displays of pioneer

life and the Nez Perce; the museum is crammed with interesting curiosities and curios.

Fishing

The Wallowa Valley area is home to several fine fishing streams, including the Wallowa, Grande Ronde, Lostine, and Imnaha Rivers. The **Joseph Fly Shoppe** (203 N. Main St., 541/432-4343, www.josephflyshop.com) is a good source for information and gear; **Winding Waters** (877/426-7238, www.windingwatersrafting.com) is a local outfitter.

Entertainment and Events

Most of the local celebrations revolve around cowboys, Native Americans, and the arts community. The **Wallowa Valley Festival of the Arts** (www.wallowavalleyarts.org) is held at the Joseph Civic Center on the first weekend of June. Along with awards for Pacific Northwest artists, there are wine-tasting parties, a silent auction, and a quick-draw competition (using pencils, not sidearms).

Held the last week of July, **Chief Joseph Days** (541/432-1015, www.chiefjosephdays.com) is a weeklong festival in Joseph that features dances, a carnival, a Grand Parade, a ranch-style breakfast, and a three-day rodeo, one of the largest in the Pacific Northwest. Also in Joseph, **Bronze, Blues, and Brews** (www.bronzebluesbrews.com) takes place in mid-August, featuring music, gallery and foundry open houses, and locally brewed beer.

A couple of times a year, Joseph hosts a low-key but talent-laden literary gathering known as **Fishtrap** (541/426-3623, www.fishtrap.org). Authors writing in different genres attend; past participants have included William Kittredge, Ursula K. LeGuin, Ivan Doig, Sandra Scofield, and Terry Tempest Williams. Writers of all levels come to read their works and discuss social issues.

Accommodations

There are few lodging options in Joseph itself; many visitors stay a few miles away at Wallowa Lake, where there's a large campground, a couple of RV parks, and several cabin resorts. But in town, for clean basic motel rooms, try the **Indian Lodge Motel** (201 S. Main St., 541/432-2651 or 888/286-5484, www.indianlodgemotel.com, $100-105), known by old-timers as "Walter Brennan's place," after the motel's original owner, the TV and movie actor.

Joseph also has a number of excellent B&Bs. **Bronze Antler Bed & Breakfast** (309 S. Main St., 541/432-0230 or 866/520-9769, www.bronzeantler.com, $149-259) is a friendly B&B in a 1925 bungalow originally built by a local sawmill supervisor who filled the Craftsman-style home with custom millwork and beautiful wood floors. The three guest rooms and one suite have private baths and luxurious linens and towels—the room appointments rival those at upscale hotels. The living and dining rooms are warmly decorated with antiques and quality furniture, adding to the comfortable atmosphere of Rocky Mountain chic.

Chandler's Inn (700 S. Main St., 541/432-9765, www.josephbedandbreakfast.com, $85-170) is a large house, long a B&B, on the edge of town. Options range from smaller rooms with a shared bath to large two-bedroom suites.

Food

The log-sided **Old Town Café** (8 S. Main St., 541/432-9898, 7am-2pm daily, $6-9) looks the part of a vintage frontier town eatery—it's a great spot for oniony hash brown potatoes topped with cheese, bacon, and homemade salsa. In nice weather, the outdoor seating is particularly appealing. **Outlaw Restaurant & Saloon** (108 N. Main St., 541/432-4321, 11am-7:30pm Mon.-Thurs., 11am-8:30pm Fri.-Sat., $8-20) offers standard American fare, but in summer there's ample outdoor seating; this is a good bet for dinner for a family. The other good dinner place is the artsy but unpretentious **Calderas** (300 N. Lake St., 541/432-0585, http://calderasofjoseph.com, 1pm-9pm Thurs.-Mon., $17-29), with sandwiches, baked parmesan chicken, butternut squash ravioli, and a good burger. When possible, Calderas uses veggies grown on their farm outside town. During the afternoon, stop by for espresso and pastries.

Embers Brewhouse (204 N. Main St., 541/432-2739, www.embersbrewhouse.com, 11am-close Mon.-Sat., noon-close Sun., $9-13) offers regional microbrews on tap plus pizza and deli sandwiches; try for a spot outside on the deck.

(**Mutiny Brewing** (600 N. Main St., 541/432-5274, 11:30am-9pm Wed.-Sun., $8-12) is a great spot for a pint of microbrew ale and a sandwich or light snack. This is a friendly establishment with a lot more heart and authenticity than many of Joseph's touristy food mills.

WALLOWA LAKE

The biggest attraction in the Wallowas is Wallowa Lake, which at 5,000 feet in elevation is the highest large body of water in eastern Oregon. This classic moraine-held glacial lake begins a mile south of Joseph on Route 82 at the east end of the Wallowa Valley, though most development is at the south end of the lake, about six miles from Joseph. Although it is beautiful, the area around the lake takes on a carnival atmosphere during the summer, with arcades, bumper boats, miniature golf, go-karts, and—for adults—parasailing. In addition to these amusement park attractions, there are lodges, a large state park with a campground, packhorse corrals, boat launches, marinas, and perhaps the **Wallowa Lake Monster,** a creature with a gentle disposition and a length varying 30-100 feet, depending on the sighting. Reports of the critter go back several centuries to Native American tales.

The lake is bordered on one side by peaks of the Eagle Cap Wilderness and on the other by rolling farmland that novelist Ethan Canin said "might have given Monet the inspiration for his palette." Be that as it may, exercise caution before you dive in for a swim. Invitingly clear, the lake waters are extremely cold and should not be experienced until August (and not much thereafter). The beach in the county park at the northern end of the lake is a good spot to test the waters.

Wallowa State Park

One of the most popular in the Oregon state

© JUDY JEWELL

The Old Town Café is a long-time favorite in Joseph.

NORTHEASTERN OREGON

© JUDY JEWELL

Wallowa Lake

park system, **Wallowa State Park** (541/432-4185, www.oregonstateparks.org) is set lakeside amid big old ponderosa pines. It's a beautiful spot and the perfect place for an outdoorsy family vacation, if you don't mind pitching your tent next to somebody's generator. Even if you're not camping here, the large lakeside day-use area is a fine place from which to enjoy the scenery. The **Wallowa Lake Marina** (541/432-9115, www.wallowalakemarina.com), located in the day-use area, rents watercraft ranging from stand-up paddleboards to motorboats and sells fishing gear. The park is moments from wilderness hiking trails and horseback riding as well as bumper boats and miniature golf. For high season, reserve a campsite several months in advance or you may be out of luck.

◖ Wallowa Lake Tramway

The gondola up Mount Howard, the **Wallowa Lake Tramway** (544/432-5331, www.wallowalaketramway.com, 9am-5:45pm daily mid-June-mid-Sept., $28 adults, $25 seniors, $22 students ages 12-17, $19 children ages 4-11), is the steepest and longest in North America—lifting passengers 3,700 feet from the edge of Wallowa Lake to the 8,200-foot summit. As the lift floats upward, the pastureland and wheat-field views near Wallowa Lake give way to forests of lodgepole pine, tamarack, and quaking aspen. On top, stay on the trails through the fragile alpine tundra so as not to damage the tiny and rare plants.

The 15-minute ride ends at the Summit Grill and Alpine Patio, with drinks and meals at the top of the peak. But forget about the snacks, knickknacks, and trinkets; the best reason for taking the trip is the view of 26 mountain peaks, including the Wallowa Range, Snake River country, and Idaho's Seven Devils area. The eight peaks of Eagle Cap Wilderness are mirrored in the lake below, and the gorges of the Snake and Imnaha Rivers stretch to the east.

The gondola operates fewer days per week and for fewer hours mid-May-mid-June and mid- to late September; check the website for the schedule during the shoulder season.

Hiking and Horseback Riding

Although many visitors hike the little trail network on Mount Howard at the top of the tram, there's a good trailhead at the end of Wallowa Lake Highway, less than one mile from the lake. From here you can hike the steep uphill trail 6 miles to Aneroid Lake, or turn around at the waterfall that's about 4 miles in. The last couple of miles, between the waterfall and the lake, are the prettiest. From the same trailhead you can catch the seven-mile trail to Chief Joseph Mountain, with good views along the way of Wallowa Lake. Expect to share the trail with horses.

If you'd rather ride a horse up one of these trails, the **Eagle Cap Wilderness Pack Station** (59761 Wallowa Lake Hwy., 541/432-4145, www.eaglecapwildernesspackstation.com) is right near the trailhead; two-mile rides start on the hour (8am-11am and 1pm-4pm, $35). A variety of longer rides are also offered.

NORTHEASTERN OREGON

© JUDY JEWELL

Saddle horses wait their riders at the Eagle Cap Wilderness Pack Station.

Accommodations and Camping

The following lodgings on Wallowa Lake reflect the special woodsy flavor of this outback locality. These accommodations are all at the south end of the lake, near the state park, which offers campsites.

The **Flying Arrow Resort** (59782 Wallowa Lake Hwy., 541/432-2951, www.flyingarrowresort.com, cabins $110-450), offers lodging in 24 cabins, ranging from one-bedroom cabins to four-bedroom houses that can sleep 14. (There's also a rustic studio cabin without kitchen for $95.) All have kitchens, fireplaces, and bathrooms, but otherwise they are all unique, so visit the website to find out which cabin matches your needs. The resort also features a swimming pool, a hot tub, a chocolate shop, a bookstore, and a market. The Flying Arrow is kid- and pet-friendly.

The **Wallowa Lake Lodge** (60060 Wallowa Lake Hwy., 541/432-9821, www.wallowalakelodge.com, $99-275) is a renovated 1923 hunting lodge on the lakefront that fairly drips with vintage atmosphere. In addition to a good restaurant, the lodge itself has 22 guest rooms in a variety of sizes and layouts. While some guest rooms are quite small, others have two bedrooms; all have private bathrooms and are decorated in a somewhat feminine style (no knotty pine). In addition, the lodge offers accommodations in eight cabins scattered around the eight-acre property. The cabins were built in the 1950s and feature knotty pine cabinets, stone fireplaces, and fully modern kitchens and bathrooms; most have lake views. It's hard to imagine a more enchanting setting. A great deal of care is taken to preserve the historic atmosphere of the lodge and the cabins, though comfort is not sacrificed.

On the quieter western side of the lake, **Trouthaven Resort** (61841 Lakeshore Dr., 541/432-2221, www.trouthavencabins.com, mid-May-mid-Sept., $100-110) is another venerable cabin resort. The cabins come in two sizes (the larger ones can sleep six) and have knotty pine paneling and a covered porch with an outdoor dining table. The Trouthaven also has a half-mile of Wallowa Lake frontage with a couple of docks; boats and fishing gear are available for rent. These cabins and this location are perfect ingredients for a family vacation; during the busy months of July and August, a five-day minimum stay is usually required.

Wallowa Lake Resort (84681 Ponderosa Ln., 541/432-2391, www.wallowalakeresort. com) rents over 30 different properties in the Lake Wallowa area, from small cabins perfect for a couple (starting at $95) to large homes that will sleep up to 10 ($260). No two are alike, so get on the website and make your selection.

Although it is not what you'd call a secret hideaway, if you're looking for a campground surrounded on three sides by 9,000-foot-high snowcapped peaks and a large clear lake, the **Wallowa State Park campground** (541/432-4185, www.oregonstateparks.org, reservations 800/452-5687 or reserveamerica.com, $20 tents, $25 RVs, $38 yurts) is for you.

Food

Most of the cabins along Lake Wallowa have kitchens, and Joseph's restaurants are just a short drive away, so even though this is a major tourist destination, there's not a vast selection of restaurants. Nonetheless, there are a couple notable places to eat. **Vali's Alpine Delicatessen** (59811 Wallowa Lake Hwy., 541/432-5691, www.valisrestaurant.com, seatings at 5 and 7pm Wed.-Sun. Memorial Day-Labor Day, 5 and 7pm Sat.-Sun. Apr.-Memorial Day, $12-17, no credit cards, reservations required) features a different fixed dinner menu each day with German and Hungarian specialties such as cabbage rolls or schnitzel (only one entrée is served each night). Stop by on Saturday and Sunday mornings (9am-11am) when freshly made doughnuts are on offer.

The dining room at the 1920s-era **◖ Wallowa Lake Lodge** (60060 Wallowa Lake Hwy., 541/432-9821, www.wallowalake.com, 8am-11:30am daily and 5pm-6pm Fri.-Tues. summer, $11-26) is beautifully preserved, though the food—steaks, pasta, fresh seafood—is up to date. Early and late in the season, restaurant hours are reduced, so call to check.

THE WALLOWA MOUNTAINS HIGH COUNTRY

The Wallowa Mountains are some of Oregon's most rugged, beautiful, and least visited: 715 square miles of this craggy backcountry are preserved as the **Eagle Cap Wilderness Area.** Glacier-torn valleys, high mountain lakes, and marble peaks are some of the rewards that long-distance hikers find on overnight treks. A few hiking trails offer recreation to day hikers. In addition, there's good fishing in streams and lakes, and in winter the heavy snowfalls attract both downhill and Nordic skiers. Forest Service campgrounds serve as bases for Wallowa Mountains exploration. For more information on recreation and camping in the Wallowas, contact the **Wallowa-Whitman National Forest** (201 E. 2nd St., Joseph, 541/426-5546, www.fs.usda.gov).

Hiking and Camping

Most Eagle Cap Wilderness Area trails are long and steep, and most alpine lakes are at least five miles from a trailhead, so opportunities for easy day hikes into the wilderness are limited. Camping is the best way to enjoy the area. Before heading out, pick up the Eagle Cap map from a Forest Service office or at local sporting goods stores. Higher elevations are usually free of snow by early July, but streams may be running high and fast until later in July.

Camping out in the Wallowa Valley and the Eagle Cap Wilderness can be as easy as pulling off Route 82 just 15 miles east of Elgin and pitching your tent at **Minam State Recreation Area** (541/551-6949, www.oregonstateparks. org, $8, no reservations) or as rigorous as using one of the following three campsites as a jumping-off point for backpacking into the high country.

Boundary Campsite (free, no water) is 5 miles south of Wallowa on County Route 515, then 2 miles south on Forest Service Road

Snow lingers in the Wallowa Mountains well into July.

163. A trailhead provides access to the dazzling grandeur of the Eagle Cap basin.

The next campsite and trailhead is **Two Pan** ($6, no water), one of the most popular gateways into the Wallowas. To get here, head south from Lostine on County Route 551 for 7 miles and down Forest Service Road 5202 for 11 miles. This is a rough and rocky washboard grade, so take your time. Firewood and vault toilets are available. Trails leave Two Pan for the Lostine River Valley and the glacial lakes at the base of Eagle Cap.

The third campsite is **Hurricane Creek** ($6, no water), three miles southwest of Joseph on Forest Service Road 8205. The Hurricane Creek trailhead leads to a hike along the east slope of the Hurricane Divide past Sacajawea Peak and the Matterhorn to the glacial lakes basin. An ambitious trek would start at Two Pan and end at Hurricane Creek. The lake basin area south of Joseph can get crowded, especially on weekends July-August.

If your budget allows for a guided adventure into the Wallowa wilds, here are two excellent services. The **Eagle Cap Wilderness Pack Station** (59761 Wallowa Lake Hwy., Joseph, 541/432-4145, www.eaglecapwildernesspackstation.com) runs many day rides to lakes and streams in the Eagle Cap high country. However, the primary focus of this operation is outfitting expeditions into the Eagle Cap backcountry. For $200 per person per day, the outfitters will furnish your complete camp, including riding horses, pack stock, a guide, wranglers, a cook, and food. You furnish only your personal gear, such as clothing, a sleeping bag, a sleeping pad, and all other personal necessities. These outfitters also offer "drop" trips, where horses and mules carry people and supplies to a lake, then leave and return at an appointed time to pack you and your gear out. This service costs $300 per person each way.

Wallowa Llamas (36678 Allstead Ln., Halfway, 541/742-2961, www.wallowallamas.com) offers a unique way to venture into the wilderness. One surefooted, even-tempered llama will carry 20 pounds of your gear; you carry the rest. The outfit offers three- to seven-day trips to Hells Canyon, Imnaha Falls, Eagle Meadows, and across the rugged Wallowas. The expeditions are designed for those with some backpacking experience or anyone in reasonably good shape. The outfitters provide tents, eating utensils, and all meals—and of course the llamas. All you'll need is a sleeping bag and pad and personal effects. Four-day excursions begin at $695.

Skiing

The recreational delights of the Wallowas are not reserved for summer only; the skiing in this alpine wonderland can be excellent. **Ferguson Ridge Ski Area** (541/426-3493, www.skifergi.com, 10am-4pm weekends and holidays, $15 adults, $10 children) is a small and laid-back downhill facility with a rope tow and T-bar that climb from a 5,100-foot base to 5,800-foot-high Ferguson Ridge. The light eastern Oregon powder, when there's enough of it, makes for good skiing. Make sure to bring a full water bottle; no water is available at the ski area. To get there, drive east from Joseph about five miles on the Wallowa Loop Highway, then follow signs south on Tucker Down Road.

For cross-country skiers, the **Sacajawea Park Cross-Country Ski Trail** challenges the ambitious. Take Hurricane Creek Road west from Joseph to the Hurricane Creek trailhead. This cross-country ski route will take you up into a basin on the northeast side of Sacajawea Peak. After two steep miles through the forest, the trail opens up into a clear area with a view of the surrounding glacial peaks.

Another popular spot is **Salt Creek Summit,** about 20 miles southeast of Joseph on Wallowa Loop Highway. The facility has five miles of marked but ungroomed ski trails and a plowed snow park.

Backcountry ski mountaineering is the focus of **Wallowa Alpine Huts** (541/398-1980, www.wallowahuts.com), which offers four- or five-day trips to several backcountry huts, including one at 7,500-foot McCully Basin within the Eagle Cap Wilderness. Ski seven miles in to a yurt base camp and spend the days exploring the high country on backcountry snowboards, telemarking skis, or randonée skis, then return to cooked meals, warm yurts, and even a sauna. Four-day trips begin at $700 and include all backcountry meals, accommodations, bedding, and guides.

Hells Canyon

⟨ HELLS CANYON NATIONAL RECREATION AREA

In 1975, Congress established the **Hells Canyon National Recreation Area** (Oxbow, OR 97828, 541/785-3395, www.fs.usda.gov), which straddles a 71-mile portion of the Snake River. The river canyon itself is preserved in the 215,223-acre Hells Canyon Wilderness Area. Most of the terrain is made up of precipitous rock walls and steep, slot-like side valleys, which, along with the wilderness designation, means that just about the only way to experience this epic landscape is on foot, horseback, or—most accessibly—by boat.

The mighty Hells Canyon is the deepest river gorge in North America. It's also one of the wildest and remotest pieces of real estate in the Lower 48. For a distance of 106 miles no bridge crosses the river, and few paved roads come even near the canyon. Between Hells Canyon Dam and Lewiston, Idaho, the Snake drops 1,300 feet in elevation in just 70 miles (in comparison, the Mississippi has an elevation change of 840 feet between Minneapolis and the Gulf of Mexico). At its deepest point, the gorge walls rise nearly 8,000 feet, deep enough to hold 47 Niagara Falls stacked atop each other.

This isolation helps to preserve some the area's greatly varied plant and animal life. From Idaho's Seven Devils Wilderness to the Snake River in Hells Canyon and back up to Oregon's Wallowa Mountains, you'll find areas that replicate most of North America's ecological zones. Cheatgrass, primroses, sunflowers, and prickly pear cactus are included in the canyon's varied botany. Bears, elk, mule deer, bighorn sheep, eagles, otters, and chukar partridges are frequently seen here. Several outfitters can steer you to the canyon's pictographs, which some sources date to 10,000 years in age. In addition to Chief Joseph and his Nez Perce nation, miners and pioneers also occupied Hells Canyon, as many turn-of-the-20th-century log cabins and shacks attest.

Hells Canyon by Vehicle

There are several ways to get to Hells Canyon from Oregon. From Baker City take Route 86 for 50 miles east to **Halfway.** Stop here to stock up on groceries and gas, continue on Route 86 another 16 miles to Oxbow Dam, and then downstream (north) 20 miles on the Idaho side of the Snake River to **Hells Canyon Dam.** A visitors center is adjacent to where rafts put in on the Snake River at the beginning of the river's Wild and Scenic stretch. This site affords a spectacular view of the canyon. Another approach is via Route 82 through the Wallowa Valley to Enterprise, Joseph, and Imnaha. From Imnaha, one of the most isolated towns in the country, take a rough, albeit recently improved, road for 24 miles to **Hat Point Lookout.** The first five miles of ascent is not for the faint of heart—the guardrail-free dirt road is vertigo-inducing. However, once on the ridgetop, the road edges to Hat Point and a view into Hells Canyon and the Snake River, a dizzying 7,000 feet below.

An altogether simpler way to glimpse the canyon is from the **Wallowa Mountain Loop Road** (a.k.a. Forest Rd. 39), which runs between Joseph and Halfway. The **Hells Canyon Lookout,** the only paved viewpoint into Hells Canyon, is 31 miles north of Halfway. The vista looks into the canyon (although there is no glimpse of the river) with interpretive displays, picnic tables, and toilets.

Hiking

More than 900 miles of trails await hikers and backpackers in the Hells Canyon National Recreation Area, and hiking is just about the only way to get to some of the canyon's remoter areas. However, it's not a hiking destination for novices. Before lacing up your hiking boots, consider that summer temperatures soar above 100°F, rattlesnakes abound, and potable water can be hard to find. Ticks and poison oak can be problems here too. Black widow and brown recluse spiders can constitute the biggest danger, however. Major trails are maintained, but others are difficult to follow. It's a good idea to talk to rangers before setting out, as this is an extremely remote and challenging wilderness. You'll also want a recent map and a trail guide.

There are long-distance riverside trails on both the Oregon and Idaho shores of the Snake River, but reaching them is a challenge. The rugged cliffs along the Hells Canyon Dam are too steep for hiking trails, although a short mile-long trail from the jet-boat launch area

© BILL MCRAE

Hells Canyon

NORTHEASTERN OREGON'S SCENIC BYWAYS

Northeastern Oregon is road-trip country, and several routes in this region are federally designated as scenic byways.

The **Wallowa Mountain Loop Road** is a scenic 54-mile drive through Hells Canyon Country. The route begins with the Joseph-Imnaha Highway, which winds past farms and canyons. Turn south on Wallowa Mountain Loop Road to the Imnaha River, then ascend into alpine forests along Dry Creek Road to Halfway. You'll come out on the south flank of the Wallowas where *Paint Your Wagon* was filmed in the 1960s and Disney's *Homeward Bound* was shot in the early 1990s. Turn east for a shoreline view of the Snake River and Hells Canyon. Closed in winter.

Explore the high country behind Sumpter by driving the **Elkhorn Drive National Scenic Byway,** which takes you northwest from Sumpter through the gold-mining territory to Granite, across the north fork of the John Day, past Anthony Lake, and on to Baker City. Because much of this road is above 5,000 feet in elevation, the loop is open only a few months of the year. The portion south of Anthony Lakes

and north of Granite is closed by snow from early November through June or early July. The Elkhorn Byway climbs higher than any other paved road in Oregon (7,392 feet), after passing North Fork John Day Campground and the junction with Blue Mountains Scenic Byway. The craggy granite peaks of the northern Elkhorns—several higher than 8,000 feet—are near this area.

The longest of eastern Oregon's scenic byways is the **Journey through Time Scenic Byway.** Departing from (or ending at) Biggs, on I-5 and the Columbia Gorge, this highly scenic route takes the back roads through the canyon-cut Columbia Plateau, extending to Baker City. The highlight of this tour is the John Day River canyon, where millennia of erosion have sculpted a dramatic gorge through layers of volcanic formations, in the process unveiling the fossil remains of ancient life, which can be seen at the various units of the John Day Fossil Beds National Monument. This route makes an excellent bike ride, especially during the spring and early fall; it's also popular with motorcyclists.

does pick its way down the Oregon side before ending precipitously. For longer hikes, you will need to start from trailheads along the ridges and hike down to the river. Hat Point is a good place to drop onto the **Oregon Snake River Trail,** on the river's western edge. The most comfortable long-distance trail on the Oregon side is the **Western Rim Trail.** There are comparatively few steep ups and downs, and daytime temperatures are much less oppressive than within the canyon. There is also plenty of shade among the rim's evergreen forests. On the other hand, the rim route has fewer water sources, so camping choices are limited. To reach the trailhead of this 37-mile trail, from Joseph, take a left onto Route 350 to Imnaha; from Imnaha follow Forest Road 4240 to Warnock Corral Trailhead. Mountain bikes are permitted on this trail.

Boating

Outfitters arrange Snake River float trips on rafts, dories, or kayaks, providing high adventure as the river bounces though 34 named rapids rated Class II-IV in the most commonly floated part of the canyon, the two- to three-day passage between Hells Canyon Dam and Pittsburgh Landing in Idaho (longer trips are available). For travelers with less time, turbine-powered jet-boat tours are also available—a less idyllic but equally exciting way to see the canyon in as little as a day. These turbine-powered flat-bottomed boats are able to maneuver shallow water and rapids, though they are also very noisy and annoying if you aren't among the passengers. The recreation area website provides a list of outfitters licensed to guide trips on the Snake River. Be sure to check the offerings available, as they are abundant. The brief selection below is just a taste of what's available and is intended to provide a guideline to prices and trips.

From the landing just below Hells Canyon Dam, **Hells Canyon Adventures** (541/785-3352 or 800/422-3568, www.hellscanyonadventures.com) offers a variety of jet-boat tours daily (Apr.-Sept.). The briefest and least expensive excursion is a two-hour afternoon jet-boat trip into the deepest part of the canyon that costs $80 adults, $55 children. A six-hour $172 tour ($85 children) leaves at 10am, runs all the principal rapids of the canyon, and includes lunch and a stop at the Kirkwood Ranch Museum, a frontier ranch at the base of the canyon. Hells Canyon Adventures offers other tours, including float trips and fishing charters. Reservations are required.

A local outfitter that specializes in white-water raft trips is **Winding Waters** (877/426-7238, www.windingwatersrafting.com). Trips of 3-6 days are offered May-October and include guide services, tent accommodations, transport to and from Joseph, a night's lodging in Joseph, and food. A three-day trip starts at $985 adults, $788 children.

If you plan to shoot the Class III and IV rapids of the Snake River on your own, you'll need a permit from the **Hells Canyon National Recreation Area office** in Oxbow (541/785-3395).

Fishing for trout, catfish, smallmouth bass, and, if you're lucky, 100-year-old sturgeon can add to the pleasure of a raft trip. **Canyon Outfitters** (P.O. Box 893, Halfway, OR 97834, 541/742-7238, www.canyonoutfitters.com) offers summer white-water float trips (4 days, $1,250) with ample time for fishing.

Camping
Of the 12 campgrounds on the Oregon side of the national recreation area, we recommend the following three. **Lake Fork Campground,** 18 miles northeast of Halfway on Forest Service Road 39, has 10 sites with drinking water, and the fishing is good at nearby Fish Lake. **Indian Crossing,** 45 miles southeast of Joseph on Forest Service Road 3960, has drinking water as well as a trailhead for backpacking into the Eagle Cap Wilderness. On the northern end of the recreational area, **Buckhorn Springs** is 43 miles northeast of Enterprise and features a great view, springwater, and berry-picking in season.

Accommodations and Food
The town of Halfway (pop. 337), 17 miles from the Oxbow Dam on the Snake River, is a popular way station for Hells Canyon-bound travelers. The ☀ **Pine Valley Lodge** (163 N. Main St., Halfway, 541/742-2027, www.pvlodge.com, $110-150) is an unexpected pleasure in the rugged Hells Canyon country. You can't get much more Old West-meets-Western chic than this! Nearly a dozen guest rooms have been created in vintage log and wood structures in downtown Halfway, and each is filled with amazing cowboy decor that's part history and part whimsy. Staying here is like settling into a really charming upscale bunkhouse. Rates include a deluxe continental breakfast.

Reasonably priced standard guest rooms can be had at the **Halfway Motel** (170 S. Main St., Halfway, 541/742-5722, www.halfwaymotel-rvpark.com, $60). Some have kitchenettes; all are close to gas, food, and shops.

Twelve miles north of Halfway, at the southern edge of the Eagle Cap Wilderness Area, the **Cornucopia Lodge** (Queen Mine Rd., 541/742-4500 or 800/742-6115, www.cornucopialodge.com, $110-170) is a great place from which to launch or conclude a backpacking trip, or just relax. The cabins and lodge are in a spectacularly scenic setting, and guests can head out on horseback rides, hikes, or fishing trips. The lodge serves meals at an extra charge ($35/day for all meals); no cooking is allowed in the cabins.

Restaurants are few and far between in this country, and it would be prudent to pack a few picnic items. Halfway has a few cafés that will cover your basic feeding needs. There's also a restaurant down at Oxbow, near the Snake River on Route 86.

Baker City

Baker City, set in a valley between the Wallowas and the Blue Mountains, is the quintessential Western ranch town, with a handsome downtown area filled with classic stone and redbrick storefronts. Ranchers hereabouts still drive their herds down the highways, and folks wave howdy to passersby. Baker City (pop. 9,700) is a friendly place that has held on to its pioneer spirit. There's lots of history here—highlighted by the nation's foremost Oregon Trail interpretive center—and with its abundant and high-quality facilities, Baker City is a good jumping-off spot for Hells Canyon, the deepest gorge in North America.

History

Baker City was named after Colonel Edward Baker, Oregon's first senator, a Union general in the Civil War, and a onetime law partner of Abraham Lincoln. In 1861 it became the hub

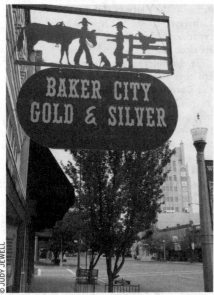

© JUDY JEWELL

Baker City is a Western town.

of the eastern Oregon gold rush, and its population swelled to 6,600, making it bigger than Boise. Baker City got its charter in 1874 and soon became known as the "Queen City" for all roads led to this commercial center. Stop by the U.S. National Bank and check out the 80.4-ounce **Armstrong gold nugget,** found in 1913. It's a remnant from the days when this wealthy raucous frontier boomtown was the biggest and most important in the region. It boasted the finest hotel between Salt Lake City and Portland—now reopened and polished to a fine patina—and even had a high school, the second in the Pacific Northwest.

West of town along Route 7 and its offshoots leading into the Elkhorn and Blue Mountains, ghost towns like Granite, McEwen, and Sumpter are remnants of the gold rush days of the 1860s. The route, which follows the twisty contours of the Powder River, is particularly pretty when the deciduous trees take on fall hues.

SIGHTS
◖ National Historic Oregon Trail Interpretive Center

Six miles east of Baker City is the 23,000-square-foot **National Historic Oregon Trail Interpretive Center** (22267 Hwy. 86, 541/523-1843, www.blm.gov/or/oregontrail, 9am-6pm daily Apr.-Oct., 9am-4pm daily Nov.-Mar., $8 adults, $4.50 seniors, children ages 15 and under free, discounts in winter). The museum is perched atop Flagstaff Hill overlooking a picturesque section of the famous frontier thoroughfare. The exhibit halls are arranged to simulate the route and experiences of pioneers on the 547-mile section of the trail within Oregon's borders. While there are impressive artifacts as well as thought-provoking historic photos and video presentations, don't think of this as another passive viewing experience. The life-size dioramas of Oregon Trail scenes, accompanied by taped renditions of immigrant voices and wagon wheels, make you feel like part of the great migration.

Theatrical entertainment, living-history exhibits, paintings, and aptly chosen pioneer diary entries recount the crossing of the Blue Mountains and the Cascades, or rafting down the Columbia into the Willamette Valley. The museum's interpretive loop articulates the immigrant's state of mind—including awe giving way to boredom across the Oregon prairie, emotional duress on a perilous river crossing, or relief while adjusting to settlement at journey's end. Attention is also given to the pioneers' effect on Native American lands and cultures.

Outside the museum, your historical reverie is sustained by living-history exhibits and the chance to stand in the actual ruts left behind by pioneer wagons at **Virtue Flat,** a two-mile walk from the center. Surrounded by the 10,000-foot Elkhorn Mountains to the west, the Blues to the south, and the craggy Eagle Cap to the northeast, the "land at Eden's gate" becomes more than just another florid phrase from a pioneer diary.

Prior to departing the Oregon Trail Interpretive Center, check out the raised relief map of northeastern Oregon. Besides getting the lay of the land, you can call up information on area attractions by pushing a button.

Baker Heritage Museum

Housed in a showcase natatorium built in 1920, the **Baker Heritage Museum** (2490 Grove St., 541/523-9308, www.bakerheritage-museum.com, 9am-4pm daily mid-Mar.-Oct., $6 adults, $5 seniors and children ages 13-17) shows off an extensive collection of furniture, vehicles, and machinery from Baker City's frontier days as well as exhibits depicting the great migration. A large collection of rocks, minerals, and stones—including a display of fluorescent rocks—will be of interest to others besides rock hounds. The museum is across from Geiser Pollman Park, which has picnic tables and playgrounds.

Eastern Oregon Museum

Ten miles northwest of Baker City in the town of Haines is the **Eastern Oregon Museum** (610 3rd St., Haines, 541/856-3233, 9:30am-4:30pm Thurs.-Sun. mid-May-mid-Sept., $2). One of the largest historical museums in this part of the state, it boasts over 10,000 artifacts. It has an outstanding collection of vintage farming equipment, mining tools and paraphernalia, and pioneer relics. The museum also has an intriguing collection of antique toys and dolls, and the grounds include a one-room school and an 1880s train depot.

SPORTS AND RECREATION
Skiing

Anthony Lakes Ski Area (541/856-3277, www.anthonylakes.com, Thurs.-Sun. and holidays, $35 adults, $29 students ages 13-18, $25 seniors 70 and older, $21 children ages 7-12, free for children ages 6 and under) is 18 miles west of Haines on the Elkhorn Scenic Byway. This ski resort offers a triple chairlift, a Nordic trail system, a day lodge, a ski shop, and ski lessons. This is Oregon's first and highest (7,000 feet) ski area. Come to this remote spot for its pristine dry powder and a family-oriented environment. The 1,100 acres of slopes offer plenty of challenge—80 percent of the runs are intermediate or expert.

During the summer, the area around Anthony Lakes is a beautiful place to hike; several trailheads sprout from the road near the ski resort.

ACCOMMODATIONS

Baker City's preeminent lodging choice is the **◖Geiser Grand Hotel** (1996 Main St., 541/523-1899 or 888/434-7374, www.geisergrand.com, $79-169), a showplace of period grandeur and refinement. Built in 1889 as the finest hotel between Portland and Salt Lake City, the Geiser Grand was totally updated and refurbished in the 1990s and again sparkles with old-fashioned charm and modern comforts. Amid Viennese chandeliers, mahogany columns, and a stained-glass skylight 40 feet above the dining room, you'll feel like you've traveled back in time to a more gracious time. For a hotel of this vintage, the standard guest rooms are large, but for a real treat you can step up to a suite—particularly one on a corner or perhaps in the cupola—and have lots of room and 10-foot-high windows on two sides to drink in the Blue Mountain views. Add fine meals at the hotel's Geiser Grill and several good restaurants within a couple of blocks, and you might want to extend your stay.

Within walking distance of downtown is a good value motel, the **Oregon Trail Motel** (211 Bridge St., 541/523-5844 or 888/523-5882, www.oregontrailmotelandrestaurant.com, $45-55). Nothing fancy, but it's a clean and pleasant place to spend the night. The adjoining restaurant is a great spot for breakfast. Just across the street, rooms at the friendly but basic **Bridge Street Inn** (134 Bridge St., 541/523-6571, $43-53) are about the same price.

The **Best Western Sunridge Inn** (1 Sunridge Ln., 541/523-6444, www.bestwesternoregon.com, $71-87) is a large motel complex with the feel of a small resort. Five motel blocks surround a nicely landscaped central garden, pool, and fitness area, which is also linked to the motel's two restaurants. Guest rooms have private patios, coffeemakers, and high-speed Internet access. The disadvantage of the Best Western is that it is near the interstate exchange, over a mile from downtown. Also out near the interstate is the **Always Welcome Inn** (175 Campbell St., 541/523-3431, www.alwayswelcomeinn.com, $78), a newer motel that offers clean comfortable rooms, an indoor pool, and—to set it apart from other interstate motels—a fossil bed out back.

Camping

The area's best camping is up in the Elkhorn Range near Anthony Lakes. **Anthony Lakes Campground** (541/523-6391, www.fs.usda.gov, $10, water, no reservations) is right at the base of the Anthony Lakes Ski Area, with campsites tucked among huge boulders a short walk from the lake. About 1 mile farther east along Forest Road 73, find **Grande Ronde Lake Campground** ($5, water, no reservations), a pretty spot at the headwaters of the Grande Ronde River.

FOOD

A great addition to Baker City's Main Street is **Zephyr Deli and Bakery** (1917 Main St., 541/523-4601, 8am-5pm Thurs.-Sun., $5-7), a hip and sociable spot for a breakfast sandwich or a salad (with as many organically grown veggies as possible), or hanging out with a cup of coffee and chatting with the locals. The orange rolls, baked fresh every morning, are worth seeking out.

Just across the street, the **Corner Brick Bar and Grill** (1840 Main St., 541/523-6099, 11am-9pm Mon.-Thurs., 11am-10pm Fri.-Sat., $10-15) is a friendly little spot with huge portions of pasta, pizza, salads, and sandwiches.

Barley Brown's Brew Pub (2190 Main St., 541/523-4266, www.barleybrowns.com, 4pm-10pm Mon.-Sat. $8-19) serves some of eastern Oregon's best brews (no small feat when you're up against the likes of Terminal Gravity). Most of its beer is only available at the pub and the Barley Brown's taproom across the street (2200 Main St.), so make a pilgrimage for a pint and enjoy well-prepared food as well. The menu goes far beyond pub grub, including steak, seafood, barbecued ribs, and pasta.

Baker City's second brewpub, **Bull Ridge Brew Pub** (1934 Broadway, 541/523-5833, 11am-9pm Mon.-Thurs., 11am-10pm Fri.-Sat, noon-8pm Sun., $9-12), brewed its first batch of craft beer—Flagstaff Hill Pale Ale—in the summer of 2013, but by then it was already a popular restaurant, serving good sandwiches and salads in the midst of some striking taxidermy. Until brewing ramps up at Bull Ridge, their taps offer some fine beers from around the state.

Earth and Vine Gallery and Wine Bar (2001 Washington Ave., 541/523-1687, 11am-9pm Mon.-Thurs., 11am-10pm Fri., 8am-11pm Sat., 8am-8pm Sun., $8-15) is, as its name suggests, a combo gallery and light restaurant. It's a bright and airy place to enjoy a drink (beer is also available, including a couple of taps from Barley Brown's) and an appetizer or sandwich. Breakfasts are good, particularly if they have fresh strawberries and waffles (available seasonally).

The **Geiser Grill** in the Geiser Grand Hotel (1996 Main St., 541/523-1899, www.geisergrand.com, 11am-2pm and 4:30pm-9pm weekdays, 7am-9am Sat.-Sun., $4-19) is easily the classiest place to eat in Baker City, if not in all of eastern Oregon. The setting is splendid—a soaring stained-glass ceiling surmounts a wood-paneled dining room sparkling with linen, crystal, and candles. The food's pretty good too, though dinners are sometimes dwarfed by the atmosphere.

Ten miles north of Baker City is the beloved **Haines Steakhouse** (910 Front St., Haines, 541/856-3639, www.hainessteakhouse.com, 4:30pm-9pm Mon. and Wed.-Fri., 3:30pm-9pm Sat., 12:30pm-9pm Sun.,

$20-30), known for its tender prime rib and authentic Western atmosphere. Antiques and cowboy Americana decorate the restaurant, enhancing what may be described as first-rate chuckwagon fare.

INFORMATION

Contact the **Baker County Chamber and Visitor Center** (490 Campbell St., 541/523-5855, www.visitbaker.com) for more information.

The *Baker City Herald* (www.bakercityherald.com) publishes a good annual travel guide to the local area. It's available free at area museums and tourist facilities.

GETTING THERE

Greyhound buses serve Baker City on runs between Portland and Boise. There are two buses daily in each direction, and the terminal is at 515 Campbell Street (541/523-5011).

Sumpter and Vicinity

In the Elkhorn Mountains west of Baker City, Sumpter is a former gold-mining town, one of many small communities in this area that hovers between ghost town and tourist town status. The first settlers were five Southerners who found gold in Cracker Creek in 1862. They built a stone cabin and christened it Fort Sumter after the South Carolina garrison that was shelled in April 1861, signaling the start of the Civil War. In 1883 the U.S. Post Office rejected the name, so locals changed it by dropping the "Fort" and adding a *p*. The heyday of gold mining in the area was 1900-1905, when over 3,000 miners worked the hard-rock mines and dredged the Powder River. By 1905 most of the easily accessed gold was gone, but dredging continued until 1954. Today, Sumpter has about 150 year-round residents—a few of whom actually still run small gold mines—and the old storefronts are now antiques shops and art galleries. A few vintage watering holes still

provide food and drink to locals and travelers alike. Sumpter is 30 miles west of Baker City and 57 miles east of John Day.

SIGHTS
Sumpter Valley Dredge State Heritage Area

This state park-managed site, the **Sumpter Valley Dredge State Heritage Area** (541/894-2486 or 800/551-6949) preserves one of three gold dredges that scooped up and sifted gold-rich Powder River gravels. With a hull 125 feet long and 52 feet wide, this is the longest and most accessible gold dredge in the country, in its day capable of chewing up 225 cubic feet (8.33 cubic yards) per minute, or an average of 100 acres of riverbed per year. Sticking out from the dredge's hull is a massive boom bearing 72 one-ton buckets. The buckets, moving like the chain of a chain saw, would bore into the riverbank and carry the loose rock back into the dredge interior. Once inside, the rock passed through a series of steel cylinders that separated the material by size, sending the smaller components deeper into the dredge. Using water and sluices, the gold was separated from the sediment, which passed through the back of the dredge along with the gravel and larger rocks and was deposited as mine tailings. In its lifetime this dredge alone made $4.5 million when gold prices were a mere $35 per troy ounce. The dredge passed to Oregon state parks in 1995, which has restored it and in summer offers interpretive displays and tours. Access to the park is free, with trails leading out into wildlife viewing areas—the orderly piles of mine tailings along the Powder River have become an unlikely wetlands habitat.

Sumpter Valley Railroad

Another piece of local history is the **Sumpter Valley Railroad** (12259 Huckleberry Loop Rd., Baker City, 541/894-2268 or 866/894-2268, www.sumptervalleyrailroad.org, $12/17.50 adults one-way/round-trip, $10/15 seniors and military, $7/11 children ages 6-16, $30/50 family), a rebuilt narrow-gauge excursion train pulled by steam engines. The railway originally ran 1890-1961 between Baker City and Prairie City, transporting logs and ore in addition to passengers. Today, passengers ride the five miles between McEwen Station and Sumpter in two vintage observation cars; a restored 1890 caboose is also part of the train. Runs depart Sumpter station at noon and 3:15pm (Sat.-Sun. Memorial Day-last weekend in Sept.).

Whitney and Granite

The Sumpter area is rich in abandoned gold rush towns. While not an official tourist site, the ghost town of **Whitney,** 12 miles up Route 7 from the junction of U.S. 26 (about 15 miles east of Prairie City), has a story to tell to those who visit its ruins. Whitney was the terminus for stage lines to the mining and cattle towns of Unity, Bridgeport, and Malheur City. Now abandoned buildings are all that remain of this bustling community of the early 1900s.

An interpretive sign just off Route 7 explains the local history.

Back-road and ghost town connoisseurs will want to stop and take a gander at the remains of **Granite** (pop. 22), Oregon's smallest incorporated town. With its false-fronted buildings of unpainted and splintered boards, Granite is a true "ghost town." Hard as it is to believe, this place once had four saloons, a 50-room hotel, several smaller hotels, a boardinghouse, a church, and a wooden jail. Founded in 1862, its mining legacy sustained the town through the 1930s. The need for miners in World War II defense industries at that time compelled President Franklin D. Roosevelt to shut down the mines. Today, people are moving back despite the lack of modern conveniences (phone service didn't arrive in Granite until 2000). Community ties are maintained by regular visits to the Granite store, where miners, retirees, and other residents meet up to keep the ghost alive.

EVENTS

On Memorial Day, Fourth of July, and Labor Day weekends, folks head to the fairgrounds for the **Sumpter Flea Market.** Collectibles, crafts, and food are arrayed in a beautiful mountain setting. This event is legendary among Oregon's bargain hunters.

ACCOMMODATIONS

The **Sumpter Stockade Motel** (129 E. Austin St., Sumpter, 541/894-2360, May-mid-Oct., $65-75) offers individually decorated rooms, including a suite with a full kitchen, in a newly built structure designed to resemble an Old West military fort complete with a pole stockade. Tent campers can set up on the lawn inside the stockade ($10 pp, $15 for 2), and there's a tiny bunkroom ($20 pp) used mainly by bicycle tourists, a surprising number of whom pass through town on cross-country tours. This is an unusual but comfy place to stay in this little town.

For more traditional guest rooms, the **Depot Inn** (179 S. Mill St., 541/894-2522 or

800/390-2522, $75) is a handsome log-built motel; rooms have fridges, microwaves, and wireless Internet.

Sumpter's original 1900 hospital is back in business as **Sumpter Bed and Breakfast** (344 NE Columbia St., 541/894-0048 or 800/287-5234, www.sumpterbb.net, $80), with six antique-filled guest rooms and a hearty breakfast that may, if you're lucky, include the inn's delectable huckleberry pancakes.

Ontario

Midway between Portland and Salt Lake City in Oregon's far east, Ontario is where "Oregon's day begins." (Indeed, it begins an hour earlier here—Ontario is on mountain time.) It's the biggest city in Malheur County, with a population of 11,000. Ontario ships over 5 percent of the nation's onions and provides a good portion of the sweet russet potatoes used for french fries by national fast-food chains. Other local crops include sugar beets, peppermint, grains, and ornamental flowers. This abundance derives from the fertile plains at the confluence of the Snake and Malheur Rivers.

History

Ontario, the town at the beginning of the Oregon section of the Oregon Trail, began as a cattle-shipping depot. The 1883 completion of the Oregon Short Line Railroad connected it to the Union Pacific and markets in the east. In 1939, reservoirs on the Snake River provided irrigation water to the otherwise parched valley, turning it into a rich agricultural region.

In 1942, President Franklin D. Roosevelt issued Executive Order 9066, which ordered the removal of 120,000 Japanese Americans from the West Coast to 10 inland concentration camps located in isolated areas of seven states. About 5,000 Japanese Americans were moved to an internment camp near Ontario. Under the leadership of Ontario mayor Elmo Smith, the eastern Oregon farming community invited internees to help fill service and farm jobs. By the end of the war, 1,000 Japanese Americans had settled in the Ontario area, giving Malheur County the largest percentage of Japanese Americans in Oregon. As a result,

Japanese surnames grace many a ranch or farmstead in eastern Oregon. Some of the migrant workers in an influx from Latin America who came to work the crops in the 1950s and 1960s also stayed to start new lives, adding yet another ethnic flavor to a cultural stew that already contained Basques and the Paiute people.

SIGHTS
Four Rivers Cultural Center
Ontario's rich mix of cultures is celebrated at the **Four Rivers Cultural Center** (676 SW 5th Ave., 541/889-8191, www.4rcc.com, 10am-5pm Mon.-Sat., $4 adults, $3 seniors and children) at Treasure Valley Community College. The four rivers—the Snake, Malheur, Owyhee, and Payette—represent the flow of people of different ethnicities into this part of Oregon: Native Americans, Basques, Hispanics, other Europeans, and Japanese. The complex includes a museum, a theater, a convention center, and a formal Japanese garden.

Snake River Crossing
Remnants of the Oregon Trail still cross this remote corner of Oregon. Museums, historic markers, and wagon-rut memorials stud the area. South of Ontario, between Nyssa and Adrian along Route 201, a roadside monument commemorates the trail's **Snake River Crossing** into Oregon. Directly across the Snake from this point was Fort Boise, a Hudson's Bay Company fur-trading fort that doubled as a landmark and trade center for often-desperate pioneers. The fort was swept away by floods years ago; the site is now part of a wildlife refuge.

Follow the Oregon Trail from Nyssa to Vale to find several other historic sites. Take Enterprise Avenue just west of Nyssa and turn right on Lyttle Boulevard; from here the paved road closely follows the tracks of the Oregon Trail to Vale.

Keeney Pass Oregon Trail Historic Site

The **Keeney Pass Oregon Trail Historic Site,** four miles south of Vale, has a display of the deep ruts cut into the earth by ironclad wagon wheels. This exhibit marks the most-used route of the wagon trains as they passed through the Snake River Valley on their way to Baker Valley to the north. From the top of this pass you can see the route of a whole day's journey on the trail to Oregon over 150 years ago. Ponder the fact that one pioneer in 10 died on this arduous transcontinental trek. In June and July, Indian paintbrush and penstemon add a dash of color to the sagebrush and rabbitbrush that surround the ruts in the trail.

Vale, the seat of Malheur County, is on the Malheur River at the spot where Oregon Trail wagon trains crossed it, 28 miles west of Ontario on U.S. 20/26. If you're intrigued by the drama of the pioneers, this little town offers an abundance of historical insight as well as evocative murals of historical scenes. On your visit to Vale, look north to **Malheur Butte** at mile marker 254. This long-extinct volcano was used as a lookout point by Native Americans watching for the wagon trains. At **Malheur Crossing,** on the east edge of Vale, the pioneers stopped to take advantage of natural hot water from underground thermal springs to bathe and do their laundry. On cool days, steam rises off the hot springs, which flow into the river between the two highway bridges. Another site of interest in Vale is the **Stone House,** one block east of the courthouse on Main Street. Built in 1872, it replaced a mud hut way station on the trail.

Farewell Bend

Twenty-two miles north of Ontario on I-84 is Farewell Bend, where travelers along the old Oregon Trail left the valley of the Snake River, which they had more or less followed from central Idaho, and climbed up into the desert uplands of eastern Oregon.

Before undertaking the strenuous journey through desert landscapes to the imposing Blue Mountains, Oregon Trail travelers usually rested at Farewell Bend, grazing livestock, gathering wood, and otherwise preparing themselves for the arduous trip ahead. Today, **Farewell Bend State Park** (www.oregonstateparks.org, $5 day use) commemorates this placid pioneer wayside with a picnic and play area, a boat launch, and a large campground (800/452-5687, $14-22).

FESTIVALS AND EVENTS

The **Vale Rodeo** is a four-day fete that takes place over the July 1-4 holiday. It's highlighted by the Suicide Race, an event held at nearby Vale Butte in which cowboys race their horses off a steep slope into an arena.

The **Obon Festival,** celebrating Ontario's Japanese heritage, is held in late June at Ontario's **Buddhist temple** (286 SE 4th St., 541/889-8562). Japanese folk dancing is the highlight of the festival.

RECREATION

Ontario-Ontario Golf Course (541/889-9022) is an 18-hole municipal course with a pro shop and a lounge, two miles west of Ontario.

ACCOMMODATIONS AND FOOD

There is a cluster of motels at I-84 Exit 376. If you're hot and tired of driving, the deluxe sheets, indoor pool, and fitness center at the **Holiday Inn Express** (212 SE 10th St., 541/889-7100, $123-153) might sound pretty good. This is the high end of what you'll find in Ontario. The **Best Western Plus Inn** (251 Goodfellow St., 541/889-2600, $99-105) is also one of the nicer places to stay in town; it has an indoor pool, an exercise room, a guest laundry, plus continental breakfast included. Some rooms have microwaves and refrigerators. The **Rodeway Inn** (615 E. Idaho Ave.,

541/889-9188, $62-76) is a good value and has a restaurant and an outdoor pool. If you want a simple, friendly, '50s-style courtyard motel well off the interstate, check out the **Ontario Inn** (1144 SW 4th Ave., 541/823-2556, www. ontarioinnmotel.com, $55-65). It's pet-friendly and even has a large fenced backyard where dogs can play.

Mexican restaurants abound in Ontario. Although **Tacos Mi Ranchito** (2520 S. Oregon St., 541/889-6130, 8am-8pm, $8) is just a simple order-at-the-counter taco joint, it's a very good one. Another good Mexican restaurant is **Casa Jaramillo** (157 SE 2nd St., 541/889-9258, 11:30am-10pm Tues.-Sat., 11:30am-10pm Sun., $6-15), an Ontario tradition since 1967. The chili verde has a local reputation, and don't forget to end your meal with deep-fried ice cream, topped with dulce de leche.

Ontario's Japanese heritage is represented at **Ogawa's Teriyaki Hut** (375 E. Idaho Ave., 541/889-2725, 11am-9pm Mon.-Fri., 4pm-9pm Sat., $3-12), which is one of the few places in this part of the state where you can get good sushi. Downtown, **Romio's** (375 S. Oregon St., 541/889-4888, 11am-2pm Mon., 11am-8pm Tues.-Wed., 11am-9pm Thurs.-Sat., noon-8pm Sun., $8-13) serves pasta, pizza, calzones, and sandwiches, including gluten-free options. Even though it's a franchised chain, it's a satisfying place for Italian American standards such as eggplant parmesan or fettuccine carbonara.

INFORMATION
Contact the **Malheur County Chamber of Commerce** (876 SW 4th Ave., 541/889-8012, www.ontariochamber.com) for more information on the area.

GETTING THERE
Greyhound buses pass through Ontario on twice-daily trips in each direction between Portland and Boise. The terminal is at 842 SE 1st Street (541/823-2567).

SOUTHEASTERN OREGON

Southeastern Oregon is a place where travelers shed their notions of what Oregon is supposed to be like. It's largely desertlike, but it has huge wetland areas. It's a little bit backcountry but also surprisingly sophisticated. It's out in the middle of nowhere, but it has a couple of the state's most charming hotels. And it does deliver on what many travelers seek: wildlife galore. Malheur National Wildlife Refuge is one of the Pacific Northwest's top birding areas, especially during the spring and fall migrations when it's easy to spot well over 50 species in a day. Hart Mountain has a refuge for pronghorn antelope, which can be seen across all of southeastern Oregon, and there are even wild mustangs living on Steens Mountain.

Although it's handy to come to southeastern Oregon prepared to camp, there are enough lodgings, mostly simple, to make your trip a little less rugged.

The area between La Pine and Lakeview has some of the most intriguing geological formations in the Pacific Northwest. Evidence of the cataclysmic forces that shaped the Columbia Plateau and the Great Basin are on display in this starkly beautiful part of the state. Fractures in the ground and wave patterns left by ancient lakes on the flanks of mountains are some of the fingerprints left by the hand of nature.

The sparsely populated sagebrush, rimrock, and grassy plains around Malheur National Wildlife Refuge and Steens Mountain are home to cattle ranches, a usually dry alkaline lake bed, and some hot springs. The tiny town of Crane has one of the few public boarding

© TIERRA CURRY

HIGHLIGHTS

◖ **Summer Lake:** Here, you're surrounded by geological curiosities such as Crack-in-the-Ground and Hole-in-the-Ground, birds, and minimally developed hot springs (page 603).

◖ **Hart Mountain National Antelope Refuge:** This refuge is home to pronghorn, along with much more wildlife, rock art, and hot springs (page 607).

◖ **Crystal Crane Hot Springs:** Here, you can actually swim in the big hot springs-fed pond (page 610).

◖ **Malheur National Wildlife Refuge:** This

wet spot in the desert supports a huge variety of bird life. Birders may get to witness the sage grouse courtship ritual (page 612).

◖ **Steens Mountain:** This fault-block mountain drops straight off to the Alvord Desert. Take your time, hike the trails, and bring binoculars—you may catch a glimpse of the local wild mustangs (page 617).

◖ **Alvord Desert:** It's hard to believe that this dry, blindingly white alkaline playa, or lake bed, is in the same state as the lush forests of western Oregon (page 619).

LOOK FOR ◖ TO FIND RECOMMENDED SIGHTS, ACTIVITIES, DINING, AND LODGING.

SOUTHEASTERN OREGON

schools in the United States. Students reside in dorms on campus because most come from ranches located many miles from town.

In the very southeast corner of the state, the area carved out by the Owyhee River is wild and beautiful, with only a handful of very small settlements.

If you're looking to get away from it all, you've found your piece of Oregon.

PLANNING YOUR TIME

If you're looking to explore the open spaces and wildlife of southeastern Oregon, be prepared

to take your time. Once you settle into the rhythm of driving, poking around, and pausing to look at a kingfisher or some pronghorn, you may find that the rest of the world seems very far away. You'll get the most out of this tour if you combine motel or hotel lodgings with camping. Likewise, you're not going to find much fine dining out here, so bring provisions for picnicking—the landscapes and vistas make for better dining ambience than a small greasy spoon.

Distances are grand out here in Oregon's Outback, as the locals have taken to calling it,

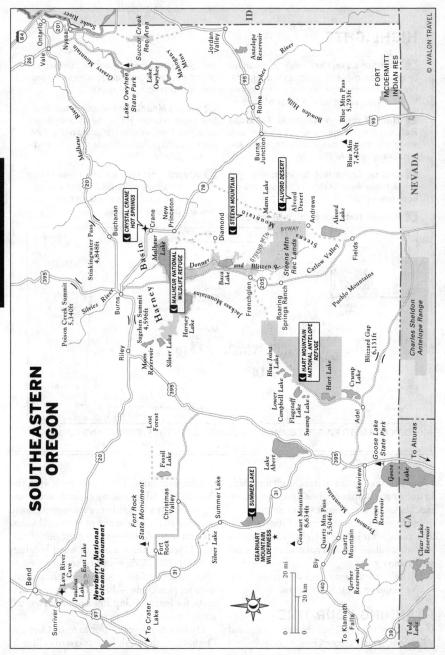

SOUTHEASTERN OREGON

© AVALON TRAVEL

20 mi

20 km

so it's a good idea to gas up frequently, especially if you're taking back roads.

This remote area of Oregon is famed for its wildlife—there are both a pronghorn and a waterfowl refuge—so be sure to bring binoculars and a wildlife guide. Southeast Oregon is also highly photogenic—landscapes are epic, geological wonders like **Fort Rock** and **Steens Mountain** are fantastic otherworldly photographic destinations, and it's worth it to plan your day to be there when the light is favorable for photography.

When you get out a map and start planning a trip across southeastern Oregon, you'll notice that there's a distinct absence of paved roads across the southern tier of the state, particularly from Plush to Frenchglen across the Hart Mountain National Antelope Refuge, just where it would be really handy to cut over to Steens Mountain. In fact, there is a gravel and hardpan dirt road through this desert landscape, and most vehicles will be able to make it across if driven slowly. If the weather is rainy or if a lot of snow has fallen, you may want to inquire locally before setting out, but the average driver in an average car has nothing to fear from this shortcut.

Lake County

One of Oregon's three largest counties, Lake County is home to just 7,900 people, or about one person per square mile. This land of open spaces and geological marvels spawns a hardy breed that clings to Old West traditions. Cowboys herd cattle on horseback, itinerant prospectors dig for color in the Quartz Mountains, and homesteaders tend to their farms in the remote outback. The county is called the Gem of Oregon partly because the region is the best place to find Oregon's official gemstone, the sunstone or "Plush diamond," a semiprecious stone found in the area north of Plush. The nickname also pays homage to the gemlike beauty of the county's wide vistas beneath skies of pastel blue.

Visitors can climb the ancient citadel of Fort Rock, camp along a high mountain stream in Fremont National Forest, or enjoy wildlife-viewing at Hart Mountain National Antelope Refuge. Because of the varied vertical topography and wind drafts, hang gliding has drawn a fair number of visitors to the cliffs around Lakeview.

The semiarid climate here is generally cool, with 250 days of sunshine per year. Summer temperatures stay in the mid-80s; winter temperatures drop to the low 30s. Precipitation averages about 16 inches per year. At higher elevations in Lake County, there are as few as 20 frost-free days per year. This area can be a harsh land with little tolerance for the foolish, so take sensible precautions like toting extra water and gas. Despite a low density of creature comforts, you'll enjoy exploring this high desert country loaded to its sandy brim with wonders found nowhere else.

History

The history of human occupation here and in the Pacific Northwest has been authenticated to as far back as 13,200 years through carbon-dating of grass sandals found in Fort Rock Cave. Early desert dwellers who roamed the Great Basin in search of game and food witnessed the eruption of Mount Mazama 6,000-8,000 years ago. Their descendants, the Northern Paiutes, were also hunter-gatherers. This Lake County indigenous group was known as the Groundhog Eaters, and they left more petroglyphs and pictographs in Lake County than in all the rest of Oregon and Washington.

The first Europeans to venture into the area were French Canadian trappers working for the Hudson's Bay Company in the early 1800s, and they were soon joined by U.S. mountain men. In 1825, Peter Skene Ogden, chief trader for the Hudson's Bay Company, made an "official" tour of the area when he sensed the threat of a U.S. incursion. John Frémont and a party guided by Kit Carson marched through here in 1843, naming Summer and Abert Lakes.

The journals kept during these expeditions noted broad valleys with grasses "belly-high to a horse." This information attracted a new cast of players: the cattle and sheep barons. With the passage of the Homestead Act in 1862, homesteaders moved in and started up more modest spreads. The white influx resulted in frequent tensions with the original occupants, often culminating in bloodshed on both sides. After the Bannock-Paiute uprising in 1878, the local Native Americans were herded up and forced onto a reservation.

In the growth spurt that followed, the town of Lakeview was chartered in 1889; it burned to the ground in 1900 and was rebuilt with brick and corrugated-iron roofs. Other hopeful hamlets with names like Arrow, Buffalo, and Loma Vista sprang up around the county, thanks to a reactivated Federal Homestead Act in 1909 that sanctioned 320 free acres per settler. Many of these tiny burgs dried up and blew away after the 1918-1920 drought. However, larger communities like Lakeview, Paisley, and Summer Lake held on. With the advent of refrigerated railroad cars, big ranchers prospered. Local farmers figured out how to irrigate and cultivate this ornery land, and those tough enough to survive eventually came to terms with life on the dry side.

ALONG ROUTE 31: LA PINE TO LAKEVIEW

A vehicle with a bit of clearance is indispensable in this region if you value your oil pan (a Subaru wagon made it to all the places described, but did suffer one flat tire along the way). Stock up on provisions in Bend or La Pine.

La Pine State Park

Located in Deschutes County, this huge state park (www.oregonstateparks.org) lies just a few miles off U.S. 97. Visitors come to the 2,333-acre park to picnic, camp, mountain bike, and fish the Fall River; it is so vast that visitors rarely see one another. The 15 miles of single-track mountain biking trails are mostly flat and perfect for beginners. Bikes can be rented at Bend and Sunriver cycle shops. The park's **campground** has 137 campsites ($22) and 10 cabins ($42 rustic, $81 deluxe) that can be reserved (800/452-5687).

Christmas Valley and Vicinity

Christmas Valley, a rather nondescript alfalfa-farming town, got its picturesque name by accident. Southeast of here, John C. Frémont spent Christmas at a lake during one of his mid-19th-century treks and called it Christmas Lake. A turn-of-the-20th-century mapmaker mistakenly affixed this name to a lake adjacent to the present-day town site, which also took on the cheery moniker. Although the expanse of sagebrush dotted with mobile homes is not immediately appealing, there are some fascinating areas nearby.

Fossil Lake is two miles east of town (head east on the Christmas Valley-Wagontire Road and turn north on Road 5-14d.). During wetter times thousands of years ago, this was a watering hole for ancient camels, enormous beavers, flamingos, mammoths, and miniature horses. It was once part of a much larger body of water in the Fort Rock basin that was perhaps 40 miles wide and 200 feet deep. The water and animals disappeared when the climate changed, but their fossilized remains are still unearthed by paleontologists on sanctioned digs. Be aware that it is illegal to remove *any* fossils from the beds without proper authorization.

Lost Forest, an unusual sight in this area, is 10 miles northeast of Christmas Valley on a very rough road. A 9,000-acre stand of ponderosa pines intermixed with the largest juniper trees in Oregon is all that is left of a grove that dates back thousands of years. Surprisingly, studies of tree rings show that this area has received on average only nine inches of rain per year for the last 600 years, half the amount normally needed to sustain the growth of ponderosa pines. A layer of pumice-like soil beneath the surface traps and retains enough moisture to allow the trees to draw water up through shorter-than-usual root systems. To reach Lost Forest, bring a detailed map (such as the Benchmark atlas for Oregon) and a high-clearance four-wheel drive vehicle before heading out. Head east on the Christmas Valley-Wagontire Road and turn north on Road 5-14c; follow signs to the Sand Dunes and Lost Forest.

This island of green is 40 miles from the nearest forest, accentuating the isolation and solitude of these stately sentinels. Many of the junipers here are over 1,000 years old. On hot summer days this place is a welcome source of shade. At any time of year the sound of the desert wind through the trees can stir contemplation. The final three-mile stretch of the approach to Lost Forest requires high vehicle clearance. To reach the area, drive 8 miles east of the Christmas Valley post office, go 8 miles north, and then 8 miles east. The forest borders the largest inland sand dunes in the state. During warm months, check yourself for ticks before leaving.

ACCOMMODATIONS AND FOOD

Although accommodations are generally more appealing at Summer Lake, Christmas Valley is not without options. The **Lakeside Terrace Motel** (1 Spruce Ln., 541/576-2309, $50) offers basic accommodations; it also serves breakfast every day and lunch Tuesday-Saturday.

◖ Summer Lake

The region surrounding **Summer Lake** sits at the interface of desert and mixed conifer forest. Abundant wildlife, geological wonders, Native American sites, and historic structures beckon further investigation. The 20-mile-long and 10-mile-wide lake is surrounded by the mountains of the Fremont National Forest and Winter Ridge.

The tiny community of Summer Lake lies on Route 32 about halfway between La Pine and Lakeview and is a good place to stop for a night or two while you explore the area. Just north of Summer Lake on Route 31, pull into **Picture Rock Turnout.** Take the trail 80 feet

SOUTHEASTERN OREGON

© BILL MCRAE

Summer Lake

CRACKS AND CAVES

Southeast of La Pine, off Route 31, lies a concentration of interesting geological features. One of the more unusual of these oddities is **Hole-in-the-Ground.** Although this 300-foot-deep indentation looks like a meteor crater, scientists believe molten lava came into contact with water here, causing a massive explosion that quarried out a 7.5-mile-diameter crater, or maar. Astronauts came here in 1966 to experience the moonlike terrain.

To find this unusual and awe-inducing sight from U.S. 97, drive 22 miles southeast on Route 31; turn left at the Hole-in-the-Ground sign. Drive 3.1 miles to the next sign. Turn right and go 1.1 miles to the final sign. Turn left and go 0.2 mile to the rim of the hole.

About 5 miles farther down Route 31 from the turnoff to Hole-in-the-Ground is **Fort Rock Cave** (a.k.a. Sandal Cave), a formation that was carved by wave action against what was once a basalt island in an immense lake. In 1938 anthropologist Luther Cressman discovered over 70 ancient sandals woven from sagebrush in the 50-foot-deep cave. Dated at almost 10,000 years old, the sandals are some of the oldest human artifacts found in the Pacific Northwest; they're now on display at the University of Oregon Natural History Museum in Eugene.

A mile east of the cave is **Fort Rock State Park** (800/551-6949, www.oregonstateparks.org), which towers 400 feet above the sagebrush plains. A series of underwater volcanic blasts created this very unusual formation when the entire area was a huge ice age lake stretching for hundreds of miles across central Oregon. Rising molten rock came into contact with mud and lake water, creating a series of massive explosions. As the ash and rock were thrown into the air, they came to rest in a perfect ring whose walls eventually reached hundreds of feet high. Fall and winter here offer wildlife-viewing par excellence; large herds of mule deer can be seen mid-November–mid-April, and pronghorn range over the alfalfa fields year-round. Many birds nest in the rocks, and golden eagles, hawks, kestrels, and peregrine falcons soar overhead. The state park offers trails and amenities for rock climbers and sightseers.

The nearby town of Fort Rock has an old-time flavor that has been accentuated by the recent restoration of homestead cabins in a pioneer village at the **Fort Rock Valley Historical Homestead Museum** (541/576-2251, www.fortrockoregon.com, 10am-4pm Fri.-Sun. mid-May-mid-Sept.).

An interesting journey down into the bowels of the earth is offered at **Derrick Cave,** 22 bumpy miles north of Fort Rock. This large lava tube is 0.5 mile long with rooms up to 40 feet wide and 60 feet high. During the Cuban missile crisis of 1962, the cave was turned into a fallout shelter. Metal doors were installed and provisions for 1,000 people were stockpiled. The supplies were later plundered by vandals, and the cave's civil defense status was eventually dropped.

If you drive eight dusty miles (the last mile a teeth-chattering ride) north of Christmas Valley on a rough Bureau of Land Management road that begins one mile east of town, you'll come to another break in terra firma that'll pique your imagination. **Crack-in-the-Ground** is about

to the southeast; behind the tallest rock is a pictograph. In the town of Summer Lake, the old **Harris School** is worth a photo. This classic one-room schoolhouse, complete with bell tower, is straight out of *Little House on the Prairie.*

The highway also passes through the **Summer Lake Wildlife Refuge** (541/943-3152, www.dfw.state.or.us, parking permit required), home to 170 species of migratory birds. Spring is the best time to see an amazing showing of waterfowl, including snow geese, avocets, black-necked stilts, and snowy plovers. An eight-mile wildlife-viewing trail around the lake is a recommended diversion at mile marker 70.

Anglers should head due west of Summer Lake to the **Thompson Valley Reservoir,** which has been known to yield large rainbow two miles long, 10-15 feet wide, and up to 70 feet deep. On hot days, it's nice and cool within this chasm. In fact, the crack is so deep that cold winter air sometimes gets trapped within and ice is preserved into summer. According to geologists, this dramatic fissure has been open for at least 1,000 years; the opening was once larger, but lava from nearby volcanoes filled it in to its present dimensions. A BLM picnic area is at one end of this curious landmark.

Five miles northwest of Crack-in-the-Ground (on rough BLM Rd. 6109C) is **Green Mountain Campground** and fire lookout, which sits high above the Derrick Cave site. This primitive campground (large enough for three cars, but without water or toilets) sits atop a small cinder cone overlooking hundreds of square miles of high desert, lava beds, and forest from 5,190 feet above sea level. In addition to Christmas Valley and Fort Rock Valley, you'll see snow-capped Diamond Peak 70 miles to the west and Wagontire Mountain 50 miles east.

© BILL MCRAE

Fort Rock

SOUTHEASTERN OREGON

trout. It's most easily reached by driving south from Silver Lake on County Road 4-12.

ACCOMMODATIONS AND FOOD

Rustic and interesting is the concept here. **Summer Lake Hot Springs** (41777 Hwy. 31, Paisley, 541/943-3931, www.summerlake-hotsprings.com, $20-175), six miles north of Paisley on the southern tip of Summer Lake, is a private operation where you can enjoy a dip in the 30-foot-long **pool** (9am-7pm daily, $10 ages 6 and over, children under 6 free, overnight guests free), housed in a rustic shed originally built in 1927 as a bathhouse for local cowboys. This hot spring resort has campsites ($20 tents, $45 RVs) on a bluff above the lake, a couple of small cabins ($85-100), and cottages ($130-175) for rent. This rustic resort is usually pretty laid-back, with an old-time Oregon hippie vibe; however, it's a popular stopover for people traveling to Burning Man, so during the week before Labor Day it can take on a bit of a party atmosphere.

The 1940s-era accommodations of the **Lodge at Summer Lake** (53460 Hwy. 31, 541/943-3993, www.thelodgeatsummerlake. com, $66-121) feature seven motel units ($66-72) and cabin and house rentals ($91-121) that sleep up to six. There is an on-site restaurant and a private bass pond.

Wildlife Refuge Campground (53447 Hwy. 31, 541/943-3152, www.dfw.state.or.us, free) is on the Ana River just north of Summer Lake on Route 31. Bird-watchers like to camp here and walk the dikes of Summer Lake looking for waterfowl.

The one local eatery that has gained a state-wide reputation is the 🍴**Cowboy Dinner Tree Steakhouse** (50836 E. Bay Rd., 541/576-2426, www.cowboydinnertree.net, 4pm-8:30pm Thurs.-Sun. June-Oct. or Fri.-Sun. Nov.-May, $27, reservations required), in a remote rustic shack 4.5 miles south of Silver Lake. You must specify when you make your reservations whether you'd like the nearly 30-ounce top sirloin steak or the chicken (and we do mean "the chicken"—an order is an entire chicken)—and no split orders are allowed. Sides include soup, salad, beans, a baked potato, dessert, and non-alcoholic beverages served in mason jars. This isn't just pretend rustic; as the sign says, "No Credit Cards—No Electricity—No Kidding." If you're too stuffed to drive after the meal, bunk down in a cabin ($120 for 2 people includes dinner).

Paisley

A few miles south of Summer Lake is the town of Paisley (pop. 244). The **Paisley Ranger Compound** features several structures built by the Civilian Conservation Corps during the Depression. Check out the pine dugout canoe carved by CCC workers for Forest Service personnel. Trout fishing on the Chewaucan River west of town and deer hunting also draw visitors. Paisley is home to the **ZX Ranch,** the

state's largest at over 1.3 million acres. The ranch property is 137 miles long and 64 miles wide.

Caves outside of Paisley have sheltered fossilized human excrement dating back about 14,400. These coprolites, as they're called, were found along with bones of horses and camels that went extinct in North America prior to 13,000 years ago.

The town's other main claim to fame is its annual **Mosquito Festival,** held the last full weekend of July.

ACCOMMODATIONS AND FOOD

If you need to stay in Paisley, the **Sage Rooms** (441 Main St., 541/943-3145, $80-85) offer basic but comfortable accommodations, and a couple of restaurants, including the historic **Pioneer Saloon** (327 Main St., 541/943-3289, 11am-9pm daily, $8-15) offer a taste of the West. Campers should head west out of downtown, up the Chewaucan River; **Marster Spring** campground ($6, drinking water) is about six miles from town on Forest Road 33.

Plan ahead to rent the historic and quite scenic **Bald Butte Lookout** cabin (541/943-3114 information, 877/444-6667 reservations, www.recreation.gov, mid-June-mid-Oct., $40, no drinking water), in the Fremont National Forest near the Gearhart Mountain Wilderness.

LAKEVIEW AND VICINITY

The "big city" in this part of the world is Lakeview (pop. 2,260), 142 miles south of La Pine on Route 31, east of Klamath Falls 96 miles on Route 140, and 139 miles from Burns on Route 395. Lakeview, the county hub, bills itself as the highest town in Oregon, at 4,800 feet in elevation.

Most of what's appealing about Lakeview lies outside the main downtown area. But if you're spending time in town, the **Schminck Memorial Museum** (128 S. E St., 541/947-3134, 11am-4pm Tues.-Sat., $3 adults, $2 seniors, children ages 12 and under free) has antiques and Native American artifacts assembled by the Oregon chapter of the Daughters of the American Revolution.

Look for hang gliders coming off 2,000-foot Black Cap Hill above the east side of Lakeview May-October. This town's fault blocks and winds have made Lakeview a center for hang-gliding enthusiasts.

You may hear stories about the local geyser, Old Perpetual, which used to erupt quite reliably in the front yard of **Hunter's Hot Springs Resort** (18088 Hwy. 395), on U.S. 395 north of town. In recent years, the geyser's been finicky, but it's worth checking to see if it's spouting.

Abert Rim

Fifteen miles north of Lakeview on U.S. 395 is the **Abert Rim,** the highest fault escarpment in the United States. The rim rises 2,000 feet above Lake Abert. This unusual body of water has no outlet and is rich in brine shrimp, which attract countless waterfowl and shorebirds. As at Summer Lake, fall is prime bird-watching season; expect thousands of plovers and other shorebirds. Due to its high alkalinity, it is hazardous to swim in the lake.

Below Abert Rim along the east shore of Lake Abert, the slope is covered with boulders, some of which sport petroglyphs. Several are located right off the highway near the geological marker. Forest Service roads lead through the North Warner Mountains to Bureau of Land Management trails up the back side of Abert Rim; obtain routing information on these obscure byways from the **Lakeview Ranger Station** (18049 Hwy. 395 N., 541/947-6300). Although reaching the rim requires an arduous journey down bumpy back roads and a steep hike up the mountain, the view from the top is spectacular. Watch for rattlesnakes in the rocks.

Gearhart Mountain Wilderness Area

About 40 miles west of Lakeview off Route 140 is the 22,000-acre roadless **Gearhart Mountain Wilderness Area.** Accessible only on foot or horseback, two major trails take adventurers into a challenging outdoor environment.

Gearhart Trail (Trail 100) incorporates 12 of the area's 16 miles of improved trails. This trail runs from **Lookout Rock** in the southeast corner of the wilderness, up over the mountain, down to **Blue Lake,** and to a trailhead on North Creek. The **Boulder Springs Trail** (Trail 100A) runs from the west side of the wilderness to a junction with the other trail 0.5 mile from the mountain summit. For maps and more information, contact the Forest Service ranger stations in Paisley, Silver Lake, or Lakeview (18049 Hwy. 395 N., 541/947-6300).

While you're in the neighborhood, you might want to visit the **Mitchell Monument** (Rte. 140 between the wilderness area and Bly), which commemorates a tragedy that occurred on May 5, 1945. Reverend Archie Mitchell and his wife were escorting five children on a picnic near Corral Creek when one of the kids discovered a bomb dropped by an incendiary balloon released by the Japanese navy. Unfortunately, the child triggered the bomb, and all but the good reverend were killed. This is the only recorded incident of World War II fatalities in the 48 contiguous states. Balloon bombs came down all over the Western states, but only Oregon recorded civilian deaths due to their detonation. The balloons were released by the Japanese in hopes of setting fire to Oregon forests.

◖ Hart Mountain National Antelope Refuge

North and east of Lakeview, **Hart Mountain National Antelope Refuge** stretches across a high plateau rising above Warner Lakes. From U.S. 395 just north of Lakeview, head east on Route 140 for 15 miles to the Plush Cutoff Road, go northeast 19 miles to Plush, and take the road up the steep west face of Hart Mountain to the refuge headquarters. The **U.S. Fish and Wildlife Service office** (18 S. G St., 541/947-3315) in Lakeview has information on the refuge.

In summer, hundreds of the agile tan-and-white pronghorn gather at sunset along the dirt road south of the refuge. The refuge is also home to bighorn sheep, mule deer, 213 species of birds, and many small mammals.

The **campground** (free, no water), a few

SOUTHEASTERN OREGON

© BILL MCRAE

pronghorn at Hart Mountain National Antelope Refuge

miles south of the refuge headquarters, features a hot spring surrounded by a cinder-block privacy wall; a dunk in the hot spring is highly recommended to loosen the stiffness from bouncing down the dirt roads to get here. Fill your water containers at the refuge headquarters.

The refuge is also a popular place for rock hounds searching for agates, fire opals, crystals, and sunstones. Check with the **chamber of commerce** (126 N. E St., Lakeview, 541/947-6040, www.lakecountychamber. org) or the ranger at Hart Mountain for more information.

Despite the name of the preserve, you won't find any antelope here; in fact, there are no wild antelope in North America, only pronghorn. Because these animals shed the outer sheaths of their horns each year, they differ from their Asian and African counterparts—true antelope—which have permanent horns. Male pronghorn have prongs, protrusions extending from their sheaths, to further distinguish them from antelope. The lingering misnomer was

bestowed on these Oregon animals by Lewis and Clark. At any rate, many scientists believe that pronghorn could be the world's fastest land mammals over a long distance, barely edging out the cheetah on distances exceeding 1,000 yards. It's said they can cruise at more than 35 mph, maintain 60 mph for half a mile, and reach 70 mph in short bursts.

Besides pronghorn, the refuge also protects a number of areas rich in prehistoric rock art. The easiest to visit is **Petroglyph Lake** (follow signs from the refuge road), where early Native Americans etched symbols and animal likenesses on a rocky cliff above a small water hole. Follow the path to the cliff's end for the best display.

Most state maps show an unpaved road between Plush and Route 205 near Frenchglen, designated a Bureau of Land Management Scenic Byway. It's about 50 miles across a frequently rough and dusty road that's equal parts gravel and hardpan, but most vehicles will make it across without problems as long as you drive slowly and carefully. Inquire locally if there has been a lot of snow or rain, as the road is not regularly maintained.

Fishing
With a name like Lake County, you'd be right to think that fishing holes are plentiful. Known for excellent trout fishing in the mountainous areas, the region is also gaining a reputation for bass, crappie, catfish, and other warm-water fishing. **Crump, Flagstaff, Anderson,** and **Campbell Lakes** in eastern Lake County provide the hottest action for crappie.

Friday Reservoir, between Adel and Plush, is stocked with Lahontan cutthroat trout, and **Rock Creek,** which flows out of the Hart Mountain National Antelope Refuge, has red-banded trout. Off U.S. 395 in western Lake County, **Goose Lake,** a few miles south of Lakeview, half in California and half in Oregon, is also home to the native red-banded trout, but it's hard to fish for this unique subspecies in the lake's shallow water. **Drews Reservoir,** 25 miles west of Lakeview on Route 140, offers excellent fishing for channel catfish—some as large as 10 pounds. In the northern section of the county, the **Chewaucan River,** which flows into Abert Lake, is heavily stocked with trout.

Rockhounding
Rockhounding is a popular hobby in Lake County. Best known for its abundance of sunstones (also known as aventurine or Plush diamonds), the area has jasper, agates, petrified wood, fire opals, wonder stones, thunder eggs, and obsidian as well. To get to the sunstone-hunting grounds, go east on Route 140 to the Plush junction and turn north. Another spot for rockhounding can be reached by taking Hogback Road just north of the upper section of the Abert Rim; the Hogback junction is about 50 miles north of Lakeview on U.S. 395. For more information visit the **Hi Desert Craft Rock Shop** (244 N. M St., 541/947-3237).

Skiing
Warner Canyon Ski Area (541/947-5001, warnercanyon.org, $32), seven miles east of Lakeview on Route 140, is a small ski area with 23 runs, one chairlift (but no lines), and over 25 miles of marked but ungroomed cross-country trails. Thanks to a mile-high base elevation and the dry southeastern Oregon climate, excellent dry powder conditions are common. The area has a day lodge near the base of the hill with a snack bar that serves breakfast and lunch. The season may start as early as mid-December and run through the end of March.

Accommodations and Food
In Lakeview, the **Fremont Inn** (524 N. G St., 541/947-2060, www.fremontinnlakecounty.com, $90-145) is a converted old folks' home with spacious, comfortable rooms. The **Best Western Skyline Motor Lodge** (414 N. G St., 541/947-2194, $106) has a pool and a hot tub as well as large guest rooms. Just north of Lakeview, **Hunter's Hot Springs Resort** (18088 Hwy. 395, 541/947-4242 or 800/858-8266, www.huntersresort.com) has basic motel rooms ($69-74) as well as an RV park and restaurant. The rooms aren't exactly luxurious, and the hot springs pool has seen better days, but it's a place to really soak in the local atmosphere.

Lakeview isn't known for its cuisine. However, **Mario's Dinner House** (9 N. F St., 541/947-3102, 5pm-9pm Tues.-Sat., $11-26) serves good steaks, salmon, prime rib, homemade breads, and other standards in a historic downtown building. It's a really popular place on the weekends, when folks drive in from surrounding areas.

Camping
Goose Lake State Park (541/947-3111 or 800/551-6949, www.oregonstateparks.org, mid-Apr.-early Oct., $20 campsite) is a big spread 15 miles south of Lakeview on U.S. 395. The campground has tent sites, RV hookups, and a boat launch on the shore of the huge lake. **Corral Creek Campground** (no water, free) is a good headquarters for an exploration of the Gearhart Mountain Wilderness, an area of high meadows, cliffs, and worn-down volcanoes. To get to the campsite, turn off Route 140 at

Quartz Mountain, 24 miles west of Lakeview, and drive north on Forest Service Road 3600.

Junipers Reservoir RV Resort (541/947-2050, www.junipersrv.com, May 1-Oct. 15 depending on weather, $30-35) is 10 miles west of Lakeview on Route 140. This private reservoir with campgrounds (including some tent sites) is situated on a working cattle ranch. Designated as one of six private wildlife-viewing areas in the state, this spread offers an excellent chance to view longhorn cattle, deer, eagles, ospreys, and coyotes.

Information
Stop by the **Lakeview Welcome Center** (126 N. E St., 541/947-6040) at the Lake County Chamber of Commerce for maps and brochures.

Steens Mountain Country

If you judge this part of southeastern Oregon by a drive-through on U.S. 20, you probably won't find it too memorable. But off the main thoroughfares are recreational retreats worthy of closer investigation. The Malheur National Wildlife Refuge is nationally recognized as one of the best bird-watching sites in the country, and Steens Mountain is famous for its stunning scenery.

BURNS
The town of Burns, named after the Scottish poet Robert Burns, was founded in 1884. By 1889 it had a population of 250, which has since grown about tenfold. A significant boost to the town's economy came in 1924 when a rail line reached Burns. Its sister city, **Hines,** was incorporated in 1930. Named after Chicago lumberman Edward Hines, this town of 1,400 residents is primarily a bedroom community for Burns.

Sagehen Hill Nature Trail
The **Sagehen Hill Nature Trail** is 16 miles west of Burns at the Sagehen rest stop on U.S. 20. This 0.5-mile nature trail has 11 stations on a route that takes you around Sagehen Hill through sagebrush, bitterbrush, and western juniper. Other plants found along the way include lupine, larkspur, owl clover, and yellowbell. The lucky early morning visitor in March and April might also catch the sage grouse courtship ritual. The male will display his plumage and make clucking noises to attract the attention of the females. The puffed-up necks and bobbing heads of these feathered philanderers are something to see. If these creatures are not visible, the views of Steens Mountain (elevation 9,733 feet) to the southeast will make the hike worthwhile.

Harney County Historical Museum
The **Harney County Historical Museum** (18 W. D St., 541/573-5618, 10am-4pm Tues.-Sat. Apr.-Sept., $5 adult, $8 couple, $3 seniors or children) started out as a brewery and then became a laundry and a wrecking yard. Descendants of local pioneer families have donated quilts, furniture, a complete kitchen, a wagon shed, and machinery to the museum. Of special interest are artifacts from pioneer Pete French's ranch.

◖ Crystal Crane Hot Springs
Spend an idyllic couple of hours at **Crystal Crane Hot Springs** (59315 Hwy. 78, 541/493-2312, www.cranehotsprings.com, 9am-9pm daily, $3.50), 25 miles southeast of Burns just west of the town of Crane. The local hot springs feed a large pond that's big enough to swim in if you have the energy. It's more likely that you'll lounge at the pond's edge and watch the coots and shoveler ducks paddling around in the adjacent cool pond. For visitors who prefer private soaking tubs ($7.50 pp per hour),

SOUTHEASTERN OREGON

steam rising from the lake at Crystal Crane Hot Springs

several bathhouses have cattle troughs filled with hot spring water. Rustic cabins ($25-67, shared bathhouse a bit of a walk away) and a camping area ($15 tents, $18 hookups) make it possible to spend the night and greet the morning with a dip in the pond.

Rockhounding

Southeastern Oregon is rockhounding country. Each year, thousands of enthusiasts flock to this far-flung corner of the state to collect fossils, agates, jasper, obsidian, and thunder eggs. The **Stinking Water Mountains,** 30 miles east of Burns, are a good source of gemstones and petrified wood.

Warm Springs Reservoir, just east of the Stinking Water Mountains, is popular with agate hunters. **Charlie Creek** and **Radar,** west and north of Burns, respectively, produce black, banded, and brown obsidians. Be sure to collect only your limit—be a rock hound, not a rock hog. Also keep in mind that it is illegal to take arrowheads and other artifacts from public lands.

Entertainment and Events

Held in Burns in early April, the **John Scharff Migratory Waterfowl Conference** (541/573-2636, www.migratorybirdfestival.com) celebrates the spring return of waterbirds to the region with lectures, movies, slides, a high-quality art show, and guided bird-watching tours, including early morning visits to the sage grouse leks, or strutting grounds. This is an excellent opportunity to learn more about birds, and it attracts some really knowledgeable and interesting people.

Accommodations

The pet-friendly **Silver Spur Motel** (789 N. Broadway, 541/573-2077 or 800/400-2077, www.silverspurmotel.net, $49-56) is a well-maintained family-owned motel on the north edge of downtown, with refrigerators and microwaves in the guest rooms.

The **Best Western Rory and Ryan Inn** (534 N. Hwy. 20, Hines, 541/573-5050 or 800/780-7234, $116-131) is newer and very comfortable, with an indoor pool and hot tub and all the extras you would expect with a hotel of this caliber.

By far the most distinctive place to stay in Burns is the **◖ Sage Country Inn** (351½ W. Monroe St., 541/573-7243, www.sagecountryinn.com, $100-115). This lovely, spacious house is set back just far enough from the main drag to make it quiet, but it's still easy to walk to restaurants in the downtown area. If frilly B&Bs turn you off, book a night in the Cattle Baron's room.

Camping

A couple of campgrounds to the north of Burns up in the Malheur National Forest are **Idlewild** and **Yellowjacket** (541/573-4300, www.fs.usda.gov, $10). Idlewild is right off U.S. 395 about 17 miles north of Burns in a pretty setting. The remoter Yellowjacket is on the shore of Yellowjacket Lake, 37 miles northwest of Burns on Forest Service Road 3745. From Burns, take County Road 127 out of town, then take Forest Road 47 to Road 37 and follow signs to the campground. Be sure to keep your food under wraps, especially meat, if you want to avoid being visited by the namesake hosts of the lake. Yellowjacket Lake is stocked with trout.

Food

Although Burns isn't known as a culinary mecca, there are a few decent places to eat in town, especially if you're hankering for a steak dinner. The **Meat Hook** (673 W. Monroe St., 541/573-7698, 4pm-9pm Mon.-Sat., $6-32) is an old-fashioned place, with large meals, including bread, salad, soup, main course, and dessert. If the timing is right, treat yourself dinner at **◖ Rhojo's** (83 W. Washington St., 541/5737656, 11am-2pm Mon.-Fri., 11:30am-2pm Sun. and 6pm-9pm Fri.-Sat., $20-25). Lunchtime sandwiches and salads are good, but the weekend nights offering two entrees (changing weekly) such as seared halibut or marinated rib eye steak, plus full fixings, including delicious vegetables, are special events in downtown Burns.

Information

For general information on the region, stop by the **Harney County Chamber of Commerce** (484 N. Broadway, 541/573-2636, www.harneycounty.com, 10am-4pm Tues.-Sat.). For information on recreation, contact the **Bureau of Land Management** office (12533 U.S. 20 W., Hines, OR 97738, 541/573-5241, 9am-5pm Mon.-Fri.). The **Emigrant Creek Ranger District** (265 U.S. 20, Hines, OR 97738, 541/573-4300, 9am-5pm Mon.-Fri.) is also nearby.

◖ MALHEUR NATIONAL WILDLIFE REFUGE

Malheur and Harney Lakes, fed by the mountain snow runoff filling the Blitzen and Silvies Rivers, have been major avian nesting and migration stopovers since prehistoric times. The contrast between the stark dry basin land, with its red sandstone monoliths and mesas, and the lush green marshes is startling. These vast marshes (the longest freshwater marsh in the western United States), meadows, and riparian areas surrounded by the eastern Oregon desert attract thousands of birds and hundreds of bird-watchers. The **Malheur National Wildlife Refuge** (36391 Sodhouse Ln., Princeton, 541/493-2612, www.fws.gov/malheur) is dominated by three fluctuating lakes—Malheur, Mud, and Harney. These are nourished by a scant eight inches of rain per year.

Refuge officials say that 250 species have been counted within its boundaries. Prime bird-watching times are spring and fall, when migratory flocks pass through. Late spring is an especially good time to visit, before summer's scorching heat. In March the first Malheur arrivals include Canada and snow geese, and in the vast Malheur Marsh, swans, mallards, and other ducks. Also look for sandhill cranes in the wet meadows. Great horned owls and golden eagles are two other early arrivals. Shorebirds are followed by warblers, sparrows, and other songbirds in spring. Red-tailed hawks can be seen swooping over the sage-covered prairies throughout spring, summer, and fall. In the late spring, ponds and canals at Malheur

© JUDY JEWELL

bird-watching at Malheur National Wildlife Refuge

occasionally host the trumpeter swan, a majestic bird with a seven-foot wingspan. This is one of the few places where you can observe this endangered species nesting. Flocks of pelicans are a summertime spectacle worth catching. See them before they head south to Mexico in the fall.

August-October is another prime time when birders might see 100 species, and lucky visitors might see the magnificent snow goose. Another fall arrival is the wood thrush, graced with one of the most beautiful songs in the bird kingdom. A September-October highlight is the concentration of greater sandhill cranes, Canada geese, and mallard ducks foraging on Blitzen Valley grain fields. The first two weeks of September are particularly nice because hunting season has yet to begin and the aspens have turned golden.

Be sure to visit the refuge headquarters in a grove of cottonwoods looking out over the huge expanse of Malheur Lake. Here you can pick up maps for the self-guided auto tour of the refuge. A short distance downhill is a small

museum where more than 250 bird specimens are beautifully arrayed. Also of interest is the charming park on the edge of the lake.

While the absolute numbers of birds at Malheur are not as great as they are at the Klamath Lakes or along the Oregon coast, the variety here is unsurpassed anywhere in the area. Among birders, however, it is the "accidental list" of 55 infrequently sighted species that makes this preserve special. Many of these "exotics" are sighted nowhere else in the region. A total of 312 different species have been sighted here over the last century.

In the late 1800s, settlers enjoyed unrestricted hunting, and at the turn of the 20th century, hunters killed thousands of swans, egrets, herons, and grebes for feathers for the millinery trade. In 1908, President Theodore Roosevelt put a stop to the slaughter by protecting the area as a bird sanctuary. The Blitzen Valley and P Ranch were added to the refuge in 1935. Today, 185,000 acres are protected.

Not everybody comes to Malheur just to watch birds—some folks come to fish.

Krumbo Reservoir is a good bet for trout or largemouth bass.

To get to the refuge, drive 25 miles south from Burns on Route 205 and then 9 miles east on the county road to Princeton. The Buena Vista Ponds are an excellent place to stop along the way.

Accommodations

A convenient though bare-bones place to stay on the refuge is the **Malheur Field Station** (34848 Sodhouse Ln., 541/493-2629, www.malheurfieldstation.org, $55-150), where you can bunk in dorm rooms (groups only, $22-30 pp), trailers, or a three-bedroom house. RV sites are also available ($19). Guests should bring bedding and towels; dorm dwellers should be prepared to share a restroom. Although most accommodations have kitchen facilities, during the peak season meals are available. Note that the trailers are the most coveted accommodations here; they're often full during spring and fall birding seasons.

Reserve a room in advance to avoid driving 35 miles to Burns for bed and board.

FRENCHGLEN

Named for famous rancher Pete French and his wealthy father-in-law Dr. Hugh Glenn, the town of Frenchglen was originally known as P Station and was part of the nearby P Ranch. Today, this historic community with its hotel, store, corral, and post office remains essentially the same as it was 50 years ago. The town is about 60 miles south of Burns on Route 205.

In Frenchglen, the ◖ **Frenchglen Hotel** (60 miles south of Burns on Rte. 205, 541/493-2825, www.oregonstateparks.org, mid-Mar.-Oct., $75-82) is an excellent place to stay while visiting Steens Mountain or Malheur National Wildlife Refuge. Built in 1914 as a stage stopover, the main hotel has eight smallish rooms with a shared bath down the hall. Just behind the hotel building are several modern rooms with private

The Frenchglen Hotel is a good place to meet birders.

© JUDY JEWELL

THE CATTLE KINGS OF EASTERN OREGON

Cattle barons, those early entrepreneurs who ran the huge livestock operations of the 19th century, have typically been portrayed as imperious characters in old Westerns. A look at the lives of three eastern Oregon cattle kings–John Devine, Pete French, and Bill Brown–paints a fuller picture.

John Devine came to Oregon in 1868 and started snapping up land by the simple method of squatting on it. He grabbed U.S. government land, Native American territory, and acreage ostensibly owned by road companies, which he quickly covered with vast herds of cattle. Part of his holding included the Alvord and the Whitehorse Ranches on the east side of the Steens. After the devastating winter of 1889-1890, during which he lost 75 percent of his stock, Devine's fortunes plummeted. He was bought out by another cattle baron, Henry Miller, and held on to just the Whitehorse Ranch until his death in 1901 at the age of 62.

Another rancher whose fate is still debated in this arid country is Pete French, an arrogant, forceful man with a bushy mustache that gave him the appearance of Wyatt Earp. Born in Red Bluff, California, in 1849, French moved to Oregon in 1873 to manage the stock ranch of Dr. Hugh Glenn in the Donner and Blitzen Valley. French married the boss's daughter, and after Glenn was murdered by his bookkeeper, French built the French-Glenn Livestock Company into one of the largest spreads in the West. At its peak, the ranch had 100,000 acres on which roamed 30,000 head of cattle and 3,000 horses. Five hundred miles of barbed wire defined this empire stretching from the Donner and Blitzen River to Harney Lake.

While he was developing the P Ranch, French earned the enmity of hundreds of local homesteaders, many of whom were evicted from their squatters' shacks. One of his enemies, homesteader Ed Oliver, rode up to French one day and shot him dead. Oliver was arrested but later acquitted by a jury of settlers.

Bill Brown was a more popular and certainly more eccentric rancher than Pete French. His Gap Ranch, headquartered a few miles east of Hampton, halfway between Brothers and Riley, was at its largest 38,000 acres spread throughout four counties. Brown didn't start out rich, and he died penniless. In between he earned and lost a number of fortunes.

His first enterprise was running a flock of 400 sheep. During that era he was so hard up he had only one sock, which he switched from one foot to the other every day. Brown added horses to his holdings with such zeal that by World War I he owned 25,000 head, many of which he sold to the U.S. Cavalry. After the war, and with the advent of mass production of automobiles, Brown lost his shirt and his land.

Many stories have been told about this balding six-footer with a square jaw and a mild manner. He never cussed, drank, or gambled, unless his faith in his store customers could be considered gambling. The operator of a shop, Brown was seldom behind the counter, relying instead on the honesty of his customers, who were asked to toss their cash in a cigar box. Another quirk was Brown's legendary habit of writing checks on anything available, from tomato-can labels to wooden slats. Local bankers had no problem cashing the "checks" for Brown's hired help or suppliers.

---

baths in the Drover's Inn, a separate unit. Ranch cooks prepare delicious family-style dinners ($22-25, reservations required) served at 6:30pm sharp; breakfast and lunch are also available. Watching thunderstorms sweep across Steens Mountain from the hotel's screened-in porch while you chat with birders from all over the West can provide after-dinner entertainment.

DIAMOND AND VICINITY
Diamond Craters

Diamond Craters have been described by scientists as the most diverse basaltic volcanic features in the United States. To tour these unique formations, drive 55 miles south of Burns on Route 205 until you reach the Diamond junction. Turn left and begin a 40-mile route ending at New Princeton on Route 78. On the way you'll

SOUTHEASTERN OREGON

see why this area is called "Oregon's Geologic Gem." There are craters, domes, lava flows, and pits that give an outstanding visual lesson on volcanism. To aid your self-guided tour, pick up the "Diamond Craters" brochure at the **Bureau of Land Management office** (12533 U.S. 20 W., Hines, 541/573-5241) in Hines.

Round Barn

While in the Diamond Craters area, stop at the Round Barn, a historic structure built in the 1870s or 1880s by rancher Pete French as a place to spend the winter breaking his saddle horses. Located 20 miles north of Diamond, the barn is 100 feet in diameter with a 60-foot circular lava rock corral inside. Twelve tall juniper poles support a roof covered with 50,000 shingles. Hundreds of cowpokes have carved their initials in the posts of this famous corral.

Just up the road from the barn, the privately owned **Round Barn Visitors Center** (541/493-2070, www.roundbarn.net, 9am-5pm daily, free), a combination gift shop, cold drink vendor, and historical museum, is worth a stop. Its architecture mirrors that of the historic barn, and the genial proprietor, a third-generation Diamond Valley rancher, leads daylong tours of the area with stops in some rather remote areas, focusing on the area's colorful history.

Accommodations and Food

Tall Lombardy poplars mark the tiny hamlet of Diamond, which is a cluster of buildings tucked in at the bottom of a hill. The focal point of the town is the **(Hotel Diamond** (541/493-1898, www.central-oregon.com/hoteldiamond, Apr.-Oct., $74-97), a wonderfully and unpretentiously restored hotel dating from the late 1800s. Don't worry about where to eat when you book a stay: breakfast, lunch, and family-style dinners (about $20) at the hotel are quite good. Reserve a seat at the table at least a day in advance so there will be plenty of food to go around.

Rancher Peter French built the Round Barn to break saddle horses.

© JUDY JEWELL

◖ STEENS MOUNTAIN

Steens Mountain, named after Major Enoch Steen, a U.S. Army officer assigned the task of building a military road through Harney County, is one of the great scenic wonders of Oregon. A 30-mile fault block, the eastern flank of the mountain rises straight up from the Alvord Desert to a row of glacial peaks. On the western side, huge gorges carved out by glaciers one million years ago descend to a gentle slope drained by the Donner and Blitzen River, which flows into Malheur Lake.

Steens Mountain has five vegetation zones, ranging from tall sage to alpine tundra. The best way to see the transition is to drive the **Steens Mountain Byway** out of Frenchglen to the top of Steens Mountain. This is the highest road in Oregon, rising to 9,000 feet in elevation. The first 15 miles of the road are gravel, and the last 9 miles are dirt. The latter section is not recommended for low-slung passenger cars. Expect to spend the entire day traveling this 59-mile byway.

Starting and ending at Frenchglen, the route up Steens Mountain, sans significant tree cover save for some beautiful aspens, evokes Alaskan alpine tundra. Multicolored low-to-the-ground wildflowers and a vast spaciousness give the feeling of being on top of the world. This impression is accentuated by standing in snow while you look 5,000 feet straight down into the sun-scorched Alvord Desert, which records just seven inches of rain annually.

The first four miles of the trek lead across the Malheur National Wildlife Refuge and up to the foothills of Steens Mountain. **Page Springs,** the first campground on the route, is a popular spot offering campsites along the bank of the Donner and Blitzen River. Approximately 13 miles beyond Page Springs is **Lily Lake,** a good place for a picnic. This shallow lake has an abundance of water lilies, frogs, songbirds, and waterfowl.

After Lily Lake, you really start to climb up the mountain to **Fish Lake, Jackman Park** (both with campsites), and viewpoints of Kiger Gorge and the East Rim. **Kiger Gorge** is a spectacular example of a wide U-shaped path left by a glacier. Blanketed in meadow grasses, quaking aspen, cottonwood, and mountain mahogany at lower elevations, tiny tundra-like flowers proliferate on the 8,000-foot viewpoint.

The **East Rim** is a dramatic example of earth-shifting in prehistoric epochs. The lava layers that cap the mountain are thousands of feet thick and formed 15 million years ago when lava erupted from cracks in the ground. Several million years later, the Steens Mountain fault block began to lift along a fault below the East Rim. The fault block tilted to the west, forming the gentler slope that stretches to the Malheur Lake Basin. At the summit (9,670 feet) on a clear day you can see the corners of four states—California, Nevada, Oregon, and Idaho.

From the summit, it's about 1 mile and 1,300 vertical feet down the slopes of Wildhorse Canyon to **Wildhorse Lake.** Expect the hike back up to the parking area to be tough—after all, you're climbing to 9,670 feet!

A good time to visit is August through mid-September—Indian summer. Nights are cold, but daytime temperatures are more pleasant than those of summertime scorchers. Later in the fall, red bushes and yellow aspens attract photographers. Some of the aspens are located at Whorehouse Meadow and are indirectly responsible for its name. Lonely shepherds would scratch love notes and erotica in the tree bark, pining away for a visit from the horse-drawn bordellos that serviced these parts. Wildlife-viewing highlights include bighorn sheep, seen around the East Rim viewpoint in summer; hummingbirds, often observed at high elevations; and hawks, which can be spotted anywhere and anytime, especially from the ridge above Fish Lake.

The area has off-highway vehicle restrictions to protect the environment. Five gates controlling access to the Steens Mountain area are located at various elevations and are opened as road and weather conditions permit. Normally, the Steens Byway is not open until early July and is closed by snow in October or November. Gas is available only in Burns, Frenchglen, and Fields. Take reasonable precautions when driving the loop: sudden storms, lightning, flash floods, and extreme road conditions can be hazardous to travelers. The loop returns to Route 205 about 10 miles south of Frenchglen.

Visit Steens Mountain the first Saturday of August for the **Chris Miller Memorial Steens Mountain Rim Run** (541/573-2636, www.steensrimrun.com), a 10K run or walk along the East Rim of Steens Mountain that starts at an elevation of 7,835 feet and finishes at above 9,700 feet.

Blitzen

Four miles south of the southern terminus of the Steens Mountain Loop Road, turn west off Route 205 to take a side trip to the ghost town of Blitzen. This eight-mile jaunt will take you to the ruins of the little town of a half-dozen dilapidated buildings, founded in the late 1800s. Blitzen was named after the Donner and Blitzen River, which flows nearby. *Donner und Blitzen* is German for "thunder and lightning," the label given this stream by Captain George Curry, who tried to cross it during a fierce thunderstorm.

Camping

As for summertime Steens weather, the 100°F temperatures in the high desert give way to 50-80°F daytime temperatures atop the mountain. Nonetheless, be aware that the summit can see severe thunderstorms and lightning, and at night the mercury can drop below freezing, even on days with high noontime temperatures.

There are three high-elevation campgrounds along the Steens Mountain Loop Road. No reservations are accepted, and sites are $8 per vehicle per night. For more info, contact the **Bureau of Land Management** (541/573-4400). **Page Springs** (year-round) is four miles southeast of Frenchglen. Close to the Malheur National Wildlife Refuge, the campground is a good headquarters for birdwatching, fishing, hiking, and sightseeing. **Fish Lake** (July 1-Nov. 15) is 17 miles east of Frenchglen. The namesake lake is stocked with eastern brook, cutthroat, and rainbow trout. Aspens surround the campsites, which

have toilets, well water, and fire pits; firewood is included in the campsite fee. Climb up on the ridge above the campground to watch hawks. **Jackman Park,** three miles east of Fish Lake, is particularly popular with backpackers, who use it as a takeoff point. It has six sites with toilets and potable water.

Another alternative is the **Steens Mountain Resort** (N. Loop Rd., Frenchglen, 541/493-2415 or 800/542-3765, www.steensmountainresort.com, $65-90 cabins, $15 tents, $30 RVs, reservations recommended), just before you get to the Page Springs campground. Views of the surrounding gorges are spectacular, and there are more amenities than at the Bureau of Land Management facilities, including showers, a small store, laundry, dumping facilities, and a public phone. Guests in the heated and air-conditioned cabins and trailers should bring towels and bed linens.

ALVORD DESERT AND VICINITY
Fields

Fields, the largest community on the east side of Steens Mountain and perhaps the friendliest place in the state, was established as a supply station in 1881, and a supply station it still is. Fields now has a gas station, a store, a café, a motel, and a B&B. All but the B&B are part of the same business, **Fields Station** (541/495-2275, www.thefieldsstation.com). The accommodations, though very simple, are perfectly sufficient and very reasonably priced; there are a couple of one-bedroom units and an old hotel that'll sleep up to 10 people ($65). The other place to stay, the **Alvord Inn B&B** (22308 Fields Dr., 541/495-2441, www.alvordinn.com, $70), is right next door and has two very comfortable and nicely decorated guest rooms. The café at Fields Station serves great milk shakes. Be sure to take a few minutes to knock around Fields; find the remains of the original Mr. Fields's stone cabin across the road from the gas pumps. If you walk a little ways past the cabin site, you may spot a great horned owl perched in a tree.

◖ Alvord Desert

About 20 miles north of Fields, the vast hard-pan playa of the **Alvord Desert** comes into view. This usually dry and stark white alkali lake bed or "playa" gets about six inches of rain per year, which quickly evaporates. It's possible to drive down to, and even on, the playa (unless it's wet, in which case it's quite slick). But rather than driving, get out of the car and walk. One popular activity here is land-sailing, which is done in a "boat" that's sort of like a go-kart with a sail.

There is a small informal camping area nestled under the east face of Steens Mountain along Pike Creek. Look for a spur road leading off to the west about 2 miles north of Alvord Hot Springs—you may also be able to spot the outhouse (voted "world's most disgusting" by one seasoned traveler). Some folks also camp on the edge of the playa.

Alvord Hot Springs

North of Fields, look for **Alvord Hot Springs,** a rustic spa recognizable by its corrugated-steel shack on the east side of the road. Two pools of hot mineral water piped in from spring runoff will warm your muscles and soak away your aches and pains at no charge. The view from the hot springs up onto the east face of Steens Mountain is magnificent.

Mickey Hot Springs

At the remote northern edge of the Alvord Desert is a little thermal basin. Don't plan to soak—the water is way too hot for that—but it's a good place to tromp around and inspect the pools and the mudflats. A little 6- to 8-foot jet of 200°F water on the north end of an ancient dry lake bed is often visible in the spring in the Alvord Desert. Also quite amazing is a 30-foot-deep hot pool. To get to **Mickey Hot Springs,** head about 10 miles north from Alvord Hot Springs, pass the Alvord Ranch, and go through a series of two sharp turns. At the second turn (a sharp left), turn onto the rough but drivable side road and head east and south. Stay to the left at the fork in the road; it's about 6.5

SOUTHEASTERN OREGON

© JUDY JEWELL

one of the few buildings in Fields, Oregon

miles from the main road to the hot springs parking area.

Mann Lake

North of the Alvord Desert, just west of the road, **Mann Lake** is a popular fishing destination. Early spring trout fishing is especially good, and the lake is the repository for the breeding stock of Lahontan cutthroat trout, a subspecies that's adapted to alkaline water. Although the lakeshore is pretty sagebrushy and unshaded, there is a campground.

OWYHEE RIVER COUNTRY

It's a long way from just about anywhere to the far southeastern corner of Oregon, but the canyons of the Owyhee are enchanting for those visitors who don't mind roughing it. If you aren't prepared to camp, you can stay in one of the two very basic motels in Jordan Valley, or come down from the north, where Ontario has more services.

Jordan Valley

This town, located almost on the Idaho border where U.S. 95 takes a sharp bend north, is mostly visited by long-haul truckers. But it's also known for its Basque heritage, which is not exactly obvious but celebrated to some small degree at the **Old Basque Inn** (306 Wroten St., 541/586-2800, 7am-2pm and 5pm-9pm Mon.-Sat., 8am-3pm Sun., $6-17), where, as in most American Basque restaurants, dinners are served family style. If you're not hopping right back into the car, you may dare to try the inn's traditional Basque Picon punch, whose main ingredient is a bitter orange cordial liqueur. If the punch sets you back, check into a room upstairs ($65). The **Basque Station Motel** (801 Main St., 541/586-2244, $65) also has basic rooms that will look pretty inviting after a long day's drive.

Owyhee River Trips

The big treat for visitors to this area is a four- to six-day raft trip down the Owyhee River.

The Owyhee River flows through steep-walled canyons in far southeastern Oregon.

© TIERRA CURRY

The river can be run only for a few weeks in the spring, and during drought years it can't be run at all. Trips start in the tiny town of Rome, east of Jordan Valley, and end at the southern edge of the Owyhee Reservoir, at the base of Leslie Gulch. Expect to pay $1,000-1,800, depending on the length of the trip. Float (with an occasional run through hair-raising rapids) through deep rugged canyons past tall rock pillars, petroglyphs, many species of birds, and a number of hot springs. The following outfitters offer Owyhee River trips: **Ouzel Outfitters** (541/385-5947 or 800/788-7238, www.oregonrafting.com), **Oregon Whitewater Adventures** (541/746-5422 or 800/820-7238, www.oregonwhitewater.com), and **Momentum River Expeditions** (541/488-2525, www.momentumriverexpeditions.com).

Succor Creek and Leslie Gulch

From Jordan Valley, head north on U.S. 95, then turn left onto Succor Creek Road and follow it to the turnoff for Leslie Gulch. Turn left to head down the relatively rough and steep 13-mile-long road through the remarkably colorful and steep-walled Leslie Gulch canyon. Along the way are a couple of trails leading up beautiful side canyons. The road ends on the shores of the Owyhee Reservoir, where there's a boat ramp and a hardscrabble camping area.

Farther north, there's a campground in a pretty area along Succor Creek. Bring your own water (and toilet paper). From the campground, wander upstream to explore the geology and wildflowers, but be sure to watch out for rattlesnakes.

SOUTHEASTERN OREGON

BACKGROUND

The Land

GEOGRAPHY

If Oregon were part of a jigsaw puzzle of the United States, it would be a squarish piece with a divot carved out of the center top. To the west is the Pacific Ocean, with some 370 miles of beaches, dunes, and headlands; to the east are the Snake River and Idaho. Up north, much of the boundary between Oregon and Washington is defined by the mighty Columbia River, while southern Oregon lies atop the upper borders of California and Nevada.

Broad rows of mountains divide the coast from the inland valleys, and western Oregon from the central and eastern parts of the state.

East of the highest central range the Columbia Plateau predominates, broken up in the northeast where mountainous features reassert themselves. In the southeast, scattered lakes dot the landscape, and fault-block mountains gently ascend on one slope, then drop sharply off. The Great Basin desert—characterized by rivers that evaporate, peter out, or disappear into underground aquifers—makes up the bottom corner of eastern Oregon. Here the seven-inch annual rainfall of the Alvord Desert seems as if it would be more at home in southeastern California and Nevada than in a state known for blustery rainstorms and lush greenery.

© BILL MCRAE

Highs and Lows

Moving west to east, the major mountain systems start with the Klamath Mountains and the Coast Range. The Klamaths form the lower quarter of the state's western barrier to the Pacific; the eastern flank of this range is generally referred to as the Siskiyous. To the north, the Oregon Coast Range, a younger volcanic range, replaces the Klamaths. The highest peaks in each of these cordilleras barely top 4,000 feet and stand between narrow coastal plateaus on the west side and the rich agricultural lands of the Willamette and Rogue Valleys on the other. Running up the west-central portion of the state is the Cascade Range, which extends from northern California up to Canada. Five of the dormant volcanoes in Oregon top 10,000 feet above sea level, with Mount Hood, the state's highest peak, at 11,239 feet.

Beyond the eastern slope of the Cascades, semiarid high-desert conditions contrast with the Coast Range rainforests and the mild, wet maritime climate that characterizes much of western Oregon. In the northeast, the 10,000-foot crests of the snowcapped Wallowas rise less than 50 miles away from the hot, arid floor of Hells Canyon, itself about 1,300 feet above sea level.

In addition to Hells Canyon, the country's biggest hole in the ground (7,900 feet maximum depth), Oregon also boasts the continent's deepest lake: Crater Lake, with a depth of 1,958 feet.

Last of the Red-Hot Lavas

Each part of the state contains well-known remnants of Oregon's cataclysmic past. Offshore waters here feature 1,477 islands and islets, the eroded remains of ancient volcanic flows. Lava fields dot the approaches to the High Cascades. East of the range, a volcanic plateau supports cinder cones, lava caves, and lava-cast forests in the most varied array of these phenomena outside of Hawaii.

The imposing volcanic cones of the Cascades and the inundated caldera that is Crater Lake, formed by the implosion of Mount Mazama

some 6,600 years ago, are some of the most dramatic reminders of Oregon's volcanic origins. More fascinating evidence can be seen up close at Newberry National Volcanic Monument, an extensive area south of Bend that encompasses obsidian fields and lava formations left by massive eruptions. (Incidentally, geologists have cited Newberry on their list of volcanoes in the continental United States most likely to erupt again.) Not far from the Lava Lands Visitor Center in the national monument are the Lava River Cave and Lava Cast Forest—created when lava enveloped living trees 6,000 years ago.

Earthquakes and Tsunamis

Scientists exploring Tillamook County in 1990 unearthed discontinuities in both rock strata and tree rings indicating that the north Oregon coast has experienced major **earthquakes** every several hundred years. They estimate that the next one could come within our lifetimes and be of significant magnitude. In this vein, Japanese scientists maintain that a 9.0 quake struck the Pacific Northwest coast in 1700, based on tsunami records indicating that 6- to 9-foot-high tidal waves hit Japan's coastline. This date is also consistent with Pacific Northwest Native American oral histories and geological evidence.

These coastal quakes are caused by subduction, which occurs when one of the giant plates that make up the earth's crust slides under another as they collide. In Pacific Northwest coastal regions, this takes place when the Juan de Fuca plate's marine layer is pushed under the continental North American plate. With virtually every part of the state possessing seismic potential that hasn't been released in many years, the pressure along the fault lines is increasing.

In coastal areas, one of the greatest dangers associated with earthquakes is the possibility of **tsunamis.** The waves are produced by an offshore quake—even one centered thousands of miles away. As a tsunami draws closer to shore, driven by the force of the quake, it takes in preceding water and builds into a series of

© BILL MCRAE

John Day Fossil Beds preserve ancient mammals in enormous drifts of volcanic ash.

waves traveling as fast as 500 miles per hour and reaching as high as 100 feet. Ever since a tsunami unleashed by Alaska's 1964 quake (measured at 14.2 feet high at the mouth of the Umpqua River) resulted in four casualties in Beverly Beach and over $1 million in damage, local authorities have made seismic preparedness a priority, with a system of warning sirens and evacuation signs pointing the way to higher ground. When the March 2011 9.0 earthquake hit Japan, coastal residents fled to higher ground; although most of the Oregon coast was spared, 8-foot waves along the southern coast damaged the harbor in Brookings.

The Great Meltdown

However pervasive the effects of seismic activity and volcanism are, they must still share top billing with the last ice age in the grand epic of Oregon's topography.

At the height of the most recent major glaciation, the world's oceans were 300-500 feet lower, North America and Asia were connected by a land bridge across the Bering Strait, and the Oregon coast was miles west of where it is today. The Columbia Gorge extended out past present-day Astoria. As the glaciers melted, the sea rose.

When that glacial epoch's final meltdown 12,000 years ago unleashed water dammed up by thousands of feet of ice, great rivers were spawned and existing channels enlarged. A particularly large inundation was the Missoula Floods, which began with an ice dam breaking up in what's now northern Idaho. Floodwaters carved out the contours of what are now the Columbia River Gorge and the Willamette Valley. Other glacial floodwaters found their outlet westward to the sea, digging out silt-ridden estuaries in the process. Pacific wave action washed this debris back up onto the land, helping to create dunes and beaches.

CLIMATE
The Rain Shadow

Oregon's location equidistant from the equator and the North Pole subjects it to weather from both tropical and polar airflows. This makes for a pattern of changeability in which calm often alternates with storm, and extreme heat and extreme cold seldom last long.

Oregon's weather system is best understood as a series of valley climates separated from each other by mountain ranges that draw precipitation from the eastbound weather systems. Moving west to east, each of these valley zones records progressively lower rainfall levels until one encounters a desert on the eastern side of the state.

Moisture-laden westerlies off the Pacific slam into the Coast and Klamath Ranges. As the mountains push the clouds higher, they drop their moisture in the form of rain or snow. That's because rising air cools 3°F for every 1,000 feet of altitude gain, and cooler air can't hold as much moisture as warm air. As a consequence, rainfall at the coast often exceeds 80 inches per year. In parts of the coastal ranges, yearly totals of well over 100 inches aren't uncommon.

By contrast, the Willamette Valley and other

inland valleys on the east side of the mountains usually record half that total.

The rain shadow effect is repeated when the Cascades catch precipitation from eastward-moving cloud masses, wringing the moisture out of the storms; consequently, the eastern side of this range often records annual rainfall totals below 10 inches.

The Coast

Wet but mild, average rainfall on the coast ranges from a low of 64 inches per year in the Coos Bay area to nearly 100 inches around Lincoln City. The Pacific Ocean moderates coastal weather year-round, softening the extremes. Spring, summer, and fall generally don't get very hot, with highs generally in the 60s and 70s, and seldom topping 90°F. Winter temperatures only drop to the 40s and 50s, and freezes and snowfall are quite rare occurrences.

Western Oregon

If there is one constant in western Oregon, it is cloudiness. Portland and the Willamette Valley receive only about 45 percent of maximum potential sunshine; more than 200 days of the year are cloudy, and rain falls an average of 150 days. While this might sound bleak, consider that the cloud cover helps moderate the climate by trapping and reflecting the earth's heat. On average, fewer than 30 days of the year record temperatures below freezing. Thus the region, despite being on a more northerly latitude than parts of Canada, has a milder climate. Except in mountainous areas, snow usually isn't a force to be reckoned with. Another surprise is that Portland's average annual rainfall of 40 inches is usually less than totals recorded in New York City, Miami, or Chicago.

The southern end of the Willamette Valley can be affected by temperature inversions. In winter, for example, warm air above the valley walls holds in the colder air below, resulting in fog. In the southern valleys, fog helps to counterbalance the region's long dry season: Ashland and Medford sometimes record only half the yearly precipitation of their neighbors to the north, as well as higher winter and summer temperatures. At the same time, these inversions can cause unwelcome pollution to linger.

While it's difficult to predict daily weather patterns in western Oregon, there are definite seasonal climatic shifts. In winter, arctic and tropical air masses collide over the Pacific, producing much of the state's rain. During the summer the clashes are less frequent. At that time, Oregon weather is more affected by Pacific Ocean temperatures and air pressure differences between inland and coastal areas.

Eastern Oregon

By contrast, the scorching deserts of eastern Oregon can give way to cold temperatures at night. This is because clear skies and a dearth of vegetation facilitate the escape of heat. Consider that on May 2, 1968, the difference between the high and low temperatures at Juniper Lake, north of the Alvord Desert in southeastern Oregon, was 81 degrees.

Mountain areas also experience extreme diurnal temperature fluctuations. Thin mountain air does not filter out ultraviolet radiation as effectively as the denser air at lower elevations, so the sun's force is accentuated at higher elevations. At night, chill spreads quickly through this thin air.

Flora and Fauna

FLORA

With 4,400 known species and varieties, Oregon ranks fourth among U.S. states for plant diversity, including dozens of species found nowhere else.

Trees

The mixed-conifer ecosystem of western Oregon—dense far-reaching forests of Douglas fir, Sitka spruce, and western hemlock interspersed with bigleaf maple, vine maple, and alder—is among the most productive woodlands in the world.

In southern Oregon, you'll find redwood groves and rare myrtle trees (prized by woodworkers and for their distinctive coloring and grain); huge ponderosa pines are a hallmark of central Oregon. A particularly striking natural display along the McKenzie River mixes red vine maple and sumacs with golden oaks and alders against an evergreen backdrop.

Eastern Oregon's desert is largely rabbitbrush, cheatgrass, sagebrush, and juniper. In the John Day backcountry of eastern Oregon, you can even find hedgehog cactus.

Just in case all the tree identification becomes overwhelming, remember a mnemonic taught to Oregon schoolchildren: The needles of a fir are flat, flexible, and friendly. Spruce needles are square, stiff, and will stick you. Hemlock needles have a hammock-like configuration, and the crown of the tree is curved as though it's tipping its hat. Finally, the ponderosa pine's platelike bark is a distinctive feature.

Of the 19 million acres of old growth that once proliferated in Oregon and Washington, less than 10 percent survive. Naturalists describe an old-growth forest as a mixture of trees, some of which must be at least 200 years old, and a supply of snags or standing dead trees, nurse logs, and streams with downed logs. Throughout this book, references are made to old-growth groves that are noteworthy for size, age, beauty, ecological significance, or ease of access. Of all the old-growth forests mentioned in this volume, **Opal Creek** in the Willamette Valley most spectacularly embodies all of these characteristics.

Coastal Plant Life

While giant conifers and a profuse understory of greenery predominate coastal forests, this ecosystem represents only the most visible part of the Oregon coast's bountiful botany. Many coastal travelers will notice **European beachgrass** (*Ammophila arenaria*) covering the sand wherever they go. Originally planted in the 1930s to inhibit dune growth, the thick, rapidly spreading grass worked too well, solidifying into a ridge behind the shoreline, blocking the windblown sand from replenishing the rest of the beach and suppressing native plants. Populations of formerly common natives such as beach morning glory, yellow abronia, gray beach pea, and American dune-grass are now much diminished. The now-endangered pink sand verbena, once abundant along the coast from British Columbia to northern California, is restricted to a few locations along central and southern Oregon coast. Herbicides, burning, and tilling have been employed in recent years to remove European beachgrass and restore the dune ecosystem to a more natural state, but progress against the pernicious weed is slow and difficult.

Freshwater wetlands and bogs, created where water is trapped by the sprawling sand dunes along the central coast, provide habitats for some unusual species. Best known among these is the **cobra lily** (*Darlingtonia californica*), which can be viewed up close just north of Florence. Also called pitcher plant, this carnivorous bog dweller survives on hapless insects lured into a specialized chamber, where they are trapped and digested.

Coastal salt marshes, occurring in the upper intertidal zones of coastal bays and estuaries, have been dramatically reduced due

© JUDY JEWELL

Trillium bloom in March.

to land "reclamation" projects such as drainage, diking, and other human disturbances. The halophytes (salt-loving plants) that thrive in this specialized environment include pickleweed, saltgrass, fleshy jaumea, salt marsh dodder, arrowgrass, sand spurrey, and seaside plantain. Coastal forests include Sitka spruce and alder riparian communities, which provide resting and feeding areas for migratory waterfowl, shore and wading birds, and raptors.

Flowers and Fruits

While not as visually arresting as the evergreens of western Oregon, the state's several varieties of berries are no less pervasive. Found mostly from the coast to the mid-Cascades, invasive **Himalayan blackberries** favor clearings, burned-over areas, and people's gardens. They also take root in the woods alongside **wild strawberries, salmonberries, thimbleberries, currants,** and **salal.** Within this edible realm, wild-food connoisseurs especially seek out the thin-leafed **huckleberry** found in the Wallowa, Blue, Cascade, and Klamath Ranges. Prime

snacking season for all these berries ranges from midsummer to mid-fall.

No less prized are the rare plant communities of the Columbia River Gorge and the Klamath-Siskiyou region. A quarter of Oregon's rare and endangered plants are found in the latter area, a portion of which is in the valley of the Illinois River, a designated Wild and Scenic tributary of the Rogue. **Kalmiopsis leachiana,** a rare member of the heath family endemic to southwestern Oregon, even has a wilderness area named after it.

Motorists will treasure such springtime floral fantasias (both wild and domesticated) such as the **dahlias** and **irises** near Canby off I-5; **tulips** near Woodburn; irises off Route 213 outside Salem; the **Easter lilies** along U.S. 101 near Brookings; **blue lupines** alongside U.S. 97 in central Oregon; **apple blossoms** in the Hood River Valley near the Columbia Gorge; **pear blossoms** in the Bear Creek Valley near Medford; **beargrass, columbines,** and **Indian paintbrush** on Cascades thoroughfares; and **rhododendrons** and **fireweed** along the coast.

East of the Cascades, the undergrowth is often more varied than the ground cover in the damp forests on the west side of the mountains. This is because sunny openings in the forest permit room for more species and for plants of different heights. And, in contrast to the white flowers that predominate in the shady forests in western Oregon, "dry-side" wildflowers generally have brighter colors. These blossoms attract color-sensitive pollinators such as bees and butterflies. On the opposite flank of the range, the commonly seen white **trillium** relies on beetles and ants for propagation, lessening the need for eye-catching pigments.

Mushrooms

Autumn is the season for those who covet wild chanterelle and matsutake mushrooms. September through November the Coast Range is the prime picking area for chanterelles—a fluted orange or yellow mushroom in the tall second-growth Douglas fir forests. In the spring, fungi lovers' hearts turn to morels. Of course, you should be absolutely certain of

sea stars

what you have before you eat wild mushrooms, or any other wild food. Farmers markets are usually good places to find an assortment of wild mushrooms.

FAUNA

Oregon's creatures great and small are an excitingly diverse group. Oregon's low population density, abundance of wildlife refuges and nature preserves, and biomes running the gamut from rainforest to desert explain this variety. Throughout the state, numerous refuges, such as the **South Slough National Estuarine Research Reserve,** the **Malheur Bird/Wildlife Refuge,** the **Jewell Preserve for Roosevelt Elk,** and the **Finley Bird and Wildlife Preserve** provide safe havens for both feathered and furry friends.

Tidepools

For most visitors, the most fascinating coastal ecosystems in Oregon are the rocky tidepools. These Technicolor windows offer an up close look at one of the richest—and

harshest—environments, the intertidal zone, where pummeling surf, unflinching sun, predators, and the cycle of tides demand tenacity and special adaptation of its inhabitants.

The natural zone where surf meets shore is divided into three main habitat layers, based on their position relative to tide levels. The **high intertidal zone,** inundated only during the highest tides, is home to creatures that can either move, such as **crabs,** or are well adapted to tolerate daily desiccation, such as **acorn barnacles** and **finger limpets, chitons, green algae,** and **limpets.** The turbulent **mid-intertidal zone** is covered and uncovered by the tides, usually twice each day. In the upper portion of this zone, **California mussels** and **goose barnacles** may thickly blanket the rocks, while ochre **sea stars** and green **sea anemones** are common lower down, along with **sea lettuce, sea palms, snails, sponges,** and **whelks.** Below that, the **low intertidal zone** is exposed only during the lowest tides. Because it is covered by water most of the time, this zone has the greatest diversity of organisms in the tidal area. Residents include many of the organisms found in the higher zones, as well as **sculpins, abalone,** and purple **sea urchins.**

Standout destinations for exploring tidepools include Cape Arago, Cape Perpetua, the Marine Gardens at Devil's Punchbowl, and beaches south and north of Gold Beach—among many other spots. Tidepool explorers should be mindful that, despite the fact that the plants and animals in the pools are well adapted to withstand the elements, they and their ecosystem are actually quite fragile, and they're very sensitive to human interference. Avoid stepping on mussels, anemones, and barnacles, and take nothing from the tidepools. In the Oregon Islands National Wildlife Refuge and other specially protected areas, removal or harassment of any living organism may be treated as a misdemeanor punishable by fines.

Gray Whales
Few sights along the Oregon coast elicit more excitement than that of a surfacing whale. The most common large whale seen from shore along the West Coast of North America is the gray whale (*Eschrichtius robustus*). These behemoths can reach 45 feet in length and 35 tons in weight. The sight of a mammal as big as a Greyhound bus erupting from the sea has a way of emptying the mind of mundane concerns. Wreathed in seaweed and sporting barnacles and other parasites on its back, a California gray whale might look more like the hull of an old ship were it not for its expressive eyes.

Some gray whales are found off the Oregon coast all year, including an estimated 200-400 during the summer, though they're most visible and numerous when migrating populations pass through Oregon waters on their way south December-February and northward early March-April. This annual journey from the rich feeding grounds of the Bering and Chukchi Seas of Alaska to the calving grounds of Mexico amounts to some 10,000 miles, the longest migration of any mammal. On the Oregon coast, their numbers peak usually during the first week of January, when as many as 30 per hour may pass a given point.

By mid-February, most of the whales will have moved on toward their breeding and calving lagoons on the west coast of Baja California.

Early March-April, the juveniles, adult males, and females without calves begin returning northward past the Oregon coast. Mothers and their new calves are the last to leave Mexico and move more slowly, passing Oregon late April-June. During the spring migration, the whales may pass within just a few hundred yards of coastal headlands, making this a particularly exciting time for whale-watching from any number of vantage points along the coast. Researchers speculate that gray whales stay close to shore as a way to help them navigate.

Seals, Sea Lions, and Otters
Pacific harbor seals, California sea lions, and Steller sea lions are frequently sighted in Oregon waters. California sea lions are the animals you might have seen in circuses. These 1,000-pound mammals are characterized by their large size and small earflaps, which seals lack. Unlike seals, they can point their rear flippers forward to give them better mobility on land. Lacking the dense underfur that covers seals, sea lions tend to prefer warmer waters.

Steller sea lions can be seen at the Sea Lion Caves. They also breed on reefs off Gold Beach and Port Orford. In the largest sea lion species, males can weigh more than a ton. Their coats tend to be gray rather than black like California sea lions. They also differ from their California counterparts in that they are comfortable in colder water.

Look for Pacific harbor seals in bays and estuaries up and down the coast, sometimes miles inland. They're nonmigratory, have no earflaps, and can be distinguished from sea lions because they're much smaller (150-300 pounds) and have mottled fur that ranges in color from pale cream to rusty brown.

Salmon and Steelhead
In recent decades, dwindling Pacific salmon and steelhead stocks have prompted restrictions on commercial and recreational fishing

SPECIES OF FISH

Touted as the best-tasting salmon, king or chinook salmon are also the largest species, sometimes weighing in at over 80 pounds. Coho or silver salmon are known among anglers as fish that fight fiercely, despite a weight of just 10-20 pounds. In 1994 the El Niño warming current inhibited coho reproduction enough to bring about a total ban on harvesting this species. That turned around after 2000, when a cautious sportfishing season reopened in Oregon.

Chum salmon (known derogatorily as "dog salmon" because Canadian and Alaskan native people thought them worthy only of being fed to their dog teams) are found only in the Miami and Kilchis Rivers near Tillamook. Two other species, sockeye and pink (or humpback) salmon, are not caught south of Washington waters, but you may see them sold in Oregon stores.

Steelhead are sea-run rainbow trout averaging 5-20 pounds whose life cycle generally resembles that of salmon—save for the fact that steelhead generally survive after spawning and may live to spawn multiple times. Runs of steelhead, often heavily supplemented by hatchery-raised fish, are found in rivers and streams up and down the coast. They provide great—if challenging—sport angling, but are not fished commercially (though you will find farm-raised steelhead in the grocery store).

in order to restore threatened and endangered species throughout the Pacific Northwest. Runs are highly variable from year to year; for more information about fish populations and fishing restrictions, see the Oregon Department of Fish and Wildlife's website (www.dfw.state.or.us).

The salmon's life cycle begins and ends in a freshwater stream. After an upriver journey from the sea of sometimes hundreds of miles, the spawning female deposits 3,000-7,000 eggs in hollows (called redds) she has scooped out of the coarse sand or gravel, where the male fertilizes them. These adult salmon die soon after mating, and their bodies then deteriorate to become part of the food chain for young fish.

Within 3-4 months, the eggs hatch into alevin, tiny immature fish with their yolk sac still attached. As the alevin exhaust the nutrients in the sac, they enter the fry stage, and begin to resemble very small salmon. The length they remain as fry differs among various species. Chinook fry, for example, immediately start heading for saltwater, whereas coho or silver salmon will remain in their home stream for 1-3 years before moving downstream.

The salmon are in the smolt stage when they start to enter saltwater. The 5- to 7-inch smolts will spend some time in the estuary area of the river or stream while they feed and adjust to the saltwater.

When it finally enters the ocean, the salmon is considered an adult. Each species varies in the number of years it remains away from its natal stream, foraging sometimes thousands of miles throughout the Pacific. Chinook can spend as many as seven years away from their nesting (and ultimately their resting) place; most other species remain in the salt for 2-4 years. Spring and fall mark the main upstream runs of the Pacific salmon. It is suspected that young salmon imprint the odor of their birth stream, enabling them to find their way home years later.

The salmon's traditional predators such as the sea lion, northern pikeminnow, harbor seal, black bear, Caspian tern, and herring gull pale in comparison to the threats posed by modern civilization. Everything from pesticides to sewage to nuclear waste has polluted Oregon waters, and until mitigation efforts were enacted, dams and hydroelectric turbines threatened to block Oregon's all-important Columbia River spawning route.

Land Animals

Oregon is home to cougars, also known as mountain lions. As human development encroaches on their territory, sightings of these large cats become more common. Although they tend to shy away from big people, they've been known to attack children and small adults. For this reason, if no other, keep your kids close to the adults when hiking.

Wild "Kiger" mustangs, descendants of horses that the Spanish conquistadors brought to the Americas centuries ago, live on Steens Mountain and are identified by their hooked ears, thin dorsal stripes, two-toned manes, and faint zebra stripes on their legs. Narrow trunks and a short back are other distinguishing physical characteristics. They sometimes can be identified from a distance by the herding instinct bred into them by the Spanish. The Kigers constitute a small percentage of the 2,000 wild mustangs in the state.

Bears

Black bears (*Ursus americanus*) proliferate in remote mountain forests of Oregon. Adults average 200-500 pounds and have dark coats. Black bears shy away from people except when provoked by the scent of food, when cornered or surprised, or when humans intrude into territory near their cubs. Female bears tend to have a very strong maternal instinct that may construe any alien presence as an attack upon their young. Authorities counsel hikers to act aggressively and defend themselves with whatever means possible if a bear is in attack mode or shows signs that it considers a hiker prey. Jump up and down, shout, and wave your arms. It may help to raise your jacket or pack to make yourself appear larger. Bears can run much faster than humans, and their retractable claws enable black bears to scramble up trees. Furthermore, bears tend to give chase when they see something running.

If you see a bear at a distance, try to stay downwind of it and back away slowly. Bears have a strong sense of smell, and some studies suggest that our body scent is abhorrent to them. Our food, however, can be quite appealing. Campers should place all food in a sack tied to a rope and suspend it 20 feet or more from the ground.

Deer, Elk, and Pronghorn

Sportspeople and wildlife enthusiasts alike appreciate Oregon's big-game herds. Big-game habitats differ dramatically from one side of the Cascades to the other, with Roosevelt elk and black-tailed deer in the west and Rocky Mountain elk and mule deer east of the Cascades. The Columbian white-tailed deer is a seldom-seen endangered species that populates western Oregon. Pronghorn reside in the high desert country of southeastern Oregon. The continent's fastest mammal, it is able to sprint at over 60 mph in short bursts. The low brush of the open country east of the Cascades suits their excellent vision, which enables them to spot predators.

Small Mammals

Many of the most frequently sighted animals in Oregon are small scavengers. Even in the most urban parts of the state, it's possible to see raccoons, skunks, chipmunks, squirrels, and opossums.

West of the Cascades, the dark-colored Townsend's chipmunks are among the most commonly encountered mammals; east of the Cascades, lighter-colored pine chipmunks and golden mantled ground squirrels proliferate in drier interior forests. The latter two look almost alike, but the stripes on the side of the chipmunk's head distinguish them from each other. Expect to see the dark brown, cinnamon-bellied Douglas squirrel on both sides of the Cascades.

Beavers

Beavers (*Castor canadensis*), North America's largest rodents, are widespread throughout the Beaver State, though they're most commonly sighted in second-growth forests near marshes after sunset. Fall is a good time to spot beavers as they gather food for winter. The beaver has long been Oregon's mascot, and for good reason: It was the beaver that drew brigades of fur trappers and spurred the initial exploration and settlement of the state. The beaver also merits a special mention for being important to Oregon's forest ecosystem. Contrary to popular belief, the abilities of Mother Nature's carpenter extend far beyond the mere destruction of trees to dam a waterway. In fact, the activities associated with lodge construction actually serve to maintain the food chain and the health of the forest.

The beaver's lodge, together with its pond, fosters a fertile web of life. Aged trees killed by the intrusion of a pond into a forest become homes for millions of insects, which provide food for woodpeckers and other birds. Fish, turtles, frogs, and snakes soon inhabit the pond and its surrounding environment, and herons, muskrats, otters, and raccoons arrive later as part of the newly emerging ecosystem. Bears, birds of prey, and deer may come to the shore to drink or feed on smaller animals. Fish may feed on mosquito larvae in the still waters. After the beavers have exhausted the nearby food supply and moved on, the pond may eventually drain and become a fertile meadow and home to yet other creatures.

The presence of beavers has other positive implications for the nearby human population. In early times, pioneers coveted the fertile soil left from a drained beaver pond. Floods and droughts are tempered in the long run by beaver activities; control of soil erosion and reduced numbers of forest fires are other positive by-products.

Banana Slugs

You won't go far in the Oregon coast woodlands or underbrush before you encounter the state's best-known invertebrates—and lots of them. There are few places on earth where these snails-out-of-shells grow as large (3-10 inches long) or as numerous. The reason is western Oregon's climate: moister than mist but drier than drizzle. This balance, combined with calcium-poor soil, enables the native banana slug and the more common European black slug to thrive.

The bane of Oregon gardeners, the eight species of nonnative slugs that have established themselves in the Pacific Northwest prey on crops and gardens. Native species generally confine themselves to forests, where they feast on indigenous plants. When these critters are not eating vegetation, you'll see them moseying along at a snail's pace on sidewalks or forest trails.

Desert Critters

Because most desert animals are nocturnal, it's difficult to see many of them. Nonetheless, their variety and exotic presences should be noted. Horned lizards, kangaroo rats, red-and-black ground snakes, kit foxes, and four-inch-long greenish-yellow hairy scorpions are some of the more interesting denizens of the desert east of the Cascade Mountains. Marine fossils dating back 225 million years have been found in eastern Oregon creek beds in an area that is now home to pronghorn and wild mustangs.

Birds

The Pacific Flyway is an important migratory route that passes through Oregon, and the state's varied ecosystems provide habitats for a variety of species, ranging from shorebirds to raptors to songbirds. The U.S. Fish and Wildlife Service has established viewpoints for wildlife- and bird-watching at 12 Oregon national wildlife refuges.

In the winter the outskirts of Klamath Falls become inundated with bald eagles. Along the lower Columbia east of Astoria and on Sauvie Island, just outside Portland, are other bald eagle wintering spots. Visitors to Sauvie Island will be treated to an amazing variety of birds. More than 200 bird species come through here on the Pacific Flyway, feeding in grassy clearings. Look for eagles here on the island's northwest side. Herons, ducks of all sorts, and geese also live on the island.

Other birds of prey, or raptors, abound all over the state. Northeast of Enterprise, near Zumwalt, is one of the best places to see hawks. Species commonly sighted include the ferruginous, red-tailed, and Swainson's hawks. Rafters in Hells Canyon might see golden eagles' and peregrine falcons' nests. Portlanders driving the Fremont Bridge over the Willamette River also might get to see peregrine falcons. Along I-5 in the Willamette Valley, look for red-tailed hawks on fence posts, and American kestrels, North America's smallest falcons, sitting on overhead wires.

Turkey vultures circle the dry areas during the warmer months. Vultures are commonly sighted above the Rogue River. In central Oregon, ospreys are frequently spotted off the Cascades Lakes Highway south of Bend, nesting atop hollowed-out snags near water (especially Crane Prairie Reservoir).

In terms of sheer numbers and variety, the coast's mudflats at low tide and the tidal estuaries are among the best birding environments. Numerous locations along the coast—including Bandon Marsh, Three Arch Rocks near Cape Meares, and South Slough Estuarine Research Reserve near Coos Bay—offer outstanding opportunities for spotting such pelagic species as pelicans, cormorants, guillemots, and puffins, as well as waders such as curlews, sandpipers, and plovers, plus various ducks and geese. Rare species such as tufted puffins and the snowy plover enjoy special protection here, along with other types of migratory birds. The **Oregon Islands National Wildlife Refuge,** which comprises all the 1,400-plus offshore islands,

reefs, and rocks from Tillamook Head to the California border, is a haven for the largest concentration of nesting seabirds along the West Coast, thanks to the abundance of protected nesting habitat.

Malheur Wildlife Refuge, in the southeast portion of the state, is Oregon's premier bird and birder retreat and stopover point for large groups of sandhill cranes, Canada and snow geese, whistling swans, and pintail ducks.

In the mountains, look for Clark's nutcracker and the large Steller's jay, whose grating voice and dazzling blue plumage often command the most attention. Mountain hikers are bound to share part of their picnic lunch with these birds. At high elevations, the quieter Clark's nutcracker will more likely be your guest.

Unfortunately, the western meadowlark, the state bird, has nearly vanished from western Oregon due to loss of habitat, but thanks to natural pasture east of the Cascades, you can still hear its distinctive song. The meadowlark is distinguished by a yellow underside with a black crescent pattern across the breast and white outer tail feathers.

History

NATIVE PEOPLES
Early Days

Long before Europeans came to this hemisphere, native peoples thrived for thousands of years in the region of present-day Oregon. A leading theory concerning their origins maintains that their ancestors came over from Asia on a land or ice bridge spanning what is now the Bering Strait. Along with archaeological evidence, shipwrecks of Asian craft on the Pacific coast also support the theory that Native Americans had Eastern Hemisphere contact. This contention has been further substantiated by facial features and dental patterns common to both peoples, as well as isolated correspondences in ritual, music, and dialect.

Despite common ancestry, the people on

the rain-soaked coast and in the Willamette Valley lived quite differently from those on the drier eastern flank of the Cascade Mountains. Those west of the Cascades enjoyed abundant salmon, shellfish, berries, and game. Broad rivers facilitated travel, and thick stands of the finest softwood timber in the world ensured that there was never a dearth of building materials. A mild climate with plentiful food and resources allowed the wet-siders the leisure time to evolve a complex culture rich with artistic endeavors, theatrical pursuits, and such ceremonial gatherings as the traditional potlatch, where the divesting of one's material wealth was seen as a status symbol. Dentalium and abalone shells, woodpecker feathers, obsidian blades, and hides

WHAT'S IN A NAME?

One rather peculiar theory of how Oregon got its name derives from a reputed encounter between Native Americans and the Spanish mariners who plied West Coast waters in the 17th and 18th centuries. Upon seeing the abalone shell earrings of the coastal Salish people, the European sailors are said to have exclaimed, *"¡Orejon!"* ("What big ears!")–later anglicized to Oregon. Others point out the similarity between the name of the state and the Spanish locales Aragon and Obregon (in Mexico). Additionally, the word *Oregon* belonged to a Wisconsin group of Native Americans who purportedly traded with Columbia River natives during salmon season.

A less fanciful explanation has it that the state's name was inspired by the English word "origin," conjuring the image of the forest primeval. The French word *ouragan* ("hurricane") has also been suggested as the source of the state's name, courtesy of French Canadian fur trappers who became the first permanent European settlers in the region during the early 19th century. In this vein, the reference to the Columbia River as the "Oregan" by some French Canadian voyageurs who came here with the "beaver brigades" of the Northwest and Hudson's Bay Companies is another possible etymological ancestor.

It was recently noted that *oregonon* and *orenogonia*, two Greek words pertaining to mountainous locales, were seen on old navigators' maps marking the area between northern California and British Columbia. Given that the famous Pacific Northwest explorer Juan de Fuca was actually Greek (born Valerianos) and that many navigators were schooled in Greece, perhaps Oregon's name originated in the Mediterranean.

---

were especially coveted. Later on, Hudson's Bay blankets were added to this list.

After contact with traders, Chinook, an amalgam of Native American tongues with some French and English thrown in, was the common argot among the diverse nations that gathered in the Columbia Gorge each year. It was at these gatherings that the coast and valley dwellers would come into contact with Native Americans from east of the Cascades. These dry-siders led a seminomadic existence, following the game and avoiding the climatic extremes of winter and summer in their region. In the southeast desert of the Great Basin, seeds and roots added protein to their diet.

The introduction of horses in the mid-1700s made hunting, especially for large bison, much easier. In contrast to their counterparts west of the Cascades, who lived in 100- by 40-foot longhouses, extended families in the eastern groups inhabited pit houses when not hunting. The demands of chasing migratory game necessitated caves or simple rock shelters.

Twelve separate nations populated Oregon.

Although these were further divided into 80 tribes, the primary allegiance was to the village. The "nation" status referred to language groupings such as Salish and Athabascan. The names of the tribes, such as Alsea or Shasta Costa, were usually derived from a word in the local argot for "the people" or from what a neighboring tribe called "them." On occasion, European explorers bestowed a name on a particular native grouping. An example of this was the "Rogue" Native American appellation. Across the region, many Native Americans were united in their worship of Spilyai, the coyote demigod. Spilyai, as well as many other animal and human figures, formed the subject of a large body of folktales that explain the origins of the land in ways that are both entertaining and insightful.

Conflicts with European Settlers

The coming of European settlers meant the usurpation of Native American homelands, exposure to European diseases such as smallpox and diphtheria, and the passing of ancient ways of life. Violent conflicts ensued on a large scale with the influx of settlers doing missionary work and seeking government land giveaways in the 1830s and 1840s. In the 1850s, mining activity in southern Oregon and on the coast incited the Rogue River Indian Wars, adding to the strife brought on by annexation to the United States.

All these events compelled the U.S. federal government to send in troops and eventually to set up treaties with Oregon's first inhabitants. The attempts at arbitration in the 1850s added insult to injury. Tribes of different—indeed, often incompatible—backgrounds were rounded up and grouped together haphazardly on reservations, often far from their homelands. In the century that followed, the evils of modern civilization destroyed much of the ecosystem on which these cultures were based. An especially regrettable result of settlement was the decline of the Columbia River salmon runs due to overfishing, loss of habitat, and pollution. This not only weakened the food chain but treated this spiritual totem of the many Native American groups along the Columbia as an expendable resource.

For a while, there was an attempt to restore the balance. In 1924 the federal government accorded citizenship to Native Americans. Ten years later the Indian Reorganization Act provided self-management of reservation lands. A decade later a court of treaty claims was established. In the 1960s, however, the government, acting on the premise that Native Americans needed to assimilate into mainstream society, terminated several reservations.

Recent government reparations have accorded many native peoples preferential hunting and fishing rights, monetary and land grants, and the restoration of status to certain disenfranchised groups. In Oregon, there are now nine federally recognized tribes and six reservations: Warm Springs, Umatilla, Burns Paiute, Siletz, Grand Ronde, and Coquille. Against all odds, their culture is still a vital part of Oregon; the 2000 census estimated that over 45,000 Oregonians are Native American. Native American gaming came to Oregon in the mid-1990s, and Native Oregonians now operate eight lucrative casinos in the state; the Confederated Tribes of Grand Ronde, owners of the phenomenally popular Spirit Mountain Casino, are among the state's biggest philanthropists.

Archaeological Perspectives

Archaeologists have unearthed all manner of Native American artifacts. One that has evoked considerable controversy is a site found at Fort Rock, east of the Cascades near Bend. Charcoals from a hearth there are thought to be more than 13,000 years old, exceeding earlier estimates of the period of human presence in the region by about 3,500 years. A sandal found at the same site dated at around 10,000 years old had been the previous standard-bearer.

Another significant find is a gallery of 5,000-year-old petroglyphs on the walls of a cave in the foothills just east of the Willamette Valley. Artifacts excavated from the site of the Oregon Country Fair near Eugene have been dated at 8,000-10,000 years of age.

Other finds include coastal and Rogue Valley digs where 9,000-year-old artifacts have been unearthed. Obsidian flaked in the Clovis style indicates that ice age people roamed the Rogue Valley as long as 11,000 years ago. The distinctive grooves in the obsidian mark it as a product of the Clovis big-game hunter culture. Researchers excavated a site at Indian Sands in Samuel H. Boardman State Park north of Brookings that yielded artifacts dating back more than 12,000 years, making it the oldest known site of human activity yet found on the coast.

In 1999 the oldest house in Oregon, and possibly the United States, was discovered on the shore of Paulina Lake. The archaeological significance of this 9,500-year-old site might eventually be rivaled by finds in several Woodburn city parks, 35 miles south of Portland. In the summer of 2000, a human hair was found in 12,000-year-old soils of an ancient wetland, along with animal bones thousands of years old.

EXPLORATION, SETTLEMENT, AND GROWTH

In the 17th and 18th centuries, Spanish, British, and Russian vessels came to offshore waters here in search of a sea route connecting the Atlantic with the Pacific. Accounts differ, but the first sightings of the Oregon coast have been credited to either Juan Rodríguez Cabrillo (in 1543) or the English explorer Sir Francis Drake (in 1579). Other voyagers of note included Spain's Vizcaíno and de Aguilar (in 1603) and Bruno de Heceta (in 1775), and Britain's James Cook and John Meares during the late 1770s, as well as George Vancouver (in 1792). Robert Gray's 1792 voyage 10 miles up the Columbia River estuary was the first U.S. incursion into the area.

In 1996, a front-page story in the London *Times* proclaimed Sir Francis Drake the first European to set foot on the coast (previously Heceta was credited with the first landing) on the basis of an archaeological find in Little Whale Cove south of Depoe Bay. Timbers from a stockade left by Drake, who is known to have beached for repairs, were purportedly found, leading to this speculation.

Sea otter and beaver pelts added impetus to the search for a trade route connecting the Atlantic and Pacific Oceans. While the Northwest Passage turned out to be a myth, the fur trade became a basis of commerce and contention between European, Asian, and eventually American governments.

U.S. Expansion in Oregon

The United States took interest the area when Robert Gray sailed up the Columbia River in 1792. The first U.S. overland excursion into Oregon was made by the Corps of Discovery in 1804-1806. Dispatched by Thomas Jefferson to explore the lands of the Louisiana Purchase and beyond, Captains Meriwether Lewis and William Clark and their party of 30 men and one woman, Sacajawea, trekked across the continent to the mouth of the Columbia, camped south of present-day Astoria during the winter of 1805-1806, and then returned to St. Louis. Lewis and Clark's exploration and mapping of Oregon threw down the gauntlet for future settlement and eventual annexation of the Oregon Territory by the United States. The expedition also initially secured good relations with the Native Americans in the West, thus establishing the preconditions to trade and the missionary influx.

Following Lewis and Clark's journey, there were years of wrangling over the right of the United States to settle in the new territory. The mere threat of British gunboats on the Columbia caused the quick departure of American John Jacob Astor's Pacific Fur Company during the War of 1812. It wasn't until the Convention of 1818 that the country west of the Rockies, south of Russian America, and north of Spanish America was open for use by U.S. citizens as well as British subjects.

During the 1820s, the Hudson's Bay Company continued to hold sway over Oregon country by means of Fort Vancouver on the north shore of the Columbia. More than 500 people settled here under the charismatic leadership of John McLoughlin, who oversaw the planting of crops and the raising of livestock. Despite the establishment of almost half a dozen Hudson's Bay outposts, several factors presaged the inevitable demise of British influence in Oregon. Most obvious was the decline of the fur trade as well as Britain's difficulty in maintaining her far-flung empire. Less apparent but equally influential was the lack of European women in a land populated predominantly by European trappers and explorers. If the Americans could attract settlers of both genders, they'd be in a position to create an expanding population base that could dominate the region.

The first step in this process was the arrival of missionaries. In 1834, Methodist soul-seekers led by Jason Lee settled near the Willamette River. Four years later, another mission was started in the eastern Columbia River Gorge. In 1843, Marcus and Narcissa Whitman's missions started up on the upper Columbia in present-day Walla Walla, Washington (until 1853, the Washington area was considered a single entity with Oregon).

THE CORPS OF DISCOVERY

For nearly two decades at the end of the 18th century, Thomas Jefferson dreamed of mounting an expedition to explore the virtually unknown North American continent west of the Mississippi River. Like others of his era, Jefferson believed in the existence of the Northwest Passage, a navigable route between the northern Pacific and Atlantic Oceans, the discovery of which would revolutionize trade between the United States and Asia and speed the growth (and increase the wealth) of the young republic. In January 1803, President Jefferson finally succeeded in securing funding from the U.S. Congress to outfit such an ambitious undertaking. Congress granted $2,500, though the eventual cost would top $38,000.

Jefferson invited his secretary, 28-year-old Meriwether Lewis, to lead the expedition, which the president named the Corps of Discovery. Its stated goals would be "to make friends and allies of the far Western Indians while at the same time diverting valuable pelts from the rugged northern routes used by [Great Britain] . . . and bringing the harvest down the Missouri to the Mississippi and thence eastward by a variety of routes." Furthermore, Lewis would be charged with mapping the territory and chronicling the people, plants, and animals encountered along the way. Lewis, in turn, asked a former Army comrade, William Clark, to cocaptain the expedition with him.

Just two months after Congress approved the request, Jefferson consummated the Louisiana Purchase, an agreement that ceded New Orleans and 820,000 square miles of France's North American territories to the United States, for $15 million—about three cents per acre. Overnight, the area of the United States doubled, and Lewis and Clark's mission assumed even greater importance.

In May 1804, after months of preparation and recruitment, the Corps set off in a large keelboat and two pirogues up the Missouri River from a base near St. Louis, then the western edge of the civilized U.S. territories. Over the next two years, their route would take them north and west, up the drainages of the Missouri River, across the Rockies, into the Columbia River system, and finally to the Pacific Ocean. The Corps, consisting of 32 men and one woman, the Shoshone Sacajawea, would spend October 1805 to May 1806 in what are today Oregon and Washington, including four wet, miserable months at Fort Clatsop near Astoria.

Along the way, Lewis and Clark charted some 8,000 miles of territory hitherto unexplored by European Americans and documented 300 species of flora and fauna previously unknown to Western science. Journals kept by Lewis, Clark, and three of their sergeants chronicle their experiences with such vividness that they still captivate readers today. The effect their journey had in accelerating westward expansion of the United States across the continent can hardly be overstated.

© BILL MCRAE

The replica of Fort Clatsop is near Astoria.

The missionaries brought alien ways and diseases for which the Native Americans had no immunity. As if this weren't enough to provoke a violent reaction, the Native Americans would soon have their homelands inundated by thousands of settlers lured by government land giveaways.

The Oregon Trail

The march across the frontier was fueled by the 640 free acres that each adult white male could claim in the mid-1840s. The westward expansion that the United States regarded as its "manifest destiny" seemed a ready solution to the problems of the 1830s, when the country was in a deep depression, with land panics, droughts, and an unstable currency. Despite Easterners' ignorance of western geography and the hardships it held, the Oregon Trail, a 2,000-mile frontier thoroughfare, was viewed with covetous eyes, especially in increasingly populous Missouri. Around Independence, Missouri, the trees thinned, the settlements ended, and the Oregon Trail began.

More than 53,000 people traversed the trail between 1840 and 1850 en route to western Oregon. In 1850, the Donation Land Act cut in half the allotted free acreage, reflecting the diminishing availability of real estate. But although a single pioneer man was now entitled to only 320 acres, and single women were excluded from land ownership, as part of a couple they could claim an additional 320 free acres. This promoted marriage and, in turn, families on the western frontier and helped to fulfill Secretary of State John C. Calhoun's prediction that American families could outbreed the Hudson's Bay Company's bachelor trappers, thus winning the battle of the West in the bedroom.

The Donation Land Act also stipulated that nonwhites could not own any part of the Oregon Territory, enabling the pioneers to seize native people's lands with impunity. The act impeded the growth of towns and industries too, as large parcels of land were given away to relatively small numbers of people, which kept the population geographically distant from one another. This was one reason why urbanization was slow in coming to the Pacific Northwest.

The Applegate Trail

Another route west was the Applegate Trail, pioneered by brothers Lindsay and Jesse Applegate in the mid-1840s. Each had lost sons several years before to drowning on the Columbia River. The treacherous rapids here had initially been the last leg of a journey to the Willamette Valley.

On their return journey to the region, the brothers departed from the established trail when they reached Fort Hall, Idaho. Veering south from the Oregon Trail across northern Nevada's Black Rock Desert, they traversed the northeast top of California to enter Oregon near present-day Klamath Falls. A southern Oregon gold rush in the 1850s drew thousands along this route.

Early Government and Statehood

There was enough unity among American settlers to organize a provisional government in 1843. Then, in 1848, the federal government decided to accord Oregon territorial status. With migration increasing exponentially from 1843 on, there was little doubt in the U.S. Congress about Oregon's viability. Still, it took frontiersman Joe Meek to coalesce popular opinion. He had first performed this role in Champoeg, at the northern end of the Willamette Valley, in 1843, when he boomed out the rallying cry for regional confederation, "Who's for a divide?," in order to force a vote on the question of whether to challenge the British claim of sovereignty in the region. Two Canadians, F. X. Matthieu and Etienne Lucier, crossed the line and won the day for the Union. In equally dramatic fashion, Meek strode into the halls of Congress fresh from the trail in mountainman regalia to argue forcefully the case for territoriality. Congress granted the petition, and Meek accompanied newly appointed territorial governor Joseph Lane to Oregon in the spring of 1849.

The Oregon Territory got off to a rousing start thanks to the California gold rush of 1849. The rush occasioned a housing boom in San Francisco and a need for lumber, and the dramatic population influx created instant markets for the agriculture of the Willamette Valley. Portland was located at the north end of the valley and 110 miles upriver from the Pacific on the Columbia, near the world's largest supply of accessible softwood timber. The young city was in a perfect position to channel goods from the interior to coastal ports. So great was the need in California for food that wheat from eastern Oregon was declared legal tender. The exchange rate started around $1 per bushel and went as high as $6. The economic benefits from the gold rush notwithstanding, Oregon lost two-thirds of its adult male population to gold fever. Many of the emigrants returned when the news of gold discoveries in southwestern Oregon came out between 1850 and 1860. The resulting influx helped establish the Rogue Valley and coastal population centers.

However, strategic importance and population growth alone do not explain Oregon becoming the 33rd state in the Union. Shortly before statehood, the Dred Scott decision had become law in 1857. This had the effect of opening the territory to slavery. While slavery didn't lack for adherents in Oregon, the prevailing sentiment was that it was neither necessary nor desirable. Because territorial status would be a potential liability to a Union on the mend, the congressional majority saw an especially compelling reason to open its doors to this new member. When nonslavery status was assured, Oregon entered the Union on Valentine's Day 1859.

Economic Growing Pains

During the years of the Civil War and its aftermath, internal conflicts were the order of the day within the state. By 1861, good Willamette Valley land was becoming scarce, so many farmers moved east of the Cascades to farm wheat. They ran into violent confrontations with Native Americans over land. Between 1862 and 1934, the Homestead Act land giveaways helped fuel these fires of resentment. Miners encroaching on Native American territory around the southern coast eventually flared into the bloody Rogue River Wars, which would lead to the destruction of most of the native peoples of the coast.

In the 1870s, cattle ranchers came to eastern Oregon, followed by sheep ranchers, and the two groups fought for dominance of the range. Just when it appeared that eastern Oregon land was ripe for agricultural promoters and community planners, the bottom fell out. Overproduction of wheat, uncertain markets, and two severe winters were the culprits. In the early 20th century a population influx created further problems by draining the water table. Thus the glory that was gold, grass, and grain east of the Cascades was short-lived. Many eastern Oregon towns grew up and flourished for a decade, only to fall back into desert, leaving no trace of their existence.

Unlike the downturn east of the Cascades, boom times were ahead for the rest of the state as the 20th century approached. In the 1860s and 1870s, Jacksonville in the south became the commercial counterpart to Portland, owing to its proximity to the Rogue Valley and south coast goldfields as well as the California border. During this period, transportation links began to consolidate, in part due to the efforts of stagecoach magnate Ben Holladay. The first stagecoach, steamship, and rail lines moved south from the Columbia River into the Willamette Valley; by the 1880s, Portland was joined to San Francisco and the east by railroad. Henry Villard was the prime champion of this effort, eventually dominating all commerce in the Pacific Northwest by channeling freight and passengers through Portland and along the Columbia. In 1900, Union Pacific magnate James J. Hill picked up where Villard left off. By selling 900,000 acres of timberland to lumber baron Frederic Weyerhaeuser at $6 per acre (with the stipulation that Weyerhaeuser build his mills close to Union Pacific tracks), he hitched the destiny of the region to the iron horse.

Progressive Politics

In the modern era, Oregon blazed trails in the thicket of governmental legislation and reform. The so-called Oregon system of initiative, referendum, and recall was first conceived in the 1890s, coming to fruition in the first decade of the 1900s. The system has since become an integral part of the democratic process.

In like measure, Oregon's extension of suffrage to women in 1912, a 1921 compulsory education law, and the first large-scale union activity in the country during the 1920s were red-letter events in U.S. history.

The 1930s were exciting years in the Pacific Northwest. Despite widespread poverty, the foundations of future prosperity were laid during this decade. New Deal programs such as the Works Progress Administration and the Civilian Conservation Corps undertook many projects around the state. Building roads and hydroelectric dams created jobs and improved the quality of life in Oregon, in addition to bolstering the country's defenses during wartime. Hydroelectric power from the Bonneville Dam, completed in 1938, enabled Portland's shipyards and aluminum plants to thrive. Low utility rates encouraged more employment and settlement, while the Columbia's irrigation water enhanced agriculture.

World War II

Thanks to Henry Kaiser's mass-production techniques, 10,000 workers were employed in the Portland shipyards. But in addition to laying the foundations for future growth, the war years in Oregon and their immediate aftermath were full of trials for state residents. Vanport—at one time a city of 45,000—grew up in the shadow of Kaiser aluminum plants and the shipyards north of Portland, but it was washed off the map in 1948 by a Columbia River flood. Tillamook County forests, which supplied Sitka spruce for airplanes, endured several massive fires that destroyed 500 square miles of trees. Along with these natural disasters, Oregon was the only state among the contiguous 48 to have a military installation (Fort Stevens, near Astoria) shelled by a Japanese submarine, to endure a Japanese bombing mission on the mainland (on Mount Emily, near Brookings), and to suffer civilian casualties when a balloon bomb exploded (near the Gearhart Mountain Wilderness Area in Lake County).

The Modern Era

With the perfection of the chain saw in the 1940s, the timber industry could take advantage of the postwar housing boom. During that decade, the state's population increased by nearly 50 percent, growing to over 1.5 million. During the 1950s and 1960s, the U.S. Army Corps of Engineers carried out a massive program of new dam projects, resulting in construction of The Dalles, John Day, and McNary Dams on the main stem of the Columbia and the Oxbow and Brownlee Dams on the Snake River. In addition, flooding on the Willamette River was tamed through a series of dams on its major tributary watersheds, the Santiam, the Middle Fork of the Willamette, and the McKenzie.

Politically, the late 1960s and 1970s brought environmentally groundbreaking measures spearheaded by Governor Tom McCall. The bottle bill, land use statutes, and the cleanup of the Willamette River were part of this legacy.

The 1990s saw the Oregon economy flourish, fueled by the growth of computer hardware and software industries here as well as a real estate market favorable to California retirees. The latter has had sociological ripple effects, with many longtime state residents feeling displaced by the transformed economy and living standards. The legalization of gambling and drastic cuts in education have provoked controversy on all sides of the political spectrum. While a retreat from long-standing legislative commitments reflects the demographics of Oregon's new arrivals as well as its changing economic climate, Oregon's physician-assisted suicide bill, extensive vote-by-mail procedures, medical marijuana initiative, and low-cost health insurance program for low-income Oregonians have sustained its maverick image.

© BILL MCRAE

Dairies are an important part of the state's economy.

Today's Economy

Until recently, logging and wood products have been the most important industries to Oregon in terms of jobs provided and revenue produced. Despite recent declines, workers are still employed in logging, sawmills, and paper production. Fishing, although it has its ups and downs, is another traditional part of the economy that has persisted.

Oregon's economy has traditionally followed a boom-bust cycle, and even though it has in recent decades diversified away from its earlier dependence on resource-based industries, the economic bust of 2008 left over 10 percent of Oregonians unemployed, second only to Michigan in unemployment rate.

The state's major manufacturing industries today include high tech, primary and fabricated metals, transportation equipment, and agricultural crops and processing. Important nonmanufacturing sectors, which account for five out of seven jobs in the state, include wholesale and retail trade; education, health, and social services; high-tech nonmanufacturing jobs such as software development; and tourism.

In agriculture, organic produce, often sold in farmers markets, and specialty products have helped many small farmers to survive. These products include nursery crops (Monrovia is the nation's largest Christmas tree nursery, and Oregon is the number one Christmas tree state); wine grapes; berries, cherries, apples, and pears; herbs and organic produce; gourmet mushrooms; and goat cheese. Oregon wineries, most of them small operations, turn out increasingly good wine, and for some this is actually a viable way to make a living. Large-scale agribusiness is also thriving with the booming food-processing and packing industries proliferating in the lower Willamette Valley and eastern Oregon.

But it must be said that Intel is the state's largest employer, and Nike, Adidas America, Columbia, and other sportswear companies have headquarters here, employing a substantial number of people in the Portland area.

ESSENTIALS

Getting There and Around

BY AIR

It is a simple enough matter getting to and getting around Oregon by air. If there is a break in the weather, the views are breathtaking. (When flying into Portland from the east, get a window seat on the left side of the plane for close-up views of Mount Hood.) The main point of entry is Portland International Airport (PDX), which is served by over a dozen airlines, but there are also airports in Redmond and Medford. If eastern Oregon is your destination, consider flying into and out of Boise, Idaho.

Horizon Air (800/547-9308, www.horizonair.com), the commuter-league farm club of Alaska Airlines, connects Portland to Redmond, Eugene-Springfield, and Medford, as well as numerous other cities around the western states. Horizon operates commuter prop planes with 10-40 seats. If you are sensitive to loud noises and pressure change, bring earplugs.

BY TRAIN

Thanks to **Amtrak** (800/872-7245, www.amtrak.com) and its high-speed Spanish-made Talgo trains, the stretch from Eugene to Vancouver, B.C., enjoys an efficient and scenic mass-transit link. Four *Cascades* trains

© BILL MCRAE

Nearly every corner of the state has some sort of bus service.

make daily round-trips between Portland and Seattle; one continues on to Vancouver, B.C. Two trains go from Portland south to Eugene daily. The **Coast Starlight** runs between L.A. and Seattle with stops in Oregon at Klamath Falls, Chemult, Eugene, Salem, and Portland.

Note that getting a sleeper on the extremely popular *Coast Starlight* requires reservations 5-11 months in advance any time of the year. Northbound passengers board in the San Francisco Bay Area and after riding all night wake up to sunrise over alpine lakes and the snowcapped Cascades. From the Cascade summit, you head down into Eugene along the beautiful Upper Willamette River.

The **Empire Builder,** which connects Portland with Chicago, shows off the Columbia River Gorge to good advantage. Trains run on the Washington side of the Columbia, giving a distant perspective on the waterfalls and mountains across the river. In summer this train stops in Glacier Park, Montana.

Amtrak also runs bus service in such corridors as Portland-Eugene and Chemult-Bend.

The latter service makes Bend accessible to *Coast Starlight* passengers who disembark in Chemult.

BY BUS

Greyhound (800/229-9424, www.greyhound.com) has cut most of its service to Oregon and now travels only along the interstate corridors of I-5 and I-84, but many smaller companies have picked up the slack. Porter, Valley Retriever, Central Oregon Breeze, Southwest and Northwest Point, and other smaller companies operate on former Greyhound routes. Visit www.tripcheck.com to find details on bus service to Oregon's cities and towns.

BY CAR

For the vast majority of visitors (and residents), the automobile is the vehicle of choice for exploring the state. Speed limits top out at 65 mph on sections of I-5 and I-84; the rest of the roads in the state have a 55 mph maximum speed limit.

Many Oregon roads are strikingly beautiful.

The magnificent scenery prompted the planning of the first paved public road in the state with the Columbia River Highway, constructed 1913-1915, now known as the Historic Columbia River Highway. The Oregon Coast Scenic Highway, U.S. 101 along the entire Oregon coast, is another internationally renowned drive. Entirely different in character, but equally stunning, is the Cascade Lakes Highway out of Bend.

Although the roads are beautiful, motorists must be sensitive to the weather and pavement conditions. Cloudbursts can cause cars to hydroplane, thick palls of fog that hang over the Willamette Valley can lead to multicar pileups, and the icy mountain roads of the Cascades and eastern Oregon also claim their share of victims.

The **Oregon Department of Transportation** advises on **road conditions** by phone (503/588-2941 out of state, 800/977-6368 within Oregon) and via the TripCheck website (www.tripcheck.com).

Gas is readily available on the main routes, but finding it can be a little trickier in remote eastern Oregon, especially after 5pm. Fill up before you leave the city. Another thing to remember is that Oregon is one of the few states that does not have self-service gasoline outlets; pull up to the pump and wait for an attendant.

Winter Driving

The first rule to follow when rain, snow, or hail make pavement slick, or when fog reduces visibility, is to slow down. From late fall to early spring, expect snow on the Cascade passes and I-5 through the Siskiyous; snow tires or chains are often required.

A **Sno-Park permit** is required to park at most ski areas and plowed parking lots leading to cross-country ski trails. Without the daily sticker or season pass in your left-hand windshield, a car left in a Sno-Park area can receive a ticket. This permit is essentially a fee levied by the state to pay for the upkeep of parking and rest areas and for snowplowing in the mountains. Pick these up at a Department of Motor Vehicles office, ski shops, sporting goods stores, and other commercial establishments. They apply to travel November 15-April 15 and cost $3 for 1 day, $20 for the season; stores selling the permits often levy an extra service fee.

If you are traveling into the mountains in the winter, make sure your car has tire chains in the trunk. During snowstorms, many mountain passes are closed to vehicles without chains, and the state patrol takes the task of enforcing this requirement very seriously.

BY BICYCLE

Oregon is user-friendly for bicyclists. In the 1970s the Oregon legislature allocated one percent of the state highways budget to develop bike lanes and encourage energy-saving bicyclists. In addition to establishing routes throughout the state with these funds, many special paths were developed with bicycle and foot access specifically in mind. For example, Eugene's Willamette River Greenway bike path system winds through a string of parks. In Portland, many streets are marked as bike corridors and signs direct cyclists to nearby destinations. A decent cyclist can easily beat a car across town during rush hour.

The **Oregon Department of Transportation** (503/986-3555, www.oregon.gov) produces some useful and free resources for cyclists, which can be ordered by phone or downloaded online. Find maps of bike trails and routing suggestions for the entire state, the Columbia Gorge, the coast, and a number of cities.

Sports and Recreation

PARK FEES AND PASSES

Oregon has more state parks than almost any other state, as well as a natural environment suited to all manner of recreational activities. In recent years, numerous state and federal parks, national recreation areas, trails, picnic areas, and other facilities have begun charging day-use fees, which are separate from overnight camping fees (the exception to this is camping at rustic campsites in national forests, which is covered by the Northwest Forest Pass). At sites that charge fees, the day-use fee is currently $5 per vehicle at state parks or federal sites. Visitors can pay for day use at individual sites or purchase one of the annual passes described here.

Oregon Pacific Coast Passport

The best deal if you plan to visit many parks along the Oregon coast, this pass covers entrance, day-use, and vehicle parking fees at all state and federal fee sites along the entire Oregon portion of U.S. 101. It does not cover the cost of camping at state parks, which is a separate fee.

Two basic Passports are available, depending on your needs and preferences. An **annual passport,** valid for the calendar year, is $35. A **five-day passport** is $10. Passports may be purchased at welcome centers, ranger stations, national forest headquarters, national memorials, and state park offices. Call 800/551-6949 to purchase an annual pass by credit card or for directions to a convenient location near you.

State Park Passes

Another option that is valid for day-use fees at Oregon's state parks that levy fees is to buy a one-year ($30) or two-year ($50) **State Park Pass.** It's available from state park offices, at day-use fee booths, and by phone (800/551-6949). See the **Oregon State Parks website** (www.oregonstateparks.org) for more details and a complete list of vendors.

Northwest Forest Pass

In response to major reductions in timber harvests and cutbacks in federal money, a revenue shortfall has made it hard to keep up trails and campgrounds at a time when the region's population has put more demand on these facilities. The **Northwest Forest Pass** ($5 for 1 day, $30 for 1 year) is a vehicle-parking pass for the use of many improved trailheads, picnic areas, boat launches, and interpretive sites in the national forests of Oregon and Washington. Funds generated from pass sales go directly to maintaining and improving the trails, land, and facilities. You will see "Northwest Forest Pass Required" signs posted at participating sites. Fees are collected at trailhead kiosks. Passes are also available at many local vendors and online at www.fs.usda.gov. You can also check this website before you head out to find out if a pass is required.

These passes are good at most Forest Service sites all over the Pacific Northwest, but they are not valid for campground fees (with the exception of rustic campsites), concessionaire-operated sites, or Sno-Parks.

Golden Passport Program

Most National Park Service sites, such as national parks and monuments, charge a fee for their use. You can pay an entrance fee at each site or park you visit, or you can purchase an annual **America the Beautiful Pass** ($80), which allows the owner to use all U.S. Forest Service, Park Service, Bureau of Land Management, and Fish and Wildlife sites, as well as developed day-use sites and recreation areas. The $10 **America the Beautiful Senior Pass** is a lifetime pass covering entrance fees for U.S. citizens over the age of 62 (proof of age required). Passport holders also get a 50 percent discount at some campgrounds, boat launches, and swimming areas. The third pass, the free **Access Pass,** is available only to those who are permanently disabled (check with the National Park Service for eligibility requirements). It offers the same benefits as the Senior Pass.

BICYCLING

While not for everybody, biking all or part of the Oregon coast is the surest way to get on intimate terms with this spectacular region. Before going, get a free copy of the **Oregon Coast Bike Route** map from the **Oregon Department of Transportation** (503/986-3555, www.oregon. gov) or from coastal information centers and chambers of commerce. This brochure features strip maps of the route, noting services from Astoria to the California border. With information on campsites, hostels, bike repair facilities, elevation changes, temperatures, and wind speed, this pamphlet does everything but map the ruts in the road.

Because the prevailing winds in summer are from the northwest, most people cycle south on U.S. 101 to take advantage of a steady tailwind. You'll also be riding on the ocean side of the road with better views and easier access to turnouts, and generally wider bike lanes and shoulders. The entire 370-mile trip (or 380 miles if you include the Three Capes Scenic Loop) involves nearly 16,000 feet of elevation change. Most cyclists cover the distance in 6-8 days, pedaling an average of 50-65 miles daily.

If you're looking for a medium to long recreational ride, check out www.rideoregonride. com, which has excellent route information for road and mountain bike rides all over the state.

A number of companies offer preplanned group bicycle trips, with everything from the bicycle to the meals and lodging included. For example, **Bicycle Adventures** (425/250-5540 or 800/443-6060, www.bicycleadventures. com) offers several coast packages, including a six-day fully supported tour from Astoria to Lincoln City for $2,745 (a budget tour with fewer fancy perks is about $2,200).

Cycle Oregon (503/287-0405 or 800/292-5367, www.cycleoregon.org) sponsors an annual weeklong supported tour of rural Oregon in September. Considered one of the best bike tours in the country, Cycle Oregon tours cover about 500 miles and attract up to 2,000 riders each year. Fees, which include all meals, showers, support, and entertainment, are around $900 per person. A mid-July weekend Cycle Oregon ride ($175 adult, $80 student) is a bit more family oriented, with a variety of daily routes ranging from 25 to 75 miles.

CAMPING
State Parks

Oregon's state parks have great amenities (including showers at most campgrounds), and given that, fees are reasonable. Fees for RV sites run about $24, tent sites about $20, yurts and rustic cabins about $40. The fee for reserving a site is $8. During the winter, camping fees drop slightly.

Most state park campgrounds have at least a couple of yurts—canvas-walled, wood-floored shelters equipped with fold-up beds, heaters, and lamps; they sleep five. Although pets have traditionally been banned from state park yurts, many parks now have at least one pet-friendly yurt.

Many state park campgrounds accept campsite reservations, and reservations are accepted for all special facilities such as cabins, yurts, and tepees. The state park system has a central **information hotline** (800/551-6949) and a website (www.oregonstateparks.org) where you can get park maps, campground layouts, rates, and other information.

Reservations for state parks can be made by phone (503/731-3411 in Portland metro area, 800/452-5687 elsewhere, 8am-7pm Mon.-Fri.). Online reservations, with a Visa or MasterCard, are handled by a private vendor, **ReserveAmerica** (www.reserveamerica.com). Reservations may be made from two days up to nine months in advance. In addition to the campsite fee, a processing fee is charged.

If you need to **cancel your reservation** three days or more before your scheduled arrival, call one of the numbers above. Two or fewer days before your trip, call the park directly to cancel your reservation. Phone numbers for all parks are found on each individual park's web page (www.oregonstateparks.org).

Sunset Bay State Park campground

Cancellation service fees and requirements for special facilities, such as yurts and cabins, may vary. Your reservation fee is nonrefundable, and a small cancellation fee will be charged if you cancel in the last two days.

National Forests

The U.S. Forest Service maintains hundreds of campsites, trails, and day-use areas. National forest campsites are usually much less developed than those at state parks; electric hookups are not available, although most campgrounds have water and vault or flush toilets. Most overnight sites charge a user fee. Fees are generally $10-18 for campsites, $5-7 for an extra vehicle. Campsites can be reserved online with a Visa or MasterCard through www.recreation.gov.

HIKING

While every corner of Oregon features hiking trails, a couple of long-distance trails deserve special notice. For 362 miles, from the Columbia River to the California border, the **Oregon Coast Trail** hugs the beaches and headlands, leading hikers into intimate contact with some of the most beautiful landscapes anywhere. Most of the trail runs through public lands, though some portions traverse easements on private parcels and the trail follows the highway and city streets in a number of places. The only coastal long-distance treks separated from U.S. 101 are the 30 miles between Seaside and Manzanita, and between Bandon and Port Orford. A free trail map and directory are available from the **Oregon State Parks information center** (800/551-6949, www.oregonstateparks.org). This pamphlet makes clear where this trail crosses open beaches, forested headlands, the shoulder of the Coast Highway, and even city streets in some towns. Be sure to bring water, particularly on northerly sections of the trail, as much of the trek is on beachfront away from a potable supply.

The other long-distance trail through the state is the Oregon portion of the **Pacific Crest Trail,** which runs from southern California to the Canadian border. The PCT through Oregon is exceptionally scenic and not too hard for sturdy, experienced backpackers; much of it runs along ridgelines, avoiding constant ups and downs.

FISHING AND HUNTING

Oregon takes a backseat to few other places when it comes to sportfishing and hunting opportunities, with varied shooting and angling possible all over the state. Rules and bag limits for both are subject to frequent change, so get a copy of the **Oregon Department of Fish and Wildlife** hunting and fishing regulations, available online (www.dfw.state.or.us) or at the agency office (4034 Fairview Industrial Dr. SE, Salem, 503/947-6000), as well as at sporting goods stores, some grocery stores (such as Fred Meyer), and other outlets.

Fishing

Fishing for trout, both wild native cutthroat and rainbows as well as planted hatchery fish, is popular all across the state. Standout areas include the Deschutes River, a blue-ribbon stream noted for its large "redband" rainbow trout, as well as excellent steelhead fishing. Other notable steelhead streams include the coastal Rogue and Umpqua Rivers, as well as the Sandy and Clackamas Rivers, right in Portland's backyard. Smallmouth bass provide excellent sport on the John Day and Umpqua Rivers, and largemouth bass draw anglers to warm-water lakes across the state.

The return of salmon and steelhead remains uneven, although it has been aided by such efforts as habitat protection, improvements to dams that make them more fish-friendly, and other conservation efforts, as well as by cyclical changes in ocean currents and nutrient levels.

Weighing into the hundreds of pounds, sturgeon is another extremely popular game fish in the larger rivers, particularly the Columbia and the Umpqua. Off the coast, bottom fishing for rockfish and other species is a year-round activity, depending on the weather. Warm ocean currents bring albacore tuna in August-September, and halibut are usually available in summer, though the season is variable and

set yearly by the Pacific Fishery Management Council.

About 1,000 fishing guides are licensed in Oregon. Fishing opportunities on your own are almost limitless, but hiring a guide can be money well spent if you're exploring unfamiliar waters or you lack a boat. Major **charter-fishing** centers on the coast include Astoria, Hammond, Warrenton, Garibaldi, Depoe Bay, Newport, Winchester Bay, Charleston, Gold Beach, Bandon, and Brookings. Charter rates vary a bit, but typical prices up and down the coast are $75-80 for a half day (5-6 hours) of bottom fishing, about $100 for a full day; $100-150 for an 8-hour salmon outing; $200-300 for 12 hours of tuna fishing; $175-200 for a 12-hour halibut charter. Inland, expect to pay at least $175-300 per person per day for guided trips for salmon, steelhead, sturgeon, and other species. Chambers of commerce in each town can also provide extensive listings.

Fishing licenses cost $16.75 (for 1 day), $31.50 (2 days), $46.25 (3 days), $58 (4 days), $59.75 (7 days), or $106.25 (full year for non-residents; $33 for Oregonians). Nonresident licenses include Combined Angling Tags (allowing the taking of salmon, sturgeon, steelhead, and halibut).

Hunting

Hunters enjoy a broad range of opportunities throughout Oregon. Shooting for upland game birds—chukar, Hungarian partridge, pheasant, grouse, and quail—can be good to excellent in eastern and central Oregon, the Cascades, and the coastal ranges. The eastern half of the state as well as the Willamette Valley, Columbia River basin, and coastal areas offer waterfowl hunting. Wild turkeys, introduced successfully on the eastern side of Mount Hood, have proliferated and are now hunted in almost every county of the state. Bigger game includes elk, black bears, cougars, black-tailed deer in western Oregon, and mule deer in the east. A limited number of special tags are also issued for pronghorn, bighorn sheep, and mountain goats.

The rules governing hunting in the state are

more complex and variable than those for fishing. Check the regulations carefully for seasons, restrictions, and bag limits, and again, consult the **Department of Fish and Wildlife's website** (www.dfw.state.or.us) for the latest information.

WHITE-WATER RAFTING

With 90,000 river miles in the state and hundreds of outfitters to choose from, neophyte rafters have an embarrassment of riches. To help navigate the tricky currents of brochure jargon and select the experience that's right for you, here's a list of rivers to run and questions to ask before going.

Raft the famous **Rogue River** June-September to avoid the rainy season and be spared current fluctuations due to dams upstream. This run is characterized by gentle stretches broken up by abrupt and occasionally severe drop-offs as well as swift currents. In fact, Blossom Bar is often cited as one of the state's consummate tests of skill for rafters. The Rogue is ideal for half- and full-day rafting trips, with most outfitters putting in near the town of Merlin and continuing downstream as far as Foster Bar. Water turbulence on the Rogue is often intensified by constricted channels created by huge boulders. Depending on the season, rafters can expect Class II, III, and IV rapids interspersed by deep pools and cascading waterfalls. At day's end, superlative campsites offer repose and the chance to savor your adventures.

Despite the dryness and isolation of Oregon's southeast corner, the **Owyhee River** has become a prime springtime destination for white-water enthusiasts. The 53 miles from Rome to the Owyhee Reservoir have two sections of exceptionally heavy rapids, but the many pools of short intense white water alternating with easy drifts make for a well-paced trip. The best times to come are May-early June. Before going, check conditions with the **Vale Bureau of Land Management District office** (541/473-3144, www.or.blm.gov/vale), because the Owyhee can only be run in years with high snowmelt. Access to rafting takeout points in

this part of the state is greatly facilitated by a four-wheel-drive vehicle.

The **John Day River** in northeastern Oregon offers an even-flowing current as it winds 175 miles through unpopulated rangeland and scenic rock formations. Below Clarno, the grade gets steep, creating the most treacherous part of the state's longest river (275 miles). The 157-mile section of the John Day that rafters, canoeists, and kayakers come to experience also has falls near the mouth that require a portage. The special charm of this Columbia tributary is the dearth of company you'll have even during the river-running seasons of late March-May and then again in November. Just watch out for rattlesnakes along the bank, and remember that the silt load in this undammed river reduces it to an unboatable trickle in summer months. Contact the **Prineville Bureau of Land Management office** (541/416-6700) for more information.

Unlike the John Day and the Owyhee Rivers, the **Deschutes River** rapids aren't totally dependent on snowmelt, and it is the busiest vacation waterway in the state. The 44 miles between Maupin and the Columbia River contain sage-covered grasslands and wild rocky canyons where you might see bald eagles, pronghorn, and other wildlife. If there's a good run of salmon or steelhead, you might also encounter plenty of fishing boats. This area averages 310 days of sunshine annually, so weather is seldom a problem except for excessively hot summer days.

Typical rafting outfitter services include meals, wetsuits or rain gear, and inflatable rafts and kayaks. Guided raft trips begin at about $50 for a half-day trip and increase to $200 and up per day for longer trips. To ensure an intimate wilderness experience, ask about the number of people in a raft and how many rafts are on the river at one time. Are there any hidden costs such as camping gear rental or added transfer charges? What is the cancellation policy? Another consideration is the training and experience of the guide. Can he or she be expected to give commentary about history, geology, and local color? You might also want to

© BILL MCRAE

windsurfer waiting for a breeze on Hood River

check about the company's willingness to customize its trips to special interests such as photography, bird-watching, or hiking.

WINDSURFING AND KITEBOARDING

Windsurfing conditions near the town of Hood River have made the Columbia River Gorge world-famous. In recent years, kiteboarding has become almost as popular. Other than the San Francisco Bay Area, no other place in the continental United States boasts summertime airflows as consistently strong as those in the gorge. Championship events and top competitors have coalesced on the shores of the river here, 60 miles east of Portland. The Columbia River runs in the opposite direction of the westerly airflows, which can cause large waves to stack up and allow windsurfers to maintain their positions relative to the shore. In short, the area offers the perfect marriage of optimal conditions and scenic beauty.

Some coastal waters are also gaining popularity for windsurfers. Floras Lake, near Port Orford, and the area around Pistol River, just south of Gold Beach, are top destinations. The latter hosts the Pistol River Wave Bash National Windsurfing Competition each June.

WINTER SPORTS

One of the silver linings to Oregon's legendary precipitation is that so much of it falls in the form of snow in the mountains. Mount Hood, for example, has been buried by as much as 100 feet of snow in a single year. That makes a lot of people happy from late fall through spring and even into summer, as Oregon snowpacks support the longest ski season in the country (at Timberline on Mount Hood), as well as snowboarding, snowmobiling, and snowshoeing. For snow reports and other updated information throughout the season, a good source is **OnTheSnow.com** (www.onthesnow.com/OR).

In addition to hundreds of miles of groomed and backcountry cross-country ski routes, alpine resorts are concentrated in the northern and central Cascades and in the state's northeast corner. A little over an hour's drive away on **Mount Hood,** Portlanders have their choice of five developed ski resorts—Mount Hood SkiBowl, Cooper Spur, Mount Hood Meadows, Timberline, and tiny Summit, the Pacific Northwest's oldest ski resort, dating to 1927. In the central Cascades, there are family-friendly **Hoodoo Ski Bowl** southeast of Salem, **Willamette Pass** southeast of Eugene, and **Mount Bachelor,** the Pacific Northwest's largest and most developed ski area, southwest of Bend. At **Mount Bailey,** near Diamond Lake in the southern Cascades, downhillers can experience snowcat skiing, a more affordable alternative to being dropped off on inaccessible slopes by helicopter. The area also offers extensive cross-country, skating, sledding, and snowmobiling terrain. Near the California border in southern Oregon, **Mount Ashland** offers downhill action in addition to 100 miles of cross-country trails.

In the northeast, skiers have their choice of **Anthony Lakes Ski Area,** between Baker City and La Grande, and **Ferguson Ridge Ski Area,** east of Joseph.

Sno-Park Permits
Note that for winter sports in many areas

November 15-April 30, you'll need to purchase a Sno-Park permit ($3 for 1 day, $20 for the season) to park your vehicle in posted winter recreation areas. Sporting goods stores, ski shops, and resorts near the slopes sell them.

Accommodations and Food

ACCOMMODATIONS
For extremely popular destinations, such as Cannon Beach and other coastal towns, plan to reserve well in advance during peak times, such as summer weekends and holidays. "Off-season" specials are a way to beat the crowds and the costs. For example, before Memorial Day and after Labor Day, room rates on the coast can drop by 25 percent or so, and in winter even by 50 percent.

While there's no sales tax in Oregon, note that a local lodging tax—ranging 6-12 percent, depending on the locale—will be added to your bill. In addition, a recently implemented 1 percent statewide "transient lodging" tax, dedicated to tourism-promotion efforts, also applies.

FOOD
Oregon has become known for its excellent restaurants, the most notable of which focus on using locally grown, raised, or gathered foods. Oregon's abundance of fresh produce, seafood, and other indigenous ingredients prompted one of the country's early apostles of haute cuisine, James Beard, to extol the restaurants and cooking of his home state. In his autobiography, *Delights and Prejudices,* he implied that Oregon strawberries, Seaside peas, Dungeness crab, and other local fare are the standards by which he judges culinary staples around the world. This cornucopia is the basis of a regional cuisine emphasizing fresh natural foods cooked lightly to preserve flavor, color, and texture.

One food that seems to be unique to Oregon is the marionberry, a purple berry whose tarter-than-blackberry taste and small seeds make it ideal for dessert fare, especially marionberry ice

cream. Oregon lamb and the seasonally available excellent fresh sturgeon, venison, and game birds are other taste treasures. Oregon specialties can be complemented with a world-class pinot noir, gourmet coffee, or microbrew.

Nonetheless, it is possible to have a bad meal in this state. In fact, the quality of the cuisine in some remote Oregon towns is a source of self-deprecating humor for the locals. And as many will tell you, there is no shortage of bland, starchy clam chowder on the Oregon coast.

LIQUOR AND MICROBREWERIES
Liquor is sold by the bottle only in state-sanctioned liquor stores, open Monday-Saturday. Many stores also keep Sunday hours. Beer and wine are also sold in grocery stores and retail outlets. Liquor is sold by the drink in licensed establishments 7am-2:30am. The minimum drinking age is 21.

Oregon has nearly 100 craft breweries making beer without preservatives or chemical additives to enhance head or color. Instead of the rice or corn used by the big outfits, the micros just use barley, malt, hops, yeast, and water. The end result is a more full-bodied, tastier brew with a distinct personality.

The reason Oregon is awash in gourmet suds owes much to the availability of top-notch ingredients—hops, barley, and clear water. Almost one-third of the world's hops are produced here in the Pacific Northwest. The Willamette Valley alone cultivates more than a dozen varieties. Add Cascade mountain water, malted barley from the Klamath basin, and Hood River-grown yeast cultures and you can see why there are more breweries and brewpubs per capita in Oregon than anywhere else in the United States.

One of the best opportunities to sample at least some of these fine brews is at the Oregon Brewers Festival, held in Portland each August.

Tips for Travelers

ENTRY REQUIREMENTS

Entry requirements are subject to change. For current information, see the **U.S. Department of State's Bureau of Consular Affairs website** (www.travel.state.gov). All visitors from abroad must be in possession of a valid passport in order to enter the United States. Also required in most cases is a round-trip or return ticket, or proof of sufficient funds for a visit and a return ticket. Visitors from most countries must also have a valid visa for entry. (See the State Department website, www.state.gov, for a current list of countries for which the visa requirement is waived.) Applicants for visitor visas should generally apply at the U.S. embassy or consulate with jurisdiction over their place of permanent residence. Although visa applicants may apply at any U.S. consular office abroad, it may be more difficult to qualify for the visa outside your country of permanent residence.

ACCESS FOR TRAVELERS WITH DISABILITIES

Oregon is generally proactive with regard to providing accessible facilities for people with disabilities, though there's always room for improvement. The great outdoors and some older buildings (lighthouses, for example), of course, can pose some insurmountable challenges, but many parks and recreation areas work to accommodate visitors with mobility issues. Many campgrounds have accessible sites.

The **Access Pass,** which allows free entry to designated federal recreation areas such as national parks and monuments, Bureau of Land Management lands, and U.S. Fish and Wildlife sites, is available to those who are blind or permanently disabled. The pass is free to qualified applicants ($10 processing fee); get details

from the **U.S. Geological Survey** (http://store.usgs.gov).

TRAVELING WITH CHILDREN

Oregon is a great place to travel with kids, with plenty of attractions and activities to keep them interested. One of the first things travelers by car will notice is the ample number of rest stops, with one every 30-60 miles or so on most major routes. In most towns and cities, public parks offer play structures and open spaces where kids can burn off some energy. Many Oregon state parks offer excellent recreational opportunities for families such as guided hikes, nature programs, and campfire presentations.

Many B&Bs discourage children. Where possible, we've indicated policies (for and against) in accommodations listings, but it's always a good idea when making a reservation to inquire as to whether the lodging is appropriate for children.

GAY AND LESBIAN TRAVELERS

In Portland, college towns such as Eugene and Corvallis, and most touristed areas, gay and lesbian visitors can expect to find progressive attitudes. In these places there are venues that specifically cater to same-sex couples; Portland's **Q Center** (4115 N. Mississippi Ave., 5037234-7837, www.pdxqcenter.org) is an LGBTQ community center. Outside of these places, one may find the attitude considerably less open and accepting; in more rural parts of the state, the attitude may be downright hostile. On the other hand, gays and lesbians live all over the state, and the relationships that these folks have built with their neighbors and coworkers often pave the way for acceptance of gay and lesbian travelers.

Health and Safety

EMERGENCY SERVICES

Throughout Oregon, dial 911 for medical, police, or fire emergencies. Most hospitals offer a 24-hour emergency room. Remember that medical costs are high here, as in the rest of the United States, and emergency rooms are the most expensive places for medical care; for nonemergency situations, look for urgency clinics. In Portland and its suburbs, the ZoomCare clinics charge about $100 for a visit, and take most insurance.

HEALTH HAZARDS
Hypothermia

In this part of the country, anyone who participates in outdoor recreation should be alert for problems with hypothermia—when your body loses more heat than can be recovered and shock ensues. The damp chill of the Pacific Northwest climate poses a greater hypothermia threat than colder climes with low humidity. In other words, it doesn't have to be freezing for death from hypothermia to occur; wind and wetness often turn out to be greater risk factors. Remember that a wet human body loses heat 23 times faster than a dry one.

One of the first signs of hypothermia is a diminished ability to think and act rationally. Speech can become slurred, and uncontrollable shivering usually takes place. Stumbling, memory lapses, and drowsiness also tend to characterize the afflicted. Unless the body temperature can be raised several degrees by a knowledgeable helper, cardiac arrhythmia or arrest may occur. Getting out of the wind and rain into a dry warm environment is essential for survival. This might mean placing the victim into a sleeping bag with another person. Ideally, a ground cloth should be used to insulate the sleeping bag from cold surface temperatures. Internal heat can be generated by feeding the victim high-carbohydrate snacks and hot liquids. Placing wrapped heated objects against the victim's body is also a good way to restore body heat. Be careful not to raise body heat too quickly, as that could also cause cardiac problems.

Measures you can take to prevent hypothermia include eating a nutritious diet, avoiding overexertion followed by exposure to wet and cold, and dressing warmly in layers of wool and polypropylene. Wool insulates even when wet, and because polypropylene tends to wick moisture away from your skin, it makes a good first layer. Gore-Tex and other waterproof breathable fabrics make for more comfortable rain gear than nylon because they don't become cumbersome and hot in a steady rain. Finally, wear a hat to prevent heat loss through your head.

Frostbite

Frostbite is not generally a major problem until the combined air and wind-chill temperature falls below 20°F. Outer appendages such as fingers and toes are the most susceptible, with the ears and nose a close second. Frostbite occurs when blood is redirected out of the limbs to warm vital organs in cold weather, and the exposed parts of the face and peripherals cool very rapidly. Mild frostbite is characterized by extremely pale skin with random splotchiness; in more severe cases, the skin will take on a gray ashen look and feel numb. At the first signs of suspected frostbite, you should gently warm the afflicted area. In more aggravated cases, immerse hands and feet in warm water. Do not massage the skin, or you risk further skin damage. Warming frostbitten areas against the skin of another person is suitable for less serious frostbite. The warmth of a campfire cannot help once the skin is discolored. As with hypothermia, it's important to avoid exposing the hands and feet to wind and wetness by dressing properly.

Poison Oak

Neither the best intentions nor knowledge from

OREGON FESTIVALS AND EVENTS

The majority of large crowd-drawing events take place June-September, but there are plenty of cool weather and ongoing activities to keep you entertained throughout the year. The free local weekly magazines are a great source for listings of events and entertainment and can be found in most of the larger burgs and college towns.

Oregon loves to celebrate its heritage, as well as its artistic and gastronomic bounty. The following seasonal sampler highlights some of the festivals and celebrations throughout the state.

In spring, two coastal gourmet affairs of note are the **Newport Seafood and Wine Festival** and the **Astoria Crab Feed and Seafood Festival.** Also around this time, Florence's **Rhododendron Festival** and Brookings's **Azalea Festival,** both on the coast, attract blossom connoisseurs.

If you have kids in tow, in June take advantage of the parades, carnival rides, air shows, and floral splendor of Portland's **Rose Festival** or the Cannon Beach **Sandcastle Festival.** You could fill up July and August with such varied musical talents as the new vaudeville acts of the **Oregon Country Fair** and the gold-record performers at Jacksonville's **Peter Britt Music Festival,** not to mention the blues icons who appear at the **Waterfront**

Blues Festival in Portland, the West Coast's largest.

During the last full weekend of July, festivalgoers can toast their appreciation of Oregon at Portland's **Oregon Brewers Festival,** where more than 60 microbreweries are showcased or at the **Annual International Pinot Noir Festival** in McMinnville, attracting master vintners from around the world. Summer festivalhoppers might also want to take in **Da Vinci Days** in Corvallis, uniting the community's scientific and artistic elements, and Portland's **Bite,** featuring the best in food.

In the fall and winter, the leading events west of the Cascades include Mount Angel's **Oktoberfest,** the **Eugene Celebration,** the **Corvallis Fall Festival,** and Thanksgiving open houses in the wine country. At Christmastime the leading events are Albany's **Victorian Parlor tours,** Portland's **Christmas Ships,** and light displays all over the state.

While most of Oregon's celebrations take place west of the Cascades, there are notable exceptions to the rule. Bird-watchers relish the Klamath Basin **Bald Eagle Conference** in February and the springtime **John Scharff Migratory Waterfowl Conference** in Burns. Highbrows can take in the summertime literary festival at **Fishtrap** in the Wallowas or rock out at the **Bend Summer Festival** in central

---

a lifetime in the woods can spare the western Oregon hiker at least one brush with poison oak. Major infestations of the plant are seldom encountered in the Coast Range but are prevalent in the Columbia Gorge. In the fall, the leaves are tinged with red. Even when the plant is totally denuded in winter, the toxicity of its irritating sap still remains a threat.

When hiking in hardwood forests, it's a good idea to wear long pants, long-sleeved shirts, and other covering. When you know you've been exposed, try to get your clothes off before the resin permeates your garments. Follow up as soon as possible by washing with Tecnu, a type of soap that seems to help remove the poison

oak oil from skin. It's available at REI and at many drugstores. If you get the rash, cortisone cream is effective at temporarily quelling the intense itching.

Giardia

Known medically as giardiasis but colloquially called "beaver fever," this syndrome afflicts those who drink water contaminated by *Giardia lamblia* parasites. Even water from cold clear streams can be infested by this microorganism, which is spread throughout the backcountry by beavers, muskrats, livestock, and other hikers. Boiling water for 20 minutes or applying five drops of chlorine, or preferably

Oregon. Rock hounds flock to summer mineral shows in the central Oregon hamlets of Madras and Prineville. Rodeo fans can whoop and holler at the venerable **Pendleton Round-Up** in September.

Such celebrations of ethnicity as Portland's **Cinco de Mayo** (one of the largest celebrations of this kind in the nation) and **Scandinavian festivals** in Astoria and Junction City express the state's diversity.

© PAUL LEVY

Oregon's music festivals are popular with locals and visitors alike.

iodine, to every quart of water and letting it sit for half an hour are simple ways to kill the giardia spores. Backpackers should use water pumps that filter out giardia and other organisms.

Mosquitoes

Mosquitoes can be a problem especially in the Cascades, the Willamette Valley, and parts of the Columbia River Gorge. West Nile virus is not common in Oregon, though every year at least a few infected mosquitoes are detected, mostly in the eastern part of the state. When mosquitoes are present, it's a good idea apply insect repellent and wear long pants and

long-sleeved shirts to reduce the chance of getting bitten. Otherwise, you may want to stay indoors during prime mosquito time, around dusk.

Ticks

Of approximately 20 species of hard ticks found in Oregon, only four species are commonly found on humans. Of these, the western black-legged tick (also known as the Pacific tick and deer tick) is the only known carrier in the western United States of the bacterium that causes the debilitating Lyme disease.

The first sign of Lyme disease is a circular rash that appears within 3-30 days at the site of the bite and gradually enlarges to several inches in diameter, clearing up at the center while staying red around the edges. The rash may be accompanied by flu-like symptoms, and it spreads all over the body in one out of two cases.

The second stage of the illness affects only about 15 percent of those infected, but the consequences can be severe. Inflammation of the nerves and covering tissues of the spinal cord and brain can often result in headaches as well as memory loss and concentration problems. The heart can also be affected, resulting in decreased heart function and fainting spells. The last stage, characterized by aching joints, occurs weeks to years after the bite.

The disease can usually be cured with a 10-day dosage of antibiotics, if it is caught early. Delay in treatment can lead to serious complications. If you see the telltale red rash days or weeks after your romp in grassy, brushy, or wooded areas, see a doctor.

A prescription for prevention is to lay the insect repellent on thickly before venturing into potentially infested areas. Also, be sure to check your body and clothing frequently during and after possible exposure. Ticks often may be found attached in the underarms, the groin, behind the knees, and at the nape of the neck.

If you find an attached tick, remove it promptly by grasping it with tweezers, as close to the skin as possible, and pulling it straight out, steadily and firmly. Don't twist it, as this increases the chance of breaking off mouth parts and leaving them embedded in your skin. Afterward, wash up with soap and water, and apply an antiseptic to the bite area. The same routine applies for the removal of ticks from pets.

Information and Services

COMMUNICATIONS AND MEDIA

The state's two largest-circulation newspapers, the **Oregonian** and the **Eugene Register Guard,** come out of the most populous cities, Portland and Eugene. The *Oregonian* is distributed statewide, while the *Register Guard* is carried in newspaper dispensers as far away as the southern coast of Oregon.

Alternatives to the big dailies are found in a number of excellent tabloids, including Portland's **Willamette Week,** the **Eugene Weekly,** Astoria's monthly **Hipfish,** and others.

Portland and Eugene also dominate the broadcast media, serving far-flung rural communities by means of electronic translators. **Oregon Public Broadcasting** (www.opb.org) is also a statewide presence both in TV and radio. Some standout TV programs of interest to visitors include the long-running *Oregon Field Guide,* which explores natural history, outdoor recreation, travel, and environmental issues; and *Oregon Art Beat,* which profiles local artists, craftspeople, and performers of all stripes.

Warm Springs Indian Reservation's KWSO (91.9 FM) is a progressive country radio station spiced with elders chanting in the morning and topical discussions on Native American issues by younger community members. Even though regional monthlies such as *Northwest Travel* and *Sunset* do not have a strictly Oregon focus, there are usually several destination pieces about the state in each edition of these magazines. **Oregon Coast** magazine confines its coverage to subjects closer to home. All these periodicals can be obtained at newsstands throughout the state.

Telephones

Oregon has three area codes. **503** is the main area code in use for the greater Portland metropolitan area, including Mount Hood and the westerly portion of the Columbia River Gorge, Astoria to Lincoln City on the coast, and Portland to Salem in the Willamette Valley; it's supplemented by **971.** The area code **541** is for the rest of the state. Note that when using a landline in Oregon, you must dial the area code, even for local calls. **Cell phone** service in some parts of Oregon—including mountainous regions, the southern coast, and the state's eastern areas—can be spotty to nonexistent.

MAPS AND TOURIST INFORMATION

Travel Oregon (775 Summer St. NE, Salem, 800/547-7842, www.traveloregon.com) is an outstanding resource for visitors and residents alike. The state-run organization maintains an informative website and produces a number of useful free maps and publications, with extensive listings of lodgings and activities, suggested itineraries, events, and more.

Nine welcome centers, located near the borders along major routes into the state, are a good first stop for newly arriving visitors. They stock literature and maps on the entire state, though their regional offerings tend to be best represented.

Other useful contacts are the **Oregon Parks and Recreation Department** (725 Summer St. NE, Salem, 503/986-0707 or 800/551-6949, www.oregonstateparks.org), the **Bureau of Land Management** (333 SW 1st Ave., Portland, 503/808-6002, www.or.blm.gov), and the **National Forest Service** (333 SW 1st Ave., Portland, 503/808-2971, www.fs.fed.us/r6). All offer free information and maps on the specific recreation areas and preserves under their respective auspices.

For members only, **AAA Oregon/Idaho** (600 SW Market St., Portland, 503/222-6734 or 800/452-1643, www.aaaorid.com) offers roadside assistance such as towing and retrieving keys locked in cars and provides tour guides and high-quality maps of the state and major towns.

Visitor information offices are all good sources for free state, regional, and town maps. Some of the best road and city maps available are those produced by AAA for their members. Particularly useful for outdoor recreation is **Oregon Road & Recreation Atlas,** a large-format book of beautiful shaded-relief maps of the entire state, published by **Benchmark Maps** (www.benchmarkmaps.com). The atlas is available in bookstores and sporting goods shops and directly from the publisher. In addition, several regional tourism authorities offer information and services for their corners of Oregon. The best sources for local information are the many chambers of commerce and visitors centers operating in communities across the state.

Trail Maps

Accurate trail and topographical maps are worth their weight in gold for hikers, mountain bikers, anglers, and other outdoors enthusiasts. A wide variety of maps, including those published by the U.S. Geological Survey can be purchased at the **Nature of the Northwest store** (800 NE Oregon St., Ste. 177, Portland, 503/872-2750, www.naturenw.org) in Portland.

Another good series of paper maps is put out by **Green Trails.** Unlike USGS maps, these maps show trail mileage and campsites. Look for them at outdoors stores and ranger stations.

RESOURCES

Suggested Reading

In addition to the titles cited in the text, Oregon-bound travelers may want to read some of these books. We advise readers to search for out-of-print books at www.powells.com.

ATLASES

Benchmark Maps. *Oregon Road and Recreation Atlas.* Medford, OR: Benchmark Maps, 2005. Use this atlas to help plan your trip or as a travel companion. You'll find that it has lots of detail and shaded relief.

Loy, William G. *Atlas of Oregon.* Eugene, OR: University of Oregon Press, 2001. Find graphic details on economics, climate, geology, and historic trails in this gorgeous detailed reference atlas.

MacArthur, Lewis. *Oregon Geographic Names.* Portland: Oregon Historical Society, 2003. This text might be physically weighty, but its alphabetic historical rundown of place-names makes for light and informative reading.

COASTAL OREGON

Gibbs, James A. *Shipwrecks of the Pacific Coast.* Portland: Binford and Mort, 1989. Endlessly fascinating and frequently heartbreaking reading from a master of Pacific Northwest maritime lore. Covers all known shipwrecks off the coasts of Oregon, Washington, and California.

McRae, W. C., and Judy Jewell. *Moon Coastal Oregon.* Berkeley: Avalon Travel Publishing, 2014. Comprised of the coastal Oregon chapters in this book with new and specific Discover, Background, and Essentials chapter for the Oregon coast.

Ostertag, Rhonda, and George Ostertag. *75 Hikes in Oregon's Coast Range.* Seattle: Mountaineers Books, 2001. A well-chosen selection of hikes along the length of the coastal ranges covers a broad variety of terrain and difficulty levels. Detailed trail descriptions and maps make this guide particularly useful.

Sullivan, William L. *100 Hikes Travel Guide: Oregon Coast and Coast Range.* Eugene, OR: Navillus Press, 2009. William Sullivan puts out the most carefully researched hiking guides in the business—we'd follow him down any trail!

EASTERN OREGON

Jackman, E. R., and R. A. Long. *The Oregon Desert.* Caldwell, ID: Caxton Press, 2003; and Jackman, E. R., John Scharff, and Charles Conkling (photographer). *Steens Mountain in Oregon's High Desert Country.* Caldwell, ID: Caxton Press, 2003. These two works are the classics for eastern Oregon. Within the volumes, history and local color fill in the east side of the state's wide-open spaces.

Kittredge, William. *Owning It All.* Saint Paul, MN: Graywolf Press, 2002. Kittredge grew up in southeastern Oregon and in these essays he reminisces and regrets some of the changes his family's ranching endeavors brought about.

Sullivan, William L. *100 Hikes Travel Guide: Eastern Oregon*. Eugene, OR: Navillus Press, 2008. Along with his usual well-researched hikes and detailed hand-drawn maps, Sullivan offers up a bit of history and a few travel recommendations.

FICTION

Davis, H. L. *Honey in the Horn*. Moscow, ID: University of Idaho Press, 2004. This reprint edition of a 1935 Pulitzer Prize-winning novel about rowdy southern Oregon settlers makes the pioneer days seem quite real.

Kesey, Ken. *Sometimes a Great Notion*. New York: Viking, 1964. One of the best novels ever about life in rural Oregon.

GENERAL INTEREST

Adams, Melvin. *Netting the Sun*. Pullman, WA: Washington State University Press, 2001. Born and raised in eastern Oregon, Adams's passion for Oregon's high desert informs this collection of haunting and beautifully written essays.

Douglas, William O. *Of Men and Mountains*. San Francisco: Chronicle Books, 1985. The final chapters of the late Supreme Court Justice's autobiography provide some redolent descriptions of life in Oregon. Particularly evocative are his descriptions of the Wallowas.

Hadlow, Robert W. *Elegant Arches, Soaring Spans: C. B. McCullough, Oregon's Master Bridge Builder*. Corvallis, OR: Oregon State University Press, 2003. Covers the dozen beautiful bridges designed by McCullough between the world wars, which he called "jeweled clasps in a wonderful string of pearls."

Jewell, Judy. *Oregon*. New York: Fodor's Compass American Guides, 2005. Read this guide before traveling to the state to complement *Moon Oregon* as your on-the-road reference. Beautiful color photos and insightful travel tips liven up this literary rendition of Oregon's greatest hits.

Tisdale, Sallie. *Stepping Westward*. New York: Holt and Co., 1991. The award-winning essayist deftly blends fact and fancy. In her treatment of the past, present, and future of the Pacific Northwest, the Portland author emphasizes a native worldview.

GUIDEBOOKS

Fanselow, Julie. *Traveling the Lewis and Clark Trail*. Helena, MT: Falcon Publishing, 2003. This guidebook for the modern-day explorer acquaints readers with what to see and do along Lewis and Clark's celebrated route from Illinois to Oregon.

Fanselow, Julie. *Traveling the Oregon Trail*. Guilford, CT: Globe Pequot Press, 2001. The adventures continue with Fanselow's scenic and informative guide to the present-day Oregon Trail.

Foster, Laura O. *Portland Hill Walks: Twenty Explorations in Parks and Neighborhoods*. Portland: Timber Press, 2005. Great walking guide with colorful commentary that will take you through Portland's neighborhoods.

Friedman, Ralph. *Oregon for the Curious*. Caldwell, ID: Caxton, 1972. Friedman was Oregon's king of the road. Of his half-dozen books, this is the most recommended. It is still the best mile-by-mile description of the state ever written.

Jones, Shawn, and Nell Nix. *Out and About: Portland with Kids*. Portland: Sasquatch Books, 2009. A must-have for those exploring Portland with children.

Vaughn, Greg. *Photographing Oregon.* Alta Loma, CA: PhotoTripUSA, 2009. Good tips on selecting subjects and setting up your shots.

HISTORY

Ambrose, Stephen. *Undaunted Courage.* New York: Touchstone Press, 1996. A classic book on the country's seminal voyage of discovery, the Lewis and Clark expedition. It gives a historical context to the explorers' journals in an entertaining, enlightening way. Read this before taking on *The Journals of Lewis and Clark* themselves. The latter work is available through many different publishers, but the antiquated grammar and archaic English make it difficult reading.

Beckham, Steven Dow, and Robert M. Reynolds (photographer). *Lewis & Clark from the Rockies to the Pacific.* Portland: Graphic Arts Center Publishing, 2002. Focusing on the second half of the expedition's outward-bound journey, this gorgeously illustrated and insightful book covers Lewis and Clark's trying months spent camped in the rainy woodlands of the northern Oregon coast.

Del Mar, David Peterson. *Oregon's Promise: An Interpretive History.* Corvallis, OR: Oregon State University Press, 2003. Something of an alternative to more traditional histories of the state, this one focuses on the diversity of the people and their varied experiences.

Federal Writers' Project (editor). *WPA Guide to Oregon.* Portland: Binford and Mort, 1940. The granddaddy of them all, this 1941 guide is the primary inspiration for *Moon Oregon.* The product of dozens of authors working in the Federal Writers' Project, this post-Depression guidebook still sets the standard for thorough coverage and vivid description. Although much of the information is dated, its rundown of pioneer history and glimpses of early 20th-century Oregon make it a valuable tool for any modern traveler. Available in many public libraries.

Friedman, Ralph. *In Search of Western Oregon.* Caldwell, ID: Caxton Press, 1991. A fascinating read, packed with anecdotes, folklore, historical details, and more, all told in Friedman's engaging style.

O'Donnell, Terrence. *Portland: An Informal History and Guide.* Portland: Oregon Historical Society, 1964. This book is widely available used, and it makes for entertaining reading.

Oregon Secretary of State (editor). *Oregon Blue Book.* Salem, OR: State of Oregon, 2009. Published biennially by the state of Oregon, this volume provides the best concise history of Oregon and a wide assortment of facts about the state. Much of the text is available at http://bluebook.state.or.us.

Robbins, William G. *Landscapes of Promise: The Oregon Story 1800-1940.* Seattle: University of Washington Press, 1999. In this fascinating environmental history of Oregon, Robbins examines ways that Oregonians have interacted with the land; he shows that Native Americans altered the landscape in a number of ways, and that the landscape encountered by early European settlers was, in some areas, highly managed.

Smith, Landon. *The Essential Lewis and Clark.* New York: Ecco Press, 2000. Covers information similar to the dynamic duo's journals, yet provides a much easier read.

NATURAL HISTORY

Alt, David, and Donald W. Hyndman. *Roadside Geology of Oregon.* Missoula, MT: Mountain Press Publishing Company, 2003. This book's mile-by-mile approach makes it a good reference to have in the car to answer your questions about Oregon's geology.

Bishop, Ellen Morris. *In Search of Ancient Oregon: A Geological and Natural History.* Portland: Timber Press, 2003. If you enjoy reading about geology, this is the book for you. Even if you are not so sure about your commitment to geological study, it's a good read with lots of illustrative photos.

Evanich, Joseph E., Jr. *Birders Guide to Oregon*. Portland: Audubon Society of Portland, 2003. A good all-around guide to the state's birdlife, with a useful breakdown of specific coastal locations and details on what species to watch for and when.

Jolley, Russ. *Wildflowers of the Columbia Gorge*. Portland: Oregon Historical Society Press, 1988. An exhaustive study of the gorge's plant species, with excellent color photos identifying 744 of the Columbia Gorge's more than 800 species of flowering shrubs and wildflowers.

Laskin, David. *Rains All the Time*. Seattle: Sasquatch Press, 1998. A fascinating inquiry into the region's rainforest-to-desert diversity.

Littlefield, Caroll D. *Birds of Malheur Refuge*. Corvallis, OR: Oregon State University Press, 1990. Recommended for serious birders.

Paulson, Dennis. *Shorebirds of the Pacific Northwest*. Seattle: University of Washington Press, 1998. For the specialist rather than the generalist, there is no better book than this richly detailed guide for distinguishing an avocet from a stilt, a plover from a curlew, and identifying any of the dozens of other species found near the water's edge. Unless you're a collector, borrow this out-of-print gem from the library.

Pojar, Jim, and Andy MacKinnon (editors). *Plants of the Pacific Northwest Coast: Washington, Oregon, British Columbia, and Alaska*. Edmonton, AB: Lone Pine Publishing, 2003. A highly regarded guide to the flora of the entire Pacific Northwest region, illustrated with excellent photos.

Sept, J. Duane. *The Beachcomber's Guide to Seashore Life in the Pacific Northwest*. Vancouver, BC: Harbour Publishing, 1999. This ideal guide for the casual and curious observer aids in understanding the intertidal zone and in identifying more than 270 species encountered there, including crabs, clams, and other mollusks, seaweeds, sea stars, sea anemones, and more.

Wallace, David Rains. *The Klamath Knot*. San Francisco: Sierra Club Books, 1984. An excellent book on the natural history of southern Oregon.

OUTDOOR RECREATION

Garren, John. *Oregon River Tours*. Portland: Garren Publishing, 1991. Detailed maps and charts make this an indispensable tool for anyone braving Oregon's white water.

Giordano, Pete. *The Soggy Sneakers Guide to Oregon Rivers*. Seattle: Mountaineers Books, 2004. An indispensable guide to Oregon's rivers, replete with maps, class ratings, gradient listings, river lengths, and best seasons to visit.

Hill, Sean Patrick. *Moon Oregon Hiking*. Berkeley: Avalon Travel Publishing, 2010. Details more than 490 hikes throughout Oregon, including hiking tips and top 10 lists of Oregon's best trails.

Stienstra, Tom. *Moon Oregon Camping*. Berkeley: Avalon Travel Publishing, 2010. Details nearly 700 campgrounds across the state, with an excellent selection on the coast. Rich with tips on gear, safety, and other topics.

Sullivan, William L. *100 Hikes in Northwest Oregon and Southwest Washington*. Eugene, OR: Navillus Press, 2006. Sullivan's excellent hiking guides also include *100 Hikes* books for the central Oregon Cascades, southern Oregon, eastern Oregon, and the Oregon coast and Coast Range.

Wozniak, Owen. *Biking Portland*. Seattle, WA: Mountaineers, 2013. Guided tours through Portland's neighborhoods, with history and interesting commentary along the way.

Internet Resources

ACCOMMODATIONS

Oregon Bed and Breakfast Guild
www.obbg.org
800/944-6196
Lists links to Oregon bed-and-breakfasts by region.

ENTERTAINMENT AND EVENTS

Oregon Arts Commission
www.oregonartscommission.org
A guide to public art, events, and galleries throughout the state.

Oregon Craft Beer
www.oregoncraftbeer.org
Proffers merchandise and features a calendar of statewide beer-related events and an extremely useful map of Oregon's microbreweries.

Oregon Wine
www.oregonwine.org
Everything you ever wanted to know about Oregon wines, wineries, and events.

Wines Northwest
www.winesnw.com
A guide to the world of wine in the great Pacific Northwest (and a useful link to guides and driving services).

HISTORY

Haunted Places
www.ghostsandcritters.com
An eerie look into Oregon's underworld. Offers advice for novice ghost hunters and info about haunted places in the state.

Oregon Historical Society
www.ohs.org
A resource for Oregon history.

OUTDOOR RECREATION AND CAMPING

ORbike
www.orbike.com
Statewide calendar of bike rides and cycling events.

Oregon Department of Fish and Wildlife
www.dfw.state.or.us
Information on fishing and wildlife in Oregon.

Oregon Hiking
www.oregonhiking.com
Information on outdoor adventures such as hiking, snowshoeing, rafting, and climbing.

Ride Oregon
www.rideoregonride.com
Bike ride options throughout the state.

State Parks
www.oregonstateparks.org
Find a state park or a campsite, make a reservation, or download brochures.

U.S. Forest Service
www.fs.usda.gov/r6
Links to national forests, camping information and reservations, ranger station contact info, maps and brochures, fees, passes, and permit info.

REGIONAL INFORMATION AND SERVICES

Central Oregon Visitors Association
www.visitcentraloregon.com
705 SW Bonnett Dr.
Bend, OR 97702
800/800-8334

Columbia River Gorge Visitors Association
www.crgva.org
800/98-GORGE (800/984-6743)

Eastern Oregon Visitors Association
www.visiteasternoregon.com
541/523-9200 or 800/332-1843

Eugene, Cascades & Coast
www.eugenecascadescoast.org
754 Olive St.
Eugene, OR 97401
541/484-5307 or 800/547-5445

Oregon Coast Visitors Association
www.VisitTheOregonCoast.com
137 NE 1st St.
Newport, OR 97365
541/574-2679 or 888/628-2101

Oregon's Mt. Hood Territory
www.MtHoodTerritory.com
150 Beavercreek Rd., Suite 305
Oregon City, OR 97045
503/655-8490 or 800/424-3002

Portland Oregon Visitors Association
www.travelportland.com
701 SW 6th Ave., Suite 1
Portland, OR 97204
503/275-8355 or 877/678-5263

Southern Oregon Visitors Association
www.southernoregon.org

Willamette Valley Visitors Association
www.oregonwinecountry.org
866/548-5018

STATEWIDE INFORMATION AND SERVICES
Travel Oregon
www.traveloregon.com
The official state tourism department's website with information about lodging, recreation opportunities, and a statewide calendar of events. It's a fun site.

TRANSPORTATION
Amtrak
www.amtrak.com
Train schedules, fares, and booking information.

Greyhound
www.greyhound.com
Schedules, fares, and booking information.

Oregon Department of Transportation
www.tripcheck.com
Great site with webcams, road conditions, public transportation, and mileage calculator.

Portland International Airport
www.flypdx.com
Portland International Airport's website provides a list of carriers, ground transport, and other useful information on the area.

Index

List of Maps

www.moon.com

DESTINATIONS | ACTIVITIES | BLOGS | MAPS | BOOKS

MOON.COM is ready to help plan your next trip! Filled with fresh trip ideas and strategies, author interviews, informative travel blogs, a detailed map library, and descriptions of all the Moon guidebooks, Moon.com is all you need to get out and explore the world—or even places in your own backyard. While at Moon.com, sign up for our monthly e-newsletter for updates on new releases, travel tips, and expert advice from our on-the-go Moon authors. As always, when you travel with Moon, expect an experience that is uncommon and truly unique.

KEEP UP WITH MOON ON FACEBOOK AND TWITTER
JOIN THE MOON PHOTO GROUP ON FLICKR

MAP SYMBOLS

▭▭▭	Expressway	◖	Highlight	✗	Airfield	⛳	Golf Course
▭▭▭	Primary Road	○	City/Town	✈	Airport	🅿	Parking Area
▭▭▭	Secondary Road	◉	State Capital	▲	Mountain	⬟	Archaeological Site
-------	Unpaved Road	⊛	National Capital	✛	Unique Natural Feature	⛪	Church
-------	Trail	★	Point of Interest			⛽	Gas Station
············	Ferry	•	Accommodation	⬙	Waterfall		Glacier
-×-×-×	Railroad	▼	Restaurant/Bar	⬥	Park		Mangrove
▬▬▬	Pedestrian Walkway	▪	Other Location	⛽	Trailhead		Reef
⟫⟫⟫⟫	Stairs	▲	Campground	⛷	Skiing Area		Swamp

CONVERSION TABLES

°C = (°F - 32) / 1.8
°F = (°C x 1.8) + 32
1 inch = 2.54 centimeters (cm)
1 foot = 0.304 meters (m)
1 yard = 0.914 meters
1 mile = 1.6093 kilometers (km)
1 km = 0.6214 miles
1 fathom = 1.8288 m
1 chain = 20.1168 m
1 furlong = 201.168 m
1 acre = 0.4047 hectares
1 sq km = 100 hectares
1 sq mile = 2.59 square km
1 ounce = 28.35 grams
1 pound = 0.4536 kilograms
1 short ton = 0.90718 metric ton
1 short ton = 2,000 pounds
1 long ton = 1.016 metric tons
1 long ton = 2,240 pounds
1 metric ton = 1,000 kilograms
1 quart = 0.94635 liters
1 US gallon = 3.7854 liters
1 Imperial gallon = 4.5459 liters
1 nautical mile = 1.852 km

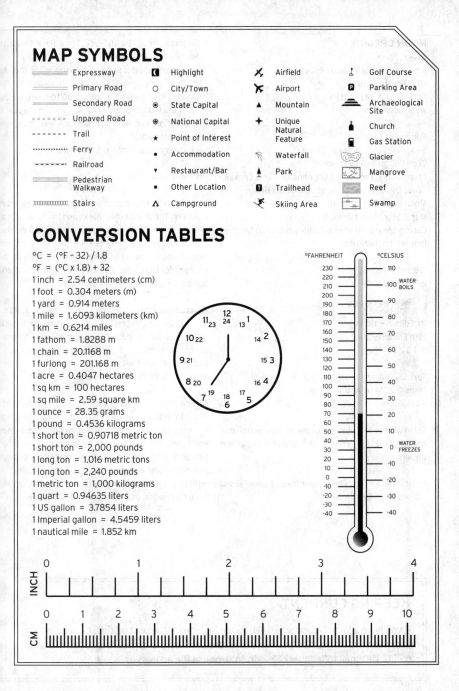

MOON OREGON

Avalon Travel
a member of the Perseus Books Group
1700 Fourth Street
Berkeley, CA 94710, USA
www.moon.com

Editor: Leah Gordon
Series Manager: Kathryn Ettinger
Copy Editor: Ashley Benning
Graphics and Production Coordinator: Lucie Ericksen
Cover Design: Faceout Studios, Charles Brock
Moon Logo: Tim McGrath
Map Editor: Albert Angulo
Cartographers: Stephanie Poulain and Brian Shotwell
Indexer: Rachel Kuhn

ISBN-13: 978-1-61238-756-7
ISSN: 1080-3394

Printing History
1st Edition – 1991
10th Edition – June 2014
5 4 3 2 1

Text © 2014 by W. C. McRae and Judy Jewell.
Maps © 2014 by Avalon Travel.
All rights reserved.

Some photos and illustrations are used by permission and are the property of the original copyright owners.

Front cover photo: a hiker near lower Proxy Falls © Grant Faint/Getty Images

Title page photo: Smith Rock State Park © Judy Jewell

Interior color photos: pages 4, 5, 6 top-left, 7 top, 8 16, 21: © Judy Jewell; pages 6 bottom and 23: © Katrina Perry; pages 7 bottom, 9 bottom-left, 12, 13 20: © Bill McRae; page 9 top: © Pam Ore; pages 9 bottom-right and 14: © Duncan Mack Murphy; page 19: © Conni Diack

Back cover photo: Ashland © Bill McRae

Printed in Canada by Friesens

Moon Handbooks and the Moon logo are the property of Avalon Travel. All other marks and logos depicted are the property of the original owners. All rights reserved. No part of this book may be translated or reproduced in any form, except brief extracts by a reviewer for the purpose of a review, without written permission of the copyright owner.

All recommendations, including those for sights, activities, hotels, restaurants, and shops, are based on each author's individual judgment. We do not accept payment for inclusion in our travel guides and our authors don't accept free goods or services in exchange for positive coverage.

Although every effort was made to ensure that the information was correct at the time of going to press, the author and publisher do not assume and hereby disclaim any liability to any party for any loss or damage caused by errors, omissions, or any potential travel disruption due to labor or financial difficulty, whether such errors or omissions result from negligence, accident, or any other cause.

KEEPING CURRENT

If you have a favorite gem you'd like to see included in the next edition, or see anything that needs updating, clarification, or correction, please drop us a line. Send your comments via email to feedback@moon.com, or use the address above.